2016/17

REFERENCE ONLY
Not to be taken aw

D1186711

THE GUIDE TO

GRANTS FOR INDIVIDUALS IN NEED

FIFTEENTH EDITION

Rachel Cain and Jennifer Reynolds

Additional research by:
Gabriele Zagnojute, Ian Pembridge, Jodie Huyton
and Denise Lillya

dsc
directory of social change

05080890

Published by the Directory of Social Change (Registered Charity no. 800517 in England and Wales)

Head office: 352 Holloway Road, London N7 6PA

Northern office: Suite 103, 1 Old Hall Street, Liverpool L3 9HG
Tel: 08450 77 77 07

Visit www.dsc.org.uk to find out more about our books, subscription funding websites and training events. You can also sign up for e-newsletters so that you're always the first to hear about what's new.

The publisher welcomes suggestions and comments that will help to inform and improve future versions of this and all of our titles. Please give us your feedback by emailing publications@dsc.org.uk.

It should be understood that this publication is intended for guidance only and is not a substitute for professional or legal advice. No responsibility for loss occasioned as a result of any person acting or refraining from acting can be accepted by the authors or publisher.

First published 1987
Second edition 1990
Third edition 1992
Fourth edition 1994
Fifth edition 1996
Sixth edition 1998
Seventh edition 2000
Eighth edition 2002
Ninth edition 2004
Tenth edition 2006
Eleventh edition 2009
Twelfth edition 2011
Thirteenth edition 2013
Fourteenth edition 2014
Fifteenth edition 2016

Copyright © Directory of Social Change 1988, 1992, 1994, 1996, 1998, 2000, 2002, 2004, 2006, 2009, 2011, 2013, 2014, 2016

All rights reserved. **No part of this book may be stored in a retrieval system or reproduced in any form whatsoever without prior permission in writing from the publisher.** This book is sold subject to the condition that it shall not, by way of trade or otherwise, be lent, re-sold, hired out or otherwise circulated without the publisher's prior permission in any form of binding or cover other than that in which it is published, and without a similar condition including this condition being imposed on the subsequent purchaser.

The publisher and author have made every effort to contact copyright holders. If anyone believes that their copyright material has not been correctly acknowledged, please contact the publisher **who will be pleased to rectify the omission.**

The moral right of the author has been asserted in accordance with the Copyrights, Designs and Patents Act 1988.

ISBN 978 1 78482 005 3

British Library Cataloguing in Publication Data
A catalogue record for this book is available from the British Library

Cover and text design by Kate Bass
Typeset by Marlinzo Services, Frome
Printed and bound by Page Bros, Norwich

Contents

Foreword

'This is the first time I've been to the foodbank – it really is the last option. I have £2.20 in my purse, and receiving a foodbank parcel means my kids will now have food and nappies until I'll next be able to receive money. If this wasn't available, I really don't know what I would have done.'

These are the words of a mum who was referred to the foodbank after fleeing domestic abuse with her three young children. Her words are echoed at foodbanks up and down the country every day.

For The Trussell Trust, the last 16 years of working with foodbanks and communities has made it clear that stories like this are real and deeply concerning. But they are not unusual.

If you had told our founder, Paddy Henderson, that by 2016 there would be a need for over one million three-day emergency food supplies in the UK in one year, he would have been stunned. It's a long way from the small project he started in a garden shed and garage in Salisbury in 2000.

He would also have been overwhelmed and humbled by the level of response to this need. From the people who have donated a tin of tuna at the end of their weekly shop, to the grant-makers and charitable trusts who have given the incredible gifts without which none of this would be possible.

Thousands of people have helped us to start making a tangible dent in UK hunger. Charities, grant-makers, businesses and ordinary people going about their daily lives are working together, and working hard, to tackle food poverty in the UK.

DSC's *The Guide to Grants for Individuals in Need* plays such a crucial role in connecting all kinds of great causes with funders who want to make life better for others.

Social change is possible. When you connect passionate, skilled people with funding and resources, and listen to the needs of people in hardship, incredible things can happen. Donations by grant-makers and the public have enabled Trussell Trust foodbanks to help tackle a shocking and previously unmet need, and – importantly – to give people suffering in silence a voice.

It has been a difficult time for the charity sector over the past year or so, but it's so important that the sector doesn't get disheartened. There has never been a more important time to focus on providing the best possible service to the people we support. This guide will help provide the vital connections that we all need to be able to stand up for, and serve, the people struggling most in the UK today.

David McAuley
Chief Executive, The Trussell Trust
www.trusselltrust.org

Preface

During what has been a troubling and challenging year for the charity sector, it has been rewarding to take part in the research for this guide and to read of the dedicated and tireless work undertaken by trustees and charity workers, both those who are paid and those volunteers who work for no monetary reward. It is a great shame that the press when they point the finger at a particular charity for 'mismanagement' or 'fraud' can have an almost unchallenged field day and spread rumours which have little foundation in fact.

The good news that the press should be communicating to the general public is the care and dedication given by those running charities to people who are struggling and who are forced to access charity funds because the state has failed to identify and/or meet their most basic needs. The press should be applauding the professionalism and excellence within the charity sector, the compassion of its volunteers and staff and the dedication of its trustees who work without pay, developing strategy, meeting ever increasing and often new demands, setting higher standards and working within strict regulatory lines (dealing with miles of red tape). This is to benefit those who are not in good health, those who are on low, or no income, those who struggle with making their benefits go around, and those who care for others – the list could go on. We could say those who are, for one reason or another, having to apply to charities for help and often through no fault of their own because there is little available from the state.

The Research Team at DSC applauds those who work to help others in disadvantaged situations financially or otherwise, and appreciates being a part of a long-established sector which has maintained its high standards and developed to accommodate an ever-changing society and its needs.

Denise Lillya
Research Team Manager, Directory of Social Change

Introduction

Welcome to the fifteenth edition of *The Guide to Grants for Individuals in Need*. The main focus of the book is to list sources of non-statutory help for people in financial need. This edition details more than 1,500 charities with £268.5 million available in grant awards, compared with charities giving £66 million in the first edition (1987).

Grants made by charities in this guide range from £10 food vouchers to larger contributions including grants for domestic items such as washing machines, wheelchairs and house adaptations, although few will cover the whole cost of these. This kind of help does not overcome long-term financial problems, but it can be extremely valuable in helping to meet immediate needs which the state does not currently cover.

This introduction looks at the charities included in this guide and how to locate them, before discussing what help is available from them and how the charities might possibly improve their giving practices. It looks briefly at other funding sources for individuals, highlights the need to explore all statutory sources available and surveys the relevant welfare reforms and cuts to local authority budgets. Ashley Wood, formerly of the Gaddum Centre, has again provided a helpful section explaining how to make your application once the relevant charities have been identified; see page xxii. We have also tried to highlight some of the key themes that have emerged from this research process in relation to the impact of welfare reforms on grant-makers and how this may affect those wishing to apply for support.

About this guide

We aim to include publicly registered charities (including those in Scotland and Northern Ireland) which give at least £500 a year to individuals in need, although most give considerably more than this.

With a few exceptions, we do not include:

▶ Organisations which give grants solely for educational purposes
▶ Organisations which give grants to members only and not to dependants
▶ Individual employer or company welfare funds
▶ Friendly societies
▶ Local branches of national charities, although they may raise money locally for cases of need
▶ Organisations only providing services (such as home visiting) rather than cash (or in-kind) grants

Many of the charities support individuals for educational causes as well. These are included in the sister guide to this book, *The Guide to Educational Grants*, which includes details of funding opportunities for all forms of education and training up to the end of a first degree, including apprenticeships, personal development and expeditions. Some charities support organisations such as community groups, and others have large financial commitments, for instance providing housing. The entries in this guide concentrate solely on the charities' social welfare grants to individuals in need.

How charities are ordered in this guide

The charities are separated into seven sections. The first six sections contain most of the grant-makers, the majority of whom make grants to individuals across the UK. Indeed, most of the money in this book is given by the charities contained in these first six sections. The final, and largest,

section of the guide contains grant-makers whose assistance is restricted to those residing in defined geographical areas. The flowchart on page xxi shows how the guide works.

1. General charities (page 1)

This section is mostly made up of charities which operate with very wide objectives, such as the relief of 'people in need', rather than serving a distinct beneficiary group based on, for example, age, profession/trade or disability. General charities are among the best known and tend to be heavily oversubscribed.

In this part of the guide – and for the first time – we have also included a subsection which lists charities whose purpose is to relieve individuals with utility debt and arrears. These charities are associated with utility providers (such as the British Gas Energy Trust) and, whilst they are generally limited to helping only the customers of a certain provider, they can operate over broad geographical areas and assist with what is a specific but common need.

2. Charities by beneficiary (page 19)

This edition of the guide has a new section featuring charities whose eligibility criteria is focused on individuals from defined beneficiary groups. The section contains alphabetically ordered subsections. Each subsection focuses on a specific group, including children and young people, older people, individuals belonging to a particular faith, and individuals whose needs are based on specific social circumstances.

3. Illness and disability charities (page 47)

These charities give grants to people (and often their families/carers) who have an illness or disability and are in financial need as a result. Some have general eligibility criteria and support individuals with any kind of illness or disability; others assist only those affected by a particular condition. Many also give advisory and other support. For a fuller list of organisations providing these functions please see 'Advice organisations', starting on page 427.

4. Armed forces charities (page 79)

This section contains exceptionally thorough charitable provision for people who have served in the forces, whether as a regular or during national service. This funding is different from the other occupational funds as they support a large percentage of the male population that is over retirement age (many of whom would have undertaken national service). These usually also provide for the widows, widowers and dependent children of the core beneficiaries. Many of these funds have local voluntary workers who provide advice and practical help and who, in turn, are backed up by professional staff and substantial resources. SSAFA, also known as The Soldiers, Sailors, Airmen Families Association (Charity Commission no. 210760), is an influential member of this sector and a model of operation for other organisations. It is often the initial contact point, and provides the application form, for many of the regimental funds.

5. Occupational charities (page 103)

This section contains charities that benefit not only the people who worked in a particular trade but also, in many cases, their widows/widowers and dependent children.

Membership or previous membership of the particular institute can be required, but many are open to non-members. Length of service can sometimes be taken into account. Many of these charities are members of the Association of Charitable Organisations, an umbrella organisation which represents this area of the sector. Some occupations are covered by a number of funds, while others do not have an established benevolent charity. Charities affiliated to trade unions can also be found in this section.

6. Livery companies, orders and membership organisations (page 195)

This section is a recent addition to the guide and focuses on charities affiliated with membership organisations, from historic livery companies and orders to more recently established bodies. Some of the charities in this section only support members of their associated institution (and often their dependants) while others administer a range of funds with varying eligibility criteria. These charities form a distinct and unique part of the grant-making sector.

Local charities (page 203)

Included in this section are those charities whose support is restricted to individuals in localised geographical areas within the UK. Northern Ireland, Scotland and Wales each have their own chapters; Scotland and Wales are divided further into regions and then into counties. Charities based in England are first organised by region, then subdivided into counties and then broken into districts/boroughs. Charities which could fall under two chapters have generally been given a full entry in one chapter and a cross reference in the other; charities relevant to three or more of the chapters have generally been included in the national section. Charitable help is unequally distributed across the UK, often with more money available in London and the south east of England than the rest of the UK. However, many of the largest cities contain at least one large charity that is able to give over £50,000 a year.

The local section starts with details on how to use this section.

Charities in Northern Ireland

Unfortunately, the section for Northern Ireland remains limited, as very little information is available at present on charities based there. It is estimated that there are between 7,000 and 12,000 charities operating in Northern Ireland. The Charity Commission for Northern Ireland expects the completion of the registration process to take several years. In the meantime, up-to-date information on the progress of registration can be found on the Charity Commission for Northern Ireland's website: www.charitycommissionni.org.uk.

How grant-making charities can help

Some charities lament the fact that the people whom they wish to support might refuse to accept charity because of a desire to maintain their independence. A charity holds

public money for the benefit of a specific group of people. As such, just as people are encouraged to access any statutory funds they can, they should also be encouraged to accept all charitable money which has been set aside for them.

However, it is not just people who are classified as 'poor' who are eligible for support from grant-making charities. Formerly known as the 'relief of sickness', this charitable purpose was re-defined under the provisions of the Charities Act 2006, and now comes under the purpose, 'the advancement of health or the saving of lives'.

The Charity Commission guidance 'The advancement of health or the saving of lives' broadened the scope of the previous guidance, 'Charities for the Relief of Sickness' (booklet CC6), meaning a wider range of activities became charitable. The following extract is from the Charity Commission guidance, which is now available on the gov.uk site:

> The advancement of health includes the prevention or relief of sickness, disease or human suffering, as well as the promotion of health. It includes conventional methods as well as complementary, alternative or holistic methods which are concerned with healing mind, body and spirit in the alleviation of symptoms and the cure of illness....
>
> The relief of sickness extends beyond the treatment or provision of care, such as a hospital, to the provision of items, services and facilities to ease the suffering or assist the recovery of people who are sick, convalescent, disabled or infirm or to provide comforts for patients.
>
> The saving of lives includes a range of charitable activity directed towards saving people whose lives are in danger and protecting life and property.

The guidance goes on to provide examples of the sorts of charities and charitable purposes which fall within this description, such as:

- *charities that provide comforts, items, services and facilities for people who are sick, convalescent, disabled or infirm;*
- *charities that promote activities that have a proven beneficial effect on health;*
- *charities set up to assist the victims of natural disasters or war.*

Charity Commission 2013

These examples focus mainly on the physical aspect of 'relief' rather than on the financial position of people who are living with an illness or disability. This is not because grants for the advancement of health are not means-tested, but simply because these charities exist to relieve a physical need rather than a financial one. There are charitable organisations that exist to carry out either or both charitable purposes; they may either deal exclusively with the financial impact that an illness or disability can have on an individual's life or concentrate on the physical aspect of 'relief', or may address both.

Many charities believe that people should not lose their life savings and standard of living to buy an essential item that they could afford, but would leave them financially vulnerable for the future. Charity Commission guidance differentiates between organisations which attempt to relieve sickness, and organisations for the relief of the sick-poor, which can only support people who are both sick and poor.

Although these are the areas charities *may* support, it would be wrong to believe that any given grant-making organisation will support all of these needs. Each charity in this guide has a governing document, stating in which circumstances people can and cannot be supported. As noted earlier, to aid the reader in identifying those charities which are of relevance to them we have broken the charities listed into sections, and we would strongly advise that individuals do not approach a charity for which they are not eligible.

Many trustees have complained to us that they receive applications that are outside their charity's scope; those which they would like to support but their governing document prevents them from doing so. These applicants have no chance of being supported and only serve to be a drain on the charity's valuable resources. With this in mind, please remember that it is not the number of charities you apply to which affects your chance of support but the relevance of them.

What types of help can be given?

Charity Commission guidance

The following guidance from the Charity Commission outlines the definition of the prevention or relief of poverty:

The prevention or relief of poverty

In the past, the courts have tended to define 'poverty' by reference to financial hardship or lack of material things but, in current social and economic circumstances, poverty includes many disadvantages and difficulties arising from, or which cause, the lack of financial or material resources.

There can be no absolute definition of what 'poverty' might mean since the problems giving rise to poverty are multi-dimensional and cumulative. It can affect individuals and whole communities. It might be experienced on a long or short-term basis.

Poverty can both create, and be created by, adverse social conditions, such as poor health and nutrition, and low achievement in education and other areas of human development.

The prevention or relief of poverty is not just about giving financial assistance to people who lack money; poverty is a more complex issue that is dependent upon the social and economic circumstances in which it arises. The commission recognises that many charities that are concerned with preventing or relieving poverty will do so by addressing both the causes (prevention) and the consequences (relief) of poverty.

Not everyone who is in financial hardship is necessarily poor, but it may still be charitable to relieve their financial hardship under the description of purposes relating to 'the

relief of those in need by reason of youth, age, ill-health, disability, financial hardship or other disadvantage.

In most cases, the commission will treat the relief of poverty and the relief of financial hardship the same. Generally speaking, it is likely to be charitable to relieve either the poverty or the financial hardship of anyone who does not have the resources to provide themselves, either on a short or long-term basis, with the normal things of life which most people take for granted.

Examples of ways in which charities might relieve poverty include:

- *grants of money*
- *the provision of items (either outright or on loan) such as furniture, bedding, clothing, food, fuel, heating appliances, washing machines and fridges*
- *payment for services such as essential house decorating, insulation and repairs, laundering, meals on wheels, outings and entertainment, child-minding, telephone line, rates and utilities*
- *the provision of facilities such as the supply of tools or books, payments of fees for instruction, examination or other expenses connected with vocational training, language, literacy, numerical or technical skills, travelling expenses to help the recipients to earn their living, equipment and funds for recreational pursuits or training intended to bring the quality of life of the beneficiaries to a reasonable standard*

The provision of money management and debt counselling advice are examples of the ways in which charities might help prevent poverty.

See also the commission's guidance on the prevention or relief of poverty for the public benefit [www.gov.uk/government/publications/charities-supplementary-public-benefit-guidance] and social inclusion [www.gov.uk/government/collections/reviews-of-the-charity-register] and its decision on AITC Foundation [www.gov.uk/government/publications/aitc-foundation].

Charity Commission 2013

One-off grants

Some charities will only give one-off cash payments. This means that they will award a single lump sum (say £50) which is paid by cheque or postal order either directly to the applicant, to the welfare agency applying on the person's behalf, or to another suitable third party. No more help will be considered until the applicant has submitted a new application, and charities are usually unwilling to give more than one such grant per person in any given year.

Recurrent grants

Other charities will only pay recurrent grants. Recurrent payments or grants in kind are disregarded when entitlement to Income Support and Pension Credit are calculated. Although this is a long-standing principle, be aware that the rules may change with the introduction of Universal Credit so it is wise to seek appropriate advice if you are in doubt.

Some charities will give either one-off or recurrent payments according to what is more appropriate for the applicant, although some charities which give small recurrent payments may also give one-off grants for irregular expenses.

Grants in kind

Occasionally grants are given in the form of vouchers or are paid directly to a shop or store in the form of credit to enable the applicant to obtain food, clothing or other pre-arranged items. Some charities still arrange for the delivery of coal.

More commonly, especially with disability aids or other technical equipment, the charity will either give the equipment itself to the applicant (rather than the money) or loan it free of charge or at a low rental price for as long as the applicant needs it. More common items, such as telephones and televisions, can also be given directly by the charity as equipment (the charity can get better trade terms than the individual).

Statutory funding

Whilst there is a wide range of types of grants that can be given and a variety of reasons why they can be made, there is one area that charities cannot support. No charitable organisation is allowed to provide funds which replace statutory funding. The reason for this is that if a charity gives £100, say, to an individual that could have received those funds from statutory sources, then it is the state rather than the individual who is benefiting from the grant.

The effectiveness of grant-making charities

While some grant-making charities, particularly national ones, produce clear guidelines, others (often local charities) do not. Based on our experience of researching this publication over the past 20 years, we would like to make some suggestions as to ways in which charities giving grants to individuals, particularly local charities, could seek to encourage greater fairness in funding:

▌ Local charities could seek to broaden their remit to meet new or more widespread needs. During 2013 the Social Fund was abolished and replaced by localised provision. We would advise charities to speak to their local authority as well as other local grant-makers in order to define what the local priorities are and see if they can adjust or develop an approach which will ensure that no groups of people will fall beneath the radar of statutory and voluntary bodies. Charities ought to guard their independence closely and should not unduly compromise on their principles in any collaborative enterprise, but they should also consider what can be gained from co-operation, including the sharing of expertise and the potential to influence public services and reduce costs. For any charities considering this route we would recommend the excellent reports produced by Child Poverty Action Group as a starting point: cpag.org.uk/policy-publications.

▌ If trustees can only meet twice a year, they should aim to cover the peak periods. Although welfare needs arise throughout the year, there are obvious peak times such as for fuel needs in the winter months.

▌ Charities should also aim to ensure that needs can be met as rapidly as possible by, for example, empowering the clerk or a small number of trustees to make payments of amounts of up to a certain limit (such as £100).

▌ Trustees should ensure that their charity is very well known in its area of benefit. We recommend that each charity (depending on its eligibility restrictions) writes to at least the following places: all welfare agencies (especially Citizens Advice); all community centres and other public meeting points; and the offices of the relevant education authority.

▌ We would also recommend that grant-making charities consider developing a website. A website is an accessible way of raising awareness of your work as well as outlining key information such as eligibility criteria, meeting dates and types of grants given. The website does not need to be overly technical and can be as simple as one page of text. There are also many free hosting sites such as Weebly (www.weebly.com) and BT Community Web Kit (www.btck.co.uk) which make expense and professional assistance unnecessary.

The Great Giving campaign and Ineligible Applications report

Over the years DSC has campaigned on a number of fronts for better grant-making. We believe that grant-makers have a responsibility that extends far beyond providing funding.

The way in which funders operate has a huge impact on the beneficiaries which their funding supports, as well as on the wider voluntary sector.

Our Great Giving campaign has grown out of these long-established beliefs. The campaign encompasses four areas:

1   A clear picture of the funding environment

2   Accessible funding for campaigning

3   An end to hidden small print

4   No ineligible applications

Although the campaign relates mainly to grant-making charities that support organisations, the four principles of the campaign extend to the charities covered in this guide. We believe that funders have a responsibility to understand the environment in which they are operating. Some funders provide little information about where money is going and what is being supported. Providing a clearer picture will enable better planning and decision-making from funders and policy makers, as well as contributing to the growing body of knowledge about the sector.

We know that most grant-makers receive more applications for funding than they can support. We also know that a significant proportion of those applications are ineligible. In some cases the fault lies with the information provided by the funder, and in some cases the fault lies with the interpretation of that information by the applicant. In our 2010 report, *Ineligible Applications*, we made some recommendations on what grant-makers can do to try and avoid receiving large numbers of ineligible applications:

▶ Provide comprehensive and accessible information: state what you do and what you want to fund, preferably online if you have a website

▶ Ensure your application guidance is clear, concise and as jargon-free as possible: encourage prospective applicants to read it

▶ Explain the application procedure clearly: what information will be required, by when and in what form

▶ Give constructive feedback, especially if the application is rejected; this should make it less likely that the applicant submits the same ineligible bid again and again

▶ Provide a clear contact point for any queries and instructions on how you prefer to be contacted

▶ Keep track of ineligible applications and analyse them periodically to see if there are any patterns: consider how the information you provide could be changed to reduce their number

In the current financial climate (which we will touch upon more in the next section) where many grant-makers have experienced a rise in demand for their services, these recommendations are particularly important. Advertising clearly what you do and how you do it will not only empower individuals to make informed decisions about their applications, but also limit the number of ineligible applications received. This will free up vital resources and ensure more time can be spent on those individuals the charity exists to support.

Further information on our research into ineligible applications and the Great Giving campaign itself can be found on our website (www.dsc.org.uk).

The impact of welfare reform

The last five years have been a landmark period of change and upheaval for the welfare state in Britain. The changes under the Welfare Reform Act 2012, as well as major shifts in the role of local government, have reshaped the landscape of social security dramatically.

During the course of research for *The Guide to Grants for Individuals 2016/17*, we have systematically analysed information from 1,500 charitable grant-makers' annual reports, accounts and websites in the field of welfare. We have corresponded with grant-makers and investigated their experiences during this time of change and discovered the implications of this altering welfare environment on both grant-makers and beneficiaries. What we have found is a continuation, and in some cases an intensification, of existing trends, and the emergence of new challenges which charities are rising to meet.

Welfare reforms

We discussed in the previous edition of this guide (Lillya *et al.* 2014) the initial impact that the Welfare Reform Act 2012 had on beneficiaries and charities under the coalition government of 2010–15. During its term in Parliament, the coalition set out its aims to make the system of benefits in the UK 'fairer and more affordable', to reduce 'poverty, worklessness and welfare dependency' and to reduce the incidence of 'fraud and error' in the benefits system (DWP 2015).

Some of the significant changes that have been made to the welfare system have included:

▶ The introduction of Universal Credit began in 2013 with the stated aim of consolidating working-age benefits in a simplified, single payment and of encouraging the transition into employment with new responsibilities for those seeking work.

▶ Disability Living Allowance started being replaced in 2013 with Personal Independence Payment.

▶ Employment Support Allowance has been offered since 2008 (in place of Incapacity Benefit, Income Support (for illness or disability) and Severe Disablement Allowance) to those suffering from 'illness or incapacity'. Claimants for Employment Support Allowance are evaluated by a Work Capability Assessment using these criteria to determine whether they are entitled to Employment Support Allowance.

▶ A housing policy, the under-occupancy penalty – more commonly known as the 'bedroom tax' – was also introduced in 2013 and has had significant welfare implications.

▶ In May 2015, the general election brought in a Conservative majority government that has continued the existing welfare strategy.

The upheaval of the welfare system, along with considerable funding pressures, sanctions for those not meeting the strict conditions of their benefit-claim requirements and a wider governmental programme of austerity have all combined to make this a difficult few years for both individuals in need and the charities serving them.

While those in secure jobs and housing may have been somewhat cushioned from the impact of this turbulence, individuals and families on a low income have suffered, as the Joseph Rowntree Foundation described:

But there is now a growing group, a subset of those in poverty, whose circumstances, both in terms of material wellbeing and security, are far worse than five or ten years ago. This group includes those whose benefits have been sanctioned or capped, people in temporary accommodation and people who have been evicted from their homes. It is a group of people whose entitlement to state support in hard times has been restricted, and whose problems frequently manifest themselves in housing crises.

MacInnes et al. 2015

It is this group of people for whom the grant-making charities in our guide are particularly important.

INTRODUCTION

Local government

There have also been seismic shifts in the role and funding of local authorities in recent years. As we reported in the previous edition of this guide, the scrapping of the Social Fund brought an end to community care grants and crisis loans, and the responsibility to provide help to those in need was devolved to local authorities, without ring-fenced funding.

Powers for local assistance were devolved to the governments of Wales and Scotland, and a transitional Local Welfare Assistance programme was funded between 2013 and 2015 in a number of local authorities in England. However, the National Audit Office (2016) reported that many local authorities were cautious in offering replacement support under this programme, citing concerns about high demand following national welfare reforms, as well as the insecurity of future funding. Some local authorities significantly reduced or even ceased local welfare provision. With core funding for local government cut by 40% over the previous Parliament, and further cuts expected during the current Parliament (LGA 2015), many local authorities have stated that they simply cannot afford to continue welfare provision without specific government funding (NAO 2016).

The NAO report found that in the areas where local welfare assistance has ceased or diminished, charities have seen an increase in demand. This finding was echoed by some grant-makers in our research. The John William Chapman Charitable Trust (2015), for example, reported in its 2013/14 annual report, that the loss of local authority crisis support has left a 'gap in resources' for many families, leading some to turn to 'short term loan companies, shopper cheques, and in some cases unregulated loan sharks'. The charity tried to fill the gap by investing more resources in its grants programme for individuals.

The uncertainty of local government provision means that the consequences for grant-makers are unpredictable. The trustees of Mrs L. D. Rope's Third Charitable Settlement (2014) reported that in 2013/14, while there had been 'no let-up in the growing number of families and individuals who are struggling to make ends meet', the charity had experienced 'a temporary pause in demand' for its furniture provision service due to the introduction of Local Welfare Assistance in the local authority. However, the trustees highlighted the insecurity of local government funding and expected that if local authority provision is stopped, 'the relentless increase in demand for help that we have seen for this programme in recent years will resume'.

The assistance available from local government varies not only from area to area, but also from year to year. Even where provision is available, there is concern about whether the funding will be available in the long term, compounded by the insecurity in funding for other local services such as social care. As expressed in the annual report for Mrs L. D. Rope's Third Charitable Settlement (2014), 'trustees have no choice but to wait and watch, standing ready for a resumption in demand for help'.

Levels of demand

A significant number of grant-making charities, although certainly not all, reported an overall rise in demand for their services in their latest annual report. The magnitude of this reported increase varied. Some charities saw a continuation of long-term growth, such as Friends of the Elderly (2015) which reported a 7% year on year growth in applications. Others experienced a steeper rise in demand, with the Royal Theatrical Fund (2014) recording a 73% increase in new applications just in the past year.

There are, of course, multiple factors which can contribute to the level of demand a charity experiences each year. Some charities attributed higher numbers of applications to a change in their publicity strategy, such as advertising services in relevant institutions or developing their online presence. Others linked the increased pressure on their services to national welfare reforms or local government cutbacks.

In order to understand more fully why demand has risen, a number of charities have stated that they are undertaking a review, consultation or specific research project to identify the needs of their beneficiaries and how best to respond, a move which should be welcomed and encouraged.

Some charities were able to keep up with the higher level of demand by increasing their grants budget, either generally or to meet need in a specific area. This was not an option for charities that reported facing the additional challenge of a squeeze on their own income alongside increased demand for their services. In response, some charities reported that they were reducing staffing levels and drawing on volunteers, or more narrowly restricting the criteria for their grants to prioritise the groups in most need or simply as a way of coping with excessive demand.

A smaller proportion of charities recorded a reduction in demand for their services. In some cases, this could be explained by exceptionally high demand in the previous year or in others by the specific nature of their grant-making policy. The trustees of the Crediton United Charities (2015) stated that there had been a noticeable decrease in grant applications due to the opening of a local food bank, serving part of the need that the charity had previously met.

Some charities also reported a rise in individuals with specific needs, such as people at risk of homelessness, or victims of domestic violence. The Fund for Human Need (2014), for example, increased by 50% its grant budget for asylum seekers, refugees and people who are homeless.

Working-age poverty

One trend that has continued and intensified since the last edition of this guide is the growth of working-age people in poverty. In 2015, the Joseph Rowntree Foundation reported that over half of all people in poverty were either in work or living with a working adult (MacInnes et al. 2015). According to the Institute for Fiscal Studies, low-income working-age households lost out more than any other group under the welfare reforms implemented by the coalition government in the last Parliament (Browne and Elming 2015).

This trend was reflected by a number of grant-making charities in our research. Grant-makers such as NABS (2015), the charity for those working in advertising and media, reported a rise in applications from those who are in work or are of working age, and others specifically highlighted the increasing numbers of people who are in employment but suffering financial difficulties. The Association of School and College Leaders Benevolent Fund (2015) stated in its annual report: 'Ninety eight per cent of cases are members who had not yet reached retirement and some of whom were mid-career with young families.'

Similarly, the annual report for the Cameron Fund (2015) highlighted this problem, stating that 'the majority of new applications now come from GPs in the early and middle years of their careers and many of these are of an extremely complex nature'.

This is a trend noted even by those charities whose beneficiaries were previously predominantly retired individuals. For example, The Chartered Secretaries' Charitable Trust (2015) noted that, while the average age of their beneficiaries overall was still 73, most new applicants in the last year were people in their 50s.

Individuals with multiple and complex needs

Coupled with this trend in working-age poverty was a continuation of the recent rise in beneficiaries with multiple issues or more complex problems and needs. Perennial: Gardeners' Royal Benevolent Society (2015) stated in its 2014 annual report that 'the increased complexity of individual cases, remarked upon last year, has continued and therefore may need to be reviewed more frequently. In many cases, the number of presenting issues initially faced by each client has also increased.'

In order to deal with more complex cases, charities may have to review the way in which they support individuals, particularly those with problems beyond the charity's own limited remit. A number of charities noted that this increased complexity had led to more time spent on each case and more accompanying administration. As pointed out in the 2013/14 annual report of the ATS and WRAC Benevolent Fund (2015), more complex cases are 'often more costly to resolve'.

The trustees of Mrs L. D. Rope's Third Charitable Settlement (2014) described a similar situation: 'the requests for help forwarded by the social and support workers can be enormously varied and it takes time to collate the information we need to understand the application and consider its merits'. The charity needed to take on more staff to deal with this extra work. Perennial: Gardeners' Royal Benevolent Society suggested that part of the problem may be attributed to changes in the benefits system:

The complexity of individual cases reported in 2012 has continued due to a combination of the ongoing changes to the benefits system and an increase needed in the assistance with initial benefits claims, both contributing to an increase in workload above the increase in client numbers.

Perennial: Gardeners' Royal Benevolent Society 2015

A number of charities are responding to increased demand or to the changing needs of beneficiaries by either providing additional training to their personnel or hiring new members of staff who are specifically qualified to deal with the range and complexity of the problems with which beneficiaries approach them. The Royal Theatrical Fund described assistance with debt advice and welfare as 'a huge growth area' following the extensive changes and reforms in welfare in recent years, and the difficulties that vulnerable individuals can face in comprehending their entitlements:

For many people attempting to understand and find their way through this barrage of complicated and diverse new information is almost an impossibility, particularly as claimants are often suffering from physical and, on occasion, psychological health problems, as well as financial concerns.

Royal Theatrical Fund 2014

The fund responded to this need by hiring a specifically qualified Welfare and Debt Advisor to assist beneficiaries, which has so far been successful:

Already the feed-back from those she has helped has been tremendous. 'You have lifted a great load from my mind', 'For the first time in many months I am now getting the correct level of benefits' and 'I can finally sleep at nights knowing that my debt problems are going to be resolved' are just three comments from recent beneficiaries' letters and emails.

Royal Theatrical Fund 2014

This kind of advice and support should be noted as a particular achievement of the charities in this guide. Several charities reported that they were able to assist beneficiaries in applying for previously unclaimed benefits to which they were entitled, improving their long-term income without even needing to make a charitable grant. RNIB, for example, stated as one of its highlights for the year in its 2013/14 annual report: 'this year we secured £14.5 million in previously unidentified welfare benefit entitlements for blind and partially sighted people' (RNIB 2014).

Partnerships and collaboration

For charities that are increasingly being approached by beneficiaries with multiple or complex needs, partnerships can provide a cost-effective way of supporting beneficiaries in a more holistic, long-term way.

Many grant-making charities already rely on other organisations or agencies, such as Citizens Advice, social workers, health professionals or occupational bodies, to refer vulnerable individuals to their services. The Non-Ecclesiastical Charity of William Moulton emphasised the benefits of grant-making charities maintaining close working relationships with other community organisations and support workers in the area to not only publicise their support but also make improvements to their practices:

Periodic meetings with the local agency support workers to ensure that the systems and processes we have adopted work to the best benefit of the needy of Newcastle.

Feedback so received is taken into account and where appropriate adjustments made.

Trustees have decided to commence discussions with local community support organisations to establish clear lines of communication and create a greater awareness of what the Charity has to offer in terms of grant aid to assist the needy of Newcastle. This process is ongoing.

Non-Ecclesiastical Charity of William Moulton 2015

Many grant-making charities have a limited, specific remit and are unable provide all the support that these beneficiaries need on their own. This concern was expressed by the trustees of The Chartered Institute of Library and Information Professionals (CILIP) Benevolent Fund (2015): 'We remain conscious that the Fund is only a "first aid" provider of help to members who are facing financial difficulties, and that, unlike some other similar funds, we are unable to give help over a longer period.'

However, the charity has overcome this problem through partnership work and collaboration: 'Fortunately, we have established excellent relationships with other, more wealthy, Benevolent Funds and charities, who sometimes will "take over" our clients in the longer term. We also have excellent working relationships with local authorities and various social services organisations.'

Many charities collaborated with other organisations that were able to offer expertise that the grant-makers themselves could not provide, such as welfare or debt advice or mental health support.

A demand for counselling or mental health support services amongst beneficiaries was recorded by a number of grant-makers in their annual report this year. Regarding the charity's helpline, NABS (2015) reported that 'calls regarding anxiety/stress and people needing emotional support have increased'. In addition, Teacher Support Network (2014) commented on the rising levels of 'stress related illness in the education workforce'. The Rowland Hill Memorial and Benevolent Fund pointed out that financial hardship can exacerbate stress or create further mental health problems amongst beneficiaries:

The threat of bailiffs knocking on the door and the stress of losing their home and not being able to pay bills has a detrimental effect on people's health and wellbeing. Long-term sickness and an unexpected happening within the family often cause financial distress and we are proud to help employees past and present at a time when they find themselves at their most vulnerable.

Rowland Hill Memorial and Benevolent Fund 2014

A large number of the grant-makers in this guide offer counselling as part of their provision to beneficiaries, many in collaboration with other partners. The need for this kind of support was expressed by PRS Members' Benevolent Fund:

In some complex cases, it's clear that people who apply to the Fund need more specialist help to resolve underlying family issues. We're planning to work with professional family psychotherapists who will be able to help with this, providing effective long-term solutions to members.

PRS Members' Benevolent Fund 2014

The Veterinary Benevolent Fund offers an exemplary programme of support for members of the profession who are dealing with mental health problems or emotional stress:

The Veterinary Surgeons' Health Support Programme provides professional advice and treatment for those suffering from mental health and addictive disease. This is tailored to the individual's needs and incorporates telephone advice, one to one counselling and referral to inpatient treatment and local support groups.

The Veterinary Benevolent Fund 2015

The programme encompasses a number of services, including working in partnership with NHS psychiatrists in a number of locations. Beneficiaries who are evaluated as being at risk are also supported to remain at work, preventing further potential hardship. Through this programme, the charity is able to offer comprehensive, co-ordinated support to beneficiaries with complex needs:

The work of the VSHSP is a vital adjunct to the financial support that we offer those in the veterinary profession who suffer with mental health problems because often our beneficiaries' financial problems are rooted in their mental health difficulties.

The Veterinary Benevolent Fund 2015

Food banks

Over the last few years there has been a proliferation of food banks across Britain and a sharp rise in demand for their services, with over 1 million people using Trussell Trust food banks alone in 2014/15 (Trussell Trust 2015).

Food banks meet the most basic, immediate needs of the most vulnerable beneficiaries. In some cases, the opening of a food bank can reduce demand for services previously provided by grant-makers, as a couple of the charities in our sample reported.

Other grant-makers, however, have taken the opportunity to provide more co-ordinated support through collaboration with food banks in their area. The trustees of the Dacorum Community Trust (2014), for example, described in their annual report how interviews with grant applicants often revealed that a client was struggling for food, a need which the trust could then meet through its partnership with the Dacorum Food Bank.

The trustees of the Deeping St James United Charities (2015) stated in their 2014 annual report that as well as offering food bank vouchers to beneficiaries, they also provided a grant for equipment and were represented on the food bank's steering group.

The Al-Mizan Charitable Trust took this a step further and established, with five partner organisations, a new food bank, providing a number of additional services:

This model of service delivery recognises that food banks provide an opportunity to reach vulnerable people, who may have little or no engagement with statutory or voluntary sector organisations, but present themselves at the food bank in crisis.

Al-Mizan Charitable Trust 2015

This demonstrates how the partnership between grant-makers and food banks (or similar organisations) can offer a real opportunity not only to provide more comprehensive support to individuals in need but also to reach vulnerable individuals who might not otherwise be identified as beneficiaries. Al-Mizan Charitable Trust (2015) reported that 3,483 people were supported by the food bank in the first six months of opening:

> Almost a quarter of guests (23.7%) stated that the main reason for accessing the food bank was due to disruptions in the benefit payments. In contrast, 27.3% of guests were from working families who could not afford the cost of living, despite being in employment.
>
> Al-Mizan Charitable Trust 2015

Grant-making – what the figures tell us

Our headline figures show that in this edition the total amount of grants awarded to individuals for welfare purposes was £268.5 million, which means that overall grant-making has remained at a similar level to the fourteenth edition.

Where possible, we obtain figures for grant totals from charity annual reports and accounts, which are available from the Charity Commission's online register. In cases where a figure for social welfare grants to individuals was not detailed in the accounts, we have made efforts to contact the charities to gather this information. For those grant-makers for which we were unable to determine a grants total, neither from accounts nor correspondence, and for those grant-makers whose incomes fell beneath the Charity Commission's threshold to submit accounts, we made an informed estimate, based on figures for income, expenditure and, where available, previous giving.

For those charities for which we have given an estimated grant total we erred on the side of caution so as to not upwardly misrepresent the amount of grants available. We were particularly considerate as to whether or not the charities gave solely to individuals for social welfare purposes. In the cases where they also gave to individuals for educational purposes and/or to organisations, we made allowances for these figures, which may have downplayed the headline figure.

The quality of information which we are able to work with as researchers has undoubtedly improved in recent years thanks to a higher number of charities offering more detailed breakdowns of their annual activity in their annual reports and accounts. Those working at the Charity Commission should be lauded for their work in promoting the Charities Statement of Recommended Practice (more often referred to as the Charities SORP). What this has meant for us is that we have been increasingly able to retrieve more precise figures for grants awarded to individuals from the accounts immediately rather than having a single, opaque figure for 'support', 'charitable activity' or 'grants', which could include a myriad of services beyond grants, as well as grants to organisations. So our information in turn has become more accurate.

Unfortunately, however, some data has remained or become more opaque. For some charities, grant-making is often lumped in along with a broad sweep of other care services and not distinguished in the accounts. Fortunately these instances were rare.

Case studies

While overall trends portray the bigger picture, case studies can provide a direct insight into the experiences of grant-making charities and beneficiaries. In order to appreciate both sides of the story, we present two case studies: one from the perspective of a grant-maker and another from the point of view of beneficiaries. The aim is, on the one hand, to understand the charity's experience of operating in the current welfare environment and the impact of its support for beneficiaries and, on the other, to demonstrate the problems beneficiaries face and the difference that a grant can make.

Case study: grant-makers

We contacted one of the larger grant-makers in our guide, the MS Society, which supports people with Multiple Sclerosis and their families and carers. We wanted to hear about their experiences of working in the context of welfare reforms and budget cuts, about the needs of their beneficiaries and about how the charity is responding to those needs:

MS Society

Multiple sclerosis is unpredictable and incurable and affects 100,000 of us in the UK. It can cause sight loss, pain, incontinence, fatigue and disability. No-one with MS can be sure when or how it will affect them next. At the MS Society we're here for everyone living with MS – to provide practical help today, and the hope of a cure tomorrow.

Welfare support can be vital for many people with MS, helping them to manage the extra costs of the condition, stay in work for longer, live independent lives and participate fully in society. MS Society research found that:

- The current welfare system too often ignores invisible symptoms like pain and fatigue and fails to recognise how MS can fluctuate.
- Over half of the people with MS surveyed who claim disability benefits said assessments do not accurately determine the impact of their condition.
- Many people are telling us that they are not getting the support they need and are having to make difficult choices, such as whether they can afford to buy basic essentials, attend hospital appointments or spend time with family and friends.
- Having MS is enough; it should not be made harder by a welfare system that doesn't make sense for people living with the condition. In September 2015 we launched a national campaign, MS: Enough, calling on the Government to recognise the reality of living with MS and make welfare make sense.

In 2015 we asked people affected by MS about their needs for financial support:

▶ They told us they wanted access to information, advice and advocacy and also direct financial support through individual support grants.

▶ 14% of the people asked told us they are finding it more difficult to get statutory funding; as the funding criteria is narrowing and they are waiting longer to obtain assessments from health and social care professionals.

▶ They said the support grants provided by the MS society had greatly improved their quality of life.

▶ Nearly half of those who responded to our research told us that as a result of receiving a grant from us they had become more aware of other issues where they needed information and advice.

Early in 2016 we will be undertaking a comprehensive review of our grants programmes and will be working with people affected by MS to co-produce our future grants offer. We will also be exploring how we can improve our welfare benefits information and signpost people with MS to access advice and advocacy services.

We are seeking to build and extend our collaborative relationships with other organisations including trusts and foundations to increase support for people affected by MS:

▶ We will increase the number of trusts and foundations we work with.

▶ We will build on established partnerships with Citizen's Advice bureaux.

▶ We will continue to provide legal services through the disability law service.

The Association of Charitable Organisations, the national UK umbrella body for Trusts and Foundations that give grants and welfare support to individuals in need is a useful information resource and source for potential collaborative partners.

Case study: beneficiaries

We contacted the Al-Mizan Charitable Trust, another of the larger grant-makers in our guide, to gain some insight into the impact of its grant-making. The case studies below tell the stories of just two of the many beneficiaries they support.

Al-Mizan Charitable Trust's beneficiaries

The Al-Mizan Charitable Trust supports people in the UK who are in poverty, regardless of faith or cultural background, with a particular focus on people and communities who are multiply disadvantaged.

The charity provides case studies of some of the beneficiaries who have received a grant, explaining the difference it made to their lives:

Vanessa left school at 16 and worked in admin and catering, before moving into care work and

starting a degree in nursing. She is a single parent to two young daughters, aged three years and eight months. Her ex-partner used to physically abuse her in front of their children, and she managed to move out last year. However, her ex-partner found out their new address and has continued to harass Vanessa and her two daughters.

Vanessa has found a new flat in a housing association, but it is unfurnished. She is keen to give her daughters a fresh start in life and after qualifying as a nurse, she will be able to offer them proper support.

The Trust provided a grant of £220 towards a cooker for Vanessa's new flat.

....

In 2007, Bilal suffered a stroke and was left in a coma for four months. When he woke up, Bilal could not move or speak for a year and has been living in a care home. Bilal feels abandoned and lonely, as neither his parents nor siblings visit him. He has made progress in his physical therapy and is now able to move the right side of his body, but struggles to move his left side.

The Trust provided a grant of £240 towards physiotherapy, so that he could receive additional support and make further progress in his recovery.

Al-Mizan Charitable Trust 2016

These are just two good examples of the grant-makers in this guide, and the vital assistance that individuals can gain from their support.

Living standards, poverty and inequality in the UK

The following article was contributed by DSC Researcher Jodie Huyton.

During the course of carrying out work for this guide the Research Team at DSC has, among other things, studied the annual reports and accounts of over 1,500 grant-making charities in the welfare field. While focusing on the potential for funding, criteria and details of grants available, it has been interesting to record the achievements and challenges of grant-making charities.

Changes made under the Welfare Reform Act 2012 have arguably pushed thousands of people further into poverty. The article highlights the major themes identified throughout our research in relation to living standards, poverty and inequality in the UK.

Food banks

The need for food banks has soared in recent years: in 2014/15 over 1 million people were fed nationwide. There is now an extensive network of food banks providing emergency food supplies for individuals in need across the UK. Rising food and fuel prices, static incomes, under-employment and changes in the benefits system are some of the reasons why an increasing number of people are being referred to food banks (Trussell Trust 2016). Food poverty is one of the starkest indicators of inequality in the UK and greater welfare cuts increase the likelihood of a food bank opening (Cooper *et al.* 2014).

Case study

The following extract is reproduced from *Below the breadline: the relentless rise of food poverty in Britain*:

Tracy lives in Ilford, Essex with her partner and baby daughter. Her partner is a teaching assistant; Tracy has been in and out of low-paid work since leaving school at 16. She also suffers from long-term depression and is currently on ESA (Employment Support Allowance). Tracy and her baby daughter came to Tower Hamlets Food Bank after being referred by her daughter's social worker. Tracy's partner is only paid during term-time, but their social security payments are paid at the same rate throughout the year. This means that during school holidays the couple receive just £6 in social security payments, which is their total weekly income ... In addition, budget cuts have meant that her partner's hours were slashed from 13 to seven a week. 'Before my maternity pay we used to have just half a meal a day ... Tracy was concerned about the quality of their food, but felt she had no choice.' Meat is so expensive these days. When I was growing up we'd only have fish fingers or something once or twice a week, and proper food the rest of the time, now it's the other way around. We only have proper meat once a month now.' 'I'm disappointed I've had to use a food bank as you want to be able to survive on your own, but at least there are people out there who help, that is nice.'

Cooper et al. 2014

Food banks are a sign of fundamental failure in society and they should not become an ever-growing feature of life in 21st century Britain – it's a step back in time and reminiscent of the soup kitchens of the Great Depression of the 1930's. According to Cooper *et al.* (2014) the government must commit to understanding the mass scale of the issue, and then set out steps to address the problem. If mistakes or lack of care in policy are not rectified many people are going to continue with their daily struggle.

Housing

Welfare cuts and a growing housing crisis continue to put a burden on people's finances and capability to stay in their homes. Between 1 July and 30 September 2015, local housing authorities received over 29,000 applications for housing assistance under the homelessness legislation of the Housing Act 1996 (Department for Communities and local government 2015). Jilani (Oxfam 2014) found that 300,000 households have experienced a cut in housing benefit, 920,000 a reduction in council tax support and 480,000 a cut in both. Furthermore, a recent survey by YouGov and Shelter found that nearly 4 million families were only one pay cheque away from losing their homes, and that 2.4 million families would lose their home immediately if they lost their jobs tomorrow (Cooper *et al.* 2014). Cooper *et al.* also identify high housing costs and stagnating wages as the causes of this situation, with people living from month to month with no money left over to save.

Debt and mental health

Many people in the UK are struggling with debt in unprecedented numbers. Debt charity StepChange warns that the number of people needing help to manage their debts has risen by 56% since 2012. More than half a million people have sought help in the past year alone, their individual debts averaging over £14,000 (StepChange 2015).

There is a well-established link between debt and mental health. Research has indicated that mental health issues can be both a consequence and catalyst of debt problems; symptoms include anxiety and stress, depression, self-harm and suicidal thoughts (Mind 2008). However, whilst the dangers of debt are well publicised, what isn't spoken about enough is the negative impact it can have on a person's mental health (Rethink 2015). According to the Money Advice Trust (2016) in a time of increased debt problems, it is vital that creditors have a robust mechanism in place for dealing with customers suffering with debt and mental health issues. Mind (2008) calls for all creditors to have procedures in place to ensure that people in debt who have mental health problems are treated fairly and appropriately.

Resilience of grant-makers

The issues raised highlight just a few of the problems that thousands of individuals in the UK face. Throughout our research we have seen how grant-makers have adapted their policies and practices in order to meet the changes in the benefits system and the complexity of cases from their beneficiaries due to welfare reforms. For example, they have made smaller grants to more people, tightened their charity's funding criteria or drawn on free reserves. In the context of the issues discussed, we hope this guide will be a source of support for individuals in need and the organisations supporting those individuals.

Advice for applicants

While there is still a large amount of money available to help applicants, the competition seems likely to remain strong. It is difficult to say how grant-makers will fare in the coming years, but it is unlikely that those who are dipping into reserves can continue to do so indefinitely, and so charities will be looking to ensure that they are making the maximum possible impact with their grants.

For those individuals applying for funding the same basic principles apply – see page xxii for Ashley Wood's excellent step-by-step guide. However, in the current climate it is worth bearing a few extra things in mind.

▶ **Check the latest criteria:** Financial pressures and rising applications have led many charities to tighten up their eligibility criteria or limit the things for which they will give. Make sure that you have the latest guidelines and read them carefully to check that you are eligible to apply and the charity can help with your specific need.

If in doubt, a quick phone call is usually welcomed and can save time for both parties in the long run.

▶ **Be open and honest when applying:** Take care to fill in any application form as fully as possible and try to be as clear and open as you can. The same applies if you need to write a letter of application. It will help grant-makers to assess your needs quickly and advise you on any other benefits or potential sources of funding for which you may be eligible.

▶ **Don't just apply to large, well-known charities:** These charities are likely to be the most oversubscribed, leaving you with less chance of success. Take the time to look for others you may also be eligible to apply for.

▶ **Apply to all appropriate charities:** Falling average amounts of grants may mean that one grant-maker cannot offer enough to cover the full cost of the item or service you need. You may have to consider applying to several charities and asking for a small contribution from each. If it has not been indicated already for any given charity in this guide whether calls are welcome or not, it is usually appropriate to make a quick phone call to establish how much they are likely to give for an individual grant.

▶ **Seek advice:** Some applications require a third-party endorsement. With advice services under increasing pressure, you may find an alternative organisation to contact in this guide; these organisations are listed on page 427. Also consider other impartial professionals who may be able to assist with an application form such as a school teacher if the application is on behalf of a child, or a medical practitioner such as a GP, consultant or therapist if the application is for a medical item or is related to a medical condition. Others who may be able to help include ministers of religion, social workers, local housing associations or probation officers. It is advisable to make a quick telephone call to the grant-maker to determine whether they can be flexible regarding who completes the application in exceptional circumstances.

Other sources of support

Whilst there are many situations in which approaching a charity might be the best option, there is, of course, a limit to the support that they can provide, individually or collectively. There are a number of alternative sources of support that should be considered in conjunction with looking at grant-makers. These are beyond the scope of this publication, but the following sections offer signposts to where to find further information.

Statutory sources

There are some funding opportunities available to individuals from the state. The exact details of these sources vary in different countries in the UK, and in some instances among different local authorities. This area is likely to become ever more confusing in the light of further budget cuts and welfare reforms. Consequently, comprehensive details are beyond the scope of this guide.

However, full details should be available from government departments such as benefits agencies and social services, as well as many of the welfare agencies listed, starting on page 427. The government's website (www.gov.uk) and the DWP website (www.dwp.gov.uk) also have a wealth of information on what is available and how to apply.

There are a number of advice organisations that may be able to offer guidance and support to people who are unsure of their benefit entitlement or who are looking for extra support in the form of a grant. It may also prove useful to visit websites such as Turn2Us (www.turn2us.org.uk) which can offer advice on statutory and non-statutory sources of funding that are either given directly to individuals or available to individuals via the charities that are working on behalf of those individuals in need.

Citizens Advice provides an online advice guide (www.adviceguide.org.uk) and offers useful information on issues relating to statutory benefits and individual entitlement. Local branches of Citizens Advice can also offer people more assistance in this area.

Food banks

Food banks exist to support people who, due to a crisis or emergency, cannot afford to feed themselves. Food banks in the UK are diverse and how they operate varies, but they are generally run by volunteers who distribute food parcels via local churches and other community organisations. In the UK, the biggest provider of emergency food relief is The Trussell Trust, which has launched more than 420 food banks nationwide, and there are many more organisations and groups also working to support people who are facing food poverty.

The way to access assistance can vary depending on the food banks in your area; however, it is usually via referral from a care professional (such as a social worker, Citizens Advice or another welfare agency) who issues the individual who is in need of assistance with a voucher. This voucher can then be redeemed in exchange for a food parcel to last usually in the range of three to five days, depending on the food bank's policy. Some food banks can also provide other support through signposting to other welfare organisations. Information on food banks in your area can be found online or alternatively you can contact your local Citizens Advice.

Money advice

Many of the grant-makers in this guide specify that, before applying for a grant, individuals should seek professional financial or debt advice first. Your local Citizens Advice can provide free money advice, as can National Debtline (mymoneysteps.org) and Debt Advice Foundation (debtadvicefoundation.org), which are both accredited by the Money Advice Service (moneyadviceservice.org.uk). Alternatively, the Money Advice Service provides an easy-to-use online search for local debt advice services, which lists Citizens Advice and other agencies that work to provide free financial advice in your area. You can also see the 'Advice organisations' on page 427 for contact details of free money advice providers.

Disaster appeals

In the event of a disaster or other humanitarian crisis the public's reaction is often to help the victims as quickly as possible, and one way to do so is to launch a disaster appeal. These are commonly set up as a public response to a well-publicised disaster, such as the London bombings in July 2005, or the South Yorkshire floods in 2007, where the public wish to show their support. They can also be established in response to a personal misfortune; The Mark Davies Injured Riders Fund, for instance, was established to support injured riders, by the parents of a talented rider killed during the Burghley Horse Trials. For comprehensive advice and guidance on whether to launch an appeal by an existing charity, assist an established charity in its efforts to help with the effects of the crisis, or set up a non-charitable appeal fund, please view the Charity Commission leaflet, CC40 *Disaster Appeals*.

Companies

Many employers are concerned to see former members of staff or their dependants living in need or distress. Few have formal arrangements, but if you send a letter or make a telephone call to the personnel manager you should be able to establish whether the company will be able to assist.

Many large and some of the smaller companies give charitable grants, although most have a policy of only funding organisations. Those that will support individuals have their own charitable foundations or benevolent funds for ex-employees, and therefore are included in this guide.

There has been a growing trend for many prominent utility companies to establish charities which give to individuals who are struggling to pay their utility bills. These charities have continued to grow and have for a number of years provided much relief to the individuals involved, lessening the financial burden on them and ensuring that no legal action will be taken against them for non-payment of bills.

Community foundations

Over recent years, community foundations have established themselves as a key community resource. According to UK Community Foundations' website, there are 48 community foundations throughout the UK which distribute around £65 million grants a year and they hold, as at January 2016, £500 million in endowed funds.

Community foundations aim to be cause-neutral and manage funds donated to them by both individuals and organisations, which are then distributed to the local communities which they serve.

Whilst most community foundations only support organisations, some also have funds available for individuals and are therefore included in this guide. The UK Community Foundations' website has a complete list and a map of community foundations (see ukcommunityfoundations.org).

Please note that, like most sources of financial support, funding for individuals is subject to frequent change. Even if your local community foundation is included in this guide, it is worth checking the availability on your local community foundation website.

Ministers of religion

There may be informal arrangements within a church, mosque, etc. to help people in need. Ministers of religion are often trustees of local charities which are too small to be included in the guide.

Hospitals

Most hospitals have patient welfare funds, but they are little-known, even within the hospitals, and so are not used as frequently as other sources of funds. It may take some time to locate an appropriate contact. Start with the trust fund administrator or the treasurer's department of the health authority.

Local organisations

Rotary Clubs, Lions Clubs, Round Tables and so on are active in welfare provision. Usually they support groups rather than individuals and policies vary in different towns, but some welfare agencies (such as Citizens Advice) have a working relationship with these organisations and keep up-to-date lists of contacts. All enquiries should be made by a recognised agency on behalf of the individual.

Orders

Historic organisations such as the Masonic and RAOB (known as Buffs) Lodges exist for the mutual benefit of their members and the wider community. Spouses and children of members (or deceased members) may also benefit, but people unconnected with these orders are unlikely to do so. Applications should be made to the Lodge where the parent or spouse is or was a member.

Hobbies and interests

People with a particular hobby or interest should find out whether this offers any opportunities for funding. Included in this guide are a number of sporting associations which exist to relieve people who are in need, but there may be many more which are not registered with the Charity Commission, or have less than £500 a year to give, but are of great value to the people they can help. It is likely that other sports and interests have similar governing bodies wishing to help their members either through making a donation or organising a fundraising event.

Educational support

This guide only deals with grants for the relief of need, ignoring grant-makers which can support individuals for educational purposes. However, many educational charities are prepared to give grants to schoolchildren for uniforms, for instance. Receiving financial support for the cost of uniforms would obviously enable parents to spend the money budgeted for that purpose on other needs, so people with children of school age should check for any educational grants available to them. For information on statutory funds, contact your local educational authority or enquire for information at the office of the individual's school. For charitable funding, this guide's sister publication, *The Guide to Educational Grants*, provides information on over 1,000 grant-making charities that give throughout the UK.

Charity shops

Some charity shops will provide clothing if the applicant has a letter of referral from a recognised welfare agency.

Getting help

Unfortunately, these methods can only offer temporary relief. Applying for grants can be a daunting experience, especially if you are unfamiliar with the process; it is probably worth starting with the help of a sympathetic advisor. Most branches of Citizens Advice have money advice workers or volunteers who are trained in money advice work. If you find that you are in financial need, try going to the nearest Citizens Advice and talk to an advisor about your financial difficulties. They may be able to help write an application to an appropriate charity, know of a welfare benefit you could claim or be able to re-negotiate some of your debt repayments on your behalf. They will certainly be able to help you minimise your expenditure and budget effectively.

Acknowledgements

Throughout this introduction, we have commented on the Charity Commission for England and Wales's guidelines and advice. Whilst we are aware that the Charity Commission for England and Wales only has rule over those countries, readers in Northern Ireland and Scotland (as well as the Isle of Man and the Channel Islands) should note that, although the exact nature of charitable law differs in these countries, the spirit and guidance remains the same throughout the UK and the Charity Commission's advice should be seen as being just as relevant.

We would like to offer a special thank you to Al-Mizan Charitable Trust, MS Society and The Trussell Trust for their contribution to this introduction.

We are extremely grateful to the many people, charity trustees, staff and volunteers, and others who have helped compile this guide. To name them all would be impossible.

A request for further information

The research for this book was done as carefully as we were able, but there will be relevant charities that we have missed and some of the information is incomplete or will become out of date. If any reader comes across omissions or mistakes in this guide, please let us know so we can rectify them. A telephone call or email to the Research Department of the Directory of Social Change (0151 708 0136; email: research@dsc.org.uk) is all that is needed. We are also always looking for ways to improve our guides and would appreciate any comments, positive or negative, about this guide, or suggestions on what other information would be useful for inclusion when we research for the next edition.

References

Al-Mizan Charitable Trust (2015), annual report and accounts 2013/14, Watford, Al-Mizan Charitable Trust

Al-Mizan Charitable Trust (2016), 'Case Studies' [web page], available at: www.almizantrust.org.uk, accessed 26 Jan 2016

Association of School and College Leaders Benevolent Fund (2015), annual report and accounts 2014, Leicester, The Association of School and College Leaders Benevolent Fund

ATS and WRAC Benevolent Fund (2015), annual report and accounts 2013/14, Winchester, The Women's Royal Army Corps Association

Browne, James and William Elming (2015), *The effect of the coalition's tax and benefit changes on household incomes and work incentives*, London, IFS

Cameron Fund (2015), annual report and accounts 2014, Richmond, The Cameron Fund

Charity Commission (2013), 'Charitable Purposes' [web page], dated September 2013, accessed 20 February 2016, available at www.gov.uk/government/publications/charitable-purposes

Chartered Secretaries' Charitable Trust (2015), annual report and accounts 2013/14, The Chartered Secretaries' Charitable Trust

CILIP Benevolent Fund (2015), annual report and accounts 2014, Gravesend, Chartered Institute of Library and Information Professionals Benevolent Fund

Cooper, N., S. Purcell and R. Jackson (2014), *Below the breadline: the relentless rise of food poverty in Britain* [online report], Church Action on Poverty, Oxfam and The Trussell Trust, www.trusselltrust.org, dated June 2014, accessed 15 January 2016

Crediton United Charities (2015), annual report and accounts 2013/14, Crediton, Crediton Relief in Need Charity

Dacorum Community Trust (2015), annual report and accounts 2013/14, Hemel Hempstead, Dacorum Community Trust

Deeping St James United Charities (2015), annual report and accounts 2014, Peterborough, Deeping St James United Charities

Department for Communities and local government (2015), *Statutory Homelessness: July to September Quarter 2015 England,* available at www.gov.uk, dated December 2015, accessed 15 January 2016

DWP (2015), *2010 to 2015 government policy: welfare reform,* Department for Work and Pensions

Friends of the Elderly (2015), annual report and accounts 2013/14, London, Friends of the Elderly

Jilani, J. (2014), *Almost 2 million of the poorest households pushed deeper into poverty by welfare cuts,* Oxfam, www.oxfam.org.uk, dated April 2014 accessed 15 January 2016

John William Chapman Charitable Trust (2015), annual report and accounts 2013/14, Doncaster, JW Chapman Earlesmere Charitable Trust

LGA (2015), *Future funding outlook for councils 2019/20: interim 2015 update,* London, Local Government Association

Lillya, Denise, Jennifer Reynolds and Gabriele Zagnojute (2014), *The Guide to Grants for Individuals in Need,* London, Directory of Social Change

MacInnes, Tom *et al.* (2014), *Monitoring poverty and social exclusion 2015,* York, Joseph Rowntree Foundation

Mind (2008), *In the Red: Debt and Mental Health* [online report], Mind, available at www.mind.org.uk, accessed 15 January 2016

Money Advice Trust (2016),'Debt and mental health' [web page], available at www.moneyadvicetrust.org, accessed 15 January 2016

Mrs L. D. Rope's Third Charitable Settlement (2014), annual report and accounts 2013/14, Woodbridge, Mrs L. D. Rope's Third Charitable Settlement

NABS (2015), annual report and accounts 2014, London, NABS

NAO (2016), *Local welfare provision: report by the Comptroller and Auditor General,* London, National Audit Office

Non Ecclesiastical Charity of William Moulton (2015), annual report and accounts 2014, North Shields, Non Ecclesiastical Charity of William Moulton

Oxfam (2016), 'Poverty in the UK' [web page], available at: policy-practice.oxfam.org.uk/our-work/poverty-in-the-uk, accessed 15 January 2016

Perennial (2015), annual report and accounts 2014, Leatherhead, Gardeners' Royal Benevolent Society

PRS Members' Benevolent Fund (2014), annual report and accounts 2014, London, PRS for Music Members' Benevolent Fund

Re-think (2015), 'Mental health and debt: knowing the facts and where to seek help', Rethink: News and views, available at www.rethink.org/news-views/2015/08/debt, dated August 2015, accessed 15 January 2016

RNIB (2014), annual report and accounts 2013/14, London, The Royal National Institute of Blind People

Rowland Hill Memorial Benevolent Fund (2014), annual report and accounts 2013/14, London, Rowland Hill Memorial Benevolent Fund

Royal Theatrical Fund (2015), annual report and accounts 2013/14, London, The Royal Theatrical Fund

Step Change Debt Charity (2015), 'A rising economic tide, but many left drowning in debt', www.stepchange.org/Mediacentre/Pressreleases, accessed 15 January 2016

Teacher Support Network (2014), annual report and accounts 2013, London, Teacher Support Network

Trussell Trust (2015), 'Trussell Trust Foodbank Statistics' [web page], available at: www.trusselltrust.org, accessed 26 Jan 2016

Trussell Trust (2016), 'What we do' [web page], available at: www.trusselltrust.org/what-we-do/how-foodbanks-work/, accessed 15 January 2016

Veterinary Benevolent Fund (2015), annual report and accounts 2014, London, Veterinary Benevolent Fund

Note: all annual reports and accounts are available on the Charity Commission for England and Wales website.

How to use this guide

Below is a typical charity entry, showing the format we have used to present the information obtained from each of the charities.

On the following page is a flowchart. We recommend that you follow the order indicated in the flowchart to look at each section of the guide and find charities that are relevant to you. You can also use the information in the sections 'About this guide' and 'How to make an application' to help inform your applications.

The Fictitious Charity

£24,000 (120 grants)

Correspondent: Ms I. M. Helpful, Charities Administrator, 7 Pleasant Road, London SN0 0ZZ (020 7123 4567; email: admin@fictitious.org.uk; website: www.fictitious.org.uk).

CC Number: 112234

Eligibility
People who live in London and are in need. Preference is given to older people and to single parent families.

Types of grants
Small one-off grants of up to £250 are given for a wide range of needs including white goods, beds and medical equipment.

Annual grant total
In 2014 the charity had assets of £132,000 and an income of £27,000. Grants to 120 individuals amounted to £24,000.

Other information
The charity also makes grants to individuals for educational purposes.

Exclusions
No grants are given for items already purchased.

Applications
Application forms are available from the charity's website. They can be submitted directly by the individual or, if necessary, by a third party such as a social worker or doctor. They are considered monthly.

Award and no. of grants
This shows the total amount given in grants during the financial year in question. Where further information was available, we have also included the total number of grants made.

Correspondent
This shows the name and contact details of the charity's correspondent. In many cases, this correspondent is the same contact listed on the charity's record at the Charity Commission; however, in cases where we could find a more appropriate correspondent on a charity's website, we have included their name here instead.

Charity Commission number
This is the number given to a charity upon registration with the Charity Commission. A small number of the grant-makers detailed in this guide are not registered charities and so do not have a Charity Commission number.

Eligibility
This states who is eligible to apply for a grant. Criteria can be based on, for example, place of residence, age, health or occupation.

Types of grants
This section specifies whether the charity gives one-off or recurrent grants, the size of grants given and for which items or costs grants are actually given. This section will also indicate if the charity runs various schemes.

Annual grant total
This shows the total amount of money given in grants to individuals in the last financial year for which there were figures available. Other financial information may be given where relevant.

Other information
This section contains other helpful or interesting information about the charity.

Exclusions
This field gives information, where available, on what the charity will not fund.

Applications
This section includes information on how to apply, who should make the application (i.e. the individual or a third party) and when to submit an application.

How to identify sources of help - a quick reference flowchart

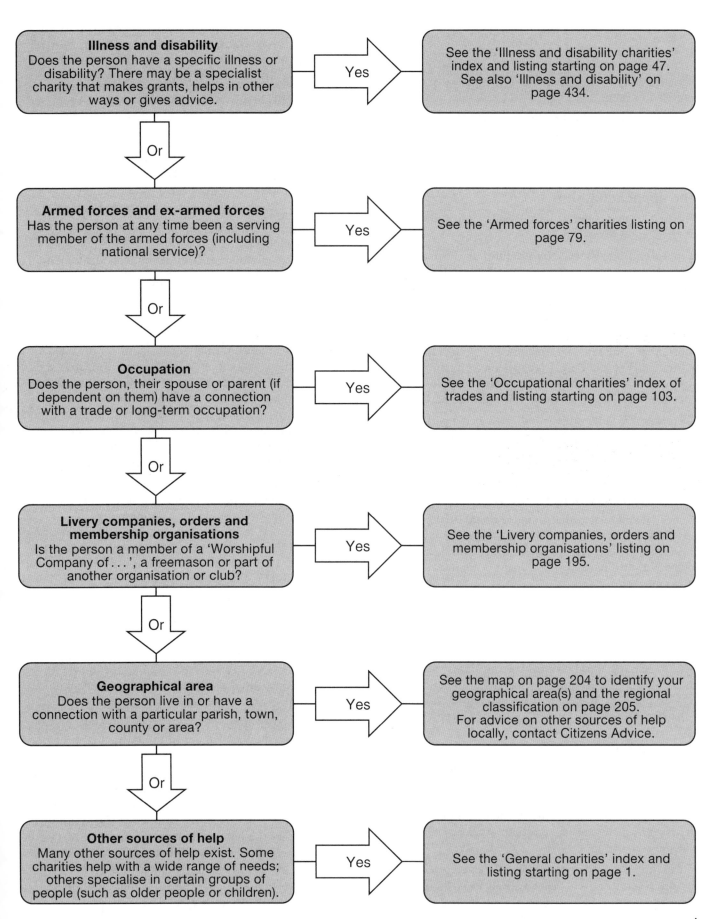

Illness and disability
Does the person have a specific illness or disability? There may be a specialist charity that makes grants, helps in other ways or gives advice.

Yes → See the 'Illness and disability charities' index and listing starting on page 47. See also 'Illness and disability' on page 434.

Or

Armed forces and ex-armed forces
Has the person at any time been a serving member of the armed forces (including national service)?

Yes → See the 'Armed forces' charities listing on page 79.

Or

Occupation
Does the person, their spouse or parent (if dependent on them) have a connection with a trade or long-term occupation?

Yes → See the 'Occupational charities' index of trades and listing starting on page 103.

Or

Livery companies, orders and membership organisations
Is the person a member of a 'Worshipful Company of . . .', a freemason or part of another organisation or club?

Yes → See the 'Livery companies, orders and membership organisations' listing on page 195.

Or

Geographical area
Does the person live in or have a connection with a particular parish, town, county or area?

Yes → See the map on page 204 to identify your geographical area(s) and the regional classification on page 205. For advice on other sources of help locally, contact Citizens Advice.

Or

Other sources of help
Many other sources of help exist. Some charities help with a wide range of needs; others specialise in certain groups of people (such as older people or children).

Yes → See the 'General charities' index and listing starting on page 1.

How to make an application

This section was contributed by Ashley Wood, former Chief Executive of the Gaddum Centre, based in Manchester.

Once the appropriate charities have been identified, the next stage is the application itself. People often find making applications difficult and those who might benefit sometimes fail to do so because of the quality of the application submitted.

This article gives guidelines both to individuals applying directly and to welfare agencies applying on behalf of individuals on how to make good, clear and relevant applications.

The application form

The first stage in submitting an application is the question of application forms.

Applications on agency letter headings or personal letters direct from the applicant, no matter how well presented, are fairly pointless if the charity being approached has a specific application form which must be completed. This obvious point is often overlooked. It is frustrating when the application is returned with a blank form requesting substantially the same information as has already been submitted. The resulting delay may mean missing a committee meeting where the application would have been considered and a considerable wait until the next one.

Entries in this guide usually indicate when a particular application form is needed, but if there is any doubt the applicant should make a preliminary telephone call to the charity.

Who submits the application?

Again, it is important that an appropriate person sends the application. The guide usually indicates whether an individual in need can apply on his/her own behalf, or whether a third party (professional or otherwise) must apply for them.

In recognition of 'empowerment' of service users, advisory bodies sometimes simply advise families of funds they can approach themselves. However, many charities require applications and forms where appropriate to be completed by, for example, a professional person who is sponsoring the application. Therefore, the individual in need may have to press the agency to make an application on his/her behalf.

The questions

When application forms are used, the questions asked sometimes cause problems, often because they don't appear relevant. Applicants sometimes fail to realise all charities are governed by criteria laid down in their trust deeds and usually specific questions are designed to ensure these criteria are met.

For example, questions concerning date and place of birth are often answered very vaguely. 'Date of birth' is sometimes answered with 'late 50's' or, even worse,

'elderly'. Such a reply reflects the appearance of the person in question and not their age! If the charity can only consider applications for those below a pensionable age, and the request was on behalf of a woman, then the above answers would be too imprecise.

Equally 'Place of birth' is sometimes answered with 'Great Britain' which is not precise enough for funds whose area of benefit is regional or local. It is always better to state the place of birth as well as town and county, even if they are different from the current home address.

Where application forms are not requested, it is essential to prepare clear, concise applications that provide:

1. A description of the person or family and the need which exists

Although applications should be concise, they must provide sufficient detail, such as:

1 The applicant's name, address, place and date of birth

2 The applicant's family circumstances (i.e. married/ partners, separated/divorced/single parent, widow/ widower, the number and ages of dependent children)

3 The applicant's financial position (i.e. breakdown of weekly income and expenditure and, where appropriate, DWP/housing benefit awarded/refused, savings, credit debts, rent/gas/electricity arrears, etc.)

4 Other relevant information, such as how the need arose (e.g. illness, loss of job, marital separation, etc.) and why other sources (especially DWP/housing departments) have not helped. If applying to a disability charity, applicants should include details of the nature and effects of the disability (although see Medical information below); if applying to a local charity, how long have they lived in the locality.

The application, which says 'this is a poor family who need their gas reconnecting', is unlikely to receive proper consideration. It is also worth mentioning that applications are dealt with in the strictest of confidence, so applicants should aim to provide as much information as is relevant. The form printed after this article may serve as a useful checklist to ensure that all relevant information is included for the particular application.

2. How much money is requested and what it will be used for

This second point appears to cause the most difficulty. Applications are often received without any indication of the amount required or without sufficient explanation as to the desired use of the money.

For example, an applicant may have multiple debts totalling over £1,000. A grant of £100 would clear one of the debts and free much-needed weekly income. So the applicant approaches a suitable charity for a grant of £100. If the applicant explains the situation clearly, trustees can see that a £100 grant in this instance would be an effective use of their charity's resources. However, if it is not made clear, trustees can only guess at the possible benefits of the grant. Because they are unwilling to take undue risks with charitable money, trustees may either turn down an incomplete application or refer it for more information, which inevitably means delays.

Charity and the state

Charities are not supposed to give grants for items that are covered by statutory sources. However, the Big Lottery and increasing reforms to the welfare state have made it much more difficult to say where statutory provision ends and charitable provision begins.

Similarly, means testing under some state provision such as Disabled Facilities Grants regulations can create shortfalls between the amount that statutory sources can and will pay, and the full costs of equipment and adaptations to properties. Sometimes, because of what can and cannot be taken into account, assessments of what families can pay appear unrealistic. Where this is the case it should be stated.

Changes arising from tightening of eligibility criteria and Community Care legislation are creating new areas of unmet need. If individuals are applying to charity because statutory provision is clearly no longer adequate, they should make it clear in the application that they have exhausted all possible statutory sources of funding but they are still left with a shortfall. A supporting reference from a knowledgeable agency may be helpful.

Where the identified need is not met, following any assessment process, applications for alternative or complementary finance should make the reasons clear.

The way that social and health care services are provided is changing. Traditionally, the state assessed an individual's need, and then provided, or arranged for those assessed services to be provided. The change gives those assessed as eligible for services, the money to purchase them themselves by way of an Individual Budget. The aim is to give more independence and choice of services purchased. It is accepted that this is a radical change for many people. Applications to charities, particularly those with social care needs may well have to reflect the services already being purchased from an individual budget, with a cogent argument as to how what is now being applied for is needed and improves quality of life.

Realism

It helps to be realistic. Sometimes families have contributed to their own situation. The applicant who admits this and seems not to expect miracles but rather seeks to plan afresh – even if with fingers crossed – will often be considered more positively than the applicant who philosophises about deprivation and the imperfections of the political regime of the day.

Likewise, the application, which tries to make the trustees feel guilty and responsible for the impending doom which is predicted for the most vulnerable members of the family unless money is given, is unlikely to impress experienced trustees, however sympathetic.

In general, be clear and factual, not moralising and emotional. In effect, a good application attempts to identify the need and promote possible resolutions.

Applications to more than one charity

Where large amounts are being sought, it can take months to send applications one at a time and wait for the outcome of each before applying to another. However, if a number of applications are being sent out together, a paragraph explaining that other charities are being approached should be included together with a commitment to return any surplus money raised. It is also worth saying if any other applications have been successful in contributing to the whole – nothing succeeds like success!

The same application should not be sent off indiscriminately. For example, if somebody is applying to a trade charity on behalf of a child whose deceased father had lengthy service in that particular trade, then a detailed description of the deceased father's service would be highly relevant. If an application for the same child was being made to a local charity, it would not.

Sometimes people who are trustees of more than one charity receive three or four identical letters, none tailored to that particular charity and none indicating that other grant-making organisations have been approached. The omission of such details and the neglect of explanations raise questions in the minds of trustees, which in the end can result in delays or even refusal.

Timing

When applying to charities, remember the time factor, particularly in cases of urgent need. Committees often sit monthly, or even quarterly. Without knowledge but with 'luck', an application can be received the day before the meeting – but if Murphy's Law operates it will always arrive the day after. For the lack of a little homework, applications may not be considered in time.

From experience, few organisations object to a telephone call being made to clarify criteria, dates of meetings or requests for application forms. So often it seems that applicants leave the whole process to chance, which leads to disillusionment, frustration and wasted time for all concerned.

Savings

When awarding a grant, most trustees take the applicant's savings into account. Some applicants may think this unnecessarily intrusive, but openness and honesty make for a better presented application and saves time. However, sometimes savings may not need to affect trustees' calculations.

For example, if a woman has a motor accident in which she was not at fault but which leaves her permanently disabled, she will receive compensation (often a one-off lump sum) through the guilty party's insurance company based on medical prognoses at the time. If her condition deteriorates faster and further than anticipated, requiring her to obtain an expensive item of equipment, it could well be argued that this should not be paid for out of the compensation awarded. The compensation was paid to cover factors such as loss of earnings potential, a reduced quality of life, reduced ability to easily fulfil basic household tasks and a general loss of future security, not to pay for unexpected and expensive pieces of equipment.

In such circumstances, the applicant should include a paragraph in the application to explain why his/her savings are not relevant to grant calculations.

In conclusion

Two final points should be borne in mind.

1. Be clear

Firstly, social care & health care professionals often resort to the use of jargon when plain English would be more effective. There appears to be two extremes; one to present a report on the basis that the trustees are not very intelligent lay people who need to be educated, or alternatively that they are all psychotherapists who need to be impressed. Usually, this only causes confusion.

2. Medical information

Secondly, medical information should not be presented without an accurate medical diagnosis to support it. Applicants' or social workers' presumptions on medical matters are not relevant. Often what is necessary is to explain why a financial need arises from a particular condition. This may be because of the rarity of the condition or the fluctuating nature of it.

The medical information should be presented by a professional in that field. The task of the applicant or the sponsor is to explain the implications of the condition.

Ashley Wood
Former Assistant Chief Executive
Gaddum Centre

Using the application form template for financial assistance

Over the page is a general-purpose application form. It has been compiled with the help of Gaddum Centre. It can be photocopied and used whenever convenient and should enable applicants (and agencies or people applying on behalf of individuals) to state clearly the basic information required by most grant-makers.

Alternatively, applicants can use it as a checklist of points to include in the letter. Applicants using this form should note the following things in particular:

1 It is worth sending a short letter setting out the request in brief, even when using this application form.

2 Because this form is designed to be useful to a wide range of people in need, not all the information asked for in the form will be relevant to every application. For example, not all applicants are in receipt of state benefits, nor do all applicants have HP commitments.
   In such cases, applicants should write 'N/A' (not applicable) in the box or on the line in question.

3 If, similarly, you do not have answers for all the questions at the time of applying – for example, if you have applied to other charities and are still waiting for a reply – you should write 'Pending' under the question: 'Have you written to any other charities? What was the outcome of the application?'

4 The first page is relevant to all applications; the second page is only relevant to people applying for school or college fees. If you are applying for clothing or books for a schoolchild then it may be worth filling out only the first page of the form and submitting a covering letter outlining the reasons for the application.

5 Filling out the weekly income and expenditure parts of the form can be worrying or even distressing. Expenditure when itemised in this way is usually far higher than people expect. It is probably worth filling out this form with the help of a professional.

6 You should always keep a copy of the completed form in case the trust has a specific query.

7 This form should not be used where the trust has its own form, which must be completed.

Application form template

Purpose for which grant is sought	Amount sought from £ this application
Applicant (name)	Occupation/School
Address Telephone no.	
Date of birth	Age	Place of birth
Nationality	Religion (if any)

☐ Single   ☐ Married   ☐ Divorced   ☐ Partnered   ☐ Separated   ☐ Widow/er

Family details: Name	Age	Occupation/School
Parents/ Partner	. . . . . .	. . . .
Brothers/Sisters/ Children	. . . . . .	. . . .
. . . .	. . . . . .	. . . .
. . . .	. . . . . .	. . . .
Others (specify)	. . . . . .	. . . .

Income (weekly)	£	p	**Expenditure** (weekly)	£	p
Father's/husband's wage	. . . . . .		Rent/mortgage	. . . . . .	
Mother's/wife's wage	. . . . . .		Council tax	. . . . . .	
Partner's wage	. . . . . .		Water rate	. . . . . .	
Income Support	. . . . . .		Electricity	. . . . . .	
Jobseeker's Allowance	. . . . . .		Gas	. . . . . .	
Employment and Support Allowance	. . . . . .		Other fuel	. . . . . .	
Pension Credit	. . . . . .		Insurance	. . . . . .	
Working Tax Credit	. . . . . .		Fares/travel	. . . . . .	
Child Tax Credit	. . . . . .		Household expenses (food, laundry etc.).	. . . . . .	
Child Benefit	. . . . . .		Clothing	. . . . . .	
Housing Benefit	. . . . . .		School dinners	. . . . . .	
Attendance Allowance	. . . . . .		Childcare fees	. . . . . .	
Disability Living Allowance	. . . . . .		HP commitments	. . . . . .	
Universal Credit	. . . . . .		Telephone	. . . . . .	
Personal Independence Payments	. . . . . .		TV rental	. . . . . .	
Maintenance payments	. . . . . .		TV licence	. . . . . .	
Pensions	. . . . . .		Other expenditure (specify)	. . . . . .	
Other income (specify)	. . . . . .				
. . . .	. . . . . .		. . . .	. . . . . .	
. . . .	. . . . . .		. . . .	. . . . . .	
. . . .	. . . . . .		. . . .	. . . . . .	

Total weekly income £   **Total weekly expenditure** £

Savings £ _____

Debts/arrears
Rent, fuels, loans, HP etc.

Has applicant received help from any other source? ☐ YES ☐ NO
(If YES, please include details below)

Specify in detail	Amount owed	Sources of grant obtained	Amount
. . . .	£	. . . .	£. . . . .
. . . .	£	. . . .	£. . . . .
. . . .	£	Other sources approached	
. . . .	£	. . . .	
. . . .	£	. . . .	

Total £ _____

Total still required £ _____

Has applicant ever received previous financial help from this charity? ☐ YES ☐ NO   If so, when?

Reason for the application

Continue on a separate sheet if necessary

For applications being submitted through a welfare agency

Name of agency . . . .

Case worker . . . .

Address. . . . .

. . . .

Telephone. . . . .

How long has the applicant been known to your department/organisation?. . . . .

For all applications

Signature: **Date:**

About the Directory of Social Change

DSC has a vision of an independent voluntary sector at the heart of social change. The activities of independent charities, voluntary organisations and community groups are fundamental to achieve social change. We exist to help these organisations and the people who support them to achieve their goals.

We do this by:

- Providing practical tools that organisations and activists need, including online and printed publications, training courses, and conferences on a huge range of topics
- Acting as a 'concerned citizen' in public policy debates, often on behalf of smaller charities, voluntary organisations and community groups
- Leading campaigns and stimulating debate on key policy issues that affect those groups
- Carrying out research and providing information to influence policymakers

DSC is the leading provider of information and training for the voluntary sector and publishes an extensive range of guides and handbooks covering subjects such as fundraising, management, communication, finance and law. We have a range of subscription-based websites containing a wealth of information on funding from charities, companies and government sources. We run more than 300 training courses each year, including bespoke in-house training provided at the client's location. DSC conferences, many of which run on an annual basis, include the Charity Management Conference, the Charity Accountants' Conference and the Charity Law Conference. DSC's major annual event is Charityfair, which provides low-cost training on a wide variety of subjects.

For details of all our activities, and to order publications and book courses, go to www.dsc.org.uk, call 08450 777707 or email publications@dsc.org.uk

General charities

This chapter includes charities which could not be categorised to a specific occupation, disability, location or beneficiary group. Many have relatively broad criteria for their grant-making.

The charities listed under 'General' can give to a wide range of people, so if individuals are unable to find help from other sources in this guide then they should be able to approach one or more of these. However, note that most of these charities still have restrictions on who they can help. Applicants should not send indiscriminate applications to any charity under the 'General' heading; rather, they should first consider whether they are eligible.

The 'Utilities' section outlines charities, mainly set up by utility companies, with the specific purpose of providing assistance to those struggling to pay their utility bills or debts. Some of these are specific to those living in a particular geographical area, while others have a broader remit.

The charities in both sections are listed in alphabetical order.

The Acorn Foundation

£27,000

Correspondent: Gill Snowdon, Correspondent, Longreach House, Jordans Way, Beaconsfield, Buckinghamshire HP9 2SP (01494 870171)

CC number: 1068004

Eligibility
People in need who live in the UK.

Types of grants
Grants are given according to need.

Annual grant total
In 2013/14 the foundation held assets of £2.2 million and had an income of £106,500. Grants totalled £64,000, of which £27,000 was awarded to individuals for welfare needs. Organisations also received funding.

Applications
Grants are made in partnership with a number of local authorities.

Other information
The foundation also works to promote the Christian faith.

The ACT Foundation

£432,000 (411 grants)

Correspondent: The Grants Manager, 61 Thames Street, Windsor, Berkshire SL4 1QW (01753 753900; fax: 01753 753901; email: info@theactfoundation. co.uk; website: www.theactfoundation. co.uk)

CC number: 1068617

Eligibility
The foundation has the aim of 'enhancing the quality of life for people in need', especially those who have physical or mental disabilities, are older or live in poverty. Applicants should be permanently resident in the UK.

Types of grants
Grants of up to £2,500 generally fall under three areas:

- building – modifications to homes (where a Disabled Facilities Grant (DFG) has already been awarded) …
- equipment – provision of specialist wheelchairs, other mobility aids and equipment including medical equipment and technology to assist independent living
- respite – help towards the cost of short-term respite breaks at registered respite centres

Grants have been given towards: specialised seating and car seats; specialised beds and sleep systems; sensory toys and equipment, room padding; communication aids, specialised software; bathroom and vehicle adaptations; stair-lifts.

The current focus is mainly on children and young adults with physical or mental disabilities in particular in the transition phase from education to adulthood.

Annual grant total

In 2013/14 the foundation had assets of £59.5 million and an income of £17.85 million. A total of £867,000 was awarded in grants, consisting of around £432,000 to 411 individuals and about £434,500 to 123 organisations.

Exclusions

Grants are not made for:
- Replacement of statutory funding
- Work, items or services already commenced, purchased or on order
- Building alterations where a Disabled Facilities Grant has not been applied for and has not been awarded
- Garden works
- Ordinary domestic items (e.g. flooring, white goods, furniture, clothing)
- Holidays
- Deposits for vehicles

Applications

Application forms are available from the website or the correspondent. They must be submitted by post, as the foundation is unable to accept email applications. Requests can be made at any time and the trustees meet four times a year (approvals may be made between meeting dates if necessary). An acknowledgement letter is sent as soon as possible – if your application is in an unacceptable form, ineligible or of a low priority you will be advised of this in the letter. All acceptable applications are assessed, if appropriate you may be contacted for further information and/or paid a personal visit. The foundation notes: 'We aim to make decisions on 95% of grant applications within two months and on all applications within three months.'

Applications should be accompanied by any required supporting documentation (qualified health professional letter, quotation and so on) and financial evidence of need, if required. If the grant is intended for building modifications, a letter of permission from the owner of the property should be attached. Applicants are advised to read the terms and conditions on the website prior to applying.

Note the following stated on the website:

> We receive many more applications than we can fund and have to prioritise our grants towards those most in need. Where it is deemed that the beneficiary, the beneficiary's family or the applying charity/organisation are able to provide the equipment from their own resources we regret that the application will not be considered.

Other information

The foundation also supports organisations and has a number of charity strategic partners.

There is an objective to increase the small grants programme by 20% in value every year. The annual report for 2013/14 states:

> Trustees are seeking to grow this area of grant making in future years and as such have increased the budget for 2014/15 by 20% to £1.2 million.

> It is the Trustees' intention to continue the expansion of direct charitable donations with the aim of covering a diverse and geographically spread cross-section of those elderly, disabled and in poverty who are in need of assistance, principally within the United Kingdom.

In addition the trustees provide assistance by the provision of accommodation to an educational project for children of shanty town dwellers in Sao Paulo, Brazil, called Meninos do Morumbi, and a £200,000 interest-free loan to Homeless International for funding housing projects in India and Malawi. During the year a further two grants were given to overseas charitable projects, totalling £36,500.

Al-Mizan Charitable Trust

£27,500 (127 grants)

Correspondent: Grants Officer, PO Box 2488, Watford WD18 1YL (email: admin@almizantrust.org.uk; website: www.almizantrust.org.uk)

CC number: 1135752

Eligibility

British citizens, those granted indefinite leave to remain in the UK and asylum seekers who are living in a condition of social or economic deprivation. Preference is given to the following groups:

- Orphans (a child who has lost either both parents or one parent who was the main bread-winner in the family)
- Children and young people under the age of 19 years (particularly those in care or who are carers themselves)
- Individuals who have disabilities, are incapacitated or terminally ill (particularly those who are severely mentally disabled)
- Single parents (particularly divorcees and widows/widowers with children)
- Estranged or isolated senior citizens
- Individuals with severe medical conditions or their families
- Ex-offenders or reformed drug addicts or alcoholics
- Victims of domestic violence and/or physical or sexual abuse
- Victims of crime, anti-social behaviour and/or terrorism

Types of grants

Mainly one-off grants, which in 2013/14 ranged from £34 to a maximum £500, with an average grant being £232. Grants are awarded with the aims of: breaking the cycle of poverty, deprivation and/or disadvantage; improving the quality of life for individuals and/or families who 'are struggling to maintain a dignified existence and positively engage in society'; relieving suffering and helping individuals/families embark on a new start following a crisis or event. They are also given to assist with education and employability. Interest-free loans can also be given.

Annual grant total

In 2013/14 the trust had assets of £150,500 and an income of £127,500. Grants totalled £39,000, of which £27,500 was awarded in 127 payments for social welfare purposes. They were distributed as follows:

Household items	71	£17,100	44%
Education and vocational training	29	£8,200	21%
Subsistence	31	£4,500	12%
Employment and enterprise	12	£3,100	8%
Medical and mobility	10	£2,400	6%
Housing	7	£1,700	4%
Other	3	£1,100	3%
Mother and baby items	5	£900	2%

Grants for purposes relating to education and employment totalled £11,300 (we have not included this in the grant total, which represents the support for social welfare needs).

Exclusions

The trust cannot help with: general appeals; applications from organisations or formal groups (except when assisting an individual or family); applicants who are not claiming all benefits for which they are eligible; applicants who have received funding from the trust in the last 12 months; applications for items or costs that have already been paid for; expenses relating to the practise or promotion of religion; debts, including rent and council tax arrears; fines or criminal penalties; university tuition fees; gap year projects; immigration costs; funeral expenses; gifts (including birthdays or festivals); holidays (however, the trust will consider funding trips for children and/or young people which 'enrich learning opportunities or very occasionally where a short vacation may serve a medical or social need'); international travel; applications for more than £500 (the trust will consider match-funding requests if the rest of the required amount is raised from other sources); products/services which contravene the ethos and values of the trust.

Applications

All applications for grant funding must be submitted using the trust's online application system. They can be submitted directly by the individual or by a third party (with the individual's permission). Only one application can be considered per household at any time. The trust states the following information on its website:

> We have developed a seven stage application process that includes an assessment of the need of the applicant based on individual social circumstances, telephone interviews and/or home-visits, analysis of the income and expenditure of applicants in relation to recognised models as well as reference and security checks.

Note that, in order to reduce administrative costs, the trust does not accept enquiries by telephone.

Other information

In 2013/14 the trust launched – along with four partner organisations – a food bank to serve the boroughs of Brent, Harrow and Ealing. The partner organisations have pledged an annual investment of £35,000 to maintain the service, as well as a range of additional services in support of individuals who are experiencing poverty. In the food bank's first year, Al-Mizan Charitable Trust contributed £10,000.

The trust has an informative website and detailed annual report with case studies.

The Bagri Foundation

£85,000

Correspondent: Mr D. Beaumont, Correspondent, 80 Cannon Street, London EC4N 6EJ (020 7280 0000; email: enquiries@bagrifoundation.org; website: www.bagrifoundation.org)

CC number: 1000219

Eligibility

People in need worldwide.

Types of grants

One-off and repeated grants according to need.

Annual grant total

In 2013/14 the foundation held assets of £14.1 million and a total income of £166,500. We estimate that the amount of grants given to individuals for welfare purposes totalled around £85,000.

Applications

Apply in writing to the correspondent.

The Biggart Trust

£9,500

Correspondent: Andrew Biggart, Trustee, Maclay Murray and Spens, 1 George Square, Glasgow G2 1AL (0330 222 0050; fax: 0330 222 0053)

OSCR number: SC015806

Eligibility

People in need, with a preference for those related to the founders of the trust and their descendants.

Types of grants

One-off and recurrent grants (half-yearly), which in previous years have ranged from £600 to £1,100.

Annual grant total

In 2013/14 the trust had an income of £11,200 and a total expenditure of £20,300. We estimate that the amount of grants given to individuals totalled £9,500, with funding also awarded to organisations.

Applications

Apply in writing to the correspondent. Applications can be submitted directly by the individual.

The Percy Bilton Charity

£155,000 (1,120 grants)

Correspondent: The Correspondent, Bilton House, 7 Culmington Road, Ealing, London W13 9NB (020 8579 2829; email: percybilton@aol.com; website: www.percybiltoncharity.org.uk)

CC number: 1094720

Eligibility

People who are on a low income and are either over 65 years old, have a physical or learning disability, or are receiving hospital or other medical treatment for a long-term illness (including mental illness).

Types of grants

One-off grants of up to £200 for specific essential items only. For example, laundry equipment, cooking and heating appliances, basic furniture, beds and bedding, floor coverings, clothing and footwear, and other essential household items.

Annual grant total

In 2013/14 the charity held assets of £22.9 million and had an income of £661,500. A total of £155,000 was awarded in 1,120 grants to individuals broken down as follows:

Home appliances	454	£73,500
Household goods/furniture	444	£61,500
Clothing and footwear	222	£20,000

The charity also distributed Christmas food parcels worth £44,000. Organisations were awarded a further £417,000 in 190 grants.

Exclusions

No payments are made towards items costing over £200, travel expenses, sponsorship, holidays, respite care, educational grants, computer equipment or software, house alterations and maintenance (including adaptations for disability facilities), debts, dishwashers, reimbursement of costs for articles already purchased, garden fencing or clearance, motor vehicle purchase or expenses, nursing and residential home fees, funeral expenses, removal expenses, medical treatment or therapy, and course fees including driving or IT lessons. No repeat grants are given within a 12-month period.

Applications

Application forms are available from the correspondent. Applications should be submitted by a social worker, community psychiatric nurse or occupational therapist, including a covering letter on local or health authority headed paper. The correspondent should be contacted by telephone to request an application form which will be sent by email. A full list of guidelines is available from the charity's website. Applicants should wait for four weeks before contacting the charity to check the progress of an application.

Note: the charity is unable to respond to applications made by anyone other than a social worker or occupational therapist or to requests which fall outside the charity's funding criteria. Applicants should also ensure that they have applied to all statutory sources and any appropriate specialist charities (e.g. employment-related funds and armed forces funds) before approaching the charity. Successful applicants should not re-apply within 12 months of receiving a grant.

Catholic Clothing Guild

£5,500

Correspondent: Carmel Edwards, Hon. Treasurer, 5 Dark Lane, Shrewsbury, Shropshire SY2 5LP (01743 243858; email: carmel.edwards@btinternet.com)

CC number: 277952

Eligibility
People in need of clothing regardless of denomination in England.

Types of grants
The Catholic Clothing Guild is a small charity which distributes new donated clothing (mainly to children). It may give small money grants when this is not possible; however, this is in exceptional circumstances as funding is limited.

Annual grant total
The 2013 accounts were the latest available at the time of writing (November 2015).

In 2013, the guild had an income of £5,700 and a total expenditure of £5,800. We estimate that the total amount of grants awarded to individuals was approximately £5,500.

Applications
Applications should be made by letter or by emailing the local branch. Telephone calls are not welcomed. Applications must be made through a welfare agency or social services. The referring agency will also receive the grants. Under no circumstances will applications be accepted by individuals.

Other information
Note: the trust is only able to assist with up to six grants per month due to limited funding.

Coats Foundation Trust

£17,500

Correspondent: Andrea McCutcheon, Coats Pensions Office, Cornerstone, 107 West Regent Street, Glasgow G2 2BA (0141 207 6800; email: cft@coats.com; website: www.coatspensions.co.uk/about-us/coats-foundation-trust)

CC number: 268735

Eligibility
People who are in need for whom there is no help available from statutory sources or from other charitable organisations.

Types of grants
One-off grants for essential items such as furniture or equipment or essential repairs.

Annual grant total
In 2013/14 the charity had an income of £1,200 and a total expenditure of £77,000. Grants are made both to individuals and organisations for social welfare and educational purposes. We estimate that the amount of grants given to individuals for social welfare purposes totalled around £17,500.

Exclusions
The charity does not have the funds to support regular payments or long-term needs such as food, rent or other day-to-day expenses.

Applications
Applications can be made using the application form, which is available to download from the website along with a financial statement, which must also be completed. Details should be provided on other sources of funding that have been applied to or from which the applicant may expect help. Any other relevant information that may help the trustees when considering the applicant's case should be included. Payments are not made to other charities as the Coats Foundation's mission is to assist individuals directly.

The Coffey Charitable Trust

£1,000

Correspondent: Christopher Coffey, Trustee, Oak Tree House, Over the Misbourne Road, Denham, Uxbridge, Middlesex UB9 5DR (01895 831381; email: coffeytrust@gmail.com)

CC number: 1043549

Eligibility
People in need in the UK.

Types of grants
Occasional one-off and recurrent grants according to need.

Annual grant total
In 2013/14 the trust had an income of £12,300 and a total expenditure of £6,500. We estimate grants to individuals for educational and social welfare purposes to be around £2,000.

Applications
Applications may be made in writing to the correspondent.

Other information
This trust mainly provides grants to Christian organisations and events.

The Cordwainers' Company Common Investment Fund

£10,500

Correspondent: John Miller, Secretary, Clothworkers' Hall, Dunster Court, Mincing Lane, London EC3R 7AH (020 7929 1121; fax: 020 7929 1124; email: office@cordwainers.org; website: www.cordwainers.org)

CC number: 261891

Eligibility
The company administers a number of small trusts, the eligibility of which varies. Specific trusts exist for people who are blind, people who are deaf and dumb, widows of clergymen, ex-servicemen and widows of those who served in the armed forces, for example.

Types of grants
Small annual grants depending on the trust and the circumstances.

Annual grant total
In 2013/14 the charity had assets of £1.9 million and an income of £74,500. Grants amounted to £26,500, of which £15,600 was awarded to organisations. Grants to individuals totalled £10,500.

The annual report states that around 70 individuals receive grants from the charity.

Applications
Apply in writing to the correspondent supported, if possible, by referrals from welfare or other charitable bodies.

Other information
The charity is also known as the Pooled Trusts.

The Dibs Charitable Trust

£5,300

Correspondent: The Trustees, Trustee Department, Coutts, 440 Strand, London WC2R 0QS (020 7663 6825)

CC number: 257709

Eligibility
People in need.

Types of grants
One-off grants for the relief of immediate distress only, usually ranging from £25 to £250. Grants are not made directly to individuals.

Annual grant total

In 2014/15 the trust had an income of £20,500 and an expenditure of £22,700. We estimate that £5,300 was given in welfare grants to individuals, with funding also awarded to charitable organisations and to individuals with educational needs.

Exclusions

No grants are given for bankruptcy fees or associated costs, overseas travel, holidays, clothing, funeral expenses or group activities. No pensions or annuities are paid.

Applications

Applications should be made in writing to 212 Business Design Centre, 52 Upper Street, London N1 0QH. Applications should be made through a local social services department or Citizens Advice and are considered throughout the year.

Monica Eyre Memorial Foundation

£1,400

Correspondent: Michael Bidwell, Trustee, 53 Oliver's Battery Road North, Winchester SO22 4JB (email: monica. eyre@gmail.com)

CC number: 1046645

Eligibility

People in need, particularly older people and people with disabilities/special needs in the UK.

Types of grants

Grants are made to enable people with low-mobility in residential care to get a holiday with essential carer support.

Annual grant total

In 2014/15 the foundation had both an income and a total expenditure of £5,800. Grants are made to individuals and organisations for a wide range of charitable purposes. We estimate that social welfare grants to individuals totalled £1,400.

Applications

Apply in writing to the correspondent.

Family Action

£175,000 (556 grants)

Correspondent: The Grants Service, 24 Angel Gate, City Road, London EC1V 2PT (020 7254 6251 (Wednesday and Thursday **only** between 2pm and 4pm); email: info@family-action.org.uk; website: www.family-action.org.uk)

CC number: 264713

Eligibility

Family Action seeks to help people 'experiencing poverty, disadvantage and social isolation across England'. Welfare grants programme aims to 'prevent an immediate crisis from spiralling and threatening the stability of families and individuals'. Help is particularly focused on people on a low income, especially those living on benefits.

Types of grants

Essential personal and household needs, such as clothing, fuel bills or household items (for example furniture or white goods). On average grants are likely to be in the region of £200–£300 (grants for holidays for women living in Greater London are likely to be in the region of £350 to a maximum of £600 per family). Support given covers the following priority areas:

Nationally

Support is given for:
- The promotion of independence and improvements of the quality of life and isolation of older people (over the age of 60)
- Disability aids that will benefit the applicant in their home, towards medical treatment or to help cover the expenses of convalescence and recuperation
- Adults (over the age of 18) with a clinical diagnosis of a mental health problem

Greater London

In the Greater London area (only) awards can be made for:
- Families or individuals who have recently experienced domestic abuse
- Young people (19–25 years of age) who are living alone
- Recuperative holidays for women living in Greater London

Local funds
- St Pancras – support for single parents with children under the age of four who are resident in the postcode areas WC1 and NW1
- Paddington – support for residents of the W2 W9 and NW8 (Westminster only) district postcode areas

Open Doors Grants Programme

In partnership with Lankelly Chase, the charity runs 'a small grants programme specifically targeting individuals and families experiencing severe and multiple disadvantage'. Applicants will not only suffer from extreme poverty, but also will be struggling with a range of other issues, such as mental health issues, homelessness, domestic abuse, sexual exploitation, substance misuse, and frequent contact with the criminal justice system. See the website for full details of the partnership.

Annual grant total

In 2013/14 the charity had assets of almost £12.3 million and an income of £20.2 million. A total of 556 grants totalling £175,000 were made for the alleviation of need. A further £137,000 was spent as 'other costs' under the educational grants advice, which we take to refer to the educational grants expenditure.

Exclusions

Funds are not available for:
- Council tax arrears
- Debts (including utility bills)
- Fines
- Rent deposits, arrears or payments
- Moving costs
- Funeral expenses (including associated expenses, such as headstones)
- Gifts (such as toys for birthdays, Christmas or other festivals)
- Repayment of Social Fund or other loans
- Bankruptcy or insolvency costs
- Items already purchased
- Citizenship applications
- Legal fees
- Passport applications
- Costs associated with employment or education
- Sponsorship
- General appeals
- Funding for projects or groups

Applications

Applications must be made online by a statutory body or voluntary organisation on behalf of the candidate.

Further details on support available can be obtained via phone or email (grants.enquiry@family-action.org.uk). Note that the grants service is only open between 9am and 5pm on Tuesday, Wednesday and Thursday.

The charity states: 'With regret we are unable to acknowledge or respond to postal enquiries unless a stamped, addressed envelope is provided.'

Other information

Family Action provides a range of advice and support services across the country – see the 'Find us' facility on the website to find your local office. Support is given to help in the areas of some of the most complex issues, including financial hardship, mental health problems, social isolation, learning disabilities, domestic abuse, or substance misuse and alcohol problems. It is aimed to improve the lives of children and families, help through the early years of child development and ensure adult mental health and well-being.

The Farthing Trust

£8,600

Correspondent: Joy Martin, Trustee, PO Box 277, Cambridge CB7 9DE (email: jmartin@bt.co.uk)

CC number: 268066

Eligibility

People in need, with a priority given to those either personally known to the trustees or recommended by those personally known to the trustees.

Types of grants

One-off and recurrent grants are given to meet 'charitable causes' in the UK and overseas.

Annual grant total

In 2013/14 the trust had assets of £2.5 million and an income of £53,000. Grants totalled £233,500, the majority of which was awarded to Christian churches and causes worldwide. Welfare grants to individuals totalled £900, all of which were made overseas, although in previous years higher sums have been granted to individuals in the UK.

Applications

Apply in writing to the correspondent. Applications can be submitted directly by the individual or through a social worker, Citizens Advice or other welfare agency. Note that applicants will only be notified of a refusal if an sae is enclosed.

The trust has previously stated that it is only able to accept about one in every one hundred of the applications it receives; therefore, success is unlikely unless a personal contact with a trustee is established.

Other information

Grants may also be available to individuals for educational needs.

The Fielding Charitable Trust

£1,000

Correspondent: Richard Fielding, Trustee, West Hall, Longburton, Sherborne, Dorset DT9 5PF (01963 210234)

CC number: 1091521

Eligibility

People in need in the UK. Preference is given to older people and people who have disabilities.

Types of grants

One-off and recurrent grants are given according to need.

Annual grant total

In 2014/15 the trust had an income of £2,000 and a total expenditure of £4,400. Grants are made to individuals and to organisations for a wide range of purposes. We estimate that social welfare grants to individuals totalled around £1,000.

Applications

Apply in writing to the correspondent.

Elizabeth Finn Care

£3.4 million (4,688 grants)

Correspondent: Elizabeth Finn Fund, Hythe House, 200 Shepherds Bush Road, London W6 7NL (020 8834 9200; fax: 020 8834 9299; email: info@ elizabethfinn.org.uk; website: www. elizabethfinncare.org.uk)

CC number: 207812

Eligibility

People who are British or Irish and have a worked in a listed profession, and their dependants. Applicants must have a low income or be claiming benefits and have less than £4,000 in savings. Applicants must also be living in Britain or Ireland for at least half of every year.

Types of grants

Recurrent grants are made towards daily living expenses. One-off grants are also available towards needs such as car expenses, household items, house repairs and adaptations, specialist equipment and help with nursing/residential fees. All grants are means-tested.

Annual grant total

In 2013/14 the charity had assets of £49.6 million. Grants were made to 4,688 individuals totalling £3.4 million.

Exclusions

Healthcare costs; computer equipment; holidays; educational costs; debts, legal fees; funeral expenses.

Applications

Applicants should contact the charity via the online enquiry form on the website to enquire about whether they are eligible. A grants leaflet containing eligibility information is also available to download via the charity's website. If the charity thinks it may be able to help, an application form will be issued. This may be submitted either directly by the individual, through a third party such as a social worker or through an organisation such as Citizens Advice or other welfare agency.

Other information

If at any stage the charity cannot help, it will try to signpost applicants to other possible sources of funding.

The Fort Foundation

£8,800

Correspondent: Edward Fort, Trustee, Fort Vale Engineering Ltd, Calder Vale Park, Simonstone Lane, Simonstone, Burnley BB12 7ND (01282 440000; email: info@fortvale.com)

CC number: 1028639

Eligibility

According to the trustees' annual report, the foundation operates throughout England and Wales and gives grants to individuals and organisations for general charitable purposes. Our research indicates that young people in Pendle Borough and district, especially those undertaking courses in engineering, may be favoured.

Types of grants

Our research suggests that one-off grants of £50–£1,000 are available.

Annual grant total

In 2014/15 the foundation had assets of £684,000 and an income of £257,500. Grants to individuals were made totalling £27,000, of which £1,500 was given for social welfare purposes, £5,300 for health needs, £2,000 for sports and £18,300 in educational support.

Exclusions

Our research suggests that awards are not made for fees.

Applications

Applications may be made in writing to the correspondent, directly by the individual. Appeals are considered at any time.

Other information

Grants are also made to organisations and small groups (£183,500 to organisations in 2014). During the year the foundation contributed £29,000 towards the funding of a report on climate change.

Friends of the Animals

£205,500 (4,157 grants)

Correspondent: Martin Gomez, Treasurer, 17A Riverway, Newport PO3 5UX (01983 810375; email: fotaiow@hotmail.com; website: www. friendsoftheanimals.co.uk)

CC number: 1000249

Eligibility

People who are in need and live on the Isle of Wight, in Portsmouth or the West Midlands.

Types of grants

Subsidised veterinary treatment, such as spaying, neutering, microchipping, inoculations and treatment of accidents.

Annual grant total

In 2013/14 the charity held assets of £158,500 and had an income of £474,000. A total of £205,500 was spent on vets' bills, with animals receiving 4,157 treatments.

Applications

Requests for assistance can be made by calling the head office on 01983 522511 (Tuesday to Saturday, 10am to 4pm) or by emailing. Include details of the area in which you live, a phone number and as much information about your enquiry as possible.

Other information

The charity's activities include the rehoming of animals and the provision of free advice and information on animal welfare, as well as loans of baskets, pens and other equipment to assist with animal care.

Friends of the Animals also supports the Farm Animal Rescue Sanctuary at Wolverton, which is home to more than 470 animals.

The Fund for the Forgotten

£25,000

Correspondent: Alexandra Taliadoros, Foundation Director, 203 Larna House, 116 Commercial Street, London E1 6NF (020 3651 4706; email: info@ beattiefoundation.com; website: www. beattiefoundation.com/ fundfortheforgotten/index.htm)

CC number: 1142892

Eligibility

People facing social injustice and inequality in the Midlands and London.

Types of grants

One-off grants of £500 to £5,000 'will be awarded to individuals facing injustice or inequality against their dignity, freedom or sanctuary'. Grants may include money for help with everyday living costs and purchasing essential household items.

Annual grant total

In 2013/14 the Jack and Ada Beattie Foundation had an income of £132,000 and charitable expenditure totalled £115,000. The accounts show that gifts and donations totalled £51,000 and we have estimated that the total amount of support given to individuals totalled around £25,000.

Applications

Initial applications are made by sending a proposal, via email, summarising your situation, the injustice/inequality you face and how it is aligned to the foundation's objectives and values. You should also explain how support from the foundation can help you.

If your proposal is successful you will be invited to submit an application form, which can be downloaded from the website. Applications must be accompanied by two references and identity documentation.

Other information

The fund is part of the registered charity, The Jack and Ada Beattie Foundation.

The R. L. Glasspool Charity Trust

£1.2 million (5,229 grants)

Correspondent: Grants Team, Second Floor, Saxon House, 182 Hoe Street, Walthamstow, London E17 4QH (020 8520 4354; email: application@glasspool. org.uk (for application requests only); website: www.glasspool.org.uk)

CC number: 214648

Eligibility

People in need who are on a low income.

Types of grants

One-off grants for white goods, beds and bedding, other household goods, clothing (including school uniforms, where other sources are not available) baby needs (if not eligible for a Sure Start Maternity Grant), travel expenses for hospital visits to family members, and as contributions towards equipment and adaptations for people with disabilities (where there has been a recommendation from an occupational health therapist). Grants are paid to the referring agency.

Only in very exceptional circumstances may grants be given for flooring, educational computer equipment, televisions, or vocational materials and training.

Grants to any one individual/family rarely exceed £750 and the average grant is around £230. Grants may be as low as £50 or (extremely rarely) as high as £5,000. Normally, not more than one grant is made to the same beneficiary in a three-year period. In practice, repeat grants are rare.

Annual grant total

In 2013/14 the trust awarded a total of £1.2 million in grants to 5,229 individuals. The grants budget for 2014/15 has been increased by 10% to £1.3 million.

Exclusions

No grants are given for loans or debts, bursaries, project funding, research or educational grants, bankruptcy and debt relief order fees, holidays, outings, respite costs, household repairs, rent in advance or deposits, funeral costs or headstones, removal costs, or equipment and adaptations that should be funded by statutory services.

Apart from in exceptional circumstances, the trust does not normally make more than one grant per individual/family. The trust will not make a grant where funding is available from another source, particularly statutory funds.

Applications

The trust has an automated application request and submitting process. To request an application form, a blank email should be sent to application@glasspool.org.uk by an organisation acting on behalf of the individual. An application form will be sent to your mailbox within an hour. Application forms should be completed and returned to the trust by email. Once your application form is accepted, you will be issued with an automated reference number. Only when you have been issued with a reference number will the Grant Team have access to your application, the team will then contact you within two to three weeks. Do not contact the trust during this time.

Under no circumstances does the trust accept applications directly from individuals. Applications must be made by an eligible organisation, which must be either: a statutory healthcare, social care or advice service; a charity that directly provides, or is contracted to provide, a statutory healthcare, social care or advice service; Citizens Advice; a prison or probation service (National Offender Management Service); or a tenancy support worker employed either by a local authority, industrial and provident society or a housing association which is registered with the Housing Corporation. The referring agency must have its own bank account and be prepared to administer the grant on behalf of the trust.

The application form is designed for applying by email only and will be rejected if received by post.

Other information

The trust is one of the few charities which operate nationally with no restrictions on its type of beneficiary. Note the following from the trust's website:

> Given the volume of applications that we receive and the limited funds available we are unable to assist in every case. The discretionary nature of the grants means we do not provide specific reasons for

rejecting an application. We do not provide feedback on applications received on an individual basis and do not have the resources to enter into correspondence regarding this.

Lady Hewley's Charity (formerly known at the Lady Hewley's Trust)

£98,500

Correspondent: Neil Blake, Correspondent, Military House, 24 Castle Street, Chester CH1 2DS

CC number: 230043

Eligibility

Present or retired ministers of the United Reformed, Congregational and Baptist churches and their widows who are in need. This is a national trust, although preference is given to applicants whose ministry is in the northern counties of England.

Types of grants

Welfare grants are given of up to a maximum of about £1,000, unless this affects benefit entitlement.

Annual grant total

In 2013/14 the trust had assets of £16.4 million and an income of almost £381,500. Grants to individuals totalled £153,000, of which £98,500 was for welfare needs. Grants made to specific groups of beneficiaries were broken down as follows:

Retired ministers	£47,000
Widows	£40,000
Ministers	£8,800
Daughters	£2,900

Grants totalling £30,500 were also made to church institutions.

Exclusions

No grants will be given when local authority funds are available.

Applications

Applications are invited through contact with respective churches at local, regional and province levels. Individual applications are considered twice a year and grants are made according to an individual's personal and financial circumstances.

The Hoper-Dixon Trust

£12,500

Correspondent: The Provincial Bursar, The Dominican Council, Blackfriars, St Giles, Oxford OX1 3LY (01865 288231; email: enquiries@hoperdixon. org.uk; website: www.hoperdixon.org. uk)

CC number: 231160

Eligibility

People in need connected with, or resident in or near, any house or pastoral centre under the direction of the Dominicans of the English Province Order of Preachers.

Types of grants

One-off and recurrent grants are given according to need, normally ranging from £100 to £1,000. Recent grants have been given to assist with: medical expenses not covered by public funds; help for those unable to work due to sickness or injury; help with unexpected expenses; relocation expenses and basic household equipment for those setting-up a new home; help for pilgrims going to Lourdes – both those who are sick and those caring for them; and the costs of attending a funeral for a close family member.

Annual grant total

In 2013/14 the trust had an income of £15,400 and a total expenditure of £27,000. We estimate that the amount of grants given to individuals totalled £12,500, with funding also awarded for educational purposes.

Applications

Applications are normally made by a Dominican Friar for the benefit of someone connected with the Order or living in the neighbourhood of a house of the Order. A list of Dominican houses and contact details is available from the English Province of the Order of Preachers website.

Third-party welfare organisations applying on behalf of an individual should contact the trust in writing or by email to enquire about possible eligibility.

The Houston Charitable Trust

£7,400

Correspondent: Mr G. Houston, Trustee, Pednor Chase, Pednor, Chesham, Buckinghamshire HP5 2SY

CC number: 1083552

Eligibility

People in need and those seeking funding for educational purposes, or for reasons relating to the advancement of the Christian faith. In practice, grants are available worldwide.

Types of grants

One-off and recurrent grants are given according to need.

Annual grant total

In 2014/15 the trust had assets of almost £327,000 and an income of £75,000.

Grants to individuals totalled £7,400, of which welfare grants amounted to £5,900. A further £1,500 was awarded to individuals for purposes relating to the advancement of the Christian faith.

The majority of grants were given to organisations, however, with Christian institutions receiving £87,500 and welfare charities another £83,000.

Applications

Apply in writing to the correspondent, although the trust has previously stated: 'unsolicited applications are not supported as the funds are already committed for the foreseeable future'.

The Johnston Family Trust

£26,000

Correspondent: B. J. S. Parsons-Smith, Aspen Cottage, Apse Manor Road, Shanklin PO37 7PN (0151 236 6666)

CC number: 207512

Eligibility

'Members of the upper and middle classes (and widows and daughters of such people) who, through no fault of their own, have fallen into impoverished circumstances.' Assistance is limited to men over 50 and women over 40.

Types of grants

Recurrent grants of around £650 a year and one-off grants of around £100 each for TV licences and birthday gifts.

Annual grant total

In 2014 the trust had an income of £20,500 and a total expenditure of £29,500. We estimate that the amount of grants given to individuals totalled around £26,000.

Applications

Apply in writing to the correspondent. Applications are considered throughout the year.

St Jude's Trust

£1,900 (5 grants)

Correspondent: Roger Millman, Trust Administrator, c/o Druces LLP, Salisbury House, London Wall, London EC2M 5PS (020 7216 5525; fax: 020 7628 7525; email: r.millman@druces.com)

CC number: 222883

Eligibility

People in need through disability or disadvantage.

Types of grants

One-off and recurrent grants are given according to need. The trust's record on the Charity Commission's website states that 'the aim is for the trust's grant alone to make a significant impact for the individual or organisation concerned'.

Annual grant total

In 2013/14 the trust had assets of over £1 million and an income of £37,000. A total of 32 grants were made totalling £26,500, including five grants to individuals totalling £1,900.

The trust's record on the Charity Commission's website notes that it aims to give 'in the region of £25,000 per annum comprising around 35 grants'.

Applications

Applications may be made in writing to the correspondent. The trustees meet twice a year. Acknowledgements are not given.

Other information

Grants are given to both organisations and individuals.

Kilcreggan Trust

£2,400

Correspondent: Kenneth Carter, Trustee, 76 Eaton Place, London SW1X 8AU (01672 514050; email: Ken@kencarter.co.uk)

CC number: 1017264

Eligibility

People in need in England and Wales.

Types of grants

One-off and recurrent grants are given according to need.

Annual grant total

In 2014/15 the trust had assets of £483,000 and an unusually high income of over £306,500 (mainly from a personal donation of £300,000 by Mr K. Carter). Charitable activities totalled £6,400 and included support for the riding school as well as 'other charities and causes'. Further breakdown was not given; therefore, we estimate that the amount of grants given to individuals totalled about £2,000.

Exclusions

The trust does not award student grants.

Applications

Apply in writing to the correspondent.

Other information

According to the trust's 2014/15 accounts, it has been supporting 'the costs of indoor riding school managed by Kilcreggan Facilities Limited for the use of the Marlborough branch of the Riding for the Disabled'. This support has now ceased, as the land used by the school was sold in 2014.

The Heinz, Anna and Carol Kroch Foundation

£87,500 (688 grants)

Correspondent: Beena Astle, Correspondent, PO Box 327, Hampton TW12 9DD (020 8979 0609; email: hakf50@hotmail.com)

CC number: 207622

Eligibility

People who are older, have a chronic illness, have fled domestic situations or are homeless and are in financial hardship.

Types of grants

One-off grants typically ranging from £100 to £500 are given towards hospital travel costs, household bills, furniture, other hospital expenses, clothing, food, medical and disability equipment, living costs, home adaptations, help in the home and so on.

Annual grant total

In 2013/14 the foundation held assets of £6.3 million and had an income of £190,000. Grants were made to 688 individuals totalling £87,500.

Exclusions

No grants are given for education or holidays.

Applications

Apply in writing to the correspondent. Most applications are submitted through other charities and local authorities. Applications should include full financial information including income and expenditure, what the grant will be used for and a why it is needed. Applicants should also state if they have approached any other charities for financial assistance and how successful they have been to date. Applications are considered monthly.

The Elaine and Angus Lloyd Charitable Trust

£6,700

Correspondent: Ross Badger, Correspondent, 3rd Floor, North Side, Dukes Court, 32 Duke Street, St James's, London SW1Y 6DF (020 7930 7797; email: ross.badger@hhllp.co.uk)

CC number: 237250

Eligibility

People 'whose circumstances are such they come within the legal conception of poverty', particularly those who require assistance due to ill health or disability. Applications from South East England may be favoured.

Types of grants

One-off and recurrent grants are given according to need. Awards have ranged up to £2,000.

Annual grant total

In 2014/15 the trust had assets of £3.1 million and an income of £107,500. A total of £110,500 was paid in grants with £6,700 awarded to individuals.

Applications

Apply in writing to the correspondent. The trustees meet regularly to consider grants.

Other information

The trust predominantly awards grants to organisations. Support may also be given for educational purposes.

The Douglas Martin Trust

£25,000

Correspondent: David Evans, Trustee, 45 Burnards Field Road, Colyton, Devon EX24 6PE (01297 553007; email: d.d.evans@btinternet.com)

CC number: 267876

Eligibility

People in need who live in southern England but only in cases personally known to the trustees. Unsolicited applications will not be responded to.

Types of grants

One-off grants typically up to £300 for items such as bedding, furniture, children's holidays, debt relief and educational grants.

Annual grant total

In 2013/14 the trust held assets of £507,000 and had an income of £34,500. A total of £30,000 was awarded in grants with around £25,000 given to individuals.

Exclusions

The trust can only support cases known to the trustees.

Applications

Applications will not be accepted unless applicants are known by the trustees or referred by an organisation known to the trustees. Organisations which have recently made successful referrals include various branches of Citizens Advice, SAFE and String of Pearls Project.

Morden College

£200,000 (116 grants)

Correspondent: Major-General David Rutherford-Jones, Clerk, Clerk's House, 19 St German's Place, Blackheath, London SE3 0PW (020 8463 8330; email: TheClerk@mordencollege.org; website: www.mordencollege.org)

CC number: 215551

Eligibility

People in need who are aged over 50, from a professional or managerial background, who have retired from paid employment either on medical grounds or because they have reached the statutory retirement age.

Types of grants

One-off grants and quarterly allowances.

Annual grant total

In 2013/14 the charity held assets of £201.5 million and had an income of £11.2 million. A total of £200,000 was awarded in donations and out-pensions to 116 individuals.

Exclusions

The trust does not give for nursing home top-up fees or any services or products which should be funded by statutory authorities. Grants are generally not awarded to individuals who have received a grant within three years.

Applications

Apply on a form available from the correspondent, online or to download from the charity's website. Applications must include details of the applicant's income and expenditure as well as their employment history. Applicants are means-tested to ensure they are in need of assistance.

Other information

Morden College is the general title used for the administration of Sir John Morden's Charity and Dame Susan Morden's Charity. Sir John Morden's Charity provides grants and accommodation for the elderly. Dame Susan Morden's Charity is primarily concerned with the advancement of religion by assisting the Church of England with the upkeep of their churches and associated activities.

The charity runs a care home for beneficiaries who are no longer capable of living independently as well as accommodation for independent and supported living.

The National Benevolent Charity

£225,500

Correspondent: Dawn Swirczek, Correspondent, National Benevolent Institution, Peter Herve House, Eccles Court, Tetbury, Gloucestershire GL8 8EH (01666 505500; email: office@ thenbc.org.uk; website: www.thenbc.org. uk)

CC number: 212450

Eligibility

The National Benevolent Charity assists people who have fallen into poverty, through no fault of their own, and who cannot escape that poverty because of age, illness, disability or some other substantial reason.

To be eligible for financial assistance an applicant must:

- Be in receipt of all state benefits and have applied to any trade or professional charity/charities that support any medical condition from which they may suffer
- Have been resident in the UK for at least 24 months
- Live in their own (owned or rented) home
- Have less than £10,000 in assets (excluding their home) if a single person and less than £15,000 if a couple
- Have a disposable income after certain expenses (such as rent or council tax) of less than £8,000 per year if a single person and less than £12,000 if a couple

Only in exceptional circumstances will people under state retirement age be assisted if, for example, they are in receipt of long-term sickness benefits or disability living allowance.

Types of grants

Regular payments and one-off grants to single people and to couples are given. Regular payments are made to supplement low incomes. In 2014 regular payments amounted to £17 per week for a single person in receipt of a state retirement pension and £22.50 for a couple. For those not in receipt of a state retirement pension, regular payments amounted to £22.50 per week for a single person and £28 for a couple.

One-off grants are given to assist with urgent costs such as fridges, cookers, heating and roof repairs, and to acquire special disability equipment, for example. Grants are also made to beneficiaries at Christmas.

Annual grant total

In 2014 the charity had assets of £12.3 million and an income of £740,500. Grants amounted to £225,500.

Of this amount, £146,500 was given in regular payments to 171 beneficiaries and £79,000 was awarded in 142 one-off grants.

Exclusions

The charity cannot help with nursing home, social or private healthcare fees. Repayments of debts will not normally be considered.

Applications

Application forms are available to download from the website, along with guidelines, or can be requested by contacting the charity. Applications should be supported by one or more referees, for example, a doctor, nurse, social worker, local clergyman or an advice worker. Applicants must include full details of their financial position; the charity's website states: 'All income is taken into consideration including DLA and attendance allowance.' Supporting documents will be required at a later date. The Welfare Committee meets to consider application every couple of months. In special cases urgent requests may be considered.

Other information

The charity also operates residential properties in Tetbury in Gloucestershire and Old Windsor in Berkshire, where it provides accommodation for people over 50 who are in financial need.

Note the following from the charity's website: 'Each year The National Benevolent Charity receives many more applications for financial assistance than it has funds available for distribution. For the time being, preference is given to applicants who do not meet the qualifications of other benevolence charities.'

Natlas Trust

£20,000

Correspondent: Joel Adler, Trustee, 32 Brampton Grove, London NW4 4AQ

CC number: 1019856

Eligibility

People in need living in the UK or Israel.

Types of grants

One-off and recurrent grants are given according to need.

Annual grant total

In 2013/14 the trust held assets of £550,000 and had an income of £121,000. We estimate that the amount of grants given to individuals totalled around £20,000, with the majority of funding awarded to organisations.

Applications

Apply in writing to the correspondent.

Newby Trust Ltd

£47,000 (355 grants)

Correspondent: Annabel Grout, Secretary, Hill Farm, Froxfield, Petersfield, Hampshire GU32 1BQ (email: info@newby-trust.org.uk; website: www.newby-trust.org.uk)

CC number: 227151

Eligibility

People in the UK with welfare needs. The trust's website states that grants are usually given to individuals who are living in poverty which is 'exacerbated by additional misfortune including bereavement, divorce, abuse, homelessness, addiction, disability or ill health'. Applicants are expected to have claimed all statutory benefits available and to have applied for any available local authority funds. Grants are only given to those with substance misuse problems if they are in recovery. Applicants should have a household income of no more than £1,500 a month.

Types of grants

One-off grants of up to £250, for items such as household essentials, furnishings, clothing and school uniforms. Grants are occasionally made to support household adaptations and mobility equipment, travel costs, training equipment, rent deposits and respite breaks in the UK.

Annual grant total

In 2013/14 the trust had assets of £18.3 million and an income of £453,500. Grants were made to 355 individuals for welfare purposes totalling £47,000. Grants were also made to organisations for the purposes of welfare, health and education.

Exclusions

The trust does not provide grants for: rent, council tax arrears, debts; bankruptcy or Debt Relief Order fees; overseas respite breaks; driving lessons. Grants are not normally made for: televisions and computers; tumble dryers and dishwashers; curtains; carpets (except in the case of medical need or families with a young child).

Grants are generally not made to those without indefinite leave to remain in the UK; however, small grants of £50 may be made to those who are destitute.

Applications

Applications can be made online on behalf of individuals in need by statutory or voluntary agencies such as social services, NHS trusts, housing associations or registered charities. Applications made directly by the individual are not accepted. Cheques are payable to the sponsoring organisation.

Full guidelines are available on the website.

Other information

Grants are also made to organisations working in education, health and welfare, as well as under a 'special category' each year.

Open Wing Trust

£4,000

Correspondent: Jennifer Kavanagh, Clerk, Flat 2, 44 Langham Street, London W1W 7AU (020 7631 3551; email: clerk@openwing.org.uk; website: www.openwing.org.uk)

CC number: 1149773

Eligibility

Individuals over the age of 18 who are living in England and Wales at the beginning of their career and those contemplating a radical re-orientation of their life's work or the deepening of an existing vision. The trustees advise: 'We expect applicants to be in a process of inner change leading to a socially engaged commitment to working with those in need.'

Types of grants

One-off grants according to need. The guidelines note:

> Trustees will consider funding specific living costs such as food and rent, training programmes, or offering support during voluntary work or an internship.
>
> The Trustees will expect clarity about what the applicant intends to do, what steps will be necessary to achieve it, and what they expect to be achieved during the period of the grant.

Annual grant total

In 2014 the trust had no income and a total expenditure of £4,200. We estimate that about £4,000 was given in grants to individuals for welfare purposes, as the trust's website states: 'We expect to fund up to three small, one-off grants a year, with an individual maximum of £2,000 (total available each year is £4,000).'

Exclusions

Grants are not made to organisations or to fund specific work. Applications are not accepted on behalf of others or from individuals who have received funding within five years of an initial grant. Note that the trust 'will not fund holidays or unspecified thinking time'.

Applications

Applicants should apply directly via an online application form on the trust's website. A CV may be attached if appropriate. Signed supporting letters from two referees must be enclosed: one from somebody who has known the applicant for at least five years, and the other from somebody who has a connection with the applicant (for example, work or study) and has known the applicant for at least two years.

Suitable applicants are invited for an interview with the trustees in London (reasonable travel expenses are covered).

Applicants will need to demonstrate commitment to their purpose, and that they are in need of financial support to make it feasible. Consult the guidance notes on the trust's website before applying to ensure that your application is in line with the aims and values of the trust.

The trustees expect to meet twice a year to consider applications, but can make decisions between meetings.

Note the following request from the trust: 'Please don't post applications to us unless absolutely necessary. Email enables all the trustees to look at the application.'

The Osborne Charitable Trust

£2,200

Correspondent: John Eaton, Trustee, 57 Osborne Villas, Hove, East Sussex BN3 2RA (01273 732500; email: john@eaton207.fsnet.co.uk)

CC number: 326363

Eligibility

People in need in the UK and overseas, especially older people and those in ill health.

Types of grants

One-off and recurrent grants are given according to need and one-off grants in kind.

Annual grant total

In 2014/15 the trust had an income of £7,200 and a total expenditure of £10,100. We estimate that around £2,200 was given in grants to individuals for social welfare purposes.

Exclusions

Grants are not made for religious or political purposes.

Applications

Our research suggests that the trust does not respond to unsolicited applications.

Other information

The trust can also make grants to individuals for educational purposes and supports organisations (especially children's charities).

Professionals Aid Council

£101,000

Correspondent: Finola McNicholl, Chief Executive, 10 St Christopher's Place, London W1U 1HZ (020 7935 0641; email: admin@professionalsaid.org.uk; website: www.professionalsaid.org.uk)

CC number: 207292

Eligibility

Professionals with a strong educational background (degree level or equivalent, or working in a professional occupation requiring that level of education). Applicants must be resident in the UK and have less than £10,000 in savings.

Types of grants

Financial assistance is available in a number of forms, mainly: weekly grants, which in 2014 supported 118 beneficiaries; help with the costs of TV licences, household insurance, road tax and car insurance; one-off grants, which are given towards the purchase of clothing, cookers, beds, household items, travel and central heating. Assistance can also be given towards the costs of respite care and, in certain circumstances, with residential and nursing home fees.

Annual grant total

In 2014 the charity had assets of £2.2 million and an income of £101,000. In total, the charity assisted 228 beneficiaries during the year, some of whom received help for educational purposes. Grants totalled £121,500, of which £101,000 was given in general assistance.

Exclusions

No grants are given for private medical fees, vet bills or pet insurance, debts, mortgage repayments, utility bills or electronic equipment.

Applications

Initial enquiries can be made using the form on the website or, alternatively, by writing to the charity's Administration Department. Grants are means-tested.

Other information

The organisation also offers advice and assistance and can signpost individuals to specific occupational charities.

Reuben Foundation

£45,500

Correspondent: Patrick O'Driscoll, Trustee, 4th Floor, Millbank Tower, 21–24 Millbank, London SW1P 4QP (020 7802 5014; fax: 020 7802 5002; email: contact@reubenfoundation.com; website: www.reubenfoundation.com)

CC number: 1094130

Eligibility

People from disadvantaged backgrounds who are in need, hardship or distress as a result of local, national or international disorder or due to social or economic circumstances.

Types of grants

One-off grants according to need, generally for healthcare and educational and training purposes.

Annual grant total

In 2014 the foundation had assets of £79.3 million and an income of £4.2 million. The vast majority of support is given to organisations (almost £3.8 million during the year, around £2 million of which was paid in scholarships through educational institutions). Grants to individuals amounted to £45,500 and, we believe, were mainly given for purposes associated with healthcare.

Applications

The website states: 'Grants will be made by invitation only and on the approval of the Trustees.' Enquiries can be made to the correspondent.

Other information

The foundation was established in 2002 as an outlet for the philanthropic giving of billionaire property investors David and Simon Reuben. The foundation was endowed by the brothers with a donation of $100 million (£54.1 million), with the income generated to be given to a range of charitable causes, particularly in the fields of healthcare and education.

The J. C. Robinson Trust No. 3

£18,000

Correspondent: Christine Howe, Barnett Wood Bungalow, Blackboys, Uckfield, East Sussex TN22 5JL (email: jcrobinsontrust3@outlook.com)

CC number: 207294

Eligibility

The trust supports older and disadvantaged people. It also provides grants for training and activities that improve the community spirit of young people in England.

Types of grants

Grants range from £50 to £1,000 according to need.

Annual grant total

In 2013/14 the trust had an income of £35,000. Grants to individuals and organisations totalled £35,500 but

further details were not disclosed in the annual report.

Applications

Apply in writing to the correspondent, including supporting documents giving evidence of need, such as a letter from a doctor or social worker. Applications should usually be made through an organisation such as Citizens Advice or through a third party such as a social worker.

Mr William Saunders Charity for the Relief of Indigent Gentry and Others

£4,600

Correspondent: St Andrew Trustees Ltd, Speechly Bircham LLP, 6 St Andrew Street, London EC4A 3LX (020 7427 6400)

CC number: 212012

Eligibility

'Indigent gentry, tutors, governesses, merchants and others' (and their dependants) who are on low incomes and live throughout England and Wales.

Types of grants

Annuities for individuals on low incomes.

Annual grant total

In 2014 the charity had an income of £9,200 and a total expenditure of £9,800. We estimate that pensions to individuals totalled £4,600, with funding also awarded to local organisations that provide care for people in need.

Applications

Apply in writing to the correspondent.

The Skinners' Benevolent Trust (formerly the Hunt and Almshouse Charities)

£35,000 (92 grants)

Correspondent: Grants Administrator, Skinners Hall, 8 Dowgate Hill, London EC4R 2SP (020 7213 0562; email: charitiesadmin@skinners.org.uk; website: www.skinnershall.co.uk)

CC number: 1132640

Eligibility

The trust provides grants of up to £200 for individuals and families in need to assist in purchasing essential household items.

Support agencies must have personal, ongoing knowledge of their client's situation and the facility to receive and monitor the money the trust provides to ensure funds are spent on the items agreed.

Applicants must be either adults over 18 and living on their own, or single/two-parent families with dependent-age children (i.e. under 18). Applications cannot be accepted from cohabiting adults with no children, or with adult children over 18. Applicants must also have already applied to a local welfare scheme – where available and if eligible – and received a decision.

The trust's main priority is to help:

▶ Those living with mental health issues
▶ Those in recovery from substance/alcohol use
▶ Victims of domestic violence
▶ Those in receipt of a state retirement pension
▶ Those who have some kind of disability or chronic illness
▶ Families with dependent-age children (under 18) and are on a very low income

Types of grants

One-off grants of up to £200 towards essential household items such as white goods, furniture or children's clothing.

Annual grant total

In 2013/14 the trust held assets of £1.6 million and had an income of £55,000. Pensions and grants to individuals totalled £35,000 with 71 people receiving a grant for an essential household item and 21 people continuing to receive a pension.

Exclusions

The trust cannot consider: applications made by individuals or organisations providing one-off support or advice; applicants who have received a grant from the charity in the previous two years; general financial assistance, including debt and utility costs; mobility or computer equipment; building work; items that have already been purchased; applications on behalf of children; applications that fall outside the trust's criteria.

Applications

Application forms are available from the Grants Administrator who can be contacted by email, phone or post. Applications must be made via referral from support agencies such as social and support services, housing associations, refuge and rehabilitation organisations, and local charities. Support workers can apply on behalf of their clients. Applications can be submitted at any time during the year and are considered on a monthly basis.

Other information

The trust has an informative website.

The Henry Smith Charity (UK)

£1 million

Correspondent: Kindred Team, 6th Floor, 65–68 Leadenhall Street, London EC3A 2AD (020 7264 4970; fax: 020 7488 9097; website: www. henrysmithcharity.org.uk)

CC number: 230102

Eligibility

Individuals are eligible to register as kindred if they are direct descendants, or adoptees, of one of the kindred previously registered (with certain date restrictions). The onus is on the individual to prove their descent. Note taken from the website: 'From June 2013, following agreement with the Charity Commission, the previous requirement for descendants of kindred to be born to married parents no longer applies.'

Clergy grants are only made to ordained clergy of the Church of England. Priority is given to those with dependants.

Types of grants

The charity manages two funds for the benefit of individuals:

Kindred Scheme grants: One-off and recurrent grants for kindred who are in financial need. Grants have included: regular financial support to kindred of retirement age on low incomes, general financial assistance to those on low incomes, grants to students, training to equip young people for employment, and grants for white goods.

Poor Clergy Fund grants: Grants are awarded to fund emergency or exceptional costs which cannot be afforded by family incomes.

Note that the charity has a Student Scheme which provides for all students taking first degrees at UK universities who are registered with this charity as kindred to be eligible for a grant from The Henry Smith Charity. Contact the office for details of the scheme.

Annual grant total

In 2014 the charity had assets of £838 million and an income of £11.5 million. Grants to individuals totalled more than £1 million, of which £613,000 was given to poor kindred and £434,000 to poor clergy.

£45,000 was spent to fund bursaries for ordinands.

Applications

To register for Kindred Scheme grants or to apply for assistance, the Kindred Team can be contacted by email: kindred@henrysmithcharity.org.uk, or telephone: 020 7264 4979 or 020 7264 4980. A helpful list of FAQs is available from the website and should be read before any contact is made.

The charity's website gives the following information regarding Poor Clergy Fund grants:

> Grants are made by the Diocesan Bishops, from a budget provided by the Charity. The Poor Clergy Fund is not therefore open to applications made directly to the Charity from individual clergy. Grants are only made to ordained clergy of the Church of England and there are specific further guidelines set down by the Charity against which Diocesan Bishops may consider individual clergy for a grant.

Other information

When Henry Smith died in 1628 he left funds to help his 'poor kindred', by which he meant descendants of his sister, who were in financial need. He did not have any children of his own. The Kindred Scheme is still in operation.

The Poor Clergy Fund now has two strands, the first of which is for individuals. The second strand is known as the Surplus of the Poor Clergy Fund and makes grants for projects which promote Christianity.

The charity also makes a large number of grants to organisations (over £26 million in 2014), much of which is further distributed to individuals.

The St Martin-in-the-Fields' Christmas Appeal Charity

£895,000 (2,768 grants)

Correspondent: Craig Norman, Clerk to the Trustees, St Martin-in-the-Fields, 6 St Martin's Place, London WC2N 4JH (020 7766 1138; email: vrfapplications@ smitf.org.; website: www.smitf.org/ christmas)

CC number: 261359

Eligibility

People in need or hardship. Priority is given to those who are in danger of becoming homeless, those who are currently homeless, destitute and/or vulnerable, and those attempting to establish or maintain a tenancy.

Types of grants

One-off grants of up to £250 are given with the aim of making a positive impact and to help alleviate distress or avert a crisis. Grants from the Vicar's Relief Fund are given to pay arrears (if they put someone at risk of homelessness) and towards deposits for a more permanent home (for those in temporary accommodation). They are also available for beds, furniture and other household items such as cookers and fridges. The Vicar's Relief Fund can also fund clothing and ordinary living expenses for those who are destitute or homeless.

Annual grant total

In 2013/14 the charity held assets of £1.4 million and had an income of £1.9 million. Grants totalled more than £1.7 million, of which £895,000 was given to individuals through the Vicar's Relief Fund. The average grant was around £220.

£840,000 was awarded to The Connection at St Martin's-in-the-Field, a charity which supports homeless people in central London, giving them 'the skills and confidence they need to rebuild their lives'.

Exclusions

No grants are made for holidays, course fees, recurring costs, holidays, respite breaks, school trips, IT equipment, medical treatment, TVs and TV licences, childcare expenses, toys, books and play equipment, administrative charges, fines and professional fees, structural renovations or specialist equipment such as wheelchairs.

Applications

An application form and a list of guidelines can be requested from the correspondent. Forms must be requested and submitted on behalf of the individual by agencies such as social services, probation services, Citizens Advice or other welfare organisations.

Note: The charity can no longer accept applications that have been handwritten or faxed and cannot send application forms to anyone other than a support worker.

Other information

The charity's very interesting website states:

In 1924, the then vicar of St Martin's, Dick Sheppard, preached at a service broadcast on the BBC. He asked the listeners from around the world to mark the holiday season by sending in a donation to support those in need. The result was phenomenal, and sparked a partnership with the BBC that has been instrumental since 1927 in helping thousands of people in need across the UK every year. The money raised goes to the St Martin-in-the-Fields Vicar's Relief Fund which gives emergency grants to people in extreme financial hardship and to The Connection at St Martin's.

With over twenty services a week, St Martin's is a place of prayer and worship for Londoners and visitors alike. Throughout the 20th century, St Martin's has played an active role in wider social, humanitarian and international issues. Architecturally, spiritually, culturally and socially, St Martin's has helped to form the world around it, including playing a part in the Anti-Apartheid Movement and the founding of many charitable

organisations, including Amnesty International, Shelter and The Big Issue.

The charity receives around 400 applications for help from the fund each month which means that sometimes even eligible applications are refused. The charity tries to ensure that the fund's resources are prioritised and fairly distributed across the UK. The trustees expect applications to be made only as a last resort.

The St Vincent de Paul Society (England and Wales)

£50,000

Correspondent: Elizabeth Palmer, Chief Executive, 9 Larcom Street, London SE17 1RX (020 7703 3030; email: info@ svp.org.uk; website: www.svp.org.uk)

CC number: 1053992

Eligibility

Anyone in need in England and Wales. Although predominantly a Catholic charity, it is completely non-denominational in its operation. Grants are only offered following a visit from a member of the society.

Types of grants

Material assistance is given in the provision of furniture, food, appliances, clothes, fuel and small financial disbursements. Friendship to anyone in need is a fundamental principle of the society; financial relief is incidental to this. During the year over 500,000 visits were made to individuals and families across England and Wales.

Annual grant total

The trust is not primarily a grant-making organisation and will only make financial assistance through the family support and befriending schemes. In 2013/14 the total expenditure in this area was £1.5 million; however, the trust does not publish separate grant figures. In previous years grants have amounted to around £50,000.

Exclusions

There are no grants available for education.

Applications

Apply in writing to the correspondent at any time. Applications can be submitted directly by the individual or through any third party, such as advice centres or probation services. The application should detail the nature of the request and relevant background information. A contact address and telephone number for the person requiring assistance must be provided to enable staff to arrange a visit as well as, if applicable, the contact

details of the person making the application.

Other information

There are around 1,050 parish groups in England and Wales, with around 10,000 members who raise and distribute income locally. The society runs six children's camps, seven holiday homes, four residential premises, as well as support centres and programmes. Considerable support is given to developing countries by SVP members in India, Sudan, South Sudan, Guyana, Grenada and Romania.

The charity's advice and support centres provide advice on issues such as debt, housing and benefits, as well as services such as counselling, training and employment support.

Mary Strand Charitable Trust

£47,500

Correspondent: Lynda Walker, Trustee, c/o Universe Media Group, Guardian Print Centre, Longbridge Road, Trafford Park, Manchester M17 1SN (0161 214 1200; email: lynda.walker@ catholicuniverse.com)

CC number: 800301

Eligibility

People who are in need due to poverty, sickness or old age.

Types of grants

One-off and recurrent grants, towards items like household goods, essential travel costs and clothing.

Annual grant total

In 2014 the trust had assets of £353,500, an income of £68,500 and a total expenditure of £130,000. Grants awarded to individuals for welfare purposes totalled £47,500.

Applications

Apply in writing to the correspondent. Applications should be submitted through a local priest, charity or welfare agency.

Other information

The trustees publish a column in each edition of The Catholic Universe, a weekly Catholic newspaper. The column contains details of deserving causes with names changed to preserve anonymity, and appeals are made for specific requirements. Donations from readers are received in answer to these appeals and then distributed.

Grants are also paid to organisations (£68,000 in 2014).

The Talisman Charitable Trust

£146,000 (147 grants)

Correspondent: Philip Denman, Trustee, Basement Office, 354 Kennington Road, London SE11 4LD (020 7820 0254; email: talismancharity@gmail.com; website: www.talismancharity.org)

CC number: 207173

Eligibility

People in the UK who are living on a very low income.

Types of grants

One-off and recurrent grants are given according to need.

Annual grant total

In 2013/14 the trust had assets of £10.4 million and an income of £205,500. Grants totalled £205,000, of which £172,000 was awarded to individuals. 147 grants to individuals for social welfare purposes amounted to £146,000 and were distributed as follows:

Housing	82	£74,500
Disablement or disability	32	£45,500
Small means or hardship	17	£14,200
Child poverty	14	£11,100
Health	2	£600

20 grants, totalling £26,000, were also made to individuals for educational purposes and organisations received a further £33,000.

Exclusions

The trust cannot accept applications made by recorded delivery or other signed-for services.

Applications

Applications should be made in writing to the correspondent through a social worker, Citizens Advice or similar third party. They should be on headed paper and include the individual's full name and address, a summary of their financial circumstances, what is needed and how much it will cost. A brief history of the case and a list of any other charities approached should also be included, as should the payment details of the third party organisation. Supporting evidence such as medical documentation, a letter from the applicant's school or written quotations would also be helpful. The trust stresses that original documentation should not be submitted, as it cannot be returned. Applications are considered throughout the year. Only successful applications will receive a reply. See the website for full guidelines on how to apply.

Other information

This trust was previously called The Late Baron F. A. D'Erlanger's Charitable Trust.

S. C. Witting Trust

£8,200

Correspondent: Christopher Gregory, Secretary, Friends House, 173 Euston Road, London NW1 2BJ (020 7663 1082; email: chris@quaker.org.uk)

CC number: 237698-10

Eligibility

Individuals in need, ordinarily resident in England, either under the age of 15 or over the age of 60.

Types of grants

One-off grants (on average of about £200) for specific items.

Annual grant total

The correspondent has informed us that the budget for welfare grants was £8,200 in 2015.

Exclusions

Grants are not made towards helping reduce debts or as loans.

Applications

Applications must be made in writing by a social worker or other key professional. They must give a short case history, reasons for need and the amount needed. Grants are only made to third party agencies, so payee details must be included. Requests are considered monthly and unsuccessful applications will not be acknowledged unless an sae is provided. The trust **does not** welcome any phone calls or emails.

Other information

Grants are also made to students who are following a course of study at university, and who are ordinarily resident in England.

This trust is linked to Friends Trust Limited (Charity Commission no. 236698).

Utilities

Anglian Water Assistance Fund

£430,000

Correspondent: Charis Grants, Anglian Water Assistance Fund, PO Box 42, Peterborough PE3 8XH (01733 421060 (Charis Grants); website: www.anglianwater.co.uk/awaf)

Eligibility

The fund can consider helping you if you are in debt with your water and/or sewerage charges to Anglian or Hartlepool Water and you are a current domestic account holder of Anglian or Hartlepool Water.

Types of grants

The fund may be able to help clear arrears of domestic water and sewerage charges by offering a number of solutions.

Annual grant total

In 2013/14 the company Anglian Water made a donation to the fund of £380,000. The fund in turn made assistance grants of £430,000. These were the figures given in the company's 2013/14 annual accounts.

Exclusions

You are not eligible to apply to the fund if you are already having water and/or sewerage charges deducted from your benefits via the Water Direct scheme.

Check the website for current exclusions before applying.

Applications

The quickest way to apply is through the online application form on the trust's website. Alternatively applicants may download the form or call the trust to receive one in the post. The fund stresses that applicants should ensure that they have included the relevant information necessary to process the application. The fund will need to see evidence of income and water debts, if applicable. If there are arrears of water/sewerage charges, the fund will always look for a full explanation of how the arrears have arisen.

The fund will write to applicants to let them know whether they have been successful or not.

Individuals who receive an award from the trust cannot apply again. Those who do not receive an award are eligible to re-apply after six months.

Other information

The Anglian Water Assistance Fund (formerly The Anglian Water Trust Fund) is administered by Charis Grants Ltd which also manages the British Gas Energy Trust, EDF Energy Trust, South East Water's Helping Hand and Affinity Water Trust.

British Gas Energy Trust

£12.2 million (16,675 grants)

Correspondent: Grants Officer, 3rd Floor, Midgate House, Midgate, Peterborough PE1 1TN (01733 421060; fax: 01733 421020; email: bget@charisgrants.com; website: www.britishgasenergytrust.org.uk)

CC number: 1106218

Eligibility

The trust helps individuals and families who are struggling to pay for their consumption of gas and electricity, with the aim of helping people to get back on their feet and remain debt free. Applications to the trust are welcomed from anyone living within England, Scotland or Wales.

Types of grants

Grants to clear gas and electricity debts and to clear other priority household debts or purchase essential household items such as:

▶ Boiler replacement
▶ Energy-efficient white goods
▶ Funeral arrears
▶ Bankruptcy/Debt Relief Order/Low Income Low Asset (Scotland) fees – these payments are known as Further Assistance Payments (FAPs)

Annual grant total

In 2014 the trust held assets of £9.2 million and had an income of £12.4 million. Grants to individuals in respect of energy debt totalled £7.4 million and grants to individuals in respect of further assistance payments totalled £4.8 million.

Exclusions

The trust cannot give loans or help with bills or items that have already been paid for. Nor can it help with the following: any household item that is not a white good; fines for criminal offences; overpayments of benefits; educational or training needs; business debts; debts to central government departments such as tax and national insurance; catalogues, credit cards, personal loans and other forms of non-secured lending; medical equipment, aids and adaptations; deposits to secure accommodation; and holidays.

Applications

The quickest way to apply is via the trust's online application form. Forms can also be downloaded from the website or requested by email or by telephoning the correspondent. A local money advice centre such as Citizens Advice may be able to provide help in completing the form. Supporting documentation is required and the assessment of applications cannot begin without it. Evidence of income can be shown via bank statements, wage slips or benefit letters. All evidence provided must be dated within three months; however, the trust can accept annual benefit letters for work pension, state pension, child benefit and Disability Living Allowance (DLA). Applicants are strongly advised to seek money advice before applying to the trust to increase the chance of a successful application.

Those in receipt of an award from the trust cannot re-apply for two years. Applicants who do not receive an award can re-apply if their circumstances change.

Other information

Grants are also made to voluntary organisations working in the field of money advice, debt counselling or energy efficiency advice.

EDF Energy Trust

£2.66 million (4,036 grants)

Correspondent: Grant Administrator, Freepost EDF Energy Trust (01733 421060; fax: 01733 421020; email: edfet@charisgrants.com; website: www.edfenergytrust.org.uk)

CC number: 1099446

Eligibility

Current domestic account holders of EDF energy (i.e. the person or people named on the bill) who are in need, hardship or other distress. The trust aims particularly to assist those who are struggling to pay for domestic electricity and/or gas services.

Types of grants

Grants are given to help clear gas and electricity debts owed to EDF energy and other suppliers. Further Assistance Payments can also be given for: bankruptcy/Debt Relief Orders; sequestration and Minimal Asset Process fees; and the purchase of essential energy efficient white goods and cookers.

Annual grant total

In 2014 the trust had assets of £618,000 and an income of almost £2.9 million. During the year, 4,036 awards were made totalling £2.66 million. Of the awards made, 3,567 amounting to £2.52 million were given to clear gas and electricity debts, and the remaining 469 – given as Further Assistance Payments – totalled £137,000.

The trust's annual report notes that: 'In 2014 the average individual energy award was £707, a 24% increase on 2013's average of £568, and the average Further Assistance Payment value was £292, an increase of 117% on 2013's total average of £134.'

Exclusions

The trust cannot assist with: loans, or bills or items already paid for; fines for criminal offences; educational or training needs; debts to central or local government departments; deposits to secure accommodation; mortgage payments; medical equipment, aids or adaptations; overpayment of benefits; business debts; credit cards, personal loans and other forms of non-secured lending; holidays; rent or council tax arrears; beds or carpets.

Applications

Apply online or by downloading an application form from the website and returning it to: FREEPOST EDF Energy Trust. Application forms can also be requested from the trust directly by telephone or email, or in writing.

All applicants are advised to seek appropriate money or debt advice from an organisation such as Citizens Advice before making an application in order to increase their chances of success. We would advise potential applicants in the first instance to consider the guidelines available from the trust's website before beginning an application.

Those in receipt of an award from the trust cannot re-apply for two years. Applicants who do not receive an award can apply again if their circumstances change. Payments for bills will be made directly to the supplier.

Other information

The trust's 2014 annual report provided the following helpful information:

> The Charity received and assessed a total of 10,144 applications during 2014, 8% of which were submitted with the support of a funded organisation (see Organisational Grants Programme). Research has shown an application supported by a funded organisation is twice as likely to succeed as an application submitted unaided.

The trust, which is administered by Charis Grants, also makes grants to organisations to support money and debt advice and fuel debt prevention services in communities.

The Severn Trent Water Charitable Trust Fund

£1.7 million (2,812 grants)

Correspondent: Grants Officer, 12–14 Mill Street, Sutton Coldfield, West Midlands B72 1TJ (0121 355 7766; email: office@sttf.org.uk; website: www.sttf.org.uk)

CC number: 1108278

Eligibility

People with water or sewage services by Severn Trent Water, or by companies or organisations which operate on behalf of Severn Trent, who are in financial difficulty and unable to pay their water charges.

Types of grants

One-off grants are given to clear or reduce water and/or sewage debt. Further assistance can be given through the purchase of essential household items or by the payment of other priority bills and debts. These grants are limited and will normally only be given if an application shows either that it will help the individual maintain a future sustainable weekly budget, or it will make an important and significant difference to the individual's quality of life. Generally, grants are paid directly to the appropriate organisation.

Annual grant total

In 2013/14 the fund held assets of £2.3 million and had an income of £4.6 million. Financial assistance to 2,812 individuals and families totalled over £1.7 million and was distributed as follows:

Water debts	£1.3 million
Debt advice/counselling	£353,000
Other household needs	£39,500
Bankruptcy orders	£11,500
Electricity	£1,700
Rent	£1,650
Gas	£1,850
Council tax	£0

Exclusions

No grants are made for court fines, catalogue debts, benefits/tax credit overpayments, personal loans or other forms of borrowing. No retrospective grants are given. Grants are usually one-off and applicants cannot re-apply within two years of receipt.

Applications

Applications can be made on the fund's website directly or you can download a form from the fund's website. Applications can be submitted at any time by the individual or through a money advice centre, Citizens Advice or similar third party, to: Severn Trent Trust Fund, FREEPOST RLZE-EABT-SHSA, Sutton Coldfield B72 1TJ.

Applicants may receive a telephone call or visit as part of the application process. Unsuccessful applicants may re-apply after six months.

Other information

The fund also made grants totalling £353,000 to organisations which provide free debt advice and debt counselling services. Although this amount was paid to organisations, it was for services to individuals selected by the fund and has been included in the total amount of grants.

South East Water's Helping Hand

£100,000

Correspondent: Customer Care Team, Customer Care Team, South East Water, Snodland, Kent ME6 5AH (0333 000 0001; email: customer.care@ southeastwater.co.uk; website: www. southeastwater.co.uk/helpinghand)

Eligibility

Domestic customers of South East Water who, through whatever difficulty, have found themselves in debt and unable to pay their water/sewerage charges.

Types of grants

Grants are initially made on a provisional basis: following the receipt of a provisional award, an applicant needs to demonstrate their commitment and ability to improve their financial sustainability and their ability to pay current and future water charges. After this period, if the applicant is judged to have taken these steps, their award will be confirmed and their debt to the company at the time of the provisional award will be cleared.

Annual grant total

Grants usually total around £100,000 per year.

Applications

Applicants may apply online on the fund's website or by completing an application form which can be obtained via download or by telephoning the fund's application request line. Applicants must attach the relevant supporting documents. Such documents include: proof of income, relevant bills and evidence of any special circumstances such as disability. The application must be made in the account holder's name.

Successful applicants may not apply again. Unsuccessful applicants may re-apply if their circumstances change.

Other information

The fund was founded by South East Water upon the dissolution of the EOS Foundation in April 2010.

United Utilities Trust Fund

£5.9 million

Correspondent: The Secretary, Emmanuel Court, 12–14 Mill Street, Sutton Coldfield B72 1TJ (0845 179 1791; email: contact@uutf.org.uk; website: www.uutf.org.uk)

CC number: 1108296

Eligibility

People in need who live in the area supplied by United Utilities Water (predominantly the north west of England).

Types of grants

Payments for water and/or sewerage charges due to United Utilities Water. The trust can also help with water or sewerage charges which are collected by other companies or organisations on behalf of United Utilities Water. In certain cases, the trust can also consider giving some help to meet other essential bills, household needs or priority debts. Payments are made directly to the supplier.

Annual grant total

In 2013/14 the trust had assets of £404,000 and an income of £7 million. Grants to individuals totalled £5.9 million.

During the year, the trust received 8,823 applications and was able to provide assistance in 5,772 cases.

Exclusions

No support is given for court fines, catalogue debts, credit cards, personal loans or other forms of borrowing; statutory loans/benefit overpayments/tax credit overpayments now being reclaimed. The fund cannot make payments towards bills already paid or purchases already made.

The trust will not normally consider more than one application from the same person.

Applications

Application forms and full guidelines are available from the website. Money advisers and other referral agents may use the online application process. Applicants may receive a phone call or a home visit as part of the assessment process. All applications will be acknowledged and applicants will be issued with a reference number which they must use when making enquiries regarding the application. Successful applicants may not re-apply for a period of two years, while unsuccessful applicants may apply again after six months.

For grants towards bankruptcy fees, a separate application form is required; call 0845 179 1791 to request one.

Other information

The trust states: 'One of the Trust's aims is to help people out of immediate financial difficulties and wherever possible through debt counselling/money advice to encourage and help financial stability in the future.' In 2013/14 grants totalling £330,000 were awarded towards debt counselling services.

Yorkshire Water Community Trust

£787,500 (1,966 grants)

Correspondent: Tasleem Salaq, Trust Officer, Freepost BD3074, Bradford BD3 7BR (0845124 24 26; fax: 01274 262265; email: info@ywct.org.uk; website: www.yorkshirewater.com/ watersure)

CC number: 1047923

Eligibility

People who are in arrears with Yorkshire Water and have at least one other priority debt, such as gas or electricity, council tax, rent or mortgage repayments. Council and housing association tenants whose water charges are included with their rent may also apply.

Types of grants

No cash grants are given. One-off payments are made to Yorkshire Water and credited to the applicant's account. The average award in 2013/14 was £401.

Annual grant total

In 2013/14 the trust had an income of £850,500 and a total expenditure of £860,500. An overall amount of £787,500 was awarded in 1,966 grants to individuals.

Exclusions

Successful applicants may not re-apply within two years.

Applications

Application forms are available from the correspondent or can be downloaded from the trust's website. Helpful guidance notes are available on the trust's website and potential applicants are advised to read these carefully before making an application. Enquiries are welcomed.

Charities by beneficiary

This chapter includes all the charities that award grants to certain groups of beneficiary (for instance based on gender or age) or to individuals in specific circumstances (such as homeless people or refugees and asylum seekers).

The categories in this chapter are ordered alphabetically. 'Children and young people' includes charities that specifically award grants to people aged 25 or under, while 'Older people' includes grant-makers that give to people aged around 55 or older. Although this reflects the criteria of some of the grant-making charities in these chapters, the exact age restrictions specified by each individual charity do vary. The 'Miscellaneous' section includes charities with specific criteria that do not fall under any of the other categories in this guide. 'Religion' includes charities that support people of a particular religious group, while charities that specifically support those in religious occupations are listed in the 'Occupational charities' chapter in this guide (see page 103).

Please note that most of the charities within any given section still have further restrictions on who they can help. Individuals who fall into a particular category (such as 'older people') should not apply to all of the charities in the relevant section, but should first consider carefully whether they are eligible for each one.

The charities under any of the categories in this chapter are by no means the only charities in this guide that will give to that particular group of beneficiaries; they are simply the only charities that specify this group as their main criteria. For example, as well as the charities under 'Specific circumstances – Asylum seekers and refugees', there will also be charities in the 'General charities' chapter, or local sections, that will give grants to asylum seekers and refugees as part of a wider set of criteria.

Index of charities by beneficiary

Children and young people

The Avenel Trust

£9,400

Correspondent: The Trustees, 77 Comiston Drive, Edinburgh EH10 5QT

OSCR number: SC014080

Eligibility

Children in need (under 18 years old) and students of nursing living in Scotland.

Types of grants

One-off grants, usually of £10 to £500, are given for safety items such as fireguards and safety gates, shoes, clothing, bedding, cots and pushchairs, money for bus passes, recreational activities for young carers and washing machines.

Annual grant total

In 2013/14 the trust had an income of £25,000 and a total expenditure of £26,500. Grants are made to individuals and organisations, it would appear, mainly for social welfare purposes. We estimate that social welfare grants to individuals totalled £9,400.

Exclusions

Grants are not given for holidays or household furnishings.

Applications

Applications are considered every two months and should be submitted through a tutor or third party such as a social worker, health visitor or teacher. Applicants are encouraged to provide as much information about their family or individual circumstances and needs as possible in their applications. Applications can only be accepted from people currently residing in Scotland.

Buttle UK – Small Grants Programme

£2.6 million (11,888 grants)

Correspondent: Hazel Sewell, Small Grants Officer, 15 Greycoat Place, London SW1P 1SB (02078287311; email: info@buttleuk.org; website: www. buttleuk.org)

CC number: 313007

Eligibility

Children under 18 years old living with parents or careers and estranged, orphaned and vulnerable young people under 20 years of age and living independently. The trustees prioritise people facing exceptional difficulties or crisis, particularly living in severe poverty or facing domestic violence, drug and alcohol misuse, estrangement, illness, distress, abuse, neglect, or behavioural or mental health issues.

Types of grants

One-off grants, for a range of essential household items or services which are critical to the well-being of a child. Grants are provided for cookers, fridges, washing machines and children's beds and bedding. Financial support is available for items of furniture, household equipment, baby necessities, and clothing. A full list of eligible and ineligible items can be found on the charity's website.

Annual grant total

In 2013/14 the charity had assets of £48.8 million and an income of around £4.3 million. A total of 11,888 grants were awarded totalling over £2.6 million.

Exclusions

The charity cannot help:

▶ People over 21 years of age
▶ Families and young people not normally resident in the UK or who are non-EU residents on a student or work visa
▶ Parents who are not the main carer for the child
▶ Young people leaving care who can access funding under the provisions of The Children (Leaving Care) Act 2000

Applications

Applications can be made online on the charity's website and should be completed by a statutory or voluntary organisation which supports the family or the individual and is capable of assessing their needs and can also administer a grant on behalf of the charity.

Contact details for applicants resident in:

England: 15 Greycoat Place, London SW1P 1SB, infor@buttleuk.org, 020 7828 7311

Scotland: PO Box 5075, Glasgow G78 4WA, scotland@buttleuk.org, 01505 850437

Wales: PO Box 2528, Cardiff CF23 0GX, wales@buttleuk.org, 029 2054 1996

Northern Ireland: PO Box 484, Belfast BT6 0YA, nireland@buttleuk.org, 028 9064 1164

Further information and guidelines are available on the charity's website.

Other information

Grants are also distributed through the BBC Children in Need Emergency Essentials Programme which the trustees administer.

The charity also runs the following initiatives:

School Fees Programme

Some children, many because of problems at home, do not thrive in mainstream education, and so fail or drop out of school entirely. The School Fees Programme funds places at schools that provide a safe and supportive environment for those at future risk of going into formal care. It enables children with medical, emotional or social difficulties to gain a stable and more supportive secondary education.

Support for Young People

The Enhanced Packages Programme provides funding of up to £2,000 for estranged young people aged 16–20. The charity's casework team works directly with young people and referrers to remove the financial barriers that stand in the way of achieving their long-term education, employment or training goals.

The Anchor Project

The first project of its kind, designed to meet the physical, emotional and developmental needs of children and young people affected by domestic violence. Note, this funding is only available for families who live in London.

Happy Days Children's Charity

See entry on page 57

Lifeline 4 Kids (Handicapped Children's Aid Committee)

£30,000

Correspondent: Roger Adelman, Correspondent, 215 West End Lane, West Hampstead, London NW6 1XJ (020 7794 1661; email: appeals@ lifeline4kids.org; website: www. lifeline4kids.org)

CC number: 200050

Eligibility

Children and young people with disabilities under the age of 19.

Types of grants

Cash grants are never given. The charity will purchase specific requested items or equipment on behalf of the individual.

The charity's website explains:

> For the individual child we provide the full spectrum of specialised equipment such as electric wheelchairs, mobility aids and varying items including specialised computers and sensory toys. We are able to give emergency and welfare appeals immediate approval within the authorised limits of our welfare sub-committee. No appeal is too large or too small for us to consider.

Annual grant total

In 2014 the charity had an income of £23,500 and an expenditure of £67,000. We estimate that around £30,000 was given in grants to individuals.

Exclusions

Funding is not normally provided for:

▶ Building or garden works
▶ Fridges, cookers or ovens
▶ Carpets/floor covering
▶ Washing machines
▶ Clothing
▶ Shoes (unless specialist)
▶ Childcare costs
▶ Transport expenses
▶ Tuition fees
▶ Driving lessons
▶ Recreational activities or holidays

Applications

Initially, apply in writing (preferably by email) to the correspondent, indicating any specific requirements and including brief factual information (such as the child's name, date of birth and health condition as well as indicating specific requirements, cost of the help sought and family contact details. If appropriate, an application form will then be sent out (you should specify whether you would prefer to receive it by email or post). The form contains questions relating to the child's medical condition and requires backup information from health professionals together with a financial statement of the applicant.

Applications are considered monthly, although urgent cases can be dealt with more quickly.

Other information

The trust also supplies equipment and items for schools, children's hospices, respite care homes and clubs for children who have a disability or are underprivileged.

The charity notes that they have been inundated with applications for iPads. Candidates are reminded that funding can only be considered for the iPad 16GB for a child over the age of five subject to specific circumstances (mainly where the request is supported by the child's school). For more details see the website or discuss this further with the charity.

Rees Foundation

£1,000

Correspondent: Sarah Millan, Director, Abberley View, Saxon Business Park, Hanbury Road, Stoke Prior, Bromsgrove B60 4AD (07964 966067; email: sarah. milan@reesfoundation.org; website: www.reesfoundation.org)

CC number: 1154019

Eligibility

Young people and adults leaving foster or residential care.

Types of grants

The foundation has a limited Crisis Fund to provide immediate financial support for emergency situations 'to help care leavers keep body and soul together'. Grants may cover rent arrears, travel costs for employment or education, equipment related to work, training or educational needs, or food or winter fuel.

Annual grant total

In 2014 the foundation had an income of £158,500 and a total expenditure of £131,000. Full accounts were not available to view on the Charity Commission's website at the time of writing (November 2015). Most of the expenditure appears to be spent on the service provision. The correspondent has informed us that the Crisis Fund is reliant on donations and can provide about £1,000 in grants in the next year, although this figure may vary.

Applications

In the first instance applicants should get in touch with the foundation to discuss their needs. There is an online 'Request Support' facility on the website.

Other information

The foundation also offers practical advice and emotional guidance on a range of matters, as well as a mentoring service and signposting.

Part of the support the foundation offers is a crowdfunding platform to support an individual's fundraising efforts.

People who are still in care may also receive help.

The Rycroft Children's Fund

£12,000

Correspondent: Mark Stirzaker, Correspondent, Lower Dunisbooth House, Lane Head, Rochdale OL12 6BH (07778 671 012; email: rycroftchildrensfund@outlook.com; website: www.rycroftchildrensfund.co. uk)

CC number: 231771

Eligibility

Children in need who live in Cheshire, Derbyshire, Greater Manchester, Lancashire, Staffordshire, South and West Yorkshire. There is a preference for children living in the cities of Manchester and Salford and the borough of Trafford. Applicants should be aged 18 or under.

Types of grants

One-off grants according to need.

Annual grant total

In 2013/14 the fund held assets of £1.2 million and had an income of £73,000. Grants totalled £24,000, of which we estimate £12,000 was given to individuals.

Exclusions

Grants are not given to individuals for education, overseas travel, individual holidays or computers.

Applications

Applications can be made through the fund's website.

Dr Meena Sharma Memorial Foundation
See entry on page 29

Eliza Shepherd Charitable Trust

£900

Correspondent: Carol Shepherd, Trustee, Southview Cottage, Islington Road, Islington, Alton, Hampshire GU34 4PR (01420 520375)

CC number: 1064464

Eligibility

Children and young people who are in need.

Types of grants

Grants are awarded according to need.

Annual grant total

In 2013/14 the trust had an income of £2,300 and a total expenditure of £1,800. Grants are made to both individuals and organisations. We estimate that the amount of grants given to individuals amounted to around £900.

Applications

Apply in writing to the correspondent.

Ellen Rebe Spalding Memorial Fund
See entry on page 29

Ethnic and national minorities in the UK

The Assyrian Charity and Relief Fund of UK

£700

Correspondent: Revd Henry Shaheen, Correspondent, 277 Rush Green Road, Romford RM7 0JL (01708 730122; email: henry.andrew.shaheen@gmail.com)

CC number: 1050419

Eligibility

People of Assyrian descent and Iraqi refugees living in the UK or worldwide who are in need, hardship or distress.

Types of grants

The fund offers food, medicine and temporary shelter to people in need. One-off and recurrent grants can be made, usually ranging between £10 and £400.

Annual grant total

In 2014/15 the trust had both an income and a total expenditure of £750. We estimate that social welfare grants to individuals totalled about £700.

Exclusions

Grants are not available for business people, political organisations, those already settled in Europe, America, Australia and Canada or those who are financially secure.

Applications

Applications can be made writing to the correspondent. They should be submitted through a social worker, Citizens Advice, welfare agency or other charity.

The German Society of Benevolence

£13,000

Correspondent: David Leigh, Correspondent, Leigh Saxton Green, 4–7 Manchester Street, London W1U 3AE

CC number: 247379

Eligibility

Older people in need who are, or were, citizens of Germany, and their dependants. Applicants must live in Greater London, Essex, Hertfordshire, Kent or Surrey.

Types of grants

Small, one-off and recurrent grants for heating, clothing and other needs.

Annual grant total

In 2013/14 the society had an income of £7,100 and a total expenditure of £14,100. We estimate that the amount of grants given to individuals totalled £13,000.

Applications

Applications are considered from individuals or from agencies acting on their behalf.

India Welfare Society

£3,200

Correspondent: Suresh Gupta, President, 11 Middle Row, London W10 5AT (020 8969 9493; email: iwslondon@hotmail.com)

CC number: 286800

Eligibility

Members of the Indian community who have membership with the society and are in need.

Types of grants

One-off and recurrent grants are given according to need for hardship and welfare purposes only.

Annual grant total

In 2014, the society had an income of £7,300 and a total expenditure of £6,600. We estimate that the total amount of grants awarded to individuals was approximately £3,200, as the society also awards grants for other charitable purposes.

Applications

Apply in writing to the correspondent.

Other information

The society also offers advice on welfare issues and runs events and social activities.

The Netherlands' Benevolent Society

£21,900 (19 grants)

Correspondent: Social Work Co-ordinator, PO Box 858, Bognor Regis, West Sussex PO21 9HS (01932 355885; fax: 01932 355885; email: info@ koningwillemfonds.org.uk; website: www.koningwillemfonds.org.uk)

CC number: 213032

Eligibility

People in need who are Dutch nationals or of Dutch extraction and living in the UK. Assistance may also be given to widows, widowers and dependants of Dutch nationals.

Types of grants

One-off grants ranging between £100 and £1,000 and regular allowances of £80 per month. In the past grants have included payments for: debts to allow someone to make a fresh start; essential home repairs; clothing; basic living items; and the costs of a training course where they lead to employment. Loans may also be made.

Annual grant total

In 2014 the trust had assets of £951,500 and an income of £44,000. Grants were made to 19 individuals (of 36 applications received) totalling £21,900.

Exclusions

Beneficiaries must not have access to financial help from other sources.

Applications

Apply on a form available from the Social Work Co-ordinator. Applications are usually made through churches, the Netherlands Embassy, the Netherlands Consulates, the Department of Work and Pensions regional offices or welfare charities. They are considered every month, except in August, at the trustees' monthly meeting, although emergency cases may be considered sooner. Information of the individual's financial situation, including details of any social security benefits, should be included. All enquiries are acknowledged.

Other information

The trust provides ongoing support, keeping in contact with applicants and beneficiaries.

The Pusinelli Convalescent and Holiday Home

£4,600

Correspondent: David Leigh, Charity Administrator, Leigh Saxton Green, 4–7 Manchester Street, London W1U 3AE (020 7486 5553; email: enquiries@lsg-ca.co.uk)

CC number: 239734

Eligibility

People who are or were German citizens and their dependants. Applicants must live in Greater London, Essex, Hertfordshire, Kent or Surrey.

Types of grants

Grants of up to £500 for families who would not otherwise be able to have a holiday.

Annual grant total

In 2013/14 the charity had an income of £6,100 and a total expenditure of £4,800. We estimate that the total amount of grants awarded to individuals was approximately £4,600.

Applications

Applications should be made to the correspondent directly from the individual or from any welfare agency on their behalf.

The Society of Friends of Foreigners in Distress

£18,000

Correspondent: Valerie Goodhart, Trustee, 68 Burhill Road, Hersham, Walton-on-Thames KT12 4JF (01932 244916; email: vkgoodhart@gmail.com)

CC number: 212593

Eligibility

People living in London or its surrounding area who are from countries which are not in the Commonwealth, the USA or which were not once part of the British Empire.

Types of grants

Pensions and one-off grants can be awarded for electrical goods, clothing, living costs, household bills, food, travel expenses and repatriation, furniture and equipment for disabilities.

Annual grant total

In 2013/14 the society had an income of £13,200 and a total expenditure of £22,000. We estimate that the amount of grants given to individuals totalled around £18,000.

Applications

Apply in writing to the correspondent at any time. Applications should be submitted by a social worker, Citizens Advice or other welfare agency.

The Spanish Welfare Fund

£7,500

Correspondent: Robert Rouse, Fund Administrator, 9 Bridle Close, Surbiton Road, Kingston upon Thames, Surrey KT1 2JW (020 8546 1817)

CC number: 273177

Eligibility

Spanish nationals in need who live in the UK and their dependants.

Types of grants

One-off and recurrent grants are given according to need.

Annual grant total

In 2014 the fund had an income of £6,500 and a total expenditure of £8,000. We estimate that the total amount of grants awarded to individuals was approximately £7,500.

Applications

Apply in writing to the correspondent.

The Swiss Benevolent Society

£20,500

Correspondent: Petra Kehr Cocks, Welfare Officer, 79 Endell Street, London WC2H 9DY (020 7836 9119; fax: 020 7379 1096; email: info@ swissbenevolent.org.uk; website: www. swissbenevolent.org.uk)

CC number: 1111348

Eligibility

Swiss citizens who are experiencing hardship and are temporarily or permanently resident in the consular district of London. In special cases, those living in other parts of the UK may also receive assistance.

Types of grants

Monthly pensions and one-off grants towards holidays, heating costs, travel to and from day centres, therapies, household equipment, telephone and TV licences, for example.

Annual grant total

In 2014 the society had an income of £57,000 and a total expenditure of £54,000. Grants to individuals totalled £20,500. Of this total, £688 was distributed to 20 individuals in pensions, and the remaining £19,700 was distributed in one-off grants to individuals.

Applications

Apply in writing to the welfare officer including proof of nationality. Applications can be submitted directly by the individual, through an organisation such as Citizens Advice or via any third party. They are considered at any time.

Other information

The trust has a welfare officer who also supports beneficiaries through: providing advice, counselling and support; offering advocacy with various agencies; co-ordinating overall care; and arranging visits from volunteers to homes, hospitals and nursing homes.

Zimbabwe Rhodesia Relief Fund

£7,000

Correspondent: Hon. W. Walker, Correspondent, PO Box 5307, Bishop Stortford, Hertfordshire CM23 3DY (01279 466121; email: denis@ mirrormedia.com)

CC number: 326922

Eligibility

Zimbabweans living worldwide who are distressed or sick.

Types of grants

One-off and recurrent grants of around £70 to £300.

Annual grant total

In 2013/14 the fund had an income of £13,800 and a total expenditure of £14,400. We estimate that the amount of grants given to individuals totalled £7,000, with Zimbabwe-based charitable organisations also receiving funding.

Exclusions

Grants are not given for educational purposes or for travel.

Applications

Apply in writing to the correspondent. Applications should be made through somebody known to the charity and include proof of past or present Zimbabwean citizenship.

Families

The Family Holiday Association

£692,000 (2,800 grants)

Correspondent: Grants Team, 3 Gainsford Street, London SE1 2NE (020 3117 0651; fax: 020 7323 7299; email: grantofficer@familyholiday association.org.uk; website: www. fhaonline.org.uk)

CC number: 800262

Eligibility

The Family Holiday Association was set up to help families, and considers a family to consist of dependent children and those who care for them. Carers can be parents, grandparents, guardians and others with caring responsibilities, such as an older child.

The family must:
▷ Be referred by someone who knows the family in a professional capacity and is aware of the family circumstances, for instance a social worker, health visitor, teacher or support worker, and who can support them until they go on the break
▷ Have at least one child in the family who is under 18 years old at the time of the holiday
▷ Be on a low income
▷ Not have had a holiday in the last four years

If the family is caring for a child who is ill or has disabilities, they should refer to The Family Fund at: www.FamilyFund. org.uk

The Family Fund is an independent charity funded by the four national governments of England, Northern Ireland, Scotland and Wales that gives grants to families living in the UK who are caring for such children aged 17 years or younger. Families in these circumstances should apply to the Family Fund before making an application to the Family Holiday Association. If the family is successful in their application to the Family Fund, they will no longer be eligible for support from the Family Holiday Association.

Types of grants

Day trips, short breaks, week-long holidays, group trips and group projects. Holidays are generally for holiday parks in the UK such as Haven or Butlins. Breaks include accommodation, linen rental (where available), entertainment passes and holiday insurance (subject to medical conditions). The charity may also make a contribution towards holiday expenses. Refer to the charity's excellent Q&A section on its website for further information.

Annual grant total

In 2013/14 the charity held assets of £1 million and had an income of £1.5 million. Holidays for a record number of 2,800 families amounted to £692,000.

Exclusions

Note the following terms and conditions taken from the fund's Q&A section of its website: 'The Family Holiday Association regrets that it is not in a position to help families with no recourse to public funds or those in receipt of foster care payments.'

If offered a break you must abide strictly by the Family Holiday Association's terms and conditions. The family and referrer must agree that:

▶ The offer cannot be transferred to another family; it is only for the family and family members named on the application form
▶ The offer is valid for a limited time: offers not taken up in time will be withdrawn
▶ The offer has no cash value: if the family has to cancel their break they cannot claim a cash alternative
▶ If the family is unable to go on the holiday the Family Holiday Association must be notified immediately
▶ The family and referring agent must complete holiday feedback forms within four weeks of returning from the holiday

Failure to meet terms and conditions may jeopardise future applications.

Applications

Applications can be made on behalf of families by charities such as Barnardo's, social workers, health visitors or other caring agencies. Note the following from the fund's website:

The referrer acts as the point of contact for the family during the holiday process, submitting the application, helping the family with holiday preparations, and dealing with any expenses offered. Many of the families we work with need support to help them prepare for their break. As we are a small team, we do not have the resources to deal directly with individual families. Any correspondence will only be sent to the referring agent who must be able to support the family throughout the holiday process.

A Family Holiday Association application form must be completed in order for an award to be considered. Applications are submitted using an online application form, available on the fund's website. Referrers are issued a unique log-in ID and password, which can be reused for multiple applications year on year. To obtain an ID and password, email GrantOfficer@ FamilyHolidayAssociation.org.uk with your name, work address, job title, phone number and email address.

School-Home Support (SHS) Service UK

£18,000

Correspondent: Welfare Fund Coordinator, 3rd Floor Solar House, 1–9 Romford Road, Stratford, London E15 4LJ (0845 337 0850; email: enquiries@shs.org.uk; website: www.schoolhomesupport.org.uk)

CC number: 1084696

Eligibility

Children and families who are working with SHS practitioners and are in need.

Types of grants

One-off payments for essential living costs and basic household items. Grants may be made for food, white goods, school uniforms, furniture and so on.

Annual grant total

In 2013/14 the charity held assets of £504,500 and had an income of £3.3 million. Our research suggests that about £18,000 is available in grants each year from the welfare fund of the charity, usually broken down into monthly budgets.

Applications

Applications must be made on behalf of families by their SHS practitioner. For more information contact the welfare fund coordinator by telephone (Mondays and Fridays only) or by email. The trustees meet four times a year.

Other information

SHS works with over 750 schools around the country helping to get children with complex needs and difficult backgrounds into school and ready to learn. Provision of human resources and services is the main activity of the charity.

Gender

Frederick Andrew Convalescent Trust

£30,500

Correspondent: Karen Armitage, Clerk to the Trustees, Andrew and Co., St Swithin's Court, 1 Flavian Road, Nettleham Road, Lincoln LN2 4GR (01522 512123; email: info@factonline.co.uk; website: www.factonline.co.uk)

CC number: 211029

Eligibility

Women who have been in paid employment at some time.

Types of grants

Grants of up to £1,000 for convalescence and domestic help, and up to £600 for therapy. Types of therapy covered include: physiotherapy, occupational therapy, speech therapy, chiropody and podiatry and counselling.

Annual grant total

In 2014 the trust had assets of £1.9 million and had an income of £72,500. Grants to individuals totalled £30,500

Applications

An initial assessment form must be completed and returned to the correspondent. The form is available from the trust's website. The trust responds to every application.

Mrs E. L. Blakeley-Marillier Charitable Fund

£14,300

Correspondent: Lynn Young, Fund Administrator, Wollen Michelmore, Carlton House, 30 The Terrace, Torquay, Devon TQ1 1BS (01803 213251; email: lynn.young@wollenmichelmore.co.uk; website: www.wollenmichelmore.co.uk)

CC number: 207138

Eligibility

Women who are over 55 who are in need and are not of the Roman Catholic faith or members of the Salvation Army. Preference is given to women from the counties of Yorkshire and Devon and in particular the towns of Scarborough and Torquay.

Types of grants

Annuities of a maximum £520 per year are paid in two instalments. Grants will not be given if the effect is to reduce income support or other benefits, or to reduce debt.

Annual grant total

In 2013/14 the fund had an income of £400 and a total expenditure of £14,500. We estimate that annuities to individuals totalled £14,300.

Applications

Application forms are available from the correspondent. Applications should be submitted directly by the individual including a general financial overview. Applications are usually considered in November and May.

The Blyth Benevolent Trust

£3,700

Correspondent: Trust Administrator, Bowman Solicitors, 27 Bank Street, Dundee DD1 1RP (01382 322267; fax: 01382 225000)

OSCR number: SC017188

Eligibility

Women aged over 60 and in need. Preference is given to people who are blind or partially sighted who have the surname Bell or Blyth, and who live in or are connected with Newport-on-Tay, Fife or Dundee.

Types of grants

Annuities are paid twice a year. A Christmas bonus may be paid, if funds permit.

Annual grant total

In 2013/14 the trust had an income of £3,200 and a total expenditure of £3,900. We estimate that the amount of grants given to individuals totalled £3,700.

Applications

Apply in writing to the correspondent. Applications should be submitted either directly by the individual or, where applicable, through a third party such as a social worker, or through an organisation such as Citizens Advice or other welfare agency.

Davenport Emergency Grant (Leamington Spa, Kenilworth or Warwick)

£4,800 (27 grants)

Correspondent: Linda Price, Grants Administrator, c/o WCAVA – Warwick District Office, 4–6 Clemens Street, Leamington Spa, Warwickshire CV31 2DL (01926 477512; email: warwickinfo@wcava.org.uk; website: www.wcava.org.uk)

Eligibility

Widows, single women over 60, and occasionally, young single women who are in need. The children (aged under 25) of these individuals may also qualify for assistance. All beneficiaries must live alone apart from school-aged children and have resided in the Midlands for at least five years. The applicant's household income should not be more than £165 a week and savings should amount to no more than £5,000.

Types of grants

One-off grants of up to £150 can be given for cookers, bath-lifts, baby equipment, carpets, telephone extensions, showers, pushchairs and so on.

Annual grant total

In 2013/14 the charity had an income of £4,000. Grants were awarded to 27 women totalling £4,800.

Applications

Applications should be made by letter, including details of status, circumstances, financial situation and a supporting statement from a GP, social worker or similar professional. Grants will only be paid to individuals via the person supporting the applications. There may be an additional payment for those in receipt of certain benefits. Contact the correspondent for further information.

Applications should be marked 'confidential'. Those from within the Warwick district should be sent to the correspondent. All other applicants in the Midlands should apply to: Baron Davenport's Charity, Portman House, 5/7 Temple Row West, Birmingham B2 5NY.

Other information

For information on Baron Davenport's Charity Trust, see page 26.

Davenport Emergency Grant (North Staffordshire)

£5,000

Correspondent: Information and Advice Service, c/o Age UK, 83–85 Trinity Street, Hanley, Stoke-on-Trent ST1 5NA (01782 286809)

Eligibility

Women (widows, singles and divorcees) who have lived in the north of Staffordshire for at least ten years and are over the age of 60. Applicants must live alone and have a low income and little or no savings.

Types of grants

One-off grants for emergencies only.

Annual grant total

Grants usually total about £5,000 a year.

Applications

This fund is now administered by Age UK, North Staffordshire. Applications should be made on a form which is available from the correspondent. Applications are considered upon receipt.

Other information

For information on Baron Davenport's Charity Trust, see page 26.

Davenport Emergency Grant (Staffordshire)

£2,000

Correspondent: Trust Administrator, Support Staffordshire, Stafford and District Office, Civic Centre, Riverside, Stafford ST16 3AQ (01785 413160; email: info@supportstaffordshire.org.uk)

Eligibility

Women who are over 60 years old and are widows, unmarried, divorcees or have been abandoned by their husbands. They must have lived in Staffordshire for at least ten years. In special circumstances, help may be given to younger women.

Types of grants

One-off and recurrent grants of up to £250 towards electrical goods, clothing, living costs, household bills, food, medical equipment, furniture, disability equipment, for help in the home and so on.

Annual grant total

Grants awarded to individuals usually total around £2,000.

Applications

Stafford District Voluntary Services (Support Staffordshire) now administers this fund. Applications should be made on a form to be submitted either directly by the individual or through an appropriate third party, such as a family member or welfare agency. Applications are usually considered upon receipt.

Davenport Emergency Grant (Stratford-upon-Avon)

£1,500

Correspondent: Helen Bowie-Simpson, Community Development Manager, Voluntary Action Stratford, Suite 3 Arden Court, Arden Street, Stratford-upon-Avon CV37 6NT (1789 298102; email: helen.bowie-simpson@vasa.org.uk)

Eligibility

Widows, and unmarried and divorced women who are over the age of 60. Applicants must:
- Live alone
- Have a total household income of no more than £165 per week and less than £5,000 in savings
- Not be in receipt of low/high rates of Attendance Allowance, middle/high rates of Disability Living Allowance, or Mobility (Car) Allowance
- Have lived in the Midlands area for at least five years

Types of grants

Small, one-off grants of up to £150 for emergencies only.

Annual grant total

Our research suggests that grants usually total about £1,500 annually.

Applications

Applications can be made directly to the correspondent but must include supporting evidence from a third party, such as a health visitor, social worker, doctor or other professional.

Other information

For information on Baron Davenport's Charity, see the following entry.

Baron Davenport's Charity

£454,500 (1,648 grants)

Correspondent: Kate Slater, Charity Administrator, Portman House, 5–7 Temple Row West, Birmingham B2 5NY (0121 236 8004; email: enquiries@barondavenportscharity.org; website: www.barondavenportscharity.org)

CC number: 217307

Eligibility

Widows, unmarried women and divorcees aged over 60 and in need; women and children abandoned by their partners; and people aged under 25 whose fathers have died. Applications will also be considered from single mothers who are under 60 years old and have limited income and school-age children living at home who are in financial need. Applicants must have lived in the West Midlands, Shropshire, Staffordshire, Warwickshire or Worcestershire area within a 60-mile radius of Birmingham town hall for at least five years. Applicants must have a net income of less than £181 per week and savings that do not exceed £10,000.

Types of grants

Recurrent grants (at the time of writing) of £260 (for women living in rented accommodation) and £290 (for owner-occupiers), paid twice annually. **Note:** grants are paid directly into beneficiaries' bank or building society accounts; applicants must have an account in their own name to be eligible.

Small, one-off grants are available for essential household items for single mothers on low incomes. Those under the age of 25 whose fathers have died are also eligible for small grants towards essential items.

Annual grant total

In 2014 the charity held assets of £33.2 million and had an income of £1.3 million. Grants totalled £1.17 million, of which £454,500 was distributed in 1,648 grants to individuals.

A further 461 grants, amounting to £715,000, were awarded to almshouses, hospices and children's charities in Birmingham and the West Midlands.

Exclusions

Applications will not be accepted from those in receipt of low/high rates of Attendance Allowance; middle/high rates of Disability Living Allowance or Mobility Allowance (or car allowance).

Applications

Except for emergency cases, applications should be made through local authority social services departments or recognised welfare agencies, although direct applications from individuals may also be considered. Application forms are available from the correspondent or to download from the website.

Applications for the spring distribution should be submitted by 15 March, and for the autumn distribution, 15 September. Grants are paid in May and November respectively. No more than one application should be submitted within 12 months.

Applications for one-off grants can be submitted at any time and are considered approximately every month. Enquiries are welcomed.

Other information

The trust and CVS regard as fatherless those whose fathers have died, and in some cases children abandoned by their fathers.

For emergency needs, see the separate regional entries of the Davenport Emergency Grant entries on page 25.

E. McLaren Fund for Indigent Ladies

£80,000

Correspondent: Rosina Dolan, Secretary, BMK Wilson, Second Floor, 90 St Vincent Street, Glasgow G2 5UB (0141 221 8004; fax: 0141 221 8088; email: rmd@bmkwilson.co.uk; website: www.bmkwilson.co.uk)

OSCR number: SC004558

Eligibility

To provide relief to widows and unmarried women in need. Preference is given to those who are above 40 years of age, and widows and daughters of Officers in the Highland Regiment or of Scotsmen.

Types of grants

Annual pensions, currently of £500 a year, are paid in May and November.

One-off grants, holidays and Christmas gifts are given according to need.

Annual grant total

In 2014 the trust had an income of £102,500 and a total expenditure of £102,000. We estimate that grants and pensions given to individuals totalled £80,000.

Applications

Apply on a form available from the correspondent or to download from the website. Applications can be made throughout the year for consideration when the trustees meet three times each year. Beneficiaries' payments are reviewed annually at the discretion of the trustees and must be signed off by a person of responsibility who can verify the applicant's financial circumstances. Beneficiaries are visited periodically.

Eaton Fund for Artists, Nurses and Gentlewomen
See entry on page 109

See entry on page 109

Francis Butcher Gill's Charity

£16,000

Correspondent: Charity Administrator, Freeths LLP Solicitors, Cumberland Court, 80 Mount Street, Nottingham NG1 6HH (0115 936 9369)

CC number: 230722

Eligibility

Unmarried or widowed women aged over 50 who are in need, who are regular attendees of Protestant Christian worship, or who would be were they not prevented by bodily infirmity. Applicants must also be of good standing and live in Nottinghamshire, although those living in Derbyshire or Lincolnshire may also be considered.

Types of grants

Pensions of £350 per quarter are given to a fixed number of pensioners. One-off grants may also occasionally be available for items such as gas fires.

Annual grant total

In 2013/14 the charity had an income £15,500 and total expenditure of £17,600. We estimate that the amount of grants given to individuals totalled around £16,000.

Applications

Application forms are available from the correspondent. Applications can be submitted through a GP or member of the clergy, or directly by the individual. If the individual is applying directly, the application must be supported by a reference from a GP or member of the clergy. Applications can be submitted at any time for consideration in March and October, or at other times in emergency situations. Applications for pensions will only be considered as a vacancy arises.

The Arthur Hurst Will Trust

£16,000

Correspondent: Official Solicitor and Public Trustee, Hythe House, 200 Shepherd's Bush Road, London W6 7NL (020 8834 9200; email: info@ turn2us.org.uk)

CC number: 207812–7

Eligibility

Women and members of the clergy who are in need and who have been forced to give up their work because of ill health. The trust also supports widows and children of clergymen.

Types of grants

One-off grants according to need.

Annual grant total

In 2014/15 the trust held assets of £737,000. The trust was transferred to Elizabeth Finn Care in 2013 and yearly grant totals are therefore not available. In past years the trust has made grants totalling around £16,000 to individuals.

Applications

Applications can be submitted directly by the individual or, where applicable, through a social worker, Citizens Advice, a welfare agency or another third party. Applications can be considered at any time, although there is not always available funding to make payments.

The Morris Beneficent Fund

£24,000 (8 grants)

Correspondent: Simon Jamison, Treasurer and Secretary, No. 10 Evendons Centre, 171 Evendons Lane, Wokingham RG41 4EH (0118 979 8653)

CC number: 256473

Eligibility

'Distressed gentlewomen' who are recommended by members of the fund. Grants are generally made to older women.

Types of grants

Recurrent grants according to need.

Annual grant total

In 2013/14 the fund had assets of £1 million and an income of £35,500.

Grants were made to eight individuals and totalled £24,000.

Applications

Application forms should be submitted by a member on behalf of the individual. No unsolicited applications will be considered.

Other information

The trustees decide each year how many annuitants can be supported, although this number rarely exceeds 20 as the trustees prefer to raise the level of grants rather than awarding a larger number of smaller annuities.

The Lilian Eveleigh Nash Foundation

£8,500

Correspondent: NatWest Trust Services, Ground Floor, Eastwood House, Glebe Road, Chelmsford CM1 1RS (01245 292445; email: nwb.charities@natwest. com)

CC number: 1043563

Eligibility

Women in need in the area comprising the dioceses of London, Southwark and Chelmsford.

Types of grants

One-off grants for the provision of permanent accommodation, maintenance, holidays and so on.

Annual grant total

In 2014/14 the trust had an income of £23,000 and a total expenditure of £53,000. Grants are made to both individuals and organisations. Grants to individuals usually amount to around £8,500.

Applications

Apply in writing to the correspondent.

Other information

The trust committee is formed of the Anglican Bishops of the Dioceses of London, Chelmsford and Southwark.

The Northern Ladies Annuity Society

£132,000 (557 grants)

Correspondent: Jean Ferry, Secretary, MEA House, Ellison Place, Newcastle upon Tyne NE1 8XS (0191 232 1518; email: jean.ferry@nlas.org.uk)

CC number: 1097222

Eligibility

Single, unmarried and widowed women who are in need, who live or have lived for a number of years in Northumberland, Tyneside, Wearside,

County Durham or Cumbria. At present only those over the state retirement age are considered. The applicant should have an annual income of less than £8,500 and savings of no more than £10,000.

Types of grants

Annuities of £1,300/£975/£650/£325 (depending on circumstances) are paid quarterly. One-off grants are also available for those in receipt of an annuity for expenses such as holidays, domestic appliances, household items and other unexpected costs. Christmas hampers are also distributed to most annuitants. The society has also distributed fuel grants during recent spells of cold winter weather.

Note that individuals who are not already in receipt of an annuity are ineligible for any other form of help from the society.

Annual grant total

In 2013/14 the society held assets of £5.4 million and had an income of £273,500. More than £132,000 was awarded in grants which were distributed as follows:

Annuities (full and half)	398	£117,500
Holiday (special grants)	26	£6,500
Hampers (special grants)	120	£5,900
General (special grants)	13	£3,000

Exclusions

The society does not give one-off grants to non-annuitants, or support students, and will ignore any such requests for assistance.

Applications

Applications to become an annuitant should be made on a form available from the correspondent. Completed forms can be submitted directly by the individual or through a third party such as Citizens Advice or a social worker. Applications are considered monthly.

Other information

In 2013/14 the society spent a further £115,000 on providing subsidised accommodation for women at 31 properties.

The Pargeter and Wand Trust

£5,000

Correspondent: Marcus Fellows, Trustee, BCOP, 1st Floor, 40B Imperial Court, Kings Norton Business Centre, Pershore Road South, Birmingham B30 3ES (0121 459 7670; email: marcus. fellows@bcop.org.uk)

CC number: 210725

Eligibility

Women who have never been married, are aged over 55 and live in their own homes. There is a preference for those living in the West Midlands area, but other areas of the country are considered.

Types of grants

Small annuities of around £300 are paid quarterly and reviewed annually. Smaller, one-off grants, usually in the range of £50 to £150, are also available.

Annual grant total

In 2014/15 the trust had an income of £11.400 and a total expenditure of £5,500. We estimate that the amount of grants given to individuals totalled £5,000.

Applications

Applications should be made via Age UK.

The Perry Fund

£47,000 (30 grants)

Correspondent: William Carter, Clerk to the Trustees, 7 Waterloo Road, Wolverhampton WV1 4DW (email: janeoliver@underhills.co.uk)

CC number: 218829

Eligibility

Annual top-up pensions are given to older women and one-off grants to women in need.

Types of grants

Annuities of around £3,000, as well as one-off grants.

Annual grant total

In 2014 the charity had assets of £666,500 and an income of £29,500. Grants to individuals totalled £47,000. Of this, £15,000 was paid in annuities to six individuals (most receiving £3,000 in the year) and £32,000 was given in one-off payments to 24 individuals.

Applications

Application forms are available from the correspondent. Applications can be submitted directly by the individual or through a third party such as a social worker, nursing home manager or welfare organisation. The trustees usually meet twice a year to consider applications.

The Royal Society for the Support of Women of Scotland (formerly known as The Royal Society for the Relief of Indigent Gentlewomen of Scotland)

£1.1 million

Correspondent: The Chief Executive, 14 Rutland Square, Edinburgh EH1 2BD (0131 229 2308; email: info@igf.org; website: www.igf.org/oldindex.htm)

OSCR number: SC016095

Eligibility

Women who are unmarried, widowed, divorced or formally separated,* who are in need and are over 50 years of age. Applicants must:

▶ Have been resident in Scotland for at least two years
▶ Show 'evidence of personal achievement in life', self-support, consideration of others, voluntary or community work or looking after family members who required care
▶ Have an annual income of less than £12,850 (from all sources, having deducted tax, housing costs and any care costs)
▶ Have savings/capital of no more than £16,000, excluding the home value

Applicants must not be co-habitant, which is defined 'in terms of Section 25 of the Family Law (Scotland) Act 2006, i.e. who are not living with a man as if they were "man and wife" or another woman as if "civil partners".'

*The society defines this as 'Separated by formal agreement or in terms of a Court Decree from their spouse or civil partner.'

Income and capital limits for admission to the roll and the level of annuities and other grants paid are regularly reviewed.

Types of grants

Annuities are paid in quarterly instalments. Beneficiaries may also receive one-off grants for TV licences, telephone rental, holidays, nursing and property maintenance, for example.

Annual grant total

In 2014/15 the society had assets of £42.7 million and an income of £1.7 million. Grants were made to 815 beneficiaries totalling £1.1 million and were distributed as follows:

Principal grants	£966,500
Supplementary grants	£110,500
Welcome grants	£26,500
Other grants	£4,200

The annual report and accounts for 2014/15 note: 'The society distributes around one million pounds per annum with strictly controlled costs on non-charitable expenditure. At present there are around 800 ladies receiving financial assistance.'

Exclusions

Women who are in long-term care or resident in nursing homes are no longer admitted.

Applications

Contact the correspondent for full details and an application form. Applications are considered quarterly in March, June, September and November by the General Committee. The website states:

> Completed forms should be lodged with the Chief Executive, in each case before the end of the preceding calendar quarter so that time is available to arrange visits, carry out checks etc. For example, for the March meeting, the application window closes on 31 December: for June on 31 March and so on, but it would help greatly if application forms are returned as soon as possible.

Other information

The society also provides support and advice across the UK through its caseworkers and English representative.

Sawyer Trust

£86,500

Correspondent: Revd Jim Brown, Trustee, PO Box 797, Worcester WR4 4BU (email: info@sawyertrust.org; website: www.sawyertrust.org)

CC number: 511276

Eligibility

Women over 50 years old who are in need through financial hardship, sickness or poor health. If there are surplus funds, men over 50 in similar circumstances may also receive assistance.

Types of grants

One-off grants of up to £500. Recent grants have been awarded for household items and fittings, removal costs, telephone bills, travel costs and rent arrears. The trustees state that they will consider a wide range of assistance but do not pay cash directly to applicants.

Annual grant total

In 2013/14 the trust held assets of £2.15 million and had an income of £61,500. Grants to individuals totalled £86,500.

Exclusions

The trust will not give funding for: luxury goods or services; parties or outings; shortfall on insurance claims, except in certain circumstances; legal expenses; credit card debt; ongoing costs; cash payments direct to individuals.

Applications

Apply on a form available from the correspondent or to download from the trust's website. Applications may be completed by the applicant or someone else on their behalf, and must be supported by an accredited third party such as Citizens Advice, a housing association, or a charitable organisation recognised by the trust. Refer to the website, or ask the correspondent for details of approved organisations. Written evidence, in the form of a bank statement, etc., must be presented as evidence of applicant's circumstances. Applications must be posted. The trustees meet monthly to consider applications.

Dr Meena Sharma Memorial Foundation

£4,000

Correspondent: Vivek Sharma, Executive, 14 Magdalene Road, Walsall, West Midlands WS1 3TA (01922629842; fax: 01922632942; email: gwalior@onetel. com; website: www.msmf.chandri.com)

CC number: 1108375

Eligibility

Children and women in the UK and India, especially those who have disabilities, are disadvantaged or underprivileged.

Types of grants

Small awards of up to £500 (generally £100–£250) are available to help children and women. Awards may include educational grants, travel expenses, and financial help to further health and other needs.

Annual grant total

In 2014/15 the foundation had an income of £22,500 and a total expenditure of £22,000. We estimate that about £5,000 was given in welfare support to individuals.

Applications

Eligible candidates should apply in writing to the correspondent via post, providing an sae. Requests should give full contact details (including email address) and reasons for seeking a grant. Applications can be made at any time. Only successful applicants are informed. The website notes: 'If you do not hear from us within six weeks of next round of meetings from your application, it has been unsuccessful. You may re-apply for next round if desired.'

Other information

Grants are also made to organisations, especially in India, and individuals are supported for educational needs (teachers, other educational professionals and medical personnel or medical students may also be supported).

The Society for the Assistance of Ladies in Reduced Circumstances

£576,000 (412 grants)

Correspondent: The General Secretary, Lancaster House, 25 Hornyold Road, Malvern, Worcestershire WR14 1QQ (0300 365 1886; email: info@salrc.org.uk; website: www.salrc.org.uk)

CC number: 205798

Eligibility

Women who live alone, have savings less than £8,000, receive a means-tested benefit, and are not eligible for help from any other charity.

Types of grants

Monthly payments towards day-to-day living expenses, TV licences and telephone rental charges. Beneficiaries are sent birthday and Christmas cards. The society can also advise on other sources of funding.

Annual grant total

In 2014 the society had assets of £29.6 million, of which £28.4 million represented the capital of the charity. Income was £886,000 and total expenditure £859,000. Payments to women in need totalled £576,000.

On average, 412 women were in receipt of payments each month. During this financial year 58 applicants were accepted as new regular beneficiaries.

Exclusions

No grants are given for education, care or nursing home fees, holidays, repayment of debts or funeral expenses. No one-off emergency grants. The charity is unable to assist students or women who work 16 hours or more a week.

Applications

Application forms are available from the correspondent. Applications can be submitted directly by the individual or through a third party such as Citizens Advice or a social worker. All details of employment history should be supplied, not just recent work history. The society requests that the following documentation is provided:

▎ A copy of the applicant's most recent council tax bill showing a 25% single occupancy discount

▎ Copies of the most recent notifications, letters and calculations of any statutory benefits, tax credits or state or occupational pensions received

▎ Payslips covering the past three months (if applicable)

▎ Statements from all bank accounts

▎ Most recent correspondence including statements or other documents relating to any arrears, overpayments, debts, loans or other money owed

If all documentation is supplied, a firm decision may be confirmed in a few days. It is advised that applicants view the society's website for a detailed list of requirements. Incomplete applications cannot be considered.

Potential applicants can call the helpline for an informal chat (0300 365 1886, Mon–Fri 9am–1pm and 2pm–4.30pm) or complete an enquiry form on the society's website, if help is required.

Other information

Grants are also made to organisations, although none were awarded in 2013/14 and there are no plans to make them for 2015. The charity no longer awards one-off grants.

The 2014 annual report states that:

> The trustees are keen to explore other possibilities for helping women out of poverty, rather than merely relieving the symptoms by making grants towards their living expenses … [they] commissioned a literature review of the barriers to women having or achieving financial independence, costing £3,000.

The society has an informative website giving details of where funding may be given for items and services not provided by the society itself.

Ellen Rebe Spalding Memorial Fund

£2,000

Correspondent: Tessa Rodgers, Secretary, PO Box 85, Stowmarket IP14 3NY (website: www.spaldingtrust. org.uk)

CC number: 209066–1

Eligibility

As specified by the fund's website, the objectives are 'to help disadvantaged women and children to adjust more easily to the pressure of modern life, and to promote those conditions of society that will enable people of different cultures and faiths to understand and appreciate one another'.

Types of grants

Grants are at the discretion of trustees and are administered monthly throughout the year. Grants are only distributed to those who intend to further the objectives of the fund.

Annual grant total

Grants awarded from this fund to individuals for social welfare purposes generally total in the region of £2,000.

Applications

Applicants should first contact the secretary.

Other information

The Ellen Rebe Spalding Memorial Fund is a linked charity to the larger Spalding Trusts. While a small amount is given in welfare grants through the Ellen Rebe fund, the majority of the Spalding Trusts' funds are spent on educational grants.

St Andrew's Society for Ladies in Need

£43,500

Correspondent: Maureen Pope, General Secretary, 20 Denmark Gardens, Ipswich Road, Holbrook, Ipswich, Suffolk IP9 2BG (01473 327408; email: mpope1@btinternet.com; website: standrewssociety.btck.co.uk)

CC number: 208541

Eligibility

Single women from a well-educated, professional or semi-professional background who are now living alone in reduced circumstances, in receipt of all relevant state benefits and with very limited savings. Applicants must be retired or unable to work and of British nationality. Preference is given to elderly women who are over 80 years of age.

Types of grants

Recurrent grants, up to a maximum of £20 a week to help with daily living expenses, are paid each quarter. Priority is given to women who are trying to maintain their own homes but grants are also given to those struggling with nursing home fees. One-off special grants are also available for heating, the cost of moving house, domestic appliances, furniture, disability aids, holidays and convalescence.

Annual grant total

In 2014 the society held assets of £1.58 million and had an income of £159,000. Grants were made to individuals totalling £43,500. The vast majority of this was given in regular grants with just £4,500 awarded in one-off special grants to meet particular short-term needs.

Exclusions

No grants are given to younger women and non-retired women who are able to

work. No assistance is given to help with the discharge of debts.

Applications

Application forms are available from the correspondent. Applications should be submitted either directly by the individual or through a social worker, Citizens Advice, other welfare agency or somebody with power of attorney. Applications should include as much background detail as possible, such as education, occupation and so on. Applications are considered at quarterly committee meetings, although urgent cases can be dealt with between meetings.

The Charles Wright Gowthorpe Fund and Clergy Augmentation Fund

£7,500

Correspondent: Lloyds Bank plc, Lloyds TSB Private Banking Ltd, UK Trust Centre, 22–26 Ock Street, Abingdon, Oxfordshire OX14 5SW (01235 232758; email: pbuktccharityadmin@lloydsbanking.com)

CC number: 213852/213853

Eligibility

(i) The Gowthorpe Fund supports widows and other women in need who live within a 12-mile radius of the Market Square, Nottingham.

(ii) The Clergy Augmentation Fund generally supports clergymen and their widows who live within a 10-mile radius of St Peter's Church, Nottingham.

Types of grants

Grants typically of around £100, paid annually in December.

Annual grant total

In 2013/14 the Gowthorpe Fund had an income of £4,700 and a total expenditure of £5,500. In the same year, the Clergy Augmentation Fund had an income of £2,800 and a total expenditure of £2,900.

We estimate that combined grants from the funds totalled £7,500; around £5,000 from the Gowthorpe Fund, and £2,500 from the Clergy Augmentation Fund.

Applications

Apply on a form available from local Church of England vicars, to be returned by the end of October. Do not write to the correspondent initially; only send the application form once it has been completed.

Miscellan-eous

The Anderson Trust

£8,000

Correspondent: Andrew Anderson, Trustee, 1 Cote House Lane, Bristol BS9 3UW (0117 962 1588)

OSCR number: SC008507

Eligibility

People who are, or were, involved in charitable activities who are in need, and their dependants.

Types of grants

One-off and recurrent grants are given according to need.

Annual grant total

In 2013/14 the trust had assets of £11.9 million and an income of £367,500. We estimate grants to individuals for social welfare purposes totalled around £34,500.

Applications

The trust states that it rarely gives to people who are not known to the trustees or who have not been personally recommended by people known to the trustees. Unsolicited applications are therefore unlikely to be successful.

Other information

Grants are also given to organisations.

East Africa Women's League (UK) Benevolent Fund

£19,000

Correspondent: Sheila Heath, Treasurer, Nobles Farm, Gatehouse Road, Holton-le-Moor, Market Rasen LN7 6AG (01673 828393; email: honsec@eawl.org.uk; website: www.considine.eclipse.co.uk/eawl/eawl.html)

CC number: 294328

Eligibility

People of UK origin who have previously lived and worked in East Africa.

Types of grants

One-off and recurrent grants are given according to need. Grants range from around £100 to £800.

Annual grant total

In 2014, the charity had income of £16,400 and outgoings of £23,500. We estimate that the amount of grants given to individuals totalled around £19,000.

Applications

Apply in writing to the Treasurer. Members of a fund subcommittee may visit applicants. The trust does not accept any unsolicited applications.

The Vegetarian Charity

£6,500

Correspondent: Susan Lenihan, Grants Secretary, PO Box 496, Manchester M45 0FL (01249 443521; email: grantssecretary@vegetariancharity.org.uk; website: www.vegetariancharity.org.uk)

CC number: 294767

Eligibility

Vegetarians and vegans up to the age of 26 who are in need. Although UK-based, the charity will consider applications from most countries.

Types of grants

One-off and recurrent grants to relieve poverty and sickness, usually ranging up to £500.

According to the website, the charity is 'keen to receive more applications from young people and parents experiencing financial hardship'. Applications for help towards school clothing, school trips, shoes, coats and other essential items for children will receive careful consideration from the trustees.

Annual grant total

In 2013/14 the charity had assets of £1.15 million and an income of £56,500. There were 51 grants paid during the year to individuals and organisations totalling £26,000. A further breakdown was not available; therefore, we estimate that the amount of grants given to individuals for relief-in-need purposes totalled around £6,500.

Exclusions

The website states: 'In the current economic climate postgraduate applications are only considered in exceptionally difficult personal circumstances.'

Applications

Application forms are available on the website or from the correspondent. They can be submitted by individuals directly or by a parent/guardian on a child's behalf, preferably by email. You will be asked to provide details of any other grants received, income and expenditure (bank statements), a CV, a covering letter, and a letter (on headed paper) from a relevant employer, doctor, social worker, carer or similar professional. Two professional references are also required to verify the applicant's commitment to a vegetarian or vegan diet.

It takes about three months to complete the consideration of an application. Requests are considered throughout the year. The trustees take into account efforts made by applicants to improve their financial situation and any evidence of employment or efforts made to find work (or conversely, reasons why they have been unable to do so, such as medical certificates) should be included.

The charity asks all communication to be via email or post.

Other information

Grants are also made to organisations which promote vegetarianism/veganism among young people (excluding business projects) and for educational purposes. The charity also offers a fully funded Vegan Cookery course for young people (aged 16–25). Applications for the cooking course open in January – see the website for further details.

The Vegetarian Charity is an amalgamation of The Vegetarian Children's Charity and The Vegetarian Home for Children and was formed in 1986.

The Eliza Haldane Wylie Fund

£16,000

Correspondent: The Trustees, Simpson and Marwick, Albany House, 58 Albany Street, Edinburgh EH1 3QR (0131 557 1545)

OSCR number: SC011882

Eligibility

People in need who are related to or associated with Eliza Haldane Wylie or her family, or are 'gentlefolk of the middle class'.

Types of grants

Small, one-off payments.

Annual grant total

In 2013/14 the fund had both an income and a total expenditure of £16,400. We estimate that the amount of grants given to individuals totalled £16,000.

Applications

Apply in writing to the correspondent.

Older people

Age Sentinel Trust

£11,900

Correspondent: Francesca Colverson, Head of Fundraising, Longreach, Clay Lane, Chichester, West Sussex PO19 3PX (020 8144 4774; email: agesentineltrust@googlemail.com; website: agesentinel.org.uk)

CC number: 1133624

Eligibility

Elderly people who are in need. Priority is given to people with dementia, particularly Alzheimer's disease, and those with other debilitating illnesses.

Types of grants

One-off and recurrent grants to support independent living. Grants have been made to individuals with medical problems for purposes such as communication devices or home adaptations.

Annual grant total

In 2013/14 the trust had an income of £51,700 and a total expenditure of £53,700. The trust awarded £23,800 to both organisations and individuals and we estimate that £11,900 of that total was awarded directly to individuals.

Applications

Apply in writing to the correspondent.

Aid for the Aged in Distress (AFTAID)

£40,500

Correspondent: Susan Elson, Trustee, 9 Bonhill Street, London EC2A 4PE (0870 803 1950; fax: 0870 803 2128; email: info@aftaid.org.uk; website: www.aftaid.org.uk)

CC number: 299276

Eligibility

UK citizens who are over 65 years old, reside in the UK, are living on a low income and have minimal savings.

Types of grants

Emergency grants for essential items to facilitate the beneficiary to maintain their independence in the familiar surroundings of their home, for example heating appliances, bedding, cookers, washing machines or other white goods, essential furniture and carpets. Grants are also made towards more expensive items such as a stair-lift, walk-in shower, motorised scooter and so on. Applications can sometimes be considered towards costs for an older carer to enjoy a respite break.

Grants are paid directly to the supplier of the goods or services.

Annual grant total

In 2014 the charity held assets of £348,500 and had an income of £74,000. Grants for older people totalled £40,500.

Exclusions

Grants cannot be made for any ongoing payments, retrospective funding, arrears or debts of any kind.

Applications

Apply on a form available through the charity's website. Applicants will initially need to fill in an online form which will automatically issue the application form by return email.

Applications can be made directly by the individual or through a welfare organisation and should include written support from a social worker, doctor or similar professional of the official care services which are personally aware of the beneficiary's situation.

The trust's annual report states that, 'an increasing number of applications that are received are having to be declined as they fall outside the charity's remit and criteria. Unfortunately, this creates additional administration costs and a drain on resources.'

Barchester Health Care Foundation

See entry on page 59

Foundations Independent Living Trust

See entry on page 48

Friends of the Elderly

£422,500

Correspondent: Supporting Friends Team, 40–42 Ebury Street, London SW1W 0LZ (020 7730 8263; fax: 020 7259 0154; email: enquiries@fote.org.uk; website: www.fote.org.uk)

CC number: 226064

Eligibility

Men and women who live in England and Wales aged 60 or over (over 50 for homeless people), with a low income and limited savings (£4,000 maximum savings for individuals) are eligible for support. The charity cannot help people living in residential care or those living in Scotland.

Types of grants

One-off grants are given for essential items such as basic furniture, flooring and household appliances. The charity can also assist with utility bills, household repairs, and adaptations and mobility aids.

The charity also distributes allowances, on a monthly or twice-yearly basis, to support older people on low incomes in maintaining their independence. Payments of regular allowances are arranged to suit the individual. The charity maintains contact with recipients of regular payments through telephone calls, letters, and cards and presents at birthdays and Christmas.

Annual grant total

In 2013/14 the charity held assets of £32.3 million and had an income of almost £23 million. Welfare grants to elderly individuals totalled £422,500.

Exclusions

Unfortunately, the charity can only help applicants living in England or Wales and cannot help those living in residential care. Grants are not available for items already purchased, council tax, rent arrears or care homes fees.

Applications

Applications should be made on a form available to download from the charity's website. Applications should be made through a third party organisation such as social services, Citizens Advice, Age UK or another welfare agency. The role of the referral organisation is to assist with the application process, providing confirmation of the applicant's circumstances and supporting the purchase of the required item or service. The charity aims to respond within two weeks of receiving the application. Unsuccessful applicants may be signposted to other possible sources of funding.

The charity welcomes enquiries from potential applicants.

Other information

The charity offers a range of care and support options for its beneficiaries through residential homes, community nursing, befriending schemes and dementia support. A main aim of the charity is to reduce the level of isolation amongst elderly people, which is something its Phoning Friends telephone service aspires to do.

In 2013/14 the charity helped older people to claim almost £76,000 in benefits they were eligible for through its provision of welfare advice and assistance. Grants were also awarded to organisations to run events and activities for older people, which totalled £24,000 and benefitted 2,366 individuals.

Home Warmth for the Aged Benevolent Fund (HWA)

£19,000

Correspondent: Mr W. Berentemfel, Fund Administrator, 19 Towers Wood, South Darenth, Dartford DA4 9BQ (01322 863836; email: w.berentemfel@btinternet.com)

CC number: 271735

Eligibility

People of pensionable age, at risk from the cold in winter who have no resources other than their state pension/income support and have savings of less than £4,000.

Types of grants

Provision of heating appliances, bedding, clothing and solid fuel. Grants are also available to pay fuel debts where the supply has been disconnected; these are one-off grants only, typically ranging between £90 and £250.

Annual grant total

In 2013/14 the charity had an income of £17,100 and an expenditure of £19,900. We estimate that the amount of grants given to individuals totalled £19,000.

Exclusions

No grants are made to people who have younger members of their family living with them.

Applications

Application forms are available from the correspondent. Applications should be submitted only through a third party such as social workers, doctors and nurses to whom grants are returned for disbursement. If there is an armed forces connection, applications should be made through SSAFA (see 'Armed forces charities' on page 79). Applications made directly by individuals are not considered. Applications are considered monthly.

Independent Age

£2.2 million

Correspondent: Advice Service, 18 Avonmore Road, London W14 8RR (0800 319 6789; fax: 020 7605 4201; email: advice@independentage.org; website: www.independentage.org)

CC number: 210729

Eligibility

People who are over the state retirement age who are lonely or isolated and find themselves in financial need. Preference is given to individuals who will benefit most from long-term support.

Types of grants

One-off grants are made towards, for example, unexpected, emergency expenses and items which it is often difficult to budget for. The association has previously stated that 'there is no definitive list of what and how much is awarded, and each grant is considered individually, on the basis of need'. Grants may be made for things like household repairs and maintenance; white goods; convalescence and respite care; spectacles and dental treatment. Parcels of clothing and toiletries are also distributed to those entering hospital and warm packs are given to help older people through the cold winter months.

Annual grant total

In 2014 the charity's assets were £149 million and it had an income of £8.1 million. The total awarded in grants was £2.2 million. The 2014 trustees' annual report and accounts provide detailed information about the charity's achievements. During that year it helped almost 6,000 older people, over 2,700 of whom received ongoing financial support, and 1,400 of whom received a personalised package of support and advice. More than 1,400 emergency packs were sent out and over £296,000 in grants for extra costs, such as mobility equipment and white goods, was spent. £5 million was the cost of the charity's advice and support services, which includes financial assistance to older people through regular payments (£1.9 million) and grants.

Applications

Financial assistance is given as part of a holistic service whereby a caseworker will work with the individual to assess and help address their issues. Initial contact should be made through the advice line (0845 262 1863) or by emailing advice@independentage.org.

The charity is no longer taking on new commitments for regular payments. Note the following from its 2013 annual report: 'Independent Age is not commencing any new regular payments going forward; it will only continue to manage the existing regular payment commitments.' The 2014 annual report endorses this with the following statement: 'We aim to review our grant criteria and other support, and continue to monitor the planned decline in the number of individual regular payments.'

Other information

The charity's vision is 'a society where older people lead the lives to which they aspire and can contribute actively to their communities'. Its mission is 'to enable older people to stay independent and live well with dignity, choice and control'.

According to its 2014 annual report:

In 2014, a comprehensive review of our services resulted in the creation of a new five-year strategy for 2015–2020. Building on our 'ABC' (Advice, Befriending and Campaigning) strategy of the past three years, this new strategy marks a major expansion and refinement of the charity's activities to ensure we put older people at the heart of all that we do and make a measurable difference to their lives.

The association provides information, advice and practical help through its network of staff and dedicated volunteers across the UK. The website

also offers a range of helpful publications (Wise Guides) relevant to older people.

The broader range of services now offered by the charity is in part due to the merger with two other older people's charities, Counsel and Care and Universal Beneficent Society.

The William Johnston Trust Fund

£35,000 (22 grants)

Correspondent: B. J. S. Parsons-Smith, Trustee, Aspen Cottage, Apse Manor Road, Shanklin PO37 7PN (0151 236 6666)

CC number: 212495

Eligibility

Older people in need who live in the UK.

Types of grants

Recurrent grants paid twice annually, usually in June and December. One-off grants towards, for example, TV licences. Birthday gifts are also awarded.

Annual grant total

In 2014 the fund held assets of £1.2 million and had an income of £39,000. Grants to 22 individuals totalled £35,000.

Applications

Apply in writing to the correspondent. Applications can be submitted directly by the individual or family member and are considered throughout the year.

Lady McCorquodale's Charity Trust

£5,500

Correspondent: Anina Cheng, Correspondent, Swan House, 17–19 Stratford Place, London W1C 1BQ (020 7907 2100; email: charity@mfs.co.uk)

CC number: 268786

Eligibility

People who are in need, with a preference for older people.

Types of grants

One-off and recurrent grants are given for day-to-day needs, such as clothing and food.

Annual grant total

In 2013/14 the trust had an income of £8,900 and a total expenditure of £12,000. As the trust's main focus is to offer funding for other charitable organisations, we estimate that individuals received a total of £5,500 from around £11,000 distributed.

Applications

Apply in writing to the correspondent. Applications can be submitted either directly by the individual or, where applicable, via a social worker, Citizens Advice or other third party.

The Muir Family Charitable Trust

£3,500

Correspondent: Simon Muir, Trustee, Angel Farm, Monks Alley, Binfield, Bracknell, Berkshire RG42 5PA (email: simonmuir@angelfarm.co.uk)

CC number: 255372

Eligibility

Older people who are in need.

Types of grants

One-off and recurrent grants ranging from £300 to £1,500.

Annual grant total

In 2013/14 the trust had an income of £7,800 and a total expenditure of £7,600. We estimate that the amount of grants given to individuals totalled £3,500, with funding also awarded to organisations based in various locations across the country.

Applications

Apply in writing to the correspondent.

Other information

The trust is also known by its registered name, The Fritillary Trust.

NBFA Assisting the Elderly

£81,000

Correspondent: Cherry Bushell, Executive Director, Floor 3, 32 Buckingham Palace Road, London SW1W 0RE (020 7828 0200; email: info@nbfa.org.uk; website: www.nbfa.org.uk)

CC number: 243387

Eligibility

For friendship breaks, applicants must be over 65 years old, on a low income, not have been on holiday for three years or more, and to be mobile enough to get on and off a coach and walk short distances.

Types of grants

Short (five-day) friendship breaks, which are run six to eight times a year. Details of current breaks are published on the website. The charity has previously given grants for pain relief equipment and low-cost emergency telephone alarms.

Annual grant total

In 2013/14 the fund had an income of £174,000 and a total expenditure of £254,500. During this financial year, the fund spent £81,000 (direct costs) on the provision of holidays for beneficiaries.

Applications

Applications for friendship breaks should be made using a form which is available from the correspondent by post, phone or email or by downloading it from the website. Applications can be made individually, as a small group or couple, with a carer (though each individual must have a separate form) or with support from a referring organisation.

Other information

The charity was formerly known as National Benevolent Fund for the Aged (NBFA).

The Roger Pilkington Young Trust

£46,000 (81 grants)

Correspondent: Ben Dixon, Trustee, c/o Everys Solicitors, Magnolia House, Church Street, Exmouth, Devon EX8 1HQ (01395 264384; email: law@ everys.co.uk)

CC number: 251148

Eligibility

People over 60 years of age whose income has been reduced through no fault of their own, through illness or accident.

Types of grants

Monthly pensions of about £45 for single people and £60 for married couples/civil partners.

Annual grant total

In 2013/14 the trust had assets of £1.5 million and an income of £64,000. Grants were made to 68 individuals and 13 married couples/civil partners totalling £46,000.

Applications

Apply on a form available from the correspondent, after the pensions are advertised.

The Florence Reiss Trust for Old People

£5,500

Correspondent: Dr Stephen Reiss, Trustee, 94 Tinwell Road, Stamford, Lincolnshire PE9 2SD (01780 762710)

CC number: 236634

Eligibility

Women over 55 and men over 60 who are in need. Priority is given to those who live in the parishes of Streatley in Berkshire and Goring-on-Thames in Oxfordshire.

Types of grants

One-off and recurrent grants are given according to need.

Annual grant total

In 2013/14 the trust had an income of £10,100 and a total expenditure of £11,700. We estimate that the total amount of grants given to individuals was approximately £5,500. The trust also gives donations to organisations concerned with the welfare of the elderly.

Applications

Apply in writing to the correspondent.

Williamson Memorial Trust

£2,300

Correspondent: Colin Williamson, Trustee, 6 Windmill Close, Ashington, Pulborough, West Sussex RH20 3LG (01903 893649; email: cpjgwilliamson@ yahoo.co.uk)

CC number: 268782

Eligibility

People who are over 65 years of age.

Types of grants

One-off grants, usually of between £20 and £100, are given as gifts (rather than maintenance). Grants are mainly given at Christmas.

Annual grant total

In 2014/15 the trust had an income of £9,100 and a total expenditure of £9,500. Grants are made to individuals and organisations for social welfare and educational purposes. We estimate that social welfare grants to individuals totalled £2,300.

Applications

Due to a reduction of its funds and the instability of its income, the trust regrets that, in order to ensure it can meet its existing commitments, very few new applications will be considered. Support will generally only be given to cases known personally to the trustees and to those individuals the trust has existing commitments with.

Religion

Christianity

The Alexis Trust

£5,300 (33 grants)

Correspondent: Prof. Duncan Vere, Trustee, 14 Broadfield Way, Buckhurst Hill, Essex IG9 5AG (020 8504 6872)

CC number: 262861

Eligibility

Members of the Christian faith.

Types of grants

Grants of between £50 and £100 are available, mostly for Christian-based activities.

Annual grant total

In 2014/15 the trust had assets of £567,500 and a total income of £45,000. Grants to 33 individuals totalled £5,300. A further £35,500 was awarded in grants to organisations.

Applications

Apply in writing to the correspondent.

The Appleton Trust (Canterbury)

£5,400 (4 grants)

Correspondent: Julian Hills, Trustee, Diocesan Board of Finance, Diocesan House, Lady Wootton's Green, Canterbury, Kent CT1 1NQ (01227 459401)

CC number: 250271

Eligibility

People in need connected with the Church of England in the diocese of Canterbury.

Types of grants

One-off grants normally ranging between £100 and £500. The trust also makes loans to members of the clergy, local parishioners and widows of clergymen for items such as cars, computer equipment and equity loans.

Annual grant total

In 2014 the trust had assets of £913,000 and an income of £31,000. Grants were made to four individuals totalling £6,600.

Exclusions

Our research suggests that grants are not given for further education.

Applications

Apply in writing to the correspondent. Applications should be submitted directly by the individual or a church organisation. They are considered every two months.

Other information

Organisations connected to the Church of England in Canterbury Diocese are also supported (three grants totalling £4,500 were given in 2012).

The Charity of Miss Ann Farrar Brideoake

£40,000

Correspondent: Alan Ware, Trustee, Cowling, Swift and Kitchin, 8 Blake Street, York YO1 8XJ (01904 625678; fax: 01904 620214)

CC number: 213848

Eligibility

Communicant members of the Church of England living within the dioceses of York, Liverpool and Manchester, who are in need. This includes parishioners, clergy and retired clergy.

Types of grants

Recurrent grants are given to help in 'making ends meet'. Support is given towards household outgoings, domestic equipment, holidays, children's entertainment and so on as well as for special medical needs. One-off payments are made in special circumstances and debt relief can be supported in exceptional circumstances.

Annual grant total

In 2013/14 the charity had an income of £74,000 and a total expenditure of £47,500. We estimate that the amount of grants given to individuals totalled £40,000.

Applications

Apply on a form available from the correspondent, to be countersigned by the local vicar as confirmation of communicant status. Applications should be submitted in April or May for consideration in July/August.

Buckingham Trust

£14,500

Correspondent: Tina Clay, Trustee, 17 Church Road, Tunbridge Wells, Kent TN1 1LG (01892 774774)

CC number: 237350

Eligibility

People in need who are missionaries or Christian workers, or people with some Christian connection. Applicants must be known to the trustees.

Types of grants

One-off and recurrent grants are given according to need.

Annual grant total

In 2013/14 the trust had assets of £734,000 and an income of £287,000. Grants were made totalling £193,500, of which £14,600 was given to individuals.

Applications

Apply in writing to the correspondent. However, the trust has previously stated that its funds are fully committed each year and not given to new applicants.

Other information

This trust also makes grants to organisations and churches.

Christadelphian Benevolent Fund

£65,500

Correspondent: Kenneth Smith, Treasurer, Westhaven House, Arleston Way, Shirley, Solihull, West Midlands B90 4LH (0121 713 7100)

CC number: 222416

Eligibility

Members of the Christadelphian body who are experiencing difficult times.

Types of grants

One-off and recurrent grants are given according to need. Interest-free loans are also available.

Annual grant total

In 2014 the trust held assets of £2.3 million and had an income of £194,000. Grants to individuals totalled £65,500 and were distributed as follows:

Fuel aid	£16,200
Annual holiday scheme	£15,200
Regular grants	£15,100
Water aid	£8,200
Compassionate grants	£7,600
Christmas grants	£3,200

A further £111,500 was paid to Christadelphian Care Homes.

Applications

Apply in writing to the correspondent. Compassionate grants are given to individuals on the basis of representations made by the ecclesia of which those individuals are members.

Charities of Susanna Cole and Others

£1,600

Correspondent: Tony Pegler, Trustee, Central England Quakers Office, Friends Meeting House, 40 Bull Street, Birmingham B4 6AF (0121 682 7575)

CC number: 204531

Eligibility

Quakers in need, with preference given to those who live within the 1910 Worcestershire boundaries or belong to Central England Area Quaker Meeting. Some favour is also given to younger children (for education). Some preference is also given to retired people on an inadequate pension.

Types of grants

One-off and recurrent grants are given according to need. Help may be given for a range of needs, including: domestic help or gardening for people with disabilities or older individuals; transport to and from meetings for worship or other Quaker gatherings; council tax; rent or accommodation fees; bills and fuel; furniture; white goods; food; clothing; convalescence or respite care; car expenses for those with limited mobility; complementary medicine; medical aids and equipment; media and communication needs, including TV licences; childcare; repairs; counselling.

Annual grant total

In 2014 the charity had an income of £12,300 and a total expenditure of £4,600. We estimate grants to individuals for social welfare purposes to be around £1,600.

Applications

It has previously been noted in the charity's annual report: 'For a new application the trustees require a letter or email from the applicant's overseer outlining the situation. To make this easier the trustees have a named trustee for each local meeting who can be consulted about the matter.'

Our research suggests that requests should be received by early March and October for consideration later in the same months.

Other information

Grants are made for both welfare and educational purposes, including training and starting work or a business.

The charity also administers the income from the Bursary Fund belonging to Central England Area Quaker Meeting, which is kept in a separate and restricted fund and is used solely to help with care home fees for elderly members or attenders of the Central England Area Quaker Meeting.

The Deakin and Withers Fund

£30,000

Correspondent: Grants Team, c/o South Yorkshire Community Foundation, Unit 3 – G1 Building, 6 Leeds Road, Sheffield S9 3TY (0114 242 4294; fax: 0114 242 4605; email: grants@sycf.org. uk; website: www.sycf.org.uk)

CC number: 1140947–2

Eligibility

Single women in the UK, whether divorced, unmarried or widowed, who are in reduced circumstances and who are members of the Church of England or of a church having full membership of the Council of Churches for Britain and Ireland. Grants are not given to women under 40 years of age and beneficiaries are usually over 55 years old.

Types of grants

Annuities of around £500 paid in December.

Annual grant total

The fund is administered by South Yorkshire Community Foundation. Grants usually total around £30,000 each year.

Applications

Application forms are available from the correspondent. Applications should be submitted directly by the individual, through a third party such as a social worker, or through an organisation such as Citizens Advice or other welfare agency.

Other information

In 2008 the Deakin Institute and the Withers Pension amalgamated and became the Deakin and Withers Fund.

The fund is linked with South Yorkshire Community Foundation.

The David Fogwill Charitable Trust

£9,000

Correspondent: Alex Fogwill, Trustee, 53 Brook Drive, Corsham, Wiltshire SN13 9AX (01249 713408; email: alex. fogwill@virgin.net)

CC number: 1062342

Eligibility

People in need who are involved in Christian outreach projects or ministry.

Types of grants

One-off and recurrent grants of up to £1,000. Support costs are usually paid to the organisations to which the Christian outreach worker is contracted.

Annual grant total

In 2013/14 the trust had an income of £15,600 and a total expenditure of £19,900. We estimate that the amount of grants given to individuals totalled £9,000, with funding also awarded to Christian organisations.

Applications

Apply in writing to the correspondent. Applications can be submitted directly by the individual or family member and should include details of the Christian activity and the organisation involved. Applications are considered in January and July.

The Four Winds Trust

£5,300

Correspondent: Simon Charters, Trustee, 64 Station Road, Drayton, Portsmouth PO6 1PJ (email: fourwindstrust1971@gmail.com)

CC number: 262524

Eligibility

Evangelists, missionaries and ministers, including those who have retired, and their widows, widowers and other dependants who are in need.

Types of grants

One-off and recurrent grants are given according to need.

Annual grant total

In 2013/14 the trust had assets of £883,500 and an income of £29,000. Grants were made totalling £27,000, of which £5,300 was distributed to individuals. Charitable and religious organisations received £26,000.

Applications

The trust states that it does not consider unsolicited applications.

The I. W. Griffiths Trust

£77,000

Correspondent: Lord Brian Griffiths of Fforestfach, Trustee, 18 Royal Avenue, London SW3 4QF (020 7774 4015)

CC number: 1090379

Eligibility

People who are, or have been, engaged in Christian mission and are in need.

Types of grants

One-off and recurrent grants are given according to need.

Annual grant total

In 2014 the trust had an exceptionally low income and a total expenditure of £81,500. Based on the previous year, we estimate that the amount of grants given to individuals totalled £77,000.

Applications

Apply in writing to the correspondent.

The Hounsfield Pension

£4,000

Correspondent: Godfrey Smallman, Charity Administrator, Wrigleys Solicitors, Fountain Precinct, Balm Green, Sheffield S1 2JA (0114 267 5594; fax: 0114 276 3176)

CC number: 221436

Eligibility

Men, unmarried women, widows and widowers who are over 50 years old, live in England or Wales, are members of the Church of England and have never received parochial relief or public assistance. The charity tries to keep the numbers of male and female beneficiaries as equal as possible.

Types of grants

Grants are fixed annually and are paid in two instalments.

Annual grant total

In 2013/14 the charity had an income of £4,900 and a total expenditure of £4,400. We estimate that the amount of grants given to individuals totalled around £4,000.

Exclusions

Applicants must reside in England or Wales.

Applications

Apply in writing to the correspondent. Only a limited number of pensions are available, and places become available at irregular intervals.

The Lind Trust

£20,000

Correspondent: Gavin Wilcock, Trustee, Drayton Hall, Drayton, Norwich NR8 6DP (email: accounts@ dacrepropertyholdings.com)

CC number: 803174

Eligibility

Individuals engaged in Christian and youth-based work.

Types of grants

One-off and recurrent grants are given according to need.

Annual grant total

In 2013/14 the trust had assets of £23.5 million and an income of £2 million. Grants and donations were made totalling £537,500, the great majority of which were made to organisations. We estimate that around £20,000 was given to individuals engaged in Christian and youth-based work for social welfare purposes.

Applications

Apply in writing to the correspondent at any time. The trust commits most of its money early, giving the remaining funds to eligible applicants.

The Morval Foundation

£60,000

Correspondent: Tricia Cullimore, Secretary, Meadow Brook, Send Marsh Road, Ripley GU23 6JR

CC number: 207692

Eligibility

Older Christian Scientists living in the UK who are members of The Mother Church, The First Church of Christ, Scientist in Boston, USA.

Types of grants

Monthly grants to allow older Christian Scientists to continue living independently in their own homes and one-off grants according to need.

Annual grant total

In 2013/14 the foundation held assets of £1.7 million and had an income of £152,500. Grants to individuals totalled £60,000 with £52,500 given in regular monthly grants and £7,500 in one-off grants.

Applications

Application forms are available from the correspondent and can be submitted directly by the individual for consideration at any time.

Other information

The foundation administers three funds: the Morval Fund, the Ruston Bequest and the New Chickering Fund.

The Mylne Trust

£24,000

Correspondent: Robin Twining, Secretary, PO Box 530, Farnham GU9 1BP (email: admin@mylnetrust.org. uk; website: www.mylnetrust.org.uk)

CC number: 208074

Eligibility

Members of the Protestant faith who have been engaged in evangelistic work, including missionaries and retired missionaries, and Christian workers whose finances are inadequate. Married ordinands with children are also supported when all other sources of funding have failed to cover their needs.

Types of grants

Annual and one-off grants for living costs and training expenses.

Annual grant total

In 2014/15 the trust had assets of £2.1 million and an income of £59,500. Grants totalled £48,500. We estimate that grants for social welfare purposes amounted to £24,000.

Exclusions

The trust cannot support individuals who are not of a Protestant denomination.

Applications

The trust notes the following helpful information on its website:

> The trust has reviewed and, in 2013, changed its policy and procedure for making grants. Most grants are now being handled with partners already in Christian mission work. (Applications based on earlier procedures, using the old application forms, will no longer be considered by the trust.)

> *Worldwide except Africa*
> In principle, the only grant applications that will be considered by direct application to the trust are those from candidates for mission work who are studying or planning to study within the UK. Such applicants are invited to contact the Clerk to the Mylne Trust at admin@mylnetrust.org.uk requesting a current application form.

> *Africa*
> There are special arrangements for applicants who are based in Africa.

We would advise potential applicants to first visit the website for more information.

The Nazareth Trust Fund

£4,400

Correspondent: Revd David Hunt, 16 Wollaton Road, Ferndown BH22 8QR

CC number: 210503

Eligibility

The trust gives support to individuals known to the trustees who promote the Christian faith and/or are Christian missionaries.

Types of grants

One-off grants ranging between £100 and £750.

Annual grant total

In 2013/14 the fund had assets of £30,000, an income of £80,000 and the grant total awarded to individuals was £4,400.

Exclusions

No support is given for individuals not known to the trustees.

Applications

Apply in writing to the correspondent. Note, however, that the trust tends only

to support individuals and organisations personally known to the trustees.

Other information

Grants are also made to organisations (£45,500 in 2013/14).

North of Scotland Quaker Trust

£5,000

Correspondent: The Trustees, Quaker Meeting House, 98 Crown Street, Aberdeen AB11 6HJ

OSCR number: SC000784

Eligibility

People who are associated with the Religious Society of Friends in the North of Scotland Monthly Meeting area, namely Aberdeen City, Aberdeenshire, Moray, Highland, Orkney, Shetland, Western Isles and that part of Argyll and Bute from Oban northwards.

Types of grants

One-off and recurrent grants are given according to need.

Annual grant total

In 2014 the trust had an income of £14,700 and a total expenditure of £30,000. Grants are made to individuals and organisations. We estimate that the amount of grants given to individuals for welfare purposes totalled around £5,000.

Exclusions

No grants are given to people studying above first degree level.

Applications

Apply in writing to the correspondent.

Other information

Grants are also given for educational purposes.

The Podde Trust

£4,000

Correspondent: Peter Godfrey, Trustee, 68 Green Lane, Hucclecote, Gloucester GL3 3QX (01452 613563; email: thepodde@gmail.com)

CC number: 1016322

Eligibility

Individuals involved in Christian work in the UK and overseas.

Types of grants

One-off and recurrent grants.

Annual grant total

In 2013/14 the trust had assets of £3,000 and an income of £46,000. There were 33 grants given to individuals totalling £8,500. The purposes for which awards were given were not specified. We estimate that the total number of grants given for welfare purposes totalled around £4,000.

Applications

Applications may be made in writing to the correspondent. Note that the trust has previously stated that it has very limited resources, and those it does have are mostly already committed. Requests from new applicants, therefore, have very little chance of success.

Other information

Organisations involved in Christian work in the UK and abroad are also supported (£36,000 was given to 40 organisations in 2013/14). The trust awards grants for charitable purposes, including the advancement of religion, of education and the relief of poverty.

The annual report and accounts for 2013/14 note the following: 'Contributions made in the past financial year include Pacific Partnership Trust working with students in New Zealand, Operation Mobilisation and TEAR Fund to name but a few.'

Retired Missionary Aid Fund

£587,000

Correspondent: Roger Herbert, Trustee, 64 Callow Hill Road, Alvechurch, Birmingham B48 7LR (0121 445 2378; website: www.rmaf.co.uk)

CC number: 211454

Eligibility

Retired missionaries from the Christian Brethren Assemblies who are in need. Help may also be given to their dependants.

Types of grants

Quarterly grants, birthday gifts and Christmas hampers.

Annual grant total

In 2013/14 the fund held assets of £1.4 million and had an income of £635,000. Grants to individuals totalled more than £587,000 and were distributed as follows:

Gifts to retired missionaries	£553,000
Earmarked gifts for retired missionaries	£20,000
Gift vouchers and Christmas hampers	£12,500
Funeral grant	£2,000

Applications

The fund only gives support to its members, who should make their circumstances known to the correspondent.

Other information

The objects of the charity are to assist retired missionaries from Christian Brethren Assemblies who are in deprived circumstances. Such missionaries have usually spent all or large proportions of their working lives serving God overseas without any salary or other fixed means of support. According to the trustees' annual report for 2013/14, the trustees have established eligibility criteria for recipients of grants, relating to such matters as their length of missionary service, ill health, and age.

Torchbearer Trust Fund

£30,000

Correspondent: Phil Burt, Secretary, Capernwray Hall, Carnforth, Lancashire LA6 1AG (01524 733908; fax: 01524 736681; email: info@capernwray.org.uk; website: www.capernwray.org.uk)

CC number: 253607

Eligibility

People engaged in full-time Christian missionary work. Preference is given to students and former students of Torchbearer Bible schools.

Types of grants

One-off and recurrent grants are given according to need.

Annual grant total

In 2013/14 the charity had assets of £132,000 and an income of £70,500. Grants totalled £60,000, a breakdown of which was not available in the accounts. We estimate that grants for social welfare purposes totalled around £30,000.

Applications

At the time of writing (August 2015) the charity stated the following on its Charity Commission record: 'All funds are fully allocated at present and so applications for funding will not receive a response.'

Other information

Grants are also available for missionary work.

The Westward Trust

£7,000

Correspondent: Alison Ironside, Trustee, 17 Green Meadow Road, Birmingham B29 4DD (0121 475 1179)

CC number: 260488

Eligibility

Quakers in who are in need and live in the UK.

Types of grants

One-off and recurrent grants can be given according to need.

Annual grant total

In 2013/14 the trust had an income of £9,400 and a total expenditure of £14,300. We estimate that the amount of grants given to individuals totalled around £7,000.

Applications

Apply in writing to the correspondent.

Other information

Grants are also made to organisations, particularly Quaker charities or projects in which members of the Religious Society of Friends are involved.

The Widows, Orphans and Dependants Society of the Church in Wales (WODS)

£85,000 (64 grants)

Correspondent: Louise Davies, Secretary, 39 Cathedral Road, Cardiff CF11 9XF (029 2034 8228; email: louisedavies@churchinwales.org.uk; website: www.churchinwales.org.uk)

CC number: 503271

Eligibility

Widows, orphans and dependants of deceased clergy of the Church in Wales only, who are living on a low income. Each year the society sets minimum income levels which each diocesan committee should aim to achieve. In 2014 these levels were set at £14,330 for widows, £13,700 for dependants and £2,600 for orphans.

Types of grants

One-off grants.

Annual grant total

In 2014 the society held assets of £749,500 and had an income of £84,000. A total amount of £83,500 was given in grants to 64 individuals.

Applications

Apply in writing to the correspondent. Applications should be made through one of the six diocesan committees of the Church in Wales. Details of the applicant's financial situation should be included.

Judaism

AJEX Charitable Foundation

See entry on page 80

Chasdei Tovim Me'oros

£2,500

Correspondent: Yoel Bleier, Trustee, 17 Durlston Road, London E5 8RP (020 8806 2406; email: tovimmeorosuk@gmail.com)

CC number: 1110623

Eligibility

People of the Jewish faith who are in need.

Types of grants

Grants given according to need.

Annual grant total

In 2013/14 the trust had an unusually low income of £3,300 and expenditure of £5,700. We estimate that the total amount of grants awarded to individuals was approximately £2,500 as the trust also awards grants to organisations. The grant total has been higher in previous years.

Applications

Apply in writing to the correspondent.

Closehelm Ltd

£41,000

Correspondent: Mr A. Van Praagh, Trustee, 30 Armitage Road, London NW11 8RD (020 8201 8688)

CC number: 291296

Eligibility

People, particularly those of the Jewish faith, who are in need.

Types of grants

Grants and loans are given to needy families for housing, medical and other costs.

Annual grant total

In 2013/14 the charity held assets of £2.5 million and had an income of £190,000 We estimate that the amount of grants given to individuals for social welfare needs totalled £41,000, with funding also awarded to individuals for educational purposes. A further £124,500 was given in grants to organisations.

Applications

Apply in writing to the correspondent.

The Engler Family Charitable Trust

£13,000

Correspondent: Mr J. Engler, Trustee, Motley Bank, South Downs Road, Bowdon, Altrincham WA14 3HB (email: jengleruk@yahoo.co.uk)

CC number: 1108518

Eligibility

Members of the Jewish faith living in England or Wales, with a particular focus on young people and the elderly.

Types of grants

Grants given according to need.

Annual grant total

In 2013/14 the trust had an income of £26,500 and a total expenditure of £27,000. We estimate that the amount of grants given to individuals totalled £13,000, with funding also awarded to Jewish organisations across England and Wales.

Applications

Apply in writing to the correspondent.

The Isaac and Annie Fogelman Relief Trust

£8,500

Correspondent: Stephen Forman, Trustee, Torrington House, 47 Holywell Hill, St Albans, Hertfordshire AL1 1HD (01727 885560; email: stephenforman@fsmail.net)

CC number: 202285

Eligibility

People of the Jewish faith aged 40 and over who live in Portsmouth and worship at the Portsmouth Jewish Synagogue.

Types of grants

One-off and recurrent grants are given according to need.

Annual grant total

In 2013/14 the trust had an income of £7,700 and a total expenditure of £9,100. We estimate that the amount of grants given to individuals totalled £8,500.

Applications

Apply in writing to: The Secretary, Portsmouth and Southsea Hebrew Congregation, The Thicket, Elm Grove, Southsea PO5 2AA. Applications are considered quarterly.

Gur Trust

£6,300

Correspondent: The Trustees, Gur Trust, 1st Floor Offices, 1 Bridge Lane, London NW11 0EA (020 8801 6038)

CC number: 283423

Eligibility

People connected to the Jewish Orthodox faith in the UK.

Types of grants

One-off and recurrent grants may be offered according to need. Note that the trust primarily aims to support education in and the religion of the Orthodox Jewish faith.

Annual grant total

In 2013/14 the trust had assets of over £1.3 million and an income of £43,000. Charitable activities totalled about £53,500; however, a further breakdown was not given. It would appear that support is mainly given for educational needs, but the information on the trust on the Charity Commission's records notes that relief in need is also supported. We estimate that relief-in-need support to individuals may have been around £6,300.

Applications

Applications may be made in writing to the correspondent. Our previous research notes the trust having stated that 'all calls for help are carefully considered and help is given according to circumstances and funds then available'.

Other information

The trust also makes grants to organisations, Talmudical colleges and to individuals for educational purposes.

The Jewish Aged Needy Pension Society

£17,500

Correspondent: Sheila Taylor, Secretary, 34 Dalkeith Grove, Stanmore, Middlesex HA7 4SG (020 8958 5390)

CC number: 206262

Eligibility

Members of the Jewish community aged 60 or over, who have known better circumstances and have lived in the UK for at least ten years or are of British nationality.

Types of grants

Up to 60 pensions of up to £10 per week for all kinds of need.

Annual grant total

In 2014 the society had assets of £426,000, an income of £55,000 and a total expenditure of £25,000. Pensions and grants totalled £17,500.

Applications

Apply in writing to the correspondent. Applications are considered quarterly.

Jewish Care Scotland

Correspondent: The Trustees, The Walton Community Care Centre, May Terrace, Giffnock, Glasgow G46 6LD (0141 620 1800; fax: 0141 620 2409; email: admin@jcarescot.org.uk; website: www.jcarescot.org.uk)

OSCR number: SC005267

Eligibility

Jewish people who live in Scotland and are in need.

Types of grants

One-off grants of £50 to £750 are given towards clothing, food, household goods, rent, holidays, equipment, and travel. The charity also runs a food bank from Mark's Deli in Glasgow.

Annual grant total

In 2014 the charity had an income of £750,500 and expended £671,000 on charitable activities. The charity's Annual Review 2015 shows that 6% (we estimate around £40,000) of funding was given towards hardship grants and support for the food bank.

Applications

In the first instance, contact the correspondent.

Other information

The board also helps with educational costs and friendship clubs, housing requirements, clothing, meals-on-wheels and counselling, for example.

Kupath Gemach Chaim Bechesed Viznitz Trust

£283,000

Correspondent: Saul Weiss, Trustee, 171 Kyverdale Road, London N16 6PS (020 8442 9604 or 0781 125 3203)

CC number: 1110323

Eligibility

Members of the Jewish faith who are in need.

Types of grants

One-off and recurrent grants are given according to need.

Annual grant total

In 2013/14 the trust held assets of £29,500 and an income of £410,500. Welfare grants to individuals amounted to £283,000, with a further £98,000 awarded to Jewish organisations.

Applications

Apply in writing to the correspondent.

The Leeds Jewish Welfare Board

£4,000

Correspondent: Liz Bradbury, Chief Executive, 311 Stonegate Road, Leeds, West Yorkshire LS17 6AZ (0113 268 4211; fax: 0113 203 4915; email: theboard@ljwb.co.uk; website: www.ljwb.co.uk)

CC number: 1041257

Eligibility

Primarily people of the Jewish faith who live in Leeds or North and West Yorkshire.

Types of grants

Grants may be given as part of a 'support package'. They are rarely given as a one-off without a full assessment of the situation. Loans may also be given and, depending on individual circumstances, may be part-grant/part-loan. A flexible approach together with budgeting advice is offered. The majority of grants are given to families with children. These may be for clothes, bedding requirements and so on. Grants are also given at Jewish festivals such as Passover. Counselling and meals-on-wheels services along with a comprehensive range of services and resources are also offered to children, families and older people primarily, but not exclusively, of the Jewish faith.

Annual grant total

In 2013/14 the board had assets of £6 million and an income of £3.5 million. Each year a small amount is reserved for grant-making purposes. We estimate that in 2013/14 grants to individuals totalled £4,000.

The organisation also spent over £3.1 million on its various other charitable services: providing activities and support for the elderly, children and their families, and people with physical and mental health problems from the Jewish community.

Applications

Applications for help can be made at any time by individuals, welfare agencies, friends or relatives. The board can respond quickly in urgent cases. The applicant will be seen by a case worker who will assess the application and gather the relevant information.

Other information

The organisation was established in 1878 as a voluntary Board of Guardians, with its main purpose being 'to hand out funds to the needy to prevent them from having to enter the workhouse'. These

days, the Leeds Jewish Welfare Board employs more than 100 staff and hundreds of volunteers, who provide support in the community.

Mercaz Torah Vechesed Ltd

£20,000

Correspondent: Joseph Ostreicher, Trustee, 28 Braydon Road, London N16 6QB (020 8880 5366; email: umarpeh@gmail.com)

CC number: 1109212

Eligibility

Members of the Orthodox Jewish community who are in need.

Types of grants

One-off grants.

Annual grant total

In 2013/14 the charity had assets of £1,000, an income of £856,500 and a total expenditure of £914,500. Grants totalled £914,500, the majority of which was distributed to Jewish organisations. We estimate that the amount of grants given to individuals amounted to £20,000.

Applications

Apply in writing to the correspondent.

Merseyside Jewish Community Care

£20,000

Correspondent: Lisa Dolan, Chief Executive, Shifrin House, 433 Smithdown Road, Liverpool L15 3JL (0151 733 2292; email: info@mjccshifrin.co.uk; website: www.merseysidejewish communitycare.co.uk)

CC number: 1122902

Eligibility

People of the Jewish faith who live in Merseyside and are in need due to poverty, illness, old age, social disadvantage, disability or mental health problems.

Types of grants

Small, one-off grants and loans to help towards medical equipment, respite breaks and basic essentials such as food and clothing. Grants are only paid on the provision of receipts for the goods/services purchased or are made directly to the supplier.

Annual grant total

In 2013/14 the charity had an income of £442,000 and a total expenditure of £407,500. The accounts had been received at the Charity Commission but were not published on its website. We estimate that as in previous years, 'relief grants' were made totalling around £20,000, for basic essentials such as food and clothing.

Applications

The individual should apply directly to the correspondent by letter or telephone.

Other information

Merseyside Jewish Community Care provide a care and welfare service for Jewish people in Merseyside.

The MYA Charitable Trust

£13,900 (8 grants)

Correspondent: Myer Rothfeld, Trustee, Medcar House, 149A Stamford Hill, London N16 5LL (020 8800 3582)

CC number: 299642

Eligibility

Jewish people in need anywhere in the world.

Types of grants

One-off and recurrent grants to people in need of financial and medical aid. Short-term interest-free loans may also be made to help with financial hardship or educational needs.

Annual grant total

In 2013/14 the trust had assets of nearly £1.4 million and an income of £245,500. There were eight grants awarded to individuals totalling £13,900.

Applications

Applications may be made in writing to the correspondent.

Other information

The charity also gives grants for educational and religious organisations. In 2013/14 a total of £561,500 was given to organisations, consisting of grants (£177,500) and an investment donation (£384,000).

The Chevras Ezras Nitzrochim Trust

£203,500

Correspondent: Hertz Kahan, Trustee, 53 Heathland Road, London N16 5PQ

CC number: 275352

Eligibility

Jewish people who are in need due to sickness, disability, financial hardship or unemployment. The trust focuses on those living in the Greater London area, although help can also be given to individuals living further away.

Types of grants

One-off and recurrent grants are available according to need. Support is also given for the provision of food items, medical supplies and clothing.

Annual grant total

In 2014 the trust had assets of £7,700 and an income of £238,500. Grants to individuals totalled £203,500.

Applications

Apply in writing to the correspondent. Applications can be made at any time.

Other information

Grants are also made to organisations for the advancement of religion, the relief of poverty and educational purposes (£26,300 in 2014).

NJD Charitable Trust

£10,000

Correspondent: Alan Dawson, Correspondent, St Bride's House, 10 Salisbury Square, London EC4Y 8EH (020 7842 7306; email: info@igpinvest. com)

CC number: 1109146

Eligibility

Members of the Jewish faith who are in need.

Types of grants

One-off and recurrent grants are given according to need.

Annual grant total

In 2014/15 the trust had assets of £129,500 and an income of £100,000. Grants were given to both organisations and individuals and totalled almost £92,000. The majority of grants were awarded to organisations. A specific breakdown of the amount awarded to individuals was not provided in the accounts; we estimate that grants to individuals totalled around £5,000.

Applications

Apply in writing to the correspondent. Applications are considered throughout the year.

Norwood

£55,000

Correspondent: Julian Anthony, Company Secretary, Broadway House, 80–82 The Broadway, Stanmore, Middlesex HA7 4HB (020 8809 8809; email: info@norwood.org.uk; website: www.norwood.org.uk)

CC number: 1059050

Eligibility

People with learning disabilities and children and families in need.

Beneficiaries are mostly Jewish although one-quarter of their clients are of mixed faith. This is a national charity but it concentrates on London and the south east of England.

Types of grants

Grants are made according to need, but no regular allowances are given. Grants towards the celebration of Jewish religious festivals, social need and occasional holidays are also made.

Annual grant total

In 2014/15 the charity had assets of £44.7 million and an income of £35.8 million. Grants total about £55,000 each year.

Applications

Potential recipients of grants are recommended by Norwood staff. Initial contact should be made by phone or emailing socialwork@norwood.org.uk.

Other information

Grants are made in conjunction with a comprehensive welfare service. Norwood provides a range of social services for Jewish children and families, including social work, day facilities, residential and foster care.

The ZSV Trust

£640,000 (600 grants)

Correspondent: Z. Friedman, Trustee, 12 Grange Court Road, London N16 5EGCC number: 1063860

Eligibility

Jewish people in need, particularly older people, refugees, orphans and families in distress.

Types of grants

One-off and recurrent grants are given according to need. Most of the trust's funds are spent on providing food parcels. Other recent grants have been given towards medical assistance, clothing, shoes and weddings.

Annual grant total

In 2014 the trust had assets of £52,000 and an income of £673,500. Grants were given to around 600 families and totalled over £640,000. They were broken down as follows:

Food parcels	£320,000
Relief of poverty	£105,000
Endowments to poor brides	£116,500
Families undergoing stress	£33,500
House repairs and utilities	£21,000
Youth activities	£12,500
Clothing and shoes	£14,000
Assistance with healthcare	£17,200

Applications

Apply in writing to the correspondent. Individuals need to apply through social services or are often recommended by Rabbis or other community leaders.

Specific circum-stances

Fund for Human Need

£23,500 (235 grants)

Correspondent: Stanley Platt, Secretary, 50 Leeds Road, Selby YO8 4HX (01757 706060; email: shplatt1@gmail.com; website: fundforhumanneed.org.uk)

CC number: 208866

Eligibility

Grants are made to refugees, asylum seekers, people who are homeless and other individuals in personal distress. The charity's website sates that 'priority is given to those who are destitute or have no income or benefits, to those who are particularly vulnerable, and to those where a small grant will make a major difference'.

Types of grants

Grants of up to £120 each. Grants are often made via another organisation but may also be made directly to individuals.

Annual grant total

In 2013/14 the charity had an income of £19,200, and a total expenditure of £33,000. Grants were made to 235 individuals totalling £23,500 and were broken down as follows:

Refugees, asylum seekers and people who are homeless	182	£18,100
Other individuals in personal distress	53	£5,500

A further six grants were made to organisations, totalling £8,600.

Exclusions

Grants are not awarded for debt repayment, educational purposes, or to individuals outside the UK. Grants are not made to organisations, apart from a small number of specific projects that the fund has worked with.

Applications

Applications may be made in writing to the correspondent or using the online application form. Applications should include details of the individual's financial situation, their reason for applying and the difference that receiving a grant would make. While applications can be made directly by an individual, it is preferred that applications are made by recognised organisation, such as a local authority or voluntary organisation, on behalf of an

individual. Grants are made on a monthly basis.

Other information

The fund's 2013/14 annual report states that the trustees have increased the number of grants made to individuals and the size of grants, due to a significant increase in grant applications and need. Grants are also made to organisations for specific projects working in disadvantaged communities.

Prisoners of Conscience Appeal Fund

£67,500

Correspondent: Kirsty Bennett, Grants Officer, PO Box 61044, London SE1 1UP (020 7407 6644; fax: 020 7407 6655; email: grantsofficer@ prisonersofconscience.org; website: www. prisonersofconscience.org)

CC number: 213766

Eligibility

Prisoners of conscience and/or their families, who have suffered persecution for their conscientiously held beliefs. The fact that the person is seeking asylum or has been a victim of civil war is not sufficient grounds in itself. The fund's website states: 'A degree of personal persecution has to be established.'

Types of grants

One-off grants ranging from £350 to £500 are given and those for immediate and urgent needs are prioritised. Grants can be given towards, for example, basic essentials such as food, clothing, toiletries and travel costs; basic furniture; counselling/therapy sessions; or medical needs.

The fund also makes family reunion grants to pay for the related costs of bringing close dependants to join eligible individuals in the UK (see the website for eligibility criteria specific to these grants).

Annual grant total

In 2014 the fund had assets of £157,000 and an income of £270,000. The fund's annual report for 2014 states that 104 grants were made to individuals and families during the year, totalling £105,500. We have taken these figures to include 11 bursaries which amounted to £38,000, and estimate relief-in-need grants to have totalled around £67,500.

Exclusions

No support is given to people who have used or advocated violence, supported a violent organisation or willingly served in the armed forces.

Applications

Applications are not considered directly from individuals but rather from approved referral organisations that apply on behalf of individuals. The fund advises the following on its website:

> You can ask your solicitor to make an application or you can contact the many local Citizens Advice Bureaux who may apply to us on your behalf. If you are in touch with any other refugee organisations or official bodies, you could also ask them to make an application. If you do not know of any organisation who might be able to assist you, please contact us grantsofficer@prisonersof conscience.org and we will try to help.

Referral agencies must register with the fund's online system in order to apply for a grant. See the website or contact the correspondent for more information.

Other information

The fund was initially established in 1962 as the relief arm of Amnesty International, but is now a charity in its own right. It is the only agency in the UK making grants specifically to prisoners of conscience – individuals who have been persecuted for their conscientiously held beliefs, provided that they have not used or advocated violence. Grant recipients include political prisoners, human rights defenders, lawyers, environmental activists, teachers and academics who come from many different countries such as Burma, Zimbabwe, Sri Lanka, Tibet, Iran, Cameroon and Eritrea.

The charity's aim is to raise and distribute money to help them and/or their families rehabilitate themselves during and after their ordeal. Financial grants cover general hardship relief, furniture, medicines, travel costs, family reunion costs, education, requalification and resettlement costs and medical treatment and counselling after torture.

The Rathbone Moral Aid Charity

£6,000

Correspondent: Carol Thompson, Clerk, Herefordshire Community Council, PO Box 181, Hereford HR2 9YN (01981 250899)

CC number: 222697

Eligibility

People who live in Herefordshire who are under 25 and in need of rehabilitation, 'particularly as a result of crime, delinquency, prostitution, addiction to drugs or drink, maltreatment or neglect'.

Types of grants

One-off and recurrent grants are given according to need.

Annual grant total

In 2014, the charity had an income of £12,100 and a total expenditure of £12,500. We estimate that the total award granted to individuals was approximately £6,000.

Exclusions

No grants are given for nursery fees.

Applications

Apply in writing to the correspondent. Individual applications are considered throughout the year. All individual applications must be supported by a welfare agency or doctor, social worker, teacher or other professional.

Other information

Grants are also made to organisations.

Six Point Foundation

£347,500 (222 grants)

Correspondent: Susan Cohen, Executive Director, 25–26 Enford Street, London W1H 1DW (020 3372 8881; email: info@ sixpointfoundation.org.uk; website: www.sixpointfoundation.org.uk)

CC number: 1143324

Eligibility

UK-resident Holocaust survivors and refugees who are of Jewish origin (whether practising or not) and have experienced Nazi persecution. To be eligible there must also be financial disadvantage. This is measured as having an income of under £10,000 per year (excluding pensions and social security payments) and assets of under £32,000 (excluding a primary residence and vehicle). Further guidance on eligibility is given on the foundation's website.

Types of grants

One-off grants for home adaptations, medical costs, short-term care, travel costs, accessibility and other items or services that enhance quality of life. Grants are only given for goods and services which are not available through other funding sources.

Annual grant total

In 2014/15 the foundation held assets of £3.9 million and had an income of £1.7 million. 128 individuals received 222 grants totalling £347,500, with organisations receiving a further £911,000.

Grants were awarded in the following categories:

Home adaptations	£114,500
Care costs	£63,500
Medical expenses	£45,000
Other purposes	£44,000
Travel costs	£25,000
Social activities	£2,700

A further £72,500 was spent on the SPF Connect Project, which delivers training for beneficiaries on using computer technology.

Exclusions

No reimbursements are given for goods or services already purchased, except in cases of absolute emergencies.

Applications

Applications are not accepted directly from individuals, but are processed through one of the foundation's partner agencies, which include Agudas, AJR, Bikur Cholim, North London Bikur Cholim, and Shalvata. Applicants or those acting on behalf of an applicant are advised contact one of these agencies to discuss an application. Enquiries can also be made to the foundation using its online enquiry submission form, or can be made in writing, by telephone or by email. Applicants may be visited at home by a social worker experienced in assessing Holocaust survivors and refugees.

Other information

The foundation has also previously awarded grants to organisations working with UK Holocaust survivors and refugees in need. In 2014/15 the foundation closed its standard grants programme to focus on individual giving; however, the foundation's small grants programme remains open to organisations. In 2014/15 18 grants were made to organisations.

The foundation also funds a project called SPF Connect, which provides training for survivors and refugees on using computer technology.

WaveLength

£32,000

Correspondent: Anny Mills, Applications Officer, 159a High Street, Hornchurch, Essex RM11 3YB (Freephone: 0800 018 2137; fax: 01708 620816; email: info@w4b.org.uk; website: www.wavelength.org.uk)

CC number: 207400

Eligibility

People whose ability to leave the house is limited, and who are isolated, lonely and in financial need.

Types of grants

The provision of radios and televisions. The society does not provide television licences unless the applicant is in receipt of, or is applying for, equipment from the charity. The charity expects applicants to make provision for any subsequent licences.

Annual grant total

In 2013/14 the charity had an income of £445,000 and assets of £2.8 million. During this financial year, the charity spent £32,000 (direct costs) on the provision of radio sets, TV rental and licences to beneficiaries.

Exclusions

No grants are given to: individuals applying on their own behalf; grant-making bodies; statutory bodies; top-up funding on under-priced contracts.

Applications

Apply on a form available directly from the correspondent or to download from the website. Applications must be submitted through a third party such as a social worker, Citizens Advice, religious organisation or other welfare agency. Applicants must be UK residents and should provide evidence such as a passport, birth certificate or citizenship document.

Note: we recommend that third parties applying on behalf of an applicant read the extensive guidelines (available from the charity's website) before an application is submitted.

Other information

The charity was known as the Wireless for the Bedridden Society until 2010.

The charity also provides equipment to charitable organisations. In 2014, 37 projects were supported, benefitting around 1,800 individuals.

Asylum seekers and refugees

Asylum Seekers Support Initiative – Short Term (ASSIST)

£49,500 (188+ grants)

Correspondent: Welfare Payments Team, c/o Victoria Hall Methodist Church, 60 Norfolk Street, Sheffield, South Yorkshire S1 2JB (0114 275 4960; email: admin@assistsheffield.org.uk; website: www.assistsheffield.org.uk)

CC number: 1100894

Eligibility

Asylum seekers who live in Sheffield.

Types of grants

Small weekly grants for food and basic living expenses, usually £20 per person. Bus passes, food vouchers, temporary accommodation and emergency support are also given.

Annual grant total

In 2013/14 the charity had assets of £203,000 and an income of £326,500. Grants were made totalling £49,500 for the following purposes:

Weekly payments	£24,500
Bus passes	£17,800
Accommodation payments	£6,600
Emergency payments	£1,100

A further £2,300 was paid to host families providing temporary accommodation.

Applications

Preliminary contact should be made with the charity.

Other information

The charity also provides advice, information, temporary accommodation and support with appointments, as well as running awareness-raising activities. In 2013/14 the charity dealt with 1,430 enquiries and supported over 230 asylum seekers.

Fund for Human Need
See entry on page 42

Homelessness

Housing the Homeless Central Fund

£52,000 (268 grants)

Correspondent: Frankie Salton-Cox, Clerk to the Trustees, 2A Orchard Road, Sidcup DA14 6RD (email: hhcfund@ gmail.com)

CC number: 233254

Eligibility

People who are either homeless or have serious accommodation problems. Priority may be given to expectant parents or those with children. Grants are given in three categories: those who are in danger of losing their home or essential services such as utilities; those caring for children in financial difficulties; those who have suffered personal setback (such as mental illness, time in prison, addiction or domestic upheaval) and who are hoping to start again in a home of their own and need basic equipment.

Types of grants

One-off grants of £100 to £300 for household items and fuel bills. Recent grants have paid for cots and beds, basic kitchen equipment, clothing, and rent arrears.

Annual grant total

In 2014/15 the fund held assets of £364,500 and had an income of £59,500. Individuals received 268 grants, totalling £52,000.

Exclusions

No recurrent grants are given or grants for holidays, medical apparatus, funeral expenses, travel costs, vehicles, educational expenses, structural improvements to property, rent deposits, toys, computers or televisions.

Applications

A professional third party such as a social worker or probation officer should request the guidelines and application form. This request should be sent on headed paper, enclosing an sae. Decisions are usually made within a week, although no grants are made in March or December. **Note:** telephone calls will not be accepted and applications must be made by a representative of a recognised third party organisation, for example Citizens Advice, social services or another welfare organisation.

People who have offended

The Michael and Shirley Hunt Charitable Trust

£14,000 (206 grants)

Correspondent: Mrs D. Jenkins, Trustee, Ansty House, Henfield Road, Small Dole, West Sussex BN5 9XH (01903 817116)

CC number: 1063418

Eligibility

Prisoners and their relatives and dependants, such as their spouses and children.

Types of grants

One-off and recurrent grants for prisoners' families' welfare needs and for travel expenses for prisoners on care leave.

Annual grant total

In 2013/14 the trust had assets of almost £6.2 million and an income of over £278,500. Grants were made to 206 individuals, totalling £14,000.

A further £66,500 was awarded to charitable organisations.

Applications

Apply in writing to the correspondent. Applications can be made directly by the individual or, where applicable, through a third party such as Citizens Advice, probation service or a social worker.

Other information

The trust also supports animal welfare causes.

Sacro Trust

£2,400

Correspondent: The Trust Fund Administrator, 29 Albany Street, Edinburgh EH1 3QN (0131 624 7270; fax: 0131 624 7269; email: info@national. sacro.org.uk; website: www.sacro.org.uk)

OSCR number: SC023031

Eligibility

People living in Scotland who are subject to a license/court order or who have been released from prison in the last two years, and their families.

Types of grants

Grants are made usually to a maximum of £300, although applications for larger sums can be considered. Grants given include those for electrical goods, clothing, furniture, driving lessons and education and training. Assistance is intended to help the individual in the process of rehabilitation.

Annual grant total

In 2013/14 the trust had an income of £83,500 and a total expenditure of £44,500. It 'awarded 41 grants totalling £4,900 to help individuals in Scotland with the process of rehabilitation'. We estimate that about £2,400 was given for social welfare needs.

Exclusions

Grants are not made where financial help from other sources is available.

Applications

Applications can only be accepted if they are made through a local authority, voluntary sector worker, health visitor or so on. The forms may be obtained from the correspondent and are considered every two months. Payments cannot be made directly to an individual, rather to the organisation making the application. Other sources of funding should be sought before applying to the trust.

Other information

The Sacro Trust is related to the Sacro organisation which provides 'community-based support to help offenders re-integrate into society and live stable, independent lives'. The organisation runs criminal justice, youth justice and mediation services,

The trust also gives grants for educational purposes. The Sacro Annual Review for 2013/14 states: 'The Sacro Trust is constitutionally separate and aims to provide small grants to individuals in the process of rehabilitation.'

Sacro (OSCR no. SC016293) provides advice and information, mediation services, criminal and youth justice services, and also conducts research and policy work. Full details of service provision are given on the trust's website. In 2013/14 it spent over £7 million in the areas of criminal justice, youth justice and community mediation. The website notes: 'Founded over 40 years ago, Sacro works independently and collaboratively within Scotland's communities to provide support, prevent conflict and challenge offending behaviour wherever the need arises.'

Lady Alice Shaw-Stewart Memorial Fund

£1,200

Correspondent: Bert Allison, Correspondent, Legal Services, Inverclyde Council, Municipal Buildings, Greenock, Inverclyde PA15 1JA (01475 712225; email: bert.allison@inverclyde. gov.uk)

OSCR number: SC019228

Eligibility
Female ex-prisoners recommended by the probation officer in the Inverclyde Council area.

Types of grants
On average one-off grants are made which total about £200 each and are given for general welfare purposes, such as electrical goods, holidays and driving lessons.

Annual grant total
In 2014/15 the fund had an income of £200 and an expenditure of £1,400. We estimate that about £1,200 was given in grants.

Applications
Applications may be made in writing to the correspondent. They should be submitted by a probation officer on behalf of the individual.

Other information
Our research suggests that the council administers about 20 other small funds for people living in Greenock, Gourock, Inverkip and Kilmalcolm.

The Sheriffs' and Recorders' Fund

£122,000 (977 grants)

Correspondent: The Secretary, c/o Central Criminal Court, Old Bailey, Warwick Square, London EC4M 7BS

(020 7248 3277 (Tue and Wed 11am–4.45pm); email: secretary@srfund. net; website: www.srfund.org.uk)

CC number: 221927

Eligibility
People on probation and families of serving prisoners in the Greater Metropolitan Area of London. The charity is also concerned with the rehabilitation of drug and alcohol abusers.

Types of grants
One-off grants towards clothing, household items, furnishings, beds and bedding, white goods, carpets, baby needs and so on. Grants to families primarily seek to enable children to enjoy holidays and other recreational activities. Support is also given for training, including vocational courses, tools and equipment or work clothing. Awards are made according to need and have ranged from £250 to £10,000.

Annual grant total
In 2013/14 the charity had assets of over £1.3 million and an income of £218,000. Grants were made to 1,284 individuals totalling £164,000. There were 977 grants totalling £122,000 for white goods and furnishing (£61,000) and clothing (£61,000).

A total of £26,000 was awarded in the provision of tools (including Bounceback donations) and a further £16,000 made for education and training purposes.

Applications
Application forms are available from the correspondent and must be submitted through probation officers or social workers. They are considered throughout the year. The website states: 'The Probation Service and other Social Welfare agencies recommend people for grants, mainly in the first weeks after release when ex-prisoners are at most risk of re-offending.'

Other information
Grants are also made for educational and training purposes and for special projects to organisations (three awards totalling £11,000 in 2013/14).

The charity's website has a list of useful organisations where support may also be available.

Illness and disability charities

There are many charities for people with illnesses or disabilities. The grant-makers detailed in this section are those that only give financial help. There are many others that provide non-financial support and advice and may be the starting point for getting financial help. For this reason we have a list of organisations which provide advice and support on page 427.

This section starts with an index of illness or disability. The entries are arranged alphabetically within each category, with charities supporting more than one illness or disability, or with broad criteria, listed at the start of the chapter. The 'Disability' section similarly lists charities which have a wide remit to support people with disabilities, rather than focusing on a specific condition. Individuals with any condition or disability, may therefore also look under these two general sections for support, as well as 'Specific conditions' or any other relevant section.

The sub-section 'Children' lists charities which give exclusively to children who have an illness or disability, with age as part of their key criteria – of course, many charities in other sections will also support children.

Similarly, the charities listed under 'Mental health' are by no means the only ones that will support those with mental health problems – rather, they are the only ones that specify this as their main criteria. Many charities with a broad remit to support those with an illness or disability will include people who have mental health problems; likewise with many of the grant-makers in the 'General charities' chapter.

Miss Ada Oliver

£1,500

Correspondent: The Trustees, c/o Marshalls Solicitors, 102 High Street, Godalming, Surrey GU7 1DS (01483 416101; email: cburnett@marshalls.uk. net)

CC number: 234456

Eligibility

People who have cancer or rheumatism and are in financial need. Preference is given for people living in Surrey.

Types of grants

Monthly and one-off grants of up to £100 are given for a variety of needs. Recent grants have been given for settling rent arrears, nursing home fees and necessities.

Annual grant total

In 2013/14 the trust had an income of £3,700 and a total expenditure of £3,200. Taking into account the fact that the charity also gives grants to organisations, we estimate that the total amount granted to individuals was £1,500.

Applications

Apply in writing to the correspondent, including details of income and circumstances. Applications can be submitted throughout the year by a social worker, Citizens Advice or other welfare agency on behalf of the individual.

The Christina Aitchison Trust

£500

Correspondent: Revd Roger Massingberd-Mundy, Trustee, The Old Post Office, The Street, West Raynham, Fakenham NR21 7AD

CC number: 1041578

Eligibility

People who are blind or have any ophthalmic disease or disability, and people who have a terminal illness and who are in need. Some preference may be given to individuals in the north east or south west of England.

Types of grants

One-off and recurrent grants to relieve blindness, ophthalmic disease or disability, and terminal illness.

Annual grant total

In 2013/14 the trust had an income of £1,900 and an expenditure of £2,200. We estimate that approximately £500 was given for relief-in-need purposes to individuals.

Applications

Application forms are available from the correspondent and should generally be submitted in March or September for consideration in April or November.

Other information

Grants are also given to individuals for educational needs and to organisations.

Clevedon Forbes Fund

£48,000 (153 grants)

Correspondent: Joan Taffs, Grants Officer, 4 Kenn Road, Clevedon BS21 6EL (01275 314777; email: joan@clevedonforbes.org; website: www.clevedonforbes.org)

CC number: 249313

Eligibility

People of limited means who are recovering from illness or who are in need of a break due to trauma or other distressing circumstances. Grants are also available for carers to have a holiday from caring for someone who is sick or who has disabilities. The majority of grants are given to individuals living in the south west but those living further afield will be considered.

Types of grants

One-off grants to those in need for convalescence or respite.

Annual grant total

In 2013/14 the trust had assets of £1.7 million and an income of £78,500. 153 grants were made to 345 individuals totalling £48,000.

Exclusions

Grants are not made for: debt relief; capital goods or the purchase of equipment; breaks outside the UK. Individuals cannot apply for another grant until a three-year period has elapsed.

Applications

Applications need to be made through a professional in the statutory or voluntary sector, such as a social worker or welfare officer. Application forms are available on the trust's website or directly from the correspondent.

Other information

A Christian gospel booklet is sent out to people receiving a grant unless there is a specific request to the contrary.

Foundations Independent Living Trust

£362,500 (406 grants)

Correspondent: Gayle Dawkes, Grants and Customer Service Assistant, The Old Co-op Building, 11 Railway Street, Glossop, Derbyshire SK13 7AG (0845 864 5210; email: gayled@foundations.uk.com; website: www.filt.org.uk)

CC number: 1103784

Eligibility

People who are elderly, vulnerable, and/or have health conditions/disabilities, who own their home or rent from a private landlord.

Types of grants

Grants for repairs, minor adaptations, home improvements, heating and insulation measures.

Annual grant total

In 2013/14 the trust held assets of £55,500 and had an income of £436,000. A total of £362,500 was awarded in 406 grants to beneficiaries. Grants ranged in value from £31 to £86,000. The average amount distributed was £212.

Applications

Apply via a local home improvement agency. Applications cannot be made directly to the trust but enquires are welcome. Local home improvement agencies are listed on the trust's website.

June and Douglas Hume Memorial Fund

£2,000

Correspondent: Jennifer McPhail, Grant Programmes Executive, Glasgow Office, Empire House, 131 West Nile Street, Glasgow G1 2RX (0141 341 4964; email: jennifer@foundationscotland.org.uk; website: www.foundationscotland.org.uk)

OSCR number: SC022910

Eligibility

Terminally ill patients who wish to spend their final days in their own home. Priority will be given to applicants from the west of Scotland and in particular the Helensburgh area.

Types of grants

One-off grants of up to £1,000 to assist patients with specialist equipment, as well as any house modifications necessary to accommodate such equipment. Grants may be used for bath and stair-lifts, reclining beds and chairs, wheelchairs and zimmers, for example.

Annual grant total

In 2013/14 the fund had an expenditure of £2,000.

Applications

Applicants should contact Jennifer McPhail on 0141 341 4964 in the first instance and an application form will be sent out to applicants, where funds are available. Applications completed by the applicant must be accompanied by a reference from a GP or consultant. Alternatively the application may be filled out directly by a medical professional. Applications are considered as they are received.

Other information

The fund is administered by Foundation Scotland.

Independence at Home

£312,000 (1,000 grants)

Correspondent: Kate Williams, Chief Executive, 4th Floor, Congress House, 14 Lyon Road, Harrow, Middlesex HA1 2EN (020 8427 7929; fax: 020 8424 2937; email: iah@independenceathome.org.uk; website: www.independenceathome.org.uk)

CC number: 1141758

Eligibility

People who have substantial disabilities or are severely ill and who live at home, or who wish to do so.

Types of grants

Grants ranging between £100 and £750 towards specific additional costs associated with living at home with a disability, including equipment and adaptations. Grants can be made towards almost any expense which is not covered by statutory provision and which is related to an individual who has disabilities living at home.

Annual grant total

In 2014/15 the trust held assets of £4.7 million and an income of £372,000. Grants were made to 1,000 individuals totalling £312,000.

Exclusions

Grants cannot be made to people living in residential care or in hospital, groups of people or organisations. Grants are not made towards medical treatment or therapies, debt relief or arrears, funeral expenses, telephone rental or call charges, televisions or licences or motor vehicles (although car adaptations may be considered).

Applications

Applications should be made by referral. Any health or social care worker, or worker for a voluntary organisation, who is supporting the client, is capable of assessing their needs and willing to act on their client's behalf and take their application forward can apply. Application forms are available on the website and should be completed and returned by post along with a letter describing your client's circumstances and medical diagnosis. For large pieces of equipment an occupational therapist's report and a quote from a builder or supplier should be included. Applications are considered on an ongoing basis. The trust accepts informal contact to prior to applications being made.

The League of the Helping Hand (LHH)

£127,000

Correspondent: The Secretary, LHH, PO Box 342, Burgess Hill RH15 5AQ (01444 236099; email: secretary@lhh.org.uk; website: www.lhh.org.uk)

CC number: 208792

Eligibility

People who have a physical disability, learning difficulty or mental health problem and are in financial need. Those who care for somebody who has disabilities, or who is older or ill may also be eligible.

Types of grants

One-off and recurrent payments. Grants of up to £250 are awarded towards essential household items, specialist equipment and carers' breaks. Quarterly gifts are available to help with daily living costs, the beneficiaries of which also receive newsletters, birthday and Christmas cards and, where possible, an annual personal visit from the Secretary.

Annual grant total

In 2014/15 the charity held assets of £2.6 million and had an income of £152,500. Grants to individuals totalled almost £127,000 and were distributed as follows:

One-off gifts	£65,000
Quarterly gifts	£52,500
Christmas gifts	£4,700
Visits	£2,300
Holidays	£2,200

Exclusions

No help is given for debts; business costs; holidays; tenancy deposits; building works; mobility scooters; wheelchairs; medical, dental or therapeutic treatments; or for education-related items.

Applications

Application forms are available to download from the trust's website. Applications must be submitted through a social worker, carers' support centre, Citizens Advice or other welfare body. If it is not possible to download the form, the correspondent should be contacted directly. An sae must be enclosed. The trustees meet every three weeks to consider applications, although emergency needs can be dealt with more quickly. Telephone enquiries are welcome.

Note: applications submitted directly by individuals will not be considered.

Other information

The charity's website gives the following information on its background: 'The League of the Helping Hand (LHH) was founded in 1908 by Miss Edith Ashby who wanted to address the suffering of those who had very little to live on. She was adamant from the first that all help should be given in the most kindly and friendly way possible.'

John A. Longmore's Trust

£13,000

Correspondent: Robin Fulton, Trustee, Turcan Connell, Princes Exchange, 1 Earl Grey Street, Edinburgh EH3 9EE (0131 228 8111; fax: 0131 228 8118)

OSCR number: SC007336

Eligibility

People who live in Scotland and have an incurable disease.

Types of grants

Annuities of around £330 are paid in two instalments. One-off grants of up to £1,000 are given to improve quality of life on a day-to-day basis. Equipment sought can be either fixed or moveable such as a wheelchair.

Annual grant total

In 2013/14 the trust had an income of £23,500 and a total expenditure of £14,300. We estimate that the amount of grants given to individuals totalled £13,000.

Exclusions

No grants are given towards holidays or house decoration.

Applications

Apply on a form available from the correspondent, to be returned with a covering letter detailing income and expenses of the household and a breakdown of how the grant will be used. Applications are considered in the third week of every month and should be submitted by the 16th of the month. **Note:** in recent years the trust has suffered from an income deficit and therefore, may not be in a position to consider new applications.

The Florence Nightingale Aid-in-Sickness Trust (FNAIST)

£229,500 (332 grants)

Correspondent: Ann Griffiths, Grants and Funding Manager, Community House, Room 35, South Street, Bromley BR1 1RH (020 7998 8817; email: ann.griffiths@fnaist.org.uk; website: www.fnaist.org.uk)

CC number: 1157980

Eligibility

People of all ages who are in poor health or convalescent or have disabilities. Preference will be given to people with professional, secretarial, or administrative qualifications or experience.

Types of grants

One-off grants are available for convalescence or respite care, medical equipment and other aids, sensory equipment, communications aids, telephone installation (or mobile phones in rare cases), computers and software, drug storage units, electric beds, household aids (for example, washing machines) and other needs to improve individuals' independent living. Partial funding may be provided where a large grant is requested.

Annual grant total

In 2014 the trust had an income of £347,000 and an expenditure of £327,500. A total of 332 grants were made to individuals amounting to £229,500.

The grants were given in the following categories:

Aid purposes	139
Respite/convalescent breaks	125
Mobility equipment	40
Miscellaneous	28

Exclusions

Grants are not usually given for:
- Car purchase or car adaptations
- Holidays, exchange visits, nursing home fees
- Debts or repayments
- General clothing
- General house furnishings
- House furnishings
- Stair-lifts
- Clothing

Under normal circumstances, grants can only be given to any one household at intervals of three years.

Applications

Application forms are available to download from the trust's website or can be requested from the correspondent. They should be submitted by Citizens Advice, other charities, a social worker, an occupational therapist, doctor, health centre worker or a similar professional with a medical background. Candidates should provide a brief medical history of the applicant and proof of the need for assistance. Applications are considered monthly, although urgent requests can be dealt with between meetings.

Other information

The annual report for 2014 states:

> Since the year end, the Trust has been dormant. Its activities are continuing in the new incorporated charity of the same name (Company number 09064489 and Charity number 1157980). The charity now operates from premises in Bromley and bookkeeping services are being provided by one of the Trustees (since 1 January 2015).

The Royal Society for Home Relief to Incurables, Edinburgh

£117,500 (200 grants)

Correspondent: Fiona Watson, Clerk and Treasurer, Scott-Moncrieff, Exchange Place 3, Semple Street, Edinburgh EH3 8BL (0131 473 3500; fax: 0131 473 3535; email: fiona.watson@ scott-moncrieff.com; website: www.scott-moncrieff.com/services/charities/ charitable-trusts)

OSCR number: SC004365

Eligibility

People throughout Scotland (normally under retirement age) who have earned a livelihood (or been a housewife) but are no longer able to continue due to an incurable illness. The society will normally consider those who have ceased employment within the last ten years.

Types of grants

Allowances are given quarterly (totalling £540 per year) to provide extra help.

Annual grant total

In 2014 the society had an income of £149,000 and an expenditure of £169,500. The society states that currently about £117,500 is available for distribution each year. Around 150 to 200 individuals are supported annually.

Exclusions

One-off grants are not provided. The society is unable to support individuals suffering from alcoholism or drug misuse, mental illness, those with learning difficulties, primary epilepsy, blindness or visual impairment and birth deformities.

Applications

Application forms are available to download from the Scott-Moncrieff website. The trustees meet four times a year to consider requests. A letter of support from the applicant's social worker or health care professional would assist the trustees.

The Strowger Trust

£10,000

Correspondent: Darren Strowger, Trustee, 9 Lower John Street, London W1F 9DZ (07767622222)

CC number: 1152108

Eligibility

People in need due to ill health, particularly young adults.

Types of grants

Grants according to need.

Annual grant total

In 2013/14 the trust had assets of £16,300 and an income of £137,000. Grants were made totalling £40,000; however, a further breakdown was not given. We estimate that about £10,000 was given in grants to individuals.

Applications

The annual report notes that 'the trust invites applications for funding of projects through various sources'. In the first instance an interest may be expressed in writing to the correspondent.

Other information

The annual report and accounts state that the trust's 'plans for the future are to continue helping charities which fall within the trust's objectives'. It would appear that grants are mainly made to organisations, although the trust's record on the Charity Commission's website notes that grants can be made to individuals.

AIDS and HIV

Eileen Trust

£140,000

Correspondent: Joyce Materego, Correspondent, Alliance House, 12 Caxton Street, London SW1H 0QS (020 7808 1172)

CC number: 1028027

Eligibility

People who have contracted HIV through NHS treatment, for example, following transfusions or a needle-stick injury. It provides financial support in the form of small regular payments or one-off payments to affected individuals and their dependants.

Types of grants

Financial help is given in three ways: regular monthly payments of £150 to £800 (in 2013/14) to contribute to meeting the additional costs of living with HIV, or to assist those who have been bereaved; single payments of £1,000 to £3,000 (in 2013/14) in response to specific requests for help; and winter payments of £1,000 (supplementary to regular payments).

Annual grant total

In 2013/14 the trust held assets of £194,00 and had an income of £157,000. Grants and payments to individuals totalled £140,000 and were distributed as follows:

Grants	£91,000
Regular payments	£33,000
Winter payments	£16,000

Applications

Applications for assistance are received in the main via the trust's case worker and from time to time by direct approach.

George House Trust

£55,500 (584 grants)

Correspondent: The Services Advisors, 75–77 Ardwick Green North, Manchester M12 6FX (0161 274 4499; fax: 0161 274 3355; email: info@ght.org.uk; website: www.ght.org.uk)

CC number: 1143138

Eligibility

People with HIV who live in the north west of England. The majority of services are provided in Greater Manchester.

Types of grants

The welfare fund provides:
- **Emergency grants:** to the trust's service users who are in immediate financial need which cannot be met

elsewhere (modest awards will normally be in the range of £10–£15)

- **Destitute payments:** to the trust's service users who have no recourse to public funds, and are therefore destitute; payments of £15 per fortnight are made to approximately 50 people and supplemented by healthy food parcels that are given out weekly by staff and volunteers
- **Standard payments:** to help people with essential household items, such as utility bills, clothing and essential household items (for example, white goods or bedding)

The trust can reimburse your public transport travel costs for coming to one to one appointments or group spaces, but you must be in receipt of basic level benefits or have no income at all to qualify.

Annual grant total

In 2013/14 the trust held assets of £1.35 million and had an income of over £1 million. Welfare grants to 584 individuals totalled £55,500.

Exclusions

Grants are not made to people without original proof of HIV diagnosis. Note that payments are not made for ordinary living expenses – your application must be for a specific item. If you are granted an item (or items) you cannot re-apply for other items for another six months.

Applications

Applications are open to anyone known to George House Trust. Appeals for standard items can be made using an online system on the trust's website (those living outside Manchester can have one sent to their home) and are considered monthly. Evidence that the individual has been diagnosed HIV positive, such as a copy of a letter from the consultant at an HIV testing clinic, should be provided and the applicant's date of birth stated. Applicants should post this evidence to the George House address, even if the application is made via the website. Where applicable, copies of bills or written estimates for goods must also be forwarded to the trust's office. Details about other types of awards can be obtained from the Service Advisers or the trust's office. If funding is a matter of emergency it is worth contacting the trust as it may be able to make a small grant straight away.

The Terrence Higgins Trust Hardship Fund

£357,000

Correspondent: Terence Higgins Trust, 314–320 Gray's Inn Road, London WC1X 8DP (020 7812 1600; fax: 020 7812 1601; email: hardshipfund@tht.org. uk; website: www.tht.org.uk)

CC number: 288527

Eligibility

People in the UK who have HIV and are in severe financial need.

Types of grants

One-off emergency grants.

Annual grant total

In 2013/14 Terence Higgins Trust held assets of £7.36 million and had an income of £19.6 million. Through its Hardship Fund, the trust awarded £357,000, supporting 2,009 people. Of this, 80% of grants were from the Necessity Fund, 'to help people in the most need pay for food, heating and transport to hospital appointments'.

Exclusions

No grants are given for council tax, rent, holiday expenses, air fares or funeral costs.

JAT

£5,000

Correspondent: Janine Clements, Director, JAT, 2A Dunstan Road, London NW11 8AA (07546 429885; email: j.clements@jat-uk.org; website: www.jat-uk.org)

CC number: 327936

Eligibility

Jewish people with HIV/AIDS.

Types of grants

One-off grants are available from the trust, which may share the cost of major items with other agencies. Past grants have been given towards the costs of Passover food, travel expenses for respite care, washing machines, cookers, moving costs and so on.

Annual grant total

The total for grants to individuals generally does not exceed £5,000 per year.

Exclusions

No grants are given towards rent, mortgage arrears, luxury items or repayments of loans, debts or credit cards.

Applications

Application forms are available from the correspondent. All referrals must be through a professional person such as a social worker, health visitor and so on. A referral must accompany every application and be on headed paper including the client's name and their date of birth; a detailed breakdown of weekly income; the details and nature of the request; the name, position and signature of the referrer; and details of whom the cheque should be made payable to. First applications require symptomatic proof of HIV diagnosis from the applicant's doctor.

The Macfarlane Trust

£2.7 million

Correspondent: Keisha Hanchard, Support Services Officer, Alliance House, 12 Caxton Street, London SW1H 0QS (020 7808 1171 or 020 7233 0057 (main number); fax: 020 7808 1169; email: keisha@macfarlane.org.uk or admin@macfarlane.org.uk; website: www.macfarlane.org.uk)

CC number: 298863

Eligibility

People with haemophilia who as a result of receiving contaminated blood products are living with HIV, and their dependants. No other people are eligible. The trust is in contact with those known to have haemophilia and to be HIV positive through infected blood products and therefore any further eligibility to register with the trust seems unlikely. Assistance is also given to the bereaved spouses or partners of an infected beneficiary.

Types of grants

One-off and recurrent grants are available towards the additional costs associated in living with HIV. Grants can be given towards health-related needs such as convalescence, respite, travel, clothes, medical care and specialist equipment. Grants are also given to primary beneficiaries towards winter fuel costs (payments of either £500 or £250) and towards supplementing the costs of children who are dependants. Payments to ensure that widows and dependants have a household income of at least £19,000 per year are also awarded.

Annual grant total

In 2013/14 the trust held assets of £4.6 million and had an income of £2.2 million. Grants to individuals totalled £3.3 million and were distributed as follows:

Widows' payments and dependants	110	£1 million
Discretionary payments	291	£993,000
Health- and mobility-related grants	113	£810,500
Dependants' supplementary payments	138	£276,000
Winter payments	294	£109,500
Grants – current year	101	£102,500

Applications

Apply on an application form available from the correspondent, although requests by letter or telephone are also considered. A medical report and supporting letter from a doctor or similar medical professional are required. Applicants must be registered with the trust in order to apply. Dates of the Grants Committee meetings are posted on the charity's website.

Positive East

£3,000

Correspondent: Alastair Thomson, Director of Finance, The Stepney Centre, 159 Mile End Road, London E1 4AQ (020 7791 2855 (Helpline); email: alastair.thomson@positiveeast.org.uk; website: www.positiveeast.org.uk)

CC number: 1001582

Eligibility

People affected by HIV who live and/or receive treatment in East London and are in need of short-term financial assistance to cover basic needs.

Types of grants

Grants of up to £25 each, up to a maximum of £50 in a year, with six months between each application. Each individual has a 'lifetime limit' of £150, after which access to the fund will be closed to them. Grants are given for one-off, HIV-related expenses, child expenses such as school uniforms or medical treatment, utility bills, the cost of travel to an essential appointment and basic necessities such as food or clothing.

Annual grant total

In 2013/14 the charity held assets of £481,500 and had a consolidated income of £1.7 million. Around £3,000 is allocated each year for emergency hardship grants.

Exclusions

Grants are not given for: legal costs; non-essential travel or travel outside London; funeral costs; ongoing non-HIV-related treatment; household goods; and credit card or other debts.

Applications

Application forms are available from the correspondent. Applications can only be made through Positive East staff and are only available to registered members of the trust (new service users will need to fill in a registration form). Forms can be submitted at any time but applicants should note that the fund is a limited resource and will not be topped up again until the end of the financial year.

Before any grant is awarded, proof will be required to demonstrate that the individual is not eligible for any other financial assistance. Equally, if the person has been the victim of a crime, a crime reference number should be included in the application.

Cancer

Brad's Cancer Foundation

£13,500

Correspondent: Susan Bartlett, Foundation Administrator, 14 Crosslands Meadow, Riverview Park, Colwick, Nottingham NG4 2DJ (0115 940 0313; email: mick@brads.org.uk; website: www.brads.org.uk)

CC number: 1103797

Eligibility

Teenagers who have cancer and related illnesses throughout the East Midlands region.

Types of grants

The provision of financial assistance to teenagers and their families, including grants towards equipment. Awards are often of £500 or under.

Annual grant total

In 2013/14 the foundation had an income of £30,000 and a total expenditure of £31,500. Note that the charitable expenditure varies each year. In the past about £13,500 has been awarded to children and young people annually.

Applications

Apply in writing to the correspondent.

Children's Leukaemia Society

£38,500

Correspondent: The Trustees, Children's Leukaemia Society, The Library, Singleton Road, Splott, Cardiff CF24 2ET (029 2045 2483; email: childrensleukaemiasociety@ hotmail.co.uk; website: www. childrensleukaemiasociety.co.uk)

CC number: 1008634

Eligibility

Children under 16 who are in need and have leukaemia. Grants are made to those living in south Wales and the West Country.

Types of grants

Gifts for children who are undergoing chemotherapy, usually in the form of an Argos voucher. The provision of holidays for children and their families following treatment.

Annual grant total

In 2013/14 the society held assets of £294,500 and had an income of £62,500. Payments for holidays and gifts to children totalled £38,500. The total

number of gifts includes 'special circumstances' gifts for terminally ill children.

Applications

Apply in writing to the correspondent.

CLIC Sargent

£1 million (5,047 grants)

Correspondent: Grants dept., Horatio House, 77–85 Fulham Place, London W6 8JA (0300 330 0803; website: www. clicsargent.org.uk)

CC number: 1107328

Eligibility

Children and young people aged 24 and under who are living in the UK and are receiving treatment for cancer.

Types of grants

One-off CLIC Sargent Standard Grants are available for children and young people who have cancer, and their families, at any time within the first 12 months of diagnosis. They are given to assist with the sudden additional costs brought about by a cancer diagnosis and can be used towards the costs of food, travel or other day-to-day expenses. For information on other types of grants which may be available, speak with a CLIC Sargent social worker.

Annual grant total

In 2013/14 the charity made 5,047 grants to young people and their families totalling £1 million. Standard grants amounted to £520,000.

Exclusions

Previous research indicates that grants are not made for the costs of treatment, medical equipment, therapies or school fees.

Applications

Through a health or social care professional, such as a CLIC Sargent social worker.

LATCH Welsh Children's Cancer Charity

£262,000

Correspondent: Ian Rogers, Trustee, LATCH Office, Children's Hospital for Wales, Heath Park, Cardiff CF14 4XW (029 2074 8858/9; fax: 029 2074 8868; email: info@latchwales.org; website: www.latchwales.org)

CC number: 1100949

Eligibility

Children who have cancer and leukaemia (including tumours) and have been referred to the Paediatric Oncology Unit at the Children's Hospital for Wales.

Types of grants

One-off and recurrent grants for children and their families who are in need of financial assistance towards, for example, travel costs to and from hospital, subsistence grants for daily expenses, utility bills, specialist equipment and other household needs (such as washing machines), childcare costs, car repairs, holidays and outings or other needs.

Annual grant total

In 2014 the charity had assets of £4.2 million and an income of £679,500. Grants were made totalling £262,0000.

Applications

Applications should be made through one of the LATCH social workers who can submit applications for consideration by the trust. More information on support given is available from other organisations, such as respite care.

The Leukaemia Care Society

£2,900 (56 grants)

Correspondent: Monica Izmajlowicz, Chief Executive, One Birch Court, Blackpole East, Worcester WR3 8SG (01905 755977; email: info@ leukaemiacare.org.uk; website: www. leukaemiacare.org.uk)

CC number: 259483

Eligibility

People with leukaemia and allied blood disorders. Financial support is open to all patients and carers who are no more than four years post-diagnosis or, if there has been bereavement, no more than two years after this.

Types of grants

Grants in the form of vouchers for a choice of three supermarkets.

Annual grant total

In 2013/14 the society held assets of £1.6 million and had an income of £899,000. There were 56 grants made towards individuals' general living costs totalling £2,900.

Exclusions

No repeat grants are made to individuals.

Applications

Applicants should first call the CARE Line on 0808 801 0444 to discuss their case and request the necessary forms. Applications usually take 14–30 days to complete. All applicants will be requested to complete an income and expenditure sheet and must provide proof of diagnosis such as a letter from their consultant.

Macmillan Cancer Support

£9.85 million (33,000 grants)

Correspondent: The Grants Team, 89 Albert Embankment, London SE1 7UQ (0808 808 0000 (free support line) or 020 7840 7840 (switchboard); fax: 020 7840 7841; website: www. macmillan.org.uk)

CC number: 261017

Eligibility

People of any age who have cancer, or who are affected by the illness, and are in financial need.

Applicants must not have capital savings of more than £8,000 per couple, or £6,000 for a single person. Household weekly disposable income (after housing costs) must not exceed: £170 for a single person, £289 for a couple, £85 for each child and £119 for each additional adult (when their income is relevant to the request). Certain benefits such as Disability Living Allowance and Attendance Allowance do not count as disposable income. These are general conditions, but Macmillan does take into account individual circumstances.

Types of grants

One-off grants of around under £300–£400 on average towards costs arising from or related to cancer or its treatment. This may include essential household items, travel to hospital, heating, clothing, furnishings, convalescence in the UK and so on.

Annual grant total

In 2014 the charity had assets of almost £65.5 million and an income of £218.4 million. Macmillan grants to 30,000 individuals totalled £9.85 million.

Exclusions

Grants are not made for daily expenses, private medical care or holidays outside the UK.

Applications

Applications should be made through a health or social care professional, such as a social worker, a district nurse or a Macmillan nurse, who will submit it to the charity on behalf of the individual. A short medical report from a medical professional should be included.

Macmillan advises that the grant request must demonstrate a clear link to the impact of cancer and its treatment. Comprehensive application guidance notes are available on the charity's website.

Applications are usually processed on the day they are received and, if successful, payments are sent out within three working days.

The Plymouth and Cornwall Cancer Fund

£14,800

Correspondent: Mr P. Harker, Honorary Secretary, Curtis Whiteford Crocker Solicitors, 87 and 89 Mutley Plain, Plymouth PL4 6JJ (01752 220587; email: admin@pccf.org.uk)

CC number: 262587

Eligibility

People in need who have cancer, or who have a dependant or relative with cancer, and live in the county of Cornwall and within a radius of 40 miles of Plymouth Civic Centre in Devon (a map is available on the charity's website) Also in-patients or out-patients of any hospital controlled by Plymouth Hospital NHS Trust.

Types of grants

One-off grants of between £10 and £400 are given to relieve hardship which is caused by cancer, for example towards the cost of travel to hospital for patients and visitors, additional clothing, bed linen, stair-lifts and telephone installations and bills.

Annual grant total

In 2013/14 the fund had an income of £60,500 and total expenditure of £57,500. The amount awarded in grants to individuals for welfare purposes totalled £14,800.

Applications

Apply in writing to the correspondent at any time. Applications should be submitted by a recognised health professional on behalf of a patient or carer. Applicants should have exhausted all other potential sources of help before approaching the fund. Further applications guidance is given on the charity's website.

Mairi Semple Fund for Cancer Relief and Research

£5,500

Correspondent: M. Sinclair, Correspondent, 4 Barhill, Glenbarr, Tarbert, Argyll PA29 6UT

OSCR number: SC000390

Eligibility

People who live in Kintyre or the Isle of Gigha and are suffering from cancer.

Types of grants

Provision of equipment and/or domestic nursing help, assistance with hospital travel costs for patients or relatives and the provision of measures to enable the 'greater privacy, quietness and dignity' of hospitalised patients with terminal cancer.

Annual grant total

In 2013/14 the fund had an income of £11,600 and a total expenditure of £11,100. We estimate that the amount of grants given to individuals totalled £5,500, with funding also awarded to projects relating to cancer research.

Exclusions

No grants are given to students for research.

Applications

Apply in writing through the doctor, nurse or church minister of the patient, at the relevant address:

(i) Minister, Killean and Kilchenzie Church, Manse, Muasdale, Tarbert, Argyll.

(ii) Doctor, The Surgery, Muasdale, Tarbert, Argyll

(iii) Nurse, The Surgery (same address as (ii)).

Carers

Carers Trust

£35,000

Correspondent: Grants Team, 32–36 Loman Street, London SE1 0EH (0844 800 4361; fax: 0844 800 4362; email: info@carers.org; website: www. carers.org)

CC number: 1145181

Eligibility

Unpaid carers in the UK, especially those who live near a Carers Trust centre.

Types of grants

One-off grants. Carers can apply for grants, usually of up to £400, to purchase equipment that will have a direct and long-term impact, not only on their caring role, but on their overall quality of life.

Annual grant total

In 2013/14 the trust had assets of £8.4 million and an income of £11.4 million. Grants to individuals totalled £70,000. We estimate that social welfare grants to individuals totalled £35,000, with funding also awarded for educational purposes.

Applications

Applications are made via your local Carers Trust centre, a list of which is available on the trust's website. Direct applications will not be considered.

The Margaret Champney Rest and Holiday Fund

£13,000

Correspondent: Gillian Galvan, General Manager, The Gate House, 9 Burkitt Road, Woodbridge IP12 4JJ (01394 388746; email: ogilviecharities@ btconnect.com; website: www. ogilviecharities.org.uk/Grants/Rest-and-holiday-fund/Funding-for-Holidays-for-Carers.html)

CC number: 211646

Eligibility

Carers, particularly those caring for a relative with severe disabilities, who need a break from their caring responsibilities. The fund's website notes that in exceptional circumstances assistance may be given 'where the carer and cared for wish to holiday together, provided they are husband and wife or partners, or an adult child caring for an aged parent or vice versa'.

Types of grants

Generally one-off grants of between £200 and £300 towards recuperative breaks. 'The primary aim is to give a complete break to a carer while the person cared for is receiving respite care.'

Annual grant total

In 2014 the fund had an income of £13,800 and a total expenditure of £14,800. We estimate that the amount of grants given to individuals totalled about £13,000.

Exclusions

Grants are not available towards regular family holidays.

Applications

Applications should be made via a social worker, community nurse or similar professional agency. They are considered at any time and should include the professional's name, job title and name and address of the organisation they represent as well as the name of the applicant and a brief summary of their circumstances. Candidates should also include full details of weekly income and expenditure, details of other agencies being approached for funding, who will care for the person while the break is being taken and the proposed holiday venue, date and likely costs.

An income and expenditure form may be downloaded from the fund's website.

Vitalise

See entry on page 62

Children

The Adamson Trust

£35,000 (79 grants)

Correspondent: Edward Elworthy, Trust Administrator, PO Box 26334, Crieff, Perthshire PH7 9AB (email: edward@ elworthy.net; website: www. theadamsontrust.co.uk/index.html)

OSCR number: SC016517

Eligibility

Children aged 17 or under who have a physical or mental disability.

Types of grants

Grants range from £150 to £5,000 and are given to help with the cost of a holiday or respite break. Grant recipients must take the trip before their 18th birthday.

Annual grant total

In 2013/14 the trust made 79 grants to individuals totalling £35,000, and a further 31 grants to organisations, amounting to £49,000.

Exclusions

No grants can be given towards the costs of accompanying adults.

Applications

Apply on a form available from the correspondent, to be returned with: details of the planned holiday; booking confirmations (if possible); and information about the child beneficiary. Supporting evidence such as a letter from the child's GP, hospital or health professional should also be attached. All applications are considered by the trustees four times a year in February, May, August and November with closing dates of 31 December, 31 March, 30 June and 30 September.

Al-Fayed Charitable Foundation

£6,500

Correspondent: The Charity Manager, Hyde Park Residence Ltd, 55 Park Lane, London W1K 1NA (email: acf@alfayed. com; website: www.the-acf.com)

CC number: 297114

Eligibility

Traumatised, impoverished and very sick children.

Types of grants

The foundation can provide 'expert medical care and unique treats', depending on need.

Annual grant total

In 2014 the foundation had assets of £80,500 and an income of £1.1 million. Grants were made totalling £1.1 million with the vast majority being given to organisations. Individual grants totalled £6,500.

Applications

Applications should be made in writing to the correspondent via post or email, including your name and contact details, an overview of why you are seeking funding and a breakdown of funds sought. If you are sending your application by post, make sure to include an sae for a response. The trustees consider applications on a monthly basis.

The Nihal Armstrong Trust

£7,000

Correspondent: Rahil Gupta, Trustee, 111 Chatsworth Road, London NW2 4BH (020 8459 6527; email: info@ nihalarmstrongtrust.org.uk; website: www.nihalarmstrongtrust.org.uk)

CC number: 1107567

Eligibility

Children living in the UK, up to and including the age of 18, with cerebral palsy. Applicants must be in receipt of means-tested benefits and be able to provide supporting evidence.

Types of grants

Grants of up to £1,000 are given towards equipment, communication aids or a particular service that will benefit children with cerebral palsy. Items/ services must not be available from the local authority.

Annual grant total

In 2013/14 the trust had an income of £8,100 and a total expenditure of £7,500 We estimate that the amount of grants given to individuals totalled around £7,000.

Exclusions

The trust does not fund holidays, refurbishment costs or household appliances. Grants are not available in the form of part-funding for equipment or services that cost more than £1,000.

Applications

Applications can be made via the trust's website and must be supported by a doctor, school, social worker, health visitor, speech, occupational therapist or physiotherapist. The trustees meet three times a year, with application deadlines falling one week before each quarterly meeting. See the trust's website for specific dates.

The trustees prefer to receive applications via the website where possible. Individuals who are sending information on equipment/services or suppliers' estimates, can forward any documents to the address provided in the 'contacts' section of the trust's website. A list of supporting documents required is available on the trust's website.

Blind Children UK (formerly National Blind Children's Society)
See entry on page 73

Brad's Cancer Foundation
See entry on page 52

Caudwell Children

£2.9 million

Correspondent: Trudi Beswick, Minton Hollins Building, Shelton Old Road, Stoke-on-Trent, Staffordshire ST4 7RY (01782 600607; fax: 01782 600639; email: charity@caudwellchildren.com; website: www.caudwellchildren.com)

CC number: 1079770

Eligibility

People under 18 years old with a disability or serious illness who live in the UK. Household income/salary (not including benefits) should be less than £45,000 gross per annum.

Types of grants

One-off and recurrent donations for mobility, sensory and sports equipment; therapy, treatment and family holidays.

Annual grant total

In 2014 the trust had assets of £6.4 million and an income of £6.3 million. Grants totalled £2.9 million.

At the time of writing (November 2015) this was the most recent financial information available for the trust.

Exclusions

No grants for: building works, fixtures and fittings; gardening and the making safe of gardens; respite care; dolphin therapy/faith healing; computers (unless specifically designed for people with special needs); iPads; motor vehicle purchase/adaptations; equipment repair or maintenance; domestic appliances; non-specialist furniture, decoration, clothing or bedding; private education; speech or occupational therapy; or legal costs.

Applications

Application forms are available to download from the website or from the correspondent. The charity uses different application forms depending upon what is being applied for. Financial details must be included. The application process can, during busy periods, take up to six months and applicants may be visited by a trustee.

Cerebra for Brain Injured Children and Young People

£156,500

Correspondent: Christopher Jones, Chief Executive, 2nd Floor, Lyric Building, King Street, Carmarthen SA31 1BD (01267 244200; email: info@ cerebra.org.uk; website: www.cerebra. org.uk)

CC number: 1089812

Eligibility

Children and young people aged 16 or under who have a neurodevelopmental disorder or condition. The condition may be of a physical nature, a learning disability or both.

Examples of the types of conditions covered include, as further specified on the website: cerebral palsy; autistic spectrum disorders; developmental disorders; seizure disorders; ADHD; traumatic brain injury; acquired brain injury; Down syndrome and other chromosomal/genetic conditions; brain abnormality or degenerative conditions; hydrocephalus; and conditions caused in utero.

This list is by no means exhaustive and applicants who are unsure as to whether they fit the criteria should contact Cerebra directly.

Types of grants

One-off grants of up to a maximum of 80% of the cost or £400, whichever is the lowest amount, of equipment or resources that would improve quality of life and which are not available from statutory agencies like social services or the NHS. Examples of grants made include those towards touch screen computers, specialist car seats, power wheelchairs, therapies, trampolines, sensory toys, and tricycles and quadricycles.

For anything where there is a medical need the trustees ask that potential applicants check with them as they may be able to help.

Annual grant total

In 2014 the charity had assets of £844,500 and an income of £4 million. Grants totalled £156,500.

Exclusions

Grants are not given for: driving lessons; motorised vehicles such as quad bikes and motorbikes; anything that could be considered a home improvement such as paint for decorating, conservatories, carpet or other flooring; garden landscaping; household items such as vacuum cleaners, washing machines, wardrobes, standard beds (special beds may be considered); vehicle purchase or maintenance; assessments; general clothing; treatment centres outside the UK; lycra suits; holidays; and educational items such as home tutors, standard teaching materials or the Son-Rise programme.

Applications

Application forms and guidance notes can be downloaded from the Cerebra website. Grants are all paid directly to the assistance provider. All applications must be accompanied by financial statements and two references: one from a medical professional and the other from someone who knows your child professionally, for example a teacher or social worker. Further guidelines on references are contained within the application form.

Challenger Children's Fund

£55,000

Correspondent: Mr T. Sellar, Trustee, Suite 353, 44/46 Morningside Road, Edinburgh EH10 4BF (07531 580414; email: info@ccfscotland.org; website: www.ccfscotland.org)

OSCR number: SC037375

Eligibility

The trust aims to help any child in Scotland under the age of 18 years living with a disability through a physical impairment of the musculoskeletal, neurological or cardio-respiratory system of the body.

The following conditions on their own, however, are not accepted: psychiatric disorders, learning disabilities, behavioural disorders, development delay, Down's Syndrome, autism, visual or hearing impairment, cancer, diabetes, epilepsy, HIV, back pain and chronic fatigue syndrome. If they are associated with a physical disability, however, consideration will be given.

Types of grants

One-off grants of up to £500. More may be granted in some circumstances.

Grants can be given towards anything which is not provided by statutory sources but is required to meet the special needs of the child. Items include clothing, apparatus, equipment, household appliances such as washing machines, furniture, travel and home or garden adaptations. In the case of a holiday grant, if it is essential that a child must be accompanied, consideration will be given to the cost.

Annual grant total

In 2013/14 the trust had an income of £80,000 and a total expenditure of £68,000. We estimate that the amount of grants given to individuals totalled around £55,000.

Exclusions

Grants cannot be made retrospectively. Only one application may be made per year.

Applications

Application forms are available from the correspondent or can be downloaded from the website. Applications should be sponsored by a social worker, GP, health visitor, district nurse or therapist. Trainee workers and community care assistants may also apply, but a qualified person must countersign the application. Grants are given to the agency sponsoring the application or the company the purchase(s) are being made from. They cannot be given direct to the child or child's family. Applications can be submitted once a year.

Children Today Charitable Trust

£129,500

Correspondent: A. Djemal, Company Secretary, 17B Telford Court, Chester Gates Business Park, Dunkirk, Chester CH1 6LT (01244 335622; fax: 01244 335473; email: info@children-today.org.uk; website: www.children-today.org.uk)

CC number: 1137436

Eligibility

Children and young people under 25 who have a disability.

Types of grants

Grants of up to £1,000 to provide vital, life-changing specialist equipment, such as wheelchairs, walking aids, trikes, educational toys, communication aids, lifting and posturepaedic sleep equipment and specially designed sensory equipment like fibre optic sprays.

Annual grant total

In 2013/14 the trust held assets of £158,000 and had an income of £499,500. Equipment grants to individuals totalled £129,500.

Exclusions

Grants are not made to organisations.

Applications

Application forms are available from the correspondent. Grants are only given for specialised pieces of equipment for individual children (not groups or schools), and applications must be made by the individual applying, their parent, or legal guardian. Applications must include: a reference from a professional such as a teacher, social worker, doctor or occupational therapist; the applicant's basic financial information; and a pro forma invoice or a quotation from the supplier of the equipment. The charity aims to deal with all applications within 28 days of receipt.

Only one application in any 12-month period.

Children's Leukaemia Society
See entry on page 52

See entry on page 52

Roald Dahl's Marvellous Children's Charity

£85,500 (258 grants)

Correspondent: Richard Piper, Chief Executive, 81A High Street, Great Missenden, Buckinghamshire HP16 0AL (01494 890465; fax: 01494 890459; email: enquiries@roalddahlcharity.org; website: www.roalddahlcharity.org)

CC number: 1137409

Eligibility

As outlined on the charity's website, the pilot programme is open to any family in the UK in which:

- There is a child or children with a serious long-term health condition (affected child or children)
- The affected child or children are eligible to receive Medium or High Rate DLA (the Care component) or the Enhanced Rate for 6 of the 12 activities in the PIP or has an equivalent level of need
- At least one affected child has yet to reach their 21st birthday
- Some form of support would help improve the emotional or psychological state of some or all of the family members (not necessarily the affected child/children)
- There are serious financial constraints that mean the family cannot access such support
- The family has not received a grant from the Stronger Families Programme in the last 12 months

Applications are welcomed from families of children with any serious condition, particularly those whose illness is undiagnosed. However, the charity cannot support children with cancer, as explained on the website: 'Levels of support for children and young people with cancer are far higher than those for other conditions and, with a small fund, we have had to take the decision to exclude families where a child has cancer.'

Types of grants

Grants are made for up to £500, for a range of purposes such as counselling sessions, play therapy, specialist equipment, respite care and so on. A list of preliminary suggestions is provided on the charity's website.

Annual grant total

In 2013/14 the charity held assets of £1.46 million and had an income of £707,000. The charity gave grants totalling £85,500, helping 258 families.

A further £404,000 was given in project and research grants and in funding for specialist children's nurses.

Exclusions

The charity is not able to fund: debts or repayment of utility bills, rent, etc.; trips outside the UK for medical treatment or holidays; educational fees; car seats, walkers, bicycles, pushchairs or mobility chairs; specialist furniture, fittings or household appliances; beds, cots, bedding or clothing; living expenses when a child is admitted to hospital away from the hometown; travel expenses to and from hospital. However, the charity provides a list of alternative sources of support for such purposes on its website.

Applications

Applications for grants must be made through established Applicant Officers such as a social worker, healthcare professional or a charity representative. For more information, refer to the grant application guidance on the website.

The Family Fund

£33.6 million (68,551 grants)

Correspondent: Sarah Duff, Grant Services Manager, Unit 4, Alpha Court, Monks Cross Drive, Huntington, York YO32 9WN (01904 621115; fax: 01904 652625; email: info@familyfund.org.uk; website: www.familyfund.org.uk)

CC number: 1053866

Eligibility

Families who are caring at home for a child or young person aged 17 or under who has a severe disability or serious illness. Eligible families must show evidence of their entitlement to one of the following: child tax credit, working tax credit, income-based job seekers allowance, income support, incapacity benefit, employment and support allowance, housing benefit and pension credit. If you do not receive any of the above, further information may be needed to complete your application. The fund also retains discretion to decline an application where a family has a significant level of capital or household income.

Types of grants

The help given must be related to the child's care needs. The top three types of grant in 2013/14 by total spend were holidays and outings (£14.2 million), computers (£6.7 million) and white goods (£4.1 million). Grants were also awarded towards: clothing and bedding; driving lessons; hospital visiting expenses; recreation and home entertainment; furniture; and floor covering. The fund is not always able to meet the full cost of every item requested due to limited funding.

Annual grant total

In 2013/14 the fund had assets of £2.2 million and made grants totalling £33.6 million to over 68,500 families.

The number of families helped was distributed across the UK as follows:

Country	No. of families
England	53,079
Scotland	7,327
Wales	4,952
Northern Ireland	3,193

Exclusions

The fund cannot provide items which are the responsibility of statutory agencies, such as medical or educational equipment or small items for daily living, such as bath aids, which are the responsibility of social services. No funding is given for general household bills, utility bills, mortgage or rent payments or household repairs. No grants are given for families receiving National Asylum Support Service payments. The fund cannot help foster carers.

Applications

Applications can be made by parents, carers or by young people aged 16 and 17 on their own behalf. Application forms and guidance notes are available to download from the fund's website or may be obtained by contacting the fund. You should tell the fund what you need to make a difference to your child/young person/family, making sure to put requests in order of importance. The application should be accompanied by photocopies of supporting documents and should be sent by post.

If you are making an application on behalf of more than one child with disability, complete an 'additional child form', which is available to download from the Family Fund website, for each child you are applying for.

The fund tries to help families raising a child or a young person with a severe disability or serious illness once every year. If you have been helped by the fund before, the decision letter confirming the grant should state when you are eligible to re-apply, which is usually after 12 months, but may be longer. If you have applied before, you may be able to re-apply through your Family Fund online account. The fund may consider early applications in certain circumstances.

For first-time applicants, the trust may arrange a home visit or a follow-up telephone call and applications are typically assessed in three to four months. For applicants who are re-applying, a decision may be made in two to six weeks. All time scales are approximate and not guaranteed. The time taken to deal with applications depends on the volume of applications and funding available at any one time.

Applicants are advised to always check the website before applying as an increased demand has seen some funds close early in recent years.

Happy Days Children's Charity

£496,500

Correspondent: Mandy Bilbrough, Holidays and Residentials Organiser, Clody House, 90–100 Collingdon Street, Luton, Bedfordshire LU1 1RX (01582 755999; email: mandy@ happydayscharity.org; website: www. happydayscharity.org)

CC number: 1010943

Eligibility

Children and young people aged 3 to 17 years (inclusive) who have special needs, i.e. children who: have disabilities; are sick; have been abused, neglected and/or disadvantaged by poverty; have a terminal illness; have lost a parent; have been involved in a traumatic incident; or are young carers. Further information is given on the charity's website. The charity can only assist families with an income of less than £26,000 a year (including all benefits but not the income from Disability Living Allowance or Carer's Allowance).

Types of grants

One-off two- to four-night respite break holidays in the UK. All funding is paid directly to the providers. The charity offers funding for one suitable adult, which may be a parent, guardian or a trusted adult (e.g. a nurse or carer). In special circumstances, the charity may choose to make alternative arrangements.

Annual grant total

In 2013/14 the charity held assets of £286,500 and had an income of £870,500. In total 17,688 children benefitted from holidays, trips and activities, with grants to individuals for these purposes totalling £496,500.

Exclusions

No extra adults are funded.

Applications

Apply on a form which is available to download from the website or from the correspondent. Applications may be submitted by a family member (a parent, guardian, grandparent or sibling) or by a GP, consultant, nurse or social worker.

Enclosed with the application should be: a photograph of the child; a copy of all benefits received (income support, child benefits, tax credits, Disability Living Allowance, Carer's Allowance, etc.); a copy of wage slips or self-employed accounts; a letter from the child's GP, hospital consultant or paediatrician addressed to Happy Days; details of weekly income and expenditure; and a respite break holiday destination list. Applicants should ensure that the form is completed with a signature. Telephone enquiries are welcomed.

Note: due to a long waiting list, it may take up to a year to 16 months before funding becomes available. Applications for children with terminal illnesses may be fast-tracked.

The Douglas Hay Trust

£45,000

Correspondent: John Ritchie, Secretary and Treasurer, Barstow and Millar CA, Midlothian Innovation Centre, Pentlandfield, Roslin, Midlothian EH25 9RE (0131 440 9030; email: johndritchie@btinternet.com; website: www.douglashay.org.uk)

OSCR number: SC014450

Eligibility

Children aged under 18 who have physically disabilities and live in Scotland.

Types of grants

One-off grants ranging from £40 to £500 towards shoes, clothes, bedding, home improvements, holidays, computers, equipment and education.

Annual grant total

In 2013/14 the trust had an income of £44,000 and a total expenditure of £52,000. We estimate grants to be in the region of £45,000.

Applications

Apply using a form available from the website or by contacting the correspondent. To be submitted through a social worker, medical practitioner or other welfare agency. Applications are considered monthly.

Make A Child Smile (formally – The UK Network for Conductive Education)

£2,500

Correspondent: John Somerset-How, Director, Purbeck Cottage, Westergate Street, Westergate, West Sussex PO20 3QS (01243 276693; email: j.somerset-how@sky.com; website: www.makeachildsmile.info)

CC number: 1062275

Eligibility

Children with cerebral palsy.

Types of grants

One-off grants are given to support children with cerebral palsy through conductive education.

Annual grant total

In 2013/14 the charity had an income of £21,000 and a total expenditure of £34,000. The charity gives grants to individuals and organisations to help towards the costs of buying therapy, services or equipment. Due to its low income, the charity was not required to submit its accounts to the Charity Commission. In previous years, grants have totalled around £9,400. We have estimated the total amount of grants made to individuals whose parents/guardians/carers are financially disadvantaged to be around £2,500.

Applications

Enquiry forms are available to download from the website and should be completed and returned to the charity by email or post. Our research suggests that applicants are visited as part of the application process.

The Power Pleas Trust

£7,500

Correspondent: Keith Berry, Trustee, 80 York Avenue, Wolverhampton WV3 9BU (01902 655962; email: admin@powerpleas.org; website: www. powerpleas.org)

CC number: 519654

Eligibility

Mainly young people, under 18 years old, with muscular dystrophy and other mobility disorders living in the Wolverhampton area.

Types of grants

Grants are given primarily towards the purchase and provision of outdoor electric powered wheelchairs and other aids.

Annual grant total

In 2013/14 the trust had an income of £4,500 and a total expenditure of £8,500. We estimate that the amount of grants given to individuals totalled £7,500.

Applications

The individual, or a family member of the individual, should apply in writing directly to the correspondent.

REACT (Rapid Effective Assistance for Children with Potentially Terminal Illnesses)

£318,000 (845 grants)

Correspondent: Grants Administrator, St Luke's House, 270 Sandycombe Road, Kew, Surrey TW9 3NP (020 8940 2575; fax: 020 8940 2050; email: react@ reactcharity.org; website: www. reactcharity.org)

CC number: 802440

Eligibility

Financially disadvantaged families caring for a child under the age of 18 living with a potentially terminal illness.

Types of grants

Grants in kind and one-off grants can be made towards domestic or medical equipment not available through a health authority, such as wheelchairs, hoists or adjustable beds, educational equipment which will aid a child's development at home or in hospital (sensory toys, communication and speech aids or computers), domestic equipment which will improve the child's quality of life (such as beds, white goods or soft furnishings) and hospital expenses (travel, food or related costs).

Week-long breaks at React holiday homes can also be offered and assistance may also be given with funeral expenses and memorial headstones. The charity says it can consider most requests; however, if you would like to check whether or not a specific item fits the criteria, the charity can be contacted by phone.

Annual grant total

In 2014/15 the charity held assets of £408,000 and had an income of £710,000. Grants totalled £352,000 and were distributed as follows:

Specialist equipment	237	£127,000
Domestic	181	£63,500
Mobile home holidays	279	£60,500
Educational	76	£34,000
Home adaptations	50	£31,500
Funeral expenses	34	£25,500
Travel and subsistence	46	£6,200
Respite holidays	52	£3,200

Exclusions

Grants are not made retrospectively (except in exceptional circumstances). Support is not given towards trips overseas, structural building works, private treatment or the purchase of vehicles.

Applications

Application forms are available to download from the charity's website or can be requested from the correspondent. Potential applicants can also ask their nurse, carer or social worker if they have a blank form available. Forms must be completed and signed by a parent/guardian and endorsed by a medical or social care professional. Supporting letters are welcome and sponsors must specifically endorse the items requested. Where applicable, quotes or exact prices for specific items should be supplied. Families are required to declare financial details and should disclose those of any other applications that have been made. The charity aims to respond to every application within 48 hours.

The Snowball Trust

£8,000

Correspondent: Pauline Blackham, Clerk to the Trustees, 11 Rotherham Road, Holbrooks, Coventry CV6 4FF (website: snowballtrust.org.uk)

CC number: 702860

Eligibility

Children and young people under 21 years old who are in poor health or who have a disability and live in Coventry and Warwickshire.

Types of grants

One-off grants, mainly for medical equipment and disability aids. Grants may be made to agencies such as schools, medical bodies or other organisations, on behalf of an individual child, to purchase equipment which can then be loaned to the child. Further information is given on the charity's website.

Annual grant total

In 2014/15 the trust had an income of £4,900 and a total expenditure of £17,500. We estimate that the amount of grants given to individuals totalled around £8,000.

Applications

Application forms are available from the correspondent or can be downloaded from the charity's website: to be submitted either by the individual or through a third party such as a special school, social worker or other welfare agency. Applications should include a firm quote for the equipment to be supplied, a letter of support from the individual's school and/or a medical professional, and confirmation of the parents'/guardians' financial need.

Variety, the Children's Charity

£459,000 (212 grants)

Correspondent: Stanley Salter, Trustee, The Variety Club Children's Charity, Variety Club House, 93 Bayham Street, London NW1 0AG (020 7428 8100; email: info@variety.org.uk; website: www.variety.org.uk)

CC number: 209259

Eligibility

Children (aged 18 and under) who have disabilities or are sick or disadvantaged. Applicants must be permanently resident in the UK.

Types of grants

Grants of between £100 and £6,000 can be made to both individuals and organisations for medical, basic care, mobility or sensory play equipment. This can include monitoring equipment, feeding tubes or hoists, or specially adapted car seats, for example.

Annual grant total

In 2014 the charity had assets of £2.6 million and an income of £7 million. Grants totalled £2.9 million, the majority of which (£2.45 million) was given to organisations. Individuals were awarded £459,000 in 212 grants during the year; 88 wheelchair grants totalled £304,000 and 124 grants for individual children, a further £154,500.

Exclusions

The charity does not fund: standard household equipment or furnishings; repayment of loans; garden adaptations; garden sheds or summerhouses; the cost of a family/wheelchair-adapted vehicle; laptops, iPads or computer hardware; maintenance or ongoing costs; travel costs; therapy sessions; reimbursement of funds already paid out; hire, rental costs or down payments; trikes, bikes or

buggies; trips abroad or holiday costs; trampolines; medical treatment; education or tuition fees.

Applications

Download the relevant application form from the website, where guidelines are also available. Note that there is a separate form for wheelchair applications. Applications can be made by parents, medical professionals, a school or organisation, hospitals and small registered charities, and must be supported by a letter from an appropriate medical professional. Two quotations for the equipment should accompany the application.

If you would like to request further information before making an application, Julie Thomas, the Grants Programme Manager can be contacted by telephone (020 7428 8120) or email (julie.thomas@variety.org.uk).

Disability

Barchester Health Care Foundation

£103,000 (128 grants)

Correspondent: Grants Management Team, Suite 304, Third Floor, Design Centre East, Chelsea Harbour, London SW10 0XF (0800 328 3328; fax: 020 7352 2229; email: info@bhcfoundation.org.uk; website: www.bhcfoundation.org.uk)

CC number: 1083272

Eligibility

Older people over the age of 65 and adults over the age of 18 with a physical or mental disability living in England, Scotland and Wales. In 2015 the main focus was on helping to combat loneliness and enable people to be active and engaged.

Types of grants

One-off grants of between £100 and £5,000 can be given according to need. The foundation specifies that applications encouraging the person's mobility, independence and improved quality of life are favoured. Awards have previously been made for specialist equipment; electric and specialist sport wheelchairs; power packs; hoists; riser/recliner chairs; stair-lifts; tricycles and mobility scooters; computers and other IT equipment and software; communication and visual aids; holidays and respite breaks; outings; transportation; home security; disability-related house, garden and car adaptations or repairs; educational grants; white goods (where related to disability/medical condition); home security; heating; storage for mobility scooters; and so on.

Annual grant total

In 2014 the foundation had assets of £86,000 and an income of £200,000. Grants to 128 individuals totalled £103,000.

Exclusions

Grants are not normally made:

▶ Retrospectively
▶ To candidates who have received a grant within the previous three years
▶ For services offered in a care home operated by Barchester Healthcare or by any other company
▶ Towards home repairs and alterations not related to disability/medical condition
▶ For property maintenance such as roof repairs, window replacements, rewiring, and other property repairs
▶ For basic household items (white goods, furniture, carpets) not related to disability/medical condition
▶ For daily living costs (rent, utility bills, clothing and so on)
▶ To repay debts
▶ For services for which the health and social care authorities have a statutory responsibility (e.g. medical and dental treatment)

Applications

Applications can be made online on the foundation's website or a form can be downloaded and submitted to the correspondent. All applications must be supported by a third party sponsor such as a health or social care professional, social worker or charity representative. The trustees meet quarterly, although applications can be dealt with in between the meetings.

Applicants can expect a response within ten weeks; however, the foundation is unable to acknowledge the receipt of postal applications.

Blesma

See entry on page 80

Elifar Foundation Ltd

£57,000

Correspondent: Paul Cawood, Trustee, 67 Clapham Common North Side, London SW4 9SB (020 7471 8702; email: info@elifarfoundation.org.uk; website: www.elifarfoundation.org.uk)

CC number: 1152416

Eligibility

People of any age with any form of physical or learning disability.

Types of grants

Grants can be made towards specialised equipment, such as wheelchairs, trikes, beds, seats and sensory equipment and toys, communication aids and specialist software, hoists and similar.

Annual grant total

In 2013/14 the foundation had an income of £23,500 and a total expenditure of £57,000. We estimate that about £55,000 was given in grants.

Exclusions

Grants are not made for:

▶ Items or work for which there is statutory funding available
▶ Building works
▶ Garden works
▶ Ordinary computers/laptops/iPads
▶ Ordinary domestic items (e.g. furniture, flooring, white goods, clothing)
▶ Ordinary or family holidays
▶ Therapies
▶ Goods already purchased, for deposits paid, or goods already on order
▶ Where it is deemed that the beneficiary or the beneficiary's family are capable of providing the equipment from their own resources

Applications

Application forms can be found on the foundation's website. They can be submitted by or on behalf of individuals, although a letter of support from a healthcare professional is required. All appeals are acknowledged.

If you are applying via post, submit your request to: c/o Shirley Baker, 21 Panmuir Road, London SW20 0PZ.

Equipment for Independent Living

£29,500 (35 grants)

Correspondent: Jan Hillman, Honorary Secretary, 19 Flanchford Road, London W12 9ND

CC number: 228438

Eligibility

People over 16 who have disabilities in the UK and overseas.

Types of grants

One-off grants towards disability equipment enabling people to obtain 'mobility, independence and earning power'. Awards are usually in the range of £100 to £1,000.

Annual grant total

In 2014 the trust had assets of £689,000 and an income of £28,500. There were 35 grants given to individuals, amounting to £29,500.

Exclusions

Normally grants are not made towards: medical equipment; course fees and materials; welfare expenditure of a non-capital nature such as holidays or moving expenses; equipment which is supplied by the NHS or social services; equipment running costs; building adaptations and decorating; household equipment (unless specially adapted for the person's disability); or private treatment, home care fees or computers (unless they are used as a speech aid or to enable the individual to earn their living).

Funds are not normally granted to cases submitted by other charities which have much larger resources than the trust.

Applications

Applicants must be referred in the first instance by a professional person involved with their welfare, for example a social worker, occupational therapist or specialist nurse. The professional person should write to the Honorary Secretary describing the applicant's circumstances and saying what equipment is needed and why. If appropriate, a full application form will then be sent out.

Applications can be submitted at any time and are considered in January, April, July and October.

Gardening for Disabled Trust

£32,500

Correspondent: The Secretary, PO Box 285, Tunbridge Wells, Kent TN2 9JD (email: info@gardeningfordisabledtrust. org.uk; website: www. gardeningfordisabledtrust.org.uk)

CC number: 255066

Eligibility

Members of the trust who wish to participate in gardening regardless of age or disability.

Types of grants

One-off grants according to need to help towards tools, raised beds, paving, labour and greenhouses.

Annual grant total

In 2014 the trust had an income of £27,500 and a total expenditure of £42,500. The total amount awarded in grants was £39,500, of which £7,000 was given to organisations.

Exclusions

No grants are given to pay for a gardener for general maintenance or for clearing or fencing.

Applications

Apply in writing to the correspondent detailing the work you would like done and an estimate of the cost of tools, materials and labour (if necessary). Applications can be submitted through the online contact form on the website. If labour is required, the applicant should provide original copies of two quotes. Applicants should also include a note from their GP, social worker or occupational therapist describing their disability. Applications are considered monthly.

Mobility Trust

£190,000

Correspondent: Anne Munn, Chief Executive, 17B Reading Road, Pangbourne, Reading, Berkshire RG8 7LR (0118 984 2588; fax: 0118 984 2544; email: mobility@mobilitytrust.org.uk; website: www.mobilitytrust.org.uk)

CC number: 1070975

Eligibility

People with severe physical disabilities due to an accident or a disease.

Types of grants

The provision of powered wheelchairs or scooters for people who are unable to obtain such equipment through statutory sources or afford it themselves. If someone is unable to walk at all and requires a powered wheelchair they should apply to their local NHS Wheelchair Service before making an application to the trust.

Note that the trust does not make direct cash grants but helps to obtain the required equipment. It states in its annual report:

> We have the expertise and knowledge to provide the best solution which includes the benefit of two years insurance cover and annual servicing and aftercare. We do not give grants as they may be used to buy cheap and unsuitable equipment which can be obtained on the internet and may do more harm than good.

Annual grant total

In 2013/14 the trust had assets of £306,000 and an income of £304,500. A total of £190,000 was spent to provide beneficiaries' equipment.

Applications

Applications must be submitted in the first instance by a letter directly by the individual or through a social worker, medical advisor or other welfare agency. The letter should explain why the person needs the equipment, detailing any disabilities and their cause. If there is a possibility of helping the person, they will be sent a form to complete.

Equipment cannot be supplied unless the candidate has had an assessment by a physiotherapist, occupational therapist or specialist engineer.

Motability

£20.5 million

Correspondent: Customer Services, Warwick House, Roydon Road, Harlow, Essex CM19 5PX (0300 456 4566; email: communications@motability.co.uk; website: www.motability.co.uk)

CC number: 299745

Eligibility

People who receive one of the following benefits: the higher-rate mobility component of Disability Living Allowance; the enhanced rate of the mobility component of the Personal Independence Payment; the War Pensioners' Mobility Supplement; the Armed Forces Independence Payment; or a government vehicle, trike or mini.

Types of grants

Assistance can be given towards 'the best value suitable solution that meets basic mobility needs'. These can include: vehicle advance payments; supplying and fitting adaptations, for instance hand controls to enable somebody with a lower body disability to drive an automatic car or hoists to load electric wheelchairs into estate cars; driving lessons for people with disabilities, or whose children or spouses have disabilities, especially people aged 16 to 24; or wheelchair-accessible vehicles for customers who wish to get in a car while seated in their wheelchair.

Annual grant total

In 2013/14 Motability had net assets of £11.6 million (excluding pension liability) and had an income of £29.5 million. Grants were made totalling £20.5 million. The majority of funding for grants, over £18.2 million, was provided by the Department for Work and Pensions and administered by Motability. Almost £2.3 million was raised and distributed independently by Motability.

Applications

Potential applicants should contact the customer services team on 0300 456 4566. The trust usually requests that potential applicants have their national insurance number to hand.

Note the following from the website: 'financial help is only awarded towards the least expensive solution that meets your mobility needs and you should also expect to contribute as much as you can afford'.

At times there may be waiting lists for some of the schemes. To find out, see

the Motability website or contact the customer services team.

The SF Charity

£11,000

Correspondent: Brenda Yong, Charitable Fund Manager, 4 Millennium Way West, Phoenix Centre, Nottingham NG8 6AS (email: brenda.yong@sfcharity.co.uk; website: www.sfcharity.co.uk)

CC number: 1104927

Eligibility

Severely disabled people of all ages. This can include people with significant sensory, physical and intellectual impairments and those with complex and challenging behavioural needs. The charity's website states that SF Charity is only able to accept applications from applicants in the counties of Nottinghamshire, Leicestershire, Derbyshire, Warwickshire and the West Midlands (primarily areas covered by the postcodes starting NG, LE, DE, CV, B, WS, WV, DY and some starting with S). There is a postcode searcher on the website.

Payments for or towards specific items or services which will make a positive difference to the quality of life of individuals or groups.

Types of grants

Applications are treated on their merit. The majority of grants given are around £1,000.

Previously, grants have been given for special clothing, footwear, mattresses and beds, indoor/outdoor wheelchairs, mobility scooters, kitchen equipment, a Meywalker and structural amendments to houses and living areas. Grants may be given for ordinary household items if it can be shown that they will have an impact on alleviating the disability rather than improving general family circumstances. Grants for UK holidays may also be considered, but applications should be submitted 6–12 months in advance of proposed holiday dates.

Annual grant total

In 2014 the charity had assets of £256,500 and an income of £62,000. Direct charitable expenditure totalled £20,500. The charity makes grants to both organisations and individuals, although a breakdown of grants was not available in the accounts. We estimate that the amount of grants given to individuals totalled £11,000.

Exclusions

No grants for: debts; education and course fees; motor vehicle purchase or expenses; nursing and residential home fees; funeral expenses; removal expenses; driving lessons; items already purchased;

therapies such as swimming with dolphins and hyperbaric therapy; alternative therapies such as reflexology, acupuncture and faith healing; iPads; or major home improvements.

Applications

Applications are welcomed from individuals, professional workers and representatives of organisations. Where the request is from a private individual, a detailed letter of support from a professional (for example, a family doctor, hospital consultant, social worker, teacher or a worker from a community or disability organisation) is essential. If applying for specialist seating, or manual or powered wheelchairs, the letter must be from an occupational therapist or physiotherapist.

Applicants should first complete a short preliminary enquiry form. This can be done online at the SF group website, or by completing the form attached to the charity's information leaflet which can be requested by phone or email. The Fund Manager will make contact within two weeks of receiving the application to discuss the request in more detail.

The Stanley Stein Deceased Charitable Trust

£15,000

Correspondent: Michael Lawson, Trustee, Burwood House, 14–16 Caxton Street, London SW1H 0GY (020 7873 1000; email: michael.lawson@ williamsturges.co.uk)

CC number: 1048873

Eligibility

People over the age of 75 or under the age of 21 who are experiencing financial hardship and people who are blind, deaf or dumb or who have a physical disability.

Types of grants

One-off and recurrent grants are given according to need.

Annual grant total

In 2013/14 the trust had an income of £11,200 and a total expenditure of £32,500. Grants are made to individuals for both social welfare and educational purposes. We estimate that social welfare grants totalled around £15,000.

Applications

Applications can be made on a form which is available from the correspondent.

Vitalise

£216,500 (403+ grants)

Correspondent: Bookings Team, 212 Business Design Centre, Upper Street, London N1 0QH (0303 3030145; fax: 020 7288 6899; email: bookings@ vitalise.org.uk; website: www.vitalise.org. uk)

CC number: 295072

Eligibility

Adults with physical disabilities and carers who might not otherwise be able to afford a break. Applicants must be aged 18 or over and must not have been on a break for over 12 months or have savings of more than £23,000. In exceptional circumstances, the charity may consider those who have been on a break in the previous 12 months. Applicants must not qualify for statutory funding.

Types of grants

Financial assistance towards the cost of a break at a Vitalise Centre. Assistance rarely covers the entire cost of a break. In 2013/14 the Joan Brander Memorial Fund was able to subsidise every break by £239.

Annual grant total

In 2013/14 the charity held assets of £6 million and had an income of £7.7 million. A total of £216,500 was expended from the Joan Brander Memorial fund and helped to subsidise breaks for 403 individuals and families.

Exclusions

Grants do not cover associated costs such as transport to and from the centre.

Applications

Both an online application form and a downloadable form are available on the website. Applications require a letter of support from a social worker or healthcare professional.

Provisional bookings must be made before completing the application form.

Bruce Wake Charity

£41,000 (36 grants)

Correspondent: Peter Hems, Trustee, c/o Grant Thornton UK LLP, Regent House, 80 Regent Road, Leicester LE1 7NH (0116 247 1234; email: wake@ webleicester.co.uk; website: www. brucewaketrust.co.uk)

CC number: 1018190

Eligibility

People who have disabilities (predominantly wheelchair users) in the UK.

Types of grants

The trustees will consider grant applications related to the provision of leisure activities for the disabled, but favour particularly applications whereby the potential beneficiaries meet one or all of the following criteria:
- The potential beneficiaries are physically disabled wheelchair users
- Improved access for wheelchair users is proposed
- A sporting or leisure activity involving disabled wheelchair users is proposed

Annual grant total

In 2013/14 the charity held assets of £8.6 million and had an income of £225,000. Grants were made to 36 individuals totalling £41,000. A further £28,000 was given for individuals through Leicester Charity Link.

Grants were made to 155 organisations totalling £412,000.

Applications

Apply in writing through a charitable organisation or equivalent recognised body. Applications should include all appropriate financial information and are considered quarterly.

The Welsh Rugby Charitable Trust

£193,000

Correspondent: Edward Jones, Hon. Secretary, 55 West Road, Bridgend CF31 4HQ (email: welshrugbycharitabletrust@gmail.com; website: www.wrct.org.uk)

CC number: 502079

Eligibility

People who have been severely injured whilst playing rugby union football in Wales, and their dependants.

Types of grants

One-off grants to help injured players regain their independence. Grants can be made towards cars, wheelchairs, hoists, domestic aids and gifts in summer (for a holiday break) and at Christmas.

Annual grant total

In 2013/14 the trust had assets of £3.6 million and an income of £212,500. Grants to individuals amounted to £193,000 and were distributed as follows:

Relief of injured players	£141,000
Summer grants	£33,000
Christmas gifts	£18,900

Applications

Apply in writing to the correspondent including the circumstances of the injury and the effect it has on the applicant's career. Information on the financial position before and after the accident should also be included. Applications are considered every two months (or sooner in emergency cases) and can be submitted either directly by the individual or by a club representative.

Players who have been seriously injured but do not have permanent disabilities are usually visited by the trust to assess the degree of need before any grant is made.

The Jonathan Young Memorial Trust

£20,000 (74 grants)

Correspondent: John Young, Trustee, 3 Hardwick Road, The Park, Nottingham NG7 1EP (0115 947 0493; email: info@ jonathan-young-trust.co.uk; website: www.joanthan-young-trust.co.uk)

CC number: 1067619

Eligibility

People who are living with a disability and would benefit from access to computer equipment. The trust operates primarily within the East Midlands (Nottinghamshire, Derbyshire, Leicestershire, Lincolnshire and South Yorkshire) but applications from anywhere in the UK will be considered. Grants are occasionally made to those who are disadvantaged by reasons other than disability.

Types of grants

Grants of £200 to £500 towards the cost of computer equipment and related types of electronic communication equipment.

Annual grant total

In 2014 the trust had an income of £11,000 and a total expenditure of £21,000. During the year 74 grants were made, which we estimate totalled £20,000.

Exclusions

The trust does not make grants for general living expenses, course or college fees, disability aids such as wheelchairs or any non-electronic items.

Applications

Applications should be made writing to the correspondent, either directly by the individual, carer or parent or through a statutory or voluntary organisation on behalf of the individual. Applications should include:

- Name, address, telephone number and age
- Background information
- The nature and extent of the disability
- Financial information – income/ expenditure and how much can be contributed towards the equipment
- Why a computer would be beneficial

- The specific equipment needed, including any software and a quotation if possible

For individuals applying directly or those applying for a family member, a supporting letter from a GP, social worker, teacher or similar should be included. Applications are considered in April and October.

Injuries

The Mark Davies Injured Riders' Fund

£20,500

Correspondent: Rosemary Lang, Administrator and Fund Co-ordinator, Lancrow Farmhouse, Penpillick Hill, Par, Cornwall PL24 2SA (01726 813156; email: rosemary@mdirf.co.uk; website: www.mdirf.co.uk)

CC number: 1022281

Eligibility

People injured in horse-related accidents (excluding professional and amateur jockeys and those injured in the horse racing industry) and their carers.

Types of grants

One-off cash grants and grants in kind according to need. Grants to beneficiaries vary from less than £100 to more than £40,000, depending on need. Assistance has recently been given in the form of travel expenses, physiotherapy, adapted motor cars, house adaptations and home and stable help.

Annual grant total

In 2014 the fund held assets of £419,500 and had an income of £98,500. Beneficial payments to individuals totalled £20,500.

Applications

Apply in writing to the correspondent at any time. All applicants are visited by a local fund volunteer to discuss their medical and financial needs. A report is then made to the trustees, who will consider whether or not to award a grant.

Headway Emergency Fund

£41,500 (About 200 grants)

Correspondent: The Fund Administrator, Unit 1, College Fields Business Centre, 16 Prince George's Road, London SW19 2PT (0115 924 0800; email: emergencyfund@headway. org.uk; website: www.headway.org.uk/ supporting-you/headway-emergency-fund)

CC number: 1025852/SC039992

Eligibility

Families and individuals coping with the practical implications of a sudden and catastrophic brain injury. Applicants should have less than £1,000 in savings.

Types of grants

Grants of up to £500 are available 'to help with an increased financial burden following a brain injury'. This may include the cost of travel to visit relatives in hospital or attend rehabilitation sessions; emergency accommodation; additional costs in the immediate aftermath of the injury; or breaks for carers (normally at a cottage in Yorkshire that Headway has access to).

Annual grant total

In 2014 the fund received 333 applications with 60% being successful. A total of about £41,500 was given to families facing hardship.

Exclusions

Support cannot be given outside the UK.

The following are excluded:

- Taxi journeys
- Food
- Debts
- Rent deposits
- Utility bills
- Everyday household expenses

Applications

Application forms can be completed online or downloaded and returned to the correspondent once completed. Only one application per survivor of a brain injury can be considered.

The Injured Jockeys Fund

£618,000 (401 grants)

Correspondent: Lisa Hancock, Chief Executive, 15 Kings Court, Willie Snaith Road, Newmarket, Suffolk CB8 7SG (01638 662246; fax: 01638 668988; email: kh@ijf.org.uk; website: www. injuredjockeys.co.uk)

CC number: 1107395

Eligibility

Jockeys who have suffered through injury, and their families. Applicants must hold (or have held) a licence to ride under the Rules of Racing, be in financial need and have obtained all state aid to which they are entitled.

Types of grants

One-off and recurrent grants to assist with medical care and to help alleviate financial problems and stress. Grants have included help with medical treatment and equipment, contributions to private medical insurance, wheelchairs, holidays, televisions and emergency cash. Assistance may also be given to help with the cost of education where children have special needs. Interest-free mortgage advances are available.

Annual grant total

In 2013/14 the fund had an income of £5.5 million. Grants to 401 injured jockeys totalled £618,000. The major grants categories were as follows:

Regular payments	£249,000
Discretionary grants	£173,500
Physiotherapy and care costs	£139,500
Medical, consultancy and operational	£161,000
Expenses for homes	£92,000
TV and Sky	£42,000
Grants for motoring, tax and insurance	£30,000

Applications

Application forms are available from the correspondent. The fund has nine almoners who cover the whole of the UK and visit potential beneficiaries to assess their needs.

Professional Footballers' Association Accident Insurance Fund

£2.3 million

Correspondent: Darren Wilson, Director of Finance, 20 Oxford Court, Bishopsgate, Manchester M2 3WQ (0161 236 0575; email: info@thepfa.co.uk; website: www.givemefootball.com)

Eligibility

Members or former members of the association in England and Wales who require medical treatment as a result of a specific injury or illness which results in their permanent total disability to play professional football.

Types of grants

Grants are to provide private medical treatment for all members and for members unable to claim under the terms of the PFA accident insurance policy due to the nature/circumstances of the injury. Grants are also given to meet operation costs which may not be covered by the insurance and free places are available at Lilleshall Rehabilitation Centre. Grants are also available to former members for treatment on injuries received as a result of their playing career.

Annual grant total

Income to the Accident Fund of the PFA was £3 million. Direct expenditure (excluding support costs and legal and professional fees) totalled almost £2.3 million in 2013/14 and can be broken down as follows:

Insurance premiums	£847,000
Medical fees and grants	£696,000
Permanent total disability	£397,000
Spire costs	£317,000
Other costs	£24,000

Applications

Application forms are available from the correspondent. Completed applications should be returned directly by the individual or by a family member/social worker on their behalf. There are no deadlines and applications are considered as they are received.

RFU Injured Players Foundation

£443,000 (136 grants)

Correspondent: Erica Preuth, Team Administrator, Rugby House, Twickenham Stadium, 200 Whitton Road, Middlesex TW2 7BA (0800 783 1518; email: EricaPreuth@RFU.com; website: www.rfuipf.org.uk)

CC number: 1122139

Eligibility

People who are seriously injured playing sport under the auspices of the Rugby Football Union.

Types of grants

Small grants of up to £5,000 per year and large grants of up to £10,000 (or higher in exceptional circumstances) for a variety of needs. Most grants are for £2,000 or less.

Grants are commonly given for home improvements to provide disability access, medical equipment and mobility aids, exercise and therapy equipment, communication aids, respite care and travel expenses.

Annual grant total

In 2013/14 the foundation held assets of £7 million and had an income of £2.1 million. A total of £443,000 was awarded to individuals; of this total, £344,000 was given in 47 large grants and £99,000 in 89 small grants.

The largest single grant given to an individual amounted to £35,000; the small grants made were all for £2,000 or less.

Exclusions

No grants are given for general household expenses such as food, clothing, utility bills or vehicle fuel costs.

Applications

Application forms for both small and large grants may be downloaded from the website. Large-grants application forms are also available from Katie Lister and can be submitted in advance so that the charity can pledge funds, enabling the purchase to be planned. Applicants

are advised to attach an estimate or invoice proving costs.

All applications will be acknowledged within five working days. Decisions on small grants are made within 14 working days. Decisions normally take between six to eight weeks for large grants of less than £20,000 and for those over £20,000, up to three months.

Contact by applicants to discuss any aspect of the application process is welcomed by the foundation.

There is a useful Q&A relating to the grants process on the website.

The Rosslyn Park Injury Trust Fund

£4,000

Correspondent: Diane McIntier, Secretary, 102 Halfway Street, Sidcup, Kent DA15 8DB (020 8302 4082; email: bridihalfwayst@talktalk.net; website: www.rosslynpark.co.uk/information/injury-trust-fund)

CC number: 284089

Eligibility

Young people who have a disability or are in poor health as a result of an injury suffered while playing sports (amateur sports). Their dependants may also receive help.

Types of grants

One-off grants for computers, special care, medical equipment, computers and disability aids. The fund has a list of recent beneficiaries on its website.

Annual grant total

In 2014 the fund had an income of £17,100 and a total expenditure of £4,200. We estimate that the amount of grants given to individuals totalled £4,000.

Applications

Apply in writing to the correspondent. Applications can be submitted by either the individual or through social services and are considered as they are received.

Mental health

The Matthew Trust

£13,000

Correspondent: Annabel Thompson, Director, PO Box 604, London SW6 3AG (020 7736 5976; fax: 020 7731 6961; email: amt@matthewtrust.org; website: www.matthewtrust.org)

CC number: 294966

Eligibility

The trust is currently running four projects with the aims of:

- Supporting children under 16 who have mental health problems
- Providing breaks for child carers
- Supporting young people aged 16–25 who have mental health problems
- Enabling people with mental health problems who are over 60 through projects, with a view to promoting their inclusion in the wider community

The priorities of the charity may change so applicants are advised to consult the website before applying.

Types of grants

One-off grants of between £50 and £250 towards counselling or medical bills; the provision of equipment and furniture to make a flat liveable; the provision of security equipment; and the provision of personal clothing items. The trust also helps with second-chance learning and skills training; travel costs for prison visits; respite breaks; and debt support in special circumstances.

Annual grant total

In 2013/14 the trust held assets of £270,000 and had an income of £51,000. Grants to individuals totalled £13,000.

Applications

Apply in writing to the correspondent through a professional agency such as a social worker, probation officer, community care worker or GP. The professional representative should also include their name and contact details on the application. Applications should include: the name, address, age and gender of the applicant; the health and age of other close family members; a summary of the mental health problem; the applicant's present circumstances; the type of support required, including costs where applicable; if the applicant has received support from the trust previously; and details of any other organisations which have been approached for support. Applications may be posted or emailed.

Note: The Matthew Trust is a 'last-stop' agency and will only consider applications when all other avenues of statutory and voluntary funding have been exhausted and then only where a care programme has been established.

The North Wales Psychiatric Fund

£12,000

Correspondent: Hilary Owen, Correspondent, Bryn Y Neuadd Hospital, Aber Road, Llanfairfechan, Gwynedd LL33 OHH (01248 682573)

CC number: 235783

Eligibility

People in North Wales who are mentally ill and are under the care of a social worker or health professional.

Types of grants

One-off grants for clothes, furniture, holidays and learning courses.

Annual grant total

In 2014 the fund had an income of £3,100 and a total expenditure of £12,700. We estimate that the amount of grants given to individuals totalled £12,000.

Exclusions

There are no grants available for the payment of debts.

Applications

Apply in writing to the correspondent through a social worker or health professional, including details of income and other possible grant sources. Applications are considered throughout the year.

Other specific conditions

Arthritis Action (Arthritic Association Treating Arthritis Naturally)

£12,000

Correspondent: Graham Weir, Company Secretary, 1 Upperton Gardens, Eastbourne, East Sussex BN21 2AA (0800 652 3188 (Freephone), 01323 408617 (general); email: info@ arthriticassociation.org.uk; website: www.arthriticassociation.org.uk)

CC number: 292569

Eligibility

People who have arthritis or a related condition, and are in financial need. Grants are only available to members of the Arthritic Association, those who are undertaking a dietary programme with the association and towards treatments associated with the programme.

Types of grants

One-off grants in kind for consultation fees, dietary supplements and remedial therapy. The 2013/14 accounts state:

> Every member following the Charity's self-management programme is entitled to a subsidised physical assessment and two subsidised treatments. Thereafter, they

are eligible to apply for non-means-tested grants to assist with subsequent fees for consultations with independent and regulated health professionals, who are registered as the Charity's Associated Practitioners. Grants to members include reimbursement of these fees and payments made direct to Associated Practitioners in respect of consultations with members.

Annual grant total

In 2013/14 the association had assets of £6.7 million and an income of £410,000. Grants paid to members towards consultation fees totalled £12,000. Research grants are also awarded to organisations.

Applications

Application forms are available from the correspondent. They can be submitted directly by the individual or through a social worker, Citizens Advice or other welfare agency. Our research suggests that requests are normally considered in January, March, July and October.

ASPIRE (Association for Spinal Injury Research Rehabilitation and Reintegration) Human Needs Fund

£126,000

Correspondent: Kim Elliott, Grants Officer, ASPIRE National Training Centre, Wood Lane, Stanmore, Middlesex HA7 4AP (020 8420 6707; email: kim.elliott@aspire.org.uk or grants@aspire.org.uk; website: www. aspire.org.uk)

CC number: 1075317/SC037482

Eligibility

People in the UK and Ireland (or EU Citizen, with indefinite leave to remain or with full refugee status) who have a spinal cord injury and are in need. Priority is given to re-establishing independent mobility.

Types of grants

One-off grants to help towards the purchase of specialist equipment, such as wheelchairs, assistive technology, mobility aids and computers, to help them increase their level of independence. The charity states that it will rarely offer full funding, but will offer part-funding and assistance with securing the remainder. Funding is given for essential items not upgrades or enhancement of existing property.

Also note the following:

> For those applying for computer equipment, where alternative computer facilities, such as local libraries and internet cafes could realistically be used,

funding for computers will rarely be available from Aspire Grants. Applications for computer equipment will prioritise those that will increase and provide access to further education or employment (additional supporting evidence may be requested).

Annual grant total

In 2013/14 the charity held assets of £2.9 million and had an income of £2.8 million. Grants to individuals totalled £126,000.

Exclusions

Grants from the fund are solely for people with acquired non-progressive spinal cord injury. The charity states that it is unlikely to fund applications for:

- Holidays
- Vehicles
- House adaptations
- Passive exercise equipment
- Secondary functions on wheelchairs, including standing functions and cosmetic features, for reasons that could be met by other means

ASPIRE will not fund repairs, maintenance, insurance, replacement of parts or contracts for equipment, or equipment already purchased or ordered.

Second-hand equipment cannot be considered, except where it is sold through a reputable business and comes with a suitable warranty.

Only one application per applicant per five-year period is accepted, unless the previous provision is insufficient due to a change in medical circumstances.

The charity will not consider applications where statutory provision has not first been explored and exhausted.

Applications

Application forms are available from the charity's website. Each application requires a supporting statement: for medical equipment applications must be supported by an occupational therapist or medical consultant to explain why the specialist equipment is appropriate; for other equipment applications must be supported by a third party (check with the Grants Officer to find out the most appropriate individual to do this in your case). The charity may request additional information or supporting evidence prior to considering an application. Completed applications will usually be considered within six weeks of receipt. Full guidelines are available on the website where there is also additional information in the form of a brochure.

Ataxia UK (formerly Friedreich's Ataxia Group)

£66,000

Correspondent: Tina Thatcher, Correspondent, Ground Floor, Lincoln House, 1–3 Brixton Road, London SW9 6DE (020 7582 1444; email: tthatcher@ataxia.org.uk; website: www.ataxia.org.uk)

CC number: 1102391

Eligibility

People who are in need and have Cerebellar Ataxia (Friedreich's Ataxia and spinocerebellar).

Types of grants

Cornberg Grants are available towards the costs of specialist equipment and home adaptations.

The Jerry Farr Travel Fellowship awards a maximum of £3,500 to fund a travel experience for one Ataxia sufferer each year.

Annual grant total

In 2013/14 the charity had assets of £755,500 and an income of £965,000. Grants to individuals totalled £66,000 with £54,000 given in Cornberg grants and £12,500 given in Jerry Farr Travel Fellowship grants.

Exclusions

People may apply only if they have not received a grant from the charity in the past three years.

Applications

For more information and to find out if you are eligible for a Cornberg grant, contact the helpline on 0845 644 0606 or email helpline@ataxia.org.uk. Closing dates for rounds of applications are displayed on the website.

Application forms for the Jerry Farr Travel Scholarship can be downloaded from the website.

The British Kidney Patient Association

£907,500

Correspondent: Fiona Armitage, 3 The Windmills, St Mary's Close, Turk Street, Alton GU34 1EF (01420 541424; fax: 01420 89438; email: info@britishkidney-pa.co.uk; website: www.britishkidney-pa.co.uk)

CC number: 270288

Eligibility

Dialysis patients and their families who are on low incomes. Grants are also made to other patients, including transplant patients and those receiving conservative care, if their health and health and quality of life is being seriously affected by their renal condition.

Types of grants

Help can be given with the costs of domestic bills such as car insurance and tax, heating costs, telephone installations and TV licences, as well as with the purchase of domestic goods like washing machines and carpets.

If an individual cannot recover the costs of travel to their local hospital through their kidney unit, the association may be able to help if they have to visit regularly and travel a long way.

The association also gives grants to individuals and families towards the costs of a basic holiday in the UK or abroad. If the cost for a holiday is modest, a grant can be used to cover the entire amount or, for more considerable amounts, can be given as a contribution towards the total.

Annual grant total

In 2014 the association had assets of £33.1 million and an income of £1.4 million. Grants totalled more than £1.8 million, of which £900,500 was given to support hospital projects and post-funding. Patient aid amounted to £931,500, with grants for social welfare purposes amounting to £907,500. Around £23,500 was given for patients' further education.

Exclusions

Grants are not made: to reimburse patients for bills already paid; for telephone bills, court fines, home improvements, the repayment of credit cards or loans, medical equipment, or council tax payments; or to help with the costs of getting ongoing dialysis. The guidelines also note: 'Whilst we don't pay for dialysis when on holiday either in the UK or abroad, it is free in European Community countries at centres which accept the European Health Insurance Card (EHIC).'

Applications

Application forms, along with guidelines, are available to download from the association's website. The form must be submitted by a renal social worker or a member of the patient's renal team, who must sign the form and attach a detailed social report on the hospital's headed paper. The association gives the following helpful information on its website: 'if there's no member of staff able to help, the BKPA's Counsellor Jacquie Fraser can be contacted by calling the main BKPA telephone number'.

The British Polio Fellowship

£28,000

Correspondent: The Support Services Team, Citibase, 44 Clarendon Road, Watford, Hertfordshire WD17 1JJ (0800 043 1935; email: info@britishpolio.org. uk; website: www.britishpolio.org.uk)

CC number: 1108335/SC038863

Eligibility

People in need who have been affected by poliomyelitis (polio) and post-polio programme and live in the UK. Carers, families and healthcare professionals may also be assisted.

Types of grants

The following grants are **only** available to members:

Welfare grants – of up to £500 are given for disability-related equipment, such as scooters, electric or manual wheelchairs, riser/recliner chairs, specialised clothing and footwear and specialist beds and mattresses. Household aids and equipment to enable independence and home as well as car adaptations can also be supported. Assistance may occasionally be given for essential home improvement and crisis prevention.

Heating grants – of up to £100 are made annually to members on a low income who are too young to qualify for the Government's Winter Fuel Payment to help with heating costs.

Holiday grants – awards of £200 on average are offered 'to enable members to find and enjoy suitable holidays in the UK and abroad by providing financial assistance'. Awards can be requested once every two years.

Annual grant total

In 2014 the fellowship had assets of £3.3 million (mainly consisting of investments) and an income of £779,000. Grants to individuals were made totalling £28,000.

Exclusions

Grants are not given for non-members, towards hospital expenses, household bills or home carers. Statutory sources such as social services' Social Fund must be exhausted before approaching the fellowship, as financial support will not be made to substitute statutory help.

Applications

Welfare and heating grant forms are available from the correspondent or a local branch welfare officer. Applications should be submitted by the individual or by an appropriate third party on their behalf and include a medical certificate or doctors note stating polio-disability. Welfare applications are considered throughout the year. Heating grants are awarded once a year in the autumn.

Holiday grant forms are available from the correspondent or by emailing Rosalind Evans at rosalindevans@ britishpolio.org.uk. They are assessed on a bi-monthly basis.

The Brittle Bone Society

£121,500

Correspondent: Patricia Osborne, Chief Executive, 30 Guthrie Street, Dundee DD1 5BS (01382 204446; email: bbs@ brittlebone.org; website: www. brittlebone.org)

CC number: 272100

Eligibility

Children and others with osteogenesis imperfecta (OI).

Types of grants

Grants in the range of £200 to £5,000 towards wheelchairs and other specialist equipment. This can include home alterations, assistance with holiday costs and laptops for children who are unable to attend school for a prolonged period. The society orders equipment directly from the manufacturer and, once received, the successful applicant is responsible for its insurance and maintenance.

The society notes that it will often not be able to fund the cost of whole items but will help raise the remaining funds on the applicant's behalf by applying to other trusts and grant-making bodies.

Annual grant total

In 2013/14 the society held assets of £333,000 and had an income of £335,000. Grants to individuals totalled £121,500 and were distributed as follows:

Wheelchair purchase	£86,000
Welfare and equipment	£30,000
Wheelchair repairs	£5,200
Holidays	£300

Exclusions

The society does not usually fund higher education, white goods or building works.

Applications

Application forms can be downloaded from the website or requested from the correspondent and should be completed and returned by post. Applications must be supported by a Letter of Support from a healthcare professional such as an occupational therapist or a physiotherapist.

The National Association for Colitis and Crohn's Disease (Crohn's and Colitis UK)

£98,500

Correspondent: David Barker, Chief Executive, 45 Grosvenor Road, St Albans AL1 3AW (01727 830038; email: info@ crohnsandcolitis.org.uk; website: www. crohnsandcolitis.org.uk)

CC number: 1117148, SC038632

Eligibility

People in need who have ulcerative colitis, Crohn's disease or related inflammatory bowel diseases (IBD). Candidates must have been resident in the UK for at least six months and be on a low income. Carers may also be supported.

Types of grants

One-off Personal Grants of up to £300 are given to individuals for items or needs arising as a consequence of Crohn's or colitis. Examples include: a washing machine or dryer; beds and bedding; a refrigerator; new clothing due to weight loss or gain; a rehabilitation holiday in the UK.

Annual grant total

In 2014 the charity had assets of £2.9 million and an income of £3.7 million. The total amount of grants given was £100,500 and was distributed to 262 individuals. We have taken these figures to also include Young Person's Grants, which are given for educational and vocational support. We estimate that social welfare grants to individuals amounted to £50,000.

Exclusions

Recurring household bills or debts cannot be considered. The charity advises on its website: 'for these you should seek help from your local Social Services, Citizens' Advice Bureau, Citizens' Advice Scotland, StepChange Debt Charity or National Debtline'.

Applications

Application forms are available to download from the charity's website, along with guidance notes. The form has two extra sections: one should be completed by a doctor to confirm the individual's illness and the other filled in by a social worker (or health visitor, district nurse, Citizens Advice advisor, or another professional person).

Completed applications should be sent to the Personal Grants Fund Secretary at: PO Box 334, St Albans, Herts AL1 2WA. Grant payments are normally made directly to the retailer/provider. See the website for details of application deadlines and subsequent Grants Panel Meeting dates. Note that, apart from in exceptional circumstances, individuals may only apply for one grant every five years.

Further information on grants can be obtained from Julia Devereux (telephone: 0800 011 4701 or 01727 759654; email: julia.devereux@ crohnsandcolitis.org.uk).

The John Lloyd Corkhill Trust

£10,000

Correspondent: Michelle Jafrate, Trust Administrator, 5 Broadway, Greasby, Wirral, Merseyside CH49 2NG (0151 678 4428; email: michelle@hoofprintsuk. com)

CC number: 216371

Eligibility

People with lung conditions who live in the metropolitan borough of Wirral.

Types of grants

Mostly for equipment (e.g. nebulisers). Help is also given towards services and amenities, for example holidays, and occasionally to buy domestic appliances such as gas fires and washing machines.

Annual grant total

In 2013/14 the charity had an income of £4,100 and an expenditure of £12,500. We estimate that grants totalled £10,000.

Applications

Clients are generally referred by their social worker or doctor and have a low income. Supporting medical evidence must be supplied. Applications are considered in June and December.

The Cystic Fibrosis Holiday Fund

£97,000 (132 grants)

Correspondent: Rachael Hutson Gormley, Secretary, 1 Bell Street, London NW1 5BY (020 7616 1300; fax: 020 7616 1306; email: info@ cfholidayfund.org.uk; website: www. cfholidayfund.org.uk)

CC number: 1088630

Eligibility

Children and young people up to the age of 25 who are diagnosed with cystic fibrosis, and their families.

Types of grants

Grants of around £250–£500 towards enabling children with cystic fibrosis to go on holidays or short trips (this may also include the child's family).

Annual grant total

In 2014 the fund had assets of £87,000 and an income of £124,000. Holiday grants totalled £96,500.

Exclusions

People who have received a grant within the previous two years cannot be assisted. The fund is usually unable to cover full costs and will not make retrospective grants (including where the trip takes place prior to the final grant approval).

Applications

Application forms can be downloaded from the fund's website, requested from the correspondent or completed line. A medical report form will be sent to applicants to be completed by their doctor/medical consultant. Applications are assessed by the fund's medical advisory panel which meets three times a year (see the website for the date of the next deadline or contact the correspondent). Note that the approval procedure can take up to a few months so applicants should leave enough time before their proposed holiday when applying.

Cystic Fibrosis Trust

£97,000

Correspondent: Trevor Man, Grants Officer, 1 Aldgate, Second Floor, London EC3N 1RE (020 3795 2184; email: helpline@cysticfibrosis.org.uk; website: www.cysticfibrosis.org.uk)

CC number: 1079049

Eligibility

People in need who have cystic fibrosis.

Types of grants

The trust offers one-off emergency grants and health and well-being grants. According to the trust's website, emergency grants are given for the following purposes:

- Grants to cover the costs of a hospital stay for those having, or being assessed for, an organ transplant (this may also include costs incurred to carers)
- Small emergency grants of up to £150 for small items such as hypoallergenic bedding, certain household repairs, unexpected travel costs, cleaning of a new home where dirt would affect health, or an annual prescription pre-payment certificate
- Grants of up to £750 towards funeral costs

Health and well-being grants, typically of £250–£350, are awarded for the purchase of items which could improve health and quality of life, such as exercise equipment, white goods, furniture for a new home or gym fees.

In some cases grants can be applied for after the cost has been incurred.

Note: the trust also provides grants for holidays, but these are administered by the Cystic Fibrosis Holiday Fund.

Annual grant total

In 2013/14 the trust held assets of £12.9 million and had an income of £10.8 million. A total of £97,000 was awarded in grants to individuals.

Exclusions

Grants are not awarded for nebulisers, computers, cars, driving lessons, major home improvements, debts or to meet ongoing costs.

Applications

Application forms are available from the correspondent or can be downloaded from the website. Applications must be supported by a social worker or other professional and should state whether the applicant has applied to other charities and the outcome, the general financial circumstances, the cost of the services or goods required and the reason for the application. Individuals or their health professionals can contact the trust for assistance before submitting an application.

Further application guidelines are provided on the trust's website.

The Dystonia Society

£1,600 (3 grants)

Correspondent: Angie Brown, Helpline and Support Manager, The Dystonia Society, 1st Floor, 89 Albert Embankment, London SE1 7TP (020 7793 3656 or 020 7793 3650 (helpline); email: info@dystonia.org.uk or support@dystonia.org.uk; website: www. dystonia.org.uk)

CC number: 1068595

Eligibility

People living with or affected by dystonia in the UK.

Types of grants

One-off and recurrent grants are given according to need. Grants do not usually exceed £300, except in special circumstances.

Annual grant total

In 2014/15 the society had assets of £541,500 and an income of £707,000. During the year three grants were made to individuals totalling £1,600.

Exclusions

Grants are not made for medical treatment or other therapies, or for items or services available from the NHS.

Applications

Our research suggests that applications can be made on a form available from the correspondent. They must be endorsed by a health or social care professional who has known the applicant for at least two years.

The Haemophilia Society (The Tanner Fund)

£500

Correspondent: Liz Carroll, Chief Executive, Wilcox House, 140–148 Borough High Street, London SE1 1LB (020 7939 0784; email: info@haemophilia.org.uk; website: www.haemophilia.org.uk)

CC number: 288260

Eligibility

People with haemophilia and related bleeding disorders, and their families.

Types of grants

One-off hardship grants of up to £200 for items relating to applicants' medical problems, such as bedding, fridges to store treatment, floor coverings and washing machines.

Annual grant total

In 2013/14 the society had assets of £948,000 and an income of £786,000. Grants made to individuals through the Tanner Fund totalled only £500 in this financial year.

Exclusions

No grants are given for debts, holidays, motor vehicles or ongoing bills such as gas or electricity.

Applications

Application forms are available from the correspondent. Applications must be completed in conjunction with a medical professional or a social worker. They are considered as received. Note that each family may only make one application a year.

The Ben Hardwick Fund

£15,000

Correspondent: Anne Auber, Co-ordinator, 12 Nassau Road, Barnes, London SW13 9QE (020 8741 8499)

CC number: 1062554

Eligibility

Children with primary liver disease, and their families, who are in need.

Types of grants

One-off and recurrent grants, usually ranging between £150 and £500, to help with costs which are the direct result of the child's illness, such as hospital travel costs, in-hospital expenses, telephone bills and childminding for other children left at home.

Annual grant total

In 2014/15 the fund had an income of £3,300 and a total expenditure of £20,900. We estimate that the amount of grants given to individuals totalled £15,000.

Applications

Apply in writing to the correspondent, usually through a hospital social worker or other welfare professional. Applications are considered at any time.

The Huntington's Disease Association

£47,500

Correspondent: Nicholas Heath, Trustee, Suite 24, Liverpool Science Park IC1, 131 Mount Pleasant, Liverpool L3 5TF (0151 331 5444; email: info@hda.org.uk; website: www.hda.org.uk)

CC number: 296453

Eligibility

People with Huntington's disease, their immediate families and those at risk, who live in England or Wales.

Types of grants

One-off grants only, typically of up to £350, although each application is considered on merit. Grants have been made for clothing, furniture, domestic equipment (such as washing machines and cookers) and flooring.

Annual grant total

In 2013/14 the association had assets of £1 million and an income of £1.4 million. Expenditure on welfare grants to individuals varies each year, and in 2013/14 totalled £47,500.

Exclusions

No grants are given towards equipment or services that should be provided by statutory services. Support will not be given for the payment of debts, loans, bills, funeral expenses, holidays or travel.

Applications

Applications can be made on a form available from the correspondent. Some grants are made through local branches and applications should be submitted through a Regional Care Adviser or other professional. Contact details for local areas can be found on the website or by contacting the Head Office by telephone.

The Hylton House Fund

£4,200

Correspondent: Grants Administrator, County Durham Community Foundation, Victoria House, St John's Road, Meadowfield Industrial Estate, Durham DH7 8XL (0191 378 6340; fax: 0191 378 2409; email: info@cdcf.org.uk; website: www.cdcf.org.uk)

CC number: 1047625–2

Eligibility

People in the North East (County Durham, Darlington, Gateshead, South Shields, Sunderland and Cleveland) with cerebral palsy and related disabilities, and their families and carers. Applicants (or their family members, if aged under 18) must be on income support or a low income or have a degree of disability in the family that creates a heavy financial demand. People who live in Burnhope and require specialist equipment due to poor health or a disability may also be assisted.

Types of grants

Grants of up to £500 are made towards specialist equipment and of up to £200 towards domestic equipment.

Our research suggests that support can be made for therapy-associated needs, such as sound and light therapy, specialist clothing or tools, communication and mobility aids, travel costs (for example taxi and rail fares to attend a specific activity if no alternative transport is available), also respite support for an individual when the needs of the person requires them to either be accompanied by an employed carer or by visiting a specialist centre where full-time extensive care is provided.

Annual grant total

In 2013/14 grants from the fund were approved totalling £8,400.

Exclusions

According to our research, awards are not generally made for:

- Legal costs
- Ongoing education
- Medical treatment
- Decorating and/or refurbishment costs (unless the work is due to the nature of the applicant's disability)
- Motor vehicle adaptations
- Motor insurance, deposits or running costs
- Televisions or DVD players
- Assessments

Only one grant can be be received in each financial year starting in April. Retrospective funding is not available.

Applications

Application forms are available to download from the foundation's website or can be requested from the correspondent. All appeals must include a reference from a social worker or health-care professional, with a telephone number and the individual's permission for them to be contacted about an application. A full breakdown of costs should also be included. A confirmation from an occupational therapist, doctor, physiotherapist or other professional advisor that the equipment requested is recommended/ suitable is also required.

Requests are generally considered in January, April, July and October and should be received before the start of the month. Urgent appeals can be considered between these dates within a month of application, but the applicant will need to request this and provide a reason why an exception to the usual policy needs to be made.

Meningitis Now (formerly known as Meningitis Trust)

£132,500

Correspondent: The Community Support Officer, Fern House, Bath Road, Stroud GL5 3TJ (01453 768000; fax: 01453 768001; email: info@ meningitisnow.org; website: www. meningitisnow.org)

CC number: 803016/SC037790

Eligibility

People in need who have meningitis or who have disabilities as a result of meningitis and reside in the UK.

Types of grants

One-off and recurrent grants towards respite care, specialist aids and equipment, specialist computers and software, travel and accommodation costs for hospital appointments, adaptations, Motability vehicles, therapeutic activities, re-education and special training, and funeral expenses and headstones.

Annual grant total

In 2013/14 the charity had assets totalling £1.3 million and an income of nearly £3.4 million. Grants for individuals totalled £265,000. This amount was not broken down; therefore we estimate that welfare awards were made totalling about £132,500.

Exclusions

Support may not be given for the following:
- Services or items which should normally be supplied by a statutory body such as the NHS or the local authority
- Home adaptations on rented property
- Holidays
- Payment of domestic bills
- Arrears such as mortgage payments
- Bedding, furniture or clothing
- Domestic appliances
- Swimming pools

Applications

Application forms are available from the correspondent or can be downloaded from the website, where criteria are also posted. An initial telephone call on 0808 801 0388 or an email to helpline@ meningitisnow.org to discuss the application process is welcomed. Applications should be submitted through a third party and are reviewed on a monthly basis. They will need to include the confirmation of the diagnosis and a supporting letter from a professional involved in the care or support of the person who had meningitis (this is **not** required for applications for funeral or headstone costs).

The Motor Neurone Disease Association

£788,000

Correspondent: Support Services, Support Services, MND Association, David Niven House, 10–15 Notre Dame Mews, Northampton NN1 2BG (01604 611802; email: support.services@ mndassociation.org; website: www. mndassociation.org)

CC number: 294354

Eligibility

People with motor neurone disease, living in England, Wales and Northern Ireland.

Types of grants

The charity offers a range of grants including those for mobility aids; adaptations to buildings; holidays; and advice and counselling. Potential applicants are advised to visit the charity's website and read through the MND Support Grant Guidance and Process information.

Annual grant total

In 2013/14 the charity held assets of £8.8 million and had an income of £16.7 million. Grants to individuals totalled £788,000. Charitable expenditure spent directly for the benefit of people affected by motor neurone disease was £10.4 million. This was spent on:
- Improving care and support – £6.3 million
- Funding and promoting research – £3.1 million
- Campaigning and raising awareness – £60.9 million

Exclusions

Retrospective funding in excess of three months and without prior agreement with the Support Services team; funeral and legal costs; emergency healthcare needs; equipment for assessment.

Applications

Application forms can be downloaded from the website. Applications must be submitted through a health or social care professional. In addition to stating what is requested, applications should include details of why the need is not met by statutory sources and where any payments should be made.

Multiple Sclerosis Society

£1.7 million

Correspondent: The Grants Team, MS National Centre, 372 Edgware Road, Cricklewood, London NW2 6ND (020 8438 0700; fax: 020 8438 0701; email: grants@mssociety.org.uk; website: www. mssociety.org.uk)

CC number: 1139257

Eligibility

People with multiple sclerosis and their families and carers, living in the UK. People living in Scotland or Northern Ireland may be subject to other conditions, contact MS Society Scotland (0131 335 4050) or MS Society Northern Ireland (028 9080 2802) for full details.

Types of grants

Individual support grant fund
One-off grants are made towards a range of needs, including: home and car adaptations; mobility aids, wheelchairs and other specialised equipment; care adaptations or driving lessons for a person with MS or their carer; disability-related removal costs; some communication aids; computers.

Short breaks and activities fund
The fund can offer grants for:
- Respite care, in the home or at a care centre or similar
- An activity (or series of activities), short break or holiday for someone with MS and/or their carer/family
- Salary costs for a professional carer needed to help someone with MS, or their carer, have a break in the home or elsewhere
- Associated costs, such as travel, accommodation and disability equipment hire
- Some alternative or complementary therapies

Carers' grant fund

Support is provided to unpaid carers of all ages for a broad range of items and for things they can do for either leisure or personal development. Examples include supporting costs towards: sports equipment; music lessons; taking part in recreational activities; helping young carers go on school trips; enabling carers to take a course to get into employment; and developing other skills such as driving. Awards may be given of up to £300 for leisure purposes and up to £1,000 for personal development, depending on the applicant's age. The society does not count Carer's Allowance as being paid. The website notes: 'We can't consider grants for adult carers (aged 25 and over) with over £23,000 in accessible household savings.'

More details about all of the above support available can be obtained from the Grants Team.

Annual grant total

In 2014 the society held assets of nearly £15.5 million and had an income of £26 million. Grants given in support of individuals totalled almost £1.7 million.

Exclusions

Applicants with more than £16,000 in savings are not eligible for regular grants and those with more than £8,000 in savings are expected to contribute towards the cost of the item. For a short break or activity grant you are not eligible if you have more than £23,000 in savings. Carers' grants cannot be made to adult (over 25-year-old) carers with savings of over £23,000.

Grants cannot be made:
▶ Retrospectively, for purchases already made
▶ For any ongoing or long-term financial commitments (such as living costs and bills)
▶ For loans, debt assistance or legal fees (except for bankruptcy or Debt Relief Order fees)
▶ Towards paying for treatments
▶ To people who have received a grant from the individual support grant fund within the last two years
▶ To people who have received a grant from the short breaks and activities fund within the last year

Statutory sources should be exhausted prior to applying to the society.

Further guidance on each of the grant programmes is given on the website.

Applications

Application forms are available to download from the website, or can be obtained from the correspondent or a local MS Society branch.

Applicants should send their completed forms by post or email to the correspondent. If there is a local branch in the applicant's area, their form will be sent on from the head office to the local branch. If the branch cannot give you a grant for the full amount, and the applicant is not able to make up the difference, they may send the application to the grants team in London or Edinburgh to consider a top-up grant. The teams can also advise on other sources of funding that may be available.

Supporting information from a health and social care professional and evidence of financial circumstances will be required. The website notes that you should allow at least eight weeks for a decision to be made.

Parkinson's UK

£90,000

Correspondent: Sarah Day, Company Secretary, 215 Vauxhall Bridge Road, London SW1V 1EJ (020 7932 1327; email: hello@parkinson's.org.uk; website: www.parkinson's.org.uk)

CC number: 258197

Eligibility

People with Parkinson's disease who are in need. From May 2015, the scheme has been suspended for a review. The Parkinson's UK website states that:

> Our previous model of offering funding didn't reach out to everyone who needed help.
>
> We couldn't promote the fund as widely as we'd like as we didn't want to encourage levels of demand that couldn't be met within the funding available.
>
> We aim to do better and do more in providing financial help.
>
> We also want to consider how we can best harness the potential in our local networks. Any new arrangements need to be fair, transparent and support those people in the most need.
>
> We'll be developing new arrangements in 2016.

Types of grants

The fund previously gave one-off grants to people with Parkinson's through the Mali Jenkins Fund, for purposes such as equipment, home adaptations, respite breaks, professional fees, domestic appliances and other household goods.

Annual grant total

In 2014 the charity had an income of £30.9 million and assets of £13.9 million. Grants to individuals totalled £90,000.

Applications

At the time of writing (October 2015), the charity is not currently accepting applications and will be developing new arrangements in 2016.

Joseph Patrick Trust

£174,000 (142 grants)

Correspondent: Robert Meadowcroft, Correspondent, c/o Muscular Dystrophy Group of Great Britain and Northern Ireland, 61A Southwark Street, London SE1 0BU (020 7803 4800; email: jptgrants@muscular-dystrophy.org; website: www.musculardystrophyuk.org/get-the-right-care-and-support)

CC number: 294475

Eligibility

People with muscular dystrophy or an allied neuromuscular condition.

Types of grants

On average about 150 one-off grants of between £200 and £1,250 are made each year to partially fund the purchase of wheelchairs (powered and manual), scooters, electric beds, trikes, computers, vehicle adaptations, riser chairs, mobile arm supports, portable aids, therapy equipment and so on. Discretionary payments can be made for funeral expenses and other emergencies.

Annual grant total

In 2013/14 the trust held assets of £272,000 and had an income of £79,000. Grants were made to 142 individuals totalling £174,000. Around 45% of the grants were made for wheelchairs.

Exclusions

Grants are not given for: holidays, household adaptations, building works or domestic appliances; equipment which has already been bought; recurring costs (e.g. wheelchair repairs); the purchase or lease of vehicles, vehicle deposits, or maintenance or repair of vehicles. No grants are given outside the UK.

Applications

Application forms are available from the correspondent or to download from the website. Applications can also be completed online but remember to send supporting documentation by post as well.

Completed forms can be submitted directly by the individual or via a third party and should be supported by an assessment and quotation for the equipment requested, confirming the need and suitability of the equipment. The assessment must be carried out by an appropriately qualified professional, such as a physiotherapist, occupational therapist or social worker. The assessment must be on headed paper. For guidance on what to include in the assessment check the trust's website.

Applications are considered six times a year. Grants can only be made payable to the supplier.

Spinal Muscular Atrophy Support UK (formerly known as The Jennifer Trust for Spinal Muscular Atrophy)

£25,000

Correspondent: Doug Henderson, Managing Director, The Jennifer Trust for Spinal Muscular Atrophy, 40 Timothy's Bridge Road, Stratford Enterprise Park, Stratford-upon-Avon CV37 9NW (01789 267520; fax: 01789 268371; email: supportservices@ smasupportuk.org.uk; website: www. smasupportuk.org.uk/information-support)

CC number: 1106815

Eligibility

Individuals diagnosed with any form of Spinal Muscular Atrophy. Note that the charity cannot give grants to people with any other condition.

Types of grants

One-off grants for equipment. The charity's website states the following: 'Items that will be considered are those that will assist people with showering, bathing, hoisting, sleeping or getting around and that will support their physical and psychological well-being and social inclusion.'

Grants do not exceed £2,500 – if the required item costs more than this, the applicant should be able to show that they are able to cover the rest of the cost from other sources of funding.

Annual grant total

In 2014/15 the charity had assets of £284,500 and an income of £690,500. Welfare and equipment grants totalled £13,500.

Exclusions

Grants are not given towards any items that have already been purchased, or any maintenance and insurance costs of equipment. Applicants are expected to have already applied to their local NHS commissioning body for funding if appropriate.

Individuals who have already received a grant from the charity in the previous three years are not eligible.

Applications

Application forms can be downloaded from the charity s website or are available from the correspondent. Forms can be submitted by email or by post. Applications can be made directly by the individual, or by a parent, carer or professional on their behalf. An acknowledgement of the application and an initial indication of eligibility will be given within two weeks, with the final decision made within two to six weeks. If the charity does not currently have funds available, the application will be assessed in the same way and the applicant will be contacted when funds are available.

Stroke Association

£200,000 (926 grants)

Correspondent: Life After Stroke Services, Stroke Association House, 240 City Road, London EC1V 2PR (0303 3033 100; fax: 020 7490 2686; email: grants.external@stroke.org.uk; website: www.stroke.org.uk)

CC number: 211015

Eligibility

People who have had a stroke and are in need. Applicants must have less than £3,000 in savings and their income must not exceed their expenditure by more than £50.

Types of grants

One-off grants of up to £300 to help improve the individual's quality of life. Grants are available towards: specialised respite care or family holidays within the UK; white goods; cooking equipment; energy bills (but not arrears); installation of telephones or other telecommunications; beds and bedding; medical or disability aids; armchairs; driving assessments or lessons; and travel costs for, for example, hospital visits.

Annual grant total

In 2014/15 the charity held assets of £22.5 million and had an income of £24.1 million. According to the charity's impact report for 2014/15, grants totalling £200,000 were given to 926 individuals under the Life After Stroke programme.

Exclusions

The trust will not fund private medical costs; labour costs (other than the installation of white goods) including item removal and structural alteration costs; nursing home fees (other than respite care); computer equipment or televisions; debts; and rent or bills arrears.

Applications

Applications should be made on a form available from a regional correspondent to be completed by a social worker, health professional or Stroke Association staff member on the individual's behalf. Regional correspondent email addresses are listed on the charity's website. Applicants should ask their health or social care professional to contact the association by email using their professional email account to receive an application form. People who are in touch with one of the charity's Life After Stroke services should ask their co-ordinator. Awards are means-tested, taking into account the total household income.

Strongbones Children's Charitable Trust

£118,000

Correspondent: Grants Officer, Unit B9 Romford Seedbed Centre, Davidson Way, Romford RM7 0AZ (01708 750599; email: Trustees@strongbones.org.uk; website: www.strongbones.org.uk)

CC number: 1086173

Eligibility

Young people under the age of 21 with scoliosis, brittle bone disease, bone cancer, arthritis or any other condition of the bone.

Types of grants

One-off grants of around of £250 – £1,000 for medical equipment, mobility aids, sensory equipment, specially adapted wheelchairs and trikes, furniture, computers/software, clothes, social activities, hospital travel and toys.

Annual grant total

In 2013/14 the trust held assets of £71,000 and had an income of £312,000. Grants to individuals totalled £118,000.

Exclusions

Holidays abroad, driving lessons, debts and bills, equipment where there has not been an assessment by an NHS physiotherapist, household appliances and furniture (excluding washing machines/dryers for incontinence).

Applications

Applicants may apply using the trust's online application form. Applications should include details of the child's condition and why a grant is needed. The trust also requires that forms are signed and accompanied by a cover letter from the child's NHS consultant, physiotherapist, GP, school nurse or social worker. Applications for funding for amounts of over £1,000 should be accompanied by a quote. Decisions can take up to three months. Families can only receive one grant in any 12-month period and unsuccessful applicants may re-apply at a later date.

Tuberous Sclerosis Association Benevolent Funds

£5,100

Correspondent: David Vaughan, Trustee, 3 Clos Y Deri, Llanedi, Pontarddulais, Swansea SA4 0XW (email: social@tuberous-sclerosis.org; website: www.tuberous-sclerosis.org)

CC number: 1039549

Eligibility

People in need who have tuberous sclerosis complex and their families and carers. Membership is usually required, forms for which are available to download from the website.

Types of grants

Grants are administered through the TSA Support Fund and can help with home adaptations; household essentials such as washing machines, carpets and flooring; short holidays with family, family visits or days out; or a holiday for a carer. The fund can also help with travel costs for those wishing to attend TSA events or for those needing to attend TSC clinics.

The Janet Medcalf Memorial Award is awarded three times a year, with each awardee receiving £300.

Note the following advice, which is taken from the TSA website: 'The amounts awarded from the Support Fund will vary depending on individual circumstances and needs. Whether your application is successful will depend on the availability of funds, the amount you need and on what you need the money for.'

Annual grant total

In 2013/14 the funds had assets of £3.4 million and an income of £405,000. Grants to individuals totalled £5,100 and were distributed as follows:

Benevolent grants	£3,000
Family days and weekends	£1,200
The Janet Medcalf Memorial Award	£900

Exclusions

The fund cannot help with costs of things that have already been ordered or paid for, recurrent or long-term costs (including living costs and bills) or costs associated with debt. There are no grants available for things which are the responsibility of a statutory service. Applicants must not re-apply within one year of a successful application being made.

Applications

Application forms and monitoring forms are available. Applications should include evidence (photocopies) of any benefits you receive and quotes for the item(s) you wish to purchase. Forms should be returned to your local TCA advisor. A list of advisors is available on the fund's website.

The fund will contact you within three weeks of receipt of application and may request a reference from a health/social care or education professional. The fund aims to notify applicants of a decision within six weeks of receipt.

Note the following from the website: 'We do not want to misinform you at any point so we recommend that your first contact should be from a support group or charity in the country where you live.' If at any point you require assistance to complete your form, your local TSA Adviser can help you.

Visual impairment

Action for Blind People

£7,500 (24 grants)

Correspondent: Anita South, Charity Administrator, Action House, 53 Sandgate Street, London SE15 1LE (020 7635 4800; email: central@ actionforblindpeople.org.uk; website: www.actionforblindpeople.org.uk)

CC number: 205913

Eligibility

People who are registered blind or partially sighted. Applicants will need to show that they have exhausted other funding options. Further guidance is given on the charity's website.

Types of grants

Grant assistance is available to 'facilitate independent living', including for assistive technology (e.g. computer assistive software, video magnifiers and accessible phones) in partnership with RNIB.

Annual grant total

In 2013/14 the charity had assets of £26 million and a total income of £20.4 million. Grants were made to 24 individuals totalling £7,500 which was given in grants to facilitate independent living and provision of assistive technology software.

Exclusions

The applicant must not have received a grant from the charity in the last three years.

Applications

Applications can be made on a form which is available from the website. The charity has a network of Independent Living Co-ordinators who can assist in finding funding and making an application. A list of action areas can be found on the charity's website or by calling 0303 123 9999.

Beacon Centre for the Blind

£500

Correspondent: Phil Thomas, Company Secretary, Wolverhampton Road East, Wolverhampton WV4 6AZ (01902 886781; email: enquiries@beaconvision. org; website: www.beaconvision.org)

CC number: 216092

Eligibility

People who are registered blind or partially sighted and live in the metropolitan boroughs of Dudley (except Halesowen and Stourbridge), Sandwell and Wolverhampton, and part of the South Staffordshire District Council area.

Types of grants

One-off grants of up to a maximum of £250 for specific items or improvements to the home. The charity also aims to facilitate employment opportunities for visually impaired people.

Annual grant total

In 2014/15 the charity had assets of £9.5 million and an income of £2.5 million. Most of the charity's expenditure, which totalled £1.8 million, is spent in relation to service provision. There were seven grants made to individuals totalling almost £1,000 for both social welfare and educational purposes.

Applications

Applications may be made in writing to the correspondent. They should state the degree of vision and age of the applicant as well as their monthly income and expenditure. Applications can be submitted through a social worker or a school, and are considered throughout the year.

Belfast Association for the Blind
See entry on page 207

Blind Children UK (formerly National Blind Children's Society)

£80,000 (47 grants)

Correspondent: Phillippa Caine, Charity Administrator, Hillfields, Reading Road, Burghfield Common, Reading, Berkshire RG7 3YG (0800 781 1444; email:

services@blindchildrenuk.org; website: www.blindchildrenuk.org)

CC number: 1051607

Eligibility

People aged up to 25 years in full-time education who are (or are eligible to be) registered blind or partially sighted and live in the UK.

Types of grants

One-off grants towards IT equipment or sensory/recreational equipment for use in the home or at school to aid with the individual's learning and development, such as computer equipment and software, screen readers or magnifiers, Braille devices, multi-sensory toys, resonance boards and so on. While there is no minimum or maximum amount available per application, only one item per applicant will be considered.

Annual grant total

In 2014 the society had assets of £4.7 million and an income of £1.9 million. Direct charitable expenditure on the Access Technology programme totalled £99,000, of which we estimate around £80,000 was given in grants to individuals. 70 applications for equipment were processed, with 47 fully funded. The charity has an annual budget of around £100,000 for grants to individuals.

Applications

In the first instance, contact the charity to discuss the child's needs. The Access Technology advisors can carry out a technology assessment in person or over the phone to help children and young people and their families to choose the right technology for their needs.

Blind Veterans UK

£1.17 million

Correspondent: Membership Department, 12–14 Harcourt Street, London W1H 4HD (0800 389 7979; email: enquiries@blindveterans.org.uk; website: www.blindveterans.org.uk)

CC number: 216227

Eligibility

Eligibility for membership takes into account both military service and sight loss.

All applicants must have served at any time in the Regular or Reserve UK Armed Forces (including National Service), or in the Merchant Navy during World War Two, or in the Polish/Indian Forces under British Command.

The trust uses its own criteria for the level of sight loss required to receive help and the charity's doctors will assess this. The website advises that 'it doesn't

matter how or when your sight loss was caused, or whether you were on active service at the time'.

Types of grants

Grants are given to allow applicants to develop their independence by a combination of training, rehabilitation, holiday and respite care. An annual support grant is given to all beneficiaries and further assistance is available for specific needs such as for: help in the garden; a domestic help allowance; healthcare needs; nursing home fees; specialist equipment; computers and other technology including reading aids; and mobility support. The charity will also help with retraining and employability issues.

Annual grant total

In 2013/14 the charity held assets of over £149 million and had an income of £27 million. A total of about £22.8 million was spent in charitable activities. The annual report states that, under the charity's welfare activities for the year, '4,293 grant transactions were completed for 1,541 beneficiaries' at a total cost of £1.17 million.

Exclusions

The charity can only assist those with a severe level of sight loss.

Applications

Application forms are available on the charity's website or from the correspondent. There is also a form on the website which allows potential applicants to request a call back from the charity for further information. Applications must include details of the applicant's service (including service number and dates of service) and details of their ophthalmic consultant. On receipt the trust will contact the respective service office and ophthalmic consultant for reports. The process can take about ten weeks.

All applicants are encouraged to get in touch with the charity to discuss their needs (Freephone 0800 389 7979).

BlindAid

£25,000 (92 grants)

Correspondent: Grant Co-ordinator, Lantern House, 102 Bermondsey Street, London SE1 3UB (020 7403 6184; fax: 020 7234 0708; email: enquiries@ blindaid.org.uk; website: www.blindaid. org.uk)

CC number: 262119

Eligibility

Blind and partially sighted people aged 18 and over who live on a permanent basis in one of the 12 central London boroughs or the City of London and

who are in receipt of means-tested benefits, with a preference for those registered blind/partially sighted.

Types of grants

One-off grants typically of up to £300 towards: computer equipment; equipment and gadgets, including talking clocks, big button phones, colour detectors, talking mobile phones and talking microwaves; and domestic items.

Annual grant total

In 2014 the charity had assets of £4.8 million and an income of £567,000. Grants to over 92 individuals totalled £25,000 and were broken down as follows:

General purpose	£23,500
Small grants	£1,500

A further £7,500 was awarded in grants to organisations.

Exclusions

Blind aid does not make grants for the following purposes: payment of outstanding debts; non-essential furniture or home goods; payment of council tax or mortgage/rent arrears; legal fees for insolvency/bankruptcy; utility bills or other household bills (including Internet connection); deposit payments for rented or leased accommodation; garden fencing or clearing; home modifications/ adaptations; educational or occupational training; medical treatment/alternative therapies; funeral expenses; removal expenses; motor vehicle purchase or maintenance; fines or arrears; pest control; fixtures or fittings (including carpets, curtains and blinds); or holidays.

Applications

There is an online application process. You may also apply on a form which is available to download or from the correspondent. Applications should be made through a third party such as a social worker or through an organisation such as Citizens Advice or other welfare agency. A supporting letter may be attached to explain the background to the case, although this is not mandatory. The trustees try to process applications within 28 days. A full list of guidelines is available to download from the website.

Only one application per person/ household can be considered in any two-year period.

Note: The trustees are no longer able to offer grants towards holidays.

Colchester Blind Society

£6,000

Correspondent: Marilyn Theresa Peck, Trustee, Kestrels, Harwich Road, Beaumont, Clacton-on-Sea, Essex CO16 0AU (01255 862062; email: info@ colchesterblindsociety.org.uk; website: www.colchesterblindsociety.org.uk/index. html)

CC number: 207361

Eligibility

People who are blind or sight impaired and live in the borough of Colchester.

Types of grants

One-off or recurrent grants according to need.

Annual grant total

In 2013/14 the society had an income of £9,500 and a total expenditure of £8,100. We estimate that the amount of grants given to individuals totalled £6,000.

Applications

Apply in writing to the correspondent.

Charity of John McKie Elliott Deceased (The John McKie Elliot Trust for the Blind)

£6,700

Correspondent: Robert Walker, Trustee, 6 Manor House Road, Newcastle upon Tyne NE2 2LU (0191 281 4657; email: bobwalker9@aol.com)

CC number: 235075

Eligibility

People who are blind or have a visual impairment and live in Gateshead or Newcastle upon Tyne.

Types of grants

One-off and repeated grants can be given according to need for specific equipment, items or services.

Annual grant total

In 2014 the charity had an income of £900 and an unusually high total expenditure of £13,700. In the past five years the charity's total spending increased from zero in 2010 to £13,700 in 2014. Grants are made to individuals for both social welfare and educational purposes. We estimate that social welfare grants amounted to £6,500.

Applications

Apply in writing to the correspondent.

Gardner's Trust for the Blind

£33,000 (70+ grants)

Correspondent: Angela Stewart, 117 Charterhouse Street, London EC1M 6AA (020 7253 3757)

CC number: 207233

Eligibility

Registered blind or partially sighted people who live in the UK.

Types of grants

One-off grants for household items. The trust also gives grants in the form of pensions.

Annual grant total

In 2013/14 the trust had assets of £3.5 million and an income of £85,000. Grants to individuals, for both social welfare and educational purposes, totalled £52,500 and were distributed as follows:

Annual grants (paid quarterly to, on average, 36 recipients)	£23,500
Education and trade grants	£19,100
General aid grants	£9,400
Music grants	£100

Exclusions

Our research indicates that no grants are made for holidays, or residential or nursing home fees. Grants are not given for loans.

Applications

Apply in writing to the correspondent. Applications can be submitted either directly by the individual or by a third party, but they must also be supported by a third party who can confirm that the applicant has a disability and that the grant is needed. They are considered in March, June, September and December and should be submitted at least three weeks before the meeting.

The Halifax Society for the Blind

£4,500

Correspondent: Lindsay Dyson, Manager, Halifax Society for the Blind, 34 Clare Road, Halifax, West Yorkshire HX1 2HX (01422 352383; email: halifaxblindsociety@gmail.com)

CC number: 224258

Eligibility

People in need who are registered blind or partially sighted and live in Calderdale. Applicants should have savings of no more than £4,000 and a disposable household weekly income of no more than £120 (after paying rent/ mortgage, council tax and utilities bills).

Types of grants

One-off grants of cash of up to £250 or equipment according to need. Grants have been given towards beds, school equipment, televisions and decorating costs.

Annual grant total

In 2013/14 the society held assets of £1.7 million and had an income of £127,000. Grants to individuals totalled £5,200.

Applications

Application forms for a grant are available from the correspondent and can be submitted when they are supported by a social worker or a rehabilitation officer. Members can also self-refer by discussing their needs with the HSB manager. Applications are considered on a regular basis.

The Anne Herd Memorial Trust

£12,500

Correspondent: The Trustees, 27 Bank Street, Dundee DD1 1RP

OSCR number: SC014198

Eligibility

People who are blind or partially sighted who live in Broughty Ferry. Applicants from the City of Dundee, region of Tayside or those who have connections with these areas and reside in Scotland will also be considered.

Types of grants

Grants are usually given for educational equipment such as computers and books. Grants are usually at least £50.

Annual grant total

In 2013/14 the trust's income (£120,500) and total expenditure (£122,500) were both unusually high. Our research suggests that the trust usually gives approximately £25,000 a year in grants for education and welfare. We estimate that grants for social welfare purposes total around £12,500.

Applications

Applications can be made in writing to the correspondent. They can be submitted directly by the individual in March/April for consideration in June.

The Kingston upon Thames Association for the Blind

£8,000

Correspondent: Della Murphy, KAB Office, Kingston Association for the Blind, Adams House, Dickerage Lane,

New Malden, Surrey KT3 3SF (020 8605 0060; email: kingstonassoc@btconnect. com; website: www. kingstonassociationforblind.org)

CC number: 249295

Eligibility

Blind and partially sighted people who live in the Royal Borough of Kingston upon Thames.

Types of grants

One-off grants of £50 to £2,000 towards the cost of holidays, travel expenses, white goods, furniture, household repairs, computers and aids like EasyReader.

Annual grant total

In 2013/14 the association held assets of £248,500 and had an income of £94,000. We estimate that around £8,000 was made in grants to individuals.

Applications

Application forms are available from the office or can be downloaded from the charity's website. If the applicant is not in receipt of income support, housing benefit, or family credit they will need to provide detailed financial circumstances. Applications are considered every other month from January onwards.

Open Sight

£8,500

Correspondent: Charity Administrator, 25 Church Road, Eastleigh, Hampshire SO50 6BL (023 8064 1244; email: info@ opensight.org.uk; website: www. opensight.org.uk)

CC number: 1055498

Eligibility

People who are visually impaired, in need and live in Hampshire, excluding the cities of Portsmouth and Southampton.

Types of grants

One-off grants of up to £500 each to aid independent living for eligible people, for example towards special equipment, aids to daily living, holiday costs and costs incurred when moving into independent living.

Annual grant total

In 2013/14 the charity had assets of £677,500 and an income of £511,500. Grants totalled £17,000. We estimate that the amount of grants given to individuals for welfare purposes totalled £8,500.

Exclusions

No grants are given for educational purposes or to groups.

Applications

Applicants should first contact the charity to be put in touch with one of their Independent Living Advisors.

The Royal Blind Society for the UK

£18,000

Correspondent: Eileen Harding, 56–61 Sea Lane, Rustington, Littlehampton, West Sussex BN16 2RQ (01903 245379; email: eileen.harding@ royalblindsociety.org; website: www. royalblindsociety.org)

CC number: 1131623

Eligibility

People who are registered blind or partially sighted and on a low income.

Types of grants

General grants are provided to blind and partially sighted people on low incomes for a wide range of purposes.

Annual grant total

In 2014 the trust held assets of £624,000 and an income of £1.1 million. Grants to individuals totalled £1,500.

The society also provided holidays and breaks for more than 2,400 beneficiaries, with £1.1 million spent providing breaks over 15 months.

Applications

Application forms are available from the correspondent or can be downloaded from the website. Applications must be submitted through a professional welfare worker who knows the applicant well, for example a social worker or similar welfare advisor. They are considered on a quarterly basis. The society offers informal advice on the application process and applicants should contact the grants co-ordinator on 01903 245379 for assistance.

The Royal National Institute of Blind People (RNIB)

£60,000

Correspondent: Grants Team, Information Resource Team, RNIB, 105 Judd Street, London WC1H 9NE (Helpline: 0303 123 9999; email: InfoResourceTeam@rnib.org.uk.; website: www.rnib.org.uk)

CC number: 226227

Eligibility

Registered or certified blind and partially sighted people who live in the UK and receive a means-tested benefit (excluding tax credits). Applicants must have been rejected for funding by their local authority for the items needed and must have savings of less than £6,000.

Types of grants

One-off grants are awarded for the following purposes only, as listed on the charity's website:

- computer accessibility software: magnification software or combined magnifier reader software, Dolphin Guide and upgrades to these. We don't currently offer grants for JAWS as this costs much more than our maximum limit and there are free alternatives (such as NVDA)
- computer dictation software (£80 maximum for Windows versions, £125 maximum for Mac versions)
- voice recorders and dictaphones (£70 maximum)
- portable and TV video magnifiers (£400 maximum)
- talking kitchen equipment including talking microwaves
- talking watches, clocks and radios (£60 maximum)
- RNIB's PenFriend 2 labelling device
- talking colour detectors (£60 maximum)
- the Alto 2 talking mobile phone (or £145 towards the cost of another talking phone or accessible smartphone)
- big button or talking landline telephones (£100 maximum)

A maximum of £500 will be given for the total value of items requested. Applicants should check the RNIB website for further details.

Annual grant total

Grants to individuals usually total around £60,000 per year.

Exclusions

Emergency grants are not available. No grants are given for recreational needs, educational costs, nursing home fees, the costs of medical treatment, telephone installation, employment needs or repeatedly accruing debts. Successful applicants cannot re-apply within three years.

Applications

Application forms are available to download from the website. Applications must be supported by a professional, such as a social worker, occupational therapist, health care visitor or a worker from a local society for the blind, who knows the personal circumstances of the applicant. Applicants must not use a GP, family member or friend as their support. Applications are considered throughout the year.

Note: if the total amount required exceeds the maximum grant amount (£500) then the rest of the funding must be secured before an application to RNIB is submitted.

The Surrey Association for Visual Impairment

£2,500

Correspondent: Bob Hughes, Chief Executive, Rentwood, School Lane, Fetcham, Leatherhead, Surrey KT22 9JX (01372 377701; fax: 01372 360767; email: info@sightforsurrey.org.uk; website: www.surreywebsight.org.uk)

CC number: 1121949

Eligibility

People who are blind or partially sighted and who live in the administrative county of Surrey.

Types of grants

Small, one-off grants are given when absolutely necessary. Grants are usually to help pay for equipment required to overcome a sight problem or a sudden domestic need. Applications from service users for small, interest-free loans are also occasionally considered.

Annual grant total

In 2013/14 the association had an income of £1.6 million and a total expenditure of £1.7 million. Full accounts were not available to view at the time of writing. The charity sets aside a budget of £5,000 each year for grants to individuals, clubs and classes, so we estimate that the amount of grants given to individuals totalled around £2,500.

Applications

Application forms are available from the correspondent. Applications can be submitted at any time by the individual or through a social worker, welfare agency, club or any recognised organisation for blind or partially sighted people.

The Swansea and District Friends of the Blind

£5,000

Correspondent: John Allan, Secretary, 3 De La Beche Street, Swansea SA1 3EY (01792 655424; email: allan.john@btconnect.com)

CC number: 211343

Eligibility

People who are registered blind and live in Swansea.

Types of grants

One-off grants which in the past have gone towards visual impairment aids such as talking watches, computers and the like. Gifts are also distributed at Christmas and Easter.

Annual grant total

In 2013/14 the trust had an income of £7,500 and a total expenditure of £59,000. We estimate that through the distribution of welfare grants, Christmas and Easter gifts, the organisation gave around £5,000 to individuals in need.

Applications

Apply in writing to the correspondent. Applications are considered on a regular basis.

Visual Impairment Breconshire (Nam Gweledol Sir Brycheiniog)

£1,000

Correspondent: Michael Knee, Secretary, 3 Beacons View, Mount Street, Brecon, Powys LD3 7LY (01874 624949; email: vibrecon@gmail.com; website: www.visualimpairment.breconshire.powys.org.uk)

CC number: 217377

Eligibility

People who have permanent and incurable eye conditions who live in Breconshire.

Types of grants

One-off grants are given for equipment or aids, services and experiences (such as holidays). The need for the grant must be related to the individual's visual impairment.

Annual grant total

In 2014/15 the charity had an income of £2,600 and a total expenditure of £3,500. We estimate that social welfare grants to individuals totalled around £1,000.

Exclusions

In general, the charity will not pay for anything that should be funded by the NHS or a local authority. Nor will it contribute towards the rental of book reading equipment and corresponding library subscriptions, or any equipment for use in care homes and similar organisations where there exists a statutory obligation or requirement to provide for client use.

Applications

Application forms, along with guidelines, are available to download from the website. They can be submitted directly by the individual, or by their relatives or carers.

Armed forces charities

Unlike other charities which are associated with occupations, the armed forces charities have been given their own section in this guide as there are many more relevant charities and they can support a large number of people. This branch of the sector is committed to helping anyone who has at least one day's paid service in any of the armed forces, including reserves and those who undertook National Service, and their husbands, wives, children, widows, widowers and other dependants.

These charities are exceptionally well organised. Much of this is due to the work of SSAFA, which has an extensive network of trained caseworkers around the country who act on behalf of SSAFA and other service charities. Many of the charities in this section use the same application procedures as SSAFA and assist a specified group of people within the service/ex-service community, while others (such as The Royal British Legion) have their own procedures and support the services as a whole.

Many service benevolent funds rely on trained SSAFA volunteer caseworkers to prepare applications, although some do have their own volunteers. Alternatively, some funds ask applicants to write to a central correspondent. In such cases, applicants may wish to follow the guidelines in the article 'How to make an application' on page xxii. Most entries in this section state whether the applicant should apply directly to the charity or through a caseworker. If in doubt, the applicant should ring up the charity concerned or the local SSAFA office.

Some people prefer to approach their, or their former spouse's, regimental or corps association. Many of them have their own charitable funds and volunteers, especially in their own recruiting areas. In other cases they will work through one of the volunteer networks mentioned above. Again, if in doubt or difficulty, the applicant should contact the regimental/corps association or local SSAFA office.

SSAFA is much more than just a provider of financial assistance. It also offers advice, support and training. It can assist members of the armed forces community on many issues, ranging from how to replace lost medals to advice on adoption. Its website (www.ssafa.org.uk) provides a wide range of information and useful links for members of the community.

Individuals connected to the armed forces should also refer to DSC's Armed Forces Charities website (www.armedforcescharities.org.uk). The website is an independent and comprehensive armed forces charity resource, created by DSC. The website contains information relevant to past or present serving members of the UK armed forces; family members or dependants; or organisations working with the UK armed forces. This free-to-access online resource allows users to search for relevant welfare support including grants, housing or other general advice and support provided by charities for the armed forces community.

ABF The Soldiers' Charity (also known as The Army Benevolent Fund)

£3.7 million (4,949 grants)

Correspondent: The Welfare Team, Mountbarrow House, 6–20 Elizabeth Street, London SW1W 9RB (020 7901 8900; fax: 020 7901 8901; email: info@ soldierscharity.org; website: www. soldierscharity.org)

CC number: 1146420

Eligibility

Members and ex-members of the British Regular Army and the Reserve Army (TA) and their dependants who are in need. Serving TA soldiers must have completed at least one year's satisfactory service, and former TA soldiers should have completed at least three years' satisfactory service.

Types of grants

Grants are awarded by the charity in seven broad areas: annuities; care home fees; bursaries (see this guide's sister publication *The Guide to Educational Grants*); holiday schemes for families under stress; special funds; general needs (grants for a wide variety of purposes which are not available from other sources, for example mobility aids such as stair-lifts); Current Operations Fund.

Annual grant total

In 2013/14 the charity had assets of £45.6 million and an income of £14.5 million. Grants totalled £7.9 million, £5 million of which was given to individuals. We estimate that the amount of grants given to individuals for educational and training purposes were awarded in the form of Individual Recovery Plan grants totalling £460,000, and for Specialist Employment Consultants totalling £847,000. This leaves £3.7 million we believe was given to individuals for social welfare purposes: £3.4 million in routine grants and the remaining £279,000 in grants from the Quick Reaction Fund (QRF).

Applications

The fund does not deal directly with individual cases. Soldiers who are still serving should contact their regimental or corps association, who will then approach the fund on their behalf. Former soldiers should first contact SSAFA or The Royal British Legion. Applications are considered at any time, but all are reviewed annually in July.

Enquiries may be made directly to the fund to determine the appropriate corps or regimental association. See also, in particular, the entries for SSAFA and The Royal British Legion.

Other information

During the year, around 23% of grants expenditure to individuals was to serving soldiers. ABF also made grants to other charities working to support service and ex-service personnel, with a focus on the following areas: care for older people; mental health and respite care; homelessness; supported housing; and education, training for employment and welfare support.

AJEX Charitable Foundation

£76,000

Correspondent: Ivan Phineas Sugarman, Trustee, Shield House, Harmony Way, Hendon, London NW4 2BZ (020 8202 2323; fax: 020 8202 9900; email: headoffice@ajex.org.uk; website: www. ajex.org.uk)

CC number: 1082148

Eligibility

Jewish ex-servicemen and women, and their dependants, who are in need.

Types of grants

One-off and recurrent grants are given according to need. Special grants are also made to cover emergencies and exceptional circumstances. Examples of special grants include the cost of stair-lifts and electric motor scooters.

Annual grant total

In 2014 the foundation held assets of £1.7 million and had an income of £123,500. Welfare grants and expenses totalled £76,000.

Applications

Application forms are available from the correspondent and should be returned directly by the individual or through a third party. Evidence of service in the British army and of Jewish religious status is required.

Other information

The foundation's website provides the following information: AJEX – The Association of Jewish Ex-Servicemen and Women spans some 80 years. Its membership includes over 4,000 individuals who served in the British Army, either during or after the Second World War.

In the 21st century, AJEX has a very important role, focusing on three main areas: remembrance for the sacrifices of the past; help for those in need in the present; and education for the future.

Blind Veterans UK
See entry on page 74

Blesma

£408,500 (1,099 grants)

Correspondent: Linda Williams, Membership Grants Assistant, 185–187 High Road, Chadwell Heath, Romford, Essex RM6 6NA (020 8590 1124; fax: 020 8599 2932; email: chadwellheath@blesma.org; website: www.blesma.org)

CC number: 1084189

Eligibility

Serving and ex-serving members of HM or auxiliary forces who have lost a limb or eye or have a permanent loss of speech, hearing or sight, and their widows/widowers.

Types of grants

One-off and recurrent grants towards, for example, wheelchairs and scooters, stair-lifts, car adaptations, gardening costs or home redecorating.

Annual grant total

In 2014 the association had an income of £3.2 million and assets of £23 million. 1,099 welfare grants were made to individuals totalling £408,500.

Exclusions

The charity does not generally issue grants for prosthetic limbs, as this should be covered by NHS provision.

Applications

Application forms are available from the correspondent. Applications can be submitted at any time, either directly by the individual or through their local Blesma representative, SSAFA, Citizens Advice or similar welfare agency.

Other information

The association provides permanent residential and respite accommodation through its residential care home in Blackpool, as well as organising a range of activities for members. Blesma also offers advice and support to members on a range of issues.

The Burma Star Association

£109,500 (215 grants)

Correspondent: Glynis Longhurst, Correspondent, 34 Grosvenor Gardens, London SW1W 0DH (020 7823 4273; email: burmastar@btconnect.com; website: www.burmastar.org.uk)

CC number: 1043040

Eligibility

People who were awarded the Burma Star Campaign Medal (or the Pacific Star with Burma clasp) during the Second World War, and their immediate dependants, who live in the UK, Republic of Ireland or other Commonwealth country.

Types of grants

One-off grants usually in the range of £200 to £1,000 towards: top-up fees for nursing, care and residential homes; respite care and holidays; domestic goods; debts; disability aids; funeral expenses; repairs and adaptations; travel costs; mobility aids and so on.

Annual grant total

In 2014 the association had assets of £821,500 and an income of £124,500. Grants to 235 individuals totalled around £109,500 and can be broken down as follows:

Nursing and residential homes	£68,500
Repairs	£17,500
Debts	£7,600
Stair-lifts and riser-recliner chairs	£5,300
Wheelchairs/electric personal vehicles	£3,300
Personal aids	£2,800
Household goods	£2,400
Communication aids	£2,000

Exclusions

No grants are available towards private medical treatment, headstones or plaques. The association does not give loans.

Applications

On an application form available from the correspondent or a local branch officer. Applications can be made by the individual or through a third party. They should either be sent directly to the correspondent or submitted via branches of the association or other ex-service organisations. Grants are made through the local branches, SSAFA, The Royal British Legion or other ex-service organisations after investigation and completion of an application form giving full particulars of circumstances and eligibility (including service particulars verifying the award of the Burma Star). Applications are considered throughout the year.

Other information

The association has 73 branches across the UK and seven overseas which offer support and advice to their local members and make small grants where possible. The contact details for local branch officers can be obtained from the correspondent.

W. J. and Mrs C. G. Dunnachie's Charitable Trust

£80,000

Correspondent: The Trustees, W. J. and Mrs C. G. Dunnachie's Charitable Trust, c/o Low Beaton Richmond, Sterling House, 20 Renfield Street, Glasgow G2 5AP (0141 221 8931; email: murdoch@lbr-city.demon.co.uk)

OSCR number: SC015981

Eligibility

People who are in poor health or who have a disability as a result of their service during the Second World War.

Types of grants

One-off and recurrent grants are given according to need.

Annual grant total

In 2013/14 the trust had an income of £84,000 and a total expenditure of £89,500. We estimate that the amount of grants given to individuals totalled £80,000.

Applications

Apply in writing to the correspondent at any time. Most applications are submitted via SSAFA or through a regimental association.

Help for Heroes

£450,000

Correspondent: Grants Team, 14 Parker's Close, Downton Business Park, Downton, Salisbury, Wiltshire SP5 3RB (01980 844354; email: grants@helpforheroes.org.uk; website: www.helpforheroes.org.uk)

CC number: 1120920, SC044984

Eligibility

Current and former members of the armed forces who have suffered a life-changing injury or illness while serving, or as a result of their service, and their dependants.

Types of grants

Immediate financial support is given through the Quick Reaction Fund (QRF). The website states that the QRF 'can essentially be used for anything that alleviates the distress caused by injury or illness'. Examples include equipment to improve home accessibility, travel costs and sporting equipment to support recovery. The QRF is delivered directly by Help for Heroes or through the services' own charities and, in urgent cases, aims to provide support within 72 hours.

Annual grant total

In 2013/14 the charity had assets of £111.3 million and an income of £37.2 million. The annual report and accounts for 2013/14 state: 'In 2014 Help for Heroes gave 936 grants to individuals with awards totalling £0.9m, and granted over £4 million in 2014 to other charities and organisations that work alongside us to support our beneficiaries.' We estimate that grants given to individuals for social welfare purposes totalled around £450,000.

Applications

Candidates are encouraged to contact the correspondent to discuss their needs and application procedure.

Other information

The charity works with the armed forces and other military charities. Funding is also given for training and educational needs and to organisations working for the benefit of members of the armed forces.

Individuals and their families or carers are welcome visit one of the 'support hubs' to receive further advice and support on a range of welfare issues. For more details and contact information of the recovery centres see the charity's website.

Huddersfield and District Army Veterans' Association Benevolent Fund

£9,900

Correspondent: Sarah Lamont, Correspondent, 10 Belton Grove, Huddersfield HD3 3RF (01484 310193)

CC number: 222286

Eligibility

Veterans of the Royal Navy, the Army and the Royal Air Force who are in need, aged over 60 years, and who were discharged from the forces 'with good character' and live in Huddersfield and part of Brighouse.

Types of grants

One-off and recurrent grants are given according to need.

Annual grant total

In 2014 the fund had an income of £28,500 and a total expenditure of £22,500. Grants to individuals totalled £9,900.

Applications

Apply in writing to the correspondent, or on a form published in the fund's applications leaflet. The leaflet is available from doctors' surgeries, local libraries and so on.

Other information

The fund also provides social activities and trips to members of the forces in the Huddersfield area, spending £5,500 for this purpose in 2014. It also has a welfare officer who can provide assistance with health and family problems and advice regarding funeral arrangements.

Lloyd's Patriotic Fund

£47,000 (100+ grants)

Correspondent: The Secretary, Lloyd's Patriotic Fund, Lloyd's, One Lime Street, London EC3M 7HA (020 7327 6144; email: communityaffairs@lloyds.com; website: www.lloyds.com/lpf)

CC number: 210173

Eligibility

Ex-servicemen and women of the Royal Navy, the Army, Royal Marines and Royal Air Force who are in need, and their dependants.

Types of grants

One-off grants, on average of about £300, can be given for essential domestic items, electric wheelchairs, home adaptations and exceptional expenses. In deserving cases grants may also be given for debt relief and help with utility bills.

Annual grant total

In 2013/14 the fund had assets of £3 million and an income of £399,500. The fund supports the welfare of individuals by making grants to organisations and through SSAFA. During the year, £40,000 was paid to SSAFA to assist individuals with essential items and equipment, and a further £6,900 was paid for annuities.

Exclusions

Note that new annuity payments are no longer considered. Existing recipients will continue to be assisted.

Applications

Applications should be made through the local SSAFA branch.

Other information

Grants are also given for educational purposes (in 2013/14 a total of £7,500 was given).

The fund works with SSAFA and other partners through which funds are administered. Various military organisations are supported, with a particular focus on those helping people who have disabilities or individuals facing poverty, illness and hardship.

The Nash Charity

£15,000

Correspondent: Clare Brennan, Peachey and Co., 95 Aldwych, London WC2B 4JF (020 7316 5200; email: cmb@peachey.co.uk)

CC number: 229447

Eligibility

Ex-service personnel who have been wounded or disabled during wartime.

Types of grants

Grants are usually paid through social services, Citizens Advice or other welfare agencies to purchase specific items.

Annual grant total

In 2013/14 the charity had an income of £13,500 and a total expenditure of £11,400. We estimate that grants totalled around £10,000.

Applications

Apply in writing to the correspondent at any time. Applications can be submitted directly by the individual or through an appropriate third party.

The Not Forgotten Association

£730,500 (10,500 grants)

Correspondent: Referral agencies, see 'Applications', 4th Floor, 2 Grosvenor Gardens, London SW1W 0DH (020 7730 2400; fax: 020 7730 0020; email: info@nfassociation.org; website: www.nfassociation.org)

CC number: 1150541

Eligibility

This charity supports service and ex-service men and women who have disabilities or who are suffering from some form of ill health. Applicants must have served in the armed forces of the Crown (or merchant navy during hostilities).

Types of grants

The association does not give financial grants direct to applicants; rather it gives help in kind in the following areas: televisions and licences for those with restricted mobility or who are otherwise largely housebound; holidays for both groups and individuals (accompanied by carers if required); and day outings to events and places of interest. The association is now including more activity and adventure breaks and outings, in light of more recent military conflicts.

Annual grant total

For the 15-month period ended March 2014, the association had an income of £1.1 million and a total expenditure of £1.3 million. Assistance to 10,500 individuals totalled £730,500 and was distributed as follows:

Holidays	£270,000
Entertainment	£187,000
Televisions	£99,500
Outings	£69,000

Exclusions

The association cannot help wives, widows or families (unless they are themselves ex-members of the forces or they are acting as carers).

Applications

Applications should be submitted through SSAFA, The Royal British Legion, Combat Stress or the Welfare Service of the Service Personnel and Veterans' Agency. These agencies will complete the common application form on behalf of the applicant and then make the appropriate recommendation to the association, with the applicant's income and expenditure details and degree of disability. Applications are considered throughout the year. Successful applicants may re-apply after three years.

Other information

The association organises two flagship events for war pensioners – its annual garden party at Buckingham Palace and a Christmas party at St James's Palace. The association is now a charitable limited company with a new registration number: 1150541. The unincorporated association has now wound up and been removed from the Central Register of Charities.

The Officers' Association

£1.61 million (604 grants)

Correspondent: Kathy Wallis, Benevolence Department, 1st Floor, Mountbarrow House, 6–20 Elizabeth Street, London SW1W 9RB (02078084160; email: k.wallis@officersassociation.org.uk; website: www.officersassociation.org.uk)

CC number: 201321

Eligibility

Officers who have held a commission in HM Forces, their widows and dependants. Officers on the active list will normally be helped only with resettlement and employment.

Types of grants

Grants fall into two main areas: regular allowances, predominantly for elderly beneficiaries on low incomes, and one-off grants towards specific items such as disability equipment. In addition, the Officers Association provides grants to bridge the gap between the fees charged for residential care and the funds that the individual can provide from personal, family and/or local authority sources.

Limited assistance may be given for education or training needs in exceptional circumstances.

Annual grant total

In 2013/14 the association had assets of £16.8 million and an income of £2.9 million. Grants were made to individuals totalling £1.6 million and were given almost exclusively for relief-in-need purposes. During the year, 458 beneficiaries received one-off payments; some of these beneficiaries also received regular help. One-off grants accounted for 52% of the total expended. The Officers Association also assisted 146 beneficiaries in 25 countries in 2013/14.

Applications

Application forms are available from the Benevolence Secretary or can be downloaded from the website. Applications can be submitted either directly by the individual or via a third party. The association has a network of honorary representatives throughout the UK who will normally visit the applicant to discuss their problems and offer advice.

Other information

The association provides a series of advice leaflets on finding accommodation in residential care or nursing homes, how to get financial assistance and how to find short-term convalescence accommodation and sheltered accommodation for older people who have disabilities. It also has an employment department to help ex-officers up to the age of 60 find suitable employment. This service is open to officers just leaving the services and to those who have lost their civilian jobs.

The association has an informative website.

For applicants in Scotland, see the next entry for the Officers' Association Scotland.

Officers' Association Scotland

£107,500 (108 grants)

Correspondent: Laura Darling, Welfare Services Administrator, New Haig House, Logie Green Road, Edinburgh EH7 4HR (0131 550 1575/1581; fax: 0131 557 5819; email: oasadmin@ oascotland.org.uk; website: www. oascotland.org.uk)

OSCR number: SC010665

Eligibility

Those 'who have held a Sovereign's Commission with embodied service in HM Naval, Military or Air Forces' who are in need, and their dependants. Ex-officers who were commissioned into the Reserve, Auxiliary, or Territorial Forces are also eligible. Applicants must be resident in Scotland at the time of their initial application, have been members of a Scottish regiment or intend to settle in Scotland.

Types of grants

Recurrent grants and one-off grants, which in the past have been used to fund

purposes such as home repairs, respite breaks, mobility aids and so on.

Annual grant total

In 2014/15 the association had assets of £6.8 million and an income of £279,000. Grants to individuals totalled £107,500, including £85,000 in annual payments to 53 beneficiaries, and £20,500 in one-off awards to 25 individuals.

Applications

Potential beneficiaries can contact the correspondent to discuss eligibility. Alternatively, applications can be initiated by sending your personal and service details to the association via the online contact form on the association's website, by email or in writing. Applications are passed to the local SSAFA branch which will contact you to progress the application.

Other information

The association runs a friendship visits programme to provide company for retired officers and their dependants who are feeling isolated.

It also offers support and advice to officers who are making the transition from service to civilian employment and for the rest of their working lives.

Poppyscotland (The Earl Haig Fund Scotland)

£775,000

Correspondent: The Trustees, New Haig House, Logie Green Road, Edinburgh EH7 4HR (0131 557 2782; fax: 0131 557 5819; email: enquiries@poppyscotland. org.uk; website: www.poppyscotland.org. uk)

OSCR number: SC014096

Eligibility

People in Scotland who have served in the UK armed forces (regular or reserve) and their widows/widowers and dependants.

Types of grants

Annual and one-off grants to overcome financial difficulties of varying complexity. Grant recipients are also given advice and support.

Annual grant total

In 2013/14 the fund had an income of £4.3 million and assets of £9.5 million. Grants made to individuals totalled £775,000.

Exclusions

Grants are not normally given towards non-priority debt, headstones or the replacement of medals. Loans are not available.

Applications

Apply in writing to the correspondent.

Other information

Other services provided by Poppyscotland include respite breaks in partnership with The Royal British Legion, as well as services and programmes to support veterans into employment. The charity also collaborates with Citizens Advice Scotland to run the Armed Services Advice Project, offering advice to armed forces veterans on a wide range of issues such as finance, housing, employment, health and benefits. The charity spent a total of £2.1 million on welfare services in 2013/14.

Poppyscotland is in many respects the Scottish equivalent of the benevolence department of The Royal British Legion in the rest of Britain. Like the Legion, it runs the Poppy Appeal, which is a major source of income to help those in need.

In 2006 the Earl Haig Fund Scotland launched a new identity – Poppyscotland – and is now generally known by this name.

The Royal British Legion

£11.1 million

Correspondent: Welfare Services, 199 Borough High Street, London SE1 1AA (Helpline: 0808 802 8080 (8am–8pm, seven days a week); email: info@britishlegion.org.uk; website: www. britishlegion.org.uk)

CC number: 219279

Eligibility

Serving and ex-serving members of the armed forces and their wives, partners, widows, children and other dependants in England, Wales, Ireland and any country overseas (for Scotland see the previous entry: Poppyscotland (The Earl Haig Fund Scotland).

Types of grants

Following a standard assessment of the beneficiary's financial situation, the Legion makes grants to individuals, either financial or by the provision of goods or services. Grants can be given for any purpose within the scope of the Royal Charter, which governs the Legion. Financial assistance offered by the Legion includes an Immediate Needs Scheme, help for homelessness and a Property Repair Loan Scheme.

Annual grant total

In 2013/14 the charity held assets of £286.2 million and had an income of £133.5 million. Welfare grants to individuals totalled £11.1 million.

There has been around a £3 million drop in grant-making from the level of giving in 2012/13. According to the annual report: 'In 2014, we spent £11 million on individual grants (2013: £14.2 million). The cost of these grants has reduced, reflecting the move towards a new model of personalised advice and support for beneficiaries.'

Exclusions

No assistance is given with business debts, legal expenses, loans or medical care.

Applications

Call the charity's helpline to be put in contact with your local welfare representative. An income and savings assessment may be required as part of the application process.

Note: Most charities for ex-servicemen and women co-operate together in their work and The Royal British Legion may also be approached through other service organisations and vice versa.

Other information

The Royal British Legion is one of the largest providers of charitable help for individuals in the country and is financed mainly by gifts from individuals, especially through its annual Poppy Day collection.

It provides a comprehensive service for advising and helping ex-servicemen and women and their dependants. Direct financial assistance is but one aspect of this work. There are over 3,000 branches of The Royal British Legion, all of which can act as centres for organising whatever help the circumstances may require. Support is available to all who served in the forces, whether in war or peace-time, as regulars or those who have done national service.

The Legion manages six cares homes in locations around the country and is dedicated to supporting the recovery of soldiers and ex-soldiers. It has pledged '£50 million over ten years, to support the Defence Recovery Capability programme for wounded, injured and sick Armed Forces men and women'. As part of the programme, in conjunction with the MoD and Help for Heroes, the Legion has taken the lead with the running of PRCs (Personnel Recovery Centres) in Edinburgh and Germany and has so far committed £27 million towards the operation of the Battle Back Centre – a sports and outdoor activity facility based at Lilleshall. Financial support has also been given to PRCs managed by Help for Heroes at Catterick, Colchester and Tidworth.

There are four break centres operated by the Legion, through which it facilitates holidays for serving and former service personnel and their families. It also provides adventure holidays for young people from service families.

Former members of the armed forces can seek support in their transition from military to civilian life through the Legion's website civvystreet.org, which 'gives beneficiaries and their partners information, advice and guidance on careers, skills and self-employment'.

More information on services provided can be found on the Legion's informative website or by calling the helpline.

Royal Military Police Central Benevolent Fund

£83,000 (279 grants)

Correspondent: Col. Jeremy Green, The Regimental Secretary, RHQ RMP, Defence College of Policing and Guarding, Postal Point 38, Southwick, Fareham, Hampshire PO17 6EJ (023 9228 4406; email: rhqrmp@btconnect. com)

CC number: 248713

Eligibility

People who are serving or have served in the Royal Military Police corps, or any of its predecessors, and their dependants.

Types of grants

One-off cash grants typically of up to £1,000, although larger grants may be available. Grants have been made towards heating, funeral expenses, household furniture, debts, clothing and bedding, mobility aids, holidays, medical needs, special chairs, removals and other needs. Christmas grants are distributed to people who have received an individual benefit grant and are over 80 years of age.

Annual grant total

In 2013/14 the fund held assets of £3.6 million and had an income of £263,000. Grants to individuals totalled £83,000 and were distributed as follows:

Individual grants	£47,000
Christmas grants	£12,500
Annuities	£12,500
Army Benevolence Fund	£11,000

Another £29,500 was awarded to military organisations.

Applications

Apply in writing to the correspondent. All applications are passed to The Royal British Legion or SSAFA, a member of whom will visit applicants to verify eligibility and financial need.

Sister Agnes Benevolent Fund

£75,500 (14 grants)

Correspondent: PA to the Chief Executive, King Edward VII Hospital, Beaumont Street, London W1G 6AA (020 7486 4319; email: info@ kingedwardvii.co.uk; website: www. kingedwardvii.co.uk)

CC number: 208944

Eligibility

People who have served in the armed forces, regardless of rank or length of service, who are uninsured and are either inpatients or outpatients at King Edward VII's Hospital Sister Agnes, and their spouses, ex-spouses, widows and widowers.

Types of grants

Means-tested grants for up to 100% of hospital fees, for both inpatient and outpatient services. In some cases, consultant fees, imaging and physiotherapy may also be covered.

Annual grant total

In 2013/14 the fund had assets of £31 million and an income of £20.5 million. Grants were made to 14 individuals totalling £75,500.

Applications

Applicants should first contact the correspondent by telephone or email.

Note: Uninsured service personnel, their spouses, ex-spouses, widows and widowers are all eligible for a 20% subsidy on their hospital bill (this is not means-tested). To claim, eligible individuals need to notify the hospital when booking their procedure.

Other information

The Sister Agnes Benevolent Fund is a restricted fund of King Edward VII's Hospital Sister Agnes. It was established in 1979 by an anonymous donation, to be held upon trust.

SSAFA (Soldiers, Sailors, Airmen and Families Association)

£11.8 million

Correspondent: The Welfare Team, Queen Elizabeth House, 4 St Dunstan's Hill, London EC3R 8AD (0845 241 7141 or 0800 731 4880 (UK Freephone); email: via an online form or info@ssafa. org.uk; website: www.ssafa.org.uk)

CC number: 210760/SC038056

Eligibility

Service and ex-service men and women who are in need and their immediate dependants.

The charity's website provides an eligibility checklist and also states: 'If you have any connection with the Armed Forces, even if it isn't covered [in the list], then it's still worth getting in touch to see if we can help.'

Types of grants

One-off grants are available for a variety of needs, for example electrically powered vehicles, white goods, household items, holidays and carers' breaks.

Annual grant total

In 2014 the charity had assets of £6.3 million and had an income of £59.5 million. Grants for welfare purposes totalled £20 million. The accounts note that 'all grants were paid to or on behalf of eligible individuals'. A total of £11.1 million was given 'on behalf of service funds and other charities', £8.1 million in 'other welfare costs' and £659,000 'from Charity funds'.

Grants are disbursed by caseworkers who work throughout the SSAFA branch network.

Exclusions

The charity does not assist with legal issues, private medical care costs, educational grants and anything the state has a statutory duty to provide.

Applications

Contact should normally be made by letter direct to the Honorary Secretary of the local branch. The appropriate address can usually be obtained from the SSAFA website, Citizens Advice, the local telephone directory (under SSAFA) and most main post offices. In case of any difficulties, the local address can be obtained from the charity's head office.

Other information

SSAFA operates throughout the UK and in garrisons and stations overseas. It is concerned with the welfare of service and ex-service men and women and their families and provides a wide range of advice and support services.

All SSAFA branches are empowered to give immediate help without reference to higher committees. Also, because of their extensive coverage of the UK, they act as agents for service and other associated funds. Indeed, SSAFA is much more of a casework organisation than a benevolent fund.

A residential home is maintained on the Isle of Wight for older ex-service personnel and their dependants. Eligible men and women can be accepted from any part of the UK. SSAFA also manages cottage homes for ex-service men and women and their spouses, some purpose-built for people with disabilities, for which residents pay no rent but make a modest maintenance payment.

Two SSAFA Norton Homes provide short-term accommodation so that families can stay nearby whilst visiting a loved one at Selly Oak Hospital in Birmingham or the Defence Medical Rehabilitation Centre at Headley Court, Surrey. The houses are designed as 'homes from home' and are both located in secure and peaceful environments.

Stepping Stone homes are provided for service families facing relationship difficulties or marital breakdown who need somewhere to live while they consider their future.

Support services for serving and ex-service prisoners, with the aim of reducing re-offending and helping prisoners resettle into society, are also available.

SSAFA provides a confidential telephone support line for serving personnel which is staffed all year round and is outside the chain of command (UK: 0800 731 4880; Germany: 0800 182 7395; Cyprus: 800 91065; Falkland Islands #6111; Rest of the world: +44 (0)1980 630854). It also continues to grow and develop its health and social care services for serving personnel around the world with specialist health centres in Leicester and Nottingham. It also provides family support groups and adoption services.

For further information on all of the services listed here, and more, go to the charity's website or visit a local branch.

Todmorden War Memorial Fund (1914/1918)

£4,500

Correspondent: Stephen Ormerod, Trustee, 2 Maitland Close, Todmorden, West Yorkshire OL14 7TG (07941 195488)

CC number: 219673

Eligibility

Veterans of the First and Second World Wars who are sick or in need and live or have lived in the former borough of Todmorden, and their dependants. Other people in need in the area of benefit can also be assisted.

Types of grants

Grants are mostly one-off; recurrent grants are very occasionally given. TV licences are given to First and Second World War families. Food vouchers, medicine, medical comforts, bedding, fuel, domestic help and convalescence expenses are also given.

Annual grant total

In 2014 the fund had an income of £3,900 and a total expenditure of £11,000. We estimate that around £4,500 was made in grants to individuals for social welfare purposes.

Applications

Apply in writing to: Mrs M. Gunton, Case Secretary, 8 Walton Fold, Todmorden, Lancashire OL14 5TE. Applications must be made through a welfare agency or similar organisation and they are considered monthly.

Other information

The fund also makes grants to organisations.

Army

Airborne Forces Security (ABFS) Fund

£209,000 (180 grants)

Correspondent: Correspondent, Regimental Headquarters, The Parachute Regiment, Merville Barracks, Colchester, Essex CO2 7UT (01206 817079; email: syfund@parachute-regiment.com)

CC number: 206552

Eligibility

Serving and former members of the Parachute Regiment, the Glider Regiment and other units of airborne forces, and their dependants.

Types of grants

One-off grants are given according to need, including: clothing, bedding, furniture and household essentials; rent, living expenses, removals; educational needs; monthly allowances; rehabilitation; and so on.

Annual grant total

In 2014 the fund had assets of £6.5 million and an income of £541,000. Grants were made to 180 individuals totalling £209,000.

Additional grants of £40,000 and £20,000 were paid to the Army Benevolent Fund and the Parachute Regiment Charity respectively.

Exclusions

Grants are not normally given for repayment of private loans, legal proceedings or fines, and purchase of private cars.

Applications

Apply in writing to the correspondent. Applications are usually made through the Army Benevolent Fund, SSAFA or The Royal British Legion.

ATS and WRAC Benevolent Fund

£211,500 (301 grants)

Correspondent: The Benevolence Secretary, ATS and WRAC Association Benevolent Fund, Unit 39 Basepoint Business Centre, 1 Winnall Road, Winchester, Hampshire SO23 0LD (0300 400 1992; fax: 0300 400 1938; email: benfund@wracassociation.co.uk; website: www.wracassociation.org.uk/benevolence)

CC number: 206184

Eligibility

Former members of the Auxiliary Territorial Service during the Second World War and members of the Women's Royal Army Corps who served up to April 1992, who are in need, and their dependants.

Types of grants

One-off grants generally up to £1,000, although requests for larger grants may be considered. The fund can also help with making up the shortfall for nursing home fees (2013/14- £40 per week) and supports some annuitants who receive regular payments throughout the year.

Note the following, taken from the fund's accounts: 'There is no minimum service requirement that would bar an applicant from receiving help, although the Trustees do set guidelines based on service to ensure that the funds continue to meet demand.'

Annual grant total

In 2013/14 the fund held assets of £6.1 million and had an income of £326,000. Grants to 301 individuals amounted to £211,500 and were distributed as follows:

Benevolent Fund	264	£189,000
Princess Royal's Memorial Fund	37	£23,000

During the year, of 336 applications received 301 met the criteria for assistance.

Grants were awarded in 25 categories, the most costly of which were assistance with debt, nursing home fee top-ups, funeral expenses, general needs, electricity powered vehicles and house repairs and/or adaptations.

Applications

All applications for financial assistance should go through the Soldiers, Sailors, Airman and Families Association (SSAFA) or The Royal British Legion caseworkers who will visit the applicants and submit whatever forms are necessary. Grants are distributed through these agencies.

Other information

If you feel that you might qualify for financial assistance, apply to your local The Royal British Legion or SSAFA office in the first instance.

The Black Watch Association

£75,000

Correspondent: The Trustees, Balhousie Castle, Hay Street, Perth PH1 5HR (01738 623214; email: bwassociation@btconnect.com; website: theblackwatch.co.uk/regimental-association)

OSCR number: SC016423

Eligibility

Serving and retired soldiers of the Black Watch, and their dependants, who are in need.

Types of grants

One-off grants are given towards rent arrears, clothing, household equipment, funeral expenses and mobility aids. There is also a holiday scheme for widows of Black Watch servicemen.

Annual grant total

In 2014 the association had an income of £151,500 and a total expenditure of £214,000. According to our research, social welfare grants amount to about £75,000 each year.

Exclusions

Our research suggests that no grants are made towards council tax arrears, loans or large debts.

Applications

The website states: 'Financial assistance is given when a report, prepared by SSAFA Forces Help, indicates a genuine need. Any grant given is authorised by an experienced Welfare Committee (who meet monthly) and is then paid to SSAFA Forces Help who administer the expenditure.' The contact details of local SSAFA branches can be found on the SSAFA website (www.ssafa.org.uk). Alternatively, SSAFA's Forcesline telephone service can be contacted from the UK by calling 0800 731 4880.

The Commandos' Benevolent Fund

£21,500

Correspondent: Michael Copland, Honorary Treasurer, PO Box 104, Selby YO8 5YY (01757 705449; email: superinfotac@gmail.com; website: commandosbenevolentfund.org.uk)

CC number: 229631

Eligibility

People who served with the Army Commandos during the Second World War, and their dependants. Unfortunately service with any other commando group does not make people eligible for help from this fund.

Types of grants

One-off grants towards hospital transport, household bills, stair-lifts, flooding costs, holidays, respite breaks, removal expenses, home adaptations, medical costs, funeral expenses and so on. The fund states that it will consider all applications on a case by case basis.

Annual grant total

In 2014 the fund had an income of £34,000 and a total expenditure of £33,500. Grants to individuals totalled £21,500.

Applications

Apply in writing, with service details, to: Assistant Secretary, PO Box 104, Selby, Yorkshire YO8 5YY; or on a form available from the website. Applications can be submitted directly by the individual or through a social worker, Citizens Advice or other welfare agency such as SSAFA. Applications should include appropriate documentation such as estimates for goods or services. Applications are considered as soon as possible after their receipt.

The Hampshire and Isle of Wight Military Aid Fund (1903)

£20,000

Correspondent: Lt Col. Colin Bulleid, Secretary, Serle's House, Southgate Street, Winchester, Hampshire SO23 9EG (01263 852933; email: secretary@hantsMAF.org; website: www.hantsmaf.org)

CC number: 202363

Eligibility

Members, or former members (and their dependants), of the British Army (whether regular, territorial, militia, yeomanry or volunteer) who are in need, and who are, or were:

a) Members or former members of any Regiment or Corps raised in Hampshire.

b) Members or former members of The Princess of Wales's Royal Regiment (Queen's and Royal Hampshire's) who were resident in Hampshire at the time of their enlistment.

Territorial Army soldiers must have had at least four years' service with a TA unit in Hampshire or operational service.

Types of grants

One-off grants for services or items such as:

- Rent arrears
- Debts/bankruptcy
- Repairs/heating
- Nursing home fees
- Funeral costs
- Respite care/holiday
- Removals/house deposit
- Travel costs
- Modifications to the home
- Electrically powered vehicles

Beneficiaries have received help with:

- Stair-lifts
- Riser chairs/beds
- Electrically powered vehicles
- Showers
- White goods
- Carpets

Annual grant total

In 2014 the fund had an income of £18,500 and a total expenditure of £30,500. We estimate that the amount of grants given to individuals totalled around £20,000.

Applications

The fund should not normally be approached directly. The following information is taken from the charity's website:

Access to assistance from the Hampshire and Isle of Wight Military Aid Fund is via a report from either SSAFA Forces Help or The Royal British Legion.

A caseworker from your chosen organisation will visit you and complete a Form A with details about your connection to the Army, financial situation, your need, and a recommendation for appropriate assistance.

You can find the contact details for your regional office on their websites: www.ssafa.org.uk or www.britishlegion.org.uk

If you are living Hampshire at the moment, use the contact details below:

Hampshire SSAFA Tel: 02380 704 978 email: secretary@hampshiressafa.org.uk

The Royal British Legion Regional Office Hampshire Tel: 023 80620900 Fax: 023 80620900 email: hampshire@britishlegion.org.uk

Other information

The fund also distributes grants and monthly allowances on behalf of the Army Benevolent Fund for nursing home top-up fees and support for individuals on a low income staying in their own homes.

The Household Division Charity

£60,000

Correspondent: Major William Style, Treasurer, Household Division Funds, Horse Guards, Whitehall, London SW1A 2AX (020 7414 2270; email: hdftreasurer@gmail.com)

CC number: 1138248

Eligibility

Current and former members of the Household Division, and their dependants, who are in need.

Types of grants

One-off and recurring grants according to need.

Annual grant total

In 2013/14 the charity held assets of almost £6.3 million some of which is permanent endowment and cannot be spent on grant-giving. It had an income of £536,000 and its charitable expenditure totalled £282,000. The charity awards grants to individuals and organisations for both social welfare and educational purposes. We estimate grants to individuals for social welfare purposes to be around £60,000.

Applications

Apply in writing to the correspondent. Applications may be submitted by the individual or by a third party such as a representative from SSAFA, Citizens Advice or other welfare organisation.

Other information

The trustees annual report for 2013/14 states:

The trustees review financial commitments regularly. The Household Division is recognised by the nation as setting an international standard of excellence. With a legacy spanning 360 years, the Household Division Charity is driven primarily to generate even greater levels of military efficiency. Resources are allocated for the promotion of 'esprit de corps' based on optimal physical and mental fitness, breadth of knowledge, competence and experience to develop courage and professional effectiveness in the face of any danger. In support of this objective, funds are allocated to further education opportunities for individuals and groups, often abroad. Resources spent on welfare and memorialisation reinforce the sense of special unity that binds all members, serving and retired, able-bodied and injured, and their families including the bereaved.

Irish Guards Charitable Fund

£53,500 (61 grants)

Correspondent: The Lt Colonel Commanding, Regimental Headquarters, Irish Guards, Wellington Barracks, Birdcage Walk, London SW1A 6HQ (020 7414 3293; email: igwebmaster@ btconnect.com; website: www. helpforirishguards.com)

CC number: 247477

Eligibility

Serving and retired officers of the Irish Guards and their dependants who are in need.

Types of grants

One-off grants according to need

Annual grant total

In 2014 the fund held assets of £2.2 million and had an income of £322,000. A total of 61 grants were awarded to individuals, amounting to £53,500.

A further £168,000 was given in 17 grants to organisations.

Applications

Apply in writing to the correspondent.

The REME Benevolent Fund

£267,000

Correspondent: William Barclay, Corps Secretary, REME Benevolent Fund, Regimental Headquarters REME, Box H075, Hazebrouck Barracks, Arborfield RG2 9NH (0118 976 3220; email: REMERHQ-Benevolence@mod.uk; website: www.reme-association.org.uk)

CC number: 246967

Eligibility

Members and former members of the REME who are in need, and their immediate dependants.

Types of grants

One-off grants usually up to £1,000 for any need; however, in exceptional circumstances larger grants may be made. Annuities and help with nursing home fees are also available.

Annual grant total

In 2014 the fund had assets of £377,000 and an income of £655,000. Grants were made to individuals totalling £267,000 and were distributed as follows:

Grants in aid – Individuals	£243,500
Annuity allowances	£21,000
Nursing home fees	£2,400

The average grant made was £432. 'Grants in aid' were made to 563 individuals.

A further £267,000 was awarded in grants to organisations, including Royal Star and Garter Homes, Erskine and Queen Alexander Hospitals and Army Benevolent Fund.

Exclusions

No grants are given for medical expenses, funeral expenses, litigation costs or debts.

Applications

Apply on a form available from the correspondent or a local branch of SSAFA or The Royal British Legion. Grants are only made through a third party (e.g. SSAFA/RBL), and applications made directly will be referred to a welfare agency for investigation. Applications are screened immediately on receipt and are either rejected on sight, referred back for more information or passed on to a committee which meets every four weeks.

Other information

The charity also makes grants to other service organisations and funds sport and recreational activities for members.

Royal Artillery Charitable Fund

£600,000

Correspondent: Lt Colonel I. A. Vere Nicoll, Secretary, Artillery House, Royal Artillery Barracks, Larkhill, Salisbury, Wiltshire SP4 8QT (01980 634309 or 01980 845698; email: rarhq-racf-welfaremailbox@mod.uk; website: www. theraa.co.uk/how-can-we-help/ra-charitable-fund)

CC number: 210202

Eligibility

Current or former members of the Royal Artillery and their dependants who are in need.

Types of grants

According to our research, one-off and recurrent grants of £250–£700 are given for essential needs, for example, household bills, kitchen and domestic equipment, rent, water rates, nursing home fees, disability equipment, clothing, council tax and utility or power bills. The website states:

> We are here to help all members of the Regimental family in need, whatever the cause and at any time in their lives. There is no geographical limit and we can assist Gunners, Gunner Veterans and their dependants throughout the world. We provide through eligibility criteria, and based on humanity, reality and flexibility speedy assistance to all members of the

Gunner Family; we judge each case on its own merits.

Annual grant total

In 2014 the fund had assets of £16.2 million and an income of £1.2 million. Individual grants totalled £643,000 distributed to 1,443 people. A further £17,700 was paid to assist in the rehabilitation of a Gunner, Ben Parkinson, who was injured in Afghanistan in 2006 (this grant was accounted as 'welfare grants to institutions').

Most of the assistance is given for general welfare, although educational costs are also supported.

Exclusions

Grants are not given towards income tax, loans, credit card debts, telephone bills, legal fees or private medical treatment.

Applications

Applications should be made through SSAFA (details of local branches can be found on SSAFA's website, telephone directories or from Citizens Advice) or other organisations, such as The Royal British Legion or Earl Haig Fund in Scotland (see Poppyscotland (The Earl Haig Fund Scotland) on page 83), Officers Association, Royal Artillery Association or other regimental charities. Applications can be considered at any time.

Other information

Grants are also given to organisations and regiments (a total of £279,500 in 2014) and for educational purposes.

The fund is the sole corporate trustee of the Royal Artillery Charitable Fund (Permanent Endowment), the Royal Artillery Benevolent Fund, the Royal Artillery Association and the Kelly Holdsworth Artillery Trust.

Royal Commonwealth Ex-Services League

£1.4 million

Correspondent: Nigel Dransfield, Haig House, 199 Borough High Street, London SE1 1AA (02032072410; email: mgordon-roe@commonwealthveterans. org.uk; website: www. commonwealthveterans.org.uk)

CC number: 231322

Eligibility

Ex-servicemen and women of the crown, their widows or dependants, who are living outside the UK. There are currently member organisations in over 40 countries throughout the world.

Types of grants

All types of help can be considered. Grants are one-off, usually ranging from £100 to £500 and renewable on application. Grants are generally for medically related costs such as hearing aids, wheelchairs, artificial limbs, food or repairs to homes wrecked by floods or hurricanes and so on.

Annual grant total

In 2014 the league held assets of £2.3 million and had an income of £1.5 million. The total amount of welfare grants was £1.4 million.

Applications

Applications are considered daily on receipt from member organisations or British Embassies/High Commissions, but not directly from individuals. Applications should include proof of military service to the crown.

Other information

The league has members or representatives in most parts of the world through whom former servicemen or their dependants living abroad can seek help. The local British Embassy or High Commission can normally supply the relevant local contact. In a Commonwealth country the local ex-service association will probably be affiliated to the league. The league's annual report, available from the Charity Commission or from the league, gives an interesting breakdown and analysis of funds allocated according to location.

The Royal Corps of Signals Benevolent Fund (formerly known as The Royal Signals Benevolent Fund)

£424,500 (565 grants)

Correspondent: Col. Terrance Canham, Secretary, RHQ Royal Signals, Griffin House, Blandford Camp, Blandford Forum, Dorset DT11 8RH (01258 482081; email: RSIGNALSHQ-RegtSec@ mod.uk; website: www.royalsignals.org/ rsbf)

CC number: 284923

Eligibility

Members and former members of the Royal Signals, regular or territorial volunteer reserve, and their widows and other dependants.

Types of grants

One-off and recurrent grants are given according to need. Grants are given towards priority debts, such as rent and utilities, mobility aids, white goods, household repairs and Christmas allowances. Applications for amounts above £800 are approved only at Welfare Committee meetings.

Annual grant total

In 2014 the fund had assets of almost £10 million and an income of more than £1.5 million. 565 grants were made during the year totalling £424,500. This included 106 grants administered on behalf of the Army Benevolent Fund, which totalled £82,500.

Exclusions

The fund does not distribute loans.

Applications

Applications should be made through SSAFA or another charitable organisation and are considered as required.

Other information

The fund also gives grants to other service charities (£44,000 in 2014).

The fund is an amalgamation of the Royal Signals Association Fund, the Royal Signals Officers Fund and the Royal Signals Corps Fund.

Royal Engineers' Association

£358,000 (1,227 grants)

Correspondent: Lt Col. Neil Jordan, Deputy Controller, Brompton Barracks, Chatham, Kent ME4 4UG (01634 822982; email: benevolence@reahq.org. uk; website: www.reahq.org.uk)

CC number: 258322

Eligibility

Past or present members of the corps, and their dependants, who are in need.

Types of grants

One-off and recurrent grants. Grants are given for a wide range of purposes including mobility aids and walk-in showers. Regular weekly allowances are made to around 140 people and Christmas cards, and in some cases monetary gifts, are sent out in November to around 1,200 people who are resident in elderly people's homes, hospitals and care homes and to those in receipt of weekly pensions. Annuities for top-up fees for nursing homes are given in exceptional circumstances.

Annual grant total

In 2014 the association had assets of £10.8 million and an income of £1.1 million. Awards to 1,227 individuals totalled £358,000 and were distributed as follows:

Grants	£266,000
Weekly allowances	£74,500
Christmas Grants	£17,700

Exclusions

No grants are given for private education, private medical fees, court or legal fees or debts.

Applications

Application forms are available from the correspondent. Applications should be submitted through SSAFA or The Royal British Legion. Applications for less than £500 will be considered at any time, while cases requiring over £500 are considered at monthly committee meetings.

Other information

Grants are also made to other affiliated charities. For example, in 2014, awards were made to SSAFA (£7,500), Veterans in Action (£3,000) and Combat Stress (£2,500).

The Royal Logistics Corps Association Trust Fund

£445,000 (1,548 grants)

Correspondent: Regimental Treasurer, RHQ The RLC, Dettingen House, Princess Royal Barracks, Deepcut, Camberley, Surrey GU16 6RW (01252 833334; email: regttreasurer@rhqtherlc. org.uk; website: www.royallogisticcorps. co.uk)

CC number: 1024036

Eligibility

People in need who have at any time served or are now serving in the Royal Logistics Corp (RLC) or its forming Corps, including the Royal Corps of Transport (RCT) and The Royal Army Services Corps (RASC). Members of the women's services and the dependants of any of the above are also eligible.

Types of grants

One-off grants towards wheelchairs and other mobility aids, house repairs, utility bills, bathroom conversions, house adaptations and so on.

Annual grant total

In 2014 the fund had assets of £30.6 million (almost exclusively consisting of investments) and an income of £2.9 million. Grants were made totalling over £1 million. The annual report and accounts specify that 'in 2014 over 2,072 benevolent or welfare cases were considered of which 1,548 received grants totalling £445,000'.

Exclusions

Grants are not made for repayment of general debts or loans.

Applications

Applications should be made through SSAFA, The Royal British Legion,

Poppyscotland or a similar welfare organisation. Grants are made to the sponsoring organisation rather than directly to the individual. Applications can be made at any time, although requests for larger amounts need to be considered by the executive committee, making them longer to process.

Other information

The fund supports the activities of the RLC, the largest Corps in the Army totalling some 12,000 regular and 3,400 soldiers in reserve. It also funds and manages the fraternal activities of the Associations of the RLC and its predecessor Corps with 80 branches.

The fund's annual report states: 'The main activity of the trust in 2014 was the continuing promotion of efficiency of the RLC and the provision of welfare and benevolence support to its dependencies, adjusting its policies and working practices to accommodate the Forming Corps Association.'

In 2014 the trustees set a budget of just over £2 million to provide support in the areas of 'benevolence, sport and adventurous training, heritage, bands and the headquarters messes, plus a range of regimental and association activities to promote the efficiency of the Corps'.

Royal Air Force

The Royal Air Force Benevolent Fund

£12.6 million (6,150 grants)

Correspondent: General Welfare Department, 67 Portland Place, London W1B 1AR (0800 169 2942; email: info@ rafbf.org.uk; website: www.rafbf.org)

CC number: 1081009

Eligibility

Past and present members of the RAF, their partners, dependent children (under the age of 18), widows and widowers. Reservists and individuals who completed National Service are also assisted.

The charity notes on its website that in order to qualify for general support, you must have less than £16,000 in savings and less than £23,250 if you require home top-up assistance.

Types of grants

Grants or loans can be given for a wide range of welfare need. Grants are given towards, for example: day-to-day living costs, such as utility bills or essential household items; welfare breaks; sickness maintenance grants; funeral costs; and emergency needs. Assistance is also given with care home fees.

Annual grant total

In 2014 the charity had assets of £122.9 million, an income of £21.7 million and a charitable expenditure of £18.7 million. The charity's Strategic Report for the year stated the following: 'Over the year, the Fund proudly considered 6,150 individual cases and spent £12.6m on all forms of welfare support to the serving and ex-serving communities.' This figure does not take into account a further £4 million spent on residential and respite care, and £2.1 million spent on housing.

Exclusions

No grants are given for private medical costs or for legal fees.

Applications

Requests for assistance can be made by contacting the charity. There is an online contact form on the website. Alternatively, assistance can also be obtained through RAFA and SSAFA. The charity runs a free helpline which potential applicants are welcome to call for advice and support on the application process. Applications are considered on a continuous basis.

Other information

The charity provides advice and assistance on a range of issues including benefits, debt advice and relationships. It also can support its beneficiaries with residential and respite care and housing. See the website for more information on the services, support and financial assistance available.

The Royal Air Forces Association

£105,000

Correspondent: Nicholas Bunting, Secretary General, 117½ Loughborough Road, Leicester LE4 5ND (0116 266 5224; fax: 0116 266 5012; email: welfare@rafa.org.uk; website: www.rafa.org.uk)

CC number: 226686

Eligibility

Serving and former members of the Royal Air Force (including National Service), and their dependants. The widows and widowers and dependants of those that have died in service, or subsequently, are also eligible for assistance.

Types of grants

Small, one-off grants when all other sources of funding have been exhausted.

Recent grants have been awarded for gas and electricity bills, clothing, bedding, electrical goods, furniture and hospital travel costs. The association may also assist with nursing, convalescent and respite care costs.

Annual grant total

In 2014 the association had assets of £26.7 million and an income of £9.9 million. Welfare grants were made totalling £105,000.

Exclusions

Credit card debts are not eligible, nor are medical fees.

Applications

Application forms are available from the relevant area welfare officer. They are contactable on the numbers below. Confirmation of RAF service is required. Applications may be submitted directly by the individual, or through SSAFA, The Royal British Legion or other welfare agency.

Northern Area	01772 426 930
Overseas Area	0044 (0) 2890 325 718
Scotland and Northern Ireland Area	0131 225 5221
South East and Eastern Area	0116 268 8784
Wales, Midland and South Western Area	01392 462 088

Other information

The association provides support and advice on state benefits, including war pensions. It also manages three Wing Breaks hotels, three sheltered accommodation facilities, and two holiday facilities.

The Royal Observer Corps Benevolent Fund

£21,500 (35 grants)

Correspondent: The Secretary, 120 Perry Hall Road, Orpington, Kent BR6 0EF (01572 768133; fax: 01689 839031; email: info@rocbf.org.uk; website: www.rocbf.org.uk)

CC number: 209640

Eligibility

All former members of the Royal Observer Corps who are in need, hardship or distress. Length of service is not a consideration, except that the person making the application must have served long enough to have received their Royal Observer Corps official number. Eligibility also extends to their widows, widowers and dependants.

Types of grants

Almost all types of grants can be considered. Typically the fund can

provide financial help for mobility aids, essential home repairs or modification, household goods and respite care.

Annual grant total

In 2014 the fund had assets of £1 million and an income of £28,500. Grants to 35 individuals were made totalling around £21,500.

Exclusions

Grants are not given towards helping reduce debts or arrears owed to government bodies.

Applications

Applicants can request help using a contact form on the charity's website. Individuals are also referred through SSAFA, The Royal British Legion, the Royal Air Forces Association or other organisations. Applications are considered on receipt and normally a decision is given within days.

Royal Navy and Marines

The Royal Naval Benevolent Trust

£2.3 million

Correspondent: The Grants Administrator, Castaway House, 311 Twyford Avenue, Portsmouth PO2 8RN (023 9269 0112; fax: 023 9266 0852; email: rnbt@rnbt.org.uk; website: www.rnbt.org.uk)

CC number: 206243

Eligibility

Members of 'The RNBT Family', serving and former Royal Navy ratings and Royal Marines other ranks, and their dependants, who are in need.

Types of grants

Grants vary in amount from under £100 up to several thousand pounds, with the average being around £626 (in 2013/14). As general guidance, the trust lists 'Categories of Need' – areas where it typically gives help – on its website. These are: medical and dental; respite breaks; house repairs; food; funerals; clothing; furniture/furnishings; mortgages; household goods; rent; energy/fuel; removals; council tax and rates; and telephones. The trust stresses that this is not a closed list.

The trust also administers regular payments of £20 per week to eligible individuals who are on very low incomes. During 2013/14 a total of 1,204 Regular Charitable Payments were administered.

Annual grant total

In 2013/14 the trust had assets of £35.1 million and an income of £5.25 million. Grants totalled £2.3 million, of which £1.3 million was given in grants and £986,000 in regular payments.

Applications

Contact the RNBT by telephone, email or letter and it will arrange for a caseworker to visit you to complete an application form.

Other information

Amongst its activities, RNBT runs a residential and nursing home for older ex-naval men (not women) namely, Pembroke House in Gillingham.

The trust has an informative website.

The Royal Naval Reserve (V) Benevolent Fund

£3,500

Correspondent: Lieutenant Yasmin Tortelli, Correspondent, M.P. 3.4, NCHQ, Leach Building, Whale Island, Portsmouth PO2 8BY (023 9262 3570)

CC number: 266380

Eligibility

Members or former members of the Royal Naval Volunteer Reserve, Women's Royal Naval Volunteer Reserve, Royal Naval Reserve and the Women's Royal Naval Reserve, who are serving or have served as non-commissioned rates. The fund also caters for wives, widows and young children of the above.

Types of grants

One-off grants only, ranging from £50 to £350. Grants have been given for gas, electricity, removal expenses (i.e. to be near children/following divorce), clothing, travel to visit sick relatives or for treatment, essential furniture and domestic equipment and help on bereavement. Schoolchildren from poor families may very occasionally receive help for clothes, books or necessary educational visits, and help can also go to eligible children with aptitudes or disabilities which need special provision.

Annual grant total

In 2014 the fund had an income of £4,400 and a total expenditure of £7,500. We estimate that around £3,500 was made in grants to individuals for social welfare purposes.

Applications

Applications may be made in writing to the correspondent directly by the individual or through the local reserve division, The Royal British Legion, SSAFA or Royal Naval Benevolent Trust, which investigates applications.

Other information

The fund also makes grants to individuals for educational needs.

The Royal Navy and Royal Marines Children's Fund

£467,000

Correspondent: Monique Bateman, Director, Castaway House, 311 Twyford Avenue, Stamshaw, Portsmouth PO2 8RN (023 9263 9534; fax: 023 9267 7574; email: rnchildren@btconnect.com; website: www.rnrmchildrensfund.org)

CC number: 1160182

Eligibility

Dependants of serving and ex-serving members of the Royal Navy, the Royal Marines, the Queen Alexandra's Royal Naval Service or the former Women's Royal Naval Service, who are under the age of 25 and are in need.

Types of grants

One-off and recurrent grants, which in 2013/14 averaged £767 per child. They are given for a range of welfare needs including food, clothing, hospital travel expenses, respite care, specialist equipment and childcare costs. Support is also available for children who have suffered bereavement or who have experienced a family breakdown or parental divorce.

Annual grant total

In 2013/14 the fund had assets of £9.4 million and an income of £1.4 million. Grants made during the year totalled £1.1 million, £467,000 of which was awarded for social welfare purposes. They were distributed in support of 1,694 children as follows:

School fees	£545,000*
Childminding and respite	£206,000
Clothing and equipment	£205,000
Extra tuition fees	£99,000*
Children's travel	£54,000
Holidays and birthdays	£2,100

*We have not included the amounts related to educational purposes in our grants total.

During the year, a further £2,000 was paid towards other charity's expenditure.

Applications

Application forms are available from the correspondent or can be downloaded from the website. Applications can be submitted directly by the individual or through the individual's school/college, SSAFA, Naval Personal Family Service, social services or another third party.

The fund can be contacted by telephone and can provide, where possible, assistance with the form's completion. Applications can be made at any time.

Other information

In August 2015 the charity was incorporated and it now has a new Charity Commission number.

The Royal Navy Officers' Charity

£260,000

Correspondent: Commander Michael Goldthorpe, Chief Executive, 70 Porchester Terrace, Bayswater, London W2 3TP (020 7402 5231; email: rnoc@arno.org.uk; website: www.arno.org.uk)

CC number: 207405

Eligibility

Officers, both in active service and retired, of the Royal Navy, Royal Marines, QARNNS and WRNS and their reserves, and their spouses, former spouses, families and dependants, who are in need.

Types of grants

One-off grants and recurrent payments. Grants have been awarded towards nursing home fees, the provision of disability or mobility aids, the replacement of white goods, home repairs and to supplement inadequate incomes.

Annual grant total

In 2014 the charity had assets of £13.7 million and an income of £1.3 million. Grants to individuals totalled £264,000, of which £260,000 was awarded in benevolence grants for social welfare purposes.

Exclusions

Grants are not normally given for private medical care or education (other than from the RN Scholarship Fund), except in very exceptional circumstances.

Applications

Application forms are available from the correspondent. Applications can be submitted either directly by the individual or through a third party such as a social worker or Citizens Advice and are considered monthly.

Other information

The Amicable Navy Society was founded on 16 May 1739 by a group of naval officers suffering from unreasonable treatment by the Admiralty. The benevolent function of the society emerged later and became its sole purpose in 1791.

In 2008, the Association of Royal Navy Officers Charitable Trust transferred its assets to the society and the charity changed its name from the Royal Naval Benevolent Society for Officers.

WRNS Benevolent Trust

£317,000

Correspondent: Roger Collings, Grants Administrator, Castaway House, 311 Twyford Avenue, Portsmouth, Hampshire PO2 8RN (023 9265 5301; fax: 023 9267 9040; email: grantsadmin@ wrnsbt.org.uk; website: www.wrnsbt.org. uk)

CC number: 206529

Eligibility

Ex-Wrens and female serving members of the Royal Navy (officers and ratings) who joined the service between 3 September 1939 and 1 November 1993 and who are in need.

Types of grants

One-off and recurrent grants. Recurrent grants are given in the following categories: general amenity; care enhancement; overseas (for beneficiaries who live overseas); weekly maintenance; and weekly support supplements. One-off grants are available towards a wide range of needs, for example: household goods and repairs; priority debts and arrears; medical aids; funeral expenses; removal and travel expenses; and rent and deposits.

Annual grant total

In 2014 the trust had assets of £3.8 million and an unusually low income of £272,000. Grants to individuals totalled £318,500, with £1,300 of this awarded for educational needs. Grants for social welfare purposes totalled £317,000.

Exclusions

People who deserted from the service are not eligible.

Applications

Applications can be made directly to the correspondent; however, the trust states the following on its website:

> The WRNS Benevolent Trust is a small Charity. We have no caseworkers of our own and therefore work mainly with The Royal British Legion (RBL) and the Soldiers, Sailors, Airmen and Families Association (SSAFA), and their caseworkers call on any applicant on our behalf. They are discreet and knowledgeable, and can give friendly support and advice on a wide variety of matters. They complete a report, which is then put before our Grants Committee for consideration.

Applications can be made directly by the individual or, with their consent, by a relative or friend.

Other information

The trust states the following on its informative website:

> One of our biggest problems is raising awareness; it is surprising how many former Wrens do not even know of our existence. If you ever hear of a former Wren who you think may be having difficulties, do please tell her about us or approach us on her behalf. Many are too proud to ask for help, but we always stress that we are their special charity and one which they may have contributed to during their time in the Women's Royal Naval Service.

Service and regimental funds

Royal Navy and Royal Marines

Royal Marines Charitable Trust Fund

RM Corps Secretary, Building 32, HMS Excellent, Whale Island, Portsmouth PO2 8ER (tel: 02392 548068; email:admin@rmctf.org.uk; website: www.rmctf.org.uk)

Royal Naval Association

General Secretary, Room 209, Semaphore Tower (PP70), HM Naval Base, Portsmouth, Hampshire PO1 3LT (tel: 02392 723747; fax: 02392 723371; email: admin@ royalnavalassoc.com; website: www. royal-naval-association.co.uk)

Women's Royal Naval Service Benevolent Trust

General Secretary, Castaway House, 311 Twyford Avenue, Portsmouth, Hampshire P02 8RN (tel: 02392 655301; fax: 02392 679040; email: generalsecretary@wrnsbt.org.uk; website: www.wrnsbt.org.uk)

Merchant Navy

Merchant Navy Welfare Board

Welfare Officer, 8 Cumberland Place, Southampton SO15 2BH (tel: 0800 121 4765; fax: 02380 634444; email: enquiries@mnwb.org.uk; website: www.mnwb.org)

Royal Alfred Seafarers Society

Weston Acres, Woodmansterne Lane, Banstead, Surrey SM7 3HB (tel: 01737 353763; fax: 01737 362678; email: enquiries@royalalfred.org.uk; website: www.royalalfredseafarers. com)

Royal Air Force

Princess Mary's Royal Air Force Nursing Services Trust

Royal Air Force High Wycombe, Buckinghamshire HP14 4UE (tel: 01494 497297)

Royal Air Force Disabled Holiday Trust

Administrator, 67 Portland Place, London W1B 1AR (tel: 020 7307 3370; email: admin@rafdht.org.uk)

Royal Air Forces Ex-POW Association Charitable Fund

Welfare Officer, 4 Barn Close, Hartford, Huntingdon, Cambridgeshire PE29 1XF (tel: 07941 044581; email: rafexpowassn@gmail. com)

Royal Observer Corps Benevolent Fund

The Secretary, 120 Perry Hall Lane, Orpington BR6 0EF (email: info@ rocbf.org.uk; website: www.rocbf.org. uk)

Army

The Adjutant General's Corps Regimental Association

The Secretary, RHQ AGC, Gould House, Worthy Down, Winchester SO21 2RG (tel: 01962 887427; website: www.rhqagc.com)

Afghanistan Trust, the Parachute Regiment

The Charity Secretary, RHQ PARA, Merville Barracks, Circular Road South, Colchester CO2 7UT (tel: 01206 817074; website: www. afghanistantrust.org)

Airborne Forces Security Fund

The Controller, Regimental Headquarters, The Parachute Regiment, Merville Barracks, Colchester, Essex CO2 7UT (tel: 01206 817079; email: syfund@ parachute-regiment.com)

Argyll and Sutherland Highlanders' Regimental Association

The Secretary, The Castle, Stirling FK8 1EH (tel: 01786 475165)

Army Air Corps Fund (post Sept 1957)

Headquarters Army Air Corps, Middle Wallop, Stockbridge, Hampshire SO20 8DY (tel: 01264 784173; email: AACHQ-RHQ-RegtSec@mod.uk)

Army Physical Training Corps Association

Regimental Secretary, HQ RAPTC, Fox Lines, Queen's Avenue, Aldershot, Hampshire GU11 2LB (tel: 01252 787161; email: raptchq-reg-sec@mod.uk; website: www.raptassociation.org.uk)

Ayrshire Yeomanry

(See Yeomanry Benevolent Fund)

Bedfordshire and Hertfordshire Regiment

(See Royal Anglian Regiment Benevolent Charity)

Berkshire and Westminster Dragoons

(See Yeomanry Benevolent Fund)

Berkshire Yeomanry

(See Yeomanry Benevolent Fund)

Blues and Royals Association

Regimental Secretary, Home HQ, Household Cavalry, Combermere Barracks, Windsor SL4 3DN (tel: 01753 755132; email: rhq-d.regsec@householdcavalry.co.uk)

Border Regiment

(See Duke of Lancaster's Regiment)

Buckinghamshire, Berkshire and Oxfordshire Yeomanry

(See Yeomanry Benevolent Fund)

Cambridgeshire Regiment

(See Royal Anglian Regiment Benevolent Charity)

Cameronians (Scottish Rifles)

(See King's Own Scottish Borders Association)

Cheshire Regiment

(See Mercian Benevolent Fund)

Cheshire Yeomanry

(See Yeomanry Benevolent Fund)

Coldstream Guards Association

Assistant Regimental Adjutant, Wellington Barracks, Birdcage Walk, London SW1E 6HQ (tel: 020 7414 3246; email: coldstreamguardspri@hotmail.com)

Connaught Rangers Association

Applications should be forwarded directly to the ABF The Soldiers' Charity, see page 80.

Corps of Army Music Trust

Corps Secretary, HQ CAMPUS, Kneller Hall, Kneller Road, Twickenham TW2 7DU (tel: 020 8744 8608; email: CAMUSHQ-Corps-Sec@mod.uk)

County of London Yeomanry (3rd)

(See Yeomanry Benevolent Fund)

Derbyshire Yeomanry

(See Yeomanry Benevolent Fund)

Devonshire and Dorset Regiment

(See the Rifles – Exeter)

Devonshire Regiment

(See the Rifles – Exeter)

Dorset Regiment

(See the Rifles – Exeter)

Dragoons:

1st King's Dragoon Guards
(See Queen's Dragoon Guards)

2nd (Queen's Bays)
(See Queen's Dragoon Guards)

3rd Carabiniers (Prince of Wales's Dragoon Guards)
(See Royal Scots Dragoon Guards Association)

4th/7th Royal Dragoon Guards
(See Royal Dragoon Guards Benevolent Fund)

5th Royal Inniskilling Dragoon Guards
(See Royal Dragoon Guards Benevolent Fund)

2nd Royal Scots Greys
(See Royal Scots Dragoon Guards Association)

3rd Dragoon Guards
(See Royal Scots Dragoon Guards Association)

6th Dragoon Guards
(See Royal Scots Dragoon Guards Association)

25th Dragoon Guards
(See Royal Scots Dragoon Guards Association)

Westminster Dragoons
(See Yeomanry Benevolent Fund)

Duke of Albany's Seaforth Highlanders

(See Queen's Own Highlanders (Seaforth and Camerons) Regimental Association)

Duke of Cornwall's Light Infantry

(See the Rifles – Bodmin)

Duke of Edinburgh's Royal Regiment

(See the Rifles – Salisbury)

Duke of Lancaster's Regiment

The Secretary, Fulwood Barracks, Preston PR2 8AA (tel: 01772 260362; fax: 01772 260583; email: INFHQ-KINGS-LANCS-RegtSec@mod.uk)

Duke of Wellington's Regiment

(See Yorkshire Regiment)

Durham Light Infantry

(See the Rifles – Durham)

East Anglian Regiment

(See Royal Anglian Regiment Benevolent Charity)

East Lancashire Regiment

(See Duke of Lancaster's Regiment)

East Yorkshire Regiment

(See Yorkshire Regiment)

Essex Regiment

(See Royal Anglian Regiment Benevolent Charity)

Fife and Forfar Yeomanry

(See Yeomanry Benevolent Fund)

Fusiliers Aid Society (Fallen Fusiliers)

City of London Headquarters, HM Tower of London, London EC3N 4AB (tel: 020 3166 6906; email: asstregsec@thefusiliers.org; website: www.fallenfusiliers.co.uk)

Glasgow Highlanders

(See Royal Highland Fusiliers Benevolent Association)

Gloucestershire Regimental

(See the Rifles – Gloucester)

The Gordon Highlanders' Association

Home HQ The Highlanders, St Luke's, Viewfield Road, Aberdeen AB15 7XH (tel: 01224 318174; email: highlandersaberdeen@btinternet.com)

Green Howards

(See Yorkshire Regiment)

Grenadier Guards Association

General Secretary, Wellington Barracks, Birdcage Walk, London SW1E 6HQ (tel: 020 7414 3225; email:regtltreasurer@grengds.com; website: www.grengds.com)

The Gurkha Welfare Trust

PO Box 2170, 22 Queen Street, Salisbury SP2 2EX (tel: 01722 323955; fax: 01722 343119; email: info@gwt. org.uk; website: www.gwt.org.uk)

Hampshire and Isle of Wight Military Aid Fund

The Secretary, Serles House, Southgate Street, Winchester SO23 9EG (tel: 01962 852933; email: secretary@hantsMAF.org)

Herefordshire Light Infantry Regiment

(See the Rifles – Shrewsbury)

Highland Light Infantry

(See Royal Highland Fusiliers Benevolent Association)

Highlanders (Seaforth, Gordons and Camerons) Regiment

(See Highlanders Association)

The Highlanders Association

Regimental Secretary, HHQ The Highlanders, Cameron Barracks, Inverness IV2 3XE

Honourable Artillery Company Benevolent Fund

Armoury House, City Road, London EC1Y 2BQ (tel: 020 7382 1537; fax: 020 7382 1538; email: hac@hac.org. uk; website: www.hac.org.uk)

Hussars:

3rd The King's Own
(See Queen's Royal Hussars)

7th Queen's Own
(See Queen's Royal Hussars)

8th King's Royal Irish
(See Queen's Royal Hussars)

10th Royal Hussars
(See King's Royal Hussars Association)

11th Hussars
(as above)

14th King's Hussars
(as above)

14th/20th King's Hussars
(as above)

20th Hussars
(as above)

23rd Hussars
(as above)

26th Hussars
(as above)

13th/18th Royal (Queen Mary's Own)
(See Light Dragoons Regimental Association Charitable Trust)

15th/19th King's Royal Hussars Regiment
(See Light Dragoons Regimental Association Charitable Trust)

The Queen's Own Hussars
(See Queen's Royal Hussars)

Queen's Royal Irish Hussars
(See Queen's Royal Hussars)

Imperial Yeomanry

(See Yeomanry Benevolent Fund)

Indian Army Association

c/o Royal Commonwealth Ex-Services League, Haig House, 199 Borough High Street, London SE1 1AA (tel: 020 3207 2413)

Inns of Court and City Yeomanry

(See Yeomanry Benevolent Fund)

Intelligence Corps Association

Building 200, Chicksands, Shefford, Bedfordshire SG17 5PR

Irish Guards Association

RHQ Irish Guards, Wellington Barracks, Birdcage Walk, London SW1E 6HQ (tel: 020 7414 3295; email: igalondonbranch@gmail.com)

King's Own Royal Border Regimental Association

(See Duke of Lancaster's Regiment)

King's Own Royal Regiment

(See Duke of Lancaster's Regiment)

King's Own Scottish Borderers Association

(See the Royal Regiment of Scotland)

King's Own Yorkshire Light Infantry Regiment

(See the Rifles – Main Office)

King's Regiment Liverpool/ Manchester

(See Duke of Lancaster's Regiment)

King's Royal Hussars Association

Unit Welfare Officer, KRH, Aliwal Barracks, Tidworth SP9 7BB (tel: 01980 656839; email: info@krh.org. uk)

King's Royal Rifle Corps

(See the Rifles – Main Office)

King's Shropshire Light Infantry

(See the Rifles – Shrewsbury)

Labour Corps

Applications should be forwarded directly to the ABF The Soldiers' Charity, see page 80.

Lancashire Fusiliers

(See Fusiliers Aid Society)

Lancashire Regiment (Prince of Wales's Royal Volunteers) Regiment

(See Duke of Lancaster's Regiment)

Lancers:

9th/12th/27th Royal Lancers (See 9th/12th Royal Lancers (Prince of Wales) Charitable Association)

16th, 5th, 17th and 21st Lancers (See Queen's Royal Lancers)

9th Queen's Royal Lancers (See 9th/12th Royal Lancers (Prince of Wales) Charitable Association)

Leinster Regiment (for those resident in UK)

Applications should be forwarded directly to the ABF The Soldiers' Charity, see page 80.

The Life Guards Association Charitable Trust

The Honorary Secretary, Combermere Barracks, Windsor SL4 3DN (tel: 01753 755229; email: LG.RegSec@householdcavalry.co.uk)

Light Dragoons Regimental Association Charitable Trust

Fenham Barracks, Newcastle upon Tyne NE2 4NP (tel: 01912 393138; email: mail@lightdragoons.org.uk; website: www.lightdragoons.org.uk)

Light Infantry

(See the Rifles – appropriate local office)

London Irish Rifles Regimental Association Benevolent Fund

Connaught House, 4 Flodden Road, Camberwell, London SE5 9LL (email:rjsk@uwclub.net)

London Regiment

Applications should be forwarded directly to the ABF The Soldiers' Charity, see page 80.

London Scottish Regiment Benevolent Fund

95 Horseferry Road, Westminster, London SW1P 2DX (tel: 020 7630 0411)

Lothian and Border Horse

(See Yeomanry Benevolent Fund)

Lovat Scouts

(See Yeomanry Benevolent Fund)

Loyal Regiment (North Lancashire)

(See Duke of Lancaster's Regiment)

Machine Gun Corps

Applications should be forwarded directly to the ABF The Soldiers' Charity, see page 80. (For Heavy Branch Machine Gun Corps see **Royal Tank Regiment Association and Benevolent Fund**)

Manchester Regiment Aid Society and Benevolent Fund

(See Duke of Lancaster's Regiment)

Mercian Benevolent Fund

Whittington Barracks, Lichfield, Staffordshire WS14 9TJ (tel: 01543 434353)

Middlesex Regiment (Duke of Cambridge's Own)

(See Princess of Wales's Royal Regiment Benevolent Fund)

Military Provost Staff Corps Association

(See Adjutant General's Corps Regimental Association)

North Staffordshire Regiment

(See Mercian Benevolent Fund)

Northamptonshire Regiment

(See Royal Anglian Regiment Benevolent Charity)

Northamptonshire Yeomanry Association (1st and 2nd Regiments)

(See Yeomanry Benevolent Fund)

Nottinghamshire and Derbyshire Regiment

(See Mercian Benevolent Fund)

'Old Contemptibles'

Applications should be forwarded directly to the ABF The Soldiers' Charity see page 80.

Oxfordshire and Buckinghamshire Light Infantry

(See the Rifles – Main Office)

Oxfordshire Yeomanry

(See Yeomanry Benevolent Fund)

Parachute Regiment

(See Airborne Forces Security Fund)

Post Office Rifles

Applications should be forwarded directly to the ABF The Soldiers' Charity see page 80.

Prince of Wales Leinster Regiment Association

Honorary Secretary, 7 Nethercombe House, Ruthin Road, Blackheath, London SE3 7SL (website: www.leinster-regiment-association.org.uk)

Prince of Wales's Own (West and East Yorkshire) Regiment

(See Yorkshire Regiment)

Princess of Wales's Royal Regiment Benevolent Fund

Benevolence Secretary, Leros TA Centre, Leros Barracks, Sturry Road, Canterbury CT1 1HR (tel: 01227 817971; email: jim.reynolds334@mod.uk)

Queen Alexandra's Royal Army Nursing Corps Association

The Secretary, AMS Headquarters, Slim Road, Camberley, Surrey GU15 4NP (tel: 01276 412754; email: regtsecqaranc@hotmail.com; website: www.qarancassociation.org.uk)

Queen's Dragoon Guards

Regimental Secretary, Maindy Barracks, Whitchurch Road, Cardiff CF14 3YE (tel: 02920 781213; fax: 02920 781384; email: adminofficer@qdg.org.uk; website: www.qdg.org.uk)

Queen's Lancashire Regiment

(See Duke of Lancaster's Regiment)

Queen's Own Buffs, The Royal Kent Regiment

(See Princess of Wales's Royal Regiment Benevolent Fund)

Queen's Own Cameron Highlanders' Regiment

(See Queen's Own Highlanders (Seaforth and Camerons) Regimental Association)

Queen's Own Highlanders (Seaforth and Camerons) Regimental Association

RHQ HLDRS, Cameron Barracks, Inverness IV2 3XD (tel: 01463 224380; email: rhqthehighlanders@ btopenworld.com; website: www. qohldrs.co.uk)

Queen's Own Yorkshire Dragoons

(See Yeomanry Benevolent Fund)

Queen's Regiment

(See Princess of Wales's Royal Regiment Benevolent Fund)

Queen's Royal Hussars

Regimental Secretary, Regent Park Barracks, Albany Street, London NW1 4AL (tel: 020 7756 2275; email: regsec@qrhussars.co.uk)

Queen's Royal Lancers

Regimental Secretary, HHQ, QRL Lancer House, Prince William of Gloucester Barracks, Grantham, Lincolnshire NG31 7TJ (tel: 01159 573195; email: qrlregsec@gmail.com; website: www.qrlassociation.co.uk)

Queen's Royal Surrey Regiment

(See Princess of Wales's Royal Regiment Benevolent Fund)

Reconnaissance Corps

(See Royal Armoured Corps War Memorial Benevolent Fund)

Rifle Brigade

(See the Rifles – Main Office)

The Rifles

Main Office: Benevolence Secretary, Peninsula Barracks, Romsey Road, Winchester, Hampshire SO23 8TS (tel: 01962 828530/01962 828126; email: benevolence@the-rifles.co.uk)

Regional offices:

Bodmin – The Keep, Victoria Barracks, Bodmin, Cornwall PL31 1EG (tel: 01208 72810; email: bodmin@the-rifles.co.uk)

Durham – Elvet Waterside, Durham City, Durham DH1 3BW (tel: 01913 865496: email: durham@the-rifles.co.uk)

Exeter – Wyvern Barracks, Exeter, Devon EX2 6AR (tel: 01392 492434; email: exeter1@the-rifles. co.uk and exeter2@the-rifles.co.uk)

Gloucester – Custom House, 31 Commercial Road, Gloucester, Gloucestershire GL1 2HE (tel: 01452 522682; email: regimental-secretary@rgbw.army.mod.uk)

London – 52–56 Davies Street, London W1K 5HR (tel: 020 7491 4936; email: london@the-rifles.co. uk)

Oxford – Edward Brooks Barracks, Cholswell Road, Shippon, Abingdon, Oxon OX13 6JB (email: oxford@the-rifles.co.uk)

Salisbury – The Wardrobe, 58 The Close, Salisbury, Wiltshire SP1 2EX (tel: 01722 414536; email: salisbury@the-rifles.co.uk)

Shrewsbury – Copthorne Barracks, Shrewsbury, Shropshire SY3 8LZ (tel: 01743 262425; email: shrewsbury@the-rifles.co.uk)

Taunton – 14 Mount Street, Taunton, Somerset TA1 3QE (tel: 01823 333434; email: taunton@the-rifles.co.uk)

Ross-Shire Buffs, Duke of Albany's Seaforth Highlanders

(See Queen's Own Highlanders (Seaforth and Camerons) Regimental Association)

Royal Anglian Regiment Benevolent Charity

RHQ Royal Anglian Regiment, The Keep, Gibraltar Barracks, Bury St Edmunds IP33 3RN (tel: 01284 752394; email: INFHQ-QUEENS-RANG-ChfClk@mod.uk; website: www.royalanglianregiment.com)

Royal Armoured Corps War Memorial Benevolent Fund

c/o RHQ Royal Tank Regiment, Stanley Barracks, Bovington Camp, Wareham, Dorset BH20 6JB (tel: 01929 403444; email: regtlsec@ royaltankregiment.org; website: www. royaltankregiment.com)

Royal Army Chaplains' Department Association

RACHD HQ, Marlborough Lines, Monxton Road Andover SP11 8HJ (tel: 01264 382104 email: ArmyCG-FIN@mod.uk)

Royal Army Dental Corps Association

Regimental Secretary, RHQ RADC, HQ AMS, The Former Army Staff College, Slim Road, Camberley, Surrey GU15 4NP (tel: 01276 412753; email: RADCRHQ@hotmail.com; website: www.radc-association.org. uk)

Royal Army Ordnance Corps Charitable Trust

(See Royal Logistic Corps Association Trust)

Royal Army Pay Corps

The Secretary, RHQ AGC Centre, Winchester, Hampshire SO21 2RG (tel: 01962 887436; email: regsec. rapc@googlemail.com; website: www. rapc.co.uk)

Royal Army Veterinary Corps Benevolent Fund

The Secretary, RHQ RAVC, HQ AMD, The Former Army Staff College, Slim Road, Camberley, Surrey GU15 4NP (tel: 01276 412749; email: regtsecravc@hotmail.com; website: www.ravc-association.org)

Royal Berkshire Regiment

(See the Rifles – Salisbury)

Royal Dragoon Guards Benevolent Fund

3A Tower Street, York YO1 9SB (email: hhq@rdgmuseum.org.uk, website: www.rdgmuseum.org.uk/ regimental-association/benevolence)

Royal Dublin Fusiliers

Applications should be forwarded directly to the ABF The Soldiers' Charity, see page 80.

Royal Electrical and Mechanical Engineers (REME) Association and Benevolent Fund

RHQ REME (H075), Hazebrouck Barracks, Arborfield RG2 9NJ (tel: 01189 763220; email:corpssec@reme-rhq.org.uk)

Royal Engineers Association

Ravelin Building, Brompton Barracks, Chatham ME4 4UG (tel: 01634 847005; email: info@reahq.org.uk; website: www.reahq.org.uk)

Fusiliers Aid Society

City of London Headquarters, HM Tower of London, London EC3N 4AB (tel: 020 3166 6906; (email: asstregtsec@mod.uk; website: www.fallenfusiliers.co.uk)

Royal Gloucestershire Hussars

(See Yeomanry Benevolent Fund)

Royal Gloucestershire, Berkshire and Wiltshire Regiment

(See the Rifles – Gloucester)

Royal Green Jackets

(See the Rifles – Main Office)

Royal Hampshire Regiment

(See Princess of Wales's Royal Regiment Benevolent Fund)

Royal Highland Fusiliers Benevolent Association

518 Sauchiehall Street, Glasgow G2 3LW (tel. 01413 320961; email: benfundsec@rhf.org.uk, website: www.rhf.org.uk).

Royal Inniskilling Fusiliers

(See Royal Irish Regiment Benevolent Fund)

Royal Irish Fusiliers

(See Royal Irish Regiment Benevolent Fund)

Royal Irish Rangers

(See Royal Irish Regiment Benevolent Fund)

Royal Irish Regiment Benevolent Fund

RHQ The Royal Irish Regiment, St Patrick's Barracks, Ballymena, BFPO 808, Northern Ireland (tel: 02825 661381; fax: 02825 661378; email: benfund@royalirishregiment. co.uk; website: www.royalirish. easynet.co.uk)

Royal Irish Rifles

(See Royal Irish Regiment Benevolent Fund)

9th/12th Royal Lancers (Prince of Wales) Charitable Association

Regimental Secretary, TA Centre, Wigston, Leicestershire LE18 4UX (tel: 01162 785425)

Royal Lincolnshire Regiment

(See Royal Anglian Regiment Benevolent Charity)

Royal Logistic Corps Association Trust

RHQ The RLC, Dettingen House, The Princess Royal Barracks, Deepcut, Camberley, Surrey GU16 6RW (tel: 01252 833334; email: regttreasurer@ rhqtherlc.org.uk)

Royal Military Academy Sandhurst Band

Applications should be forwarded directly to the ABF The Soldiers' Charity, see page 80.

Royal Munster Fusiliers Charitable Fund

Applications should be forwarded to the ABF The Soldiers' Charity, see page 80.

Royal Norfolk Regimental Association

(See Royal Anglian Regiment Benevolent Charity)

Royal Northumberland Fusiliers

(See Fusiliers Aid Society)

Royal Regiment of Fusiliers (post 1968)

(See Fusiliers Aid Society)

Royal Regiment of Scotland

Regimental Secretary, The Castle, Edinburgh EH1 2YT

Royal Scots Dragoon Guards Association

The Castle, Edinburgh EH1 2YT

Royal Scots Fusiliers

(See Royal Highland Fusiliers Benevolent Association)

Royal Sussex Regiment

(See Princess of Wales's Royal Regiment Benevolent Fund)

Royal Tank Regiment Association and Benevolent Fund

RHQ Royal Tank Regiment, Stanley Barracks, Bovington, Dorset BH20 6JA (tel: 01929 403331; email: regtlsec@royaltankregiment.org; website: www.royaltankregiment.com)

Royal Ulster Rifles Benevolent Fund

(See Royal Irish Regiment Benevolent Fund)

Royal Warwickshire Regimental Association

Area Headquarters, St John's House, Warwick CV34 4NF (tel: 01926 491653; email: rrfhqwark@btconnect. com)

Royal Welsh Fusilier Comrades' Association

Secretary, RHQ The Royal Welsh, Maindy Barracks, Cardiff CF14 3YE (tel: 02920 781207; fax: 02920 781357; email: rhgroyalwelsh@hotmail.co.uk)

Royal Welsh Benevolent Fund

Secretary, RHQ The Royal Welsh, Maindy Barracks, Cardiff CF14 3YE (tel: 02920 781207; fax: 02920 781357; email: rhgroyalwelsh@hotmail.co.uk)

Scots Guards Association

2 Clifton Terrace, Edinburgh EH12 5DR (tel: 01313 371084)

Seaforth Highlanders' Regiment

(See Queen's Own Highlanders (Seaforth and Camerons) Regimental Association)

Sharpshooters Yeomanry

(See Yeomanry Benevolent Fund)

Sherwood Foresters

(See Mercian Benevolent Fund)

Sherwood Rangers Yeomanry

(See Yeomanry Benevolent Fund)

Small Arms School Corps Comrades' Association

HQ SASC, Land Warfare Centre, Imber Road, Warminster, Wiltshire BA12 0DJ (tel: 01985 222496)

Somerset Light Infantry

(See the Rifles – Taunton)

South Lancashire Regiment (Prince of Wales's Volunteers)

(See Duke of Lancaster's Regiment)

South Staffordshire Regiment

(See Mercian Benevolent Fund)

Special Air Service Association

PO Box 35051, London NW1 4WF (tel: 020 7756 2408; email: assn@ marsandminerva.co.uk; website: www. marsandminerva.co.uk)

Staffordshire Regiment

(See Mercian Benevolent Fund)

Staffordshire Yeomanry

(See Yeomanry Benevolent Fund)

Suffolk Regiment

(See Royal Anglian Regiment Benevolent Charity)

Sussex Regiment

(See Princess of Wales's Royal Regiment Benevolent Fund)

Ulster Defence Regiment Benevolent Fund

Applications should be submitted through one of four regional contact centres of Aftercare Service: www. aftercareservice.org

Welsh Guards Afghanistan Appeal

RHQ Welsh Guards, Wellington Barracks, Birdcage Walk, London SW1E 6HQ (tel: 020 7414 3291; email: DINF-FtGds-WG-OffMgr@ mod.uk)

West Riding Regiment

(See Yorkshire Regiment)

West Yorkshire Regimental Association

(See Yorkshire Regiment)

Wiltshire Regiment

(See the Rifles – Salisbury)

Women's Royal Army Corps Benevolent Fund

Applications should be submitted through your local branch of SSAFA or regional The Royal British Legion office.

Worcestershire Regiment

(See the Mercian Benevolent Fund)

Worcestershire and Sherwood Foresters Regiment

(See the Mercian Benevolent Fund)

Yeoman of the Guard – Queen's Bodyguard

(See Yeomanry Benevolent Fund)

Yeoman Warders

(See Yeomanry Benevolent Fund)

Yeomanry Benevolent Fund

Honorary Secretary, 4 Harolds Close, Leafield, Witney OX29 9PU (tel: 01993 878516;) This fund covers all Yeomanry Regiments.

York and Lancaster Regiment

(See Yorkshire Regiment)

Yorkshire Hussars

(See Yeomanry Benevolent Fund)

Yorkshire Regiment

RHQ, 3 Tower Street, York YO1 9SB (tel: 01904 461013; email: RHQYORKS-OffrRec@mod.uk)

All-service funds

Funds marked with a (*) also have an entry in the main 'Armed forces charities' section on page 79.

*Association of Jewish Ex-Servicemen and Women (AJEX)

Shield House, Harmony Way, London NW4 2BZ (tel: 020 8208 2323; website: www.ajex.org.uk)

Fund dedicated to the welfare of Jewish veterans and their dependants.

British Korean Veterans (1981) Relief Fund

c/o The Royal British Legion, 199 Borough High Street, London SE1 1AA (tel: 020 3207 2150)

Fund for the relief of distress amongst men and women who served with the British Forces during the Korean Campaign between June 1950 and July 1954 who are holders of, or are entitled to, the British Korean Medal or United Nations Medal, and their widows and dependants. Applicants need not be members of the British Korean Veterans Association to qualify for assistance.

*British Limbless Ex-Service Men's Association (BLESMA)

General Secretary, 185–187 High Road, Chadwell Heath, Romford RM6 6NA (tel: 020 8590 1124; fax: 020 8599 2932; email: ChadwellHeath@blesma.org; website: www.blesma.org)

To promote the welfare of all those of either sex who have lost a limb or limbs, or one, or both eyes, whilst in service or as a result of service in any branch of Her Majesty's Armed Forces or auxiliary forces and to assist needy dependants of such limbless ex-servicemen and women. It will also help those ex-servicemen and women who suffer amputation of a limb or limbs after service.

*Burma Star Association

Benevolence Secretary, 34 Grosvenor Gardens, London SW1W 0DH (tel: 020 7823 4273; email: burmastar@ btconnect.com; website: www. burmstar.org.uk)

Grants for men and women who served with His Majesty's or Allied Forces or in the Nursing Services during the Burma campaign and are Burma Star medal holders.

Canadian Veterans' Affairs

Welfare Officer, Department of Veterans' Affairs, Canadian High Commission, MacDonald House, 1 Grosvenor Square, London W1K 4AB (tel: 020 7258 6339)

Support for Canadian veterans, and their widows and dependants, living in the UK.

Chindits Old Comrades Association

Capt. B K Wilson, Secretary and Welfare Officer, c/o The TA Centre, Wolsley House, Fallings Park, Wolverhampton WV10 9QR

The aim of the association is to provide advice and aid (including, in appropriate cases, financial aid) to people who served in Burma with the Chindit Forces in 1943 and 1944, and their widows.

Ex-Services Mental Welfare Society (Combat Stress)

Tyrwhitt House, Oaklawn Road, Leatherhead KT22 0BX (tel: 0800 138 1619; email: contactus@combatstress. org.uk; website: www.combatstress. org.uk)

The society is the only organisation specialising in helping those of all ranks of the armed services and merchant navy suffering from combat related psychological injury caused by the traumatic events they have experienced in service. Remedial treatment is offered at three centres in Surrey, Shropshire and Ayrshire. The society also has a network of welfare officers who visit at home or hospital, and can help with war pensions and appeals. Information packs on request.

The Far East Prisoners of War (FEPOW) Trust Funds

c/o The Royal British Legion, 199 Borough High Street, London SE1 1AA (tel: 020 3207 2133)

Support for people who were FEPOW and their spouses, widows/widowers and dependants from the Far East Prisoner of War Fund and the FEPOW Central Welfare Fund.

Forces Pensions Society

68 South Lambeth Road, London SW8 1RL (tel: 020 7820 9988; email: memsec@forpen.co.uk; website: www. forcespensionsociety.org)

This society provides advice on all aspects of Armed Forces Pensions Schemes. No financial assistance is given.

Irish Ex-Service Trust

c/o The Royal British Legion, 199 Borough High Street, London SE1 1AA (tel: 020 3207 2030)

This is a government fund for those ex-service persons of the British Armed Forces who are resident in Northern Ireland or the Republic of Ireland, and their dependants. The trust makes one-off and recurrent grants for a variety of needs, particularly in those cases that might not normally be considered by other trusts/welfare organisations.

Joint Committee of the Order of St John and British Red Cross

c/o The Royal British Legion, 199 Borough High Street, London SE1 1AA (tel: 0845 772 5725)

Help is available mainly by grants administered through other voluntary organisations, for War Pensioners and their widows/widowers, primarily those disabled in the First and Second World Wars and the subsequent recognised conflicts, but not including Falklands War, the Gulf War 1990/91 or service in Northern Ireland.

*Lloyd's Patriotic Fund

c/o Welfare Department, SSAFA Forces Help, 19 Queen Elizabeth Street, London SE1 2LP (tel: 0800 731 4880)

The fund aims to help former members of the armed forces and their dependants who are in need. Grants will be given to a limited number of cases for one-off single grants for those with chronic illness or living in poverty, or in need of respite holidays.

National Ex-Prisoners of War Association

59 Pinkwell Lane, Hayes UB3 1PJ (tel: 07968 991714; website: www. prisonerofwar.org.uk)

To relieve poverty and sickness among members of all ranks of the forces or nursing services and who during such service were prisoners of war in any theatre of war, and their widows and dependants.

Normandy Veterans Association Benevolent/ Welfare Fund

General Secretary, 53 Normandy Road, Cleethorpes, South Humberside DN35 9JE (tel: 01472 600867)

The purpose of the fund is to give practical help to members, and to dependants of veterans, whose circumstances require it.

*Not Forgotten Association

4th Floor, 2 Grosvenor Gardens, London SW1W 0DH (tel: 020 7730 2400; fax: 020 7730 0020; email: info@nfassociation.org; website: www. nfassociation.org)

Provides recreational facilities for wounded service and disabled ex-service men and women as follows: TV sets (applicants whose mobility is severely restricted), TV licences, holidays, day outings and, for those confined to care homes, in-house entertainments.

Please note: the Association is unable to make cash grants, undertake welfare casework or assist widows.

*Officers' Association

First Floor, Mountbarrow House, 6–20 Elizabeth Street, London SW1W 9RB (tel: 0845 873 7153; website: www.officersassociation.org. uk)

The association awards regular and one-off financial help and advice to those in distress at home. Help is also provided towards care home third party shortfalls. Advice papers are also available on Care in the Community Legislation, Pension Credit and associated benefits, and accommodation such as care homes and sheltered accommodation.

*Officers' Association Scotland

New Haig House, Logie Green Road, Edinburgh EH7 4HR (tel: 01315 572782; website: www.oascotland.org.uk)

The association aims to relieve distress among all those who have at any time held a Sovereign's Commission with embodied service in HM Naval, Military, or Air Forces, and among their wives, widows, husbands, widowers, children and dependants. This includes ex-officers who were commissioned into the Reserve, Auxiliary, or Territorial Forces. Applicants must be resident in Scotland at the time of their initial application or have been members of a Scottish Regiment. Financial assistance is available through the Benevolence Service and help to ex-officers looking for employment is given through the Employment Service.

*Poppyscotland (Earl Haig Fund Scotland)

New Haig House, Logie Green Road, Edinburgh EH7 4HR (tel: 01315 572782; fax: 01315 575819; email: enquiries@poppyscotland.org.uk; website: www.poppyscotland.org.uk)

Head of Charitable Services: Gary Gray; Benevolence Secretary: Capt. Jim Macfarlane.

To relieve financially all ex-servicemen and women in need residing in Scotland, and their dependants. Poppyscotland also assists Merchant Seamen who have served in a war environment and Polish ex-servicemen provided, in both cases, they are resident in Scotland. Grants may be given either following an annual review or as an individual one-off payment.

Prisoners Families Fund

c/o Welfare Department, SSAFA Forces Help, 19 Queen Elizabeth Street, London SE1 2LP (tel: 0800 731 4880)

This fund makes grants for essential household items and children's clothing where a prisoner's family is struggling as a result of imprisonment.

The corporation provides financial help to widows, children and other dependants of officers and men of the armed forces who are in need, in the form of continuing allowances and grants, including education grants or bursaries.

Special Forces Benevolent Fund

c/o Brig Roger Dillon, D Group, 23 Grafton Street, London W1S 4EY (tel: 020 7318 9210)

Grants and pastoral support to 1939–1945 members of Special Operations Executive and their dependants.

Veterans Aid

40 Buckingham Palace Road, London SW1W 0RE (tel: 0800 012 6867; email: info@veterans-aid.net; website: www.veterans-aid.net)

This organisation provides advice and assistance to homeless or 'pending' homeless ex-service personnel and their families in the UK and overseas. Help can be given in the form of food, clothing and shelter. Assistance is also given with drug, alcohol and gambling addictions and issues around mental health.

War Widows Association of Great Britain

c/o The Royal British Legion, 199 Borough High Street, London SE1 1AA (tel: 0845 241 2189; email: info@warwidows.org.uk; website: www.warwidowsassociation.org.uk)

The association, formed in 1971 to improve conditions for all service widows and their dependants, works with government departments and service and ex-service organisations to help with all matters of its members' welfare. The association does not make grants.

Occupational charities

This section begins with an index of categories of occupation, which are listed alphabetically.

First, the charities with wide occupational criteria, including trade unions, are listed. Whether members or not, individuals should check for any trade unions listed that cover their area of work, as they will sometimes have resources available for non-member workers in their sector, as well as benevolent funds and other support for members.

Following this section, the charities are arranged alphabetically within each occupational category. Grant-makers include both independent charities and benevolent funds associated with particular professional bodies.

Many of the grant-making charities listed here support not only members of a particular occupation, but also their dependants (such as parents, children and partners). This may present additional options to explore when identifying a relevant occupational category.

Being a member of a particular profession or trade is not necessarily enough to be eligible for support – charities may also specify further criteria, so do read the entries in each section carefully.

We have grouped together certain occupations to make relevant charities easier to identify. For example, 'Hospitality and retail' includes charities with general criteria supporting employees in these industries, as well as charities which support a very specific branch of occupation within this sector.

We have placed all 'Medical and health' workers in the same category, as again there are charities that support workers generally and some that will only support certain specific occupations. The 'Food and drink provision' section contains many different individual roles within the industry and similarly, the 'Skilled crafts and trades' section includes charities covering a wide range of occupations.

Some sectors have been further divided into sub-categories of occupation, such as 'Arts and Culture' or 'Public and government sector', which firstly lists charities with broad criteria within this sector, followed by sub-sections for 'Civil service', 'Emergency services', 'Prison services' and 'Social services'.

In some cases, paid employment is not necessary – for example, under 'Sports' there are some grant-making charities that support amateur sports people. In this edition, charities concerning clergy and missionaries have been listed under 'Religion' in this chapter; for charities that give based on religious group rather than religious occupation, refer to the chapter 'Charities by beneficiary'.

Please also note that charities which specify both occupation and location are still mainly listed under the appropriate occupational heading, but those with a very specific location (such as the 'Manx Marine Society', for example) may be listed in the relevant geographical chapter instead.

The National Association of Co-operative Officials (NACO) Benevolent Fund

£6,600

Correspondent: Lynne Higginbottom, Finance/Administration Manager, 6A Clarendon Place, Hyde, Cheshire SK14 2QZ (0161 351 7900; fax: 0161 366 6800; email: info@naco.coop; website: www.naco.coop)

CC number: 262269

Eligibility

Those who are in need who are: members and former members of the association; members'/former members' dependants; and the widows and children of deceased members.

Types of grants

One-off grants of up to a maximum of £1,000.

Additional grants of up to £2,500 are available to a spouse/civil partner (or another nominated person) upon the death of a member whilst in membership to help with bereavement costs and funeral expenses.

Annual grant total

In 2014 the association had an income of £16,000 and a total expenditure of £6,800. Note that financial figures vary each year. We estimate that about £6,600 was awarded in grants to individuals.

Applications

Application forms are available to download from the association's website. They can be submitted directly by the individual including details of personal finance. Applications are considered at executive meetings, dates of which are available online.

Prospect Benevolent Fund

£84,000 (82 grants)

Correspondent: The Finance Officer, New Prospect House, 8 Leake Street, London SE1 7NN (020 7902 6600; fax: 020 7902 6667; email: enquiries@ prospect.org.uk; website: www.prospect. org.uk)

Eligibility

Members and retired members of the union (and the former Institution of Professional Civil Servants), and their dependants, who are experiencing financial problems.

Types of grants

Generally one-off grants with recurrent grants not exceeding £1,500. The trustees aim to relieve immediate problems and often point applicants to other channels and agencies for long-term solutions. Grants are usually sent to the applicant, but for speed and/or reliability, some awards are sent direct to the utility/body owed money. Occasionally this is processed through an agency or second party (such as a welfare officer, debt counsellor, branch officer or relative).

The union also makes death benefit grants to dependants of a deceased member (except retired members) which is equal to five times the higher national rate annual subscription. In 2015 this sum was £1,057.80.

Annual grant total

In 2014 the fund held assets of £582,000 and had an income of £19,900. Grants for welfare support were made to five individuals totalling £5,100. An additional £79,000 was given in 77 death grants, from a separate fund.

Exclusions

The fund does not make loans.

Applications

Application forms are available from the correspondent. They can be submitted directly by the individual or through the employer's welfare officers or branch representatives. Applications are considered throughout the year and generally are processed quickly.

Public and Commercial Services Union Benevolent Fund

£130,000

Correspondent: Gavin Graham, Fund Administrator, PCS Member Benefits, Freepost BFH 1003, 160 Falcon Road, London SW11 2LN (020 7801 2810 or 020 7801 2601, option 3; fax: 020 7801 2852; email: membenefits@pcs.org.uk; website: www.pcs.org.uk/en/about_pcs/ member_benefits/finance/benevolent_ fund.cfm)

Eligibility

Members and associate members of the union who are suffering severe financial hardship, through sickness, family troubles or other problems. Applications will be rejected if the individual is not a fully paid-up member, or associate member, of the union. Candidates must have been members for at least six months.

Types of grants

One-off grants to a maximum of £500 in any 12-month period.

Annual grant total

Previously around £130,000 has been distributed in benevolence services.

Exclusions

Grants are not given for:

- Private debts and credit card overdrafts
- Medical treatment
- Education costs
- Legal expenses
- Strike action

Loans are not provided.

Applications

Application forms are available from the correspondent or can be downloaded from the Public and Commercial Services Union website. Completed applications should be submitted either directly by the individual/family member, or through a third party (such as a union representative) and may be emailed or posted. They are reviewed weekly.

There For You (UNISON Welfare)

£608,000

Correspondent: Tina Willis, Casework Team, UNISON Centre, 130 Euston Road, London NW1 2AY (08000857 857; email: thereforyou@unison.co.uk; website: www.unison.org.uk/welfare)

CC number: 1023552

Eligibility

Financial help is given to UNISON members and in certain circumstances former members of NALGO can apply. Partners/dependants of deceased members can apply in their own right.

Types of grants

One-off grants for individuals experiencing unforeseen difficulties such as redundancy, illness, bereavement or relationship breakdown. Recent awards have been given to help with household bills, travel costs, childcare, school uniforms, winter fuel costs, furniture, domestic appliances, funeral expenses, disability aids and so on. Emergency grants are available when there is a crisis and money is needed quickly. For example, if an individual has been forced to leave their home and is in need of food and temporary shelter. Weekly grants for up to twelve weeks may be considered if the applicant is in a temporary period of reduced income, especially if they have considerable debt.

Funding is also available for holidays, convalescence and respite breaks under the charity's Wellbeing Breaks scheme.

There is also a small grants programme which provides targeted assistance to those on the lowest income. These accounted for 43% of all applications received in 2014. Unsurprisingly, given the massive hike in fuel costs witnessed in recent years, winter fuel applications accounted for 63% of all applications.

Uptake for school uniform grants reduced for the second year running and a review of how the programme is promoted will be undertaken in 2015. The trustees state in their annual report: 'Overall, the programme continues to be a major success story and evidence clearly shows that awareness of the charity has increased as a result.'

Annual grant total

In 2014 the trust had assets of £5.8 million, an income of £1.2 million and a total charitable expenditure of £1.2 million. Grants were made totalling £608,000 and can be broken down as follows:

Short-term weekly assistance	£142,000
Priority debt	£83,000
Household – white goods and furniture	£78,500
Special payments e.g. rent deposits, hospital travel	£70,000
Utilities costs	£52,000
Clothing	£32,000
Funeral expenses	£31,000
Household maintenance and services	£28,500
Bankruptcy	£26,500
Wellbeing breaks	£24,500
Emergency crisis payments	£13,000
Disability, health, medical	£12,000

Exclusions

Grants are generally not given for educational costs, private medical treatment, legal fees, car purchase or income lost due to industrial action.

Applications

Individuals should first contact their branch welfare officer or secretary who will help them to fill in an application form. Applications are usually processed within two weeks, although urgent requests can be dealt with more quickly, sometimes within 48 hours. People who are having difficulty contacting their local branch may submit the form, available from the website, directly to the national office.

Note that there are separate application forms for welfare grants and well-being breaks.

Other information

The charity, previously known as UNISON Welfare, provides support and advice on a variety of issues including personal debt and state benefits.

UNITE the Union Benevolent Fund

£94,000

Correspondent: Steven Skinner, Trustee, Unite, 128 Theobald's Road, London WC1X 8TN (020 7611 2500; email: stephen.skinner@unitetheunion.org; website: www.unitetheunion.org/how-we-help/memberoffers/benevolentfund)

CC number: 228567

Eligibility

Members, former members, employees or ex-employees of the union and their dependants.

Types of grants

One-off grants of between £100 and £1,000 to people who have fallen on hard times through being absent from work through prolonged sickness, retirement through ill health, family bereavements or a change in domestic circumstances. Grants have included payment towards a riser/recliner for person with back problems, help to somebody dismissed while on sick leave, heating grants for older people, Christmas bonuses for people who are elderly or have young children, and general assistance with bills.

Annual grant total

At the time of writing (November 2015), the latest accounts available were from 2013. In 2013 the fund had an income of £109,000 and a total expenditure of £162,000. It had assets of £1.1 million which mainly consisted of investments and was, therefore, not available for distribution. Grants totalling £94,000 were made to individuals for social welfare purposes.

Exclusions

Help with legal fees, educational grants and credit card bills is not usually available.

Applications

Apply on a form available from the correspondent or to download from the website. Applications can be submitted by post or by email to applications@unitebf.org and relevant supporting documents such as doctors letters, bank statements, payslips, etc., should also be attached to the application. Applications are considered every other month.

Arts and culture

Equity Charitable Trust

£111,500 (122 grants)

Correspondent: Kaethe Cherney, Acting Secretary, Plouviez House, 19–20 Hatton Place, London EC1N 8RU (020 7831 1926; fax: 020 7242 7995; email: kaethe@ equitycharitabletrust.org.uk; website: www.equitycharitabletrust.org.uk)

CC number: 328103

Eligibility

Professionals in the field of entertainment, who are eligible for an Equity card. The trust typically assists those who are unable to work due to an illness or accident, although individuals who are experiencing financial hardship due to an emergency may also be eligible.

Types of grants

One-off grants to help with financial emergencies. Grants can assist with many needs – from utility bills and home repairs, to convalescent care and healthcare costs. Each case is considered on its merits and the trust tries to make grants in proportion to the individual's need.

Annual grant total

In 2013/14 the trust had assets of £10.7 million and an income of £448,000. Grants totalled £346,000, £102,500 of which was awarded to organisations. Grants made to individuals amounted to £243,000 and included £131,500 paid in education and training grants to 40 people. Welfare and benevolence grants to 122 individuals totalled £111,500.

Exclusions

The trust cannot help amateur performers, musicians or drama students.

Applications

Applications can be made using a form, which is available to download from the website or on request by emailing rosalind@equitycharitabletrust.org.uk or by calling 020 7831 1926. They are considered at Welfare Committee meetings every six weeks.

Other information

As part of an application, beneficiaries are able to speak with an experienced money advisor who can help to find other sources of funding, including state benefits.

Though the trust usually only provides one-off payments, a page on its informative website lists organisations that may be able to help with regular financial assistance.

The Guild of Motoring Writers Benevolent Fund

Correspondent: Elizabeth Aves, Correspondent, 23 Stockwell Park Crescent, London SW9 0DQ (020 7737 2377; email: benfundadmin@gomw.co. uk; website: www.gomw.co.uk)

CC number: 259583

Eligibility

Motoring writers, journalists, photographers, broadcasters or web editors, who are in need and are, or have been, members of the guild. Their dependants may also be supported.

Types of grants

Mainly loans to help with short-term financial difficulties such as those experienced following redundancy or injury. Loans may in some cases be converted to grants at the discretion of the trustees.

Annual grant total

In 2014 the fund had assets of £572,500 and an income of £29,500. While the charity did not make any grants to individuals during the year, loans totalling £17,800 were made to beneficiaries. Loans may occasionally be converted to grants.

Applications

Apply in writing to the correspondent at any time. Applications can be made either directly by the individual or through a third party.

Other information

See also the entry for Ben – The Automotive Industry Charity, which supports anyone who has worked in the motor industry.

The Evelyn Norris Trust

£32,500 (43 grants)

Correspondent: Kaethe Cherney, Acting Secretary, Plouviez House, 19–20 Hatton Place, London EC1N 8RU (020 7831 1926; fax: 020 7242 7995; email: kaethe@ equitycharitabletrust.org.uk; website: www.equitycharitabletrust.org.uk/ evelynnorris.php)

CC number: 260078

Eligibility

Members or ex-members of the concert or theatrical profession who are older, sick, have a disability or are otherwise in need.

Types of grants

One-off grants of up to £700 towards convalescence or recuperative holidays following illness, injury or surgery.

Annual grant total

In 2014 the trust had assets of £821,000 and an income of £45,500. Grants to 43 individuals totalled £32,500.

Exclusions

No grants are given for student/ education course fees.

Applications

Application forms are available to download from the website, although the trust advises potential applicants to call or email first to discuss eligibility details and the application process. Applications are considered monthly and can be submitted directly by the individual or through a social worker, Citizens Advice, welfare agency or any third party. Applications should include any relevant financial or personal information.

Other information

Grants have also been made to residential homes (two grants of £1,000 each in 2014).

The Royal Opera House Benevolent Fund

£126,000 (45 grants)

Correspondent: Cheng Loo, Secretary, Benevolent Fund, Royal Opera House, Covent Garden, London WC2E 9DD (020 7212 9128; email: ben.fund@roh. org.uk; website: www.roh.org.uk/about/ benevolent-fund)

CC number: 200002

Eligibility

People who work, or have worked, for the Royal Opera House or Birmingham Royal Ballet, and their widows, widowers, partners or children. Applicants do not have to have contributed to the fund in order to receive help.

Note: In previous years, it has been required that applicants have an annual income of no more than £10,000 if single and £15,000 if married; although this is not currently stated on the fund's website or in its accounts, such limits may still apply.

Types of grants

Grants range from £50 per month to £3,000 as a one-off grant. Monthly allowances are towards food and clothing. One-off grants have been given towards essential building repairs, second-hand furniture, medical and care fees, dentures, glasses, home equipment, medical costs and MOT repairs. Interest-free loans are also available.

Annual grant total

In 2013/14 the fund held assets of £7.3 million and had an income of £126,000. A total of £126,000 was awarded in 45 grants to individuals and was distributed as follows:

Monthly allowances	32	£118,000
Other grants	13	£8,000

Applications

Apply on a form available from the correspondent, providing details of your income and expenditure. Applications should be submitted directly by the individual for consideration on receipt.

Other information

The fund continues to support Capita Services, a counselling and legal advice service for employees, as well as the ROH Occupational Health Unit. The fund's Welfare Officer also makes visits to support some beneficiaries.

The Royal Theatrical Fund

£230,500 (204 grants)

Correspondent: Sharon Lomas, Secretary, West Suite, 2nd Floor, 11 Garrick Street, London WC2E 9AR (020 7836 3322; fax: 020 7379 8273; email: admin@trtf.com; website: www. trtf.com)

CC number: 222080

Eligibility

People who have professionally practised or contributed to the theatrical arts (on stage, radio, film or television or any other medium) for a minimum of seven years, who are in need, and the dependants of such people.

Types of grants

Monthly allowances and one-off grants towards domestic bills, shortfalls in nursing and residential fees, car tax, stair-lifts, computers, insurance, TV licences and so on. Winter fuel allowances and occasional gifts are also awarded.

Annual grant total

In 2013/14 the fund held assets of almost £7.1 million and had an income of £503,000. Grants to 204 individuals totalled £230,500 and were distributed as follows:

Monthly allowances	£86,000
One-off grants/gifts and birthday and Christmas gifts	£97,000
Nursing home/residential/ convalescent/home care	£47,500

Birthday and Christmas gifts totalled £15,500 and a winter fuel allowance of £200 was also awarded to each beneficiary.

Exclusions

No grants are made to students or towards courses or projects.

Applications

Apply using the form on the fund's website. Alternatively in writing to the correspondent, making sure to include: a letter outlining your financial difficulties and how the fund may be able to help; any other relevant information; a letter of support from your GP or hospital, or a current medical certificate; and a full CV or details of your theatrical career. Applications can be submitted at any time. The Welfare Committee meets on a monthly basis to consider applications. Telephone enquiries are welcome.

Other information

In cases where the fund cannot assist, the Welfare Committee may choose to refer the applicant to another suitable fund or organisation.

The fund also works to provide advice relating to state benefits and emotional support for beneficiaries who are lonely or isolated.

Acting, theatre and film

The Actors' Benevolent Fund

£565,500

Correspondent: Stuart Crozier, 6 Adam Street, London WC2N 6AD (020 7836 6378; fax: 020 7836 8978; email: office@ abf.org.uk; website: www. actorsbenevolentfund.co.uk)

CC number: 206524

Eligibility

Professional actors and theatrical stage managers who are unable to work because of an accident, sickness or old age.

If you are a dancer, a singer or a variety performer or if you are a member of the theatrical profession and have children under 19 there are other charities which may be able to help. Phone the office for advice.

Types of grants

Weekly allowances; grants paid monthly, in summer and at Christmas; hampers; and winter heating grants. During the year the fund also provided assistance with general household expenses, the cost of replacing household equipment, mobility aids, physiotherapy, osteopathy, the shortfall of nursing home fees and holiday and funeral costs.

Annual grant total

In 2014 the fund had assets of £22.4 million and an income of £1.7 million Grants to individuals totalled £565,500.

Exclusions

No grants are available to students. Grants are unlikely to be made for credit card debts, loans or private dental or medical treatment, which should be covered by the NHS, although the fund will consider such applications.

Applications

Apply online or on a form available from the correspondent or to download from the fund's website. Applications should be submitted directly by the individual and include a detailed CV and, if appropriate, the applicant's Spotlight link, Equity number or IMDB entry. If applying due to ill health or an accident, a recent doctor's letter giving details of the individual's condition should be included. It may also be helpful to include any Benefit Agency letters which confirm the level of benefits received. Applications are considered on the last Thursday of each month and forms should be submitted by the Friday before a meeting.

In cases of emergency, where potential beneficiaries need their application to be considered before the next scheduled meeting contact the fund's office on 020 7836 6378 for advice.

Other information

The Actors' Benevolent Fund also provides advice on welfare and debt and supports its beneficiaries through visits, telephone calls and birthday cards.

The fund occasionally approaches other theatrical charities on behalf of applicants, if given permission to do so. There is a list of charities with which the fund has links available on its helpful website.

The Actors' Children's Trust (TACT)

£148,500

Correspondent: Robert Ashby, General Secretary, 58 Bloomsbury Street, London WC1B 3QT (020 7636 7868; email: robert@tactactors.org; website: www. tactactors.org)

CC number: 206809

Eligibility

Children (aged under 21) of professional actors who are in financial need with a particular focus on children with special needs, learning disabilities or long-term illnesses or those facing family crisis.

One or both parents must be a professional actor. If the actor-parent is now doing other work, acting must still have formed the majority of the paid work in their career to date. **Note:** The trust cannot help those who have solely worked in variety, amateur dramatics or as an extra.

Types of grants

One-off and recurrent grants may be given for help with essential furnishings, utility bills (where this will benefit the children), holidays, childcare costs, clothing, daily essentials and special equipment. Additional grants at Christmas and crisis grants are also available.

Annual grant total

In 2013/14 the trust had assets of £6.8 million and an income of £697,000. Grants for educational and welfare purposes were made to 131 families, with 212 children between them. Grants were made totalling £296,500 with an average spend per child being £1,400. We estimate that about £148,500 was given for welfare needs.

Exclusions

Grants are not usually given for private school fees; however, the trust may consider making a grant if private education would be beneficial to the child i.e. due to special educational needs or family situation. TACT does not pay independent school fees.

Applications

Application forms may be filled in online, downloaded and printed from the charity's website or requested from the correspondent. Applicants are strongly advised to contact the charity to discuss their situation before making an application. Applications can be submitted at any time either by the individual or a parent. Awards are decided in July each year.

Other information

The annual report for 2013/14 states:

> The two largest areas of funding continued to be education including extra-curricular activities (music lessons and exams, dance, drama, sports, and so on) and childcare. Smaller areas of funding include school transport, holidays, crisis relief, clothing and uniform, sports kit, and performing arts kit.

Note that on 31 March 2014 the trustees closed a small related charity, TACT Education Fund, which awards student grants to older children of actors, and transferred its activity, assets and liabilities to TACT, as a restricted endowment with its income applied for the same purposes.

The trust also provides support for specialist tuition, extra-curricular activities, play schemes, school trips and groups and sports clubs, for example. Maintenance grants of £1,200 per year

are offered to higher education students of professional actors.

Grand Order of Water Rats Charities Fund

£17,500

Correspondent: Mike Martin, Secretary, 328 Gray's Inn Road, London WC1X 8BZ (020 7278 3248; email: charities@gowr.net; website: www.gowr. net)

CC number: 292201

Eligibility

People, and their dependants, who have been involved in a theatrical profession for at least seven years and are in need.

Types of grants

One-off and recurrent grants are given according to need.

Annual grant total

At the time of writing (November 2015), the latest accounts available were from 2013. In 2013 the fund had assets of £1.7 million and an income of £79,500. Grants to both organisations and individuals totalled £35,000. We estimate that the amount of grants given to individuals totalled £17,500.

Exclusions

No grants are given towards student fees, education, taxes, overdrafts, credit card bills or bank loans.

Applications

Apply in writing to the trustees.

Other information

The charity also gives grants to organisations.

The Scottish Cinematograph Trade Benevolent Fund

£15,000

Correspondent: Fund Administrator, Grant Thornton UK LLP, Scottish Legal Life Building, 95 Bothwell Street, Glasgow G2 7JZ (0141 223 0000; email: information@sctbf.co.uk; website: www. sctbf.co.uk)

OSCR number: SC001786

Eligibility

People in need who are/have been working in the cinema industry in Scotland for at least two years.

Types of grants

One-off and recurrent grants for general living costs, household essentials, Aid Call systems and convalescence.

Annual grant total

In 2014 the fund had an income of £5,300 and an expenditure of £23,500. Our research suggests that in previous years grants have totalled about £15,000.

Applications

Apply in writing to the correspondent. Applications can be submitted either directly by the individual or through a third party, for example, a social worker, Citizens Advice or other welfare agency.

Other information

The fund also offers advice on state benefits and pensions and employs a welfare visitor.

The Theatrical Guild

£79,000 (57 grants)

Correspondent: Laura Hannon, Office Manager, The Theatrical Guild, 11 Garrick Street, London WC2E 9AR (020 7240 6062; email: admin@ttg.org. uk; website: www.ttg.org.uk)

CC number: 206669

Eligibility

People who work, or have retired from working, either backstage or front-of-house in a professional theatre. Financial support may be given where accident, ill health or other circumstances have prevented the applicant from working. In special cases, support may be given to working members of the profession and to one-parent families who are prevented from accepting a job due to the cost of childcare.

Types of grants

One-off and recurring grants are typically given for bills, equipment, special medical needs and retraining costs. Applicants typically seek help when they are unable to work through accident, ill health, emergency or some other reason.

Annual grant total

In 2013 the charity had an income of £146,000 and a total expenditure of £102,500. Grants to 57 beneficiaries totalled £79,000 and were given for both social welfare and educational purposes.

At the time of writing (November 2015) these were the most recent accounts available.

Exclusions

No grants are given for the repayment of credit card debt. Help cannot be given to drama students, amateur performers or anyone who has not worked or does not currently work in a professional theatre.

Applications

Application forms can be downloaded from the website or requested by calling or emailing the office. Applications can be submitted either directly by the individual, through a third party such as a social worker or through an organisation such as Citizens Advice. They are considered monthly, with the exception of August and December. Those seeking emergency assistance should contact the office directly by email or phone.

Other information

The guild also offers counselling, welfare support and educational sponsorship.

Artists

The Artists' General Benevolent Institution

£365,000 (123 grants)

Correspondent: Brad Feltham, Secretary, Burlington House, Piccadilly, London W1J 0BB (020 7734 1193; email: info@ agbi.org.uk; website: www.agbi.org.uk)

CC number: 212667

Eligibility

Professional artists, i.e. painters, sculptors, illustrators, art teachers at A-level or above, who live in England, Wales and Northern Ireland, who have earned their living (or a major part of it) from art and cannot work due to accident, illness or old age, and their dependants. Widows and orphaned children of artists are also eligible for assistance.

Types of grants

One-off and recurrent grants to artists who through old age, illness or accident are unable to work and earn. Grants cover a wide range of items and uses, such as domestic and utility bills, repair of equipment or replacement of worn-out items, help to cover costs of car replacements, visits to family and friends and respite care. Recent grants have been awarded towards the costs of specialist equipment to help an artist with eyesight problems, as well as contributions towards the upkeep of a studio and household utility bills for an artist with a progressive illness.

Annual grant total

In 2013/14 the charity had an income of £525,500 and a total expenditure of £549,000. Grants to 123 professional artists in need amounted to £365,000.

Exclusions

The fund cannot help with career or legal difficulties, loss of earnings due to poor sales, etc., expenses associated with exhibitions, or (except in exceptional circumstances) student fees.

Applications

Applications should initially be in writing, including a full CV listing all training, qualifications, exhibitions in professional galleries and teaching experience (if any) at GCSE, A-level or above. They can be submitted directly by the individual, through a recognised referral agency such Citizens Advice, or by a doctor, social worker, etc. The secretary visits most potential beneficiaries in order to carry out an assessment and to collect original works, as well as letters from two referees and a doctor or consultant (if applicable). The council meets to consider applications regularly throughout the year. Enquiries from potential applicants are welcomed.

The Eaton Fund for Artists, Nurses and Gentlewomen

£168,500 (348 grants)

Correspondent: Anne Murray, Correspondent, PO Box 528, Fleet GU51 9HH (020 3289 3209; email: admin@eatonfund.org.uk; website: www. eatonfund.org.uk)

CC number: 236060

Eligibility

Artists, including painters, potters, sculptors and photographers but not performing artists; nurses, including SRN, SEN, medical carers and dental nurses who are in employment or retired; and women over 18, who are in need of financial assistance.

Types of grants

One-off grants for artist's materials and equipment; picture framing for an exhibition; wheelchairs; and the setting up of a new home due to disability, family breakdown or homelessness.

Annual grant total

In 2013/14 the fund had assets of £8.7 million and an income of £302,500. Grants were made to 348 individuals totalling £168,500.

Exclusions

Grants are not given for educational fees, recurring expenses such as mortgage repayments, rent, fuel or phone bills, special diets, care home fees, private treatments or to clear debt.

Applications

Application forms are available to download from the website or can be requested from the correspondent. Forms can be submitted directly by the individual but the charity also asks that a supporting letter from an appropriate third party, such as a doctor or social worker, is included as well as evidence of

benefit if you are in receipt of any. Relevant documents such as invoices or quotations should also be sent with the form. Applications are considered six times a year and applicants will be notified of the decision within a month of the application deadline. For more information on specific application deadlines see the 'calendar' section on the charity's website.

The fund advises that an application is more likely to be successful where:
- Detailed background information is given about the applicant and their specific need
- Applicants have also applied to other charities for assistance when requesting sums of more than £400

The Scottish Artists' Benevolent Association

£20,000

Correspondent: Lesley Nicholl, Secretary, 2nd Floor, 5 Oswald Street, Glasgow G1 4QR (0141 248 7411; fax: 0141 221 0417)

OSCR number: SC011823

Eligibility

Scottish artists in need and their dependants.

Types of grants

Regular or one-off grants according to need. Single payments can also be made to cover emergency situations. Grants are mainly given to people who are older or in poor health.

Annual grant total

In 2014/15 the association had an income of £32,000 and an expenditure of almost £33,000. We estimate that the amount of grants given to individuals for social welfare purposes totalled around £20,000.

Applications

Application forms are available from the correspondent. Applications should be submitted directly by the individual.

The Miss M. O. Taylor and Alexander Nasmyth Funds

£10,000

Correspondent: The Miss M. O. Taylor Trust Fund/Alexander Nasmyth Fund, Royal Scottish Academy, The Mound, Edinburgh EH2 2EL (0131 225 6671; email: info@royalscottishacademy.org; website: www.royalscottishacademy.org)

OSCR number: SC007352 and SC004198

Eligibility

Scottish artists of established reputation, mainly in painting, sculpture, architecture or engraving, who are in need. To be eligible you must have had some previous experience of success in the profession, namely, have exhibited and sold work with a recognised gallery or institution.

Types of grants

One-off payments of up to £1,000. Grants are means-tested.

Annual grant total

The Nasmyth Fund is registered separately from the Taylor Fund which is held as a fund within the Royal Scottish Academy (RSA). In 2013/14 the Nasmyth Fund had an income of £13,000 and an expenditure of £9,300.

We estimate that the amount of grants given to individuals from both funds combined will usually exceed £10,000.

Applications

Application forms are available from the correspondent. Awards are made once a year and the deadline is usually early June, check the website for the exact date.

Dance

The Dance Teachers' Benevolent Fund

£6,000 (9 grants)

Correspondent: Lynn Chandler, Trustee, 32 Wingate Road, London W6 0UR (01603 619166; email: info@dtbf.co.uk; website: www.dtbf.co.uk)

CC number: 278899

Eligibility

Dance teachers or ex-dance teachers who are experiencing short or long-term hardship. Applicants are normally expected to be a registered member of one of the recognised examining bodies, or to have acquired a minimum of eight years' experience as a professional dance teacher.

Types of grants

Grants for clothing, household items, medical treatment and so on. Recurrent grants may be given to applicants living on a low income and loans may also be considered.

Annual grant total

In 2013/14 the fund held assets of £485,500 and had an income of £38,500. Monthly and one-off grants to nine dance teachers totalled £6,000.

Applications

Contact the fund directly to discuss whether they may be able to provide assistance.

Other information

The fund was founded in 1979 by a group of dance teachers drawn from all the major dance bodies. As it relies entirely on donations for income, the fund has organised numerous fundraising galas and events since its formation.

The International Dance Teachers' Association Ltd Benevolent Fund

£13,000 (16 grants)

Correspondent: Keith Holmes, Secretary, International House, 76 Bennett Road, Brighton, East Sussex BN2 5JL (01273 685652; fax: 01273 674388; email: info@idta.co.uk; website: www.idta.co.uk)

CC number: 297561

Eligibility

Members and former members of the association, other dancers, former dancers, teachers or former teachers of dance, employees or former employees of the association, and their dependants who are affected by hardship. Support is mainly given in cases where individuals are unable to teach or work due to sickness, injury or disability.

Types of grants

According to our research, one-off grants ranging from £100 to £5,000 are available. Support is of benevolent nature for people in need during times of crisis or ill health rather than to develop career.

Annual grant total

In 2014 the fund had assets of £185,500 and an income of £72,500. Grants were made to 16 individuals totalling £13,000.

Applications

Applications are available from the correspondent.

Other information

The fund also organises various dancing events and may sponsor dance-related organisations.

The Royal Ballet Benevolent Fund

£71,500

Correspondent: Clementine Cowl, Charity Manager, Royal Opera House, Covent Garden, London WC2E 9DD (01273 234011; email: info@rbbf.org.uk; website: www.rbbf.org.uk)

CC number: 207477

Eligibility

People who have been employed in a ballet or contemporary dance company as a dancer, dance teacher, choreographer, choreologist or as an independent dance artist for at least five years. In certain circumstances, the fund may consider people who do not fit this criteria e.g. people who have had their careers prematurely ended by injury.

Types of grants

One-off grants and regular payments are available to relieve any form of hardship. This includes financial assistance to older people on a low income, aids for people with a disability, help with the transition from dance to another career, or specialist surgery/therapy for injured dancers. Typical grants cover items such as supplementary pensions, disability equipment and adaptations; and medical treatment and care.

Annual grant total

In 2013/14 the fund held assets of £4.9 million and had an income of £233,000. Grants and allowances totalled £71,500.

Exclusions

There are no grants available for students training to be dancers. The fund cannot help dancers whose careers have not been within ballet and contemporary dance companies, for example dancers whose main career has been in musical theatre.

The fund does not normally pay off credit card debts.

Applications

Application forms are available from the correspondent or to download from the website. Applications should be submitted directly by the individual along with a professional CV. The form may be completed by someone else on behalf of the applicant but the applicant must sign it. An assessment of the applicant's income based on earnings from work or benefits and an assessment of the applicant's expenditure should be submitted as supporting evidence. Confirmation of the applicant's professional details must be provided by at least one referee. The trustees meet four times a year to consider applications.

The trustees welcome informal enquiries to discuss an application prior to the submission of a formal application.

Other information

The fund offers non-financial assistance in the form of advice services and home visits.

There is an informative website, with links to other agencies offering similar assistance.

Entertainment

The Concert Artistes' Association Benevolent Fund

£20,000

Correspondent: Barbara Daniels, Trustee, 3 Malm Close, Rickmansworth, Herts WD3 1NR (01923 771030; email: office@thecaa.org)

CC number: 211012

Eligibility

Members of the association, and their dependants, who are in need. Applicants must have held their membership for at least two years (or five years if over 40 at the time of joining).

Types of grants

One-off and recurrent grants are given according to need. Grants have previously been given towards the payment of household bills, dentures, hearing aids, glasses, disability equipment and electrical goods. Monthly grants may also be distributed to pensioners.

Annual grant total

In 2013/14 the fund had an income of £20,000 and a total expenditure of £20,500. We estimate that the amount of grants given to individuals totalled around £20,000.

Applications

Application forms are available from the correspondent. Applications should be submitted directly by the individual. Applications are considered on an ongoing basis.

Royal Variety Charity

£91,000 (69 grants)

Correspondent: Giles Cooper, Chair, Brinsworth House, 72 Staines Road, Twickenham, Middlesex TW2 5AL (020 8898 8164; email: enquiries@royalvarietycharity.org; website: www.eabf.org.uk)

CC number: 206451

Eligibility

Entertainment artistes, performers and other people who have been associated with the entertainment professions, and their dependants.

Types of grants

Regular top-up pensions and one-off grants for expenditure that eases financial hardship and improves quality of life, such as removals, medical treatment, travel costs, funeral costs and food vouchers.

Annual grant total

In 2014 the charity had assets of £8 million and an income of £2.45 million. Grants and pensions totalled around £91,000. Recurrent grants were given to 47 families totalling £69,500 and single payments were made to 22 individuals totalling £21,500. One-off grants were made in: Greater London (41%); North West (21%); South East (10%); Wales (8%); Anglia (6%); Midlands, Yorkshire and Humberside (6% each); North East (2%); Europe, rest of the world (Australia), Scotland and South West (0% each).

Applications

Applicants should contact the correspondent by email or telephone. Applications should include details of the applicant's difficulties, as well as evidence of their career in the entertainment industry. Requests for support are considered every couple of months.

Other information

Formerly known as The Entertainment Artistes' Benevolent Fund, the charity changed its name in June 2015. The charity's major fundraising event of the year is the Royal Variety Performance.

The charity also has its own residential and nursing care home for older entertainment professionals and supports its residents.

The Scottish Show Business Benevolent Fund

£20,000

Correspondent: Mandy Barnes, President, Caledonian Suite, 70 West Regent Street, Glasgow G2 2QZ (0141 255 0508; email: info@ssbf.co.uk; website: www.ssbf.co.uk)

OSCR number: SC009910

Eligibility

Members of The Show Business Association (and their dependants) who are in need, and their widows/widowers.

Types of grants

One-off and recurrent grants towards, for example, clothing, fuel, living expenses, funeral costs, TV rental and licences and holidays to Blackpool.

Annual grant total

In 2014/15 the fund had an income of £19,400 and an expenditure of £25,500. We estimate that the amount of grants given to individuals totalled around £20,000.

Applications

Apply in writing to the correspondent.

Music

The English National Opera Benevolent Fund

£25,000

Correspondent: Christian Francis, Fund Administrator, 118 Dartford Road, Dartford DA1 3EX (020 7845 9267; email: cfrancis@eno.org; website: www.eno.org)

CC number: 211249

Eligibility

People who are or have been employed by the English National Opera and/or Sadler's Wells Companies and are in need.

Types of grants

Applicants for recurrent grants must be over 58 years old and payments are normally towards telephone, TV and insurance costs. One-off support is considered on a case by case basis. Grants normally range between £150 and £3,000. Loans are also available.

Medical/dental treatment is not normally supported, except where delay would affect a performing career. The fund will help with payments for treatment which is not generally available through the NHS.

Annual grant total

In 2013/14 the charity had an income of £20,000 and a total expenditure of £29,000. We estimate that the amount of grants given to individuals totalled around £25,000.

Applications

Applications should be submitted directly by the individual on a form available from the correspondent, to be considered quarterly.

The Incorporated Association of Organists' Benevolent Fund

£9,000

Correspondent: Michael Whitehall, Hon. Secretary and Treasurer, 180 Lynn Road, Wisbech, Cambridgeshire PE13 3EB (01945 463826; email: michael@whitehalls.plus.com; website: www.iaobf.com)

CC number: 216533

Eligibility

Organists and/or choirmasters who are members/former members of any association or society affiliated to the Incorporated Association of Organists and their dependants who are in need.

Types of grants

One-off and recurrent grants are given according to need.

Annual grant total

In 2014 the fund had an income of £19,000 and a total expenditure of £18,500. We estimate that social welfare grants to individuals totalled around £9,000. Funding is also awarded to dependants of members or former members of the IAO to assist with pipe-organ course or examination fees.

Applications

Application forms are available from the correspondent or can be downloaded from the fund's website. Applications can be made by the individual but should be countersigned by the secretary of the applicant's local organists' association. They should be submitted by 31 March for consideration at the trustees' annual meeting in May. In urgent cases the secretary may obtain approval at other times.

ISM Members' Fund (The Benevolent Fund of The Incorporated Society of Musicians)

£90,000 (67 grants)

Correspondent: Deborah Annetts, Correspondent, 4–5 Inverness Mews, London W2 3JQ (020 7221 3499; email: membership@ism.org; website: www.ism.org)

CC number: 206801

Eligibility

Members and former members of the society and their dependants who are in need.

Types of grants

One-off and recurrent grants are given according to need.

Annual grant total

In 2013/14 the society had assets of £3.5 million and an income of £181,000. Grants were made to 67 individuals totalling £90,000.

Exclusions

No grants are given towards professional training.

Applications

Application forms are available from the correspondent. Applications should be submitted directly by the individual at

any time. An initial informal discussion with the primary contact would be beneficial. Applications are considered by a committee which assesses the needs of each applicant and decides on the nature and amount of financial support given.

Other information

The fund provides an outsourced telephone counselling service which is available to all members and their families.

The Musicians Benevolent Fund

£1.5 million

Correspondent: Help and Advice Team, 7–11 Britannia Street, London WC1X 9JS (020 7239 9100; email: info@helpmusicians.org.uk; website: www.helpmusicians.org.uk)

CC number: 228089

Eligibility

The fund can help if you: are a working professional musician; are retired and your principal career was in music; work in a related music profession; or (in some circumstances) are a dependant or partner of a musician. The fund defines a professional musician as:

> Someone who has earned their living substantially from music for a significant portion of their working life. We define 'working life' to be from the start of a career (i.e. the end of formal education, usually minimum age 18) to state pension age, or to the age at which a crisis occurs. This would normally be more than three years.

To qualify, you must be directly involved in the production of music, or in work for which the main qualification is a high level of music training.

Additionally, you must be able to show the fund that you are in financial need and be either resident in the UK, having spent the majority of your working life as a musician in the UK, or – if you are not currently living in the UK – have been resident in the UK for a minimum of three consecutive years having made an active contribution to British music.

Financial help is not normally given to individuals with savings of more than £16,000. For older and retired musicians, this limit is £20,000, however.

Types of grants

Support is given to professional musicians who are facing an unexpected crisis, a long-term illness or disability, or to help cope with retirement. The type of support given depends on the personal circumstances of the applicant. Contact the fund or see its informative website for more details.

Annual grant total

In 2014 the charity had assets of £59.2 million and an income of almost £5.1 million. During the year, financial assistance was given to 983 musicians to help with continuing care or in retirement, amounting to £1.5 million.

Exclusions

The fund is not able to assist amateur musicians or people whose paid musical work is clearly secondary to another career.

Applications

Contact the fund by calling the helpline (0800 082 6700) or by email (help@helpmusicians.org.uk). If the fund feels it can help, you will be asked to complete a simple form, providing details of you, your career, your finances and the problem you are facing. You will be asked to provide details of a musical referee who can vouch for your career and status as a professional musician, as well as some evidence of finances, such as bank statements. Once the fund has received all the paperwork, it will aim to give a decision within ten working days and, if it is able to offer you support, will try to arrange a visit to your home within eight weeks of agreeing to help, in order to assess your application and personal needs better. In a 'real emergency' a response may be made more quickly.

In the case of the fund being unable to help, it will try to signpost you in the direction of somebody who can.

Other information

The following information is taken from the fund's annual report:

> The charity supports musicians with a mix of advice, guidance and financial support... This support falls into 3 categories:
> ▶ musicians at the point of entering the profession
> ▶ musicians in their working lives who hit a serious crisis, illness or accident
> ▶ musicians in retirement or later life

The fund's trained team can offer advice on a range of issues, including welfare advice, and can help put you in touch with other sources of support, such as debt advice services or medical specialists. Part of the way it offers support is through its successful home visiting scheme. The fund also runs a Talent Programme and the Music Students Health Scheme for young musicians, more details of which are available on the website.

The Performing Rights Society Members' Benevolent Fund (PRS Members' Fund)

£402,000 (1,125 grants)

Correspondent: John Logan, General Secretary, 2 Pancras Square, London N1C 4AG (020 3741 4067; email: fund@prsformusic.com; website: www.prsformusicfund.com)

CC number: 208671

Eligibility

Songwriters and composers of music who are or were members of the Performing Rights Society, and their dependants (including of deceased members), who are in need and/or unable to work because of old age, illness, accident or disability. Members must have held membership for seven years or more.

Types of grants

The fund offers a variety of grants and loans:

- One-off grants – towards unexpected costs, such as repair or replacement of furniture, specialist equipment or deposits for individuals moving home due to vulnerability
- Regular grants – up to £20 a week to help with general living expenses for those who are receiving benefits but still cannot maintain basic standards of living. Grants can also be given for expenses like gas or heating bills, telephone costs, TV rental and TV licences. Recipients of regular grants also receive Christmas gifts or bonuses
- Holidays for those in need of a break after a difficult period
- Short-term low interest loans to those experiencing an unexpected financial crisis

Annual grant total

While accounts for 2014 were not available from the Charity Commission at the time of writing (November 2015), the charity's annual review for 2014 was available on its website. In 2014 a total of 1,125 grants amounting to £402,000 were made to individuals for welfare purposes. This included: 41 grants totalling £29,000 towards unexpected costs (including repair or replacement of household items and rent or deposits for vulnerable people); 50 grants totalling £27,500 towards winter fuel bills; weekly grants to 474 people, as well as each receiving vouchers at Christmas; holidays or day trips for 55 people.

The charity received 811 applications during the year.

It made 36 low-interest loans totalling almost £373,000 altogether. A grant of £5,000 was also made to the British Association for Performing Arts Medicine for beneficiaries to access specialist health assessments and treatments.

Exclusions

The fund will not help:

- With the cost of buying a home
- To promote any commercial venture
- Composers who do not have any other employment
- Towards payments as an advance against future royalties

Applications

Application forms can be downloaded from the fund's website or requested from the correspondent. In cases of claims based on illness, a medical or GP's report is required. The committee generally meets on a monthly basis to consider applications.

All applications are means-tested in line with DWP income and savings criteria. Recipients of regular support are paid a visit by the fund at least once a year.

Other information

As well as offering financial assistance the fund can make referrals for specialist financial advice as well as provide specialist health assessments in conjunction with their partners, the British Association for Performing Arts Medicine. The fund also provides sheltered accommodation and runs a career counselling service.

The Royal Society of Musicians of Great Britain

£739,000

Correspondent: Penny Ryan, Accountant, 10 Stratford Place, London W1C 1BA (020 7629 6137; fax: 020 7629 6137; email: enquiries@royalsocietyofmusicians.co.uk; website: royalsocietyofmusicians.co.uk)

CC number: 208879

Eligibility

Current, former or beginning professional musicians and their families who are in need because of illness, an accident or age. Membership of the society is not a requirement, although some priority may be given.

Types of grants

One-off and recurrent grants from £50 to £5,000. Loans of musical instruments are also available.

Annual grant total

In 2013/14 the society had assets of £18.7 million and an income of

£2.2 million. Grants made to individuals totalled £739,000.

Exclusions

Grants are not given to students or people whose only claim for relief arises from unemployment.

Applications

Apply in writing to the correspondent. Enquiries from welfare organisations are welcomed as is the identification of need from any concerned individual. Normally, applications will need to be supported by a member of the society (a copy of the current membership list is supplied to applicants). Requests for assistances are considered monthly.

Other information

The society is a charity for musicians, run by musicians. Specialist advice is also available from honorary officers, which include medical consultants. If unable to help, the society may refer applicants to other relevant organisations.

Writing

The Authors' Contingency Fund

£17,500

Correspondent: Sarah Baxter, Contracts Advisor and Literary Estates, 84 Drayton Gardens, London SW10 9SB (020 7373 6642; email: SBaxter@societyofauthors.org; website: www.societyofauthors.org)

CC number: 212406

Eligibility

Professional authors in the UK and their dependants. Grants are also made to professional poets and their dependants and female journalists.

Types of grants

One-off grants usually of between £500 and £750, to relieve a temporary financial emergency.

Annual grant total

In 2014 the fund had an income of £25,000 and a total expenditure of £25,500. Social welfare grants to individuals totalled £17,500.

Exclusions

The trust cannot help with the following:

- Grants to cover publication costs
- Grants to authors who are in financial difficulty through contributing towards publication costs
- Tuition fees
- General support whilst writing a book

Applications

Application forms and guidelines are available from the fund's website. Applications should be submitted to the correspondent. The assessment process usually takes around three weeks.

Other information

The fund, in conjunction with the John Masefield Memorial Trust, makes grants to British poets and administers the Margaret Rhondda Awards to support women journalists.

Francis Head Award

£25,000

Correspondent: Sarah Baxter, Contracts Advisor and Literary Estates, 84 Drayton Gardens, London SW10 9SB (020 7373 6642; email: sbaxter@societyofauthors. org; website: www.societyofauthors.org)

CC number: 277018

Eligibility

Professional writers (writing in the English language) who were born in the UK and are over the age of 35. The focus of the trust is primarily on those who are temporarily unable to support themselves or their dependants due to illness, accident or disability, although the trust's website does state that 'the terms of the trust are reasonably wide'.

Types of grants

Emergency grants usually ranging from £1,000 to £2,000.

Annual grant total

In 2014 charity had an income of £23,000 and a total expenditure of £30,000. We estimate that grants totalled £25,000.

Exclusions

No grants are given to cover publication costs, tuition fees or general maintenance whilst writing a book. Support is also unavailable to authors who are in financial difficulty because they have invested money in publication costs.

Applications

Apply on a form available from the correspondent or to download from the trust's website. Applications can be submitted directly by the individual and should include a covering letter explaining the circumstances prompting the application. A decision is usually made within three weeks.

Peggy Ramsay Foundation

£115,500

Correspondent: Neil Adleman, Trustee, Hanover House, 14 Hanover Square, London W15 1HP (020 7667 5000; fax: 020 7667 5100; email: prf@harbottle.

com; website: www. peggyramsayfoundation.org)

CC number: 1015427

Eligibility

Playwrights who are resident in the British Isles (UK, Republic of Ireland, the Channel Isles and the Isle of Man) who have had at least one full length play in English professionally produced for a run for an audience of adults or young people (see exclusions). The website specifies: 'By full length the Trustees usually mean a play of more than one hour and that a run implies performance for more than one week.'

Types of grants

One-off grants. Individual grants never ordinarily exceed a standard commissioning fee. Grants are sometimes made for equipment, such as laptops, and for expenditure which makes writing possible.

Annual grant total

In 2014 the foundation had assets of £5.95 million and an income of £227,000. During the year, 94 grants were made to individuals totalling £231,000. We estimate that social welfare grants to individuals amounted to £115,500.

Exclusions

The website states the following information:

> The Trustees will not accept as qualification books for musicals, pantomime scripts, puppet plays, foreign language plays, translations or school plays. Adaptations and plays intended primarily for younger audiences are accepted only in special circumstances which imply wider originality.
>
> Plays in other media and scripts for film or television are not a qualification but are relevant in a CV.
>
> The Foundation does not support production costs or any project which does not have a direct benefit to individual playwrights or writing for the stage. Commissioning costs are usually considered as part of production costs. Fees for training or courses of any kind are not supported. Scripts, publicity material and reviews should not be sent. References are not needed.

Applications

Apply by writing a short letter to the correspondent, which should explain the need, the amount requested and the way in which the amount would be spent. A full CV 'not limited to writing' should also be sent.

Applicants are also asked to provide answers to the following questions:

▸ When and where the first professional performance of a play of theirs took place?
▸ Who produced the play which qualifies them for a grant?

▸ When and where was their qualifying play produced, how long was it, what was its approximate playing time and has it been revived?
▸ For that production were the director and actors all professionals engaged with Equity contracts?
▸ Did the audience pay to attend?

Scripts and publicity material must not be included, and references are not needed. The trustees meet quarterly and, although applications are dealt with between meetings, it may take six to eight weeks before a definitive answer is received.

The Royal Literary Fund

£1 million (227 grants)

Correspondent: Eileen Gunn, Chief Executive, 3 Johnson's Court, Off Fleet Street, London EC4A 3EA (020 7353 7159; email: eileen.gunn@rlf.org.uk; website: www.rlf.org.uk)

CC number: 219952

Eligibility

Authors of published work of literary merit and their dependants. You are eligible to apply for help from the RLF if you have commercially published several works in the UK for a general readership and are suffering financial hardship. The work must be written in English. Books stemming from a parallel career as an academic or practitioner are not eligible.

Types of grants

One-off (outright) grants, instalment grants and pensions. Instalment grants and pensions are awarded over a three and five year period respectively. Pensions are reviewed for renewal after the five year period.

Recent examples of beneficiaries include:
▸ A writer of books for children suffered from ME. She had recently had a baby and lost some of her regular paid work. Her husband had also lost his job. The committee made her an annual grant
▸ An elderly poet and his wife lived on a tight budget. Urgent repairs had been needed to their house and their savings had been depleted. The committee made him an annual pension
▸ An award-winning writer of science fiction had taken time out from fiction to work on screenplays. This had not been a success and he had lost vital income. The committee made him a grant

Annual grant total

In 2013/14 the fund had assets of over £137 million and an income of £2.2 million. Grants and pensions totalled £1 million.

Exclusions

No grants are given for projects or work in progress. The trust does not make loans. Books stemming from a previous academic or practitioner career do not count.

Applications

Application forms are available from the correspondent. The form requests that details of the applicant's income and expenditure are listed. A member of staff will subsequently arrange to meet with new applicants at their homes. Applicants are asked to supply copies of their published work which is then read by two members of the committee who decide on the question of literary merit. When requesting an application form applicants are asked to provide a list of their publications, including names of publishers, dates and whether they were the sole author. If this is approved, a grant/pension may be made based on an assessment of need.

Other information

One grant was paid to the Royal Society of Literature (£10,000).

The Society of Authors Pension Fund

£13,200

Correspondent: The General Secretary, c/o The Society of Authors, 84 Drayton Gardens, London SW10 9SB (020 7373 6642; email: info@societyofauthors.org; website: www.societyofauthors.org)

CC number: 212401

Eligibility

Authors over 65 who have been a member of the Society of Authors for at least ten years.

Types of grants

Annual grants of £1,800 which are paid in quarterly instalments.

Annual grant total

In 2014 the fund had assets of £687,000 and an income of £36,000. Grants were made to individuals totalling £13,200.

Applications

Apply in writing to the correspondent when vacancies are announced in the society's journal.

Business, financial services and insurance

The AIA Educational and Benevolent Trust

£3,500

Correspondent: Mr T. Pinkney, Staithes 3, The Watermark, Metro Riverside, Tyne And Wear NE11 9SN (0191 493 0272; fax: 0191 493 0278; email: trust. fund@aiaworldwide.com; website: www. aiaworldwide.com)

CC number: 1118333

Eligibility

Fellows and associates of the institute, and their close dependants, who are in need.

Types of grants

One-off grants according to need.

Annual grant total

In 2014 the trust had an income of £3,520 and a total expenditure of £7,000. We estimate that social welfare grants to individuals totalled £3,500. Grants are also given to those wishing to undergo education and training in accountancy.

Applications

Make application on a form available from the trust's website which should be printed and posted to the correspondent. Applications are received on an ongoing basis.

The Baltic Exchange Charitable Society

£84,000 (35 grants)

Correspondent: Richard Butler, Secretary, St Mary Axe, London EC3A 8BH (020 7283 6090; fax: 020 7283 6133; email: richard.butler@baltic-charities.co.uk)

CC number: 277093

Eligibility

Employees and ex-employees of member companies of the Baltic Exchange as well as companies in the oilseeds trade, and their dependants, who are in need. Assistance is available only to those who have joined as a member of the society.

Types of grants

Annual grants and emergency or one-off grants. One-off grants have recently been awarded towards physiotherapy, respite and care home fees, legal support, grave maintenance and gardening. Fuel payments were also made during exceptionally cold weather. Recurrent grants are paid quarterly to help with living expenses. In 2014 Christmas gifts were distributed to all beneficiaries. Loans may also be offered.

Annual grant total

In 2014 the society had an income of £179,500 and a total expenditure of £240,000. Grants to 35 individuals totalled £84,000, of which £66,000 was awarded in quarterly payments to 13 members and their dependants and £18,000 in special one-off grants.

Applications

Application forms are available from the correspondent. Applications can be submitted at any time.

Other information

At the end of the year, outstanding loans to beneficiaries amounted to £365,500.

The Bank Workers Charity

£601,500

Correspondent: The Client Advisor, Pinners Hall, 105–108 Old Broad Street, London EC2N 1EX (0800 023 4834 (helpline); email: info@bwcharity.org.uk; website: www.bwcharity.org.uk)

CC number: 313080

Eligibility

Current and former employees of banks in the UK, and their dependants, who are in need. The charity seeks to help those in financial need due to 'bereavement, ill health or disability and those in crisis situations who need help to get back on their feet'.

Types of grants

Regular grant payments for those on limited incomes; limited help with residential and nursing home fees; contributions towards the cost of wheelchairs, scooters, mobility aids and domestic appliances; carers' respite breaks and some family holidays; in special cases, assistance with telephone bills and TV licenses; grants towards house repairs and maintenance. The charity aims to 'provide support for people in need based on early intervention, rather than picking up the pieces at crisis point'.

Annual grant total

In 2013/14 the charity had assets of £47.7 million and an income of

£1.7 million. Cash grants totalled £767,000, broken down as follows:

Families	£308,500
Retirees	£293,000
Child education	£165,500

We take the amount given for 'families' and 'retirees' to represent welfare support awarded.

In 2013/14 the charity had assets of £47.7 million and an income of £1.7 million. Cash grants totalled £767,000, broken down as follows:

Families	£308,500
Retirees	£293,000
Child education	£165,500

We take the amount given for 'child education needs' to represent educational support awarded.

In 2013/14 the charity had assets of £47.7 million and an income of £1.7 million. Cash grants totalled £767,000, broken down as follows:

Families	£308,500
Retirees	£293,000
Child education	£165,500

We take the amount given for 'child education needs' to represent educational support awarded.

Exclusions

Non-priority debts; private medical fees; home improvements, except when essential repairs are needed to ensure independent living, safety and security. People who have worked in the insurance or stock broking industries are generally not helped.

Applications

Contact the charity's Client Advisors in the first instance to discuss making an application and learn about support available. The trustees meet quarterly to consider new cases.

Other information

The charity also provides support in three main areas – home, money and well-being. They have client advisors who offer information, advice and guidance covering a range of issue as well as offering independent and confidential counselling. The cost of service delivery and client support amounted to over £1.1 million, which constitutes about 70% of the overall expenditure.

In 2014/15 the charity has planned to distribute about £900,000 in grants.

The Chartered Accountants' Benevolent Association

£676,000 (292 grants)

Correspondent: Donna Cooper, Grants Co-ordinator, 8 Mitchell Court, Castle Mound Way, Rugby CV23 0UY (0800 107 6163(24hr helpline); email: donna. cooper@caba.org.uk; website: www.caba. org.uk)

CC number: 1116973

Eligibility

Chartered Accountants' Benevolent Association (CABA) provides advice and practical support to current and former ICAEW chartered accountants and their families; ICAEW chartered accountants; retired ICAEW chartered accountants; spouses and life partners; active ACA students; those living overseas. Visit the website for full information.

Types of grants

One-off and recurrent grants towards daily living costs, respite care, household essentials and so on. The association also provides interest-free loans.

Annual grant total

In 2014 the association held assets of £103.6 million and had an income of £4.8 million. Financial assistance to individuals totalled £676,000.

Applications

Initial contact can be made by calling the 24 hour helpline or by using the live chat feature on the association's website.

Other information

The association offers a wide range of support and advice on issues such as accessing state benefits, debt and financial problems and stress management. Services are free and only the direct financial support is means-tested.

The Chartered Certified Accountants' Benevolent Fund

£15,600 (8 grants)

Correspondent: Hugh McCash, Honorary Secretary, 2 Central Quay, 89 Hydepark Street, Glasgow G3 8BW (0141 534 4045; email: hugh.mccash@ accaglobal.com; website: www.accaglobal. com/gb/en/member/membership-benefit/ benevolent-fund/apply-assistance.html)

CC number: 222595

Eligibility

Members, and former members, of the ACCA, and their dependants.

Types of grants

Grants in 2014/15 ranged from £9 to £2,500. Recurrent grants are available to help with stair-lifts, telephone bills, holidays, TV rental and so on; one-off grants in tragic circumstances to help beneficiaries get back on their feet; and low-interest or interest-free loans on property.

Annual grant total

In 2014/15 the fund held assets of £3.5 million and had an income of £239,500. Grants to eight individuals totalled £15,600.

Exclusions

Grants are not generally available for the education of children.

Applications

Apply on a form available from the correspondent or downloadable from the website. Applications can be submitted directly by the individual or through a social worker, Citizens Advice, welfare agency or other third party. They are considered at meetings held every two or three months.

The Chartered Institute of Management Accountants Benevolent Fund

£99,000

Correspondent: Caroline Aldred, Secretary, CIMA Benevolent Fund, The Helicon, One South Place, London EC2M 2RB (020 8849 2221; email: benevolent.fund@cimaglobal.com; website: www.cimaglobal.com)

CC number: 261114

Eligibility

Past and present CIMA members and their dependants anywhere in the UK and the world.

Types of grants

One-off grants for specific needs such as television licence/rental, telephone rental, motor insurance/tax, disability aids, some repairs and necessary household items such as fridges, cookers, etc. Grants are also made for medical bills for members outside the UK. Regular grants are also made to help meet basic living costs. Interest-free loans may be provided in exceptional circumstances.

Annual grant total

In 2014 the fund had assets of £2.1 million and an income of £110,000. Grants to 44 individuals totalled £109,000, mostly for social welfare purposes. We have estimated the figure for social welfare grants to be around £99,000.

Exclusions

No grants are given to enhance property, for investment in business ventures, or for private medical care (however, assistance may be given to members living outside the UK who do not have access to state-funded medical treatment or medical insurance and have large medical bills).

Applications

Applications can be made on a form available from the correspondent or to download from the website. Applications can be submitted directly by the individual or through a recognised referral agency (Citizens Advice, doctor, social worker and so on), or through a third party. Anybody wishing to discuss a possible application informally can contact the Secretary 'in complete confidence'.

Other information

The charity can also signpost people to relevant services and provide support from a welfare officer.

Educational grants are also made for dependent children. CIMA has another charity, the General Charitable Trust Fund, which funds the advancement of education in accountancy and related topics.

The Corn Exchange Benevolent Society

£35,500 (30 grants)

Correspondent: Richard Butler, Secretary, The Baltic Exchange, 38 St Marys Axe, London EC3A 8BH (020 7283 6090; email: richard.butler@baltic-charities.co.uk; website: www.baltic-charities.co.uk)

CC number: 207733

Eligibility

Members of the society and their dependants who are in need. Limited funds are also available for non-members who work or have been engaged in any aspect of grain trading in England and Wales (corn, grain, seed, animal feed stuffs, pulses, malt, flour or granary-keeping trades) and their dependants.

Types of grants

Quarterly grants are available to help towards day-to-day living costs. Recent one-off grants have been awarded towards essential household items, hospital travel costs, mobility aids and help with general living expenses. Christmas gifts are made to all beneficiaries. In 2014 special grants were also paid towards heating costs during periods of cold weather.

Annual grant total

In 2014 the society had an income of £97,000 and a total expenditure of £96,500. Grants to 30 individuals totalled £35,500. Of this, £19,200 was given in quarterly payments, with the remaining 16,100 awarded in special grants to beneficiaries.

Applications

Apply on a form available from the correspondent or to download from the website. Applications can be submitted directly by the individual or through a social worker, Citizens Advice or other welfare agency. Applicants are required to provide full details of their income and expenditure.

Initial approaches by phone, email or in writing are also welcomed.

The CTBI – The Salespeople's Charity

£523,500 (256 grants)

Correspondent: Mandi Leonard, Secretary, 2 Fletcher Road, Ottershaw, Chertsey, Surrey KT16 0JY (01932 429636; email: info@salespeoplescharity.org.uk; website: www.salespeoplescharity.org.uk)

CC number: 216538

Eligibility

People in the UK who are in need and have worked as a sales representative/agent promoting or selling to the trade for at least five years, and their dependants. Sales must be business to business and involve the representative visiting client sites to sell or promote goods or services to the trade (rather than the public). Applicants must be in financial need and may be in work, retired, have been made redundant or be unable to work due to ill health or disability.

Types of grants

Recurrent grants and gifts in kind. One-off grants are also given towards respite breaks, disability aids, home adaptations and urgent maintenance work, TV licences, Christmas and birthday payments and support with critical one-off payments. Gifts in kind have included vouchers for high street stores and food hampers.

Annual grant total

In 2014 the charity had an income of almost £602,000 and a total expenditure of £636,000. Grants to 256 beneficiaries totalled £523,500 and were distributed as follows:

Quarterly benefit, birthday and Christmas payments	£423,500
Hampers and food vouchers	£51,500
One-off grants	£32,000
TV licences, phones, etc.	£14,500
Respite	£1,900
Gifts	-

Exclusions

No help is given to those engaged in 'van sales', retail, telesales or general selling to the public.

Applications

Applications should be made on a form available from the correspondent or on the charity's website. Applications should include evidence of employment in commercial sales and be submitted either directly by the individual or through a third party. Applicants may be visited by a volunteer to discuss their application further. The trustees meet five times a year to consider applications, although emergency payments can be made quickly in cases of extreme hardship.

The Charles Dixon Pension Fund

£19,000

Correspondent: Richard Morris, Trustee, The Society of Merchant Venturers, Merchants' Hall, The Promenade, Clifton Down, Bristol BS8 3NH (0117 973 8058; email: enquiries@merchantventurers.com)

CC number: 202153

Eligibility

Merchants who are in reduced circumstances, are over 60 years of age, and live in Bristol, Liverpool or London.

Types of grants

Pensions, usually between £500 and £2,000 a year.

Annual grant total

In 2013/14 the fund had an income of £8,500 and a total expenditure of £20,500. We estimate that welfare grants to individuals totalled £19,000.

Applications

Application forms are available from the correspondent. Applications can be submitted directly by the individual or, where applicable, through a social worker, Citizens Advice, other welfare agency or a third party such as a clergyman. They are dealt with as received.

The George Drexler Foundation

£38,000

Correspondent: Nicola Extance-Vaughan, Correspondent, 35–43 Lincolns Inn Fields, London WC2A 3PE (020 7869 6080; email: info@georgedrexler.org.uk; website: www.georgedrexler.org.uk)

CC number: 313278

Eligibility

Former employees of the Ofrex Group and their dependants. Other people formerly employed in commerce and their families may be considered.

Types of grants

One-off and recurrent grants for the relief of poverty.

Annual grant total

In 2013/14 the foundation had assets of nearly £6.5 million and an income of £260,000. Grants to individuals to relieve poverty totalled £38,000. Grants totalling £174,500 were made for educational purposes, consisting of £74,500 given to individuals and £100,000 to The Royal College of Surgeons of England for educational facilities and tutors.

Exclusions

Support is not given for:
- Overseas students
- Volunteering
- Part-time study
- Study abroad
- Medical electives
- Gap year projects
- Non-UK citizens

Applications

The foundation accepts applications between 1 January and 30 April. Applications must be submitted using an online system on the foundation's website. Outside these dates appeals are not accepted or processed. Successful and unsuccessful applicants are notified of the outcome by letter/email in June.

Other information

For UK citizens who have a direct (personal or family) link with commerce – candidates (or their parents or grandparents) must have worked in or owned a commercial business. Our research suggests that this does not include professional people, such as doctors, lawyers, dentists, architects or accountants. Selected Medical Schools and Schools of Music apply by invitation only.

Alfred Foster Settlement

£15,500

Correspondent: Graham Prew, Correspondent, Barclays Bank Trust Co. Ltd, Executorship and Trustee Service, Osborne Court, Gadbrook Park, Rudheath, Northwich CW9 7UE (01606 313118)

CC number: 229576

Eligibility

Current and former employees of banks and their dependants who are in need.

Types of grants

One-off grants of £250–£1,000 according to need.

Annual grant total

In 2013/14 the charity had assets of £867,500, an income of £35,500 and awarded over £31,000 in grants. Further breakdown was not given; therefore, we estimate that about £15,500 was given in welfare-related awards.

Applications

Applications may be made in writing to the correspondent. They can be submitted directly by the individual or through the employee's bank or to their local regional office.

Other information

The charity also makes grants to individuals for educational purposes.

The Ruby and Will George Trust

£15,000

Correspondent: Damien Slattery, Administrator, 125 Cloverfield, West Allotment, Newcastle upon Tyne NE27 0BE (0191 266 4527; email: admin@rwgt.co.uk; website: www.rwgt.co.uk)

CC number: 264042

Eligibility

People who are employed in commerce, and their dependants, who are in need. Preference is given to people who live in the North East.

Types of grants

One-off or recurrent grants for items which are needed but cannot be afforded.

Annual grant total

In 2013/14 the trust had assets of £3.7 million and an income of £74,000. A total of 38 grants were made to individuals during the year, amounting to £61,500. The annual report and accounts state that: 'The vast majority of the income generated by the trust's assets is paid out by means of either one-off or continuing grants, these being predominantly made to those in either secondary or further education.' With this in mind, we estimate that grants for social welfare purposes totalled around £15,000.

Applications

The trust has an online application process, although its annual report also states that 'those without access to the internet are also provided with the means to submit paper-based applications where appropriate'. Applicants will need to prove their commerce connection and their income and expenditure. Two references are required. The trust considers applications four times a year. The precise dates of these meetings, and of deadline dates for applications, can be found on the website.

The Institute of Financial Accountants' and International Association of Book-Keepers' Benevolent Fund

£7,500

Correspondent: Christopher Brown, Correspondent, Brantwood, Post Office Corner, Sutton, Ipswich IP9 2TJ (01473 327361; email: secretary@ifaiabbenfund.org.uk; website: www.ifaiabbenfund.org.uk)

CC number: 234082

Eligibility

Past and present members of the institute or the association, their dependants, and all current IFA and IAB students.

Types of grants

Grants, usually one-off, 'where there is a critical situation that affects daily life'.

Annual grant total

In 2013/14 the fund had an income of £18,900 and a total expenditure of £15,500. We estimate that social welfare grants to individuals totalled £7,500, with funding also awarded to individuals for educational purposes.

Exclusions

No recurrent or ongoing payments are made where they could be considered to 'be in lieu of a steady income'.

Applications

Application forms are available from the correspondent or to download from the website. Applications can be submitted directly by the individual or on their behalf by a family member. Details of the individual's income and expenditure, as well as any relevant supporting evidence (for example, bank statements, pay slips, tax return forms, proof of rent or mortgage payments) should be included. Every application is considered on its merits.

Other information

The trustees may choose to support the educational needs of those who are pursuing professional qualifications of the IFA or IAB when the fund has surplus income.

The Insurance Charities

£862,000

Correspondent: Annali-Joy Thornicroft, CEO and Company Secretary, 20 Aldermanbury, London EC2V 7HY (020 7606 3763; fax: 020 7600 1170; email: info@theinsurancecharities.org.uk; website: www.theinsurancecharities.org.uk)

CC number: 206860

Eligibility

People who have been engaged in any aspect of the UK or Irish insurance industry, normally for at least five years, and their dependants. Support is given where there is a case of financial hardship, illness, disability or distress.

Types of grants

One-off grants for essential items (such as equipment to help someone with reduced mobility, an adaptation to a property which is not financed by local or central government, the replacement of an appliance or some essential property maintenance) and repeated assistance are both considered.

Annual grant total

In 2013/14 the charity had assets of £31.25 million and an income of nearly £1.3 million. Grants were made to 251 individuals totalling £920,000. This figure includes £58,000 – the contribution made by the Paul Golmick Fund towards grants, which we take to represent awards for educational purposes. The remainder of awards, which we take to be for social welfare needs, totalled £862,000. Note that the trustees may decide to use money from the general fund to support educational needs as well, in which case this figure may be lower.

Applications

If you think you may qualify for help, in the first instance you should complete an initial form, which can be filled in online, downloaded and emailed or printed off and posted to the charity. The Grants Committee meets quarterly to consider awards.

Other information

The charity also provides loans and offers money advice service.

According to the website:

> The Paul Golmick Fund is a Trust, separate from The Insurance Charities, which promotes the maintenance and education of those under the age of 24, and primarily under the age of 18, who reside in the UK or Ireland and have at least one parent/guardian in insurance.

The Liverpool Merchants' Guild

£910,500 (315 grants)

Correspondent: Trusts and Estates Team, Moore Stephens LLP, 110–114 Duke Street, Liverpool L1 5AG (0151 703 1080; fax: 0151 703 1085; email: info@liverpoolmerchantsguild.org.uk; website: www.liverpoolmerchantsguild.org.uk)

CC number: 206454

Eligibility

People over 50 years old who have been employed in a professional, supervisory, clerical capacity (or self-employed people) and their dependants who live on Merseyside (or who have lived there for a continuous period of at least 15 years) and are in need or distress.

Types of grants

Annual pensions of £200 upwards, paid twice yearly. One-off grants of up to £5,000 for items of exceptional expenditure, such as equipment or adaptations to support independent living.

Annual grant total

In 2014 the guild had assets of almost £36 million, £27 million of which represents permanent endowment and is not available for grant-making. There is also a restricted legacies fund of almost £1.2 million included in the assets figure. The guild's income was £1 million and grants were made totalling £910,500 which included £798,500 given in pensions and £112,000 given in grants.

Exclusions

Manual workers and their dependants.

Applications

Apply on a form available from the correspondent or to download from the website. Applications must be countersigned by two unrelated referees and include all relevant supporting documentation – refer to the website for details. They can be submitted at any time and are considered every three months.

Note: Applicants wishing to apply for a one-off grant will need to fill in the standard application form and a supplementary grants form (also available on the website).

Other information

The Liverpool Merchants' Guild was instituted in the year 1880 for the purpose of taking over and managing a fund bequeathed by the will of Catherine Wright, of Liverpool, who died in the month of September 1868.

Catherine Wright by her will bequeathed the sum of £10,000 to the trustees for the purpose of founding an institution to be called Wright's Institution, the object of which was to grant pensions to people who had been unable to make adequate provision for their declining years.

The name was changed in 1880 to Liverpool Merchants' Guild and in 2006 a Royal Charter was granted replacing the original of 1914.

The Lloyd's Benevolent Fund

£190,500 (29 grants)

Correspondent: Raymond Blaber, Secretary, Lloyd's Benevolent Fund, 1 Lime Street, London EC3M 7HA (020 7327 6453; email: raymond.blaber@lloyds.com)

CC number: 207231

Eligibility

People who work or have worked in the Lloyd's insurance market anywhere in the world (and their dependants).

Types of grants

One-off or recurrent grants can be given towards relieving general hardship.

Annual grant total

In 2013/14 the fund held assets of £10.5 million and had an income of £291,500. Grants to 29 beneficiaries totalled £190,500.

Exclusions

No assistance is given for underwriting members of Lloyd's. School fees or medical costs will not be covered.

Applications

Application forms are available from the correspondent. Applications can be submitted by the individual or through a social worker, Citizens Advice, other welfare agency or other third party. They are considered throughout the year.

London Metal Exchange Benevolent Fund

£5,000

Correspondent: Marcos Castro, Company Secretary, The London Metal Exchange Ltd, 56 Leadenhall Street, London EC3A 2DX (020 7264 5555; email: marcos.castro@lme.com)

CC number: 231001

Eligibility

People in need who are members of, or have been connected with, the London Metal Exchange, and their dependants.

Types of grants

One-off and recurrent grants are given according to need.

Annual grant total

In 2013/14 the fund had an income of £1,000 and a total expenditure of £5,700. We estimate the total amount of grants given to individuals for welfare purposes to be in the region of £5,000.

Applications

Application forms are available from the correspondent.

Pawnbrokers' Charitable Institution

£66,000

Correspondent: Mrs K. Way, Correspondent, 184 Crofton Lane, Orpington BR6 0BW (01689 811978)

CC number: 209993

Eligibility

Pawnbrokers in need who have been in the business for at least five years, and their dependants. Help is primarily given to people over 60 but assistance may also be available to younger people if there is sufficient need.

Types of grants

Regular payments, Christmas gifts, equipment and one-off grants to meet emergency needs for those on a low income who cannot manage on a state pension.

Annual grant total

In 2013/14 the institution had an income of £102,000 and an expenditure of £120,500. Welfare grants totalled £66,000.

Applications

Application forms are available from the correspondent.

The Prime Charitable Trust

£6,000

Correspondent: Pauline Weller, Correspondent, Federation of Small Businesses, Sir Frank Whittle Way, Blackpool FY4 2FE (01253 336000; email: admin@prime-charitable-trust.co.uk; website: www.prime-charitable-trust.co.uk)

CC number: 328441

Eligibility

Members or former members of the National Federation of Self-Employed and Small Businesses Ltd and their family and dependants, who due to illness or incapacity are unable to maintain themselves.

Types of grants

One-off and recurrent grants are given according to need.

Annual grant total

In 2013/14 the trust had an income of £6,100 and a total expenditure of £6,700. We estimate that social welfare grants to individuals totalled £6,000.

Applications

Apply in writing to the correspondent.

H. J. Rawlings Trust

£4,900

Correspondent: Trust Administrator, Liverpool Charity and Voluntary Services, 151 Dale Street, Liverpool L2 2AH (0151 227 5177; website: www.charitycheques.org.uk)

CC number: 265690

Eligibility

People in need, with a preference for current and former employees of John Holt and Company (Liverpool) Ltd and their dependants.

Types of grants

One-off and recurrent grants are given according to need.

Annual grant total

In 2013/14 the trust held assets of £987,000 and had an income of £32,000. Grants totalled £17,900, of which £4,900 was received by individuals for welfare needs, with the remainder awarded to local organisations.

Applications

Apply in writing to the correspondent.

Scottish Chartered Accountants' Benevolent Association

£60,000

Correspondent: Robert Linton, Correspondent, Robert Linton and Co., c/o ICAS 2nd Floor, 7 West Nile Street, Glasgow G1 2PR (0141 301 1788; email: scaba@robertlinton.co.uk; website: www.icas.com/our-charitable-work/scaba-scottish-chartered-accountants-benevolent-association)

OSCR number: SC008365

Eligibility

Members of the Institute of Chartered Accountants of Scotland who are in need, and their dependants.

Types of grants

One-off and recurrent grants and loans for a variety of needs. Previously grants have been given for hospital travel costs, house repairs, general living expenses, mobility aids, retraining and home help.

Annual grant total

In 2014 the association had an income of £211,000 and an expenditure of £162,500. Our research suggests that grants usually total about £120,000 each year. We estimate that about £60,000 was given for welfare needs.

Applications

An initial letter or telephone call should be made to the correspondent.

Other information

Grants are also given for educational purposes.

Sears Group Trust

£122,000 (147 grants)

Correspondent: Gary Branston, Secretary to the Directors, Capita Employee Benefits, Hartshead House, 2 Cutlers Gate, Sheffield S4 7TL (0114 273 7331; email: gary.branston@capita.co.uk)

CC number: 1022586

Eligibility

Employees, former employees and their dependants of any company that is, or has been, associated with Sears Ltd, who are in financial need.

Types of grants

One-off and recurrent grants are given according to need. Recurrent grants are made to top up low incomes. Recent one-off grants have been awarded towards respite care, decorating, beds, televisions and kitchen appliances. The trust also owns a number of pieces of mobility equipment which may be gifted or loaned to individuals. Entitlement to recurrent grants is reviewed every three years.

Annual grant total

In 2013/14 the trust held assets of £9.7 million and had an investments income of £377,500. Individuals received a total of £122,000 in 147 grants; 132 of which were annual grants, the remaining 15 were one-off. Organisations received a further £5,000.

Exclusions

No grants are given for bankruptcy or funeral costs.

Applications

Initial contact should be made with the correspondent who will arrange for a visit from one of the trust's welfare visitors. The visitor will assess the applicant and make a recommendation to the trustees. The trustees meet to consider applications two to three times per year; however, applications can be processed between meetings.

Other information

In 2013/14 the trust's welfare visitors made more than 1,375 home calls to pensioners and former Sears employees, to whom they were able to offer advice on applications for statutory benefits.

The Stock Exchange Benevolent Fund

£647,500

Correspondent: James Cox, Secretary, 10 Paternoster Square, St Pauls, London EC4M 7DX (020 7797 1092/3120; fax: 020 7374 4963; email: enquiries@sebf.co.uk; website: www.sebf.co.uk)

CC number: 245430

Eligibility

Members and ex-members of the Stock Exchange and their dependants.

Types of grants

Annuities and one-off grants are given according to need. Grants have been made for medical equipment, motor repairs and household essentials.

Annual grant total

In 2014 the fund held assets of £22.7 million and had an income of £1.1 million. Grants were made totalling £647,500, of which £473,000 was given in pensions to 69 individuals and £174,000 in one-off grants.

Applications

An application form is available from the correspondent or to download from the website. Applications are considered quarterly, usually on the first Tuesday of March, June, September and December, although emergency grants can be made between meetings. Forms should be submitted two months before the next meeting.

Other information

The fund tries to keep in regular contact with its beneficiaries and is there to offer advice and support if needed.

Stock Exchange Clerks Fund

£77,500 (44 grants)

Correspondent: Mr A. Barnard, Correspondent, 1–5 Earl Street, London EC2A 2AL (020 7797 4373 or 01245 322985; email: deanaball44@gmail.co.uk)

CC number: 286055

Eligibility

Former members of the fund and former employees of the London Stock Exchange or member firms of the London Stock Exchange, who are in need, and their dependants.

Types of grants

Monthly payments to help with living costs. One-off grants towards medical equipment, mobility costs, household goods and funeral expenses. Most beneficiaries also receive a Christmas food parcel.

Annual grant total

In 2014 the fund had an income of £39,000 and assets of £1.1 million. Grants were made to 44 individuals totalling £77,500.

Applications

Application forms are available from the correspondent. Applications can be submitted at any time by the individual or through a third party. New applicants are visited by the fund's Liaison Officer who will then make a report to the trustees.

Any information concerning individuals who were previously employed in the industry and who may be in need of assistance can be given in complete confidence to either the correspondent or any of the trustees.

UCTA Samaritan Benefit Fund Society

£73,500

Correspondent: Peter Brennan, Trustee, The Cottage, Dairy House Lane, Dunham Massey, Altrincham WA14 5RD (0161 265 3462; email: pjbfca@gmail.com)

CC number: 1071037

Eligibility

Commercial travellers and their dependants in the UK who are in need.

Types of grants

One-off and recurrent grants are given according to need.

Annual grant total

In 2014 the society had assets of £215,500 and an income of £89,000. Welfare grants to individuals totalled £73,500.

Applications

Application forms are available from the correspondent.

Other information

The charity continues to locate potential beneficiaries using the internet and the diligence of the trustees.

Construction

Builders' Benevolent Institution

£57,500

Correspondent: The Secretary, 12 Shepherds Walk, Chestfield, Kent CT5 3NB (01227 791623; email: bbi@fmb.org.uk; website: www.bbi1847.org.uk)

CC number: 212022

Eligibility

Those who are or who have been master builders (employers in the building industry), and their dependants. Applicants with less than ten years' experience are not eligible, nor are those who have been employees.

Types of grants

Mostly pensions and Christmas vouchers. Occasionally, the charity distributes one-off grants towards the cost of necessary items such as home alterations and urgent house repairs. The charity notes that the average length of time over which beneficiaries receive support is around 15 years.

Annual grant total

In 2014 the institution had assets of £1.1 million and an income of £79,500. Grants were made totalling £57,500 and were distributed as follows:

Pensions	£52,000
Christmas gift vouchers	£5,000
Temporary relief	£800

Applications

Apply on a form available from the correspondent, submitted directly by the individual, through a social worker, Citizens Advice, other welfare agency or third party. Applications are considered throughout the year.

Other information

The charity has a Welfare Advisor who visits beneficiaries regularly to offer support and to assist with applications for state benefits.

The Chartered Institute of Building Benevolent Fund

£73,500

Correspondent: Franklin MacDonald, Secretary, 1 Arlington Square, Downshire Way, Bracknell, Berkshire RG12 1WA (01344 630780; email: fmacdonald@ciob.org.uk; website: www.ciob.org.uk)

CC number: 1013292

Eligibility

Members of the institute and their dependants who are in real need.

Types of grants

One-off and recurrent grants for a variety of daily living costs such as household bills or essential travel for work. Grants are also provided for food and clothing for children living at home and in hardship.

Annual grant total

In 2014 the fund had assets of £1 million and an income of £104,500. Grants made to individuals for social welfare purposes totalled £73,500.

Exclusions

The fund does not cover: membership fees; medical treatment; legal costs; business-related costs; educational costs; personal or business debts; purchase of motor vehicles.

Applications

Initially contact the fund by phone or email. You may then be asked to complete an application form to provide more details of your daily outgoings.

The Lighthouse Club

£399,000 (337 grants)

Correspondent: Bill Hill, Chief Executive, 51 Church Road East, Crowthorne, Berkshire RG45 7NF (0161 429 0022; email: info@lighthouseclub.org; website: www.lighthouseclub.org)

CC number: 1149488

Eligibility

People, or dependants of people, who work or have recently worked in the construction industry, or in an industry associated with construction (e.g. civil engineering, demolition or design), in the UK or Republic of Ireland. Applicants should usually have worked in the industry for at least two years, although not necessarily consecutively.

Types of grants

Recurrent grants to help towards living costs for those in need through accident, disability or ill health and for those in need because a member of their family (who was in the construction industry) has died or has a fatal illness. One-off grants are also available towards essential items or services, such as a new bed, a replacement washing machine, funeral costs and school uniforms.

Annual grant total

In 2014 the fund had assets of £601,000 and an income of £1.1 million. Grants were made to 337 individuals totalling almost £399,000. Of those, 174 received regular support while 163 received one-off support.

Applications

In the first instance contact the charity by telephone, or contact a branch welfare officer (a list of local branches is available on the fund's website) to discuss an application.

Other information

In 2013 the Lighthouse Construction Industry Charity was formed following a merger of the two charities The Lighthouse Club and the Lighthouse Club Benevolent Fund. 2014 was the charity's first full financial year.

The Lighthouse Club now provides a 24/7 construction industry helpline, which can be contacted by calling 0845 605 1956.

According to the charity's website, it can help to access advice on a range of matters including:

- Occupational health and wellbeing issues as an employee or an employer (Through [the charity's] partners Constructing Better Health)
- Support and advice for sufferers of stress and addiction related illness
- Advice on matters ranging from divorce to employment
- Advice on specific tax related issues concerning employment within the construction sector (Through [the charity's] partners RIFT)
- Help to manage and reschedule debt
- Help to understand the benefits system and entitlement, especially if caring for others
- Support on career changes, especially after accident or injury preventing return to your original job

The charity also plans to develop a strategy for making grants for educational purposes.

LionHeart (The Royal Institution of Chartered Surveyors Benevolent Fund)

£466,000

Correspondent: Dawn Shirley, Office Administrator, Surveyor Court, Westwood Way, Coventry CV4 8BF (0845 603 9057; fax: 024 7647 4701; email: dshirley@lionheart.org.uk; website: www.lionheart.org.uk)

CC number: 261245

Eligibility

Members and former members of the Royal Institution of Chartered Surveyors (or organisations it has merged with) and their dependants. Applications are welcome from people in the UK and those living overseas. Applicants should visit the website for current eligibility criteria and are advised to contact one of the charity's support officers if in any doubt as to their suitability to apply for a grant. Support officers can also help with information and advice on the charity's other services.

Types of grants

One-off and recurrent grants and loans are given towards: essential domestic appliances, furnishings, re-decorations and property repairs; living expenses; care in the community, residential and nursing care; respite care and holidays; and medical aids, adaptations and equipment for children with disabilities and the elderly. Additional financial help is also available for those most in need at Christmas.

Annual grant total

In 2014/15 the charity had assets of £18.9 million and an income of £1.9 million. Grants to individuals for social welfare purposes totalled £466,000, excluding support costs.

Applications

Application forms can be downloaded from the charity's website. Evidence of RICS membership or details of the member of whom the applicant is a dependant should be provided. Applications are considered quarterly, although urgent cases can be considered between meetings.

Other information

The fund offers grants, confidential advice, counselling, befriending, information and help in kind to members of the profession and their dependants on a range of social welfare, financial, legal, employment and property-related matters. A helpline is operated on 0845 603 9057.

The trustees' 2014/15 annual report states that there are plans to increase services, most notably with: the launch of a new online talking therapies service; the development of additional workshops; launching a new donor and fundraising programme together with a new programme for legacies; and a large scale survey of members to find out from them what other services they would like to see offered and how they would like to access them.

It is also planned to develop the charity's donor strategy alongside a more proactive fundraising plan, which together with a legacy fundraising plan will help secure funding into the future as services are developed and expanded. This will be complemented by ongoing and improved work with firms and the continued development of the charity's links with RICS.

Scottish Building Federation Edinburgh and District Charitable Trust

£10,000

Correspondent: Fiona Watson, Charity Accounting Services, Scott-Moncrieff (Secretaries and Treasurers), Exchange Place 3, Semple Street, Edinburgh EH3 8BL (0131 473 3500; email: fiona. watson@scott-moncrieff.com; website: www.scott-moncrieff.com/services/ charities/charitable-trusts/scottish-building-federation-edinburgh)

OSCR number: SC029604

Eligibility

People in reduced circumstances who have been involved with the building trade in the City of Edinburgh or the Lothians, and their dependants. There is a particular emphasis on people who have been owners or senior employees of companies (supervisory grade, e.g. site agents, or above).

Types of grants

One-off grants according to need.

Annual grant total

In 2014 the trust had an income of £51,500 and a total expenditure of £57,000. We were able to establish that grants are made to individuals for both social welfare and educational purposes, but we were unable to determine a precise figure for awards made during the year. The trust is administered by Scott-Moncrieff, whose website provides the following information: 'The Trust invites applications from persons in reduced circumstances, who should complete and return the form below. In

the region of £10,000 is available for this purpose per annum.'

Applications

Applications can be made using the appropriate form, which is available to download from the Scott-Moncrieff website.

Education and training

Church School Masters and Mistresses' Benevolent Institution

£14,000

Correspondent: Di Cara, Secretary, 3 Kings Court, Harwood Road, Horsham RH13 5UR (01403 250798; email: info@ cssbi.org.uk; website: www.cssbi.org.uk)

CC number: 207236

Eligibility

Current or former teachers/lecturers and those in teacher training who are members of the Church of England or another recognised Christian denomination and their dependants who are in need.

Types of grants

One-off grants according to need.

Annual grant total

In 2013/14 the institution had assets of £2.6 million and an income of £156,000. Grants totalled £29,500. We estimate that of this, £14,000 was distributed in welfare grants to individuals, with the remainder awarded to individuals for educational purposes.

Applications

Application forms can be downloaded from the charity's website. Applications should be submitted directly by the individual or a family member. Applications are considered upon receipt.

Other information

The following was taken from the institution's website: 'Since the first meeting in 1857 when a benevolent fund was established, the CSSBI has supported Church of England teachers who "fell on hard times".' Today the CSSBI is actively looking for those individuals from all Christian denominations who would benefit from support.

The Educational Institute of Scotland Benevolent Fund

£125,000

Correspondent: The General Secretary, Educational Institute of Scotland, 46 Moray Place, Edinburgh EH3 6BH (0131 225 6244; fax: 0131 220 3151; email: enquiries@eis.org.uk; website: www.eis.org.uk)

OSCR number: SC007852

Eligibility

Members of the institute suffering from financial hardship due to unexpected illness, long-term health problems or a sudden change in financial circumstances, and their widows/ widowers and dependants. Applicants must have held a full membership for at least one year prior to application.

Types of grants

One-off and recurrent grants towards, for example, daily living costs, television licences, telephone rental, hairdressing and holidays. Emergency grants may also be available to members who have had an arrestment on their salary, who face eviction, or who have had their gas or electricity cut off.

Annual grant total

In 2013/14 the fund had an income of £164,000 and a total expenditure of £135,500. We estimate that grants totalled around £125,000.

Applications

Apply on a form available from a local Benevolent Fund Correspondent. Individual contact details are available from the EIS website. The correspondent may arrange a visit to discuss an application and can offer help to applicants completing the form.

The Headmasters' Association Benevolent Fund

£6,000

Correspondent: Andrew Smetham, Trustee, The Water Barn, Water Meadow Lane, Wool, Wareham BH20 6HL (01929 463727)

CC number: 260303

Eligibility

Widows and dependants of deceased secondary school headmasters who were members of the association. Help is also given to secondary school headmasters and ex-headmasters who are, or were, members of the association and are in urgent need of assistance. Eligibility is restricted to those who were members of the former association prior to its amalgamation with the Association of Headmistresses in 1978.

Types of grants

One-off and recurrent grants are given according to need. Loans are also available.

Annual grant total

In 2014 the fund had an income of £20,600 and a total expenditure of £6,300. We estimate that the amount of grants given to individuals totalled £6,000.

Applications

Apply in writing to the correspondent. Applications are considered as they arrive.

HM Inspectors of Schools' Benevolent Fund

£4,000

Correspondent: Clive Rowe, Trustee, Hassocks House, 58 Main Street, Newtown Linford, Leicester LE6 0AD (01530 243989; email: rowe.clive@sky. com)

CC number: 210181

Eligibility

Present and retired HM Inspectors of schools in England and Wales and their dependants who are in need or distress.

Types of grants

One-off grants of £500 to £5,000 and loans of up to £10,000.

Annual grant total

In 2014 the fund had an income of £16,500 and a total expenditure of £24,500. We estimate that the amount of grants given to individuals for welfare purposes amounted to around £4,000, with loans also available.

Applications

Apply in writing to the correspondent, either directly by the individual or through a third party such as a friend or colleague. Applications are considered as they arise and should include the applicant's financial situation and, for example, arrangements for repaying loans.

Other information

The fund also provides pastoral support, including advice, for its beneficiaries.

IAPS Charitable Trust

£1,500 (6 grants)

Correspondent: Richard Flower, Secretary, 11 Waterloo Place, Leamington Spa, Warwickshire CV32 5LA (01926 887833; email: rwf@ iaps.uk; website: iaps.uk/about/our-charities)

CC number: 1143241

Eligibility

Members, retired members and the dependants of current, retired or deceased members of Independent Association of Prep Schools (IAPS). Support may also be given to association employees or, with the consent of the directors, anyone connected with education.

Types of grants

One-off grants are available according to need to relieve general hardship.

Annual grant total

In 2014/15 the trust had assets of £1.2 million and an income of £558,500. Grants totalled £54,500, of which £28,500 was given to individuals. A breakdown of grants distributed was not included in the annual report and accounts; however, they did provide the following information:

> The restricted funds were used to make bursary grants to support the on-going education of four children in senior schools, **benevolent grants to support six individuals** and Harrison fund grants to twenty eight children so that they could attend courses. Two further children were assisted by grants from unrestricted funds.

We estimate benevolent grants to individuals to have totalled around £1,500.

Applications

Applications can be made in writing to the correspondent. They are considered at termly meetings, although urgent cases can be considered in between these meetings.

Other information

In 2012 the IAPS Benevolent Fund and the IAPS Bursary Trust, and in 2013 the IAPS Orchestra Trust, merged with the trust allowing to extend its work.

The trust is also known as 'itrust'.

The National Association of Schoolmasters Union of Women Teachers (NASUWT) Benevolent Fund

£337,000 (1,021 grants)

Correspondent: Legal and Casework Team, NASUWT, Hillscourt Education Centre, Rose Hill, Rednal, Birmingham B45 8RS (0121 453 6150 (8.30am - 5.30pm); email: legalandcasework@mail. nasuwt.org.uk; website: www.nasuwt.org. uk)

CC number: 285793

Eligibility

Members, former members and their dependants (including of deceased members) who have fallen on hard times because of illness, bereavement, an accident or loss of employment through dismissal or redundancy. Members should have paid a subscription to the union. Note that candidates should have less than £5,000 in savings and investments (though this limit may be waived in extenuating circumstances).

Types of grants

One-off and recurrent grants or interest-free loans can be given according to need. Support is given in monthly grants of £86, holiday grants (£200 for adults and £125 for dependants under the age of 18), convalescence grants of £500, living expenses, for specific needs (for example, household equipment or council tax arrears), also in educational support to schoolchildren (£125 for those under the age of 16 and £150 for those aged over 17). Grants have also been given to people with terminal illnesses to visit relatives, for the services of an occupational therapist to assess disability home conversion needs, for a purchase of a converted vehicle for a member who is paralysed and a monthly grant to a member's widow with no occupational pension.

Annual grant total

In 2014 the fund had assets of £2 million and an income of £304,000. Grants to 1,021 individuals totalled £337,000. The accounts further specify that benevolent loans converted to grants totalled £5,700.

Exclusions

Support is not available for:
- Private health care or dental treatment
- Private school fees or educational courses
- Assistance with curriculum-based field trip
- Legal fees

- House purchase
- Repayment of money owed to friends or family
- Repayment of student loans or student living expenses

Assistance is not given if it would affect the applicant's entitlement to means-tested state benefits.

Applications

Potential applicants should either contact their local association secretary or the correspondent to arrange a meeting with a benevolence visitor. The visitor will complete an application form with the individual and submit a recommendation to the benevolence committee. The committee normally meets monthly to consider new applications; however, emergency cases can be processed more quickly.

Other information

Grants totalling £18,600 were also made to 44 NASUWT Federations during the year.

The fund also provides members with a range of other advice and support services.

Recourse

£64,000

Correspondent: Julian Stanley, Group Chief Executive, Teacher Support Network, 40A Drayton Park, London N5 1EW (020 7697 2772; email: enquires@recousre.org.uk; website: www.recourse.org.uk)

CC number: 1116382

Eligibility

People working in adult, further and higher education who have less than £6,000 in savings. Applicants must be working or have worked in further or higher education for at least two days a week and for at least one term.

Types of grants

Grants for energy bills, mortgage repayments, food, council tax, childcare costs, house repairs, special needs equipment, care home fees, clothing, white goods, furniture and removal costs.

Annual grant total

In 2013 the charity had an income of £490,000. We estimate that grants totalling £64,000 were awarded during the year based on previous giving. At the time of writing (November 2015) the latest information available was from 2013.

Exclusions

No grants are given for student teachers, student loans, private school fees, educational course fees, school trips,

unsecured debts, house purchases or private medical treatment.

Applications

Applicants should contact the charity by phone or email in the first instance for an application form. The charity will also provide financial advice.

Other information

Recourse also offers information and advice, telephone counselling and online coaching.

The Association of School and College Leaders Benevolent Fund

£12,400 (40+ grants)

Correspondent: Carole Baldam, Secretary, 130 Regent Road, Leicester LE1 7PG (0116 299 1122; fax: 0116 299 1123; email: carole.baldam@ascl.org.uk; website: www.ascl.org.uk/about-us/social-responsibility/benevolent-fund.html)

CC number: 279628

Eligibility

Current or former members of the association and their dependants (including dependants of deceased members). Retired employees of the association are also supported.

Types of grants

One-off and recurrent grants are available according to need. Support can be given in cases of a serious accident, redundancy, chronic illness, disability or other unexpected circumstances. Single payments are usually made towards treatment or equipment relating to disability or illness and to help with general household needs. Low interest loans are available as well. The trustees also organise holiday gifts and social engagements with isolated elderly beneficiaries.

Annual grant total

In 2014 the fund had assets of £648,500 and an income of £54,500. According to the 2014 accounts, grants of £120 were made, along with donations of £9,900 and flowers and gifts totalling £2,400. Over 40 beneficiaries were assisted during the year.

Applications

Apply in writing to the correspondent. Candidates are normally paid personal visits by the trustees to assess the case.

Other information

The association was previously known as The Secondary Heads Association Benevolent Fund.

Schoolmistresses' and Governesses' Benevolent Institution

£130,500 (163 grants)

Correspondent: Sarah Brydon, Director and Secretary, SGBI Office, Queen Mary House, Manor Park Road, Chislehurst, Kent BR7 5PY (020 8468 7997; email: enquiries@sgbi.net)

CC number: 205366

Eligibility

Women who work, or have worked, as a schoolmistress, matron, bursar, secretary or librarian in the private sector of education. Self-employed teachers may also receive assistance.

Types of grants

All types of help including annuities and one-off grants towards telephone bills, TV licences, household items, clothing, medical needs, holidays and mobility equipment. Grants typically range from £50 to £500. Loans may also be available.

Annual grant total

In 2013/14 the charity held assets of £4.15 million and had an income of £1.4 million. Grants to 163 individuals totalled £130,500 and were distributed as follows:

Annuities	£96,000
General cash grants	£12,200
General needs	£5,800
Holiday and occupational	£4,900
Household expenses	£4,200
Mobility	£2,600
Telephone	£1,800
Medical	£1,700
Television	£1,300
Clothing	-

Applications

Application forms are available from the correspondent. Applications should be submitted at any time directly by the individual or family member.
Applications are considered monthly.

Other information

The institution arranges annual visits to beneficiaries by its case manager. 'The beneficiaries are considered to be members of The SGBI "family" and the visits by the case manager are intended to strengthen the links and encourage a sense of "belonging".'

Queen Mary House, a residential home which can accommodate around 40 women, is run by the institution.

Scottish Secondary Teachers' Association Benevolent Fund

£4,000

Correspondent: The General Secretary, West End House, 14 West End Place, Edinburgh EH11 2ED (0131 313 7300; email: info@ssta.org.uk; website: www.ssta.org.uk)

OSCR number: SC011074

Eligibility

Members and retired members of the association and, in certain circumstances, their dependants and families who are in need. Spouses and partners of deceased members are also supported.

Types of grants

One-off and recurrent grants (generally limited to a period of six months) to help members through a period of long-term illness or other difficulty. The fund notes that support is most often given 'in cases of financial hardship but can also be used to meet for requests where the member is not actually experiencing financial difficulties but for whom additional funds would be useful'; one example includes a grant for a member to visit an ill friend at hospital.

Annual grant total

In 2014 the fund had an income of £9,700 and an expenditure of £4,700. We estimate that around £4,000 was given in grants to individuals.

Applications

Apply in writing to the correspondent. Applications can be submitted directly by the individual or through a third party. Applicants are asked to provide details of their financial circumstances.

The Society of Schoolmasters and Schoolmistresses

£4,500

Correspondent: The Case Manager, Queen Mary House, Manor Park Road, Chislehurst, Kent BR7 5PY (020 8468 7997; email: enquiries@societyofss.org.uk; website: societyofss.org.uk)

CC number: 206693

Eligibility

Schoolmasters or schoolmistresses (employed/retired) of any independent or maintained school who have ten years of continuous service, and their dependants.

Types of grants

One-off and recurrent grants of up to a maximum of £600 per year. Grants are normally made to retired schoolmasters or schoolmistresses who have no adequate pension, but exceptions can sometimes be made for younger teachers. One-off grants have previously been given for purposes such as household items, nursing home fees and medical expenses.

Annual grant total

In 2014 the society had an income of £8,000 and a total expenditure of £4,900. We estimate that around £4,500 was made in grants to individuals for social welfare purposes.

Exclusions

Grants are not usually given to anyone who has savings of more than £16,000.

Applications

Application forms are available from the correspondent. Applications can be submitted directly by the individual. They are considered quarterly.

Teacher Support Network

£144,500

Correspondent: Grants Team, 40A Drayton Park, London N5 1EW (England – 0800 056 2561, Wales – 0800 855088; email: enquiries@teachersupport.info; website: www.teachersupport.info)

CC number: 1072583

Eligibility

Serving, former or retired teachers or lecturers (including further education and higher education), and their dependants (including widows or widowers) who live in a household with less than £4,000 in savings and realisable assets and own no more than one home. All candidates should have been assessed by a Teacher Support Network Group debt counsellor and not received more than £3,000 in financial assistance from the group over the last seven years from the date of the application.

Types of grants

One-off grants of between £300 to £3,000 are aimed to help with short-term financial emergencies, including due to illness or injury. Support is given towards a range of needs, such as clothing, removal costs, rent, council tax, utility bills, special needs equipment, funeral costs, also to help stay in or get back to work. Assistance towards household repairs will be considered for those who have retired. Payments are normally made to third parties/service providers, not the applicants.

Annual grant total

At the time of writing (November 2015) the latest financial information available was from 2013. In 2013 the charity had assets of £6.7 million and an income of £3.6 million. A total of £144,500 was awarded in welfare grants.

The charity's main focus for grants continues to be help with expenses that are fundamentally important to the daily functioning of teachers and their families.

Exclusions

Student teachers are not eligible for financial support and student loans are not made. Grants are not given for private school fees, educational course fees, school trips, unsecured debts, house purchases, care home fees, holidays, white goods, furniture or private medical treatment. Assistance is not generally awarded for non-priority debt, although advice is available.

Applications

Applicants are invited to contact the grants team to discuss their needs and the application procedure. Applications can be made online directly by the individual and are considered once a week, usually on Wednesdays. They are means-tested so financial information is needed, alongside other supporting documentation proving the need (such as bank statements for the last three months, three quotes for the service required or bills/evidence of arrears). On average, the application process takes around six to eight weeks.

Other information

Grant-making is just one aspect of the work of this charity. In 1999, it established Teacher Support Line (formerly Teacherline), 'providing day-to-day support for teachers in both their personal and professional lives'. Services include coaching, counselling, advice, information and financial assistance. Individuals may also be signposted to other bodies for help.

Energy

BP Benevolent Fund

£9,500 (9 grants)

Correspondent: Peter Darnell, Fund Administrator, BP Benevolent Fund Trustees Ltd, 4 Woodside Close, Shermanbury, Horsham RH13 8HH (01403 710437; email: peter.darnell@uk.bp.com)

CC number: 803778

Eligibility

Former employees of BP plc or subsidiary or associated companies and the dependants of such people.

Types of grants

One-off and recurrent awards according to need. Occasional hardship grants of up to a maximum of £750.

In 2014 grants were paid for a variety of reasons including: a replacement back door; roof repairs; a water heater; a bathroom adaptation; white goods; household items and furnishings; window replacements; a bath-lift; and a mattress and bedding.

Annual grant total

In 2014 the fund had assets of over £1.2 million and an income of £41,000. Awards were made to help nine individuals and totalled £9,500.

The fund also provides interest-free loans. The trustees approved three new loans totalling £7,000 in 2014.

Applications

Apply in writing to the correspondent.

The Electrical Industries Charity

£378,000

Correspondent: Jill Nadolski, Correspondent, 36 Tanner Street, London SE1 3LD (020 3696 1710; website: www.electricalcharity.org)

CC number: 1012131

Eligibility

Employees and former employees of the UK electrical and electronic industries and allied sciences, including: electrical contracting and facilities management; electrical and electronic manufacturing; wholesaling, distribution and retail; electrical and mechanical engineering; lighting industry; generation, distribution and supply of electrical power, including nuclear and renewable energy.

Types of grants

Grants are available for a wide range of needs, including home repairs, disability adaptations, mobility equipment and everyday essentials such as heating and food. In certain cases, the charity may also be able to offer financial assistance for carers' respite breaks.

Annual grant total

In 2013/14 the charity held assets of £6 million and had an income of £1.6 million. Grants to individuals totalled £378,000.

Exclusions

Grants are not normally given to cover the costs of private medical care, educational fees, bankruptcy fees, nursing/residential fees or for headstones or funeral plaques.

Applications

Application packs and a list of guidelines are available to download from the website or by calling the charity's helpline. Applicants must provide the latest letter/statement from the benefits or pensions office or their current payslip, copies of their latest bank statements from current and savings accounts and, if a specific item is required, two or three estimates. Medical equipment normally requires an occupational therapy assessment, which can be discussed at a later date. Enquiries are welcomed.

Other information

The Electrical Industries Charity was formerly known as the Electrical and Electronics Industries Benevolent Association (EEIBA). It also provides a confidential helpline, debt advice, respite for carers and careers advice and outplacement.

Engineering

The Chartered Institution of Building Services Engineers' Benevolent Fund

£54,000 (53 grants)

Correspondent: Janet Wigglesworth, Chief Executive's Secretary, CIBSE Services Ltd, Delta House, 222 Balham High Road, London SW12 9BS (020 8675 5211; fax: 020 8673 3302; email: benfund@cibse.org; website: www.cibse.org/cibse-benevolent-fund)

CC number: 1115871

Eligibility

Members and former members of the institution (and their dependants) who are in need.

Types of grants

Regular (quarterly) payments to supplement pensions and other income sources. One-off grants towards the cost of special equipment such as stair-lifts or equipment which will enable the individual to work from home and major one-off bills such as essential repairs to the home. Help may also be given in the form of waived CIBSE subscriptions.

Annual grant total

In 2014 the fund held assets of nearly £568,000 and had an income of £61,000. Grants to 53 individuals totalled £54,000.

Exclusions

Private health care or education.

Applications

Apply in writing or by contacting the helpline or your local almoner. Applications can be submitted at any time either directly by the individual or through a social worker, Citizens Advice or other welfare agency. An almoner will visit the applicant to obtain details. Applications are considered on receipt.

Other information

The fund's regional almoners visit applicants to assess circumstances, as well as providing advice.

The Chemical Engineers Benevolent Fund

£11,500

Correspondent: Jo Downham, Finance Manager, c/o The Institution of Chemical Engineers, Davis Building, 165–189 Railway Terrace, Rugby, Warwickshire CV21 3HQ (01788 578214; email: info@benevolentface.org; website: www.benevolentface.org)

CC number: 221601

Eligibility

Current and former chemical engineers and their immediate dependants. This includes all chemical engineers worldwide, not only members or former members of the Institution of Chemical Engineers.

Types of grants

One-off and recurrent grants, and loans, for example, towards medical treatment, special equipment, nursing home fees, special education needs and general expenses.

Annual grant total

In 2014 the fund had assets of £432,000 and an income of £48,500. Grants to individuals totalled £11,500.

Exclusions

The fund is able to support costs arising from the pursuit of postgraduate chemical engineering studies, but is not cannot fund postgraduate living expenses, tuition fees or any costs associated with undergraduate study.

Applications

Applicants should fill out an initial form from the charity's website, which can be completed online or sent by post to the trustees. This should preferably be done directly by the person who will benefit from the support, but in exceptional circumstances, applications may be made by a nominated person on behalf of the individual (for further information, contact the fund). If the initial request is successful, applicants will receive an email within two days inviting them to make a full application. Full applications are considered at regular trustee meetings, the dates of which will be provided on submitting an application. In exceptional circumstances, urgent requests may be dealt with sooner.

The Benevolent Fund of the Institution of Civil Engineers

£507,000 (159 grants)

Correspondent: Lindsay Howell, Caseworker, 5 Mill Hill Close, Haywards Heath, West Sussex RH16 1NY (01444 417979 or 0800 587 3428 (free 24 hour helpline); email: info@icebenfund.com; website: www.icebenfund.com)

CC number: 1126595

Eligibility

Members and former members of The Institution of Civil Engineers (ICE), and their dependants, who are in need.

Types of grants

One-off grants towards: medical and disability aids; equipment to help with independent living; house repairs or maintenance; residential and nursing home care; carers' breaks and respite care; essential domestic appliances; furnishings. Emergency grants in times of crisis and monthly payments to people out of work and on very limited income are also available.

The charity's website states: 'All applications are treated sympathetically and are means-tested. The ICE Benevolent Fund operates worldwide.'

Annual grant total

In 2014 the charity had assets of £15.3 million and an income of £1.2 million. Grants were made to a total of 168 individuals (148 in the UK and 20 overseas) totalling £516,000, including support for nine students. There was no breakdown of support in the accounts but the majority of awards are made for social welfare purposes. We have estimated the amount awarded to individuals for welfare purposes to be around £507,000.

Applications

Application forms are available from the website or the correspondent. They can be submitted directly by the individual or through a third party, such as a social worker, Citizens Advice or other welfare agency, solicitor, close relative or a similar party. Supporting documents should also be included (this will help to speed up the consideration process, but the charity states that 'you should not

delay sending your application if you have not got everything to hand immediately'). If you are unsure about your eligibility or support available, do not hesitate to get in touch with the charity.

Other information

The fund owns properties in West Sussex and has nomination rights to the Hanover Housing Association which it uses to help current and former members and their families who are facing difficult circumstances and need somewhere to live. Educational support is given to student members who have disabilities or are otherwise disadvantaged.

It also runs a 24-hour helpline (0800 587 3428) which offers support and advice on a wide range of issues, including counselling, stress management, relationship problems, financial troubles, parenting, illness and well-being and work life. Face-to-face support can also be arranged. There is the 'Back to Work' scheme operating providing advice and coaching for people who have been out of work for at least three months.

The Institution of Engineering and Technology Benevolent Fund (IET Connect)

£644,000

Correspondent: Christine Oxland, Chief Executive, Napier House, 24 High Holborn, London WC1V 6AZ (020 7344 5498; email: ietconnect@theiet.org; website: www.ietconnect.org)

CC number: 208925

Eligibility

Members and former members, including those of the Institution of Electrical Engineering and the Institution of Engineering and Technology, and their dependants.

Types of grants

The 2013/14 trustees' annual report details the support provided:

Assistance is offered in the form of grants of money where a financial need has been identified and may be either one-off for a specific purpose such as an adaptation of a house or a regular grant, perhaps on a monthly basis for a fixed period. Some of the items include routine expenses which are not met by State provision such as respite breaks, television licences, telephone charges, transport costs and essential replacement household items. Where possible regular grants are avoided as they can lead to a dependency rather than the individual trying to resolve their situation in the longer term. The preference is to give a larger initial sum, where appropriate, to help get the person

or family back on their feet or to give them breathing space to resolve their difficulty and move forward independently.

Those struggling to pay their IET membership can contact the IET membership department directly on +44 (0)1438 765 678

Annual grant total

In 2013/14 the fund held assets of £20.7 million and had an income of £1.2 million. Grants to individuals amounted to £644,000 (an increase of £175,000 on the previous year).

Exclusions

The fund is unable to fund items retrospectively.

Applications

Application forms are available from the correspondent.

Other information

The fund has reformulated its policies and is now pursuing a more preventative strategy through its activities. The objectives of the charity are set out in its 2013/14 accounts:

IET Connect provides information, advice, support and financial assistance, to IET members and former members and their dependants in times of need. (Its remit includes former members of the Institution of Electrical Engineers and its former constituent institutions and their dependants.) It helps individuals and families, many of whom are affected by accident, illness, disability, unemployment and redundancy and bereavement. The creation of the Speirs Fund in 2010 has broadened the objectives of the Charity and enabled it to begin to develop services primarily to help individuals and families affected by disability, and in particular carers.

Applicants are advised to visit the fund's very accessible, useful and informative website.

The Benevolent Fund of the Institution of Mechanical Engineers (IMechE) – known as Support Network

£223,000

Correspondent: Maureen Hayes, Casework and Support Officer, 1–3 Birdcage Walk, Westminster, London SW1H 9JJ (020 7304 6816; fax: 020 7973 1262; email: info@ supportnetwork.org.uk; website: www. supportnetwork.org.uk)

CC number: 209465

Eligibility

Past and present members of the Institution of Mechanical Engineers, and their dependants, who are in need.

Former members must have paid subscription fees for at least five years. Priority is given to those on low incomes who qualify for means-tested state benefits.

Types of grants

One-off grants and loans are available towards a variety of needs, including house repairs and adaptations, medical equipment, domestic appliances, beds and bedding, furniture, respite care, holidays and carers' breaks. Recurrent grants are also available to help with living expenses.

Annual grant total

In 2014 the charity had assets of £21.7 million and an income of £1.2 million. All grants to individuals were listed as relief of poverty and totalled £278,500. Although educational/training grants are not separately listed, this may be because most of the criteria for educational/training grants appear to include a financial qualification as well. We estimate social welfare grants to have totalled around £223,000.

Exclusions

No grants are given for school fees, business ventures, private medical treatment or the payment of debts.

Applications

In the first instance, contact the correspondent by phone, letter, email or fax. You will be asked a few questions about your situation and, if the fund is able to help, then an application form will be sent for you to complete.

Other information

Support Network offers a range of support and advice services which also include student grants, sheltered housing and residential care, and help with job seeking.

Free expert advice is available through a telephone helpline run by the charity's partner organisation, Advice Express. For advice on 'all sorts of everyday problems and queries' call 01275 376029 (Monday-Friday 8am-8pm and 9am – noon on weekends), mentioning that you are calling from the IMechE. There are also financial and legal advice helplines, more details of which are available from the website.

Institution of Plant Engineers Benevolent Fund

£12,500

Correspondent: Nicholas Humphrey, Trustee, 87 Overdale, Ashtead KT21 1PX (01372 277775; email: nick.jones87@ btopenworld.com)

CC number: 260934

Eligibility

Members/former members of the institution, and their dependants living in England, Scotland and Wales.

Types of grants

One-off grants according to need. Most grants are given to people who are financially stressed through serious illness, unemployment or bereavement. For example, support for a young member no longer able to work due to multiple sclerosis.

Annual grant total

In 2014 the fund had an income of £13,500 and a total expenditure of £12,800. We estimate that the total amount of grants awarded to individuals was approximately £12,500.

Applications

Apply in writing to the correspondent. Applications can be submitted directly by the individual or by a relative or close friend. They are considered in March, July and November.

The ISTRUCTE (Institution of Structural Engineers) Fund

£48,500 (17 grants)

Correspondent: Dr Susan Doran, Secretary, International HQ, 47–58 Bastwick Street, London EC1V 3PS (020 7235 4535; email: benfund@istructe.org; website: www. istructe.org)

CC number: 1049171

Eligibility

Members of the institution and their dependants who are in financial difficulties due to circumstances such as: unemployment; illness, an accident or disability; family problems; difficulties during retirement; or bereavement.

Types of grants

One-off and recurrent grants and loans up to a maximum of £12,000 per year towards, for example, home repairs, household equipment, property adaptations, disability equipment, carers' breaks and daily living costs for those on very modest incomes. Where appropriate, the fund will also pay the annual subscription fee of the beneficiary, as well as their fee to Engineering Council UK.

Annual grant total

In 2014 the fund had assets of £2.47 million and an income of £72,500. Grants were made to 17 individuals totalling £48,500.

Exclusions

No grants are given for private health care. If the fund settles debts for a beneficiary, it will not usually pay any subsequent debts. The fund will not normally help members' children over the age of 21 or any individuals legally separated or divorced from a member. Grants are assessed by the Benefits Consultant to ensure that the beneficiary's entitlement to statutory benefits will not be reduced.

Applications

Apply on a form, available to request by emailing the correspondent, which can be submitted by the individual or an appropriate third party. The fund likes to visit applicants before any grant is made.

Note: In cases of genuine emergency, the fund can pay up to £500, as a loan, normally within days.

The Matthew Hall Staff Trust Fund

£235,000 (194 grants)

Correspondent: Elaine Hanna, Secretary, AMEC, Booths Hall, Chelford Road, Knutsford WA16 8QZ (01565 683281)

CC number: 1019896

Eligibility

Former employees of Matthew Hall (1992) plc who are over the age of 65, suffering financial hardship and have completed at least two years of service, and their dependants. The spouses of deceased former employees who had completed between two and ten years of service are also eligible.

Types of grants

One-off and recurrent grants are given according to need.

Annual grant total

In 2014/15 the fund held assets of £2 million and had an income of £49,500. A total of £235,000 was made in 194 grants to 92 former employees.

Applications

Apply in writing to the correspondent. The trustees meet at least twice a year, normally in July and December, to consider applications.

Other information

The fund was founded using a gift from Bertram Baden, the then owner of the company.

Environment and animals

Environmental Health Officers Welfare Fund

£5,000

Correspondent: Graham Jukes, Chief Executive, Chadwick Court, 15 Hatfields, London SE1 8DJ (020 7928 6006; email: membership@cieh.org; website: www. cieh.org)

CC number: 224343

Eligibility

Past and present members of Chartered Institute of Environmental Health Officers, Association of Public Health Inspectors or The Guild of Public Health Inspection who are in need (and their dependants).

Types of grants

One-off and recurrent grants are given according to need.

Annual grant total

In 2014 the fund had an income of £220 and a total expenditure of £5,300. We estimate that the amount of grants given to individuals totalled around £5,000.

Applications

Initial enquiries should be made by telephone or through the contact form on the CIEH website. Applications should then be forwarded through the regional or branch secretary.

Gamekeepers' Welfare Trust

£11,800 (11 grants)

Correspondent: Helen Benson, Chief Executive and Charity Manager, Keepers Cottage, Tanfield Lodge, West Tanfield, Ripon, North Yorkshire HG4 5LE (01677 470180 (helpline) or 01677 47010; email: enquiries@thegamekeeperswelfaretrust. com or gamekeeperwtrust@btinternet. com; website: www.thegamekeepers welfare trust.com)

CC number: 1008924

Eligibility

Gamekeepers and those in similar occupations who are in need, and their dependants.

Types of grants

One-off and recurrent grants are given according to need. Some recent examples of support include housing assistance, home help, travel, medical equipment and aids, access to work vehicles,

veterinarian assistance and small gifts and flowers.

Annual grant total

In 2014 the trust had assets of £154,000 and an income of £54,500. Welfare support totalled £13,300, including £11,800 in grants to individuals. During the year the trust received 11 formal applications and supported all of them.

Applications

Application forms are available from the correspondent or can be found on the website. They can be submitted at any time.

Other information

Educational assistance is also given to people who wish to enter the career in gamekeeping; however, no such awards were made in 2014. Awards may also be made to organisations.

RSABI (Royal Scottish Agricultural Benevolent Institution)

£506,000

Correspondent: The Welfare Team, The Rural Centre, West Mains of Ingliston, Newbridge, Midlothian EH28 8LT (0300 111 4166 (helpline); fax: 0131 472 4156; email: rsabi@rsabi.org.uk; website: www. rsabi.org.uk)

OSCR number: SC009828

Eligibility

People who have been engaged for at least ten years, full-time in a land-based occupation in Scotland, and their dependants. Applicants should be either retired or unable to work, on a low income (RSABI does not include non-means-tested disability benefits when calculating qualifying income) and have limited savings (£12,000 for a single applicant, £16,000 for couples) or be facing a crisis due to ill health, accident or bereavement

Qualifying occupations include: agriculture, aquaculture, crofting, forestry, fish-farming, gamekeeping, horticulture, rural estate work and other jobs that depend on the provision of services directly to these industries.

Types of grants

The charity offers:
- Recurring payments ranging between £700 and £900 (or between £1,100 and £1,400 in case of partnered/joint beneficiaries) made twice a year on a bi-annual basis to those on limited income and little or no savings. The charity can provide help with fuel and heating expenses, TV licences and seasonal bonuses and so on to older people and those who are unable to

work. RSABI welfare staff ensure that individuals receive their full entitlements to any other benefits due and will help and advise with other difficulties such as care services, housing or similar matters
- One-off grants for specific essential items, such as home repairs and modifications, disability aids, essential transport costs, car tax or insurance (where personal transport is essential) and respite breaks
- Awards to help individuals meet a particular crisis in their lives – by way of direct help, payments to suppliers (for example energy providers) and/or supermarket shopping vouchers (£25–£75 per person)
- In special circumstances, Centenary Fund awards to help individuals 'where a significant improvement in their quality of life, or that of their carers, can be achieved'

There are 'Essential needs packages' up to £250 available to assist with the costs of household appliances, furniture, floor covering and other home necessities.

Annual grant total

In 2013/14 the charity had assets of £10.7 million (which includes restricted and endowment funds) and an income of £1.3 million.

Grants to individuals totalled around £526,000. The annual report for 2013/14 further specifies that 1563 payments were processed to 498 distinct beneficiaries. From the total, £356,000 was made in 'Basic Benefit Grants' and £170,000 was paid in 'Single Grants to 46 individuals', of which £90,000 was paid through the designated 'Weather 2012 Fund' (covering 28 families) and £8,200 through 'Centenary Fund'.

The support was allocated as follows:

Annual beneficiaries	£341,000
Weather 2012	£89,000
Single grants	£78,000
TV licences	£13,000
Centenary and Christmas grants	£5,000

The amount awarded for educational purposes was not specified in the accounts; therefore, we estimate that it could have totalled around £20,000, this leaving about £506,000 awarded for welfare needs. During the year the charity took on 26 individuals as new annual beneficiaries.

Exclusions

Grants are not made to help with:
- Business expenses
- Repayment of loans, overdrafts or credit facilities
- Setting up any debt arrangement

Applications

Preliminary application forms are available from the correspondent or can be downloaded from the website. They can be submitted directly by the individual or through a third party (such as a social worker or Citizens Advice) and are considered at any time. The charity's website states:

> We will let you know as soon as possible after receiving the Form whether or not we may be able to help you. If we can, one of our Welfare Officers will arrange to visit at a suitable time and will help you to complete our formal Application for Assistance Form and discuss how RSABI may best be able to help.

Candidates are also encouraged to contact the charity to discuss their application.

Other information

The trustees' annual report for 2013/14 notes that 'while welfare support and guidance remain the trustees principal focus, consideration is, and will be, given to educational or training-related activities… particularly where these might help raise awareness of the charity'.

RSABI also offers advice on benefits, support available from other organisations, provide guidance through key life events, such as bereavement, serious illness, redundancy or retirement, and offer home visits by welfare officers to provide ongoing support and friendship. A confidential listening and support service for Scotland's farming and land-based community – GATEPOST -is operated by the charity. Call 0300 111 4166 – Monday-Friday, 9am-5pm.

Weather 2012 Fund was instigated in December 2012 when The Prince's Countryside Fund made funds available to the farming charities in the UK to help farmers who were struggling through the winter months as a result of the extreme weather throughout that year.

Agriculture
The Bristol Corn Trade Guild

£3,500

Correspondent: Richard Cooksley, Correspondent, Portbury House, Sheepway, Portbury, Bristol BS20 7TE (01275 373539; email: richard@bcfta.com; website: www.bcfta.org.uk/theguild.php)

CC number: 202404

Eligibility

People who have a connection with the corn, grain, feed, flour and allied trades and are in need. Dependants of such people are also eligible. Current and former members of the Bristol Corn and Feed Trade Association may be favoured.

Types of grants

One-off grants generally between £200 and £800 can be given towards medical equipment or specialist treatment, repairs and household essentials, also as food vouchers. Recurrent grants can be made for utility bills.

Annual grant total

In 2014 the guild had an income of £8,500 and a total expenditure of £7,400. We estimate that grants totalled around £3,500.

Applications

Apply in writing to the correspondent. Applications can be submitted directly by the individual or through a social worker, Citizens Advice or other welfare agency.

Other information

Members and former members of the Bristol Corn and Feed Trade Association are also invited to various activities organised by the guild, for example, sporting events or Christmas lunch.

East Sussex Farmers' Union Benevolent Fund

£12,700

Correspondent: Gordon Fowlie, Trustee, Farthings, North Road, Ringmer, Lewes, West Sussex BN8 5JP (01273 812406; email: fowlie.family@btinternet.com)

CC number: 271188

Eligibility

People in need who are farmers, farmworkers or their dependants, with priority for those who live in the county of East Sussex. When funds are available, eligible people living in Kent, Surrey and West Sussex may also be supported.

Types of grants

One-off and recurrent grants are given according to need.

Annual grant total

In 2013/14 the fund had assets of £1.6 million and an income of £38,000. Grants to individuals totalled £12,700.

Applications

Apply in writing or by telephone to the correspondent.

The Sir Percival Griffiths' Tea-Planters Trust

£7,000

Correspondent: Stephen Buckland, Trustee, Duncan Lawrie Ltd, Wrotham Place, High Street, Wrotham, Sevenoaks, Kent TN15 7AE (020 7201 3065)

CC number: 253904

Eligibility

People who are or have been involved in tea planting in India, live in the UK and are in need. Dependants of such people are also eligible.

Types of grants

Our research suggests that one-off and recurrent grants of up to £3,000 are available to help with general living expenses. Single payments include those for assistance with medical equipment, electrical goods and so on.

Annual grant total

In 2014 the trust had an income of £2,100 and a total expenditure of £7,300. We estimate that the amount of grants given to individuals totalled around £7,000.

Applications

Application forms are available from the correspondent. They should include details of career in India (dates, tea garden and so on) and can be submitted at any time either directly by the individual or through a third party, such as a social worker, Citizens Advice, or another welfare agency.

The Royal Agricultural Benevolent Institution

£1.2 million

Correspondent: Head of Welfare, Shaw House, 27 West Way, Oxford OX2 0QH (01865 724931; fax: 01865 202025; email: info@rabi.org.uk; website: www.rabi.org.uk)

CC number: 208858

Eligibility

Farmers, farm managers, farm workers and their dependants. Applicants should usually have less than £10,000 in savings. Retired applicants must normally be aged at least 65 and have worked full-time in the industry for at least ten years. These qualifications may be waived if the applicant has been forced to give up work due to illness or disability.

There is an emergency fund available for working farmers and farm workers who are experiencing exceptionally difficult circumstances of a temporary nature.

Types of grants

One-off grants and regular financial assistance. Grants can be given towards white goods, disability equipment, TVs and licences, telephone rental, Lifelines, help in the home, care home fees, replacement boilers and so on. Emergency relief is available for essential domestic expenses in times of financial difficulty. Emergency grants have also been made in the past to assist farmers who have struggled with flooding and the foot and mouth outbreak.

The institution can also pay for temporary help on the farm if the individual or an immediate dependant is seriously ill or has an accident. Grants may also be made through the Gateway Project which offers vocational training grants to enable farmers and their immediate family to gain qualifications to enable them to increase the farm income.

Annual grant total

In 2014 the institution had assets of more than £62 million and had an income of £6.5 million. Direct grants awarded totalled £1.2 million.

Exclusions

No grants can be given towards business debts and expenses, medical expenses or private education costs.

Applications

Enquiries can be made by telephoning the helpline on 0300 303 7373 or by letter or email to the correspondent either directly by the individual or through a social worker, Citizens Advice or other third party.

All new applicants for regular assistance will be visited by one of the institution's regional welfare officers. The grants committee meets every six weeks to consider applications, although emergency needs can be fast-tracked.

Other information

The institution also operates two residential homes, one in Bury St Edmunds and one in Burnham on Sea and also associated sheltered flats for older members of the farming community.

The RABI Welfare Team 'are fully trained in all complexities of the state benefits system' and can advise people on pension credits and other state entitlements. There is a flyer about the Welfare Department and the work they do on the institution's informative website.

Rural, Agricultural and Allied Workers' Benevolent Fund

£5,000

Correspondent: Fund Administrator, Food and Agriculture, UNITE, 128 Theobald's Road, Holborn, London WC1X 8TN (020 7611 2500)

Eligibility

Rural and agricultural members of the organisation (now a trade group within Unite the Union).

Types of grants

One-off grants with an average value of £150. In some cases recurrent support may be given.

Annual grant total

The amount varies, but usually never more than £5,000 per year.

Exclusions

This fund does not award grants to individuals who are not current union members within the agricultural section.

Applications

Potential applicants should contact their local branch official.

Animal care

Veterinary Benevolent Fund

£154,000 (51+ grants)

Correspondent: Vanessa Kearns, Administration Manager, British Veterinary Association, 7 Mansfield Street, London W1G 9NQ (020 7908 6385; fax: 020 7980 4890; email: info@ vetlife.org.uk; website: www.vetlife.org. uk)

CC number: 224776

Eligibility

Veterinary surgeons who are or have been on the register of the Royal College of Veterinary Surgeons (RCVS) and are ordinarily resident in the UK, and their dependants.

Types of grants

Regular monthly payments for people living on a low income and one-off grants of up to a maximum of £1,000 towards TV licences, telephone line rental, additional heating costs, car tax and insurance, holidays, medical equipment, disability aids and so on. The fund has previously noted an increasing trend towards providing more one-off support with less demand for recurrent grants. Short-term, interest-free loans may also be made to tide beneficiaries over in times of crisis.

Annual grant total

In 2014 the fund had assets of £6.8 million and an income of £533,500. Grants to beneficiaries totalled £154,000 comprising £117,000 in regular payments to 51 individuals and around £37,000 in special gifts, usually at Christmas time. A further £2,600 was paid in loans to two people.

Exclusions

No grants are given towards:
- Support to anyone before they have qualified and are on the RCVS register
- The cost of studying veterinary medicine as a second degree
- Business or partnership debt
- Mandatory training courses
- Indemnity insurance
- Private education
- Private medical care or care home fees
- Repaying loans to family and friends
- Improvements and repairs to rented property
- Support to individuals simply because they are unemployed

Applications

Application forms are available from the VBF office or can be downloaded from the Vetlife website and should be submitted with bank statements for the last three months and other supporting documentation (such as a copy of a letter from the DWP with details of any state benefits received, recent mortgage/ rent statement and copies of letters from creditors regarding arrears, if there are outstanding debts). Two references are required. A decision may be made immediately or VBF may request that one of their representatives make a home visit before a decision is reached. Applicants may be visited or asked to provide further information before a decision is made, although an immediate payment may be made for those in need of urgent help.

Other information

Alongside the benevolent fund the charity also runs a helpline, mental health support programme and the Vetlife website. They can also provide advice on a wide range of issues, including debt and welfare benefits. The fund owns four bungalows at Burton near Christchurch (Dorset) which are available 'for deserving veterinary surgeons and their families'.

Fishing

Fishermen's Mission

£513,000

Correspondent: David Dickens, Secretary and Chief Executive, Fishermen's Mission Head Office, Mather House, 4400 Parkway, Fareham, Hampshire PO15 7FJ (01489 566910; email: enquiries@fishermensmission.org. uk; website: www.fishermensmission.org. uk)

CC number: 232822

Eligibility

Commercial fishermen, including retired fishermen, and their wives and widows who are experiencing unforeseen tragedy or hardship.

Types of grants

Immediate one-off payments to widows of fishermen lost at sea. There are also other individual grants to alleviate cases of hardship (e.g. provision of basic furniture for impoverished older fishermen). Grants are almost always one-off.

Annual grant total

In 2013/14 the charity held assets of £9.3 million and had an income of £3.2 million. Welfare payments were made totalling £513,000.

Applications

Apply in writing to the correspondent or the local superintendent, either directly by the individual or through a social worker, Citizens Advice or other welfare agency. Record of sea service and names of fishing vessels and/or owners is required.

Other information

Grant-making is a small part/area of this charity's activities. It also has a team of welfare staff who provide advice and assistance to fishing communities throughout the UK. In addition they assist injured or ill fishermen and, where appropriate, arrange for them to receive enhanced medical attention, and, finally, source emergency accommodation and catering facilities where there is no alternative provision.

Forestry

Forest Industries Education and Provident Fund

£2,000

Correspondent: Jane Karthaus, Trustee, Woodland Place, West Street, Belford, Northumberland NE70 7QA (01668 213693; email: info@edwardmills.co.uk; website: www.confor.org.uk/AboutUs/Default.aspx?pid=150)

CC number: 1061322

Eligibility

Members of the Forestry and Timber Association (or Confor) and their dependants who are in need, hardship or distress (for example, due to illness, death or injury). Members must have been involved with the association for at least one year.

Types of grants

One-off grants are made towards expenses for those experiencing hardship.

Annual grant total

In 2014 the fund had an income of £6,200 and an expenditure of £4,000. We estimate that welfare grants totalled around £2,000.

Exclusions

Retrospective funding is not given.

Applications

Application forms are available from the fund's website or can be requested from the correspondent.

Other information

Anyone can join Confor who has an interest in trees, woodlands or timber. Grants are also made for educational purposes.

The fund's website also directs beneficiaries to other potential sources of help: The Institute of Chartered Foresters' Educational and Scientific Trust and The Royal Forestry Society.

The New Forest Keepers Widows Fund

£9,000

Correspondent: Richard Mihalop, 17 Ferndale Road, Marchwood, Southampton SO40 4XR (023 8086 1136; email: newforestkwfund@gmail.com)

CC number: 1016362

Eligibility

Retired keepers of the New Forest and their dependants who are in need, or the dependants of deceased keepers who are in need.

Types of grants

One-off and recurrent grants ranging from £50 to £2,500.

Annual grant total

In 2013/14 the fund had an income of £15,000 and a total expenditure of £9,400.

Applications

Apply in writing to the correspondent directly by the individual or family member. Applications can be submitted at any time.

Horticulture

Gardeners' Royal Benevolent Society (Perennial)

£363,000

Correspondent: Sheila Thomson, Director of Services, 115–117 Kingston Road, Leatherhead, Surrey KT22 7SU (0800 093 8510; email: info@perennial. org.uk; website: www.perennial.org.uk)

CC number: 1155156, SC040180

Eligibility

People who are, or have been, employed or self-employed in the horticultural industry in the UK and their spouses/partners, widows/widowers and other immediate dependants. This includes qualified and unqualified gardeners, nursery workers, landscapers, garden centre employees, arboriculturists, people running their own small businesses and others in the industry who are in necessitous circumstances, such as financial difficulties, illness, disability and so on.

Types of grants

The charity offers the following help:

- One-off grants towards a variety of needs, including: mobility aids; holidays; travel and transport costs; property adaptations and maintenance; domestic appliances; debt clearance; personal items; housing needs; housing benefit top-up; day-to-day living costs; energy bills; funeral expenses; community alarms; pet care; furniture and fittings
- Regular quarterly allowances payable on a long-term basis (in some cases for life), usually to those over retirement age
- Assistance and top-up for care home fees ranging from £10 to £100 per week
- Perennial also distributes grocery vouchers, makes winter fuel payments and provides referrals to food banks

Annual grant total

In 2014 the charity had assets of £46.9 million and an income of £3.5 million. The consolidated accounts state that a total of about £490,000 was spent in grants and benefit payments to beneficiaries, including restricted income funds and designated funds (this appears to include support and administration costs).

The notes on 'Designated Funds' state that grants and benefit payments from The Lironi Training Fund totalled £61,000, from The Good Samaritan Welfare Fund – £186,000, and from 1839 Regular Beneficiary Fund – £183,000.

The notes on 'Restricted Funds' show that grants and benefit payments from The Children's Fund totalled £51,000 and from the Clients Grants Fund – £9,000.

The 'Our Financial Assistance & Special Circumstances' section in the accounts notes that £176,000 was paid from The Regular Beneficiary Fund, £167,000 from The Good Samaritan Welfare Fund and over £41,000 from The Lironi Training Fund. The Children's Fund was established to provide both educational and welfare support; therefore, we add half of this amount towards the welfare expenditure and calculate the annual total amount of grants given for welfare purposes to be around £363,000.

The biggest part of the charity's expenditure is spent in providing advice and advocacy services, including debt advice (£959,000 in 2014).

Exclusions

Help is not available for maintaining council or other rented property. Grants are not usually awarded where statutory provision is available.

Applications

Initial contact should be made to the charity via phone, email or post, either directly by the individual or through a third party/any welfare organisation. The charity's website states: 'When someone gets in touch with us, we aim to make telephone contact with them within three working days of receiving their contact details. This is usually followed up with a home visit from a caseworker or debt adviser within two weeks.'

The caseworker will make an initial assessment and fill in an application form with the prospective client (or their parent if the applicant is the child of a horticulturalist).

Other information

In 2010 this charity merged with the Royal Fund for Gardeners' Children. From 2014 the charity had a change in its legal status – became a company limited by guarantee and was registered with the Charity Commission. It continues to be registered with the Office of the Scottish Charity Regulator.

The charity's website notes: 'Perennial provides free and confidential advice, support and financial assistance to people of all ages working in, or retired from horticulture. This help extends to spouses, partners and children.'

To access help get in touch with the charity via email or phone: general advice at 0800 093 8543, services@perennial.org.uk (educational activities at training@perennial.org.uk); debt advice at 0800 093 8546.

Grants are also available to individuals for education and training purposes.

Food and drink provision

The Bakers' Benevolent Society

£9,300

Correspondent: Suzanne Pitts, Clerk to the Society, The Mill House, 23 Bakers Lane, Epping, Essex CM16 5DQ (01992 575951; fax: 01992 561163; email: bbs@ bakersbenevolent.co.uk; website: www. bakersbenevolent.co.uk)

CC number: 211307

Eligibility

People in need who have worked in the baking industry and its allied trades and are now retired and their dependants and widows.

Types of grants

Recurrent grants to top-up a low income. One-off grants are also available towards items such as mobility aids, Lifelines and telephone rental, and household essentials.

Annual grant total

In 2013/14 the society had assets of £1.4 million and an income of £487,500. Grants and pensions to individuals totalled £9,300.

Applications

Application forms are available from the correspondent. Applications should be submitted either directly by the individual or a family member or through an appropriate welfare agency. Applications should include details of occupational history, age and financial circumstances. Applications are considered upon receipt.

Other information

The charity's website states that 'The Bakers' Benevolent Society is an Almshouse Charity that was founded in 1832 and has had Sheltered accommodation in Epping, Essex for more than 30 years.'

Barham Benevolent Foundation

£10,200 (15 grants)

Correspondent: Michael Cook, Trustee, 8 Stumps End, Bosham, Chichester, West Sussex PO18 8RB (01243 573993; email: mcook1158@googlemail.com)

CC number: 249922

Eligibility

People who have been employed in the dairy business, and their dependants, who are in need.

Types of grants

One-off grants according to need. In some circumstances the foundation will support the costs of holidays and provide assistance with accommodation expenses.

Annual grant total

In 2013/14 the foundation had assets of £5.3 million and an income of £163,000. Total expenditure amounted to £130,500 and included 'Legal & professional expenses' of £47,000.

Grants totalled £74,500, of which those to individuals amounted to £27,000. The annual report for the year stated: 'During the year the Foundation made welfare payments to 15 former employees of the Dairy trade amounting to a total of £10,240.' It would appear that these payments were distributed through the National Dairymen's Benevolent Institution (NDBI).

Applications

Apply in writing to the correspondent.

Other information

Most funding given by the foundation goes towards supporting education relating to the dairy industry.

The Benevolent (formerly The Wine and Spirits Trades' Benevolent Society)

£340,000

Correspondent: Pam Jarrett, Office Manager, 39–45 Bermondsey Street, London SE1 3XF (020 7089 3888; fax: 020 7089 3889; email: support@ thebenevolent.org.uk; website: www. thebenevolent.org.uk)

CC number: 1023376

Eligibility

People living in the UK who have worked for more than five years, or 20% of their life, directly or indirectly, in the drinks industry – whether 'in a pub, brewery, bar, distillery, off licence, trade press publication, warehouse or in an office based role at a company producing, distributing, marketing or selling primarily alcohol'. Those applying for financial assistance are expected to have limited income and savings.

Types of grants

Regular beneficial grants towards general living expenses of up to £65 paid monthly and one-off grants of up to £250 for a variety of items, including cookers, fridges, other household furniture, structural repairs, respite breaks, electric scooters and stair-lifts. Grants are given in exceptional cases for funeral costs. The society also makes Christmas gift donations and gives grants towards TV licence fees. Cases are assessed on an individual basis.

Annual grant total

In 2014 the charity had an income of £690,000 and a total expenditure of £1 million. Accounts were not available to view from the Charity Commission, but, based on previous years, we estimate that the amount of grants given to individuals totalled around £340,000.

Exclusions

No grants are given towards business equipment.

Applications

Apply on a form available from the correspondent or to download from the charity's website, along with application guidelines. Applications are considered throughout the year and should include history of employment within the drinks industry. All new beneficiaries are visited by one of the charity's welfare officers to assess the best form of support. Contact the charity with any queries or support needed with completing the application form.

Other information

The society, formerly known as 'The Wine & Spirits Trades' Benevolent Society', also provides sheltered housing and offers personal welfare support and advice.

E. F. Bulmer Benevolent Fund

£73,000 (260 grants)

Correspondent: Janet Hill, Welfare Manager, Fred Bulmer Centre, Wall Street, Hereford HR4 9HP (01432 271293; email: efbulmer@gmail.com; website: www.efbulmer.co.uk)

CC number: 214831

Eligibility

Former employees of H P Bulmer Holdings plc (before it was acquired by Scottish and Newcastle plc) or its subsidiary companies for a period of not less than one year, or their dependants, who are in need. Grants are occasionally made to other individuals in need in Herefordshire.

Types of grants

One-off grants, typically up to £500, are awarded according to need. Some top-up pensions are made from a historic list but the fund is not considering new pension applicants.

Annual grant total

In 2013/14 the fund held assets of £13.1 million and had an income of £383,500. Grants to 260 individuals totalled £73,000 and were distributed as follows:

Pension supplements	144	£28,000
One-off grants to H P Bulmer pensioners	62	£26,500
One-off grants to other individuals	54	£18,500

A further £151,000 was awarded in grants to 67 organisations.

Applications

H. P. Bulmer pensioners and former employees should direct their initial enquiries to the Welfare Manager, preferably by email. Individuals with no connection to H. P. Bulmer should direct their requests to James Grrenfield, Administrator; however, applications must be made through a recognised organisation such as social services, Citizens Advice or other reputable organisations. Applicants are encouraged to consider the information noted on the fund's website before applying. The fund aims to inform eligible applicants of the outcome as soon as possible after the trustees' meeting. Ineligible applicants will not receive a reply.

Other information

The fund maintains the Fred Bulmer centre which provides facilities and accommodation for other charities.

Butchers' and Drovers' Charitable Institution (BDCI)

£183,500

Correspondent: Tina Clayton, Vice Clerk to the Trustees, Butchers' and Drovers' Charitable Institution, 105 St Peter's Street, St Albans, Hertfordshire AL1 3EJ (01727 896094; email: info@bdci.org.uk; website: www.bdci.org.uk)

CC number: 1155703

Eligibility

People in the UK, who work or have worked in any aspect of the meat industry whether wholesale, retail or otherwise, and their widows, widowers, partners and dependent children. Applicants will normally have worked within the industry for at least ten years and will often be retired or medically certified unfit to work.

Types of grants

The charity gives assistance in two ways:
- One-off awards can be made towards heating bills, mobility aids, white goods, house repairs and clothing, for example

- Small grants are given to top up nursing home fees

The charity also supports some beneficiaries with pensions.

Annual grant total

In 2014 the charity had assets of £10.8 million and an income of £701,000. Grants totalled £183,500 and were distributed as follows:

Pensions	£98,000
One-off grants	£83,500
Nursing home top-up	£2,000

During the year, 85 applications for assistance were considered by the Grants Committee, with 70 being approved.

Applications

Application forms can be requested from the correspondent or downloaded from the charity's website. They can be submitted directly by the individual or through a third party, such as a social worker, Citizens Advice or other welfare agency. Applications require the following information: the applicant's name, date of birth, address and phone number; details of other people living with the applicant; the presence of any children; the applicant's connection with the meat trade; financial details, including the income of the applicant and also, if applicable, their partner; details of the applicant's ownership of their own business, if applicable; the applicant's weekly expenditure; the type of assistance sought (i.e. financial, nursing or residential care). Applicants must provide proof of their connection with the meat trade as well as financial details. Applications are considered at bi-monthly meetings.

Other information

The charity also provides residential accommodation to those in need.

The Fishmongers' and Poulterers' Institution

£19,200

Correspondent: Roy Sully, Secretary, Butchers' Hall, 87 Bartholomew Close, London EC1A 7EB (020 7600 4106; email: fpi@butchershall.com; website: www.butchershall.com)

CC number: 209013

Eligibility

People in need who are, or have been, involved in the processing, wholesale and retail in fish and poultry trades for at least ten years, and their dependants.

Types of grants

Pensions and one-off grants. In 2014 one-off grants were given for needs such as the purchase of white goods, replacement windows and assistance with care costs.

Annual grant total

In 2014 the institution had assets of £672,000 and an income of £31,500. Grants to individuals totalled £19,200 of which £18,300 was given in pensions and £980 in one-off grants.

Applications

Application forms are available from the correspondent. Applications can be submitted directly by the individual or through a third party. The institution points out in its 2014 annual report that many applications are received through intermediary bodies such as The Royal British Legion or Care and Repair agencies. They are considered three times a year.

GroceryAid

£2.5 million

Correspondent: Welfare Team, Unit 2, Lakeside Business Park, Swan Lane, Sandhurst, Berkshire GU47 9DN (01252 875925; email: welfare@groceryaid.org. uk; website: www.groceryaid.org.uk)

CC number: 1095897

Eligibility

To qualify for assistance applicants must have worked for a minimum of ten years in the UK grocery industry (including food manufacturing, wholesaling and retailing in all its aspects and the retail off-licence trade) and be able to demonstrate a degree of financial hardship.

The trustees may make an exception to the ten year rule for people who have hit an immediate but short-term crisis and require a one-off grant. In this event the qualifying period of employment is five years. If you or your partner currently work in any part of the grocery industry, from the largest factory through the supply chain to the smallest of stores, and you have over five years' service then you may be eligible for a one-off grant.

All applications will be considered on a case-by-case basis.

Types of grants

The charity offers help in the following ways:

▶ Regular payments for those who are struggling to get by
▶ An emergency one-off grant to help with a short-term crisis
▶ Essential household appliances
▶ Mobility items that bring independence
▶ Befriending for those socially isolated

Annual grant total

In 2014/15 the charity held assets of £13.4 million and had an income of over £6.5 million. Quarterly grants were made totalling over £2.5 million, with a further £920,000 spent on the provision of goods and services. Charitable expenditure was distributed as follows:

Quarterly payments	£2.5 million
Christmas hampers	£189,500
Emergency assistance	£153,000
Basic essentials	£138,500
One-off payments	£133,000
Mobility	£134,000
Welfare Helpline	£91,500
Birthday vouchers and TV licences	£35,000
Telephone response systems	£17,000
Respite for carers	£14,000
Beneficiary outings	£14,000

Applications

Application forms are available from the correspondent or to download from the website. Applications can be submitted by post or email, directly by the individual, through a social worker, Citizens Advice, other welfare agency, or via a third party such as a relative. Applications are considered throughout the year. Applicants will be visited, if possible, by a welfare assessor who will carry out a more detailed assessment of their needs.

Other information

In February 2012 Caravan and the Sweet Charity, the charity for the confectionary trade, merged to form GroceryAid.

A welfare helpline (0808 802 1122) is also operated for all staff from the grocery industry, whether or not they are eligible for financial help from the charity.

Licensed Trade Charity

£453,000

Correspondent: Helpline Team, Heatherley, London Road, Ascot, Berkshire SL5 8DR (0808 801 0550; fax: 01344 884703; email: support@ supportandcare.org; website: www. supportandcare.org)

CC number: 230011

Eligibility

People in need who are working, or have worked, in the licensed drinks industry, including their spouses/partners and dependent children. To qualify for assistance applicants should have worked in the trade for a minimum of five years continuously at some time in their working lives.

Types of grants

Recurrent grants are given to those on a very low income to help with utility bills, food costs, hospital travel expenses and other essential living expenses. One-

off grants are also made towards: urgently needed equipment, such as household appliances and mobility aids; household improvements like door widening, stair-lifts and ramps; convalescent care and nursing costs for those recovering from illness; winter fuel grants; and funeral expenses.

Annual grant total

In 2014 the charity had assets of £56.3 million and an income of £19.95 million. Welfare grants to individuals totalled £453,000.

Exclusions

Grants are not generally made for fees for educational courses, student maintenance, and student loan repayments. Support is not given for top-up fees for residential care or for private medical treatments.

Applications

In the first instance get in touch with the charity to discuss your needs.

Other information

The charity also operates an independent school in Ascot and SEN schools in Oxford and Hassocks, and offers bursaries to students whose parents have worked in the licensed drinks industry amounting to around £427,000 in 2014.

The charity's website offers advice and information on a range of issues, such as housing, money problems, education and health needs. Educational grants can also be made for families.

The Benevolent Society of the Licensed Trade of Scotland

£151,500

Correspondent: Chris Gardner, Chief Executive, 79 West Regent Street, Glasgow G2 2AW (0141 353 3596; fax: 0141 353 3597; email: chris@bensoc.org. uk; website: www.bensoc.org.uk)

OSCR number: SC005604

Eligibility

Members of the society and people who have been employed full-time in the licensed trade in Scotland for at least three years.

Types of grants

Annual pensions usually of up to £640. Each pensioner also receives a substantial Christmas and holiday gift. One-off grants are also available for temporary emergencies.

Annual grant total

In 2013/14 the society had an income of £433,000 and a total expenditure of £399,000. Grants and donations to individuals totalled £151,500.

Applications

Apply to the correspondent, who can be contacted in writing, by telephone or email, or through the website. Applications can be made directly by the individual or through a social worker, Citizens Advice or other welfare agency. The BEN can offer help to applicants who need assistance to complete an application.

Other information

Pensioners are visited at least once a year.

The Liverpool Provision Trade Guild

£6,500

Correspondent: The Trustees, The Liverpool Provision Trade Guild, c/o KBH Accountants Ltd, 255 Poulton Road, Wallasey CH44 4BT (0151 638 8550)

CC number: 224918

Eligibility

Members of the guild and their dependants who are in need. If funds permit, benefits can be extended to other members of the provision trade on Merseyside who are in need and their dependants.

Types of grants

Recurrent grants of £400 to £900 paid monthly, half-yearly or annually.

Annual grant total

In 2013/14 the guild had an income of £3,600 and a total expenditure of £7,000. We estimate that the amount of grants given to individuals totalled £6,500.

Applications

Applications should be made directly to the correspondent by the individual. Meetings are held in May and December to discuss applications.

The National Association of Master Bakers, Confectioners and Caterers Benevolent Fund

£20,000

Correspondent: The Secretary, 21 Baldock Street, Ware, Hertfordshire SG12 9DH (01920 468061; email: info@craftbakersassociation.co.uk; website: www.craftbakersassociation.co.uk)

CC number: 206691

Eligibility

Former master bakers and their families who are in need.

Types of grants

Quarterly grants to help towards living costs such as gas, electricity and telephone bills. One-off grants are also available for specific items such as wheelchairs and household adaptations.

Annual grant total

In 2014 the fund had an income of £16,700 and a total expenditure of £30,500. We estimate that the amount of grants given to individuals totalled around £20,000, with funding also awarded to organisations.

Exclusions

No grants are given for business debt or towards nursing home fees.

Applications

Application forms are available from the correspondent. Applications should be submitted by the individual or through a recognised referral agency such as a social worker, Citizens Advice or doctor. Applications are usually considered on a monthly basis.

The National Federation of Fish Friers Benevolent Fund

£2,200

Correspondent: The General Secretary, New Federation House, 4 Greenwood Mount, Meanwood, Leeds LS6 4LQ (0113 230 7044; fax: 0113 230 7010; email: mail@federationoffishfriers.co.uk; website: www.federationoffishfriers.co.uk)

CC number: 229168

Eligibility

Members or former members of the federation and their dependants (whether subscribers to the fund or not).

Types of grants

One-off grants in the range of £150 to £300 for necessities and convalescent holidays in the UK.

Annual grant total

In 2014 the fund had an income of £1,100 and a total expenditure of £2,500. We estimate that the total amount of grants awarded to individuals was approximately £2,200.

Exclusions

No grants are available for debts due to poor business practice, or to organisations.

Applications

Application forms are available from the correspondent. Applications can be submitted by the individual, through a recognised referral agency (such as a social worker, Citizens Advice or AFF Associations/branches) or by the individual's family, and are considered throughout the year.

Other information

The fund maintains several convalescent homes.

The Provision Trade Charity

£61,000

Correspondent: Mette Barwick, Secretary, 17 Clerkenwell Green, London EC1R 0DP (020 7253 2114; fax: 020 7608 1645; email: secretary@ptbi.org.uk; website: www.ptbi.org.uk)

CC number: 209173

Eligibility

People in need in the provision and allied trade, and their dependants. Applicants are normally retired and must have been employed in the trade for a number of years.

The provision trade covers the following: bacon; pork; canned meat/fish; and dairy products.

Types of grants

Recurrent grants are issued quarterly. Summer and winter gifts and one-off grants can also be awarded, where appropriate. One-off grants may also be issued to assist with special purchases or home improvements.

Annual grant total

In 2014 the charity had an income of £66,000 and a total expenditure of £63,000. We estimate that grants totalled £61,000. At the time of writing (November 2015) no accounts were available to view.

Exclusions

The charity does not provide loans.

Applications

Application forms can be downloaded from the charity's website and may be returned by email or post. Applications are usually considered in February, May, August and November. They can be submitted directly by the individual, through a social worker, Citizens Advice, other welfare agency or through a relation or friend. Prospective beneficiaries are visited by the charity's welfare visitor.

Other information

This charity was founded as the Cheesemonger's Benevolent Institution in 1835 'for pensionary relief of indigent or incapacitated members of the Provision Trade and their widows'. The charity is also referred to as PTBI.

The Scottish Association of Master Bakers' Benevolent Fund

£13,500

Correspondent: Grants Administrator, Atholl House, 4 Torphichen Street, Edinburgh EH3 8JQ

OSCR number: SC010444

Eligibility

Members or ex-members of the Scottish Association of Master Bakers and their families who are in need. Other members of the Scottish baking industry may also be supported.

Types of grants

One-off grants of up to £700 towards electrical goods, household repairs, repayment of small debts and so on.

Annual grant total

In 2013/14 the fund had an income of £18,500 and a total expenditure of £15,000. We estimate that the amount of grants given to individuals totalled £13,500.

Applications

Application forms are available from the correspondent.

Scottish Grocers' Federation Benevolent Fund

£9,000

Correspondent: Pete Cheema, Chief Executive, Federation House, 222–224 Queensferry Road, Edinburgh EH4 2BN (0131 343 3300; fax: 0131 343 6147; email: info@scotgrocersfed.co.uk; website: www.scottishshop.org.uk/about/benevolent-fund)

OSCR number: SC014216

Eligibility

Past members or employees of the grocery trade in Scotland who are in need.

Types of grants

One-off grants or recurrent grants, distributed quarterly, usually totalling around £900 a year.

Annual grant total

In 2014 the fund had an income of £16,200 and a total expenditure of £9,400. Though the website states that 'around £14,000 is distributed annually', we estimate that during this financial year social welfare grants to individuals totalled £9,000.

Applications

Apply on a form available from the correspondent or to download from the website. Applicants are then visited to assess the most appropriate form of help.

Other information

Each beneficiary has an almoner appointed to them so that any special needs can be met and their welfare can be monitored.

The Sir John Edwin and Arthur Mitchell Fund

£33,000

Correspondent: Ms H. Woodall, Administrator, Mitchells & Butlers, 27 Fleet Street, Birmingham B3 1JP (0121 498 4129; website: www.mbtrusts.org.uk)

CC number: 528922

Eligibility

Employees and former employees of Mitchells & Butlers, Six Continents and Bass Companies, in brewing, licensed retailing or catering.

Types of grants

Recurrent and one-off grants to pay essential bills or buy essential household items, assistance with property deposits, home adaptations for people with disabilities, convalescent and respite breaks, wheelchairs and aids, counselling, etc.

Annual grant total

In 2013/14 the fund held assets of £1.4 million and had an income of £49,000. Grants totalling £26,500 were made to The Licensed Trade Charity to fund former employees of Mitchells & Butlers with a further £6,500 given in grants directly to six individuals.

Exclusions

Top-up fees for residential care, private medical treatment or retrospective funding of items/services already purchased.

Applications

Applications are made through Licensed Trade Support and Care, part of the Licensed Trade Charity, which provides support to current and former brewery and licensed trade workers where it is needed. An application can be made by contacting the helpline on 01344 898550 or by using the contact form on the website.

Other information

The fund supplies money to beneficiaries through the umbrella welfare organisation Licensed Trade Support and Care. This organisation provides a holistic support service offering benefit, housing and debt advice as well as financial assistance.

Hospitality and retail

ABTA LifeLine (The ABTA Benevolent Trust)

£43,500 (28 grants)

Correspondent: Isabel O'Riordan, Business and Marketing Assistant, 30 Park Street, London SE1 9EQ (020 3693 0171; email: lifeline@abtalifeline.org.uk or apatel@abta.co.uk; website: www.abtalifeline.org.uk)

CC number: 295819

Eligibility

People in need who are or have been employed by ABTA members, ABTA itself or other organisations within the industry who are engaged in the sale of ABTA products, and their dependants.

Types of grants

One-off and recurrent grants unrestricted in size. Grants have been awarded for mobility equipment, disability and health needs, children's expenses, funeral costs, emergency home repairs, assistance with daily living costs and respite breaks for carers. Loans may also be available. The charity's lifeline stretches far and wide and nothing is too big or too small to be considered.

The charity advises:

> Whilst we do not help with paying off debts, we may be able to help with priority debts (rent, mortgage, utility bills). The charity will request that you first seek guidance from the Citizens Advice Bureau. The CAB can help you plan and budget according to your needs, and provide advice on how to tackle the debts that you have.
>
> In exceptional circumstances, and where there is a clear need, we may be able to provide an immediate payment to help relieve the pressure.
>
> We may, also in exceptional circumstances, be able to help the parent of someone working in travel. Both the parent and the person applying on behalf of the parent will need to be assessed.

Annual grant total

In 2014 the charity had assets of £530,500 and an income of £119,500. Grants were made to 28 individuals totalling £45,500, including two loans totalling £5,300, which were later written off, and a bursary of £2,000. During the year the charity received a total of 42 applications.

Exclusions

The charity generally does not have any restrictions in relation to their grant criteria, except it cannot help with business costs including those arising from the failure of a company. Statutory help and assistance from other appropriate authorities or supportive agencies should be exhausted before applying for a grant from the charity.

Applications

Application forms are available from the correspondent or can be downloaded from the website. They should be submitted either directly by the individual, through a third party, such as a social worker, or through an organisation, such as Citizens Advice.

Other information

The charity also offers The ABTA Lifeline Bursary in memory of Colin Heal to assist 'an individual in [the] travel community who does not have the means to further their education and develop their career potential within the industry'. The bursary was established in partnership with Travel Weekly.

The British Office Supplies and Services Federation Benevolent Fund

£46,500 (173 grants)

Correspondent: Liz Whyte, Administrator, 2 Villiers Court, Meriden Business Park, Copse Drive, Coventry CV5 9RN (0845 450 1565; email: liz@bossfederation.co.uk; website: www.bossfederation.co.uk)

CC number: 279029

Eligibility

People who work or have worked in the stationery, office products and office machines sector (and their dependants) who are in need due to ill health, disability or loneliness, or are unable to work, are struggling to support a family or are otherwise in financial need.

Types of grants

One-off grants according to need are given towards, for example, wheelchairs, property repair, school uniforms. Regular quarterly payments are also made.

Annual grant total

In 2014 the fund had an income of £69,500 and assets of £942,000. Grants made to 173 individuals for social welfare purposes totalled £46,500.

Applications

Applicants should contact the fund by telephone for an initial consultation, after which an appointment will be made for a member of the fund to visit the applicant at home for further information and to assess the situation.

Other information

This fund was previously known as The British Office Systems and Stationery Federation Benevolent Fund.

The Guild of Registered Tourist Guides Benevolent Fund

£12,000

Correspondent: Elizabeth Keatinge, Administrator, c/o GRTG, The Guild House, 52D Borough High Street, London SE1 1XN (01980 623463)

CC number: 211562

Eligibility

Institute registered (blue badge) guides who are in need and have been qualified for at least one year, and former and retired guides who have been qualified for five years or more. The dependants of guides qualified for at least five years may also be eligible for support.

Types of grants

One-off grants to relieve need and enable a guide to work. Grants can be up to £700, but are normally between £300 and £400.

Annual grant total

In 2014 the fund had an income of £19,700 and a total expenditure of £9,100. We estimate that the amount of grants given to individuals totalled £7,000.

Exclusions

Grants are not given for debts or private hospital care.

Applications

Apply in writing to the correspondent, including the tourist board with which the applicant was registered, whether any statutory bodies have been approached and details of the specific need. Applications can be made directly by the individual or through a third party. They can be considered at any time. Each trustee has a portfolio of clients and is responsible for checking how the beneficiaries are getting on, sometimes through home visits.

Hospitality Action

£595,000 (703+ grants)

Correspondent: The Grants Team, 62 Britton Street, London EC1M 5UY (020 3004 5507; fax: 020 7253 2094; email: help@hospitalityaction.org.uk; website: www.hospitalityaction.org.uk)

CC number: 1101083

Eligibility

Former and current workers in the hospitality industry in the UK, and their dependants. Applicant must be either currently working, have worked for one continuous year in the past five years, or have worked for seven years in their lifetime in the UK.

The individuals or the company they work for would need to have been involved in the direct provision of food, drink or accommodation away from home. Applicants must have limited savings. People who are suffering from a life altering illness, domestic violence, experience poverty, are in bereavement or older people who find themselves isolated are all assisted.

Types of grants

According to the Hospitality Action website, the charity offers:

- Essential Needs Grants – 'towards the cost of an item or need considered essential for the well being or improving the quality of life of the applicant'
- Crisis Grants – usually for a maximum of one year 'to assist with the general living costs to applicants of working age who have suffered a sudden loss of income due to bereavement, illness or injury'
- Top-up Grants – 'to assist with their general living costs to ensure that an adequate standard of living is achieved'
- Winter Fuel Grants – £100 to pay essential fuel bills

Loans are also available.

Annual grant total

In 2014 the charity held assets of £8.45 million and had an income of £1.35 million. Welfare grants totalled 595,000 and were distributed as follows:

Essential needs grants	510	£343,000
Top-up grants	73	£89,500
Short-term crisis grants	120	£87,500
Christmas grants	Not specified	£26,500
Other grants	Not specified	£16,200
Winter fuel grants	Not specified	£15,500
Family members' scheme	Not specified	£8,100
TV licence and phone grants	Not specified	£7,100
Volunteers' expenses	Not specified	£1,400

Exclusions

Funding is not available towards the following:

- Education-related costs, such as private school fees, fees for educational courses, student maintenance, and student loan repayment
- Most private medical treatments
- Residential care fee shortfalls

▶ Legal costs
▶ Property repairs/adaptations where equity release is a viable option

The charity cannot consider a grant for an item until all statutory sources of funding have been tried. Only one grant per applicant can be made in any twelve month period.

Applications

Application forms are available from the website and can be returned by post or email. Consideration normally takes about two weeks and all applicants are informed of the outcome in writing. The application must include the candidates NI number, work history, reasons for application, payee details and quotes (if applicable) and be signed. Supporting letter on headed paper must be provided. There are detailed and helpful application guidance notes on the charity's website.

The annual report notes:

> Applicants are required to complete a Hospitality Action application form unless a referring organisation has already supplied much of the relevant information. All applications need to be supported by an appropriate independent organisation such as Social Services, Citizens Advice Bureaux or charities such as British Legion, Help the Aged, etc. A copy of the grant rules is sent out on request by the Grants & Advisory Team.

The website notes: 'If you have any questions about any part of this form or what we require please don't hesitate to get in touch on 020 3004 5500.'

Other information

The charity was established and formerly known as the Hotel and Catering Benevolent Association (HCBA).

Hospitality Action runs The Ark Foundation Programme which offers seminars on drugs and alcohol misuse. The organisation has a Family Members scheme – a free scheme open to anyone who is over pension age and has worked within the hospitality industry in the UK for at least seven years. Christmas hampers and gift vouchers are offered to the members.

Johnson Charitable Trust

£23,500

Correspondent: Yvonne Monaghan, Trustee, Johnson Service Group plc, Johnson House, Abbots Park, Monks Way, Preston Brook WA7 3GH (01928 704600; email: enquiries@jsg.com)

CC number: 216974

Eligibility

Employees and ex-employees of the Johnson Group plc and their dependants.

Types of grants

One-off and recurrent grants are given according to need.

Annual grant total

In 2013/14 the trust held assets of £1.7 million and had an income of £49,000. Allowances, grants and Christmas hampers to individuals totalled about £23,500 and were distributed as follows:

Christmas hampers	£14,700
Widows/widowers allowance and gifts	£8,900
Physiotherapy	£200

Costs paid towards a pensioners' lunch amounted to a further £300.

Applications

Apply in writing to the correspondent.

The National Federation of Retail Newsagents Convalescence Fund

£9,800

Correspondent: Michael Jenkins, Administrator, Yeoman House, Sekforde Street, Clerkenwell Green, London EC1R 0HF (020 7017 8855; email: michael@nfrn.org.uk; website: www.nfrn.org.uk)

CC number: 209280

Eligibility

Members of the federation and their spouses. Other people in the retail news agency trade who are not members of the federation are not eligible.

Types of grants

One-off grants for convalescent holidays.

Annual grant total

In 2014 the fund had an income of £14,900 and a total expenditure of £9,300. We estimate that the amount of grants given to individuals totalled around £9,800.

Applications

Apply in writing to the correspondent or by contacting the NFRN helpline on 0800 121 6376 (020 7017 8880 from a mobile phone) or emailing helpline@nfrn.org.uk. Applications can be submitted directly by the individual, through a third party such as a social worker, or through a district office of the federation. They are considered at any time.

Retail Trust

£953,500

Correspondent: Grants Manager, Marshall Hall, Marshall Estate, Hammers Lane, London NW7 4DQ (0808 801 0808; email: helpline@retailtrust.org.uk; website: www.retailtrust.org.uk)

CC number: 1090136

Eligibility

People in need who have worked in the retail, wholesale, manufacturing and distribution trades – qualification varies depending on whether retired/redundant/carer/of working age but no longer in retail. For full details visit the charity's website. Applicants who are unsure if they qualify should contact the support line.

Types of grants

Examples of items the trust will help with:

▶ Disability aids and adaptations
▶ Funeral costs
▶ Prevention of homelessness (rent/mortgage arrears and rent deposit)
▶ Council tax arrears
▶ Essential household furniture
▶ Food vouchers
▶ Prevention of fuel poverty (help with heating bills, and boiler replacements)
▶ Bankruptcy and debt relief order fees (these are exceptional cases)

Annual grant total

In 2013/14 the trust held assets of £33.5 million and had an income of £9.8 million. Grants to individuals totalled £953,500.

Exclusions

No grants are given for private medical treatment, legal fees, most personal debts or for items purchased prior to the application.

Applications

Apply on a form available to complete online. The application requirements are quite specific and potential applicants are advised to follow the information provided by the trust on its website. On average, applications take three weeks to process from the date all the required documentation is supplied, although in some cases this make take longer.

Other information

Retail Trust runs a helpline for its beneficiaries (Freephone 0808 801 0808) and in 2013/14 there was a 33% increase in first time calls.

The trust also has sheltered and extra-care accommodation in locations across England as well as a care home in Scotland. See the trust's informative website for more details.

Information and communication

The Book Trade Charity

£128,000

Correspondent: David Hicks, Chief Executive, The Foyle Centre, The Retreat, Abbots Road, Kings Langley, Hertfordshire WD4 8LT (01923 263128 or 01329848731; fax: 01923 270732; email: david@btbs.org or info@booktradecharity.org; website: www.booktradecharity.org)

CC number: 1128129

Eligibility

People in need who have worked in the book trade in the UK for at least one year (normally publishing/distribution/book-selling), and their dependants.

Types of grants

One-off grants and regular monthly grants of up to £2,000 a year. Grants are normally to supplement weekly/monthly income and for recuperative holidays. Other support is given in a variety of ways, for example, assistance with telephone and television rental, medical aid, aids for people with disabilities and house repairs/redecoration. Grants are also given to help retrain people from the book trade who have been made redundant. Support is also available to assist young people to join the trade where their financial circumstances might otherwise prevent this, including contributions towards interview costs, travel and subsistence. This support may also be available to those undertaking internships in the industry.

Annual grant total

In 2014 the charity had assets of nearly £5.7 million consisting for the most part of land and buildings and, therefore, not available for grant-giving, and an income of £543,000. Grants were made totalling £130,000, of which £128,000 was awarded in social welfare grants (including £7,000 in medical costs).

During the year the charity received 75 applications for welfare support and supported 53 of those. Regular beneficiaries were reviewed. In total 81 beneficiaries were assisted in the year.

Regular support	52 (45 – for full 12 months)	£76,000
Housing/rent arrears/debt	17	£15,000
Disability, medical and nursing home fees (including £6,000 for the support of one exceptional, specific project funded by restricted donations)	4	£13,000
Christmas one-off grants	46	£9,000
Travel and car costs	8	£7,800
Household, including carpets and white goods	13	£5,500
Holidays and clothing	3	£2,000
Retraining and redundancy support, computers	7	£1,800

Applications

Application forms are available from the correspondent or the charity's website. They can be submitted by the individual or through a recognised referral agency (a social worker, Citizens Advice, doctor and so on). They are considered as they arrive.

Other information

The charity can offer support to 'individuals and families in need with help to address and ameliorate the impact of':

- Low household income and savings, debt and insolvency
- Unemployment and redundancy
- Health and medical aid not easily or normally provided by the NHS
- Being a carer
- Emergencies and unforeseen circumstances
- Accidents, illness or bereavement
- Housing difficulties and homelessness

The BT Benevolent Fund

£770,000

Correspondent: Mike Pearce, Treasurer and Accountant, Room 323, Reading Central Telephone Exchange, 41 Minister Street, Reading RG1 2JB (020 8726 2145; email: benevolent@bt.com; website: www.benevolent.bt.com)

CC number: 212565

Eligibility

Present or past (whether pensionable or not) British Telecom Group employees and present or future BT Group pensioners, and their dependants. The fund's website specifies: 'Past BT employees may include workers from Telecoms side of former GPO.'

Types of grants

One-off grants are given towards: household appliances; disability aids; home adaptations; convalescence; carers' breaks; funeral costs; and debt arrears, especially when there is a risk of eviction

and small children are involved. Weekly grants, which in 2014 ranged between £5 and £25 per week, are available to older former employees, and their dependants, who are living on a low income. Recipients of weekly grants are also eligible to receive a £100 one-off Christmas grant.

Annual grant total

In 2014 the fund had assets of £3.4 million and an income of £1.3 million. Grants totalled £770,000, of which £547,000 was given in single grants and £223,000 in weekly grants to 228 regular beneficiaries.

Applications

Contact the correspondent for more information. The website notes that it is helpful if individuals who are in receipt of a BT pension have their pension number to hand.

Current BT employees should, in the first instance, contact the Employee Assistance Programme (EAP) by calling 0800 917 6767.

Other information

The fund also operates a 'contact scheme' to provide advice and support for BT pensioners who are over 75 years old.

The Chartered Institute of Journalists Orphan Fund

£9,700

Correspondent: Dominic Cooper, Trustee, Institute of Journalists, 2 Dock Offices, Surrey Quays Road, London SE16 2XU (020 7252 1187; email: memberservices@cioj.co.uk)

CC number: 208176

Eligibility

Orphaned children of institute members who are in need, aged between 5 and 22 and in full-time education.

Types of grants

Monthly grants (plus birthday/Christmas/summer holiday payments) are given.

Annual grant total

In 2014 the fund had assets of £2.4 million and an income of £100,500. Grants to individuals totalled £19,400 for both welfare and education. We have estimated that grants to individuals for social welfare purposes totalled around £9,700.

Applications

Applications may be made in writing to the correspondent.

Other information

This fund also gives grants for educational purposes.

The Charity Commission's records note that the fund's website is www.cioj.co.uk; however, it did not seem to work at the time of writing.

The Chartered Institute of Library and Information Professionals (CILIP) Benevolent Fund

£5,700 (Around 10 grants)

Correspondent: Eric Winter, Secretary, 19 Cricketers Drive, Meopham, Gravesend DA13 0AX (020 7255 0648; email: eric.winter@cilip.org.uk; website: www.cilip.org.uk)

CC number: 237352

Eligibility

Members and former members of the CILIP and their dependants. This includes former members of the Library Association and the Institute of Information Scientists who may not have chosen to become members of CILIP.

Types of grants

One-off grants only for 'unusual or unexpected expenses that may be causing anxiety and hardship'. Grants are given towards, for example, urgent house repairs, household equipment, unexpectedly large heating bills, overdrafts or debts that have accumulated due to illness and so on. Interest-free loans are also available.

Annual grant total

In 2014 the fund held assets of £156,500 and had an income of £30,500. Welfare grants to around ten individuals totalled £5,700.

Exclusions

No grants are given to students. The fund is not able to offer recurrent grants or pension top-ups.

Applications

Applicants should either write to or telephone the correspondent and outline their difficulties. A visit will then be arranged to discuss the circumstances in more detail. The trustees meet three or four times a year to consider applications, although urgent requests can be dealt with more quickly.

Other information

While the fund can only offer short-term help, it has built up relationships with a number of charities and other bodies that it may refer beneficiaries to for further support.

The Cinema and Television Benevolent Fund

£766,000 (6,334 grants)

Correspondent: Welfare Department, 22 Golden Square, London W1F 9AD (0800 138 2522; email: welfare@ctbf.co.uk; website: www.ctbf.co.uk)

CC number: 1099660

Eligibility

People who have worked behind the scenes in the cinema, film and commercial television industries in the UK for two years in any capacity, i.e. production, exhibition, distribution, administration or transmission of film or commercial television. Help is also available to dependants.

Applicants should have less than £10,000 in savings, must be in receipt of all state benefits applicable to their situation, must have received debt counselling from Citizens Advice or one of the large free debt advice agencies and must have exhausted statutory options. If applicable, a Disabled Facilities Grant must have been applied for from the local authority.

Types of grants

Recurrent payments and one-off grants for a wide range of needs, for example, towards white goods, televisions, disability aids/special equipment, disability adaptations and home repairs.

Annual grant total

In 2014/15 the fund held assets of £31.5 million and had an income of £3.2 million. Grants to individuals totalled £766,000. The following are the grant categories and amounts distributed:

Regular monthly grants	£383,000
Other grants	£75,000
Support to Glebelands and Broccoli Cloisters residents	£62,000
JBA grants	£34,000
Christmas gifts and hampers	£31,000
Cold weather grants	£24,000
Birthday grants	£24,000
National Care Plan	£22,000
Household appliances	£21,000
Grants from restricted reserves	£14,000
Utilities	£12,000
TV licences	£10,000
Mobility aids	£10,000
Assistance with rent and mortgages	£7,000
Medical	£3,000
Loans	£3,000

Exclusions

The fund is not able to assist individuals who have been employed solely by the BBC on a full-time basis. No grants are given for educational purposes (except in exceptional circumstances).

Applications

Application forms are available from the fund's website or welfare department. Applications are considered on an ongoing basis and should be submitted either directly by the individual or through a third party such as a social worker. Supporting documents must be submitted. These include an up-to-date CV, any documentation that proves employment (such as a payslip), DWP letters showing government benefits, local authority letters showing housing and council tax benefits, letters/bills from creditors, any other relevant paperwork and documentation relating to other funding sources, for example Disabled Facilities Grant applications. Applicants are advised to visit the charity's very helpful website for full details.

Other information

The fund owns and manages a home for the elderly at Glebelands, which gives priority to those who have worked in the world of film, cinema and television. For more information contact the fund or go to the Glebelands website (www.glebelands.org).

The most significant announcement of the year, according to the trustees' annual report, was from the welfare department launching the National Care Plan in March 2014. The charity's partnership with Anchor Trust will offer discounted care in Anchor's 96 residential care homes in England to both current and potential beneficiaries and the parents of those working in the film and television industries.

The Grace Wyndham Goldie (BBC) Trust Fund

£3,300 (2 grants)

Correspondent: Cheryl Miles, Secretary, BBC, Room M1017, Broadcasting House, Cardiff CF5 2YQ (029 2032 2000; website: www.bbc.co.uk/charityappeals/about/grants/grace-wyndham-goldie)

CC number: 212146

Eligibility

Individuals currently or previously engaged in broadcasting, and their dependants.

Types of grants

One-off grants are given to help relieve 'short-term domestic hardship' not covered by assistance from other sources.

Annual grant total

In 2014 the fund had assets of £1.3 million and an income of £52,500. The fund made 20 grants totalling £29,500, the vast majority of which were given for educational purposes. A total of two welfare grants were given, amounting to £3,300.

Exclusions

Grants are not given for medical, nursing or care home fees, funeral expenses or holidays.

Applications

Application forms are available to download from the fund's page on the BBC website. Applicants are asked to provide full information about the circumstances supporting their application. All applications are considered in confidence. Completed forms should be returned to: Trustees, Grace Wyndham Goldie (BBC) Trust Fund, BBC Pension and Benefits Centre, Broadcasting House, Cardiff CF5 2YQ.

Iprovision (formerly The Institute of Public Relations Benevolent Fund)

£16,000 (35 grants)

Correspondent: Ruth Ritchie, Iprovision Administrator, c/o CIPR Public Relations Centre, 52–53 Russell Square, London WC1B 4HP (020 8144 5536; email: administrator@iprovision.org.uk; website: www.cipr.co.uk/iprovision)

CC number: 242674

Eligibility

Members of the institute and dependants of members or deceased members. The website states that the following are eligible for support:

> Anyone who is a current full Member of CIPR; a Fellow; retired full Member or Fellow Member; an Associate Member of CIPR for at least one year; a Student Member of CIPR for at least one year; a past CIPR who was in membership for at least five years; a CIPR permanent member of staff (whether full-time or part-time) with at least one year of service; a former CIPR permanent member of staff (whether full-time or part-time) for at least five years; and close dependants of all the above categories.

Types of grants

One-off and recurrent grants are given according to need as well as interest-free loans. Grants can cover white goods, daily living expenses, unexpected one-off costs, and help can be given towards the costs of respite breaks, etc. Members receiving support may be entitled to abatement of membership fees for up to a year.

Annual grant total

In 2014 the fund had assets of £846,500 and an income of £59,500. 35 grants and repayable grants were awarded to 16 members in need. Grants totalled

£16,000 and repayable grants totalled £18,000.

Exclusions

No grants are given for CIPR annual subscriptions, business costs or debts.

Applications

Initially contact the administrator in writing, by phone or by email outlining your situation and explaining how you think Iprovision could help you. The administrator will then contact you personally, so make sure to include your contact details. You will be asked to complete the application form, which is available to download from the website, and to provide some financial details. The trustees meet to consider applications every three months, but if the need is urgent decisions may be made between meetings.

Note: If you are contacting the administrator by post, mark your envelope 'Private and Confidential'.

The Market Research Benevolent Association

£22,300 (28 grants)

Correspondent: Danielle Scott, Secretary and Treasurer, 11 Tremayne Walk, Camberley, Surrey GU15 1AH (0845 652 0303; email: info@mrba.org.uk; website: www.mrba.org.uk)

CC number: 274190

Eligibility

People who are or have been engaged in market research and their dependants.

Types of grants

Generally one-off grants for people in need. Funding has been given towards the costs of wheelchairs and other medical equipment, convalescence and other medical expenses, and emergency house and car repairs. Interest-free loans are also available.

Annual grant total

In 2013/14 the association held assets of almost £507,000 and had an income of almost £32,000. Grants totalling £19,000 were awarded to 22 individuals, with a further £3,300 in loans converted to grants. Loans totalling £12,000 were made to eight individuals.

Applications

Applicants should contact the correspondent by phone or by email to be assigned to an MRBA Regional Manager and sent an application form. The regional manager will then contact the applicant and offer assistance throughout the application process. When completed, the application form will be the subject of a summary report which will then be reviewed by the

MRBA Committee, which meets every six weeks. The regional manager will then inform the applicant on whether and how the association is able to assist. Urgent cases can be fast-tracked.

Other information

The association also provides advice, often in partnership with other organisations, as well as debt and bereavement support.

NABS

£170,000

Correspondent: Support Team, 6th Floor, 388 Oxford Street, London W1C 1JT (0800 707 6607; email: support@nabs.org.uk; website: www.nabs.org.uk)

CC number: 1070556

Eligibility

People who work or have worked in advertising, marketing, marketing services and related industries, and their dependants.

Types of grants

One-off and repeated assistance is given according to need. The annual report for 2014 provides the following information:

> Grants for all beneficiaries are more targeted and focus on making a definitive difference as we continue to move away from providing long-term support. Grants for new applicants have largely been directed towards household utilities, rehoming and staving off homelessness...

Annual grant total

In 2014 NABS had assets of £5.3 million and an income of almost £4.9 million. Grants totalled £170,000.

Applications

In the first instance, contact the charity's Advice Line (0800 707 6607) or email support@nabs.org.uk.

The charity's website states that 'even if we're not able to offer you direct financial assistance, we're always available to give practical advice and support on the next step towards resolving financial issues'.

Other information

The society provides a wide range of advice, support, networking and career guidance for members of the advertising and media industry, including a telephone helpline, career coaching and workshops and a working parents programme. It also owns Peterhouse, a comprehensive retirement complex containing a registered care home.

The Newspaper Press Fund (Journalists' Charity)

£290,000 (150–200 grants)

Correspondent: David Ilott, Director, Dickens House, 35 Wathen Road, Dorking, Surrey RH4 1JY (01306 887511; fax: 01306 888212; email: enquiries@ journalistscharity.org.uk; website: www. journalistscharity.org.uk)

CC number: 208215

Eligibility

Practising and former journalists and their dependants who are in need because of sickness, an accident or other unforeseen circumstances. There are no age restrictions.

Types of grants

One-off grants normally in the range of £250 and £500 but all cases are decided on their merits. Regular payments may be provided on a weekly or monthly basis.

Annual grant total

In 2014 the charity had assets of £11.4 million and an income of £1.6 million. It would appear that full accounts were not available to view at the time of writing. Our research indicates that, normally, around 150–200 awards are made each year totalling around £300,000, with a small amount given for educational purposes.

Exclusions

The charity states that its 'aim is to give financial support in times of need however it cannot subsidise those who, in the long term, find it difficult to make a living from journalism unless through illness or other misfortune'. Grants are not offered to subsidise an existing lifestyle. Awards are not generally given towards holidays (although support may be given for convalescence or respite breaks) and it is unlikely that support will be given towards care home fees. Only in exceptional circumstances will help be given towards medical fees. Assistance is not given for the payment of credit card debts, bank loans, legal costs or fines, or for anything that is available through the state. Loans are not offered.

Applications

Application forms can be requested from the correspondent. They can be submitted directly by the individual or a family member. Applications should include details of the career in journalism and are considered monthly. Our research suggests that the consideration process may take around two to six weeks.

Other information

The fund also runs residential and care homes in Dorking.

NewstrAid Benevolent Society

£885,000

Correspondent: Alexander Henry Van Straubenzee, Welfare Manager, Suites 1&2, Thremhall Estate, Start Hill, Bishop's Stortford CM22 7TD (01279 879569; fax: 01371 873816; email: oldben@newstraid.org.uk; website: www. newstraid.org.uk)

CC number: 1116824

Eligibility

People who have been employed in newspaper and magazine distribution in the UK and who have fallen on hard times, and their immediate dependants. Distribution means people who deal with newspapers and magazines from the time they leave the printing press until they reach the reader. All applications are assessed on their merits but the society states that normally applicants should have been connected with the trade for a minimum of ten years.

Types of grants

Annual payments and one-off grants for various items including household appliances, special chairs, mobility aids, small repairs and disability equipment. The charity offers interest-free loans to home owners in respect of costly repairs, repayable on the sale of their property.

Annual grant total

In 2014 the charity had assets of £9 million and an income of £2.2 million. £885,000 was given in grants to individuals for welfare purposes.

Exclusions

No grants are given for private medicine or school or college fees.

Applications

Initial contact should be made by calling the welfare team or by submitting an enquiry form available to download from the website. The application will then be followed up by a telephone call from the welfare team.

NUJ Extra

£61,000

Correspondent: Lena Calvert, Fund Administrator, Headland House, 308–312 Gray's Inn Road, London WC1X 8DP (020 7843 3705; fax: 020 7837 8143; email: lenac@nuj.org.uk; website: www.nuj.org.uk/work/nuj-extra)

CC number: 1112489

Eligibility

Members and former members of the National Union of Journalists and the dependants of deceased members. Applicants must have paid at least one year's full subscription to the NUJ. **Note:** current members are only eligible for short-term assistance.

Types of grants

One-off grants are given for: urgent bills, mainly rent and utilities; wheelchairs; beds; domestic goods; medical equipment; and minor home adaptations. Bills or rent payments will generally be made directly to the supplier or landlord. Recurrent grants are available to top up the income of those living on a state pension and/or other benefits. The value of recurrent grants is set at an annual meeting. Christmas bonus grants are also made.

Annual grant total

In 2014 the charity held assets of £2.35 million and had an income of £65,000. Grants to individuals totalled £61,000. 20 beneficiaries received recurrent grants.

Exclusions

No grants are given for legal expenses, private medical treatment or private education. Help is unlikely to be available for consumer debts. Members who left owing the union contributions are not eligible for help. Applicants are expected to have claimed all available benefits before applying.

Applications

Application forms are available from the correspondent or to download from the website. Applications can be submitted by the individual or through an NUJ welfare officer or other third party. Applicants are required to provide details of their personal income and expenditure. Requests are considered throughout the year.

Other information

NUJ Extra is an amalgamation of charities previously known as National Union of Journalists Members in Need Fund and National Union of Journalists Provident Fund.

Legal professions

The Barristers' Benevolent Association

£89,500

Correspondent: Susan Eldridge, The Secretary, 14 Gray's Inn Square, London WC1R 5JP (020 7242 4761; fax: 020 7831 5366; email: susan@the-bba.com; website: www.the-bba.com)

CC number: 1106768

Eligibility
Past or present practising members of the Bar in England and Wales, and their spouses, former spouses and dependants.

Types of grants
Assistance may be provided by way of a grant or loan, or a combination of the two. Grants include small amounts of cash, regular food vouchers, payment of specific bills such as TV licences, car tax, telephone bills, or the purchase of equipment or medicine not available from the NHS.

Annual grant total
In 2014 the association had assets of £10.4 million and an income of £590,000. Grants totalled £178,500 and are awarded both for social welfare and educational purposes. We estimate that social welfare grants amounted to £89,500.

Exclusions
Our research indicates that no grants were made to those who, when qualified, went straight into commerce.

Applications
Application forms are available to download from the website.

The Chartered Institute of Legal Executives' Benevolent Fund

£2,200

Correspondent: Valerie Robertson, Charities and CSR Officer, The Chartered Institute Of Legal Executives, Kempston Manor, Manor Drive, Kempston, Bedford MK42 7AB (01234 845763; email: vrobertson@cilex.org.uk; website: www.cilex.org.uk)

CC number: 295527

Eligibility
Members and former members of the institute (including associates, fellows and student members), and their families or dependants. Help is particularly aimed at those who have become unemployed through old age, illness or other circumstances. Applicants must have been a member of CILEX for at least one year before applying.

Types of grants
One-off grants ranging between £100 and £1,000 can be given for specific purposes, for example, utility bills (such as telephone or fuel bills), nursing/residential care, medical equipment and so on.

Annual grant total
In 2014 the fund had an income of £3,500 and an expenditure of £2,400. We estimate that grants totalled £2,200.

Exclusions
Grants are not given to assist with student course fees, outstanding judgement debts, tax bills or bankruptcy. Although grants are not given towards membership fees or the cost of joining CILEX, members who have been made redundant can contact the membership department to arrange spreading the cost over a year or moving to a different grade of membership.

Applications
Further details on the application procedure can be requested from the correspondent or accessed on the institute's website. Applications should be submitted directly by the individual or a dependant and can be considered at any time.

Other information
The fund also offers information, practical advice and advocacy services.

Faculty of Advocates 1985 Charitable Trust

£135,000

Correspondent: Gaynor Adam, Secretariat Officer, Advocate's Library, Parliament House, Edinburgh EH1 1RF (0131 226 5071; website: www.advocates.org.uk/index.html)

OSCR number: SC012486

Eligibility
Widows, widowers, children or former dependants of deceased members of the Faculty of Advocates and members who are unable to practise by reason of permanent ill health.

Types of grants
Single grants, annuities or loans appropriate to the circumstances.

Annual grant total
In 2013/14 the trust had an income of £182,500 and a total expenditure of £151,000. We estimate that welfare grants totalled around £135,000.

Applications
The trust is regularly publicised among members and applications are often informal, by word of mouth via a trustee. Alternatively applications may be made in writing to the correspondent.

The Incorporated Benevolent Association of the Chartered Institute of Patent Attorneys

£22,000

Correspondent: Derek Chandler, Secretary, 3rd floor, 95 Chancery Lane, London WC2A 1DT

CC number: 219666

Eligibility
British members and former members of the institute, and their dependants.

Types of grants
One-off and recurrent grants or loans according to need.

Annual grant total
In 2013/14 the association had assets of £1 million and an income of £85,000. Grants to individuals totalled £22,000 and were made for social welfare purposes only.

Applications
Apply in writing to the correspondent, marked 'Private and Confidential'. Applications can be submitted at any time. Where possible, grants are provided via a third party.

Other information
The association also makes grants for educational purposes; however, based on the annual reports and accounts available to view from the Charity Commission, it would appear that there have been no grants of an educational nature made for some time.

The Pritt Fund

£4,000

Correspondent: Liverpool Law Society, The Cotton Exchange Building, Second Floor, Edmund Street, Liverpool L3 9LQ (0151 236 6998; email: charities@liverpoollawsociety.org.uk; website: www.liverpoollawsociety.org.uk)

CC number: 226421

Eligibility
Solicitors or clerks of solicitors, who are in need and have practised in the city of Liverpool or within the area of Liverpool Law Society, and their dependants.

Types of grants

One-off and recurrent grants are given according to need.

Annual grant total

In 2013/14 the fund had an income of £14,000 and a total expenditure of £4,400. We estimate that the amount of grants given to individuals totalled £4,000.

Applications

Application forms are available from the correspondent.

The Scottish Solicitors' Benevolent Fund (incorporating The Scottish Law Agents' Society Benevolent Fund)

£17,000 (25 grants)

Correspondent: Michael Sheridan, Secretary, c/o Sheridans Solicitors, 166 Buchanan Street, Glasgow G1 2LW (0141 332 3536; fax: 0141 353 3819; email: secretary@slas.co.uk; website: www.slas.co.uk)

OSCR number: SC000258

Eligibility

People in need who are or were members of the solicitors' profession in Scotland and their dependants. Typical beneficiaries include solicitors unable to practise due to ill health, and the spouses and children of deceased solicitors who have been unable to make adequate provision for their families.

Types of grants

One-off and recurrent grants are given according to need. A standard award is £500 for a period of six months.

Annual grant total

In 2013/14 the fund had assets of £283,500, an income of £8,500 and awarded 25 grants to 15 individuals totalling £17,000. Of these, seven grants were made to six individuals from the Tod Endowment restricted fund.

Applications

Application forms are available to download from the fund's website. Applicants should include their financial details and details of two referees. This document is then considered in detail, so as to determine the suitability of the individual's circumstances. A decision is then made on whether the grant application has been successful and, where appropriate, the level of award.

Other information

The trustees' annual report for 2013/14 provides the following information:

The fund is intended to assist solicitors qualified in Scotland, or their dependants, who are in need of financial assistance and whose circumstances meet the criteria set by the trustees for the payment of grants. In light of this overarching objective, the Benevolent Fund Committee does not set annual objectives.

Manufacturing

Ben – The Automotive Industry Charity

£662,000 (2,310 grants)

Correspondent: Welfare Team, Lynwood Court, Lynwood Village, Rise Road, Sunninghill, Ascot SL5 0AJ (01344 876770; email: careservices@ben.org.uk; website: www.ben.org.uk)

CC number: 297877

Eligibility

People who are resident in the UK or the Republic of Ireland who are employed or were formerly employed in the automotive industry, or its associated or allied trades or industries, and their dependants.

Types of grants

Most grants for household items or essential bills are of less than £500, although grants of up to £2,000 are available for larger items such as disability adaptations or specialist equipment. Grants are given towards essential household items, wheelchairs, adaptations and help towards children's costs such as essential school trips, clothing and specialist equipment.

Annual grant total

In 2013/14 the charity had assets of £21.8 million and an income of £13.4 million. A total of 2,310 grants were made amounting to £662,000. Of this amount, £645,500 was given in 2,246 one-off discretionary payments and the remaining £16,200 was paid in 64 regular grants.

The grants figure includes payments amounting to £29,000 which were paid to individuals on behalf of other organisations.

Exclusions

BEN cannot assist with top-up fees for people in care homes, property repairs or improvements (except heating and adaptations for a person with disabilities), private education costs, private medical costs and medications, or costs associated with bankruptcy.

Applications

Individuals, or somebody referring an individual, can contact the charity directly via the helpline (01344 876770), email (careservices@ben.org.uk), text (07781 472622), the online contact form, or by post. The charity requires a referral form to be completed, providing details of the individual's situation and the help they require. In order to confirm eligibility for assistance, the following documentation must be supplied: evidence of the connection with the motor industry (for example, a copy of a payslip, P45, contract or a letter from an employer); and proof of address/ residency status (such as a household bill or statement dated within the last three months). Referral forms can be downloaded from the website and returned to BEN by email (careservices@ben.org.uk) or by post.

The website notes the following helpful advice: 'If you are having difficulty providing proof of your eligibility then you can contact HMRC on 03000 560 616 to request a record of your employment history (within the motor trade only) by asking for a Subject Access Request.'

Other information

BEN offers free support and advice on a broad range of issues through its welfare team. Each of the following five regions has its own welfare officer assigned: Scotland and Northern Ireland; North of England; Midlands and Wales; East of England; South of England.

The fund also runs care centres, more details of which are available from the fund's informative website.

Vehicle Builders and Repairers Association Benevolent Fund

£2,300

Correspondent: David Hudson, Administrator, c/o Vehicle Builders' and Repairers' Association Ltd, Belmont House, Gildersome, Leeds LS27 7TW (0113 253 8333; fax: 0113 238 0496; email: vbra@vbra.co.uk; website: www.vbra.co.uk)

CC number: 225924

Eligibility

Present and former members, and employees of members, of the Vehicle Builders and Repairers Association who are in need, and their dependants. Applicants must have been a member or employee of a member for at least five years.

Types of grants

One-off and recurrent grants are given according to need.

Annual grant total

In 2014 the fund had an unusually low income of £47 and a total expenditure of £2,600. We estimate that the amount of grants given to individuals totalled £2,300.

Applications

Application forms are available from the correspondent.

Other information

The fund is also known as the H T Pickles Memorial Benevolent Fund.

Marine occupations

The Corporation of Trinity House, London

£30,200 (28+ grants)

Correspondent: Graham Hockley, Secretary, Trinity House, Tower Hill, London EC3N 4DH (020 7481 6914; email: graham.hockley@thls.org; website: www.trinityhouse.co.uk)

CC number: 211869

Eligibility

Mariners and their dependants.

Types of grants

The charity operates 18 almshouses at Walmer, Kent and makes provision for regular payments to up to 60 annuitants. Other direct support is made through occasional one-off grants to former seafarers and their dependants.

Annual grant total

The charity's significant assets are no reflection of the money available for grant-making which is a very small part of its activities.

In 2013/14 the corporation had assets of £201.4 million and an income of more than £8 million. Grants were made to 28 retired seafarers in financial need at a rate of £676 per year. This totalled £24,500. A further £11,500 was awarded in grants to individuals, some of which was distributed for educational purposes. We estimate that grants for social welfare purposes totalled around £5,700.

The vast majority of the charity's grants expenditure was distributed to organisations, with more than £1.5 million awarded during the year.

Applications

Enquiries regarding welfare grants can be made via email to the secretary.

Other information

The following information is taken from the corporation's website: 'The safety of shipping, and the well being of seafarers, have been our prime concerns ever since Trinity House was granted a Royal Charter by Henry VIII in 1514.'

Today there are three distinct functions:
- The General Lighthouse Authority (GLA) for England, Wales, the Channel Islands and Gibraltar. The remit is to provide Aids to Navigation to assist the safe passage of a huge variety of vessels through some of the busiest sea-lanes in the world
- A charitable organisation dedicated to the safety, welfare and training of mariners
- A Deep Sea Pilotage Authority providing expert navigators for ships trading in Northern European waters

The Furness Seamen's Pension Fund

£12,000

Correspondent: Heather O'Driscoll, Administrator, Waltons Clark Whitehill, Oakland House, 38–42 Victoria Road, Hartlepool, Cleveland TS26 8DD (01429 234414; email: heather.odriscoll@waltonscw.co.uk)

CC number: 226655

Eligibility

Seamen in need who are 50 or over and live in the borough of Hartlepool or the former county borough of West Hartlepool, or who had their permanent residence there during their sea service. All applicants must have served as seamen for at least 15 years and with some part of the sea service in vessels registered in Hartlepool, West Hartlepool or the Port of Hartlepool, or vessels trading to/from any of these ports.

Types of grants

Quarterly pensions.

Annual grant total

In 2013/14 the fund had an income of £10,000 and a total expenditure of £12,200. We estimate that pensions totalled £12,000.

Applications

Applications should be made on a form available from the correspondent. Advertisements have previously been placed in the Hartlepool Mail when vacancies are available.

The Guild of Benevolence of The Institute of Marine Engineering Science and Technology

£202,500

Correspondent: Mr A. Muncer, Chair, Aldgate House, 33 Aldgate Street, London EC3N 1EN (020 7382 2644; email: guild@imarest.org; website: www.imarest.org/guild)

CC number: 208727

Eligibility

Past and present members of the institute and guild, certified marine engineers, past and present employees of the institute or guild, and the dependants of the above.

Types of grants

Regular weekly grants of around £25 are given to supplement a low income. One-off grants, to a maximum of £4,000, are also available for disability aids, debt relief, reasonable nursing home fees, funeral costs, home maintenance and respite care. All regular beneficiaries receive a Christmas gift of £100.

Annual grant total

In 2013/14 the charity had assets of £1.4 million and an income of £107,500. Grants to individuals totalled £202,500.

Exclusions

No grants are given for educational costs.

Applications

Application forms are available from the correspondent or to download from the website. Evidence of service or qualifications as a marine engineer must be produced if not already a member of the Institute of Marine Engineers, as well as full disclosure of financial situation. Applicants should expect a visit by a guild representative who will assess their needs and assist in completing the application form. Applications are considered by trustees every eight weeks, although in cases of emergency can be considered between meetings.

Other information

The charity's website provides the following background information: 'The guild originated from the fund set up in 1912…in co-operation with the Daily Chronicle to help families of the engineer officers of the RMS Titanic that sank on 15 April 1912, after striking an iceberg in mid-Atlantic.'

Since 1989 the guild has administered the Marine Engineers' Benevolent Fund.

The guild is a constituent charity of the Merchant Navy Welfare Board (MNWB) and receives referrals from a number of charities including SSAFA, The Royal British Legion, the Officers' Association, Occupational Benevolent Funds Association and Royal Merchant Navy Schools Foundation, as well as local social services.

The Marine Society and Sea Cadets

£607,000

Correspondent: Claire Barnett, Company Secretary, 202 Lambeth Road, London SE1 7JW (020 7654 7011; fax: 020 7928 8914; email: info@ms-sc.org; website: www.ms-sc.org)

CC number: 313013/ SC037808

Eligibility

Professional seafarers, active or retired, serving in the Royal Navy, the British Merchant Navy or fishing fleets or any other maritime career persons who are serving in the navies, merchant navies or fishing fleets, members of the Sea Cadet Corps.

Types of grants

It is the society's policy to help where financial hardship is evident. Assistance is aimed to improve the conditions of life of seafarers and their dependants in need by reason of their social and economic circumstances. Interest-free loans rather than grants are given where the need is short-term and the applicant expects to be earning again. Support is also given through bursaries, scholarships, one-off grants and loans towards educational and training needs.

Annual grant total

In 2013/14 the charity had assets of £23.7 million and an income of £15.3 million. Grants totalled £3.8 million and consisted of £2.6 million given to organisations and £1.2 million to individuals. Note that the charity states that 'individual grants given are small and not material within the overall total'. As the accounts did not specify the proportion of awards given for educational and for welfare purposes we have divided the £1.2 million figure between the two.

Exclusions

Recurrent grants are not made.

Applications

Application forms are available from the correspondent and are considered as they arrive.

Other information

Grants are also made to sea cadet units and support can be given to 'nautical or other schools or training establishments which are charities or to other

organisations established for charitable purposes'. In addition grants are provided to volunteers to allow upkeep or purchase of uniforms on promotion or for wear and tear during the year.

The Ann Molyneux Charity

£20,000

Correspondent: John Wilson, Trustee, Liverpool Seafarers Centre, 20 Crosby Road South, Liverpool L22 1RQ (0300 8008085; email: john.wilson@ liverpoolseafarers.org.uk)

CC number: 229408

Eligibility

Seafarers and their widows living in the city of Liverpool. Preference for men who sailed from the city for most of the last five years that they were at sea. Applicants must be in receipt of benefits.

Types of grants

Pensions of £200 a year (paid quarterly).

Annual grant total

In 2013/14 this charity had an income of £20,500 and a total expenditure of £21,500. Previously grants have totalled around £20,000 a year.

Applications

Application forms are available from Liverpool Parish Church and Our Lady and St Nicholas. Applications should be accompanied by the seafarer's discharge books, details of income and a testimonial from a person of good standing in the community.

Nautilus Welfare Fund

£171,500 (200+ grants)

Correspondent: Mike Jess, Secretary, Trinity House Hub, Webster Avenue, Mariner's Park, Wallasey CH44 0AE (0151 346 8840; email: welfare@ nautilusint.org; website: www. nautiluswelfarefund.org)

CC number: 218742

Eligibility

Former seafarers with significant career at sea, and their dependants.

Types of grants

One-off grants towards household items, medical expenses, home repairs and adaptations, removal expenses, essentials for independent living or mobility aids. Regular payments of up to £12 a week are normally paid in quarterly instalments to supplement state/ employment pensions.

Annual grant total

In 2014 the fund had assets of £22.7 million and an income of £2.5 million. Grants were made totalling about £171,500, of which £130,500 was given in regular awards to 204 merchant mariners and the remaining £41,100 was distributed in one-off grants.

Applications

Application forms are available from the fund's website or the correspondent. They can be submitted directly by the individual or through a third party, such as SSAFA. Proof of sea-service, medical and birth certificates, also details of the individual's income and expenditure, bills and so on are required to support the application. Requests for funding are normally processed within two weeks. Candidates will usually be visited by the fund's own caseworker from local area or a person from SSAFA. Caseworkers can also be contacted for advice or assistance in applying for a grant.

Other information

The fund also manages the Mariners Park welfare complex in Wallasey, which accommodates independent older seafarers and their dependants in bungalows and flats, and older seafarers and their dependants assessed for residential or nursing care in the Mariners Park Care Home. The management and maintenance of this site takes up a large proportion of the fund's income.

The fund is continually developing its holistic welfare service offering advice and other services suited to each individual beneficiary's needs.

In 2014 all grant beneficiaries received quarterly information, offering support on topics such as benefits and security. All beneficiaries are visited in their first year of receiving a grant.

There are caseworkers based in Merseyside, Hull/Grimsby and Southampton/Portsmouth.

The Ropner Centenary Trust

£18,000 (31 grants)

Correspondent: Alan Theakston, Trustee, 15 The Green, High Coniscliffe, Darlington, County Durham DL2 2LJ (01325 374249; email: alantheakston@ btinternet.com)

CC number: 269109

Eligibility

Present and former maritime employees who are in need, and their dependants. Preference is generally given to people living in the North East of England and particularly those who have worked for Ropner Shipping Company Ltd.

Types of grants
One-off and recurrent grants are given according to need.

Annual grant total
In 2013/14 the trust had assets of £1 million and an income of £33,500. 31 individuals received grants totalling £18,000.

Applications
Apply in writing to the correspondent. Applications are considered annually, although urgent requests can be dealt with between meetings.

Other information
Grants are also paid to organisations with similar aims (£12,000 in 2013/14).

Royal Institution of Naval Architects

£34,500 (1,699 grants)
Correspondent: Trevor Blakeley, Chief Executive, 8–9 Northumberland Street, London WC2N 5DA (020 7235 4622; email: hq@rina.org.uk; website: www.rina.org.uk)

CC number: 211161

Eligibility
Members and their dependants who are in need.

Types of grants
One-off grants for a variety of needs.

Annual grant total
In 2013/14 the charity had assets of £9.5 million and an income of £2.2 million. Grants were made totalling £34,500. Grant-making is a very small part of this charity's activities.

Applications
Apply in writing to the correspondent.

Other information
The Royal Institution of Naval Architects is an internationally renowned professional institution whose members are involved at all levels in the design, construction, maintenance and operation of marine vessels and structures. Members of RINA are widely represented in industry, universities and colleges, and maritime organisations in over ninety countries. The charity also runs training schemes and bursaries.

The Royal Liverpool Seamen's Orphan Institution (RLSOI)

£112,500
Correspondent: Linda Cotton, Secretary, 2nd Floor, Tower Building, 22 Water Street, Liverpool L2 1BA (0151 227 3417 or 07747 607062 (mobile); email: enquiries@rlsoi-uk.org; website: www.rlsoi-uk.org)

CC number: 526379

Eligibility
Children of deceased British merchant seafarers, who are of pre-school age or in full-time education (including further and higher education). Help can also be given to seafarers who are at home caring for their family alone.

Types of grants
Discretionary awards for general living expenses and monthly maintenance grants. Support can be provided throughout the child's education.

Annual grant total
In 2014 the charity had assets of £2.8 million and an income of £222,500. Grants to individuals totalled £225,500 for both welfare and educational purposes. During the year a total of 80 individuals were supported, including 16 new beneficiaries. The breakdown between educational and welfare support was not specified; therefore, we estimate that about £112,500 was awarded for welfare needs.

Applications
Application forms are available from the correspondent and can be submitted at any time. They should also be downloadable from the charity's website (at the time of writing (August 2015) forms were being revised and not accessible online). Each application is considered on its own merits.

Other information
Support is given to both educational and welfare causes. While the proportions given for each cause were not specified, all grants are given to children and young people who are in attendance at school and further or higher education institutions. The charity's website also provides links to other organisations helping seafarers.

In 2013 the charity came to an arrangement with the Royal Merchant Navy Education Foundation whereby they would in future take over the support of beneficiaries in further education. In 2014 two students have been transferred following the agreement.

Sailors' Society

£51,000
Correspondent: Welfare Fund Manager, 350 Shirley Road, Southampton SO15 3HY (023 8051 5950; email: bkidd@sailors-society.org; website: www.sailors-society.org)

CC number: 237778

Eligibility
Merchant seafarers and their dependants who are in need.

Types of grants
Emergency grants to ease financial hardship. Monthly payments are also made from the Leith Aged Mariners' Fund (OSCR no. SC003014) – 19 ex-seafarers or their dependants residing in the UK were supported through regular awards of £52 in 2014.

Annual grant total
In 2014 the society had assets of £17 million and an income of £3.7 million. Welfare grants awarded to individuals totalled £38,000. A total of £13,000 was accounted for as the 'Leith Aged Mariners' Fund commitment'.

Applications
In the first instance contact the correspondent via email.

Other information
The society maintains a network of chaplains at the various key ports around the world who carry out ship visiting routines and minister to seafarers. It also provides centres and clubs for seafarers and associated maritime workers at strategic seaports. International disaster relief is also given and organisations are supported.

The society runs Sir Gabriel Wood's Mariners' Home for retired seafarers and those who have worked in maritime-related industries in Greenock, Scotland to provide accommodation and care.

Educational support is also given to intending seafarers.

Sailors' Children's Society

£291,500
Correspondent: Deanne Thomas, Chief Officer, Francis Reckitt House, Newland, Cottingham Road, Hull HU6 7RJ (01482 342331; fax: 01482 447868; email: info@sailorschildren.org.uk; website: www.sailorschildren.org.uk)

CC number: 224505

Eligibility
Seafarers' children under the age of 18 who are in full-time education and

whose families are in severe financial difficulties. One of the child's parents must have served in the Royal or Merchant Navy or in the fishing fleets, including on ferries, tankers, cruise ships or cargo boats.

Applicants must be in receipt of Housing Benefit or Council Tax Benefit (other than single person's 25% discount or disablement reduction), with the following information given on the website: 'All the families we help are on a means-tested benefit which ensures we only help those in most need.'

Types of grants

The charity provides financial assistance in a number of ways, including:

- Monthly child welfare grants – designed to boost income and enable families to provide basic essentials
- Clothing grants – payable per child twice a year to help children start off the new school year and, secondly, to buy a new winter coat and shoes
- Christmas grants – to help to buy a special Christmas present
- Emergency heating grants – in the event of extreme winter weather
- Special grants – one-off grants are given in extreme cases to provide, for example, furniture for a child's bedroom
- Caravan holidays – the charity owns eight caravans at seaside resorts across the UK. Travel grants are given to help with the costs of public transport or fuel expenses

Annual grant total

In 2013/14 the charity had assets of £2 million and an income of £676,000. We believe that grants to individuals for welfare purposes totalled £291,500 and were distributed as follows:

Monthly grants to families	£212,500
Clothing grants	£54,000
Holiday grants	£13,800
Special grants	£6,800
Christmas grants	£4,100

A further £17,700 was awarded in grants for home computers.

Applications

Application forms are available from the correspondent and require details about children, and the individual's income and expenditure. Copies of relevant certificates, for example, birth certificates and proof of seafaring service should also be provided. Applications can be submitted directly by the individual or through a social worker, Citizens Advice, other welfare agency, or through seafaring organisations. Applications are considered every other month, beginning in February.

Other information

The charity, which was previously known as Sailors' Families' Society, has

an informative website where more details can be found.

The charity notes that even if it is unable to help an individual directly, it may be able to direct them to another organisation that may be able to assist.

Sailors' Orphan Society of Scotland

£40,000

Correspondent: Joyce Murdoch, Administrator, 18 Woodside Crescent, Glasgow G3 7UL (0141 353 2090; fax: 0141 353 2190; website: www. sailorsorphansociety.co.uk)

OSCR number: SC000242

Eligibility

Dependants of seafarers who are or may be in a position of need either through disadvantage or through death or incapacity of one or both of their parents. Support is also given to disadvantaged young people within seafaring communities in Scotland.

Children must be under 16 or in full-time education if over 16.

Types of grants

Monthly grants of around £80 per child as well as two additional payments in July and December. One-off grants may also be paid at the trustees' discretion.

Annual grant total

In 2013/14 the charity had an income of £56,000 and a total expenditure of £51,000. We estimate that grants totalled around £40,000.

Applications

Apply on a form available to download from the charity's website. Applications should include a reference from a third party who can confirm the disadvantage suffered or the death or incapacity of a parent.

Scottish Nautical Welfare Society

£60,000

Correspondent: Gail Haldane, Administrator, 937 Dumbarton Road, Glasgow G14 9UF (0141 337 2632; email: ghaldane@snws.org.uk; website: www. snws.org.uk)

OSCR number: SC032892

Eligibility

Active, retired or disabled seafarers with ten years in service who are in need and their widows.

Types of grants

Recurrent quarterly grants of £156.

Annual grant total

In 2013/14 the charity had an income of £121,000 and a total expenditure of £120,000. We estimate that grants totalled £60,000.

Applications

Apply in writing to the correspondent.

Other information

This society was established in April 2002 as an amalgamation of Glasgow Aged Seamen Relief Fund, Glasgow Seaman's Friend Society and Glasgow Veteran Seafarers' Association.

The charity also runs a social club and a range of social events for former seafarers.

Seamen's Hospital Society

£123,000 (290 grants)

Correspondent: Peter Coulson, General Secretary, 29 King William Walk, Greenwich, London SE10 9HX (020 8858 3696; fax: 020 8293 9630; email: admin@ seahospital.org.uk; website: www. seahospital.org.uk)

CC number: 231724

Eligibility

Current or retired merchant seafarers and fishermen who are in need, and their dependants. Applicants must be seafarers with significant service at sea, except where accident or illness has interrupted intended long-term commitment. They may have worked anywhere in the UK and be of any nationality.

Types of grants

One-off grants can be given towards medical treatment and disability aids/ equipment (such as wheelchairs, riser recliner chairs, stair-lifts and installation of disability access), household essentials (white goods, beds, carpets), home repairs and alterations, maintenance costs, utility bills, holidays, convalescence and respite breaks, clothing, priority debts, sometimes funeral expenses. The society's website states that 'there are no rigid rules about what you can get a grant for. We look at each case individually and assess the overall situation.'

Annual grant total

In 2014 the society had assets of almost £9 million and an income of £495,500. Grants were made to 290 individuals totalling £123,000, and were broken down as follows:

General grants	212	£105,000
Physiotherapy	57	£13,400
Patient expenses	21	£4,600

Patient expenses consisted of support with travel or accommodation for individuals using the Dreadnought Medical Services at Guy's and St Thomas' NHS Foundation Trust in London, where merchant seafarers are treated with priority.

Exclusions

Grants are not normally given towards study or retraining costs. Our research suggests that members and former members of the Royal Navy are not eligible.

Applications

Application forms are available to download from the society's website or can be requested from the correspondent. They should be completed in conjunction with a caseworker, such as representatives from SSAFA, Shipwrecked Mariners' Society, Citizens Advice or the Fishermen's mission. If you are not already in contact with a caseworker contact the society to arrange assistance. Candidates will need to include full information of sea service and specify details of the support required. The society welcomes informal contact prior to submitting applications to discuss eligibility, need and so on.

Other information

The society supports Dreadnought patients at Guys and St Thomas' Hospital in London as well as running various regional health and fitness programmes for seafarers. It also helps to fund the Seafarers Advice and Information Line (SAIL) (0845 741 3318, admin@sailine.org.uk), which provides advice and information on a wide range of issues.

Grants are also made to other maritime charitable institutions with the same or similar objectives (£262,500 in 2014).

The Shipwrecked Fishermen and Mariners' Royal Benevolent Society

£1.4 million (2,267 grants)

Correspondent: The Grants Team, 1 North Pallant, Chichester, West Sussex PO19 1TL (01243 787761; fax: 01243 530853; email: grants@ shipwreckedmariners.org.uk; website: www.shipwreckedmariners.org.uk)

CC number: 212034

Eligibility

Fishermen, mariners and their widows and dependants, who are on a low income, especially those who are over 60 or in poor health. Priority is given to widows with young children. There is a minimum sea service of five years for

one-off grants and ten years for regular payments, although this is reviewed periodically to reflect employment patterns. Applicants must be in receipt of all the state benefits they are entitled to.

Types of grants

Mainly regular grants of £676 a year (usually to people aged over 60). One-off grants are available for those who do not qualify for regular support for help towards white goods, beds and bedding, household repairs, rent deposits, utility bill arrears, bankruptcy charges and as contributions towards the installation of stair-lifts and electrically powered vehicles. Immediate grants are given to widows and children left in need following the death of a serving fisherman or mariner. Death benefit grants are also given to the widows of life members of the society. Where appropriate, financial assistance may be offered to survivors of shipwrecks landed on the coasts of the UK or Ireland.

Annual grant total

In 2013/14 the society held assets of £25.1 million and had an income of £1.8 million. A total of 2,267 grants were awarded, amounting to £1.4 million. Most of these grants were given as regular payments.

Exclusions

Applications for assistance are only accepted from eligible applicants residing in the UK and Ireland.

Applications

Application forms are available from the correspondent or can be downloaded from the website. Applications can be submitted by the individual or through a third party and are considered on a weekly basis.

Other information

This charity was founded in 1839 with the object of:

> Giving relief and assistance to the widows and orphans of fishermen; and of mariners, members of the society, who lose their lives by storms and shipwreck on any part of the coasts of the United Kingdom, while engaged in their lawful occupations; and also to render necessary assistance to such mariners, soldiers, or other poor persons as suffer shipwreck upon the said coasts.

Shipwrecks still occur and the society is called upon to help but its main activity today is to provide financial assistance to retired or incapacitated fishermen and mariners and their dependants who are in need.

The society is one of the largest maritime charities in the UK and administers grants on behalf of some other funds such as the Royal Seamen's Pension Fund, the Hull Fishermen's Trust Fund and a subsidiary charity, the Fleetwood Fishing Industry Benevolent Fund. It manages the payment of grants from Trinity House, London, a fellow maritime charity.

The society also has an extensive network of honorary agents (volunteers), who conduct case work, fundraising activities and distribute grants to beneficiaries around the country.

The Tyne Mariners' Benevolent Institution

£96,500 (145 grants)

Correspondent: Janet Littlefield, Correspondent, Hadaway and Hadaway, 58 Howard Street, North Shields, Tyne and Wear NE30 1AL (0191 257 0382; email: janetl@hadaway.co.uk)

CC number: 229236

Eligibility

Former merchant seamen who live in Tyneside (about five miles either side of the River Tyne) and their widows. Applicants must be: (a) at least 55 years old and have served at least five years at sea; (b) under the age of 55, but unable to work owing to ill health; or (c) the widows of such people.

Types of grants

Recurrent grants. In 2014 pensioners received payments of £43 per calendar month, with additional payments of £75 at Christmas and Easter.

Annual grant total

In 2014 the institution held assets of £1.25 million and had an income of £256,000. Pensions and Christmas gifts to 145 individuals totalled £96,500.

Applications

Application forms are available from the correspondent. Applications should be submitted either directly by the individual or through a social worker, Citizens Advice or other welfare agency. Applications can be considered at any time.

Other information

The institution also administers and maintains the Master Mariners Homes in Tynemouth, providing 30 homes for beneficiaries.

Medicine and health

The 1930 Fund for District Nurses

£28,000

Correspondent: Mia Duddridge, Administrator, The Trust Partnership, 6 Trull Farm Buildings, Tetbury, Gloucestershire GL8 8SQ (01285 841904; fax: 01285 841576; email: 1930fund@ thetrustpartnership.com; website: www. 1930fundfornurses.org)

CC number: 208312

Eligibility

Qualified nurses who have worked in the community as a district nurse, community nurse, school nurse, health visitor, community midwife or community psychiatric nurse, and who are in need. Those applying for monthly or quarterly payments must hold a bank account solely in their own name.

Types of grants

One-off grants typically ranging from £100 to £300 for a variety of needs, including bathroom and kitchen equipment, household essentials, mobility aids, spectacles, dentures and specialist equipment. The fund also provides recurrent grants to help with living expenses, which are paid monthly or quarterly.

Annual grant total

In 2013/14 the fund held assets of £1.9 million and had an income of £57,500. Recurrent and one-off welfare grants totalled £28,000.

Exclusions

No grants are given for care home fees, educational fees, private healthcare, payment of debt, payment of rent/ council tax or for expenses incurred before the grant is received.

Successful applicants of one-off grants may not re-apply within a year.

Applications

Apply on a form available from the correspondent or to download from the website. Applications can be submitted directly by the individual or through a family member, social worker, Citizens Advice or other welfare agency. They are considered at quarterly meetings. Applicants are required to supply evidence of having worked as a nurse, such as copies of any nursing certificates or qualifications and, if applicable, a recent payslip. A third party applying on behalf of a nurse should include a letter of endorsement from an approved

authority. If the application is for home adaptations, repairs or the purchase of specific items, a copy of the invoice or quote must be supplied.

The fund welcomes enquiries.

Other information

The fund, which was founded in 1930 by a Mr Ernest Cook, has an informative website.

It also runs a telephone befriending service.

Avenel Trust
See entry on page 19

Barbers' Amalgamated Charity
See entry on page 181

The Benevolent Fund for Nurses in Scotland

£200,000

Correspondent: Mrs A. Davidson, Liaison Officer, Mitchell Edwards, Chartered Accountants, 24A Ainslie Place, Edinburgh EH3 6AJ (07584 322257; email: admin@bfns.org.uk)

OSCR number: SC006384

Eligibility

Current and former nurses, midwives or student nurses who have worked, were trained in or have otherwise substantial connection with Scotland and are experiencing financial difficulties.

Types of grants

Quarterly grants to applicants with limited income due to illness or disability, or those with minimal level of their pension. One-off grants towards general welfare needs, furnishing or home adaptations are also given.

Annual grant total

In 2014 the fund had an income of £221,500 and an expenditure of £213,000. We estimate that the amount of grants given to individuals totalled around £200,000.

Applications

Application forms are available from the correspondent and can be submitted by the individual directly or through a recognised referral agency (such as a social worker, Citizens Advice, doctor and so on). They are considered upon receipt. The fund may decide to visit potential beneficiaries.

Berkshire Nurses and Relief-in-Sickness Trust
See entry on page 348

The Birmingham and Three Counties Trust for Nurses

£11,000

Correspondent: David Airston, 16 Haddon Croft, Halesowen B63 1JQ (0121 602 0389; email: ruthmadams_45@ msn.com)

CC number: 217991

Eligibility

Nurses on any statutory register, who have practiced or practice in the City of Birmingham and the counties of Staffordshire, Warwickshire and Worcestershire.

Types of grants

One-off or recurrent grants according to need. Grants are given to meet the costs of heating, telephone bills, cordless phones for the infirm, household equipment, household repairs, car repairs, electric scooters, wheelchairs, medical equipment and personal expenses such as spectacles and clothing. Grants are also made for convalescent care, recuperative holidays and to clear debt.

Annual grant total

In 2013/14 the trust had an income of £8,700 and a total expenditure of £16,000. Assistance in previous years has mostly been given for welfare purposes, although grants for educational needs are also made. We estimate that social welfare grants totalled around £11,000.

Applications

Applications can be made on a form available from the correspondent. They can be submitted either directly by the individual or through a friend, relative or a social worker, Citizens Advice or other welfare agency. Details of financial status, including the individual's income and expenditure, reasons for application, and health status, where relevant, should be included. Applications are considered throughout the year

Applicants are visited by a trustee (where distance allows) for assessment. Supportive visiting continues where considered necessary.

BMA Charities Trust Fund

£21,500 (30 grants)

Correspondent: Marian Flint, Principal Officer, BMA House, Tavistock Square, London WC1H 9JP (020 7383 6142; email: info.bmacharities@bma.org.uk; website: bma.org.uk/about-the-bma/what-we-do/bma-charities)

CC number: 219102

Eligibility

Medical doctors, medical students, and their dependants who are in financial need due to illness or unemployment, whether or not they are BMA members. All beneficiaries must be in receipt of their full state benefit entitlement.

Types of grants

One-off grants for specific items in times of crisis, such as disability equipment, rent, utility bills, travel expenses and retraining costs. Support can be given to refugee and asylum seeking doctors to meet the costs of taking the PLAB exams and GMC registration. Applicants who are in work can normally only apply for assistance with paying for GMC retention fees or medical defence insurance. For medical students in immediate need, there is a maximum grant amount of £500.

Annual grant total

In 2014 the fund had assets of over £4.6 million and an income of £283,500. Grants to individuals from the Hastings Fund were authorised to a total of £31,500 but amounted to £21,500 in the accounts, made to 30 beneficiaries (including 22 refugee doctors, two other doctors and six medical students in financial need).

During the year, a further £125,000 was awarded to 55 beneficiaries from the Medical Education Fund and £30,000 to two external charities.

Exclusions

The fund does not help with legal fees, private medical treatment or career development projects. There are no general grants for 'living costs' or to 'maintain lifestyles'.

Applications

Application forms are available from the correspondent and can be submitted at any time. Two personal references are required, one of which must be from a doctor. The trustees meet to consider applications four times a year.

Other information

The BMA Charities Trust Fund incorporates the Hastings Benevolent Fund and the Medical Education Fund.

The fund can make referrals to its licensed money advisor for those applicants who are troubled by debt. Support is also given to medical charities and those organisations that help medical practitioners.

The website states: 'The Trustees are particularly keen to help doctors achieve or remain in work so that they are self-supporting and not dependent on the State and to help medical students who are in danger of having to withdraw from their course because of lack of funds.'

The British Dental Association Benevolent Fund (BDA Benevolent Fund)

£169,000 (97+ grants)

Correspondent: Ms S. Mitchell, General Manager, 64 Wimpole Street, London W1G 8YS (020 7486 4994; email: administrator@dentistshelp.org; website: www.bdabenevolentfund.org.uk)

CC number: 208146

Eligibility

Dentists resident in the UK who are or have been on the UK dental register and their dependants. Students at UK dental schools who are members of the association can also be supported. Applicants must be on a low income and have little in the way of savings.

Types of grants

One-off grants towards purposes such as specialist equipment, car or home adaptations, essential household items, support with Christmas expenditure, TV licences and telephone bills, clothing and school uniforms. Regular monthly grants may also be made to assist with living costs, and assistance may be given to help those returning to work following illness, such as the costs of retraining or professional fees. Loans may also be offered.

Annual grant total

In 2014 the fund had assets of £5.7 million and an income of almost £311,000. Grants were made totalling £169,000. The annual report states that 30 new applicants requested assistance, and 97 dentists and their families were supported in the year. In addition, a further £165,500 was paid in interest-free loans.

Exclusions

The fund cannot provide support towards:

- Private health care and medical insurance
- Private education
- Legal fees

- HMRC payments
- Repayment of loans from family or friends
- Business debts

Support will not be given to individuals with substantial savings, investment or property.

Applications

The fund advises that potential applicants initially contact the fund by email or telephone to discuss whether they are eligible for support. Applications can then be made on a form available from the correspondent or to download from the website. Applicants will then be visited by the General Manager or a trustee, and their application will be considered at a bi-monthly Executive Committee meeting. Emergency grants can be made within a couple of days when the need is urgent.

Other information

Every beneficiary receiving regular support from the fund is visited once a year to review their needs.

The Cameron Fund

£115,000

Correspondent: David Harris, Company Secretary, BMA House, Tavistock Square, London WC1H 9HR (020 7388 0796; email: info@cameronfund.org.uk; website: www.cameronfund.org.uk)

CC number: 261993

Eligibility

Current and former registered general practitioners and their families and dependants. Doctors on postgraduate specialty training who have successfully completed the training or those who only completed it partially, due to unforeseen circumstances, are also considered.

Types of grants

One-off and recurrent grants towards essential living costs, rent, nursing home fees, help for pensioners and so on. Each application is considered on its own merits. Our research suggests that grants are generally of up to £3,000. Interest-free loans are also available.

Annual grant total

In 2014 the charity had assets of £5.8 million and an income of £349,000. The trustees' annual report notes that new applications for assistance were received from 139 individuals and grants and loans, including Money Advice, were authorised totalling £319,500 to 191 beneficiaries. Grants totalled around £229,500. The accounts did not specify how much was given in support of welfare needs; therefore, we estimate that welfare assistance totalled around £115,000.

Exclusions

Grants cannot be made towards items which should be provided through statutory sources. Student grants are only given to families previously supported by the charity.

Applications

Application forms can be found on the charity's website or requested from the correspondent. Applications can be made directly by individuals or on their behalf. Referrals from Local Medical Committees and other organisations or individuals who may know of someone who might benefit from support from the charity are also welcome. Applicants are invited to get in touch with the correspondent if they are unsure about the eligibility or the application procedure.

Further information, detailing assets, debts, the individual's income and expenditure and any other documentation which illustrates the financial circumstances of the applicant are requested and references may be required. Additional information is often requested to ensure utmost accuracy. A trustee may visit the applicant before agreeing a grant. Applicants should have started the process of claiming state and/ or local authority benefits.

Note: signed application forms can be returned in an unstamped envelope addressed to FREEPOST CAMERON.

Other information

Grants are also made for education and training purposes. There is also a specific scheme to assist children (over the age of 18) of existing and former beneficiaries with living expenses relating to first degree or vocational training. Financial, legal, career advice and counselling are also offered.

The trustees' annual report for 2014 notes: 'Close relations are fostered with other medical benevolent funds and with BMA Charities, which enables a more concerted and appropriate response to be made to those applicants who may be eligible for assistance from other charities.'

It is further stated: 'The potential beneficiaries who are eligible to be considered for support comprise over 39,000 general medical practitioners in the United Kingdom and their dependants, together with GP trainees and retired GPs.'

The Care Workers Charity

£7,000

Correspondent: Dr Asif Raja, Trustee, c/o SummerCare, 38/40 Ceylon Road, Westcliff on Sea, Essex SS0 7HP (0845 601 9055; email: grants@ thecareworkerscharity.org.uk; website: www.cpbenevolentfund.org.uk)

CC number: 1132286

Eligibility

Current and former employees of the care profession (who work/have worked in a registered domiciliary, residential care, or supported living service) and their dependants who are in need. Current workers must have worked in the care industry for one continuous year. Former workers must have worked in the industry for a total of three continuous years out of the past five; six continuous years in the past ten years; or more than ten years service during their lifetime. Applicants must have limited savings and resources.

Types of grants

One-off grants, for purposes such as furniture, medical equipment, housing repairs or alterations and funeral costs. For further information, refer to the guidance on the charity's website.

Annual grant total

In 2014 the fund had assets of £49,500 and an income of £51,500. Grants to individuals totalled £7,000

Exclusions

No grants are given for debts or arrears (apart from in exceptional cases where the applicant has been referred by a welfare agency who can confirm that the situation has arisen from a recent life-changing circumstance or an unforeseen loss of income, and that all other sources of support have been exhausted). Nor are grants given for: bankruptcy or debt relief order fees; statutory sick pay shortfall; future payments or bills; reimbursement for items already purchased; education-related costs such as school fees, fees for educational courses, student maintenance and student loan repayments; most private medical treatments; or shortfalls in care fees.

Applications

Apply on an application form available to download from the website. Applications should also include supporting evidence such as a letter from your ex-employer to confirm your length of service, bank statements for the last three months and evidence to suggest the reason for your application. Detailed guidelines on completing the application form are also available on the website.

At the time of writing (November 2015) the fund's website states that: 'At present applications are taking 6–8 weeks to be assessed. If your application is of an extremely urgent nature then please contact the office in the first instance before applying.'

Other information

The charity was previously known as The Care Professionals Benevolent Fund.

Cavell Nurses' Trust

£399,500 (640 grants)

Correspondent: Welfare Team, Grosvenor House, Prospect Hill, Redditch, Worcestershire B97 4DL (01527 595999; email: admin@ cavellnursestrust.org; website: www. cavellnursestrust.org)

CC number: 210571

Eligibility

Working and retired nurses, midwives and healthcare assistants, as well as student nurses, suffering hardship, through illness, disability, accidents and family breakdowns. Applicants should hold no more than £4,000 in savings.

Types of grants

One-off and recurrent grants towards, for example, household repairs and equipment, current utility and telephone bills, specialist aids, convalescence and respite breaks. Regular grants range from £10 to £30 per week.

Annual grant total

In 2014 the trust had assets of £2.8 million and had an income of £464,000. Grants to individuals totalled £399,500. In the year, 640 grants were made, including 222 new beneficiaries.

Exclusions

No grants are given for debt repayment, holidays, bankruptcy fees, funeral expenses, educational costs or nursing home fees.

Applications

An initial short eligibility form, which is available on the trust's website, may be completed first to see if your application is likely to be funded. A member of the welfare team will then contact you to discuss your circumstances and application. Applications may also be made by post or by telephone, and can be made either by the individual or by a referring agency.

Other information

Previously known as NurseAid, the trust also provides advice and support on issues such as domestic violence, isolation and loneliness.

Chartered Physiotherapists' Benevolent Fund

£87,000 (77 grants)

Correspondent: Simone Tomlinson, Correspondent, Chartered Society of Physiotherapy, 14 Bedford Row, London WC1R 4ED (020 7306 6642; email: mbf@csp.org.uk; website: www.csp.org.uk)

CC number: 219568

Eligibility

Members, past members, assistant members and student members of the society.

Types of grants

One-off and recurrent grants (of £150 per month in 2013) to help with living expenses, household repairs, heating bills and road tax (where car use is essential).

Annual grant total

In 2014 the society had assets of £2.2 million and an income of £120,500. Grants were made to 77 individuals totalling £87,000.

Exclusions

No grants are given towards the payment of debts or when statutory help is available. Grants cannot be made to those who hold capital exceeding the maximum figure used by the Department of Work and Pensions to decide on benefit eligibility.

Applications

Application forms are available from the correspondent. They should be submitted directly by the individual or by a third party such as a carer or partner. Applications are considered in January, April, July and October.

Cheltenham Aid-in-Sickness and Nurses Welfare Fund (Gooding Fund)
See entry on page 404

The Benevolent Fund of the College of Optometrists and the Association of Optometrists

£132,000

Correspondent: David Lacey, Administrative Secretary, PO Box 10, Swanley, Kent BR8 8ZF (01322 660388; email: davidlacey293@btinternet.com)

CC number: 1003699

Eligibility

Current and retired members of the optical profession and their dependants.

Types of grants

Regular monthly payments to elderly or ill members towards bills and other living expenses. One-off grants are occasionally given towards costly items or expenditure such as house repairs, wheelchairs and holidays. Christmas grants are also given. For younger practitioners unable to work, the fund may assist with professional fees. Grants usually range from £20 to £200.

Annual grant total

In 2013/14 the fund held assets of £1.3 million and had an income of £79,500. Grants to individuals totalled £132,000.

Exclusions

No grants are given to students.

Applications

Application forms are available from the correspondent and a financial form must be completed. Applications are considered all year round and applicants are usually visited by a member of the profession.

Eaton Fund for Artists, Nurses and Gentlewomen
See entry on page 109

The Ethel Mary Fletcher Fund For Nurses

£2,800

Correspondent: Miss H. Campbell, Vice-President, Cricket Green Medical Practice, Room 2, 2nd Floor, 75–79 Miles Road, Mitcham, Surrey CR4 3DA (020 8685 1945; email: enquiries@rbna.org.uk; website: www.rbna.org.uk)

CC number: 209887

Eligibility

Registered, or retired, state nurses over 40 years of age who are sick and have a disability and who live in the UK.

Types of grants

Pensions are given.

Annual grant total

In 2014 the fund had an income of £3,600 and an expenditure of £3,100. Grants totalled approximately £2,800.

Applications

Application forms are available from the correspondent. Applications are considered quarterly.

Forth Valley Medical Benevolent Trust

£1,200

Correspondent: The Administrator, Forth Valley Medical Benevolent Trust, Meeks Road Surgery, 10 Meeks Road, Falkirk FK2 7ES (01324 619930)

OSCR number: SC000014

Eligibility

Medical practitioners and their families or relatives living in Forth Valley who are in need.

Types of grants

One-off grants according to need.

Annual grant total

In 2014/15 the trust had an income of £3,200 and an expenditure of £2,500. The charity supports both educational and general welfare causes; therefore, we estimate that grants for welfare purposes totalled about £1,200.

Applications

Applications may be made in writing to the correspondent.

Other information

Educational needs are also supported.

Junius S. Morgan Benevolent Fund

£270,000 (164 grants)

Correspondent: Shirley Baines, Grant Administrator, Rathbone Trust Company Ltd, 1 Curzon Street, London W1J 5FB (020 7399 0110; email: grantadmin@juniusmorgan.org.uk; website: www.juniusmorgan.org.uk)

CC number: 1131892

Eligibility

Registered nurses and auxiliaries (including midwives and retired nurses) who have practised in the UK for a minimum of five years and find themselves in financial hardship due to illness, death of a family supporter, marriage breakdown, unforeseen expenditure or debt, and so on.

Types of grants

One-off grants of up to £1,500 and recurrent payments for a variety of purposes, including electricity and fuel bills, telephone charges, household renewal costs (decorating, furniture or furnishings), television rental and licence fees, home adaptations and repairs to those with disabilities, and so on.

Annual grant total

In 2014 the fund had assets of £2.8 million and an income of £450,000. Grants were made to 164 individuals totalling £270,000. The average grant was of £1,167 per person.

Exclusions

Grants are not normally given towards educational fees, residential/nursing home fees, holidays or respite care, funeral costs, bankruptcy fees and to carers or student nurses.

Applications

Applications may be submitted online on the fund's website or are available to download together with full application guidelines. All requests must be supported by an independent third party (such as a social worker, care worker, Citizens Advice, GP and so on) who is acting in a professional capacity. Applications should also include bank statements for the last three months and a copy of the most recent statement of the applicant's savings account. Awards are considered on a fortnightly basis and applicants will be notified of a decision in writing.

The NHS Pensioners' Trust

£59,500 (224 grants)

Correspondent: Frank Jackson, Director, PO Box 456, Esher KT10 1DP (01372 805760; email: nhsptinfo@gmail.com; website: www.nhspt.org.uk)

CC number: 1002061

Eligibility

i) Any person who has retired from service in any capacity in the NHS in England, Wales or Scotland; ii) any person who has retired from service in England, Wales or Scotland for any of the related health service organisations or caring professions prior to the creation of the NHS; and iii) any person who is the wife, husband, widow, widower or other dependant of those specified above.

Types of grants

Grants of up to £350 are given for general upkeep to ease financial difficulty in cases of hardship, including the cost of living with disability, aids and equipment, repairs to the home and fuel bills. Larger grants can be considered in particular circumstances. Grants are one-off, but individuals can re-apply in the following year.

Annual grant total

In 2014/15 the trust held assets of £872,000 and had an income of £30,500. Grants to 224 individuals totalled £59,500.

Exclusions

No grants are paid for top-up fees in nursing or residential accommodation.

Applications

Apply on a form available from the correspondent following receipt of an sae. Applications containing supporting information and/or the backing of social work agencies will be processed more quickly. Third party agencies may apply on behalf of individuals and may use their own application forms. A trust's representative may follow up applications to verify information.

Other information

Advice services are also available from the trust.

The Nurses' Memorial to King Edward VII Edinburgh Scottish Committee

£60,000

Correspondent: Secretaries and Treasurers, Johnston Smillie Ltd, Chartered Accountants, 6 Redheughs Rigg, Edinburgh EH12 9DQ (0131 317 7377; email: info@nursesmemorial.org. uk; website: www.nursesmemorial.org. uk)

OSCR number: SC023963

Eligibility

Nurses or midwives with a strong connection to Scotland (including nurses who have worked in Scotland, or Scottish nurses working outside Scotland) who are retired, ill or otherwise in need.

Types of grants

One-off and monthly grants towards accommodation charges, domestic bills, equipment and to supplement inadequate income.

Annual grant total

In 2014 the charity had an income of £73,500 and a total expenditure of £113,500. Between 50 and 60 nurses are usually supported each year, with grants totalling around £60,000.

Applications

Apply on a form on the charity's website or available from the correspondent. Details of present financial and other circumstances should be included.

Pharmacist Support

£268,000

Correspondent: Diane Leicester-Hallam, Correspondent, 5th Floor, 196 Deansgate, Manchester M3 3WF

(0808 168 2233; email: info@ pharmacistsupport.org; website: www. pharmacistsupport.org)

CC number: 221438

Eligibility

You are eligible to apply for assistance if you are a pharmacist, a widow or widower of a pharmacist or a retired pharmacist and either you or your partner have been registered as a pharmacist with the General Pharmaceutical Council or RPSGB. Any member of a pharmacist's family who is dependent on you for financial support is eligible to apply. MPharm students at a university in Great Britain and pre-registration trainees are also eligible to apply for support.

Types of grants

The charity offers four types of grants:

▷ Health and well-being grants are given to support 'mental or physical quality of life'. Funding is typically given for respite care, counselling and therapies, convalescence, home help during convalescence, particular disability aids and for contributions towards residential and nursing home fees

▷ One-off grants are awarded for unexpected expenses such as essential car or home repairs, winter fuel bills or the purchase of a washing machine, for example

▷ Recurrent grants act as 'top-ups' for those on very low incomes who 'are finding it difficult to make ends meet without getting into debt'. Recipients of these grants are often widows/widowers or retired pharmacists

▷ Student hardship grants are for pharmacy students who are facing extreme financial hardship due to unforeseen circumstances such as family issues, ill health or bereavement

Interest-free loans are also available.

Annual grant total

In 2014 the charity held assets of £14.2 million and had an income of £444,500. Grants totalling £268,000 were made to individuals for social welfare purposes.

Assistance is also given to pharmacists dealing with issues of addiction through the Health Support Programme. In 2014 grants paid directly from the charity to assist individuals through recovery totalled £59,000, with a further £39,000 paid to the charity's partner, Action on Addiction, to fund their support services for individuals.

Exclusions

There are no grants available for pharmacy technicians or pharmacy assistants. Support is not available in Northern Ireland.

Applications

Application forms can be downloaded from the charity's website, or are available from the correspondent. Applications will be considered year round and can be submitted either directly by the individual or through a social worker, Citizens Advice, other welfare agency, or other third party on behalf of an individual. The charity recommends that applicants make contact informally before applying in order to discuss eligibility and needs.

Other information

Pharmacist Support, formerly known as the Royal Pharmaceutical Society's Benevolent Fund, offers a range of services, information and specialist advice for pharmacists, former pharmacists and their families.

In partnership with Action on Addiction, the charity runs its Health Support Programme, which seeks to support pharmacists who are dealing with addiction and dependency issues through the provision of qualified addiction specialists. Those requiring more information on the Health Support Programme should call 0808 168 5132.

To talk to a trained volunteer about any work- or home-related issues (including stress, bullying, ill health, financial worries, bereavement and anxiety about exams), call the Listening Friends telephone helpline on 0808 168 5133.

General enquiries can be made by calling 0808 168 2233.

The Queen's Nursing Institute

£115,000 (445 grants)

Correspondent: Joanne Moorby, Welfare and Grants Officer, 1A Henrietta Place, London W1G 0LZ (020 7594 1400; fax: 020 7490 1269; email: mail@qni.org.uk; website: www.qni.org.uk)

CC number: 213128

Eligibility

Queen's Nurses (district nurses who were trained by the QNI between 1887 and 1967) and community nurses who have worked in the community for a minimum of three years. The majority of beneficiaries are community nurses who are no longer able to work because of illness, age or disability.

Types of grants

One-off and recurrent grants ranging from help with household essentials, building repairs and adaptations to specialist aids and equipment.

The institute states:

> We will consider almost any request, but help is usually given, for example, with the provision of essential household items, building repairs or adaptations, respite care, specialist equipment such as walk-in baths, stair lifts, electric wheelchairs and amenity bills. In certain cases, the QNI may make regular quarterly payments to clients.

Annual grant total

In 2014 the institute had assets of more than £10 million and an income of nearly £2.4 million. Welfare support was given to 445 individuals totalling £115,000.

Exclusions

Grants are not made for:
- Residential or nursing home fees
- Debt
- Cost of medical treatment
- Funeral expenses

Applications

Application forms are accessible on the institute's website. You will need a copy of your latest bank statement and a utility bill too. Applications are accepted from nurses, their friends, family or professionals and voluntary organisations supporting them. Initial contact may also be made to Joanne Moorby (020 7549 1405; joanne.moorby@qni.org.uk) to discuss the application. Requests can be made at any time.

Other information

Educational assistance is also given to nurses. The institute undertakes campaigning, lobbying and various projects. Organisations are also supported (nine grants totalling £38,500 in 2014).

Debt and other advice services are available – see information on the website.

The RCN Foundation

£216,000 (318 grants)

Correspondent: Grants Manager (Hardship or Educational), 20 Cavendish Square, London W1G 0RN (020 7647 3645; email: rcnfoundation@rcn.org.uk; website: www.rcnfoundation.org.uk)

CC number: 1134606

Eligibility

Registered or retired nurses, midwives, HCAs and health visitors in the UK, and their families in times of need, to help 'get their lives and careers back on track'. Student nurses may also be assisted in exceptional circumstances.

Types of grants

The fund makes one-off grants to assist at a time of financial shortfall. Examples of how the foundation can assist are listed on its website:
- a rental payment where there is a shortfall in Housing Benefit entitlement
- a respite break following a period of illness or caring for a sick relative
- payment of a utility service, such as gas or water, during a period of reduced income
- short-term childcare costs when a relationship has broken down and this facilitates remaining at work
- funding for disability equipment needed due to illness
- costs of essential household items when fleeing domestic violence

The foundation stresses that this list is not exhaustive and that individuals should make contact to see if it may be able to offer assistance.

Annual grant total

In 2014 the foundation had assets of £29.4 million and an income of £1 million. Grants during the year amounted to £466,000, of which organisations received £94,000. Of the £372,000 given to individuals, £216,000 was in benevolent grants.

Exclusions

No grants are given to: repay consumer debts; for private medical treatment; for awards for family members; or for top-up fees for care homes.

Applications

If you wish to apply for funding, contact the foundation to request an application form by calling 020 7647 3882 or by emailing rcnfoundation@rcn.org.uk. The aim is to process applications within approximately 30 working days.

Other information

Previously known as The Royal College of Nursing Benevolent Fund, the purpose of the foundation is to enable nurses and nursing to improve the health and well-being of the public through:
- Benevolent funding
- Education and training bursaries
- Supporting the development of clinical practice and the improvement of care
- Developing practice to enable people and communities to make positive choices about their own health and well-being
- Promoting research

The Royal College of Midwives Trust

£53,000

Correspondent: Benevolent Fund Administrator, Royal College of Midwives, 15 Mansfield Street, London W1G 9NH (0300 303 0444; fax: 020 7312 3536; email: info@rcm.org.uk; website: www.rcm.org.uk)

CC number: 275261

Eligibility

Midwives, former midwives and student midwives who are in need. Preference is given to those who are members of the RCM or who have served as members of staff with the RCM or RCM Trust Ltd for at least five years.

Types of grants

Usually one-off grants for emergency or other unexpected needs (typically £50 to £200). Grants are given, for instance, towards the cost of a wheelchair, removal expenses, furniture, personal items and childcare costs.

Annual grant total

In 2014 the trust had assets of £3.4 million and an income of £680,000. Support to members totalled £53,000.

Exclusions

The trust's website notes that 'unfortunately, the fund is not large enough to provide regular financial support, nor can it act as a top-up for low salaries or student midwives' bursaries, although it is able to advise on other sources of help'. However, Christmas grants are routinely paid to long-standing elderly midwife members on low incomes.

Applications

Apply on a form available from the correspondent or to download from the website. Applications should be submitted either directly by the individual or through a third party such as a nursing organisation.

Other information

The trust engages in a range of other activities such as providing information, advice and support to members as well as running educational programmes and conferences and undertaking campaigning work. The trust's total charitable expenditure amounted to almost £2.8 million in 2014.

The Royal Medical Benevolent Fund (RMBF)

£360,500

Correspondent: The Casework Department, 24 King's Road, Wimbledon, London SW19 8QN (020 8540 9194; email: help@rmbf.org; website: www.rmbf.org)

CC number: 207275

Eligibility

Doctors who have held GMC Registration, and their dependants, who are on a low income and unable to support themselves due to illness, disability, bereavement or being over state retirement age. Medical students experiencing unforeseen financial hardship, and their dependants.

Types of grants

Assistance is given to doctors, medical students and their dependants. Help ranges from financial assistance in the form of grants and interest-free loans to a telephone befriending scheme for those who may be isolated and in need of support. Assistance is tailored to the individual's needs. Support includes:

- One-off grants to help with costs such as home adaptations or specialist vehicles for those with disabilities
- Interest-free loans or grants to help where eligible applicants are in financial need
- Specialist money and debt management advice to renegotiate debts and secure all eligible state benefits
- Regular monthly grants towards day-to-day living costs
- Back-to-work awards for those returning to work following a period of illness (including retraining costs, professional fees and occasionally childcare costs)
- Top-up for residential care fees, extra care costs
- Support for medical students in exceptional financial hardship
- Support for refugee doctors retraining in the UK

The charity aims to help its beneficiaries to 'become more independent and self-sufficient again wherever possible, whilst maintaining longer term support for those for whom this is needed'.

For more detailed information on eligibility for financial help check the financial support section of the charity's helpful website or get in touch with the caseworkers.

Annual grant total

In 2013/14 the charity had assets of £28.8 million and an income of £1.5 million. Amounts paid to individuals were made totalling £721,500. The breakdown between educational and welfare support was not given; therefore, we estimate that about £360,500 was given for welfare causes.

The charity aims to provide a total of at least £720,000 each year to its beneficiaries. The key objective to March 2015 was to provide about £750,000 in financial support.

Exclusions

The following are excluded:

- Private health care and medical insurance/fees
- Legal fees
- HMRC payments
- Debts to relatives or friends
- Private education

Applications

For an application pack and further information, get in touch with the correspondent by email or phone. Applications can be submitted either directly by the individual or through a third party, for example a social worker, Citizens Advice, other welfare agency, medical colleague or other medical and general charities.

Two references are required (at least one of which should be from a medical practitioner). All applicants are visited before a report is submitted to the Case Committee, which meets every two months (although emergency assistance may be given). The income/capital and expenditure are fully investigated, with similar rules applying as for those receiving Income Support.

Other information

Every year the RMBF helps hundreds of doctors, medical students and their dependants in a variety of ways. Voluntary visitors liaise between beneficiaries and the office. The fund has an informative website.

The charity also provides specialist information and advice for doctors through the Support4Doctors website (www. support4doctors.org) on a range of areas, including career, health, employment, money management and practical issues.

The Royal Medical Foundation

£47,500 (29 grants)

Correspondent: Helen Jones, Caseworker, RMF Office, Epsom College, College Road, Epsom, Surrey KT17 4JQ (01372 821010; email: rmf-caseworker@epsomcollege.org.uk; website: www.royalmedicalfoundation.org)

CC number: 312046

Eligibility

Doctors (registered with the GMC) and their dependants who are in need. Doctors who have qualified outside the UK and are currently GMC registered may also apply, although they should have worked in the UK for at least three years prior to making an application.

Types of grants

One-off grants, monthly pensions and maintenance grants of £500 to £15,000. Previous applications have included support for doctors with debt problems, fall-out from divorce or suspension, re-training expenses, practical financial support during/after rehabilitation, help with essential domestic bills, respite breaks, home alterations for the elderly or people with disabilities and nursing home fees.

Annual grant total

In 2013/14 the foundation made 42 grants totalling £122,000. This included grants amounting to £47,500 made to 29 individuals for what we consider to be social welfare purposes. Grants made during the year were distributed as follows:

Financial assistance with educational expenses	12	£48,000
Short-term payments or one-off grants where urgent assistance is required	23	£30,000
Financial assistance with educational expenses at Epsom College	1	£27,000
Regular payments to medical practitioners and their widows/widowers	4	£16,900
Other grants	2	£700

Applications

There is an online financial assistance request form on the foundation's website. For more information contact the correspondent. Applicants must have applied for any state benefits to which they may be entitled before an application can be considered and will be visited by the caseworker as part of the application process. The foundation's board meets quarterly, in January, April, July and October and applications should be submitted well in advance (specific dates are listed on the website).

Other information

The Royal Medical Foundation is a charity founded by Dr John Propert in 1855 and administered by Act of Parliament. Its original objects were to provide an asylum for qualified medical practitioners and their spouses and to found a school for their sons. Today, the foundation's aims and objectives are to assist registered doctors and their families who are in financial hardship. Practical assistance is given in three ways:

- Provision of regular payments to their widows, widowers and their children
- Provision of one-off grants when emergency help is required and
- In exceptional circumstances, assistance with school fees for sons or daughters of registered doctors enabling them to maintain educational stability at times of distress caused by illness, bereavement or financial need in their family

The foundation is managed by a board of directors drawn from various professions and is located at Epsom College.

The Society for Relief of Widows and Orphans of Medical Men (The Widows and Orphans)

£52,500

Correspondent: Charlotte Farrar, Secretary, Lettsom House, 11 Chandos Street, Cavendish Square, London W1G 9EB (01837 83022; email: info@widowsandorphans.org.uk; website: www.widowsandorphans.org.uk)

CC number: 207473

Eligibility

Support is given in the following order of priority:

(i) necessitous dependants of deceased members of the society

(ii) necessitous members of the society

(iii) necessitous dependants of members of the society

(iv) necessitous medical practitioners not being members of the society and their dependants.

Types of grants

Our research suggests that one-off and recurrent grants from £500 to £3,000 and holiday gifts are available to help families in the time of hardship. Support can be given towards household items, home repairs and alterations, debt repayments, disability aid, utility bills, also holiday expenses and so on.

Annual grant total

In 2014 the society had assets of £5.9 million and an income of £181,500. Grants to 25 individuals totalled £105,000. All grant recipients, except for one orphan, were regular practitioners or their dependants. We estimate that relief-in-need awards totalled around £52,500.

Exclusions

Grants are not normally made towards nursing home fees, loans, long-term assistance or second degrees.

Applications

Application forms (separate for different types of applicants) can be found on the society's website or requested from the correspondent. They can be submitted directly by the individual or a family member. Note that applications **must** be submitted via post.

Other information

Support is also given for educational needs.

The Society of Chiropodists Benevolent Fund

£23,000

Correspondent: Helena Basarab-Horwath, Honorary Secretary, 1 Fellmongers Path, Tower Bridge Road, London SE1 3LY (020 7234 8635; email: hb@scpod.org)

CC number: 205684

Eligibility

Members/former members of the society or one of its constituent bodies and their dependants.

Types of grants

One-off grants according to need, usually ranging from £50 to £1,000. Interest-free loans may also be made in appropriate cases.

Annual grant total

In 2014 the fund had assets of £1 million and an income of £29,500. Grants to individuals totalled £17,000 and included Christmas grants of £250 to 18 members or dependants. A further £6,000 was expended on paying the annual subscription fees of 16 members who were experiencing financial difficulties and has been included in the grant total.

Applications

Apply on a form available from the correspondent, which should be submitted directly by the individual or through a third party.

Other information

The charity also makes payments of subscriptions or grants to a charity offering similar benefits to members of the society, former members, or deceased members and relatives.

The Society of Radiographers Benevolent Fund

£2,800

Correspondent: Benevolent Fund Trustees, 207 Providence Square, Mill Street, London SE1 2EW (020 8545 9944; email: help@sor.org; website: www.sor.org)

CC number: 326398

Eligibility

Past and present members of the society and their dependants in need.

Types of grants

One-off grants towards, for example, stair-lifts, retraining, orthopaedic beds, house adaptations, car repairs, healthcare travel costs, long-term residential care, computer equipment and washing machines.

Annual grant total

In 2013/14 the fund had an income of £9,200 and a total expenditure of £3,100. We estimate that welfare grants to individuals totalled £2,800.

Exclusions

There are no grants available for further education or to repay debts.

Applications

Applicants must complete an application form and a financial circumstances form, both of which are available on request from the correspondent or to download directly from the fund's website. Applications can be submitted by the individual or through a third party such as a colleague or relative.

The Somerset Local Medical Benevolent Fund

£23,000

Correspondent: Dr Harry Yoxall, Secretary to the Trustees, Somerset LMC, The Crown Medical Centre, Crown Industrial Estate, Venture Way, Taunton TA2 8QY (01823 331428; email: lmcoffice@somersetlmc.nhs.uk; website: www.somersetlmc.co.uk)

CC number: 201777

Eligibility

General medical practitioners who are practising or have practised in Somerset and their dependants who are in need.

Types of grants

One-off or recurrent grants according to need. Grants have included a contribution to the locum costs of a young GP undergoing a cardiac procedure and a donation towards the costs of a doctor absent from work to care for a sick relative. The trustees may also make a death-in-service payment to the dependants of any practising GP working in Somerset.

Annual grant total

In 2013/14 the fund had an income of £20,000 and a total expenditure of £28,500. The accounts for the year had not been published on the Charity Commission's website due to the low income but grants are normally distributed amongst: doctors and their dependants; doctors in distress; and donations to medical charities. We estimate that grants to individual doctors and their dependants for social welfare purposes totalled around £23,000.

Applications

Apply in writing to the correspondent. Applications can be submitted directly by the individual or by any person on their behalf.

The Trained Nurses Annuity Fund

£18,500

Correspondent: Miss H. Campbell, Correspondent, Cricket Green Medical Practice, 75–79 Miles Road, Mitcham, Surrey CR4 3DA (020 8685 1945; email: enquires@rbna.org; website: www.rbna.org.uk)

CC number: 209883

Eligibility

Nurses aged 40 or over who have disabilities and have at least three years' service. Applications are made through third-party organisations such as Citizens Advice, SSAFA or Care of the Elderly.

Types of grants

Annuities and occasionally one-off grants. Each year beneficiaries of recurrent grants send a short report explaining whether their financial circumstances have changed and whether they are still in need of assistance. Annuities are paid twice-yearly in July and December.

Annual grant total

In 2014 the fund had an income of £15,600 and a total expenditure of £19,200. We estimate that around £18,500 was made in grants to individuals.

Exclusions

No grants are given for education or house improvements.

Applications

Application forms are available from the correspondent. These should normally be submitted by doctors or social workers along with a doctor's certificate or by the individual. Referrals may also be made through a third party such as Citizens Advice, Age UK, SSAFA, etc. Applications are considered at quarterly executive meetings and payments are made in July and December.

The West Sussex County Nursing Benevolent Fund

£2,800

Correspondent: Rod Shepherd, Trustee, Sheen Stickland LLP, 7 East Pallant, Chichester PO19 1TR (email: rod.shepherd@btinternet.com)

CC number: 234210

Eligibility

Nurses who are or have been engaged in community nursing in West Sussex and are in financial need. Beneficiaries must also be in poor health, convalescing or have disabilities. The fund may also assist general or specialist nurses, both retired and serving, if such a need arises.

Types of grants

One-off and recurrent grants are given according to need. Gifts are also distributed at Christmas.

Annual grant total

In 2014 the fund had an income of £700 and an expenditure of £3,000 We estimate that the amount of grants given to individuals totalled £2,800.

Applications

Application forms are available from the correspondent. Applications can be submitted directly by the individual, or through a third party such as a social worker, Citizens Advice or other welfare agency.

Mining and quarrying

The Coal Industry Social Welfare Organisation

£810,500

Correspondent: Vernon Jones, Secretary, The Old Rectory, Rectory Drive, Whiston, Rotherham, South Yorkshire S60 4JG (01709 728115; fax: 01709 839164; email: mail@ciswo.org.uk; website: www.ciswo.org.uk)

CC number: 1015581

Eligibility

Widows and families of miners who have died as a result of industrial accident or disease (mainly pneumoconiosis). Help is also available to mineworkers and their dependants who are experiencing financial difficulties.

Types of grants

- General hardship grants towards, for example, buying a motorised wheelchair, specialist equipment and home adaptations
- Grants to the dependants of miners who have died as a result of their work
- Grants to miners who are in hospital as a result of their work, up to a maximum amount per year
- Grants of up to a maximum amount for miners who have to travel to an outpatients centre as a result of an accident at work

Annual grant total

In 2014 the charity held assets of £32.6 million (£20 million of which represents endowment funds) and had an income of £4.1 million. Grants were made totalling £1 million (including educational grants) and were distributed as follows:

Hardship grants	£397,000
Regulation cases	£329,000
Education grants	£217,500
Special needs	£55,000
Social intervention fund	£13,000
Durham project	£10,000
Christmas voucher scheme	£4,500
Other grants	£2,000

Applications

Apply in writing to the correspondent for consideration by the trustees. The charity usually sends one of its own social workers to visit the individual to assess their needs and assist with the application form.

Other information

The following information is taken from the charity's informative and helpful website:

> CISWO is a National Charity which has a focus on the key role of delivering community and personal welfare services within mining and former mining communities.

> CISWO is a responsive team-based charity positively impacting upon the lives of over 500,000 coalfield residents through a wide range of services delivered by professional, experienced and dedicated staff.

> CISWO is committed to building community capacity through a range of One-Stop-Shops, IT learning opportunities; facilitating life long learning; raising achievement with under 5's support; and after-school clubs.

> CISWO dedicates resources to empowering individuals and communities to combat social exclusion, by facilitating such activities as advocacy, group support provision, outreach employment services and credit unions, in order to address deprivation, unemployment and disaffection.

CISWO also focuses 'on the wider community regeneration agenda, offering advice and support to 350 miners' welfare schemes (recreational charities,) administrative services to 30 regional charities, and engaging in partnership work to stimulate local initiatives towards regeneration'.

The charity also operates seven convalescence homes throughout the UK and a comprehensive social work service.

From January 2010 the Coal Industry Benevolent Trust merged with the Coal Industry Social Welfare Organisation, which now administers the charity.

The Coal Trade Benevolent Association

£141,000 (299 grants)

Correspondent: Nicholas Ross, Secretary, Unit 6 Bridge Wharf, 156 Caledonian Road, London N1 9UU (020 7278 3239; email: coalbenev@ btconnect.com; website: www. coaltradebenevolentassociation.org)

CC number: 212688

Eligibility

Non-manual workers of the coal industry in England and Wales who have worked in the production or distribution sectors and allied trades, and their dependants.

Types of grants

Weekly payments to supplement a low income and help with telephone costs, televisions, respite holidays, birthday and Christmas cheques and shopping vouchers. One-off grants are also available towards capital items such as stair-lifts, special bathrooms, washing machines, carpets and other items. Further special fuel payments have been distributed to regular beneficiaries during periods of exceptionally cold weather.

Annual grant total

In 2014 the association had an income of £238,000 and a total expenditure of £315,500. Grants to 299 beneficiaries amounted to £141,000.

Applications

Apply on a form available from the correspondent for consideration throughout the year.

Other information

CTBA supports a network of volunteer case visitors in branches across the country. These volunteers act as the association's way of keeping in touch with its beneficiaries, with individuals receiving personal visits at least twice a year.

The Institute of Quarrying Educational Development and Benevolent Fund

£24,500 (7 grants)

Correspondent: Benevolent Fund Secretary, McPherson House, 8A Regan Way, Chetwynd Business Park, Chilwell, Nottingham NG9 6RZ (0115 945 3885; email: mail@quarrying.org; website: www.quarrying.org)

CC number: 213586

Eligibility

Members or former members of the Institute of Quarrying and/or their dependants.

Types of grants

One-off grants ranging from £100 to £2,500. No recurrent grants are made although most beneficiaries successfully re-apply each year.

Annual grant total

In 2013/14 the fund held assets of £1.1 million and had an income of £30,500. Grants totalling £24,500 were made to seven long-term beneficiaries.

Exclusions

People who are involved in the quarrying industry but are not members of the institute cannot be considered.

Applications

Apply in writing to the correspondent.

Other information

The fund also supports projects which advance the education and research of quarrying.

The Institution of Materials, Minerals and Mining – Benevolent Fund

£38,500

Correspondent: The Honorary Secretary, The Member's Benevolent Trust, 1 Carlton House Terrace, London SW1Y 5DB (020 8299 4905; email: mbt@iom3.org; website: www.iom3.org)

CC number: 207184

Eligibility

Members of the institute and former members and their dependants who are in need.

Types of grants

One-off and recurrent grants in the range of £250 and £3,500. One-off grants in kind are also made. Grants are for general household needs, furniture, security installations, medical aids and adaptations, clothing, respite breaks and school uniforms. The charity is also keen to help unemployed and redundant members with travel costs, subscriptions, relocation costs and short course fees (where this will widen the scope for re-employment).

Annual grant total

In 2014 the fund had assets of £1.5 million and an income of £71,500. Grants to individuals totalled £38,500.

Applications

Requests for assistance are preferred in writing and application forms can be requested from the Honorary Secretary. Once returned there is a preliminary review of the completed form. This is usually followed by a visit to the applicant by an established regional visitors or a trustee to talk through the application. Following the visit, the board assesses each application thoroughly and makes its decision.

Mining Institute of Scotland Trust

£12,500

Correspondent: Keith Donaldson, Hon. Secretary/Treasurer, 14/9 Burnbrae Drive, Edinburgh EH12 8AS (0131 629 7861; website: www.mining-scotland.org/trust.htm)

OSCR number: SC024974

Eligibility

Former members of the Mining Institute of Scotland (MIS) and members or former members of IMM who live in Scotland or who worked in connection with Scottish mining matters for at least five consecutive years. The dependants of eligible people can also be supported.

Types of grants

One-off and repeated hardship grants of up to £1,000 a year. Widows of members can receive Christmas and summer holiday grants.

Annual grant total

In 2014 the trust had an income of £33,000 and a total expenditure of £43,000. Our research suggests that the trust has about £25,000 available to give in grants each year, for both education and social welfare purposes.

Applications

Applications for assistance can be made in writing to the correspondent.

Other information

Organisations are also supported.

North East Area Miners' Social Welfare Trust Fund

£20,000

Correspondent: Vincent Clements, Secretary, Coal Industry Social Welfare Organisation, 6 Bewick Road, Gateshead, Tyne and Wear NE8 4DP (0191 477 7242; email: vincent.clements@ciswo.org.uk; website: www.ciswo.org.uk)

CC number: 504178

Eligibility

People in need living in Durham, Northumberland and Tyne and Wear who are or have been employed by the coal industry, and their dependants.

Types of grants

One-off grants according to need. The fund aims to improve beneficiaries' health, social well-being and conditions of living.

Annual grant total

In 2013/14 the fund had assets of £3.25 million and an income of £309,500. Grants were made totalling £46,500. Out of this sum a total of £25,500 was given to individuals (including £700 approved and paid in 2015). We estimate that about £20,000 was given for social welfare needs.

The fund continued to help miners and people from former mining communities to afford convalescent holidays spending £155,500 to assist individuals in the year.

Applications

Applications may be made in writing to the correspondent. They can be submitted directly by the individual or through a social worker, Citizens Advice or other welfare agency. Requests are usually considered four times a year.

Other information

The fund also makes grants to mining charities. It also provides group holidays for its beneficiaries and revenue/capital costs relating to the day to day running of the Sam Watson Rest Home. Educational and training support may also be given, although it would appear that most support is awarded for general social welfare needs.

The North Staffordshire Coalfield Miners' Relief Fund

£6,000

Correspondent: Susan Jackson, Correspondent, c/o Coal Industry Social Welfare Organisation, 142 Queens Road, Penkhull, Stoke-on-Trent, Staffordshire ST4 7LH (01782 744996)

CC number: 209616

Eligibility

Mineworkers or retired mineworkers who worked in the North Staffordshire coalfield (including Cheadle), and their widows or dependants. The mineworker must have suffered an industrial accident or disease or died as a result of their duties.

Types of grants

One-off grants according to need.

Annual grant total

In 2013/14 the fund had an income of £2,800 and a total expenditure of £13,300. We estimate that the amount of grants given to individuals totalled around £6,000.

Applications

Apply in writing to the correspondent or by telephone either directly by the individual or via a third party such as a social worker, Citizens Advice or other welfare agency. Applications are considered throughout the year.

Other information

Grants are also made to organisations.

The Nottinghamshire Miners' Welfare Trust Fund

£113,500

Correspondent: Donald Brookes, Secretary, CISWO, Welfare Offices, Berry Hill Lane, Mansfield, Nottinghamshire NG18 4JR (01623 625767; email: donald. brookes@ciswo.org.uk)

CC number: 1001272

Eligibility

Members of the mining community in Nottinghamshire who are in need, and their dependants.

Types of grants

One-off and recurrent grants are given to improve health and living conditions. Recent grants have been given for bathroom alterations, mortgage repayments, stair-lifts, wheelchairs, scooters, beds and bedding, furniture and replacement boilers. Holiday grants of £100 to £250 are also available.

Annual grant total

In 2014 the fund had assets of £3.6 million and an income of £121,000. Grants were made totalling £113,500 and were distributed as follows:

Personal welfare and hardship grants	£96,500
Holiday grants	£16,500
Convalescent grants	£500

Applications

Application forms are available from the correspondent. Applications should be submitted directly by the individual or through a third party such as the Coal Industry Social Welfare Organisation (CISWO), Citizens Advice, social worker or similar welfare organisation. Applications are considered regularly throughout the year. Some applicants may be visited by a CISWO social worker.

Other information

Grants are also made to organisations (£5,600 in 2014).

Warwickshire Miners' Welfare Trust Fund Scheme

£4,700

Correspondent: David Thomas, Administrator, CISWO, 142 Queens Road, Stoke-on-Trent ST4 7LH (01782 744996; email: david.thomas@ciswo.org. uk)

CC number: 519724

Eligibility

People who work or have worked within the coal mining industry in Warwickshire, and their dependants. Widows, widowers and relatives of the deceased miners are eligible to apply.

Types of grants

Our research suggests that one-off grants from £50 to £1,500 can be given towards convalescent holidays, hospital visits, electrical appliances (such as cookers and vacuum cleaners), carpets, beds and other furniture, wheelchairs, stair-lifts, scooters and medical reports for industrial diseases.

Annual grant total

In 2014 the fund had an income of £14,600 and a total expenditure of £9,500. We estimate that individual grants totalled around £4,700.

Exclusions

According to our research, death grants are not provided and support is not given to people who have received redundancy pay in the last ten years. Awards will not be given for any purpose for which the DWP will pay.

Applications

Apply in writing to the correspondent. Applications can be submitted at any time directly by the individual or through a third party, for example, a social worker, Citizens Advice or other welfare agency. Candidates should include weekly income and medical proof from a doctor (if applicable).

Other information

Organisations in old coalfield areas are also supported.

Public and government sector

British Association of Former United Nations Civil Servants Benevolent Fund

£20,000

Correspondent: John Miller, Clerk to the Trustees, 4 Roebuck Rise, Purley-on-Thames, Reading, Berks RG31 6TP (01963 250206; email: jbmiller83@gmail. com; website: www.bafuncs.org/ benevolent.html)

CC number: 297524

Eligibility

Former employees of the United Nations organisation or its specialised agencies, and their dependants who are in need.

Types of grants

One-off grants, grants in kind and loans of between £100 and £500. Grants can be made towards a wide range of needs, including remedial medical and surgical attention, respite care to release a family carer, aids for people with disabilities, household aids for older people, assistance towards transport costs for Hospital out-patient visits; or visits by family or a BAFUNCS member to a hospitalised patient, convalescent visits to family and remedial holidays, loans or grants to meet short-term emergencies.

Annual grant total

In 2014 the fund had an income of £11,100 and a total expenditure of £22,500 We estimate that the total amount of grants awarded to individuals was approximately £20,000.

Applications

Application forms are available on the website and are normally referred to an appropriate BAFUNCS registered welfare officer for immediate follow-up. Applications are considered throughout the year.

Other information

The fund is also known by its short title, 'BAFUNCS Benevolent Fund'.

City of London Benevolent Association

£5,500

Correspondent: Philippa Sewell, Administrator, City of London, Town Clerk's Department, PO Box 270, Guildhall, London EC2P 2EJ (020 7332 1425; email: philippa.sewell@ cityoflondon.gov.uk; website: www. cityoflondon.gov.uk)

CC number: 206643

Eligibility

People in need who are, or have been, members of the Court of Common Council, and their dependants.

Types of grants

One-off grants according to need.

Annual grant total

In 2013/14 the charity had an income of £11,100 and a total expenditure of £6,000. We estimate that grants totalled around £5,500.

Applications

Initial contact should be made with the administrator.

Environmental Health Officers Welfare Fund
See entry on page 130

See entry on page 130

Civil Service

Assist Fund (formerly known as the Century Benevolent Fund)

£51,000

Correspondent: The Correspondent, PO Box 62849, London SE1P 5AE

CC number: 251419

Eligibility
Employees and ex-employees of the Government Communications Bureau and its associated organisations, and their dependants.

Types of grants
One-off or recurrent grants and loans towards telephone bills, house repairs and so on.

Annual grant total
In 2013/14 the fund had assets of £1.6 million and an income of £198,000. Grants to individuals totalled £51,000.

Applications
Apply in writing to the correspondent, although applications are often made by word of mouth. Applications are generally considered four times a year, but exceptions can be made in urgent cases.

The Charity for Civil Servants

£2.67 million (4,250 grants)

Correspondent: Help and Advisory Services, Fund House, 5 Anne Boleyn's Walk, Cheam, Sutton, Surrey SM3 8DY (0800 056 2424; fax: 020 8240 2401; email: help@foryoubyyou.org.uk; website: www.foryoubyyou.org.uk)

CC number: 1136870

Eligibility
Serving and former staff of the Civil Service, and their dependants, who are in need. Individuals who work for organisations directly funded by a government department may also be eligible to apply.

Types of grants
Grants, loans and allowances according to need. Grants have recently been given for: essential household bills; utilities; appliances; childcare; daily living expenses; heating repairs; home adaptations; the relief of priority debts such as rent or council tax arrears; bereavement costs (funeral costs, cremation charges and solicitor's fees); hospital visiting costs; nursing home fees; mobility equipment (hoists, ramps, mobility scooters, walking aids and wheelchairs).

Annual grant total
In 2014 the charity had assets of £40.3 million and an income of £8.8 million. Grants to individuals totalled almost £2.7 million and were distributed as follows:

Reduced or low incomes	£1.2 million*
Poor or inappropriate living arrangements	£507,000
Debt	£427,000
Ill health	£219,000
Bereavement	£198,000
Immobility	£92,000
Emergency situations	£25,000

*This figure includes £216,000 paid in allowances (ongoing payments) to individuals.

Exclusions
The charity does not help employees of the NHS, the armed forces or local authorities. Funding is not available towards: items that have already been bought or bills that have already been settled; non-priority debt, such as a payday loan; purchasing a property; education costs; and legal expenses or fines. Grants are not normally awarded to cover medical costs.

Applications
Apply by completing the online application form. The charity runs a Freephone help service (0800 056 2424 or help@foryoubyyou.org.uk, open every working day, 8.30am-5pm) which provides advice and information as well as assistance with completing applications.

Other information
In addition to its grant-making, the charity runs services to give advice on, for example, money issues, stress and depression, carers' support, domestic abuse and mental well-being. More details of the full range of services are available on the website.

The Overseas Service Pensioners' Benevolent Society

£119,500 (98 grants)

Correspondent: David Le Breton, Secretary, 138 High Street, Tonbridge, Kent TN9 1AX (01732 363836; email: bensoc@ospa.org.uk; website: www.ospa.org.uk)

CC number: 235989

Eligibility
Retired members of the Overseas Service Pensioners' Association, and their dependants, who are in need. In certain circumstances those with other relevant service in the Overseas Civil Service or in a former British dependent (colonial) territory can be supported as well as the dependants of such people.

Types of grants
Grants of up to £1,500 are usually paid quarterly to help with general living expenses. Occasionally single grants are given for special needs and towards holidays. All cases are reviewed annually.

Annual grant total
In 2014 the society had an income of around £69,000 and an expenditure of £136,500. Grants to individuals totalled £119,500, of which £11,500 was given in grants for holidays and one-off needs. During the year 98 cases of support (121 people) were recorded.

The society notes that over half of the beneficiaries are Zimbabwe Public Service pensioners, or their dependants, living mainly in Zimbabwe and South Africa.

Exclusions
Grants are not normally made for residential care or nursing home fees.

Applications
Application forms can be requested from the correspondent. They can be submitted directly by the individual or by a third party, such as a close relative or legal representative.

Emergency services

Ambulance Services Benevolent Fund

£30,500

Correspondent: The Director, 12 Ensign Business Centre, Westwood Way, Coventry CV4 8JA (024 7798 7922; email: Director@asbf.co.uk; website: www.asbf.co.uk)

CC number: 800434

Eligibility
Serving and retired ambulance personnel and their immediate dependants who are in need.

Types of grants
One-off grants to assist with such items as special medical equipment, mobility aids, home adaptations and temporary financial crises due to sickness, domestic circumstances, bereavement, etc.

Annual grant total

In 2013/14 the fund held assets of £400,000 and had an income of £35,000. Grants to individuals totalled £30,500.

Exclusions

No grants are given for items which have already been purchased.

Applications

Application forms are available to download from the fund's website and should be completed and returned by post to the director. Alternatively, you can write to the director to request a hard copy. If applying for specialised aids or equipment, supporting evidence from a recognised health practitioner will be required to confirm needs and to show suitability of the equipment to meet your needs. The fund aims to decide on requests within ten working days.

Avon and Somerset Constabulary Benevolent Fund

£20,500

Correspondent: Caroline Peters, Administrator, Police Headquarters, PO Box 37, Valley Road, Portishead, Bristol BS20 8QJ (01275 816905; email: caroline.peters@avonandsomerset.police. uk)

CC number: 1085497

Eligibility

Mainly serving and retired members of the Avon and Somerset Constabulary who are in need. Their dependants may also be supported.

Types of grants

One-off grants, ranging from £500 to £2,000, for equipment and house repairs, travel costs for hospital visits and holidays (in extreme cases). Interest-free loans are also available to cover debts or other urgent needs.

Annual grant total

In 2014 the fund had assets of £992,000 and an income of £65,500. Grants and donations to individuals and organisations totalled £41,000. We estimate that welfare grants to individuals totalled £20,500.

Exclusions

No grants are given for private medical treatment, legal representation or private education.

Applications

Applications must be submitted with a report and recommendation by a force welfare officer. They can be considered at any time.

Blackstock Trust

See entry on page 224

The British Fire Services Association Members Welfare Fund

£16,500

Correspondent: David Stevens, Secretary and Treasurer, 9 Brooksfield, South Kirkby, Pontefract, West Yorkshire WF9 3DL (01977 650245; email: welfare. bfsa@btinternet.com)

CC number: 216011

Eligibility

Fire-fighters and ex-fire-fighters who have held BFSA membership, and their dependants.

Types of grants

The Members Welfare Fund assists members, ex-members and their dependants. Assistance may be in the form of one-off grants to aid the purchase of mobility items, electrical appliances, furniture or repairs. Alternatively the Management Committee of the fund may consider long-term maintenance grants, to those on limited income.

Annual grant total

In 2014 the fund had an income of £19,000 and total expenditure of £18,800. We estimate that the amount of grants given to individuals totalled around £16,500.

Applications

Apply in writing to the correspondent, including details of your income and expenditure and a record of fire service employment. Applicants are usually visited at home by a representative of the fund to assess their needs.

The Cumbria Constabulary Benevolent Fund

Correspondent: Federation Representative, Cumbria Constabulary Police Headquarters, 1 The Green, Carleton Hall, Penrith, Cumbria CA10 2AU (01768 217073; fax: 01708 217425; email: fiona.richardson@ cumbria.police.uk)

CC number: 505994

Eligibility

Members and former members of the Cumbria Constabulary in need, and their widows and dependants.

Types of grants

One-off cash grants ranging from £250 to £750, usually for the purchase of medical equipment.

Annual grant total

The fund now makes grants through the North West Police Benevolent Fund.

Applications

Apply in writing to the correspondent directly by the individual or family member. Although grants are made through the North West Police Benevolent Fund, applications are still accepted through the Cumbria Constabulary federation department.

Other information

The charity joined the North West Police Benevolent Fund in 2013.

Essex Police Support Staff Benevolent Fund

£3,500

Correspondent: Barry Faber, Trustee, Essex Police Headquarters, PO Box 2, Chelmsford, Essex CM2 6DA (01245 452597; email: jan.pyner@essex.pnn. police.uk)

CC number: 269890

Eligibility

People in need who work or worked full-time or part-time for Essex Police Authority, and their dependants.

Types of grants

One-off grants or loans for essential needs such as travel expenses for hospital visits and unforeseen bills such as car repairs.

Annual grant total

In 2014/15 the fund had an income of £8,200 and a total expenditure of £3,700. We estimate that the total amount of grants awarded to individuals was approximately £3,500.

Exclusions

No grants are given towards medical treatment.

Applications

Individuals should apply via the benevolent fund representative of their division or subdivision of Essex Police Authority. Applications are considered quarterly, although this can be sooner in emergencies.

The Fire Fighters Charity

£234,000

Correspondent: Christine Goonan, Director, The Fire Fighters Charity, Level 6, Belvedere, Basing View, Basingstoke, Hampshire RG21 4HG (01256 366566; fax: 01256 366599; email: info@ firefighterscharity.org.uk; website: www. firefighterscharity.org.uk)

CC number: 1093387

Eligibility

The charity may be able to assist:

- serving Fire and Rescue Service (FRS) personnel
- former FRS personnel (having served for at least five years before retiring, being made redundant after two years, or retired because of illness or injury)
- works firefighter or former works firefighter that meets the criteria determined by the Trustees
- employee of The Fire Fighters Charity or former employee with at least five years' service/retired on the grounds of illness or injury
- any dependant of any person falling within the above categories*
- any person engaged on, or assisting in the management or provision of a Fire Services Youth Scheme
- any active Fire and Rescue Service volunteer

* dependants can be: a spouse or partner living in the same household for at least two years; a former spouse who has not remarried; a widow or widower; a child treated as a child/an assumed parental role; or anybody who is maintained by the beneficiary, wholly or partially.

Types of grants

The charity looks to assist its beneficiaries by providing practical solutions to meet their needs. The majority of these solutions are one-off and the type of solution can vary depending on the beneficiary's situation. In some cases this may be a monetary solution in the form of a grant or the charity may assist practically by purchasing the solution (for example, equipment or home adaptations that are required due to disability/ill health). Assessments are made under either a health or general category and the cost of the solution can vary according to the needs of the beneficiary.

Annual grant total

In 2013/14 the charity held assets of £26.7 million and had an income of £8.3 million. We believe financial support to beneficiaries amounted to £234,000, with one-off solutions amounting to £227,500 and continuing support a further £6,200.

Exclusions

The charity cannot finance private medical care, pay off debts or cover funeral or repatriation costs. The charity does not provide loans to beneficiaries, pay university/educational fees or residential care nursing fees. Statutory provision must be exhausted in the first instance.

Applications

Note the following from the charity's annual report:

> Over recent years the Charity has sought to move away from purely making grants and the level of assistance in this manner has now substantially reduced. This has taken place alongside the introduction of the Beneficiary Support Service and assistance is now focused on providing active solutions to enable and empower individuals to have increased control over their personal circumstances. The grant application process has now ceased, however, a small number of beneficiaries will require ongoing support from grants, but this is now administered through the Beneficiary Support Service.

Call 0800 389 8820 to access any of the charity's services.

Other information

The charity also runs rehabilitation and recuperation centres at locations in Devon, the Lake District and West Sussex.

For more information, including access to self-help factsheets, visit the charity's informative website.

St George's Police Children Trust (formerly St George's Police Trust)

£145,000 (Over 2,000 grants)

Correspondent: The Trust Administrator, St Andrews, Harlow Moor Road, Harrogate, North Yorkshire HG2 0AD (01423 504448; email: enquiries@thepolicetreatmentcentres.org; website: www. stgeorgespolicechildrentrust.org)

CC number: 1147445/SC043652

Eligibility

Children and young people in full-time education of serving or retired officers who were members of a police force covered by the trust (see 'Other information') and who are now deceased or have been incapacitated whilst on duty and can no longer work. Young people not in full-time education who have lost a police officer parent, but who are unable to earn their own living as a result of having special needs, may also be eligible.

Note: usually, to be eligible, the police officer parent must have donated to the trust whilst serving.

Types of grants

One-off and recurrent grants. The amount awarded is dependent upon household income and the potential need or hardship. Registration grant of £100 is given to all eligible applicants, before the full consideration at the trustees' meeting.

The trust offers:

- **St George's Police Children Trust Grants** – available to eligible beneficiaries in full-time education to statutory school leaving age, or up to the end of the school year in which they turn 19 years of age
- **Weekly Support Allowances** – to children satisfying the above criteria
- **Seasonal Gifts** – awarded twice yearly in summer and at Christmas
- **Special Needs Grants** – to children who are deemed to be classed as having a special need, i.e. are in receipt of the 'children's award' as defined in the police pensions regulations (poof of receipt will be required)
- **Ex-Gratia Grants** – to children and young people in full-time education and school leaving age towards trade tools when leaving school to start work; this includes musical instruments and necessary text books, amongst other things
- **Further Education Grants** – £1,500 a year to eligible beneficiaries aged of 18–25 for any form of further education, including first degree, HNC, HND or NVQ level 4. A course can be supported up to a maximum of four years

One-week respite holidays at the trust's holiday home in Harrogate are available to all current and future beneficiaries.

The website informs:

> Weekly maintenance allowances and grants approved by the Trustees will be back dated to the date of the event giving rise to the application, or where the date of the event giving rise to the application is more than twelve months previously, to a maximum of twelve months preceding the date of the application.

Annual grant total

In 2014 the trust had assets of over £12 million and an income of £908,000. Grants were made totalling £247,000, including awards to 2,231 children in full-time education and further 68 individuals undertaking further education. We estimate that support for children in education other than further totalled about £145,000.

Exclusions

People in education beyond first degree level cannot be assisted. Grants are not made for gap year activities. If you are applying for a Further Education Grant after a gap year, note that application can only be considered after a single gap period from education of not more than one year. The trust does not pay allowances or grants where the beneficiary is in work and earning money.

Applications

Application forms are available to download from the website or can be requested from Police Federation representatives or Police Force Benevolent Funds. They have to be submitted via the police force in which the parent served and **not** directly to the trust. This is usually done through the police federation office, the occupational health and welfare department or occasionally the force benevolent fund. Request should be accompanied by relevant documentation. Applications are considered on a quarterly basis in February, May, August and November.

Other information

The website notes that the foundation for The St George's Police Children Trust was laid by Catherine Gurney who opened Northern Police Orphanage in 1898 'for the care and welfare of Northern Police Force children who had lost one or both parents'. In the second half of the 20th century the orphanage was closed and St George's Fund and the Northern Police Orphans Trust, both providing grants to police officers' children, were formed. The two charities merged in 2006 to form St George's Police Trust.

In 2013 the trade and assets not restricted by permanent endowment of the St George's Police Trust were transferred to the St George's Police Children Trust which has been granted a linking order between the two charities. The St George's Police Children Trust acts as the corporate trustee of the St George's Police Trust, which remains registered with the Charity Commission (Charity Commission no. 1147445–1).

The trust covers the following police forces: Cheshire; Cleveland; Cumbria; Derbyshire; Durham; Greater Manchester Police; Humberside; Lancashire; Lincolnshire; Merseyside; Northumbria; North Wales; North Yorkshire; Nottinghamshire; Police Service of Scotland; South Yorkshire; Staffordshire; West Mercia; West Yorkshire. The accounts state that 'the number of serving police officers in this catchment area is now approximately 63,000 and the number of police officers making the voluntary donation is around 37,000 (the number of retired police officers is likely to be similar)'.

Hampshire Ambulance Service Benevolent Fund

£6,800

Correspondent: Phil Pimlott, Correspondent, 29 Beech Avenue, Lane End, High Wycombe HP14 3EQ (01494 881986)

CC number: 1041811

Eligibility

Serving and retired members of Hampshire Ambulance Service/South Central Ambulance Service NHS Trust and their dependants.

Types of grants

One-off grants according to need.

Annual grant total

In 2013/14 the fund had an income of £4,400 and a total expenditure of £7,000. We estimate that welfare grants to individuals totalled £6,800.

Applications

Apply in writing to the correspondent.

The Hampshire Constabulary Welfare Fund

£41,500

Correspondent: Paul Robertson, Trustee, Hampshire Constabulary Welfare Fund, Federation House, 440 The Grange, Romsey Road, Romsey SO51 0AE (023 8067 4397; email: hampshire@polfed.org; website: www. hampshirepolfed.org.uk/services/welfare. htm)

CC number: 291061

Eligibility

Members, pensioners and civilian employees of the Hampshire Constabulary and their dependants. Assistance may also be available to special constables injured during police duty.

Types of grants

One-off and recurrent grants or loans to help support people experiencing family crisis or recovering from injury or illness. Past grants have been given towards stair-lifts, bath-lifts, wheelchairs, respite holidays and general living costs.

Annual grant total

In 2013/14 the fund held assets of £512,500 and had an income of £261,500. Grants totalled £41,500 and were distributed as follows:

Widows and children's Christmas gifts	£16,100
Assistance and grants	£13,500
Gifts to sick members, wreaths and donations	£9,700
Loans now written off as grants	£2,000

Applications

Application forms are available to download from the Hampshire Police Federation website. Applicants are requested to provide at least two quotes for grants above £2,000 and one quote for amounts below £2,000. If a grant is for medical purposes, applicants should provide as much relevant information as possible, such as medical reports, occupational therapy reports and other supporting information. Details of any other agencies or charities that have been approached for funding must be provided. Applications are considered on a regular basis and eligible applicants may be contacted for further information. Urgent applications can be fast-tracked.

Other information

The trust also donates to other charitable trusts and organisations which support police officers. In 2013/14 the Police Convalescent Home received £147,500 from the fund.

Humberside Police Welfare and Benevolent Fund

£18,000

Correspondent: Humberside Police Welfare and Benevolent Fund, Humberside Police, Courtland Road, Hull HU6 8AW (08456060 222; email: webmail@humberside.pnn.police.uk; website: www.humberside.police.uk)

CC number: 503762

Eligibility

Serving and retired officers of the Humberside Police and retired officers from other forces who live in Humberside, and their partners and dependants; and civilian employees of Humberside Police Authority, retired civilian employees and their partners and dependants.

Types of grants

One-off and recurrent grants of up to £500. Loans are also available.

Annual grant total

In 2014 the fund had an income of £17,300 and a total expenditure of £19,400. We estimate that the amount of grants given to individuals totalled £18,000.

Applications

Apply in writing to the correspondent at any time, either through the branch/divisional representative or the headquarters.

Metropolitan Police Benevolent Fund

£191,500 (45 grants)

Correspondent: William Tarrant, Correspondent, Charities Section, 10th Floor, Metropolitan Police Services, Empress State Building, Empress Approach, London SW6 1TR (020 7161 1667; email: william.tarrant@met.police.uk)

CC number: 1125409

Eligibility

Current and former officers of the Metropolitan Police, and their dependants, who are in need due to illness, injury, financial difficulties and so on.

Types of grants

Generally one-off grants according to need. Support can be given for bereavement expenses, building repairs and alterations, furniture and other household necessities, payment of debts and so on. Interest-free loans are also offered.

Annual grant total

In 2014 the fund had assets of £4 million and an income of almost £2 million. Grants to 45 individuals totalled £191,500. Charitable activities totalled £1.95 million and were broken down as follows:

Police Rehabilitation Centre	£1.4 million
Metropolitan and City Police Orphans Fund	£325,000
Officers and former officers of the Metropolitan Police, and their dependants.	£191,500

A further £385,000 was provided in 39 loans.

Applications

The individual should apply directly to the correspondent in writing. Applications are considered throughout the year.

Other information

Since 2008 the charity is an amalgamation of four former charities (Metropolitan Police Convalescent Home Fund, Metropolitan Police Widows' and Widowers' Fund, Metropolitan Police Relief Fund and Metropolitan Police Combined Fund).

Grants are also made to other organisations supporting police officers and their families. Officers are also allowed free access to Flint House – the police rehabilitation centre in Goring.

Metropolitan Police Civil Staff Welfare Fund

£44,000

Correspondent: William Tarrant, Charities Officer, Charities Section, Metropolitan Police Service, 10th Floor (East), Empress State Building, Lillie Road, London SW6 1TR (020 7161 1667; email: william.tarrant@met.police.uk)

CC number: 282375

Eligibility

Members and past members of the Metropolitan Police Staff and the Metropolitan Police Authority and their families and dependants who are in need through poverty, hardship or distress.

Types of grants

One-off grants ranging from £400 to £3,600 and loans from £200 to £4,000 (2013/14 figures).

Annual grant total

In 2013/14 the fund held assets of £250,000 and had an income of £29,500. Welfare grants to individuals totalled £44,000. Loans amounted to a further £32,500.

Exclusions

Grants are unlikely to be made towards private healthcare, private education fees, legal costs, business debts or bills that have already been paid.

Applications

Application forms are available from the correspondent. Applications should be submitted directly by the individual or, where applicable, through a social worker, Citizens Advice or other welfare agency.

The North Wales Police Benevolent Fund

£18,500

Correspondent: Mel Jones, Assistant Secretary, North Wales Police Federation, 311 Abergele Road, Old Colwyn, Colwyn Bay LL29 9YF (01492 805404; email: mel.jones@nthwales.pnn.police.uk)

CC number: 505321

Eligibility

Members and former members of the North Wales Police Force, former members of previous forces amalgamated to form the North Wales Police, and their families and immediate dependants who are in need.

Types of grants

One-off and recurrent grants are given according to need. Grants are also made at Christmas.

Annual grant total

In 2013/14 the fund had an income of £14,800 and a total expenditure of £18,800, both of which were unusually high (total expenditure usually ranges between around £2,500 and £4,600). We estimate that the amount of grants given to individuals totalled £18,500.

Applications

Apply in writing to the correspondent. Applications are considered quarterly, although urgent appeals can be considered as they arrive.

The North West Police Benevolent Fund

£104,000

Correspondent: Jackie Smithies, Trustee, St Michael's Lodge, Northcote Road, Langho BB6 8BG (01254 245571; email: jsmithies@gmpf.polfed.org; website: www.nwpbf.org)

CC number: 503045

Eligibility

Serving and retired officers of Cheshire Constabulary, Greater Manchester Police, Lancashire Constabulary, Merseyside Police and previous police forces amalgamated within the constituent forces, together with their dependants, who are in a condition of need and hardship. Former officers of the above forces may be considered at the trustees' discretion.

In 2011 the fund was joined by National Crime Agency (NCA) (previously known as Serious Organised Crime Agency – SOCA). From September 2013 Cumbria Constabulary also became a member.

Types of grants

One-off or recurrent grants and interest-free loans are given for convalescence, medical and disability equipment (but not for private health care) or to help in other cases of need arising from unforeseen circumstances.

In the event of death of a serving police officer a grant of £5,000 is paid to the dependent family.

Orphaned children of the police officers are supported through the St George's Police Children's Trust (see a separate entry).

Annual grant total

In 2014 the fund had assets of £6 million and an income of over £2 million. Welfare grants were made totalling £104,000. Support was given in the following categories:

Death benefits	£55,000
Serving Officers	£29,500
Pensioners	£13,000
Attendance at convalescent homes	£4,200
Christmas grants to pensioners and widows	£250

The fund also provided 41 interest-free loans totalling £139,500.

Exclusions

No grants available for private health, education or legal fees.

Applications

Application forms are available from the correspondent. Requests are usually made through a force welfare officer or a member of the management committee. Our research suggests that requests for assistance are generally considered each month and should be submitted by the second Wednesday in January or by the first Wednesday in any other month.

Other information

The fund does not give grants to organisations but does contribute to other police funds and convalescent homes. Members are also able to use the police treatment centres or holiday lodges. See the website for further details.

Northern Ireland Police Fund

£1.7 million

Correspondent: The Secretary, Maryfield Complex, 100 Belfast Road, Holywood BT18 9QY (028 9039 3556; email: admin@nipolicefund.org; website: www. nipolicefund.org)

Eligibility

Serving and retired police officers in Northern Ireland, and their dependants, who have been directly affected by terrorist violence whether on or off-duty. This includes those with serious physical and/or psychological injuries which would be considered sufficiently serious to warrant the award of an IOD Band 2 medical discharge, as determined by an occupational physician. The applicant must also be able to demonstrate that the IOD was a result of the individual being the directly intended target of terrorist attack. Applications are also considered from the families of officers who have committed suicide if a causal link can be established between a direct attack on the officer and their subsequent death.

Types of grants

Our research indicates that regular grants are given to those on a very low income and one-off grants are administered through a number of separate schemes. Contact the correspondent for more information.

Annual grant total

At the time of writing (November 2015) the fund's website, which usually displays the fund's financial and other information, was under construction.

In the past, the previous NIPF website provided the following information:

> Its remit is to provide support to those police officers injured as a result of terrorist violence, and their families, and the widows, children and parents of officers killed in terrorist incidents. The Fund has an annual budget of £1.8m per year for the provision of these services.

In previous years, grants have totalled £1.7 million.

Exclusions

Once an application has been approved the applicant must wait 12 months before re-applying. Applicants cannot re-apply for the same item if their first request has been declined nor can applications be split into separate parts to avoid the capping of awards.

Applications

Contact the correspondent for more information.

Other information

The fund was established in 2001 following the Patten Report into policing in Northern Ireland.

The Police Dependants' Trust Ltd

£300,000 (108 grants)

Correspondent: Gill Scott-Moore, Chief Executive Officer, 3 Mount Mews, High Street, Hampton, Middlesex TW12 2SH (020 8941 6907; fax: 020 8979 4323; email: office@pdtrust.org; website: www. pdtrust.org)

CC number: 1151322

Eligibility

Dependants of current or former police officers who have died from injuries received in the execution of duty, and current or former police officers incapacitated as a result of injury received in the execution of duty, or their dependants. Eligible officers include:

- Members of the British Transport Police
- Members of the Civil Nuclear Constabulary
- People who are performing temporary overseas or central police force who enjoy a statutory right of reversion to such a police force
- Special Constables appointed for any such police area

- Police cadets appointed to undergo training with a view to becoming members of such police forces

Grants are **not restricted** to those individuals who are living in the UK – if you have moved but would otherwise be eligible you can still apply.

Types of grants

One-off grants in the range of around £200 to £9,000. The following welfare grants are available:

- Assistance Grants – awarded to those whose income (after accommodation costs) falls below a defined level, enabling incapacitated officers and police dependants to enjoy a reasonable standard of living
- Special Purpose Grants – made in a variety of situations but most commonly to incapacitated officers for customised adaptations to their car or for special equipment to ease their disability and enable them to remain in their own homes
- Bereavement Grants – these can also be made where necessary to assist with the immediate costs that arise when a police officer is killed on duty
- Residential Care Grants – considered to assist with incidental expenses associated with residential care

Support can include awards towards furniture and household appliances, essentials, for example, food and clothing, set-up costs to help getting into rented accommodation or to participate in sports and hobbies.

Annual grant total

In 2013/14 the trust had assets of £25.6 million and an income of over £1.4 million. There were 117 grants made totalling £327,000, of which 108 awards were other than educational. Support was allocated as follows:

Special purpose grants	£315,500
Children support grants	£11,500

Assistance grants	73
Special purpose grants	34
Education grants	9
Other (bereavement, residential care)	1

There was no breakdown given of the amounts given in educational grants and welfare grants. We have estimated the welfare grants to be around £300,000.

During the year the Management Committee considered a total of 246 applications for assistance, including 53 new applications and five urgent appeals (dealt with immediately).

Exclusions

Cash is not normally given (unless in exceptional circumstances and at the discretion of trustees).

Grants are not normally awarded to individuals to:

- Help where state assistance or statutory services are available
- Repay debts

- Cover legal expenses such as county court costs and solicitors' fees
- Help in the form of a loan
- Assist with medical care
- Help where the impact of an injury was temporary (unless exceptional circumstances apply)

Applications

Application forms are available on the trust's website or from the correspondent. They can be submitted at any time but all applicants must first register with the trust. Supporting materials may be required. Applications are generally considered every two months although urgent cases can be addressed between meetings. Generally applications are received, processed and concluded within twelve weeks.

Other information

The Police Dependants' Trust was founded in 1966 as a response to the deaths of three police officers who were shot while on duty in London. An anonymous donation of £100,000 was offered to the Home Office Minister to establish a permanent trust. It offers support to both welfare and educational needs.

The trust's activities have been transferred to The Police Dependants' Trust Ltd (Charity Commission no. 1151322), registered in March 2013. It has previously operated as Police Dependants' Trust (Charity Commission no. 251021). The new entity maintains the same objectives.

The website notes that the trust 'also administers the National Police Fund, which shares broadly the same eligibility criteria i.e. financial support is provided to the families/dependants of police officers who have been killed or injured on duty, and this support is provided on the basis of need'. The National Police Fund provides grants to:

- Police dependants who are in further education (university degree or vocational qualification)
- Widows and orphans of police officers who were below inspector level at the time of their death or medical retirement (through the Mary Holt Fund)
- Police benevolent funds or sports/social clubs
- Police charities and other bodies which assist the police services

Port of London Authority Police Charity Fund

£6,000

Correspondent: Chair to the Board of Trustees, 14 Bedford Close, Rayleigh,

Essex SS6 7QR (01268 777061; email: barry.smith@potll.com)

CC number: 265569

Eligibility

Former officers who have served in the port authority's police force, and their dependants.

Types of grants

One-off grants are given to help with unforeseen bills, household items, holidays and so on.

Annual grant total

In 2013/14 the fund had an income of £780 and a total expenditure of £6,500. We estimate that the amount of grants given to individuals totalled £6,000.

Applications

Apply in writing to the correspondent, clearly stating the need for financial assistance. Applications are considered at quarterly meetings, or sooner if the need is urgent.

The Royal Ulster Constabulary – Police Service of Northern Ireland Benevolent Fund

£400,000

Correspondent: Fund Administrator, Police Federation for Northern Ireland, 77–79 Garnerville Road, Belfast BT4 2NX (028 9076 4215; email: benevolentfund@policefedni.com; website: www.rucgc-psnibenevolentfund.com)

IR number: XN 48380

Eligibility

Members and former members of the Royal Ulster Constabulary, and their dependants. The main objectives of the charity are to look after serving PSNI officers, widows/widowers, other dependants, injured officers and those with disabilities, pensioners and former members who are not pensionable and parents of deceased officers, all experiencing financial hardship or difficulties. Eligibility relates to financial hardship but 'the bottom line is simply that a case of need must be identified'.

Types of grants

One-off and recurrent grants and interest-free loans according to need. The charity offers a wide range of assistance, including adventure holidays for children, short breaks for widows, convalescence for injured officers, purchase of medical aids, wheelchairs and stair-lifts, household goods, medical

equipment and other necessities, and other financial help as required.

Annual grant total

Previously about £800,000 has been spent supporting the beneficiaries. We divide this figure between educational and welfare causes as no further details are available.

Exclusions

Grants for NHS treatment are not normally made. Our research suggests that loans for debt cases cannot be supported.

Applications

Initial contact should be made in writing to the charity. Eligible applicants will then be advised on further application process. Candidates are visited by the representatives of the charity who then present the case to the management committee, which meets on the first Wednesday of each month. Each Regional Board has an appointed Benevolent Fund Representative. Applicants will be required to provide full financial breakdown and quotes where possible.

Other information

The charity also supports beneficiaries for educational causes and maintains eight apartments in Portrush and eight holiday cottages in Kesh, allowing beneficiaries to 'enjoy a short break away from the difficulties imposed on them by their own circumstances or environment'.

Note that the administration of all Police Dependants' Trust applications from Northern Ireland is also in the hands of the charity.

Additional help is offered by a number of other organisations, details of which can be found on the Northern Ireland Police Family Assistance website (www.northernirelandpolicefamilyassistance.org.uk).

Sussex Police Welfare Fund

£55,500

Correspondent: Lorna Stagg, Correspondent, Sussex Police Headquarters, Malling House, Church Lane, Lewes, East Sussex BN7 2DZ (101 ext.544133; email: spct@sussex.pnn.police.uk; website: www.sussex.police.uk)

CC number: 257564

Eligibility

Members of the Sussex Police Welfare Fund who are in need, and their dependants.

Types of grants

One-off grants towards, for example, hospital travel and parking costs, emergency accommodation, essential household items, mobility problems and emergency childcare. Assistance is also given to facilitate mediation and initial legal advice.

Discretionary loans may be given to serving officers subscribing to the fund who are facing financial difficulties. Loans are repayable from salary at source per pay period. Any assistance agreed will usually be paid directly to the provider of a service requested by a member.

Annual grant total

In 2014 the fund held assets of £1.6 million and had an income of £169,000. Grants were paid totalling £55,500. Though the fund's Charity Commission record states that it also makes grants to organisations, we estimate that all grants expenditure went to individuals.

Applications

Apply by calling, emailing or writing to the fund. Your case will be dealt with by an adviser who will work with you to address your problems. If it is deemed appropriate they will prepare an anonymous application to the fund for financial assistance. The adviser then presents your application at a monthly meeting and advocates on behalf of the applicant. More urgent requests can be considered between the monthly meetings.

Other information

The fund owns a bungalow in Dorset which is available to members in need of a recuperative break.

West Yorkshire Police (Employees) Benevolent Fund

£12,000

Correspondent: Pat Maknia, Finance Department, PO Box 9, Wakefield, West Yorkshire WF1 3QP (01924 292841; email: diane.nelson@westyorkshire.pnn. police.uk)

CC number: 701817

Eligibility

Employees and ex-employees of the West Yorkshire Police Force or the West Yorkshire Metropolitan County Council under the direct control of the Chief Constable who are in need, and their widows, orphans and other dependants.

Types of grants

One-off and repeated grants are given according to need.

Annual grant total

In 2013/14 the fund had an income of £3,200 and an unusually high total expenditure of £12,200. We estimate that the amount of grants given to individuals totalled £12,000.

Applications

Apply in writing to the correspondent. The trustees' meetings are held every three months, although urgent cases can be considered at any time.

Wiltshire Ambulance Service Benevolent Fund

£2,500

Correspondent: Andrew Newman, Treasurer, 82 Dunch Lane, Melksham, Wiltshire SN12 8DX (07966 534713; email: charliecopter@msn.com)

CC number: 280364

Eligibility

Serving and retired members of the Wiltshire Ambulance Service and their dependants.

Types of grants

One-off and recurrent grants are given according to need.

Annual grant total

In 2014/15 the fund had an income of £17,700 and a total expenditure of £20,500. We estimate that the amount of grants given to individuals totalled around £2,500.

Applications

Applicants should contact their station's benevolent fund representative, who will then contact the chair on their behalf.

Other information

The fund also owns and supports three properties that provide convalescence.

Prison services

The Edridge Fund

£52,000 (138 grants)

Correspondent: The Secretary, Edridge Applications, 4 Chivalry Road, London SW11 1HT (020 3397 7025; email: office@edridgefund.org; website: www. edridgefund.org)

CC number: 803493

Eligibility

Members and ex-members of the probation service and CAFCASS who are (or were) eligible to be members of NAPO and their bereaved partners, spouses and dependants.

Types of grants

Financial and welfare support, generally in a one-off grant, to alleviate cases of distress and hardship. Applications are assessed individually and grants are designed to help towards the applicant's specific requirements.

Annual grant total

In 2014 the fund had assets of £202,500 and an income of £58,500. Grants to individuals totalled £52,000.

During the year, the fund received 165 applications, of which 138 were successful.

Applications

Apply on a form available from the correspondent, a local representative or to download from the fund's website. The fund prefers to receive applications via email. If the applicant is sending the application from a home email, it must be sent to office@edridgefund.org. If it is being sent from the applicant's probation, prison or CAFCASS address, it can be sent securely to edridge.applications@edridge.cjsm.net (this address cannot be used from a home email address). Applicants wishing to send a handwritten scanned copy, must send a.pdf file; otherwise, handwritten applications must be sent by ordinary post.

Applications are usually dealt with by the trustees within three weeks; however, in 'extreme' cases of emergency, decisions can be made much more quickly.

Note: If applicants do not wish their local representative to be aware of their application it should be stated clearly on their form. If an applicant has not received an email or letter of acknowledgement within five working days of submitting their application, the fund should be contacted through its voicemail.

Scottish Prison Service Benevolent Fund

£15,000

Correspondent: Scottish Prison Service Benevolent Fund, HMP Glenochil, King O Muir Road, Glenochil FK10 3AD

OSCR number: SC021603

Eligibility

Scottish prison officers, both serving and retired, and their families who are in need.

Types of grants

One-off and recurrent grants are given according to need.

Annual grant total

In 2014/15 the fund had an income of £25,000 and an expenditure of £35,500. We estimate that the amount of grants given to individuals totalled around £15,000.

Applications

Apply in writing to the correspondent.

Social services

The Social Workers' Benevolent Trust

£35,500 (83 grants)

Correspondent: The Honorary Secretary, 16 Kent Street, Birmingham B5 6RD (email: info2014@swbt.org; website: www.swbt.org)

CC number: 262889

Eligibility

Social workers who hold a professional social work qualification and are experiencing financial difficulties, and their dependants. Unqualified social workers may also be considered depending upon the nature and length of their employment.

Types of grants

One-off grants of up to a maximum of £500 are given for specific debts and other needs.

Annual grant total

In 2013/14 the trust held assets of £216,500 and had an income of £42,000. Grants to individuals totalled £35,500. Of 108 applications received, 83 were successful.

Exclusions

No grants for: daily living costs; social work training; private health care; private education; or private social care. Grants are not normally given to individuals who have received a grant in the last year.

Applications

Apply on a form available from the correspondent or to download from the website. Applications should be submitted directly by the individual and are considered bi-monthly.

Religion

Frances Ashton's Charity

£51,000 (56 grants)

Correspondent: Georgina Fowle, Administrator, Beech House, Woolston,

North Cadbury, Somerset BA22 7BJ (fax: 01732 520159)

CC number: 200162

Eligibility

Serving and retired Church of England clergy, or their widows/widowers, who are in need.

Types of grants

One-off grants of between £150 and £880. The charity has a number of areas of priority including emergency, medical or care needs.

Annual grant total

In 2014 the charity had assets of £1.77 million and an income of £75,000. Grants were made to 56 individuals totalling £51,000.

Exclusions

Grants are not given towards: property purchase; school fees or higher education costs (unless the child has disabilities); sabbatical expenses; credit card debts and loans; general living expenses; parochial expenses.

Applications

Application forms are available from the correspondent. Applications should be submitted directly by the individual, usually by the beginning of June each year. Applications are considered at the autumn meeting of the trustees but urgent cases may be dealt with when they arise.

Other information

The charity also makes grants to the charity Royal London Society (£95 in 2014), to support ex-offenders in need.

The Bible Preaching Trust

£7,000

Correspondent: Richard Mayers, Secretary and Treasurer, 34 Barleyfields, Didcot OX11 0BJ (01235 799219; email: richard.mayers@tesco.net)

CC number: 262160

Eligibility

Ministers of the Evangelical Christian faith who are in need. Theological students may occasionally benefit.

Types of grants

Usually one-off grants ranging from £250 to £2,000.

Annual grant total

In 2013/14 the trust had an income of £8,300 and a total expenditure of £7,200. We estimate the grant total to be £7,000.

Exclusions

Funding is not given for social causes, group projects, or to any person who

cannot agree to the trust's doctrinal statement.

Applications

Apply either by recommendation or by letter, after which application forms and trust deed extracts are then sent out. The trustees' meetings are held every four months at which applications will be considered. 'Mass-targeting' applications or those outside the terms of the trust may not be answered.

The Bishop of Lincoln's Discretionary Fund

£17,000

Correspondent: Revd Sally-Anne McDougall, Trustee, The Bishop's Office, The Old Palace, Minster Yard, Lincoln LN2 1PU

CC number: 1022582

Eligibility

Ministers of the Church of England who live and work in the Diocese of Lincoln, and their dependants.

Types of grants

One-off grants of around £25–£450 according to need. Grants are usually to assist sick clergy and their families and for holiday expenses.

Annual grant total

In 2014 the fund had an income of £13,300 and a total expenditure of £17,200. We estimate that the amount of grants given to individuals totalled £17,000.

Applications

Apply in writing by the individual or one of the other local bishops to the Bishop of Lincoln. Applications are considered throughout the year.

The Chasah Trust

£13,000

Correspondent: Richard Collier-Keywood, Trustee, Glydwish Hall, Fontridge Lane, Etchingham, East Sussex TN19 7DG (01435 882768; email: lck07@hotmail.com)

CC number: 294898

Eligibility

Missionaries who are known to the trustees, or are a contact of the trustees.

Types of grants

One-off and recurrent grants to support Christian work.

Annual grant total

In 2013/14 the trust had assets of £29,500 an income of £45,500. Grants to individuals totalled £13,000. A further

£15,900 was awarded to religious organisations.

Applications

Apply in writing to the correspondent.

The Church of England Pensions Board

£111,000

Correspondent: Lee Marshall, Chief of Staff, 29 Great Smith Street, London SW1P 3PS (020 7898 1802; email: pensions@churchofengland.org; website: www.cofe.anglican.org/about/cepb)

CC number: 236627

Eligibility

Retired clergy and licensed lay workers of the Church of England, their widows, widowers and dependants.

Types of grants

Allowances for those participating in the retirement housing scheme and to clergy widows and widowers to supplement their low income. The standard of 'low income' is reviewed annually. Our research suggests that no new grants are made for assistance with private nursing or retirement care.

Annual grant total

In 2014 the board had assets of almost £116 million and an income of almost £23.9 million. A total of £111,000 was awarded in grants.

Applications

Application forms can be requested from the correspondent.

Other information

The charity's main concern is the administration of the pension scheme and the provision of supported housing and nursing care. It operates seven such complexes across the country. The charity also runs a retirement housing scheme which offers mortgages and loans to assist those vacating 'tied' housing.

The charity is known by a number of working names: Bishop Morley College, Church Workers Pension Augmentation Fund, Clergy (Widows and Dependants) Pensions Augmentation Fund, Clergy Pensions Augmentations Fund, Clergy Retirement Housing Trust, Clergy Widows and Dependants Pensions Augmentation Fund, Suffolk Clergy Housing Trust and The Rev Joshua Case Trust.

The Clergy Rest Fund

£31,000 (23 grants)

Correspondent: Hugh MacDougald, Administrator, Wickworth Sherwood LLP, Minerva House, 5 Montague Close, London SE1 9BB (020 7593 5000; website: www.wslaw.co.uk)

CC number: 233436

Eligibility

Church of England clergy who are in need.

Types of grants

One-off grants ranging from £500 to £1,500 for a variety of needs.

Annual grant total

In 2014 the fund had an income of £43,000 and a total expenditure of £56,500. Grants were made to 23 individuals totalling £31,000.

Applications

Apply in writing to the correspondent.

Other information

The fund also makes grants to institutions connected with the Church of England.

The Collier Charitable Trust

£7,000

Correspondent: Michael Blagden, Secretary, Cherry Tree Cottage, Old Kiln Lane, Churt, Farnham, Surrey GU10 2HX (01428 717534)

CC number: 251333

Eligibility

Retired Christian missionaries and teachers in the UK and overseas.

Types of grants

One-off and recurrent grants of around £300 each. The trust may also provide accommodation.

Annual grant total

In 2014 the trust had an income of £22,000 and a total expenditure of £83,000. Our research indicates that generally grants to individuals take up between 5–10% of the total charitable expenditure, with grants to organisations given priority. We have estimated that around £7,000 was given in grants to individuals.

Applications

Apply in writing to the correspondent.

Other information

Grants are also made to organisations, mostly those which are known to the trustees.

The Cornwall Retired Clergy, Widows of the Clergy and their Dependants Fund

£4,800

Correspondent: Sophie Eddy, Director of Finance, Truro Diocesan Board of Finance Ltd, Church House, Woodland Court, Truro Business Park, Threemilestone TR4 9NH (01872 274351; email: finance@truro.anglican.org)

CC number: 289675

Eligibility

Widows, widowers and dependants of deceased members of the clergy who live in, or have worked in, the diocese of Truro. Retired Anglican clergy who are in need and have links with Truro are also eligible for support.

Types of grants

Grants are one-off and occasionally recurrent according to need. Recent grants have ranged from £50 to £500 and included funding for dentist's fees, spectacles, travel to hospital and assistance with equipment for people with disabilities.

Annual grant total

In 2014 the fund had an income of £12,600 and a total expenditure of £5,100. We estimate that the total amount of grants awarded to individuals was approximately £4,800.

Exclusions

No grants are given for assistance with school fees or university fees.

Applications

Apply in writing to the correspondent. Applications can be submitted directly by the individual or through a relative or a carer. They are usually considered monthly.

Lord Crewe's Charity

£28,500 (28 grants)

Correspondent: Clive Smithers, Clerk Manager, Rivergreen Centre, Aykley Heads, Durham DH1 5TS (0191 383 7398; email: enquiries@lordcrewescharity.co.uk; website: www.lordcrewescharity.org.uk)

CC number: 1155101

Eligibility

Church of England clergy and their dependants who are in need in the dioceses of Durham and Newcastle. Grants may be given more generally to people in need who live in the area of benefit, with preference to people resident in parishes where the charity owns land or has the right of presentation to the benefice.

Types of grants

One-off and recurrent grants are given according to need in specific instances of hardship and to assist clergy moving out of church housing on retirement.

Annual grant total

In 2014 the charity had assets of £39 million and an income of £38.1 million (which includes a transfer of assets, liabilities and undertakings of the old charity worth £36.9 million). A total of 28 grants, amounting to £28,500, was paid in support of clergy in hardship and to assist clergy moving out of church housing when they retire. Additionally £15,900 was spent as 'miscellaneous charitable giving', which may also include support for general welfare purposes. Further 118 educational grants were made totalling £173,000.

Exclusions

Applicants who are not members of clergy are not supported and the trustees ask not to be contacted by people who do not fit the criteria.

Applications for church buildings and church projects are not assisted (except in the very small number of parishes in which the charity holds property or has rights of presentation).

Applications

The charity's website states that there is no 'application form or an open application procedure for grants. ... The charity works directly with its beneficiaries and with a number of partner organisations.' The application round opens in March and continues until July. Grants are considered in the first two weeks of August and the outcome is communicated to the applicant by the end of the month. Consult the website for the latest updates on awards available.

Other information

From 2014 the charity has become a charitable incorporated organisation and changed its registered charity number (previously 230347).

Small annual grants are made to organisations (annual sums specified in the trust deed totalling £7,000 were paid in 2014) and support is also given for welfare purposes. Payments are made to Lincoln College of Oxford to be applied in scholarships, fellowships and hardship grants (£150,000 in 2014 consisting of 11 undergraduate scholarships, 12 graduate scholarships, a postdoctoral fellowship, and the provision of hardship funds for undergraduates). No other institution can be supported in the same way. During the year an award of £120,000

was also made to the Diocese of Newcastle:

> For a package of approved projects to support clergy through services including pastoral care and counselling, mentoring, continuing ministerial development, support for engagement in parishes in areas of high deprivation, and the replacement of inefficient boilers and improvement of central heating systems control in clergy housing with higher than average fuel costs.

A linked charity, Lord Crewe's Library and Archives Trust (Charity Commission no. 1155101–2) has been established to own the libraries and archives collections currently held at Durham Cathedral, Durham University, the North East Religious Learning Resource Centre, and the Northumberland Records Office.

In 2014 the trustees continued the previously set grants programme for another year while undertaking a full evaluation of activities undertaken. The evaluation will then inform the trustees' consideration of whether to operate any further three-year programme, and if so what its contents should be.

Anne French Memorial Trust

£61,000

Correspondent: Christopher Dicker, Administrator, Trustee Training and Support Ltd, Hill House, Ranworth, Norwich NR13 6AB (01603 270356; email: cdicker@hotmail.co.uk)

CC number: 254567

Eligibility

Members of the Anglican clergy in the diocese of Norwich.

Types of grants

Holiday and other relief-in-need grants as well as training costs for clergy and young people.

Annual grant total

In 2013/14 the trust had assets of £7.3 million and an income of £256,500. Grants to individuals totalled approximately £60,000 and were broken down as follows:

Gifts to clergy	£39,000
Youth and training	£11,000
Training of the clergy	£11,000

Applications

Apply in writing to the correspondent.

Other information

The charity has a close association with the Bishop of Norwich Fabric Fund Trust and the Norwich Diocesan Board of Finance Ltd.

The Fund for the Support of Presbyters and Deacons

£200,000

Correspondent: Revd Gareth Powell, Secretary, Methodist Church House, 25 Marylebone Road, London NW1 5JR (020 7486 5502; email: stipends@ methodistchurch.org.uk; website: www. methodist.org.uk)

CC number: 1132208

Eligibility

Retired ministers and deacons of the Methodist church who are in need, and their dependants. Grants can also be made to enable ministers and deacons who are in need as a result of illness or impairment to continue to work where otherwise they would have to retire.

Types of grants

One-off grants to meet all kinds of needs including unexpected household expenditure (for example, the replacement of boiler/cooker/washing machine), gardening costs, property maintenance and repairs, bills, re-carpeting, redecorating and medical needs (such as stair-lifts, mobility scooters, opticians and dental costs). Grants of up to £4,800 are also available for residential care fees. Grants are also awarded for adaptation, equipment or other expenditure which enables ministers to sustain or return to ministry or training.

Annual grant total

In 2013/14 a breakdown of grants was not available. In previous years, however, grants to individuals have totalled around £200,000.

Applications

Apply in writing to the correspondent at any time.

Other information

The fund is part of the Methodist Church in Great Britain.

Gibbons Charity

£19,000

Correspondent: Noel Fryer, Correspondent, 12 Shrewsbury Street, Hodnet, Market Drayton, Shropshire TF9 3NP (01630 684007; email: noelfryer@the-fryers.com)

CC number: 215171

Eligibility

Shropshire Church of England clergy and retired clergy and their widows, widowers, spouses, divorced partners and children who face hardship.

Types of grants

One-off and recurrent grants are given according to need.

Annual grant total

In 2014 the charity had an income of £5,900 and a total expenditure of £19,600. We estimate that the total amount of grants awarded to individuals was approximately £19,000; however, in previous years grants have totalled £2,000–£3,000.

Applications

Apply in writing to the correspondent.

The Glasgow Society of the Sons and Daughters of Ministers of the Church of Scotland

£25,500 (15 grants)

Correspondent: Fiona Watson, Charity Accounting Services, Scott-Moncrieff, Exchange Place, 3 Semple Street, Edinburgh EH3 9BL (0131 473 3500; email: fiona.watson@scott-moncrieff.com; website: www.scott-moncrieff.com/services/charities/charitable-trusts/glasgow-society-of-the-sons-and-daughters)

OSCR number: SC010281

Eligibility

Children of deceased ministers of the Church of Scotland, who are in need.

Types of grants

One-off and recurrent grants are given according to need. Annual grants are made with an extra payment prior to Christmas.

Annual grant total

In 2013/14 the charity had an income of £57,500 and a total expenditure of £68,500.

The charity is administered by Scott-Moncrieff, whose website stated the following:

> £45,000 is available for distribution during the year. Last year, 15 children of deceased Ministers were supported, each receiving between £1,075 and £2,310. Eight grants were made in connection with educational and training ranging from £1,350 to £2,030 per annum. One grant was also made out of a separate fund in connection with applications which fell outwith the criteria indicated above but were nevertheless for educational purposes.

We estimate that the amount of grants given to individuals for social welfare purposes totalled around £25,500.

Applications

Application forms are available from the correspondent or to download from the website. Applications from children of deceased ministers may be submitted at any time.

The Arthur Hurst Will Trust

See entry on page 27

H. E. Knight Charitable Trust

£10,000

Correspondent: Aubrey Curry, Trustee, 14 Bramley Gardens, Whimple, Exeter EX5 2SJ (01404 822295; email: aubrey.curry31@btinternet.com)

CC number: 283549

Eligibility

Individuals involved in missionary Christian work and spiritual teaching in the UK.

Types of grants

Ongoing support for Christian workers. Grants of up to £500 are awarded.

Annual grant total

In 2014/15 the trust had an unusually high income of £24,500 and a total expenditure of £26,000. We estimate that the total amount of grants awarded to individuals was approximately £10,000 as the trust also awards grants to other voluntary organisations that support and facilitate religious activities.

Applications

Apply in writing to the correspondent. Note, the trust has stated that the majority of its funds go to missionaries known to the trustees and as such, other applicants are unlikely to be successful. The trust does not accept unsolicited applications.

The Lancashire Infirm Secular Clergy Fund

£107,500 (94 grants)

Correspondent: Revd Simon David, Correspondent, Hawksworth, High Wray Bank, High Wray, Ambleside, Cumbria LA22 0JD (01539 433160; email: simon.hawksworth@hotmail.co.uk)

CC number: 222796

Eligibility

Catholic secular clergy of the dioceses of Liverpool, Salford and Lancaster who are unable, through age or illness, to attend to their duties of office and are in need.

Types of grants

Annual grants mostly of £1,300 each although smaller grants of around £600 are also available.

Annual grant total

In 2013/14 the fund held assets of £3.6 million and had an income of £235,000. Grants to members of clergy who are ill totalled £107,500.

Applications

Apply using a form available from the correspondent.

The Leaders of Worship and Preachers Trust

£7,400

Correspondent: Adrian Needham, Executive Officer, PO Box 2352, Watford WD18 1PY (01923 231811; fax: 01923 296899; email: lwptoffice@lwpt.org.uk; website: www.lwpt.org.uk)

CC number: 1107967

Eligibility

Preachers and leaders of worship, and their dependants, who are in need.

Types of grants

One-off and weekly grants for a broad range of needs.

Annual grant total

In 2013/14 the trust had assets of £582,500 and an income of £848,000. Grants totalled £11,200, of which £7,400 was given in financial assistance to individuals facing hardship.

Applications

Application forms are available to download from the website. There are three parts: Part A – personal information form; Part B1 – application for a weekly grant; and Part B2 – application for a lump sum grant. Part A should be completed along with either Part B1 or Part B2, depending on the applicant's need.

Other information

The website states the following information:

> Depending on need, grants may be offered toward care at one of the Westerley Christian Care Homes managed by LWP Homes, which aim to provide the best in time of need for people looking for actively Christian residential care in retirement. They offer an excellent quality of life; at a price that represents good value for the high quality of care and accommodation provided; in an atmosphere of Christian family values with daily prayers and regular celebrations of Holy Communion. To find out more about LWP Homes Westerley Christian Care Homes, visit their website [www.lwphomes.org.uk].

Sylvanus Lysons Charity

£22,000 (51 grants)

Correspondent: Mr A. Holloway, 8–12 Clarence Street, Gloucester GL1 1DZ (01452 522047)

CC number: 202939

Eligibility

Widows and dependants of the clergy of the Church of England in or retired from the diocese of Gloucester who are in need.

Types of grants

One-off grants according to need.

Annual grant total

In 2013/14 the charity had an income of £383,500 and a total expenditure of £400,500. Individuals received 51 grants totalling £22,000. A further 38 grants were awarded to organisations, totalling £302,500.

Applications

Apply in writing to the correspondent, directly by the individual, for consideration usually in March, July, September and November.

Ministers' Relief Society

£24,000

Correspondent: Alan Lathey, Trustee, 2 Queensberry Road, Penylan, Cardiff CV23 9JJ

CC number: 270314

Eligibility

Protestant ministers, their widows and dependants who are in need, especially due to old age or disability. Children of deceased ministers generally must be under the age of 21 and of 'genuine evangelical and protestant convictions' to be eligible.

Types of grants

One-off and recurrent grants can be given according to need. In the past grants have been given to: ministers who are retired or have disabilities, and their widows, with inadequate income or savings; specific emergencies, such as serious illness, removal costs, enforced resignation or dismissal by congregation; candidates and students seeking vocational training in the ministry.

Annual grant total

In 2014 the society had an income of £17,600 and a total expenditure of £25,000. We estimate that the amount of grants given to individuals for social welfare purposes totalled around £24,000.

Applications

Application forms are available from the correspondent and can be submitted directly by the individual.

Other information

The charity is also known as the Society for the Relief of Necessitous Protestant Ministers, their Widows and Orphans.

The Pyncombe Charity

£14,000

Correspondent: Rita Butterworth, Administrator, Wingletye, Lawford, Crowcombe, Taunton TA4 4AQ (01984 618388; email: joeandrita@waitrose.com)

CC number: 202255

Eligibility

Serving Anglican clergy under 70 years of age and their immediate families who are resident with them, who are in financial need resulting from a serious illness, an injury or special circumstances.

Types of grants

Small, one-off grants.

Annual grant total

In 2013/14 the charity had an income of £17,200 and an expenditure of £15,600. We estimate that the amount of grants given to individuals totalled £14,000.

Exclusions

No grants are given towards educational expenses.

Applications

Applications must be made through the diocesan bishop on a form available from the correspondent. Applications should be submitted by April. No direct applications can be considered and the charity has told us the majority of the direct applications received are ineligible. **Note:** it is important that the financial impact of the applicant's circumstances is clearly stated and quantified in the application.

Other information

The charity also makes donations to Pyncombe Educational Foundation and towards the repairs and maintenance of Poughill parish church.

The Rehoboth Trust

£16,500

Correspondent: Shakti Singh Sisodia, Trustee, 71 Rydal Gardens, Hounslow TW3 2JJ (020 8893 3700; website: www. rehobothtrust.org.uk)

CC number: 1114454

Eligibility

Christian ministers or retired ministers who are in need. Grants are prioritised geographically in the following order: the county of Newport; the area comprising the counties of Torfaen, Monmouth, Caerphilly and Blaenau Gwent; the rest of Wales.

Types of grants

Grants given according to need.

Annual grant total

In 2014 the trust had an income of £34,500 and a total expenditure of £33,000. We estimate that the amount of grants given to individuals totalled £16,500. No accounts were available to view at the time of writing.

Applications

Apply in writing to the correspondent.

Other information

Grants are also made to organisations.

The Retired Ministers' and Widows' Fund

£31,000 (38 grants)

Correspondent: Bill Allen, Administrator, 7 Wendover Lodge, Church Street, Welwyn, Hertfordshire AL6 9LR (01438 489171; email: billallen1960@gmail.com; website: www. retiredministers.org.uk)

CC number: 233835

Eligibility

Retired ministers, and ministers' widows of Presbyterian, Independent (including Unitarian, Free Christian, Congregational and the United Reformed) and Baptist churches, who live in England and Wales and are on a low income. In 2013/14 this was defined as those with an income (not including state benefits) of less than £5,200 (£7,800 for married couples) and savings not exceeding £40,000. The savings limit for one-off grants is £10,000, although any of these limits may be disregarded in exceptional circumstances, such as when an application is made by a resident of a nursing home.

Types of grants

Bi-annual payments, which in 2013/14 totalled £670 a year for widows and single ministers and £930 a year for married ministers. Christmas gifts are also awarded. One-off grants of up to £375 may also be awarded to help in an emergency. Priority will be given to those already registered with the charity.

A maximum of two one-off grants may be received in a four year period by any single beneficiary.

Annual grant total

In 2013/14 the fund held assets of £759,000 and had an income of £36,500. Welfare grants, including Christmas gifts, to 38 individuals (19 in England and 19 in Wales) totalled £31,000. No one-off grants were awarded during the year.

Applications

Application forms are available from the correspondent. Applications can be submitted by the individual but should be signed by a local minister.

Other information

This fund has its origins in 1733.

George Richards' Charity

£15,000

Correspondent: Dr Paul Simmons, Correspondent, Flat 96, Thomas More House, Barbican, London EC2Y 8BU (020 7588 5583)

CC number: 246965

Eligibility

Church of England clergy who are in need and their widows and dependants. Preference is given to older people and those in poor health.

Types of grants

One-off and recurrent grants for heating expenses, household costs, travel, education, clothing, Christmas gifts and medical care. Pensions are available for those who have been forced to retire early from active ministry and are on a low income.

Annual grant total

In 2014 the charity had an income of £22,500 and a total expenditure of £16,000. Grants are made to individuals in need and we estimate the total amount given in this financial year to be around £15,000.

Exclusions

No grants are given for repaying debts.

Applications

Apply on a form available from the correspondent, including details of all sources of income. Applications should be submitted directly by the individual. They are usually considered twice a year.

The Sheffield West Riding Charitable Society Trust

£4,900

Correspondent: Malcolm Fair, Diocesan Secretary, Diocesan Church House, 95–99 Effingham Street, Rotherham, South Yorkshire S65 1BL (01709 309100; email: malcolm.fair@sheffield.anglican. org; website: www.sheffield.anglican.org)

CC number: 1002026

Eligibility

Clergymen of the Church of England in the diocese of Sheffield who are in need. Also their widows, orphans or distressed families, and people keeping house, or who have kept house, for clergymen of the Church of England in the diocese or their families.

Types of grants

One-off and recurrent grants, usually of £100 to £1,000.

Annual grant total

In 2014 the trust had an income of £13,900 and a total expenditure of £10,100. We estimate that social welfare grants to individuals totalled £4,900.

Applications

An application form is available from the correspondent.

Other information

Welfare grants are also made to the clergy, house-keepers and disadvantaged families in the diocese.

The Henry Smith Charity (UK)
See entry on page 13

The Society for the Relief of Poor Clergymen

£18,000 (37 grants)

Correspondent: The Treasurer, SRPC, 312 Waterside Court, Millpond Place, Carshalton, Surrey SM5 2JT (020 3652 0551; email: treasurer@srpc-aid.com; website: srpc-aid.com)

CC number: 232634

Eligibility

Evangelical ordained ministers and accredited lay workers and their dependants or widows/widowers in the Church of England, the Church in Wales, the Church of Ireland and the Scottish Episcopal Church.

Types of grants

One-off grants to help with illness or financial support when it can be shown that the illness has caused distress and hardship to the individual or family.

Annual grant total

In 2014 the society had an income of £23,000 and a total expenditure of £21,000. According to the charity's website, 37 grants were awarded in the year. We estimate that the amount of grants given to individuals totalled around £18,000.

Exclusions

Grants are not given towards school fees or normal travel expenses.

Applications

Apply on a form available to download from the website. Applications can be submitted directly by the individual or through a third party without the knowledge of the individual and in confidence if the individual is not inclined to apply. Completed forms should be returned by email to secretary@srpc-aid.com or by post to The Secretary, SRPC, c/o CPAS, Unit 3, Sovereign Court One, Sir William Lyons Road, University of Warwick, Science Park, Coventry CV4 7EZ.

Sons and Friends of the Clergy

£1.3 million

Correspondent: The Rt Revd Graeme Knowles, Registrar, 1 Dean Trench Street, Westminster, London SW1P 3HB (020 7799 3696; email: enquiries@ clergycharities.org.uk; website: www. clergycharities.org.uk)

CC number: 207736

Eligibility

The charity's record on the Charity Commission states: 'The charity provides financial assistance to clergy of the Anglican communion in the UK, Eire and the diocese in Europe (and elsewhere if working for a UK-based missionary society) and their widows/ widowers and dependants.'

Types of grants

See also the 'Applications' section. In the past, funding has been given to assist with, for example: bereavement expenses; children's car seats; child maintenance; clothing; contact grants for maintaining contact with children after separation or divorce; counselling; debts; financial management courses; heating expenses; holidays; hospital travel; medical expenses; nursing home fees; ordinands; removals and resettlement for clergy/ retired clergy; retirement housing; and sabbaticals and retreats.

Annual grant total

In 2014 the charity had assets of £89.1 million and an income of £4 million. During the year, 1,332 grants were awarded to individuals and four to organisations totalling £2.1 million. Grants for welfare purposes amounted to £1.3 million and were distributed as follows:

General welfare	£599,000
Holidays	£403,000
Resettlement and house expenses	£185,000
Christmas	£77,500
Debt	£36,500
Bereavement	£27,000

The figures in this table may also include funding awarded to organisations.

An additional £817,000 was given for educational purposes.

Exclusions

Exclusions are usually described on the charity's website. Contact the correspondent for more information.

Applications

At the time of writing (November 2015) the charity was in the process of updating its website. A message posted on 2 March 2015 read: 'We are currently in the process of updating our website. For information about grants please telephone (020 7799 3696) or email (enquiries@clergycharities.org.uk)'.

Other information

According to the charity's website:

The charity was founded in 1655 by a group of merchants in the City of London and clergymen who were all sons of the cloth. During the Commonwealth, persecution of clergy who had remained loyal to the Crown was widespread and many who had been deprived of their livings by Cromwell were destitute. The charity's foundation dates from a recognition by a body of sons of clergymen that action was required to meet a pressing need among clergy families for charitable help. The charity's present name is often felt to be a misleading one, but it is in fact an accurate description of its founding fathers.

The Foundation of Edward Storey

£157,500 (272 grants)

Correspondent: Timothy Burgess, Clerk to the Trustees, Storey's House, Mount Pleasant, Cambridge CB3 0BZ (01223 364405; email: info@edwardstorey.org.uk; website: www.edwardstorey.org.uk)

CC number: 203653

Eligibility

'Financially unsupported' (i.e. single, separated, divorced or widowed) women who fall into either of two qualifying categories:

a) Women over 40 living within the county of Cambridgeshire

b) Widows, ex-wives or dependants of Church of England clergy; women priests, deacons or deaconesses of the Church of England; clergywomen, missionaries, or other women with a close professional connection with the Church of England.

Types of grants

One-off grants or recurrent grants and pensions (which are annually reviewable and renewable). Pensions to older lay women are also occasionally available (only to those over 60). Some grants are issued with contractual terms of repayment. Christmas gifts may also be issued to residents or individuals in the local community.

Annual grant total

In 2013/14 the foundation held assets of £14.5 million and had an income of £1.4 million. Grants to individuals totalled £157,500 and were distributed as follows:

Parish grants	212	£89,500
Clergy widow pensions	22	£23,000
Clergy widow grants	15	£23,000
Parish pensions	23	£22,000

A grant of £500 was also awarded to one organisation in 2013/14.

Applications

Application forms are available from the correspondent. Applications can be submitted directly by the individual or a family member (if sponsored by a suitable third party), through a third party such as a social worker, Diocesan Widows' Officers, Diocesan Visitors, clergy and so on, or through an organisation such as Citizens Advice or other welfare agency. Applicants may be visited by the foundation's Grants Officer. Applications are considered on a regular basis.

Other information

The foundation also manages sheltered accommodation and a residential home based across four different sites.

Tancred's Charity for Pensioners

£22,000

Correspondent: Andrew Penny, Clerk, Forsters, 31 Hill Street, London W1J 5LS (020 7863 8522; email: andrew.penny@forsters.co.uk)

CC number: 229936

Eligibility

Men and women aged 50 or over who are UK citizens and clergy of the Church of England or Church in Wales, or who have been commissioned officers in the armed forces.

Types of grants

Annual pensions of around £2,250 a year are paid quarterly to a limited number of beneficiaries.

Annual grant total

In 2014 the charity had an income of £23,000 and a total expenditure of £28,000. Pensions to individuals totalled £22,000. At the year's end, the charity was assisting ten pensioners, all of whom were retired clergymen including one retired army chaplain.

Applications

Apply in writing to the correspondent. Individuals may apply at any time, but applications can only be considered when a vacancy occurs, which is approximately once a year.

Other information

The charity is administered along with the Tancred's Educational Foundation.

The Thornton Fund

£2,800

Correspondent: Dr Jane Williams, Trustee, 93 Fitzjohn Avenue, Barnet EN5 2HR (020 8440 2211; email: djanewilliams@dsl.pipex.com)

CC number: 226803

Eligibility

Ministers and ministerial students of the Unitarian church and their families who are in need.

Types of grants

One-off grants, usually ranging from £250 to £1,500. In the past grants have been given towards convalescence, counselling, the replacement of equipment not covered by insurance, and taxis for somebody unable to drive for medical reasons.

Annual grant total

In 2014 the fund had an income of £20,500 and a total expenditure of £11,300. Grants are made to individuals for both welfare and educational purposes, and occasionally to Unitarian and Free Christian churches for special projects. We estimate that social welfare grants to individuals totalled £2,800.

Applications

Apply in writing to the correspondent through a third party such as a minister. Requests are considered on an ongoing basis.

The Wells Clerical Charity

£3,700

Correspondent: Ven. Nicola Sullivan, Trustee, 6 The Liberty, Wells, Somerset BA5 2SU (01749 670777; email: general@ bathwells.anglican.org)

CC number: 248436

Eligibility

Clergy of the Church of England who have served in the historic archdeaconry of Wells, and their dependants, who are in need.

Types of grants

One-off grants according to need.

Annual grant total

In 2014 the charity had an income of £9,000 and a total expenditure of £7,600. Grants are made to individuals for both social welfare and educational purposes. We estimate that social welfare grants totalled £3,700.

Applications

Apply in writing to the correspondent.

The Widows' Fund

£58,000

Correspondent: John Cook, Correspondent, Kingsmead, Upton Road, Prenton CH43 7QQ (0151 652 4943)

CC number: 248657

Eligibility

Protestant ministers over 60 and their widows, widowers and children who are in need. Ministers who have been prevented from continuing in their ministries due to poor health or disability may also qualify for assistance.

Types of grants

Recurrent grants to supplement a low income and one-off emergency grants for specific purposes.

Annual grant total

In 2014 the fund had an income of £24,500 and a total expenditure of £58,500. We estimate that grants awarded totalled £58,000. At the time of writing (November 2015) no accounts were available to view.

Applications

Apply in writing to the correspondent.

The Charles Wright Gowthorpe Fund and Clergy Augmentation Fund

See entry on page 30

Sciences and technology

The Architects' Benevolent Society

£607,000 (307 grants)

Correspondent: Robert Ball, Chief Executive, 43 Portland Place, London W1B 1QH (020 7580 2823; fax: 020 7580 7075; email: help@absnet.org.uk; website: www.absnet.org.uk)

CC number: 265139

Eligibility

People engaged or formerly engaged in the practice of architecture, and their dependants. This includes (but is not limited to) architects, assistants, technicians and technologists and landscape architects.

Types of grants

Recurrent monthly grants, one-off grants and interest-free loans.

Annual grant total

In 2013/14 the society held assets of £20.8 million and had an income of £1.4 million. Grants and gifts to 307 individuals totalled £607,000.

Exclusions

No educational grants.

Applications

A short application form is available from the correspondent or to download from the website. Applications can be submitted directly by the individual or through a social worker, Citizens Advice or other welfare agency. Once received, the society will arrange a visit by one of their welfare officers. Applications are considered throughout the year.

Other information

Details of the grants available and the awards procedure are contained within the trustees' annual report for 2013/14. Grants are made to those who need help on a regular basis and gifts are provided for specific essential items that a person would otherwise be unable to afford. Interest-free loans are sometimes made where a beneficiary may be able to repay the society at some time in the future.

The committee works in close co-operation with two full-time welfare officers who visit most beneficiaries in person annually and as a result have first-hand knowledge of the circumstances of each case. Assessments and recommendations are prepared by the welfare team for consideration by the committee. Visiting people in their own homes is believed to be an essential part of the assistance given to people in need and visiting is written into the charity's constitution as one of the basic ways in which help is provided.

The welfare officers keep up to date with the latest information on state benefits in order to be able to give advice on subjects such as universal credit, and with colleagues in other professional benevolent funds.

The society can provide financial assistance very rapidly in cases of pressing need and is able to do so within 24 hours when necessary. In this regard the welfare team works closely with the chair of the case committee who is authorised to agree urgent applications for financial help between committee meetings. The society's trained welfare officers can offer support and information on various issues, including those relating to the state's benefit system.

The Benevolent Fund administered by the Institute of Physics

£23,000 (19 grants)

Correspondent: Simon Kellas, Correspondent, Institute of Physics, 76 Portland Place, London W1B 1NT (020 7470 4843; email: simon.kellas@iop. org; website: www.iop.org)

CC number: 209746

Eligibility

Physicists and members of their family in need, whether members of the institute or not.

Types of grants

One-off and recurrent grants are given according to need.

Annual grant total

In 2014 the fund held assets of £1.5 million and had an income of £26,000. Grants to 19 individuals totalled £23,000.

Applications

Apply in writing to the correspondent, marked 'Private and confidential'. The committee meets periodically through the year although emergency cases can be considered more urgently.

Other information

The benevolent fund also provides free access to legal advice; see the Institute of Physics website for details.

John Murdoch's Trust

£4,000

Correspondent: The Trust Administrator, c/o The Royal Bank of Scotland plc, Eastwood House, Glebe Road, Chelmsford, Essex CM1 1RS

OSCR number: SC004031

Eligibility

People in need who are over the age of 50 and have pursued science, in any of its branches, either as amateurs or professionals.

Types of grants

Our research suggests that yearly allowances and one-off grants, on average of about £200–£1,000, are offered. Awards are given for general relief-in-need purposes not for scientific needs.

Annual grant total

In 2013/14 the trust had an income of £44,000 and an expenditure of 31,500. Our research indicates that the annual total amount of grants given to individuals varies but is usually in the range of about £4,000 a year.

Applications

Application forms are available from the correspondent. Grants are normally considered twice a year.

The Royal Society of Chemistry Benevolent Fund

£76,500

Correspondent: Benevolent Fund Team, Thomas Graham House, Science Park, Milton Road, Cambridge CB4 0WF (01223 432227; website: www.rsc.org/awards-funding/funding/benevolent-fund)

CC number: 207890

Eligibility

People who have been members of the society for the last three years, or ex-members who were in the society for at least ten years, and their dependants, who are in need.

Types of grants

The fund can provide a range of support depending on the individual's circumstances. Forms of support include: regular monthly grants to assist with essential living costs and medical expenses; one-off grants for unexpected expenses such as a fridge or car repair; one-off grants towards redecoration and home adaptations; and support with respite breaks for carers.

Annual grant total

In 2014 the Benevolent Fund had an expenditure of £153,000 and grants were made for both social welfare and educational purposes. We estimate that social welfare grants to individuals totalled £76,500.

Exclusions

Anything which should be provided by the government or local authority is ineligible. Retrospective funding cannot be given.

Applications

Individuals should, in the first instance, contact the correspondent to discuss their situation. An application form will then be sent. The fund's webpage states: 'As part of assessing and supporting your application, we will ask that all sources of relevant state benefits have been explored.' The fund may also be able to signpost to other sources of potential support. Applications can be submitted by post or electronically and require information on the individual's personal and financial circumstances. If there are difficulties in completing an application form, the benevolent fund team can be contacted for assistance. The fund's advisor reviews applications to ensure all relevant information has been gathered and as a final check for eligibility. Following this, applications are presented to the Benevolent Fund's Grants Committee, which meets four times a year.

Other information

The society also provides advice and guidance services.

UBA Benevolent Fund

£52,000

Correspondent: Elaine Price, Fund Manager and Secretary, Unit CU1, Warrington Business Park, Long Lane, Warrington WA2 8TX (01925 633005; email: info@tnibf.org; website: www.tnibf.org)

CC number: 208729

Eligibility

Past and present employees of United Kingdom Atomic Energy Authority, British Nuclear Fuels, Amersham International or any successor/spin-off organisation who are in need, and their dependants.

With the many changes that have taken place in the Nuclear Industry, the fund now helps people in a wide range of organisations which are linked back to the original eligible organisations. Contact the fund if you are unsure of your eligibility.

Types of grants

Financial assistance is given to cover both short and long-term problems. Typical examples of assistance might be help with everyday things like essential appliances or household repairs. Interest-free loans are also available.

Annual grant total

In 2013/14 the fund held assets of £3.1 million and had an income of £74,500. Welfare grants and allowances to individuals totalled £52,000 and a further £13,500 was given in interest-free loans.

Exclusions

Grants are not given for private health care (excluding convalescence and residential home fees) or private education.

Applications

Application forms are available from the correspondent. Applications may be channelled through the network of local representatives, located at or near the organisations' sites; direct to the fund's office; or through other charities or similar bodies.

Secretarial and administration

The Chartered Secretaries' Charitable Trust

£54,500 (108 grants)

Correspondent: Elizabeth Howarth, Charities Officer, Saffron House, 6–10 Kirby Street, London EC1N 8TS (020 7612 7048; email: icsacharities@icsa.org.uk; website: www.icsa.org.uk/about-us/charitable-trust)

CC number: 1152784

Eligibility

Members and former members, graduates, students, employees or former employees of the institute, and their dependants, who are in need and live in the UK, Eire and associated territories. Note that there are more detailed conditions on the range and extent which govern eligibility.

Types of grants

Weekly allowances and regular support according to need, for example towards telephone line or mobile rental, broadband, white goods, house repairs, rental for emergency alarm systems and TV rental and licences. One-off grants are given for specific items and services, often paid directly to the supplier, including those for clothing, dental work, medical aids, clearance of debts, decorating or property repairs. Interest-free loans are also considered.

Annual grant total

In 2013/14 the trust had assets of £5.58 million and an income of £32,500. During the year, the trust assisted 108 beneficiaries and welfare support was given totalling £61,500, including £7,100 in interest-free loans. Grants were distributed as follows:

Allowances	£26,500
Grants	£17,200
Telephone line, mobile rental and broadband subscription payments	£5,800
ICSA subscriptions	£3,000
Emergency alarms	£2,100

Included in these figures are Christmas gifts totalling £7,000 and winter grants amounting to £5,000.

Applications

Application forms are available from the correspondent. Requests can be made throughout the year. Institute members (volunteers) visit beneficiaries, where necessary. Contact the correspondent if assistance in making the application is required.

Other information

The current body was established in 2013 to bring together three charities. The trustees' annual report and accounts for 2013/14 states: 'The ICSA Benevolent Fund, the ICSA Education and Research Foundation and the ICSA Prize Fund were successfully brought together from 1 August 2013 into one new charitable company named "The Chartered Secretaries' Charitable Trust".'

There are prizes offered to highest achieving students in ICSA examinations (in 2013/14 awards were made totalling around £1,700).

Skilled crafts and trades

The Barbers' Amalgamated Charity

£8,000

Correspondent: Col. P. Durrant, Clerk, The Worshipful Company of Barbers, Barber-Surgeons' Hall, 1A Monkwell Square, Wood Street, London EC2Y 5BL (020 7606 0741; email: clerk@barberscompany.org; website: www.barberscompany.org)

CC number: 213085

Eligibility

Poor, generally older, members of the medical, barber or hairdressing professions and their dependants.

Types of grants

Annual pensions.

Annual grant total

In 2013/14 the charity had an income of £13,100 and a total expenditure of £8,200. We estimate that the amount of grants given to individuals totalled £8,000.

Applications

Apply in writing to the correspondent directly by the individual or via a family member, or through an organisation such as Citizens Advice or other welfare agency. Applications are considered throughout the year.

The Bespoke Tailors' Benevolent Association

£91,000 (48 grants)

Correspondent: Elizabeth Fox, Secretary, 65 Tierney Road, London SW2 4QH (07831 520801; email: Elizabeth.Fox@ukgateway.net)

CC number: 212954

Eligibility

'Journeyman tailors and tailoresses' and their near relatives who were employed in the bespoke (made to measure) tailoring trade. Preference is given to past and present members of the institute but help can be given to other eligible applicants.

Types of grants

Small, one-off grants and regular allowances. Previously, allowances have been in the region of £20 a week.

Annual grant total

In 2013/14 the charity had an income of £126,000 and total assets of £2.8 million. During the year, the charity provided grants of £91,000 to 48 beneficiaries.

Applications

Application forms are available from the correspondent. Applications should preferably be submitted through a social worker. However, those submitted directly by the individual or through another third party will be considered.

Other information

In late 2012 the Tailors Benevolent Institute and the Master Tailors Benevolent Association merged to form the Bespoke Tailors Benevolent Association.

The British Antique Dealers' Association Benevolent Fund

£5,000

Correspondent: Mark Dodgson, Secretary, 20 Rutland Gate, London SW7 1BD (020 7589 4128)

CC number: 238363

Eligibility

Members and former members of the association who are in need, and their dependants.

Types of grants

One-off or recurrent grants ranging from £100 to £2,000 for needs such as assistance with household bills.

Annual grant total

In 2014 the fund had an income of £8,500 and a total expenditure of £5,400. We estimate that the total amount of grants awarded to individuals was approximately £5,000.

Applications

Application forms are available from the correspondent. Applicants should provide two references from members or former members of the association. Applications are considered on a regular basis.

The British Jewellery, Giftware and Finishing Federation Benevolent Society

£34,000 (62 grants)

Correspondent: Lynn Snead, Secretary, Federation House, 10 Vyse Street, Hockley, Birmingham B18 6LT (0121 236 2657; email: enquiries@batf.uk.com; website: www.thebenevolentsociety.co.uk)

CC number: 208722

Eligibility

People in financial need or who have a disability who have worked in the industries covered by the federation, and their dependants. Eligible trades are jewellery manufacture and distribution, giftware, surface engineering and travel goods and fashion accessories industries.

Types of grants

One-off grants are given towards the provision of essential items such as cookers, washing machines, fridges, freezers, bedding, winter clothing, telephone rental, television licence fees and household repairs. Recurrent grants are also paid to those on a low income. Interest-free loans may also be awarded.

Annual grant total

In 2014 the society had assets of £790,500 and an income of £97,000. Grants were made to 62 individuals totalling £34,000.

Applications

Apply on a form on the charity's website. The charity can offer assistance with completing the form if needed. Applications can be submitted either directly by the individual or through a social worker, Citizens Advice, welfare agency or other third party. Applications are considered at quarterly trustee meetings, but urgent requests may be dealt outside meetings. The charity visits applicants where possible.

Other information

In 2014 the charity also provided a day out at Blenheim Palace for local beneficiaries.

The Ceramic Industry Welfare Society

£6,000

Correspondent: The Secretary, Unity Trades Union, Hillcrest House, Garth Street, Stoke-on-Trent ST1 2AB (01782 272755)

CC number: 261248

Eligibility

People in need who are or have been employed in the ceramics industry, or widows of former employees.

Types of grants

Recurrent grants are fixed at £45 per six week period depending on the circumstances of the applicant as confirmed by the society's representative through a personal visit.

Annual grant total

In 2014 the society had an income of £4,500 and a total expenditure of £6,700. We estimate that the amount of grants given to individuals totalled £6,000.

Exclusions

No grants are payable beyond 12 months of the date of retirement.

Applications

Apply in writing to the correspondent.

The Cotton Industry War Memorial Trust

£117,500 (190 grants)

Correspondent: Peter Booth, Secretary, Stables Barn, Coldstones Farm, Bewerley, Harrogate HG3 5BJ (01423 711205; email: ciwmt@btinternet.com)

CC number: 242721

Eligibility

People in need who have worked in the cotton textile industry in the north west of England. This includes weaving, spinning and dyeing. Cotton industry workers who were badly injured while fighting for HM Forces in wartime may also be eligible.

Types of grants

Convalescence arrangements are made for people who are in poor health or who have suffered injury due to their work in the cotton textiles industry. The trust makes arrangements for beneficiaries' convalescence at commercial hotels in Blackpool. One-off grants may also be awarded for specific needs.

Annual grant total

In 2014 the trust held assets of almost £6.7 million and had an income of £322,500. The trust arranged convalescence for 193 individuals through the trust's Convalescent Scheme, totalling £116,000. Three one-off grants were made to individuals in need, totalling £1,200. A further £123,500 was awarded to organisations.

Exclusions

People who have worked with clothing, footwear, hosiery and other man-made fabrics are not eligible.

Applications

Application forms are available from the correspondent. Note that the correspondent cannot send forms directly to applicants, only to employers, trade unions, SSAFA or similar welfare agencies for them to pass on to potential beneficiaries. Applicants must show that they have worked in the textile industry and provide medical evidence if claiming assistance due to employment injury or disability. Applications are considered quarterly.

Other information

The trust gives substantial grants to educational bodies to assist eligible students in furthering their textile studies, to other bodies which encourage recruitment into or efficiency in the industry and to organisations furthering the interests of the industry by research and so on. Grants are also made to charitable organisations.

The Fashion and Textile Children's Trust

£85,000

Correspondent: Grants Co-ordinator, Office 1 and 2, J411/412 The Biscuit Factory, 100 Clements Road, London SE16 4DG (0300 123 9002; fax: 020 7691 9356; email: grants@ftct.org.uk; website: www.ftct.org.uk)

CC number: 257136

Eligibility

Children and young people under 18 years old whose parents or full-time carer work or have worked (within the last nine years) in the UK fashion and textile retailing and manufacturing industry.

Types of grants

See the trust's website for full details of grants available. The trust concentrates its grant-giving on supporting children in their education; however, it also makes well-being grants for children and young people who have illness, disabilities, behavioural and psychological problems, or who are facing various social issues. Grants are usually given towards needs such as: essential items including clothing, bedding and white goods; therapies; respite activities; mobility equipment; specialist clothing; and home adaptations.

Annual grant total

In 2013/14 the trust had assets of £8.5 million and an income of £591,500. Grants to children for purposes associated with their well-being amounted to £85,000.

Applications

First contact the Grants Co-ordinator by telephone or by using the online enquiry form to discuss your child's needs and to see if the trust may be able to assist. You should have evidence of your connection to the trade to hand (P45/P60/an employer's letter/an NI letter). If the Grants Co-ordinator feels that the trust may be able to help, an application form will be sent to you. It may be returned at any time and the trust can offer assistance with completing it. Supporting evidence, which must be provided, is listed on the website.

The Feltmakers Charitable Foundation

£10,500

Correspondent: Maj. J. T. H. Coombs, Clerk to the Trustees, Post Cottage, The Street, Greywell, Hook, Hampshire RG29 1DA (01256 703174; email: jcpartnership@btopenworld.com; website: www.feltmakers.co.uk)

CC number: 259906

Eligibility
Employees or former employees of the hat trade who are in need.

Types of grants
Annual pensions.

Annual grant total
In 2013/14 the foundation had assets of £547,000 and an income of £55,000. Support for pensioner hatters totalled £11,000, of which pensions amounted to £10,500.

A further £25,000 was awarded to 14 charitable organisations.

Applications
Applicants must be nominated in the first place by their employer or former employer or, in exceptional circumstances, by a welfare organisation.

Other information
The foundation supports current and historical research into felt making and the general promotion of the trade. During 2013/14, the foundation contributed £5,500 in support of the Feltmaker Awards.

Footwear Friends

£65,500 (194 grants)

Correspondent: Gabi O'Sullivan, Secretary, Footwear Benevolent Society, 5th Floor, 15–16 Margaret Street, London W1W 8RW (020 7323 2362; email: info@footwearfriends.org.uk; website: www.footwearfriends.org.uk)

CC number: 222117

Eligibility
People who are working or have worked in the boot trade and footwear industry, usually for a minimum of five years, and their dependants.

Types of grants
One-off grants and recurrent payments. Grants are available for, for example, hardware, appliances, furnishings, special equipment for people with disabilities or essential repairs. Funding is also available towards convalescent holidays. Recurrent grants may be paid once every six months, or seasonally at Christmas and mid-year.

Annual grant total
In 2014/15 the society held assets of £1.2 million and had an income of £128,500. Financial assistance to 194 individuals totalled more than £65,500.

Christmas grants	£16,800
One-off grants	£16,300
Mid-year grants	£16,100
Half yearly allowances	£7,200
December bonus grants	£6,100
Christmas grants	£2,500
Holiday grants	£700

Applications
Apply on a form available from the correspondent or to download from the society's website. Applications can be completed by the individual or a third party. If completed by the individual, it must be verified by someone who has known the applicant for some time, who works in a professional capacity and is not related to the applicant; or a third party acting on behalf of the applicant, for example a welfare adviser.

Other information
Also known as the Footwear Benevolent Society and formerly as The Boot Trade Benevolent Society.

The Hugh Fraser Foundation (Emily Fraser Trust)

£30,000

Correspondent: Heather Thompson, Administrator, Turcan Connell, Princes Exchange, 1 Earl Grey Street, Edinburgh EH3 9EE (0131 228 8111; email: ht@turcanconnell.com)

OSCR number: SC009303

Eligibility
People in need who work or worked in the drapery, printing, publishing, bookselling, stationery and newspaper and allied trades and their dependants. The trustees consider applications particularly from individuals who are or were in the employment of House of Fraser Ltd, Scottish Universal Investments Ltd and Paisleys.

Types of grants
One-off grants of £100 to £4,000.

Annual grant total
In 2013/14 the trust had an income of £2.3 million and a total expenditure of £1.6 million. We estimate that the amount of grants given to individuals totalled around £30,000, with funding mainly awarded to organisations.

Applications
Apply in writing to the correspondent. The trustees meet on a quarterly basis and applications should be received three months before funding is required.

Note: the foundation's focus is on making grants to charitable organisations and only rarely, and in exceptional circumstances, will the trustees consider applications from individuals and their dependants.

The Furniture Makers' Company

£121,000 (175 grants)

Correspondent: Damilola Bamidele, Grants and Education Manager, 4th Floor, Furniture Makers' Hall, 12 Austin Friars, London EC2N 2HE (020 7256 5954; fax: 020 7256 5155; email: grantsandeducation@furnituremakers.org.uk; website: www.furnituremakers.org.uk)

CC number: 1015519

Eligibility
Current and former employees of the furnishing industry and their dependants who are in financial need. Applicants must have worked in the industry for a minimum of two years.

Types of grants
One-off grants averaging around £500 towards the needs associated with living costs, healthcare, education, or rest and recuperation. This may include, for example, the purchase of scooters, recliner chairs, TV licences, the installation of walk-in showers, central heating and telephone lines, the payment of rent arrears, interior decorating costs and so on. Quarterly annuities are £195 per quarter per beneficiary.

The Edenfield Holiday Scheme enables beneficiaries with ten years' experience in the industry to take respite breaks or holidays.

The charity states that 'there has been a greater tendency to help with grants rather than annuities'.

Annual grant total
In 2013/14 the charity held assets of £8.2 million and had an income of £611,000. Welfare grants to individuals totalled £121,000 and were distributed as follows:

Quarterly grants	£86,500
One-off grants	£34,500

There were 120 annuitants receiving support and 55 individuals receiving one-off grants to meet a specific need. No grants were made through the Edenfield Holiday Scheme in the year. A further £38,500 was awarded in student bursaries and for other needs.

Exclusions

Currently grants cannot be made for the following:

◗ Assistance towards the clearance of consumer credit debt
◗ Bankruptcy fees, including Low Income Low Asset routes and Debt Relief Orders
◗ Legal costs
◗ Private education fees (except in cases of disability)
◗ Replacement of statutory funding
◗ Non-essential home improvements
◗ Ongoing financial assistance, except in the case of annuities
◗ Loans of any kind
◗ Memorial stones
◗ Holidays (except through the Edenfield Holiday Scheme)

Applications

An application form is available to download from the charity's website. Once completed, forms should be posted or emailed to the correspondent. Documentary evidence of your employment within the UK furnishing industry will be required. The charity welcomes enquiries.

Other information

Bursaries are given to university students in order to complete their MA qualifications in Furniture Making and Design.

The charity states that the majority of people helped with welfare grants are over the age of 70.

The GPM Charitable Trust

£5,000

Correspondent: Keith Keys, c/o 43 Spriggs Close, Clapham, Bedford MK41 6GD (07733 262991; email: gpmcharitabletrust@tiscali.co.uk; website: www.gpmtrust.org)

CC number: 227177

Eligibility

Workers, former workers and their dependants in the printing, graphical, papermaking and media industries.

Types of grants

Grants have been made: to help with the purchase of mobility aids; to finance home improvements to enable applicants to remain in their own homes; and towards the cost of a respite or convalescent break.

Annual grant total

In 2013/14 the trust had an income of £7,700 and a total expenditure of £23,500. Grants are made to individuals and organisations for both social welfare and educational purposes. We estimate

that social welfare grants to individuals totalled £5,000.

During the year, the trust continued working with the Bookbinders Charitable Society on a refurbishment project for applicants in sheltered accommodation.

Applications

An application form can be downloaded from the website or requested from the correspondent. It must be printed and completed in black ink before being returned to the trust. The dates of application deadlines for subsequent trustee meetings are listed on the website.

Other information

Formed in 2001, the trust brought together the former Lloyd Memorial and NATSOPA (National Society of Operative Printers and Assistants) trusts. The Sheridan Trust, a Manchester-based printing charity, joined in 2010.

Hair and Beauty Benevolent

£100,000

Correspondent: HABB, 1st Floor, 9 Cheam Road, Ewell Village, Surrey KT17 1SP (01737 212494; email: info@ habb.org; website: www.habb.org)

Eligibility

Members and former members of the hairdressing and beauty industries and their dependants.

Types of grants

One-off and recurrent grants to those in need. Grants have been made for house adaptations, mobility aids, TV licences and holidays. In some cases regular financial assistance may be given.

The HABB children's welfare fund also provides one-off and recurrent grants. Grants have been made for monthly pocket money to children from low-income families as well as one-off grants for specialist equipment, holidays, school uniforms, bedding and Christmas/ birthday payments.

Annual grant total

HABB is not registered with the Charity Commission and so limited financial information was available. HABB's website notes that its fund needs '£150,000 a year to meet our existing commitments to beneficiaries and to take new requests for assistance on board.' We estimate that each year, grants to individuals total around £100,000. The fund currently supports more than 100 adults and children.

Exclusions

No assistance with non-priority debts or bankruptcy fees. The trust cannot help

those who have not worked in the profession since 1970.

Applications

Application forms are available to download from HABB's website or can be requested by writing or telephone from the correspondent. In order to process the application HABB will need to know: what help is needed, why the help is needed, the applicant's length of involvement in the industry and when they last worked in the industry. If it was the applicant's partner who worked in the industry, this information should be provided on them. After this initial enquiry HABB will notify eligible applicants, who can then download an application form from the website which should be returned along with copies of bank statements and proof of work in the industry.

Applications are decided on the second Tuesday of each month. All applicants will be informed of the decision in writing. Regular beneficiaries will have their cases reviewed annually.

Other information

HABB has been sponsored by a number of corporate partners including well known names such as L'Oreal, Wella and Schwarzkopf.

Institute of Clayworkers Benevolent Fund

£3,500

Correspondent: Francis Morrall, Trustee, British Ceramic Confederation, Federation House, Station Road, Stoke-on-Trent, Staffordshire ST4 2SA (01782 571846; email: francism@ceramfed.co. uk)

CC number: 212300

Eligibility

People in the clay-working industry, namely current and former employees of the British Ceramic Confederation member companies and members and ex-members of the institute, and their dependants. Applicants will normally be unable to work due to ill health or an accident.

Types of grants

Recurrent pensions and one-off grants, usually of £250. Our research indicates that in exceptional cases where applicants have been identified by other charitable bodies as being in extreme need, larger grants may be given.

Annual grant total

In 2014 the fund had an income of £3,000 and a total expenditure of £3,900. We estimate the annual total amount of grants given to individuals to be around £3,500.

Applications

Apply in writing to the correspondent. Applications should include age, length of service, date of termination of employment (if applicable), brief description (two or three sentences) of circumstances leading to application, and brief testimonial (a sentence or two) from a supervisor/manager, if appropriate. Our research suggests that the fund only accepts applications made through a former employer and not usually those made directly by the individual. Requests may be made at any time.

Leather and Hides Trades' Benevolent Institution

£63,500 (63 grants)

Correspondent: Karen Harriman, Secretary, 143 Barkby Road, Leicester LE4 9LG (0116 274 1500; email: karenharriman@btconnect.com; website: www.lhtbi.org.uk)

CC number: 206133

Eligibility

People who work or have worked in the leather trade (i.e. in the production of leather or in the handling of hide and skin) for ten years or more. Applicants are usually over 60, although people under 60 may also be considered. Bereaved spouses are also eligible to apply.

Types of grants

Currently, annuities of between £260 and £1,240 a year are paid quarterly. Grants towards residential or nursing home fees, special one-off payments for equipment and Christmas hampers.

Annual grant total

In 2014 the charity had assets of £844,000 and an income of £51,500. Annuities (paid to around 63 beneficiaries) and grants were made totalling more than £63,500.

Applications

Apply on a form available from the correspondent or through the charity's website. Applications can be submitted directly by the individual or through a social worker, Citizens Advice or other welfare agency. Applications can be considered at any time.

Note: Recurrent grants are subject to annual review.

The National Caravan Council (NCC) Benevolent Fund

£10,000

Correspondent: Mrs S. Amey, Trustee, PO Box 1421, Woking GU22 2ND (email: info@nccbf.org.uk; website: www.nccbf.org.uk)

CC number: 271625

Eligibility

People in need who are, or have been, employed in the caravan industry, and their dependants.

Types of grants

Normally one-off grants ranging from £200 to £2,500, although occasionally recurrent grants may be given. Smaller grants have been given to help with maintenance or unexpected bills, and larger ones have been made to help provide the likes of building adaptations or heating.

Annual grant total

In 2013/14 the fund had an income of £8,700 and a total expenditure of £11,700. We estimate that the amount of grants given to individuals totalled £10,000.

Applications

Apply on a form available from the correspondent including details of employment within the caravan industry. Applications can be submitted directly by the individual or through an appropriate third party.

Other information

The fund was established in 1976 by six key caravan industry leaders, 'initially to help those current, past or retired employees who have been involved with the caravan industry'. In 2010 the fund changed its status so it could support people in need from outside the caravan industry.

Through a partnership with Happy Days Children's Charity (1010943), the fund owns a touring caravan and a caravan holiday home which it uses to give disadvantaged children and their families the opportunity to enjoy a holiday experience.

The Printing Charity

£566,500

Correspondent: Henry Smith, Grants Officer, First Floor, Underwood House, 235 Three Bridges Road, Crawley, West Sussex RH10 1LS (01293 542820; fax: 01293 542826; email: info@ theprintingcharity.org.uk; website: www.theprintingcharity.org.uk)

CC number: 208882

Eligibility

People who have worked for at least three years in the printing profession, graphic arts or allied trades, and their dependants, who are in need. A list of eligible trades can be found on the charity's website.

Types of grants

One-off grants of about up to £2,000 (depending on the type) and recurrent payments of up to £25 per week. The website gives exact details of types and amounts available and this includes: bereavement allowance; care home top-up fees; communication aids; home adaptation; independent living help; mobility aids; miscellaneous; nursing home top-up fees; respite breaks; residential care; day centre fees; care service at home. Home repairs and adaptations, household items, bankruptcy fees, travel costs to and from the hospital and also emergency relief for people affected by natural disasters are also supported.

During extremely cold winters winter fuel allowances of £75 are sent those who receive regular assistance from the charity.

Annual grant total

In 2014 the charity had assets of £36.75 million and an income of £1.6 million. Grants were made to 530 individuals totalling £758,500 and can be broken down as follows:

Regular financial assistance	£332,500
One-off grants	£202,000
Future Proposals schemes	£114,500
Educational bursaries	£46,000
Nursing home grants	£32,000
The Prince's Trust partnership	£31,500

We take the amounts given as regular financial assistance, one-off grants and nursing home grants to represent social welfare support to individuals. Future Proposals schemes and the Prince's Trust partnership relate to programmes aimed at education and employment and are targeted at younger people.

Exclusions

Examples of what is not funded include:

▶ Grants for study or training overseas
▶ Grants for non-accredited or non-recognised training or education courses
▶ Grants above the charity's limits
▶ Holidays (with the exception of respite care breaks for the carer or person being cared for)
▶ To replace items or money that has been stolen unless the item is related to mobility or independent living
▶ Payments for parking fines or speeding tickets or any other fine imposed by the courts

- Legal fees or costs associated with solicitors' letters or interviews or any other kind of legal representation
- Applicants with high levels of savings that are over and above the set thresholds (for further information on this contact the correspondent)
- School fees unless there is a statemented educational need
- Pensions

Applications

Application forms and guidelines are available from the charity's website. Further information on the application process can also be received by contacting the correspondent. Assistance is means-tested so applicants should be prepared to make a full declaration of their finances, including state benefits and funding from other charitable sources. Applications can be made by individuals directly or through a welfare agency at any time.

The charity advises potential applicants to contact them before submitting an application. The Grant Officer's direct contacts are: 01293 649368, henry@theprintingcharity.org.uk.

The charity aims to acknowledge all applicants and assess the case within 15 working days.

Other information

The charity also provides sheltered homes for older people at Basildon and Bletchley and gives education and training help to individuals.

The trustees are looking to ensure that at least 51% of their support is given to people outside London and the South-East. The website states: 'We want to have an even greater impact and have committed to helping 2,000 people in 2017.'

Rainy Day Trust

£126,500 (174 grants)

Correspondent: Nicola Adams-Brown, Charity Administrator, British Home Enhancement Trade, 10 Vyse Street, Hockley, Birmingham B18 6LT (0121 237 1130; email: info@rainydaytrust.org. uk; website: www.rainydaytrust.org.uk)

CC number: 209170

Eligibility

People who are in need and have worked in the hardware/DIY, housewares, pottery and glass, brushware, builders merchants, garden supply and allied trades – normally for at least five years. The majority of beneficiaries are over 60 years old but younger individuals may also be eligible for assistance. The spouse or widower of an employee can also apply.

Types of grants

One-off grants towards, for example, mobility equipment and installation, travel expenses to see distant relatives, TV licences, nursing home and residential care fees, funeral expenses, assistance with utility bills, food hampers at Christmas, household equipment and so on. Recurrent grants may be given for healthcare costs.

Annual grant total

In 2014 the trust had assets of £1.8 million and an income of £165,500. Grants were made to 174 individuals totalling £126,500. These were broken down as follows:

Quarterly pensions	£85,500
Other grants	£29,000
Christmas hampers/grants	£4,400
Telephone grants	£3,900
Holiday grants	£1,700
TV licence grants	£1,100
Funeral grants	£1,000

Exclusions

No grants are given to children, or to people working in the steel and motor industries.

Applications

Apply on a form available from the correspondent or to download from the trust's website. Applications are considered at any time.

Other information

The trust visits the majority of beneficiaries every 12–18 months to review their needs.

The Scottish Hide and Leather Trades' Provident and Benevolent Society

£9,000

Correspondent: David Ballantine, Charity Administrator, c/o Mitchells Roberton Solicitors, George House, 36 North Hanover Street, Glasgow G1 2AD (0141 552 3422; fax: 0141 552 2935; email: info@mitchells-roberton.co. uk)

OSCR number: SC004504

Eligibility

People of retirement age who have worked in the Scottish hide and leather trades.

Types of grants

The society exists principally to provide pensions to its members. It also pays pensions to the widows and widowers of members who have survived their pensionable spouse. Donations equivalent to the annual pensions are also paid to people who have been employed in the trades but who are not members. Very occasionally one-off payments of about £100 to £200 are made for specific purposes, usually for the replacement of household equipment, such as a washing machine, fridge and so on.

Annual grant total

In 2014 the society had an income of £9,700 and a total expenditure of £9,500. We estimate that the amount of grants given to individuals totalled £9,000.

Applications

Most applicants have been recommended by other members of the society or local organisations.

The Silversmiths and Jewellers Charity

£57,500

Correspondent: Julie Griffin, Secretary, PO Box 61660, London SE9 9AN (020 8265 9288; email: info@thesjcharity.co. uk; website: www.tsjc.org.uk)

CC number: 205785

Eligibility

People in need who are, or have been, employed in any sector of the gold and silver smithing trade or the jewellery trade, and their dependants.

Types of grants

Quarterly payments, summer gifts (£50 in 2014), Christmas gifts (£200 in 2014) and Christmas hampers are given to regular grantees. One-off grants are also made for special needs such as domestic goods, furniture, bedding and hospital travel costs.

Annual grant total

In 2014 the society had an income of £195,000 and a total expenditure of £144,000. It has assets of £1.9 million which mainly consists of investments and are not available for distribution. Grants totalling £57,500 were made to individuals for social welfare purposes. 65 beneficiaries received regular grants during the year and three one-off grants were also made.

Applications

Apply on a form on the charity's website or in writing to the correspondent, including the details of the applicant, a summary of why the grant is needed and the amount required. Applications can be submitted directly by the individual or through a social worker, Citizens Advice or other welfare agency.

Other information

This charity was previously known as the Goldsmiths', Silversmiths' and Jewellers' Benevolent Society.

The Society of Motor Manufacturers and Traders Charitable Trust Fund

£3,000

Correspondent: Jenny Wallbank, Administrator, SMMT, 71 Great Peter Street, London SW1P 2BN (020 7344 9267; email: charitabletrust@smmt.co.uk; website: www.smmt.co.uk)

CC number: 209852

Eligibility

People in need who are associated with the motor industry, and their dependants.

Types of grants

One-off and recurrent grants are given according to need.

Annual grant total

In 2014 the fund had an income of £131,000 and a total expenditure of £78,800. Payments due to BEN for beneficiaries totalled £3,000.

Applications

Apply in writing to the correspondent.

Other information

During the year, grants were not given directly to individuals by the fund, but rather, they were made payable to BEN (Motor and Allied Trades Benevolent Fund), 'to cover the cost of specific contributions to a number of its beneficiaries'. The fund's annual report states that:

> Since 1990 under an informal arrangement, BEN have assisted in the administration of trust beneficiaries' income payments. This relationship arose as BEN was able to provide an existing structure within which the suitability for payment of prospective SMMT Charitable Trust Fund beneficiaries could be assessed.

In 2014 an additional payment of £25,000 was made to BEN, contributing to its refurbishment programme.

The fund also seeks to help 'young persons where such assistance would enable them to gain employment in the automotive sector'. Therefore, in 2014 the Foyer Federation, a charity that focuses on youth development, received £41,400 from the fund towards an automotive project for 70 beneficiaries. The fund's annual report states that 'the trustees were very pleased with the results of the 2014 Foyer Federation project, and have since agreed to make a further grant to the Federation for a continuation of the project into 2015'.

The Textile Benevolent Association (1970)

£13,000

Correspondent: Sandra O'Hara, Administrator, 156 Alnwick Road, London SE12 9BS (020 8851 8728)

CC number: 261862

Eligibility

People in need who are employees and former employees of: wholesalers and retailers engaged in the textile trade; and of manufacturers in the trade which distribute to retailers as well as manufacture. The wives, widows, husbands and widowers of such people can also benefit.

Types of grants

Grants are towards holidays, winter fuel bills, clothing, cookers, washing machines and so on.

Annual grant total

At the time of writing (November 2015), the latest financial information available was from 2012/13.

In 2012/13 the association had an income of £1,800 and a total expenditure of £69,000. We estimate that the total amount of grants awarded to individuals was approximately £13,000 based on previous giving.

Applications

Apply on a form available from the correspondent, usually via employers, doctors or social services.

The Timber Trades Benevolent Society

£111,500

Correspondent: Ivan Savage, General Manager, Masons Croft, 19 Church Lane, Oulton, Stone ST15 8UL (084489222 05; email: info@ttbs.org.uk; website: www.ttbs.org.uk)

CC number: 207734

Eligibility

People who have worked for a minimum of 10 (or five in exceptional circumstances) years for a firm selling timber commercially, such as timber merchants, importers or exporters or agents and their dependants. Note the society does not cover carpenters or joiners.

Types of grants

Grants have been awarded towards heating installation, adaptation of cars for use by people with disabilities, domestic appliances, phone rentals, TV rental or licences, hampers, funeral costs house repairs or essential car

maintenance. Winter fuel grants (£300 in 2013) are also made. Regular allowances are paid quarterly (£150 per quarter).

Annual grant total

In 2014 the society had assets of £3 million and an income of £277,000. Grants to individuals totalled £111,500 and were broken down as follows:

Regular payments	£39,500
Winter fuel payments	£30,000
Christmas gifts	£17,200
Telephone rental	£13,200
TV Licences and sets	£4,200
Occasional grants	£4,000
Spring gifts	£2,700
Holiday grants	£600

Exclusions

No grants are made towards care or nursing home fees. The society will not support furniture manufacturers and carpenters servicing the building trade.

Applications

Application forms are available from the correspondent. Applications can be submitted directly by the individual or through a social worker, Citizens Advice, welfare agency or other third party. They are considered on a regular basis.

The Tobacco Pipe Makers and Tobacco Trade Benevolent Fund

£222,500 (Around 200 grants)

Correspondent: Ralph Edmondson, Secretary, 2 Spa Close, Brill, Aylesbury, Buckinghamshire HP18 9RZ (01844238655; fax: 020 8663 0949; email: info@tobaccocharity.org.uk; website: www.tobaccocharity.org.uk)

CC number: 1135646

Eligibility

People who have been engaged for a substantial period of time in the manufacture, wholesale or retail sections of the tobacco industry, and their dependants, who are in need. Both full-time and part-time workers are eligible for assistance. Applicants should have no more than £12,000 in savings/capital (not including property).

Types of grants

Recurrent payments and one-off grants, mainly for household items, television licences and house repairs. Grants are also given to help with winter fuel costs and at birthdays and Christmas.

Annual grant total

In 2013/14 the fund held assets of £6.2 million and had an income of £391,500. Grants to made to around 200 individuals totalled £222,500 and were distributed as follows:

Pensions and general relief	£82,000
Maintenance grants	£58,000
One-off grants	£38,000
Welfare assistance	£18,400
TV rentals and licences	£12,800
Christmas and birthday gifts	£13,900
House insurance	£900

Applications

Application forms are available from the correspondent or to download from the website. They can be submitted directly by the individual or through a social worker, Citizens Advice, welfare agency or other third party. Applicants are asked to provide details of the length of their service in the tobacco trade, financial position and whether they own their own home. Applications are considered regularly throughout the year.

Other information

The fund was formed in April 2010 as a result of a merger between the Tobacco Trade Benevolent Association, the Worshipful Company of Tobacco Pipe Makers and Tobacco Blenders Benevolent Fund. The fund works alongside other charities such as GroceryAid, The Royal British Legion and SSAFA to help achieve its objectives.

Beneficiaries are visited regularly and are provided with a point of contact.

Grants are also awarded to charitable organisations.

The National Benevolent Society of Watch and Clock Makers

£140,000 (144 grants)

Correspondent: Anne Baker, Secretary, 19 Illett Way, Faygate, West Sussex RH12 0AJ (020 8288 9559; email: sec@ nbswcm.org; website: www.nbswcm.org)

CC number: 206750

Eligibility

Members of the UK watch and clock trade and their widows/widowers and dependants that are in need. Generally grants are given to those with an income below £15,000 although the trustees have the discretion to act outside this guideline in certain circumstances.

Types of grants

Help is usually offered in the form of quarterly grants (£150 per quarter in 2013/14), Christmas payments (£200 in 2013/14) and 'heating' gifts (£100 in March 2014).

Annual grant total

In 2013/14 the society held assets of £2.86 million and had an income of £108,000. Grants to individuals totalled £132,500 and were distributed to 144 beneficiaries as follows:

Grants in aid	£88,000
Heating and seasonal gifts	£44,000
Television licence fees	£1,000

Exclusions

Grants are not usually awarded for individual items such as disability aids or home adaptations; however, the charity's website states that 'if an individual has a requirement for these and cannot find the funds, their income may be such that they qualify for a recurrent grant'.

Applications

Applications for grants should be made by contacting the secretary, providing the applicant's full name, address, telephone number and any relevant details. The secretary will then send an application form. Completed forms should be submitted by individuals or, if they require assistance, through a family member, social worker, welfare agency or Citizens Advice.

Sports

The Football Association Benevolent Fund

£26,000 (43 grants)

Correspondent: Richard McDermott, Secretary, Wembley Stadium, Wembley, PO BOX 1966, London SW1P 9EQ (0844 980 8200 ext. 6575; email: richard. mcdermott@thefa.com)

CC number: 299012

Eligibility

People who have been involved in Association Football in any capacity, such as players and referees, and their dependants, who are in need. The fund interprets people involved in football as broadly as possible, although it tends not to support professional footballers, passing their details on to the occupational benevolent funds which they can apply to.

Types of grants

One-off and recurrent grants ranging from £250 to £2,000 are given to meet any need.

Annual grant total

In 2014 the fund held assets of £4.6 million and had an income of £114,000. Grants were made to 43 individuals totalling £26,000.

Applications

Application forms are available from the correspondent. Applications should be made through the County Football Associations. They are considered on a regular basis.

The Grand Prix Mechanics Charitable Trust

£22,000

Correspondent: Fiona Miller, Administrator, The Old Bakehouse, Little Street, Sulgrave, Oxfordshire OX17 2SG (07770 371332; email: fiona@ gpmechanicstrust.com; website: www. gpmechanicstrust.com)

CC number: 327454

Eligibility

Past and present Grand Prix mechanics and their dependants who are in need.

Types of grants

One-off and recurrent grants towards medical costs, bills, living expenses and so on.

Annual grant total

In 2013/14 the trust had an income of £149,000 and an expenditure of £103,000. Welfare grants totalled around £22,000.

In accordance with usual practice, the trustees met their objectives by making donations of £47,000 to charitable causes. The largest donation during the year was a £25,000 donation to BEN (the Automotive Industry Charity). Grants to individuals are estimated at around £22,000.

Applications

Apply in writing to the correspondent or via the online contact form. The trustees' grant-making policy has been to generally consider making donations by way of direct funding to individuals and also by way of grants to charitable organisations. The trustees consider donation at their Appeals and Awards Committee meetings and also bi-annual trustee meetings. The trustees continue to monitor the requirements of potential beneficiaries and provides advice and guidance to beneficiaries, as well as providing financial support.

The Hornsby Professional Cricketers Fund Charity

£47,000 (46 grants)

Correspondent: The Revd Michael Vockins, Secretary, Birchwood Lodge, Birchwood, Storridge, Malvern, Worcestershire WR13 5EZ (01886 884366)

CC number: 235561

Eligibility

Former professional cricketers and their dependants who are in need.

Types of grants

Recurrent grants of around £240, paid monthly, and special payments at Christmas (£700 in 2013/14), in mid-summer or for heating allowance. One-off payments may be given to help with a particular or urgent need. Assistance may also be given towards medical costs and special equipment such as electric wheelchairs and stair-lifts.

Annual grant total

In 2013/14 the charity held assets of £455,500 and had an income of £35,000. Almost £47,000 was awarded in payments, which were distributed as follows:

Monthly allowances	9	£25,000
Heating allowance	7	£7,000
Winter allowances	9	£6,300
Summer allowances	10	£6,300
Former WHMF recipients	5	£2,100
Special grants	1	£200

Applications

Apply in writing to the correspondent. Applications can be submitted either directly by the individual or by a county cricket club or similar association. Decisions are made at trustee meetings three times each year.

The League Managers Benevolent and Community Fund Trust

£40,000

Correspondent: The Trustees, In The Game, League Managers Association, National Football Centre, Newborough Road, Needwood, Burton upon Trent DE13 9PD (01283 576350; email: lma@lmasecure.com; website: www.leaguemanagers.com)

CC number: 1016248

Eligibility

Members of the League Managers Association who are in need and their wives, widows and children.

Types of grants

One-off and recurrent grants are given according to need.

Annual grant total

In 2014/15 the charity had an income of £11,800 and a total expenditure of £115,000. Due to its low income, the charity was not required to submit its accounts to the Charity Commission. We estimate that the amount of grants given to individuals totalled £40,000.

Applications

Apply in writing to the correspondent. Applications are considered throughout the year.

Other information

The trust is otherwise known as In The Game.

The charity's Community Fund aims to encourage outreach and involvement in grassroots and community football projects.

PGA European Tour Benevolent Trust

£213,500 (15 grants)

Correspondent: Jonathan Orr, Administrator, PGA Building, Wentworth Drive, Virginia Water, Surrey GU25 4LX (01344 840400; email: cduffain@europeantour.com; website: www.europeantour.com/tourgroup/benevolenttrust/index.html)

CC number: 327207

Eligibility

Members and former members of the PGA European Tour and other people whose main livelihood is, or has been, earned by providing services to professional golf, and their dependants.

Types of grants

One-off or recurrent grants according to need. In 2014 grants ranged from £2,400 to £35,000.

Annual grant total

In 2014 the trust had assets of £846,000 and an income of £86,000. A total of £213,500 was awarded to 15 individuals.

Applications

Apply in writing to the correspondent at any time. Applications can be submitted directly by the individual or through a social worker, Citizens Advice, other welfare agency or another third party.

The Professional Billiards and Snooker Players Benevolent Fund

£25,000

Correspondent: Lisa Bray, World Snooker Ltd, 75 Whiteladies Road, Clifton, Bristol BS28 2NT (0117 317 8210; email: lisa.bray@worldsnooker.com)

CC number: 288352

Eligibility

Current or retired professional snooker or billiards players who are members of the World Professional Billiards and Snooker Association, and their dependants, who are in need.

Types of grants

One-off grants and interest-free loans according to need. Trustees currently prioritise one-off payments on the death of players, payments to cover the private medical insurance policies of those who are ill or have suffered an injury related to the sport and the provision of loans for specific purposes to be repaid over a set period of time.

Annual grant total

In 2013/14 the fund had an income of £25,000 and a total expenditure of £32,000. Grants to individuals totalled £25,000.

Loans totalling £20,400 were also provided to three current and former players.

Applications

Application forms are available from the correspondent. Personal and financial details and medical evidence should be included where appropriate. Applicants for loans will be asked to identify how the loan will be repaid.

Professional Footballers' Association Benevolent Fund

£562,000

Correspondent: Darren Wilson, Director of Finance, 20 Oxford Court, Bishopsgate, Manchester M2 3WQ (0161 236 0575; email: info@thepfa.co.uk; website: www.thepfa.com/thepfa/finance)

CC number: 1056012

Eligibility

Current and former members of the association in England and Wales who are experiencing financial hardship and are on a low income, and their dependants.

Types of grants

One-off grants in the range of £50 to £2,000 to help relieve financial hardship. Where appropriate, general advice regarding financial management and options concerning further education may be offered. There is also funding available in the event of the death of any member while under contract, up to a maximum of £1 million.

Annual grant total

In 2013/14 the Benevolent Fund had an income of £297,000. A total of £562,000 was awarded in grants to individuals.

Exclusions

No grants are made for cars, holidays or to set up businesses. Loans are not available to former members and there are no recurrent grants.

Applications

Application forms are available from the correspondent. Completed applications should be returned directly by the individual or by a family member/social worker on their behalf. There are no deadlines and applications are considered as they are received.

Other information

See also the entry for the Professional Footballers' Association Accident Insurance Fund.

Racing Welfare

£113,000

Correspondent: The Welfare Team, 20B Park Lane, Newmarket, Suffolk CB8 8QD (01638 560763 (head office) or 0800 630 0443 (helpline); fax: 01638 565240; email: info@racingwelfare.co.uk; website: www.racingwelfare.co.uk)

CC number: 1084042

Eligibility

People in need who are, or have been, employed in the thoroughbred horse-racing and breeding industry, and their dependants. Applicants must have worked in the industry for at least five years (with the exception of anyone who has had a work-related accident and/or is under the age of 25).

The charity has estimated the overall number of people working in the industry to be 18,600 and staff retired – 14,000.

Types of grants

One-off and recurrent grants can be made according to specific need. Throughout the years the majority of funding has been given in the form of quarterly benefits to older people on minimum income; however, now,

although existing beneficiaries are still supported, the charity 'no longer makes these awards to new applicants preferring more specific financial assistance to address individual need'.

Support can be given to help with disability aids and equipment, house adaptations, bedding, clothing, food, medical expenses, car adaptations, drugs rehabilitation, retraining and so on. Grants have also been given in response to sudden, unexpected events, such as family deaths, disease diagnoses, assaults, or loss of employment. In most cases, funds will be paid directly to service providers, rather than to individual beneficiaries.

Annual grant total

In 2014 the charity had assets of £13.3 million and an income of £2.4 million. Grants to individuals in need were made totalling £113,000. The charity notes that 'the largest number of grants [were] given to assist people suffering ill health, disability, accidents and injuries'. A total of £44,000 was spent on quarterly grants.

Exclusions

Note that:

> Racing Welfare no longer makes loans to individuals as it recognises that this is not the most appropriate way to assist someone already in financial difficulty. Instead, the team will signpost for specialist debt and budgeting advice before deciding if a grant is appropriate.

Applications

Application forms are available from a Welfare Officer at most racing centres or from the correspondent. Candidates are normally visited by the Welfare Officer before the application is considered by the trustees. Individuals are encouraged to get in touch with the charity to discuss their application and available help.

Payments are normally paid directly to service providers rather than individuals.

Other information

The charity's main activity is the provision of support and guidance through its welfare officers based all over the country who offer information and advice, including on financial and personal issues, health and housing. There is a 24-hour helpline (0800 630 0443) offering advice. The charity also provides housing services, runs a holiday scheme for older beneficiaries and those with disabilities, continues to fund sporting events and sports centre memberships for those in need, and has a life skills programme at the Northern Racing College, British Racing School and National Stud, for young people between the ages of 16 and 19.

A small number of grants may be made to organisations that offer services to people who work in, or are retired from, racing (£92,000 in 2014).

The Referees' Association Members' Benevolent Fund

£5,500

Correspondent: The Clerk to the Trustees, 63 Hazel Road, Rubery, Birmingham B45 9DY (024 7642 0360; fax: 024 7667 7234; email: ra@ footballreferee.org; website: the-ra.org)

CC number: 800845

Eligibility

Members and former members of the association in England and their dependants who are in need.

Types of grants

One-off and recurrent grants to relieve an immediate financial need such as hospital expenses, convalescence, clothing, living costs, household bills, medical equipment and help in the home.

Annual grant total

In 2014/15 the fund had an income of £14,700 and a total expenditure of £5,800. We estimate that the amount of grants given to individuals totalled £5,500.

Applications

Apply on a form available from the correspondent or to download from the fund's website. Applications should be submitted directly by the individual for consideration at any time.

The RFL Benevolent Fund (Try Assist)

£51,500

Correspondent: Steve Ball, General Manager, Red Hall, Red Hall Lane, Leeds, West Yorkshire LS17 8NB (0844 477 7113; email: info@tryassist.co.uk; website: www.rflbenevolentfund.co.uk)

CC number: 1109858

Eligibility

People who play or assist, or who have played or assisted, in the game of Rugby League in the UK or for a team affiliated to an association primarily based in the UK and their dependants. Beneficiaries should be in hardship or distress, in particular, as a result of injury through playing or training, or when travelling to or from a game or training session.

Types of grants

Hardship grants, also donations towards special vehicles and repairs, home modifications, furniture, wheelchairs, gym equipment, computers, hotel accommodation, travel, physiotherapy, home appliances, educational courses and Christmas presents.

Annual grant total

In 2014 the fund had assets of £521,500 and an income of £224,000. We believe social welfare grants to have totalled around £51,500.

Applications

In the first instance, contact the correspondent.

Other information

Grants are also made for educational purposes.

Transport and storage

The Transport Benevolent Fund

£622,000 (3,613 grants)

Correspondent: Vicky Jennings, Secretary, Transport Benevolent Fund, New Loom House, 101 Back Church Lane, London E1 1LU (0300 333 2000; fax: 0870 831 2882; email: help@tbf.org.uk; website: www.tbf.org.uk)

CC number: 1058032

Eligibility

Employees and former employees of the public transport industry who are in need (often due to being sick, having a disability/disabilities, or convalescent), their partners and dependants. Only members of the benevolent fund are supported.

Types of grants

Grants are to meet unexpected one-off situations, where help is not available from other sources. They can be given towards medical equipment, complementary medical treatments (up to a maximum of £250 per 12-month period) and other needs.

Loans are only available to beneficiaries of the Staff Welfare Fund who are able to make repayments through regular deductions from their salary.

Annual grant total

In 2013/14 the fund had assets of £4.4 million, an income of £2.7 million and a total expenditure of £2.6 million. Grants to individuals amounted to £622,000. The majority of grants were made from the Transport Benevolent

Fund, with £27,000 paid from the Transport for London Staff Welfare Fund. Grants were distributed as follows:

Hardship	3,458	£566,000
Medical equipment and mobility aids	108	£51,000
Convalescence	46	£4,000
Medical treatment	1	£1,000

A further £1.2 million was spent on the provision of services.

Exclusions

The fund is not normally able to assist with dental or optical treatment, funeral costs, short-term absence from work (generally less than two weeks), replacement of possessions or medical operations. Continuing support is not offered except in particular cases (e.g. loans of medical equipment). No institutions, organisations or companies are supported except in relation to payment for services for beneficiaries.

Applications

By writing to or emailing the fund with a description of your claim outlining your need, how it arose and how much you are asking for. Applications are considered monthly or when required.

Other information

The fund's website gives the following information on its background and purpose:

> The Transport Benevolent Fund (TBF) was founded in 1923 by the predecessors of Transport for London (TfL) to relieve cases of necessity among its members and to meet their needs for convalescence or surgical equipment. The needs of staff today take a very different form, but there is still need, hardship and distress among those who work in the public transport industry (or are retired from it) and TBF is still there to help when things are not going so well.

TBF also manages the TfL Staff Welfare Fund.

Legal and financial advice are also offered to beneficiaries, including in the areas of debt management and bankruptcy.

The trustees are continuing to extend their work in Scotland.

This charity produces an excellent annual trustees' report detailing its objectives, strategies, activities, achievements and performance for the financial year.

Air

The Air Pilots Benevolent Fund

£9,900

Correspondent: Chris Spurrier, Trustee, Cobham House, 9 Warwick Court,

Gray's Inn, London WC1R 5DJ (020 7404 4032; fax: 020 7404 4035; email: office@airpilots.org; website: www.airpilots.org)

CC number: 212952

Eligibility

Members of The Honourable Company of Air Pilots and those who have been engaged professionally as air pilots or air navigators in commercial aviation and their dependants.

Types of grants

One-off and recurrent grants ranging between £250 and £2,000. Grants and loans can be made to assist in the rehabilitation of people after accidents or to enable them to regain licences.

Annual grant total

In 2013/14 the fund had assets of £748,000 and an income of £57,000. Grants were made totalling £44,500 and consisted of:

PPL scholarship via Air Pilots Trust	£9,000
Occasional grants	£8,800
Flying instructor development bursaries via E&TC	£7,800
Flying scholarship for people with disability	£7,000
Ray Jeffs gliding scholarships	£4,000
Inner London schools gliding	£3,900
City University bursary via Air Safety Trust	£3,000
Regular grants	£1,100

We take it that 'regular' and 'occasional' grants, totalling £9,900, included more social-welfare-related requests.

Exclusions

The fund cannot give 'grant or loan money for the repayment of debts or long-term expenses such as school fees, prolonged medical care or for obtaining professional pilots' licences and ratings'.

Applications

Requests for support should be made on the 'Application for Financial Assistance' form. Appeals are reviewed at the quarterly meetings, although immediate grants may be made (the fund's office should be contacted directly if there is such an urgent need).

The fund works closely with the other aviation trusts for individuals (both military and civilian). If an applicant has approached another such trust, they should say so in their application to this fund.

Other information

The charity was previously called The Guild of Air Pilots Benevolent Fund and provides both educational and welfare support.

The fund is administered by The Honourable Company of Air Pilots which is also managing Air Safety Trust and Air Pilots Trust.

People who want to become pilots or wish to gain further qualifications in the aviation industry are supported by The Honourable Company of Air Pilots.

The British Airline Pilots' Association Benevolent Fund (BALPA)

£23,500

Correspondent: Antoinette Girdler, BALPA House, 5 Heathrow Boulevard, 278 Bath Road, West Drayton UB7 0DQ (020 8476 4029; email: tonigirdler@balpa.org)

CC number: 229957

Eligibility

Current or retired British commercial airline pilots, flight engineers and winchmen, and their dependants.

Types of grants

One-off and recurrent grants and interest-free loans. The fund prefers to give grants for specific needs such as electricity bills, school books for children and so on.

Annual grant total

In 2013/14 the charity had assets of £1.6 million and an income of £34,000. Grants totalled £47,000 and interest-free loans were made to the sum of £12,000. We estimate that grants for social welfare purposes totalled around £23,500.

Exclusions

Grants are not given for school fees.

Applications

Apply in writing to the correspondent to request an application form. Applications are considered quarterly.

Land

Associated Society of Locomotive Engineers and Firemen (ASLEF) Hardship Fund

£14,000

Correspondent: The General Secretary, ASLEF, 77 St John Street, Clerkenwell, London EC1M 4NN (020 7324 2400; fax: 020 7490 8697; email: info@aslef.org.uk; website: www.aslef.org.uk)

Eligibility

Members of ASLEF, and their dependants, who are in need.

Types of grants

One-off grants can be given according to need.

Annual grant total

In 2014 the fund had assets of £1.5 million and an income of £89,000 in contributions from over 18,000 members. Grants to individuals totalled £14,000.

Applications

Apply in writing to the correspondent.

The Railway Benefit Fund

£324,000

Correspondent: Abigail Smith, Executive Director, Electra Way, Crewe, Cheshire CW1 6HS (01270 251316; email: info@railwaybenefitfund.org.uk; website: www.railwaybenefitfund.org.uk)

CC number: 206312

Eligibility

Current and former railway staff, and their dependants, who are in need.

Types of grants

One-off and repeated grants of £100 to £1,500. The main types of grants are:

> Single benevolent grants – one-off grants provided to meet specific needs, for example, to assist with the costs of convalescence, disability equipment, funeral expenses, debts and arrears, minor house repairs and household equipment

> Annuities – paid quarterly to people on a low income

> Residential care grants – paid monthly to 'top up' care home fees

> Webb Fund grants – paid quarterly to assist the parents of underprivileged dependent children

> Childcare grants are one-off payments given towards clothing, footwear, school projects and the initial costs of entering higher education

Annual grant total

In 2014 the fund had assets of £3.5 million and an income of £484,500. Grants for welfare purposes totalled £324,000 and were distributed as follows:

Single benevolent grants	329 grants	£278,000
Quarterly grants	190 beneficiaries	£38,000
Webb Fund grants	Ten families	£5,100
Other charitable grants	85 beneficiaries	£2,200
Residential care grants	One beneficiary	£745

An additional £4,400 was given in childcare grants. We have taken these to be for purposes relating to education and have, therefore, not included them in the grant total for social welfare.

The 329 single benevolent grants were broken down again according to purpose:

Funeral expenses	52	£100,000
Disability equipment	37	£45,500
Debts and arrears	54	£36,000
Minor house repairs	31	£32,000
Household equipment	40	£24,000
Other	104	£20,500
Convalescence	11	£10,700

Applications

Applications are available to download from the website, or can be requested by telephone, via the 'Contact Us' form on the website, or by emailing welfare@railwaybenefitfund.org.uk. The form should be completed and returned to the charity, along with evidence of railway employment and the relevant documents detailed on the form, to the following address: FREEPOST, RRBA-KSXA-RYAE, RBF, Electra Way, Crewe CW1 6HS. Applications can be submitted directly by the individual or by another person and are reviewed by the Benefits Committee monthly.

The Railway Housing Association and Benefit Fund

£700

Correspondent: Anne Rowlands, Chief Executive, Bank Top House, Garbutt Square, Darlington DL1 4DR (01325 482125; email: info@railwayha.co.uk; website: www.railwayha.co.uk)

CC number: 216825

Eligibility

People who are working or who have worked in the railway industry, and their dependants, in England, Scotland and Wales.

Types of grants

One-off grants towards house repairs, care attendants, respite care, essential household items, aids and adaptations and general financial assistance.

Annual grant total

In 2013/14 the charity held almost £26.5 million in assets and had an income of £6.1 million. Grants to individuals totalled £700.

Applications

The association has transferred the administration of its grants to the Railway Benefit Fund and potential applicants should contact them directly at: Electra Way, Crewe Business Park, Crewe, Cheshire CW1 6HS – 01270 251316. However, the association is happy to help and advise any individual who wishes to discuss their case prior to making an application.

Other information

The association's primary concern is the management of affordable accommodation for the benefit of older people in need.

Removers Benevolent Association

£9,500

Correspondent: The Grants Officer, The British Association of Removers, Tangent House, 62 Exchange Road, Watford, Hertfordshire WD18 0TG (01923 699480; fax: 01923 699481; email: rba@bar.co.uk; website: www.bar.co.uk)

CC number: 284012

Eligibility

People in need who are or have been employed for a minimum of two years by a member or former member of the British Association of Removers Ltd, and their dependants.

Types of grants

One-off grants, usually in the range of £250 to £750, to help those experiencing a temporary period of financial difficulty due to an illness or other difficulties. Occasionally, recurrent grants may be given.

Annual grant total

At the time of writing (November 2015) the latest financial information available was from 2013. In 2013 the association had an income of £15,800 and a total expenditure of £10,000. We estimate that grants totalled about £9,500.

Applications

Apply in writing to the correspondent. Applications should be made by a member of the company the employee has worked for on behalf of the candidate. They are considered upon submission.

RMT (National Union of Rail, Maritime and Transport Workers) Orphan Fund

£150,000

Correspondent: Collin Sharpe, Administrator, Unity House, 39 Chalton Street, London NW1 1JD (020 7387 4771; fax: 020 7387 4123; email: info@rmt.org.uk; website: www.rmt.org.uk)

Eligibility

Children of deceased members of the union who are under the age of 22.

Types of grants

Current grants are made of £12 per week per child under the age of 16 and £12.75 per week per child continuing to receive full-time education between the ages of

16 and 22, payable on the member's death.

Annual grant total

Generally around £150,000 is distributed in grants each year.

Applications

Application forms are available from the local union branch or to download from the union's website. For children over the age of 16 in full-time education an education certificate should also be attached. Applications should be made through the local union branch and must be endorsed by the branch secretary. Grants are made quarterly, in March, June, September and December.

Other information

The union also provides accident, retirement, death and demotion benefits and grants for union members or their widows/widowers. More details are available on the website.

The Road Haulage Association Benevolent Fund

£3,000

Correspondent: Sheikh Ali, Road Haulage Association, Roadway House, The Rural Centre, Newbridge EH28 8NZ (0131 333 4900; email: s.ali@rha.uk.net; website: www.rha.uk.net)

CC number: 1082820

Eligibility

Current and former members and employees/ex-employees of the association, and their dependants.

Types of grants

One-off grants according to need.

Annual grant total

In 2014 the fund had assets of £896,000 and an income of £27,000. Expenditure on 'charitable cases' totalled £3,000, all of which we believe was given in support of individuals.

Exclusions

Grants are not usually awarded towards holidays (unless there are exceptional circumstances).

Applications

Application forms are available from the correspondent. Applications should be submitted directly by the individual or through a social worker, Citizens Advice or other third party. Applications are considered throughout the year.

Mail

The Rowland Hill Memorial And Benevolent Fund

£320,500

Correspondent: Mary Jeffery, Manager, Room 412, Royal Mail, 185 Farringdon Road, London EC1A 1AA (0800 232 1762; email: rowland.hill.fund@royalmail.com; website: www.rowlandhillfund.org)

CC number: 207479

Eligibility

People in need who have been employed by the Royal Mail, Post Office, Parcelforce Worldwide, Romec or associated companies, for at least six months (full or part-time, not casual); retired employees in receipt of a Royal Mail pension; and people who no longer work for Royal Mail or Post Office and have not yet retired, but will receive a Royal Mail pension when they do. If none of the above apply, you must be able to prove that you were employed by Royal Mail or Post Office Ltd. The direct dependants of such people may also be eligible for assistance. Applicants must have less than £12,000 in savings.

Types of grants

One-off grants of up to £5,000 but usually less than £1,000 for disability aids, house adaptations, hospital travel costs, funeral expenses, medical equipment, essential household items and increasingly, personal debt. Beneficiaries must be experiencing financial hardship due to unforeseen circumstances. Recurrent cost of living grants and help with nursing home fees are also available to older people. Loans are also available to Royal Mail Group employees to help short-term crises and are repaid from salary.

Annual grant total

In 2013/14 the fund held assets of £4.2 million and had an income of £542,500. Grants to individuals totalled £320,500 and were distributed as follows:

Lump sum grant payments	£292,500
Cost of living grants	£22,500
Home fees	£5,600

Applications

Call the free 24 hour helpline operated by Royal Mail (0800 688 8777, selecting option 1, then option 4). A trained advisor will conduct a telephone assessment (approximately 40 minutes in length) to discuss what you are applying for and request details of income, expenditure and any savings and documentary evidence that supports your application. This includes recent bank statements, details of Royal Mail service, medical evidence and cost estimates, if appropriate. They will then, with your agreement, prepare a report of the case for the trustees' consideration.

People applying through a third party such as a social worker or Citizens Advice may apply via telephone or in writing to the correspondent, including as much background information and supporting documentation as possible. The fund also accepts SSAFA Form A and will ask for bank statements.

Other information

The fund's sister organisation is POOBI, the Post Office Orphans Benevolent Institution, which helps Royal Mail families with children who are in need. They can be contacted by calling 020 7239 2295.

The National Federation of Sub-Postmasters Benevolent Fund

£70,000 (49 grants)

Correspondent: George Thomson, General Secretary, Evelyn House, 22 Windlesham Gardens, Shoreham-by-Sea, West Sussex BN43 5AZ (01273 452324; fax: 01273 465403; email: benfund@nfsp.org.uk; website: www. nfsp.org.uk)

CC number: 262704

Eligibility

Serving or retired sub-postmasters/sub-postmistresses, full-time employees of the NFSP, and the dependants of the above in the event of a breakdown in health, bereavement or domestic distress.

Types of grants

One-off and recurrent grants are given according to need. Support can be given in for a wide range of requirements, for example towards installing equipment in the post office to help the applicant work, holiday expenses for people with disability or those convalescing, for home or car adaptations, specific items or equipment to aid medical conditions or disability.

Annual grant total

In 2014 the fund had assets of £1.17 million and an income of £66,000. Grants totalled £70,000, including nine one-off grants and 11 beneficiaries receiving recurrent assistance.

Applications

Application forms are available from the fund's website or can be requested from the correspondent. They can be submitted directly by the individual or through another welfare charity. Applications are usually considered

quarterly, but emergency cases can be dealt with as they arise.

Other information

The fund also provides access to a one-on-one counselling service with qualified counsellors who offer counselling and emotional support following a traumatic incident in life (such as an illness or trauma reaction after an attack/raid) as well as on other issues affecting sub-postmasters/mistresses, their immediate family members and sub-post office staff.

Water

The London Shipowners' and Shipbrokers' Benevolent Society

£21,500 (10 grants)

Correspondent: Richard Butler, Secretary, 20 St Dunstan's Hill, London EC3R 8HL (020 7283 6090; email: richard.butler@baltic-charities.co.uk)

CC number: 213348

Eligibility

Shipowners and shipbrokers and their dependants.

Types of grants

Annual cost of living grants, paid quarterly, as well as special grants at Christmas and during periods of cold weather. One-off and emergency grants are also available.

Annual grant total

In 2014 the society had assets of £1.1 million and an income of £32,000. Grants to ten individuals amounted to £21,500. Of this, £17,400 was distributed in quarterly payments to beneficiaries and £4,100 was awarded in special grants.

Applications

Application forms are available from the correspondent. Applications can be submitted at any time either directly by the individual or a family member, through a third party such as a social worker, or through an organisation such as Citizens Advice or other welfare agency. The applicant must provide full details of income and expenditure.

Other information

The society can also provide advice and counselling.

Voluntary sector

WRVS Benevolent Trust

£8,600 (4 grants)

Correspondent: Honorary Secretary, PO Box 567, Tonbridge TN9 9LS (07894 060 517; email: enquiry@wrvsbt.org.uk; website: www.wrvsbt.org.uk)

CC number: 261931

Eligibility

Individuals who have volunteered or worked for the WVS, WRVS or Royal Voluntary Service and are on a relatively low income.

Types of grants

One-off grants ranging from £50 to £6,000. Recent grants have been made for washing machines and other household items, personal alarms, contribution towards an electric wheelchair, household adaptations and dental treatment. Grants also cover the installation of electrical or white goods and the removal of old equipment.

Annual grant total

In 2014 this charity had an income of £43,500 and total expenditure of £27,500. Grants to four individuals for social welfare purposes totalled £8,600.

Applications

Applications should be made on a form available to download from the website, and are considered all year round. Applications can be made directly by the individual, or by a friend or family member on their behalf.

Livery companies, orders and membership organisations

This chapter includes the charities which award grants to members of a particular association or organisation. This chapter is divided into four sub-sections.

'Livery companies' are listed first. These are some of the oldest charities in the UK, originally set up as guilds by members of the same craft, trade or profession. With a historic connection to the City of London and in some aspects analogous to an early sort of trade union, the companies were originally responsible for training and regulation of their profession, with their halls providing a site for meetings and socialising. The existing Worshipful Companies all continue to practice charitable giving as an integral part of their work – often in the form of benevolence to members of their profession or trade, like those featured in this guide, but often more broadly to the wider community too.

'Orders' lists charities which generally support members of their particular order and their dependants.

'Sports clubs' includes charities which give grants to members of particular clubs, but please note that other sports charities are listed in the 'Occupational charities' chapter. The 'Other' section includes membership organisations that do not fit into any of the above categories.

All of the charities in each section are listed in alphabetical order.

Please note that trade unions are listed in a sub-section of the 'Occupational charities' chapter.

Index of livery companies, orders and membership organisations

Livery companies

The Worshipful Company of Engineers Charitable Trust Fund

£600

Correspondent: Anthony Willenbruch, Clerk, Wax Chandlers' Hall, 6 Gresham Street, London EC2V 7AD (020 7726 4830; fax: 020 7726 4820; email: clerk@ engineerscompany.org.uk; website: www. engineerstrust.org.uk)

CC number: 289819

Eligibility

Professional engineers who have been engaged in engineering at chartered engineer level in industry and commerce and who are in need. Existing members of the Worshipful Company of Engineers, retired members, or their spouses, widows/widowers, children, orphans and others dependants.

Types of grants

Grants are generally of up to £1,000 and can be given for various welfare purposes.

Annual grant total

In 2014 the trust had assets of £1.5 million and an income of £116,000. The annual report for the year stated: 'Monetary prizes to the value of £21,900 (2013 £16,000) were made to seven (2013 six) individuals and grants to a total value of £632,700 (2013 £11,735) were made to individuals and organisations.' Unlike those for 2013, these accounts did not include a breakdown of grants awarded and so we were unable to determine an exact figure for social welfare grants to individuals. In previous years, these have accounted for only a small amount of grants made, totalling around £600.

Applications

Applications should be made in writing to the clerk and should provide as much detail about the individual's circumstances as possible.

Other information

The trust also awards annual prizes for excellence in engineering and supports engineering research. Support can be given to organisations concerned with engineering or organisations in the City of London that further the interest of the history, traditions and customs of the city.

The Worshipful Company of Farriers' Charitable Trust 1994

£800

Correspondent: The Clerk, 19 Queen Street, Chipperfield, Kings Langley, Herts WD4 9BT (01923 260747; fax: 01923 261677; email: theclerk@wcf.org. uk; website: www.wcf.org.uk/charity. php)

CC number: 1044726

Eligibility

Registered farriers, their widows and dependants who are in need.

Types of grants

One-off and recurrent grants are given according to need. Grants are usually given to people who are unable to work through injury or sickness.

Annual grant total

In 2013/14 the trust had assets of £1.6 million and an income of £65,000. Grants were made to individuals totalling £800.

Applications

Apply in writing to the clerk. Applications are considered eight times a year.

The Honourable Company of Master Mariners and Howard Leopold Davis Charity

£71,500

Correspondent: The Clerk, HQS Wellington, Temple Stairs, Victoria Embankment, London WC2R 2PN (020 7836 8179; fax: 020 7240 3082; email: info@hcmm.org.uk; website: www. hcmm.org.uk/activities/charitable-giving)

CC number: 1127213

Eligibility

British master mariners, navigating officers of the merchant navy, and their wives, widows and dependants who are in need.

Types of grants

One-off and quarterly grants are given according to need.

Annual grant total

In 2014 the charity had an income of £104,500 and a total expenditure of £153,000. At the time of writing (November 2015) the charity's annual report and accounts were not yet available to view online at the Charity Commission. Based on previous years, we estimate that the amount of grants given to individuals for both social welfare and educational purposes totalled around £143,000.

Applications

In the first instance, applications should be made to The Merchant Navy Welfare Board or SSAFA. Members of the company who are seeking assistance should instead apply directly to the correspondent.

Other information

This charity is an amalgamation of four separate funds: the Education Fund, the Benevolent Fund, the London Maritime Institution and the Howard Leopold Davis Fund.

The Worshipful Company of Launderers Benevolent Trust

£2,900 (3 grants)

Correspondent: Terence Winter, Clerk, Launderers' Hall, 9 Montague Close, London SE1 9DD (020 7378 1430; fax: 020 7378 9364; email: clerk.launderers@ btconnect.com; website: www.launderers. co.uk)

CC number: 262750

Eligibility

Existing and retired members of the laundry industry and their dependants.

Types of grants

Grants can be paid annually (towards fuel bills); bi-annually (fuel bills and a summer grant); or monthly (towards general living expenses).

Annual grant total

In 2013/14 the trust had assets of £597,000 and an income of £46,000. Grants totalled £31,500, of which £2,900 was given in monthly grants to three individuals from the General Fund.

Applications

Apply in writing to the correspondent.

Other information

The trust is made up of three portfolios: The General Fund; The Arthur Kennedy Fund; and The Launderers' and Cleaners' Education Fund. The Launderer and Cleaners' Education Fund offers the Travelling Scholarship, which is available once every two years. Most of the trust's grant-making is to organisations.

The Worshipful Company of Scientific Instrument Makers

£7,100

Correspondent: The Clerk, Glaziers Hall, 9 Montague Close, London SE1 9DD (020 7407 4832; email: theclerk@wcsim.co.uk; website: www.wcsim.co.uk)

CC number: 221332

Eligibility

Members and past members of the company and their dependants.

Types of grants

One-off grants according to need. Grants have been used, for example, for bereavement and funeral costs.

Annual grant total

In 2013/14 the charity held assets of £2.3 million and had an income of £74,500. Grants to individuals for educational purposes totalled £51,000 and for social welfare purposes totalled £7,100.

Applications

Apply in writing to the correspondent.

Other information

The majority of the charity's charitable work is concerned with educational scholarships.

Orders

The Cheshire Provincial Fund of Benevolence

£20,000

Correspondent: Christopher Renshaw, 6 Auden Close, Ewloe, Deeside, Clwyd CH5 3TY (01244 534343; email: enquiries@cheshiremasons.co.uk)

CC number: 219177

Eligibility

Freemasons of Cheshire and their dependants who are in need.

Types of grants

One-off and recurrent grants are given according to need.

Annual grant total

In 2013/14 the fund had assets of £4.2 million and an income of £221,500. Grants were made totalling £155,000, of which £77,000 was given to Masonic institutions. Individuals and charities received £77,500. We estimate that welfare grants to individuals totalled around £20,000.

Applications

Apply in writing to the correspondent.

Other information

Freemasons in Cheshire have also supported the Teddies for Loving Care Appeal (TLC), which provides teddies for children visiting A&E departments in Cheshire hospitals. On average around 12,000 bears are donated every year.

Grants to non-Masonic charities are also made in the following areas: youth opportunities; vulnerable people; hospices; emergency grants; medical research.

The Coventry Freemen's Charity

£558,000 (2,811 grants)

Correspondent: David Evans, Clerk to the Trustees, Abbey House, Manor Road, Coventry CV1 2FW (024 7625 7317; email: john@foxevans.co.uk; website: www.foxevans.co.uk)

CC number: 229237

Eligibility

Freemen and their dependants, and the widows, widowers and other former dependants of deceased freemen, who are in need and live within the existing boundary of the city of Coventry or within seven miles of St Mary's Hall, Coventry.

Types of grants

One-off and recurrent grants.

Annual grant total

In 2014 the charity had assets of almost £13.5 million and an income of £806,500. Grants totalled £558,000 and were distributed to 2,811 beneficiaries as follows:

Freemen and women	2,213	£439,500
Freemen's widows	586	£116,000
Special cases	12	£2,600

Grants for relief in need totalled £2,600.

Applications

Application forms are available from the correspondent and can be submitted directly by the individual.

Grand Charitable Trust of the Order of Women Freemasons

£6,600

Correspondent: The Secretariat, 27 Pembridge Gardens, London W2 4EF (020 7229 2368; email: enquiries@owf.org.uk; website: www.owf.org.uk)

CC number: 1059151

Eligibility

Women freemasons who are in need.

Types of grants

One-off and recurrent grants to help towards medical, household and living expenses.

Annual grant total

In 2013/14 the trust held assets of £720,000 and had an income of £177,500. Grants were made to individuals totalling £7,900.

The trust's grant-making activities mainly focused on funding for organisations, with The Adelaide Litten Charitable Trust, which owns sheltered housing properties, receiving £54,000, and outside charities a further £155,500.

Applications

Apply in writing to the correspondent, usually through the local Lodge. The trustees meet regularly throughout the year to consider applications.

Other information

The trust is administered through The Order of Women Freemasons which was established as 'The Honourable Fraternity of Ancient Masonry' in 20 June 1908. 'Its first Grand Master and driving force was a man – the Rev. Dr. William Frederick Cobb. However, since 1912, the Grand Masters have all been women.' The group altered its name in 1958 to avoid confusion with a similarly named organisation, and has kept it ever since.

The Grand Charity (of Freemasons under the United Grand Lodge of England)

£3.5 million (1,527 grants)

Correspondent: Laura Chapman, Freemasons Hall, 60 Great Queen Street, London WC2B 5AZ (020 7395 9261; fax: 020 7395 9295; email: info@the-grand-charity.org; website: www.grandcharity.org)

CC number: 281942

Eligibility

Any freemason, past or present (under the United Grand Lodge of England) in need, their widows, and their immediate dependants.

As a general guide, almost anyone in receipt of pension credit or another means-tested benefit is likely to be eligible; however, assets and capital (not including the home) will be taken into account.

Queries regarding eligibility should be directed towards your Lodge Almoner, Provincial Grand Almoner or the

Freemasonry Cares helpline (080003560 90).

Types of grants

Grants are usually made for essential daily living costs and are expected to last for a minimum period of 12 months. In certain circumstances, one-off grants may be made for specific items. Emergency grants may also be made in exceptional circumstances.

Annual grant total

In 2012/13 the charity had assets of £64.5 million and an income of £13.7 million. Masonic relief grants totalled £3.5 million. Of 2,173 applications, 1,527 were successful. At the time of writing (November 2015) the information provided was the latest available.

Exclusions

There is no limit to the number of grants an individual may receive over their lifetime, although usually only one grant per year will be made.

Applications

Applicants should first contact their Lodge Almoner or Provincial Grand Almoner who will provide support throughout the application process. Applications can be submitted at any time and a decision is usually reached within four to eight weeks of receipt. The charity has now adopted the use of a joint application form with the Royal Masonic Trust for Girls and Boys and the Masonic Samaritan Fund. The form is designed to make it easier for an applicant to seek support from more than one charity for different types of need at the same time. Details on required supporting documentation can be found on a checklist attached to the form.

For further information on emergency grants, the visiting brother should contact the Director of Masonic Relief Grants.

Current grant recipients will receive a review form prior to the anniversary of the initial application.

Other information

The charity also manages the Relief Chest Scheme. Each 'relief chest' is used to accumulate funds collected by a Lodge, Chapter or Province for charitable purposes. These are then used by the individual Lodges to distribute grants to charities and individuals in need. Applications for these funds should be made through the relevant Lodge, Chapter or Province.

In 2002, the charity took over responsibility for the Transferred Beneficiaries Fund, which makes regular payments to former beneficiaries of the Royal Masonic Benevolent Institution Annuity Fund. This fund is not open to new applications for assistance.

Practical help and financial support for individuals in times of personal distress and for local charities are also given independently of the Grand Charity by individual Lodges and Provincial Grand Lodges. Addresses are available from the correspondent.

The separate entries within this section for the Royal Masonic Benevolent Institution and the New Masonic Samaritan Fund may also be helpful. There is also the Masonic Trust for Girls and Boys, which helps children of any age (including adopted children and step-children) of Freemasons under the United Grand Lodge of England. Details of the Masonic Trust for Girls and Boys and its application criteria can be found in our sister publication, *The Guide to Educational Grants*.

The Grand Lodge of Ancient, Free and Accepted Masons of Scotland

£155,000 (previously)

Correspondent: The Trustees, c/o Freemasons Hall, 96 George Street, Edinburgh EH2 3DH (0131 225 5577; fax: 0131 225 3953; email: curator@ grandlodgescotland.org; website: www. grandlodgescotland.com)

OSCR number: SC001996

Eligibility

Members and their dependants, and the widows and dependants of deceased members.

Types of grants

One-off and recurrent grants which are usually used to assist with the cost of day-to-day living expenses.

Annual grant total

In 2013/14 the charity had an income of £659,500 and a total expenditure of £410,500. Our research indicates that benevolence grants usually total around £155,000; however, considering that the figures for the year's income and expenditure were unusually low, the actual sum of these grants may have also been lower.

Applications

Application forms are available from the correspondent, or you can approach your local Lodge directly.

Other information

The charity also makes grants to individuals for educational purposes, as well as to organisations, and runs care homes for older people.

The Leicester Freemen's Estate

£4,000 (6 grants)

Correspondent: Lynda Bramley, Administrator, Estate Office, 32 Freemen's Holt, Old Church Street, Leicester LE2 8NH (0116 283 4017; email: office@leicesterfreemen.com; website: www.leicesterfreemen.com)

CC number: 244732

Eligibility

Needy freemen of Leicester and their widows who are elderly or unwell.

Types of grants

Monthly payments and Christmas hampers.

Annual grant total

In 2014 the estate held assets of £6 million and had an income of £243,000. Payments and Christmas hampers to two freemen and four widows totalled £4,000.

Applications

Application forms are available from the correspondent and proof of status as a freeman/widow of a freeman should be included. Applications can be submitted directly by the individual and are considered monthly. Beneficiaries' eligibility is reviewed annually.

Other information

The charity also provides accommodation for needy freemen and their widows. Application forms are available from the above address. Social events for residents and non-residents were arranged throughout the year.

The New Masonic Samaritan Fund

£5.7 million (1,976 grants)

Correspondent: Peter Smith, 60 Great Queen Street, London WC2B 5AZ (020 7404 1550; email: info@msfund.org.uk; website: www.msfund.org.uk)

CC number: 1130424

Eligibility

Freemasons, their families, dependants and widows or surviving partners who are in both financial and medical need.

Types of grants

One-off grants towards medical, respite, mobility and dental care. Grants have recently been awarded towards, for example, stair-lifts, wet-room installations, home care and dentures.

Annual grant total

During the eighteen months between September 2013 and March 2015 the fund held assets of £65.8 million and had an income of £5.9 million. Grants to individuals totalled £5.7 million. During the period 1,976 applications were approved.

Exclusions

No grants can be made towards treatment which has already been provided privately, or which can be made through the NHS without undue delay or hardship.

Applications

Potential applicants should initially contact the fund by phone. An Almoner or Visiting Brother will be appointed to assist with every application. Application forms will be sent to the Almoner/ Visiting Brother. Once completed and returned a decision is usually made within four weeks. An eligibility checker is also available on the fund's website.

Other information

To access the MSF Counselling Careline, call 020 7404 1550. One of the team will assess the caller's eligibility and will then provide a Freephone number through which the helpline can be accessed.

Norfolk (Le Strange) Fund

£6,300

Correspondent: Russell Carter, Trustee, Brick Kiln Farm, Cross Road, Starston, Harleston, Norfolk IP20 9NH (01379 854600; email: rcarter@carrotech.com)

CC number: 209020

Eligibility

Freemasons of the Province of Norfolk and their dependants.

Types of grants

Grants are made to Freemason families according to need.

Annual grant total

In 2014 the charity had an income of £13,700 and a total expenditure of £26,400. We estimate that relief-in-need grants to individuals totalled about £6,300.

Applications

Applications may be made in writing to the correspondent. They are considered every two months. The charity does not respond to unsuccessful applications made outside its area of interest and prefers applicants to enquire and apply by post or email, rather than by phone.

Other information

Funding is also awarded to Masonic charities and to individuals for educational purposes.

The Royal Antediluvian Order of Buffaloes, Grand Lodge of England War Memorial Annuities

£20,000

Correspondent: The Secretary, Grove House, Skipton Road, Harrogate, North Yorkshire HG1 4LA (01423 502438; email: hq@raobgle.org.uk; website: www.raobgle.org.uk)

CC number: 220476

Eligibility

Members of the Order who are elderly or who have disabilities and their dependants.

Types of grants

Annuities, although the Grand Lodge may have other charitable funds available for one-off grants.

Annual grant total

In 2013/14 the charity had an income of £11,500 and a total expenditure of £27,000. We estimate grants totalled around £20,000.

Applications

Applications should be made through the Member's Lodge. All assistance originates at the local Lodge level; if its resources are inadequate, the Lodge may then seek assistance at provincial or ultimately national level. For dependants of deceased members it is necessary to state the Lodge to which the member belonged. If its name and number is known the correspondent will probably be able to identify a current local telephone number or address. If only the place is known this may still be possible, but not in all cases (particularly when the Lodge concerned does not belong to this Grand Lodge group).

Other information

This fund was established by the Grand Lodge of England as a tribute to members of the order who died during the First World War.

The Grand Lodge also runs two convalescent homes; one in Harrogate and the other in Paignton.

Royal Masonic Benevolent Institution

£40,000

Correspondent: David Innes, Chief Executive, Royal Masonic Benevolent Institution, 60 Great Queen Street, London WC2B 5AZ (020 7596 2400; fax: 020 7404 0724; email: enquries@rmbi.org.uk; website: www.rmbi.org.uk)

CC number: 207360

Eligibility

Freemasons (usually over 60 years of age, unless unemployed due to incapacity) of the English Constitution (England, Wales and certain areas overseas) and their dependants.

Types of grants

Christmas gifts and annuities.

Annual grant total

In 2013/14 annuities and grants amounted to £40,000.

Applications

Applications are usually submitted through the Lodge of the relevant freemason.

Other information

The institution runs 17 homes catering for around 1,000 older freemasons, in addition to 145 sheltered residences. The charity also has an advice and support team, with welfare visitors covering the whole of England and Wales, who visit beneficiaries and offer guidance and support on a range of issues.

The Town Moor Money Charity

£65,000

Correspondent: Richard Grey, Correspondent, Moor Bank Lodge, Claremont Road, Newcastle upon Tyne NE2 4NL (0191 261 5970; email: admin@freemenofnewcastle.org; website: www.freemenofnewcastle.org)

CC number: 248098

Eligibility

Freemen of Newcastle upon Tyne, Northumberland and Durham and their widows and children who are in need.

Types of grants

One-off and recurrent grants are given according to need. Grants are means-tested and paid in June and December.

Annual grant total

In 2013/14 the charity had an income of £24,000 and a total expenditure of £81,500. We estimate grants to individuals totalled around £65,000.

Applications

Application forms are available in April and October from the senior steward of the appropriate company. They are usually considered in May and November.

Sports clubs

The Auto Cycle Union Benevolent Fund

£63,000 (62 grants)

Correspondent: The Auto Cycle Union Benevolent Fund, ACU House, Wood Street, Rugby, Warwickshire CV21 2YX (01943 878666; email: admin@acu.org.uk; website: www.acu.org.uk)

CC number: 208567

Eligibility

Past and present members of the Auto Cycle Union, and their dependants, who are in need through accident, illness or hardship in England, Scotland or Wales.

Types of grants

One-off and recurrent grants. Loans may also be available.

Annual grant total

In 2014 the fund held assets of £2.5 million and had an income of £111,000. Grants were made to 62 individuals totalling £63,000.

Applications

Application forms are available from the local ACU officer or centre. Applications should be made directly by the individual and include details on current income and expenses. They are considered monthly. In very special circumstances the committee has the power to make emergency payments pending full information.

Other information

A full list of ACU clubs and centres is available on the website.

British Motor Cycle Racing Club Benevolent Fund

£6,500

Correspondent: Mike Dommett, CEO, Unit D2, Seedbed Centre, Davidson Way, Romford, Essex RM7 0AZ (01708 720305; fax: 01708 720235; website: www.bemsee.net/ben-fund)

CC number: 213308

Eligibility

Members of the club and their dependants who are in need, with a particular focus on those who have been injured while riding.

Types of grants

One-off grants towards subsistence, travel and, as is the case most often, towards medical care and equipment costs.

Annual grant total

In 2014 the trust had an income of £8,600 and a total expenditure of £7,000. We estimate that the amount of grants given to individuals totalled £6,500.

Applications

Apply in writing to the correspondent. Applications can be submitted at any time, either directly by the individual or through a third party such as a spouse or friend.

British Racing Drivers Club (BRDC) Benevolent Fund

£23,500 (9 grants)

Correspondent: Ruth Ritchie, Facilitator, 42 Baskerville, Malmesbury SN16 9BS (07714701351; email: BRDCbenevolentfund@brdc.co.uk; website: www.brdc.co.uk)

CC number: 1084173

Eligibility

Members of the BRDC and their families and dependants or people involved with motor racing generally and their families and dependants.

Types of grants

One-off and recurrent grants are given according to need. For example, grants have previously been awarded for mobility aids, contributions to care costs and counselling.

Annual grant total

In 2013/14 the fund had assets of £548,500 and an income of £28,000. Grants were made to nine individuals totalling £23,500.

Applications

Applications can be made using an initial enquiry form on the charity's website, or in writing to the correspondent, including details of income and expenditure, assets and liabilities. Applications can be submitted directly by the individual, by an organisation such as Citizens Advice or through a third party such as a social worker. There are no deadlines and applications are considered at trustee meetings.

Other information

During 2008/09 the British Racing Drivers Club (BRDC) Benevolent Fund merged with the British Motoring Sport Relief Fund and the assets of the latter have been transferred under the control of the trustees of the BRDC Benevolent Fund.

The charity's facilitator and social worker can offer advice about benefits and accessing further support.

Sussex County Football Association Benevolent Fund

£6,500

Correspondent: Michael Brown, Trustee, 10 Hillcrest, Brighton BN1 5FN (01273 708587; email: mike.jbrown@ntlworld.com; website: www.sussexfa.com)

CC number: 217496

Eligibility

Members of Sussex county FA clubs and their relatives or dependants.

Types of grants

One-off or recurrent grants to support players and officials affiliated to Sussex County FA who have suffered a football-related injury and, as a result, find themselves in financial hardship.

Annual grant total

In 2013/14 the fund had an income of £11,500 and a total expenditure of £6,800. We estimate that the amount of grants given to individuals totalled £6,500.

Exclusions

Claims for one week's incapacity should only be submitted in very exceptional circumstances as they are not considered necessitous.

Applications

Application forms are available from the correspondent. Requests for application forms must be received by the secretary within 14 days of the injury and then completed and returned within a further 28 days.

Applications must include a full disclosure of financial and general circumstances alongside a medical certificate.

Other

Catenian Association Benevolent and Children's Fund

£83,500

Correspondent: Mark Allanson, Trustee, The Catenian Association, 2nd Floor, 1 Park House, Station Square, Coventry CV1 2FL (024 7622 4533; email: senadmin@thecatenians.com; website: www.thecatenians.com)

CC number: 214244

Eligibility
Members of the association and their dependants who are in need.

Types of grants
One-off and recurrent grants are given according to need. Loans are also available.

Annual grant total
In 2013/14 the fund held assets of £6.55 million and had an income of £278,500. Grants totalled £83,500, with a further £382,000 paid in non-secured loans. In the past about 20–30 grants have been made annually.

Applications
Applications can be made in writing to the correspondent. The trustees meet to consider applications four times a year, although urgent applications may be considered between the meetings.

Other information
The website states:

The Catenian Association is an international body of proudly Catholic laymen who meet at least once a month in local units called Circles, to enjoy each other's company and thereby strengthen their family life and faith through friendship. It is open to practising Catholic laymen from the age of 18 years.

There is a separate Catenian Association Bursary Fund Ltd (Charity Commission no. 1081143) providing Catholics aged 16–24 'to take part in community-based projects at home and abroad, which have a clear benefit for others as well as for the participant'.

The fund is administered by the Catena Trustees Ltd.

Conservative and Unionist Agents' Benevolent Association

£47,000

Correspondent: Sally Smith, Hon. Secretary CABA, Conservative Campaign Headquarters, 30 Millbank, London SW1P 4DP (020 7984 8172 (Tuesdays 11am–5pm); email: sally.smith@conservatives.com; website: www.conservativeagentscharity.org.uk)

CC number: 216438

Eligibility
Retired and serving Conservative Party agents and their dependants.

The charity's website specifies that it assists:

Deserving persons holding office as an Agent or who formerly served as an Agent for a minimum of ten years and who are or have been full or Associate members of the National Society of Conservative and Unionist Agents, and their dependants

and the dependants of such deceased Members of the Society.

Types of grants
Recurrent grants to help with living costs which, at the time of writing, range from £50 to £300 per month. The website also states:

In addition beneficiaries receive a holiday grant, a seasonal grant at Christmas and a heating allowance. CABA provides a TV, and for those under 75, pays for a licence. Telephone rental or an IT grant is also payable as appropriate. Beneficiaries can, if they choose, be reimbursed for the cost of the Daily Telegraph Voucher scheme.

Applications for grants for white goods, household repairs and other specific requests are also considered from regular beneficiaries and on a one-off basis.

Annual grant total
In 2013/14 the charity had assets of £2.8 million and an income of £92,500. Grants totalled £57,000, of which we estimate around £10,000 was made for educational purposes, leaving £47,000 for social welfare.

Exclusions
Grants cannot be made for nursing home fees, nor are loans given. The charity is not able to provide support to serving or retired Conservative Party staff who are not qualified agents.

Applications
Initial enquiries can be made by post, email or telephone to the correspondent, who will then discuss the possibilities available for the applicant. A member of the management committee or a local serving agent will then visit the applicant to discuss their application and their need for support, which is based on an assessment of household income and other circumstances. Every beneficiary is reassessed annually, either in winter or summer.

Other information
The majority of the association's grants are made for relief-in-need purposes but some help is given to the children of deceased members for the costs of education.

Local charities

This section lists local charities that award grants to individuals for welfare purposes. The information in the entries applies only to welfare grants and concentrates on what the charity actually does rather than on what its governing document allows it to do.

Regional classification

We have divided the UK into 12 geographical areas, as numbered on the map on page 204. Scotland, Wales and England have been divided into unitary or local authorities, in some cases grouped in counties or regions. On page 205 you can find the list of unitary or local authorities within each county or area. (Please note: not all of these unitary authorities have a grant-making charity included in this guide.)

The Northern Ireland section has not been subdivided into smaller areas. Within the other sections, charities are ordered as follows:

Scotland

▷ First, the charities which apply to the whole of Scotland, or at least two areas in Scotland, are listed.
▷ Second, Scotland is further divided into electoral board areas, and then again into council areas.
▷ Should an entry apply for at least two council areas, it will appear in in the appropriate electoral board section.

Wales

▷ First, charities which apply to the whole of Wales, or at least two areas of Wales, are listed.

▷ Second, Wales is sub-divided into four regions. The entries which apply to the whole region, or to at least two local government areas within it, appear first.
▷ Third, the charities are listed under the relevant local government division.

England

▷ First, charities which apply to the whole of England, or at least two regions within it, are listed.
▷ Second, England is divided into nine regions. The entries which apply to the whole region, or to at least two counties within it, appear first.
▷ Third, the regions are divided into counties.
▷ The counties are sub-divided into relevant local government areas.

London

▷ First, the charities which apply to the whole of Greater London, or to at least two boroughs are listed.
▷ The charities serving London are further sub-divided into the relevant boroughs.

Within each geographical category, the charities are listed alphabetically.

To be sure of identifying every relevant local charity, look at the charities in each relevant category in the following order:
1 Unitary or local authority (for England, Scotland and Wales) or borough (for Greater London)
2 County (for England)
3 Region (for England, Wales and, in some cases, Scotland)
4 Country (for England, Northern Ireland, Scotland and Wales).

For example, if you live in Liverpool, first establish which region Merseyside is in by looking at the map on page 204. Then, having established that Merseyside is in region 9, North West, look under the 'Geographical areas' list on page 205 and find the page where the entries for Merseyside begin. First, look under the heading for Liverpool to see if there are any relevant charities. Then work back through the charities under Merseyside generally, the charities under North West generally, and then charities listed under England generally.

Having found grant-makers covering your area, read any other eligibility requirements carefully. While some charities can and do give grants for any need for people in their area of benefit, most have other, more specific criteria which potential applicants must meet in order to be eligible.

Geographical areas

Northern Ireland

Belfast Association for the Blind

£8,000

Correspondent: R. Gillespie, Hon. Secretary, 30 Glenwell Crescent, Newtownabbey, County Antrim BT36 7TF (028 9083 6407)

IR number: XN45086

Eligibility

People who are registered blind in Northern Ireland. Consideration may also be given to those registered as partially sighted.

Types of grants

One-off grants (generally up to £350) for towards holidays, house repairs, visual aids and so on

Annual grant total

We have no current information for this charity. Previously around £16,000 has been given in grants to individuals for both educational and social welfare purposes.

Applications

Applications may be made in writing to the correspondent, through a social worker. Requests can be considered throughout the year.

Other information

Grants can also be made to organisations and to individuals for educational purposes. The association can also assist the research of causes, cure and prevention of blindness.

The Belfast Central Mission

£15,000

Correspondent: Janet Sewell, Community Services Manager, Grosvenor House, 5 Glengall Street, Belfast BT12 5AD (028 9024 1917; fax: 028 9024 0577; email: info@ belfastcentralmission.org; website: www. belfastcentralmission.org)

IR number: XN46001

Eligibility

Children, young people and the elder who are in need and live in Greater Belfast.

Types of grants

One-off gifts of food parcels and toys at Christmas to children, families and older people. Our research shows that around 3000 toy parcels and 1600 food parcels are distributed every Christmas. Short breaks and holidays for elderly people are offered each year.

Annual grant total

According to our research, approximately £15,000 worth of donations and gifts in-kind are available annually.

Applications

Application forms are available from the correspondent. Grants are normally decided in October and November.

Other information

This charity also runs advice centres and residential homes. It organises social gatherings and companionship to older people and runs a mentoring scheme for young people who have been residents of BCM's Supported Housing Project.

Belfast Sick Poor Fund

£5,000

Correspondent: Grants Officer, c/o Bryson House, 28 Bedford Street, Belfast BT2 7FE (028 9032 5835; fax: 028 9043 9156)

Eligibility

Families in Northern Ireland with children aged under 18 who are in poor health or who have a disability and are in receipt of benefits or on a low income and who are in need.

Types of grants

One-off grants ranging from £50 to £200 for necessities and comforts.

Annual grant total

Grants usually total about £5,000 each year.

Applications

Apply in writing to the correspondent by a social worker or other health professional. The fund cannot accept self-referrals. Applications should include: background information on the applicant with a breakdown of needs; why the request is being made; how a grant will benefit the applicant; details of income and expenditure on a weekly or monthly basis; and details of other sources of financial assistance and outcomes of any applications.

Other information

The fund derives its income from BBC Children in Need who have been a long-term sponsor.

Church of Ireland Orphans and Children Society for Counties Antrim and Down

£70,000

Correspondent: Charity Administrator, Church of Ireland House, 61–67 Donegall Street, Belfast BT1 2QH (028 9082 8830; email: office@diocoff-belfast.org; website: connor.anglican.org)

Eligibility

Orphaned children who live in the counties of Antrim or Down and who are members of the Church of Ireland.

Types of grants

Annual grants of up to £500 and one-off bereavement grants of £1,000 to a family on the death of a parent.

Annual grant total

Around £70,000 is available each year. No other information was available at the time of writing (August 2015).

Exclusions

No grants are given to applicants living outside the beneficial area.

Applications

Applications can be made at any time through the clergy of the parish in which the individual lives. Direct applications cannot be considered.

The Community Foundation for Northern Ireland

Correspondent: Grant Programmes Team, Community House, Citylink Business Park, Albert Street, Belfast BT12 4HQ (028 9024 5927; email: info@ communityfoundationni.org; website: www.communityfoundationni.org)

IR number: XN 45242

Eligibility

People in need in Northern Ireland. The foundation manages a number of funds providing support to local organisations, communities and individuals. Specific eligibility criteria will vary for separate funds.

Types of grants

Grants from David Ervine and the Women's Fund may provide support to individuals (the applicants are strongly advised to consult the website to ensure that the funding is available to individuals at a particular time when they wish to apply).

The Thomas Devlin Foundation operates solely for the benefit of people leaving school and developing their career in the arts field.

Annual grant total

In 2014/15 grants to individuals were only made from the Thomas Devlin Foundation for education in the arts.

Applications

Applications can be made online on the foundation's website. The standard application form consists of two parts – one is completed in the first instance and the second is emailed to the applicant to be filled in within the following two weeks and returned along with supporting documentation.

Like with all community foundations, funds are likely to open and close at short notice. See the website for latest updates before starting an application.

Other information

The foundation states on its website:

> Through our own small grants programme and by distributing grants on behalf of a range of organisations and private individuals and families, we are enabling community organisations across Northern Ireland to make a difference to peoples lives, built on the fundamental principles of peace building, social justice, equality and cultural diversity.

Grants are largely made to community groups and organisations and most funds will not fund individuals.

Occasionally new funds aimed specifically at individuals may open.

Northern Ireland Police Fund
See entry on page 169

Presbyterian Old Age Fund, Women's Fund and Indigent Ladies Fund

£148,500 (99 grants)

Correspondent: The Secretary, Presbyterian Church in Ireland, Assembly Buildings, 2–10 Fisherwick Place, Belfast BT1 6DW (028 9032 2284; fax: 028 9041 7303; email: bsw@ presbyterianireland.org; website: www. pcibsw.org)

Eligibility

Needy, elderly (over 60 years of age) or ill members of the Presbyterian Church in any part of Ireland. Applicants will normally be living at home, have an income of less than £12,000/17,500 euro per year, be in receipt of some type of state benefit, have less than £16,000/20,000 euro in savings, have no significant support from their family members and have medical needs requiring extra expenditure (some, albeit not all, of the above criteria need to be satisfied).

Types of grants

Annual grants were of £1,360 paid in quarterly instalments. Special gifts of £340 were sent to every beneficiary in the run up to Christmas. One-off grants are also made to help in cases of immediate financial need.

Support can be given for equipment, services or activities, including travel allowances to visit relatives or attend a funeral, household equipment, clothing and beddings, specialist medical or disability aids, home security, heating appliances and boilers, home insulation, respite care and a wide range of other needs.

Annual grant total

In 2014 a total of 99 people were assisted (42 in Old Age Fund, 40 in Women's Fund and 17 in Indigent Ladies' Fund) totalling £148,500 (£62,500 from the Old Age Fund, £58,500 from the Women's Fund and £27,500 from the Indigent Ladies' Fund).

Exclusions

Requests normally covered by statutory sources are not supported.

Applications

Apply in writing to the correspondent. Applications should be supported by a minister and are usually considered in January, April, June and October.

Other information

The Church's Board of Social Witness runs a full social care programme spanning family and childcare, older people's services, criminal justice, learning difficulties, mental health and disability.

The Presbyterian Orphan and Children's Society

£289,000

Correspondent: Dr Paul Gray, Executive Secretary, Glengall Exchange, 3 Glengall Street, Belfast BT12 5AB (028 9032 3737; email: paulgray1866@gmail.com; website: www.presbyterianorphanandchildrens society.org)

CC number: NIC101444

Eligibility

Young people aged 23 or under who are in full or part-time education, living in Northern Ireland and Republic of Ireland, and are in need. Beneficiaries are usually from single parent families. One parent must be a Presbyterian.

Types of grants

Regular grants are paid each quarter. The website states: 'The amount of regular quarterly grant is calculated on a per family basis and is in line with grant scales which are increased regularly to include increases in inflation.'

Depending on financial resources, a summer grant and a Christmas grant is paid to each family; in 2014 these were £110 each. Exceptional grants are also given to help with, for example, basic clothing, repayment of debts, funeral expenses and general household expenditure. These grants are usually of around £300, although in exceptional circumstances may be awarded up to £500 (however, in 2014 grants averaged £437).

Annual grant total

In 2014 the charity had assets of £10.4 million and an income of £786,500. Grants to children amounted to £578,000 and were given for both social welfare and educational purposes. We estimate social welfare grants to have totalled around £289,000.

The annual report and accounts included the following information: 'Around 730 children in 389 families were helped through regular grants' and '124 exceptional grants (the highest number for some time) were paid'.

Applications

Applications are to be made by Presbyterian clergy; forms are available from the correspondent or to download from the website.

The Royal Ulster Constabulary – Police Service of Northern Ireland Benevolent Fund

See entry on page 170

Sunshine Society Fund

£5,000

Correspondent: David Mahaffy, Grants Administrator, c/o Bryson House, 28 Bedford Street, Belfast BT2 7FE (028 9032 5835; fax: 028 9043 9156)

Eligibility

Families in Northern Ireland with children aged under 18 who are ill, disabled or facing financial hardship.

Types of grants

One-off grants for necessities and comforts. Only a small number of grants (no more than 20) are made each year.

Annual grant total

Around £5,000 is available each year for grants.

Applications

Apply in writing to the correspondent by a social worker or other health care professional. Applications should include: background information on the applicant with a breakdown of needs; why the request is being made; how a grant will benefit the applicant; details of income and expenditure on a weekly or monthly basis; and details of other sources of financial assistance and outcomes of any applications.

Scotland

General

The Association for the Relief of Incurables in Glasgow and the West of Scotland

£137,500

Correspondent: Trust Administrator, BMK Wilson Solicitors, 90 St Vincent Street, Glasgow G2 5UB (0141 221 8004; fax: 0141 221 8088; email: anita@ bmkwilson.co.uk; website: www. bmkwilson.co.uk/our-practice/links)

OSCR number: SC014424

Eligibility

People over 18 years of age in financial need with long-term illnesses who are living at home. Applicants must be living in Glasgow or the West of Scotland.

Types of grants

Quarterly pensions. One-off grants of up to £400 for specific needs, such as telephone installation, washing machines and cookers.

Annual grant total

In 2014 the charity had an income of £322,000 and a total expenditure of £164,000. Welfare grants to individuals totalled £137,500.

Exclusions

The charity will only assist individuals whose incurable condition is 'the result of a contracted/untreatable disease and not due to a congenital state or the result of an accident'. Further detail on specific conditions is given in the charity's guidance notes, available online or by request from the correspondent. Grants are not given to clear debts or towards holidays.

Applications

Applications must be made through a social worker, Citizens Advice or another welfare agency on a form available from the correspondent. The applicant's GP must confirm their medical condition. Applications are considered quarterly with deadlines 14 days prior to each meeting.

Barony Charitable Trust

£2,000

Correspondent: Agnes Cunningham, Trustee, Canal Court, 40 Craiglockhart Avenue, Edinburgh EH14 1LT (0845 140 7777)

OSCR number: SC021091

Eligibility

People in need through age, ill health, financial hardship or disability who live in Edinburgh and Central Scotland.

Types of grants

One-off grants of around £100, possibly up to £250 in exceptional circumstances. Recent grants have included support for people trying to make a fresh start, the purchase of disability aids such as wheelchairs or hoists and contributions towards the cost of a carer to accompany an individual on holiday.

Annual grant total

In 2014/15 the trust had an income of £950 and a total expenditure of £2,100. We estimate that the amount of grants given to individuals totalled around £2,000.

Applications

Application forms are available from the correspondent and should be submitted preferably through a recognised referral agency such as a GP, health visitor, priest or minister, social worker or care worker. Details of what the money is for, how it will help and any other funding applied for should also be included in the application.

Other information

Note, this trust is linked to the Barony Housing Association and applications from their area of activity receive priority.

Challenger Children's Fund
See entry on page 56

The Craigcrook Mortification

£30,000 (34 grants)

Correspondent: Fiona Watson, Manager, Charity Accounting Services, Scott-Moncrieff, Exchange Place, 3 Semple Street, Edinburgh EH3 8BL (0131 473 3500; email: fiona.watson@scott-moncrieff.com; website: www.scott-moncrieff.com/services/charities/charitable-trusts)

OSCR number: SC001648

Eligibility

People in need who are over 60 and were born in Scotland or have lived there for more than ten years.

Types of grants

Pensions of between £1,000 and £1,500 per annum payable in half-yearly instalments. One-off payments are not available.

Annual grant total

In 2014 the charity had an income of £30,500 and an expenditure of £62,000. The charity's webpage states: 'At present there are 34 pensioners who each receive between £1,000 and £1,500 per annum payable in half-yearly instalments.' There is £30,000 available for distribution each year.

Exclusions

Assistance is not normally given to those living with relations or in nursing homes.

Applications

At the time of writing (September 2015), the charity's webpage states that the application process is currently suspended. Check the website or contact the correspondent for current information.

William Hunter Old Men's Fund

£15,000

Correspondent: The Trustees, c/o Edinburgh Chamber of Commerce, 2nd Floor, Ardmore House, 40 George Street, Edinburgh EH2 2LE (0131 221 2999)

OSCR number: SC010842

Eligibility

Older men in need who were born in Scotland and are of Scottish parentage and who are/were merchants, manufacturers or master tradesmen.

Types of grants

Recurrent grants paid twice a year of £370 for people under 80, and £385 for those over 80.

Annual grant total

In 2013/14 the fund had an income of £14,800 and a total expenditure of £38,500. We estimate that the amount of grants given to individuals totalled around £15,000.

Applications

Apply in writing to the correspondent.

Key Trust

£50,000

Correspondent: The Trustees, c/o Key Housing, 70 Renton Street, Glasgow G4 0HT (0141 342 1890; email: info@ keycommunitysupports.org)

OSCR number: SC006093

Eligibility

People living in Scotland who are in need due to age, ill health or disability.

Types of grants

One-off grants according to need. Grants have been given to help people setting up home, for example, towards furnishings, such as carpets and to enable people to gain independence and 'experience more out of life'.

Annual grant total

In 2013/14 the trust had an income of £58,000 and a total expenditure of £52,500. We estimate that the amount of grants given to individuals totalled £50,000; however, expenditure seems to vary significantly each year and in previous years has been far less (£300 in 2011/12 and £11,300 in 2012/13).

Applications

Application forms are available from the correspondent and can be submitted either directly by the individual or through a social worker, Citizens Advice or other welfare agency.

Lennox Children's Trust

£8,000

Correspondent: Lennox Children's Trust, c/o Citizens Advice, Bridgend House, 179 High Street, Dumbarton G82 1NW (01389 744690)

OSCR number: SC023740

Eligibility

Children who are in need through poverty, neglect, behavioural or psychological disorders, physical or mental disability, and who live in the Dunbartonshire area.

Types of grants

One-off and recurrent grants are given according to need. Grants have been given for disability aids, educational and medical equipment and toys.

Annual grant total

In 2013/14 the trust had an income of £11,100 and total expenditure of £8,800. We estimate that the amount of grants given to individuals totalled £8,000.

Applications

Application forms are available from the correspondent. Applications should be submitted by a third party with a connection to the child.

Lockerbie Trust

£6,500

Correspondent: Trust Administrator, Farries Kirk and McVean, Dumfries Enterprise Park, Heathhall, Dumfries DG1 3SJ (01387 252127; fax: 01387 250501)

OSCR number: SC019796

Eligibility

People in need who live in Lockerbie.

Types of grants

One-off grants are up to £500. Annual payments may be considered but only in exceptional circumstances.

Annual grant total

In 2013/14 the trust had an income of £17,500 and an expenditure of £14,300. We estimate that about £6,500 was awarded in grants to individuals.

Exclusions

According to our research, educational grants are not awarded where Scottish Office grants are available.

Applications

Application forms can be requested from the correspondent. They can be submitted directly by the individual. Candidates should note that the availability of grants from other sources will be taken into account in assessing applications. Generally grants are decided quarterly, in February, June, August and November.

Other information

Organisations and groups or societies are also supported.

The George McLean Trust

£8,600

Correspondent: Grants Administrator, Blackadders Solicitors, 30–34 Reform Street, Dundee DD1 1RJ (01382 229222; fax: 01382 342220; email: enquiries@ blackadders.co.uk)

OSCR number: SC020963

Eligibility

People in need who are living with a mental or physical disability and reside in Fife and Tayside. Older people may also qualify for assistance.

Types of grants

Grants typically range between £100 to £1,000 and are made towards convalescence, hospital expenses, electrical goods, clothing, holidays, travel expenses, medical equipment, nursing fees, furniture, disability aids and help in the home.

Annual grant total

In 2014/15 the trust had an income of £48,500 and a total expenditure of £43,000. We estimate that the amount of grants given to individuals totalled £8,600, as grants are also made to local organisations.

Exclusions

No grants are made towards helping reduce debts.

Applications

Application forms are available from the correspondent. Applications can be submitted directly by the individual or through any third party. They are considered monthly.

Other information

Approximately 20% of the trust's expenditure goes to individuals, with much of the rest going to local charitable organisations. This is flexible, however, as the trustees consider where funding is needed most.

Annie Ramsay McLean Trust for the Elderly

£3,000

Correspondent: The Trustees, Blackadders Solicitors, 30–34 Reform Street, Dundee DD1 1RJ (0131 222 8000; email: toni.mcnicoll@blackadders.co.uk)

OSCR number: SC014238

Eligibility

Elderly people aged 60 or over, who live in Fife and Tayside.

Types of grants

One-off and recurrent grants of £100 to £1,000 towards needs such as convalescence, travel expenses, furniture, clothing, medical and disability equipment, electrical goods, holidays, nursing home fees, help in the home, household items, electrically operated chairs, motorised scooters and so on.

Annual grant total

In 2013/14 the trust had an unusually high income of £257,500 and a total expenditure of £45,000. We estimate that grants awarded to individuals totalled around £3,000 as the trust awards most of its grants to organisations.

Exclusions

No grants are given towards helping reduce debts.

Applications

Application forms are available from the correspondent. Applications can be submitted directly by the individual or thorough any third party. They are considered monthly.

James Paterson's Trust and Nursing Fund

£17,000

Correspondent: The Fund Administrator, Mitchells Roberton Solicitors, George House, 36 North Hanover Street, Glasgow G1 2AD (0141 552 3422; fax: 0141 552 2935; email: info@mitchells-roberton.co.uk)

OSCR number: SC017645

Eligibility

Women who have worked in cotton factories or mills in the Glasgow area, consisting of the district of the City of Glasgow and the contiguous districts of Dumbarton, Clydebank, Bearsden and Milngavie, Bishopbriggs and Kirkintilloch, East Kilbride, Eastwood and Renfrew.

Types of grants

Our research suggests that grants are given to pay primarily for short-term convalescent accommodation and occasionally for medical expenses and private accommodation in any private hospital. Grants are usually one-off payments of around £250.

Annual grant total

In 2013/14 the fund had an income of £34,000 and a total expenditure of £18,400. We estimate that grants totalled around £17,000.

Applications

Applications may be made in writing to the correspondent. They can be submitted directly by the individual or through a social worker, Citizens Advice or other welfare agency. Requests are considered throughout the year.

Radio Clyde Cash for Kids

£709,000 (28,237 grants)

Correspondent: The Grants Officer, Radio Clyde Cash for Kids, 3 South Avenue, Clydebank Business Park, Glasgow G81 2RX (0141 204 1025; email: cashforkids@radioclyde.com; website: www.clydecashforkids.com)

OSCR number: SC003334

Eligibility

Children under the age of 16 who are in need by reason of ill health, disability, financial hardship or other disadvantage and live within the geographical areas to which Radio Clyde broadcasts (west central and south-west Scotland).

Applications are accepted from families in the following local authority areas: Glasgow, Argyll and Bute, North Ayrshire, South Ayrshire, East Ayrshire, East Dunbartonshire, North Lanarkshire, South Lanarkshire, West Dunbartonshire, Inverclyde, Renfrewshire, East Renfrewshire and Dumfries and Galloway.

Types of grants

Christmas family grants of £25 per child. Awards are intended to help pay for Christmas presents, Christmas dinner or winter clothing. Grants are normally paid to a third party supporter, usually a social work department, health centre, housing association, recognised voluntary organisation or a person in authority such as a headteacher, doctor or member of the clergy.

Annual grant total

In 2014 the charity had an income of £1.4 million and a total expenditure of £1.7 million. Grants amounted to £1.3 million though, as the accounts for the year were not available to view, we were unable to determine how much of this total was awarded to individuals. Our research indicates that, in previous years, grants to individuals have amounted to £709,000.

Applications

Applications can be made online on the charity's website. After completing the form applicants should print the confirmation page and pass it to their referee for an endorsement. All applications should be referred by a third party such as Citizens Advice, a housing association, a social work department, a headteacher, GP or member of the clergy. The referee must be willing to accept payment on behalf of the applicant. Applicants are usually notified of the decision by email. An email address must be provided.

Applications tend to open for a month in early October, check the website for the exact dates.

Other information

Details of the scheme are broadcast on Radio Clyde in the run up to Christmas. Grants are also awarded to groups organising a trip to the pantomime or Christmas parties with Santa, and to organisations or for various projects for the benefit of children (including summer, special and community grants) throughout the year.

Radio Forth Cash for Kids

£200,000

Correspondent: Emma Kemp, Manager, Radio Forth, Forth House, Forth Street, Edinburgh EH1 3LE (0131 475 1332; email: emma.kemp@radioforth.com; website: www.forthonline.co.uk)

OSCR number: SC041421

Eligibility

Children under the age of 18 who suffer from sickness, have a disability or are disadvantaged and live in Edinburgh, Fife and the Lothians.

Types of grants

Grants are given according to need. Support can be given towards clothing, travel costs for medical reasons, hospital expenses and medical and disability equipment and so on. At the time of writing (August 2015), the charity is running an appeal with focus on providing beds for children who currently do not have a bed of their own.

Annual grant total

Grants have previously totalled around £200,000.

Exclusions

Generally holidays are not funded except for in exceptional circumstances.

213

Applications

Application forms are available from the correspondent or to download from the charity's website. A letter of support is required from a GP, health visitor, social worker, occupational therapist or other professional involved with the child who can support the claim. Applications need to be accompanied by at least three monthly bank statements from the child's parents/guardians. The trustees meet several times a year to consider requests which should be submitted at least a month in advance to the meeting (specific dates of the meetings can be requested from the correspondent). All applicants are notified of the outcome.

Other information

The charity is a part of Bauer Radio's Cash for Kids Charities (Scotland) and serves the East Central Scotland and Edinburgh area.

Groups and small charities are also supported.

Radio Tay Cash for Kids

£75,000

Correspondent: Lynda Macfarlane, Charity Co-ordinator, Cash for Kids, 6 North Isla Street, Dundee DD3 7JQ (01382 423263 or 01382 423285; email: lynda.macfarlane@radiotay.co.uk; website: www.tayfm.co.uk)

Eligibility

Children and young people aged under 18 who are in need and live within Radio Tay's transmission area (Dundee, Angus, Perth and North East Fife).

Types of grants

One-off grants of £50 to £5,000 for a range of needs.

Annual grant total

All funds raised go towards helping children in the Radio Tay transmission area, with a focus on 'improving quality of life, personal development & the fulfilment of aspirations'. Around 30,000 children are assisted each year, with funding also available for organisations. We estimate grants to individuals total around £75,000 each year.

Exclusions

Grants are not made to pay salaries or rent.

Applications

Application forms can be downloaded from the website or requested from the correspondent. Applications must be submitted with a supporting letter, proof of incomings/outgoings and at least two written quotes. Grants are awarded quarterly, typically in February, May,

August and November, with applications to be submitted by the previous month.

Dr John Robertson Sibbald Trust

£10,000

Correspondent: The Trustees, c/o Brodies LLP, 15 Atholl Crescent, Edinburgh EH3 8HA (0131 228 3777)

OSCR number: SC001055

Eligibility

Adults living in Scotland who have an incurable disease and who are in financial need.

Types of grants

Usually £140 a year payable in two instalments in May and November. Occasional one-off grants are given in exceptional circumstances.

Annual grant total

In 2013/14 the trust had an income of £5,800 and a total expenditure of £10,800. We estimate grants that awarded to individuals totalled around £10,000.

Applications

Application forms are available from the correspondent. Applications should be accompanied by a certificate from a surgeon or physician giving full details of the disease and certify that in their opinion it is incurable. As much background information about the applicant as possible is also required which can be in the form of a letter from a social worker or friend describing the family circumstances and giving other personal information. Applications should be submitted by 15 November for consideration in late November/early December.

Mrs S. H. Troughton Charitable Trust

£2,400

Correspondent: Anina Cheng, Swan House, 17–19 Stratford Place, London W1C 1BQ (020 7907 2100; email: charity@mfs.co.uk)

CC number: 265957

Eligibility

People in need who receive a pension and live on the estates of Ardchattan in Argyll, and Blair Atholl.

Types of grants

One-off and repeated grants.

Annual grant total

In 2013/14 the trust had an income of £11,900 and a total expenditure of £395,500. Due to the trust's low income,

it was not required to submit its accounts to the Charity Commission and so we were unable to determine the reason for its exceptionally high expenditure (in 2012/13 total expenditure was £17,000). In the past, the majority of grant funding has been awarded to organisations rather than to individuals. In 2011/12 – the only year's accounts we were able to view – grants to individuals totalled £2,400.

Exclusions

Grants are not given to people whose income is £1,000 above their personal allowance for income tax.

Applications

Apply in writing to the correspondent at any time. Applications can be submitted by the individual or, where applicable, via a third party such as a social worker or through an organisation such as Citizens Advice or other welfare agency. Unsuccessful applications will not be acknowledged.

Ayrshire

East Ayrshire

Miss Annie Smith Mair Bequest

£6,500

Correspondent: c/o Head of Democratic Services, East Ayrshire Council, Council Headquarters, London Road, Kilmarnock KA3 7BU (01563 576093; email: admin@east-ayrshire.gov.uk; website: www.east-ayrshire.gov.uk)

OSCR number: SC021095

Eligibility

People in need who live, or were born in, Newmilns.

Types of grants

One-off grants usually in the range of £50 to £1,000, towards clothing, household essentials, minor house or garden maintenance work/adaptations, mobility and personal aids, short breaks and small donations for living expenses.

Annual grant total

In 2013/14 the charity had an income of £200 and a total expenditure of £7,000. We estimate that the amount of grants given to individuals totalled £6,500.

Applications

Apply on a form available from the correspondent or from the East Ayrshire Council website. Applications can be made directly by the individual or through a GP, social worker, Citizens Advice or other welfare agency.

Note: if an application is being made on health grounds alone, a GP's certification of need will also be required.

Other information
The trust is administered by East Ayrshire Council and in recent years, has aided more than 100 people through its grant-making activities.

Archibald Taylor Fund

£14,000

Correspondent: Gillian Hamilton, Democratic Services Officer, East Ayrshire Council, Council Headquarters, London Road, Kilmarnock KA3 7BU (01563 576093; email: admin@east-ayrshire.gov.uk; website: www.east-ayrshire.gov.uk/Home.aspx)

OSCR number: SC019308

Eligibility
People who are either living in Kilmarnock, or were born there, and are in need of special nursing, convalescent treatment at the coast or in the country; or a holiday during convalescence. Applicants must be in financial need.

Types of grants
Grants are given for the provision of special nursing or convalescent treatment and convalescent holidays of up to three weeks. Previous awards have ranged from £250 to £1,000. Support can also be given for beneficiaries to be accompanied on holiday by a carer or companion.

Annual grant total
In 2013/14 the charity had an income of £2,000 and a total expenditure of £17,200. We estimate that the amount of grants given to individuals totalled £16,500.

Exclusions
Funding will not be given for holidays abroad (it can only be given for holidays within the UK and Ireland), unless there are exceptional circumstances to support doing so.

Applications
Application forms are available from the correspondent or can be downloaded from the East Ayrshire website. Requests are considered throughout the year. Applicants should be recommended for this by a GP. The following should be submitted with the application: household income, employer's certificate of earnings and/or a benefit award letter and a declaration by the applicant's GP.

Completed forms should be returned to: Head of Democratic Services, East Ayrshire Council Headquarters, London Road, Kilmarnock KA3 7BU. The Democratic Services Officer can answer queries by telephone, and help can be given to complete the application form and make holiday arrangements.

Central Scotland

Clackmannanshire
The Spittal Trust

£7,000

Correspondent: Revenue Services, Kilncraigs, Greenside Street, Alloa FK10 1EB (01259 450000; email: benefits@clacks.gov.uk; website: www. clacksweb.org.uk/community/ spittaltrust)

OSCR number: SC018529

Eligibility
People in need who are of a 'deserving character' and have lived in Alloa for at least ten years immediately before applying to the trust.

Types of grants
Although all requests will be considered, assistance is mainly given in small, one-off grants for essential household goods such as beds, bedding, electric cookers and washing machines.

Annual grant total
In 2013/14 the trust had an income of £380 and a total expenditure of £7,700. We estimate that the amount of grants given to individuals totalled £7,000.

Applications
Application forms are available to collect from the Clackmannanshire Council reception office or can be downloaded from the council's website. The trust also requires proof of income and, if necessary, evidence of any medical conditions. Application deadlines are at the end of February, May, August and November for consideration in March, June, September and December. Exact dates of trustee meetings are advertised on the website.

Falkirk
The Anderson Bequest

£10,000

Correspondent: The Trustees, c/o Johnston and Co., 13 Register Street, Bo'ness, West Lothian EH51 9AE (01506 822112)

OSCR number: SC011755

Eligibility
People in need who live in Bo'ness.

Types of grants
Annual grants, normally of around £150 per year.

Annual grant total
In 2013/14 the charity had an income of £29,000 and a total expenditure of £24,500. Our research tells us that usually around £10,000 is given in grants to individuals each year.

Applications
Apply in writing to the correspondent.

Stirling
The George Hogg Trust

£8,000

Correspondent: Secretary, Tayview, Main Street, Killin, Perthshire FK21 8UT

OSCR number: SC001890

Eligibility
People who live in Killin and are in need.

Types of grants
One-off and recurrent grants are given according to need. For example, a recent grant of £200 was given towards an electric wheelchair.

Annual grant total
In 2013/14 the income of the trust was £18,600 and the charitable expenditure was £9,400. We estimate that the amount of grants given to individuals totalled £8,000.

Applications
Apply in writing to the correspondent via a third party such as a local doctor or minister. There are no deadlines and applications are normally considered at the Annual General Meeting.

Dumfries and Galloway

The Holywood Trust

£25,500

Correspondent: Richard Lye, Trust Administrator, Hestan House, Crichton Business Park, Bankend Road, Dumfries DG1 4TA (01387 269176; fax: 01387 269175; email: funds@holywood-trust. org.uk; website: www.holywood-trust. org.uk)

OSCR number: SC009942

Eligibility
Primarily young people aged 15 to 25 living in the Dumfries and Galloway region, with a preference for those who

are mentally, physically or socially disadvantaged.

The website further states:

> Our focus is primarily on young people aged 15 – 25 years, however we will consider grants for younger vulnerable children if they are preventative measures in relation to health or social disadvantage, or if a child has an exceptional talent and requires funding to further this.

Types of grants

The trust supports a large number of individual young people by making small grants to improve their lives. Grants are usually in the range of £50 to £500 and can be given towards, for example, the purchase of household items for a young person leaving care.

Annual grant total

In 2013/14 the trust had an income of £2.1 million and a total expenditure of £1.8 million. We were unable to determine the amount given in grants during the year; however, in previous years, grants to individuals have amounted to £99,000, with around 26% awarded for social welfare purposes.

Exclusions

Our research indicates that no grants are given towards carpets or accommodation deposits. Retrospective (backdated) awards are not made.

Applications

Application forms can be downloaded from the website, where a helpful application Q&A can also be found, or can be requested from the correspondent. The application guidelines provide the following advice: 'It will always be helpful to have a supporting letter from a third-party who knows you in a formal capacity. Depending on your circumstances the third-party could be a Social Worker, support worker, college tutor, sports coach, etc.' At least four weeks should be allowed for an application to be processed. Normally only one grant is made per beneficiary per year.

John Primrose Trust

£2,600

Correspondent: The Trustees, 1 Newall Terrace, Dumfries DG1 1LN

OSCR number: SC009173

Eligibility

People in need who live in Dumfries and Maxwelltown or have a connection with these places by parentage.

Types of grants

Our research suggests that grants of £100–£150 are given twice a year to 10–20 older people.

Annual grant total

In 2014/15 the trust had an income of £16,400 and a total expenditure of £10,600. We estimate that the amount of grants given to individuals for social welfare purposes totalled around 2,600.

Applications

Application forms are available from the correspondent. They are generally considered in June and December.

Other information

The trust awards grants to both individuals and organisations for educational and social welfare purposes.

Dunbarton-shire and Argyll and Bute

Argyll and Bute

Glasgow Bute Benevolent Society

£32,000

Correspondent: Charity Administrator, Ardmore, 15 Crichton Road, Rothesay, Isle of Bute

OSCR number: SC016182

Eligibility

People in need who live in Bute, particularly the elderly. The length of time a person has lived in Bute and how long they have been connected with the area is taken into consideration.

Types of grants

Our research suggests that the society does not award grants as such – suitable applicants are admitted to the Society's Roll of Pensioners and receive a pension payable half-yearly and a Christmas bonus payment. The half-yearly pension is usually of about £50 and the value and availability of the bonus depends on income available.

Annual grant total

In 2014 the society had an income of £35,000 and an expenditure of £33,000. We estimate that support to individuals totalled around £32,000.

Exclusions

People in receipt of parochial help are not supported, unless in extraordinary circumstances.

Applications

Application forms are available from the correspondent. Candidates should provide a supporting recommendation by a minister of religion, doctor, solicitor or other responsible person.

Other information

Small grants for educational purposes may be made on rare occasions.

Fife

The Bruce Charitable Trust

£18,000

Correspondent: The Trustees, The Bruce Charitable Trust, c/o Pagan Osborne, 106 South Street, St Andrews KY16 9QD (01334 475001)

OSCR number: SC014927

Eligibility

People who are older, in need, infirm or distressed who live in the burgh of Cupar.

Types of grants

One-off grants of up to £400.

Annual grant total

In 2013/14 the trust had an income of £55,500 and a total expenditure of £40,500. We estimate that the amount of grants given to individuals totalled £18,000, with funding also awarded to local organisations.

Applications

Apply in writing to the correspondent including the applicant's date of birth, postal address and reason for request. Applications should be made by an organisation such as Citizens Advice or through a third party such as a social worker.

Other information

The trust also funds local organisations and charities, youth groups, cultural, educational and recreational facilities.

The Fleming Bequest

£20,000

Correspondent: Elizabeth Calderwood, Administrator, Pagan Osborne, 106 South Street, St Andrews, Fife KY16 9QD (01334 475001; fax: 01334 476322; email: elcalderwood@pagan.co.uk)

OSCR number: SC016126

Eligibility

People living in the parish of St Andrews and St Leonards in the town of

St Andrews who are older, in poor health or in financial difficulty.

Types of grants

One-off grants, up to around £300. Grants are awarded towards clothing, carpets, fridge/freezers, special chairs and other essential household needs.

Annual grant total

In 2013/14 the trust had an income of £18,500 and an expenditure of £24,500. We estimate that the amount of grants given to individuals totalled around £20,000.

Applications

Apply in writing to the correspondent preferably through a social worker, Citizens Advice or similar welfare agency. Applications are considered at any time and should include details of the applicant's postal address, date of birth and reason for the request.

The St Andrews Welfare Trust

£10,000

Correspondent: Elizabeth Calderwood, Administrator, Pagan Osborne, 106 South Street, St Andrews, Fife KY16 9QD (01334 475001; fax: 01334 476322)

OSCR number: SC008660

Eligibility

People in need who live within a four-mile radius of St Andrews.

Types of grants

One-off grants of up to £400 are given towards carpeting, cookers, clothing, fireguards and so on.

Annual grant total

In 2014 the trust had an income of £27,500 and an expenditure of £18,800. Our research tells us that around £10,000 is given to individuals and about £4,000 to organisations each year.

Exclusions

No grants are given for educational purposes, such as gap year projects.

Applications

Apply in writing to the correspondent through a social worker, Citizens Advice or other welfare agency. Applications should include applicant's date of birth, postal address and reason for request and are considered throughout the year.

Other information

Grants are also given to playgroups and senior citizen Christmas teas.

Glasgow

The Glasgow Care Foundation

£150,000

Correspondent: The Secretary, Orkney Street Enterprise Centre, 18–20 Orkney Street, Glasgow G51 2BX (0141 445 2736; email: info@ glasgowcarefoundation.org; website: www.glasgowcarefoundation.org)

OSCR number: SC000906

Eligibility

Residents of Glasgow who have lived in the city for a minimum of five years and are in need by reason of age, ill health, disability, financial hardship or other disadvantage.

Types of grants

Grants are given for essential support to those in need where support is not available through local authorities or other agencies. Support is given for items such as essential white goods e.g. cookers, fridges, freezers, washing machines, beds and bedding, basic furniture, children's clothing and holidays mainly in the UK.

Annual grant total

In 2013/14 the foundation had an income of £324,000 and a total expenditure of £317,500. We estimate that the amount of grants given to individuals totalled around £150,000, with local organisations also receiving funding.

Exclusions

People who are living in care are not eligible.

Applications

Applications can be made online, only through a recognised agency working in the community such as social services. Note the following for online applications:

If applying online for the first time, you will need to register first to obtain a unique password which you can then use in subsequent online applications. If you have already registered and have been given a password then you can go directly to complete the online application form.

The foundation's welfare officers visit and investigate all cases. Any previous successful applications to the foundation will be taken into account.

Other information

The foundation was formerly known as the City of Glasgow Society of Social Service.

The Andrew and Mary Elizabeth Little Charitable Trust

£51,500

Correspondent: Ronnie Munton, Administrator, Low Beaton Richmond Solicitors, Sterling House, 20 Renfield Street, Glasgow G2 5AP (0141 221 8931; fax: 0141 248 4411; email: gabrielle@lbr-law.co.uk)

OSCR number: SC011185

Eligibility

People in need whose sole source of income is income support, disability benefit or pension, who live in the city of Glasgow.

Types of grants

One-off and recurrent grants are given according to need.

Annual grant total

In 2013/14 the trust had an income of £85,500 and a total expenditure of £64,500. Typically grants to individuals account for 80% of the trust's charitable expenditure and grants to organisations the remaining 20%. Therefore, we estimate that individuals received a total of £51,500.

Applications

Apply writing to the correspondent, to be submitted through social services. Applications should include financial details and are considered monthly.

The Trades House of Glasgow

£199,000

Correspondent: The Clerk, Administration Centre, North Gallery – Trades Hall, 85 Glassford Street, Glasgow G1 1UH (0141 553 1605; email: info@ tradeshouse.org.uk; website: www.tradeshouse.org.uk)

OSCR number: SC040548

Eligibility

People in need who live in Glasgow, especially those receiving only a pension.

Types of grants

One-off grants of up to £5,000 are given.

Annual grant total

In 2013/14 the charity had assets of £22 million and an income of £1.1 million. Grants to individuals totalled £219,000, of which £199,000 was given for social welfare purposes. Bursaries and educational grants to individuals totalled a further £19,800.

Applications

Apply in writing to the correspondent.

Other information

Guilds and Craft Incorporations are the Scottish equivalent of the craft guilds or livery companies, which developed in most of the great cities of Europe in the Middle Ages. Over the years many of the House's political and legal duties have been transferred to other bodies, but the charitable functions and concern for the future of Glasgow remain. The assistance of the needy, the encouragement of youth and support for education, particularly the schools and the further education colleges in developing craft standards, are now its chief objects.

The Trades House also operates the Drapers Fund which distributes £50,000 annually to children in need who are under the age of seventeen. The fund has its own application form, which is available to download from the charity's website.

The Ure Elder Trust

£6,500

Correspondent: Trust Administrator, Maclay Murray and Spens LLP, 1 George Square, Glasgow G2 1AL (0330 222 0050)

OSCR number: SC003775

Eligibility

Widows in need who live in Glasgow, especially Govan.

Types of grants

Annual grants paid twice a year plus a bonus at Christmas.

Annual grant total

In 2014 the trust had an income £9,500 and a total expenditure of £7,100. We estimate that around £6,500 was made in grants to individuals.

Applications

Application forms are available from the correspondent. They can be submitted directly by the individual or through a third party and are normally considered in April and October.

Grampian

Grampian Police Diced Cap Charitable Fund

£20,000

Correspondent: The Secretary, Grampian Police, Queen Street, Aberdeen AB10 1ZX (email: secretary@ dicedcap.org; website: www.dicedcap. org)

OSCR number: SC017901

Eligibility

People in need who live in the Grampian police force area.

Types of grants

One-off and recurrent grants to improve the health and well-being of any deserving individuals.

Annual grant total

In 2013/14 the fund had an income of £81,500. Grants usually total about £50,000, although most of this is given to organisations. We estimate that around £20,000 each year is given to individuals for social welfare purposes.

Applications

Apply in writing to the correspondent.

Aberdeen and Aberdeenshire

Aberdeen Indigent Mental Patients' Fund

£10,000

Correspondent: Fund Administrator, Peterkins Solicitors, 100 Union Street, Aberdeen AB10 1QR (01224 428000)

OSCR number: SC003069

Eligibility

People who live in Aberdeen and are, or have been, mentally ill on their discharge from hospital.

Types of grants

One-off and recurrent grants are given according to need.

Annual grant total

In 2014/15 the fund had an income of £4,600 and an unusually high expenditure of £15,000. We estimate that around £10,000 has been awarded in grants to individuals.

Applications

Apply in writing to the correspondent.

The Aberdeen Widows' and Spinsters' Benevolent Fund

£40,000

Correspondent: Trust Administrator, c/o Raeburn Christie Clark and Wallace, 12–16 Albyn Place, Aberdeen AB10 1PS (01224 332400)

OSCR number: SC002057

Eligibility

Widows and unmarried women over 60 years of age who live in the city or county of Aberdeen; in cases of special need and where surplus income is available, those between 40 and 60 are considered.

Types of grants

Generally yearly allowances of up to £360 paid in two instalments in June and December.

Annual grant total

In 2013/14 the fund had an income of £64,500 and a total expenditure of £58,000. Grants usually total around £40,000.

Applications

Application forms are available from the correspondent.

James Allan of Midbeltie's Fund for Widows

£65,000

Correspondent: Michael Macmillan, Administrator, Burnett and Reid, 15 Golden Square, Aberdeen AB10 1WF (01224 644333; fax: 01224 632173; email: mdcmillan@burnett-reid.co.uk)

OSCR number: SC003865

Eligibility

Widows who live in Aberdeen and are in need.

Types of grants

Recurrent yearly allowances of around £300 a year payable in two instalments in May and November.

Annual grant total

In 2013/14 the charity had an income of £74,500 and a total expenditure of £84,500. We estimate that grants totalled £70,000.

Applications

Application forms are available from the correspondent. Applications can be submitted either directly by the individual, through a third party such as a social worker or through an organisation such as Citizens Advice or another welfare agency. Applications are usually considered in April and October.

The George, James and Alexander Chalmers Trust

£42,000

Correspondent: Trust Administrator, c/o Storie Cruden and Simpson Solicitors, 2 Bon Accord Crescent, Aberdeen AB11 6DH (01224 587261; fax: 01224 580850; email: info@storiecs.co. uk)

OSCR number: SC008818

Eligibility

Women living in Aberdeen who have fallen on hard times as a result of misfortune and not through any fault of their own.

Types of grants

Recurrent grants of about £450 a year, payable in half-yearly instalments.

Annual grant total

In 2013/14 the trust had an income of £352,500 and a total expenditure of £109,000. Grants are estimated to have totalled around £42,000.

Applications

Application forms are available from the correspondent.

Other information

Regular grants are also made to organisations.

The Gordon Cheyne Trust Fund

£20,000

Correspondent: Trusts Administrator, Raeburn Christie Clark and Wallace, 12–16 Albyn Place, Aberdeen AB10 1PS (01224 332400; fax: 01224 332401)

OSCR number: SC012841

Eligibility

Widows and daughters of deceased merchants, shopkeepers and other businessmen who are elderly natives of Aberdeen or who have lived there for at least 25 years.

Types of grants

Annual allowances of around £400 are paid twice yearly.

Annual grant total

In 2013/14 the charity had an income of £26,500 and a total expenditure of £31,000. We estimate that the amount of grants given to individuals totalled around £20,000.

Applications

Apply on a form available from the correspondent via a social worker, Citizens Advice or other welfare agency.

The Donald Trust

£15,000

Correspondent: Trusts Administrator, Raeburn Christie Clark and Wallace, 12–16 Albyn Place, 52–54 Rose Street, Aberdeen AB10 1PS (01224 332400; email: info@raeburns.co.uk)

OSCR number: SC0158844

Eligibility

People in need who live in the city of Aberdeen and former county of Aberdeen. 'Advanced age, lack of health, inability to work, high character and former industry are strong recommendations.'

Types of grants

Annuities of around £400 a year, paid in two instalments.

Annual grant total

In 2014 the trust had an income of £21,000 and a total expenditure of £21,000. We estimate that annuities totalled around £15,000.

Exclusions

Generally, people under the age of 60 are not eligible.

Applications

Application forms are available from the correspondent. Applications should be submitted through a third party such as a social worker. They are considered twice a year.

Garden Nicol Benevolent Fund

£4,000

Correspondent: The Trustees, c/o Peterkins Solicitors, 100 Union Street, Aberdeen AB10 1QR (01224 428000)

OSCR number: SC007140

Eligibility

Women in need who 'having been in a position of affluence have, by circumstances beyond their control, been reduced to comparative poverty'. Applicants must both have been born and be living in the city or county of Aberdeen.

Types of grants

One-off and recurrent grants are given according to need.

Annual grant total

In 2013/14 the fund had an income of £10,000 and a total expenditure of £4,500. We estimate that the amount of grants given to individuals totalled £4,000.

Applications

Apply in writing to the correspondent.

The Jopp Thomson Fund

£16,000

Correspondent: Fund Administrator, Ledingham Chalmers LLP, 52–54 Rose Street, Aberdeen AB10 1HA (01224 408408; email: mail@ledinghamchalmers.com)

OSCR number: SC009106

Eligibility

People in need through age, ill health or disability. Preference is given for widowed and single women living in Aberdeenshire and those whose name or maiden name is Thomson or Middleton.

Types of grants

Annuities of around £500 paid in two instalments to each beneficiary to be used at their discretion.

Annual grant total

In 2013/14 the fund had an income of £45,000 and an expenditure of £19,300. Previously around £16,000 has been awarded in grants.

Applications

Application forms are available from the correspondent. They can be submitted directly by the individual or through a third party and are considered in April each year.

Other information

This fund is an amalgamation of the Henry John Jopp Fund and the Jessie Ann Thomson Fund.

The Mary Morrison Cox Fund

£14,000

Correspondent: The Trustees, 18 Bon-Accord Crescent, Aberdeen AB11 6XY (01224 573321)

OSCR number: SC007881

Eligibility

People in need who live in the parish of Dyce, Aberdeen. Preference is given to older people and people living with disabilities.

Types of grants

One-off grants, ranging from £100 to £400, to help with general living expenses.

Annual grant total

In 2013/14 the fund had an income of £12,900 and a total expenditure of £14,700. We estimate that the amount of grants given to individuals totalled £14,000.

Applications

The fund has a list of potential beneficiaries to whom it sends application forms each year, usually in November. In order to be added to this list, applicants should contact the correspondent.

Miss Caroline Jane Spence's Fund

£25,000

Correspondent: Trust Administrator, c/o Mackinnons, 14 Carden Place, Aberdeen AB10 1UR (01224 632464; fax: 01224 632184; email: aberdeen@ mackinnons.com)

OSCR number: SC006434

Eligibility
Widows or unmarried females living within the city or county of Aberdeen who are in need.

Types of grants
Recurrent grants are made.

Annual grant total
In 2013/14 the charity had an income of £99,500 and a total expenditure of £95,000. In previous years grants to individuals have totalled around £25,000.

Exclusions
No grants are made where statutory funding is available.

Applications
Application forms are available from the correspondent. Applications can be submitted either directly by the individual, or through a social worker, Citizens Advice or other welfare agency or other third party. Applications are considered in November, January and April.

Other information
Grants are also made to organisations.

Highlands and Na h-Eileanan Siar (Western Isles)

Dr Forbes Inverness Trust

£6,000

Correspondent: David Hewitson, Secretary and Treasurer, Munro and Noble Solicitors, 26 Church Street, Inverness IV1 1HX (01463 221727; fax: 01463 225165; email: legal@munronoble. com)

OSCR number: SC005573

Eligibility
People with a medical or similar need who live in the former burgh of Inverness or immediately surrounding areas to the south of the Beauly/ Inverness Firth.

Types of grants
Generally one-off grants to help with the cost of medical treatment and equipment, convalescence or a period of residence in a nursing home, food, clothing and travel expenses to visit sick relatives. Help has also been given with holidays for people who, from a medical point of view, would benefit from it.

Annual grant total
In 2013/14 the trust had an income of £10,700 and a total expenditure of £7,500. We estimate that the amount of grants given to individuals totalled around £6,000.

Applications
Application forms are available from the correspondent. Applications should be submitted by the individual or through a recognised referral agency (e.g. social worker, Citizens Advice or doctor) or other third party. Forms are considered throughout the year and must be signed by the applicant's doctor. Supporting letters can also help the application.

The Highland Children's Trust

£10,000

Correspondent: Trust Administrator, 105A Castle Street, Inverness IV2 3EA (01463 243872; email: info@hctrust.co. uk; website: www.hctrust.co.uk)

OSCR number: SC006008

Eligibility
Children and young people in need who are under 25 and live in the Highlands.

Types of grants
One-off grants of £50 to £500 are available for the following purposes:
- Student hardship funding – small grants to assist students at college or university who are finding it hard to manage financially
- School or educational trips – for children attending Highland schools who cannot afford the whole cost of a trip
- Family holidays – for families who would not normally be able to go on holiday, the trust runs a scheme which enables the children of a family to have a holiday accompanied by an adult. A copy of the current holiday scheme can be obtained by application to the administrator
- Educational items for children with special educational needs – help can

be given in certain circumstances to help with the cost of educational equipment

Annual grant total
Our research indicates that this trust awards around £20,000 a year for both education and welfare purposes. We estimate that grants for social welfare total around £10,000.

Exclusions
Grants are not given for postgraduate study, to pay off debts, nor to purchase clothing, footwear, food, furniture or cars, etc. Holidays abroad are not considered for the holiday scheme.

Applications
Application forms can be requested from the correspondent in writing or by email, or can be downloaded from the website, where guidelines are also given. They can be submitted at any time either directly by the individual or through a social worker, Citizens Advice or other welfare agency. Applicants under the age of 18 must have their form counter-signed by their parent or guardian.

The William MacKenzie Trust

£20,000

Correspondent: Trust Administrator, 26 Lewis Street, Stornoway, Isle of Lewis HS1 2JF (01851 702335)

OSCR number: SC001598

Eligibility
People who are older or in poor health and live in Stornoway.

Types of grants
One-off grants to enable individuals to continue living in their own homes. Grants have been given for house adaptations, reclining chairs and domestic equipment such as washing machines.

Annual grant total
In 2013/14 the trust had an income of £40,000 and a total expenditure of £48,500. We estimate that the amount of grants given to individuals totalled £20,000, with organisations also receiving funding.

Applications
Apply in writing to the correspondent. Applications can be submitted directly by the individual or, where applicable, through a social worker, Citizens Advice or other welfare agency.

Lothian

Capital Charitable Trust

£16,000

Correspondent: The Trustees, Capital Charitable Trust, c/o Aitken Nairn WS, 7 Abercromby Place, Edinburgh EH3 6LA (0131 556 6644; email: reception@aitkennairn.co.uk)

OSCR number: SC004332

Eligibility

People in need who live in the Edinburgh and Lothians area.

Types of grants

Small, one-off grants of about £10 to £20 for clothes, decorating, household goods and other general welfare needs.

Annual grant total

In 2012/13 the trust had an income £23,000 and a total expenditure of £22,000. In the past grants have totalled about £16,000.

At the time of writing (November 2015) this was the latest financial information available.

Applications

Our research shows that application forms can be obtained from the Lothian Regional Council Social Work Departments and other responsible bodies who will forward them to the correspondent. Applications are not accepted directly from the individual.

The Robert Christie Bequest Fund

£40,000

Correspondent: Fund Administrator, Gibson McKerrell Brown LLP, 14 Rutland Square, Edinburgh EH1 2BD (0131 228 8319; email: enquiries@g-m-b.co.uk)

OSCR number: SC000465

Eligibility

People over 60 who are in need, live in Edinburgh, Midlothian, East Lothian or West Lothian and have an acutely painful disease.

Types of grants

Annual allowances are given according to need.

Annual grant total

In 2013/14 the fund had an income of £117,000 and a total expenditure of £112,500. We estimate that the amount of grants given to individuals totalled around £40,000.

Applications

Application forms are available from the correspondent. Applications can be submitted directly by the individual or through a social worker, Citizens Advice or other welfare agency. Applications are usually considered twice a year.

The Ecas (Access/ Holiday Fund)

£30,000

Correspondent: Janice Todd, Administrator, Norton Park, 57 Albion Road, Edinburgh EH7 5QY (0131 475 2344; email: administrator@ecas-edinburgh.org; website: www.ecas-edinburgh.org)

OSCR number: SC014929

Eligibility

People who are long-term and significantly disabled through impairment of the musculoskeletal, neurological or cardio-respiratory systems of the body, living in Edinburgh and the Lothians.

Types of grants

One-off grants of up to a maximum of £750. Recent grants have been given for washing machines, fridge-freezers, cookers, laptops, iPads, furniture, car adaptations, sheds and flooring. The fund also awards grants of up to £1,000 towards holidays, or £1,500 where two or more carers are required.

Annual grant total

In 2014/15 the fund had an income of £191,000 and a total expenditure of £324,500. We estimate that the amount of grants given to individuals totalled £30,000.

Exclusions

There are no grants available for bills, debts, wheelchairs, scooters or small pieces of domestic equipment. Funding is not given to pay for items which have already been bought.

People with the following conditions on their own do not meet the criteria for participation in Ecas activities: psychiatric disorders, learning difficulties, behavioural disorders, developmental delay, Down's syndrome, autism, visual or hearing impairment, cancer, diabetes, epilepsy, HIV, back pain and chronic fatigue syndrome.

Applicants must wait for two years before re-applying for a one-off grant, or four years before re-applying for a holiday grant.

Applications

Apply on a form available from the correspondent or to download from the website. Applications must be supported by a social worker or health care professional. A short GP report may also be required. Applications can be made at any time but individuals should allow around six weeks (12 weeks for holiday applications) for the administration of any grant. Further application guidance is provided on the charity's website. Applications may be fast-tracked in extenuating circumstances, in which case applicants should contact the charity.

Any application for funds for maintenance or repair for battery-packs, power-chairs or scooters must be accompanied by evidence of third party insurance.

Applicants requesting computer equipment will be asked to contact Ecas for assessment.

Note: The fund tends to purchase items and holidays directly from the supplier. If an item is eligible for only part-funding, Ecas will not release funds until the rest of the money has been raised.

Other information

Ecas also runs classes – ranging from art and craft, to yoga, swimming and ICT – as well as a 'facilitated friendship' scheme and the Ecas Befriending Project, all of which aim to improve the quality of life for people living with physical disabilities.

Edinburgh and Lothian Trust Fund

£70,000

Correspondent: Janette Scappaticcio, Trust Administrator, 1st Floor, 14 Ashley Place, Edinburgh EH6 5PX (0131 555 9100; fax: 0131 555 9101; email: grants@eltf.org.uk; website: www.eltf.org.uk)

OSCR number: SC031561

Eligibility

Individuals in need who live in the city of Edinburgh and the Lothians. Priority is given where there is a serious illness of the individual or in the family.

Grants from the Edinburgh Fire Fund are also made to individuals and families resident in the City of Edinburgh council area who have been affected by fire, either through physical or psychological trauma or through damage to their home. Applicants must be in receipt of state benefits or on a low income (less than the living wage of £14,287 per annum).

Types of grants

One-off grants of up to £200 where they will be of real benefit to the family or individual in need, such as for clothing and household essentials.

For individuals or families affected by fire, grants will be considered for compensating damage to household items (not structural damage) and support for psychological trauma (such as counselling).

Annual grant total

In 2013/14 the trust had an income of £137,500 and a total expenditure of £172,000. We estimate that the amount of grants given to individuals totalled £70,000.

Exclusions

No grants are given for electrical equipment, white goods, holidays (except in special circumstances), students' fees/equipment or the repayment of debt. Only one application will be considered in a year.

Applications to the Fire Fund will only be accepted for fires that have occurred within the last month. Grants will not be given for structural damage to property. Grants are not given for household items if the applicant has appropriate insurance, but support with counselling or therapy will be considered.

Applications

Grants for individuals in need can be applied for using a form on the website. Applications will only be accepted from a professional in the local authority, social services, hospital or voluntary sector agency. They are considered monthly. Grants are made to the applicant agency.

Grants from the Edinburgh Fire Fund can be applied for using a form on the website. Applications must be made by the affected individual, and verified by a third party such as a social worker or medical professional.

Other information

The charity was formerly known as Edinburgh Voluntary Organisations' Trust.

The charity also makes grants to organisations working in social welfare and administers grants to individuals on behalf of the Ponton House Trust.

The Merchant Company Endowments Trust (formerly known as The Edinburgh Merchant Company Endowments Trust)

£123,000

Correspondent: The Secretary and Chamberlain, The Merchant Hall, 22 Hanover Street, Edinburgh EH2 2EP (0131 220 9284; fax: 0131 220 4842; email: info@mcoe.org.uk; website: www.mcoe.org.uk)

OSCR number: SC002002

Eligibility

'Decent, indigent men and women' who are over the age of 55 and have lived or worked in the city of Edinburgh or in Midlothian. Help may also be given to younger individuals who are certified on medical grounds as unable to earn their living.

Types of grants

Assistance can be given in the form of a cash grant, bi-annual pension, gift or appliance, as well as provision and care support.

Annual grant total

In 2013/14 the trust had an income of £843,000 and an expenditure of £480,000. According to the accounts £123,000 was awarded in grants and donations however the amount allocated to individuals was not specified.

Applications

Application forms are available from the correspondent. The trust employs an almoner who assesses need and reports to the trust prior to any grant being made.

Other information

The trust also provides almshouse accommodation.

Edinburgh

The Airth Benefaction Trust

£12,500

Correspondent: Douglas Hunter, Trust Administrator, HBJ Gateley, Exchange Tower, 19 Canning Street, Edinburgh EH3 8EH (0131 228 2400; email: info@gateleyuk.com)

OSCR number: SC004441

Eligibility

People in need in Edinburgh.

Types of grants

Recurrent grants and pensions.

Annual grant total

In 2013/14 the trust had an income of £2,900 and a total expenditure of £14,700. We estimate that the amount of grants given to individuals totalled £12,500.

Applications

Application forms are available from the correspondent. Applications should be submitted either directly by the individual or through a third party such as a social worker. These should be returned no later than 30 September for consideration in December. Beneficiaries are invited to re-apply each year.

Alexander Darling Silk Mercer's Fund

£22,000

Correspondent: Gregor Murray, Secretary and Chamberlain, The Merchant Company, The Merchant Hall, 22 Hanover Street, Edinburgh EH2 2EP (0131 220 9284; fax: 0131 220 4842; email: gregor.murray@mcoe.org.uk; website: www.mcoe.org.uk)

OSCR number: SC036724

Eligibility

Unmarried or widowed women, over 55, who live in Edinburgh or who have worked in Edinburgh in the manufacture or sale of textile garments for women and children. Preference is given to women bearing the surname Darling, Millar, Small or Scott and to women born in the town of Lanark. Unfortunately, women who have only been involved in the manufacture and sale of textiles for men do not qualify for these grants.

Types of grants

Recurrent grants every six months to support living costs. The fund also helps with the cost of white goods for qualifying people over the age of 55.

Annual grant total

In 2013/14 the fund had an income of £56,500 and a total expenditure of £40,500. We estimate that the amount of grants given to individuals totalled £22,000.

Applications

Applications should be made in writing to the secretary of the Merchant Company, either directly by the individual or through a third party such as a social worker or Citizens Advice. Every written application is followed up by a visit by the almoner, during which a declaration regarding the applicant's financial circumstances is required.

The Edinburgh Royal Infirmary Samaritan Society

£19,000

Correspondent: Charity Administrator, 7 Fountainhall Road, Edinburgh EH9 2NL

OSCR number: SC004519

Eligibility

Patients of NHS hospitals in Edinburgh who are in need.

Types of grants

Specific sums of money for clothing, bills, travel expenses or other help for the families and dependants of patients while in these hospitals or on leaving. Grants range between £5 and £150.

Annual grant total
In 2013/14 the society had an income of £19,100 and a total expenditure of £20,100. We estimate that the amount of grants given to individuals totalled £19,000.

Applications
Application forms are available from the correspondent and should be submitted through a medical social worker based at Edinburgh Royal Infirmary Social Work Department. Applications are considered fortnightly.

The Edinburgh Society for Relief of Indigent Old Men

£30,000

Correspondent: Trust Secretary, c/o Lindsays, Caledonian Exchange, 19A Canning Street, Edinburgh EH3 8HE (0131 229 1212; fax: 0131 229 5611; email: edinburgh@lindsays.co.uk)

OSCR number: SC005284

Eligibility
Older men of good character resident in Edinburgh, who usually have no pension apart from statutory sources, have capital of £3,000 or less and are experiencing hardship or disability. Under exceptional circumstances, men under 65 will be considered.

Types of grants
Monthly payments, normally of around £50.

Annual grant total
In 2013/14 the society had an income of £55,000 and a total expenditure of £61,500. Grants usually total around £30,000.

Applications
Apply in writing to the correspondent.

EMMS International – Hawthornbrae

£9,100

Correspondent: Charity Administrator, 7 Washington Lane, Edinburgh EH11 2HA (0131 313 3828; email: info@emms.org; website: www.emms.org)

OSCR number: SC032327

Eligibility
People resident within the Edinburgh city boundary who are recovering from an illness and are of 'good character'

who have insufficient funds to pay for a holiday for themselves.

Types of grants
Grants of up to £300 for adults and £150 for children (under 16) for recuperative holidays. Grants to one family will not exceed £900.

Annual grant total
In 2014 the fund had assets of £395,000 and an income of £15,500. Grants totalling £9,100 were made to individuals.

Exclusions
The charity cannot give grants towards spending money.

Applications
Application forms are available from the correspondent. Applications must be sponsored by a social worker, health visitor or minister and be supported by a medical reference from a GP. Applications are considered throughout the year on a first come first served basis and usually take up to six to eight weeks to process.

Other information
EMMS International also runs a bursary scheme for medical students undertaking electives in mission schools and hospitals.

The William Brown Nimmo Charitable Trust

£20,000

Correspondent: Grants Administrator, MHD Law LLP, 45 Queen Charlotte Street, Leith, Edinburgh EH6 7HT (0131 555 0616; fax: 0131 553 1523; email: fiona.marshall@mhdlaw.co.uk)

OSCR number: SC001671

Eligibility
Older women living on a low income who were born, and permanently live, in Leith or Edinburgh.

Types of grants
Annual grants of around £165.

Annual grant total
Grants to individuals in need total about £20,000 each year. The trustees usually accept several new beneficiaries a year, but this is dependent on available income and existing beneficiaries failing to re-qualify for a grant. In 2013/14 the trust had an income of £36,500 and a total expenditure of £39,000.

Applications
Apply on a form only available from 1 June the correspondent. It should be returned by 31 July for consideration in September/October. Applicants are visited.

Police Aided Clothing Scheme (Edinburgh)

£20,000

Correspondent: Scheme Administrator, Operational Support, St Leonard's Police Station, 14 St Leonard's Street, Edinburgh EH8 9QW (0131 662 5792; email: EdinburghDCU@scotland.pnn.police.uk)

OSCR number: SC011164

Eligibility
Underprivileged children between the ages of 5 and 18 who live in the area administered by City of Edinburgh Council. In exceptional circumstances adults may be assisted.

Types of grants
In-kind gifts of socks, shoes, sweatshirts, coats and jackets or other clothing/footwear.

Annual grant total
In 2013/14 the charity had an income of £78,000 and a total expenditure of £89,500. Each year about £20,000 is spent to support individuals in need. We have been informed that this amount is not set and may be higher, depending on need.

Exclusions
The charity does not make cash grants and does not provide assistance towards school uniforms.

Applications
Initial enquiries should be made in writing or by phone to the Operational Support unit. All applicants are visited in their homes by a police officer in uniform to complete an application.

Orkney and Shetland

Shetland Charitable Trust

£383,000

Correspondent: Ann Black, Chief Executive, 22–24 North Road, Lerwick, Shetland ZE1 0NQ (01595 744994; email: mail@shetlandcharitabletrust.co.uk; website: www.shetlandcharitabletrust.co.uk)

OSCR number: SC027025

Eligibility
People who are vulnerable due to age, ill health, disability or financial hardship and have been resident in Shetland for more than a year.

Types of grants

One-off hardship grants are made from the Social Assistance Fund. Christmas grants are also given.

Annual grant total

In 2013/14 the trust had an income of £10.4 million and assets of £229 million. Social Assistance grants to individuals totalled £1,000 and Christmas grants totalled £382,000.

£29,500 was also paid in grants from the Arts Grants Scheme which makes grants to both individuals and organisations; however, a breakdown was not available.

Applications

Applications for Christmas grants tend to open in September of each year; check the website before contacting the trust to ensure applications are being accepted. Applicants for the social assistance grants should contact the duty social worker on 01595 744400.

Other information

The trust also has a number of grant schemes for organisations.

Renfrewshire

Inverclyde

Gourock Coal and Benevolent Fund

£4,200

Correspondent: Mr S. Baldwin, Trustee, 38 Taymouth Drive, Gourock, Renfrewshire PA19 1HJ

OSCR number: SC009881

Eligibility

People in need who live in the former burgh of Gourock. There is a preference for older people, especially people who live on their own.

Types of grants

Gas and electricity vouchers are available and coal deliveries can also be made.

Annual grant total

In 2013/14 the fund had an income of £4,900 and a total expenditure of £4,500. We estimate that the total amount of grants awarded to individuals was approximately £4,200.

Applications

Apply in writing to any minister or parish priest in the town, or the local branch of the WRVS (not to the correspondent). Applications are normally considered in December and can be submitted either directly by the individual or through a social worker, Citizens Advice or other welfare agency.

Scottish Borders

The Blackstock Trust

£12,000

Correspondent: Trust Secretary, Pike and Chapman, 36 Bank Street, Galashiels TD1 1ER (01896 752379)

OSCR number: SC014309

Eligibility

People who are elderly or sick, or people who have disabilities and live in the counties of Roxburgh, Berwick and Selkirk.

Serving and retired British police officers and their dependants who have been injured or incapacitated while serving as a police officer.

Types of grants

Financial assistance (usually up to £500) for accommodation, maintenance or welfare, short holiday breaks, respite care and the provision of amenities.

Annual grant total

In 2013/14 the trust had an income of £30,500 and a total expenditure of £26,000. We estimate that the amount of grants given to individuals totalled £12,000, with funding also awarded to Scottish organisations with similar charitable purposes.

Applications

Apply in writing to the correspondent, including details of financial position (income and capital).

Tayside

The Mair Robertson Benevolent Fund

£4,600

Correspondent: The Trustees, 144 Nethergate, Dundee DD1 4EB

OSCR number: SC007435

Eligibility

Older women living in Dundee and Blairgowrie who are suffering from financial hardship.

Types of grants

One-off grants of up to about £300.

Annual grant total

In 2013/14 the fund had an income of £9,500 and a total expenditure of £9,600. We estimate that the amount of grants given to individuals totalled £4,600.

The fund also makes grants to charities based locally in Blairgowrie and Dundee.

Applications

Application forms are available from the correspondent. Applications can be submitted directly by the individual or, where applicable, through a social worker, Citizens Advice, other welfare agency or other third party.

The Gertrude Muriel Pattullo Trust for Handicapped Boys

£3,200

Correspondent: Private Client Team, Blackadders Solicitors, 30–34 Reform Street, Dundee DD1 1RJ (01382 229222; fax: 01382 342220; email: enquiries@ blackadders.co.uk)

OSCR number: SC015505

Eligibility

Boys aged 18 or under who are living with a physical disability and have resided in the city of Dundee or the county of Angus.

Types of grants

Gifts in-kind and one-off cash grants are given. In the past, grants have been given for electrical goods, clothing, hospital expenses, holidays, medical and disability equipment, travel expenses, furniture, nursing fees and home help.

Annual grant total

In 2013/14 the trust had an income of £5,300 and a total expenditure of £6,700. We estimate that the amount of grants given to individuals totalled £3,200, with funding also awarded to organisations.

Exclusions

No grants are given towards repayment of debts.

Applications

Application forms are available from the correspondent. They can be submitted directly by the individual or, where applicable, through a social worker, Citizens Advice or other welfare agency.

The Gertrude Muriel Pattullo Trust for Handicapped Girls

£3,400

Correspondent: Private Client Team, Blackadders Solicitors, 30–34 Reform Street, Dundee DD1 1RJ (01382 229222; email: enquiries@blackadders.co.uk)

OSCR number: SC011829

Eligibility

Girls aged 18 years or under who have physical disabilities and live in the city of Dundee or the county of Angus.

Types of grants

One-off grants ranging from £100 to £500 have been given for electrical goods, clothing, hospital expenses, holidays, medical and disability equipment, travel expenses, furniture, nursing fees and home help.

Annual grant total

In 2013/14 the trust had both an income and a total expenditure of around £7,100. We estimate that the amount of grants given to individuals totalled £3,400, with funding also awarded to local organisations.

Exclusions

No grants are given for the repayment of debts.

Applications

Apply on a form available from the correspondent at any time. Applications can be submitted directly by the individual or through a social worker, Citizens Advice, or other welfare agency. Applications are considered monthly.

The Gertrude Muriel Pattullo Trust for the Elderly

£3,100

Correspondent: Private Client Team, Blackadders Solicitors, 30–34 Reform Street, Dundee DD1 1RJ (01382 229222; fax: 01382 342220; email: enquiries@ blackadders.co.uk)

OSCR number: SC004966

Eligibility

Older people (i.e. generally those of state pensionable age), especially those living with a disability, resident in the city of Dundee and county of Angus.

Types of grants

One-off grants are given for general welfare purposes. Funding is available towards, for example, medical services, appliances and comforts not available from the NHS, home nursing and holidays. The trust also assists with the provision of accommodation, furnishings and clothing.

Annual grant total

In 2013/14 the trust had an income of £5,200 and a total expenditure of £6,300. We estimate that the amount of grants given to individuals totalled £3,100, with funding also awarded to organisations.

Exclusions

No grants are given for debt repayment.

Applications

Application forms are available from the correspondent. They can be submitted either directly by the individual or through a third party such as a social worker.

Angus
Angus Council Charitable Trust

£3,300

Correspondent: Head of Legal and Democratic Services, Democratic Services, Resources Directorate, Angus House, Orchardbank Business Park, Forfar, Angus DD8 1AF (0845 277 7778; email: accesslawcommittee@angus.gov. uk; website: www.angus.gov.uk/info/ 20033/councillor_information/130/ charitable_trusts/2)

OSCR number: SC044695

Eligibility

Residents of Angus who are in need, including the wards of: Kirriemuir and Dean; Brechin and Edzell; Forfar and District; Monifieth and Sidlaw; Carnoustie and District; Arbroath East and Lunan and West and Letham; Montrose and District; as well as Angus-wide.

Types of grants

Pensions and one-off grants of up to £1,000. Loans may also be offered. The purposes of funds available in each ward may vary; applicants should check the charity's website or contact the correspondent for further information.

Residents of Forfar may also apply to Strangs Mortification, which gives heating grants as well as one-off grants. Applicants must have lived in Forfar for at least two years and be in receipt of housing benefit.

Annual grant total

In the charity's first financial period, from 1 August 2014–31 March 2015, it had assets of £543,500 and a total income of £8,000. Grants were awarded to both individuals and organisations totalling £6,600; we estimate that the amount of grants given to individuals totalled £3,300.

Applications

Apply on a form available to download from the charity's website or from ACCESS offices or libraries. Applications to Strangs Mortification from those who live in Forfar must be approved by a social worker, health professional or minister, from whom an application form can also be obtained.

Other information

The Angus Council Charitable Trust was formed on 1 August 2014, consolidating 97 registered charities and 42 non-registered trusts, the largest of which is Strangs Mortification.

Grants are also awarded to organisations meeting the charity's objectives.

The Colvill Charity

£8,000

Correspondent: Trusts Administrator, Thorntons Law LLP, Brothockbank House, Arbroath DD11 1NJ (01241 872683; fax: 01241 871541; email: arbroath@thorntons-law.co.uk)

OSCR number: SC003913

Eligibility

People who are in need and live in the town of Arbroath and the parish of St Vigeans and the surrounding area.

Types of grants

Annual grants of up to about £100 are given to older people. Special one-off grants of up to about £250 are also available for specific medical or household needs.

Annual grant total

In 2013/14 the charity had an income of £37,000 and a total expenditure of £32,000. Our research tells us that grants to individuals usually total £8,000 per year, although the total for grants may have been higher during this financial year.

Applications

Application forms are available from the correspondent. Applications should be submitted directly by the individual or through a social worker, Citizens Advice or other welfare agency. Applications can be made at any time, although requests for regular grants are usually assessed once a year.

The Angus Walker Benevolent Fund

£5,700

Correspondent: T. Duncan and Co., Solicitors, 192 High Street, Montrose, Angus DD10 8NA (01674 672533)

OSCR number: SC008129

Eligibility

People in need who live in Montrose.

Types of grants

One-off grants.

Annual grant total

In 2013/14 the fund had an income of £20,000 and a total expenditure of £5,900. We estimate that the amount of grants given to individuals totalled £5,700.

Applications

By formal application via a trustee, local district councillors, the Minister of Montrose Old Church or the Rector of St Mary's and St Peter's Episcopal Church, Montrose.

Dundee

Broughty Ferry Benevolent Trust

£14,000

Correspondent: The Trustees, 12 Tircarra Gardens, Broughty Ferry, Dundee DD5 2QF

OSCR number: SC010644

Eligibility

People in need living in Broughty Ferry, Dundee, who are not in residential care.

Types of grants

One-off grants according to need.

Annual grant total

In 2014/15 the trust had an income of £15,000 and a total expenditure of £16,000. We estimate that the total amount of grants awarded to individuals was approximately £14,000.

Applications

Application forms are available from the correspondent. Applications can be submitted either directly by the individual or through a social worker, Citizens Advice or other welfare agency.

The Margaret and Hannah Thomson Trusts

£9,000

Correspondent: Trust Manager, Thorntons Solicitors, Whitehall House, 33 Yeaman Shore, Dundee DD1 4BJ (01382 229111; email: dundee@thorntons-law.co.uk)

OSCR number: SC000276

Eligibility

Firstly, people in need who live in Dundee and were wounded during the Second World War, and their spouses. Secondly, ex-employees (or their dependants) of the carpet making industry in Dundee who were employed for at least 20 years and are in need of financial assistance for whatever reason.

Types of grants

Recurrent grants of £360 per year.

Annual grant total

In 2014/15 the trust had an income of £11,500 and a total expenditure of £10,500. We estimate grants to individuals totalled £9,000.

Applications

Apply in writing to the correspondent. Applications can be submitted either directly by the individual or through a social worker, Citizens Advice or other welfare agency.

Perth and Kinross

The Andrew Anderson Trust

£34,500

Correspondent: Trusts Administrator, Miller Hendry, 10 Blackfriars Street, Perth PH1 5NS (01738 637311; fax: 01738 638685; email: info@millerhendry.co.uk)

CC number: 212170

Eligibility

Women in need who live in the parish of Kinnoull or Perth and who belong to the established Church of Scotland.

Types of grants

Grants are limited to a maximum of £500 per person each year.

Annual grant total

In 2013/14 the trust had an income of £6,600 and a total expenditure of £8,700. We estimate that the amount of grants given to individuals totalled £8,000.

Applications

Apply on a form available from the correspondent at any time.

Mrs Agnes W. Carmichael's Trust (incorporating Ferguson and West Charitable Trust)

£2,300

Correspondent: Alison Hodge, Administrator, Watson & Lyall Bowie, Union Bank Building, Coupar Angus, Perthshire PH13 9AJ (01828 628395; email: legalservices@wandlb.co.uk)

OSCR number: SC004415

Eligibility

People with disabilities or other health problems, older people and other defined groups of people in need.

Types of grants

Grants of £50 to £250. Donations, loans, gifts and pensions are also given.

Annual grant total

In 2013/14 the trust had an income of £4,500 and total expenditure of £4,800. We estimate that the amount of grants given to individuals totalled around £2,300, with funding also given to organisations.

Applications

Application forms are available from the correspondent. Applications should give details of the individual's financial circumstances. Deadlines are in November and applications are considered in December.

Other information

The trust also supports older people's organisations.

The Neil Gow Charitable Trust

£16,000

Correspondent: Trust Administrator, c/o Miller Hendry, 10 Blackfriars Street, Perth PH1 5NS (01738 637311; email: info@millerhendry.co.uk)

OSCR number: SC012915

Eligibility

People in need who live in the district of Perth and Kinross or the immediate neighbourhood.

Types of grants

Annuities of around £90 each, paid quarterly.

Annual grant total

In 2013/14 the trust had an income of £10,800 and a total expenditure of £17,400. We estimate that the amount of grants given to individuals totalled £16,000.

Applications

Apply in writing to the correspondent.

The Guildry Incorporation of Perth

£31,000

Correspondent: Lorna Peacock, Secretary, 42 George Street, Perth PH1 5JL (01738 623195; email: guildryperth@btconnect.com; website: www.perthguildry.org.uk)

OSCR number: SC008072

Eligibility

People in need who live in Perth.

Types of grants
One-off and recurrent grants usually ranging between £100 and £500.

Annual grant total
In 2014/15 the charity had an income of £209,000. In previous years around £80,000 was given in grants to individuals, of which approximately £31,000 was given for welfare purposes, namely weekly pensions (£18,000); quarterly pensions (£8,500); and fuel allowances (£4,800).

Applications
Application forms can be requested from the correspondent. They are considered at the trustees' meetings on the last Tuesday of every month.

Scones Lethendy Mortifications

£20,000

Correspondent: The Treasurer, King James VI Hospital, Hospital Street, Perth PH2 8HP (01738 624660)

OSCR number: SC015545

Eligibility
People in need who live in the burgh of Perth and are poor descendants of Alexander Jackson, or with the surname Jackson and other people who are in need (Jackson Mortifications)

Types of grants
Grants usually of around £65 a quarter.

Annual grant total
In 2013/14 the charity had an income of £18,400 and a total expenditure of £22,000. We estimate that the amount of grants given to individuals totalled around £20,000.

Applications
Apply on a form available from correspondent. There is a waiting list to which applications will be added, although successful applicants are judged on need rather than when they applied.

Other information
Another similar trust is the Cairnie Mortification: Recurrent grants lasting for ten years can be given to two young men, starting when they are near the age of 14. Priority is given to those who are direct descendants of Charles Cairnie or any of his five brothers, otherwise grants can be given to people with the surname Cairnie.

Wales

General

Gwalia Housing Trust

Correspondent: Trust Administrator, 7–13 The Kingsway, Swansea SA1 5JN (0800 012 1080; email: ght@gwalia.com; website: www.gwaliatrust.org.uk)

CC number: 700822

Eligibility

Tenants of Gwalia who are supported by a neighbourhood housing officer or floating support worker and clients of Gwalia Care and Support who are supported by a floating support worker.

Types of grants

One-off grants for housing-related needs such as furniture and white goods. Tenants of Gwalia can apply for grants of up to £500, which can also be given for carpets (if there is no other flooring is in the property). Individuals who are under the Gwalia Care and Support Scheme can apply for a grant of up to £300.

Annual grant total

In 2013/14 the trust had assets of £2.4 million and an income of £50,500. The Group Welfare Fund was closed during this period but has now re-opened and is accepting applications. In previous years the trust has made grants totalling around £15,000.

Applications

Application forms are available from the trust's website. All applicants must have a letter of support from and must be signed off by either the neighbourhood housing officer or a floating support worker.

Other information

The trust provides housing for people in necessitous circumstances, particularly older people, people recovering from mental illness, people who have been homeless, students and people living with disabilities.

The trust also makes grants through its Community Development Fund through which grants of up to £750 are available to assist communities living in Gwalia's residential or non-residential accommodation and who are identified as being in need of financial assistance to improve their quality of life or living environment.

Mid Wales

Powys

The Montgomery Welfare Fund

£2,400

Correspondent: Edward Humphreys, 2 Rowes Terrace, Pool Road, Montgomery SY15 6QD (01686 668790; email: ejhumphreys1@gmail.com)

CC number: 214767

Eligibility

People in need who live permanently in the ecclesiastical parish of Montgomery (not the county).

Types of grants

One-off grants ranging from £25 to £100. Reapplications can be made. Grants cover a wide range of needs.

Annual grant total

In 2013/14 the fund had an income of £4,100 and a total expenditure of £2,600. We estimate that the total award granted to individuals was approximately £2,400.

Exclusions

No grants are given to pay rates, tax or other public funds.

Applications

Apply in writing to the correspondent.

Other information

Grants can also be given to individuals for education, 'development in life' and so on.

North Wales

Conwy

Conwy Welsh Church Acts Fund

£2,500

Correspondent: Catherine Dowber, Financial Administrator, Head of Financial Services, Conwy County Borough Council, Bodlondeb, Conwy LL32 8DU (01492 576201; email: welshchurchactsfund@conwy.gov.uk; website: www.conwy.gov.uk/doc.asp?cat=2972&doc=14371)

Eligibility

People in need living in the county borough of Conwy.

Types of grants

One-off grants ranging from £50 to £2,000, for the relief of poverty and sickness, elderly people, the blind and visually impaired, the advancement of religion, the advancement of literature and the arts, medical and social research, those on probation, and the relief of emergencies and disasters.

Annual grant total

Our research tells us that the fund generates approximately £10,000 per annum for distribution, which is divided between individuals (for both welfare and educational purposes) and organisations.

Exclusions

Grants are not made to individuals for sport or tuition fees.

Applications

Application forms are available from the correspondent. Applications should be submitted directly by the individual or through a third party. The closing date for applications is the first week in May or October, for consideration in June/July or November/December respectively.

Other information

The fund has its origins in The Welsh Church Act of 1914.

There is a page about the fund on the Conwy County Borough Council website.

The Evan and Catherine Roberts Home

£3,600

Correspondent: Ken Owen, Trustee, 81 Bryn Avenue, Old Colwyn, Colwyn Bay LL29 8AH (01492 515209; email: kenowen@uwclub.net)

CC number: 244965

Eligibility

People over the age of 60 who live within a 40-mile radius of the Bethesda Welsh Methodist Church in Old Colwyn, with preference for members of the Methodist Church. Those living in parts of Conwy, Denbighshire, Flintshire and Gwynedd are eligible.

Types of grants

One-off grants ranging from £50 to £150.

Annual grant total

In 2013/14 the charity had an income of £1,400 and a total expenditure of £3,900. We estimate that the amount of grants given to individuals totalled £3,600

Applications

Application forms are available from the correspondent.

Denbighshire

Freeman Evans St David's Day Denbigh Charity

£3,300 (7 grants)

Correspondent: Medwyn Jones, Town Clerk, Denbigh Town Council, Town Hall, Crown Square, Denbigh LL16 3TB (01745 815984; email: townclerk@ denbightowncouncil.gov.uk)

CC number: 518033

Eligibility

People in need who live in Denbigh and Henllan, particularly those who are older, have disabilities or an illness.

Types of grants

One-off grants according to need, including towards disability aids, furniture, carpets, travel costs, home adaptations, funeral costs, debt repayments, Christmas gifts and so on. The charity appears to pay to service/ item providers rather than making direct cash payments to individuals.

Annual grant total

In 2013/14 the charity had assets of £155,500, an income of £34,000 and a total expenditure of almost £100,000. Grants were made totalling £97,000 and consisted of 32 awards. Awards for social welfare purposes were paid to organisations on behalf of individuals and we believe that there were seven relief-in-need grants to individuals totalling £3,300.

Applications

Applications may be made in writing to the correspondent, either directly by the individual or through a third party, such as a social worker, Citizens Advice or other welfare agency. The trustees meet regularly throughout the year to consider applications.

Other information

Organisations are also supported and assistance is given to individuals for educational purposes.

Elizabeth Williams Charities

£6,500

Correspondent: Alison Alexander, Administrator, Arfon Cottage, 19 Roe Parc, St Asaph, Denbighshire LL17 0LD (01745 583798; email: alison.alexander@ btinternet.com)

CC number: 216903

Eligibility

People in need who live in the communities of St Asaph, Bodelwyddan, Cefn and Waen in Denbighshire.

Types of grants

One-off grants, generally between £50 and £100, are given as Christmas bonuses for people who are older, to families with parents suffering serious illnesses and for particular needs.

Annual grant total

In 2013/14 the charity had an income of £6,700 and a total expenditure of £6,900. We estimate that the amount of grants given to individuals totalled £6,500.

Exclusions

Grants are not given for aid that can be met specifically by public funds, for private education or if the grant would affect a claimant's benefit from the DWP.

Applications

Apply in writing to the correspondent, either directly by the individual or, where applicable, through a social worker, Citizens Advice or other welfare agency. Applications can also be submitted via a trustee. Applications are generally considered in November, although specific cases can be considered at any time.

Gwynedd

The Freeman Evans St David's Day Ffestiniog Charity

£35,000

Correspondent: Mr Maldwyn Evans, Trustee, NatWest Bank plc, Meirionnydd Business Centre, Bridge Street, Dolgellau, Gwynedd LL40 1AU (01341 421242; email: maldevans@aol.com)

CC number: 518034

Eligibility

People who are older, in poor health or who have disabilities and live in the districts of Blaenau Ffestiniog and Llan Ffestiniog as they were prior to the 1974 reorganisation.

Types of grants

One-off and recurrent grants for home adaptations, specialist chairs, stair-lifts, electric wheelchairs and phone Lifelines.

Annual grant total

In 2014/15 the charity had an income of £40,000 and a total expenditure of £43,500. We estimate that the amount of grants given to individuals totalled £35,000.

Applications

Applications can be submitted in writing directly by the individual or, where applicable, through a recognised referral agency such as a social worker, minister of religion, councillor, Citizens Advice or doctor. Applications are considered by the trustees twice a year, although urgent cases can be dealt with between meetings.

Isle of Anglesey

Anglesey Society for the Welfare of Handicapped People

£5,000

Correspondent: Robert Jones, Administrator, 8 Gorwel Deg, Rhostrehwfa, Llangefni, Anglesey

CC number: 218810

Eligibility

People living in Anglesey who have tuberculosis or any other disease, illness or disability.

Types of grants

One-off or recurrent grants according to need.

Annual grant total

In 2014, the charity had an income £2,800 and a total expenditure of £5,200. We estimate the grant total to be £5,000.

Applications

Apply in writing to the correspondent.

Other information

The charity also makes grants to organisations.

Wrexham

The Jones Trust

£25,000

Correspondent: Patricia Williams, Secretary, 33 Deva Way, Wrexham LL13 9EU (01978 261684)

CC number: 229956

Eligibility

People who are sick, convalescing, have disabilities or who are infirm in the city of Wrexham.

Types of grants

Grants for respite care in residential and nursing homes and convalescence. Grants for appliances and surgical aids not readily available through the health service are also considered.

Annual grant total

In 2014 the trust had an income of £39,000 and total expenditure of £33,000. We estimate that the amount of grants given to individuals totalled around £25,000.

Applications

Apply in writing to the correspondent.

Ruabon and District Relief-in-Need Charity

£800

Correspondent: James Fenner, 65 Albert Grove, Ruabon, Wrexham LL14 6AF (01978 820102; email: jamesrfenner65@ tiscali.co.uk)

CC number: 212817

Eligibility

All people who are considered to be in need who live in the county borough of Wrexham, which covers the community council districts of Cefn Mawr, Penycae, Rhosllanerchrugog and Ruabon.

Types of grants

One-off and recurrent grants. Previously grants have been made towards installation of a telephone, heating costs, children's clothing, cookers, furniture, musical instruments, electric wheelchairs, clothing for adults in hospital, travel costs for hospital visits and books and travel for university students.

Annual grant total

In 2014 the charity had an income of £3,100 and an expenditure of £1,700. The accounts were not required at the Charity Commission because of the low income. We estimate that grants for social welfare totalled approximately £800.

Exclusions

Grants are not given for instigating bankruptcy proceedings. Loans are not given.

Applications

Apply in writing to the correspondent either directly by the individual or a family member, through a third party such as a social worker or teacher, or through an organisation such as Citizens Advice or a school. Applications are considered on an ongoing basis.

The Wrexham and District Relief in Need Charity

£18,000

Correspondent: Frieda Leech, Correspondent, Holly Chase, Pen Y Palmant Road, Minera, Wrexham LL11 3YW (01978 754152; email: clerk. wpef@gmail.com)

CC number: 236355

Eligibility

People in need who live in the former borough of Wrexham or the communities of Abenbury, Bersham, Bieston, Broughton, Brymbo, Esclusham Above, Esclusham Below, Gresford, Gwersyllt and Minera in Wrexham.

Types of grants

One-off or recurrent grants according to need typically ranging from £40 to £500. Grants have been given towards the costs of maternity necessities, household equipment, wheelchairs, clothing and a stair-lift, for example.

Annual grant total

In 2014 the charity had an income of £17,800 and a total expenditure of £18,600. We estimate that the amount of grants given to individuals totalled £18,000.

Applications

Apply in writing to the correspondent. Applications should be submitted directly by the individual, or by a third party, and should include full details of the applicant's weekly income and expenditure together with the cost of the item required where applicable. Applications are considered throughout the year.

South East Wales

Cardiff

Cardiff Citizens Charity

£3,000

Correspondent: Liza Kellett, Administrator, The Community Foundation in Wales, 24 St Andrews Crescent, Cardiff CF10 3DD (029 2037 9580; email: mail@cfiw.org.uk; website: www.cfiw.org.uk)

CC number: 206549

Eligibility

People in need who live in the city of Cardiff.

Types of grants

One-off grants in the range of £100 to £400 for funeral expenses, clothes, specialist computer software, household appliances and so on.

Annual grant total

In 2013/14 the charity had an income of £4,300 and a total expenditure of £4,600. According to the accounts for the Community Foundation in Wales, grants from this charity totalled £3,000.

Exclusions

No grants are made for educational purposes.

Applications

Application forms are available from the correspondent. Applications should be submitted through a recognised referral agency (such as a social worker, Citizens Advice or doctor) or other third party. Evidence of weekly/monthly expenditure must be submitted. The trustees meet twice yearly to consider applications.

Other information

This charity was formerly known as the Cardiff Charity for Special Relief. The charity is now administered by the Community Foundation in Wales.

The Duffryn Trust

£5,800

Correspondent: Mr D. Williams, Trustee, 89 Cyncoed Road, Cardiff CF23 5SD (029 2048 4554; email: david.williams85@btinternet.com)

CC number: 1031718

Eligibility

People in need with a preference for those who live in Cardiff.

Types of grants

One-off and recurrent grants are given according to need.

Annual grant total

In 2014/15 the trust had an income of £24,500 and a total expenditure of £11,900. We estimate that the amount of grants given to individuals totalled £5,800, with funding also awarded to Christian organisations.

Applications

Apply in writing to the correspondent.

Other information

The trust supports evangelical churches and missionary organisations.

Merthyr Tydfil

Merthyr Mendicants

£3,000

Correspondent: Allen Lane, 4 Georgetown Villas, Georgetown, Merthyr Tydfil, Mid Glamorgan CF48 1BD (01685 373308)

CC number: 208105

Eligibility

People in need who live in the borough of Merthyr Tydfil.

Types of grants

One-off grants according to need. Grants have been given towards medical equipment not available from the National Health Service (providing it is recommended by a medical authority); Christmas parcels; holidays for children; telephone helplines for incapacitated people; and help with domestic equipment such as cookers, refrigerators, washing machines, bedding and beds.

Annual grant total

In 2014 the charity had an income of £10,900 and a total expenditure of £13,300. We estimate that social welfare grants to individuals totalled £3,000. Grants are also given to organisations and for educational purposes.

Applications

Apply in writing to the correspondent, including information on the individual's sources of income. Applications can be submitted directly by the individual or through a social worker, Citizens Advice or other welfare agency.

Monmouthshire

Monmouth Charity

£2,900

Correspondent: Andrew Pirie, Trustee, Pen-y-Bryn, Oakfield Road, Monmouth NP25 3JJ (01600 716202; email: carol@pirie.info)

CC number: 700759

Eligibility

People who are in need and live within an ten-mile radius of Monmouth town.

Types of grants

One-off grants usually up to a maximum of £500.

Annual grant total

In 2013/14 the charity had an income of £10,200 and a total expenditure of £11,000. Grants are made to individuals and organisations for a wide range of charitable purposes, including for the relief of poverty, disability and education. We estimate that social welfare grants to individuals totalled £2,900.

Applications

The charity advertises in the local press each September/October and applications should be made in response to this advertisement for consideration in November. Emergency grants can be considered at any time. There is no application form. Applications can be submitted directly by the individual or through a social worker, Citizens Advice or other welfare agency.

The Monmouthshire County Council Welsh Church Act Fund

£0

Correspondent: Joy Robson, Head of Finance, Monmouthshire County Council, Innovation House, PO Box 106, Magor, Caldicot (01633 644657; email: davejarrett@monmouthshire.gov.uk; website: www.monmouthshire.gov.uk)

CC number: 507094

Eligibility

People living within the boundaries of Monmouthshire county council who are in need. Grants are also given to discharged prisoners and their families.

Types of grants

Grants of money or payment for items, services or facilities. Accommodation can be provided to older people who need it because of infirmities or disabilities. People who are visually impaired may also be given access to charitable homes and holiday homes.

Annual grant total

In 2013/14 the fund had assets of £4.7 million and an income of £166,000. There were no social welfare grants made to individuals during the year.

Applications

Apply using a form available from the correspondent at any time. Applications are considered seven times a year.

Other information

The fund also makes grants to organisations.

Torfaen

The Cwmbran Trust

£17,000

Correspondent: Kenneth Maddox, Secretary, c/o Meritor HVBS (UK) Ltd, Grange Road, Cwmbran, Gwent NP44 3XU (01633 834040; email: cwmbrantrust@meritor.com)

CC number: 505855

Eligibility

People in need living in the town of Cwmbran, Gwent.

Types of grants

One-off and recurrent grants are awarded for a wide variety of educational and welfare purposes, such as stair-lifts, home-study courses, equipment, repairs, computer equipment, wheelchairs, holidays, debt clearance, removal costs, building renovation, funeral costs, travel expenses and respite care. Grants usually range between £100 and £3,000.

Annual grant total

In 2014 the trust had assets of £2.35 million and an income of £98,500. Grants were made to 33 individuals totalling £19,500 for educational and welfare purposes. The majority of funding for individuals is given for social welfare purposes.

Applications

Applications may be made in writing to the correspondent. They can be submitted directly by the individual or through a social worker, Citizens Advice, welfare agency or other third party. Applications are usually considered in March, May, July, October and December.

Other information

The trust also makes grants to organisations (£59,500 to 18 organisations in 2014).

Vale of Glamorgan

The Cowbridge with Llanblethian United Charities

£19,200

Correspondent: Clerk to the Trustees, 66 Broadway, Llanblethian, Cowbridge CF71 7EW (01446 773287; email: h. phillips730@btinternet.com)

CC number: 1014580

Eligibility

People in need who live in the town of Cowbridge with Llanblethian.

Types of grants

The provision of items, services or facilities that will reduce the person's need.

Annual grant total

In 2013/14 the charity had an income of £30,000 and a total expenditure of £22,500. Grants totalled £20,000, of which £19,200 was awarded for social welfare purposes. A further £400 was paid in educational grants to students and £500, which we believe was received by organisations, was given for the general benefit of the Cowbridge area.

Applications

Apply in writing to the correspondent. Applications can be submitted directly by the individual or through a welfare agency.

South West Wales

Pembrokeshire

Haverfordwest Freemen's Estate

£8,500

Correspondent: The Clerk, R. K. Lucas and Son, The Tithe Exchange, 9 Victoria Place, Haverfordwest, Pembrokeshire SA61 2JX (01437 762538)

CC number: 515111

Eligibility

Hereditary freemen of Haverfordwest aged 18 years and over.

Types of grants

One-off grants according to need.

Annual grant total

In 2013/14 the estate had an income of £18,400 and a total expenditure of £18,000. We estimate that the amount of grants given to individuals totalled £8,500, with funding also awarded to local organisations.

Applications

Freemen must be enrolled by the chair of the local authority. The honour is hereditary being passed down through the male or female line.

The William Sanders Charity

£20,000

Correspondent: Julia Phillips, Administrator, 11 Freemans Walk, Pembroke, Dyfed SA71 4AS

CC number: 229182

Eligibility

Widows and unmarried women in need who live within a five-mile radius of the parish of St John's, Pembroke Dock.

Types of grants

Christmas grants typically ranging from £25 to £40. They are available in November and December each year.

Annual grant total

In 2013/14 the charity had an income of £9,500 and a total expenditure of £22,300. We estimate that the amount of grants given to individuals totalled around £20,000.

Applications

Apply in writing to the correspondent. Applications can be submitted directly by the individual or by a family member.

The Tenby Relief-in-Need and Pensions Charity

£25,500 (120 grants)

Correspondent: Clive Mathias, Clerk to the Trustees, Lewis Lewis and Co., County Chambers, Pentre Road, St Clears, Carmarthen SA33 4AA (01994 231044; email: clive@lewislewis.co.uk)

CC number: 231233

Eligibility

Older people in need who live in the community of Tenby.

Types of grants

Pensions of £17 a month to help relieve financial difficulties. Most beneficiaries will also receive a small Christmas bonus of £20. Usually, once a grant has been agreed it will be paid indefinitely.

Annual grant total

In 2014 the charity held assets of £743,500 and had an income of £31,500. Grants to 120 individuals totalled £25,500.

Applications

Application forms are available from the correspondent. Applications should be submitted directly by the individual or a family member.

William Vawer

£2,300

Correspondent: R. K. Lucas, Administrator, R. K. Lucas and Son, 9 Victoria Place, Haverfordwest, Pembrokeshire SA61 2JX (01437 762538)

CC number: 213880

Eligibility

People in need who live in the town of Haverfordwest.

Types of grants

Pensions to existing pensioners. Other grants to those in need, hardship or distress.

Annual grant total

In 2013/14 the charity had an income of £6,600 and a total expenditure of £2,500. We estimate that the total amount of grants awarded to individuals was approximately £2,300.

Applications

Apply in writing to the correspondent.

East Midlands

General

The John Heggs Bates' Charity for Convalescents

£13,000

Correspondent: Barbara Amos, Correspondent, 1 Mill Lane, Leicester LE2 7HU (0116 204 6620; email: barbara.amos@stwcharity.co.uk)

CC number: 218060

Eligibility

'Necessitous convalescents' and their carers who reside in Leicester, Leicestershire and Rutland.

Types of grants

One-off grants of £100 to £600 for convalescence breaks.

Annual grant total

In 2014 the charity had an income of £12,000 and a total expenditure of £13,400. We estimate that the amount of grants given to individuals totalled £13,000.

Applications

Application forms are available from: Leicester Charity Link, 20A Millstone Lane, Leicester LE1 5JN. Applications should be submitted through a social worker, Citizens Advice, doctor or church and are considered throughout the year.

The Brooke Charity

£2,800

Correspondent: Barbara Clemence, Trustee, Old Rectory Farm, Main Street, Brooke, Oakham, Leicestershire LE15 8DE (01572 770558)

CC number: 221729

Eligibility

People in need who live in the parish of Brooke or the adjoining parishes of Oakham, Braunston, Ridlington and Morcott, with priority given to the sick, elderly and children.

Types of grants

One-off grants to relieve financial difficulty, usually in the range of £50 to £250, and for items and services which will improve a person's daily life.

Annual grant total

In 2013/14 the charity had an income of £4,200 and a total expenditure of £5,900. We estimate that the amount of grants given to individuals totalled £2,800, with funding also awarded to local organisations.

Applications

Apply in writing to the correspondent. Applications can be submitted directly by the individual or, where applicable, through a social worker, Citizens Advice or other welfare agency. They are considered at any time.

Jordison and Hossell Animal Welfare Charity
See entry on page 267

The Leicester Charity Link

£874,000 (4,299 grants)

Correspondent: James Munton, Director of Operations, 20A Millstone Lane, Leicester, Leicestershire LE1 5JN (0116 222 2200; fax: 0116 222 2201; email: info@charity-link.org; website: www.charity-link.org)

CC number: 1078271

Eligibility

People in need who live in the city of Leicester and the vicinity, which includes the whole of Leicestershire and Rutland, as well as Northamptonshire. Beneficiaries have included those on a low income or experiencing hardship, vulnerable families, people who are homeless and the elderly.

Types of grants

One-off grants and occasionally recurrent grants or pensions. The charity makes payments from its own funds, administers funds on behalf of other charities and puts potential beneficiaries into contact with funds and charities which may be able to help.

Grants are available for a wide range of needs, although the charity most commonly funds essential, everyday items such as beds, cookers and, in emergencies, food. Recent grants for larger items have included stair-lifts and specialist wheelchairs.

Goods and services are received by the charity and delivered directly to applicants.

Annual grant total

In 2013/14 the charity held assets of £460,500 and had an income of £1.25 million. A total of 4,299 grants was awarded to individuals, amounting to £874,000.

Aside from making grants from its own funds, the charity also secured 283 awards totalling £278,500 for individuals and organisations from other donors.

Exclusions

It is expected that all statutory funding sources are explored before applying.

Applications

Individuals are referred through other organisations, such as charities and health, social or educational agencies, using an application form available on the website. The charity's website notes:

> We use a network of local organisations that are in the community working with individuals and families in need. Using organisations already in place keeps our overheads to a minimum, increases the efficiency of our services and ensures that we get the help to those who need it when they need it most.

While the charity aims provide support within 20 days, urgent help on the same day can also be given if the charity is contacted by telephone.

Other information

The charity also makes small grants to organisations (three grants totalling £450 in 2013/14).

The charity supports a food bank in conjunction with Leicester City Council, St Martin's House, Tomorrow Together and FareShare. Those working with vulnerable individuals or families wishing to access the food bank should telephone (0116 222 2200) or download an application form from the website.

Leicestershire Coal Industry Welfare Trust Fund

£16,000

Correspondent: Peter Smith, Trustee, Miners Offices Unit 12, The Springboard Centre, Mantle Lane, Coalville, Leicestershire LE67 3DW (01530 832085; email: leicesternum@ukinbox.com)

CC number: 1006985

Eligibility

Miners and their dependants connected with the British coal mining industry in the Leicestershire area.

Types of grants

The fund aims to promote and improve applicants' health, social well-being and living conditions. Grants can be given towards holidays, special needs assistance, house repairs, heating systems, house conversions, electrical equipment and so on.

Annual grant total

In 2014 the fund had an income of £7,800 and a total expenditure of £33,000. Note that both the income and the expenditure vary each year. We estimate the annual total amount of grants given to individuals to be around £16,000.

Applications

Apply in writing to the correspondent. Applications should include details of mining connections, residence in Leicestershire and dependence on the mineworker (in the case of children). The trustees meet throughout the year to discuss applications.

Other information

Grants are also given to organisations.

The Leicestershire County Nursing Association

£38,000

Correspondent: Edward Cufflin, Treasurer, Charles Stanley, Mercury Place, St George Street, Leicester LE1 1QG (0116 366 6200; email: ed. cufflin@charles-stanley.co.uk)

CC number: 216594

Eligibility

Retired district nurses and people who are sick and in need, who live in Leicestershire or Rutland (excluding the city of Leicester). Priority is given to retired district nurses.

Types of grants

One-off grants of up to £3,000 for any need. Recent grants have been given towards hospital costs, bedding and convalescence.

Annual grant total

In 2013/14 the association had assets of £1.4 million and a total income of £55,000. The grant total awarded to individuals was approximately £38,000.

Applications

Apply in writing to the correspondent. Applications can be submitted directly by the individual in the case of retired district nurses or through Leicester Charity Link in other cases.

Other information

The charity also makes grants to organisations.

Richard Smedley's Charity

£2,000

Correspondent: Maurice Ward, Robinsons Solicitors Co., 21–22 Burns Street, Ilkeston, Derbyshire DE7 8AA (0115 932 4101; email: Maurice.Ward@geldards.com)

CC number: 221211

Eligibility

People in need who live in the parishes of Breaston, Dale Abbey, Draycott with Church Wilne, Heanor, Hopwell, Ilkerton, Ockbrook and Risley (all in Derbyshire) or of Awsworth, Bilborough, Brinsley, Greasley and Strelley (all in Nottinghamshire).

Types of grants

One-off grants generally in the range of £50 to £350 are given towards items such as furniture, washing machines, mobility aids, clothing and carpets.

Annual grant total

In 2014 the charity had an income of £9,300 and a total expenditure of £4,600. We estimate that the amount of grants given to individuals for social welfare purposes totalled £2,000.

Applications

Application forms are available from the correspondent and should be submitted either directly by the individual or through a social worker, Citizens Advice or other welfare agency. Applications can be submitted at any time and are usually considered quarterly.

Other information

Grants are also made to organisations.

Derbyshire

Amber Valley

Alfreton Welfare Trust

£3,800

Correspondent: Celia Johnson, 30 South Street, Swanwick, Alfreton, Derbyshire DE55 1BZ (01773 609782; email: celiajohnson2001@hotmail.com)

CC number: 217114

Eligibility

People in need who live in the former urban district of Alfreton in Derbyshire, namely, the parishes of Alfreton, Ironville, Leabrooks, Somercotes and Swanwick.

Types of grants

One-off grants of up to £200. Our research indicates that previous grants have included hospital travel expenses, provision of necessary household items and installation costs, recuperative holidays, relief of sudden distress (such as theft of pension or purse, funeral costs, marital difficulties), telephone installations and to cover outstanding bills. Support can also be given to people with disabilities (including help to buy wheelchairs and so on).

Annual grant total

In 2013/14 the trust had an income of £2,400 and a total expenditure of £4,000. We estimate that the amount of grants given to individuals totalled £3,800.

Exclusions

Grants are not given to organisations and groups or for educational purposes.

Applications

Apply in writing to the correspondent. Applications can be made directly by the individual and are considered throughout the year.

Chesterfield

The Chesterfield General Charitable Fund

£2,500

Correspondent: Keith Pollard, Trustee, 266 Old Road, Chesterfield, Derbyshire S40 3QN (01246 221872; email: kmfp2@gmx.co.uk)

CC number: 511375

Eligibility

People in need who live in the parliamentary constituency of Chesterfield.

Types of grants

One-off and recurrent grants usually ranging from £200 to £800.

Annual grant total

In 2013/14 the fund had both an income and an expenditure of £5,200. We estimate that the amount of grants given to individuals totalled around £2,500, with local organisations also receiving funding.

Applications

Apply in writing to the correspondent. Applications are considered quarterly and should be made directly by the individual concerned.

Arthur Townrow Pensions Fund

£108,000

Correspondent: P. King, Secretary, PO Box 48, Chesterfield, Derbyshire S40 1XT (01246 560560; email: p.king15@sky.com; website: www.townrowfund.org.uk)

CC number: 252256

Eligibility

Women in need who are unmarried or widows, over 40 years of age and live in the Chesterfield and North-East Derbyshire areas. The fund specifies that the applicant should be 'of good character' and be a member of the Church of England or a Protestant dissenting church that acknowledges the doctrine of the Holy Trinity. Applicants should have an income of £8,000 or less.

Types of grants

Recurrent grants of £60 a month (£720 per annum). One half of the pensions granted must be paid to unmarried women and widows living in Chesterfield, Bolsover or North East Derbyshire. The remaining grants may be paid anywhere in England but only to eligible unmarried women over the age of 40.

Annual grant total

In 2013/14 the fund held assets of £3.8 million and had an income of £140,500. Grants to individuals totalled £108,000.

Applications

Application forms are available from the correspondent. Applications should be submitted either directly by the individual or through a third party.

Other information

Arthur Townrow was a Chesterfield based miller who left a bequest to be used to support widows and unmarried women who are on low incomes.

Derby

The Liversage Trust

£82,000

Correspondent: Yvonne Taylor, General Manager, The Board Room, London Road, Derby DE1 2QW (01332 348199; fax: 01332 349674; email: info@liversagetrust.org; website: www.liversagecourt.org/charitable-grant-giving)

CC number: 1155282

Eligibility

Grants are made to subsidise almshouse residents and Liversage Court residents, as well as to local people in need and organisations. Subsidies for almshouse residents include Christmas bonuses and winter fuel allowances.

Types of grants

Cash grants for the relief of poverty, usually limited to a maximum of £150 although most grants are of between £30/£40 and £150. Grants can be made towards clothing, food or consumer durables.

Annual grant total

The charity incorporated and re-registered with the Charity Commission in January 2014. In 2014/15 the charity had assets of £19.2 million, an income of £2 million and made grants to individuals of £82,000.

Exclusions

Usually only one grant per applicant within a two-year period, although the trustees do have discretion in cases of crisis.

Applications

Apply on a form available from the charity's website or the correspondent. Applications should be submitted through a recognised referral agency such as a social worker, Citizens Advice or GP; they are considered throughout the year.

Other information

The charity's main concern is the management of almshouses and the care home, Liversage Court.

The Spondon Relief-in-Need Charity

£16,000

Correspondent: Lynn Booth, Secretary and Treasurer, PO Box 5073, Spondon, Derby DE21 7JZ (01332 678533; email: info@spondonreliefinneedcharity.org; website: www.spondonreliefinneedcharity.org)

CC number: 211317

Eligibility

People who live in the ancient parish of Spondon within the City of Derby.

Types of grants

One-off grants in-kind for items such as beds, white goods (fridges, freezers, etc.), carpets, furniture, cookers and childcare. Gifts are also made at Christmas.

Annual grant total

In 2014 the charity had assets of £706,000 and an income of £29,500. Grants totalled £22,500, of which we believe £16,000 was given for social welfare purposes.

During the year, educational grants to individuals amounted to around £3,100 and at least two grants of more than £1,000 were made to organisations, totalling £3,600.

Exclusions

No grants are made for the relief of rates and taxes, or any expenses usually covered by statutory sources.

Applications

The charity's website gives the following advice: 'For more details please write or email us explaining why you think we can help you. Please provide your full contact details with your enquiry.'

Derbyshire Dales

The Ernest Bailey Charity

£350

Correspondent: Ros Hession, Community Engagement Officer, Community Development Department, Derbyshire Dales District Council, Town Hall, Bank Road, Matlock DE4 3NN (01629 761302; email: ros.hession@derbyshiredales.gov.uk; website: www.derbyshiredales.gov.uk)

CC number: 518884

Eligibility

People in need, sickness, old age or distress who live in Matlock and district (this includes Bonsall, Cromford, Darley Dale, Matlock and Matlock Bath, Northwood, Rowsley (part of),

Starkholmes, South Darley and Tinkersley).

Types of grants

Most applications have been from local groups, but individuals in need and those with educational needs are also supported. Each application is considered on its merits. Grants to individuals are one-off and usually to a maximum of £250.

Annual grant total

In 2013/14 the charity had an income of £1,900 and an expenditure of £1,600. The website notes that 'in 2014 a total of a £1,350 was awarded between 16 recipients'. We estimate that social welfare grants to individuals totalled about £350.

Applications

Application forms are available online or can be requested from the correspondent. They can be submitted online or via post, directly by the individual and/or can be supported by a relevant professional. Most recently the submission deadline was in October. Requests should include costings (total amount required, funds raised and funds promised). Previous beneficiaries may apply again, with account being taken of assistance given in the past.

Other information

Organisations are also supported. Educational grants are also given.

The Margaret Harrison Trust

£3,000

Correspondent: Alexandra Mastin, Trustee, 273 Chesterfield Road, Matlock, Derbyshire DE4 5LE (01629 259357)

CC number: 234296

Eligibility

'Gentlewomen of good character' aged 50 or over who have lived within a 15-mile radius of St Giles Parish Church, Matlock for at least five years.

Types of grants

Small quarterly pensions.

Annual grant total

In 2014 the trust had an income of £4,700 and an expenditure of £3,600. Grants usually total around £3,000 per year.

Applications

Application forms are available from the correspondent.

High Peak
The Mary Ellen Allen Charity

£2,400

Correspondent: Tony Lawton, Correspondent, 8 Spinney Close, Glossop SK13 7BR (01457852434; email: tony@tlawton.co.uk)

CC number: 512661

Eligibility

People over 60 who are in need and live in the former borough of Glossop (as it was in 1947). There is a preference for those who have lived in the area for at least five years in total.

Types of grants

About 15 one-off grants a year in the range of £50 to £500.

Annual grant total

In 2013/14 the trust had an income of £4,400 and a total expenditure of £7,100. We estimate that the amount of grants given to individuals totalled £2,400, with funding also awarded to local organisations.

Applications

Apply in writing to the correspondent through a social worker, Citizens Advice or other welfare agency where applicable, or directly by the individual. Applications can be submitted at any time for consideration in January, April, July and October.

The Bingham Trust

£19,500

Correspondent: Emma Marshall, Secretary, Unit 1, Tongue Lane Industrial Estate, Dew Pond Lane, Buxton SK17 7LN (01298 600591; email: binghamtrust@aol.com; website: www. binghamtrust.org.uk)

CC number: 287636

Eligibility

People in need, primarily those who live in Buxton, Derbyshire (SK17 postcode area). Most applicants from outside Buxton are rejected unless there is a Buxton connection.

Types of grants

One-off grants ranging from £200 to £1,500. Grants are made to individuals for a wide variety of needs, including further education. Grants made to individuals are usually by cheque made out to the provider of the service or goods.

Annual grant total

In 2013/14 the trust had assets of £4.45 million and an income of £191,000. During the year a total of 130 organisations and individuals were supported totalling £174,000. Grants to individuals totalled £39,000. There was no breakdown of how much was awarded in educational/social welfare grants and we estimate the total amount of welfare grants to be around £19,500.

Exclusions

The trust cannot provide:

- Support for higher educational purposes – university and college level
- Grants to repay existing debts
- Grants for businesses, profit-making organisations (even if they are not actually making a profit)

In exceptional circumstances assistance may be given for people in higher education who suffer from disabilities for the purchase of specialised equipment.

Applications

Application forms are available from the website or may be requested from the correspondent and returned via post or email (with no additional attachments). Appeals by letter are also accepted but may take longer to proceed. The trust states that 'usually, applications look better if they are posted or sent by email as a letter attachment'. Individuals not applying via any organisation or charity must send a supporting letter from a third party, such as social worker, or someone from a charity or community organisation who knows their circumstances, or a doctor or minister. Applications are considered during the first two weeks of January, April, July and October and should be received before the end of the previous month.

Queries can be made to the correspondent via the email address given or on 07966 378 546.

The website states: 'All applications are acknowledged either by letter or email. If you do not receive an acknowledgment, you can assume that we have not received your application. If you do not hear from us within one month of our meeting, you can assume that your application has not been funded.'

Other information

The trust gives primarily to organisations. Special consideration is given to those involved with research into arthritis, anywhere within Britain.

John Mackie Memorial Ladies' Home

£4,300

Correspondent: David Wellens, Trustee, Axholme, Woodbourne Road, New Mills, High Peak, Derbyshire SK22 3JX (01663 742246; email: dhw111@hotmail.com)

CC number: 215726

Eligibility

Widows, unmarried women and divorcees, who are members of the Church of England, are over 50 and are in need. Applicants must have a connection with the parish of New Mills.

Types of grants

Christmas gifts in the region of £60 to around 80 individuals. Applicants will not receive help if they re-marry.

Annual grant total

In 2014 the charity had an income of £3,200 and a total expenditure of £4,500. We estimate that the amount of grants given to individuals totalled £4,300.

Applications

Apply in writing to the correspondent, with (i) evidence of the birth, marriage and death of the applicant's husband, (ii) references from three house owners, confirming her character, respectability and needy circumstances, (iii) proof that she has a small income and (iv) evidence that she is a member of the Church of England. Applications can be submitted either directly by the individual or through a third party. Applications are considered throughout the year.

North East Derbyshire

Dronfield Relief in Need Charity

£800

Correspondent: Dr Anthony Bethell, Trustee, Ramshaw Lodge, Crow Lane, Unstone, Dronfield, Derbyshire S18 4AL (01246 413276)

CC number: 219888

Eligibility

People in need who live in the ecclesiastical parishes of Dronfield, Holmesfield, Unstone and West Handley.

Types of grants

One-off grants, up to a value of £100, towards household needs (such as washing machines), food, clothing, medical appliances (such as a nebulizer) and visitors' fares to and from hospital.

Annual grant total

In 2014 the charity had an income of £3,600 and an expenditure of £3,300. We estimate that about £800 was given to individuals for social welfare purposes.

Exclusions

Support is not given for rates, taxes and so on.

Applications

Applications may be made in writing to the correspondent through a social worker, doctor, member of the clergy of any denomination, a local councillor, Citizens Advice or other welfare agency. The applicants should ensure they are receiving all practical/financial assistance they are entitled to from statutory sources.

Other information

Grants are also given to local organisations and for educational purposes.

Leicester-shire

Thomas Monke

£1,000

Correspondent: Christopher Kitto, Correspondent, 29 Blacksmiths Lane, Newton Solney, Burton-on-Trent, Staffordshire DE15 0SD (01283 702129; email: chriskitto@btinternet.com)

CC number: 214783

Eligibility

People in need who live in Austrey, Measham, Shenton or Whitwick, especially older people over the age of 75 who live alone.

Types of grants

One-off and recurrent grants are awarded (up to a maximum of the £200) according to need. Financial help is mainly given to older people who need modest support, for example with fuel costs or hospital travel expenses.

Annual grant total

In 2014 the charity had an income of £4,000 and an expenditure of £4,400. We estimate that the amount of grants given to individuals for social welfare purposes totalled around £1,000.

Applications

Application forms are available from the correspondent and should be submitted directly by the individual before 31 March, in time for the trustees' yearly meeting held in April.

Other information

The charity also supports young individuals for educational and training needs. Organisations may also be assisted. Educational support is, however, the primary concern.

The Nicholson Memorial Fund (The Rosehill Trust)

£5,000

Correspondent: The Clerk to the Trustees, The Nicholson Memorial Fund (Rosehill Trust), 20A Millstone Lane, Leicester LE1 5JN (0116 222 2200; fax: 0116 222 2201; email: info@charity-link.org; website: www.charity-link.org/trust-administration/trusts-we-support)

CC number: 1000860

Eligibility

Young people and children 'who are delinquent, deprived, neglected or in need of care' in Leicestershire or Rutland.

Types of grants

One-off grants according to need.

Annual grant total

In 2013/14 the fund had an income of £12,100 and a total expenditure of £10,500. We estimate that welfare grants to individuals totalled £5,000, with funding also awarded to local organisations and for educational purposes.

Exclusions

One grant per two year period, except in exceptional circumstances.

Applications

Apply on a form available from Leicester Charity Link website.

Other information

Leicester Charity Link, the administrator of this fund, provides a wide range of support and advice to people in need.

The Thomas Stanley Shipman Charitable Trust

£34,500

Correspondent: Andrew York, Secretary to the Trustees, 6 Magnolia Close, Leicester LE2 8PS (0116 283 5345; email: andrew_york@sky.com)

CC number: 200789

Eligibility

People in need who live in the city and county of Leicester.

Types of grants

One-off and recurrent grants for living expenses and gifts at Christmas.

Annual grant total

In 2013/14 the trust held assets of £1.4 million and had an income of £55,500. Financial assistance for individuals was distributed as follows:

Grants administered by Leicester Charity Link	£15,000
Christmas gifts	£10,600
Grants and assistance to the elderly	£9,200

Individuals received a total of £34,500 from the trust, £15,000 of which was awarded in discretionary payments through Leicester Charity Link.

A further £14,300 was given to local organisations.

Exclusions

The trust does not usually provide educational grants due to lack of resources, and in light of its other objectives.

Applications

Apply in writing to the correspondent. Applications can be made either directly by the individual or, where applicable, via a relevant third party such as a social worker, Citizens Advice or other welfare agency, or through Leicester Charity Link. The trustees meet twice-yearly, normally in November and June. Applications should be submitted in mid-October and mid-April for consideration.

Charnwood

Babington's Charity

£9,500

Correspondent: Helen McCague, Trustee, 14 Main Street, Cossington, Leicester, Leicestershire LE7 4UU (01509 812271)

CC number: 220069

Eligibility

People in need in the parish of Cossington, Leicestershire.

Types of grants

One-off and recurrent grants are given according to need. Support includes assistance to people with disabilities and older people towards adequate heating expenses, household equipment and hospital travel costs. Help is offered to families suffering from hardship and other parishioners in distress.

Annual grant total

In 2014 the charity had an income of £40,500 and a total expenditure of £40,000. In previous years grants have on average amounted to about 61% of the charity's total expenditure and on average about 78% of the overall grant-making was made to students and individuals. We estimate that about £19,000 was given to individuals, of which about £9,500 was awarded for welfare needs.

At the time of writing (September 2015) the latest accounts were not available to view on the Charity Commission's website.

Applications

Applications may be made in writing to the correspondent. The trustees meet at least twice a year.

Other information

The charity gives to individuals and organisations for both education and social welfare purposes.

The Loughborough Welfare Trusts

£13,300

Correspondent: Lesley Cutler, Administrator, Bird Wilford and Sale Solicitors, 20 Churchgate, Loughborough LE11 1UD (07765934117; email: loughweltrsts@fsmail.net)

CC number: 214654

Eligibility

People in need who live in Loughborough and Hathern.

Types of grants

One-off and recurrent grants are given to people on low income for decoration costs, second-hand fridges, holidays and cookers, for example. Grants are also made towards clothing for primary schoolchildren under the age of 11.

Annual grant total

In 2014 the trust had an income of £34,000 and a total expenditure of £34,000. Welfare grants to individuals totalled £13,300, of which £6,500 was distributed for relief-in-need purposes and £6,800 for relief in sickness.

Applications

Apply in writing to the correspondent for consideration in January, March, May, July, September or November.

Other information

The trust administers Edgar Corah Charity, John Storer Education Foundation, The Reg Burton Fund, Loughborough Adult Schools, Herrick Charities, and The Loughborough Community Chest.

Mountsorrel Relief in Need Charity

£57,000

Correspondent: Rachel White, Benefit Secretary, c/o KDB Accountants and Consultants Ltd, 21 Hollytree Close, Hoton, Loughborough LE12 5SE (0793 1129 360; email: mountsorrelunitedcharities@outlook.com; website: www.mountsorrelunitedcharities.com)

CC number: 217615

Eligibility

People in need who have lived in the parish of Mountsorrel for at least six months.

Types of grants

One-off grants towards essential needs. Grants towards Charnwood Lifeline are available.

The charity states: 'We offer help in a variety of ways with electrical household products, garden maintenance, decorating, carpeting, mobility equipment (that is not supplied by Social Services), i.e. mobility scooters, hospital travel expenses and many of other areas of need.'

The charity also runs foot care services and provides one-off or ongoing grants for gardening needs (offered at the beginning of the season, i.e. April – November).

Annual grant total

In 2014 the charity had an income of £131,500 and a total expenditure of £120,500. Full accounts were not available to view on the Charity Commission's website at the time of writing (November 2015). We estimate that grants awarded to individuals totalled about £57,000, based on previous grant-making patterns. Grants are also awarded to organisations.

Applications

Contact the correspondent who will visit you in your home and help you to complete the application form. You will need to provide some financial details.

Other information

This is one of the two funds, together with Mountsorrel Educational Fund (Charity Commission no. 527912), administered under the Mountsorrel United Charities (Charity Commission no. 1027652) name.

The H. A. Taylor Fund

£16,500

Correspondent: Alexander Munton, Clerk to the Trustees, Leicester Charity Link, 20a Millstone Lane, Leicester LE1 5JN (0116 222 2200; email: info@charity-link.org; website: www.charity-link.org)

CC number: 516428

Eligibility

People in need who have been in resident in the parish of Syston for at least one year.

Types of grants

One-off grants, usually ranging from £50 to £1,000, towards a range of purposes, such as travel costs, furniture, clothing, fuel, household repairs, medical treatment, books and course fees, mobility aids and telephone and television expenses.

Annual grant total

In 2013/14 the fund had an income of £24,000 and a total expenditure of £28,500. We estimate that the amount of grants given to individuals totalled £14,000, with funding also awarded to organisations.

Exclusions

Applicants should not re-apply within two years of receiving a grant, apart from in exceptional circumstances.

Applications

Application forms are available from Syston and District Volunteer Centre, Syston Health Centre and Syston Library or can be downloaded from the website. They can be submitted at any time either through a third party or directly by the individual and are considered every two months.

Other information

Grants are also given to organisations.

Wymeswold Parochial Charities

£2,200

Correspondent: Mrs J. Collington, Correspondent, 94 Brook Street, Wymeswold, Loughborough, Leicestershire LE12 6TU (01509 880538; email: jocollington@sky.com)

CC number: 213241

Eligibility

People in need who have lived in Wymeswold for two years prior to application.

Types of grants

One-off grants are given for educational and relief-in-need purposes. Winter gifts

are given to pensioners, widows and widowers. One-off awards are also given to people who are ill.

Annual grant total

In 2014/15 the charity had an income of £4,500 and an expenditure of £4,700. We estimate that about £2,200 was given to individuals for social welfare purposes.

Applications

Applications may be made in writing to the correspondent at any time.

Other information

Educational needs are also assisted.

Harborough

Valentine Goodman Estate Charity

£10,000

Correspondent: John Stones, Trustee, Blaston Lodge, Blaston Road, Blaston, Market Harborough LE16 8DB (01858 555688)

CC number: 252108

Eligibility

People in need who live in the parishes of Blaston, Bringhurst, Drayton, East Magna, Hallaton or Medbourne.

Types of grants

One-off or recurrent grants according to need.

Annual grant total

In 2014 the charity had an income of £16,700 and an expenditure of £10,400. Grants made totalled approximately £10,000.

Applications

Apply in writing to the correspondent. Grants are distributed in February each year.

Illston Town Land Charity

£7,000

Correspondent: Mr J. Tillotson, Correspondent, Warwick House, 5 Barnards Way, Kibworth Harcourt, Leicester LE8 0RS (0116 279 2524)

CC number: 246616

Eligibility

People in need who live in the town of Illston in Leicestershire.

Types of grants

Grants towards the costs of council tax charges.

Annual grant total

In 2013/14 the charity had an income of £7,500 and a total expenditure of £7,000. We estimate that welfare grants to individuals totalled £7,000.

Applications

Apply in writing to the correspondent.

Keyham Relief in Need Charity

£15,000

Correspondent: David Witcomb, Trustee, Tanglewood, Snows Lane, Keyham, Leicester LE7 9JS (0116 259 5663)

CC number: 215753

Eligibility

People who live in the parish of Keyham (Leicestershire) and are in need. Applications from people who do not live in the area but have strong connections to residents in Keyham have previously been considered.

Types of grants

One-off grants according to need.

Annual grant total

In 2014 the charity had an income of £18,500 and a total expenditure of £35,000. We estimate that the amount of grants given to individuals totalled £15,000.

Applications

Applications should be made in writing to the correspondent and submitted directly by the individual. If the applicant does not live in Keyham, information about their connection with residents should be provided with the application.

Other information

The charity's primary source of funding is rental income from the four cottages it owns.

The Market Harborough and The Bowdens Charity

£21,500

Correspondent: James Jacobs, Steward, 10 Fairfield Road, Market Harborough, Leicestershire LE16 9QQ (01858 419128; email: admin@mhbcharity.co.uk; website: www.mhbcharity.co.uk)

CC number: 1041958

Eligibility

People in need who have lived within Market Harborough area for at least six months. The guidance notes state: 'The charity prefers prevention to palliatives.

It wishes to foster self-help and the participation of those intended to benefit; enable less advantaged people to be independent, gain useful skills and overcome handicaps; and encourage volunteer involvement.'

Types of grants

One-off grants are given for financial emergencies, for example, to older people or single parents who are in urgent need of a replacement for a broken down washing machine or cooker.

Annual grant total

In 2014 the charity had assets of £17.6 million and an income of £645,500. Grants were awarded to 38 individuals totalling around £21,500 (grants of £1,000 and over were awarded to five individuals totalling £8,800; grants of less than £1,000 were awarded to 33 individuals totalling £12,800).

Exclusions

Applicants must have exhausted all other areas of assistance before applying to the trust. Individuals who have received a grant from the charity in the previous 12 months will not normally be eligible for assistance.

Applications

Application forms are available from the correspondent or can be downloaded from the charity's website. They should normally be supported by a third party, such as a social worker, Citizens Advice or other welfare agency. Potential applicants are invited to contact the correspondent directly for further guidance.

Other information

Support is also given to individuals for educational purposes, to organisations, institutions and towards preservation of historical churches in the area.

Hinckley and Bosworth

Poor's Platt

£19,000

Correspondent: Jim Munton, Clerk to the Trustees, 20A Millstone Lane, Leicester LE1 5JN (0116 222 2200; email: info@charity-link.org; website: www.charity-link.org/trust-administration/trusts-we-support/the-poors-platt)

CC number: 503580

Eligibility

People in need in the ancient parish of Barwell, Leicestershire.

Types of grants

One-off grants of between £50 and £500 are given according to need.

Annual grant total

In 2014 the charity had an income of £24,000 and an expenditure of £19,700. We estimate that the amount of grants given to individuals totalled around £8,500.

Applications

Applications can be made through Leicester Charity Link using its application form (available to access from the Barwell parish council website) or in writing to the correspondent. Awards are considered quarterly, normally in March, June, September and December. The deadline for the submission is the 15th of the preceding month. Only one grant may be awarded in any 12-month period.

Other information

Grants are also available for various organisations, projects and schools in the area of benefit.

Thomas Herbert Smith's Trust Fund

£5,100

Correspondent: Andrew York, 6 Magnolia Close, Leicester LE2 8PS (0116 283 5345; email: andrew_york@sky.com)

CC number: 701694

Eligibility

People who live in the parish of Groby in Leicestershire.

Types of grants

One-off and recurrent grants, usually ranging from £100 to £500.

Annual grant total

In 2013/14 the fund had an income of £17,000 and a total expenditure of £20,500. Grants are made to individuals and organisations for both social welfare and educational purposes. We estimate that the amount of grants given to individuals for social welfare purposes totalled £5,100.

Applications

Applications can be made using a form available from the correspondent. They can be submitted either directly by the individual, or through a social worker, Citizens Advice or other third party, and are considered throughout the year.

Leicester

The Leicester Aid-in-Sickness Fund

£11,000

Correspondent: Mark Dunkley, Correspondent, Shakespeare Martineau, Two Colton Square, Leicester LE1 1QH (0116 254 5454; email: mark.dunkley@shma.co.uk)

CC number: 219785

Eligibility

People living in the City of Leicester, who are in poor health and financial need.

Types of grants

One-off grants, generally ranging between £20 and £125.

Annual grant total

In 2013/14 the fund had an income of £12,600 and a total expenditure of £11,700. We estimate that the amount of grants given to individuals totalled £11,000.

Applications

Apply in writing to the correspondent. Applications are usually considered quarterly.

Alex Neale Charity

£3,000

Correspondent: Maurice Kirk, Administrator, 6 Ervin Way, Queniborough, Leicester LE7 3TT (0116 260 6851; email: mrakirk@btinternet.com)

CC number: 260247

Eligibility

Older people in need who live in the parish of Queniborough.

Types of grants

Grants towards gas and electricity bills.

Annual grant total

In 2014, the charity had an income of £2,800 and a total expenditure of £3,300. We estimate that the total amount of grants awarded to individuals was approximately £3,000.

Applications

The trustees publicise the grants, usually every two years, in The Queniborough Gazette. An application form is then available from the correspondent. The trust may ask for copies of fuel bills for the two years prior to application, and then a grant would be made towards the costs of these bills.

The Parish Piece Charity

£5,500

Correspondent: Revd Canon Barry Naylor, Trustee, St Martins House, 7 Peacock Lane, Leicester LE1 5PZ (email: magwill26@ntlworld.com)

CC number: 215775

Eligibility

People in need who live in the parish of St Margaret in Leicester. Priority is usually given to older people and people with disabilities.

Types of grants

One-off grants and small pensions. Grants have been given for heating costs and electrical appliances.

Annual grant total

In 2014/15 the charity had an income of £11,000 and a total expenditure of £11,600. We estimate that welfare grants to individuals totalled £5,500, with funding also awarded to local organisations.

Applications

Apply in writing to the correspondent or via Leicester Charity Link using their standard application form.

St Margaret's Charity

£1,500

Correspondent: Revd Canon Barry Naylor, Trustee, St Martins House, 7 Peacock Lane, Leicester LE1 5PZ (email: magwill26@ntlworld.com)

CC number: 234626

Eligibility

People in need who live in the city of Leicester.

Types of grants

One-off grants, usually ranging from £25 to £100.

Annual grant total

In 2014/15 the charity had an income of £4,400 and a total expenditure of £3,100. We estimate that the amount of grants given to individuals totalled £1,500, with funding also awarded to local organisations.

Applications

Applications must be made through a welfare organisation such as Leicester Charity Link.

Melton

Melton Mowbray Building Society Charitable Foundation

£10,000

Correspondent: Martin Reason, Trustee, Melton Mowbray Building Society, Leicester Road, Melton Mowbray LE13 0D3 (01664 414141; fax: 01664 414040; email: m.reason@mmbs.co.uk; website: www.mmbs.co.uk/index.cfm?id=167&navid=98)

CC number: 1067348

Eligibility

Individuals in need who live within a 30-mile radius of Melton Mowbray – particularly young people, vulnerable adults, elderly people, people with disabilities and people with mental illness.

Types of grants

One-off grants in the range of £100 and £250, to provide, for example: opportunities for children from disadvantaged backgrounds; means of preparing young people for adult life; and help for those suffering from disabilities.

Annual grant total

In 2014/15 the foundation had an income of £16,600 and total expenditure of £21,300. We estimate that the amount of grants given to individuals totalled £6,000, with local organisations receiving around £14,000.

Exclusions

Grants are not made for expeditions or overseas travel.

Applications

Apply in writing to the correspondent. Applications should be submitted either directly by the individual or a family member, through a third party such as a social worker or teacher, or, where applicable, through an organisation such as Citizens Advice or a school. Applications should include details of the cash value sought, the nature of the expense, the reason for application and the location of the applicant. Applications are considered at meetings held on a quarterly basis.

Other information

On its website the foundation pledges to 'commit at least 33% and up to 50% of the annual contribution made by the Melton Mowbray Building Society to either kickstart a community project within the catchment area or to establish an enduring activity or initiative for the benefit of the community'.

The Melton Mowbray Building Society has a helpful page about the foundation on its website.

Oadby and Wigston

The Oadby Educational Foundation

£0

Correspondent: Rodney Waterfield, Hon. Secretary and Treasurer, 2 Silverton Road, Oadby, Leicester LE2 4NN (0116 271 4507; email: rodatthegnomehouse@talktalk.net)

CC number: 528000

Eligibility

People in need in the parish of Oadby only.

Types of grants

One-off and recurrent grants in the range of £50 and £200.

Annual grant total

In 2014 the foundation had assets of £1.3 million and an income of £49,000. Grants totalled £56,000, all of which was given for educational or religious purposes to individuals and organisations.

Applications

Applications should be made in writing to the correspondent and can be submitted either through a social worker, Citizens Advice or other welfare agency, or directly by the individual.

Northamptonshire

Litchborough Parochial Charities

£3,200

Correspondent: Maureen Pickford, Trustee, 18 Banbury Road, Litchborough, Towcester NN12 8JF (01327 830110; email: maureen@mojo1904.plus.com)

CC number: 201062

Eligibility

People in need who live in Litchborough.

Types of grants

Pensions are given to widows and grants are made to assist pensioners with heating bills.

Annual grant total

In 2014/15 the charity had both an income and total expenditure of £6,500.

Grants are made to individuals for both social welfare and educational purposes. We estimate that social welfare grants to individuals totalled £3,200.

Applications

Apply in writing to the correspondent.

The Nottingham Annuity Charity

£13,500

Correspondent: David Simmons, Correspondent, c/o Intermediate Housing Team, Nottingham Community Housing Association Ltd, 12–14 Pelham Road, Sherwood Rise, Nottingham NG5 1AP (0115 844 3404; email: david. simmons@ncha.org.uk; website: www. ncha.org.uk)

CC number: 510023

Eligibility

People in need who live in Nottinghamshire, with a preference for widows and unmarried women.

Types of grants

Regular yearly allowances of around £200 are paid in quarterly grants.

Annual grant total

In 2013/14 the charity had an income of £15,000 and a total expenditure of £14,100. We estimate that pensions totalled £13,500.

Applications

Applications should be made on a form available from the correspondent to be submitted either directly by the individual or through an appropriate third party such as a social worker, Citizens Advice or other welfare agency. Applications are usually considered quarterly.

Daventry

The Chauntry Estate

£2,700

Correspondent: Rita Tank, Walnut Tree Cottage, Main Street, Great Brington, Northampton NN7 4JA (01604 770809; email: ritatank40@yahoo.com)

CC number: 200795

Eligibility

Older people in need who live in the parish of Brington.

Types of grants

One-off grants to relieve sudden distress or illness, for example, towards travel expenses for visits to hospital, food, fuel and heating appliances, and aids not provided by health authorities.

Annual grant total

In 2014/15 the charity had an income of £10,800 and a total expenditure of £11,200. Grants are made to individuals and organisations for both social welfare and educational purposes. We estimate that social welfare grants to individuals totalled £2,700.

Applications

Apply in writing to the correspondent.

The Daventry Consolidated Charity

£6,500

Correspondent: Maggie Dowie, Correspondent, PO Box 7692, Daventry, Northamptonshire NN11 1DW (email: daventryconsolidatedcharity@gmail.com)

CC number: 200657

Eligibility

People in need who live in the borough of Daventry.

Types of grants

One-off grants for a specific need. Examples include a special chair for a child with cerebral palsy, travel to hospital 45 miles from home and help with the costs of adaptations to a motability vehicle.

Annual grant total

In 2014 the charity had an income of £21,000 and a total expenditure of £13,600. We estimate that the total amount of grants awarded to individuals was approximately £6,500.

Exclusions

There are no grants available towards helping reduce debts or for ongoing expenses.

Applications

Apply in writing to the correspondent. The trustees meet three times a year in March, July and November. Applications must include financial circumstances and the specific purpose for the grant. Relevant information not included will be requested if required.

Other information

The charity also makes grants to organisations.

The United Charities of East Farndon

£2,600

Correspondent: Cameron Fraser, Trustee, Linden Lea, Main Street, East Farndon, Market Harborough LE16 9SJ (01858 464218; email: fraser_cameron@ hotmail.com)

CC number: 200778

Eligibility

Families in need who live in East Farndon.

Types of grants

One-off cash grants of up to £50 are provided for travel expenses to hospital, fuel grants towards electricity, disability equipment, living costs and household bills.

Annual grant total

In 2014 the charity had an income of £6,900 and a total expenditure of £10,800. Grants are made to individuals and organisations for both social welfare and educational purposes. We estimate that social welfare grants to families totalled £2,600.

Applications

Applications can be made in writing to the correspondent and can be submitted directly by the individual or by a family member. They are considered as they are received.

The Yelvertoft and District Relief-in-Sickness Fund

£5,000

Correspondent: Richard Atterbury, Trustee, Crick Lodge, Crick, Northampton NN6 7SN (01788 822247)

CC number: 285771

Eligibility

People in need who live in the parishes of Yelvertoft, West Haddon, Crick, Winwick, Clay Coton or Elkington, who are sick, convalescent, disabled or infirm.

Types of grants

Small, one-off grants for wheelchairs, walkers and the like.

Annual grant total

In 2014 the fund had an income of £8,300 and a total expenditure of £5,400. We estimate that the amount of grants given to individuals totalled £5,000.

Applications

Apply in writing to the correspondent. Applications should be submitted directly by the individual, a relative or district nurse, and can be considered at any time.

Kettering

Church and Town Allotment Charities and others

£6,000

Correspondent: Anne Ireson, Kettering Borough Council, Council Offices, Bowling Green Road, Kettering NN15 7QX (01536 534398; email: anneireson@kettering.gov.uk)

CC number: 207698

Eligibility

Widows, widowers and single people over the age of 60 who live alone in Kettering or Barton Seagrave and who are in receipt of retirement pension.

Types of grants

Grants of £25 towards winter fuel bills.

Annual grant total

In 2012/13 the charity had an income of £14,800 and a total expenditure of £12,200. We estimate that welfare grants to individuals totalled £6,000, with funding also awarded to individuals for educational purposes.

At the time of writing (November 2015) the information provided was the latest available.

Applications

The charity places advertisements in local newspapers in November each year, after which an application form can be applied for from the correspondent. Applications are considered in November. Applicants must include details of income, status, age and address.

Other information

Educational grants are available for over 16s who live in Kettering and Barton Seagrave.

The Desborough Town Welfare Committee

£2,600

Correspondent: Ann King, Hon. Secretary, 190 Dunkirk Avenue, Desborough, Kettering, Northamptonshire NN14 2PP (01536 763390; email: paulineginns41@btinternet.com)

CC number: 235505

Eligibility

People who are older, sick or in need and living in Desborough.

Types of grants

One-off and recurrent grants, paid mainly at Christmas.

Annual grant total

In 2013/14 the committee had an income of £6,800 and an expenditure of £5,300. We estimate that the amount of grants given to individuals totalled £2,600, with funding also awarded to local organisations.

Applications

Apply in writing to the correspondent, for consideration within two to three months.

The Stockburn Memorial Trust Fund

£8,000

Correspondent: Andy Sipple, Correspondent, 62 Pipers Hill Road, Kettering, Northamptonshire NN15 7NH (01536 524662; email: andy.sipple@btinternet.com)

CC number: 205120

Eligibility

People in need who live in the borough of Kettering.

Types of grants

One-off grants according to need.

Annual grant total

In 2014 the trust had an income of £9,000 and a total expenditure of £8,700. We estimate that the amount of grants given to individuals totalled £8,000.

Applications

Apply in writing to the correspondent through a social worker, Citizens Advice or other welfare agency. Applicants should include details of age, address, telephone number, financial situation and health circumstances.

Northampton

St Giles Charity Estates

£26,000

Correspondent: Anthony Lainsbury, Administrator, 5 Barrock Close, Southwaite, Carlisle CA4 0LL, Nicholas Rothwell House, 290 Harborough Road, Northampton NN2 8LR (01604 841882; fax: 01604 850845; email: info@nicholasrothwell.co.uk; website: www.nicholasrothwell.co.uk/grants)

CC number: 202540

Eligibility

People in need who live within the borough of Northampton.

Types of grants

St Giles Charity makes one-off grants for the benefit of needy people residing in Northamptonshire. Grants are given to individuals and families towards, for example, helping to fund individual household requirements such as carpets/washing machines and so on. Grants are always made for a specific purpose, not as a financial top up.

The trustees state that because the charity's funds are limited they tend to make smaller to medium-sized grants. They also may give only a partial grant on condition that the remainder of the amount required is raised from other sources.

Annual grant total

In 2014 the charity had assets of £3.3 million and an income of £691,000 most of which came from residents' fees. Grants were made totalling £56,000 and were given to both individuals and organisations. We estimate the amount given to individuals was around £26,000.

Exclusions

Grants cannot be made in certain circumstances, for instance:
- Applications from, or on behalf of, people residing outside Northampton
- For building projects, staffing costs, etc.
- For educational course fees, expenses, or materials
- For gap year projects, overseas expeditions, etc.
- For the repayment of debts, arrears of council tax or rent, or other payments to public bodies
- For funeral expenses

General funding grants are not made to other charities and organisations.

Applications

Note that staff at Nicholas Rothwell House **cannot** deal with personal or telephone enquiries. General enquiries may be made by email to the charity administrator at: tonylains43@gmail.com

Applicants may be asked to complete an application form available from the administrator, or downloaded from the charity's website.

Due to the quarterly cycle of meetings, applications can sometimes be held for up to three months until the next meeting occurs. However, urgent cases may be dealt with between meetings, at the discretion of the trustees.

Applications by individuals and families, which **must** be supported by a social care agency or similar organisation, are considered by the charity's grants committee, which meets quarterly, usually in February, May, August, and November.

Other information

The charity's main activity is the provision of almshouses and the support of Nicholas Rothwell House, a specially designed and purpose-built complex dedicated to providing both short and long-term residential care.

Coles and Rice Charity

£10,500

Correspondent: Marina Eaton, Wilson Browne Solicitors, 4 Grange Park Court, Roman Way, Northampton NN4 5EA (01604 876697; email: meaton@ wilsonbrowne.co.uk)

CC number: 238375

Eligibility

People in need who are over the age of 55 and have lived in the borough of Northampton for at least five years. However, the charity also makes one-off grants to younger people in need.

Types of grants

Annual pensions to elderly people around £200 paid in quarterly instalments. One-off grants of up to about £500 may be provided.

Annual grant total

In 2014 the charity had an income of £12,500 and an expenditure of £11,200. We estimate that around £10,500 was given in individual grants.

Applications

Application forms are available from the correspondent. They can be submitted either directly by the individual or through a social worker and are usually considered in March and November.

The Eleemosynary Charity of Giles Heron

£3,500

Correspondent: George Benson, Trustee, Brunton House, Wall, Hexham NE46 4EJ (01434 681203; email: office@ chestersestate.co.uk)

CC number: 224157

Eligibility

People in need who live in the parish of Wark and Simonburn.

Types of grants

One-off grants ranging from £100 to £500.

Annual grant total

In 2014/15 the charity had an income of £15,700 and a total expenditure of £15,200. Grants are made to individuals and organisations for both social welfare and educational purposes. We estimate that the amount of grants given to individuals for social welfare purposes totalled £3,500.

Applications

The individual should apply directly to the correspondent in writing.

The John and Mildred Law Fund

£15,000

Correspondent: Jane Forsyth, Clerk to the trustees, Wilson Browne, 4 Grange Park Court, Roman Way, Grange Park, Northampton NN4 5EA (01604 876697; email: jforsyth@qswblaw.com)

CC number: 1121230

Eligibility

People in need who live in the borough of Northampton.

Types of grants

One-off grants of up to £1,000 according to need.

Annual grant total

In 2013/14 the fund had an income of £32,000 and a total expenditure of £35,000. We estimate that the amount of grants given to individuals totalled around £15,000.

Applications

Apply in writing to the correspondent. The trustees meet twice a year to consider applications in May and November.

The Henry and Elizabeth Lineham Charity

£29,500 (55 55 grants)

Correspondent: Angela Moon, Clerk to the Trustees, Hewitsons LLP, Elgin House, Billing Road, Northampton NN1 5AU (01604 233233; email: mail@ hewitsons.com)

CC number: 205975

Eligibility

Women in need who are at least 55 and live in the borough of Northampton.

Types of grants

Annuities, currently £512 per annum, are paid half-yearly in June and December.

Annual grant total

In 2014 the charity held assets of £1.27 million and had an income of £48,500. During the year, 55 individuals received £29,500 in annuities.

Applications

Apply in writing to the correspondent. Beneficiaries are usually nominated by one of the trustees, mostly councillors or ex-councillors.

The Northampton Municipal Church Charities

£50,000

Correspondent: Jane Forsyth, Administrator, Wilson Browne Solicitors, 4 Grange Park Court, Roman Way, Grange Park, Northampton NN4 5EA (01604 876697; email: jforsyth@wilsonbrowne.co.uk)

CC number: 259593

Eligibility

People in need who live in the borough of Northampton.

Types of grants

People aged over 55 are eligible for quarterly payments of £85 and a Christmas voucher of £45. People of any age can receive one-off grants of up to a maximum of £500.

Annual grant total

In 2013/14 the charity had an income of £275,000 and an expenditure of £283,500. Grants to individuals for social welfare purposes usually total around £50,000.

Exclusions

The Charity is unable to assist with debt.

Applications

Apply on a form available from the correspondent, including details of age, residence, income, assets and expenditure. Applications can be submitted either directly by the individual or through a third party such as a social worker, Citizens Advice or other welfare agency. They are considered on a regular basis.

Other information

The charity runs a sheltered housing scheme at St Thomas House in St Giles Street, Northampton. It is warden controlled and has 17 small flats for people over 55. The charity's income must firstly be used for maintaining St Thomas House, secondly for the benefit of residents, and thirdly for the relief in need of people who live in Northampton.

The Page Fund

£7,000

Correspondent: Wilson Browne, Clerk to the Trustees, Wilson Browne Solicitors, 4 Grange Park Court, Roman Way, Northampton NN4 5EA (01604 876697; fax: 01604 768606; email: jforsyth@wsqblaw.com)

CC number: 241274

Eligibility

People in need who live in the borough of Northampton or within five miles of the Guild Hall and have done so for more than five years. Preference is given to older people, and to those with a sudden and unforeseen drop in income, for example widows following the death of a husband.

Types of grants

Pensions of around £1,000 per year for people who have experienced a reduction in income due to widowhood or old age.

Annual grant total

In 2013/14 the fund had an income of £32,500 and a total expenditure of £31,500. We estimate that 7,000 was awarded in grants to individuals. Most of the charity's expenditure is awarded to organisations.

At the time of writing (November 2015) no accounts were available to view.

Exclusions

Applicants must have lived in the Northampton area for at least five years.

Applications

Application forms are available from the correspondent. Applications can be submitted directly by the individual or through a social worker, Citizens Advice or other welfare agency. They are accepted at any time and are usually considered in May and November.

South Northamptonshire

Blakesley Parochial Charities

£2,100

Correspondent: Derek Lucas, Secretary/ Treasurer, Bradworthy, Main Street, Woodend, Towcester, Northamptonshire NN12 8RX (01327 860517; email: deelucas@uwclub.net; website: www. blakesley-village.co.uk/Blakesley Northants/Parochial_Charities.html)

CC number: 202949

Eligibility

People in need who live in Blakesley.

Types of grants

One-off and recurrent grants are given according to need. Grants are given towards the fuel bills of older people and as pensions to widows. Christmas cheques are also given to older people, widows or those suffering from illness. Vouchers are awarded 'to those who have made a contribution to the general community'.

Annual grant total

In 2014 the charity had an income of £4,200 and a total expenditure of £4,500. We estimate that welfare grants to individuals totalled around £2,100.

Applications

Applications may be made in writing to the correspondent at any time. The trustees normally meet in December to consider Christmas grants.

Other information

The charity also makes grants for educational purposes and to local organisations.

The Brackley United Feoffee Charity

£14,200

Correspondent: Irene Bennett, 24 Broad Lane, Evenley, Brackley NN13 5SF (01280 703904; email: caryl.billingham@ tesco.net)

CC number: 238067

Eligibility

People in need who live in the ecclesiastical parish of Brackley (which consists of the town of Brackley and the village of Halse only).

Types of grants

The charity gives funding to a wide range of causes, including the distribution of Christmas donations to around 60 elderly residents of Brackley. Grants made during 2013/14 included: the purchase of second hand furniture for people who had been recently rehoused; assistance with carpets and white goods for people who had been rehoused and were on very low incomes; the purchase of special equipment for a child with cerebral palsy; the purchase of domestic equipment to help a child with severe asthma; assistance with the unexpected and additional hospital travel costs for a person suffering from cancer; assistance with the purchase of school uniforms.

Annual grant total

In 2013/14 the charity had an income of £33,500 and a total expenditure of £35,000. Relief-in-need grants totalled £14,200.

Applications

Applications can be made in writing to the correspondent preferably by the individual or through a social worker, Citizens Advice or other welfare agency. The trustees meet every three to four months.

Other information

The charity awards grants to individuals and organisations for both educational and social welfare purposes.

The Harpole Parochial Charities

£4,000

Correspondent: Mary Burt, Trustee, 16 Garners Way, Harpole, Northampton NN7 4DN (01604 831365)

CC number: 202568

Eligibility

People in need who have lived in Harpole for more than seven years, with a preference for those over 65.

Types of grants

Recurrent grants ranging from £25 to £30.

Annual grant total

In 2014 this charity had an income of £8,000 and a total expenditure of £4,600. We estimate that the amount of grants given to individuals totalled around £4,000.

Applications

Application forms are available from the correspondent. You should include details of financial status, benefits and income. Applications can be submitted either directly by the individual or through a relative. They are considered in December and should be submitted in November.

The Pattishall Parochial Charities

£8,000

Correspondent: The Clerk to the Trustees, 59 Leys Road, Pattishall, Towcester NN12 8JY (01327 830583; website: pattishallparish.org.uk/parish-council/pattishall-charities)

CC number: 204106

Eligibility

People in need who have lived in the parish of Pattishall for at least three years. Preference is given to people who are over 65.

Types of grants

The 15 oldest applicants for the Widows' and Widowers' pension receive monthly payments of £30. Others can apply separately to receive grants for fuel at Christmas (currently £65 per household). Grants of between £15 and £500 are available for one-off needs within the community and have been given towards, for example, provision of a downstairs toilet and a contribution towards a child's playgroup fees.

Annual grant total

In 2014 the charities had an income of £9,200 and a total expenditure of £8,300. We estimate that pensions and grants to individuals totalled £8,000.

Applications

Apply in writing to the correspondent, making sure to include details of age, marital status and the length of time the applicant has been resident in the parish. Applications are usually considered in November for fuel grants, July for pensions, and throughout the year for other grants. Applications can be submitted either directly by the individual or by anybody who hears of a need. Receipts (copies will do) should be included for the cost of travel for hospital visits and estimates for the purchases of large equipment, such as wheelchairs.

Other information

'Each year the charity clerk will advertise around Pattishall and on the website for new applicants. In an effort to help identify those who would benefit from a grant, members of the parish are requested to bring forward names to the attention of the clerk.'

The Roade Feoffee and Chivall Charity

£9,000

Correspondent: Michael Dowden, Trustee, 67 High Street, Roade, Northampton NN7 2NW

CC number: 202132

Eligibility

People in need who live in the ancient parish of Roade.

Types of grants

One-off grants usually ranging from £15 to £100. Past grants have been given at Christmas time and for such things as travel expenses to visit relatives in hospital.

Annual grant total

In 2014 the charity had an income of £24,500 and a total expenditure of £19,900. We estimate that welfare grants to individuals totalled £9,000.

Applications

Apply in writing to the correspondent, specifying the reason for the application.

Nottingham-shire

The Mary Dickinson Charity

£19,500 (32 grants)

Correspondent: Nigel Cullen, Clerk to the Trustees, Freeths LLP, Cumberland Court, 80 Mount Street, Nottingham NG1 6HH (0115 936 9369; email: anna.chandler@freeths.co.uk)

CC number: 213884

Eligibility

Older people in need who live in the city or county of Nottingham. Preference is given to Christians.

Types of grants

Pensions are given to a fixed number of older people. One-off grants may also be available for emergency items such as replacing gas fires and safety alarm and telephone systems.

Annual grant total

In 2014 the charity had assets of £1.3 million and an income of £39,500. Pensions and grants to individuals amounted to £19,500.

Applications

Application forms are available from the correspondent. Applications can be submitted through a GP or member of the clergy, or directly by the individual. If the individual is applying directly, the application must be supported by a reference from a GP or member of the clergy. Applications can be submitted all year round and are considered in March, June, September and December, although emergency cases can be considered at any time.

The Fifty Fund

£33,000 (134 grants)

Correspondent: Craig Staten-Spencer, Administrator, Nelsons Solicitors, Pennine House, 8 Stanford Street, Nottingham NG1 7BQ (0115 989 5251)

CC number: 214422

Eligibility

People in need who live in Nottinghamshire.

Types of grants

Monthly payments and one-off grants to help with debts, household and white goods.

Annual grant total

In 2014 the fund had assets of almost £8.1 million and an income of £288,500.

Grants to individuals were made totalling £33,000. Five individuals received regular support and 129 individuals received one-off grants.

Exclusions

No grants are given for education, sponsorship, holidays, house moving costs, bonds or rents in advance.

Applications

Applications, in writing to the correspondent, can be submitted either by the individual or through a recognised referral agency (such as a social worker, Citizens Advice or doctor) or other third party. Applications are considered at quarterly meetings through the year.

Other information

Grants are also made to organisations (£142,500 to 61 organisations in 2014). The accounts note that at trustees' meetings, 'the level of income not utilised is considered and, if considered appropriate, funds are donated to charities with similar aims to The Fifty Fund on the basis that such funds are used to help individuals and families in need and who are resident in Nottinghamshire'.

The John William Lamb Charity

£15,100

Correspondent: Nina Dauban, Chief Executive, Nottinghamshire Community Foundation, Pine House B, Southwell Road West, Rainworth, Mansfield NG21 0HJ (01623 620202; fax: 01623 620204; email: enquiries@nottscf.org.uk; website: www.nottscf.org.uk)

CC number: 221978

Eligibility

People in need who have been living for at least one year within the city of Nottingham, or within 20 miles of the Nottingham Exchange, with a preference for older people.

Types of grants

Annuities are paid quarterly. One-off grants are also available.

Annual grant total

In 2013/14 the charity had assets of £955,500 and an income of £36,500. Annuities to individuals totalled £15,100 and were distributed as follows:

Annuities	26	£12,500
One-off grants	-	£2,600

Applications

Apply in writing to the correspondent. Applicants will be visited by a member of the trust.

Other information

The fund is administered by Nottinghamshire Community Foundation.

Long Bennington Charities

£4,500

Correspondent: Nicola Brown, Trustee, 61 Main Road, Long Bennington, Newark, Nottinghamshire NG23 5DJ (01400 282458; email: secretarylbcharities@yahoo.co.uk)

CC number: 214893

Eligibility

People in need who live in the parish of Long Bennington.

Types of grants

One-off grants according to need. Grants have previously been given for garden maintenance and disability aids.

Annual grant total

In 2014 the charity had an income of £6,600 and a total expenditure of £4,800. We estimate that welfare grants to individuals totalled £4,500.

Applications

Applications should be made in writing to the correspondent directly by the individual or through a third party.

Municipal General Charities for the Poor

£9,500 (55+ grants)

Correspondent: Michael Gamage, Clerk, Payne and Gamage Solicitors, 48 Lombard Street, Newark, Nottinghamshire NG24 IXP (01636 640649)

CC number: 217437

Eligibility

People who live in the parishes of Coddington, Collingham, Farndon, Hawton, Holme, Langford, Newark or Winthorpe and are in need by reason of youth, age, ill health, disability, financial hardship or other disadvantage.

Types of grants

One-off grants of £200–£300 are mainly given towards household items such as cookers, washing machines, furniture and other household equipment. Christmas gifts of £80 each are also available.

Annual grant total

In 2014 the charity had assets of £1.65 million and an income of £35,000. Grants to individuals totalled £9,500, including £4,400 in Christmas gifts of £80 to 55 individuals.

Applications

Application forms are available from the correspondent. They should be submitted through a social worker, Citizens Advice or other welfare agency. Awards are normally considered at quarterly meetings and must include details of the particular need.

Other information

The charity also makes grants to organisations and is responsible for administration of a number of charitable funds.

The New Appeals Organisation for the City and County of Nottingham

£33,000

Correspondent: Phil Everett, Joint Chair, 4 Rise Court, Hamilton Road, Nottingham NG5 1EU (0115 960 9644 (answering service); email: enquiries@newappeals.org.uk; website: www.newappeals.org)

CC number: 502196

Eligibility

People in need who live in the city and county of Nottingham.

Types of grants

One-off grants ranging from £50 to £2,000 to meet needs which cannot be met from any other source. For example, wheelchairs, white goods, flooring, beds and bedding, rise/recliner chairs, adapted vehicles, holidays, sensory stimulation equipment, computers and other electrical goods. Christmas gifts are also given to elderly and homeless people. Much of the money is raised for specific projects or people.

Annual grant total

In 2013/14 the organisation had an income of £123,000 and a total expenditure of £71,000. We estimate that £33,000 was given in grants to individuals, with funding also awarded to local schools and organisations.

Exclusions

The trust does not usually help with debt arrears, building works, wages, educational costs, foreign travel for students or requests from outside Nottingham.

Applications

Application forms are available from the correspondent. Applications should ideally be made through a social worker, Citizens Advice, medical establishment or other welfare agency, although those submitted directly by the individual are considered. Applications are considered on the first Monday of each month.

The Nottingham Children's Welfare Fund

£2,600

Correspondent: Gwen Derry, Trustee, 37 Main Road, Wilford, Nottingham NG11 7AP (0115 981 1830)

CC number: 215445

Eligibility

Children and young adults under 18, with priority given to children who live in Nottinghamshire, especially in Nottingham and particularly those who have lost either or both of their parents.

Types of grants

One-off grants of around £50 to £75. Recent awards have been made for domestic appliances, furniture, furnishings, clothing, toys and contributions to school trips and family holidays.

Annual grant total

In 2013/14 the fund had an income of £1,800 and a total expenditure of £2,800. We estimate that the total amount of grants awarded to individuals was approximately £2,600.

Applications

Apply on a form available from the correspondent: to be submitted by social services, the probation service or another welfare agency or third party such as a teacher. Applications are usually considered four times a year.

The Nottingham General Dispensary

£20,000

Correspondent: Nigel Cullen, Clerk to the Trustees, Cumberland Court, 80 Mount Street, Nottingham NG1 6HH (0115 901 5558; fax: 0115 901 5500; email: anna.chandler@freeths.co.uk)

CC number: 228149

Eligibility

People who are in poor health, convalescent or who have disabilities and live in the county of Nottinghamshire.

Types of grants

One-off grants ranging from £20 to £1,000 are given for a variety of needs, including home adaptations, mobility equipment, medical aids, hospital travel costs, computer equipment, holidays and respite breaks.

Annual grant total

In 2013/14 the charity had an income of £44,500 and a total expenditure of

£54,500. We estimate that the amount of grants given to individuals for social welfare purposes, paid either directly or through other organisations, totalled around £20,000. The charity usually sets aside an additional annual donation of £10,000 for the Nottingham Self Help Projects Funds. Accounts were received but not available to view on the Commission's website.

Exclusions

No grants are given where funds are available from statutory sources. No recurrent grants are made.

Applications

Apply in writing to the correspondent through a social worker, Citizens Advice, other welfare agency or a professional, for example, a doctor or teacher. Individuals can apply directly via an application form available from the correspondent but must include supporting medical evidence and details of the costs of the items or facilities needed. Applications are considered all year round although requests for grants exceeding £1,000 may take longer.

The Perry Trust Gift Fund

£11,000

Correspondent: Anna Chandler, Correspondent, c/o Freeths LLP, Cumberland Court, 80 Mount Street, Nottingham NG1 6HH (0115 901 5562)

CC number: 247809

Eligibility

In order of preference: (a) people in need who have lived in the city of Nottingham for at least five years; (b) people in need who have lived in Nottinghamshire for at least five years. Grants are mainly given to older people with low incomes but some help is also available to younger people in need.

Types of grants

One-off grants of up to £200 towards, for example, electric bills, clothing, living costs, household bills, food, furniture, disability equipment and help in the home.

Annual grant total

In 2013/14 the fund had an income of £12,500 and a total expenditure of £11,200. We estimate that the amount of grants given to individuals totalled £11,000.

Applications

Application forms are available from the correspondent. Applications can be made through a third party such as a social worker, Citizens Advice or other welfare agency. Grants are made in either May or November. Successful applicants may apply again in another year if necessary.

The Puri Foundation

£1,600 (1 grant)

Correspondent: Nathu Ram Puri, Trustee, Environment House, 6 Union Road, Nottingham NG3 1FH (0115 901 3000; website: www.purico.co.uk/charitable_functions)

CC number: 327854

Eligibility

Individuals in need living in Nottinghamshire who are from India (particularly the towns of Mullanpur near Chandigarh and Ambala). Employees/past employees of the Melton Medes Group Ltd, Blugilt Holdings or Melham Inc. who are in need, and their dependants, are also eligible. The trust wants to support people who have exhausted state support and other avenues, in other words to be a 'last resort'.

Types of grants

One-off and recurrent grants are given according to need, for items such as furniture or clothes. The maximum donation is usually between £150 and £200.

Annual grant total

In 2013/14 the foundation had assets of nearly £3.2 million and an income of £345,000. Grants were made totalling £284,500, with a major grant of £227,000 being given to Puri Foundation for Education in India. Grants to two individuals were listed in the accounts totalling £3,200, one of them being for 'general support' and two for 'education and cultural' purposes.

Applications

Applications may be made in writing to the correspondent, either directly by the individual or through a social worker.

Other information

Note that the vast majority of charitable giving is in grants to organisations. Individual support is given occasionally. Educational grants can also be made.

The West Gate Benevolent Trust

£81,000

Correspondent: Stephen Carey, Secretary, 17 Storcroft Road, Retford, Nottinghamshire DN22 7EG (01777 707677)

CC number: 503506

Eligibility

People in need who live in Nottinghamshire.

Types of grants

One-off grants ranging from about £50 to £5,000. For example, recent grants have been given for washing machines, holidays and travel to visit relatives in hospital.

Annual grant total

In 2013/14 the trust had an income of £82,500 and a total expenditure of £83,500. Grants awarded to individuals totalled £81,000.

Applications

Applications cannot be made by individuals directly, but only through a third party such as a social worker or Citizens Advice.

Bassetlaw

The Sir Stuart and Lady Florence Goodwin Charity

£9,000

Correspondent: Grants Administrator, Bassetlaw District Council, Finance Department, Queen's Buildings, Potter Street, Worksop, Nottinghamshire S80 2AH (01909 533249; email: goodwin.charity@bassetlaw.gov.uk)

CC number: 216902

Eligibility

People over 60 who are need and live in the former rural district of East Retford. Consideration may be given to younger applicants.

Types of grants

One-off grants to improve quality of life. Recent grants have been given for medical equipment such as nebulisers, access ramps, walk-in baths and mobility scooters.

Annual grant total

In 2013/14 the charity had an income of £8,500 and a total expenditure of £9,300. We estimate grants to individuals totalled around £9,000.

Applications

Apply in writing to the correspondent. Applications can be submitted directly by the individual or through a third party such as Age Concern or social services. Grants will only be made to the person raising the invoice, not the individual.

Mansfield
The Brunts Charity

£12,800

Correspondent: H. Hawkins, Correspondent, Brunts Chambers, 2 Toothill Lane, Mansfield, Notts NG18 1NJ (01623 623055)

CC number: 213407

Eligibility
Older people over 60 who are in need and have lived in the former borough of Mansfield (as constituted in 1958) for at least five years.

Types of grants
Regular allowances in the form of small pensions. Christmas gifts are also available.

Annual grant total
In 2014/15 the charity had assets of £12.9 million and an income of £789,000. During the year £300 was given in pensions, along with a grant of £1,800 from the Christmas gifts account, A further £10,700 in Christmas gifts was awarded to residents and £3,100 was given in other grants.

Applications
Application forms are available from the correspondent. Applications should be submitted directly by the individual. Applications are considered regularly.

Other information
The charity's main concern is the provision of almshouses for elderly residents in financial difficulty. It also makes grants to local organisations.

Warsop United Charities

£1,600

Correspondent: Jean Simmons, Trustee, Newquay, Clumber Street, Warsop, Mansfield, Nottinghamshire NG20 0LX

CC number: 224821

Eligibility
People in need who live in the urban district of Warsop (Warsop, Church Warsop, Warsop Vale, Meden Vale, Spion Kop and Sookholme).

Types of grants
Our research suggests that one-off grants for necessities and quarterly grants to about 60 individuals are made.

Annual grant total
In 2014 the charity had an income of £6,000 and a total expenditure of nearly £7,000. We estimate that the amount of grants given to individuals for social welfare purposes totalled around £1,600.

Applications
Applications may be made in writing to the correspondent. The trustees meet three or four times a year.

Other information
Grants are also made for educational purposes. Both individuals and organisations can be supported.

Newark and Sherwood
The John and Nellie Brown Farnsfield Trust

£6,200

Correspondent: Alan Dodd, Trustee, Roan House, Crabnook Lane, Farnsfield, Newark NG22 8JY (01623 882574; email: alan@alandodd.force9.co.uk)

CC number: 1078367

Eligibility
People in need who live in Farnsfield in Nottinghamshire and the surrounding area.

Types of grants
Grants are given according to need.

Annual grant total
In 2013/14 the trust had an income of £5,000 and a total expenditure of £26,000. Grants are made to individuals and organisations for both educational and social welfare purposes. We estimate that social welfare grants to individuals totalled £6,200.

Applications
Apply in writing to the correspondent.

The Coddington United Charities

£6,500

Correspondent: Mr A. Morrison, Clerk to the Trustees, 26 Kirkgate, Newark, Nottinghamshire NG24 1AB (01636 700888)

CC number: 1046378

Eligibility
People in need who live in the parish of Coddington.

Types of grants
One-off grants for individuals resident in the charity's almshouses and for general relief in need.

Annual grant total
In 2014 the charity had an income of £24,500 and a total expenditure of £14,000. We estimate that the amount of grants given to individuals totalled £6,500 with funding also awarded to local organisations.

Applications
Apply in writing to the correspondent. Applications can be submitted at any time, either through a third party such as a social worker or Citizens Advice or directly by the individual.

The Mary Elizabeth Siebel Trust

£60,500 (53 grants)

Correspondent: Frances Kelly, Secretary to the Trustees, Tallents Solicitors, 3 Middlegate, Newark, Nottinghamshire NG24 1AQ (01636 671881; fax: 01636 700148; email: frances.kelly@tallents.co.uk)

CC number: 1001255

Eligibility
People over 60 years of age who are in poor health and live within a 12-mile radius of Newark Town Hall.

Types of grants
One-off grants ranging from £50 to £2,500. The trust aims to enable individual applicants to live in their own homes e.g. help with the cost of stair-lifts, essential home repairs, aids for disabled people, care at home, relief for carers and so on.

Annual grant total
In 2013/14 the trust had assets of £2.77 million, an income of £114,000 and a total expenditure of £120,500. Grants were made to 53 individuals totalling £60,500.

Applications
Application forms are available from the correspondent. Applications can be submitted at any time but must be endorsed by a recognised third party such as a doctor or social worker. Individuals are usually visited by the charity's assessor who will then make a recommendation to the trustees. The trustees meet every two months to consider applications.

Other information
Grants are also made to organisations (£5,500 in 2013/14).

Nottingham

Nottingham Gordon Memorial Trust for Boys and Girls

£9,100

Correspondent: Anna Chandler, Charity Administrator, Cumberland Court, 80 Mount Street, Nottingham NG1 6HH (0115 901 5562; email: anna.chandler@freeths.co.uk)

CC number: 212536

Eligibility

Children and young people under the age of 25 who are in need, hardship or distress and live in Nottingham or the area immediately around the city. Preference can be given to individuals who are of the former Nottingham Gordon Memorial Home for Destitute Working Boys.

Types of grants

One-off grants are made for baby essentials, clothing, bedding, electrical goods (mainly cookers and washing machines), basic equipment for people with disabilities and family holidays and trips. Grants are also given to those who are fleeing domestic violence or re-building their lives after a relationship breakdown.

Annual grant total

In 2014 the trust had assets of £1.2 million and an income of £47,500. A total of £35,500 was awarded to individuals. The total amount of grants included £12,000 in 'educational grants to assist a number of students with the cost of education', £6,200 'to individuals and organisations taking part in trips both in the UK and overseas', £5,400 'to organisations in order to assist a number of individuals' and £2,800 'was awarded to Nottingham Scout Association which was distributed to 14 Explorer Scouts who had been selected to take part in the World Scout Jamboree in Japan'. We estimate that about £9,100 was given for social welfare purposes.

Applications

Application forms are available from the correspondent. They can be submitted through the individual's school, college, educational welfare agency, a health visitor, social worker, probation officer or similar professional. Our research suggests that individuals, supported by a reference from their school/college, can also apply directly. The trustees meet twice a year, although applications can be considered all year round.

Other information

The trust also supports organisations in the Nottingham area (£7,600 in 2014) and provides educational support for individuals.

The Thorpe Trust

£13,500

Correspondent: Mandy Kelly, Administrator, Actons Solicitors, 20 Regent Street, Nottingham NG1 5BQ (email: mandy.kelly@actons.co.uk)

CC number: 214611

Eligibility

Widows and unmarried women in need who live within a mile radius of Nottingham city centre. The recipients must be the widows or fatherless daughters of clergymen, gentlemen or professional people or of people engaged (otherwise than in a menial capacity) in trade or agriculture.

Types of grants

Recurrent grants according to need.

Annual grant total

In 2013/14 the trust had an income of £14,900 and a total expenditure of £13,700. We estimate that the amount of grants given to individuals totalled £13,500.

Applications

Application forms are available from the correspondent. Applications can be submitted directly by the individual or, where applicable, through a social worker, Citizens Advice or other welfare agency. They are considered once during the summer and at Christmas.

Rushcliffe

Bingham United Charities 2006 (formerly known as Bingham United Charities)

£2,000

Correspondent: Susan Lockwood, 23 Douglas Road, Bingham, Nottingham NG13 8EL (01949 875453; email: lockwoodsue79@gmail.com)

CC number: 213913

Eligibility

People in need who live in the parish of Bingham.

Types of grants

Grants can be given for a wide range of purposes.

Annual grant total

In 2014/15 the charity had an income of £9,400 and a total expenditure of £8,300. Grants can be given to individuals and organisations for both social welfare and educational purposes. We estimate that social welfare grants to individuals totalled £2,000.

Exclusions

Applicants must live in Bingham and be able to show need, hardship or distress.

Applications

Application forms are available from the secretary. Those applications which are supported by a professional, medical, or social care agency can often be dealt with more quickly.

Rutland

The Rutland Dispensary

£3,500

Correspondent: Correspondent, 31 Springfield Way, Oakham, Leicestershire LE15 6QA (01572756120; email: angelaandfrancis@talktalk.net)

CC number: 230188

Eligibility

People who are poor, old or sick and live in Rutland.

Types of grants

One-off and recurrent grants, usually in the range of £100–£250. Support is mainly given to relieve medical needs not covered by the NHS.

Annual grant total

In 2014 the charity had an income of £2,900 and an expenditure of £3,700. We estimate the annual total amount of grants given to individuals to be about £3,500.

Applications

Apply in writing to the correspondent. Applicants should include details of any medical conditions and their general circumstances.

The Rutland Trust

£3,500

Correspondent: Richard Adams, Clerk, 35 Trent Road, Oakham, Rutland LE15 6HE (01572 756706; email: adams@apair.wanadoo.co.uk)

CC number: 517175

Eligibility

People who have disabilities who live in Rutland and are in need.

Types of grants

Our research indicates that one-off and repeated grants, usually ranging between £50 and £400, are given to buy medical equipment.

Annual grant total

In 2013 the trust had an income of £20,000 and a total expenditure of £14,000. Grants are made for social welfare and educational purposes and to organisations. We estimate that grants awarded to individuals for social welfare purposes totalled around £3,500.

At the time of writing (November 2015) this was the most recent financial information available for the trust.

Applications

Our research suggests that an initial telephone call is recommended.

West Midlands

General

Beacon Centre for the Blind

See entry on page 73

The W. E. Dunn Trust

£61,500 (368 grants)

Correspondent: David Corney, Chair, The Trust Office, 30 Bentley Heath Cottages, Tilehouse Green Lane, Knowle, Solihull B93 9EL (01564 773407; email: wedunn@tiscali.co.uk)

CC number: 219418

Eligibility

People who are in need and live in the West Midlands, particularly Wolverhampton, Wednesbury, north Staffordshire and the surrounding area. Preference is given to people who are very old or very young, who the trust recognises as possibly being the least able to fund themselves.

Types of grants

One-off grants usually ranging from £50 to £200.

Annual grant total

In 2013/14 the trust had assets of £4.9 million and an income of £173,500. Individuals received a total £65,000 in 383 awards, including £61,500 paid in 368 grants for what we consider to be social welfare purposes. They were distributed as follows:

Clothing and furniture	185	£26,500
Domestic equipment	110	£22,000
Social and welfare	28	£6,000
Radio, TV and licences	40	£5,800
Education	15	£3,600*
Convalescence and holidays	5	£1,000

*We have not included this figure for educational awards in the grants total.

A further £105,500 was given in 154 grants to organisations.

Exclusions

Grants are not made to settle or reduce debts already incurred.

Applications

Applications should be made in writing via a social worker, Citizens Advice or other welfare agency. The trustees meet on a regular basis to consider applications.

Grantham Yorke Trust

£6,800

Correspondent: Christine Norgrove, Charities Administrator, SGH Martineau, 1 Colmore Square, Birmingham B4 6AA (email: christine. norgrove@sghmartineau.com)

CC number: 228466

Eligibility

People who are under 25 and were born in the old West Midlands Metropolitan County area (basically: Birmingham, Coventry, Dudley, Redditch, Sandwell, Solihull, Tamworth, Walsall or Wolverhampton).

Types of grants

One-off grants according to need.

Annual grant total

In 2013/14 the trust had assets of £6.8 million and an income of £249,500. Grants totalled £183,000, of which £169,500 was given to organisations. A total of 38 grants were awarded to individuals, for both social welfare and educational needs, amounting to £13,600. We estimate that welfare grants to individuals totalled £6,800.

Applications

Applications can be made on a form available from the correspondent. They can be submitted directly by the individual or via a relevant third party such as a social worker, Citizens Advice or other welfare agency, in February, May, August and November for consideration in the following month.

The James Frederick and Ethel Anne Measures Charity

£5,800

Correspondent: Laura Reid, Clerk to the Trustees, EFG Harris Allday, 33 Great Charles Street, Birmingham B3 3JN (0121 214 2340)

CC number: 266054

Eligibility

The following criteria apply:
1. Applicants must usually originate in the West Midlands
2. Applicants must show evidence of self-help in their application
3. Trustees have a preference for disadvantaged people
4. Trustees have a dislike for applications from students who have a full local authority grant and want finance for a different course or study
5. Trustees favour grants towards the cost of equipment
6. Applications by individuals in cases of hardship will not usually be considered unless sponsored by a local authority, health professional or other welfare agency

Types of grants

One-off or recurrent grants, usually between £50 and £500.

Annual grant total

In 2013/14 the charity had assets of £1.1 million and an income of £31,000. A total of 37 grants were made, amounting to £23,000. The charity gives to individuals and organisations for both social welfare and educational purposes. We estimate that the amount of grants given to individuals for social welfare purposes totalled £5,800.

Applications

Applications should be made in writing to the correspondent and be sponsored by a local authority, health professional or other welfare agency. No reply is given to unsuccessful applicants unless an sae is enclosed.

The Newfield Charitable Trust

£32,000 (135 grants)

Correspondent: Mary Allanson, Clerk, Rotherham and Co. Solicitors, 8–9 The Quadrant, Coventry CV1 2EG (024 7622 7331; fax: 024 7622 1293; email: m.allanson@rotherham-solicitors.co.uk)

CC number: 221440

Eligibility

Girls and women (under the age of 30) who are in need of care and assistance and live in Coventry or Leamington Spa.

Types of grants

The trust's objects are stated as: 'The relief of the physical, mental and moral needs of, and the promotion of the physical, social and educational training' of eligible people. Most grants are of under £500 and are given towards, for example: clothing, both school and general; beds and bedding; and essential household items.

Annual grant total

In 2014/15 the trust had assets of £1.6 million and an income of £58,000. Grants totalled £33,000, of which £32,000 was awarded to individuals for social welfare purposes. They were distributed as follows:

General	101	£24,000
Clothing	34	£8,300
Educational	2	£800

We have not included the figure for educational awards in the grants total.

Exclusions

Grants are not made for arrears or utility bills.

Applications

Our research indicates that applicants should write to the correspondent to request an application form. Applications are accepted from individuals or third parties e.g. social services, Citizens Advice, school/college, etc. A letter of support/reference from someone not a friend or relative of the applicant (i.e. school, social services, etc.) is always required. Details of income/expenditure and personal circumstances should also be given. Applications are considered eight times a year.

The Norton Foundation

£10,400 (139 grants)

Correspondent: The Correspondent, The Norton Foundation, 50 Brookfield Close, Hunt End, Redditch B97 5LL (01527 544446; email: correspondent@nortonfoundation.org; website: www.nortonfoundation.org)

CC number: 702638

Eligibility

Young people aged under 25 who live in Birmingham, Solihull, Coventry and Warwickshire. Applicants must be 'in need through some aspect of disadvantage defined as: in care or in need of rehabilitation, lapsing into delinquency, suffering from maltreatment or neglect, or whose potential is not yet realised due to circumstances beyond their control'.

Types of grants

One-off grants are given towards clothing, household items and, occasionally, holidays. Grants of up to £500 can be made, although they usually range between £50 and £250.

Annual grant total

In 2013/14 the foundation had assets of £4.9 million and an income of £154,500. Grants totalled £88,500, of which £55,000 was awarded to organisations. A total of 161 grants were made directly to individuals totalling £12,000. They were distributed as follows:

Household	106	£8,100
Clothing	32	£2,200
Education and training	22	£1,600*
Holidays	1	£75

*The figure for educational grants was not included in the grants total.

In addition, £22,000 was paid in block discretionary grants to 19 'sponsors' for redistribution to individuals. Sponsors included South Birmingham Young Homeless Project (£14,000), St Basil's Centre (£4,000) and Action for Children (£1,000).

Applications

Applications should be made in writing and contain all the information described in the guidance notes, which are available from the website. Applications must be submitted through a social worker, Citizens Advice, probation service, school or other welfare agency, and should be typed or printed, if possible. They are considered on a monthly basis.

Note: the foundation's website gives the following helpful tips on making applications:

What are the trustees looking for in ALL applications?

- information should be specific and to the point
- evidence on the causes of the current situation or need
- what other efforts are being made to solve the problem
- a clear indication of what difference the grant will make

Other information

The foundation's website also lists helpful information on why applications fail:

- the trustees are not convinced by the case being presented
- too many assumptions and unrealistic aspirations
- the amount requested is outside the range for the grant being applied for
- the bid was to fund long-term commitments
- financial information was insufficient and inadequate
- the contact details were insufficient for the trustees to obtain further information

The Persehouse Pensions Fund

£11,000

Correspondent: Clive Wheatley, Correspondent, 12A Oakleigh Road, Stourbridge, West Midlands DY8 2JX (01384 379775; email: clive.wheatley@virginmedia.com)

CC number: 500660

Eligibility

Elderly or distressed people belonging to the upper or middle classes of society who were born in the counties of Staffordshire or Worcestershire, or people who have lived in either county for ten years or more, and have been 'reduced to poverty by misfortune'.

Types of grants

Mainly pensions, but occasional one-off grants.

Annual grant total

In 2013/14 the charity had an income of £12,500 and a total expenditure of £11,700. We estimate that welfare grants to individuals totalled £11,000.

Applications

Application forms are available from the correspondent and can be submitted directly by the individual.

The Samuel Smith Charity, Coventry

£26,500

Correspondent: Elizabeth Martin, 44 Madeira Croft, Coventry CV58NY (024 76419622; email: lizmartin44@live.co.uk)

CC number: 240936

Eligibility

People who live in Coventry and the ancient parish of Bedworth and are in need.

Types of grants

Pensions and one-off grants.

Annual grant total

In 2014 the charity had an income of £40,000 and a total expenditure of £43,000. Grants totalled £26,500 and were distributed as follows:

Pensioner grants	£21,000
Payments in lieu of coal	£2,800
May gifts	£1,600
Christmas gifts to pensioners	£1,200
Bibles	£200
Relief in need	£200

During the year, 104 pensioners received recurrent grants.

Applications

Applications can be made in writing to the correspondent, but most beneficiaries are referred by the charity's almoner. The trustees meet three times a year to consider applications.

Other information

This charity has merged with Spencer's Charity – City of Coventry Warwickshire (Charity Commission no. 212935) which was removed from the central register of charities in August 2014. We are informed by the solicitor acting for both charities in the merger, that the charity will be renamed 'Samuel Smith's and Spencer's Charities' in the near future.

The Anthony and Gwendoline Wylde Memorial Charity

£2,100

Correspondent: Kirsty McEwen, Clerk to the Trustees, c/o Higgs and Sons Solicitors, 3 Waterfront Business Park, Dudley Road, Brierley Hill, West Midlands DY5 1LX (01384327322; email: kirsty.mcewen@higgsandsons.co.uk; website: www.wyldecharity.weebly.com)

CC number: 700239

Eligibility

People in need in the areas of Dudley and Staffordshire, with a preference for residents of Stourbridge (West Midlands) and Kinver (Staffordshire) – area defined by the DY7 and DY8 postcodes.

Types of grants

One-off grants, generally in the range of £50–£500.

Annual grant total

In 2013/14 the charity had assets of £876,000 and an income of £47,500. Grants were made totalling £30,500 and consisted of 25 awards to organisations totalling £26,000 and 18 awards to individuals totalling £4,300. We estimate that the amount of grants given to individuals for social welfare purposes totalled about £2,100.

Exclusions

The website states that 'grants are not normally made to other grant giving organisations'. Applications from areas outside the beneficial area may only be considered in exceptional circumstances. Support is not given where statutory help should be sought, towards bills or debts.

Applications

Applications should be made online on an appropriate form on the charity's website, but may also be submitted via post. Small grants (up to £750) can be dealt with quickly whilst larger awards (over £750) can only be approved at the trustees' meetings, which are held twice a year. There are separate forms. Concise supporting documentation may be attached, if appropriate/required.

Other information

The charity was created by a Trust Deed dated 6 April 1988, in memory of Anthony and Gwendoline Wylde. It awards grants for educational and general welfare needs, and to local organisations.

The website notes: 'Typically, a significant proportion of the small grants will be from individuals, and for educational purposes, and the larger grants tend to be from local organisations, although every application is considered on its merit.'

Herefordshire

All Saints Relief-in-Need Charity

£2,100

Correspondent: Douglas Harding, Trustee, 6 St Ethelbert Street, Hereford HR1 2NR (01432 267821; email: carodoug@hotmail.co.uk)

CC number: 244527

Eligibility

Individuals in need who live in the city of Hereford, with a preference for those resident in the ancient parish of All Saints.

Types of grants

One-off grants. However, the charity typically prefers to give items rather than cash sums.

Annual grant total

In 2013/14 the charity had an income of £7,600 and a total expenditure of £5,500. We estimate that welfare grants to individuals totalled £2,700, with funding also awarded for educational purposes.

Applications

Application forms are available from the correspondent.

Hereford Municipal Charities

£14,800

Correspondent: Clerk to the Trustees, 147 St Owen Street, Hereford HR1 2JR (01432 354002; email: herefordmunicipal@btconnect.com)

CC number: 218738

Eligibility

People in need who live in the city of Hereford.

Types of grants

One-off grants of up to £200. Grants are given to help with household equipment, clothes, educational equipment, emergencies and so on.

Annual grant total

In 2014 the charity had an income of £332,000 and a total expenditure of £252,000. At the time of writing (September 2015) the latest accounts were not available to view on the Charity Commission's website. Much of the charity's expenditure is allocated to the running of its almshouses. In the past grants to individuals have totalled about £32,500 on average with social welfare support totalling around £14,800.

Exclusions

Debts or nursery fees.

Applications

Application forms are available from the correspondent and should be submitted directly by the individual or through a relevant third party. Applications are considered five times a year but can be authorised between the trustees' meetings if they are very urgent. Applicants are normally interviewed.

Other information

The charity also offers almshouse accommodation. There are two separate funds (eleemosynary and educational) administered by the Grants Committee.

The Hereford Society for Aiding the Industrious

£2,200

Correspondent: Sally Robertson, Secretary, 18 Venns Close, Bath Street, Hereford HR1 2HH (01432 274014 – Thursdays only; email: hsaialms@ talktalkbusiness.net)

CC number: 212220

Eligibility

People in need who live in Herefordshire (particularly the city of Hereford) and are trying to better themselves by their own efforts. The early history of the society involved aid to the 'industrious poor' and those who would not make an effort to help themselves were excluded. This is reflected today with priority being given to individuals who are trying to obtain training to get back to work, often as mature students. Grants will be considered when a person is required to fund a gap between formal education and training for a career. The society also considers applications from girl guides and boy scouts for assistance with the cost of camp, but need must be proved in all cases.

Types of grants

Grants or interest-free loans, usually of £50 to £1,000, according to need.

Annual grant total

In 2013/14 the charity had assets of £1 million and an income of £131,000. Grants are given to individuals and organisations for both social welfare and educational purposes. During the year, grants to individuals totalled £4,500. We estimate that social welfare grants to individuals amounted to £2,200.

An additional £7,800 was given to organisations.

Applications

Application forms are available from the correspondent. Applicants are interviewed by the secretary. Trustees usually meet on the third Monday of every month.

Other information

The trust's main areas of activity are grants and loans to individuals and maintaining almshouses. Donations are also given to Herefordshire charities for specific projects rather than for running costs.

The Herefordshire Community Foundation (known as Herefordshire Foundation)

£2,500

Correspondent: Dave Barclay, Director, The Fred Bulmer Centre, Wall Street, Hereford HR4 9HP (01432 272550; email: info@herefordshirefoundation.org; website: www.herefordshirefoundation.org)

CC number: 1094935

Eligibility

People who are in need and live in Herefordshire.

Types of grants

Grants are given according to need.

Annual grant total

In 2013/14 the foundation had assets of £3.4 million and an income of £1.8 million. The majority of grants are awarded to organisations, although a breakdown of grants made during the year was not included in the annual report and accounts. Previous research suggests that approximately £5,000 is given each year to individuals for both welfare and educational purposes.

Applications

HCF administers a number of different funds. These all have specific application processes and criteria.

The foundation's website gives the following information:

> Applications should be addressed to 'Herefordshire Community Foundation' and if a grant is awarded the applicant will be advised of which fund (or funds) it came from it. It is rare for any of these funds to make an award of more than £1,000.

> Applications for under £1,000 are welcomed as a 'free-format' letter but this of course should include some standard information such as contact details, what is the grant to be used for and when, a budget/costs and why the grant is needed. Please contact us if you wish to discuss details before you apply.

The Norton Canon Parochial Charities

£2,500

Correspondent: Mary Gittins, Ivy Cottage, Norton Canon, Hereford HR4 7BQ (01544 318984)

CC number: 218560

Eligibility

People in need who live in the parish of Norton Canon.

Types of grants

One-off and recurrent grants are given according to need.

Annual grant total

In 2014 the charity had an income of £21,500 and a total expenditure of £52,000. The figure for total expenditure is unusually high and, as the charity was not required to submit its accounts to the Charity Commission due to its low income, we were unable to determine the reason for this. Our research suggests that grants usually total around £10,000 per year and are given to both individuals and organisations for educational and welfare purposes. We have estimated social welfare grants to individuals to total around £2,500.

Applications

Apply in writing to the correspondent at any time.

Shropshire

The Lady Forester Trust

£51,000 (138 grants)

Correspondent: Janet McGorman, Correspondent, Willey Park, Broseley, Shropshire TF12 5JJ (01952 884318)

CC number: 241187

Eligibility

People living in of the county of Shropshire who are sick, disabled, convalescent or infirm with priority given to inhabitants of the ancient borough of Wenlock.

Types of grants

One-off grants for medical equipment, nursing care, travel to and from hospitals and other medical needs not otherwise available on the NHS.

Annual grant total

In 2014 the trust held assets of £5.2 million and had an income of £153,000. Grants to 138 individuals totalled £51,000.

Grants to organisations totalled £69,000.

Exclusions

No retrospective grants are made, nor are grants given for building repairs/alterations, home/garden improvements or household bills.

Applications

Application forms are available from the correspondent. Applications should be made through a doctor (or Social Services in exceptional circumstances) and are considered on a quarterly basis.

The Gorsuch, Langley and Prynce Charity

£25,000 (246 grants)

Correspondent: Pamela Moseley, Administrator, 116 Underdale Road, Shrewsbury SY2 5EF

CC number: 247223

Eligibility

People in need who live in the parishes of Holy Cross (the Abbey) and St Giles in Shrewsbury.

Types of grants

One-off and recurrent grants usually ranging from £50 to £500. Grants have been given towards furniture, carpets, washing machines, cookers, fridges, baby clothes and cots. Christmas gifts are also given.

Annual grant total

In 2014 the charity had assets of £1 million and an income of £41,500. During the year the charity gave grants to 230 individuals and families, as well as to four local primary schools. The total amount of grants given was £36,500, although a breakdown of distribution was not available from the accounts. We estimate that the amount of grants given to individuals and families totalled £25,000.

Applications

Apply in writing to the correspondent through a social worker, healthcare professional, Citizens Advice or other welfare agency such as Home-Start. Applications should include details of the full the amount required and why it is needed. They are considered on a regular basis.

The Basil Houghton Memorial Trust

£4,200

Correspondent: Julia Baron, Trustee, c/o Community Council Building, The Creative Quarter, Shrewsbury Business Park, Shrewsbury SY2 6LG (01743 360641; email: houghton.trust@ shropshire-rcc.org.uk; website: www. basilhoughtontrust.org.uk)

CC number: 1101947

Eligibility

People with learning disabilities who are in need and live in Shropshire.

Types of grants

One-off grants usually of no more than £350. Grants should be additional to any services provided by statutory bodies. Typically, grants have been made towards travel expenses, achieving individuals' goals, the provision of life-improving items and services, and as contributions towards holidays.

Annual grant total

In 2014/15 the trust had an income of £13,500 and a total expenditure of £8,900. We estimate that the amount of grants given to individuals totalled £4,200 with funding also awarded to local organisations.

Exclusions

Applicants for individual grants must be resident in Shropshire or Telford and Wrekin.

Applications

Application forms are available from the correspondent. The trustees meet quarterly in March, June, September and December.

Other information

The website notes that the trust 'was established with an endowment from Mrs Doris Houghton and named after her son, the late Basil Houghton of Shrewsbury, who himself had a learning disability.'

The Thompson Pritchard Trust

£16,500

Correspondent: Dr Len Hill, Trustee, Radbrook Stables, Radbrook Road, Shrewsbury SY3 9BQ (01743 236863)

CC number: 234601

Eligibility

Individuals who live in Shropshire and have medically related and disability-related expenses and problems. Preference is given to those who have recently been discharged from hospital.

Types of grants

One-off grants of up to £300 are given towards: medical equipment (and repairs); convalescent treatment; domestic equipment which affects health such as washing machine or fridge repairs; expenses incurred during illness, including treatment; and travel and occasional accommodation for relatives during major operations.

Annual grant total

In 2014 the trust had an income of £20,500 and a total expenditure of £17,600. We estimate that the amount of grants given to individuals totalled £16,500.

Exclusions

No recurrent grants or grants towards purchasing, repairing or maintaining buildings or to pay off debts.

Applications

Application forms are available from the correspondent. Applications for small grants can be submitted at any time either directly by the individual or through a relevant third party such as a social worker, Citizens Advice or other welfare agency. More advice is available from the trust.

Shropshire

Alveley Charity

£10,000

Correspondent: Rachel Summers, Correspondent, MFG Solicitors LLP, Adam House, Birmingham Road, Kidderminster, Worcestershire DY10 2SH (01562 820181; email: rachel. summers@mfgsolicitors.com)

CC number: 1026017

Eligibility

People in need who live in the parishes of Alveley or Romsley.

Types of grants

One-off grants according to need.

Annual grant total

In 2013/14 the charity had an income of £19,000 and a total expenditure of £18,800. Part of the charity's activities involves the 'maintenance of property owned by the charity'; therefore, we estimate that the amount of grants given to individuals totalled around £10,000.

Applications

Applications may be made in writing to the correspondent, either directly by the individual or through a social worker, Citizens Advice or other welfare agency.

Other information

The charity also maintains properties.

The Ellen Barnes Charitable Trust

£5,000

Correspondent: Mark Woodward, Administrator, Crampton Pym and Lewis, The Poplars, 47 Willow Street, Oswestry, Shropshire SY11 1PR (01691 653301; email: info@crampton-pym-lewis.co.uk; website: www.crampton-pym-lewis.co.uk)

CC number: 217344

Eligibility

People in need who live in Weston Rhyn or adjoining parishes.

Types of grants

Although the trust's income is mainly used to run six almshouses, one-off grants are considered.

Annual grant total

In 2014, the trust had an income of £23,500 and a total expenditure of £31,000. We estimate that the total amount of grants awarded to individuals was approximately £5,000.

Applications

Applications can be made in writing to the correspondent either directly by the individual or through a social worker, Citizens Advice, doctor or other welfare agency. Applications are considered throughout the year.

Other information

The trust's main activity is the provision of almshouses.

The Bridgnorth Parish Charity

£800

Correspondent: Elizabeth Smallman, Trustee, 37 Stourbridge Road, Bridgnorth WV15 5AZ (01746 764149; email: eeesmallman@aol.com)

CC number: 243890

Eligibility

People in need who live in the parish of Bridgnorth, including Oldbury, Quatford and Eardington.

Types of grants

Our research suggests that one-off grants are given according to need, including, for example, towards funeral expenses and heating costs.

Annual grant total

In 2014 the charity had an income of £8,100 and a total expenditure of £1,700. Note that the expenditure varies each year and in the past has fluctuated from £0 to £9,400. We estimate that the total amount of grants awarded to individuals for social welfare purposes was approximately £800.

Applications

Applications may be made in writing to the correspondent either directly by the individual or through a doctor, nurse, member of the local clergy, social worker, Citizens Advice or other welfare agency.

Other information

The charity also awards grants for educational purposes and to organisations.

Telford and Wrekin
The Charity of Edith Emily Todd

£7,000

Correspondent: Mary Ayres, Administrator, 4 Willmoor Lane, Lilleshall, Newport, Shropshire TF10 9EE (01952 606053)

CC number: 215058

Eligibility

People over the age of 60 who are in need and who live in the ecclesiastical parish of Lilleshall.

Types of grants

Pensions of £15 a month with a bonus payment at Christmas time.

Annual grant total

In 2013/14 the charity had an income of £8,300 and a total expenditure of £7,000. We estimate that the amount of grants given to individuals totalled £7,000.

Applications

Applications should be made in writing directly by the individual to the correspondent. Applications are considered on receipt.

Staffordshire

Malam-Heath Fund

£3,500 (10 grants)

Correspondent: Sally Grieve, Grants Officer, Staffordshire Community Foundation, Communications House, University Court, Staffordshire Technology Park, Stafford ST18 0ES (01785 339540; email: sally.grieve@ staffsfoundation.org.uk; website: www. staffsfoundation.org.uk)

Eligibility

In order to qualify for a grant from the Malam-Heath Fund applicants must: be aged over 18; be resident in Stoke-on-Trent, or a neighbouring area that identifies more with Stoke-on-Trent than other areas, such as Kidsgrove, Biddulph or Cheadle; be unable to finance the holiday themselves and be in financial need; need a holiday as part of recuperation or respite, or relief from a recent traumatic event.

Note that all payments will be made directly to the holiday company/hotel and that there will be no direct payments to applicants.

Types of grants

Awards are as follows: single person for one week holiday – £150; single person for two weeks holiday – £300; a couple for one week holiday – £300; and a couple for two weeks holiday – £600.

Annual grant total

In 2013/14 the fund had assets of £298,500, an income of £11,800 and awarded 10 grants amounting to £3,500 in total to individuals. A further 17 grants were awarded to charitable organisations, totalling £16,900, for day trips and Christmas parties. The accounts state that 380 individuals benefitted from the fund in 2013/14, either through an individual grant or participation in a community activity.

Exclusions

It is unlikely that an individual would benefit from an award in consecutive years.

Applications

Application forms and guidance can be downloaded as part of an application pack from Staffordshire Community Foundation's website.

Applications will be considered at quarterly panels, the dates of which are published on the website. Applicants should allow at least four weeks between the panel and the date of the holiday. Applications should be countersigned by a medical professional.

Other information

Since 2009, the Malam-Heath Fund has been administered by the Staffordshire Community Foundation. It was previously listed as a separate fund in this guide but has now been removed from the Central Register of Charities.

The fund now also makes grants to community organisations to provide day trips for people who are not comfortable being away from home for longer than one day.

Staffordshire Community Foundation

£73,000 (149 grants)

Correspondent: The Grants Team, Communications House, University Court, Staffordshire Technology park, Stafford ST18 0ES (01782683030; email: office@staffsfoundation.org.uk; website: www.staffsfoundation.org.uk)

CC number: 1091628

Eligibility

Each of the funds has its own eligibility criteria. Visit the foundation's website for further information.

Types of grants

Bishop Stramer Fund for Individuals – small grants are made on an individual basis to older, (50+) or ill individuals who are in need of support to help them or their carers to provide specific facilities.

Children's' Holiday Fund – grants are available for recuperative, respite and educational holidays to children aged between 4 and 17 years who are resident in Stoke-on-Trent.

The John Flock Bentilee Empowerment Fund has been set up specifically for residents in Bentilee and will provide practical support to empower people in the small things in life that can really make a difference such as driving lessons or short training courses.

Malam-Heath Fund for Individuals – provides grants for people living in Stoke-on-Trent who are in need of a holiday for reasons such as convalescence or recovery but who are unable to finance it themselves.

Youth Endeavour Fund – provides grants to young people aged 14–25 to help them break down barriers that may stop them achieving their full potential.

Annual grant total

In 2013/14 the foundation had an income of £827,500 and a total expenditure of £817,500. Grants were made to 149 individuals totalling £73,000. A further 251 grants were made to organisations totalling £603,000.

Applications

There are five different grants available for individuals which are listed on the website under the 'Grants' tab. Applications can be made online or for some funds application forms can be downloaded and emailed or returned by post.

The Strasser Foundation

£3,800

Correspondent: The Trustees, c/o Knights Solicitors, The Brampton, Newcastle-under-Lyme, Staffordshire ST5 0QW (01782 619225; email: afhjb@fsmail.net)

CC number: 511703

Eligibility

Individuals in need in the local area of Stoke-on-Trent and Newcastle-under-Lyme, with a preference for North Staffordshire.

Types of grants

Usually one-off grants for a specific cause or need, to help relieve poverty.

Annual grant total

In 2014/15 the foundation had an income of £10,100 and a total expenditure of £16,000. We estimate that the amount of grants given to individuals for social welfare purposes totalled around £3,800.

Applications

Applications may be made in writing to the correspondent. The trustees meet quarterly. Applications are only acknowledged if an sae is sent.

Other information

The foundation also makes grants to organisations and to individuals for educational purposes.

East Staffordshire

The Burton-on-Trent Nursing Endowment Fund

£5,000

Correspondent: Marilyn Arnold, Correspondent, 141 Newton Road, Burton-on-Trent, Staffordshire DE15 0TR (01283 567900)

CC number: 239185

Eligibility

People in need who live in the former county borough of Burton-on-Trent.

Types of grants

One-off grants towards, for example, chiropody treatment, bedding, removal costs, electric scooter batteries, fridges, freezers and childcare provision.

Annual grant total

In 2014 the fund had an income of £6,600 and a total expenditure of £5,300. We estimate that the amount of grants given to individuals totalled £5,000, with funding also awarded to organisations.

Applications

Application forms are available from the correspondent. Applications can come directly from the individual or through a recognised referral agency (social worker, Citizens Advice, local GP and so on).

Consolidated Charity of Burton upon Trent

£34,500 (116 grants)

Correspondent: John Southwell, Clerk, Dains LLP, 1st Floor, Gibraltar House, Crown Square, First Avenue, Burton-on-Trent DE14 2WE (01283 527067; fax: 01283 507969; email: clerk@consolidatedcharityburton.org.uk; website: www.consolidatedcharityburton.org.uk)

CC number: 239072

Eligibility

People who live in Burton upon Trent and the neighbouring parishes of Branston, Outwoods and Stretton and are in need.

Types of grants

One-off grants are awarded up to a maximum of £400 for essential items such as cookers, fridge freezers, washing machines, carpets, furniture, bedding, mobility aids and school uniforms.

Annual grant total

In 2014 the charity had assets of £12.7 million and an income of £457,000. Grants made during the year totalled £119,500, of which £49,000 was given to organisations working in the local area. In total, £70,500 was awarded to individuals for purposes relating to social welfare and education. 116 welfare grants were made, amounting to £35,500.

Exclusions

Grants are not awarded for the relief of debt.

Applications

Applications can be made using a form which is available online or to download from the website. They must be supported by a support worker or another appropriate professional (such as a social worker, probation officer, tenancy support worker or health visitor). Letters of support should contain, in detail, the reason why the individual needs assistance and should state the items that are needed clearly. They should be signed by the supporting professional and submitted on headed paper. Applications are considered on an ongoing basis by the Small Grants Committee.

Other information

The charity also runs 32 almshouses in the local area.

Lichfield

The Lichfield Municipal Charities

£11,800 (33 grants)

Correspondent: Simon James, Correspondent, Ansons LLP Solicitors, St Mary's Chambers, 5 Breadmarket Street, Lichfield, Staffordshire WS13 6LQ (01543 267980; email: sjames@ansonsllp.com)

CC number: 254299

Eligibility

Individuals in need who live in the city of Lichfield (as it was pre-1974).

Types of grants

One-off grants according to need.

Annual grant total

In 2014 the charity had assets £2.2 million and an income of £91,500 Grants were made to 33 individuals totalling £11,800 and to two organisations totalling £1,600.

Applications

Application forms are available from the correspondent. The trustees meet four times a year in March, June, September and December.

Michael Lowe's and Associated Charities

£39,500 (254 grants)

Correspondent: Simon James, Clerk to the Trustees, Ansons LLP Solicitors, 5–7 Breadmarket Street, Lichfield, Staffordshire WS13 6LQ (01543 267995; email: sjames@ansonsllp.com)

CC number: 214785

Eligibility

People in need who live in the city of Lichfield, particularly older people and those requiring help in an emergency.

Types of grants

One-off grants of up to £600 for domestic items, special chairs, school uniforms, wheelchairs and so on. People who are over 70 and living on a low income can also apply for fuel grants. The trustees may require the recipient to make a contribution of 10% towards the cost of any item provided. Gifts in the form of second hand furniture are also distributed.

Annual grant total

In 2013/14 the charity held assets of £1.7 million and had an income of £116,000. Grants to individuals totalled £39,500 and were distributed as follows:

| Other grants | 95 | £27,500 |
| Fuel grants | 159 | £12,000 |

The charity spent a further £7,300 running the Furniture Transfer Scheme, which redistributes second hand furniture to families recommended by local welfare agencies. Grants to organisations amounted to a further £19,900.

Applications

Application forms are available from the correspondent. Applications are considered on their own merits and individuals are usually interviewed before any grant is awarded. Beneficiaries of the Furniture Transfer Scheme are usually recommended to trustees through a local welfare organisation. The trustees meet on average five times a year to consider grant applications, although special meetings may be called to deal with urgent requests.

Other information

Applicants are visited and may also be directed to other relevant organisations or services for welfare support.

Newcastle

The Newcastle-under-Lyme United Charities

£3,000

Correspondent: Caroline Horne, Civic Offices, Merrial Street, Newcastle-under-Lyme, Staffordshire ST5 2AG (01782 742232; email: caroline.horne@ newcastle-staffs.gov.uk)

CC number: 217916

Eligibility

People in need who live in the borough of Newcastle-under-Lyme (as it was before 1974).

Types of grants

Small donations are given at Christmas.

Annual grant total

In 2013/14 the trust had an income of £4,100 and a total expenditure of £3,200. We estimate that the amount of grants given to individuals totalled £3,000.

Exclusions

No grants are given to older people living in sheltered housing.

Applications

Apply in writing to the correspondent. Applications should be submitted either directly by the individual or via a friend or family member. They are considered in October each year. The circumstances of beneficiaries are assessed on an annual basis by trustees.

South Staffordshire

The Enville Village Trust

£2,200

Correspondent: Richard Jones, Trustee, Batfield House, Batfield Lane, Enville, Stourbridge, West Midlands DY7 5LF (01746 780350; email: enville.trusts@ btinternet.com)

CC number: 231563

Eligibility

People in need who live in the parish of Enville, with a preference for older people.

Types of grants

One-off grants ranging from £50 to £150. Grants may not always be given directly to individuals; sometimes they may be used to provide a service to individuals, which they cannot themselves afford. Grants have been given for telephone installation/ connection (including an emergency contact line), emergency medical help, optician bills for partially sighted people, special dental treatment, travel to hospital, food parcels, clothing and fuel in winter.

Annual grant total

In 2013/14 the trust had an income of £2,300 and a total expenditure of £2,400. We estimate that the total award given to individuals was approximately £2,200.

Applications

Apply in writing to the correspondent. Applications can be submitted either directly by the individual or through a social worker, the vicar of the parish church or the village welfare group. They are considered at any time.

Stafford

Church Eaton Relief-in-Need Charity (Church Eaton Charities)

£8,500

Correspondent: Stephen Rutherford, Trustee, 5 Ashley Croft, Church Eaton, Stafford ST20 0BJ (01785 823958)

CC number: 216179

Eligibility

People in need who have lived in the parish of Church Eaton for at least two years. In exceptional circumstances grants may be available to those living immediately outside the parish.

Types of grants

Support is generally given towards the heating costs or in provision of coal during the winter season. Grants are also available for other items, equipment or services, for example, TV licences, Lifeline telephones and so on.

Annual grant total

In 2014 the charity had an income of £10,000 and a total expenditure of £9,000. We estimate that grants totalled around £8,500.

Applications

Apply in writing to the correspondent. Applications are considered upon receipt.

Staffordshire Moorlands

The Carr Trust

£40,000

Correspondent: Tina Mycock, Correspondent, St Luke's Church of England, Fountain Street, Leek, Staffordshire ST13 6JS (01538 373306; email: stlukesleek@hotmail.co.uk)

CC number: 216764

Eligibility

Residents of Leek, mainly older people, who are in need.

Types of grants

Mainly pensions, usually of around £20 a month towards items, services and facilities that will help to reduce need or hardship. One-off grants are also available and most beneficiaries receive a Christmas bonus.

Annual grant total

In 2014 the trust had an income of £19,000 and a total expenditure of £42,000. We estimate that the amount of grants given to individuals totalled around £35,000.

Applications

Apply in writing to the correspondent. An advert about the grants appears in a local paper in March each year. The trustees require details of the applicant's age, marital status, income, savings and details of any property owned.

Other information

The Carr Trust administers three charities – the Charity of Charles Carr, the Charity of Elizabeth Flint for the Poor and the Charity of William Carr.

Tamworth

Beardsley's Relief-in-Need Charity

£7,000

Correspondent: Derek Tomkinson, Trustee, 'Torview', 95 Main Road, Wigginton, Tamworth, Staffordshire B79 9DU (01543 255612; email: enquries@tomkinsonteal.co.uk)

CC number: 214461

Eligibility

People in need who live in the borough of Tamworth.

Types of grants

One-off grants and loans for health and welfare purposes.

Annual grant total

In 2013/14 the charity had an income of £12,700 and a total expenditure of £14,300. We estimate that the amount of grants given to individuals totalled £7,000, with funding also awarded to local organisations.

Applications

Applications should be made in writing to the correspondent, either directly by the individual or, where applicable, through a social worker, Citizens Advice or other welfare agency.

The Rawlet Trust

£6,000

Correspondent: Christine Gilbert, 47 Hedging Lane, Wilnecote, Tamworth B77 5EX (01827 288614; email: christine. gilbert@mail.com)

CC number: 221732

Eligibility

People in need who live in the borough of Tamworth.

Types of grants

One-off and recurrent grants towards disability facilities, holidays, bibles for children and Home Link telephone expenses. Grants for educational purposes are also available for young people under the age of 25 who have parents resident in the area.

Annual grant total

In 2014/15 the trust had an income of £24,500 and a total expenditure of £25,500. Grants are made to individuals and organisations for both social welfare and educational purposes. We estimate that social welfare grants to individuals totalled £6,000.

Applications

Apply using the application form available from the correspondent. Applications should be submitted either directly by the individual or through a third party such as a social worker or Citizens Advice. The clerk or one of the trustees will follow up applications if any further information is needed. The trustees meet in January, April, July and October to consider applications.

Tamworth Municipal Charity

£2,600

Correspondent: Anthony Goodwin, Trustee, Tamworth Borough Council, Marmion House, Lichfield Street, Tamworth, Staffordshire B79 7BZ (01827 709212)

CC number: 216875

Eligibility

People in need who live in the borough of Tamworth.

Types of grants

One-off grants towards, for example, equipment, household items and hospital travel costs.

Annual grant total

In 2014 the charity had an income of £2,000 and an expenditure of £2,000. We estimate that grants totalled around £900, with funding also awarded to organisations.

Applications

Apply in writing to the correspondent.

Other information

Grants may also be given to organisations.

Warwick-shire

The J. I. Colvile Charitable Trust

See entry on page 403

The South Warwick-shire Welfare Trust

£10,000

Correspondent: Valerie Grimmer, Clerk, 62 Foxes Way, Warwick CV34 6AY (01926 492226; email: valerie.grimmer@ sky.com)

CC number: 235967

Eligibility

People who are sick and in need and live in Warwick district or the former rural district of Southam.

Types of grants

One-off grants of £25 to £400 for items, services or facilities to alleviate suffering or assist recovery for people who are sick, convalescent, disabled or infirm. Grants are awarded towards holidays, cookers, carpets, white goods and home aids, for example.

Annual grant total

In 2014 the trust had an income of £9,700 and a total expenditure of £11,000. We estimate that the amount of grants given to individuals totalled £10,000.

Exclusions

Grants are not repeated and are not given for relief of taxes or other public funds.

Applications

Application forms are available from the correspondent. They can be submitted through a social worker, Citizens Advice or other welfare agency, or through a doctor, church official or similar third party. Applications are considered in January, April, July and October and should be submitted in the preceding months. Details of income/expenditure must be disclosed on the application form.

North Warwickshire

Relief-in-Need Charity of Simon Lord Digby and Others

£6,000

Correspondent: Juliet Bakker, Administrator, The Vicarage, High Street, Coleshill, Birmingham B46 3BP (01675 462188)

CC number: 237526

Eligibility

People in extreme hardship who live in the parish of Coleshill.

Types of grants

One-off grants are given according to need. Our research shows that in the past grants have been made, for example, to an individual with multiple sclerosis towards the cost of an electric reclining/rising chair and to the family of an eight-year-old with leukaemia for help with extra expenses.

Annual grant total

In 2014 the charity had an income of £11,700 and an expenditure of £13,800. We estimate the annual total amount of grants given to individuals to be around £6,000.

Applications

Apply in writing to the correspondent. Applications are usually decided in March and November, although decisions can be made more quickly in an emergency. They can be submitted directly by the individual or through a social worker, Citizens Advice or other welfare agency. Candidates are requested to provide as much detail as possible including information about applications to other organisations/charities.

Other information

Organisations may also be supported.

Rugby

The Bilton Poor's Land and Other Charities

£5,600

Correspondent: Robin Walls, Trustee, 6 Scotts Close, Rugby CV22 7QY (email: biltoncharities@outlook.com)

CC number: 215833

Eligibility

People in need who live in the ancient parish of Bilton (now part of Rugby). Preference is given to older people and those referred by social services.

Types of grants

One-off grants, generally of between £15 and £250. Cash grants of £20 per person are also made to older people at Christmas.

Annual grant total

In 2014/15 the charity had assets of £595,500 and an income of £64,500. Grants totalled £11,200 and were made to 198 individuals and organisations. We estimate that the amount of grants given to individuals amounted to £5,600.

Applications

Applications can be made in writing to the correspondent, by the individual or through a third party such as a minister, although applications are often forwarded by social services. They are considered three times a year.

Sir Edward Boughton Long Lawford Charity

£25,000

Correspondent: Debbie Groves, Clerk to the Trustees, 7 College Road, Willoughby, Rugby, Warwickshire CV23 8BN

CC number: 237841

Eligibility

People in need who live in the parish of Long Lawford or Rugby. Applicants for pensions must have lived in the parish for the last five years.

Types of grants

Pensions of £10 a month and Christmas bonuses of £40. One-off grants are awarded for various welfare purposes, including disability aids, TV licences and stair-lifts. Small awards have also been made for swimming classes.

Annual grant total

In 2014 the charity had assets of £1.6 million and an income of £123,000. Grants to individuals totalled £24,500, of which £14,900 was given to 94 individuals in pensions and Christmas bonuses, and £9,400 was given to individuals in one-off grants.

A further £46,000 was given in grants to local schools and organisations.

Applications

Apply on a form available from the correspondent, to be considered by the trustees every three months, usually February, May, August and November.

Rugby Relief in Need Charity

£2,800

Correspondent: Carol Patricia Davies, 14 School Street, Long Lawford, Rugby, Warwickshire CV23 9AU (01788 544630)

CC number: 217987

Eligibility

People in need who live in the ancient parish of Rugby, which includes the parishes of St Andrew's and St Matthew's.

Types of grants

Christmas vouchers to the elderly of the parish. Some one-off grants may be made in cases of emergency.

Annual grant total

In 2013/14 the charity had an income of £3,400 and a total expenditure of £2,900. We estimate that vouchers and social welfare grants to individuals totalled £2,800.

Applications

Apply in writing to the correspondent. Applications are generally considered three or four times a year, although urgent cases can be considered at any time.

Stratford

Mayor's Fund Society of Stratford-upon-Avon

£2,500

Correspondent: Ros Dobson, Trustee, 155 Evesham Road, Stratford-upon-Avon, Warwickshire CV37 9BP (01789 293749; email: themayorsfund@yahoo.com; website: www.themayorsfund.webs.com)

CC number: 220136

Eligibility

Older people in need who live in the former borough of Stratford-upon-Avon.

Types of grants

One-off and recurrent grants are usually given in the form of grocery vouchers.

Annual grant total

In 2013/14 the fund had an income of £4,000 and a total expenditure of £2,800. We estimate that the total amount of grants awarded to individuals was approximately £2,500 which was paid to an average of 45 beneficiaries.

Applications

Apply in writing to the correspondent. Applications can be submitted directly by the individual or through a social worker, Citizens Advice, other welfare agency or other third party such as a member of the clergy. They should include a general summary of income, other relief received (for example housing benefits) and financial commitments.

Municipal Charities of Stratford-upon-Avon – Relief in Need

£20,000

Correspondent: Ros Dobson, Clerk to the Trustees, c/o 6 Guild Cottages, Church Street, Stratford-upon-Avon, Warwickshire CV37 6HD (01789 293749; email: municharities@yahoo.co.uk or municharities@btinternet.com; website: www.municipal-charities-stratforduponavon.org.uk)

CC number: 214958

Eligibility

People in need, generally older people of state pensionable age, who have been living in the town of Stratford-upon-Avon for at least 18 months. People immediately outside the area of benefit may be supported in exceptional circumstances.

Types of grants

One-off and recurrent grants in the range of £100–£500 towards essential living expenses. Support can be given for food, fuel, clothing, items of furniture and household equipment (such as beds, support chairs, cookers, microwaves, fridges, freezers or washing machines), mobility aids and unexpected household bills.

Annual grant total

In 2014 the charity had assets of £80,500 and an income of £52,500 (including a £51,500 transfer from Charity of William Tyler). Grants from the relief-in-need fund totalled £99,500, including £45,000 given to almshouses. A total of £900 was given in educational grants. We estimate that about £20,000 was awarded to individuals.

Exclusions

Grants are not given for the repayment of debts, rent and council tax arrears, rental deposits and where support is available from statutory sources.

Applications

Application forms are available from the correspondent. They should include details of the financial circumstances of the applicant (income and savings). When applying for financial assistance in connection with a specific health condition, applicants are asked to include a letter from a GP, occupational therapist, social worker or similar professional to support the application. Requests for help are considered throughout the year.

Candidates are encouraged to contact the correspondent to clarify any questions or to discuss their case.

Other information

The Stratford-upon-Avon Municipal Charities is an amalgamation of seven different charities in the local area. A big part of the charity's activities is the provision of almshouse accommodation. Welfare support is given from the relief-in-need fund. Educational grants are also occasionally provided.

Note the following taken from the charity's website: 'As is the case with many other grant-making organisations, the funds available for distribution are limited. With an increasing number of applications being received, the Trustees have decided to award this year's grant for a specific need only.'

Warwick

The Barford Relief-in-Need Charity

£3,500

Correspondent: Terry Offiler, 14 Dugard Place, Barford, Warwick CV35 8DX (01926 624153)

CC number: 256836

Eligibility

People in need who live in the parish of Barford.

Types of grants

One-off cash grants and gifts in kind are given towards 'any reasonable need', including hospital expenses, electric goods, convalescence, living costs, household bills, holidays, travel expenses, medical equipment, nursing fees, furniture, disability equipment and help in the home.

Annual grant total

In 2014 the charity had an income of £11,400 and a total expenditure of £14,200. Grants are made to individuals and organisations for both social welfare and educational purposes. We estimate that social welfare grants to individuals totalled £3,500.

Applications

Applications can be made in writing to the correspondent, directly by the individual or a family member. One of the trustees will then visit the applicant to obtain all necessary information. Applications are usually considered in May and October.

Austin Edwards Charity

£2,600

Correspondent: Jackie Newton, Receiver, 26 Mountford Close, Wellesbourne, Warwick CV35 9QQ (01789 840135; website: www.austinedwards.org.uk)

CC number: 225859

Eligibility

People living in the old borough of Warwick (generally the CV34 postcode).

Types of grants

Grants, generally of no more than £300, are given for relief in need.

Annual grant total

In 2014/14 the charity had both an income and a total expenditure of £10,800. Grants are made to individuals and organisations for both social welfare and educational purposes. We estimate that social welfare grants to individuals totalled £2,600.

Applications

Apply in writing to the correspondent stating the purpose of the grant and the amount required, as well as details of any other charities approached with the same request. The individual's name and address must be supplied with the application. The trustees usually hold one meeting annually in July but will consider applications throughout the year.

Other information

The charity was named after Mr Austin Edwards who lived and worked in Warwick as a photographic manufacturer in the early years of the twentieth century. As a councillor of the borough of Warwick, he remained deeply interested in Warwickians and Warwick affairs generally. He gave generously to the Corporation of Warwick throughout his life.

Hatton Consolidated Fund (Hatton Charities)

£2,200

Correspondent: Mrs M. Sparks, Clerk, Weare Giffard, 32 Shrewley Common, Shrewley, Warwick CV35 7AP (01926 842533; email: bsparks1@talktalk.net)

CC number: 250572

Eligibility

People in need who live in the parishes of Hatton, Beausale or Shrewley. Applications from outside these areas will not be considered.

Types of grants

One-off grants, usually in the range of £50–£500. Awards include those towards travel expenses to patients at convalescent homes, clothing and footwear, bedding, fuel costs, other household necessities and payments in case of sudden distress, sickness or unexpected loss. Loans may also be available.

Annual grant total

In 2013/14 the fund had an income of £10,100 and a total expenditure of £8,800. We estimate that grants awarded to individuals for social welfare purposes totalled around £2,200.

Exclusions

Our research suggests that grants are not given to schoolchildren. Support is not made to cover council tax and other taxes or where public funds should be sought first.

Applications

Applications may be made in writing the correspondent, directly by the individual or a family member.

Other information

Grants are given to both organisations and individuals for educational and social welfare purposes.

The Kenilworth United Charities

£6,000

Correspondent: Clerk to the Trustees, Damian J. Plant and Co., 29b Warwick Road, Kenilworth, Warwickshire CV8 1HN (01926 857741)

CC number: 215376

Eligibility

People in need who live in the ancient parish of Kenilworth.

Types of grants

Generally grocery vouchers given to one-parent families. One-off grants have also been made towards white goods.

Annual grant total

In 2014 the charity had an income of £17,800 and a total expenditure of £23,800. We estimate that the total amount of grants awarded to individuals was approximately £6,000.

Applications

Application forms are available from the correspondent. Applications are considered quarterly, although urgent cases will receive special consideration.

Other information

The charity also funds almshouses and the Citizens Advice office in Kenilworth.

The King Henry VIII Endowed Trust – Warwick

£1,000 (1 grant)

Correspondent: Jonathan Wassall, Clerk and Receiver, 12 High Street, Warwick CV34 4AP (01926 495533; email: jwassall@kinghenryviii.org.uk; website: www.kinghenryviii.org.uk)

CC number: 232862

Eligibility

People who live in the former borough of Warwick. The area of benefit is roughly the CV34 postcode but exceptions apply; see the full list of eligible areas in the guidelines on the trust's website or contact the correspondent for clarification.

Types of grants

One-off grants can be given for general welfare purposes, according to need. Awards are usually made only if a previous application to The Warwick Relief in Need Charity has been unsuccessful.

Grants are intended to be supplementary and applicants are expected to raise additional funds themselves. Payments are normally made upon submission of receipts.

Annual grant total

In 2014 the trust had assets of £28.8 million and an income of £1.37 million. Two grants to individuals totalled £2,100, one of which we estimate to be for social welfare needs. The money for charitable activities is generated from the permanent endowment.

Exclusions

Grants are not made where support should be provided by the local or central government. Funding is not given retrospectively.

Applications

Application forms are available from the correspondent or from the trust's website. Applications should provide full details of the costs involved and the time schedule of the activity, where relevant. Awards are considered on a quarterly basis, usually in March, June, September and December. The closing dates for applications are the beginning of March/June and the second half of August/November. You will normally hear the outcome of your application within a week of the relevant meeting. In urgent cases applications can be fast-tracked ('emergency' should be specified in the application).

Other information

The income is distributed to the historic Anglican churches in Warwick (50%), Warwick Independent Schools Foundation for allocation in scholarships and bursaries (30%), and to organisations and individuals in the town (20%). Town grants to 33 organisations totalled £195,000, the foundation received £335,500 and the churches were awarded £544,000 in 2014.

Note that the trust states in its 'Guidelines to Assist Applications':

> Where the trust believes that there are more suitable charities within the town to assess applications it will either forward the application directly to another charity or recommend that the applicant approaches them directly. Young people under 24 years old applying for support at university or college will be referred directly to the Warwick Apprenticing Charities.

Leamington Relief-in-Sickness Fund

£2,000

Correspondent: Hillary Holland, Trustee, 55 West Street, Warwick CV34 6AB (01926401168; email: hilaryholland2@gmail.com)

CC number: 216781

Eligibility

People suffering from ill health and expectant mothers who live in the former borough of Leamington Spa and the neighbourhood, and are in need. People with disabilities or mental health problems are especially welcomed.

Types of grants

One-off grants only from around £25, including help with fuel debts, television licences, baby necessities, food for special diets, fares for visiting hospitals or sick relatives, replacement locks after a burglary, children's clothing, repairs to washing machines and so on.

Annual grant total

In 2013/14 the fund had an income of £4,000 and a total expenditure of £4,500. We estimate that the amount of grants given to individuals totalled around £2,000.

Exclusions

Applicants can only receive one grant each year.

Applications

Apply in writing through a social worker, Citizens Advice, health visitor, doctor, probation service, Mind or other welfare agency. Applications submitted by individuals will not be acknowledged or considered. Applications are considered throughout the year.

Warwick Combined Charity

£21,000 (39 grants)

Correspondent: Christopher Houghton, Clerk to the Charity, c/o Moore and Tibbits Solicitors, 34 High Street, Warwick CV34 4BE (01926 491181; fax: 01926 402692; email: choughton@ moore-tibbits.co.uk; website: www. warwickreliefinneed.org.uk)

CC number: 256447

Eligibility

People in need who live in the town of Warwick.

Types of grants

One-off grants of up to £1,000 towards, for example, washing machines, beds, mattresses, vacuum cleaners, carpets, holidays and home repairs.

Annual grant total

In 2014 the charity had an income of £159,000 and made grants totalling £100,500. Grants to 39 individuals totalled £21,000. A further £79,500 was awarded in grants to 12 organisations.

Applications

Apply on a form available from the correspondent or to download from the charity's website. Applications are normally submitted through social services or a similar welfare organisation and should be accompanied by a covering letter providing details of the applicant and the nature of the need. They are considered by the trustees at quarterly meetings.

West Midlands

Jordison and Hossell Animal Welfare Charity

£2,200

Correspondent: Sally Reid, Trustee, Whitestones, Haselor, Pellham Lane Alcester, Warwickshire B49 6LU (01789 488942; email: sallyreid@me.com)

CC number: 515352

Eligibility

People in the Midlands who are on low incomes and are in need of financial assistance in meeting vets' bills for their pets.

Types of grants

One-off grants, usually of up to £500, are made towards unpredictable vets' bills.

Annual grant total

In 2013/14 the charity had an income of £1,700 and a total expenditure of £2,400. We estimate that grants totalled around £2,200.

Exclusions

Support is not given with vets' bills for larger animals such as horses and farm animals. Grants are not made to support the continuing care of a pet.

Applications

Apply in writing to the correspondent. Applications must be made by the vet in question or a third party such as Citizens Advice, rather than by the individual applicant. The charity does not deal with applicants directly. Evidence that the applicant is on benefits is required.

Pedmore Sporting Club Trust Fund

£2,800

Correspondent: The Secretary, Nicklin and Co. LLP, Church Court, Stourbridge Road, Halesowen, West Midlands B63 3TT (email: psclub@pedmorehouse. co.uk; website: www. pedmoresportingclub.co.uk)

CC number: 263907

Eligibility

People in need who live in the West Midlands.

Types of grants

One-off grants have included those for medical care equipment, travel to and from hospital, wheelchairs, other access aid and IT equipment. Grants are

normally paid directly to the service/ item provider, not the individual. Christmas and Easter parcels are given to senior citizens.

Annual grant total

In 2014 the charity had assets of £287,000 and an income of £41,500. Grants to individuals totalled £2,800.

Exclusions

The charity is unable to help with general living costs.

Applications

Our research indicates that candidates for the holiday food parcels should be recommended by a member of the sporting club. Other applications can be made in writing to the correspondent. The trustees meet quarterly and may interview the candidates.

Other information

Grants are mainly made to organisations, preferably local (£29,500 in 2014).

The Eric W. Vincent Trust Fund

£2,100 (25 grants)

Correspondent: Janet Stephen, Clerk, PO Box 6849, Stourbridge DY8 9EN (email: vttrust942@gmail.com)

CC number: 204843

Eligibility

People in need living in the West Midlands, within a 20-mile radius of Halesowen.

Types of grants

Grants of around £100 can be made for clothing, furniture, hospital travel expenses, equipment and holidays. In 2014, grants to individuals averaged £86.

Annual grant total

In 2013/14 the fund had assets of £1.4 million and an income of £45,000. Grants were made to 14 individuals totalling £1,200. A further £28,500 was awarded in grants to 63 organisations.

Exclusions

The trust does not make loans or give grants for gap year projects or to pay off debts.

Applications

Trustees normally meet bi-monthly. Applications should be in writing through a health professional, social worker, Citizens Advice or other welfare agency. Applications will not be considered if they are not made through a relevant third party. Details of financial circumstances must be included.

Other information

Small grants (generally under £1,000) are also made to organisations.

Birmingham

The Freda and Howard Ballance Trust

£2,000

Correspondent: The Trustees, Blackhams, Lancaster House, 67 Newhall Street, Birmingham B3 1NR (0121 233 0062; email: mstocks@blackhams.com)

CC number: 513109

Eligibility

People who are in need and live in Birmingham.

Types of grants

One-off grants usually ranging from £50 to £200. In the past, grants have been given for clothing, furniture and disability aids. Grants are occasionally made for educational purposes.

Annual grant total

In 2013/14 the trust had an income of £3,500 and a total expenditure of £5,000. Grants are made to individuals and organisations and, occasionally, for educational purposes as well as for social welfare. We estimate that social welfare grants to individuals totalled £2,000.

Applications

Apply using the form, which is available from the correspondent. A letter giving brief details of the application is required before an application form is sent out. Applications can be made either directly by the individual or via a third party such as a charity, social worker or Citizens Advice. They are usually considered quarterly.

The Richard and Samuel Banner Trust

£4,600

Correspondent: Anne Holmes, Administrator, Veale Wasbrough Vizards LLP, Second Floor, 3 Brindley Place, Birmingham B1 2JB (0121 227 3705)

CC number: 218649

Eligibility

Men and widows who are in need and live in the city of Birmingham.

Types of grants

Grants of up to £100, usually for clothing.

Annual grant total

In 2013/14 the trust had an income of £10,100 and a total expenditure of £9,700. We estimate that welfare grants totalled £4,600, with funding also awarded to individuals for educational purposes.

Applications

Applicants must be nominated by a trustee, doctor or the Council for Old People. Applications are considered on 1 November and grants are distributed immediately after this date.

Other information

The trust can also give apprenticeship grants to male students under 21, but this is done through certain colleges; applicants should not apply directly.

The Thomas Bromwich Trust

£18,200 (62 grants)

Correspondent: Christine Norgrove, Correspondent, Shakespeare Martineau, 1 Colmore Square, Birmingham B4 6AA (0121 214 0487)

CC number: 214966

Eligibility

People in need living in Handsworth (that is, the ecclesiastical parishes of St Mary, St Andrew, St James, St Michael, St Peter and the Holy Trinity, Birdfield and St Paul, and Hanstead); Great Barr (that is, the ecclesiastical parish of St Margaret), or Perry Barr (that is, the ecclesiastical parishes of St John the Evangelist, Perry Barr, St Luke, Kingstanding, and St Matthews and Perry Beeches).

Types of grants

One-off grants towards electric goods, clothing, household bills, food and help in the home.

Annual grant total

In 2014/15 the charity held assets of £1.1 million had an income of £31,000. Grants to 62 individuals totalled £18,200.

Applications

Applications should be made in writing to the correspondent either directly by the individual or through a social worker, Citizens Advice or other welfare agency. Applications are considered at any time.

Friends of Home Nursing in Birmingham

£3,600

Correspondent: Mrs J. Burns, Hon. Treasurer, 46 Underwood Road, Handsworth Wood, Birmingham B20 1JS (0121 686 5565; email: jaybee46@btinternet.com)

CC number: 218182

Eligibility

Sick and older people who live in Birmingham city and who are patients nursed at home by the district nurse.

Types of grants

The charity provides goods, equipment and occasional monetary grants which are not available from other sources. In the past this has included digital thermometers, a dressing trolley, cameras and films for ulcer recordings, and part of the cost of holidays. Grants are usually one-off and range from £50 to £500. No grants are made for double glazing or electrical work.

Annual grant total

In 2014 the charity had an income of £6,700 and a total expenditure of £4,600. We estimate that welfare grants to individuals totalled £2,200, with funding also given for educational purposes.

Applications

Apply in writing, via a district nurse, to the correspondent. Applications can be submitted at any time, for consideration in the spring and autumn. The charity has previously stated that if a real case of need occurs they can deal with it as soon as possible.

The Handsworth Charity

£4,100

Correspondent: Dipali Chandra, Administrator, 109 Court Oak Road, Birmingham B17 9AA (email: info@ handsworth-charity.com; website: www. handsworth-charity.com)

CC number: 216603

Eligibility

People in need who live in the parish of Handsworth (now in Birmingham). A map of the beneficial area is available on the website.

Types of grants

One-off grants of up to £500 according to need. Grants are given towards essential household items such as bedding, carpets, cookers, fridges and for small property repairs.

Annual grant total

In 2014 the charity had an income of £24,000 and a total expenditure of £8,500. We estimate that the amount of grants given to individuals totalled £4,100, with funding also awarded to organisations whose work benefits the residents of Handsworth.

Applications

Application forms are available to download from the website. Forms must be submitted through a recognised referral agency that is willing to act as a sponsor throughout the application process. The trustees meet three times a year, normally in mid-March, mid-July and mid-November. Applications should be received by the charity in the month before a meeting.

Note: Successful applicants are expected to provide receipts of items purchased with the grant awarded. Sponsoring agencies are expected to accept some responsibility in making sure the grant is spent on its intended purposes.

The Harborne Parish Lands Charity

£49,000

Correspondent: Sharon Murphy, Grants Officer, 109 Court Oak Road, Harborne, Birmingham B17 9AA (0121 426 1600; email: sharon.murphy@hplc.org.uk; website: www.hplc.org.uk)

CC number: 219031

Eligibility

People in need who live in the ancient parish of Harborne, which includes parts of Harborne, Smethwick, Bearwood and Quinton. A map of the old parish is available to view on the website and individuals are advised to check that they reside in the area of benefit before making an application.

Types of grants

One-off grants of up to £700 are available for essential household items. Applications for carpets are only eligible if there is a health and safety issue and grants for washing machines are made only to families.

Annual grant total

In 2013/14 the charity held assets of £15 million and had an income of £1.3 million. Grants were made totalling £263,500, of which £49,000 was awarded to individuals.

Exclusions

Grants are not made in cash and cannot be used to pay debts such as utility bills or rent arrears.

Applications

Application forms are available from the Grants Officer by email or by telephone on 0121 426 1600.

Other information

The charity also runs five almshouses with around 100 residents.

The CB and AB Holinsworth Fund of Help

£150

Correspondent: Sanjeev Bhopal, Administrator, Birmingham City Council, Legal and Democratic Services, PO Box 15992, Birmingham B2 2UQ (0121 675 4673; email: sanjeev.bhopal@ birmingham.gov.uk)

CC number: 217792

Eligibility

People in need who live in or near to the city of Birmingham and are sick or convalescing.

Types of grants

One-off grants ranging from £50 to £300. Grants are given towards the cost of respite holidays, travelling expenses to and from hospital, clothing, beds and carpets.

Annual grant total

In 2014/15 the fund had an income of £6,800 and a total expenditure of £300. We estimate that the total amount of grants awarded to individuals was approximately £150.

Exclusions

Generally grants are not given for bills or debt.

Applications

Application forms are available from the correspondent. Applications are considered throughout the year and should be submitted through a social worker, Citizens Advice or other welfare agency. Confirmation of illness is needed, for example a letter from a doctor, consultant or nurse.

Other information

Grants are also given to organisations.

The King's Norton United Charities

£2,500

Correspondent: Canon Rob Morris, Trustee, The Parish Office, 81 The Green, Kings Norton, Birmingham B38 8RU (0121 458 3289; email: parishoffice@kingsnorton.org.uk; website: www.knuc.org.uk)

CC number: 202225

Eligibility

The charity is able to assist only those who live within the boundary of the Ancient Parish of Kings Norton, formerly in Warwickshire and Worcestershire, now in Warwickshire and the West Midlands. This area includes the current Church of England Parishes of Kings Norton, Cotteridge, Stirchley, parts of Bournville, Balsall Heath, Kings Heath, Moseley (St Anne's and St Mary's), Brandwood, Hazelwell, Highters Heath, Wythall, West Heath, Longbridge, Rubery and Rednal.

Types of grants

The charity's annual report states that grants are usually of between £50 and £350 and are typically for one-off purchases of essential household items, for short-term bridging support or for educational needs such as help with fees or to cover unforeseen expenses. The trustees may consider making larger grants in specific cases.

Annual grant total

Our research indicates that social welfare grants usually total around £2,500, with funding also awarded for educational purposes. At the time of writing (November 2015) the charity's 2013 annual report and accounts were the most recent available.

Applications

The trustees prefer to receive requests for grants through organisations or agencies working on behalf of families or individuals in need. An organisation or individual applying on another's behalf will then be expected to take responsibility and to account for the correct use of the grant.

The trustees meet twice each year to consider grant requests and to distribute regular amounts to the discretionary funds of the incumbents of member parishes. Other selected organisations or agencies, based within the Ancient Parish of King's Norton and who assist in relieving genuine poverty or hardship, may also be awarded discretionary grants. Grant applications for smaller amounts (currently up to £250) may also be agreed and paid by the chair, vice-chair and treasurer on behalf of the main meeting.

Charity of Harriet Louisa Loxton

£7,700 (23 grants)

Correspondent: Maureen Morris, Administrator, 67 Sutton New Road, Erdington, Birmingham B23 6QT (0121 675 2501)

CC number: 702446

Eligibility

People in need who live in Birmingham, particularly older people, children and individuals with disabilities.

Types of grants

Our research suggests that one-off grants can range from £100 to £2,000, although

269

WEST MIDLANDS – WEST MIDLANDS

the average award is generally around £400. Previously grants have been given for purposes such as essential household items, central heating and an electric scooter.

Annual grant total

In 2013/14 the charity had assets of £1.7 million and an income of £27,000. A total of £12,000 was awarded in 23 grants.

Exclusions

According to our research, grants are not available to pay off debts, relieve public funds or towards the community charge.

Applications

Application forms are available from the correspondent. The trustees normally meet four times a year to consider applications. Note that applications must be made by a social worker (or an equivalent agency) and may take some considerable time to process. Immediate decisions on applications cannot be given.

Other information

The charity was established from proceeds of the sale of Icknield, a property donated to the city by Harriet Louisa Loxton for use as a home for older people.

Organisations can also be supported at the approval by the advisory panel and general purposes committee.

The Newman Trust Homes

£8,700 (27 grants)

Correspondent: Judy Dyke, Trustee, Tyndallwoods Solicitors, 29 Woodbourne Road, Harborne, Birmingham B17 8BY (0121 693 2222; email: jdyke@tyndallwoods.co.uk)

CC number: 501567

Eligibility

People who are in need, hardship or distress who live, or have formerly lived, in the City of Birmingham. Grants are primarily paid to benefit people who are older, people with housing difficulties and people living within the area of Handsworth and its immediate vicinity.

Types of grants

One-off and recurrent grants are given according to need.

Annual grant total

In 2013/14 the charity held assets totalling £820,000 and had an income of £34,000. Grants were made to 27 individuals totalling £8,700.

Exclusions

No funding is given for funerals.

Applications

Application forms are available from the charity. Applicants are encouraged to detail any additional information they believe may assist the trustees in their decision.

Sands Cox Relief in Sickness Charity

£4,300

Correspondent: Ann Andrew, Trustee, 12 Hayfield Gardens, Moseley, Birmingham B13 9LE (email: pjcombellack@aol.com)

CC number: 217468

Eligibility

People who live in Birmingham and are in need due to illness, disability or other difficulties.

Types of grants

One-off grants of up to £200 are available according to need.

Annual grant total

In 2013/14 the charity had an income of around £7,600 and an expenditure of £8,800. We estimate that individual grants totalled around £4,300.

Applications

Apply in writing to the correspondent. Applications can be made either directly by the individual or through a responsible person, for example, a trustee, doctor or social services professional.

Other information

The charity also makes grants to local organisations.

Sutton Coldfield Municipal Charities

£23,000 (26 grants)

Correspondent: John Hemming, Grants Manager, Lingard House, Fox Hollies Road, Sutton Coldfield, West Midlands B76 2RJ (0121 351 2262 (Tuesday to Thursday, 9am to 4pm); fax: 0121 313 0651; email: info@suttoncharitabletrust. org; website: www.suttoncoldfield charitabletrust.com)

CC number: 218627

Eligibility

People who are in need and have lived in the four electoral wards of Sutton Coldfield (New Hall, Four Oaks, Trinity and almost all of Vesey) for at least five years.

Types of grants

One-off grants are given to individuals, usually in the range of £100 and £1,500. Grants are given to assist with, for

example, the purchase of essential household equipment, to help people who have disabilities, to help people suffering from long-term health problems, and to meet other needs.

Annual grant total

In 2013/14 the charity had assets of £48.8 million and an income of £1.8 million. Grants totalled £1.6 million, the vast majority of which was awarded to organisations. Grants were made to individuals totalling £45,500, of which £23,000 was given in 26 grants for social welfare purposes.

Exclusions

Our research indicates that grants are not given to people in receipt of benefits from other sources, for example social services, family, DWP and so on.

Applications

Applications can be made on a form available from the correspondent. The form requires applicants to provide information on their family, income and expenditure, and details of what the grant is needed for. If the application is for help with medical assistance, the applicant's doctor or health visitor may be asked for a supporting letter. Following the form being completed and returned to the charity, the Almshouse Manager will make contact to arrange a visit to discuss the application. Applications are considered by the trustees, who meet regularly to consider requests. Applicants will be notified of the trustees' decision during the week following their meeting. No reasons will be given for applications that have been unsuccessful. Contact the correspondent for more information.

Other information

The principal objectives of the charity, which is also known as the Sutton Coldfield Charitable Trust, are the provision of almshouses, the distribution of funds and other measures for the alleviation of poverty and other needs of inhabitants and organisations within the boundaries of the former borough of Sutton Coldfield.

The Yardley Great Trust

£31,000

Correspondent: Karen Grice, Clerk to the Trustees, 31 Old Brookside, Yardley Fields Road, Stechford, Birmingham B33 8QL (0121 784 7889; email: enquiries@ygtrust.org.uk; website: www. ygtrust.org.uk)

CC number: 216082

Eligibility

People living in the ancient parish of Yardley in the city of Birmingham. This includes the wards of Yardley, Acocks

Green, Fox Hollies, Billesley, Hall Green and part of the wards of Hodge Hill, Shard End, Sheldon, Small Heath, Sparkhill, Moseley, Sparkbrook and Brandwood. (A map is produced by the trust outlining the beneficial area.)

Types of grants
One-off grants towards washing machines, fridges, cookers, clothing, beds and bedding and household furniture.

Annual grant total
In 2014 the trust held assets of £8.8 million and had an income of £2.3 million. Welfare grants to individuals amounted to £31,000. A further £35,500 was awarded to organisations.

Exclusions
No grants are given towards the relief of rates, taxes or for items that should be met by local authorities, health authorities or social services. No grants are given for educational purposes, home improvements (redecoration excepted) or school uniforms.

Applications
Applications should be made through referral agents such as Neighbourhood Offices and Citizens Advice offices. A list of authorised referral agencies is available on the trust's website.

Other information
The trust also provides second hand furniture through a partner organisation, Ladywood Furniture Project, and manages sheltered accommodation, care and nursing homes for elderly people.

Coventry
The Children's Boot Fund

£4,500

Correspondent: Janet McConkey, Chair, 123A Birmingham Road, Coventry CV5 9GR (024 7640 2837; email: martin_harban@btconnect.com)

CC number: 214524

Eligibility
Schoolchildren in the city of Coventry between the ages of 4 and 16.

Types of grants
Grants for school footwear for children in need. No other type of award is given. Grants are made directly to footwear suppliers in the form of vouchers. Normally only one child per family can be awarded a grant within one year, but exceptions for families in difficult circumstances may be made. Twins are usually given an award each. People

leaving school may receive a grant for shoes to attend interviews.

Annual grant total
In 2013/14 the fund had assets of £49,500 and an income of £33,500. A total of around £4,500 was spent in direct charitable expenditure. Grants are only made for school footwear.

Applications
Application forms are available from schools in the area. They should be made by the parents/guardians and supported by the headteacher of the child's school. Applications from social care services are also considered. Applicants are required to list their benefits and income. Requests are considered four times a year.

General Charity (Coventry)

£127,500

Correspondent: V. Tosh, Clerk to the Trustees, General Charities Office, Old Bablake, Hill Street, Coventry CV1 4AN (024 7622 2769; email: cov.genchar@btconnect.com)

CC number: 216235

Eligibility
People in need living in the city of Coventry.

Types of grants
One-off grants in kind and recurrent grants, but not cash grants. Regular payments of around £45 a quarter can be given to a maximum of 650 pensioners over the age of 60.

Annual grant total
In 2014 the charity had assets of £9.7 million and a total income of £1.5 million, of which £542,500 was in restricted funds. Grants totalled £1.3 million and, of this amount, we believe £127,500 was given to individuals for social welfare purposes. Pensions amounting to £80,500 were paid to, on average, 403 older people, and relief-in-need grants totalled £47,000.

Exclusions
Our research suggests that regular cash grants are not given.

Applications
Applications should normally be made through social workers, probation officers, Citizens Advice or other welfare agencies.

Other information
The charity consists of the charities formerly known as The Relief in Need Charity, Sir Thomas White's Pension Fund and Sir Thomas White's Educational Foundation. The trustees are

also responsible for the administration of Lady Herbert's Homes and Eventide Homes Ltd providing accommodation for the elderly in the city of Coventry.

Most of the charity's assistance is given to organisations. Support is also given to individuals for educational purposes.

John Moore's Bequest

£3,000

Correspondent: Ian Cox, Sarginsons Law LLP, 10 The Quadrant, Coventry CV1 2EL (02476553181)

CC number: 218805

Eligibility
People in need, generally older people, living in the city of Coventry.

Types of grants
Grants of up to £20 given in December.

Annual grant total
In 2013/14 the charity had an income of £4,800 and a total expenditure of £3,000. We estimate that around £3,000 was made in grants to individuals for social welfare purposes.

Applications
The charity's trustees each select around 25 recipients either directly or through local churches.

The Tansley Charity Trust

£2,200

Correspondent: Lara Knight, Correspondent, Governance Services, Room 59, Council House, Earl Street, Coventry CV1 5RR (email: lara.knight@coventry.gov.uk)

CC number: 505364

Eligibility
Women over 50 years old who are in poor health and live in the city of Coventry.

Types of grants
One-off grants of up to £200. In the past, grants have been given towards the purchase of clothing, household items and the payment of bills.

Annual grant total
In 2013/14 the trust had an income of £6,400 and a total expenditure of £2,500. We estimate that the amount of grants given to individuals totalled £2,200.

Exclusions
No grants are given for council tax or tax payable to HMRC.

Applications

Application forms are available from the correspondent. Applications can be submitted by the individual or through a recognised referral agency (e.g. a social worker, Citizens Advice or doctor). Grants are considered twice a year.

The Tile Hill and Westwood Charities for the Needy Sick

£6,500

Correspondent: John Ruddick, Clerk, 4 Poundgate Lane, Coventry CV4 8HJ (024 7646 6917; email: john.ruddick@bttj.com)

CC number: 220898

Eligibility

People who are both sick and in need and live in the parish of Westwood and parts of the parish of Berkswell, Kenilworth and Stoneleigh and elsewhere within a three and a half-mile radius of 93 Cromwell Lane, Coventry.

Types of grants

One-off grants according to need. The charity is often able to provide assistance where a potential beneficiary 'falls between the cracks' of other providers.

Annual grant total

In 2014 the charity had an income of £21,500 and a total expenditure of £14,000. We estimate that the amount of grants given to individuals totalled £6,500.

Applications

Apply in writing to the correspondent.

Doctor William MacDonald of Johannesburg Trust

£2,400

Correspondent: Jane Barlow, Trustee, Lord Mayor's Office, Council House, Earl Street, Coventry CV1 5RR (024 7683 3047; email: jane.barlow@coventry.gov.uk)

CC number: 225876

Eligibility

People in need who live in the city of Coventry.

Types of grants

One-off grants, typically of between £50 and £200, are made for welfare purposes.

Annual grant total

In 2014/15 the trust had an income of £3,200 and a total expenditure of £2,500. We estimate that the amount of grants given to individuals totalled £2,400.

Exclusions

No grants are made for the relief of debt.

Applications

Apply in writing to the correspondent. Applications can be submitted directly by the individual or through a third party such as a social worker.

Dudley

The Badley Memorial Trust

£49,500 (126 grants)

Correspondent: Christopher Williams, Clerk to the Trustees, 16 Manderville Gardens, Kingswinford DY6 9QW (01384 294019; email: badleymemorial@yahoo.com)

CC number: 222999

Eligibility

People in need who are in poor health, convalescent or who have disabilities and live in the former county borough of Dudley (as constituted in 1953). In certain cases the present metropolitan boroughs of Dudley and Sandwell may be included.

Types of grants

One-off grants have been made towards medical aids, clothing, beds/bedding, heating appliances, domestic appliances, televisions, radios, fuel, respite holidays and adaptations for people with disabilities. Recurrent grants are only given in exceptional cases.

Payments are made directly via cheque to the providers of goods or services, no cash payments are made to applicants.

The average grant in 2014/15 was £393.

Annual grant total

In 2014/15 the trust held assets of £1.5 million and had an income of £65,000. A total of £49,500 was distributed in 126 grants to individuals.

Exclusions

Grants are not given to pay off debts or for educational fees.

Applications

Application forms are available from the correspondent. Applications should be submitted directly by the individual or, where applicable, through a social worker, Citizens Advice, other welfare agency or a third party such as a relative, doctor or member of the clergy. Applications are considered quarterly. Those of an urgent nature may be dealt with more quickly by an authorised trustee.

Other information

Although none were awarded in 2014/15, the trust also makes grants to organisations.

The Dudley Charity

£3,200

Correspondent: David Hughes, Trustee, 53 The Broadway, Dudley, West Midlands DY1 4AP (01384 259277; email: dudleycharity@hotmail.co.uk; website: www.dudleyrotary.org.uk/dudleycharity.html)

CC number: 254928

Eligibility

People in need who live in the town of Dudley (as constituted prior to 1 April 1966) and its immediate surroundings, including Netherton.

Types of grants

One-off grants in the range of £100 to £250. Examples of the types of grants considered are: payments to relieve sudden distress; expenses for visiting people in hospitals or correctional facilities; assistance in meeting gas or electricity bills; the provision of furniture, bedding, clothing, food and other household appliances; the supply of tools, payment for training or equipment for recreational pursuits; respite care; contributions towards wheelchairs and scooters; and food for special diets, medical or other aids and nursing requisites or comforts. Weekly allowances may also be given for a limited period.

Annual grant total

In 2013/14 the charity had an income of £6,400 and a total expenditure of £6,500. We estimate that the amount of grants given to individuals totalled £3,200 with funding also awarded to local organisations.

Applications

Application forms are available from the correspondent or from the charity's webpage. Applications can be submitted directly by the individual or through a third party such as a social worker. They are normally considered monthly.

Other information

The charity was formed in 1987 through the amalgamation of a number of small charities in Dudley. The charity's website notes: 'The earliest of these charities dates back to 1659 founded under the will of Jasper Cartwright that with two others became known as The Bread Charities.'

The Reginald Unwin Dudley Charity

£1,400

Correspondent: David Hughes, Trustee, 53 The Broadway, Dudley, West Midlands DY1 4AP (01384 259277; email: rududley@hotmail.com; website: www.dudleyrotary.org.uk/rududley.html)

CC number: 217516

Eligibility

People in need who live in Dudley.

Types of grants

One-off grants of up to around £200. Since the charity began grant-making in 1980, it has provided funding for items such as clothing, household appliances, respite holidays, funeral expenses, course fees, nebulizers, computers, software and wheelchairs, for example.

Annual grant total

In 2013/14 the charity had an income of £3,100 and a total expenditure of £1,500. We estimate that the amount of grants given to individuals totalled £1,400.

Applications

Application forms are available from the correspondent or from the charity's page on the Dudley Rotary website. The application is more likely to succeed if accompanied with a supporting letter detailing the nature of the need for a grant.

Other information

The charity was originally established in 1904 by Reginald Unwin Dudley, who was a silk mercer in Dudley. 'Originally the charity was called The Reginald Unwin Dudley Highland Road Homes' and consisted of four houses for elderly residents, which were sold in 1980 when the charity was organised into its current form.

The Palmer and Seabright Charity

£9,700

Correspondent: Susannah Griffiths, Clerk to the Trustees, c/o Wall James Chappell, 15–23 Hagley Road, Stourbridge, West Midlands DY8 1QW (01384 371622; email: sgriffiths@wjclaw.co.uk)

CC number: 200692

Eligibility

People in need who live in the borough of Stourbridge.

Types of grants

One-off and weekly grants according to need.

Annual grant total

In 2014 the charity had assets of £278,500 and an income of £39,500. Grants were made totalling £16,700 (including £2,600 in Christmas grants). We estimate that social welfare grants to individuals amounted to £9,700.

Applications

Applications can be made on a form available from the correspondent. Applications can be submitted either directly by the individual or a family member, through a third party such as a social worker or teacher, or through an organisation such as Citizens Advice or a school.

The Edwin John Thompson Memorial Fund

£6,000 (1 grant)

Correspondent: David Thompson, Trustee, Long House Office, 56 High Street, Albrighton, Wolverhampton WV7 3JQ (01902 372036)

CC number: 213690

Eligibility

People in need who live in the County Borough of Dudley or any other local district, area or administrative unit within a radius of fifteen miles from Dudley Town Hall.

Types of grants

One-off and recurrent grants are given according to need, especially to young people to help them improve their skills and to those who are sick and needy. This may include scholarships to local young people and equipment for people with disabilities.

Annual grant total

In 2013/14 the fund had assets of £714,500 and an income of £28,000. Grants were made totalling £18,200, the majority of which (£12,200) was given to organisations. During the year one individual received a grant of £6,000.

Applications

Applications can be made in writing to the correspondent.

Other information

Grants are largely made to organisations.

Chris Westwood Charity

£59,000 (58 grants)

Correspondent: Martyn Morgan, Trustee, Quality Solicitors Talbots, 63 Market Street, Stourbridge DY8 1AQ (01384 445850; email: martynmorgan@ talbotslaw.co.uk; website: www.chriswestwoodcharity.co.uk)

CC number: 1101230

Eligibility

Children and young people under the age of 25 with physical disabilities, who live in Stourbridge or the surrounding areas (typically within a 50-mile radius).

Types of grants

Typical examples of support have included: special exercise equipment to assist in regaining and maintaining mobility; wheelchairs, special mobility chairs and lifting equipment; and contributions towards the cost of home modifications, to improve access, or provide specialised facilities that may be required.

Annual grant total

In 2014 the charity had an income of £69,000 and an expenditure of £59,000. All of this expenditure was given in financial assistance, in the form of 58 grants for individuals with the charity spending no money on governance or accountancy costs.

Applications

Apply in writing to the correspondent. Applications should detail: the name, age and address of the family and, where applicable, the school attended; background information and the reason for the request; a detailed quotation prepared after an assessment by the supplier; details of the financial position of the family; and details of any funds already raised. Applications should also be supported by a suitable professional person detailing the applicants medical condition and any advantages the proposed equipment purchase would bring. The charity aims to respond to requests within 48 hours. Grants are made by cheque paid directly to the supplier.

Sandwell

The Chance Trust

£1,300

Correspondent: Revd Ian Shelton, Trustee, 192 Hanover Road, Rowley Regis B65 9EQ (0121 559 1251; email: ianshelton232@hotmail.co.uk; website: www.warleydeanery.co.uk)

CC number: 702647

Eligibility

People in need in the rural deaneries of Warley and West Bromwich (the area covered by the southern parts of Sandwell borough).

Types of grants

One-off grants, usually ranging from £50 to £400, can be given according to need.

Annual grant total

In 2013/14 the trust had an income of £2,800 and a total expenditure of £2,700. Grants are made to individuals for social welfare and educational purposes. We estimate that social welfare grants to individuals totalled £1,300.

Exclusions

Grants are not normally provided where statutory funding is available.

Applications

Apply in writing to the correspondent. Applications should specify the need and the amount required. They are usually considered in January and July.

The Fordath Foundation

£6,400

Correspondent: John Sutcliffe, Trustee, 33 Thorneyfields Lane, Stafford ST17 9YS (01785 247035; email: fordath-foundation@ntlworld.com)

CC number: 501581

Eligibility

People who are in need and live in the Metropolitan Borough of Sandwell. Preference is given to older people and those in poor health.

Types of grants

One-off grants to meet a specific expense. Grants are also available for educational needs.

Annual grant total

In 2014 the foundation had an income of £6,800 and a total expenditure of £6,600. We estimate that the amount of grants given to individuals totalled £6,400.

Applications

Applications are usually only considered if they are made through Sandwell Social Services, Citizens Advice or a similar organisation. They should include brief details of the individual's circumstances. They are considered throughout the year, funds permitting.

George and Thomas Henry Salter Trust

£7,300 (27 grants)

Correspondent: Mrs J. Styler, Lombard House, Cronehills Linkway, West Bromwich, West Midlands B70 7PL (0121 553 3286)

CC number: 216503

Eligibility

People who are in need and live in the borough of Sandwell.

Types of grants

One-off grants, usually in the range of £50 to £1,000, are given towards clothing and household equipment, for example.

Annual grant total

In 2013 the trust had assets of £1.5 million and an income of £35,000. Grants amounted to £26,000, of which £11,400 was given to 15 organisations and 27 individuals for relief-in-need purposes. These grants averaged £272. Based on this average, we estimate that individuals were awarded around £7,300 for social welfare needs.

At the time of writing (November 2015) these were the most recent accounts available for the trust.

Applications

An application form is available from the correspondent.

Walsall

W. J. Croft for the Relief of the Poor (commonly known as W. J. Croft Charity)

£2,000

Correspondent: Matthew Underhill, Clerk to the Trustees, Legal and Democratic Services, Council House, Lichfield Street, Walsall WS1 1TW (01922 654369 or 01922 654766; email: charities@walsall.gov.uk; website: cms.walsall.gov.uk/charities)

CC number: 702795

Eligibility

Residents of the borough of Walsall.

Types of grants

The charity stresses that limited funds mean it can only offer small grants.

Annual grant total

Grants from the charity usually total around £2,000.

Exclusions

Property deposits, taxes, rent arrears, mortgage payments and utility bills.

Applications

Apply on a form available to download from the Walsall council website or by telephoning the council to receive a copy by post.

Walsall Wood (Former Allotment) Charity

£9,200

Correspondent: Craig Goodall, Democratic Services, Walsall Council, Council House, Lichfield Street, Walsall WS1 1TW (01922 654765; email: goodallc@walsall.gov.uk; website: www.walsall.gov.uk/charities)

CC number: 510627

Eligibility

Residents of the borough of Walsall.

Types of grants

The remit of the charity is wide, but awards are typically made for clothing and footwear, white goods and furniture.

Annual grant total

In 2013/14 the charity had an income of £22,500 and a total expenditure of £18,700. We estimate that grants for social welfare purposes totalled around £9,200.

Exclusions

Grants are not made for the relief of taxes, public funds, rent arrears or utility bills.

Applications

A form is available to download from the council website and can also be requested from the correspondent by telephone. It is helpful, but not essential, to submit supporting evidence along with an application. This can include proof of income, such as a wage slip, benefit letter or bank statement, or a supporting letter from a professional familiar with the applicant's case. The trustees meet around six times a year.

Other information

The charity is administered by the Walsall Council Democratic Services team, which also administers a number of other funds.

Wolverhampton

The Bushbury United Charities

£4,800

Correspondent: Harold Hilton, Administrator, Dallow and Dallow, 23 Waterloo Road, Wolverhampton, West Midlands WV1 4TJ (01902 420208)

CC number: 242290

Eligibility

People in need living in the ancient parish of Bushbury.

Types of grants

Annual grants paid at Christmas.

Annual grant total

In 2014 the charity had an income of £6,500 and a total expenditure of £5,000. We estimate that the total amount of grants awarded to individuals was approximately £4,800.

Applications

Apply in writing to the correspondent.

Worcester-shire

Charities of Susanna Cole and Others

See entry on page 35

The Worcestershire Cancer Aid Committee

£11,300

Correspondent: Anthony T. Atkinson, Trustee, c/o Kennel Ground, Gilberts End, Hanley Castle, Worcestershire WR8 0AS (01684 310408)

CC number: 504647

Eligibility

People with cancer who live in the old county of Worcestershire.

Types of grants

One-off and recurrent grants and loans, including grants in kind to assist cancer patients in financial distress with home nursing, transport to hospital, specialist equipment and so on.

Annual grant total

In 2013/14 the committee had an income of £35,500 and a total expenditure of £27,000. Grants to both individuals and organisations amounted to over £22,500. Of this, we estimate that social welfare grants to individuals totalled £11,300.

Applications

Applicants must be referred by a medical professional, a hospice senior staff member or a social worker, etc. Applications are normally considered within one week.

Malvern Hills

The Ancient Parish of Ripple Trust

£3,000

Correspondent: John Willis, Secretary, 7 Court Lea, Holly Green, Upton-upon-Severn, Worcestershire WR8 0PE (01684 594570; email: willis.courtlea@ btopenworld.com)

CC number: 1055986

Eligibility

People in need, hardship or distress living in the parishes of Ripple, Holdfast, Queenhill and Bushley.

Types of grants

Small, one-off cash grants are made. Repeated Christmas grants can also be made to older people.

Annual grant total

In 2014/15 the trust had an income of £13,400 and an expenditure of £12,600. We estimate that grants for individuals for social welfare purposes totalled about £3,000.

Applications

Applications may be made in writing to the correspondent. Our research suggests that the trustees meet twice a year to consider appeals and the funds are advertised locally before these meetings.

Other information

The trust gives to both individuals and organisations and for educational and welfare purposes. The trust's record on the Charity Commission's website notes that 50% of the net income is paid to the trustees of the Ripple Ecclesiastical Charity (Charity Commission no. 1059002) for the repair of the St Mary's Church, Ripple.

Worcester

Armchair

(254 grants)

Correspondent: Steve Hines, Manager, Grevis Cottage, Lower Dingle, Malvern WR14 4BQ (01905 456080; fax: 01905 456080; email: armchair@ talktalkbusiness.net; website: www. armchairworcester.co.uk)

CC number: 702078

Eligibility

People in need who have no savings and live in the city of Worcester (generally, within three-mile radius).

Types of grants

The charity collects, recycles and provides good quality second-hand furniture at low cost (£33 per item in 2014/15) to families and individuals. Furniture provided includes beds, wardrobes, tables/chairs, desks and so on.

Annual grant total

In 2014/15 the charity had assets of £69,500, an income of £27,000 and a total expenditure of £39,500, all of which has been spent on the overheads required for the distribution of second-hand furniture – the charity's main activity.

During the year the charity received 725 donated items and delivered them to 184 people and families (on average four items each).

Exclusions

The charity cannot provide electrical goods, carpets, clothing, bedding, kitchen utensils and similar items.

Applications

Applications should be submitted through local authorities, a social worker, Citizens Advice or other welfare agency. They are considered all year round. If the need is urgent it should be specified in the application.

Other information

The trustees' annual report from 2014/15 notes that 'occasionally, gifts are collected from just outside the city but due to limited resources, the need to economise on fuel, and to achieve a low carbon footprint, all deliveries of household items are within the city boundary'.

The Mary Hill Trust

£3,800

Correspondent: Andrew Duncan, Clerk, 16 The Tything, Worcester WR1 1HD (01905 731731; email: a.duncan@wwf.co. uk)

CC number: 510978

Eligibility

People in need who live within the boundaries of the city of Worcester.

Types of grants

One-off grants ranging from £50 to £500.

Annual grant total

In 2014, the trust had an income of £8,200 and a total expenditure of £8,100. We estimate that the total amount of grants awarded to individuals was approximately £3,800 as the trust also awards grants to organisations.

Applications

Applications should be made in writing to the correspondent either through a third party such as a social worker, Citizens Advice or other welfare agency, or directly by the individual. Applications from individuals are considered upon receipt. Applicants should include as many financial details as possible, for example income and weekly outgoings.

The United Charities of Saint Martin

£1,600

Correspondent: Michael Bunclark, 4 St Catherine's Hill, London Road, Worcester WR5 2EA (01905 355585)

CC number: 200733

Eligibility

People in need who live in the parish of St Martin, Worcester.

Types of grants

One-off grants and pensions are given according to need.

Annual grant total

In 2014 the charity had an income of £6,400 and a total expenditure of £6,600. Grants are made to individuals for social welfare and, our research suggests, for educational purposes. We estimate that social welfare grants to individuals totalled £1,600.

Applications

Apply in writing to the correspondent.

Other information

The charity also supports the maintenance of the parish church of St Martin and St Peter on London Road, Worcester.

The Henry and James Willis Trust

£8,400

Correspondent: John Wagstaff, Clerk, The Laurels, 4 Norton Close, Worcester WR5 3EY (01905 355659)

CC number: 201941

Eligibility

People who are convalescing and live in the city of Worcester.

Types of grants

One-off grants to allow convalescents to spend six weeks at the seaside or other health resort. Travel costs, accommodation and, in special cases, the cost of a carer are included. Patients are usually asked for a small weekly contribution.

Annual grant total

In 2013/14 the trust had an income of £7,100 and a total expenditure of £8,600. We estimate that the amount of grants given to individuals totalled £8,400.

Applications

Apply on a form available from the clerk. Applications can be submitted directly by the individual or, where applicable, through a social worker, Citizens Advice or other welfare agency.

Worcester Consolidated Municipal Charity (Worcester Municipal Charities)

£81,500 (341 grants)

Correspondent: Maggie Inglis, Office Manager, Kateryn Heywood House, Berkeley Court, The Foregate, Worcester WR1 3QG (01905 317117; fax: 01905 619979; email: admin@wmcharities.org.uk; website: www.wmcharities.org.uk)

CC number: 205299

Eligibility

People in need who live in the city of Worcester.

Types of grants

One-off grants of £20 to £1,000. Support is mainly given towards household essentials and personal items, such as white goods, carpets, electrical items, beds, baby necessities, clothing and so on, also funeral costs, debt relief and holidays.

Pensions are also provided to residents in need. Through the DWAS scheme applications can be made for white goods – further details on the scheme are available on the Worcester Council website (www.worcester.gov.uk/discretionary-welfare-assistance-scheme).

Annual grant total

In 2014 the charity had assets of £15.2 million and an income of £1.7 million. There were 341 grants made directly by the charity to individuals in need totalling £81,500 (all under £1,000). Further 418 grants were administered through the Discretionary Welfare Assistance Scheme (DWAS) scheme totalling £161,500.

Note that a significant proportion of the charity's income is spent on maintaining the almshouses.

Exclusions

Grants are not given where help is available from family/friends or statutory sources. Previous recipients of a grant from the charity are generally ineligible to apply again.

Applications

Applications have to be made through a social worker, health visitor, Citizens Advice or other welfare agency. Candidates should have exhausted any statutory sources before applying to the charity. Application forms can be accessed online and are considered monthly. The deadline for applications is 12 noon the Thursday before each monthly meeting – for dates of these see the charity's website.

Other information

The charity also provides grants to organisations and maintains almshouses in Worcester. In 2014 a total of 10 grants to organisations totalled £252,500.

The same body of trustees administers Worcester Consolidated Municipal Charity (Charity Commission no. 205299) and Worcester Municipal Exhibitions Foundations (Charity Commission no. 527570), which provides educational grants to individuals and organisations.

The annual report and accounts state:

> In 2013 the Government Social Fund which provided help to poor people in an emergency was all but wound up and replaced in Worcester by the DWAS (Discretionary Welfare Assistance Scheme). The charity agreed to act as agents and in 2014 bought white goods to the value of over £160,000, greatly reducing the number of grants requested. However, the Government has now announced that the scheme will end in 2016 and the charities are joining others in lobbying against this decision.

Wychavon

John Martin's Charity

£111,500 (886 grants)

Correspondent: John Daniels, The Clerk to the Trustees, 16 Queen's Road, Evesham, Worcester WR11 4JN (01386 765440; email: enquires@johnmartins.org.uk; website: www.johnmartins.org.uk)

CC number: 527473

Eligibility

People resident in Evesham, Worcestershire, who are in need.

Note: People who are suffering from chronic ill health living in designated parishes close to Evesham may also be able to apply for assistance with the costs of medical aids, equipment, etc. These parishes are listed on the charity's website.

Types of grants

Grants are available for the benefit of children, families, individuals, people who have disabilities and people who are on low incomes or who are in financial difficulty due to a variety of circumstances. Grants are considered for a range of purposes including essential household items, medical and mobility equipment, utility bills, gaps in income payments and school uniforms (for children aged 4–18 who live with a parent/guardian in the town).

Heating Award – Pensioners aged 63 and over may also apply for an award towards their heating costs. Criteria may be downloaded from the website and are also advertised throughout the town and in the Evesham Journal in November.

Annual grant total

In 2014/15 the charity had assets of £22.3 million and an income of £743,500. Grants were made to individuals and organisations totalling £657,500 and were distributed as follows:

Purpose	Grants to individuals	Grants to organisations/ schools
Promotion of education	£257,500	£75,000
Relief in need	£111,500	£99,500
Health and other charitable purposes	£9,600	£29,000
Religious support	£8,200	£67,000

Exclusions

Payments are never considered for council tax or fines. The charity cannot replace statutory benefits or supply equipment that is normally available from statutory sources.

Applications

Application forms are available from the correspondent or as a download from the website, where criteria is also posted. Applications can be submitted directly by the individual or through a social worker, Citizens Advice or other welfare agency. All applications are subject to a financial assessment and evidence of income and housing costs must be provided. The charity's office can be contacted to discuss an individual's request and circumstances.

Other information

Grants are also made to organisations and to individuals for educational purposes. The charity has an informative website.

Randolph Meakins Patty's Farm and the Widows Lyes Charity

£2,500

Correspondent: Lesley Houghton, Orchard House, Main Street, Cropthorne, Pershore, Worcestershire WR10 3LT (01386 860217)

CC number: 500624

Eligibility

People in need who live in the village of Cropthorne, Worcestershire.

Types of grants

As well as general social welfare grants, parcels are distributed at Christmas.

Annual grant total

In 2013/14 the charity had an income of £4,200 and a total expenditure of £5,200. Grants are made to individuals for a wide range of purposes. We estimate that

social welfare grants to individuals totalled £2,500.

Applications

Apply in writing to the correspondent.

Pershore United Charities

£1,600

Correspondent: Cllr Christopher Parsons, Correspondent, Town Hall, 34 High Street, Pershore, Worcestershire WR10 1DS (01386 561561)

CC number: 200661

Eligibility

People in need who live in private or rented accommodation (not residential or nursing homes) in the parishes of Pershore and Pensham. Priority is given to older people and people in need who have lived in the town for several years.

Types of grants

Recurrent and occasionally one-off grants to help with heating costs at Christmas.

Annual grant total

In 2014/15 the charity had an income of £5,100 and a total expenditure of £3,500. We estimate that the amount of grants given to individuals totalled £3,300 with funding also awarded to local organisations.

Applications

Apply in writing to the correspondent. Applications are considered in October.

Wyre Forest

The Kidderminster Aid In Sickness Fund

£22,500

Correspondent: Rachel Summers, Clerk to the Trustees, c/o M. F. G. Solicitors, Adam House, Birmingham Road, Kidderminster DY10 2SH (01562 820181; email: rachel.summers@ mfgsolicitors.com; website: kaisf.org.uk)

CC number: 210586

Eligibility

People who are in sick, infirm, convalescent, or in need of rest or domestic help, are in financial need, and live in the borough of Kidderminster.

Types of grants

One-off grants typically ranging between £100 and £2,000 towards, for example, fuel expenses, equipment, furniture, beds and bedding.

Annual grant total

In 2014 the fund had an income of £18,000 and an expenditure of £45,000. We estimate grants to individuals to have totalled £22,500, with grants also awarded to organisations.

Applications

Apply in writing to the correspondent or on a form available for download from the fund's website. Application forms must be accompanied by a Supporting Information form and can be considered at any time.

East of England

General

The Hunstanton Convalescent Trust

£4,500
CC number: 218979

Eligibility

People who are on a low income, physically or mentally unwell and in need of a convalescent or recuperative holiday, with a preference for those living in Norfolk, Cambridgeshire or Suffolk.

Types of grants

Grants ranging from around £100 to £350 are given to provide or assist towards the expenses of recuperative holidays, including for carers. The trust can sometimes provide other items, services or facilities which will help the individual's recovery.

Annual grant total

In 2013/14 the trust had an income of just £1,000 and a total expenditure of nearly £5,000. We estimate that the amount of grants given to individuals totalled around £4,500.

Applications

Apply on a form available from the correspondent, through a social worker, GP or other welfare/medical professionals. Applications should be submitted at least one month before the proposed holiday. The full board of trustees usually meets in January, June and September.

Mrs L. D. Rope's Third Charitable Settlement

£395,000 (1,855 grants)
CC number: 290533

Eligibility

People in need who live in eastern Suffolk, particularly in the parish of Kesgrave or the town of Ipswich, as well as small areas in Essex and Norfolk.

Types of grants

One-off grants or vouchers according to need. Grants may be given for items such as food, clothing, household appliances, carpet, or for essential applications (possibly visa compliance or bankruptcy protection). The average size of grants to individuals in east Suffolk during 2013/14 was £210.

Annual grant total

In 2013/14 the charity had both an income and a charitable expenditure of £1.4 million. During this financial year, 1,855 grants were awarded to individuals totalling £395,000. The majority of these grants were distributed to people living in the charity's local area of eastern Suffolk (£415,000 in 1,842 grants), with the remainder received by individuals living in other parts of East Anglia.

The charity also awarded 146 grants to organisations to the sum of £768,500.

Exclusions

Grants are not given for individuals working overseas, debt relief, health/palliative care or educational fees. Only in exceptional cases will more than one grant be awarded to the same individual or family in any one year.

Applications

Apply in writing to the correspondent preferably through a social worker, Citizens Advice or another agency with whom the charity works. Apply in a concise letter, saying what is needed and how charity may be able to help. It helps to include details of household income (including benefits), expenses, and a daytime telephone number.

Although the majority of applicants are referred by a local professional, unsolicited applicants are carefully reviewed.

Cambridgeshire

The Foundation of Edward Storey
See entry on page 178

City of Cambridge

The Cambridge Community Nursing Trust

£3,500

Correspondent: Jan Croft, Correspondent, 38 Station Road West, Whittlesford, Cambridge CB22 4NL (01223 835412; email: enquiries@ cambridgecommunitynursingtrust.co.uk; website: www.cambridgecommunity nursingtrust.co.uk)

CC number: 204933

Eligibility

People in need who live in the boundaries of the city of Cambridge.

Types of grants

Grants of up to around £300 are given to provide extra care, comforts and special aids which are not available from any other source.

Annual grant total

In 2014 the trust had an income of £15,300 and a total expenditure of £3,700. We estimate that the total amount of grants awarded to individuals was approximately £3,500.

Exclusions

Grants are not made to assist with debts.

Applications

Applications should be made by a professional on behalf of the individual, using the referral form on the trust's website. The receipt of applications will be acknowledged as soon as possible. The trustees meet regularly throughout the year and may consider applications between meetings to enable a swift response. The correspondent is happy to speak to potential applicants over the telephone before an application is submitted.

City of Peterborough

The Florence Saunders Relief-in-Sickness Charity

£2,700

Correspondent: Paula Lawson, Correspondent, 36 Tyndall Court, Commerce Road, Peterborough PE2 6LR (01733 343275; email: paula.lawson@ stephensonsmart.com)

CC number: 239177

Eligibility

People in need who are in poor health, convalescent, or who have disabilities and live in the former city of Peterborough.

Types of grants

One-off grants typically range between £100 and £500, and have been awarded to assist with hospital expenses, convalescence, holidays, travel expenses, electrical goods, medical equipment, furniture, disability equipment and help in the home.

Annual grant total

In 2013/14 the charity had an income of £7,000 and a total expenditure of £5,700. We estimate that the amount of grants given to individuals totalled £2,700, with funding also awarded to local organisations.

Exclusions

No grants are given for the repayment of debts.

Applications

Apply in writing to the correspondent. Applications should be submitted either directly by the individual or, where applicable, through a third party such as a family member, social worker or other welfare agency. Applications are considered at trustees' meetings, usually held three times per year.

East Cambridgeshire

Thomas Parson's Charity

£2,500

Correspondent: The Clerk, Hall Ennion and Young, 8 High Street, Ely, Cambridgeshire CB7 4JY (01353 662918; email: john@heysolicitors.co.uk; website: www.thomasparsonscharity.org.uk)

CC number: 202634

Eligibility

People in need who live in the city of Ely.

Types of grants

One-off and occasionally recurrent grants to relieve financial hardship and towards medical needs.

Annual grant total

In 2013/14 the charity had assets of £9.3 million and an income of £265,000. Grants were made to four individuals, totalling £2,500. A further 4 grants were awarded to organisations, totalling £9,500.

Applications

Apply in writing to the correspondent. Applications can be submitted either directly by the individual, or through a social worker, Citizens Advice or other welfare agency. Applicants should include as much detail about their financial situation and their need for the grant as is possible. Applications are considered monthly.

Swaffham Bulbeck Relief-in-Need Charity

£4,000

Correspondent: Cheryl Ling, 43 High Street, Swaffham Bulbeck, Cambridge CB25 0HP (01223 813885)

CC number: 238177

Eligibility

People in need who live in the parish of Swaffham Bulbeck.

Types of grants

One-off and annual grants.

Annual grant total

In 2014 the charity had an income of £9,700 and a total expenditure of £8,200. We estimate that the amount of grants given to individuals totalled around £4,000.

Applications

Apply in writing to the correspondent.

Fenland

Feoffee Charity (Poor's Land)

£2,200

Correspondent: Brian Hawden, Administrator, Brian Hawden and Co. Solicitors, The Coach House, Chatteris, Cambridgeshire PE16 6PX (01354 692133; email: b.hawden@sky.com)

CC number: 202150

Eligibility

People who are 'poor and needy' and have lived in Chatteris for at least ten years.

Types of grants

Grants of around £25 are given annually in January.

Annual grant total

In 2014/15 the charity had an income of £5,600 and a total expenditure of £4,600. Taking into account that the charity also gives grants to organisations, we estimate that the total amount of grants awarded to individuals was approximately £2,200.

Applications

Apply in writing to the correspondent, or upon recommendation of a trustee.

The Leverington Town Lands Charity

£9,000

Correspondent: Rosemary Gagen, Clerk to the Trustees, 78 High Road, Gorefield, Wisbech, Cambridgeshire PE13 4NB (01945 870454; email: levfeoffees@aol. com)

CC number: 232526

Eligibility

People in need who live in the parishes of Leverington, Gorefield or Newton.

Types of grants

One-off grants towards, for example, glasses, new teeth or household appliances.

Annual grant total

In 2013/14 the charity held assets of £951,500 and had an income of £45,500. One-off grants to individuals totalled £9,000.

Applications

Application forms are available from the correspondent. Applications are considered in May and November.

The Upwell (Cambridgeshire) Consolidated Charities

£4,700

Correspondent: Ronald Stannard, Correspondent, Riverside Farm, Birchfield Road, Nordelph, Downham Market, Norfolk PE38 0BP (01366 324217; email: ronstannard@waitrose. com)

CC number: 203558

Eligibility

People in need who are over 65 (unless widowed) and live in the parish of Upwell (on the Isle of Ely) and have done so for at least five years.

Types of grants

Grants, which in previous years have ranged between £10 and £40, are given at Christmas.

Annual grant total

In 2014 the charity had an income of £5,700 and a total expenditure of £4,900. We estimate that the amount of grants given to individuals totalled £4,700.

Applications

Apply in writing to the correspondent. Applications should be submitted directly by the individual and are considered in November.

Elizabeth Wright's Charity

£2,100

Correspondent: Dr Iain Mason, Trustee, 13 Tavistock Road, Wisbech, Cambridgeshire PE13 2DY (01945 588646; email: i.h.mason60@gmail.com)

CC number: 203896

Eligibility

People who live in the parish of Wisbech St Peter, Cambridgeshire.

Types of grants

One-off grants for essential items to offset hardship or cope with long-term illness.

Annual grant total

In 2014 the charity had assets of over £1 million and an income of £41,000. Grants were made totalling £41,500, of which £2,100 was given to 'families in need known to social services'. A total of £13,300 was paid in grants 'in the categories of Education and Youth work involving music, art and religious tuition and provision of books and materials'.

Applications

Applications can be made in writing to the correspondent. They can be submitted directly by the individual at any time. The trustees usually meet quarterly.

Huntingdonshire

Huntingdon Freemen's Trust

£1,400

Correspondent: Karen Clark, Grants Officer, 37 High Street, Huntingdon, Cambridgeshire PE29 3AQ (01480 414909; email: info@huntingdonfreemen. org.uk; website: www. huntingdonfreemen.org.uk)

CC number: 1044573

Eligibility

People in need resident in Huntingdon (normally for at least one year).

Types of grants

The trust can help people 'who cannot afford to help themselves and who have basic needs that are not met by public services', including children, families, pensioners and people with disabilities. Applicants may be working or in receipt of benefits – the need is determined on an individual basis. Examples of support given include mobility aids, domestic appliances, furniture and carpets (particularly where young children are involved), adaptations and so on.

According to the annual report, 'relief in need is applied to a number of sub-categories, such as medical, children, elderly, unemployment/low income and domestic violence needs'.

Annual grant total

In 2013/14 the trust had assets of £15.8 million and an income of about £438,500. The accounts state that relief-in-need grants were made totalling £125,500. Christmas meals and trips for older people totalled £1,400 (this was listed under 'Significant individual projects over the year'). There was no further breakdown between individual and organisational grants; therefore, welfare support may be higher.

Exclusions

The trust cannot substitute services that should be provided by the state but may supplement them. Relief-in-need support is not normally the payment of rent, council tax, debts, fines or funerals.

Applications

Individuals (other than students) should apply in writing to the correspondent. Potential applicants are invited to get in touch with the trust or drop by to discuss their needs. The website states: 'We are always open to suggestions of how we could provide more help, so if you have an idea drop in for a chat!'

Consideration procedure will involve visiting the applicants' homes to assess their needs and financial circumstances. If you have a support worker, it would be helpful if they liaised with the trust. Applications are considered at monthly meetings.

South Cambridgeshire

The Samuel Franklin Fund Elsworth

£16,900

Correspondent: Serena Wyer, Clerk to the Trustees, 5 Cowdell End, Elsworth, Cambridge CB23 4GB (01954 267156; email: serena.wyersff@gmail.com; website: www.samuelfranklinfund.co.uk)

CC number: 228775

Eligibility

People who live in the parish of Elsworth and suffer from poverty, hardship or illness. Preference is given to older people, children and people with disabilities.

Types of grants

Grants are made at Trinity and Christmas and can also be made according to need e.g. special equipment for people who have disabilities or, in appropriate cases, help with funeral expenses. Our research indicates that they usually range between £10 and £1,000.

Annual grant total

In 2014 the fund had an income of £22,500 and a total expenditure of £42,500. Due to its low income, the fund was not required to submit its accounts to the Charity Commission and so a breakdown of grants awarded during the year was not available to view. In recent years, grants for social welfare purposes have totalled around £16,900.

Applications

In the first instance, contact the clerk or one of the trustees.

Thomas Galon's Charity

£2,600

Correspondent: Linda Miller, Clerk, 21 Thistle Green, Swavesey, Cambridge CB24 4RJ (01954 202982; email: thomasgaloncharity@swavesey.org.uk; website: www.swavesey.org.uk/thomas_galon_charity)

CC number: 202515

Eligibility

People in need who live in the parish of Swavesey. Preference is given to those who are over 70, single or widowed; married couples when one partner reaches 70; and widows and widowers with dependent children up to 18 years old.

Types of grants

An annual gift, to be agreed in November, for people in need. One-off grants for hospital travel expenses, fuel costs and other needs.

Annual grant total

In 2014 the charity had an income of £9,000 and a total expenditure of £5,200. We estimate that the amount of grants given to individuals totalled £2,600, with funding also awarded to local organisations.

Exclusions

No grants are given for capital projects such as buildings.

Applications

Apply in writing to the correspondent for consideration in November. Grants will be delivered in December.

John Huntingdon's Charity

£10,600

Correspondent: Jill Hayden, Charity Manager, John Huntingdon House, Tannery Road, Sawston, Cambridge CB2 3UW (01223 492492; email: office@ johnhuntingdon.org.uk; website: www. johnhuntingdon.org.uk)

CC number: 1118574

Eligibility

People in need who live in the parish of Sawston in Cambridgeshire.

Types of grants

Grants can be given for essential household items such as cookers, washing machines or beds. Assistance is also given towards school uniforms, school trips and sometimes nursery or playgroup fees.

Annual grant total

In 2014 the charity had assets of £8.6 million and an income of £393,000. Grants to individuals totalled £21,000 and are given for both social welfare and educational purposes, but a breakdown of distributions was not included in the annual report and accounts. We estimate that social welfare grants to individuals totalled £10,600.

Applications

In the first instance, call the charity's office to arrange an appointment with one of its support workers.

The Ickleton United Charities (Relief-in-Need Branch)

£8,800

Correspondent: John Statham, Trustee, 35 Abbey Street, Ickleton, Saffron Walden, Essex CB10 1SS (01799 530258)

CC number: 202467

Eligibility

People in need who live in the Parish of Ickleton, Cambridgeshire.

Types of grants

One-off grants of around £40 towards fuel costs and necessities, and gift vouchers at Christmas. The charity often pays for Lifelines (emergency telephone links for older people and people with disabilities) for those who require them.

Annual grant total

In 2014 the charity had an income of £9,800 and a total expenditure of £9,200. We estimate that the amount of grants given to individuals totalled £8,800.

Applications

Apply in writing to the correspondent. Applications should be submitted directly by the individual.

Pampisford Relief-in-Need Charity

£3,000

Correspondent: Dennis Beaumont, 4 Hammond Close, Pampisford, Cambridge CB22 3EP (01223 833653)

CC number: 275661

Eligibility

People in need who live in the parish of Pampisford, particularly children and young people, older people and individuals who have a disability. In exceptional circumstances support may be given to otherwise eligible candidates who live immediately outside the parish.

Types of grants

Christmas gifts or individual grants of up to £250 for items, services or other specific requirements. Contributions are also made for the improvement of village amenities, which can then be enjoyed by the parishioners, particularly the elderly, the young and people with disabilities.

Annual grant total

In 2014 the charity had an income of £14,900 and an expenditure of £14,200. About £3,000 is available each year for individuals.

Applications

Apply in writing to the correspondent. Applications can be made directly by the individual at any time.

Lincolnshire

Committee For Kesteven Children in Need (KCIN)

£7,500

Correspondent: Alexandra Howard, Trustee, Nocton Rise, Lincoln LN4 2AF (01522 791217; email: enquiries@kcin. org; website: www.kcin.org)

CC number: 700008

Eligibility

Children/young people up to the age of 16 who live in Kesteven (Lincolnshire) and are in need.

Types of grants

One-off and recurrent grants of up to £500. Examples of previous grants include clothing, educational holidays, days out, prams/pushchairs, beds/sheets, fireguards, second-hand washing machines, educational toys and playschool fees.

Annual grant total

In 2014 the charity had an income of £15,000 and a total expenditure of £11,000. We estimate that the amount of grants given to individuals totalled around £7,500. Grants are also made to organisations.

Applications

The charity acts purely on referrals from professionals, such as social workers, health visitors, teachers, education officers and similar. Applications should include the family situation, the age of the child and his/her special needs. Applications are considered throughout the year.

Edward Hunstone

£6,500 (20 grants)

Correspondent: Tony Bradley, Correspondent, 58 Eastwood Road, Boston, Lincolnshire PE21 0PH (01205 364175)

CC number: 214570

Eligibility

Older gentlemen and those with disabilities who are in need and live in Lincolnshire.

There is a preference for descendants of Edward Hunstone, the Gedneys of Bagarderly – Lincolnshire, Robert Smith of Saltfleetby – Lincolnshire or the Woodliffes of Toft Grange – Lincolnshire.

Particular mention is also made of retired clergymen, members of HM Forces, farmers and farm labourers.

Types of grants

Recipients receive £325 per year, paid in two instalments of £162.50 in April and October. The assistance will be given as long as the trustees consider necessary or until the death of the recipient.

Annual grant total

In 2014 the charity had assets of £42,500 and an income of £30,000. Grants to 20 beneficiaries totalled £6,500 during the year.

Exclusions

Grants are not given to women.

Applications

Application forms are available from the correspondent. They can be submitted directly by the individual or through a social worker, Citizens Advice or other welfare agency. Appeals are considered in May each year and should be received by 30 April; urgent applications can be considered at other times. Two references are required with each application.

Kitchings General Charity

£8,800

Correspondent: Mrs J. Smith, Secretary, 42 Abbey Road, Bardney, Lincoln LN3 5XA (01526 398505)

CC number: 219957

Eligibility

People in need who live in the parish of Bardney, Southrey, Tupholme or Bucknall.

Types of grants

One-off grants are available to relieve hardship or distress and may include holidays/respite care for people with disabilities (mostly at a special home at Sandringham), specialised nursing equipment, including wheelchairs, funeral expenses and household essentials, such as carpets, flooring and bedding. Grants are usually in the range of £200–£500 but can be of up to £2,000.

Pensions are available to eligible widows of Southrey (£10 per week).

Annual grant total

In 2014 the charity had assets of £13,400 and an income of £36,500. Grants made for welfare purposes included widows' pensions (£1,100) and unspecified grants (£15,400). We estimate that the amount of grants given to individuals for social welfare purposes totalled around £8,800 (including the pensions).

Applications

Applications may be made in writing to the correspondent and should include some basic background details about the applicant and the nature of need. Our research indicates that applications are normally considered in May, October and January.

The Lincoln General Dispensary Fund

£6,500

Correspondent: Michael Bonass, Administrator, Durrus, Scothern Lane, Dunholme, Lincoln LN2 3QP (01673 860660)

CC number: 220159

Eligibility

People who are in poor health, convalescent or who have disabilities and live within the ten-mile radius of the Stonebow (Lincoln).

Types of grants

One-off grants of up to around £250 to alleviate suffering or aid recovery. Our research tells us that past grants have been given for orthopaedic beds, alarm systems and recuperative holidays.

Annual grant total

In 2014 the fund had an income of £11,200 and a total expenditure of £13,700. We estimate that the amount of grants given to individuals totalled £6,500. Funding was also given to local organisations.

Exclusions

No grants are given for building adaptations, debts already incurred or anything that could be provided by public funds.

Applications

Application forms are available from the correspondent and should be submitted through a recognised social or medical agency. Applications are considered throughout the year.

Lincolnshire Community Foundation

£1,600

Correspondent: Sue Fortune, Grants Manager, 4 Mill House, Moneys Yard, Carre Street, Sleaford, Lincolnshire NG34 7TW (01529 305825; email: lincolnshirecf@btconnect.com; website: www.lincolnshirecf.co.uk)

CC number: 1092328

Eligibility

Generally, residents of Lincolnshire who are in need; however, different funds have different eligibility criteria attached. See types of grant section.

Types of grants

The type and amount of grant available depends on the fund being applied to. See the foundation's website for more information on open funds.

Annual grant total

In 2014 the foundation had assets of £5.7 million and an income £664,500. Grants are mainly made to organisations. We estimate that around £1,600 was awarded to individuals for welfare purposes through The Colin Batts Family Trust, which also gives to local organisations and to promote opportunities for young people.

Exclusions

Grants cannot be awarded retrospectively.

Applications

See the foundation's website for more information on the funds it operates and how to apply for assistance.

Lincolnshire Police Charitable Fund

£18,000

Correspondent: Amanda Watson, Correspondent, c/o Police Federation Office, Lincolnshire Police Headquarters, Nettleham, Lincoln LN2 2LT (01522 558303; email: charitable.fund@lincs.pnn.police.uk)

CC number: 500682

Eligibility

People in need who are present or former employees of Lincolnshire Police Authority, and their dependants. Former employees of other Police Authorities who have retired and now live in Lincolnshire may also qualify for assistance.

Types of grants

One-off grants according to need.

Annual grant total

In 2013/14 the fund held assets of £167,000 and had an income of £40,000. Grants to individuals totalled £18,000 and were distributed as follows:

Medical, travel and expenses	£10,500
General cases	£4,000
Death grant	£2,400
Christmas gifts	£700
Fruit, flowers and donations	£600

A further £3,000 was awarded in grants to four organisations.

Applications

Application forms are available from the Welfare Officer. Applications can be submitted directly by the individual or, where applicable, through a social worker, Citizens Advice or other welfare agency.

Boston

The Frampton Town Lands and United Charities

£2,400

Correspondent: Mark Hildred, Correspondent, Moore Thompson, Bank House, Broad Street, Spalding, Lincolnshire PE11 1TB (01775 711333)

CC number: 216849

Eligibility

People in need who have lived in the ancient parish of Frampton for at least five years. Preference is usually given to older people (aged over 65) and recently bereaved widows.

Types of grants

One-off grants towards electricity bills, Christmas gifts for older people and so on.

Annual grant total

In 2013/14 the charity had an income of £8,700 and an expenditure of £9,700. We estimate that welfare grants to individuals totalled £2,400, with funding also awarded to local organisations and for educational purposes.

Applications

Apply in writing to the correspondent. Applications are normally considered in October.

The Sutterton Parochial Charity Trust

£6,500

Correspondent: Deirdre McCumiskey, Correspondent, 6 Hillside Gardens, Wittering, Peterborough PE8 6DX (01780 782668; email: deirdre. mccumiskey@tesco.net)

CC number: 234839

Eligibility

People in need who live in the parishes of Sutterton or Amber Hill.

Types of grants

One-off grants of around £50.

Annual grant total

In 2014/15 the trust had an income of £11,600 and a total expenditure of £13,500. We estimate that the amount of grants given to individuals totalled £6,500 with funding also awarded to local organisations.

Applications

Application forms are available from the correspondent which can be submitted directly by the individual or a family member. Applications for Christmas grants should be received by the end of November for consideration in early December.

The Swineshead Poor Charities

£5,500

Correspondent: Lynne Richardson, Correspondent, 27 Sorrel Drive, Spalding, Lincolnshire PE11 3GN (01775 762977; email: lynne@hmtg.co.uk)

CC number: 216557

Eligibility

People in need who live in the parish of Swineshead.

Types of grants

One-off and recurrent grants and loans according to need.

Annual grant total

In 2014/15 the charity had an income of almost £24,000 and a total expenditure of £12,100. We estimate that the amount of grants given to individuals totalled £5,500, with organisations also receiving funding.

Applications

Apply in writing to the correspondent.

East Lindsey

Addlethorpe Parochial Charity

£6,900

Correspondent: Maggie Boughton, Clerk, The Willows, Mill Lane, Addlethorpe, Skegness, Lincolnshire PE24 4TB (01754 760644; email: addlethorpeparishcouncil@gmail.com)

CC number: 251412

Eligibility

People who are sick, convalescent, disabled or infirm, and who live in the parish of Addlethorpe, or who previously lived in Addlethorpe and now live in an adjoining parish. Applicants must be either living on a low income, with limited savings or investments of less than £10,000, or have a disability or illness that renders them unable to work.

Types of grants

Support is given on an annual basis to assist with heating costs. One-off grants are given towards funeral expenses, household repairs and other necessities. Grants have also been given for hospital or doctor's visits.

Annual grant total

In 2013/14 the charity had an income of £6,400 and a total expenditure of £7,100. We estimate that the amount of grants given to individuals totalled £6,900.

Applications

Apply in writing to the correspondent. Applications can be submitted either directly by the individual or a family member, through a third party such as a social worker, or through an organisation such as Citizens Advice or other welfare agency. Applications must state that they are living on a reduced income and that savings/investments are below £10,000. Applications are considered on an ongoing basis.

The Spilsby Poor Lands Charity

£2,600

Correspondent: Mrs J. Tong, Clerk, Rosedale Lodge, Ashby Road, Spilsby, Lincolnshire PE23 5DW (01790 752885)

CC number: 220613

Eligibility

People of retirement age in need who have lived in Spilsby for at least five years.

Types of grants

Grants of up to £25 are made twice a year in June and December.

Annual grant total

In 2014, the charity had an income of £2,900 and a total expenditure of £2,800. We estimate that the total amount of grants awarded to individuals was approximately £2,600.

Applications

Application forms are available from the correspondent. Applications must be submitted directly by the individual and are considered in June and December. Applicants must state how long they have lived in Spilsby.

The Stickford Relief-in-Need Charity

£4,700

Correspondent: Katherine Bunting, Clerk, 28 Wide Bargate, Boston, Lincolnshire PE21 6RT (01205 351114; fax: 01205 356018)

CC number: 247423

Eligibility

People in need who live in the parish of Stickford.

Types of grants

One-off and recurrent grants for relief-in-need purposes, towards school uniforms, and bonuses at Christmas.

Annual grant total

In 2014 the charity had an income of £16,900 and a total expenditure of £19,600. Grants are made to both individuals and organisations for a range of purposes. We estimate that the amount of grants given to individuals for social welfare needs totalled £4,700.

Applications

Applications can be made in writing to the correspondent. They should be submitted directly by the individual and are considered all year.

Lincoln

The Charity of John Dawber

£13,000

Correspondent: Helen Newson, Administrator, Andrew and Co. Solicitors, St Swithin's Court, 1 Flavian Road, Lincoln LN2 1HB (01522 512123; email: helen.newson@andrew-solicitors.co.uk)

CC number: 216471

Eligibility

People in need who live in the city of Lincoln or the parish of Bracebridge.

Types of grants

The charity has ceased making payments of annuities and Christmas grocery vouchers. They plan to make grants which will be of benefit to the community and are hoping to work with Lincoln City Council to address these needs.

Annual grant total

In 2013/14 the charity had assets of £1.47 million and an income of £44,000. During the year six grants were made, although a breakdown of grants to individuals and organisations was not provided. Charitable expenditure total during the year totalled £25,000.

Applications

Apply in writing to the correspondent. There are no deadlines for applications.

The Lincoln Municipal Relief-in-Need Charities

£33,000

Correspondent: M. Bonass, Clerk, Durrus, Scothern Lane, Dunholme, Lincoln LN2 3QP (01673 860660; email: m.bonass213@btinternet.com)

CC number: 213651

Eligibility

People in need who live in the city of Lincoln.

Types of grants

One-off grants of up to £500 each according to need.

Annual grant total

In 2013/14 the charity held assets of £801,000 and had an income of £38,500. Grants to individuals totalled £33,000 and were distributed as follows:

Various individuals	£30,200
Quarterly payments	£2,800

Exclusions

No grants are given that: should be covered by public funds; contribute to the fabric of buildings; or help to reduce debts that have already been incurred. Recurrent grants are not made.

Applications

Applications are generally only accepted through recognised social or medical agencies and are considered at any time. Requests for more than £500 must be approved at a quarterly trustee meeting.

North East Lincolnshire

Sir Alec Black's Charity

£4,300 (12 grants)

Correspondent: Stewart Wilson, Trustee, Wilson Sharpe and Co., 27 Osborne Street, Grimsby, North East Lincolnshire DN31 1NU (01472 348315; email: sc@wilsonsharpe.co.uk)

CC number: 220295

Eligibility

Fishermen and dockworkers who are sick and poor, who live in the borough of Grimsby. Grants are also available to people employed by Sir Alec Black during his lifetime.

Types of grants

One-off and recurrent grants are given according to need.

Annual grant total

In 2013/14 the charity had an income of £97,000 and a total expenditure of £86,000. Grants to 12 fishermen and dockworkers totalled £4,300 and grants to 25 charitable organisations totalled £60,000.

Applications

Apply in writing to the correspondent. The trustees meet twice a year, in May and November, to consider applications.

Grimsby Sailors and Fishing Charity

£25,000

Correspondent: Duncan Watt, Charities Administrator, 1st Floor, 23 Bargate, Grimsby, South Humberside DN34 4SS (01472 347914; fax: 01472 347914; email: duncan.watt4@gmail.com)

CC number: 500816

Eligibility

Primarily the children of Grimsby fishermen lost at sea or dying ashore while still fishermen. However, help may also be available to other beneficiaries living in Grimsby and the surrounding area, at the trustees' discretion.

Types of grants

Weekly and quarterly grants to support children of deceased fishermen while they are still in full-time education. Weekly grants are usually around £13 and quarterly grants range from £100 to £250.

Annual grant total

In 2014 the charity had an income of £570,500 and a total expenditure of £365,500. The majority of the charity's expenditure is spent on providing and maintaining almshouses. We estimate that the amount of grants given to individuals totalled £25,000. Full accounts were not available to view from the Charity Commission at the time of writing (November 2015).

Applications

Application forms are available from the correspondent or from the Port Missioner. Applications should be submitted directly by the individual or through an appropriate welfare agency. They are considered when received.

North Kesteven

The Navenby Town's Farm Trust

£4,500

Correspondent: Leonard Coffey, Secretary, 17 North Lane, Navenby, Lincoln LN5 0EH (01522 810273)

CC number: 245223

Eligibility

People in need who live in the village of Navenby.

Types of grants

One-off grants according to need.

Annual grant total

In 2014/15 the trust had an income of £19,000 and a total expenditure of £19,300. Grants are made to individuals and organisations for both social welfare and educational purposes. We estimate that social welfare grants to individuals totalled £4,500.

Exclusions

No grants can be given to individuals resident outside the village.

Applications

Apply using a form available from the correspondent, the village post office, or the local newsagents. Applications are considered in September. Urgent applications may occasionally be considered at other times. Unsolicited applications are not responded to.

North Lincolnshire

The Beeton, Barrick and Beck Relief-in-Need Charity

£3,800

Correspondent: Mrs A. Lawe, Correspondent, Barrow Wold Farm, Deepdale, Barton-upon-Humber, North Lincolnshire DN18 6ED (01469 531928)

CC number: 234571

Eligibility

People in need who are over 60 and live in the parish of Barrow-upon-Humber.

Types of grants

Christmas vouchers and one-off grants for a variety of purposes, such as travel costs to hospital.

Annual grant total

In 2013/14 the charity had an income of £4,300 and a total expenditure of £4,000. We estimate that the amount of grants given to individuals totalled £3,800.

Applications

Application forms are available from the correspondent.

Blue Coat Charity

£21,500

Correspondent: Keith Ready, Market Place, Barton-upon-Humber, North Lincolnshire DN18 5DD (01652 632215; email: mail@keithready.co.uk)

CC number: 237891

Eligibility

People in need who live in Barton-upon-Humber.

Types of grants

One-off grants, usually in the form of vouchers which can be spent locally. The charity has given grants towards the purchase of footwear, clothing, bedding, food and other essential items.

Annual grant total

In 2013/14 the charity had an income of £31,000 and a total expenditure of £25,000. Grants were made to individuals totalling £21,500.

Applications

Apply in writing to the correspondent. Unless urgent, applications are considered each November and awarded in December.

South Holland

The Moulton Poor's Lands Charity

£6,900

Correspondent: Richard Lewis, Clerk, c/o Maples and Son Solicitors, 23 New Road, Spalding, Lincolnshire PE11 1DH (01775 722261)

CC number: 216630

Eligibility

People in need, generally older people, who live in Moulton village and the surrounding areas (near Spalding in Lincolnshire).

Types of grants

Grants can be paid in cash or in kind. Relief-in-need grants are generally paid following a severe accident, unexpected loss or misfortune. The charity can provide bereavement grants and pension credits, among other needs.

Annual grant total

In 2014 the charity had assets of £928,500 and an income of £34,500. During the year £7,100 was awarded in grants, the majority of which we believe was to individuals for welfare purposes. We estimate that educational grants to individuals amounted to no more than £200.

Applications

Applications may be made in writing to the correspondent, usually through a trustee. Appeals are normally considered in April and December.

Spalding Relief-in-Need Charity

£16,600

Correspondent: R. Knipe, Clerk and Solicitor, Dembleby House, 12 Broad Street, Spalding, Lincolnshire PE11 1ES (01775 768774; email: patrick.skells@ chattertons.com)

CC number: 229268

Eligibility

People in need who live in the area covered by the district of South Holland. Preference is given to residents of the urban district of Spalding and the parishes of Cowbit, Deeping St Nicholas, Pinchbeck and Weston.

Types of grants

The charity can provide one-off and recurrent grants, usually in the range of £100 to £400. Support is given towards various items, services and facilities, including awards for furniture and domestic appliances, rent arrears and other debts, children's clothing and so on. Residents of the almshouses can be helped with the cost of TV licence.

Annual grant total

In 2014 the charity had assets of £1.3 million and an income of £50,000. Grants totalled £30,500, £500 of which was donated to an organisation (Age UK Spalding). Grants to individuals amounted to £30,000 and were distributed as follows:

Individuals	£25,500*
TV licences for almshouse residents	£2,300
Annual grants to individuals	£1,500

*We have estimated that, of this figure, around £12,700 was given in grants for educational purposes.

Exclusions

Grants are not intended to be made where support can be obtained from statutory sources.

Applications

Application forms can be requested from the charity. They can be submitted directly by the individual or assisted by a social worker/Citizens Advice/other welfare agency, if applicable. Grants are considered fortnightly. Payments are normally paid directly to suppliers.

The Surfleet United Charities

£2,700

Correspondent: Leanne Barlow, Clerk, Crimond, Hedgefield Hurn, Gosberton, Spalding, Lincolnshire PE11 4JE (01775 750183)

CC number: 215260

Eligibility

Retired people in need who have lived in the parish of Surfleet for over ten years (exceptions will be made on the age restriction in cases of extreme need).

Types of grants

Normally grants are given as Christmas gifts each year of £15 (individuals) and £25 (couples). Other one-off grants are available according to need.

Annual grant total

In 2014 the charity had assets of £728,500 and an income of £697,500. Grants to the elderly and poor totalled £2,700.

Applications

Apply in writing to the correspondent. Applications can be submitted directly by the individual and are normally considered in November.

The Sutton St James Foundation for Education and the Poor (The Sutton St James United Charities)

£3,200

Correspondent: Keith Savage, Clerk to the Trustees, Lenton Lodge, 94 Wignals Gate, Holbeach, Spalding, Lincolnshire PE12 7HR (01406 490157; email: keithsavage@btinternet.com)

CC number: 527757

Eligibility

People in need who have lived in the parish of Sutton St James and the surrounding area for at least three years.

Types of grants

One-off and recurrent grants are given according to need. Previously grants have been given for funeral expenses and to help people who have been evicted.

Annual grant total

In 2014/15 the charity had an income of £22,000 and a total expenditure of £13,000. We estimate the amount awarded to individuals for social welfare purposes to be around £3,200.

Applications

Application forms are available from the correspondent or the village post office. Applications are only considered where all other available avenues have been explored.

South Kesteven

Deeping St James United Charities

£19,600

Correspondent: Julie Banks, Clerk, The Institute, 38 Church Street, Deeping St James, Peterborough PE6 8HD (01778 344707 (Tues/Thurs 9am-12pm); email: dsjunitedcharities@btconnect.com; website: www.dsjunitedcharities.org.uk)

CC number: 248848

Eligibility

People in the parish of Deeping St James (including Frognall) who are in need, hardship or suffer from ill health, disability or are otherwise disadvantaged. There are no fixed income limits for applications.

Older residents of the parish who are in receipt of a state pension, have lived in the parish for at least two years, and are in need, can also apply for assistance from St Thomas' Day Charity.

Types of grants

One-off and recurrent grants are given according to need are given for a variety of purposes such as clothing, hospital travel expenses, household equipment and repairs, white goods, carpets, bathroom conversions for older people, special equipment or services (for example foot care), pre-paying prescriptions, food, bills, heating installations or bereavement support. Interest-free loans may also be made. In partnership with Deeping Men's Group funds are provided for mobility aid, such as wheelchairs, beds, hoists and so on.

St Thomas' Day Charity offers small cash grants to older residents of the parish who are in need.

Annual grant total

In 2014 the charity had assets of £2.7 million and an income of £98,000. Grants totalled £31,500, the vast majority of which was given to individuals. Grants to individuals for social welfare purposes amounted to £19,600 and were distributed as follows:

Relief in need	£13,500
Relief in sickness	£3,100
Grants from St Thomas' Day Charity*	£3,000

*These grants were awarded to 121 people during the year.

An additional £6,100 was awarded for educational purposes and organisations were awarded £5,700.

Applications

Application forms can be requested from the correspondent or collected from the Institute. Awards are generally considered at the start of March, June, September and December.

Application forms for St Thomas Day grants are available to download online, from the local post office, and are also printed in the Deepings Advertiser in November. The awards are made on or around 21 December. Grants are limited to one application per household.

The Farmers' Benevolent Institution

£5,700

Correspondent: J. Andrew, Administrator, c/o Duncan and Toplis, 3 Castlegate, Grantham, Lincolnshire NG31 6SF (01476 591200; fax: 01476 591222; email: duncan.andrew@duntop.co.uk)

CC number: 216042

Eligibility

People living within a 15-mile radius of Grantham who have 'been owners or occupiers of land, but who from losses or other untoward circumstances have become destitute'. Applicants must be over 60 if they have been a subscriber of the fund for ten years or more. Otherwise they should be over 65.

Types of grants

Annual payments of around £150 and a supplementary payment at Christmas.

Annual grant total

In 2014/15 the charity had an income of £4,700 and a total expenditure of £6,300. We estimate that the total amount of grants awarded to individuals was approximately £6,000.

Applications

Apply in writing to the correspondent.

Haconby Poor's Money and Others

£3,100

Correspondent: Sally Burton, Trustee, 36 Headland Way, Haconby, Bourne, Lincolnshire PE10 0UW (01778 571441; email: sally.burton@tiscali.co.uk)

CC number: 218589

Eligibility

People in need who live in the parish of Haconby and Stainfield.

Types of grants

One-off and recurrent grants are given according to need. Grants have been given as Christmas gifts to people aged over 60, help with home alterations for disabled people and towards funeral expenses and hospital travel costs.

Annual grant total

In 2014 the charity had an income of £4,100 and a total expenditure of £3,300. We estimate that the amount of grants given to individuals totalled £3,100.

Applications

Apply in writing to the correspondent. Applications can be submitted directly by the individual or through a third party such as a social worker, Citizens Advice, welfare agency or neighbour.

West Lindsey

Willingham and District Relief-in-Sickness Charity

£3,000

Correspondent: Linda Summers, Windyridge, Pilham Lane, Corringham, Gainsborough, Lincolnshire DN21 5RB (01427838705; email: lindasummers@ btinternet.com)

CC number: 512180

Eligibility

People in need who live in the parishes of Corringham, Heapham, Kexby, Springthorpe, Upton or Willingham.

Types of grants

Grants of money or providing or paying for items, services or facilities which help those in need.

Annual grant total

In 2014 the charity had an income of £5,900 and an expenditure of £3,000. We estimate that grants totalled around £3,000.

Applications

Apply in writing to the correspondent by 1 April or 1 October for meetings at the end of those months.

Norfolk

Benevolent Association for the Relief of Decayed Tradesmen, their Widows and Orphans

£5,200

Correspondent: Nicholas Saffell, Administrator, c/o Brown and Co., The Atrium, St George's Street, Norwich, Norfolk NR3 1AB (01603 629871; fax: 01603 616199; email: nick.saffell@brown-co.com)

CC number: 209861

Eligibility

People who are in need and live in Norwich or the parishes of Costessey, Earlham, Hellesdon, Catton, Sprowston, Thorpe St Andrew, Trowse with Newton and Cringleford. Preference is given to those who have carried on a trade in the area of benefit and their dependants.

Types of grants

One-off and recurrent grants are given according to need.

Annual grant total

In 2014/15 the charity had an income of £5,600 and a total expenditure of £5,500. We estimate that the amount of grants given to individuals totalled £5,200.

Exclusions

The charity does not assist with bankruptcy fees.

Applications

Apply in writing to the correspondent.

The Shelroy Trust

£7,300

Correspondent: Jenny Bevan, Grants Manager, Norfolk Community Foundation, St James Mill, Whitefriars, Norwich NR3 1TN (01603 623958; fax: 01603 230036; email: jennybevan@ norfolkfoundation.com)

CC number: 327776

Eligibility

Residents of East Norfolk or Norwich who are in need. It would appear that a considerable proportion of support for individuals is given to assist people who have disabilities.

Types of grants

One-off grants, usually ranging from £200 to £500, to help with a specific need. Hampers are also distributed at Christmas to people who are isolated,

older, bereaved, single parents or are otherwise in need.

Annual grant total

In 2013/14 the trust had assets of £908,500 and an unusually high income of £1.75 million, the vast majority of which was received thanks to a bequest. This was a factor in the trust's unusually high grants total for the year, which amounted to £1.6 million.

The trust principally makes grants to organisations, although in the year it also assisted 19 individuals who have disabilities or who were facing disadvantage and distributed an additional 108 Christmas parcels to individuals in need. Two young people who were carrying out humanitarian projects were also supported. We were unable to determine an exact figure for grants to individuals but estimate that those for social welfare purposes totalled around £7,300.

Exclusions

The trust does not assist with bankruptcy costs.

Applications

Applications can be made in writing to the correspondent at any time. Individuals applying for grants must provide full information and two referees are required. Applications can be made directly by the individual or through a social worker, Citizens Advice or other third party. They are considered at the trustees' quarterly meetings in March, June, September and December. The trust is not able to reply to unsuccessful applicants unless an sae is provided.

Breckland

The Banham Parochial Charities

£5,000

Correspondent: Brian Harper, Trustee, 6 Pound Close, Banham, Norwich NR16 2SY (01953 887008)

CC number: 213891

Eligibility

People in need who live in the parish of Banham.

Types of grants

One-off grants according to need. Grants have been given towards such things as heating bills, fuel, clothing and 'illness needs'.

Annual grant total

In 2014 the charity had an income of £11,600 and a total expenditure of £10,300. We estimate that social welfare grants to individuals totalled £5,000, with grants also awarded to individuals for educational purposes.

Applications

Apply in writing to the correspondent. Applications can be considered at any time.

The East Dereham Relief-in-Need Charity

£2,800

Correspondent: Derek Edwards, Correspondent, Lansdown House, 3 Breton Close, Dereham NR19 1JH (01362 695835; email: dae.air-arch@talktalk.net)

CC number: 211142

Eligibility

People in need who live in East Dereham.

Types of grants

One-off and recurrent grants ranging from £35 to £100 including payments of coal and clothing vouchers.

Annual grant total

In 2013/14 the charity had an income of £29,000 and a total expenditure of £5,800. We estimate that the amount of grants given to individuals totalled £2,800, with funding also awarded to local organisations.

Applications

Apply on a form available from the correspondent, submitted either directly by the individual or through a social worker, Citizens Advice or other welfare agency.

Swaffham Relief in Need Charity

£1,800

Correspondent: Richard Bishop, Town Clerk, The Town Hall, Swaffham, Norfolk PE37 7DQ (01760 722922; email: reliefinneed@swaffhamtowncouncil.gov.uk; website: swaffhamtowncouncil.gov.uk)

CC number: 1072912

Eligibility

People in need who have lived in Swaffham for at least 12 months. In exceptional circumstances, the trustees may decide to aid someone who is resident outside Swaffham or only temporary resident in the area.

Types of grants

Grants have been given for a number of reasons, for example to help with school uniforms, to provide disability access facilities or mobility scooters, towards central heating, to relieve long-term debt

or to assist with basic home start up facilities. Help is given where applicants are in need because of illness or disability, loss of work, emergencies and so on.

Annual grant total

In 2013/14 the charity had an income of £5,300 and a total expenditure of £7,800. We estimate that about £1,800 was given in grants to individuals for social welfare purposes.

Exclusions

Typically, an applicant is eligible for one grant in three years. The website also states: 'The Charity does not exist to copy or replace other forms of assistance for which you may be able to legitimately claim from the State.'

Applications

Application forms are available from the correspondent. The charity may arrange a visit to the applicant as part of the application process and may contact a GP, vicar, priest, or care worker familiar with the applicant's situation. The trustees meet six times a year to consider applications – in January, March, May, July, September and November.

United Eleemosynary Charity (Old Buckenham Charities)

£3,000

Correspondent: Jenny Sallnow, Administrator, Arianne, Attleborough Road, Old Buckenham, Attleborough, Norfolk NR17 1RF (01953 860166)

CC number: 206795

Eligibility

People in need who live in Old Buckenham, Norfolk. Preference for pensioners (over 65) but other groups are also considered.

Types of grants

Normally recurrent grants in coal or cash in lieu for those without coal fires, although other needs may also be addressed. Grants are usually £50 or equivalent and distributed yearly in early December. Cases considered to be of exceptional need may be given more. There is a reserve of money to help those in emergencies throughout the year.

Annual grant total

In 2014 the charity had an income of £5,000 and an expenditure of £3,100. We estimate that around £3,000 was given in grants to individuals.

Applications

Application forms are available from the correspondent, following posted notices around the parish each autumn.

Requests are usually considered in early November and can be submitted either directly by the individual or through a third party, such as any of the trustees. Any relevant evidence of need is helpful, but not essential.

King's Lynn and West Norfolk

The Calibut's Estate and the Hillington Charities

£4,600

Correspondent: William Tawn, Trustee/Chair, 2 Wheatfields, Hillington, King's Lynn, Norfolk PE31 6BH (01485 600641)

CC number: 243510/243511

Eligibility

People in need, usually over the age of 65, who live in Hillington or East Walton.

Types of grants

One-off and recurrent grants, generally ranging from £25 to £100.

Annual grant total

In 2014 the charity had a combined income of £5,100 and a total expenditure of £4,800. We estimate that the amount of grants given to individuals totalled around £4,600.

Income from the charity is divided evenly, with the trustees of the Parish of East Walton receiving one half for distribution to individuals in need, and the trustees of the Parish of Hillington receiving the other.

Exclusions

Owner occupiers are not eligible for support.

Applications

Apply in writing to the correspondent. Applications should be submitted directly by the individual. Applications are considered in November.

The Gaywood Poor's Fuel Allotment Trust

£3,800

Correspondent: Marjorie Lillie, Trustee, 'Edelweiss', Station Road, Hillington, King's Lynn, Norfolk PE31 6DE (01485 600615; email: glno2ac@btinternet.com)

CC number: 209364

Eligibility

Elderly people who are in need and live in the parish of Gaywood in Norfolk.

Types of grants

Grants to help with fuel costs.

Annual grant total

In 2013/14 the charity had an income of £4,400 and a total expenditure of £4,000. We estimate that the amount of grants given to individuals totalled around £3,800.

Applications

Apply in writing to the correspondent through social services.

The Hundred Acre Charity – Dolcoal

£7,000

Correspondent: Ronald Stannard, Correspondent, Riverside Farm, Birchfield Road, Nordelph, Downham Market PE38 0BP (01366 324217; email: ronstannard@waitrose.com)

CC number: 208301

Eligibility

People in need who live in Downham Market, Downham West, Stow Bardolph or Wimbotsham.

Types of grants

Fuel and food vouchers.

Annual grant total

In 2014 the charity had an income of £7,800 and a total expenditure of £7,600 We estimate that the amount of grants given to individuals totalled £7,000.

Applications

Apply in writing to the correspondent, after local advertisements are placed in shops in the village. Applications can be submitted directly by the individual and are usually considered at the end of November.

The King's Lynn and West Norfolk Borough Charity

£12,000

Correspondent: Kathleen Moorhouse, Correspondent, 1 Cedar Court, Rareridge Lane, Bishops Waltham, Hampshire SO23 1DX (01489896366; email: katebeale@hotmail.com)

CC number: 243864

Eligibility

People who live in the borough of King's Lynn and West Norfolk and are in need, hardship or suffer from illness or disability.

Types of grants

One-off grants of up to £300 are available towards, for example, furniture, beds, washing machines, carpets, bedding, cookers, electric scooters and other essentials.

Annual grant total

In 2014 the charity had an income of £9,600 and an expenditure of £13,000. We estimate that grants made to individuals totalled around £12,000.

Exclusions

Grants are not given to relieve public funds.

Applications

Application forms are available from the correspondent. They should be submitted through a social worker, Citizens Advice or other welfare agency. Requests are usually considered in March, June, September and December and should be received in the preceding month.

The Marham Poor's Allotment

£22,000

Correspondent: Wendy Steeles, Trustee, Jungfrau, The Street, Marham, Kings Lynn, Norfolk PE33 9JQ (01760 337286; email: gary@tax.uk.com)

CC number: 236402

Eligibility

People of a pensionable age who are in need and live in Marham village.

Types of grants

One-off vouchers usually of around £35 for food and fuel, to be spent in local shops.

Annual grant total

In 2013/14 the charity had an income of £27,000 and a total expenditure of £25,500. Welfare grants to individuals totalled almost £22,000 and were distributed as follows:

Food vouchers	£15,500
Fuel vouchers	£6,500

Applications

Apply in writing to the correspondent. Applications are considered in October and vouchers distributed in November.

Marshall's Charity

£9,900

Correspondent: Lynda Clarke-Jones, Clerk to the Trustees, The Barn, Main Street, Littleport, Cambridgeshire CB6 1PH (01353 860449; email: littleportpc@btconnect.com)

CC number: 202211

Eligibility

Widows in need who live in the parish of Welney.

Types of grants

Grants of £125 paid quarterly.

Annual grant total

In 2014 the charity held assets of £2.2 million and had an income of £56,000. Quarterly payments to individuals totalled £9,900.

Applications

Apply in writing to the correspondent. The list of recipients is reviewed quarterly.

The Harold Moorhouse Charity

£7,500

Correspondent: Christine Harrison, Trustee, 30 Winmer Avenue, Winterton-on-Sea, Great Yarmouth NR29 4BA (01493 393975; email: haroldmoorhousecharity@yahoo.co.uk)

CC number: 287278

Eligibility

Individuals in need who live in Burnham Market in Norfolk only.

Types of grants

One-off grants are made ranging from £50 to £200 for heating, medical care and equipment, travel to and from hospital, educational equipment and school educational trips.

Annual grant total

Our research suggests that this charity gives around £15,000 to individuals each year, for both educational and welfare purposes.

Applications

Applications can be made in writing to the correspondent. Applications should be submitted directly by the individual in any month.

Sir Edmund de Moundeford Charity

£9,800

Correspondent: Barry Hawkins, The Estate Office, 15 Lynn Road, Downham Market, Norfolk PE38 9NL (01366 387180)

CC number: 1075097

Eligibility

Older individuals who live in Feltwell and are in need.

Types of grants

Grants are given at Christmas for heating. They can also be made to assist residents of the charity's almshouses.

Annual grant total

In 2014 the charity had assets of £6.2 million and an income of £130,000. Grants totalled £19,100, including £5,000 awarded to a local playgroup. Individuals received grants totalling £14,100 for both social welfare and educational purposes. They were distributed as follows:

Fuel grants (Christmas)	£9,600
Student grants	£2,800
School leavers	£1,600
Almshouse tenants	£200

We have not included the figures for educational assistance in our grant total.

Applications

Applications can be made writing to the correspondent either directly by the individual or through an organisation such as Citizens Advice or a school. Applications are considered at meetings held quarterly.

The Northwold Combined Charities and Edmund Atmere Charity

£2,700

Correspondent: Helaine Wyett, Administrator, Pangle Cottage, Church Road, Wretton, King's Lynn PE33 9QR (01366 500165; email: hwyett@tiscali.co. uk)

CC number: 270227

Eligibility

People in need who live in the parish of Northwold.

Types of grants

One-off grants according to need. Aids for people with disabilities are also loaned by the charity.

Annual grant total

In 2014 the charity had an income of £2,900 and a total expenditure of £2,700. We estimate that the total amount of grants awarded to individuals was approximately £2,700.

Applications

The individual should apply directly to the correspondent in writing.

South Creake Charities

£2,600

Correspondent: Sarah Harvey, Clerk, Byanoak, Leicester Road, South Creake, Fakenham, Norfolk NR21 9PW (01328 823391; email: sccharities@hotmail.co. uk)

CC number: 210090

Eligibility

People in need who live in South Creake.

Types of grants

According to our research, mostly recurrent annual grants towards fuel of between £35 and £100 per year are available.

Annual grant total

In 2013/14 the charity had an income of £5,700 and a total expenditure of £5,500. We estimate that grants awarded to individuals for social welfare purposes totalled around £2,600.

Exclusions

Grants are not given to people in work.

Applications

Applications may be made in writing to the correspondent. They can be submitted directly by the individual and are considered in November (any requests should be received before the end of October).

The United Walsoken and Baxter Charities

£7,000

Correspondent: Derek Mews, Clerk, 7 Pickards Way, Wisbech, Cambridgeshire PE13 1SD (01945 587982)

CC number: 205494

Eligibility

Older people in need who have lived in the parish of Walsoken for at least two years.

Types of grants

Small, one-off grants and gifts in kind.

Annual grant total

In 2014 the charity had an income of £10,800 and a total expenditure of £7,800. We estimate that the amount of grants given to individuals totalled £7,000.

Applications

Apply in writing to the correspondent. Applications can be submitted directly by the individual.

North Norfolk

The Blakeney Twelve

£14,000

Correspondent: Christopher Scargill, Trustee, 24 Kingsway, Blakeney, Holt NR25 7PL (01263 741020)

CC number: 276758

Eligibility

Individuals who are older, in ill health or who have disabilities and who live in the parish of Blakeney, Morston or the surrounding district.

Types of grants

One-off and recurrent grants, donations of coal and the payment of insurance.

Annual grant total

In 2013/14 the trust had an income of £18,100 and a total expenditure of £14,400. We estimate that the amount of grants given to individuals totalled £14,000.

Applications

Apply in writing to the correspondent.

The Pentney Charity

£7,800

Correspondent: Emma Greeno, Administrator, 19 Westfields, Narborough, King's Lynn, Norfolk PE32 1SX (email: emmagreeno@aol. com)

CC number: 212367

Eligibility

People over 65 who have lived in the parish of Pentney for the last two years are eligible for fuel grants. Other people in need may also apply for help.

Types of grants

One-off grants of £50 to £150 for fuel costs, travel to and from hospital, funeral expenses, medical expenses, disability equipment, clothing and household bills.

Annual grant total

In 2013/14 the charity had an income of £12,500 and a total expenditure of £16,200. We estimate that the amount of grants given to individuals totalled £7,800, with funding also awarded to local organisations.

Exclusions

No grants are given where help is available from the social services.

Applications

Apply in writing to the correspondent either directly by the individual; through a social worker, Citizens Advice or other welfare agency; or by a third party on behalf of the individual, for example a neighbour or relative. Applications are usually considered twice a year.

Saxlingham United Charities

£5,000

Correspondent: Julie Queen, Correspondent, 22 Henry Preston Road, Tasburgh, Norwich NR15 1NU (01508 470759; email: saxlingham.uc@gmail.com)

CC number: 244713

Eligibility

People who live in the parish of Saxlingham and are in need. Our research suggests that applicants should generally be older people over the age of 70 and must have lived in the parish for at least five years.

Types of grants

Our research indicates that the charity offers recurrent grants for coal and electricity of £50–£100 and one-off grants for widows and widowers.

Annual grant total

In 2013/14 the charity had an income of £9,600 and a total expenditure of £10,100. These are the highest figures in the past five years. We estimate grants for social welfare purposes totalled around £5,000.

Applications

Applications may be made in writing to the correspondent. They can be submitted directly by the individual and are usually considered in October.

Norwich

Norwich Consolidated Charities

£197,500 (319 grants)

Correspondent: David Walker, Clerk to the Trustees, 1 Woolgate Court, St Benedicts Street, Norwich NR2 4AP (01603 621023; email: info@ norwichcharitabletrusts.org.uk; website: www.norwichcharitabletrusts.org.uk)

CC number: 1094602

Eligibility

People on low incomes who are permanent residents of the City of Norwich. Grants are generally only made to those with dependants, unless the application is supported by a social worker.

Types of grants

One-off grants, typically in the range of £50 to £500, are made for welfare purposes. They can be given to help with the purchase of essential household items (cookers, fridges, beds and carpets, for example), taking out a Debt Relief Order, or applying for a personal bankruptcy order.

Annual grant total

In 2014 the charity had assets of £31.8 million and an income of £1.9 million. Grants were made totalling £852,000. Of this amount, £400,000 was awarded to organisations and a further £115,500 to residents of the charity's almshouses, Doughty's, for care charges. A total of 319 grants were made to other individuals amounting to £197,500.

Applications

Applications should be made on a form available from the correspondent. They can be submitted either through a social worker, Citizens Advice, other welfare agency or directly by the individual. Telephone or write to the office to confirm eligibility. Generally, applicants will be asked to attend an interview or will be visited by a representative of the charity.

Norwich Town Close Estate Charity

£120,000

Correspondent: David Walker, Clerk to the Trustees, 1 Woolgate Court, St Benedicts Street, Norwich NR2 4AP (01603 621023; email: info@ norwichcharitabletrusts.org.uk; website: www.norwichcharitabletrusts.org.uk)

CC number: 235678

Eligibility

Freemen of Norwich and their families who are in need.

Types of grants

The charity provides annual pensions as well as one-off grants, generally for 'extraordinary and often unexpected items' as well as general relief in need. Examples may include decorating costs, house repairs, replacement of boiler, carpets, spectacles and dental work. Grants are occasionally given for holiday costs.

Annual grant total

In 2014/15 the charity had assets of £23.3 million and an income of £909,500. Grants were made totalling £842,500, of which about £120,500 was given for welfare purposes. A total of 142 individuals benefitted across all categories. All grants were broken down as follows:

Other bodies	£578,500
Education	£125,500
Pensions	£98,500
Relief in need	£18,500

TV licences	£3,000

Applications

Application forms are available from the correspondent. They are considered throughout the year. Applicants living locally will usually be required to attend an interview.

The website notes: 'Detailed conditions apply to many of these grants – contact us and we can tell you if you are eligible.'

South Norfolk

Diss Parochial Charity

£7,200

Correspondent: Sylvia Grace, Honorary Clerk, 2 The Causeway, Victoria Road, Diss IP22 4AW (01379 650630)

CC number: 210154

Eligibility

People in need who live in the town and parish of Diss.

Types of grants

One-off grants, ranging between £30 and £200, are made for a range of welfare purposes, including bereavement support (usually £150 each), funeral expenses and gifts to bereaved individuals at Christmas.

Annual grant total

In 2014 the charity had assets of £795,000 and an income of £30,000. Awards to individuals were distributed as follows:

Bereavements	£3,800
Individuals	£3,400*
Bereavement Christmas grants	£500

*Previously the majority of grants to individuals have been welfare-related, with a couple of awards made for educational purposes.

An additional £400 was awarded to schools in the area of benefit.

Applications

Applications can be made in writing to the correspondent. They can be made directly by the individual or through a third party, for example DWP, Citizens Advice, Diss Health Centre or Diss Town Hall, and are considered upon receipt.

Suffolk

The Martineau Trust

£30,000

Correspondent: Roger Lay, Clerk, 5 Princethorpe Road, Ipswich, Suffolk IP3 8NY (01473 724951; email: clerk@ martineautrust.org.uk; website: www. martineautrust.org.uk)

CC number: 206884

Eligibility

People living in Suffolk who have incurred expenses as a result of an illness or disability.

Types of grants

The trust makes approximately 100 one-off grants a year. These may cover the whole cost of an item or be a contribution to a larger sum. Grants have been made towards new wheelchairs; transport costs for parents visiting children in hospital; clothing for a cancer patient; a bath-lift; a gas cooker for a family affected by a disability; and a new bed and mattress for a cancer patient. Further examples are available on the trust's website.

Annual grant total

In 2013/14 the trust had an income of £20,500 and a total expenditure of £34,500. We estimate that the amount of grants given to individuals totalled £30,000.

Exclusions

Grants are not normally made for: holidays and breaks for families, childcare costs, alternative treatment therapies, such as acupuncture, normal household running expenses, repayment of debts, retrospective grants, or for anything not relating to an illness or disability.

Applications

Application forms are available from the correspondent or can be downloaded from the website. They must be completed by a suitable third party, such as a social worker, health visitor, nurse, doctor or charity welfare officer.

Mrs L. D. Rope's Second Charitable Settlement

£30,000 (23 grants)

Correspondent: Crispin Rope, Trustee, Crag Farm, Boyton, Near Woodbridge, Suffolk IP12 3LH (01473 333288)

CC number: 275810

Eligibility

People in need, with a preference for people who are resident in Suffolk.

Types of grants

One-off and recurrent grants ranging from £50 to £10,000. Grants are given for the relief of poverty and for the support of religion and education. Almost all grants are made to charities or organisations with which the trust has long-term connections or at the recommendation of members of the late founders' families.

Annual grant total

In 2013/14 the charity made 84 grants totalling £157,000, 23 of which were made to individuals. During this year the charity had a total income of £158,500, an expenditure of £165,000 and assets of £667,000. Grants to individuals including the support of pastoral work in the UK was around £30,000.

Applications

The trust does not invite unsolicited applications.

Babergh

The Charity of Joseph Catt

£3,600

Correspondent: Keith Bales, Trustee, 34 Cattsfield, Stutton, Ipswich IP9 2SP (01473 328179)

CC number: 213013

Eligibility

People in need who live in the parish of Stutton only.

Types of grants

One-off grants and loans are given to help with fuel, hospital travel expenses, convalescent holidays, household goods and clothing.

Annual grant total

In 2014 the charity had an income of £11,300 and a total expenditure of £7,500. Grants are made to individuals for a range of purposes. We estimate that social welfare grants totalled £3,600.

Applications

Applications can be submitted by the individual or through a recognised referral agency (e.g. social worker, Citizens Advice or doctor).

Sudbury Municipal Charities

£2,100

Correspondent: Adrian Walters, Clerk, Longstop Cottage, The Street, Lawshall, Bury St Edmunds IP29 4QA (01284 828219; email: a.walters@sclc.entadsl. com)

CC number: 213516

Eligibility

Older people (generally those over 70) who are in need and live in the borough of Sudbury.

Types of grants

Ascension Day and Christmas gifts, usually in the range of £10 to £30. Grants for special cases of hardship are also available.

Annual grant total

In 2014, the charity had an income of £6,000 and a total expenditure of £4,500. We estimate that the total amount of grants awarded to individuals was approximately £2,100.

Applications

Grants are usually advertised in the local newspaper when they are available.

Forest Heath

George Goward and John Evans

£3,500

Correspondent: Laura Williams, 8 Woodcutters Way, Lakenheath, Brandon, Suffolk IP27 9JQ (07796 018816; email: laurawill@btinternet.com)

CC number: 253727

Eligibility

People who are in need, hardship or distress and live in the parish of Lakenheath, Suffolk.

Types of grants

One-off grants, usually in the range of £25 to £300, can be given according to need.

Annual grant total

In 2014 the charity had an income of £35,500 and a total expenditure of £27,000. At the time of writing (November 2015) the charity's annual report and accounts for the year were not yet available to view on the Charity Commission register. In previous years, we have estimated social welfare grants to individuals to have totalled around £3,500.

Exclusions

Help is not normally given for the relief of public funds.

Applications

Applications can be made in writing to the correspondent. They can be submitted either directly by the individual or through a third party, such as a family member, social worker, teacher, or an organisation, such as Citizens Advice, for example. Applications should generally be submitted by February and August for consideration in March and September, respectively. Candidates should provide brief details of their financial situation and include receipts for the items purchased.

The Mildenhall Parish Charities

£15,000

Correspondent: Vincent Coomber, Clerk, 22 Lark Road, Mildenhall, Bury St Edmunds IP28 7LA (01638 718079)

CC number: 208196

Eligibility

Pensioners, widowers and widows in need who live in the parishes of Mildenhall and Beck Row.

Types of grants

The majority of the charity's giving is achieved through annual payments of £10 per person. One-off cash grants of up to £500 are given towards travelling expenses to hospital, assistance to people who are preparing to enter into a trade or profession. Subscriptions to homes or hostels are also available for people who are infirm or homeless.

Annual grant total

In 2014 the charity had an income of £15,500 and total expenditure of £16,500. Grants of around £15,000 were made to individuals.

Applications

Apply in writing to the correspondent either directly by the individual or through a recognised third party. Applications are considered three times a year.

Ipswich

John Dorkin Charity

£6,500

Correspondent: Jay Harvey, Trustee, Kerseys Solicitors, 20 Back Hamlet, Ipswich, Suffolk IP3 8AJ (email: office@ johndorkincharityipswich.co.uk; website: www.johndorkincharityipswich.co.uk)

CC number: 209635

Eligibility

People in need who live in the ancient parish of St Clement, Ipswich (a map of the area of benefit is provided on the charity's website). Preference for the widows and children of seamen.

Types of grants

One-off cash grants of about £200 towards electrical goods, essential household items and furniture, clothes, holidays, hospital travel costs and so on.

Annual grant total

In 2014, the charity had an income of £12,500 and a total expenditure of £13,600. Taking into account that the charity also gives grants to organisations, we estimate that the total amount of grants awarded to individuals was approximately £6,500.

Exclusions

No grants are given to applicants resident outside the beneficial area.

Applications

Apply in writing to the correspondent at any time, giving details of financial circumstances. Applications can be submitted through a third party such as a social worker, or through an organisation such as Citizens Advice or other welfare agency, and are considered twice a year.

Mid Suffolk

Mendlesham Town Estate Charity

£5,300

Correspondent: Shirley Furze, Clerk, Beggars Roost, Church Road, Mendlesham, Stowmarket, Suffolk IP14 5SF (01449 767770; website: mendlesham.onesuffolk.net)

CC number: 207592

Eligibility

People who are in need and live in the parish of Mendlesham (Suffolk), particularly the elderly and those who are suffering from a sickness or hardship.

Types of grants

One-off grants can be given towards, for example, heating, hospital visiting and associated special needs, including bereavement costs.

Annual grant total

In 2014 the charity had an income of £9,400 and an expenditure of £10,800. We estimate that individual grants totalled around £5,300.

Applications

Apply in writing to the correspondent. Applications can be submitted directly by the individual or through a third party, such as a social worker or Citizens Advice.

The Stowmarket Relief Trust

£68,500 (138 grants)

Correspondent: Colin Hawkins, Correspondent, Kiln House, 21 The Brickfields, Stowmarket, Suffolk IP14 1RZ (01449 674412; email: colinhawkins08@aol.com)

CC number: 802572

Eligibility

People in need who live in the town of Stowmarket and its adjoining parishes including the parish of Old Newton with Dagworth.

Applicants must have approached all sources of statutory benefit. People on Income Support will normally qualify. People in full-time paid employment will not normally qualify for assistance, but there are possible exceptions. People with substantial capital funds are also ineligible.

Types of grants

Normally one-off, but recurrent grants have been given in special circumstances. Recent grants have been made for the purchase and repair of white goods; payment of modest arrears (rent, council tax, electricity, gas, water and telephone charges); payment of bankruptcy fees and debt relief orders; repayments resulting from the overpayment of state benefits; carpets and floor coverings; beds, bedding and household furniture; electric wheelchairs and riser/recliner chairs; living/household expenses; car repairs; medical aids; and, clothing and footwear. Grants generally range from about £15 to £700, although in exceptional circumstances awards may exceed £1,000.

Annual grant total

In 2013/14 the trust had assets of £1.5 million and an income of £68,500. Grants were made to 138 individuals totalling £37,500. A further £500 was awarded to one organisation.

Applications

Application forms are available from the correspondent. Applications should be submitted through a third party such as a social worker, probation officer, Citizens Advice or doctor. Applications are considered at trustee meetings held three times a year, although urgent cases can be dealt with between meetings.

St Edmundsbury

The Pakenham Charities for the Poor

£2,800

Correspondent: Sally Smith, Clerk, 5 St Mary's View, Pakenham, Bury St Edmunds IP31 2ND (01359 232965; email: sally@sallysmithbooks.co.uk; website: www.pakenham-village.co.uk/Main/PakenhamCharities.htm)

CC number: 213314

Eligibility

People in need who live in Pakenham.

Types of grants

Annual fuel grants and one-off payments of around £20 to £1,250 for particular needs. In the past, grants have been awarded for alarms for people who are elderly, disability equipment, medical equipment, hospital expenses, clothing and travel expenses. The charity makes special provision for small annual fuel grants to residents who are older, in ill health or who have disabilities.

Annual grant total

In 2014 the charity had an income of £5,800 and a total expenditure of £5,800. We estimate that the amount of grants given to individuals totalled £2,800, with funding also available for organisations which benefit residents of Pakenham.

Applications

Apply in writing to the correspondent either directly by the individual, through a third party such as a social worker, or through an organisation such Citizens Advice or other welfare agency. Applications are considered in early December and should be received by 30 November.

The Risby Fuel Allotment

£3,000

Correspondent: Penelope Wallis, Trustee, 3 Woodland Close, Risby, Bury St Edmunds IP28 6QN (01284 81064)

CC number: 212260

Eligibility

People in need who live in the parish of Risby.

Types of grants

Annual grants, primarily to buy winter fuel but also for other needs.

Annual grant total

In 2013/14 the charity had an income of £7,300 and a total expenditure of £7,200. Our research tells us that grants are made predominantly for relief-in-need purposes. They are also made to organisations. We estimate that social welfare grants to individuals totalled £3,000.

Exclusions

Applications made by individuals outside the specific area of interest (the parish of Risby) are not acknowledged.

Applications

Apply in writing to the correspondent.

The Stanton Poor's Estate Charity

£4,500

Correspondent: Michael Ronchetti, Trustee, 1 Grundle Close, Stanton, Bury St Edmunds, Suffolk IP31 2DX (01359 251535)

CC number: 235649

Eligibility

People in need who live in the parish of Stanton and are in receipt of means-tested benefits. Grants can be made in special cases of need or hardship outside these criteria at the trustees' discretion.

Types of grants

Grants generally range between £40 and £90, although larger applications may be considered. Applications are considered for both full and part-funding.

Annual grant total

In 2014/15 the charity had an income of £4,800 and a total expenditure of £4,700. We estimate that the amount of grants given to individuals totalled £4,500.

Applications

Apply in writing to the correspondent, for consideration in November.

Suffolk Coastal

Aldeburgh United Charities

£2,800

Correspondent: Lindsay Lee, Administrator, Moot Hall, Market Cross Place, Aldeburgh IP15 5DS (01728 452158; email: aldeburghtc@moothall1.fsnet.co.uk)

CC number: 235840

Eligibility

People in need who live in the town of Aldeburgh. The charity describes its beneficiaries as 'senior citizens, people in specific sensitive situations, young and young minded people and people in the development stage of life's experience'.

Types of grants

One-off and recurrent grants are given according to need.

Annual grant total

In 2014 the charity had an income of £3,300 and an expenditure of £5,900. We estimate that around £2,800 was given in grants to individuals during the year.

Applications

Apply in writing to the correspondent.

The Dennington Consolidated Charities

£2,300

Correspondent: Peter Lamb, Clerk, 2 The Coach House, The Square, Dennington, Woodbridge, Suffolk IP13 8AB (01728 638897; email: peterlamb54@googlemail.com)

CC number: 207451

Eligibility

People in need who live in the village of Dennington.

Types of grants

One-off and repeated grants according to need towards, for example, travel expenses for hospital visiting of relatives, telephone installation for emergency help calls for people who are elderly and infirm, and annual Christmas grants to older people. Grants usually range from £50 to £250.

Annual grant total

In 2014 the charity had an income of £16,700 and a total expenditure of £9,400. Grants are made to individuals for social welfare and educational purposes, and to organisations. We estimate that social welfare grants to individuals totalled £2,300.

Exclusions

The trust does not make loans, nor does it make grants where public funds are available unless they are considered inadequate.

Applications

Apply in writing to the correspondent. Applications are considered throughout the year and a simple means-test questionnaire may be required by the applicant. Grants are only made to people resident in Dennington (a small village with 500 inhabitants). The charities do not respond to applications made outside this specific geographical area.

Dunwich Town Trust

£18,400

Correspondent: Angela Abell, Trustee, The Old Forge, St James Street, Dunwich, Saxmundham, Suffolk IP17 3DU (01728 648107; email: dttchair@btinternet.com; website: www. dunwichtowntrust.org)

CC number: 206294

Eligibility

People in need who live in the parish of Dunwich.

Types of grants

Support with winter fuel costs, care alarms for older and vulnerable people, travelling costs, medical expenses (not covered by the NHS), home help, emergency needs and any other costs to help out in difficult circumstances. Awards can range from £600 to £3,500, depending on need.

Annual grant total

In 2014 the trust had assets of over £2.5 million and an income of £99,500. Grants to individuals totalled about £18,400 and were awarded as follows:

Winter grants	£10,000
General relief	£4,400
Unrestricted fund	£2,600
Contact care alarms	£2,000

No grants were given for welfare purposes in 2014 but they have been made in the past and we anticipate grants being made in the future.

Applications

Application forms can be requested from the correspondent or downloaded online. They should be returned two weeks prior to a meeting of the trustees – dates of these are published on the trust's website.

For winter grants 'the trust does not rely on individual applications, but on a list which is compiled each year using local information and candidates put forward by trustees'.

The Melton Trust

£9,500

Correspondent: Anthony Thompson, Trustee, Melton Rectory, Station Road, Melton, Woodbridge IP12 1PX (07952 992945; email: meltontrust.suffolk@ googlemail.com)

CC number: 212286

Eligibility

The present policy of The Melton Trust is to encourage applications from individuals who are residents of Melton, Suffolk (the Ecclesiastical Parish Boundary, not the present smaller Civil Parish), directly or through support organisations such as Suffolk CC Children's Centre, Citizens Advice, SNAP, Social Services, and also applications from organisations that seek to alleviate or prevent hardship of the residents of Melton, Suffolk.

Types of grants

One-off and recurrent grants are given according to need.

Annual grant total

In 2014 the trust had an income of £11,000 and an expenditure of £9,900. Grants totalled approximately £9,500.

United Charities Town and Poor's Branch

£2,800

Correspondent: David Mantell, Clerk, Rosecroft Farm, Chediston Green, Chediston, Halesworth, Suffolk IP19 0BB (01986 785440; email: dpmantell@gmail. com; website: www.chediston.suffolk. gov.uk)

CC number: 206742

Eligibility

People in need who live in the civil parish of Chediston.

Types of grants

One-off and recurrent grants are given according to need ranging from £5 to £100. Grants are given for alarm systems for older people, hospital transport and as Christmas gifts to all pensioners and children in full-time education.

Annual grant total

In 2013/14 the charity had an income of £3,900 and a total expenditure of £3,100. We estimated that grants totalled £2,800.

Applications

Apply in writing to the correspondent. Applications are considered throughout the year, although mainly in November. The trust has no formal application procedure as requests are usually made personally to the trustees.

Walberswick Common Lands

£3,700

Correspondent: Michelle Webb, Clerk, 7 Adams Lane, Walberswick, Southwold, Suffolk IP18 6UR (01502 725014; email: clerkwclc@gmail.com; website: walberswick.onesuffolk.net/walberswick-common-lands-charity)

CC number: 206095

Eligibility

People in need who live in Walberswick village.

Types of grants

Grants include quarterly payments to individuals, Christmas bonuses and one-off awards of £35–£1,200 towards a range of needs, including gardening, veterinary expenses, domestic appliances, emergency repairs, hospital visiting, telephone rental and television licence payments, access adaptations and travel expenses. Personal loans are also available.

Annual grant total

In 2014 the charity had assets of £253,000 and an income of £165,000. Educational grants to individuals totalled almost £400 and grants for social welfare purposes – £3,700.

Exclusions

Funding is not given for expenses that should be covered by statutory sources (such as benefits) or that could reasonably be expected to be funded from another source (for example, employment or sponsorship).

Applications

Applications should be made in writing to the correspondent. Requests can be made directly by individuals or on their behalf and must include details of the items required and a justification of the request. Consideration may take about two months. Applications are generally considered in February, April, June, August, October and December. Candidates are normally interviewed.

Waveney

Carlton Colville Fuel or Poor's Allotment

£12,000

Correspondent: Keith Vincent, Trustee, 23 Wannock Close, Carlton Colville, Lowestoft, Suffolk NR33 8DW (01493 852411)

CC number: 242083

Eligibility

People in need who live in the ancient parish of Carlton Colville. Preference is given for older people who only receive the basic state pension and have limited savings.

Types of grants

Recurrent grants for fuel and heating costs.

Annual grant total

At the time of writing (November 2015) the latest financial information available was from 2013. In 2013 the charity had an income of £18,000 and a total expenditure of £14,500. We have estimated that around £12,000 was given in grants to individuals.

Applications

Application forms are available from the correspondent. They can be submitted directly by the individual or through a social worker, Citizens Advice or other welfare agency.

Corton Poor's Land Trust

£4,300

Correspondent: Claire Boyne, Administrator, 48 Fallowfields, Lowestoft NR32 4XN (01502 733978; email: claire. murray4@tesco.net)

CC number: 206067

Eligibility

People in need who live in the ancient parish of Corton.

Types of grants

Grants are given for various needs and in Christmas gifts for older people. Previously support has included funding for chiropody treatment, taxi fares to hospital, payment for home alarm installation and rent.

Annual grant total

In 2013/14 the trust had an income of £20,100 and a total expenditure of £8,900. We estimate that the amount of grants given to individuals totalled around £4,300.

Applications

Apply in writing to the correspondent. Applications can be submitted at any time directly by the individual or by an appropriate third party.

Gisleham Relief in Need Charity

£2,700

Correspondent: Elizabeth Rivett, Trustee, 2 Mill Villas, Black Street, Gisleham, Lowestoft, Suffolk NR33 8EJ (01502 743189; email: elizabethrivett@hotmail.co.uk)

CC number: 244853

Eligibility

People in need who live in the parish of Gisleham.

Types of grants

One-off and recurrent grants are given according to need, but usually averaging about £50. Recent grants have been given for household bills, travel expenses and disability aids.

Annual grant total

In 2013/14 the charity had an income of £3,100 and a total expenditure of £2,900. We estimate the grant total given to individuals was approximately £2,700.

Applications

Apply in writing to the correspondent. Applications should be submitted directly by the individual. Applications are considered at any time.

Kirkley Poor's Land Estate

£19,500

Correspondent: Lucy Walker, Clerk to the Trustees, 4 Station Road, Lowestoft, Suffolk NR32 4QF (01502 514964; email: kirkleypoors@gmail.com; website: kirkleypoorslandestate.co.uk)

CC number: 210177

Eligibility

Individuals in need who live in the parish of Kirkley.

Types of grants

One-off grants ranging from £50 to £300. Vouchers of £20 are available to pensioners each winter to help towards the cost of groceries.

Annual grant total

In 2013/14 the charity had assets of over £2 million and an income of £88,000. Grants were made totalling £60,500 and were distributed as follows:

Grants to organisations	£35,500
Grocery voucher scheme	£19,500
Grants to individuals (education)	£5,300

Applications

Applications can be made writing to the correspondent.

Lowestoft Fishermen's and Seafarers' Benevolent Society

£33,000

Correspondent: H. Sims, Secretary, 10 Waveney Road, Lowestoft, Suffolk NR32 1BN (01502 565161; fax: 01502 514382; email: lowestoftfpo@tiscali.co.uk; website: infolink.suffolk.gov.uk/kb5/suffolk/infolink/service.page?id=gRkUDSP_dqM)

Eligibility

Widows, children and dependants of fishermen and seamen lost at sea from Lowestoft vessels, who are in need.

Types of grants

One-off grants have previously been made for funeral costs, mobility aids and household adaptations.

Annual grant total

Grants generally total between £30,000 and £36,000 a year. Both monthly payments and one-off grants are made.

Applications

Apply in writing to the correspondent.

The Reydon Trust

£4,100

Correspondent: H. Freeman, Administrator, 22 Kingfisher Crescent, Reydon, Southwold, Suffolk IP18 6XL (01502 723746; email: h_freeman1@sky.com)

CC number: 206873

Eligibility

People in need who live in the parish of Reydon.

Types of grants

One-off grants towards hospital expenses, clothing, food, travel costs and disability equipment. Vouchers are also given as gifts at Christmas time.

Annual grant total

In 2014/15 the trust had assets of almost £29,000 and an income of almost £27,000. We estimate that one-off welfare grants to individuals totalled £4,100, including £3,700 in Christmas vouchers. Funding was also awarded to local organisations and for educational purposes, with charitable expenditure totalling £22,000.

Applications

Apply in writing to the correspondent. Applications can be submitted either directly by the individual, through a third party such as a social worker or via a doctor or health centre. They are considered upon receipt.

London

General

The Arsenal Foundation

£4,200

Correspondent: Svenja Geissmar, Director and Trustee, Highbury House, 75 Drayton Park, London N5 1BU (020 7704 4000; fax: 020 7704 4001)

CC number: 1145668

Eligibility

People in need including those injured whilst playing sport, or their dependants who live in Greater London, with a preference for Islington and Hackney. The charity also supports the provision of recreational activities to those in need.

Types of grants

Grants and loans according to need.

Annual grant total

In 2012/13 the foundation had assets of £1.3 million and an income of £2.1 million. Grants to individuals totalled £8,300 and are given for both social welfare and educational purposes. We estimate social welfare grants to individuals to have totalled £4,200. A further £492,000 was also given in grants to organisations. At the time of writing (November 2015) the latest accounts available were from 2012/13.

Applications

Apply in writing to the correspondent.

Other information

The foundation has also supported Save the Children's international campaigns to provide emergency disaster relief and educational and recreational opportunities for disadvantaged children in China, West Java and Syria.

BlindAid

See entry on page 74

The Charity of Sir Richard Whittington

£242,000 (213 grants)

Correspondent: Mahvish Inayat, Grants Officer, Worshipful Company of Mercers, Mercers' Hall, Ironmonger Lane, London EC2V 8HE (020 7776 7235; email: mahvishi@mercers.co.uk; website: www.mercers.co.uk/grants-elderly-individuals)

CC number: 1087167

Eligibility

Elderly London residents who are on a low income. Applicants must be over the age of 60, although priority will be given to older and more frail applicants.

Types of grants

Regular grants of £1,140, paid quarterly, mainly for essential household goods.

Annual grant total

In 2013/14 the charity held assets of £85.2 million and had an income of £2.6 million. Grants to 213 individuals totalled £242,000.

A further £308,500 was awarded to organisations.

Applications

Application forms may be requested by contacting the correspondent. The application must be submitted by an appropriate agency, such as social services, a registered charity, member of the clergy, etc., who must also provide a reference. This is followed by a home visit from a member of the Mercers' Company. The charity welcomes enquiries.

Note the following from the charity's website: 'our list of beneficiaries is currently full, so we are adding new applicants to a waiting list for future consideration'.

Other information

The Mercers' Company website provides the following background information on the charity:

> The Charity of Sir Richard Whittington is the amalgamation of both The Charity of

Sir Richard Whittington and Lady Mico's Almshouse Charity.

> The Charity of Sir Richard Whittington was founded in 1424 under the will of Richard Whittington (1354–1423) who was Mayor of London four times and Master of the Mercers' Company three times.

> Lady Mico's Almshouses were founded under the bequest of Lady Jane Mico, widow of Sir Samuel Mico, Alderman and Mercer. In 1690 almshouses for eight elderly women were built opposite St Dunstan's Church, Stepney.

The charity still owns almshouses at Whittington College, Felbridge, Surrey and at Stepney, London.

Cripplegate Foundation

£56,500

Correspondent: Kristina Glenn, Director, 13 Elliott's Place, Islington, London N1 8HX (020 7288 6940; email: grants@cripplegate.org.uk; website: www.cripplegate.org)

CC number: 207499

Eligibility

Residents of the Borough of Islington who are facing exceptional hardship. The Resident Support Scheme (also known as RSS) targets those 'most at risk and vulnerable'. Residents who can apply for a budgeting loan from the Social Fund are expected to apply for a loan before applying to the Resident Support Scheme. Applicants must also be in receipt of specified benefits. Full details of eligibility criteria are available from the Cripplegate Foundation website.

Types of grants

The RSS may be able to assist with, for example: payments for the purchase of essential household items; payments towards a shortfall in rent caused by the bedroom tax, for example; payments for removal expenses; help with living expenses for those affected by crisis or disaster; help managing a council tax bill. In the case of a crisis or disaster, assistance can be given in the form of grocery vouchers or help with help to connect or maintain access to gas or electricity supplies. The scheme does not make cash payments and the form of payment varies depending on the type of assistance.

Annual grant total

In 2014, the foundation had assets of £37 million and a total income of £2.5 million. Grants made to individuals under the foundation's Islington Resident Support Scheme totalled £56,500.

Exclusions

The scheme cannot fund: clothing (except when someone is fleeing their home rapidly, is in a case of disaster such as a flood/fire, or needs help to start work); minor structural repairs; furniture and household items (for those living in private rented furnished accommodation or those placed in furnished temporary accommodation where these are the responsibility of the landlord); specialist disability equipment, adaptations or recliner chairs; wheelchairs or mobility scooters; debts; or funeral expenses.

Note: 'If you have no money because of a failure by Job Centre Plus or the DWP to pay benefit, you cannot apply to the RSS for help.' Instead contact Job Centre Plus for a crisis loan.

Applications

Applications for the Resident Support Scheme can only be made online through designated access points, a list of which is available from the Cripplegate website. Only one application needs to be made to receive assistance from any of the funds.

Other information

From 2 April 2013 Cripplegate Foundation joined with Islington Council to deliver the new Resident Support Scheme, which brought together a number of different funds to help those facing exceptional hardship. These are: discretionary housing payments; payments previously made through the Social Fund by the Department of Work and Pensions (DWP); Islington Council's new welfare provision for council tax relief in exceptional circumstances; and Cripplegate Foundation's former Grants to Resident's Scheme.

Financial assistance is only one way in which the scheme offers support to those most in need. The scheme also aims to help improve the long-term circumstances of the residents it assists, through benefit checks and referrals to specialist services in the fields of money advice, education or employment opportunities, for example. More details are available from the website.

The foundation also works with many local organisations supporting vulnerable residents in the community.

Emanuel Hospital

£64,500 (49 grants)

Correspondent: Clerk to the Trustees, Town Clerk's Office, Corporation of London, PO Box 270, Guildhall, London EC2P 2EJ (020 7332 1399; email: natasha.dogra@cityoflondon.gov.uk; website: www.cityoflondon.gov.uk)

CC number: 206952

Eligibility

People who are of 60 years of age or older, who are in need and who have lived in the London boroughs of Kensington and Chelsea, Hillingdon or Westminster for at least two years.

Types of grants

Pensions of around £1,200 a year are paid in monthly instalments along with a Christmas 'bonus' (£125 per person in 2013/14). One-off grants are also available for essential household items.

Annual grant total

In 2013/14 the charity had assets of £2.2 million and an income of almost £83,000. Grants were made totalling over £64,500, of which £62,500 was given in pensions to 47 beneficiaries and £1,900 in two one-off grants.

Applications

Application forms can be obtained from the City of London website and should be returned along with evidence of income such as benefit award notices, a copy of your birth certificate and two written testimonials confirming your eligibility and need for assistance, at least one of which must be from someone other than a friend or relative. Applications should be submitted directly by the individual.

Other information

The charity publicises its activities and details of pension vacancies in local papers, through welfare agencies and churches within the beneficial areas.

Sir John Evelyn's Charity

£16,000

Correspondent: Colette Saunders, Clerk, Clerk's Office, Armada Court Hall, 21 Macmillan Street, Deptford, London SE8 3EZ (020 8694 8953)

CC number: 225707

Eligibility

People in need who are in receipt of state benefits and live in the ancient parish of St Nicholas and St Luke (Deptford, South East London).

Types of grants

Grants for various needs, for example, household equipment or recuperative holidays. Pensioners are awarded regular payments as well as grants for holidays and outings.

Annual grant total

In 2013 the charity had assets of £2.8 million and an income of £72,000. Grants to individuals totalled £16,000 and were broken down as follows:

Payment to pensioners	£7,600
Pensioner outings and holidays	£5,600
Miscellaneous grants to individuals	£250

The 2013 accounts were the latest available at the time of writing (November 2015).

Applications

Application forms are available from the correspondent. They are considered every two months.

Other information

Organisations and community projects are also supported.

The Hornsey Parochial Charities

£25,000

Correspondent: The Clerk to the Trustees, PO Box 22985, London N10 3XB (020 8352 1601; fax: 020 8352 1601; email: hornseypc@blueyonder.co.uk; website: www.hornseycharities.com)

CC number: 229410

Eligibility

People in need who have lived in the ancient parish of Hornsey in Haringey or in Hackney for at least 12 months. There are maps showing the area of benefit on the charity's website.

Types of grants

Grants are made for clothing, bedding and other essential items, as well as to assist with the costs of heating and lighting.

Annual grant total

In 2014 the charity had an income of £60,000 and a total expenditure of £54,000. At the time of writing (November 2015) the charity's annual report and accounts for the year were not available to view in their entirety. In previous years, we have estimated social welfare grants to individuals to have totalled around £25,000.

Exclusions

Grants cannot be made to individuals living outside the area of benefit.

Applications

Application forms are available to download from the website, where dates of trustees' meetings can also be found. Forms should be completed and returned to the correspondent.

Other information

Grants are also made for educational purposes and to organisations.

Mary Minet Trust

£14,000

Correspondent: The Mary Minet Trust, PO Box 53673, London SE24 4AF (07906 145 199; email: admin@maryminettrust. org.uk)

CC number: 212483

Eligibility

People who are living with a disability, sickness or infirmity and reside in the boroughs of Southwark or Lambeth.

Types of grants

One-off grants towards convalescence holidays, disability aids, medical equipment and household items such as washing machines, fridges, cookers, essential furniture, carpets, clothing, beds and bedding.

Annual grant total

In 2013/14 the trust had an income of £15,000 and a total expenditure of £14,500. We estimate that the amount of grants given to individuals totalled £14,000.

Applications

Applications for individuals are invited from sponsoring organisations, social workers, housing officers and other involved professionals. Applications should be made on the trust's application form, available by contacting the trust by email or telephone. Payments are made to the sponsoring organisation to ensure that the money is spent appropriately, and are paid by BACS transfer. Applications from families and friends, interested parties or the individual in need will be considered only in exceptional circumstances and supporting information will be required. Applications are considered quarterly.

The Saint George Dragon Trust

£8,200

Correspondent: Di Emmerson, Trustee, 12 Lindsay Close, Epsom, Surrey KT19 8JJ (0777 963 6677; email: di. emmerson1@gmail.com)

CC number: 275674

Eligibility

People in need who live in Greater London and are moving, or have recently moved, from supported housing into independent accommodation.

Types of grants

One-off grants ranging from £100 to £400 for buying essential household equipment and furniture. Small grants of £50 to £100 are also available for the purchase of essential items following a move. Applicants should not be eligible for a Community Care grant or support from the Social Fund and have only minimal resources. (A rare exception may be where a very low Community Care grant has been awarded – see Applications section.)

Annual grant total

In 2013/14 the trust had an income of £8,100 and a total expenditure of £8,700. We estimate that the amount of grants given to individuals totalled £8,200.

Exclusions

Grants are not made to students or to 'able young people'.

Applications

Apply in writing, through a social, housing or welfare worker. Applications should be typed, wherever possible, and should be made on headed notepaper of the organisation through which the application is being made. Guidance can be obtained by emailing: SGDT@barraball.com.

ScotsCare

£386,500 (900+ grants)

Correspondent: Willie Docherty, Chief Executive, 22 City Road, London EC1Y 2AJ (020 7240 3718; email: info@ scotscare.com; website: www.scotscare. com)

CC number: 207326

Eligibility

Scottish people, and their children and widows, who are in need, hardship or distress and live within a 35-mile radius of Charing Cross. Beneficiaries are usually in receipt of state benefits.

Types of grants

As well as giving weekly allowances (£87 per month) to people over the age of 60 who are on low incomes, ScotsCare also gives support on a one-off basis to help with, for example: essential household items; family trips at Christmas and in summer; and children's items, such as clothing and school uniforms.

Annual grant total

In 2013/14 the charity had assets of £45.6 million and an income of more than £2 million. Grants to individuals amounted to £417,000, of which we believe £386,500 was for social welfare purposes.

Exclusions

No grants are made for debts or for items that have already been purchased.

Applications

There is an online ScotsCare application request form on the website. Alternatively, call the Freephone helpline on 0800 652 2989; the ScotsCare team is there to give advice from Monday to Thursday 9am-5pm and on Friday 9am-4pm.

Other information

In addition to making grants, ScotsCare also offers a range of services for beneficiaries in the areas of advocacy, employment and training, families, health, housing, money management, mental health, socialising and substance misuse.

Society for the Relief of Distress (SRD)

£19,000

Correspondent: Caroline Armstrong, Honorary Treasurer, 21 Hartswood Road, London W12 9NE (website: www. reliefofdistress.org.uk)

CC number: 207585

Eligibility

People in need who live in one of the London boroughs.

Types of grants

One-off grants, usually of up to £150 (average grant around £95), for 'relieving distress'. Grants may be given towards essential household items, clothing and similar needs. Payments are made to the applicant body, not the individual.

Annual grant total

In 2014 the society had an income of £21,000 and an expenditure of £19,500. We estimate that about £19,000 was awarded in grants.

Exclusions

Grants are very rarely given towards general financial support, holidays, further education or debt repayment.

Applications

Applications must be made through a social worker, Citizens Advice, registered charity, NHS, church or similar organisation. Requests submitted by individuals will not be considered. Grants are considered throughout the year, normally on the third Wednesday of each month (except August) and applications should be received up to 48 hours before a meeting. There is no formal application form, instead the following information needs to be supplied: name, address and date of birth of the individual; a concise summary of personal circumstances and financial position (including benefits received); particular items needed or expenses to be incurred; other sources of funding secured or applied to; and any other relevant or special circumstances.

The South London Relief-in-Sickness Fund

£6,000

Correspondent: Ozu Okere, Clerk, Room 111, Town Hall, Wandsworth High Street, London SW18 2PU (020 8871 6035; fax: 020 8871 6036; email: ookere@wandsworth.gov.uk; website: www.wandsworth.gov.uk)

CC number: 210939

Eligibility
People in need through disability or ill health who live in the boroughs of Lambeth and Wandsworth.

Types of grants
One-off grants of up to £300, towards, for example, furniture, furnishings, clothing, holidays and medical equipment.

Annual grant total
In 2014 the fund had an income of £13,800 and a total expenditure of £13,100. We estimate that the amount of grants given to individuals totalled £6,000, with funding also awarded to organisations.

Exclusions
No grants are given towards taxes or debts.

Applications
Application forms are available to download from the charity's website. Applications should be made through a social worker, Citizens Advice or other welfare agency. Requests are considered quarterly (normally in March, June, September and December). Full guidelines are available from the correspondent.

St John Southworth Fund

£2,100

Correspondent: Mary Gandy, Grants Administrator, Caritas Westminster, Vaughan House, 46 Francis Street, London SW1P 1QN (020 7798 9063; email: caritasgrants@rcdow.org.uk; website: rcdow.org.uk/caritas/st-john-southworth-fund)

CC number: 233699

Eligibility
People in need in in Hackney, Tower Hamlets and Islington Deaneries. The fund is hoping to cover more of the Diocese of Westminster in the near future.

Types of grants
One-off grants of around £500 to assist those in poverty, in danger of homelessness, with disabilities, and so on.

Annual grant total
In 2014 the fund made grants to individuals totalling £2,100. However during this period the fund was being re-organised and therefore not accepting any new applications. In previous years the fund has made grants to individuals totalling around £55,000. The fund re-opened in Easter 2015 and is accepting applications on a rolling basis.

Applications
Contact the correspondent or your local priest for further information.

Other information
Note: The website www.rcdow.org.uk states:

> Established in 2007, the St John Southworth Fund has supported the work of parishes, organisations and projects across a range of issues including poverty, homelessness, old age and infirmity and children with disabilities or in danger of deprivation; it also gives grants direct to individuals.
>
> The Fund is not a separate charity but is part of Westminster Diocese. It was created by the amalgamation of a large number of existing legacies and trusts held within the Diocese, some dating back as far as the 19th century. However, with the creation of Caritas Westminster as the social action agency for the Diocese, the St John Southworth Fund now comes under the Caritas umbrella. Its operational procedures are therefore being changed to address poverty and deprivation more effectively in partnership with the ongoing development of Caritas Westminster.
>
> While these changes are taking place, grant giving has been suspended and no new applications are currently being accepted. Further information about the changes and when applications may re-open will be given [on the fund's website] as soon as they are known.

Barnet

The Mayor of Barnet's Benevolent Fund

£12,400

Correspondent: Ken Argent, Grants Manager, The London Borough of Barnet, Building 4, North London Business Park, Oakleigh Road South, London N11 1NP (020 8359 2020; email: ken.argent@barnet.gov.uk; website: www.barnet.gov.uk/citizen-home/council-tax-and-benefits/grants-and-funding/grants-for-individuals.html)

CC number: 1014273

Eligibility
People who are on an income-related statutory benefit (such as Income Support or Child Tax Credit), have lived in the London borough of Barnet for at least a year and are in need, hardship or distress. Children, young people, older people and individuals with disabilities are particularly supported.

Types of grants
Small, one-off grants of up to £200 are given towards essential household items, appliances (for example, cooker, refrigerator or washing machine), furnishing or equipping a new property, children and baby necessities, clothing items for adults where there is an exceptional need, small, one-off debts (such as telephone bills), the cost of school uniforms (up to £60) and for any other necessities arising from an unforeseen financial crisis. Up to two awards per applicant are provided.

Annual grant total
In 2013/14 the fund had an income of £15,700 and a total expenditure of £15,400. Both figures are the highest in the past five years. Most support is given in relief-in-need grants; therefore, we estimate that welfare grants to individuals totalled around £12,400.

Applications
Applications have to be made in writing to the correspondent via post or email. Applications can be submitted directly by the individual or through a third party, such as a social worker, health visitor or an advice agency. Candidates should provide full details of their name, address, contact number, confirmation and length of residence in the borough, number and ages of the family members, family income, a proof of entitlement to a benefit, a summary of the applicant's circumstances, details of support requested, a quotation for any items required and information on other sources of funding approached. Consideration takes about a month and

the outcome is communicated by a letter. Payments are not made to the applicant directly, but to the school or supplier.

Other information

Grants are also given for school uniforms.

The Finchley Charities

Correspondent: Jean Field, Office Manager, 41A Wilmot Close, East Finchley, London N2 8HP (020 8346 9464; fax: 020 8346 9466; email: info@ thefinchleycharities.org; website: www. thefinchleycharities.org)

CC number: 206621

Eligibility

People in need who live in the former borough of Finchley.

Types of grants

One-off grants only.

Annual grant total

In 2014 the charity had an income of £1.4 million and a total expenditure of £990,000. The amounts given to individuals was not specified; however our research suggests that grant-making to individuals is sporadic and often limited to modest sums.

Exclusions

Grants are not made for educational purposes.

Applications

Apply in writing to the correspondent either directly by the individual or through a social worker, Citizens Advice or other welfare agency. Applications must include details of the amount being asked for and the reason for the application.

Other information

The charity's main concern is the provision of 156 flats for people in Finchley aged 55 and over who have insufficient funds to purchase their own property and have been resident in the London borough of Barnet for at least five years.

Awards are made to local churches and organisations helping people in the area of benefit.

Jesus Hospital Charity

£6,600

Correspondent: Simon Smith, Administrator, Ravenscroft Lodge, 37 Union Street, Barnet, Hertfordshire EN5 4HY (020 8440 4374; email: info@ jesushospitalcharity.org.uk; website: www.jesushospitalcharity.org.uk)

CC number: 1075889

Eligibility

People in need who live in the former district of Barnet, East Barnet and Friern Barnet.

Types of grants

One-off grants between £100 and £1,000 towards, for example, Lifeline rentals, winter clothing, shoes, food vouchers, fridges/freezers, beds, gas cookers and utensils for single parent families and couples living on low incomes; and holidays for people with disabilities.

Annual grant total

In 2014 the charity held assets of £11.3 million and had an income of £627,500. Relief-in-need grants to individuals totalled £6,600, of which £5,200 was given to residents of the charity's almshouses and £1,400 to other individuals.

A further £34,500 was given in grants to organisations.

Applications

Application forms can be downloaded from the charity's website. Applications are considered by the trustees who meet every other month. Applicants may be visited by the clerk.

Other information

The charity maintains 54 almshouses in the Chipping Barnet and Monken Hadley area.

Eleanor Palmer Trust

£17,500

Correspondent: Fred Park, Clerk to the Trustees, 106b Wood Street, Barnet, Hertfordshire EN5 4BY (020 8441 3222; email: info@eleanorpalmertrust.org.uk; website: www.eleanorpalmertrust.org.uk)

CC number: 220857

Eligibility

People in need who live in the former urban districts of Chipping Barnet and East Barnet, This includes those living within the postal codes of EN4, EN5 N11 and N14. Applicants must have lived within the area for at least two years prior to the submission of your application.

Types of grants

One-off grants of up to £1,000 towards, for example, carpets, furniture and clothing. Items or services are purchased directly from the supplier. No cash grants are made.

Annual grant total

In 2013/14 the trust held assets of £4.6 million and had an income of £1.6 million. Grants from the trust's relief-in-need fund totalled £62,000 with £44,500 given to organisations and £17,500 given to individuals.

Other grants amounting to £14,500 were awarded to elderly residents of homes managed by the trust.

Exclusions

No grants are available towards educational purposes, bankruptcy fees, medical costs, taxes or debts.

Applications

Application forms are available from the correspondent. Applications are considered every two months. Applications should include details of the applicant's circumstances and income, the items or service required, and details of any other local charities to which the applicant has applied for assistance. The clerk visits applicants in order to assess need if this has not been done recently by a local charity.

Other information

The trust is named after Eleanor Palmer and was founded through the charitable bequest she made in 1558, just months before Queen Elizabeth I was crowned Queen of England.

The trust concentrates on running almshouses and a residential home for older people.

The Valentine Poole Charity

£37,500

Correspondent: Victor Russell, Clerk, Forum Room, Ewen Hall, Wood Street, Barnet, Hertfordshire EN5 4BW (020 8441 6893; email: vpoole@btconnect. com; website: www.valentinepoole.org. uk)

CC number: 220856

Eligibility

People in need who live in the former urban districts of Barnet and East Barnet (approximately the postal districts of EN4 and EN5).

Types of grants

One-off grants are given towards essential items such as household goods, children's clothing, travel and food costs. Pensions of £120 to £150 a month are made to older people. Christmas grants are also made to families at Christmas.

Annual grant total

In 2014 the charity had assets of £645,500 and an income of £67,500. Grants totalled £47,500. During the year, £26,500 was paid in pensions to older people and Christmas grants to 25 families totalled £2,400. Grants totalling £10,600 were also made to individuals. We believe the majority of these were made for relief-in-need purposes and we estimate that around £2,000 was given for the 'advancement of life'. In all, we estimate that the amount of grants given to individuals for social welfare purposes amounted to £37,500. A further £8,000 was paid in grants to organisations.

Applications

Application forms are available from the correspondent and are considered in March, July and November. Applications should be submitted by a social worker, Citizens Advice or other third party or welfare agency, not directly by the individual.

Bexley

Bexley Mayor's Benevolent Fund

£2,000

Correspondent: Dave Easton, Administrator, Mayors Office, London Borough of Bexley, Civic Offices, 2 Watling Street, Broadway, Bexleyheath, Kent DA6 7LB (020 3045 3678; email: mayors.office@bexley.gov.uk)

Eligibility

People in need who live in the borough of Bexley.

Types of grants

Grants, usually in the range of £50 to £100, for a variety of needs (for example towards an electric wheelchair for an individual with disabilities and to buy new clothes for an older person whose home had been damaged in a fire). There can be an immediate response in emergency cases.

Annual grant total

An exact grant total figure was not available but is usually around £2,000 per year.

Applications

Apply in writing to the correspondent. In practice, many applications are referred by the council's social services department who also vet all applications from individuals. Applications can be submitted at any time.

Bromley

Bromley Relief-In-Need Charity

£300

Correspondent: Revd Anne Jablonski, Trustee, 9 St Pauls Square, Bromley BR2 0XH (email: vicar@ bromleyparishchurch.org; website: bromleyrelief.weebly.com)

CC number: 262591

Eligibility

People in need who live in the ancient borough of Bromley, although there is some discretion to make grants within the wider area of the modern borough of Bromley.

Types of grants

One-off grants of up to £300. Grants have previously been made for purposes including bedding, decorating costs, travel costs, disability equipment and so on.

Annual grant total

In 2013 the charity had an income of £2,500 and a total expenditure of £400. We estimate that the total amount of grants awarded to individuals was approximately £300.

At the time of writing (November 2015) the information provided was the latest available.

Applications

Applications should be made on a form available to download from the website or from the correspondent. All applications must be made through a professional third party, such as social worker, health worker, religious leader, other welfare organisation and so on.

The Hayes (Kent) Trust

£9,300 (23 grants)

Correspondent: Andrew Naish, Trustee, 2 Warren Wood Close, Bromley BR2 7DU (020 8462 1915; email: hayes. kent.trust@gmail.com)

CC number: 221098

Eligibility

People in need who live in the parish of Hayes.

Types of grants

One-off grants, in the region of £75–£1,500, are given according to need.

Annual grant total

In 2014/15 the trust had assets of over £1 million and an income of £49,000. Grants were awarded totalling £35,500, of which £16,500 was given to 28 individuals, allocated as follows:

Relief in need	22	£8,900
Advancement of education	5	£6,900
Relief in sickness	1	£400

The trust also awarded £19,500 to 12 organisations: £10,600 for educational purposes (five organisations); £8,000 for relief in sickness (five organisations); and £700 for relief-in-need purposes (two organisations).

Applications

Applications can be made in writing to the correspondent. They should include the full name of the applicant, postal address in Hayes (Kent), telephone number, email, date of birth, and details of why support is required. Applications may include any supporting information and can be made at any time either directly by the individual or through a third party, such as a social worker, Citizens Advice or other welfare agency.

Other information

The trust is an amalgamation of the following charities: The Poors Land Cottage Charity; The Poors Land Eleemosynary Charity; The Hayes (Kent) Educational Foundation.

Camden

Hampstead Wells and Campden Trust

£275,000 (3,284 grants)

Correspondent: Sheila Taylor, Director and Clerk, 62 Rosslyn Hill, London NW3 1ND (020 7435 1570; fax: 020 7435 1571; email: grant@hwct.co.uk; website: www.hwct.org.uk)

CC number: 1094611

Eligibility

People who are sick, convalescent, disabled, infirm or in conditions of need, hardship or distress and who live in the former metropolitan borough of Hampstead. Grants to individuals, whether one-off payments or pensions, can only be made to residents of the former Metropolitan Borough of Hampstead (the area of benefit, a map of which is available on the website). A temporary stay in Hampstead, or in hospital in the area is not in itself a sufficient qualification.

Types of grants

In addition to pensions (£15 per week at the time of writing), one-off grants of up to £1,000 are given for a range of purposes including holidays, clothing, help with debts, removals and transport, furniture, gas, electric, fuel, TV and telephone bills and medical purposes. Kitchen starter packs and birthday and Christmas hampers are also given.

Annual grant total

In 2013/14 the trust had assets of £16.4 million and an income of £554,000. A total of 3,187 grants were made to individuals for social welfare purposes, totalling £199,500, in addition to 97 pensions, totalling £75,500.

Organisations were awarded 155 grants, amounting to £231,000, whilst ten educational grants to individuals totalled a further £2,600.

Exclusions

Grants are not made for: the payment of taxes, including council tax; the payment of fines; course or school fees.

Applications

Applications are accepted on behalf of individuals and families from any local constituted group, departments/units of Camden Council or the health service, a housing association, advice agency or other voluntary agency where the individual or family is known. The applying organisation must be willing to receive and account for any grant offered. The trust prefers to receive applications via the appropriate forms, which are available to download from the website; however, it also accepts applications in letter form. There is a list of essential information which must be included in any letter application on the website. The trust's website also gives the following advice: 'The application will be strengthened if details are given of the financial effects of disability on any member of the household.'

Other information

The trust's website lists additional eligibility criteria for individuals wishing to apply for a pension.

St Andrew Holborn Charities

£133,500

Correspondent: Anna Paterson, Grants Officer, 5 St Andrew Street, London EC4A 3AB (020 7583 7394; email: charity@standrewholborn.org.uk; website: www.standrewholborn.org.uk)

CC number: 1095045

Eligibility

People in need resident in a defined area of Holborn (applicants should call the charity or check the website for confirmation of the beneficial area). The charity's website states: 'Only applicants living off a low disposable income will be considered i.e. those on jobseekers allowance, income support, Disability Living Allowance.' In the case of annual awards, an applicant's savings will be taken into consideration.

Types of grants

One-off grants of up to £500 are given towards household items and clothing. Annual awards, which in 2014 were awarded in two £350 instalments in May and November, are given to older people, people who have long-term illness or chronic disabilities, and young widows and widowers who have children.

Annual grant total

In 2014 the charity had assets of £10.7 million and an income of £382,000. Grants totalled £292,000, of which £167,000 was given to individuals. Annual awards to 144 individuals amounted to £100,500 and we estimate social welfare grants to individuals to have totalled an additional £33,000.

Exclusions

Grants are not made for holidays apart from in exceptional circumstances.

Applications

Application forms can be downloaded from the website, where guidelines can also be found. Following the submission of an application, applicants will be visited by the charity's Grants Officer, who will discuss the application and produce a report for the trustees. Two trustees will then consider the application and the Grants Officer will inform the applicant of their decision. The majority of applications take 21 days. Only one application may be considered per individual in a twelve-month period, and only two per individual in a three-year period.

The website gives the following additional information: 'All grants for household items will be bought from Argos in Grays Inn Road or from IKEA, unless the applicant is known to other agencies i.e. Housing Support, a Housing Association etc. when a cheque can be made out to that organisation.'

Other information

This charity is the result of an amalgamation of three trusts: The City Foundation, The Isaac Duckett's Charity and The William Williams Charity. Grants are also given to organisations.

St Giles-in-the-Fields and Bloomsbury United Charity

£900 (9 grants)

Correspondent: Pam Nicholls, Clerk to the Trustees, The Rectory, 15A Gower Street, London WC1E 6HW (020 7323 1992; email: pam.nicholls@london.anglican.org; website: www.stgilescharities.org.uk)

CC number: 1111908

Eligibility

People in need who live in the ancient parishes of St Giles in the Fields and St George's Bloomsbury. A map of the area of benefit is available on the website. In exceptional cases, the trustees may assist an individual outside the area of benefit.

Types of grants

One-off grants, towards the purchase of white goods, furniture, bedding, clothing, medical equipment and to cover the costs of restorative holidays.

Annual grant total

In 2014 the charity had an income of £42,500 and assets of almost £1.6 million. Grants to individuals, including annuities, totalled £900, although more has been given in previous years.

Applications

At the time of writing (November 2015), the website states the following information: 'Please be advised that we are temporarily unable to accept ANY new applications from individuals seeking financial support or organisations seeking small grants. We hope to resume grant making later in 2015.'

Applicants should check the website or contact the charity for updated information.

Other information

The charity also provides almshouse accommodation, consisting of eight flats, for women over the age of 60 in the Covent Garden area.

The St Pancras Welfare Trust

£29,000 (214 grants)

Correspondent: John Knights, Secretary to the Trustees, St Pancras Welfare, PO Box 51764, London NW1 1EA (020 7267 8428; email: thesecretary@spwt.org.uk; website: www.spwt.org.uk)

CC number: 261261

Eligibility

People in need or who are sick, convalescent, disabled or infirm who live in the old Metropolitan Borough of St Pancras (postal districts NW5, most of NW1, parts of N6, N19 NW3 and WC1). If you are unsure of whether you live in a qualifying area you can check using the street directory on the trust's website. Applicants must have the support of a sponsoring agency. The trust does not accept direct applications.

Types of grants

One-off grants, typically between £100 and £300, for a wide range of needs. Grants may be in the form of cash or vouchers.

Annual grant total

In 2013/14 the trust held assets of almost £777,000 and had an income of £37,000. Grants to individuals totalled £29,000. The trust's grant-making activities benefitted in all at least 194 children and 233 adults.

Exclusions

No grants are made for educational purposes, computers, utility bills, statutory payments or rent arrears.

Applications

Apply on an application form available from the trust's website, with an accompanying cover letter. The trustees will only consider applications made through statutory bodies such as social services or community organisations like Citizens Advice. Applications are considered in March, June, September and December and should be received two weeks prior to the meeting.

Other information

According to the trustees' annual report for 2013/14:

> During the year ending March 2014 the trustees received 94 eligible applications of which 91 were supported. A further 123 applications were made to our Christmas/ winter voucher programme that aims to reach the neediest families when the pressure on budgets is most severe. Three applications were received from projects seeking help in areas of work that complement the aims of the trust.

The trust occasionally makes small grants of less than £1,000 to local organisations.

Stafford's Charity

£66,500 (95+ grants)

Correspondent: Anna Paterson, Grants Officer, 5 St Andrew Street, London EC4A 3AB (020 7583 7394; email: stafford@standrewholborn.org.uk or charity@standrewholborn.org.uk; website: www.standrewholborn.org.uk/charities)

CC number: 206770

Eligibility

People in need who have lived in the Holborn locality, centred on the ancient parish of St Andrew Holborn now comprising of the guild church of St Andrew Holborn and the parishes of St George the Martyr, Queen Square and St Alban the Martyr Holborn for at least three years (a map of the area of benefit is provided on the charity's website). Applicants must be living off a low disposable income (such as those on jobseekers allowance, income support, Disability Living Allowance, etc.).

Preference may be given to the elderly, chronically disabled and long-term sick of any age (evidence of disability is required) and young widows or widowers with children.

Types of grants

Annual awards for people on a low income (less than £75 a week for a single person, or less £120 for a couple). In 2014, annual awards were £700 each, paid in two instalments of £350 in May and November. One-off grants are also available to people on a low income for kitchen appliances, furnishings, carpets, medical equipment, clothing, redecoration costs and other household items or needs.

Annual grant total

In 2014 the charity had assets of £6.7 million and an income of £216,000. The charity awarded grants to individuals totalling £66,500, consisting of £65,500 in annual awards to 95 beneficiaries and £815 in one-off grants. A further £28,500 was given in grants to organisations.

Exclusions

No new application will be considered unless a year has elapsed since the last one and no grants are given for holidays (unless in exceptional circumstances).

The recipients of annual award will lose the entitlement if they move into a residential home. Individuals will also lose their annual award if they move outside the area of benefit.

Applications

Application forms are available to download from the website or can be requested from the correspondent. Applications can be submitted at any time. All new applicants are visited by the Grants Officer.

Other information

Note the following information from the charity's website: 'All grants for household items will be bought from Argos in Grays Inn Road or from IKEA, unless the applicant is known to other agencies i.e. Housing Support, a Housing Association etc. when a cheque can be made out to that organisation.'

City of London

The Aldgate Freedom Foundation

£16,200

Correspondent: Michael Sonn, Administrator, 140 Hall Lane, Upminster, London RM14 1AL (01708 222482)

CC number: 207046

Eligibility

Older people, generally aged over 65, who are in need and live in the parish of St Botolph without Aldgate or the area to the boundary of the Portsoken ward.

Types of grants

Our research suggests that one-off and recurrent grants of £200 a year, plus a £30 Christmas gift, are available, as well as relief-in-need grants.

Annual grant total

In 2014 the foundation had assets of £1.7 million and an income of £45,500. Grants to individuals, including Christmas bonuses, totalled £16,200.

Applications

Application forms are available from the correspondent. They can be submitted directly by the individual, through a social worker, Citizens Advice or through a councillor or an alderman. Details of income/capital/expenditure and length of residence in the parish must also be included. Requests for support can be considered at any time.

Other information

Grants are also given to organisations or hospitals within the city and towards the maintenance of St Botolph's church.

The Mitchell City of London Charity

£16,800 (26 grants)

Correspondent: Lucy Jordan, Clerk to the Trustees, Ash View, High Street, Orston, Nottingham NG13 9NU (0845 600 1558; email: mitchellcityoflondon@gmail.com)

CC number: 207342

Eligibility

Individuals of state pension age who are in need and who live or work, or have lived or worked, in the City of London for at least five years. Widows of men so qualified may also apply.

Types of grants

Pensions, which in 2013/14 were paid at £400 per annum, in quarterly sums of £100. Gifts are also given at Christmas (£150) and on the Queen's birthday (£75).

Annual grant total

In 2013/14 the charity held assets of £1.9 million and had an income of £77,000. Pensions and welfare grants totalled £16,800, to the benefit of 26 older individuals.

Applications

Application forms are available from the correspondent and should include details of the applicant's income and expenditure. Applications can be submitted directly by the individual or through an organisation such as Citizens Advice. They are considered in March, June, September and November.

Other information
The charity is one half of the Mitchell City of London Charity and Educational Foundation. The Educational Foundation also makes grants.

City of Westminster

The Charity of A. J. G. Cross

£6,800

Correspondent: Michael Horsley, Administrator, 4 Chester Square, London SW1W 9HH (020 7730 8889)

CC number: 210466

Eligibility
People who are sick and in need and live in South Westminster (i.e. south of Oxford Street).

Types of grants
One-off grants of up to £150 for purposes including heating costs, clothing, holidays and furnishings.

Annual grant total
In 2013/14 the charity had an income of £7,200 and a total expenditure of £7,100. We estimate that the amount of grants given to individuals totalled £6,800.

Exclusions
No grants are given towards arrears.

Applications
Application forms are available from the correspondent. Applications should be submitted through a third party such as a social worker. The charity does not deal directly with the individual.

The Hyde Park Place Estate Charity (Civil Trustees)

£8,300

Correspondent: Shirley Vaughan, Clerk, St George's Hanover Square Church, The Vestry, 2a Mill Street, London W1S 1FX (020 7629 0874; email: hpppec@ stgeorgeshanoversquare.org; website: www.stgeorgeshanoversquare.org)

CC number: 212439

Eligibility
People in need who are residents of the City of Westminster.

Types of grants
One-off grants, usually in the range of £50 and £500, to individuals and families for all kinds of need, including those of an educational nature.

Annual grant total
In 2013/14 the charity had assets of £12.9 million and an income of £498,000. Grants totalled £154,000, of which £16,600 was awarded to around 120 individuals. The charity makes grants for both social welfare and educational purposes. We estimate that the amount of grants given to individuals for social welfare purposes totalled around £8,300.

Exclusions
Our research indicates that refugees and asylum seekers are not eligible.

Applications
All applications should be made through a recognised third party/organisation and include a case history and the name, address and date of birth of the applicant. Applications are considered on an ongoing basis.

Strand Parishes Trust

£24,900

Correspondent: Frank Brenchley-Brown, Clerk to the Trustees, 169 Strand, London WC2R 2LS (020 7836 3205; email: sptwestminster@aol.com)

CC number: 1121754

Eligibility
People who live and/or work in the London borough of the City of Westminster, with preference for the parish of St Clement Danes and St Mary le Strand.

Types of grants
One-off grants and pensions.

Annual grant total
In 2014 the trust had assets of £6.5 million and an income of £202,000. Pensions were made to 40 individuals totalling £24,100 and a further £750 was given in grants to four individuals.

A further £163,000 was made in grants to organisations.

Exclusions
No grants are given for expeditions, electives, non-residents of Westminster or asylum seekers.

Applications
Application forms are available from the correspondent. Applications must be made through a sponsoring organisation i.e. social services or Citizens Advice.

Other information
The Isaac Duckett's Charity, St Mary le Strand Charity and St Clement Danes Parochial Charities were amalgamated with other charities to form the Strand Parishes Trust.

The United Charities of St Paul's, Covent Garden

£4,000

Correspondent: Maggie Rae, Flat 9, 19 Henrietta Street, London WC2E 8QH (020 7379 6080; email: mrae@clintons. co.uk)

CC number: 209568

Eligibility
People in need who live in the city of Westminster.

Types of grants
One-off grants ranging from £50 to £120. Grants can be paid directly or through hospitals, health authorities, family service units or an early intervention service.

Annual grant total
In 2013/14 the charity had an income of £4,500 and a total expenditure of £4,250. We estimate that the amount of grants given to individuals totalled £4,000.

Exclusions
Tuition fees and holidays are not funded.

Applications
Apply in writing to the correspondent.

Other information
Funding is occasionally awarded to organisations.

Westminster Almshouses Foundation

£106,000

Correspondent: Cristina O'Halloran, Clerk to the Trustees, 7 Allandale Place, Orpington, Kent BR6 7TH (020 7828 3131; email: cristina@ westminsteralmshouses.com; website: www.westminsteralmshouses.com)

CC number: 226936

Eligibility
People in need who live in the London Borough of Westminster. Limited support is available to those living elsewhere in Greater London and to women living elsewhere in the UK.

Types of grants

One-off grants averaging around £500, as well as pensions. Grants are typically offered for help in obtaining cookers, washers, microwaves, as well as children's clothing and equipment.

Annual grant total

In 2014 the foundation had assets of £27.3 million and an income of £756,000. Pensions and grants to individuals for welfare purposes totalled £106,000.

Applications

Application forms are available from the correspondent. Forms must detail your request, current circumstances and how this award will help you towards self-sufficiency. Decisions are made quickly once all the necessary information is acquired.

Other information

The foundation's main activity is providing almshouse accommodation in central London for people over the age of 60 who are in need. The foundation also makes educational grants.

The Westminster Amalgamated Charity

£33,000 (254 grants)

Correspondent: Julia Moorcroft, Grants Administrator, School House, Drury Lane, London WC2B 5SU (020 7395 9460; fax: 020 7395 9479; email: wac@3chars.org.uk; website: www.w-a-c.org.uk)

CC number: 207964

Eligibility

People in need who live, work or study in the old City of Westminster (the former Metropolitan Borough of Westminster) or those who have previously lived or worked in the area for a total of five years or more.

Note: the old City of Westminster is that area, covered by Westminster Council, which is situated south of Oxford Street.

Types of grants

One-off grants ranging from £100 to £350 towards: clothing; essential household items (furniture, white goods, kitchen equipment); holidays for individuals aged 60 and over (taken in the UK only); and decorating and flooring costs. Payments will be made to the sponsor or a designated retailer.

Annual grant total

In 2014 the charity had assets of £7 million, most of which represents permanent endowment and is not available for grant-giving. It had an income of £307,000. Grants to 204 individuals (205 applications considered)

totalled £33,000 and were distributed as follows:

Discretionary	79	£15,800
Household	59	£9,600
Clothing	58	£5,000
Holidays	7	£2,600
Other	1	£50

Grants to 43 organisations totalled £200,000.

Exclusions

No grants for: TVs; CD/DVD players; mobile phones; computers/software; educational needs; holidays abroad; debt repayment or fees. No retrospective grants.

Applications

Application forms are available from the correspondent or can be downloaded from the website. Applications must be submitted through a recognised referral agency such as Social Services, Citizens Advice, hostel worker, etc.; and be accompanied by a supporting statement. The supporting statement should include all of the details which explain the individual's need, for example: family circumstances; medical, domestic or behavioural issues; the extent of your agency's involvement with the applicant and why assistance is sought. Applications will usually take four to six weeks to process.

Other information

The charity regularly publishes and updates the amount of money available for distribution on its website.

Croydon

Croydon Relief in Need Charities

£10,800 (1 grant)

Correspondent: Mr W. Rymer, Clerk to the Trustees, Elis David Almshouses, Duppas Hill Terrace, Croydon CR40 4BT (020 8774 9382; email: billrymer@croydonalmshousecharities.org.uk; website: www.croydonalmshousecharities.org.uk)

CC number: 810114

Eligibility

Residents of the London Borough of Croydon who are in conditions of need, hardship or distress (including ill health).

Types of grants

One-off grants according to need.

Annual grant total

In 2014, the charity had an income of £111,000 and a total expenditure of £135,000. During the year, only one grant of £10,800 was awarded to an

individual in respect of the Sequal Trust. The charity mainly makes grants to organisations (£110,000 in 2014).

Applications

Apply in writing to the correspondent.

Other information

The charity is linked to The Croydon Almshouse Charities, which runs two almshouses in the area.

Ealing

Acton (Middlesex) Charities – Relief in Need Fund

£1,200

Correspondent: Lorna Dodd, Clerk to the Trustees, c/o St Mary's Parish Office, 1 The Mount, Acton High Street, London W3 9NW (020 8992 8876; email: acton.charities@virgin.net; website: www.actoncharities.co.uk)

CC number: 211446

Eligibility

People in need who have lived in the former ancient parish of Acton for at least three years. (The John Perryn Relief in Need Charity fund considers awards from applicants who have lived in the parish for less than three years.)

Types of grants

One-off grants for the purchase furniture, white goods and other essential items of household equipment or other needs. Payments are made directly to suppliers.

Small awards are also available 'to encourage local talent', including help with mounting exhibitions if the group or artist is involved is in the Acton area.

Annual grant total

In 2014 the charity had an income of £7,200 and an expenditure of £1,200. The Acton (Middlesex) Charities' website notes that during the year a total of about £1,200 was given in relief-in-need grants (including the awards through John Perryn Relief in Need Fund).

Exclusions

Anyone outside the area of benefit (there is a helpful map on the charity's website). Grants are not given for courses in private schools or institutions.

Applications

Application forms are available from the charity's website or the correspondent; however, referrals **must be** made by a professional third party, such as a doctor, district and health visitor or social services.

Note that any correspondence should be made via post or email only. The charity advises that 'a quick response is not always possible'. The trustees meet twice a year.

Further details on support for artists can be obtained from the correspondent.

Other information

This charity, together with Acton (Middlesex) Educational Charity (Charity Commission no. 312312) form part of the Acton (Middlesex) Charities, administered by the same body of trustees. The charities provide welfare, educational and arts grants and also support local schools and carnivals. The website states that 'in present times the charities try to help where other local services fail'.

During 2014 a total of £1,900 was paid to local organisations and artists (Athawes Art Gallery Fund).

The Ealing Aid-in-Sickness Trust

£2,500

Correspondent: Anita Sheehan, c/o William Hobbayne Community Centre, St Dunstan's Road, London W7 2HB (020 8810 0277; email: hobbaynecharity@btinternet.com; website: www.williamhobbaynecharity.co.uk)

CC number: 212826

Eligibility

People in need who live in the old metropolitan borough of Ealing (this includes Hanwell, Ealing, Greenford, Perivale and Northolt but not Southall or Acton), and are incurring extra expense due to long- or short-term illness.

Types of grants

One-off grants according to need.

Annual grant total

In 2013/14 the trust had an income of £3,100 and a total expenditure of £2,600. We estimate that the amount of grants given to individuals for social welfare purposes totalled £2,500.

Applications

Application forms are available from the correspondent. Applications should be made through a third party such as a social worker or an organisation such as Citizens Advice.

The Eleemosynary Charity of William Hobbayne

£5,200 (44 grants)

Correspondent: Anita Sheehan, Administrator, The William Hobbayne Centre, St Dunstan's Road, London W7 2HB (020 8810 0277; email: hobbaynecharity@btinternet.com; website: www.williamhobbaynecharity.co.uk)

CC number: 211547

Eligibility

Primarily people in need who live in the civil parish of Hanwell. Very limited funds are also available for people with a medical condition who live in Hanwell, Perivale, Northolt, Greenford and Central Ealing.

Types of grants

One-off grants for clothing, furniture and domestic appliances. Grants are paid directly to the sponsors or suppliers.

Annual grant total

In 2013/14 the charity held assets of almost £3.2 million and had an income of £207,500. Welfare grants to 44 individuals totalled £5,200, with 22 local organisations receiving a further £30,500.

Applications

Application forms are available from the correspondent. Applications should be submitted through a sponsoring organisation such as a local health centre, church, outreach organisation or social services. Applications are considered on a monthly basis although urgent cases can be dealt with more quickly.

Other information

The charity owns the William Hobbayne Centre which runs activities and events for local people over the age of 50. It also has an outreach worker who, aside from encouraging grant applications, organises Christmas toy collections in more affluent parts of Hanwell for redistribution to families with difficult financial circumstances.

Enfield

The Edmonton Aid-in-Sickness and Nursing Fund

£5,700

Correspondent: David Firth, Hon. Secretary, 9 Crossway, Bush Hill Park, Enfield EN1 2LA (020 8127 1949)

CC number: 210623

Eligibility

People in need who are in poor health and live in the old borough of Edmonton (mainly N9 and N18).

Types of grants

One-off grants usually up to £300. In the past, grants have been awarded towards clothing, furniture, household necessities, convalescence, household bills and debts and medical equipment not covered by NHS provision.

Annual grant total

In 2014 the fund had an income of £7,000 and a total expenditure of £6,000. We estimate that the amount of grants given to individuals amounted to £5,700.

Exclusions

The charity will not subsidise public funds, therefore applicants should have sought help from all public sources before approaching the trust.

Applications

Apply in writing to the correspondent either directly by the individual or through social services, Citizens Advice or other welfare agency. Applications can be received at any time.

The Old Enfield Charitable Trust

£170,000

Correspondent: Personal Grants Administrator, The Old Vestry Office, 22 The Town, Enfield, Middlesex EN2 6LT (020 8367 8941; email: enquiries@toect.org.uk; website: www.toect.org.uk)

CC number: 207840

Eligibility

People in need, hardship or distress who live within the ancient parish of Enfield. There is an 'eligibility checker' on the charity's website.

Types of grants

One-off grants are given to help with unexpected expenses, including the replacement or provision of household goods and furniture, items associated with needs of individuals who have disabilities or chronic illnesses and, in exceptional circumstances, bills. Around 150 regular quarterly grants are made to people on a low income in financial need.

Annual grant total

In 2013/14 the charity had an income of £599,000 and a total expenditure of £640,000. At the time of writing (November 2015) the annual report and accounts for the year were not yet available to view on the Charity Commission's online register.

The charity's website states: 'In a typical year The Old Enfield Charitable Trust administers around £250K in discretionary grants to families, individuals and community groups residing and living within the boundary of the Ancient Parish.' In previous years, social welfare grants to individuals have accounted for around £170,000 of grants made.

Exclusions

The trust will not provide support where local authority or central government should be assisting. Our research suggests that grants are not normally given to people who are homeless.

Applications

Application forms are available from the correspondent or can be completed online on the website. Supporting evidence, which is listed on the website, must be submitted before an application can be considered.

Other information

The charity makes community grants to local organisations and individuals can also receive financial assistance to help with educational needs. The charity also administers Ann Crowe's and Wright's Almshouse Charity which owns almshouses that are let to people who are in need and already resident in the ancient parish of Enfield.

Greenwich

Greenwich Charities of William Hatcliffe and The Misses Smith

£43,500

Correspondent: Linda Clayton, Clerk to the Trustees, Greenwich Hatcliffe Charities, PO Box 70569, London SE9 9DT (email: linda_clayton@outlook.com)

CC number: 227721

Eligibility

People over the age of 55 who live within a five-mile radius of the almshouses operated by the charity.

Types of grants

One-off grants to help older people remain independent in their own homes and Christmas grants of £100 to almshouse residents.

Annual grant total

In 2013/14 the charity had an income of £160,000 and a total expenditure of £184,000. Grants totalled £43,500 and

consisted of £1,600 given in Christmas gifts and the remainder awarded in one-off grants.

Applications

Apply in writing to the correspondent. The 2013/14 accounts note that 'applicants are referred to the charity by Age UK and other relevant bodies, or may self-refer'.

Other information

The charity also provides almshouse accommodation for elderly residents in the ancient parish of East Greenwich.

The Greenwich Charity

£4,300

Correspondent: Raymond Crudgington, Administrator, c/o Grant Saw Solicitors, Norman House, 110–114 Norman Road, London SE10 9EH (020 8858 6971; email: thegreenwichcharities@gmail.com; website: thegreenwichcharities.com)

CC number: 1074816

Eligibility

People in need who live in Greenwich.

Types of grants

One-off and recurrent grants are given according to need.

Annual grant total

In 2014/15 the charity had an income of £9,100 and a total expenditure of £8,900. We estimate that the amount of grants given to individuals totalled £4,300, with funding also awarded to local organisations.

Applications

Apply in writing to the correspondent, by post or email.

The Woolwich and Plumstead Relief-in-Sickness Fund

£6,200

Correspondent: Dave Lucas, Correspondent, Royal Borough of Greenwich, The Woolwich Centre, 35 Wellington Street, Woolwich, London SE18 6HQ (020 8921 5261; email: dave.lucas@royalgreenwich.gov.uk)

CC number: 212482

Eligibility

People in need who have a physical illness or disability and live in the parishes of Woolwich and Plumstead. When funds allow, applications may be accepted from people living in the borough of Greenwich.

Types of grants

One-off grants ranging between £50 and £500 towards meeting a specific need or a contribution towards the total cost.

Annual grant total

In 2014/15 the fund had an income of £13,000 and a total expenditure of £12,800. We estimate that the amount of grants given to individuals totalled £6,200, with funding also awarded to local organisations.

Exclusions

No grants are given to help with debts, utility bills, recurrent expenditure, structural works or rent. Support for recurring items is not usually provided.

Applications

Application forms are available from the correspondent and should be submitted either directly by the individual or through a health visitor, district nurse, social services or other welfare agency. The application should include: the applicant's income and expenditure; a supporting letter from a health professional confirming the diagnosis and the resulting problems; and the reason why a grant is needed. Applications can be dealt with as and when received.

Hackney

Hackney Benevolent Pension Society

£5,200

Correspondent: Frances Broadway, Trustee, 39 Sydner Road, London N16 7UF (020 7254 6145; email: fm.broadway@gmail.com)

CC number: 212731

Eligibility

People who are older and in need, and who have lived in Hackney for at least seven years.

Types of grants

Gifts of around £30 are given to pensioners at Christmas, on their birthday and at the society's annual general meeting in November. Payments are delivered in person through home visits.

Annual grant total

In 2013/14 the society had an income of £5,500 and a total expenditure of £5,200. We estimate that the amount of grants given to individuals totalled £5,000.

Applications

Apply in writing to the correspondent.

The Hackney Parochial Charities

£11,000

Correspondent: Sarah Bennett, Correspondent, c/o Trust Partnership, 6 Trull Farm Buildings, Trull, Tetbury, Gloucestershire GL8 8SQ (020 3397 7805 or 01285 841900; email: sarah.bennett@ thetrustpartnership.com or office@thetrustpartnership.com; website: www.hackneyparochialcharities.org.uk)

CC number: 219876

Eligibility

People in need who live in the former metropolitan borough of Hackney (as it was before 1970).

Types of grants

The charity states that grants to individuals are usually made for the purchase of clothing and essential household equipment, although grants can be given for many other welfare purposes, such as bedding, furniture and medical and travel expenses for hospital visits. Grants have also been given for widows with small children and single parent families and for gifts at Christmas for children in need.

Grants are one-off, generally of £100–£250, although individuals can apply annually.

Annual grant total

In 2013/14 the charity had assets of £5.7 million and an income of £250,000. Grants were made totalling £122,000, most of which appears to be given to organisations. We estimate that about £22,000 was given to individuals for both social welfare and educational needs.

Exclusions

The following are not supported:
- Overseas trips
- Family holidays (apart from project applications for group trips)
- Debt of any kind
- Statutory charges
- Rent
- Rates
- Gas, electricity or telephone charges

Additional exclusions apply to organisations.

Applications

Applications can be made on a form available on the website or requested from the correspondent. Grants for individuals are considered by the trustees by email on a monthly or bi-monthly basis. Requests must be made through a supporting agency, such as a church or a social worker, details of whom need to be added to the form. Individuals must provide evidence of their postal address, such as a copy of a utility bill.

Other information

In 2008 the charity took over the administration of Hackney District Nursing Association; however, no grants were made out of the Hackney District Nursing Association's funds during the year.

The annual report notes that 'the trustees also make regular small grants to the local ministers' discretionary sick and needy funds to enable the local clergy to assist poor local people, who are in urgent need, without having to make a formal application for a grant each time'.

The Lolev Charitable Trust

£3.9 million

Correspondent: Abraham Tager, Trustee, 14A Gilda Crescent, London N16 6JP

CC number: 326249

Eligibility

People who are sick or in need who live in Hackney and the surrounding area.

Types of grants

The trust's annual report states: 'Assistance is given according to circumstances and available finance.'

Note: See other information.

Annual grant total

In 2013 the trust had assets of £14,500 and had an income of £4.2 million. Grants to individuals totalled £3.9 million.

At the time of writing (November 2015) this was the most recent financial information available for the trust.

Applications

Applications by individuals must be accompanied by a letter of recommendation by the applicant's minister or other known religious leader.

See also 'Other information'.

Other information

At the time of writing (November 2015) this was the only information available on the trust. We were unable to contact the correspondent for more details. Potential applicants are advised to write to the correspondent to confirm eligibility criteria and the types of grants available before submitting an application.

Hammersmith and Fulham

Dr Edwards and Bishop King's Fulham Charity

£122,000

Correspondent: Jonathan Martin, Clerk to the Trustees, Percy Barton House, 33–35 Dawes Road, London SW6 7DT (020 7385 9387; fax: 020 7610 2856; email: clerk@debk.org.uk; website: www. debk.org.uk)

CC number: 1113490

Eligibility

People in need who are on low incomes and live in the old Metropolitan Borough of Fulham. This constitutes all of the SW6 postal area and parts of W14 and W6.

Types of grants

One-off grants according to need are made towards essential items of daily living, including kitchen appliances, beds, furniture and clothing (including school uniforms), carpets, flooring, decorating materials, baby items, furnishings, cleaning or cleaning equipment, or essential medical equipment.

Annual grant total

In 2013/14 the charity had assets of almost £9.3 million and an income of £438,000. A total of 197 grants were made to individuals totalling £123,000 (including educational/training grants). The annual report suggests that the vast majority was given for welfare need. In the past about 1% of support has been given for educational needs; therefore we deduct about £1,200 and estimate that around £122,000 was given for welfare causes.

Exclusions

According to the website, the charity does not:
- Normally help those who are homeowners
- Help those not in the area of benefit
- Give cash grants (unless they are to be administered by an agency)
- Give grants retrospectively or pay arrears on utility bill
- Provide funds for funerals
- Provide wheelchairs or electric scooters
- Provide computer equipment of any sort, unless you are housebound
- Provide dishwashers
- Provide laminate flooring

311

▶ Provide grants for equipment where government, or local government, or any other agency is required to provide that equipment by law

The charity prefers not to satisfy repeat requests and is extremely unlikely to help requests for which funding may be available from other places. Our research suggests that postgraduate courses are not funded.

Applications

Application forms are available from the correspondent or on the charity's website. Applications must be submitted in hard copy either directly by the individual or through a third party. Though, it is important to note that individuals applying directly for a grant will be visited at home by the Grants Administrator.

The committee which considers relief-in-need applications, including educational grant applications, meets ten times a year, roughly every four or five weeks. The charity suggests that applications should be submitted around two or three weeks before the next meeting.

Applicants are welcome to get in touch with the charity prior to making a formal appeal.

Other information

The charity gives money to both individuals and organisations, with its main responsibility being towards the relief of poverty rather than assisting students.

There are also Summer Schemes whereby funding is given to help with 'organised activities and day trips for young local people from challenging backgrounds, over the July and August school holidays'. Assistance for longer trips – provided the destination venues are reputable, reasonably priced, and within the UK – may also be given under the scheme. In 2013/14 funding totalling £21,000 to eight local groups either to run community play schemes, or to finance trips (within the UK) for underprivileged children.

In 2013/14 the overall support was distributed between organisations (50%), relief-in-need grants (43%) and Summer Schemes (7%).

It is stated on the website that 'educational grant uptake in the year was minimal, despite increased provision by the charity' during 2013/14.

Fulham Benevolent Society

£3,600

Correspondent: Angela Rogers, Trustee, 4 Maltings Place, London SW6 2BT (020 7736 6128)

CC number: 207938

Eligibility

Elderly people, young children and people with special needs who are in need of temporary financial assistance, and live in the metropolitan borough of Fulham.

Types of grants

One-off and recurrent grants are given according to need.

Annual grant total

In 2014/15 the society had an income of £5,700 and a total expenditure of £7,500. We estimate that the amount of grants given to individuals totalled £3,600, with funding also awarded to local organisations.

Applications

Apply in writing to the correspondent. Applications should be submitted through a third party such as social services, Citizens Advice, general practitioner or minister of religion.

Haringey

The Tottenham District Charity

£86,500

Correspondent: Carolyn Banks, Secretary, 7th Floor, River Park House, 225 High Road, London N22 8HQ (email: charities@virginmedia.com; website: www.tottenhamdistrictcharity. org.uk)

CC number: 207490

Eligibility

People in need, especially the elderly, who have lived in the urban district of Tottenham (as constituted on 28 February 1896, which is largely the postal districts of N15 and N17) for at least three years prior to applying.

Types of grants

One-off grants and pensions. Grants of up to £400 are available towards, for example: basic household furniture or items; white goods; clothing; hospital visits; indirect educational expenses such as transport costs; recuperative holidays; or home decoration or repairs. Lifetime pensions totalling £260 a year (two payments of £130) are awarded to people over the age of 65.

Annual grant total

In 2014/15 the charity held assets of £2.57 million and had an income of £143,500. Grants to individuals totalled £86,500 and were distributed as follows:

Pensions	£51,000
Grants	£35,500

Exclusions

No grants are given for bills or debts.

Applications

Application forms are available from the correspondent or can be downloaded from the charity's website. Applications should be submitted through, or with the support of, an organisation such as social services, the Citizens Advice, or other welfare agency. Applications for grants should include information and costs of the specific items required (website, catalogue page, etc.). The charity aims to make decisions on applications within a month. Organisations supporting successful applicants are required to find suitable shops that will accept the charity's cheque. The charity does not normally make cheques out to individuals directly unless proof of purchase has been submitted.

Harrow

Mayor of Harrow's Charity Fund

£5,000

Correspondent: Nana Asante, Councillor, c/o Independent Labour Group Office, Middlesex Suite North, PO Box 2, Civic Centre, Station Road, Harrow HA1 2UH (020 8424 1154)

CC number: 219034

Eligibility

People in need who live in the borough of Harrow.

Types of grants

One-off grants usually up to a maximum of £150 are given for basic items such as beds, food, heating appliances, cookers, clothing and so on. Grants are also given towards holidays/school trips for children.

Annual grant total

In 2013/14 the fund had an income of £5,100 and a total expenditure of £5,600. We estimate that the total amount of grants awarded to individuals was approximately £5,000.

Applications

Application forms are available from the correspondent. Most applications come through a social worker, Citizens Advice or other welfare agency, although this does not preclude individuals from applying directly. Applications are considered at any time. Applicants must demonstrate that the individual/family is experiencing financial hardship and that the grant will alleviate ill health or poverty or improve essential living conditions. Grants are paid directly to the supplier or through a third party.

Hillingdon

The Harefield Parochial Charities

£3,000

Correspondent: John Ross, Chair, 11 Burbery Close, Harefield, Uxbridge UB9 6QP (01895 823058; fax: 01895 823644; email: hpc@harefieldcharities.co.uk; website: www.harefieldcharities.co.uk)

CC number: 210145

Eligibility
People in need who live in the ancient parish of Harefield, especially those who are older or in poor health.

Types of grants
The trustees have previously stated in their annual report that grant-making is minimal and usually limited to coal allocation grants made each Christmas by cheques to elderly residents. Occasionally modest support may be given for clothing, food, furniture, convalescence, home help, educational needs, hospital travel expenses, medical equipment and disability aids.

Annual grant total
In 2014 the charity had an income of £133,500 and a total expenditure of £87,000. We estimate that grants totalled around £3,000.

Full accounts for 2014 were not available to view at the time of writing.

Exclusions
Grants are not given towards 'relief of rates, taxes or other public funds'.

Applications
Apply in writing to the correspondent. Applications can be made directly by the individual or through a social worker, Citizens Advice or other welfare agency.

Other information
The charity also provide alms accommodation for older women and families in need. People entering a trade or undertaking apprentices are also supported.

The Hillingdon Partnership Trust

£10,000

Correspondent: John Matthews, Chief Executive, Room 22–25, Building 219, Epsom Square, Eastern Business Park, London Heathrow Airport, Hillingdon, Middlesex TW6 2BW (020 8897 3611; email: johnmatthewshpt@lineone.net; website: www.hillingdonpartnershiptrust.com)

CC number: 284668

Eligibility
People in need who live in the borough of Hillingdon.

Types of grants
Occasional one-off grants or gifts of equipment, furniture, clothes and toys. Partners have also donated hampers around Christmas time. The 2013/14 annual report notes that the trust does not have the resources to act as a typical grant-making body, but instead:

> Channels appeals to its business supporters on behalf of needy organisations and, exceptionally, individuals, and our business partners may then provide funds for an applicant. Occasionally, we may meet a need by arranging the purchase of necessary items and arranging delivery direct to an applicant, using funds held in reserve or generated through a number of fundraising activities.

Annual grant total
In 2013/14 the trust had assets of £17,400, an income of £148,000 and a total expenditure of £149,000. Cash contributions and in-kind gifts totalled almost £144,000, the majority of which was awarded to local organisations. We estimate that individuals benefitted from gifts in-kind to the value of £10,000.

Applications
Application forms are available from the correspondent.

Other information
The trust is a formal grouping of businesses and people in business who have come together as volunteers, either as representatives of local companies or as individuals. Essentially, the trust acts as a broker between business and the community and tries to match projects in need of funding with a company wishing to sponsor a local activity. As such, grant-making to individuals is only a small part of the trust's overall activities.

Uxbridge United Welfare Trusts

£90,000 (221 grants)

Correspondent: Mrs J. Duffy, Grants Officer, Woodbridge House, New Windsor Street, Uxbridge UB8 2TY (07912 270937; email: grants.officer@uuwt.org; website: www.uuwt.org)

CC number: 217066

Eligibility
People in need due to financial circumstances, health problems, age and so on who live in or have a very strong connection with the Uxbridge area. The area of benefit covers Cowley, Harefield, Hillingdon, Ickenham and Uxbridge.

Types of grants
One-off grants can be given for services or specific goods, such as furniture, household equipment, clothing, baby equipment, and help with fuel bills, for example.

Annual grant total
In 2014 the charity had assets of £10.7 million and an income of £514,000. Grants to individuals totalled £102,500, of which £90,000 was given in 221 grants for hardship relief.

Exclusions
Our research suggests that grants are not given for rent or rates. Funding is not available where help could be obtained from the statutory sources.

Applications
Application forms can be requested from the correspondent. They can be submitted directly by the individual or through a social worker, Citizens Advice or educational welfare agency, if applicable. Awards are considered each month. A trained member of staff will visit applicants for an interview to better assess their case.

Other information
Grants are also awarded for educational purposes and may be given to support organisations. The charity also runs almshouses.

Islington

Richard Cloudesley's Charity

£96,000

Correspondent: Melanie Griffiths, Director, Office 1.1, Resource for London, 365 Holloway Road, London N7 6PA (020 7697 4094; email: info@richardcloudesleyscharity.org.uk; website: www.richardcloudesleyscharity.org.uk)

CC number: 205959

Eligibility
People in need who are sick or disabled and live in the ancient parish of St Mary's Islington (roughly the modern borough, excluding the area south of the Pentonville and City Roads). A map of the area of benefit is available on the charity's website.

Types of grants

One-off grants, for a wide range of purposes, with the aim of relieving poverty and distress for those who are in need.

Annual grant total

In 2013/14 the charity held assets of £44.7 million and had an income of £1.55 million. Welfare grants made to individuals totalled £96,000. Of this total, £1,200 were made via the Cripplegate Foundation and £95,000 under the Interim Welfare Grants Programme 2013/14, delivered by Cloudesley Trusted Partners.

Exclusions

No help for debts, education, computers, childcare, funeral expenses or for money that has been stolen.

Applications

Check the charity's website for up-to-date information. Under the interim welfare grants scheme, applications should be made to one of the charity's Welfare Grants Programme Trusted Partner organisations. The charity does not currently accept direct applications but can give further information and refer individuals to the appropriate partner agency.

Other information

During 2013/14, the charity reviewed its welfare grants programme in response to welfare reforms and the programme is now administered in-house, rather than by the Cripplegate Foundation as in previous years. An interim grants programme ran throughout 2013/14, working with other voluntary organisations, Cloudesley Partners, to agree grants on the charity's behalf. This interim programme was extended until June 2015 after which the foundation plans to launch a new welfare grants programme.

Grants are also made to local churches and to organisations working to promote the health of those living in poverty within the beneficiary area.

Lady Gould's Charity

£24,500 (48 grants)

Correspondent: Graeme Andrew Couch, Clerk, Bircham Dyson Bell, 50 Broadway, Westminster, London SW1H 0BL (020 7783 3769; fax: 020 7222 3480; email: andycouch@bdb-law.co.uk; website: www.ladygouldscharity.org)

CC number: 234978

Eligibility

People in need who live in Highgate (i.e. the N6 postal district and part of the N2, N8, N10 and N19 districts). A reference map and street index is available on the

website. Most grantees are in receipt of income support and housing benefit, although the charity may also consider applications from people earning under £10,000 a year.

Types of grants

One-off grants generally ranging from £200 to £500, although more is available in exceptional circumstances. Grants are given for clothing, furniture, furnishings, baby necessities and white goods. Grants to help towards reducing debts and for holidays are available but will only be given in very needy cases. It is not usual for an individual or family to receive more than one grant in a year.

Annual grant total

In 2014 the charity made grants totalling £24,500 to 48 applicants.

During the year the average grant was £508 per person.

Exclusions

Grants are rarely made for educational or recreational purposes or for debt relief.

Applications

Application forms are available to download from the website. Applications should be accompanied by a supporting statement from a social worker, GP or other recognised body. If this is not possible attach evidence of your entitlement to benefits, such as a housing benefit letter. Applications can be submitted directly by the individual or through a third party such as a social worker, Citizens Advice or other welfare agency. They are considered at any time.

The St Sepulchre (Finsbury) United Charities

£39,500

Correspondent: Elias Poli, Administrator, Smithfield Accountants LLP, 117 Charterhouse Street, London EC1M 6AA (020 7253 3757; email: elias@smithfield-accountants.co.uk)

CC number: 213312

Eligibility

People over 60 who are in need who live in the old London Borough of Finsbury.

Types of grants

Quarterly pensions and one-off grants.

Annual grant total

In 2013/14 the charity held assets of £2.7 million and had an income of £66,500. Grants to individuals totalled £39,500, of which £21,500 was given in quarterly pensions and £18,000 in one-off grants. A further £11,500 was given

to organisations operating within the charity's catchment area.

Applications

In April 2013 the charities joined the new Islington Resident Support Scheme, which is delivered through a partnership between Cripplegate Foundation and Islington Council. Applications to the scheme can only be made online through a designated access point. See the Cripplegate Foundation website (cripplegate.org) for a list of access points and more details on the scheme.

Kensington and Chelsea

The Campden Charities

£1.1 million

Correspondent: Christopher Stannard, Clerk, Studios 3&4, 27A Pembridge Villas, London W11 3EP (020 7243 0551 or 020 7313 3797; website: www. campdencharities.org.uk)

CC number: 1104616

Eligibility

Individuals applying for funding must: have been continuously living in Kensington for at least two years (there is a helpful area of benefit map on the website); be a British or European citizen or have indefinite leave to remain; live in rented accommodation and not be a homeowner; be in receipt of benefits, including housing benefits, or in low paid work.

Types of grants

Grants are given to relieve financial hardship. Examples include grants to assist older people with the replacement of household appliances and with bills.

Annual grant total

In 2014/15 the charity had assets of £143.4 million and an income of £2.9 million. During the year, the charity made grants to both individuals and organisations for social welfare and educational purposes. Of £1.9 million awarded, £1.5 million was given to individuals and £405,000 to organisations. Grants to individuals for social welfare purposes amounted to almost £1.1 million.

Exclusions

Previous research indicates that the charity will not give funding for: direct payment of council tax or rent; debt repayments; fines or court orders; foreign travel or holidays; career changes; personal development courses; postgraduate studies; computers; individuals whose immediate goal is self-employment; goods and services catered for by central government.

Applications

The charity's website advises that eligible applicants living in the area of benefit should call 020 7243 0551 to apply.

Other information

The charity provides debt advice for all of its beneficiaries through its partnership with Nucleus (nucleus.org.uk).

The Kensington and Chelsea District Nursing Trust

£45,500 (121 grants)

Correspondent: Margaret Rhodes, Clerk to the Trustees, 13B Hewer Street, London W10 6DU (020 8969 8117; email: kcdnt@tiscali.co.uk)

CC number: 210931

Eligibility

People who are in need who have lived for at least two years in the borough of Kensington and Chelsea. Beneficiaries have included people who are physically or mentally ill, people who have disabilities, or people who have been rehoused after rehabilitation from substance abuse. Grants are given in exceptional circumstances to people who are in need outside the beneficiary area.

Types of grants

One-off grants of up to £1,000 for domestic appliances, medical and nursing aids and equipment, beds, bedding and other furniture and clothing. Heating allowances may also be made.

Annual grant total

In 2013/14 this trust had an income of £82,500 and total expenditure of £69,500. Grants to 121 individuals totalled £45,500. A further £5,500 was given in grants to organisations.

Exclusions

Grants are not given for payment of salaries, rents, court orders or fines.

Applications

Application forms are available from the correspondent. Applications must be submitted through a social worker, Citizens Advice or other welfare agency and are considered each month.

Kingston upon Thames

Chessington Charities

£2,000

Correspondent: Mrs L. Roberts, Correspondent, St Mary's Centre, Church Lane, Chessington, Surrey KT9 2DR (07540 144016; email: stmaryschessington@hotmail.co.uk)

CC number: 209241

Eligibility

People in need who live in the parish of St Mary the Virgin, Chessington. Applicants must have lived in the parish for at least one year.

Types of grants

Grants are usually one-off in the range of £30–£250. Awards may include those given to older people (with low income) at Christmas and for specific items, such as special food, furniture, medical equipment, electrical goods and clothing.

Annual grant total

In 2014 the charity had both an income and total expenditure of £8,500. We estimate grants for individuals for social welfare purposes to have totalled around £2,000.

Exclusions

Grants are not given to pay debts. The area of benefit is only the parish of St Mary the Virgin and excludes the rest of the Chessington postal area.

Applications

Application forms are available from the correspondent. Applications should be submitted either directly by the individual or through a social worker, Citizens Advice or other agency. A home visit will be made by a trustee to ascertain details of income and expenditure and to evaluate the need. Applications for Christmas grants for older people must be received by 1 November and are distributed in this month. Other applications are considered throughout the year.

Other information

Grants are also given to local organisations which help older people or people with disabilities. Educational grants are also available for individuals.

The Hampton Wick United Charity

£5,000

Correspondent: The Clerk, Hunters Lodge, Home Farm, Redhill Road, Cobham, Surrey KT11 1EF (01932 596748; email: info@hwuc.org.uk; website: hwuc.org.uk)

CC number: 1010147

Eligibility

People who are in need and live in the parishes of St John the Baptist in Hampton Wick, St Mark in Teddington, and St Mary with St Alban in Teddington. Beneficiaries are usually in receipt of a state benefit and proof of this may be required.

Types of grants

Relief-in-need grants have been give towards, for example: the purchase of a wheelchair; travelling expenses to enable the recipient to visit relatives in hospital; certain items of medical equipment not available on the NHS; heating repairs; the purchase of furniture; the purchase of a television set; school uniforms.

Annual grant total

We have no current information on the grant-giving of this charity. At the time of writing (October 2015) financial information had not been submitted to the Charity Commission for any of the years listed on the charity's online record.

We know that previously over £20,000 a year was awarded to individuals in educational and welfare grants. Grants are also awarded to organisations. We estimate that the amount given to individuals for social welfare purposes is around £5,000.

Applications

In the first instance, contact the Clerk.

Lambeth

The Clapham Relief Fund

£15,500 (57 grants)

Correspondent: Shirley Cosgrave, Clerk to the Trustees, PO Box 37978, London SW4 8WX (email: enquires@ claphamrelieffund.org; website: claphamrelieffund.org)

CC number: 1074562

Eligibility

People in need who live in Clapham. A map of the area of benefit is available on the website.

Types of grants

One-off grants under £500 towards domestic appliances, beds and bedding, redecoration, clothing and convalescent holidays, for example. Recurrent grants can be made for a limited period to meet a particular need. Christmas gifts may also be distributed. Cheques cannot normally be made out to individuals, but rather to sponsors, or, if this is not possible, to the supplier on receipt of an estimate or page from a catalogue.

Annual grant total

In 2014 the fund had an income of £26,000 and a total expenditure of £29,500. Grants to individuals totalled £15,500. Of 57 grants awarded during the year, 55 were one-off grants and the remaining two were Christmas distributions.

A further £7,200 was awarded to organisations which benefit residents of Clapham.

Exclusions

No grants will be given where sufficient help is available from public sources. Support will only be given to permanent residents of Clapham. Grants are not usually given for debts and living expenses.

Applications

Application forms are available to download from the website. Applications should include details of monthly income and outgoings and verification by a sponsor. They can be submitted either directly by the individual, through a welfare agency or by a third party such as a district nurse, charitable agency worker, parish priest or doctor. Applications are considered at trustee meetings held four times a year, usually in March, June, September and December, although in exceptional circumstances they may be considered more urgently. Application forms should be submitted during the last week of the month before meetings. Emergency grants of up to £300 can be awarded between meetings.

Other information

The fund has an informative website.

Lewisham

The Deptford Pension Society

£6,000

Correspondent: Mike Baker, Administrator, 144 Farnaby Road, Shortlands, Bromley BR1 4BW (020 8402 0775; email: mjpbaker@hotmail.co.uk)

CC number: 219232

Eligibility

People over the age of 60 in receipt of supplementary benefits who have lived in the former London borough of Deptford for at least seven years.

Types of grants

Pensions of £15 per month (with a bonus payment in December) to around 30 individuals.

Annual grant total

In 2014 the society had an income of £6,500 and a total expenditure of £6,400. We estimate that the amount of grants given to individuals totalled £6,000.

Applications

Application forms are available from the correspondent and are considered bi-monthly. Applications can be submitted either directly by the individual or a family member, through a third party such as a social worker, or through an organisation such as Citizens Advice or other welfare agency. The application form must be signed by the individual.

The Lee Charity of William Hatcliffe

£14,000 (35 grants)

Correspondent: Anne Wilson, PO Box 7041, Bridgnorth, Shropshire WV16 9EL (07517 527849; email: annewilsontc@hotmail.co.uk)

CC number: 208053

Eligibility

People in need in Lewisham, with preference to those living in the ancient parish of Lee, who are in need, hardship or distress.

Types of grants

Regular allowances.

Annual grant total

In 2013 the charity had an income of £50,000. Grants were made to 35 individuals totalling £14,000. This was the latest information at the time of writing (October 2015).

Applications

Apply in writing to the correspondent. Many applications come via partner agencies in Lewisham.

Other information

Grants are also made to organisations. During the year grants totalled £32,000 to 12 organisations.

Lewisham Relief in Need Charity

£2,200

Correspondent: The Finance and Administration Manager, Clerk's Office, Lloyd Court, Slagrove Place, London SE13 7LP (020 8690 8145; email: admin@lpcharities.co.uk; website: www.lpcharities.co.uk)

CC number: 1025779

Eligibility

People in need, including those who are who are older, disadvantaged or who have disabilities and who live in the ancient parish of Lewisham, which does not include Deptford or Lee.

Types of grants

Small, one-off grants of up to £500 for essential items such as kitchen equipment, beds or carpets. Small Christmas gifts are also awarded – in 2013/14 gifts of £25 were awarded to 14 individuals.

Annual grant total

In 2013/14 the charity had assets of £975,000 and an income of £130,000. Grants and gifts to individuals totalled £2,200.

Exclusions

No grants are made towards the payment of bills.

Applications

Apply in writing to the correspondent either directly by the individual, through a third party such as a social worker, or through an organisation such as Citizens Advice or other welfare agency. Applications should include as much supporting information as possible to enable the trustees to make informed decisions about why the individual is in need. Applications are considered throughout the year.

Other information

The charity is primarily engaged in providing sheltered accommodation for the elderly at its almshouse, Lloyd Court. It also makes grants to small organisations aiding the people of Lewisham.

Merton

Wimbledon Guild of Social Welfare (Incorporated)

£19,000

Correspondent: Helen Marti, Welfare Administrator, Guild House, 30–32 Worple Road, Wimbledon, London SW19 4EF (020 8946 0735; email: info@wimbledonguild.co.uk; website: www.wimbledonguild.co.uk)

CC number: 200424

Eligibility

Individuals in need who live primarily in Wimbledon but also in the borough of Merton. The charity's activities focus on ageing well, supporting mental health and fighting poverty.

Types of grants

Small, one-off grants (averaging around £300) according to need towards kitchen equipment, children's clothing, household bills, emergency household repairs, exam entrance fees, mobility scooter batteries and so on. The guild also distributes gifts in-kind, including furniture, food and Christmas toys and also gives emergency cash grants.

Annual grant total

In 2013/14 the charity had assets of £6.1 million and an income of £1.8 million. Charitable activities totalled £1.2 million. The charity's website states that the Small Grants Programme provides about £19,000 in small grants.

Exclusions

Grants will not normally be given to anyone who has been a recipient in the previous year.

Applications

Application forms are available from the correspondent or to download from the website. Applications are considered every other month. Upcoming meeting dates can be found on the website. Applications must be received a week before the date of each meeting, except when applying for an emergency food grant.

Other information

The charity also runs clubs, classes and a furniture recycling service.

Redbridge

The Ethel Baker Bequest

£4,200

Correspondent: Revd Charles Neil Spencer, Trustee, 18 Chestnut Walk, Woodford Green IG8 0TE (020 8530 4916; email: neil@woodfordbaptist.org)

CC number: 270274

Eligibility

People in need who live in the parish of Woodford Baptist Church in the London borough of Redbridge. In the case of any excess income, applications from those living outside the area who have attended or are connected with the church will be considered.

Types of grants

One-off and recurrent grants are given according to need.

Annual grant total

In 2013/14 the charity had an income of £1,400 and a total expenditure of £4,200. We estimate that the amount of grants given to individuals totalled £4,200.

Applications

Apply in writing to the correspondent, although the trust states that its funds are already allocated.

Richmond upon Thames

The Barnes Workhouse Fund

£19,300

Correspondent: Miranda Ibbetson, Director, PO Box 665, Richmond, Surrey TW10 6YL (020 8241 3994; email: mibbetson@barnesworkhousefund.org. uk; website: www.barnesworkhousefund. org.uk)

CC number: 200103

Eligibility

People in need who live in the ancient parish of Barnes (this broadly corresponds to the SW13 postcode area).

Types of grants

Grants are limited to £350 for any one individual in any one year. Grants are given for a wide range of needs including: utility bills; furniture, including beds; carpets; washing machines; cookers; home computers; medical needs and therapy; removal costs; funeral expenses; bankruptcy costs; and holiday expenses. They are also given for individuals who are experiencing a crisis or emergency, and to replace stolen property.

Annual grant total

In 2014 the fund had assets of £10 million and an income of £617,000. Grants totalled £207,000, the majority of which was awarded to organisations. Individuals received grants amounting to almost £33,000; of this amount £19,300 was given for social welfare needs and the remaining £13,500 for educational purposes.

During the year, the fund awarded 88 grants to individuals for social welfare purposes. This included 18 grants which, at the time of the annual report and accounts being produced, had been awarded but not yet paid.

Exclusions

Our research shows that grants are not generally made to people who are homeless, as the scheme requires applicants to be resident in Barnes.

Applications

Application forms are available from the correspondent and must be submitted through a referral agency. This could be Citizens Advice, a social worker or your housing association, for example. Small grants for individuals are considered immediately, whereas requests of a more complex nature are considered at the next trustees meeting. These meetings are held in January, March, May, September and November and, for consideration at one of these meetings, applications must be received by the fund by the 6th of the preceding month.

Note: A home visit from two of the trustees may be suggested in order to determine the full extent of the applicant's need.

Other information

The Barnes Workhouse Fund provides sheltered accommodation for around 40 residents at its almshouse, Walsingham Lodge, in Barnes.

The fund has an informative website and annual report, which each provide in great detail information on the fund's activities and its history.

The Hampton and Hampton Hill Philanthropic Society

£6,000

Correspondent: Joan Barnett, Trustee, Waverley, Old Farm Road, Hampton, Middlesex TW12 3RL (020 8979 0395)

CC number: 208992

Eligibility

People in need in St Mary's and All Saints', Hampton or St James, Hampton Hill.

Types of grants

Grants of about £200 each are made to people who have suddenly come into financial need.

Annual grant total

In 2013/14 the charity had an income of £8,300 and a total expenditure of 6,800. Priority is given to making grants to individuals, with any surplus funds donated to local organisations.

Applications

Apply in writing to the correspondent.

The Hampton Fuel Allotment Charity

£746,500 (1,977 grants)

Correspondent: Carole Swinburne, Grants Manager, 15 High Street, Hampton, Middlesex TW12 2SA (020 8941 7866; fax: 020 8979 5555; website: www.hfac.co.uk)

CC number: 211756

Eligibility

People who are in poor health or financial need and live in the ancient parish of Hampton. Priority is given to applicants from Hampton but grants may also be made to those living in the remainder of the former borough of Twickenham. Applicants must either work part-time or be on a low wage; in receipt of state benefits; in receipt of help with rent or council tax; or have children who receive free school meals.

Types of grants

One-off grants are given for heating costs and other household essentials such as fridges, cookers, washing machines, wheelchairs and special medical equipment. Grants are made directly to the supplier and, in the case of fuel grants, credited to the applicant's account.

Annual grant total

In 2013/14 the charity had assets of £53 million and an income of £2 million.

Grants to individuals in need totalled £746,500 and were distributed as follows:

Fuel grants	1,775	£686,500
Essential equipment and furniture	202	£45,000
Careline telephone equipment	115	£15,000

Exclusions

The charity is unlikely to support: private and further education; building adaptations; holidays (except in cases of severe medical need); decorating costs, carpeting or central heating; anything which will replace statutory funds.

Applications

Application forms are available to download from the website. They can also be obtained from the charity's office at 15 High Street, Hampton; the Greenwood Centre at School Road, Hampton Hill; Twickenham Citizens Advice; and the outreach service (which the charity funds) at The White House, The Avenue, Hampton. Applications should be submitted by post either directly by the individual or by a third party. Applications for fuel grants are considered every two months. Those for essential household items are reviewed weekly and should be verified through a letter of support from a welfare professional such as a social worker or housing officer. If this is not possible, the charity will visit the applicant at home.

Note the following from the charity's most recent accounts: 'We no longer accept new applications for "Careline" units.'

Other information

The charity was created following the 1811 Enclosure Act by the granting of 10.14 acres of land for producing a supply of fuel for the poor of the ancient parish of Hampton. Subsequently the land was rented out for nurseries. In 1988, the land was sold for development and the sale proceeds formed the financial base for the current work of the charity.

As well as awarding grants for fuel and essential equipment and furniture the charity also offers school journey grants for children in their penultimate or final year of junior school 'to enable them to participate in the school journey arranged before they transfer to secondary school'. Interested parties should first discuss this with the child's school. More details are available on the charity's informative website.

It is worth noting that the local authority's local assistance scheme provides similar support for those requiring white goods or furniture, but this scheme is restricted to those on benefits; it does not extend to those who

are working, but on low pay. This charity takes a different approach and according to the trustees' annual report for 2013/14, they have seen a tangible increase over the last year in the number of working families on low income who have been eligible for a fuel grant and support with white goods and furniture. The Grants Team continues to work with schools and other agencies to promote the existence of the fuel grants. The trustees also recognise that families and individuals on low income are struggling with increasing fuel costs and food bills. For this reason, the trustees agreed to increase the level of fuel grants by around 20%, and this took effect from 1 July 2014.

The Richmond Aid-in-Sickness Fund

£6,800

Correspondent: Juliet Ames-Lewis, Director, 8 The Green, Richmond, Surrey TW9 1PL (020 8948 4188; email: info@richmondcharities.org.uk; website: www.richmondcharities.org.uk)

CC number: 200434

Eligibility

People in need who live in the borough of Richmond.

Types of grants

One-off grants of up to £250 towards, for example, fuel costs, extra bedding, nightwear and the costs of special equipment.

Annual grant total

In 2014 the fund had an income of £5,500 and a total expenditure of £7,000. We estimate that the amount of grants given to individuals totalled £6,800.

Applications

Applications should be submitted through social services, Citizens Advice or other organisations such as Richmond Community Mental Health Resource Centre. Payments are received in February, May, August and November.

Richmond Charities Almshouses (formerly known as The Henry Smith Charity (Richmond)

£2,000

Correspondent: Juliet Ames-Lewis, Director, The Richmond Charities, 8 The Green, Richmond, Surrey TW9 1PL (020 8948 4188; email: info@ richmondcharities.org.uk; website: www. richmondcharities.org.uk)

CC number: 200431

Eligibility

People experiencing hardship or distress who lived in Richmond upon Thames for at least five years.

Types of grants

One-off grants of up to £250. Recently the greatest number of grants have been made to unemployed single parents, towards children's clothing and fuel bills.

Annual grant total

Grants usually total around £2,000 per year.

Applications

Apply in writing to the correspondent, from referring bodies such as social services, health authority or Citizens Advice. Applications are considered at regular trustees' meetings.

Other information

The Richmond Charities also administer other funds including the Richmond Aid in Sickness Fund and the Richmond Philanthropic Society (see separate entries).

Richmond Parish Lands Charity (RPLC)

£141,000

Correspondent: Sharon La Ronde, Grants Director, The Vestry House, 21 Paradise Road, Richmond, Surrey TW9 1SA (020 8948 5701; fax: 020 8332 6792; email: grants@rplc.org.uk; website: www.rplc.org.uk)

CC number: 200069

Eligibility

People who are in need or suffering from ill health or hardship in the TW9 TW10 or SW14 areas of Richmond, Ham, Sheen and Mortlake. Applicants must have lived in the area for at least six months prior to application and have no other possible sources of help. Older people must be in receipt of a means-tested benefit to qualify for a winter heating grant.

Types of grants

Crisis Grants

Awards of up to £250, mostly for household goods, bills, debts, food and clothing. Grants of £60 towards heating bills are available to older people.

Winter Fuel Grants

Over 500 payments in winter fuel grants are distributed in January to pensioners in receipt of benefits to assist with energy bills. In 2014/15 the payment was set to be £100 per household.

Annual grant total

The charity is a grant-maker and housing provider. In 2013/14 it had assets of £85.7 million and an income of £1.86 million. Grants were made to over 1,000 individuals totalling £267,000. Grants for welfare purposes totalled £141,000, consisting of Crisis Grants (£89,000) and Winter Fuel Grants (£52,000).

Applications

Contact the correspondent or visit the charity's website for further information.

Application forms for fuel grants are distributed through local agencies including GP surgeries.

Crisis grants are made to individuals in extreme need following a referral from local agencies, such as Richmond Borough support teams or the Citizens Advice, Social Services, Age UK Richmond and the Community Mental Health Team. Applications are not accepted from individuals directly.

Other information

Grants are also made to organisations – 'regular core funding to charities with a proven track record of serving local community needs' and also project or strategic funding. In 2013/14 assistance was given to 106 organisations totalling over £1 million. The charity also provides educational support to individuals as well as organisations (£273,000 was distributed to schools, organisations and individuals in 2013/14).

The Barnes Relief in Need Charity (BRINC) (Charity Commission no. 200318) is also administered by the Richmond Parish Lands Charity. BRINC seeks to help people in need who are resident in SW14 and also supports local organisations. BRINC and the RPLC use the same application forms, which are held by referral agencies.

The charity has an informative website.

The Richmond Philanthropic Society

£18,000

Correspondent: Juliet Ames-Lewis, Director, 8 The Green, Richmond, Surrey TW9 1PL (020 8948 4188; email: info@richmondcharities.org.uk; website: www.richmondcharities.org.uk)

CC number: 212941

Eligibility

People in need who live in the borough of Richmond, including Kew, Petersham and Ham (post codes TW9 and TW10).

Types of grants

Small, one-off grants of up to £250 for white goods, prams, beds and bedding, TV licences, rent arrears and fuel bills. Christmas hampers are distributed to elderly people who have been recommended by care workers and district nurses.

Annual grant total

In 2014 the society had an income of £14,600 and a total expenditure of £19,400. We estimate that the amount of grants given to individuals totalled £18,000.

Exclusions

No grants are given for educational purposes or for the payment of council tax. There are no cash grants available.

Applications

Applications should be made through Citizens Advice, social services, district nurses, health visitors or other established third parties and are considered regularly.

Other information

Richmond Charities took over the administration of the society in October 2010.

In previous years, the society has also chosen to award grants to organisations, to help reach as many individuals as possible through specific projects.

Southwark

The Camberwell Consolidated Charities

£45,000 (133 grants)

Correspondent: Janet McDonald, Correspondent, London Borough of Southwark, Level 2, Hub 5, PO Box 64529, London SE1P 5LX (020 7525 7511; email: janet.mcdonald@southwark.gov.uk)

CC number: 208441

Eligibility

Primarily older people in need who have lived in the former parish of Camberwell for at least two years. Priority is given to those whose income is on or around the minimum state pension.

Types of grants

Annual pensions, the rates of which vary each year (in 2013/14 pensions stood at £352 per person or £530 per couple). Hardship grants are also available for emergency items.

Annual grant total

In 2013/14 the charity held assets of £1.2 million and had an income of £45,500. Payments to 133 individuals totalled £45,000, all but £80 of which was awarded in pensions to older people.

Applications

Application forms are available from the correspondent. Vacancies are advertised in the local press and by social services, Age UK and so on.

Rotherhithe Consolidated Charities

£105,000

Correspondent: John Clarke, Administrator, Amwell House, 19 Amwell Street, Hoddesdon, Hertfordshire EN11 8TS (01992 444466)

CC number: 211980

Eligibility

Recurrent grants are made primarily to widows who are in need and have lived in the ancient parish of Rotherhithe for at least ten years. Help is also given for the general benefit of those in need who live in the parish.

Types of grants

One-off grants for relief in need, Christmas donations and the provision of holidays. Annual pensions are also provided to widows in need.

Annual grant total

In 2014 the charity had assets of almost £4.2 million and an income of £95,000. Grants totalled £105,000 and were broken down as follows:

Holiday grants	£65,000
Stipend grants	£34,500
Other grants	£5,600

Applications

Apply in writing to the correspondent.

Other information

Grants are also made to organisations (£7,800 in 2014).

Southwark Charities

£99,500

Correspondent: Chris Wilson, Clerk to the Trustees, Charities Office, Edward Edwards House, Nicholson Street, London SE1 0XL (020 7593 2000; email: clerk@southwarkcharities.org.uk; website: www.southwarkcharities.co.uk)

CC number: 1137760

Eligibility

Older people in need who have lived in the former metropolitan borough of Southwark for at least five years.

Types of grants

Quarterly pensions (£180 per annum in 2014), a Christmas bonus (£50 in 2014) and one-off grants (up to £200) towards the cost of holidays.

Annual grant total

In 2014 this charity had assets of £23.8 million, an income of almost £687,000. Support for individuals totalled £99,500 of which £32,000 was awarded in pensions, £49,500 in holiday grants and £17,700 in Christmas gifts and parties. There are currently 180 people receiving pensions.

Applications

Apply in writing to the correspondent, either directly by the individual, via a third party or through a social worker, Citizens Advice or other welfare agency.

Other information

The charity's main objective is the maintenance of a number of almshouses for the benefit of older people who are in financial difficulties. The assets of the charity therefore bear no relation to the amount available for grant-giving.

The Mayor of Southwark's Common Good Trust (The Mayor's Charity)

£6,000 (37 grants)

Correspondent: Eric Bassett, Treasurer, 90 Sunnywood Drive, Haywards Heath RH16 4PB (01444 412812; email: eric.bassett@btinternet.com)

CC number: 280011

Eligibility

People in need who live in the borough of Southwark and the immediate surrounding area.

Types of grants

One-off grants, averaging around £160 each, for essential kitchen items, medical equipment, clothing, furniture and household items.

Annual grant total

In 2014/15 the trust had an income of £29,500 and a total expenditure of £30,000. The following information was taken from the trustees' report for 2014/15: 'Grants made in the year exceeded £4,500 in over 30 cases of individual application. Grants made were either direct through the provision of required items, or through other organisations who administered awards.'

Applications

Apply in writing to the correspondent. Applications can be made either directly by the individual or, where applicable, through a social worker, Citizens Advice or other third party such as a family member, MP or doctor. Applications should include full details of family/financial/health background and details of other sources of funds, including whether a previous application has been made to this trust. Trustees may visit applicants to assess needs and to determine the best course of action.

Other information

The trust works alongside local community groups.

The United Charities of St George the Martyr

£163,500

Correspondent: Paul Leverton, Clerk, Marshall House, 66 Newcomen Street, London SE1 IYT (020 7407 2994; email: stgeorge@marshalls.org.uk)

CC number: 208732

Eligibility

Older people in need in the parish of St George the Martyr (in north Southwark SE1).

Types of grants

Pensions and Christmas parcels. Pensions currently total £150 per annum. One-off grants according to need, usually of up to £300, towards kitchen equipment, furnishing, flooring, mobility aids, accompanied transport to medical and dental treatments, easy-fitting slippers and shoes, and illuminated magnifying lenses. The charity also funds holidays and outings for its beneficiaries.

Annual grant total

In 2014 the charity held assets of £7.85 million and had an income of £328,500. Financial assistance for individuals totalled £163,500 and were distributed as follows:

Pensioner holiday costs	£78,500
Pensions	£38,500
Pensioner trips and outings	£27,000
Christmas hampers and parties	£16,600
Sundry purchases for pensioners	£1,800
Grants	£900
Relief in need	£600

In 2014, 219 individuals received a pension and a Christmas hamper.

Applications

Apply in writing to the correspondent. The charity has previously stated that its grants and pensions are fully committed but that any new applications will be kept on file.

Other information

The charity also has a welfare visitor, who is able to visit beneficiaries and potential beneficiaries in their own homes.

St Olave, St Thomas and St John United Charity

£214,500

Correspondent: Angela O'Shaughnessy, 6–8 Druid Street, off Tooley Street, London SE1 2EU (020 7407 2530; email: st.olavescharity@btconnect.com)

CC number: 211763

Eligibility

People in need who live in Bermondsey (part SE1 and all SE16).

Types of grants

Individuals over the age of 70 can receive a birthday gift of £100 a year and a further grant towards holidays once every year or every two years. Depending on additional income, other one-off grants can be made for a wide variety of needs, including clothes, musical instruments and holidays.

Annual grant total

In 2013/14 the charity had assets of £14.3 million and an income of £384,500. Grants totalled £260,500, of which £46,000 was awarded to organisations. Grants to individuals – all of which were awarded for social welfare purposes – totalled £214,500.

Applications

Applications should be made in writing to the correspondent and are considered four times a year.

Sutton

Cheam Consolidated Charities

£2,500

Correspondent: Nola Freeman, Trustee, St Dunstan's Church, Church Road, Cheam, Surrey SM3 8QH (020 8641 1284)

CC number: 238392

Eligibility

People in need who live in Cheam. Preference is given to older people.

Types of grants

One-off and recurrent grants, of £50 to £200.

Annual grant total

In 2014 the charity had an income of £4,700 and a total expenditure of £5,200. We estimate that the amount of grants given to individuals totalled £2,500, with funding also awarded to organisations.

Applications

Apply in writing to the correspondent, usually for consideration at the start of May and November. Applications can be made either directly by the individual, or via a social worker, Citizens Advice or other welfare agency.

Sutton Nursing Association

£11,000

Correspondent: John Helps, Administrator, 28 Southway, Carshalton SM5 4HW (020 8770 1095; email: admin@skingle.co.uk)

CC number: 203686

Eligibility

People who are in poor health, require financial assistance and live in the London borough of Sutton or the surrounding area.

Types of grants

One-off grants of up to £500 for domestic items, specialised equipment (such as phones or buggies), furniture, beds, holiday expenses (including insurance), gym sessions, rent arrears, respite care, carpets, disability and other medical aids, computer equipment, clothing and school uniforms, Christmas gifts and so on.

Annual grant total

In 2014 the association had an income of £22,000 and a total expenditure of £23,500. Grants are mainly made through various organisations. We estimate that support to individuals totalled around £11,000.

Exclusions

Recurrent grants and matters relating to ongoing liabilities are not considered.

Applications

Applications are normally made through a social worker, Citizens Advice or other welfare agency. They are considered on a bi-monthly basis and should include as much information as possible, including estimated costs, funds available from other sources secured or applied to and the ability of the individual to contribute.

Other information

The association also makes grants to the community nursing services, hospitals and local organisations.

Tower Hamlets

Bishopsgate Foundation

£41,500

Correspondent: Geoff Wilson, Director of Finance, Bishopsgate Institute, 230 Bishopsgate, London EC2M 4QH (020 7392 9253; email: enquiries@ bishopsgate.org.uk; website: www. bishopsgate.org.uk)

CC number: 1090923

Eligibility

Pensioners over the age of 60 who live and work, or have lived or worked, in the parishes of St Botolph without Bishopsgate; Christchurch, Spitalfields; and St Leonard's, Shoreditch – all within the borough of Tower Hamlets.

Types of grants

Recurrent grants plus a Christmas bonus.

Annual grant total

In 2013/14 the foundation held assets of £22.5 million and had an income of £2.3 million. Pensions to individuals totalled £41,500, with local charitable organisations receiving a further £40,000.

Applications

Application forms are available from the correspondent. Applications can be submitted either directly by the individual or, where applicable, through a social worker, Citizens Advice or other welfare agency. There are no deadlines and applications are considered as and when a vacancy arises.

Other information

The foundation's principal activity is the running of the Bishopsgate Institute and library. As well as making top-up pension grants, it runs monthly lunches, a Christmas lunch and day trips for elderly individuals, and offers funding for local organisations.

Help-in-Need Association (HINA)

£4,000

Correspondent: The Trustees, Students Union Building, St Bartholomew's and Royal London, School of Medicine and Dentistry, Stepney Way, Whitechapel, London E1 2AD (email: president@ blhina.org)

CC number: 285585

Eligibility

Individuals in need living in Tower Hamlets, the City of London, Hackney, Newham, Waltham Forest, Redbridge, Barking and Dagenham, Havering or Essex.

Types of grants

One-off grants of up to £175 each for a specified purpose.

Annual grant total

The 2011/12 accounts were the latest available at the time of writing (November 2015).

In 2011/12 the association had an income of £8,000 and a total expenditure of £8,000. We estimate that the total amount of grants awarded to individuals was approximately £4,000, as the association also awards grants to organisations.

Applications

Application forms are available on the association's website. Applications must be submitted via a third party such as a social worker, GP, support worker, etc., who should also include a supporting letter and any relevant supporting documentation. Additional documents may be uploaded along with the application form.

The Henderson Charity

£16,000

Correspondent: Philip Hendry, Administrator, Flat 8, Masters Lodge, Johnson Street, London E1 0BE (020 7790 1793; email: philipehendry@gmail. com)

CC number: 1012208

Eligibility

Older people who live in the hamlet of Ratcliff and the parish of St George's-in-the-East, Stepney. Applicants must be longstanding residents of the beneficial area and there is a maximum income requirement.

Types of grants

Small pensions of around £20 a month.

Annual grant total

In 2013/14 the charity had both an income and expenditure of around £18,000. We estimate that the amount of grants given to individuals amounted to £16,000.

Applications

Vacancies are normally advertised locally through social services and appropriate welfare agencies. When a pension is available, application forms can be obtained from social services or the correspondent.

Stepney Relief-in-Need Charity

£16,700 (29 grants)

Correspondent: Mrs J. Partleton, Clerk to the Trustees, Rectory Cottage, 5 White Horse Lane, Stepney, London E1 3NE (020 7790 3598; email: jeanpartleton194@btinternet.com)

CC number: 250130

Eligibility

People in need who live within the old metropolitan borough of Stepney.

Types of grants

One-off grants, usually of £100 to £500, are considered for a wide range of needs, including household items, clothing, holidays where individuals will benefit from a short break, convalescence costs following discharge from hospital, hospital travel expenses and mobility aids.

Annual grant total

In 2013/14 the charity had both an income and total expenditure of £30,500. Grants were awarded totalling £17,500, of which we believe around £16,700 was given for social welfare purposes. In total, 31 grants were made to individuals during the year for both social welfare and educational needs.

Exclusions

No grants are made towards the repayment of loans, rent, council tax or utility bills.

Applications

An application form is available from the correspondent and may be submitted either directly by the individual or through a relative, social worker or other welfare agency. The trustees usually meet four times a year, but some applications can be considered between meetings at the chair's discretion.

Wandsworth

The Wandsworth Combined Charity

£9,000

Correspondent: R. Cooles, 179 Upper Richmond Road West, East Sheen, London SW14 8DU (020 8876 4478)

CC number: 210269

Eligibility

People in need who live in the London borough of Wandsworth. The current funding themes for welfare are to relieve poverty or need of the elderly, to provide education or training to help residents irrespective of age, to become better equipped to enter the world of work and to tackle crime and anti-social behaviour, particularly amongst those who feel marginalised

Types of grants

One-off grants of up to £1,500 may be made.

Annual grant total

In 2013/14 the charity had an income of £7,800 and a total expenditure of £9,500. We estimate grants to individuals were around £9,000.

Exclusions

The grant cannot be used to fund work that is the responsibility of statutory agencies, statutory organisations, such as local authorities and schools, purely commercial ventures, political campaigns or concerns, religious organisations where the activities benefit only those of a particular faith, individuals, spending that has already taken place.

Applications

Apply in writing to the correspondent. Applications should be submitted through voluntary or community groups or registered charities.

Other information

Grants are also made to organisations working in the local area.

North East

General

Alderman Worsley Bursary

£4,500

Correspondent: Hugh McGouran, Administrator, Tees Valley Community Foundation, Wallace House, Falcon Court, Preston Farm Industrial Estate, Stockton-on-Tees TS18 3TX (01642 260860; email: info@ teesvalleyfoundation.org; website: www. teesvalleyfoundation.org)

CC number: 1111222

Eligibility

Students from Thornaby-on-Tees intending to study on a full-time undergraduate degree at any UK university.

Types of grants

Bursary of up to £4,500.

Annual grant total

Annual award of up to £4,500.

Applications

Application forms can be found on the Tees Valley Community Foundation website, once the application round begins.

Other information

This charity is administrated by the Tees Valley Community Foundation.

The Olive and Norman Field Charity

£17,000

Correspondent: Paddy Chapman, Chair, British Red Cross Society, Carrick House, Thurston Road, Northallerton DL6 2NA (01609 772186; email: olive&norman@redcross.org.uk; website: oliveandnorman.co.uk)

CC number: 208760

Eligibility

People who are in poor health, convalescent or who have disabilities and live in the following local government areas: the boroughs of Darlington, Hartlepool, Middlesbrough, Redcar and Cleveland, and Stockton-on-Tees; Durham County Council; York City Council; North Yorkshire County Council; and former North Riding of Yorkshire.

Types of grants

One-off grants, usually in the range of £100 to £350, are given towards services, items or facilities that aid the recovery or improve quality of life. Applications are considered on an individual basis, but previous grants have been used for purposes including the purchase of specialist equipment, a holiday for a family coping with illness and white goods for an individual leaving hospital.

Annual grant total

In 2014 the charity had an income of £24,000 and a total expenditure of £19,700. We estimate that the amount of grants given to individuals totalled around £17,000.

Exclusions

Grants cannot be given to pay for bills or any outstanding arrears.

Applications

Application forms are available from the charity's website or from the correspondent. Applications should be submitted through a supporting professional, such as a doctor or other health professional, social worker, housing officer, Citizens Advice officer or other similar agency. Applications are usually considered at quarterly trustee meetings. Applications should be received ten days prior to a meeting, the dates of which are posted on the charity's website. Grants are made to the supporting agency.

The Greggs Foundation

£104,500 (918 grants)

Correspondent: David Carnaffan, Grants Manager, Fernwood House, Clayton Road, Jesmond, Newcastle upon Tyne NE2 1TL (0191 212 7626; email: greggsfoundation@greggs.co.uk; website: www.greggsfoundation.org.uk)

CC number: 296590

Eligibility

People in need who live in the north east of England (Northumberland, Tyne and Wear, Durham and Teesside). Priority is given to children and families.

Types of grants

Grants of up to £150 and are given for essential items such as white goods, furniture, baby equipment, flooring, clothing and school uniforms. The maximum grants for certain items are detailed on the website.

Annual grant total

In 2014 the foundation held assets of £14.4 million and had an income of £2 million. 918 hardship grants to individuals totalled £104,500. Of this grants made directly from the foundation amounted to £130,000, and £71,000 came from the foundation's charitable partners. £96,000 of this was given in block grants directly to social organisations to make grants on the foundation's behalf.

Various other causes received a total of £1.1 million (excluding supporting costs).

Exclusions

Grants are not given to cover unspecified costs, loan repayments, bankruptcy fees, holidays, funeral expenses, medical equipment or computer equipment.

Applications

The foundation now uses an online application form. In exceptional circumstances, if you cannot use the online form contact the trust to make other arrangements. Applications should be made through a welfare agency, such as social services, probation services,

Citizens Advice, victim support, health, disability and housing associations, or other similar organisations. Applications submitted directly by the individual will not be considered. The foundation asks that applicants do not send any additional information as this will not be considered.

Applications received by Friday at 4pm will be processed in the following week. If the applicant does not receive a reply after three weeks it can be assumed that the application has been unsuccessful.

Other information
Through the Hardship Fund, the Greggs Foundation administers funds on behalf of a number of other local charitable trusts, including the Brough Benevolent Association, the Barbour Trust, the 1989 Willan Trust, the Chrysalis Trust, the Hadrian Trust, the Joicey Trust, the Sir James Knott Trust and the Rothley Trust.

Note: only one form from each applicant should be submitted to the joint trusts, as the payment will be made from joint funds.

The foundation also has separate grants programmes for organisations.

Lady Elizabeth Hastings' Non-Educational Charity

£138,000 (145 grants)

Correspondent: Andrew Fallows, Clerk, Carter Jonas, 82 Micklegate, York YO1 6LF (01904 558220; email: leh. clerk@carterjonas.co.uk; website: www. ladyelizabethhastingscharities.co.uk)

CC number: 224098

Eligibility
People who are in need and live in the ecclesiastical parishes of Collingham with Harewood, Ledsham with Fairburn or Thorp Arch. Clergy and former clergy who are working or have worked in the former counties of Yorkshire, Westmorland, Cumbria and Northumberland, and their dependants. Maps showing the boundaries of the areas of benefit are provided on the charity's website.

Types of grants
One-off grants for welfare purposes or payment of relevant items or services.

Annual grant total
In 2013/14 the charity held assets of £15.9 million and had an income of £542,000. A total of 117 clergy, and their dependants, as well as other individuals in need, received a combined £138,000 in grants from the Non-Educational Charity. Grants were also given for the maintenance of churches in the beneficiary area.

A further 203 grants were made from the Educational Foundation, totalling £118,000.

Applications
Apply in writing to the correspondent.

Other information
The trust is managed by and derives its income from the Lady Elizabeth Hastings Estate Charity. Half of the charity's income goes is distributed to the Non-Educational Charity and the other half to the Education Foundation.

The John Routledge Hunter Memorial Fund

£3,000

Correspondent: Mary Waugh, Dickinson Dees Solicitors, One Trinity, Broad Chare, Newcastle upon Tyne NE1 2HF (0191 279 9000)

CC number: 225619

Eligibility
People who live in Northumberland and Tyne and Wear (north of River Tyne) who have (or recently have had) chest, lung or catarrhal complaints.

Types of grants
Grants of £200 to £500 towards a two or three week recuperative holiday in a hotel in Lytham St Annes or Southport (including rail travel expenses, bed, breakfast, evening meal and £25 in cash). Holidays are taken between Easter and September.

Annual grant total
In 2013/14 the fund had an income of £15,400 and a total expenditure of £13,400. Our research suggests that the fund is currently focused on making grants to organisations and we estimate that around £3,000 was made in grants to individuals.

Applications
Application forms are available from the correspondent. They should be supported by a certificate signed by a doctor. Applications should be submitted directly by the individual and are considered from January to April.

Sherburn House Charity

£152,000 (827 grants)

Correspondent: Stephen Black, Administration Manager, Ramsey House, Sherburn Hospital, Durham DH1 2SE (0191 372 2551; fax: 0191 372 0035; email: admin@sherburnhouse.org; website: www.sherburnhouse.org)

CC number: 217652

Eligibility
People in 'extreme social and financial need' who live in the North East of England between the rivers Tweed and Tees.

Types of grants
One-off grants according to need.

Annual grant total
In 2013/14 the charity held assets of £30.6 million and had an income of £1.7 million. During the year, the charity made 827 relief-in-need grants which totalled £152,000. Of this amount, just over £1,000 was awarded to residents of the charity's care homes.

In other grants, £1,300 was given for educational purposes and a further £300,000 was received by 127 organisations.

Exclusions
Applicants must wait two years before re-applying. No grants are awarded for floor covering (apart from in exceptional circumstances), central heating, driving licences, telephones or telephone arrears, specialist medical equipment, funeral expenses or holidays (apart from in exceptional circumstances) or where there is an apparent surplus of income over expenditure.

Applications
At the time of writing, the charity's preferred method of application-making via its online form had been disabled. However, a form is also available to download from the website. Applications must be made through a welfare agency such as social services, probation services, Citizens Advice or other organisation. The applicant must disclose weekly household income and expenditure, explaining any excess of income over expenditure. Applications are normally assessed on a monthly basis.

Note: if a grant is successful, only one item will be awarded. Cheques are paid to the welfare agency on behalf of the applicant. Agencies have one month to use a grant before it is withdrawn. A full list of application guidelines is available to download from the website.

Other information
The charity also runs residential care, sheltered housing and independent accommodation for elderly people, more details and application packs for which are available from its informative website.

John T. Shuttleworth Ropner Memorial Fund

£34,000

Correspondent: Brenda Dye, Grants Manager, County Durham Community Foundation, Victoria House, St Johns Road, Meadowfield Industrial Estate, Durham DH7 8XL (0191 378 6340; fax: 0191 378 2409; email: brenda@cdcf.org.uk; website: www.cdcf.org.uk)

CC number: 1047625

Eligibility

Sick, elderly or disabled individuals and their carers in the Tees Valley area who are in need of respite care, or who need temporary support following hospitalisation, bereavement or because of dependency treatment. Applicants must live in Darlington, Hartlepool, Middlesbrough, Redcar and Cleveland or Stockton-on-Tees.

Types of grants

Grants of up to £1,000 for recuperative or respite care, home help assistance, bereavement-related costs, travel and accommodation for individuals (and for their families) undergoing dependency treatment at a clinic or centre away from their place of residence.

Annual grant total

In 2013/14 the charity made grants to individuals totalling £34,000.

Exclusions

Only one grant per family per financial year. Retrospective grants will not be made. No grants are given for medical equipment or treatment, or nursing care.

Applications

Application forms are available to download from the Durham Community Foundation website. A reference from a social or healthcare professional is required.

County Durham

John T. County Durham Community Foundation

£57,000

Correspondent: Barbara Gubbins, Chief Executive, Victoria House, Whitfield Court, St John's Road, Meadowfield Industrial Estate, Durham DH7 8XL (0191 378 6340; email: info@cdcf.org.uk; website: www.cdcf.org.uk)

CC number: 1047625

Eligibility

People who are in need and live in County Durham or Darlington.

Types of grants

One-off grants, usually of between £50 to £2,000, are awarded. In 2013/14 grants were given towards, for example, beds and bedding, cots, white goods, carpets, disability equipment and respite holidays. See the website for details of open funds and the types of grants they offer.

Annual grant total

In 2013/14 we believe welfare grants to individuals totalled around £57,000.

Exclusions

No grants are made towards medical treatment, nursing care or anything which is the responsibility of social services or the NHS. Grants are not made retrospectively.

Applications

See the website for information on open funds, guidelines and application procedures.

Other information

The foundation also makes grants to organisations working to benefit its local area.

Lord Crewe's Charity
See entry on page 173

The Sedgefield District Relief in Need Charity (The Sedgefield Charities)

£6,300

Correspondent: John Hannon, Clerk to the Trustees, East House, Mordon, Stockton-on-Tees, County Durham TS21 2EY (01740 622512; email: east.house@btinternet.com)

CC number: 230395

Eligibility

People in need who live in the parishes of Bishop Middleham, Bradbury, Cornforth, Fishburn, Mordon, Sedgefield and Trimdon, in County Durham.

Types of grants

One-off grants, including those for furnishings, bedding, medical requisites, mobility aids, hospital travel costs, transport for people with disabilities, living expenses and respite care. Loans may also be available.

Annual grant total

In 2014 the charity had an income of £20,500 and a total expenditure of £26,500. We estimate that the amount awarded to individuals for social welfare purposes totalled around £6,300.

Applications

Applications can be made in writing to the correspondent. They can be submitted directly by the individual or through a social worker, Citizens Advice, welfare agency or other third party, such as a carer or relative. They are considered as they arise.

Other information

The charity gives to individuals and organisations and awards grants for both educational and social welfare purposes.

The Teesside Emergency Relief Fund
See entry on page 415

John T. Wright Funk Fund

£3,000

Correspondent: Barbara Gubbins, County Durham Community Foundation, Victoria House, Whitfield Court, St John's Road, Meadowfield Industrial Estate, Durham DH7 8XL (0191 378 6340; email: info@cdcf.org.uk; website: www.cdcf.org.uk)

CC number: 1047625

Eligibility

Families in Darlington or County Durham.

Types of grants

Hardship grants of up to £500 to help keep families together or to support families in crisis. Grants are made for the purchase of essential domestic equipment and furniture.

Annual grant total

Grants usually total in excess of £3,000 to £5,000 each year.

Exclusions

The fund does not assist with bankruptcy fees or debt and will not make retrospective grants.

Applications

Application forms are available to download from the County Durham Community Foundation website. Applications can be completed by the individual or by a representative on the applicant's behalf, if necessary. A reference from a social worker or professional advisor in a related field should also be attached. Forms must be completed and signed. Guidance notes can also be downloaded from the County Durham Foundation's website. A telephone interview with a representative of the foundation may be conducted to determine eligibility. The grants team can be contacted for additional guidance.

Northumberland

Lord Crewe's Charity
See entry on page 173

Morpeth Dispensary

£2,500

Correspondent: Michael Gaunt, Trustee, 15 Bridge Street, Morpeth, Northumberland NE61 1NX (01670 512336; email: alison@ brumellandsample.f2s.com)

CC number: 222352

Eligibility
People who are sick and poor and live in or around Morpeth.

Types of grants
Grants are one-off and range from £40 to £300 including those for new washing machines, household bills, cookers, decorating costs, clothing, furniture and so on.

Annual grant total
In 2014 the charity had an income of £3,200 and an expenditure of £4,600. We estimate that the amount of grants given to individuals totalled around £2,200.

Applications
Apply in writing to the correspondent at any time through a third party such as a social worker, GP, Citizens Advice or other welfare agency. Applications must include detail of the applicant's age, whether a single parent, whether on benefits, their address and any details regarding health matters. Grants are made directly to the third party, not the applicant.

Other information
Grants are also made to organisations to provide additional help at Christmas, for instance a trip to the theatre at Christmas for those individuals meeting the eligibility criteria.

Tyne and Wear

Gateshead

The Gateshead Relief-in-Sickness Fund

£900

Correspondent: Rachel Ray, Correspondent, Thomas Magnay and Co., 8 St Mary's Green, Whickham, Newcastle upon Tyne NE16 4DN (0191 488 7459; email: rachelray@ thomasmagnay.co.uk)

CC number: 234970

Eligibility
People who are in poor health, convalescent or who have disabilities and live in the borough of Gateshead.

Types of grants
One-off grants towards providing or paying for items, services or facilities, which will alleviate need or assist with recovery, and are not readily available from other sources. In the past, grants have been given to adapt a bathroom for a boy with learning and physical disabilities and for computers and talking typewriters for people who are registered blind.

Annual grant total
In 2014 the fund had an income of £2,600 and a total expenditure of £1,000. We estimate that grants totalled £900.

Applications
Apply in writing to the correspondent. Applications can be submitted directly by the individual or through a social worker, Citizens Advice or other welfare agency.

Newcastle upon Tyne

The Non-Ecclesiastical Charity of William Moulton

£28,500

Correspondent: George Jackson, Clerk to the Trustees, 10 Sunlea Avenue, North Shields NE30 3DS (0191 251 0971; email: jgeorgelvis@blueyonder.co.uk)

CC number: 216255

Eligibility
People in need who have lived within the boundaries of the city of Newcastle upon Tyne for at least the past 12 months.

Types of grants
Grants typically range between £50 and £200 for general household/personal needs such as washing machines, cookers, furniture, clothing and so on.

Annual grant total
In 2014 the charity held assets of £1.3 million and had an income of £33,800. Financial assistance to individuals totalled £28,500 and was distributed as follows:

Payments, gifts and donations	£23,500
Mothers' Union holiday grants	£5,000

Exclusions
No grants are given for education, training or rent arrears.

Applications
Application forms are available from the correspondent. Applications should be submitted through a social worker, Citizens Advice or other welfare agency and are considered monthly.

Other information
The charity also makes grants to local organisations although none were awarded during 2014.

The Thomas Thompson's Poor Rate Gift

£3,500

Correspondent: Carol Farquhar-Johnston, Correspondent, Newcastle City Council, Civic Centre, Newcastle NE1 8QH (0191 211 6287; email: carol.s.farquhar-johnston@newcastle.gov.uk)

CC number: 253846

Eligibility
People in need who live in Byker.

Types of grants
One-off grants for items such as washing machines, furniture and cookers. Grants have also been given to replace Christmas presents and children's bikes which have been stolen.

Annual grant total
In 2013/14 the charity had an income of £4,300 and a total expenditure of £3,900. We estimate that £3,500 was given in grants to individuals.

Applications
Apply in writing to the correspondent, for consideration throughout the year. Grants to replace stolen property are usually submitted through Victim Support.

North Tyneside

Wallsend Charitable Trust

£2,000

Correspondent: The Secretary, North Tyneside Council, 16 The Silverlink North, Newcastle upon Tyne NE27 0BY (0191 643 7006)

CC number: 215476

Eligibility

People over 60 who are on or just above state benefit income levels and live in the former borough of Wallsend.

Types of grants

One-off grants ranging between £10 and £500 to help meet extra requirements including, washing machines, fridge-freezers, carpets, home decoration, safety and security measures and medical equipment.

Annual grant total

In 2014 the trust had an income of £49,800 and a total expenditure of almost £10,000. The majority of the trust's charitable expenditure is generally given to organisations with similar objects. We estimate that the amount of grants given to individuals totalled around £2,000.

Exclusions

The trust will not help with continuing costs such as residential care or telephone rentals and will not help a person whose income is significantly above state benefit levels. Applicants must have exhausted all statutory avenues such as DWP, social services department and so on.

Applications

Apply in writing to the correspondent either directly by the individual or through a social worker, Citizens Advice or other welfare agency or third party, such as a friend or relative. Applications are considered quarterly in April, July, September and December. They must include details of the purpose of the grant and an estimate of the cost.

Other information

Grants are given to organisations provided that the majority of members meet the same criteria that apply to individuals.

Sunderland

Houghton-le-Spring Relief in Need Charity

£2,000

Correspondent: Brian Scott, Correspondent, 28 Finchale Close, Houghton-le-Spring, Tyne and Wear DH4 5QU (0191 584 1608; email: rectorpinnington@gmail.com)

CC number: 810025

Eligibility

People in need living in the parishes of Bournmoor, South Biddick and West Rainton in County Durham, the parishes of Hetton and Warden Law in Tyne and Wear, or those parts of the borough of Sunderland and the parish of Framwellgate Moor, which formerly constituted part of the ancient parish of Houghton le Spring.

Types of grants

One-off and recurrent according to need.

Annual grant total

In 2014/15 the charity had an income of £1,400 and a total expenditure of £2,200. We estimate that the amount of grants given to individuals totalled £2,000.

Applications

Apply in writing to the correspondent.

George Hudson's Charity

£19,500

Correspondent: Peter Taylor, Secretary, 19 John Street, Sunderland SR1 1JG (0191 567 4857; fax: 0191 510 9347; email: petertaylor@mckenzie-bell.co.uk)

CC number: 527204

Eligibility

People under the age of 18 whose father has died or is unable to work and are living in Sunderland, with first preference to children of seafarers or pilots belonging to the Port of Sunderland, and in second preference to those born and resident in the ancient township of Monkwearmouth.

Types of grants

The charity gives pocket money, Christmas bonuses and clothing vouchers.

Annual grant total

In 2013/14 the charity had assets of £584,000 and an income of £41,000. £13,400 was given in monthly allowances and Christmas bonuses to 55 children. £9,300 was given in clothing and footwear grants and a further £125 was used to distribute Easter confectionary for beneficiaries.

Applications

Application forms are available from the correspondent. Applications are considered every other month.

The Sunderland Guild of Help

£7,000

Correspondent: Norman Taylor, Chair, 4 Toward Road, Sunderland, Tyne and Wear SR1 2QG (0191 567 2895 (only on Wednesdays 9.30am – 4pm); fax: 0191 567 2895; email: info@guildofhelp.co.uk; website: www.guildofhelp.co.uk)

CC number: 229656

Eligibility

People in need who live in Sunderland.

Types of grants

Support is given for the advancement of health and the relief of poverty. In special circumstances, refurbished goods have been given to those most in need in the form of beds, washing machines and fridges.

Annual grant total

In 2013/14 the guild had an income of £9,700 and a total expenditure of £7,600. We estimate that the amount of grants given to individuals totalled £7,000.

Exclusions

New goods or goods made to order cannot be supplied. Applications requesting money or loans will be rejected.

Applications

Applications can only be considered if they are submitted through a social worker or professional familiar with the guild's system. They should include an income and expenditure statement and are considered throughout the year.

Other information

The guild administers funds including the Sunderland Queen Victoria Memorial Fund 1901 and the Sunderland Convalescent Fund.

In addition, the guild also acts as an enabling charity through its premises on Toward Road, Sunderland where other small charities are provided with accommodation at rents that reflect their charitable status.

The Sunderland Orphanage and Educational Foundation

£13,000

Correspondent: Peter Taylor, Partner, McKenzie Bell, 19 John Street, Sunderland SR1 1JG (0191 567 4857; fax: 0191 510 9347; email: petertaylor@ mckenzie-bell.co.uk)

CC number: 527202

Eligibility

Young people under the age of 25 who are resident in or around Sunderland who have a parent who has disabilities or has died, or whose parents are divorced or legally separated.

Types of grants

Allowances are given for clothing and pocket money. Grants are also made to students.

Annual grant total

In 2013/14 the foundation had an income of £23,500 and a total expenditure of £27,500. Grants are made to individuals for both social welfare and educational purposes. We estimate that social welfare grants totalled around £13,000.

Applications

Applications should be made in writing to the correspondent. They are considered every other month.

North West

General

The Cotton Districts Convalescent Fund and the Barnes Samaritan Charity

£25,000

Correspondent: Nicholas Stockton, Secretary, c/o Cassons Chartered Accountants, Rational House, 64 Bridge Street, Manchester M3 3BN (0845 337 9409; fax: 0845 337 9408; email: manchester@cassons.co.uk; website: www.cotton-districts.co.uk)

CC number: 224727

Eligibility

People in need who have a severe/long-term illness, are convalescent or who have a disability and live: in the counties of Lancashire and Greater Manchester; the districts of Craven, North Yorkshire and High Peak, Derbyshire; the districts of Macclesfield and Warrington in Cheshire; or the district of Calderdale, West Yorkshire.

Types of grants

The charity makes grants to enable a subsidised convalescent holiday of one week to be taken at hotels in Blackpool and St Annes. Applicants are expected to pay an amount towards the cost of a week's half-board holiday with the fund paying the difference. Alternatively, the charity may instead make a contribution of £200 towards the costs of a holiday elsewhere in the UK. Consideration will be given to making a grant towards the costs of a special needs holiday proposed by the applicant (for example where nursing or other care is required).

Monthly grants not exceeding £45 per month are also available towards living costs for those who are in poor health, convalescent or who have a disability.

Annual grant total

In 2014 the charity had assets of £1.1 million, an income of £47,500 and a total expenditure of £28,500. Payments to beneficiaries totalled £25,000.

Applications

Apply in writing to the secretary, providing details of your financial and medical circumstances. The application should be accompanied by a supporting letter from a sponsor, such as a doctor or social worker, confirming these medical and financial circumstances.

Note: the trustees have previously stated that due to a lack of income, future grant-making will be limited.

Other information

This charity was previously known as The Cotton Districts Convalescent Fund.

The Grant, Bagshaw, Rogers and Tidswell Fund

£11,500

Correspondent: Lawrence Downey, Correspondent, Ripley House, 56 Freshfield Road, Formby, Liverpool L37 3HW (01704 879330; email: lawrencedowney@btconnect.com)

CC number: 216948

Eligibility

Older people in need who live, or were born in, Liverpool, the Wirral, Ellesmere Port or Chester.

Types of grants

Small pensions are paid half-yearly. Occasional one-off grants may also be given.

Annual grant total

In 2013/14 the fund had an income of £14,100 and a total expenditure of £12,100. We estimate that the amount of grants given to individuals totalled £11,500.

Applications

Application forms are available from the correspondent. Applications should be returned by 28 February and 30 October for consideration in April and December respectively.

Gregson Memorial Annuities

£2,700

Correspondent: Alison Houghton, Brabners Chaffe Street, Horton House, Exchange Flags, Liverpool L2 3YL (0151 600 3443; email: alison.houghton@ brabnerscs.com)

CC number: 218096

Eligibility

Female domestic servants who have been in service for at least ten years in Liverpool, Southport, Malpas and the surrounding area and who cannot work now for health reasons.

Types of grants

Annuities of about £300 a year, payable in two six-monthly instalments.

Annual grant total

In 2013/14 the charity had an income of £3,400 and a total expenditure of £2,900. We estimate that the total award granted to individuals was approximately £2,700.

Applications

Applications in writing to the correspondent are considered throughout the year.

Lancashire County Nursing Trust

£13,500

Correspondent: Hadyn Gigg, Trustee, Plumpton House, Great Plumpton, Preston PR4 2NJ (01772 673618; email: hadyngigg@yahoo.co.uk; website: www. lcnt.org.uk)

CC number: 224667

Eligibility

Retired nurses who are in need and have been employed in Lancashire, south Cumbria or Greater Manchester. Grants are also given to people who are in need in the area, including adults or children who are in ill health or who have disabilities. Most of the trust's income is for the benefit of retired nurses.

Types of grants

One-off grants of up to £500. Support for retired nurses can be for any purpose but funding for people who are in need or ill health is generally focused on household or medical equipment that improves quality of life.

Annual grant total

In 2014 the trust had an income of £15,000 and a total expenditure of £14,600. We estimate grants to individuals for social welfare purposes to be in the region of £13,500.

Applications

Apply in writing to the correspondent. Applications can be submitted directly by the individual or through health and social work professionals, charities or other welfare organisations.

Cheshire

John Holford Charity

£12,000

Correspondent: Kerris Owen, Clerk to the Trustees, Parish Office, St Peter's Church, The Cross, Chester CH1 2LA (07794654212; email: jholfordcharity@ gmail.com; website: www. johnholfordcharity.org)

CC number: 223046

Eligibility

People in need who live in the parishes of Astbury, Clutton, Congleton and Middlewich.

Due to local authority changes the list of eligible parishes has been extended and now also includes: Alsager, Brereton, Church Lawton, Eaton, Goostrey, Holmes Chapel, Hulme Walfield, Mow Cop, North Rode, Odd Rode, Rode Heath, Sandbach, Smallwood, Swettenham and Wheelock.

Types of grants

One-off and recurrent grants for a variety of needs, ranging from £100 to £2,500.

Annual grant total

In 2014 the charity had an income of £186,000 and an expenditure of £96,000. At the time of writing (November 2015) full accounts could not be viewed, but in previous years grants to individuals and organisations totalled £23,000 on average. We estimate that about £12,000 is given to individuals.

Exclusions

According to our research, grants are not given for education or medical treatment.

Applications

Applications can be made online on the charity's website. Alternatively an application form can be downloaded from the website or requested from the correspondent. They can be submitted by the individual or through a social worker, carer, Citizens Advice, other welfare agency or also a relative. Two letters of support are required. Requests are considered on a regular basis.

Other information

Organisations are also supported.

Lindow Workhouse Charity

£7,700

Correspondent: John Fallows, Correspondent, 1 Thornfield Hey, Wilmslow, Cheshire SK9 5JY (01625 533950; email: lwt@jfallows.org.uk)

CC number: 226023

Eligibility

People in need who live in the ancient parish of Wilmslow.

Types of grants

One-off grants to help with, for example, fuel bills, equipment repairs, property repairs. Any cases of real need are considered.

Annual grant total

In 2013/14 the charity had an income of £10,800 and a total expenditure of £15,600. We estimate that about £7,700 was awarded to individuals for social welfare purposes.

Exclusions

Grants are not made towards relief of rates, taxes or other public funds.

Applications

Application may be made in writing to the correspondent at any time. They can be submitted directly by the individual or a family member, through a third party (such as a social worker or teacher), or through an organisation (such as Citizens Advice or a school).

Other information

Our research suggests that children with special educational needs are also supported.

Municipal General Charities for the Poor
See entry on page 249

Cheshire East

The Congleton Town Trust

£5,000

Correspondent: Jo Money, Clerk, c/o Congleton Town Hall, High Street, Congleton, Cheshire CW12 1BN (01260 270908; email: info@congletontowntrust. co.uk; website: www.congletontowntrust. co.uk)

CC number: 1051122

Eligibility

People in need who live in the town of Congleton (this refers only to the area administered by Congleton Town Council).

Types of grants

Grants, usually in the range of £200 and £3,000, are given to individuals in need or to organisations that provide relief, services or facilities to those in need.

Annual grant total

In 2014 the trust had an income of £24,500 and a total expenditure of £21,000. Grants are made to individuals and organisations for both social welfare and educational purposes. We estimate that social welfare grants to individuals totalled £5,000.

Applications

We would advise potential applicants to, in the first instance, contact the correspondent for more information. This can be done using the online form on the website.

Macclesfield and District Relief-in-Sickness Charity

£2,800

Correspondent: Peter Womby, Trustee, Oak Crescent, Leek Old Road, Sutton, Macclesfield, Cheshire SK11 0JA (01260 252220)

CC number: 501631

Eligibility

People who are sick, convalescent, disabled or infirm and live in Macclesfield, the rural district of Macclesfield or the urban district of Bollington.

Types of grants

One-off grants only for necessary items such as washing machines, telephone installation, removals or specialist wheelchairs and especially for health-related items that would improve the quality of the applicant's situation.

Annual grant total

In 2013/14 the charity had an income of £2,700 and a total expenditure of £3,000. We estimate that the amount of grants given to individuals totalled around £2,800.

Applications

Applications must be made through a local social services office, doctor's surgery or other welfare agencies and they should verify the need of the applicant.

Cheshire West and Chester

Chester Municipal Charities

£46,000

Correspondent: Sharon Green, Administrator, The Bluecoat, Upper Northgate Street, Chester CH1 4EE (01244 403277; email: sharon.green@chestermc.org.uk)

CC number: 1077806

Eligibility

Residents of Chester who are in need due to age, ill health, disability or financial hardship.

Types of grants

Mainly one-off grants for relief-in-need purposes.

Annual grant total

In 2014 the charity had assets of £14.4 million and an income of £364,000. Grants totalled £182,500 and were awarded to individuals for welfare and educational purposes and to organisations. We estimate that social welfare grants to individuals totalled £46,000.

Applications

An application form is available from the correspondent.

Other information

The charity also manages almshouses.

The Chester Parochial Charity

£14,900

Correspondent: Kerris Owen, Clerk, Parish Office, St Peter's Church, The Cross, Chester CH1 2LA (07794 654212; email: cprncharity@gmail.com)

CC number: 1001314

Eligibility

People in need who live in the city of Chester.

Types of grants

One-off grants, usually ranging from £50 to £1,000, are given for furniture, washing machines, cookers, electrical items, clothing, school uniform, carpets, and so on. A supermarket vouchers scheme is also available to help low-income families, mainly over the Christmas period.

Annual grant total

In 2013/14 the charity had an income of £39,500 and a total expenditure of £23,000. At the time of writing (October 2015) the charity's accounts were not yet available to view on the Charity Commission; however, the charity's record tells us that trustees awarded grants to the sum of £14,900.

Applications

Application forms are available from the correspondent. Applications can be made directly by the individual, through a recognised referral agency or through a third party such as a family member. All applicants will be visited by a trustee who will then report back to the subcommittee for a final decision. Applications are considered at any time.

Frodsham Nursing Fund

£3,200

Correspondent: Joan Pollen, Trustee, 22 Fluin Lane, Frodsham WA6 7QH (01928 731043; email: andrewfaraday@hotmail.com)

CC number: 503246

Eligibility

People in need who are sick, convalescent or living with disabilities and are resident in the town of Frodsham.

Types of grants

One-off grants according to need. Past grants have been given for items such as bedding, clothing, medical aids, heating and other domestic appliances. Temporary relief may also be provided to those caring for somebody who is sick or disabled.

Annual grant total

In 2013/14 the fund had an income of £3,000 and a total expenditure of £3,500. We estimate that social welfare assistance for individuals totalled around £3,200; however, the fund's expenditure tends to vary significantly from year to year.

Applications

Apply in writing to the correspondent, either directly by the individual or on their behalf by a doctor, nurse or social worker. Applicants should briefly state their circumstances and what help is being sought.

The Ursula Keyes Trust

£13,800 (16 grants)

Correspondent: c/o Dot Lawless, Administrator, Baker Tilly, The Steam Mill Business Centre, Steam Mill Street, Chester CH3 5AN (01244 505100; website: www.ursula-keyes-trust.org.uk)

CC number: 517200

Eligibility

People in need, especially those with a medical condition, who live in the area administered by Chester District Council and in particular those within the boundaries of the former City of Chester and the adjoining parishes of Great Boughton and Upton.

Types of grants

One-off grants towards, for example, washing machines for families in need or computers for children with disabilities.

Annual grant total

In 2014 the trust had assets of £4.6 million and had an income of £308,500. Grants to 16 individuals totalled £13,800.

A further £145,000 was given in grants to organisations.

Exclusions

No grants are given to repay debts or loans or to reimburse expenditure already incurred.

Applications

Apply in writing to the correspondent. A summary form is available to download from the website and should be submitted along with your application. Applications must be supported by a social worker, a doctor (if relevant) or another professional or welfare agency.

Applications are usually considered at the end of January, April, July and October and should be received at least four weeks in advance to be certain of consideration at any particular meeting.

Cumbria

Barrow Thornborrow Charity

£4,300

Correspondent: Fred Robinson, Trustee, The Parrock, Stankelt Road, Silverdale, Carnforth LA5 0TW

CC number: 222168

Eligibility

People who have disabilities or are sick and live, or were born in, the former county of Westmorland, the former county borough of Barrow, the former rural districts of Sedbergh and North Lonsdale, or the former urban districts of Dalton-in-Furness, Grange and Ulverston.

Types of grants

One-off grants towards items, services or facilities which are calculated to alleviate suffering and assist recovery and are not available from other sources. In previous years grants have been awarded for household equipment, travel expenses in case of hospitalisation, clothing, computer aids and assistance with essential property repairs.

Annual grant total

In 2014 the charity had an income of £3,300 and a total expenditure of £4,000. We estimate that the amount of grants given to individuals totalled £3,500.

Applications

Apply in writing to the correspondent including details of the applicant's circumstances. Applications can be submitted through a social worker, Citizens Advice or other welfare agency.

Cumbria Community Foundation

£5,300

Correspondent: The Grants Team, Cumbria Community Foundation, Dovenby Hall, Cockermouth, Cumbria CA13 0PN (01900 825760; fax: 01900 826527; email: enquiries@ cumbriafoundation.org; website: www. cumbriafoundation.org)

CC number: 1075120

Eligibility

People resident in Cumbria. Other restrictions including geographical and age-related restrictions pertain depending upon the fund being applied to.

Types of grants

One-off and recurrent grants for various welfare needs, equipment, fuel bills, household adaptations and independent living and homelessness.

Annual grant total

In 2013/14 the foundation made 19 grants to individuals totalling £10,700. We estimate that the amount of grants given to individuals for social welfare purposes amounted to around £5,300.

During the year, more than £1.9 million was awarded to organisations in 232 grants.

Applications

The foundation administers numerous funds that give grants to individuals, they have differing eligibility criteria. Applicants should check the website for full details of each scheme and how to apply.

Other information

The foundation administers funds for both individuals and organisations, some of which may open and close regularly.

Lakeland Disability Support

£16,500

Correspondent: Brenda Robinson, Trust Secretary, 46 Victoria Road North, Windermere, Cumbria LA23 2DS (01539 442800; website: www.amblesideonline. co.uk/clubs/lds/main.html)

CC number: 1102609

Eligibility

People with physical disabilities who live in South Lakeland, Cumbria.

Types of grants

Grants ranging from £200 to £5,000 towards, for example, the cost of respite care, garden access, special education, or equipment such as electric scooters, special chairs or computers.

Annual grant total

In 2014 the charity had an income of £185,000 and a total expenditure of £47,500. Grants to individuals totalled £16,500, with a further £23,500 awarded to local organisations.

Exclusions

No grants are given for long-term care provision.

Applications

Application forms are available from the correspondent or to download from the charity's website. Applications may be made by the individual or a third party and should be accompanied by a reference from a carer, doctor or social worker. Applications are considered quarterly in March, June, September and December. Successful applicants should wait for 12 months before re-applying.

Allerdale

The Bowness Trust

£2,000

Correspondent: Richard Atkinson, Trustee, Milburns Solicitors, Oxford House, 19 Oxford Street, Workington, Cumbria CA14 2AW (01900 67363; fax: 01900 65552)

CC number: 502323

Eligibility

People in need who live in Workington and live at home (not in institutions).

Types of grants

Grants are made to individuals for a wide range of charitable purposes.

Annual grant total

In 2013/14 the trust had an income of £7,100 and had a total expenditure of £2,400. We estimate that the total amount of grants awarded to individuals was £2,000.

Applications

Apply in writing to the correspondent.

Carlisle

Carlisle Sick Poor Fund

£5,500

Correspondent: Lynne Rowley, Correspondent, 15 Fisher Street, Carlisle, Cumbria CA3 8RW

CC number: 223124

Eligibility

People living in Carlisle and its neighbourhood who are in financial hardship due to ill health.

Types of grants

One-off grants of up to £200 are given towards bedding, food, fuel, medical aids and equipment, convalescence, holidays and home help.

Annual grant total

In 2014 the fund had an income of £8,900 and an expenditure of £11,400. We estimate the annual total amount of grants given to individuals to be around £5,500.

Applications

Application forms are available from the correspondent.

Other information

Support is also given to local organisations providing care and relief to people who are sick and in need.

Eden

Crosby Ravensworth Relief in Need Charities

£4,100

Correspondent: George Bowness, Trustee, Ravenseat, Crosby Ravensworth, Penrith, Cumbria CA10 3JB (01931 715382; email: gordonbowness@aol.com)

CC number: 232598

Eligibility

People in need who have lived in the ancient parish of Crosby Ravensworth for at least 12 months. Preference is given to older people.

Types of grants

One-off and recurrent grants. Grants may include coal vouchers, usually of around £30, to senior citizens and a basket of fruit (or other gift) to people who have been in hospital. Grants can also be given to local students entering university if they have been educated in the parish.

Annual grant total

In 2013 the charity had an income of £13,600 and a total expenditure of £16,900. We estimate that social welfare grants to individuals totalled around £4,100.

At the time of writing (November 2015) this was the most recent financial information available.

Applications

Applications may be made in writing to the correspondent, submitted directly by the individual. They should include details of the applicant's financial situation. Applications are normally considered in February, May and October.

Other information

Grants are also awarded to individuals for educational and training purposes and to organisations.

South Lakeland

The Ambleside Welfare Charity

£34,500

Correspondent: Michael Johnson, Clerk to the trustees, 11 The Green, Bolton-le-Sands, Carnforth LA5 8FD (01539 431656; email: lakesparishclerk@yahoo.co.uk)

CC number: 214759

Eligibility

People in need who live in the parish of Ambleside, especially those who are ill.

Types of grants

One-off and recurrent grants are given according to need. Help is also given to local relatives for hospital visits.

Annual grant total

In 2014 the charity had an income of £51,000 and a total expenditure of £42,500. Welfare grants amounted to £34,500.

Applications

Apply in writing to the correspondent.

Agnes Backhouse Annuity Fund

£3,400 (65 grants)

Correspondent: James Hamilton, Trustee, Temple Heelis Solicitors, 1 Kent View, Kendal, Cumbria LA9 4DZ (01539 723757)

CC number: 224960

Eligibility

Unmarried women (including widows) aged over 50 who live in the parish of Ambleside who are in need.

Types of grants

Recurrent grants, usually of around £50.

Annual grant total

In 2014 the fund had assets of £736,000 and an income of £26,500. total expenditure of £15,500. Annuities paid to 65 individuals totalled £3,400.

Applications

Apply in writing to the correspondent.

Other information

In 2013/14 the fund made a grant of £31,000 to Age UK (South Lakeland). The majority of funds were used to assist poorer members of the local community and those with mental health issues (over the age of 50) with the aim of reducing the number of admissions to hospital during the winter months. Grants were used for such items as washing machines, mobility scooters, boilers and external handrails.

The Jane Fisher Trust

£3,400

Correspondent: Kath Marsden, Secretary, 9 Benson Street, Ulverston, Cumbria LA12 7AU (01229 585555; fax: 01229 584950; email: kathmarsden@hotmail.co.uk)

CC number: 225401

Eligibility

People in need over 50 and people who have disabilities, who have lived in the townships of Ulverston and Osmotherly

or the parish of Pennington for at least 20 years.

Types of grants

Small monthly payments. No lump sum grants have been made for many years.

Annual grant total

In 2013/14 the trust had an income of £2,600 and a total expenditure of £3,600. We estimate that the amount of grants given to individuals totalled around £3,400.

Applications

Application forms are available from the correspondent. Applications are considered when they are received. They must include details of income, capital, age, disabilities, marital status and how long the applicant has lived in the area.

Greater Manchester

J. T. Blair's Charity

£23,000

Correspondent: Anne Hosker, Director of Finance, Gaddum Centre, Gaddum House, 6 Great Jackson Street, Manchester M15 4AX (0161 834 6069; email: info@gaddumcentre.co.uk; website: www.gaddumcentre.co.uk)

CC number: 221248

Eligibility

People over 65 who live in Manchester and Salford and are in need.

Types of grants

Weekly pensions of up to £10 are paid at four-weekly intervals.

Annual grant total

In 2013/14 the charity had an income of £21,500 and a total expenditure of £25,500. We estimate that the amount of grants given to individuals totalled £23,000.

Applications

Application forms are available from the correspondent. Applications should be submitted by a social worker or other professional person. The trustees meet three or four times a year. Applicants should contact the charity for specific deadlines. Those in receipt of a pension are visited at least once a year.

The Community Foundation for Greater Manchester (Forever Manchester)

£3,500

Correspondent: The Grants and Awards Officer, 2nd Floor, 8 Hewitt Street, Manchester M15 4GB (0161 214 0940; email: info@forevermanchester.com; website: forevermanchester.com)

CC number: 1017504

Eligibility
People in need who live in Greater Manchester.

Types of grants
Grants are usually one-off.

Annual grant total
In 2013/14 the foundation had assets of £9.6 million and an income of over £3 million. Grants were made totalling £1.3 million, of which £6,900 was given to individuals. Further breakdown was not available; therefore, we estimate that about £3,500 was given for welfare purposes.

Applications
Visit the foundation's website and contact the foundation for details of grant funds that are currently appropriate for individuals to apply for. The website states: 'Please contact our awards team on 0161 214 0940 to discuss deadline dates, eligibility and criteria and to receive guidelines and an application pack.'

Other information
The Community Foundation for Greater Manchester manages a portfolio of grants for a variety of purposes which are mostly for organisations, but there also are a select few aimed at individuals. Funds tend to open and close throughout the year as well as new ones being added – check the website for up-to-date information on currently operating schemes.

Manchester District Nursing Institution Fund

£14,200 (60 grants)

Correspondent: Katherine Malin-August, Correspondent, Gaddum Centre, Gaddum House, 6 Great Jackson Street, Manchester M15 4AX (0161 834 6069; email: info@gaddumcentre.co.uk; website: www.gaddumcentre.co.uk/trust-funds-more-info)

CC number: 235916

Eligibility
People on low income with health-related needs in the cities of Manchester and Salford or the borough of Trafford.

Types of grants
One-off grants. It is important that the request is directly related to the health issue of the applicant and is not related to a general condition of poverty.

Annual grant total
In 2014 the fund had assets of £846,500 and an income of £28,000. The accounts note that in the year a total of 80 applications were considered and 60 grants made totalling £14,200. Further £10,000 was paid to the Gaddum Centre.

Financial figures include the LTRSS.

Exclusions
Grants are not made for funeral expenses, rates, taxes or other public funds, bills, debts or fines.

Applications
Application forms and guidance can be obtained from the correspondent. All requests must be made by a sponsor from a recognised social and/or health agency or an appropriate third party professional. Our research suggests that the trustees meet monthly and the deadline for any meeting is the first Wednesday of the month.

Other information
The fund incorporates The Levenshulme Trust for the Relief of Sickness and Suffering (LTRSS) the objective of which is to help people resident in the postcode Manchester 19 who have health-related problems.

Bolton

The Bolton and District Nursing Association

£2,300

Correspondent: David Wrennall, Trustee, Bolton Guild of Help, Scott House, 27 Silverwell Street, Bolton BL1 1PP (01204 524858; email: guildofhelp@btconnect.com)

CC number: 250153

Eligibility
People who are sick, convalescing, have disabilities or who are infirm and live in the area of Bolton Metropolitan Borough Council.

Types of grants
One-off grants are made for items and services, such as the provision of medical equipment, disability equipment and convalescence.

Annual grant total
In 2014 the charity had an income of £3,200 and a total expenditure of £2,500. We estimate that the amount of grants given to individuals totalled £2,300.

Applications
Application forms are available from the correspondent. Applications can be submitted directly by the individual or through a third party such as a social worker, health visitor or welfare agency. Initial telephone enquiries are encouraged to establish eligibility.

The Bolton Poor Protection Society

£900

Correspondent: The Trustees, Bolton Guild of Help, Scott House, 27 Silverwell Street, Bolton BL1 1PP (email: guildofhelp@btconnect.com)

CC number: 223099

Eligibility
People in need who live in the former county borough of Bolton.

Types of grants
One-off grants are given for emergencies and all kinds of need, ranging from £25 to £50.

Annual grant total
In 2014 the charity had both an income and a total expenditure of £900. We estimate that grants totalled around £900.

Applications
Initial telephone enquiries are encouraged to establish eligibility. Application forms are sent out thereafter.

The Louisa Alice Kay Fund

£49,500 (245 grants)

Correspondent: Tracey Wallace, Secretary, Bolton Guild of Help (Inc.), Scott House, 27 Silverwell Street, Bolton BL1 1PP (email: guildofhelp@btconnect.com)

CC number: 224760–1

Eligibility
People in need who live in Bolton.

Types of grants
One-off grants for emergencies and relief in need, mostly for replacing household equipment and furniture.

Annual grant total

In 2014 grants were made to 245 individuals totalling £49,500 and were distributed in the following areas:

Washing machines	£17,900
Cookers	£12,900
Beds/furniture	£7,200
Other assistance	£5,800
Fridges/freezers	£5,700

Applications

Application forms are available from the correspondent. Applications can be submitted either directly by the individual or a family member, through a third party such as a social worker, or through an organisation such as Citizens Advice or other welfare agency. Applicants will sometimes be interviewed before a grant is awarded.

Other information

The fund is the main subsidiary of the Bolton Guild of Help Incorporated.

Bury

The Bury Relief-in-Sickness Fund

£4,300

Correspondent: Gill Warburton, Trustee, The Royal Bank of Scotland plc, PO Box 26, 40 The Rock, Bury, Lancashire BL9 0NX (0161 797 8040)

CC number: 256397

Eligibility

People living in the metropolitan borough of Bury who are in poor health, convalescent or who have disabilities.

Types of grants

One-off grants towards convalescence, medical equipment and necessities in the home which are not available from other sources.

Annual grant total

In 2014 the fund had an income of £2,600 and a total expenditure of £4,600. We estimate that the total amount of grants awarded to individuals was £4,300.

Applications

Apply in writing to the correspondent.

The Mellor Fund

£4,500

Correspondent: Gillian Critchley, Trustee, 17 Marle Croft, Whitefield, Manchester M45 7NB

CC number: 230013

Eligibility

People who are sick or in need and live in Radcliffe, Whitefield or Unsworth.

Types of grants

One-off grants towards fuel, food and clothing, domestic necessities, medical needs, recuperative breaks and so on. Recurrent grants are generally not given.

Annual grant total

In 2014 the fund had an income of £4,700 and a total expenditure of £4,900. We estimate that around £4,500 was made in grants to individuals for social welfare purposes.

Applications

Apply in writing to the correspondent. Applications can be submitted directly by the individual or through a social worker, Citizens Advice, other welfare agency or a relative, and should include brief details of need, resources, income and commitments. Applications are considered when received.

Manchester

The Crosland Fund

£9,500

Correspondent: John Atherden, Correspondent, Manchester Cathedral, Victoria Street, Manchester M3 1SX (0161 833 2220)

CC number: 242838

Eligibility

People affected by hardship who live in the City of Manchester.

Types of grants

One-off grants given quarterly, usually to the sum of £40 to £50. Grants are typically given for basic necessities such as clothing, food, bedding, furniture, repairs and household materials. Children's Christmas presents may also be given.

Annual grant total

In 2013/14 the fund had an income of £7,000 and a total expenditure of £10,000. We estimate that welfare grants to individuals totalled £9,500.

Applications

Apply in writing to the correspondent. Applications must be submitted through a recognised organisation, for example, a social worker, Citizens Advice or other welfare agency. They are considered in February, May, August and November.

The Dr Garrett Memorial Trust

£4,000

Correspondent: Anne Hosker, Administrator, Gaddum Centre, Gaddum House, 6 Great Jackson Street, Manchester M15 4AX (0161 834 6069; email: amh@gaddumcentre.co.uk; website: www.gaddumcentre.co.uk)

CC number: 1010844

Eligibility

Families or groups in need who live in Manchester.

Types of grants

Grants are given towards the cost of convalescence or holidays for individual families and groups.

Annual grant total

In 2013/14 the trust had an income of £11,100 and a total expenditure of £10,700. We estimate that the amount of grants given to individuals totalled £4,000, with funding also awarded to local organisations.

Exclusions

Applicants should not have had a funded holiday during the past three years.

Applications

Application forms are available from the correspondent and should be completed by a sponsor from a recognised social or health agency. Applications must be submitted by the end of April each year.

Other information

The trust also provides information and advice on a range of social and health care issues.

The Manchester Relief-in-Need Charity and Manchester Children's Relief-in-Need Charity

£42,500

Correspondent: Anne Hosker, Administrator, Gaddum Centre, Gaddum House, 6 Great Jackson Street, Manchester M15 4AX (0161 834 6069; email: amh@gaddumcentre.co.uk; website: www.gaddumcentre.co.uk)

CC number: 224271 and 249657

Eligibility

People in need who live in the city of Manchester and are over 25 (Relief-in-Need) or under 25 (Children's Relief-in-Need).

Types of grants

One-off grants for domestic appliances, furniture, clothing, heating and fuel bills, and other general necessities. Cheques are made out to the supplier of the goods or services.

Annual grant total

In 2013/14 the charities had a combined income of £82,000. Welfare grants to individuals totalled around £42,500; Manchester Relief-in-Need awarded 163 grants amounting to over £29,500 and the Manchester Children's Relief-in-Need an estimated £13,000.

Exclusions

Debts are very rarely paid and council tax and rent debts are never met. Normally an individual may only receive one grant in any 12-month period.

Applications

Application forms are available from the correspondent and should be completed by a sponsor from a recognised social or health-related agency. The trustees meet during the last week of every month. Applications must be received by the 15th of the month.

Other information

Grants are also made to organisations.

Oldham

The Sarah Lees Relief Trust

£1,800

Correspondent: Catherine Sykes, Trustee, 10 Chew Brook Drive, Greenfield, Oldham OL3 7PD (01457 876606; email: cathiesykes@btinternet.com)

CC number: 514240

Eligibility

People living in Oldham who are sick, convalescent, disabled or infirm.

Types of grants

One-off grants of up to £500 and gifts in kind.

Annual grant total

In 2014/15 the trust had an income of £3,200 and a total expenditure of £2,000. We estimate that the amount of grants given to individuals totalled £1,800

Exclusions

No grants are given for items, services or facilities that are readily available from other sources.

Applications

Apply in writing to the correspondent through a social worker or other recognised welfare agency. The trustees meet three times a year, but urgent requests will be considered in between the meetings.

Rochdale

The Norman Barnes Fund

£5,000

Correspondent: S. Shahid, Clerk to the fund, Finance Services, Floor 2, Number One Riverside, Smith Street, Rochdale OL16 1XU (01706 924713; email: committee.services@rochdale.gov.uk; website: www.rochdale.gov.uk/the_council/charitable_trusts.aspx)

CC number: 511646

Eligibility

People over the age of 60 who live in Rochdale, Castleton, Norden or Bamford.

Types of grants

One-off grants according to need. There is no limit to the number of applications or the amount that can be applied for.

Annual grant total

In 2014/15 the fund had an income of £12,700 and a total expenditure of £10,400. We estimate that the amount of grants given to individuals totalled £5,000 with funding also awarded to local organisations.

Exclusions

No payments for tax, council tax, or other statutory payments, except where relief or assistance is already provided out of public funds.

Applications

Application forms are available to download from the Rochdale council website or by contacting the correspondent. It is recommended that applicants include a supporting comment from a doctor, social worker, Age UK representative or some other relevant professional. Requests for items or services should include written quotations. Standard items like fridges or cookers will be ordered directly by the trustees. For grants greater than £250, the support of an officer of Rochdale Council's Social Services Department is required.

Heywood Relief-in-Need Trust Fund

£2,800

Correspondent: The Trustees, c/o 94 Whalley Road, Clayton-le-Moors, Accrington BB5 5DY (email: phoenixtrust@outlook.com)

CC number: 517114

Eligibility

People in need who live in the former municipal borough of Heywood are eligible. In exceptional cases applications may be considered from those who are only temporarily located within the borough.

Types of grants

One-off grants usually ranging from £50 to £400. Grants have been given to help with fuel arrears, clothing and furniture.

Annual grant total

In 2013/14 the fund had an income of £8,000 and a total expenditure of £5,800. We estimate that the amount of grants given to individuals totalled £2,800.

Exclusions

No grants are awarded to pay council tax, public funds or other taxes. No repeat grants are given.

Applications

Apply in writing to the correspondent. Applications should be supported by a social worker, health visitor or similar professional.

Other information

Donations/subscriptions are also made to organisations which provide services or facilities to people in need who live in Heywood.

The Rochdale Fund for Relief-in-Sickness

£7,600

Correspondent: Susan Stoney, Trust Administrator, The Old Parsonage, 2 St Mary's Gate, Rochdale OL16 1AP (01706 644187; email: law@jbhs.co.uk; website: www.rochdalefund.org.uk)

CC number: 222652

Eligibility

People living in the borough of Rochdale (including Wardle, Littleborough, Middleton, Heywood, Norden, Birtle, Milnrow and Newhey) who are in poor health, convalescent or who have disabilities. Help may also be given to those whose physical or mental health is likely to be impaired by poverty, deprivation or other adversity.

Types of grants

One-off grants according to need. The trustees will consider any requests for items which will make life more comfortable or productive for the individual. For example, recent grants have been given towards wheelchairs, hoists, IT equipment, house adaptations, special leisure equipment, medical aids, washing machines, cookers, clothing, beds, bedding and respite breaks.

Annual grant total

In 2013/14 the fund had assets of £1.5 million and an income of £50,000. Grants were made totalling around £33,000, of which £25,000 was awarded to organisations and £7,600 was given to specific families.

Exclusions

Grants are not given for the payment of debts, including utility bills, council tax and HMRC payments or to help with hardship not directly related to, or caused as a result of, sickness.

Applications

Application forms are available from the correspondent or to download from the website. Applications can be made either directly by the individual (if no other route is available) or through a social worker, Citizens Advice, other welfare agency or other third party such as a doctor. Whether completed by the individual or a third party all applications must be supported by a letter from a recognised body or person such as social services or a doctor.

Other information

The fund's website states that they may also make grants to organisations, 'both statutory and voluntary, to assist them in providing equipment, services or facilities which may alleviate the suffering, or promote the recovery of, persons who qualify'.

Rochdale United Charity

£3,500

Correspondent: Saddleworth Parish Council, Saddleworth Parish Council, Civic Hall, Lee Street, Uppermill, Oldham OL3 6AE (01457 876665; website: parishcouncil.saddleworth.org/contact.html)

CC number: 224461

Eligibility

People in need who live in the ancient parish of Rochdale (the former county borough of Rochdale, Castleton, Wardle, Whitworth, Littleborough, Todmorden and Saddleworth).

Types of grants

One-off grants typically ranging from £50 to £250. Grants have been awarded for the provision of domestic appliances such as fridges and cookers, medical aids and equipment, telephones, televisions or radios for the lonely or housebound and towards the costs of arranging recuperative holidays.

Annual grant total

In 2013/14 the charity had an income of £9,700 and a total expenditure of £7,800.

We estimate that the amount of grants given to individuals totalled £3,500, with local organisations also receiving funding.

Exclusions

No grants are given for the relief of rates, taxes or other public funds. No recurrent grants.

Applications

Application forms are available from the correspondent. Applications should be submitted through a social worker, GP, health visitor, Citizens Advice or other welfare agency. Applications are usually considered quarterly.

Salford

The Booth Charities

£2,000

Correspondent: Jonathan Aldersley, Administrator, Butcher and Barlow LLP, 3 Royal Mews, Gadbrook Road, Northwich, Cheshire CW9 7UD (01606 334309; email: jaldersley@butcher-barlow.co.uk)

CC number: 221800

Eligibility

People who are retired, over 60, on a basic pension, live in the city of Salford and are in need.

Types of grants

Annual pensions of up to £105 and one-off grants towards TV licences.

Annual grant total

In 2013/14 the charity had an income of £962,000 and a total expenditure of £1.7 million. The charity's main area of activity is providing grants to organisations. Accounts were not available to view at the time of writing, but we estimate that the amount of grants given to individuals totalled around £2,000.

Applications

Application forms are available from the correspondent. Applications for one-off grants must be made by social services, ministers of religion, doctors and so on. Distribution meetings are held regularly throughout the year.

Stockport

Sir Ralph Pendlebury's Charity for Orphans

£1,700

Correspondent: Stephen Tattersall, Correspondent, Lacy Watson and Co., Carlyle House, 107–109 Wellington Road South, Stockport SK1 3TL

CC number: 213927

Eligibility

Orphans who have lived, or whose parents have lived, in the borough of Stockport for at least two years and who are in need.

Types of grants

Our research suggests that recurring payments, usually of £5 or £6 a week, plus clothing allowances twice a year are available. Support can also be given for holidays. The main priority for the charity is relief in need.

Annual grant total

In 2014 the charity had an income of £9,800 and a total expenditure of £3,600. We estimate that around £1,700 was awarded in grants for welfare needs.

Applications

Applications can be made in writing to the correspondent. They should be made by a parent/guardian.

Other information

Grants are also made for educational purposes.

Sir Ralph Pendlebury's Charity for the Aged

£3,500

Correspondent: Stephen Tattersall, Administrator, Lacy Watson and Co., Carlyle House, 107–109 Wellington Road South, Stockport, Cheshire SK1 3TL (0161 477 7400; email: help@lacywatson.co.uk)

CC number: 213928

Eligibility

People above pensionable age who have lived in the borough of Stockport for at least two years and are in necessitous circumstances.

Types of grants

Small grants to elderly people.

Annual grant total

In 2014 the charity had an income of £7,600 and an expenditure of £7,300. We estimate that the amount of grants given to individuals totalled around £3,500.

Applications

Apply in writing to the correspondent.

Other information

Grants may also be made to organisations.

Wigan

The Golborne Charities – Charity of William Leadbetter

£5,400

Correspondent: Paul Gleave, 56 Nook Lane, Golborne, Warrington WA3 3JQ (01942 727627; email: p.gleave56@ hotmail.com)

CC number: 221088

Eligibility

People in need who live in the parish of Golborne as it was in 1892.

Types of grants

One-off grants usually between £70 and £100, although larger sums may be given. Grants are usually cash payments, but are occasionally in-kind, for food, bedding, fireguards, clothing and shoes, for example. Help can also be given with hospital travel and necessary holidays.

Annual grant total

In 2014/15 the charity had an income of £6,600 and a total expenditure of £7,300. Grants are made to individuals for both social welfare and educational purposes. We estimate that social welfare grants to individuals totalled £5,400.

Exclusions

Loans or grants for the payments of rates are not made. Grants are not repeated in less than two years.

Applications

Apply in writing to the correspondent through a third party such as a social worker or a teacher, or via a trustee. Applications are considered at three-monthly intervals. Grant recipients tend to be known by at least one trustee.

The Lowton United Charity

£2,000

Correspondent: John Naughton, Secretary, 51 Kenilworth Road, Lowton, Warrington WA3 2AZ (01942 741583)

CC number: 226469

Eligibility

People in need who live in the parishes of St Luke's and St Mary's in Lowton.

Types of grants

One-off grants at Christmas and emergency one-off grants at any time.

Annual grant total

In 2014/15 the charity had an income of £7,300 and a total expenditure of £6,300. Our research suggests that grants for individuals total about £4,000 each year. About a half is given at Christmas for relief-in-need purposes and the rest are given throughout the year. We estimate that the amount of grants given to individuals for welfare purposes totalled about £2,000.

Applications

Applications are usually accepted through the rectors of the parishes or other trustees.

Other information

Some assistance may also be given to organisations. Educational support is also given to individuals.

Isle of Man

Manx Marine Society

£5,000

Correspondent: Capt. R. Cringle, 10 Carrick Bay View, Ballagawne Road, Colby, Isle of Man IM9 4DD (01624 838233)

Eligibility

Seafarers, retired or disabled seafarers and their widows, children and dependants, who live on the Isle of Man. Young Manx people under 18 who wish to attend sea school or become a cadet are also eligible.

Types of grants

One-off and repeated grants of up to £400 are given according to need.

Annual grant total

Our research suggests that around £5,000 is awarded to individuals for social welfare purposes each year.

Applications

Application forms are available from the correspondent. Applications are considered at any time and can be submitted either by the individual, or through a social worker, Citizens Advice or other welfare agency.

Other information

The trustees also award grants for educational purposes.

Lancashire

Baines's Charity

£4,600

Correspondent: Duncan Waddilove, Correspondent, 2 The Chase, Normoss Road, Blackpool, Lancashire FY3 0BF (01253 893459; email: duncanwaddilove@hotmail.com)

CC number: 224135

Eligibility

People in need who live in the areas of Blackpool, Fylde or Wyre.

Types of grants

One-off grants ranging from £100 to £250. Requests are considered on their merits.

Annual grant total

In 2014 the charity had an income of £20,500 and a total expenditure of £18,900. We estimate that the amount paid in grants to individuals for welfare purposes was £4,600.

Applications

Application forms are available from the correspondent. They can be submitted either directly by the individual or through a social worker, Citizens Advice or other welfare agency. Applications are considered upon receipt.

Other information

Grants can be made to individuals and organisations for both welfare and educational purposes, including support to schools. The charity works in conjunction with John Sykes Dewhurst Bequest (Charity Commission no. 224133).

The charity's charitable objects include the ancient townships of Carleton, Hardhorn-with-Newton, Marton, Poulton and Thornton.

Daniel's and Houghton's Charity

£12,000

Correspondent: Miss H. Ryan, Brabners Chaffe Street LLP, 7–8 Chapel Street, Preston PR1 8AN (01772 823921; fax: 01772 201918; email: helen.ryan@ brabners.com)

CC number: 1074762

Eligibility

People in need who live in Lancashire with preference given to those living in Preston, Grimsargh, Broughton, Woodplumpton, Eaves, Catforth, Bartle, Alston or Elston.

Types of grants

One-off and recurrent grants are given according to need.

Annual grant total

In 2013/14 the charity had a total income of £28,500 and a total expenditure of £25,000. We estimate that grants paid during the year totalled £12,000.

Exclusions

No grants are given for items or services where statutory funds are available.

Applications

Apply in writing to the correspondent.

Other information

Grants are also made to organisations.

The Goosnargh and Whittingham United Charity

£4,500

Correspondent: John Bretherton, Clerk to the Trustees, Lower Stanalea Farm, Stanalea Lane, Goosnargh, Preston PR3 2EQ (01995 640224)

CC number: 233744

Eligibility

Older people in need who live in the parishes of Goosnargh, Whittingham and Barton.

Types of grants

One-off and recurrent grants are given according to need.

Annual grant total

In 2014 the charity had an income of £7,000 and a total expenditure of £4,700. We estimate that the amount of grants given to individuals totalled £4,500.

Applications

Apply in writing to the correspondent. Applications should be submitted directly by the individual or family member.

The Harris Charity

£2,000

Correspondent: David Ingram, Secretary, c/o Moore and Smalley, Richard House, 9 Winckley Square, Preston PR1 3HP (01772 821021; email: harrischarity@mooreandsmalley.co.uk; website: theharrischarity.co.uk)

CC number: 526206

Eligibility

People in need under the age of 25 who live in Lancashire, with a preference for the Preston district.

Types of grants

One-off grants of £100 to £5,000 for electrical goods, travel expenses and disability equipment, for example.

Annual grant total

In 2013/14 the charity had assets of £3.7 million and an income of £123,500. Grants totalled £87,000 and were mainly made to organisations. We were able to establish that the amount of grants given to individuals totalled £4,000, but we were unable to determine how they were distributed.

Exclusions

No grants are made for course fees or to supplement living expenses.

Applications

The trustees advertise for applications in the local press twice a year in March and September. Applications must be made using the form, which is available to download from the website, where guidance can also be found. The completed form should be returned to the trust and accompanied by supporting references from a responsible referee such as a school, college, social services, vicar, priest or minister. Applications must be submitted by 31 March or 30 September, with successful applicants notified in July and January respectively.

Other information

The original charity known as the Harris Orphanage Charity dates back to 1883. A new charitable scheme was established in 1985 following the sale of the Harris Orphanage premises in Garstang Road, Preston. The charity also supports charitable organisations that benefit individuals, recreation and leisure and the training and education of individuals.

Peter Lathom's Charity

£5,800

Correspondent: Christine Aitken, Clerk, 13 Mallard Close, Aughton, Ormskirk L39 5QJ (0151 520 2717)

CC number: 228828

Eligibility

People in need who live in West Lancashire.

Types of grants

One-off grants.

Annual grant total

In 2014 the charity had assets of £1.5 million and an income of £50,000. The charity supports individuals and organisations through three funds: Lathom Educational Foundation; the Welfare Fund; and the Estate or Mixed Account.

During the year, one individual was supported with a grant of £500 from the Welfare Fund. In addition, individuals received grants totalling £10,500 from the Estate or Mixed Account. We estimate that individual grants from this fund for social welfare purposes totalled around £5,300.

Applications

Applications can be made using a form available from the correspondent. Grants are awarded in November/December of each year.

Blackburn with Darwen

The W. M. and B. W. Lloyd Trust

£22,500

Correspondent: John Jacklin, Trustee, Gorse Barn, Rock Lane, Tockholes, Darwen, Lancashire BB3 0LX (01254 771367; email: johnjacklin@homecall.co.uk)

CC number: 503384

Eligibility

People in need who live or have been educated in the old borough of Darwen, Lancashire. Preference is given to single parents.

Types of grants

One-off and recurrent grants are given according to need. Awards are usually of £50–£7,500 can include awards for medical equipment. Our research indicates that educational grants are given priority over social or medical grants.

Annual grant total

In 2014/15 the charity had an income of £90,500 and a total expenditure of £99,500. At the time of writing (September 2015) full accounts were not yet received by the Charity Commission. In the past about 90% of the overall expenditure was spent in grants to organisations and individuals. We estimate that the amount of grants given to individuals for welfare purposes totalled around £22,500.

Applications

Applications may be made in writing to the correspondent. They should be supported by a relevant third party, such as a social worker, doctor, minister or someone who knows the applicant and can endorse their application for help. Applications are considered quarterly, in March, June, September and December. There is also an Emergency Committee capable of making awards at short notice. Applicants are advised to enquire about the other funds (detailed in this entry) administered by the trustees and available to people living in Darwen.

Other information

Grants are made to both individuals and organisations for educational and social welfare purposes.

The trustees also administer the following funds:
- **The Peter Pan Fund** – for the benefit of people with mental disabilities
- **The Darwen War Memorial and Sick Poor Fund** – originally to help war widows and dependants after the First

World War and the sick poor of Darwen

- ▶ **The Darwen Disabled Fund** – originally designed to assist with the social welfare of people with physical disabilities in Darwen
- ▶ **The Ernest Aspin Donation** – to support sporting activities and in particular training and educating young people in sports
- ▶ **The T P Davies Fund** – for the benefit of the residents of Darwen
- ▶ **Darwen Probation Volunteers Fund** – supporting people in Darwen who have come under the probation and after care service, and their families

Blackpool

The Blackpool Ladies' Sick Poor Association

£22,500

Correspondent: Patricia Dimuantes, Correspondent, 22 James Avenue, Blackpool FY4 4LB (01253694228; email: SAND_GROWN@MAC.COM)

CC number: 220639

Eligibility

People in need who live in Blackpool.

Types of grants

Food vouchers are distributed monthly. Special relief grants can be made for immediate needs such as rent, second-hand cookers and washers, clothing, heaters, fireguards, stair gates and so on.

Annual grant total

In 2013/14 the association held assets of £407,000 and had an income of £9,500. Grants to individuals totalled £22,500 with £13,500 given for general relief and £8,500 given for special relief.

Applications

Applications must include proof of extreme hardship and must be in writing via health visitors, social workers, Citizens Advice or other welfare agencies such as Age Concern, Mind and so on. Health visitors and social workers can write to the association's treasurer directly, otherwise letters should be sent to the correspondent. Applications are considered all year round, excluding August.

Other information

The association occasionally makes grants to organisations with similar objectives.

The Swallowdale Children's Trust

£8,600 (71 grants)

Correspondent: Alexa Alderson, Secretary, PO Box 1301, Blackpool FY1 9HD (07919 154952; email: secswallowdale@hotmail.co.uk; website: www.swallowdaletrust.co.uk)

CC number: 526205

Eligibility

People who live in the Blackpool area who are under the age of 25.

Types of grants

Assistance is given in the form of payments to third parties or vouchers towards, for example: beds and bedding for children whose parents have lost their home; clothing for young people; and safety equipment in a home to protect young children.

Annual grant total

In 2013/14 the trust had assets of £1 million and an income of £39,500. Grants made during the year amounted to £43,500. Of this total, £9,000 was given to Lancashire Outward Bound, £1,700 to Life Education and £1,000 to Windmill Group. 71 grants to individuals for the relief of hardship totalled £8,600, and no grants were made to individuals for educational purposes.

The annual report for the year also states: 'In association with the Blackpool Gazette the Trust held a '£25,000 Give Away' to promote the aims of the Trust. This had a very positive response and helped a large number of individuals and organisations.'

Applications

Applications must be supported by an independent or professional third party such as a social worker or teacher. An application form is available to download from the website. It should be completed and signed by the relevant parties before being returned to the correspondent. The trustees meet on a bi-monthly basis.

Hyndburn

The Accrington and District Helping Hands Fund

£5,500

Correspondent: The Secretary, Tithe Cottage, 4 Grindleton Road, West Bradford, Clitheroe BB7 4TE (01200 422062; email: maryann.renton2@btinternet.com)

CC number: 222241

Eligibility

People living in the former borough of Accrington, Clayton-le-Moors or Altham, who are in poor health and are either supported by benefits or are on a low income.

Types of grants

One-off grants usually ranging from £100 to £300 towards the cost of: (i) special foods and medicines, medical comforts, extra bedding, fuel and medical and surgical appliances; (ii) the provision of domestic help; (iii) convalescence (iv) provision of mobile physiotherapy service. Grants are usually paid directly to the supplier.

Annual grant total

In 2014 the fund had an income of £12,300 and a total expenditure of £5,800. We estimate that the amount of grants given to individuals totalled £5,500.

Applications

Application forms are available from the correspondent and should be submitted either directly by the individual or through a social worker, Citizens Advice or other welfare agency. Applications should include evidence of income and state of health, as well as estimates of what is required.

Lancaster

James Bond/Henry Welch Trust

£4,300

Correspondent: Jane Glenton, Secretary, c/o Democratic Services, Lancaster City Council, Town Hall, Dalton Square, Lancaster LA1 1PJ (01524 582068; email: jglenton@lancaster.gov.uk)

CC number: 222791

Eligibility

People in need who live in the area covered by Lancaster City Council and have diseases of the chest/lung and early forms of phthisis. Children with disabilities and other special needs are also eligible.

Types of grants

One-off and recurrent grants typically ranging from £100 to £500 towards, for example, computer equipment, household essentials and holidays.

Annual grant total

In 2014/15 the trust had an income of £10,000 and an expenditure of over £11,500. We estimate that the amount of grants given to individuals totalled £5,500, with funding also awarded to local organisations.

Applications

The trust's home visitor will visit the individual and complete the form. Applications can be submitted at any time.

The Cottam Charities

£15,000

Correspondent: Emma Edwards, Administrator, Blackhurst Swainson Goodier Solicitors, 3 and 4 Aalborg Square, Lancaster LA1 1GG (01524 32471; email: eje@bsglaw.co.uk)

CC number: 223936 and 223925

Eligibility

People in need who are over 50 and have lived in the parish of Caton-with-Littledale for at least five years.

Types of grants

One-off grants ranging from about £100 to £140.

Annual grant total

In 2013/14 both charities had a combined income of £18,100 and a combined expenditure of £15,800. We estimate that grants totalled around £15,000.

Applications

Apply in writing to the correspondent directly by the individual or family member by mid-November for consideration in November/December each year. Applicants must re-apply each year.

Other information

The support is provided by two charities – Edward Cottam Charity (Charity Commission no. 223936) and Alice Cottam Charity (Charity Commission no. 223925).

The Gibson, Simpson and Brockbank Annuities Trust

£3,200

Correspondent: Emma Edwards, Administrator, Blackhurst Swainson Goodier Solicitors, 3 & 4 Aalborg Square, Lancaster LA1 1GG (01524 32471; fax: 01524 386515; email: eje@bsglaw.co.uk; website: www.bsglaw.co.uk)

CC number: 223595

Eligibility

Unmarried women or widows in need (with an income of less than £1,000 from sources other than their state pension), who are over 50 years old and have lived in Lancaster for the last three years.

Types of grants

Quarterly grants.

Annual grant total

In 2014 the trust had an income of £7,300 and a total expenditure of £3,400. We estimate that the amount of grants given to individuals totalled £3,200.

Applications

Application forms are available from the correspondent. Applications should be submitted directly by the individual. Applications are usually considered every three months.

The Lancaster Charity

£2,100

Correspondent: Philip Oglethorpe, Clerk to the Trustees, William Penny's, Regent Street, Lancaster LA1 1SG (01524 842663; email: lancastercharity@btconnect.com; website: www.lancaster-charity.org.uk)

CC number: 213461

Eligibility

People over 60 who are in need and have lived in the old city of Lancaster for at least three years. People under 60 may be considered if they are unable to work to maintain themselves due to age, accident or infirmity.

Types of grants

Top-up pensions according to need.

Annual grant total

In 2014, the charity had an income of £203,500 and a total expenditure of £216,000. During the previous year, payments totalling £2,100 were made to pensioners. The majority of income is spent on maintaining the charity's almshouses. At the time of writing (November 2015) no updated accounts were available to view.

Applications

Application forms are available from the correspondent. Applications are considered when vacancies occur.

Pendle

Nelson District Nursing Association Fund

£4,000

Correspondent: Joanne Eccles, Administrator, Democratic and Legal Services, Pendle Borough Council, Nelson Town Hall, Market Street, Nelson, Lancashire BB9 7LG (01282 661654; email: joanne.eccles@pendle.gov.uk)

CC number: 222530

Eligibility

Sick or poor people who live in Nelson, Lancashire.

Types of grants

One-off grants according to need, ranging from £50 to £500.

Annual grant total

In 2014/15 the fund had an income of £4,100 and a total expenditure of £4,500. We estimate that the total amount of grants awarded to individuals was approximately £4,000.

Applications

Apply in writing to the correspondent. Applications can be submitted directly by the individual or through a social worker, Citizens Advice or other welfare agency. All applicants will be visited by the association's welfare officer as part of the assessment process.

Merseyside

The Girls' Welfare Fund

Correspondent: Mrs S. O'Leary, Trustee, West Hey, Dawstone Road, Heswall, Wirral CH60 4RP (email: gwf_charity@hotmail.co.uk)

CC number: 220347

Eligibility

Girls and young women (usually aged 15 to 25) who are in need and were born, educated and live in Merseyside. Applications from other areas will not be acknowledged.

Types of grants

One-off and repeated grants are given according to need. Grants usually range from £50 to £750.

Annual grant total

In 2014 the fund had an income of £8,700 and a total expenditure of £4,700. At the time of writing (November 2015) the fund's Charity Commission record described its activities as: 'to assist young women, of non-vocational education, in buying equipment or materials to help gain a qualification and achieve independence'. We have taken this to reflect that grants exclusively for social welfare purposes are not currently a priority for the fund.

Exclusions

Grants are not made to charities that request funds to pass on and give to individuals.

Applications

Apply in writing to the correspondent or by email. Applications can be submitted directly by the individual or through a social worker, Citizens Advice, other welfare agency or college/educational establishment. Applications are considered quarterly in March, June, September and December, and should include full information about the college, course and particular circumstances.

Other information

The charity also gives grants to organisations benefitting girls and young women on Merseyside, and to eligible individuals for leisure, creative activities, sports, arts and education.

The Liverpool Caledonian Association

£14,500

Correspondent: David Johnson, Correspondent, 46 Primrose Lane, Helsby, Frodsham WA6 0HH

CC number: 250791

Eligibility

People of Scottish descent, or their immediate family, who are in need and who live within a 15-mile radius of Liverpool Town Hall. The association states: 'generally speaking we do not welcome applications from people who have fewer than one grandparent who was Scots born'.

Types of grants

Regular monthly payment of annuities, heating grants and a limited number of Christmas food parcels. The usual maximum grant is £50.

Annual grant total

In 2014 the association had an income of £12,000 and a total expenditure of £15,200. We estimate that grants totalled around £14,500.

Exclusions

Holidays are generally excluded.

Applications

Apply in writing to the correspondent either directly by the individual, through a social worker, Citizens Advice, or other welfare agency or through any other third party. Applications are considered at any time and applicants will be visited.

The Liverpool Ladies' Institution

£5,000

Correspondent: David Anderton, Trustee, 15 Childwall Park Avenue, Childwall, Liverpool L16 0JE (0151 722 9823; email: d.anderton68@btinternet. com)

CC number: 209490

Eligibility

Single women in need who were either born in the City of Liverpool or live in Merseyside. Preference is given to women who are members of the Church of England, and to older women.

Types of grants

Recurrent grants.

Annual grant total

In 2014 the institution had an income of £3,700 and a total expenditure of £5,300. We estimate that the amount of grants given to individuals totalled £5,000.

Applications

Application forms are available from the correspondent. Applications should be submitted, at any time, through a social worker, Citizens Advice or other welfare agency. The trust has previously stated that it receives a lot of inappropriate applications.

Liverpool

Channel – Supporting Family Social Work in Liverpool

£8,000

Correspondent: Rebecca Black, Trustee, 38 Brick Kiln Lane, Rufford, Ormskirk L40 1SZ (01704823408; email: beccavblack@hotmail.com)

CC number: 257916

Eligibility

Families with young children, elderly or disabled people, who live in Liverpool and are in need.

Types of grants

One-off grants of no more than £100 for childcare, clothing, food, furniture and kitchen equipment.

Annual grant total

In 2013/14 the charity had an income of £7,900 and a total expenditure of £8,500. We estimate that welfare grants to individuals totalled £8,000.

Applications

Applications can only be made through a social worker, health worker or voluntary agency, who should contact the correspondent for advice on funding, an application form and guidelines. Applications are considered on an ongoing basis.

Liverpool Corn Trade Guild

£3,000

Correspondent: Ian Bridge, Trustee, 1A St Johns Road, Southport PR8 4JP (01704 565596)

CC number: 232414

Eligibility

Members of the guild and their dependants who are in need. If funds permit benefits can be extended to former members and their dependants. Membership is open to anyone employed by any firm engaged in the Liverpool Corn and Feed Trade.

Types of grants

One-off and recurrent grants are given according to need. Loans may also be provided.

Annual grant total

At the time of writing (November 2015) the latest financial information available was from 2013. In 2013 the charity had an income of £7,500 and an expenditure of £3,300. We estimate that the amount of grants given to individuals totalled around £3,000.

Applications

Apply in writing to the correspondent. Applications can be made directly by the individual.

Liverpool Wholesale Fresh Produce Benevolent Fund

£5,000

Correspondent: Thomas Dobbin, Correspondent, 207 Childwall Road, Liverpool L15 6UT (0151 722 0621; email: t.dobbin@virginmedia.com)

CC number: 1010236

Eligibility

People in need, who are or have been associated with the Liverpool fruit, veg or flower trade either as importers or wholesalers, and their families.

Types of grants

One-off and recurrent grants usually ranging from £50 to £80.

Annual grant total

In 2014/15 the fund had an income of £3,100 and a total expenditure of £22,000. We estimate that the total amount granted to individuals was approximately £5,000 as the fund also awards grants to organisations and provides other types of finance.

Applications

Apply in writing to the correspondent.

Other information

The fund has stated that it predominantly makes grants to local charities in Merseyside due to a dwindling number of applications from individuals connected with the fresh produce trade.

Sefton

Southport and Birkdale Provident Society

£19,300 (108 grants)

Correspondent: Ian Jones, Treasurer, 12 Ascot Close, Southport PR8 2DD (01704 560095)

CC number: 224460

Eligibility

People in need who live in the metropolitan borough of Sefton.

Types of grants

One-off grants in kind only after social services have confirmed that all other benefits have been fully explored. Grants have been awarded towards clothing, bedding, cookers, washing machines and other basic household needs.

Annual grant total

In 2014 the society had an income of £26,000 and a total expenditure of £29,500. Grants to individuals amounted to £19,300.

During the year, the society received 122 applications, of which one was declined, six cancelled and 115 were agreed and paid. Of these, 7 grants totalling £10,000 were awarded to charitable organisations.

Exclusions

No cash payments are made. Grants are not given for education, training experience, rental deposits, personal debt relief or hire purchase. Medical services are not supported.

Applications

Apply in writing to the correspondent with as much information on family background and the reasons for the request as possible. Applications should be submitted through social services and are considered at any time.

Wirral

The Christ Church Fund for Children

£3,200

Correspondent: Robert Perry, Trustee, 28 Beresford Road, Prenton CH43 1XG (email: rperry4851@aol.com)

CC number: 218545

Eligibility

Children in need up to the age of 17 whose parents are members of the Church of England and who live in the county borough of Birkenhead. Preference is given to children living in the ecclesiastical parish of Christ Church, Birkenhead.

Types of grants

Grants for any kind of need, but typically for bedding, furniture, clothing and trips.

Annual grant total

In 2013/14 the fund had an income of £3,600 and a total expenditure of £3,500. We estimate that social welfare grants to individuals totalled £3,200.

Applications

Apply in writing through a recognised referral agency (for example, a social worker or Citizens Advice) or other third party. Applications are usually considered quarterly (around January, April, September and December), but emergency applications can be considered at any time.

The Conroy Trust

£1,900

Correspondent: Tom Bates, Administrator, 22 Waterford Road, Prenton, Wirral CH43 6UU (0151 652 2128)

CC number: 210797

Eligibility

People in need who live in the parish of Bebington.

Types of grants

Bi-monthly payments to regular beneficiaries and one-off grants for special needs. Grants usually range from £50 to £300.

Annual grant total

In 2014 the trust had an income of £5,200 and a total expenditure of £4,100. We estimate that social welfare grants to individuals totalled £1,900, with funding also awarded to organisations.

Exclusions

No grants are made for educational purposes.

Applications

The individual should apply directly to the correspondent in writing.

The Maud Beattie Murchie Charitable Trust

£13,000

Correspondent: Anthony Bayliss, Duncan Sheard Glass, Castle Chambers, 43 Castle Street, Liverpool L2 9TL (0151 243 1209)

CC number: 265281

Eligibility

Retired members of Beattie stores who are in need and people in need who live on the Wirral.

Types of grants

One-off and recurrent grants are given according to need. Grants to organisations are mostly recurrent.

Annual grant total

In 2013/14 the trust had an income of £29,000 and a total expenditure of £34,500. Grants were made totalling £26,000, of which we estimate £13,000 was awarded to individuals and the remainder to charitable organisations.

Exclusions

No grants are given for educational purposes.

Applications

Applications should be made through Wirral Social Services. Awards are made twice a year.

Other information

The trust also makes grants to charitable organisations.

The West Kirby Charity

£19,500

Correspondent: Jane Boulton, Cobblestones, 2 The Roscote, Wallrake, Heswall, Wirral CH60 8QW (07773 449123; email: ajaneboulton@btinternet.com)

CC number: 218546

Eligibility

People in need who have lived in the old urban district of Hoylake (Caldy, Frankby, Greasby, Hoylake, Meols and West Kirby) for at least three years. Preference is given to older people and people who have a disability.

Types of grants

Pensions of about £20 a month.
Christmas gifts and one-off grants are
also made to non-elderly locals.

Annual grant total

In 2014 the charity had an income of
£24,000 and a total expenditure of
£20,000. We estimate that the amount of
grants given to individuals totalled
around £19,500.

Applications

Application forms are available from the
correspondent. Applications are usually
considered quarterly.

South East

General

The Argus Appeal

£34,500

Correspondent: Elsa Gillio, Fundraising Co-ordinator, Argus House, Crowhurst Road, Hollingbury, Brighton BN1 8AR (01273 544465; email: elsa.gillio@ theargus.co.uk; website: www.theargus. co.uk/argusappeal)

CC number: 1013647

Eligibility

People in need, particularly older people and underprivileged children, who live in the Sussex area.

Types of grants

One-off and recurrent grants are given according to need and food parcels for older people. Past grants have been made to purchase computers for hospitalised children to enable them to continue with their school work and to purchase specially adapted trikes for four children with disabilities. More than 750 Christmas hampers and food vouchers were given to pensioners and low income families in 2014.

Annual grant total

In 2014 the charity held assets of £334,000 and had an income of £163,000. Grants to individuals totalled more than £34,500, of which £14,000 went towards the provision of food parcels for older people and people in need. The remaining £20,500 was given in 11 one-off grants and donations to families.

A further £68,000 was awarded to local organisations.

Applications

Apply in writing to the correspondent including details on who you are, what you do, how much is needed, how it will be spent and what has been done so far to raise the necessary funds.

The Stanley Foster Charitable Trust

£1,000

Correspondent: John Graham, Trustee, 4 Meadowcroft, Bromley BR1 2JD (020 8402 1341)

CC number: 1085985

Eligibility

People in need in south east England.

Types of grants

One-off grants of up to £1,000 mainly for medical support.

Annual grant total

In 2014/15 the trust had both an income and a total expenditure of £21,600. The trust's Charity Commission record describes its activities as: 'Makes grants to national and local charities, organisations, and individuals known to the trustees. The individual element is a minor part of its disbursements.' We estimate that the amount of grants given to individuals amounted to no more than £1,000.

Applications

Grants are only made to individuals known to the trustees. The majority of grants are made to organisations.

Hitcham Poor Lands Charity

£3,300

Correspondent: Donald Lindskog, Trustee, Little Orchard, Poyle Lane, Burnham, Slough SL1 8JZ (01628 605652; email: d.lindskog@tiscali.co.uk)

CC number: 203447

Eligibility

People in need who live in the parishes of Hitcham, Burnham or Cippenham.

Types of grants

Gifts in kind including furniture, white goods and school uniforms. Grants are available towards the costs of school trips and carers' holidays. Around 300

Christmas parcels are distributed each year.

Annual grant total

In 2013/14 the charity had an income of £7,600 and a total expenditure of £7,000. We estimate that the amount of grants given to individuals totalled £3,300, with funding also awarded to local organisations.

Applications

Apply in writing to the correspondent. Applications can be submitted directly by the individual or through a third party such as Citizens Advice or a social worker. There are no deadlines for applications and they are considered frequently.

Other information

The charity supports The Burnham Lighthouse Project and Thames Hospice Care, which operate in the local area.

The B. V. MacAndrew Trust

£5,500

Correspondent: Roger Clow, Trustee, 4th floor, Park Gate, 161–163 Preston Road, Brighton, East Sussex BN1 6AF (01273 562563)

CC number: 206900

Eligibility

People in need who live in East and West Sussex.

Types of grants

One-off grants for a variety of needs including emergencies and household appliances.

Annual grant total

In 2013/14 the trust had an income of £10,600 and a total expenditure of £11,500. We estimate that the amount of grants given to individuals totalled £5,500, with funding also awarded to local organisations.

Exclusions

The trustees are unable to assist with bankruptcy fees or debts.

Applications

Apply in writing to the correspondent at any time including the amount required and the name of the person the cheque is to be made out to. Applications can be made either through a third party such as a social worker or through an organisation such as Citizens Advice or other welfare agency. Applications are usually considered a month following receipt.

MidasPlus

£8,400

Correspondent: Michael Wylie, Trustee, 20 Island Close, Staines-upon-Thames TW18 4YZ (01784 440300 or 07803706440; email: info@midasplus.org.uk; website: www.midasplus.org.uk)

CC number: 1110699

Eligibility

Community groups and individuals who have lived in Surrey and Middlesex and surrounding areas for at least six months. The charity usually supports those 'who demonstrate a need that cannot be fulfilled elsewhere'.

There is a particular emphasis on people from: Addlestone, Ashford (Middlesex), Camberley, Cobham, Feltham, Hampton, Heathrow, Hounslow, Isleworth, Richmond, Shepperton, Staines-upon-Thames, Stanwell, Sunbury-on-Thames, Teddington, Twickenham, West Drayton and Wraysbury.

Types of grants

Awards (generally include those for medical and disability aids, such as wheelchairs or scooters, holidays, equipment, carpeting, communication aids, garden and home adaptations and any other items to help those who are disadvantaged due to low income, ill health, disability or other reason.

Annual grant total

In 2013/14 the charity had assets of £23,000 and an income of £30,500. There were 14 grants made totalling £16,700 to individuals and organisations. A further breakdown was not given; we estimate that the amount of grants given to individuals totalled about £8,400.

Exclusions

Grants cannot be made to:
- People planning to move out of the area of benefit
- Those who have received three grants in the past
- Pay for general living costs
- Pay off debts
- Buy floor coverings of any type (unless there are very exceptional circumstances)
- Buy non-essential items

Running costs of organisations are not supported either.

Applications

Application forms can be found on the charity's website. Candidates are required to submit a letter of support from their GP confirming their hardship, need or distress. The website states that 'your application will be acknowledged as soon as it has been received and you should expect to hear the outcome of your application within four weeks'.

Other information

Organisations and community groups are also assisted.

The Victoria Convalescent Trust

£104,500 (386 grants)

Correspondent: Mrs A. Perkins, Grants Co-ordinator, 11 Cavendish Avenue, Woodford Green, Essex IG8 9 DA (020 8502 9339)

CC number: 1064585

Eligibility

People in medical need of convalescence, recuperative and respite care with a preference to people living in Surrey and Croydon. A small proportion of support is also given for general relief in need with a preference for women resident in the Greater London area.

Types of grants

Grants of up to £400 are available for services, items or equipment and awards up to £900 for recuperative holidays and respite care.

Annual grant total

In 2014 the trust had an income of £116,000 and a total expenditure of £148,500. Grants to individuals totalled £104,500. Out of that sum, £89,500 was for convalescence and respite purposes and £15,200 given in sundry grants.

Applications

Application forms are available from the correspondent. Applications must be submitted through a social worker, a health care worker or a welfare agency or another professional worker and will be considered every month. Medical and social reports supporting the need for a break must be provided.

Other information

Some support is given to women living in Greater London for vital equipment and services.

The trust incorporates Victoria Convalescent Trust Fund, King Edward VII Children's Convalescent Trust Fund and Princess Mary Memorial Trust Fund.

The Vokins Charitable Trust

£500

Correspondent: Trevor Vokins, Trustee, 56 Hove Park Road, Hove, East Sussex BN3 6LN (01273 556317)

CC number: 801487

Eligibility

People who live in Brighton and Hove and East and West Sussex, particularly people with disabilities or those suffering from ill health.

Types of grants

One-off and recurrent grants are given according to need. The trust also provides mobility scooters to individuals who are 'less abled'.

Annual grant total

In 2014 the trust had an income of £10,000 and a total expenditure of £1,200. Grants are made to both individuals and organisations. We estimate that the amount of grants given to individuals totalled around £500.

Applications

Apply in writing to the correspondent.

Whitton's Wishes (The Kathryn Turner Trust)

£50,000

Correspondent: Kathryn Turner, Founder and Trustee, Unit 3, Suffolk Way, Abingdon, Oxfordshire OX14 5JX (01235 527310; email: kathrynturnertrust@hotmail.co.uk)

CC number: 1111250

Eligibility

Children, young people, the elderly and people with disabilities/special needs in the area of the old county of Middlesex. Grants can also be made in relieving the need, suffering and distress of members and former members of the services, their wives, husbands, widows, widowers and dependants.

Types of grants

Grants towards the costs of equipment and other support.

Annual grant total

In 2013 the trust had an income of over £200,500 and a total expenditure of £200,000. Grants are made to organisations and individuals for both social welfare and educational purposes. We estimate that the amount of grants given to individuals for social welfare purposes totalled around £50,000.

The 2013 accounts were the latest available at the time of writing (November 2015).

Applications

Apply in writing to the correspondent.

Other information

The trust's registered name is The Kathryn Turner Trust.

Bedfordshire

Bedford

Bedford Municipal Charities

£13,000

Correspondent: Lynn McKenna, Administrator, Bedford Borough Council, Committee Services, Borough Hall, Cauldwell Street, Bedford MK42 9AP (01234 228193; email: lynn. mckenna@bedford.gov.uk)

CC number: 2005566

Eligibility

People in need who live in the borough of Bedford.

Types of grants

Pensions, grants towards fuel bills and other necessities, occasional one-off grants for special purposes and Christmas bonuses.

Annual grant total

In 2014/15 the charity had an income of £23,000 and a total expenditure of £16,300. We estimate grants to individuals totalled around £13,000.

Applications

Apply in writing to the correspondent. Applications can be submitted directly by the individual or through an appropriate third party. Individual applicants may be visited to assess the degree of need.

The Norah Mavis Campbell Trust

£6,300

Correspondent: Lynn McKenna, Correspondent, Bedfordshire Borough Council, Committee Services, Borough Hall, Cauldwell Street, Bedford MK42 9AP (01234 228193; email: lynn. mckenna@bedford.gov.uk)

CC number: 1073047

Eligibility

Elderly people in need who reside in the Bedford Borough Council area.

Types of grants

Grants are given according to need.

Annual grant total

In 2013/14 the trust had an income of 2,500 and a total expenditure of £12,800, which is a first major grant after three years of no expenditure. We estimate that about £6,300 was given to individuals.

Applications

Apply in writing to the correspondent.

Other information

The trust also provides additional benefits for residents at the Puttenhoe Home in Bedford. Grants are made to both individuals and organisations.

The Ravensden Town and Poor Estate

£2,600

Correspondent: Alison Baggott, Trustee, Westerlies, Church End, Ravensden, Bedford MK44 2RN (01234 771919; email: alisonbaggott@btinternet.com)

CC number: 200164

Eligibility

Older people who are in need and live in the parish of Ravensden.

Types of grants

One-off and recurrent grants are given according to need.

Annual grant total

In 2014, the estate had an income of £2,300 and a total expenditure of £2,800. We estimate that the total amount of grants awarded to individuals was approximately £2,600.

Applications

Apply in writing to the correspondent. Applications can be submitted directly by the individual. They are usually considered in November, although urgent cases can be responded to at any time.

Other information

This charity also gives grants to a local school.

Central Bedfordshire

Clophill United Charities

£3,300

Correspondent: Gillian Hill, Clerk, 10 The Causeway, Clophill, Bedford MK45 4BA (01525 860539)

CC number: 200034

Eligibility

People who live in the parish of Clophill and are in need. Older people and individuals with disabilities are particularly supported.

Types of grants

One-off and recurrent grants are given according to need.

Annual grant total

In 2014 the charity had an income of £10,700 and a total expenditure of £13,600. We estimate that welfare grants to individuals totalled around £3,300.

Exclusions

Grants are not given where statutory funds are available.

Applications

Application forms can be obtained from the correspondent. The trustees normally meet every two months.

Other information

Grants are also made to organisations and to individuals for educational purposes.

Dunstable Poor's Land Charity

£4,500

Correspondent: Yvonne Beaumont, Clerk to the Trustees, Grove House, 76 High Street North, Dunstable, Bedfordshire LU6 1NF (01582 660008; email: dunstablecharity@yahoo.com; website: www. associationofdunstablecharities.co.uk)

CC number: 236805

Eligibility

People, usually pensioners, who live in the parish of Dunstable.

Types of grants

Small grants are made annually on Maundy Thursday, mostly to older people on a low income.

Annual grant total

In 2014, the charity had an income of £5,100 and a total expenditure of £4,700. We estimate that the total amount of grants awarded to individuals was approximately £4,500.

Applications

Potential applicants should first contact the correspondent by telephone for information on how to apply for a grant.

Flitwick Combined Charities

£5,400

Correspondent: David Empson, Trustee, 28 Orchard Way, Flitwick, Bedford MK45 1LF (01525 718145; email: deflitwick8145@aol.com; website: www.flitwickcombinedcharities.org.uk)

CC number: 233258

Eligibility

People in need who live in the parish of Flitwick.

Types of grants

Usually one-off grants for 'services or facilities to reduce hardship or distress'. The charity states: 'We also help the elderly in the community and are always looking for more people who genuinely require help, regardless of their situation.'

Annual grant total

In 2013/14 the charity had an income of £11,100 and a total expenditure of £10,000. We estimate that grants for social welfare purposes totalled about £5,400.

Applications

Application forms are available from the charity's website or the correspondent. The charity's website states:

> To apply for Relief In Need, applications must be made to the Trustees either directly, through the website or personally. Applications are periodically reviewed throughout the year.
>
> Anything not covered by these forms should be sent to us as a short paragraph outlining the reasons for the request and how any money will be spent, **using the contact us form**, following which we will then be in touch for extra information.

The trustees' meetings are held three times a year and the dates are publicised on the website. Applications need to be submitted at least two weeks in advance of the meeting.

Other information

There are three charities (The Deacons Dole, The Poors Moor and The Town Lands Charity) collectively known as Flitwick Combined Charities. The objectives of the trustees are to provide both educational and relief-in-need help.

Mary Lockington Charity

£3,400

Correspondent: Yvonne Beaumont, Clerk, Grove House, 76 High Street North, Dunstable, Bedfordshire LU6 1NF (01582 660008; email: dunstablecharity@yahoo.com; website: www.associationofdunstablecharities.co.uk)

CC number: 204766

Eligibility

Individuals living in the parishes of Dunstable, Leighton Buzzard and Hockliffe who are in need, for example due to hardship, disability or sickness.

Types of grants

One-off grants towards items, services or facilities.

Annual grant total

In 2013/14 the charity had an income of £12,300 and a total expenditure of £7,100. Taking into account that the charity also gives grants to organisations that provide facilities for those in need, we estimate that the amount of grants awarded to individuals totalled approximately £3,400.

Applications

Application forms are available from the correspondent or can be downloaded from the website. Applicants are usually referred by health professionals or other local organisations.

Other information

The charity also contributes to the upkeep of almshouses and makes grants to local organisations.

The Sandy Charities

£3,500

Correspondent: P. Mount, Clerk, Woodfines Solicitors, 6 Bedford Road, Sandy, Bedfordshire SG19 1EN (01767 680251; email: pmount@woodfines.co.uk)

CC number: 237145

Eligibility

People who live in Sandy and Beeston and are in need.

Types of grants

One-off grants only, ranging from £100 to £1,000, are given towards motorised wheelchairs, decorating costs and children's clothing, for example.

Annual grant total

In 2013/14 the charity had an income of £7,700 and a total expenditure of £15,300. Grants are made to individuals and organisations for both social welfare and educational purposes. We estimate that social welfare grants to individuals totalled £3,500.

Applications

Apply in writing to the correspondent who will supply a personal details form for completion. Applications can be considered in any month, depending on the urgency for the grant; they should be submitted either directly by the individual or via a social worker, Citizens Advice or other welfare agency.

Berkshire

The Berkshire Nurses and Relief-in-Sickness Trust

£53,500 (138 grants)

Correspondent: Rosalind Pottinger, Honorary Secretary, 26 Montrose Walk, Calcot, Reading RG31 7YH (0118 901 0196; email: berksnursestrust@virginmedia.com)

CC number: 205274

Eligibility

1. People in need through sickness or disability who live in the county of Berkshire and those areas of Oxfordshire formerly in Berkshire.

2. Nurses and midwives employed as district nurses in the county of Berkshire and those areas of Oxfordshire formerly in Berkshire; people employed before August 1980 as administrative and clerical staff by Berkshire County Nursing Association.

Types of grants

One-off grants are given only towards household expenditure, holidays, some medical aids, special diets, clothing, wheelchairs, electronic aids for people with disabilities, hospital travel costs, prescription season tickets and so on.

Annual grant total

In 2014/15 the trust held assets of £1.6 million and had an income of £67,500. A total of £53,500 was distributed in 138 grants to individuals. A further £1,700 was given in grants to two organisations.

Exclusions

No grants are given for rent or mortgage payments, community charge, water rates, funeral bills, ongoing payments such as nursing home fees or any items thought to be the responsibility of statutory authorities.

Applications

Application forms are available from the correspondent. Applications should be made through a social worker, Citizens Advice or other welfare agency known to the trustees and supported by a member of the statutory authorities. They are not accepted directly from members of the public.

Other information

The trust states in its 2014/15 annual report that ' the trust also provides funding for local caring organisations, such as hospices and good neighbour schemes, where funds allow.'

The Slough and District Community Fund

£3,000

Correspondent: David Nicks, Trustee, 7 Sussex Place, Slough SL1 1NH (01753 577475; email: dave.nicks@btinternet.com)

CC number: 201598

Eligibility
People who are in need and live in Slough, New Windsor and Eton.

Types of grants
One-off grants according to need. Grants are typically awarded for household essentials, clothing, food and fuel costs, child and baby expenses and the like.

Annual grant total
In 2014 the fund had an income of £3,700 and a total expenditure of £3,100. We estimate that the amount of grants given to individuals totalled £3,000.

Applications
Application forms are available from the correspondent.

Other information
This charity was formed by the amalgamation of 'All Good Causes' and 'The Slough Nursing Fund'.

Reading

John Sykes Foundation

Correspondent: Vickie Randall, Chief Executive, 23/24 Market Place, Reading RG1 2DE (0118 903 5909; email: mail@johnsykesfoundation.org; website: johnsykesfoundation.org)

CC number: 1156623

Eligibility
Individuals who live in and around Reading who are in need of help and support. A map showing the area of benefit can be found on the foundation's website.

Types of grants
Grants are given to individuals for purposes relating to arts and culture, education, science and sport (the details of which can be found in *The Guide to Educational Grants*), as well as for needs relating to health and disability. The website provides the following information:

Health
The charity will support individuals who have a genuine need for medical support. It may be a piece of equipment

to help everyday life or specialist treatment that may be out of reach.

Disability
Life may have been changed by a disability or it may be a part of everyday life. The foundation wants to support individuals who may need help as a result of a disability or support when facing a newly diagnosed condition.

The foundation has four grant programmes and states on its website: 'Each grant is not currently time specific. The individual grants are structured with a grant total therefore it's important to apply to the correct grant programme.' The four grant programmes are: Minster – grants of £500 or less; Abbey – grants of £2,500 or less; Forbury – grants of £5,000 or less; and Maiwand – grants of £10,000 or less. It is important that applicants apply to the programme that is appropriate for the amount needed.

Annual grant total
John Sykes Foundation was registered in April 2014 and, at the time of writing (November 2015), had not yet submitted any accounts to the Charity Commission. We were therefore unable to gather any financial information for the foundation.

Applications
Application forms can be downloaded from the website and should be completed and returned to the foundation's office by post or email. When your application is submitted, you will be sent a notification to confirm it has been received. Your application will be assessed by the trustees and you will be informed whether it has been taken forward to the next stage. Applicants who are unsuccessful at this point will also be notified. If your initial application is successful, you will either be invited to the foundation's office or visited in your home to discuss your application, financial details, your reason for applying and what you hope to achieve. Following this meeting, you will be informed verbally of the foundation's decision and will receive confirmation in writing.

Note: As the foundation is a newly registered grant-maker and is in the early stages of its development, we would advise potential applicants to consider the information on the website thoroughly before beginning an application.

Other information
The foundation's informative website provides the following information: 'The foundation established by John Sykes in 2014 aims to help, support, and transform the lives of people living in and around the Reading area. John not

only has a passion for business but his hometown of Reading too.'

Reading Dispensary Trust

£27,000 (92 grants)

Correspondent: Walter Gilbert, Clerk, 16 Wokingham Road, Reading RG6 1JQ (0118 926 5698; email: admin.rdt@btconnect.com; website: www.readingdispensarytrust.org.uk)

CC number: 203943

Eligibility
People in need who are in poor health, convalescent or who have a physical or mental disability or illness and live in Reading and the surrounding area (within a seven-mile radius of the centre of Reading).

Types of grants
One-off grants of on average around £200 for a wide range of needs including beds and bedding; counselling; clothing and footwear; computer equipment and software; cooking equipment; course fees; food vouchers; furniture and carpets; glasses; instruments; holidays; travel and respite care; house and garden adaptations; repairs and redecoration; therapeutical assessments; play schemes; white goods and equipment; removals; baby and child equipment; disability and access equipment; play equipment; and wheelchairs and scooters.

Annual grant total
In 2014 the charity had assets of £1.3 million and an income of £49,000. Grants totalled £29,000, of which £1,500 was awarded to five organisations. During the year, 94 grants were made to individuals, the vast majority of which were for social welfare purposes. Of this total, two grants were also made towards the purchase of computer equipment and software. We estimate that social welfare grants totalled around £27,000.

Exclusions
The charity cannot fund services or goods which are available from statutory sources.

Applications
Application forms can be downloaded from the website, along with guidelines. Applications are usually made through doctors, nurses, social workers or voluntary organisations. Grant applications are considered on the 2nd Tuesday of each month. Further information can be obtained by contacting the Clerk (the office is open on Tuesday and Thursday mornings only, although answerphone messages can be left outside these times).

Other information

The charity's annual report states: 'Grants usually represent only part of the claimed amount or need. Sometimes these are part paid by other Charities.'

St Laurence Relief-in-Need Trust

£1,900 (7 grants)

Correspondent: Jason Pyke, Treasurer, Vale and West, Victoria House, 26 Queen Victoria Street, Reading RG1 1TG (0118 957 3238; email: mail@ valewest.com)

CC number: 205043

Eligibility

People in need or hardship who live in the ancient parish of St Laurence in Reading. Surplus money can be given to people living in the county borough of Reading.

Types of grants

One-off and annual grants are awarded according to need. Our research suggests that the minimum grant is £100.

Annual grant total

In 2014 the trust held assets of £134,000 and an income of £57,500, mainly from the related Church Lands and John Johnson's Estate Charities. Grants to seven individuals totalled £1,900.

Exclusions

Grants are not made to students for training and research purposes or to people not resident in the area of benefit.

Applications

Apply in writing to the correspondent. Applications can be made directly by the individual or through a third party (such as a social worker or Citizens Advice), including details of required help and the place of residence. Requests are considered twice a year, usually in April and November.

Other information

The trust gives predominantly to organisations (£54,000 to 34 organisations in 2014).

Slough

The Datchet United Charities

£3,200

Correspondent: Anita Goddard, 25 High Street, Datchet, Slough SL3 9EQ (01759 541933)

CC number: 235891

Eligibility

People in need who live in the ancient parish of Datchet.

Types of grants

Grants of £15 to £1,500 are given for clothing, fuel bills, living costs, food, holidays, travel expenses and household bills. Christmas vouchers are also distributed.

Annual grant total

In 2013/14 the charity had assets of £844,000 and an income of £28,500. Grants to individuals totalled £3,200 and were distributed as follows:

Christmas vouchers	£2,400
Family assistance	£800

An additional £7,500 was awarded to local organisations.

The charity also spent £4,800 as part of its 'People to Places' transport scheme.

Applications

Apply in writing to the correspondent either directly by the individual or through a social worker, Citizens Advice or other welfare agency. All applicants will be visited by a social worker.

Other information

The organisation owns a day centre which local groups are able to use free of charge. Loans of medical equipment are also available.

West Berkshire

The Newbury and Thatcham Welfare Trust

£2,400

Correspondent: Jacqui Letsome, Correspondent, Volunteer Centre West Berkshire, 1 Bolton Place, Northbrook Street, Newbury, Berkshire RG14 1AJ (07917 414376; email: ntwt@hotmail. com; website: www. newburyandthatchamwelfaretrust.org)

CC number: 235077

Eligibility

People in financial need who are sick, disabled, convalescent or infirm and live in the former borough of Newbury as constituted on 31 March 1974 and the parishes of Greenham, Enborne, Hamstead Marshall, Shaw-cum-Donnington, Speen and Thatcham.

Types of grants

One-off grants of up to £250. Grants given include those for medical aids, food, holidays, respite care, travel, special equipment, TV licences, furniture and appliances.

Annual grant total

In 2014 the trust had an income of £3,500 and a total expenditure of £2,600. We estimate that the amount of grants given to individuals totalled around £2,400.

Exclusions

Grants are not given towards housing or rent costs and debts.

Applications

Apply on an application form available to download from the website, to be submitted either through a social worker, Citizens Advice or other welfare agency or through a third party on behalf of an individual such as a doctor, health visitor or other health professional. They can be considered at any time and may be submitted by email or post.

Windsor and Maidenhead

Sunninghill Fuel Allotment Trust

£7,200

Correspondent: The Clerk, Sunninghill Trust, PO Box 4712, Ascot SL5 9AA (01344 206320; email: help@ thesunninghilltrust.org; website: thesunninghilltrust.org)

CC number: 240061

Eligibility

People in need who live in the parish of Sunninghill.

Types of grants

One-off grants ranging from about £100 to £1,000. Recent awards have been made to relieve sudden distress, to purchase essential equipment or household appliances and to cover utility bills.

Annual grant total

In 2013/14 the trust had an income of £513,000 and a total expenditure of £92,000. Grants to individuals totalled £7,200. A further £69,500 was awarded in grants to organisations.

Exclusions

Grants are not made for retrospective purposes.

Applications

Apply in writing to the correspondent, via post or email, outlining the need for the grant, where assistance has so far been sought, why funding is not available elsewhere, the urgency of the grant and the difference it will make. All applications will be acknowledged and the trust aims to inform applicants of eligibility within 12 weeks. Urgent applications may be processed with priority. Applicants may be visited by a trustee.

Other information

The majority of the trust's charitable giving is to organisations.

Wokingham
The Earley Charity

£5,700

Correspondent: Jane Wittig, Clerk to the Trustees, Liberty of Earley House, Strand Way, Earley, Reading RG6 4EA (0118 975 5663; fax: 0118 975 2263; email: enquiries@earleycharity.org.uk; website: www.earleycharity.org.uk)

CC number: 244823

Eligibility

People in need who have lived in Earley and the surrounding neighbourhood for at least six months. Applicants must be living in permanent accommodation and have UK citizenship or have been granted indefinite leave to remain in the UK.

In order to check whether you live within the area of benefit, see the map available on the website. If in doubt, get in touch with the correspondent to confirm.

Types of grants

One-off grants are given for the purchase of a specific item, equipment or service. Grants have been given for household goods, such as washing machines, cookers, fridges/freezers, beds and bedding, other furniture, kitchen appliances, and also mobility aids (wheelchairs, scooters, etc.) and sensory equipment. In the past, support has also been given towards gardening tools, specialist computer software, laptops, computers and counselling sessions. Grants do not normally exceed £400, but larger sums may be given for specialist medical or therapeutic equipment and, occasionally, for essential building work and repairs.

Annual grant total

In 2014 the charity had assets of £13.1 million and an income of £1.2 million. Grants totalled £325,000, of which £7,200 was given in 29 awards to individuals. We were able to establish that grants are given to individuals for both social welfare and educational purposes, but we were unable to determine the proportion of the grants total that was attributed to each (the correspondent has previously informed us that the trustees 'do not record separately the amount awarded' in educational grants). We estimate that

social welfare grants to individuals totalled £5,700.

Exclusions

Grants are not given to:
- Those who are planning to move out of the area of benefit
- People who have been awarded a grant within the last two years
- Individuals who have received 3 grants in the past
- Pay for general living costs
- Cover repayment of debts
- Help with non-essential items
- Buy floor coverings and carpets (unless in very exceptional circumstances)

Applications

Application forms can be requested from the correspondent. They can be submitted either directly by the individual or through a social worker, Citizens Advice or other welfare agency. Applications for grants under £500 and applications for grants over £500 are considered at separate meetings around five times each year. The dates of these meetings, along with application submission deadlines, are published on the charity's website.

Other information

Grants are also made to organisations and local voluntary and community groups.

The charity's website notes that currently the main focus is on various community initiatives and projects aimed at older people.

The Polehampton Charity

£4,500 (3 grants)

Correspondent: Miss E. Treadwell, Assistant Clerk to the Charity, 114 Victoria Road, Wargrave, Berkshire RG10 8AE (0118 934 0852; email: polehampton.applications@gmail.com; website: www.thepolehamptoncharity.co.uk)

CC number: 1072631

Eligibility

People in need who live in the former ecclesiastical parishes of St Mary the Virgin in Twyford and St James the Great in Ruscombe.

Types of grants

The website notes: 'Charitable Grants are made for assistance in the case of personal hardship or special need where financial resources are not available.'

This may include items, such as clothing, domestic appliances, holidays, medical equipment, furniture and equipment for people with disabilities.

Our research suggests that awards are generally in the range of £100–£250.

Educational grants are made to help with the cost of 'books and tools which are essential for the completion of courses of training at university, college, or other recognised educational establishments, including apprenticeships'.

Annual grant total

In 2014 the charity had assets of £2.9 million and an income of £96,000. Grants were made totalling about £41,500. Awards to individuals totalled £7,200. The trustees' annual report notes that £2,700 was given in 10 grants to individuals for educational purposes and £4,500 in three awards – for other needs.

Applications

Applications should be made in writing to the correspondent, including full details of the applicant and their need and giving full costings. They can be submitted directly by the individual or a family member, through a third party (such as a social worker or teacher), or through an organisation (such as Citizens Advice or a school). Applications can be made at any time and are considered at trustee meetings (there are three meetings a year – in February, May and October).

Other information

The charity supports both individuals and organisations for social welfare and educational purposes. Awards to organisations during 2014 totalled £34,000 (£27,000 in grants to schools for equipment and resources and £7,200 in grants to organisations and groups).

The Wokingham United Charities

£2,500

Correspondent: P. Robinson, Clerk, 66 Upper Broadmoor Road, Crowthorne, Berkshire RG45 7DF (01344 351207; email: peter.westende@btinternet.com; website: www.westende.org.uk)

CC number: 1107171

Eligibility

People in need who live in the civil parishes of Wokingham, Wokingham Without, St Nicholas, Hurst, Ruscombe and that part of Finchampstead known as Finchampstead North.

Types of grants

One-off grants towards household items, utility arrears and clothing.

Annual grant total

The annual report and accounts for 2013/14 did not include a figure for grants made from the Relief-in-Need Charity. In previous years, grants have totalled around £5,000 and we have estimated those for social welfare purposes to have amounted to £2,500.

Exclusions

The charity is unable to fund items that are the obligation of the state or local authority.

Applications

Apply using a form available from the correspondent or website. Applications can be submitted directly by the individual although most often, grants are delivered through a social worker, school liaison officer or similar third party.

Other information

Wokingham United Charities 'is an amalgamation of some 21 Wokingham local charities – which date back to being some of the oldest charities in England'.

The organisation's Almshouse Charity runs sheltered accommodation for elderly people in the area. The charity's almshouses at Westende are made up of 27 two-person flats and any income generated is reinvested into the property for the benefit of residents.

The organisation has an informative website.

Buckinghamshire

Aylesbury Vale

Charity of Elizabeth Eman

£50,500 (119 grants)

Correspondent: John Reddington, Clerk, Horwood and James LLP, 7 Temple Square, Aylesbury, Buckinghamshire HP20 2QB (01296 487361; email: enquiries@horwoodjames.co.uk; website: www.emans.co.uk)

CC number: 215511

Eligibility

Due to the expansion of the charity both men and women regardless of their marital status living in Aylesbury Vale are eligible. Priority may still be given to people born in Aylesbury.

Types of grants

Allowances of £111 per quarter, paid at the end of March, June, September and December. Grants are for life.

Annual grant total

At the time of writing, the latest accounts available were from 2013. In 2013 the charity had assets of £647,500 and an income of £61,000. Annuities to 116 pensioners totalled £50,500.

Applications

Applications can be made online through the charity's website. Alternatively, potential applicants can print out the form or request one from the correspondent. If you need any assistance call 01296 487361 and ask for Sue Batchelor who will be able to help. Applicants will be informed about the outcome of their application in about a month following the submission.

Other information

The trustees note in their annual report from 2013 that 'the trust is continuously seeking new beneficiaries because income invariably exceeds expenditure'.

Thomas Hickman's Charity

£48,000

Correspondent: John Leggett, Clerk, Parrott and Coales, 14–16 Bourbon Street, Aylesbury, Buckinghamshire HP20 2RS (01296 318500; email: doudjag@pandcllp.co.uk)

CC number: 202973

Eligibility

People who live in Aylesbury town and are in need, hardship or distress.

Types of grants

One-off grants are given according to need.

Annual grant total

In 2014 the charity had an income of £641,000 and a total expenditure of £678,500. A total of 144 grants were made to individuals, amounting to £63,500, although a breakdown of distribution by purpose was not included in the annual report. We estimate that around £48,000 was awarded to individuals for welfare purposes.

Applications

Application forms can be requested from the correspondent. They should be submitted either directly by the individual or through a third party, such as a family member, social worker, school or Citizens Advice. The trustees meet on a regular basis and applications are considered as they arise.

Other information

The charity also provides almshouses to the elderly, supports individuals with their education and makes grants to organisations.

The Stoke Mandeville and Other Parishes Charity

£52,500

Correspondent: Caroline Dobson, Administrator, 17 Elham Way, Aylesbury HP21 9XN (01296 431859; email: smandopc@gmail.com; website: smandopc.org)

CC number: 296174

Eligibility

People in need who live in the parishes of Stoke Mandeville, Great Missenden and Great and Little Hampton. Applicants should have been resident in the area of benefit for at least two years.

Types of grants

At the time of writing, the charity listed the following types of grants on its website:

- Lifeline alarms – available for older residents of Stoke Mandeville parish and provided by Aylesbury Vale Housing Trust
- Senior railcards – reimbursement for cost of a senior citizens railcard, available for residents of Stoke Mandeville parish aged 60 and over
- Senior citizens Christmas grant – an annual grant available to residents of Stoke Mandeville aged 70 and over

Annual grant total

In 2014 the charity had assets of £1.9 million and an income of £90,500. We believe welfare grants totalled about £52,500, comprising £10,700 in Christmas grants, £4,200 in senior railcards and £37,500 in other grants.

Applications

Applications can be made using the relevant form available to download from the website.

Other information

Grants are also made to support residents of the parishes of Stoke Mandeville, Great Missenden and Great and Little Hampton who are studying at college or university, and to enable children resident in Stoke Mandeville to attend school trips.

Chiltern

Amersham United Charities (Amersham and Coleshill Almshouse Charity)

Correspondent: Mrs C. Atkinson, Clerk to the Trustees, 25 Milton Lawns, Amersham, Buckinghamshire HP6 6BJ (01494 723416)

CC number: 205033

Eligibility

People in need who are resident in the parishes of Amersham and Coleshill, Buckinghamshire.

Types of grants

One-off grants to relieve people who are in need, hardship or distress.

Annual grant total

In 2014 the charity had assets of £243,000 and an income of £56,000. The latest accounts state: 'The Trustees have made gifts to various parties in line with the objectives of the Young Persons and Poor Fund during the year.'

The correspondent has previously informed us that, although no grants have been made in recent years, the charity is open to applications from individuals for relief in need and education.

Applications

Applications may be made in writing to the correspondent.

Other information

The main work of the charity is the administration and management of 13 almshouses. Grants can be made through the Young Persons and the Poor Fund.

Milton Keynes

The Ancell Trust

£2,000

Correspondent: Karen Phillips, Secretary, 78 London Road, Stony Stratford, Milton Keynes MK11 1JH (01908 563350; email: karen.phillips30@hotmail.co.uk)

CC number: 233824

Eligibility

People in need in the town of Stony Stratford.

Types of grants

Occasional grants to people in need, including those for healthcare or travel costs.

Annual grant total

In 2014/15 the trust had an income of nearly £8,000 and a total expenditure of £12,400, which is the highest in the past five years. Accounts were not required to be submitted to the Charity Commission due to the low income. We estimate that about £2,000 was given to individuals for welfare purposes.

Applications

Applications may be made in writing to the correspondent at any time.

Other information

The trust owns the sports ground in Stony Stratford, which provides cricket, football, bowls, croquet and tennis facilities.

Our research suggests that grants are given to students for books and may also be awarded for other training needs, including apprenticeships. Support is occasionally given to individuals for welfare purposes and to organisations or groups.

Catherine Featherstone

£4,600

Correspondent: Karen Phillips, Secretary, 78 London Road, Stony Stratford, Milton Keynes, Buckinghamshire MK11 1JH (01908 563350; email: karen.phillips30@hotmail.co.uk)

CC number: 242620

Eligibility

People in need who live in the ancient parish of Wolverton. Preference is given to persons who attend church regularly.

Types of grants

One-off and recurrent grants ranging from £150 to £500. Recent grants have been given for household bills, food, medical and disability equipment, electrical goods, living costs and home help.

Annual grant total

In 2014, the charity had an income of £8,900 and a total expenditure of £9,800. Taking into account that the charity also gives grants to organisations and other voluntary bodies, we estimate that the amount of grants awarded to individuals totalled approximately £4,600.

Applications

Application forms are available from the correspondent. Applications should be submitted either directly by the individual or through a social worker, Citizens Advice or other welfare agency. Applications are considered in March, July and October.

South Buckinghamshire

The Iver Heath Sick Poor Fund

£3,000

Correspondent: John Shepherd, Trustee, Loch Luichart, Bangors Road North, Iver SL0 0BN (01753 651398)

CC number: 231111

Eligibility

People who are sick, convalescing, physically or mentally disabled or infirm and who live in the Iver Heath ward of the parish of Iver and part of the parish of Wexham.

Types of grants

Usually one-off grants for clothing, medical needs, home help, fuel, lighting, chiropody and other necessities, although recurrent grants will be considered.

Annual grant total

In 2014 the fund had an income of £3,800 and a total expenditure of £3,300. We estimate that social welfare grants to individuals totalled £3,000.

Applications

Apply in writing to the correspondent. Applications are considered twice a year in spring and autumn, although in emergencies they can be considered at other times.

Stoke Poges United Charity

£4,000

Correspondent: Anthony Levings, Clerk, The Cedars, Stratford Drive, Wooburn Green, High Wycombe HP10 0QH (email: anthony@levings123.wanadoo.co.uk; website: www.stokepogesparishcouncil.gov.uk/village-charities)

CC number: 205289

Eligibility

People who are in need and live in the parish of Stoke Poges and the surrounding area.

Types of grants

According to our research, grants of £30 to £1,500, can be given for clothing, food, household necessities, medical care and equipment. During the year, grants were given to assist with the costs of: a wet room for an older couple; saving a car from bailiffs; a holiday; car tax and insurance; and school uniform.

Annual grant total

In 2014 the charity had an income of £58,000 and a total expenditure of £13,100. During the year, grants totalled £12,800, of which £4,000 was for social welfare purposes.

Exclusions

The charity cannot give regular or frequent grants and the guidance notes also state that 'it is unlikely the Charity will meet the cost of goods already purchased or replace items already provided within what manufacturers would reasonably expect their life span to be'.

Applications

An application form is available to download from the Stoke Poges parish council website. It should be completed and returned to: Mike Dier, 34 Hazell Way, Stoke Poges SL2 4DD. There is also the option of applying for a grant online via the website. The guidance notes, which are available to download along with the application form, state: 'If you need any assistance with completion, please contact our Chairman, Trevor Egleton 01753 646090 or Mike Dier 01753 642886'.

Other information

See the Stoke Poges parish council website for more information.

The Tracy Trust

£14,500

Correspondent: Jim Cannon, Trustee, 21 Ingleglen, Farnham Common, Slough, Bucks SL2 3QA (01753 643930; email: cannassoc@msn.com)

CC number: 803103

Eligibility

People of a pensionable age who are in need and live in the parish of Hedgerley.

Types of grants

One-off grants towards medical and welfare needs, such as spectacles, chiropody, hospital travel costs, aid alarms, TV licenses, stair-lifts and other related equipment or assistance.

Annual grant total

In 2014/15 the trust had an income of £17,700 and a total expenditure of £15,200. We estimate that £14,500 was given in grants to individuals.

Applications

Apply in writing to the correspondent.

Wycombe

The High Wycombe Central Aid Society

£4,400

Correspondent: Stuart Allen, Secretary, Central Aid, West Richardson Street, High Wycombe, Buckinghamshire HP11 2SB (01494 535890; email: office@central-aid.org.uk; website: www.central-aid.org.uk)

CC number: 201445

Eligibility

People in need, and those in receipt of benefits, who live in the old borough of High Wycombe. The charity will also help ex-service personnel and their dependants.

Types of grants

Mainly one-off grants in kind and gift vouchers to a maximum of £100. Recent grants have been given for food, clothing and furniture.

Annual grant total

In 2013/14 the society had assets of £416,500 and an income of £183,500. Grants totalled £4,400 and were distributed to families through the society's furniture warehouse.

Exclusions

No grants are given towards council tax.

Applications

Apply in writing to the correspondent including details of income, savings, family situation and a quote for the goods needed along with any relevant supporting documents. Applications can be submitted through a social worker, Citizens Advice or other welfare agency and are considered on a monthly basis.

Other information

The society has a second-hand furniture warehouse and clothes and soft furnishings store (Tel: 01494 443459, Email: furniture@central-aid.org.uk).

Radnage Charity

£5,000

Correspondent: Ian Blaylock, Clerk to the Trustees, Hilltop, Green End Road, Radnage, High Wycombe, Buckinghamshire HP14 4BY (01494 483346)

CC number: 201762

Eligibility

People in need who live in the parish of Radnage.

Types of grants

One-off and recurrent grants of around £50 to £200. Grants have been given towards food and hospital visits.

Annual grant total

In 2014 the charity had an income of £10,200 and a total expenditure of £10,300. We estimate that the amount of grants given to individuals totalled £5,000 with local organisations also receiving funding.

Applications

Apply in writing to the correspondent either directly by the individual or, where applicable, through a social worker, Citizens Advice or other third party.

Other information

The charity also contributes to the upkeep of the village's twelfth-century parish church.

Wooburn, Bourne End and District Relief-in-Sickness Charity

£16,000

Correspondent: Dorothea Heyes, Correspondent, 11 Telston Close, Bourne End, Buckingham SL8 5TY (01628 523498)

CC number: 210596

Eligibility

People who live in the parishes of Wooburn, Bourne End, Hedsor or parts of Little Marlow who are sick, convalescent, physically or mentally disabled or infirm.

Types of grants

One-off grants and gift vouchers in the range of £50 to £400 for telephone installation, help with nursing costs, convalescence, holidays, home help and other necessities. All items for which a grant is requested must have a direct connection with the applicant's illness.

Annual grant total

In 2014 the charity had an income of £24,500 and a total expenditure of £19,300. We estimate that the amount of grants given to individuals totalled around £16,000.

Exclusions

No recurrent grants are given.

Applications

Apply in writing to the correspondent through a doctor, health visitor, priest or other third party. Applications are considered throughout the year and should contain details of the nature of illness or disability.

East Sussex

The Derek and Eileen Dodgson Foundation

£15,000

Correspondent: Ian Dodd, Clerk to the Trustees, 8 Locks Hill, Portslade, Brighton and Hove BN41 2LB (01273 419802; email: ianwdodd@gmail.com)

CC number: 1018776

Eligibility

People in need over 55, who live in East and West Sussex, with a strong preference for connections with Brighton and Hove.

Types of grants

Generally, one-off grants or loans of up to £1,000 are made, mainly to older people. Most of the funds are given to local non-governmental organisations to pass on to individuals.

Annual grant total

In 2013/14 the foundation held assets of £2.1 million and had an income of £116,000. We estimate that social welfare grants to individuals amounted to around £15,000. Grants in total were £62,000 and are also given for educational purposes and to organisations.

Applications

Application forms are available from the correspondent. Applications can be submitted either directly by the individual or through a social worker, Citizens Advice or other third party.

The Doctor Merry Memorial Fund

£3,500

Correspondent: Ronald Pringle, Friston Corner, 3 Mill Close, East Dean, Eastbourne, East Sussex BN20 0EG (01323 423319; email: ronpringle@hotmail.com)

CC number: 213449

Eligibility

People who are ill and who live in East Sussex.

Types of grants

One-off grants for nursing home care and medical equipment.

Annual grant total

In 2013/14 the fund had an income of £6,400 and a total expenditure of £7,300. We estimate that the amount of grants given to individuals totalled £3,500 with funding also awarded to local organisations.

Applications

Individuals should apply via their doctor on a form available from the correspondent. Applications are considered throughout the year.

Other information

The fund was established in 1922 as commemoration to a Dr Merry, who died of exhaustion while caring for the people of Eastbourne during a flu epidemic.

The Mrs A. Lacy Tate Trust

£9,700

Correspondent: The Trustees, Heringtons Solicitors, 39 Gildredge Road, Eastbourne, East Sussex BN21 4RY (01323 411020)

CC number: 803596

Eligibility

People in need who live in East Sussex.

Types of grants

One-off and recurrent grants are given according to need.

Annual grant total

In 2013/14 the trust had assets of £688,500 and an income of £56,000. Grants were made to 76 individuals totalling £19,500. We estimate that the amount of grants given to individuals for social welfare purposes totalled around £9,700.

Applications

Applications can be made in writing to the correspondent.

Other information

Grants are also made to individuals for educational purposes and to organisations.

City of Brighton and Hove

The Brighton District Nursing Association Trust

£1,700

Correspondent: Anthony Druce, Hon. Secretary, 15 Mill Drive, Henfield, West Sussex BN5 9RY (01273 686811)

CC number: 213851

Eligibility

People in need who are in poor health, convalescent or who have a disability and live in the county borough of Brighton and Hove. Support is also given to those who are engaged in, or

have been engaged in, domiciliary nursing in the former county borough of Brighton.

Types of grants

One-off grants for items in respect of medical treatment and for convalescence; some limited allowances for nurses may also be available.

Annual grant total

In 2014, the trust had assets of almost £2.4 million and an income of £56,000. Grants to individuals totalled £1,700, with a further £42,500 awarded in grants to 13 organisations.

Applications

Apply in writing to the correspondent: preferably supported by a doctor or health visitor. Applications are considered quarterly, although emergency grants of up to £250 may be awarded between meetings in urgent cases.

The Brighton Fund

£41,000

Correspondent: The Secretary, Brighton and Hove City Council, Democratic Services, Room 121, Kings House, Hove, East Sussex BN3 2LS (01273 291067 or 01273 291077; email: brightonfund@brighton-hove.gov.uk; website: www.brighton-hove.gov.uk)

CC number: 1011724

Eligibility

Individuals in need (primarily people over the age of 60) who live in Brighton and Hove administrative boundary and are in need, hardship or distress.

Types of grants

Small, one-off cash grants according to need, including those for household items, medical equipment and subsistence. Christmas gifts of £75 in the form of gift vouchers are also made to a list of beneficiaries.

Annual grant total

In 2013/14 the fund had assets of almost £1.3 million. Grants were paid totalling £53,500 – a total of £19,500 to residents over the age of 60, around £24,500 to residents under the age of 60, and £9,300 to residents outside the Brighton area but within the Brighton and Hove city area. Awards are made to individuals for both educational and social welfare purposes. We estimate grants made for welfare needs totalled about £41,000.

Exclusions

Only in exceptional circumstances support can be made to someone who is resident outside the Brighton area, or who is only temporarily resident within there. Applications from individuals applying on their own behalf are not accepted.

Applications

Application forms are available from the correspondent or the fund's website and must be submitted through a third party, such as a social worker, health visitor, minister or teacher. Applications are considered upon receipt. It usually takes around two to three weeks to receive a decision (unless additional information from the applicant is required).

Other information

The fund also supports people under the age of 60, including towards educational needs. The annual report specifies that 'the trustees after meeting the administration costs of the charity apply the remaining income 70% to residents over 60 and 30% to residents under 60'.

The Mayor of Brighton and Hove's Welfare Charity

£4,600

Correspondent: Michael Hill, Administrator, Selborne Centre, 5 Selborne Place, Hove, East Sussex BH3 3ET (01273 779432; email: hill. michael4@sky.com)

CC number: 224012

Eligibility

Individuals in need living in the old borough of Hove and Portslade.

Types of grants

One-off grants of up to a maximum of £250.

Annual grant total

In 2014/15 the charity had an income of £3,300 and a total expenditure of £4,800. We estimate that the amount of grants given to individuals totalled £4,600.

Exclusions

No retrospective grants are made.

Applications

Apply on a form available from the correspondent along with full guidelines. Applications should be submitted directly by the individual or a relevant third party, for example, a friend, carer or professional (social worker, health visitor). Grants are considered bi-monthly, in January, March, May, July, September and November. No money is given directly to the applicant, but rather directly to settle invoices. The committee will only consider one grant for each applicant and successful applicants should not re-apply.

Hastings

The Catharine House Trust

£38,000 (131 grants)

Correspondent: Richard Palim, Administrator, Ridge Cottage, New Cut, Westfield, Hastings, East Sussex TN35 4RL (email: catharinehouse@ btinternet.com)

CC number: 801656

Eligibility

Older individuals and people who have disabilities or are in poor health, who live in the borough of Hastings.

Types of grants

One-off grants of up to £400. Funding is available for medical equipment and treatment; household goods when they are essential for maintaining health (but not general furniture); respite breaks for the client or carer; and relevant courses for instruction.

Annual grant total

In 2013/14 the trust had an income of £36,500 and an expenditure of £38,500. Individuals received 131 welfare grants, amounting to £38,000.

Exclusions

Usually only one application is accepted per person.

Applications

Apply in writing to the correspondent, supported by a written statement from a medical professional or social worker. Most applications are made through NHS trusts, local authority social services departments and other charities.

The Hastings Area Community Trust

£42,000 (397 grants)

Correspondent: Anthony Bonds, Administrator, Bolton Tomson House, 49 Cambridge Gardens, Hastings, East Sussex TN34 1EN (01424 718880; website: www.reliefhastings.moonfruit. com)

CC number: 1002470

Eligibility

People in need who are under 60 and live in Hastings borough and Rother district who are on a very low income and have children, or who have medical reasons for not working.

Types of grants

One-off grants mainly in the form of payments to suppliers for essential household needs, including white goods, beds, fuel costs, clothing and baby items.

Annual grant total

In 2013/14 the trust held assets of £532,500 and had an income of £72,500. Grants to 397 individuals totalled £42,000.

Exclusions

No grants are given for carpets, curtains or televisions.

Applications

Application forms are available from the correspondent. Applications can only be accepted from a recognised referral agency (e.g. social worker, Citizens Advice or recognised advice agency) and are considered throughout the year. The trust encourages applicants who wish to telephone to leave a message on the answer phone if there is no reply as messages are listened to daily.

Other information

The trust also provides accommodation and administration services to other local charities and organisations.

William Shadwell Charity

£4,000

Correspondent: C. Morris, Correspondent, 4 Barley Lane, Hastings TN35 5NX (01424 433586)

CC number: 207366

Eligibility

People in need who are sick or in need and live in the borough of Hastings.

Types of grants

One-off and recurrent grants.

Annual grant total

In 2014 the charity had both an income and a total expenditure of £8,400. We estimate that the amount of grants given to individuals totalled £4,000, with funding also awarded to local organisations.

Exclusions

No grants are given for the payment of debt, taxes and so on.

Applications

Apply in writing to the correspondent. Applications should be submitted in March and September for consideration in April and October, but urgent cases can be considered at any time. Applications can be submitted directly by the individual or through a third party.

Rother

The Battle Charities

£2,800

Correspondent: Timothy Roberts, Correspondent, 1 Upper Lake, Battle, East Sussex TN33 0AN (01424 772401; email: troberts@heringtons.net)

CC number: 206591

Eligibility

People in need who live in Battle and Netherfield, East Sussex.

Types of grants

Grants are usually made towards fuel and children's clothing, and range from £50 to £200.

Annual grant total

In 2013, the charity had an income of £3,000 and a total expenditure of £3,000. We estimate that the total amount of grants awarded to individuals was approximately £2,800.

Applications

Apply in writing to the correspondent. Applications can be sent directly by the individual or family member, through an organisation such as Citizens Advice or through a third party such as a social worker. Full details of the applicant's circumstances are required.

Essex

The Colchester Catalyst Charity

£226,000

Correspondent: Stephanie Grant, Administrator, Colchester Catalyst Charity, 3 Dedham Vale Business Centre, Manningtree Road, Dedham, Colchester, Essex CO7 6BL (01206 323420; email: info@colchestercatalyst.co.uk; website: www.colchestercatalyst.co.uk)

CC number: 228352

Eligibility

People in north east Essex who are living with a disability or sickness.

Types of grants

One-off and recurrent grants for respite care and specialist therapy. Funding is also given towards wheelchairs, mobility scooters and other mobility aids, special beds, pressure relieving mattresses and cushions, computers for specific needs and communication aids. Grants are paid directly to the supplier or an appropriate registered charity. Where appropriate, a loan or part-funding of an item may be awarded.

Annual grant total

In 2013/14 the charity had an income of £364,500 and a total expenditure of £425,500. Grants to individuals totalled £226,000 and were distributed as follows:

Respite care	£134,500
Special individual needs	£88,000
Equipment pools	£3,700

A further £139,500 was awarded to organisations.

Exclusions

Funding will not be given for items already purchased or where there is an obligation for provision by a statutory authority. The charity states that it does not take responsibility for the insurance, maintenance and repairs of any items funded. Grants towards replacement vehicles will only be considered where evidence of a replacement fund is available.

Applications

Application forms are available from the correspondent or to download from the charity's website. Applications should include supporting statements, professional assessments by an appropriate professional practitioner (GP, occupational therapist, district nurse) and any quotes or estimates. The charity may request further professional assessments before a grant is made.

Other information

Applications for respite care and counselling are administered through the charity's partners, a full list of which is available on the website.

Grants are also made to charitable organisations for the same purposes.

Braintree

Helena Sant's Residuary Trust Fund

£2,800

Correspondent: Malcolm Willis, Trustee, Greenway, Church Street, Gestingthorpe, Halstead, Essex CO9 3AX (01787 469920; email: willis.malcolm@gmail.com)

CC number: 269570

Eligibility

People in need who live in the parish of St Andrew with Holy Trinity, Halstead who have at any time been a member of the Church of England.

Types of grants

One-off cash grants are given according to need.

Annual grant total

In 2014 the fund had an income of £5,500 and a total expenditure of £5,800.

As half of the fund's charitable expenditure goes towards religious and other charitable work in the parish, we estimate that the amount of grants given to individuals totalled around £2,800.

Exclusions

Grants are not given to pay rates, taxes or public funds.

Applications

Applications can be submitted in writing to the correspondent directly by the individual, through an organisation such as Citizens Advice or through a third party such as a social worker. Applications are considered at any time.

Brentwood

Ecclesiastical Charity of George White

£2,500

Correspondent: Revd Robert Wallace, Trustee, c/o St Peter's Parish Office, Claughton Way, Hutton, Brentwood, Essex CM13 1JS (01277 262864; email: dawn_shaxon@btconnect.com; website: www.huttonchurch.org.uk)

CC number: 208601

Eligibility

People in need who live in the parish of All Saints with St Peter, Hutton. Particular favour is given to children, young adults and older people. The usual length of residency is seven years.

Types of grants

Pensions and one-off grants usually in the range of £100 and £400 towards necessary living expenses.

Annual grant total

In 2014 the charity had an income of £5,400 and a total expenditure of £5,600. We estimate that the amount of grants given to individuals totalled around £2,500.

Applications

Apply in writing to the correspondent at any time. Applications can be submitted either directly by the individual, through a third party such as a social worker, or through an organisation such as Citizens Advice or other welfare agency. They are considered at any time.

Other information

The charity also makes grants towards the repair of the church fabric in the two local parish churches.

Chelmsford

Broomfield United Charities

£2,800

Correspondent: Brian Worboys, Trustee, 5 Butlers Close, Chelmsford CM1 7BE (01245 440540; email: woollards@ theworboys.freeserve.co.uk)

CC number: 225563

Eligibility

People in need who live in the civil parish of Broomfield.

Types of grants

One-off grants according to need and vouchers at Christmas.

Annual grant total

In 2014/15 the charity had an income of £5,700 and an expenditure of £5,600. We estimate that the amount of grants given to individuals totalled £2,200, with funding also awarded to local organisations.

Applications

Apply in writing to the correspondent directly by the individual for consideration at any time.

Kay Jenkins Trust

£2,600

Correspondent: Diana Tritton, Trustee, Hole Farmhouse, Great Leighs, Chelmsford, Essex CM3 1QR (01245 361204; email: dstritton@yahoo.com)

CC number: 241344

Eligibility

People in need, especially older or disabled people, who live in Great and Little Leighs.

Types of grants

One-off, mainly small, grants to help with household expenditure, medical aids and equipment. Occasionally up to £1,000 is given for a large item. No loans are made.

Annual grant total

In 2014/15 the charity had a low income and a total expenditure of £2,800. We estimate that grants totalled around £2,600.

Applications

Apply in writing to the correspondent directly by the individual or through a relative. Grants are considered throughout the year.

The Springfield United Charities

£8,000

Correspondent: Nick Eveleigh, Administrator, Civic Centre, Duke Street, Chelmsford, Essex CM1 2YJ (01245 606606)

CC number: 214530

Eligibility

Individuals in need living in the parish of Springfield.

Types of grants

One-off grants according to need.

Annual grant total

In 2013/14 the charity had an income of £12,400 and a total expenditure of £8,800. We estimate that around £8,000 was made in grants to individuals for social welfare purposes.

Applications

Apply in writing to the correspondent.

Harlow

The Harlow Community Chest

£3,300

Correspondent: Chris Sheldrick, Trustee, c/o K. P. Dispatch, Joseph House, Harolds Road, Harlow, Essex CM19 5BJ (01279 428247; email: harlowcommunitychest@virginmedia. com)

CC number: 252764

Eligibility

Individuals and families in financial need, particularly where a small financial contribution will help to prevent a spiral of debt. Applicants must live in Harlow.

Types of grants

One-off grants. Grants have been made for payment of outstanding utility bills for people with special needs, clothing (for unemployed young people attending a job interview, for example), household items, funeral expenses, removal costs, lodging deposits and nursery fees. Small emergency grants are also available.

Annual grant total

In 2013/14 the charity had an income of £8,000 and a total expenditure of £3,600. We estimate that the amount of grants given to individuals totalled £3,300.

Exclusions

No grants are given for housing rents or rates. Only one main grant to an individual/family can be made in any one year.

Applications

Application forms are available from the correspondent. Applications should be submitted through a recognised referral agency such as a social worker, welfare organisation or doctor. Applications are considered on a monthly basis. Emergency payments can be made between meetings.

Tendring

Henry Smith's Charity (Ancient Parish of Dovercourt)

£2,500

Correspondent: Janet Elliot, 20 Kilmaine Road, Dovercourt, Harwich, Essex CO12 4UZ (01255 503020)

CC number: 246792

Eligibility

People who are in need and live in the ancient parish of Dovecourt and the parish of Harwich Peninsula.

Types of grants

The charity does not normally give direct grants, rather it provides goods such as domestic items, clothing, bedding, food, and pay towards fuel costs, if requested. Our research suggests that one-off payments may be of up to £100.

Annual grant total

In 2013/14 the charity had an income of £2,600 and a total expenditure of £2,700. We estimate that support to individuals totalled around £2,500.

Applications

Apply in writing to the correspondent for consideration at any time. Applications should contain family details and be submitted through a third party, such as Citizens Advice or other welfare agency, or a priest who can recommend the applicant. After receiving a letter, the trustees usually visit the applicant.

Thurrock

East Tilbury Relief in Need Charity

£4,300

Correspondent: Reginald Fowler, Treasurer, 27 Ward Avenue, Grays, Essex RM17 5RE (01375 372304)

CC number: 212335

Eligibility

People in need who live in the parish of East Tilbury.

Types of grants

One-off and recurrent grants have been given towards hospital visits and to children in need.

Annual grant total

In 2014 the charity had an income of £7,300 and an expenditure of £8,800. We estimate that about £4,300 was given in grants to individuals in need.

Applications

Applications may be made in writing to the correspondent, to be considered in November.

Other information

The charity also makes grants to organisations operating in the local area.

Uttlesford

Hatfield Broad Oak Non-Ecclesiastical Charities

£5,800

Correspondent: Martin Gandy, Correspondent, Carters Barn, Cage End, Hatfield Broad Oak, Bishop's Stortford, Hertfordshire CM22 7HL (01279 718316)

CC number: 206467

Eligibility

People in need who live in Hatfield Broad Oak.

Types of grants

One-off and recurrent grants ranging from £20 to £25.

Annual grant total

In 2014 the charity had an income of £7,000 and a total expenditure of £11,900. We estimate that the amount of grants given to individuals totalled around £5,800.

Applications

Apply in writing to the correspondent directly by the individual or family member.

Other information

The charity's Charity Commission record states that it also assists with housing accommodation.

The Saffron Walden United Charities

£37,500

Correspondent: Jim Ketteridge, Clerk to the Trustees, c/o Community Hospital, Radwinter Road, Saffron Walden, Essex CB11 3HY (01799 526122; email: alfredjames.ketteridge@ntlworld.com)

CC number: 210662

Eligibility

People in need who live in the former borough council of Saffron Walden including the hamlets of Little Walden and Sewards End.

Types of grants

One-off grants in kind and gift vouchers. A range of help is considered including, for example, electrical goods, convalescence, clothing, household bills, food, holidays, travel expenses, furniture, disability equipment and nursery fees.

Annual grant total

In 2014 the charity had assets of £1.2 million and an income of almost £43,000. Grants to individuals totalled £37,500.

Exclusions

No grants are given for credit card debt.

Applications

Apply in writing to the correspondent either directly by the individual, through a third party such as a social worker, or through an organisation such as Citizens Advice or other welfare agency. Applications are considered as they arrive.

Thaxted Relief-in-Need Charities

£2,100

Correspondent: Michael Hughes, Correspondent, Yardley Farm, Walden Road, Thaxted, Essex CM6 2RQ (01371 830642; email: michaelbhughes@hotmail.co.uk)

CC number: 243782

Eligibility

People in need who live in the parish of Thaxted.

Types of grants

One-off and recurrent grants are given according to need.

Annual grant total

In 2014 the charity had an income of £27,000 and a total expenditure of £27,500. We estimate that around £2,100 was made in grants to individuals.

Applications

Apply in writing to the correspondent.

Other information

The main priority for the charity is to maintain its almshouses. A small number of grants are also made to local organisations.

Hampshire

Hampshire Football Association Benevolent Fund

£6,500

Correspondent: Robin Osborne, Chair, Winklebury Football Complex, Winklebury Way, Basingstoke, Hampshire RG23 8BF (01256 853000)

CC number: 232359

Eligibility

People in need who have been injured while playing football, and others who have 'done service' to the game of football. Applicants must be playing for a team affiliated with Hampshire Football Association.

Types of grants

One-off and recurrent grants, usually ranging from £50 to £1,000 according to need.

Annual grant total

In 2014 the charity had an income of £4,200 and a total expenditure of £6,700. We estimate that the amount of grants given to individuals totalled £6,500.

Applications

The club secretary must apply to Hampshire Football Association or the Area Benevolent Officer for an application form on behalf of the applicant. The application should be completed by the applicant and endorsed by the secretary of the club.

A doctor's certificate clearly stating the nature of the injury and probable period of incapacitation must accompany each application. Completed application forms should be returned to the county office or the Area Benevolent Officer.

The Hawley Almshouse and Relief-in-Need Charity

£8,200

Correspondent: The Secretary, Trustees' Office, Ratcliffe House, Hawley Road, Blackwater, Camberley, Surrey GU17 9DD (01276 33515; email: hawleyalmshouses@btconnect.com; website: www.hawleyalmshouses.org.uk/relief-in-need)

CC number: 204684

Eligibility

People in need who live in the area covered by Hart district council and Rushmoor borough council. Beneficiaries are generally women aged 60 or over and men aged 65 or over.

Types of grants

Generally one-off grants for needs that cannot be met from any other source. Examples of grants made in recent years include: funding towards school trips for low income families; one-off help with utility bills; rent deposits; purchase of special equipment for disabled people; and contributions to specialist medical assessments. The charity's website states: 'the trust only has a limited amount of funds and therefore the trustees are not able to help with every request received'.

Annual grant total

In 2014/15 the charity had assets of £1.7 million and an income of £131,500. Grants to individuals totalled almost £28,000.

Applications

An initial contact form can be completed on the website by the individual or by an appropriate third party such as a social worker or close family member. It should include a brief summary of the problem and how a grant may be able to help. The charity will then make contact to discuss the applicant's situation and whether they may qualify.

Other information

The charity also provides warden-operated individual accommodation for elderly people in the area.

The Portsmouth Victoria Nursing Association

£18,400

Correspondent: Susan Resouly, Secretary, Southlands, Prinsted Lane, Prinsted, Emsworth, Hampshire PO10 8HS (01243 373900; email: PVNAcharity@gmail.com)

CC number: 203311

Eligibility

People in need who are sick and live in the areas covered by the Portsmouth City Primary Care Trust, the Fareham and Gosport Primary Care Trust and the East Hampshire Primary Care Trust.

Types of grants

One-off grants of up to £750 towards medical equipment, household essentials, special clothing and respite care.

Annual grant total

In 2014 the association held assets of £24,500 and had an income of £46,000. Grants to individuals totalled £18,400 with £16,900 given to patients and £1,500 given to nurses.

Exclusions

Items that should be provided by the NHS will not be funded.

Applications

All applications must be made through the community nursing staff and help is confined to those on whom the nurses are in attendance. Referrals are made by the district nurses on a form which is considered by the committee at monthly meetings.

The Lord Mayor of Portsmouth's Charity

£22,000

Correspondent: Toni Shaw, Administrator, Dame Mary Fagan House, Chineham Court, Lutyens Close, Basingstoke, Hampshire RG24 8AG (01256 776127; email: info@hantscf.org.uk; website: www.hantscf.org.uk)

CC number: 1100417–2

Eligibility

Contact the correspondent for current details. Formerly this charity funded individuals in need who lived in the city of Portsmouth, or former residents who lived in Havant, Waterlooville, Fareham or Droxford.

Types of grants

One-off grants.

Annual grant total

This is now a linked charity to the Hampshire and Isle of Wight Community Foundation; however, we could not find any information in the foundation's accounts for this particular charity's activities. The accounts did state that the Lord Mayor of Portsmouth's Charity had assets amounting to almost £505,000. In the past we know that the charity awarded around £22,000 in grants.

Applications

Apply in writing to the correspondent.

Other information

Grants are also made to local organisations.

Basingstoke and Dean

The Kingsclere Welfare Charities

£5,500

Correspondent: Roy Forth, Correspondent, PO Box 7721, Kingsclere, Newbury RG20 5WQ

(07796423108; email: kclerecharities@aol.co.uk)

CC number: 237218

Eligibility

People in need who live in the parishes of Ashford Hill, Headley and Kingsclere.

Types of grants

The provision or payment for items, services or facilities such as medical equipment, expenses for travel to hospital and grants to relieve hardship. Grants are mostly one-off, but recurrent grants can be considered. They range from around £100 to £2,500.

Annual grant total

In 2014 the charity had an income of £5,200 and a total expenditure of £5,700. We estimate that the amount of grants given to individuals would be around £5,500.

Applications

Apply in writing to the correspondent. Applications are considered in February, April, June, September and November.

East Hampshire

Bordon Liphook Haselmere Charity

£70,000

Correspondent: Sue Nicholson, Administrator, Room 29, The Forest Centre, Pinehill Road, Bordon, Hampshire GU35 0TN (01420 477787; email: info@blhcharity.co.uk; website: www.blhcharity.co.uk)

CC number: 1032428

Eligibility

People in need who live in north-east Hampshire and south-west Surrey.

Types of grants

One-off grants of between £50 and £3,000 can be awarded. The trustees consider a wide range of applications including those for heating and rent arrears.

Annual grant total

At the time of writing (November 2015), the latest financial information available was from 2013. In 2013 the charity had an income of £148,000 and a total expenditure of £111,500. Full accounts were not published online. Based on previous research we estimate that the amount of grants given to individuals for social welfare purposes in the year 2013 was in the region of £70,000.

Applications

Apply on a form available from the correspondent or to download from the website. Applications can be made either directly by the individual or through a social worker, Citizens Advice, other welfare agency, health visitor or district nurse. Applications are considered monthly and the charity reserves the right to commission a case worker's report.

Other information
The charity raises money through its three charity shops – Bordon Care, Haslemere Care and Liphook Care and provides support to both individuals and organisations.

Fareham
The Fareham Welfare Trust

£11,500

Correspondent: Anne Butcher, Correspondent, 44 Old Turnpike, Fareham, Hampshire PO16 7HA (01329 235186)

CC number: 236738

Eligibility
People in need who live in the ecclesiastical parishes of St Peter and Paul, St John and Holy Trinity, all in Fareham. Preference is given to widows in need.

Types of grants
One-off and recurrent grants of up to around £250 a year. Grants have been given for clothing, furniture, food, cookers, washing machines and other essential electrical items.

Annual grant total
In 2013/14 the trust had an income of £12,700 and a total expenditure of £11,800. We estimate that the amount of grants given to individuals totalled £11,500.

Applications
Applications should be submitted through a recognised referral agency (e.g. a social worker, health visitor, Citizens Advice or doctor) or trustee. Applications are considered throughout the year. Details of the individual's income and circumstances must be included.

The Earl of Southampton Trust

£12,300

Correspondent: Sue Boden, Clerk, 24 The Square, Titchfield PO14 4RU (01329 513294; email: earlstrust@yahoo.co.uk; website: eost.org.uk)

CC number: 238549

Eligibility
People in need who live in the ancient parish of Titchfield (now subdivided into the parishes of Titchfield, Sarisbury, Locks Heath, Warsash, Stubbington and Lee-on-Solent). Groups catering for people who are in need are sometimes considered.

Types of grants
One-off grants in the range of £25 and £1,000 are given for a wide range of purposes including, for example, furnishings, food, payment of household bills, household appliances, rent arrears, transport, holidays, respite care, and medical equipment.

Annual grant total
In 2013/14 the trust had assets of £1.65 million and an income of £99,500. Grants amounted to £15,300 and were given for a wide range of purposes. We estimate educational grants (for uniforms and child holiday care) to have totalled around £500, and social welfare grants around £12,300. A further £2,500 was awarded to organisations.

Exclusions
The trust will not supply items or services which should be provided for by the state.

Applications
Application forms can be downloaded from the trust's website and must be submitted through a recognised agency (social services, a health visitor, etc.). Applications must include details of medical/financial status and are usually means-tested. They are normally considered on the last Tuesday of every month, although in the event of extreme urgency requests can be fast tracked between meetings.

Other information
The trust runs almshouses and a day centre for older people.

Gosport
Thorngate Relief-in-Need and General Charity

£3,200

Correspondent: Kay Brent, 16 Peakfield, Waterlooville PO7 6YP (023 9226 4400; email: kay.brent@btinternet.com)

CC number: 210946

Eligibility
People in need who live in Gosport.

Types of grants
One-off grants usually of between £100 and £500.

Annual grant total
In 2013/14 the charity had an income of £11,200 and a total expenditure of £12,900. Grants are made to individuals and organisations for a wide range of purposes. We estimate that social welfare grants to individuals totalled £3,200.

Exclusions
No grants are made towards legal expenses.

Applications
Apply using a form available from the correspondent. Applications can be made either directly by the individual or through a social worker, Citizens Advice, Probation Service or other welfare agency.

New Forest
Dibden Allotments Fund

£169,500 (1,138 grants)

Correspondent: Valerie Stewart, Clerk to the Trustees, 7 Drummond Court, Prospect Place, Hythe, Southampton SO45 6HD (023 8084 1305; email: dibdenallotments@btconnect.com; website: daf-hythe.org.uk)

CC number: 255778

Eligibility
People in need who live in the parishes of Hythe, Dibden, Marshwood and Fawley in Hampshire. Individuals should have lived in the Waterside area for at least 12 months.

Types of grants
One-off grants are made, according to need, for the relief of hardship or distress. Grants to individuals can take many forms, such as vouchers for food, clothes or household items, or the supply of white goods or furniture.

Shoe Vouchers Scheme – mainly for children and older people, towards the costs of shoes at a number of participating local shoe retailers.

Garden Support Scheme – run in conjunction with a number of local gardeners to assist older people and people who have disabilities with essential work in their gardens, such as grass cutting and hedge trimming, between March and November.

Annual grant total
In 2013/14 the fund had assets of £9.5 million and an income of £391,500. Grants totalled £264,000, of which organisations were awarded £94,000. Grants to individuals amounted to £170,500, and were distributed as follows:

General	245	£104,000
Garden support scheme	159	£43,500
Shoe project	734	£22,000
Education	2	£700*

*We have not included the figure for educational grants in our grant total.

Exclusions

The fund's website states: 'It would be unusual for an individual to receive more than a single grant in any one year or for goods already provided to an individual by the Fund to be replaced within what a manufacturer would consider to be "a reasonable period of use".'

Applications

Application forms are available on the fund's website, where the fund's criteria, guidelines and application process are also posted. It is helpful to supply a supporting statement from a professional such as a health or social worker, midwife or teacher.

Shoe Vouchers Scheme – Vouchers are distributed mainly through schools and organisations working with older people, although people who don't have contact with either can apply using the same process as for a general grant (as described above).

Garden Support Scheme – Applications can be made at any time via letter or telephone call, although the fund encourages individuals wishing to join the scheme to make contact during January and February.

Other information

Grants are also made to charitable and voluntary organisations.

The Sway Welfare Aid Group

£17,600 (33 grants)

Correspondent: Jeremy Stevens, Treasurer, Driftway, Mead End Road, Sway, Lymington, Hampshire SO41 6EH (01590 681500 or 01590 682843; email: info@swaghants.org.uk; website: www. swaghants.org.uk)

CC number: 261220

Eligibility

Individuals and families in need who live in the parish of Sway (Hampshire) and its immediate neighbourhood.

Types of grants

One-off grants towards: household equipment; rent (to avoid eviction); bereavement costs; hospital travel costs; heating bills; essential decorating costs and home repairs; insulation; reasonable recreational equipment; disability aids; and support with unexpected crises.

Help may also be given towards training courses and school trips.

Annual grant total

In 2013/14 the group had assets of £187,000, an income of £21,000 and expenditure of £22,000. During the year the group helped 22 people with heating grants totalling £9,700 and provided a further 11 grants to individuals and families totalling £7,900.

Applications

Apply in writing to the correspondent or by personal introduction.

Other information

The group runs a lunch club for people living on their own. It also has a team of volunteer drivers that can help local residents who have difficulty in getting to, for example, hospital appointments.

Organisations can also be supported – in 2013/14 Sway Over Sixties Club (£360) and New Forest Basics Bank (£750) have been supported.

Portsmouth

The Montagu Neville Durnford and Saint Leo Cawthan Memorial Trust

£5,000

Correspondent: Toni Shaw, Chief Executive, Hampshire and Isle of Wight Community Foundation, Dame Mary Fagan House, Chineham Court, Lutyens Close, Basingstoke, Hampshire RG24 8AG (01256 776127; email: info@hantscf.org.uk; website: www.hantscf.org.uk)

CC number: 1100417–1

Eligibility

People over 60 who are in need and who live in the city of Portsmouth. Preference is given to ex-naval personnel and their dependants/widows.

Types of grants

Annual grants.

Annual grant total

The fund was transferred from Portsmouth city council to Hampshire and Isle of Wight Community Foundation along with 12 other funds known as the Portsmouth City Community Fund in a strategic move to manage the funds together and leverage match funding for the benefit of the community.

Applications

Application forms are available from the correspondent. Grants are made to the RNBT for redistribution.

E. C. Roberts Charitable Trust (Roberts Trust)

£100

Correspondent: Revd Wendy Kennedy, Administrator, First Floor, Peninsular House, Wharf Road, Portsmouth PO2 8HB (023 9289 9668; email: wendy.kennedy@portsmouth.anglican.org)

CC number: 1001055

Eligibility

Children in need who live in the city of Portsmouth, with a preference for those who are orphans, blind or have a disability.

Types of grants

One-off or recurrent grants according to need, including clothing and other essentials.

Annual grant total

In 2014 there was a significant drop in the income of the charity and consequently its expenditure. Income was just £330 and total expenditure £102. Note that the expenditure varies significantly each year and in the past five years has fluctuated from £0 to £36,000.

Applications

Apply in writing to the correspondent. Applications can be submitted either directly by the individual or through a third party, for example, a social worker, Citizens Advice or other welfare agency. Requests for assistance are considered upon receipt.

Other information

Organisations may also be supported.

Rushmoor

The Farnborough (Hampshire) Welfare Trust

£2,800

Correspondent: M. Evans, Correspondent, Bowmarsh, 45 Church Avenue, Farnborough, Hampshire GU14 7AP (01252 542726; email: evans.bowmarsh@ntlworld.com)

CC number: 236889

Eligibility

People in need who live in the urban district of Farnborough, Hampshire.

Types of grants

One-off and recurrent grants mainly to older people at Christmas. Grants are generally between £20 and £50.

Annual grant total

In 2014, the charity had an income of £3,700 and a total expenditure of £3,100. We estimate that the total amount of grants awarded to individuals was approximately £2,800.

Applications

Apply in writing to the correspondent: to be submitted either directly by the individual or by a third party. Applications are usually considered in early December.

Southampton

The Southampton (City Centre) Relief-in-Need Charity

£9,800

Correspondent: Linda Page, Correspondent, 12 Westgate Street, Southampton SO14 2AY (02380638968)

CC number: 255617

Eligibility

People in need who live in the ecclesiastical parish of Southampton (in practice, the city centre).

Types of grants

One-off grants usually ranging from £50 to £100. The charity supplies a leaflet detailing the types of grants it can give.

Annual grant total

In 2014 the charity had an income of £9,400 and a total expenditure of £10,000. We estimate that the amount of grants given to individuals totalled £9,800.

Exclusions

No grants are given towards rent, debts or council tax.

Applications

Apply in writing to the correspondent submitted through a social worker, Citizens Advice, health visitor or other welfare agency. Applications are considered quarterly, usually in March, June, September and December; those made directly by the individual will not be considered.

Southampton and District Sick Poor Fund and Humane Society (Southampton Charitable Trust)

£5,100

Correspondent: Rachel Doran, Administrator, c/o BDO LLP, Arcadia

House, Maritime Walk, Southampton SO14 3TL (email: rachel.doran@bdo.co.uk)

CC number: 201603

Eligibility

People who are sick and poor and live in Southampton and the immediate surrounding area. Grants and certificates are also awarded to people for saving or attempting to save someone from drowning or other dangers.

Types of grants

Our research suggests that one-off grants, usually ranging from £50 to £250, are available for bedding, food, fuel and specialist equipment to alleviate an existing condition or to assist with day-to-day living.

Annual grant total

In 2014 the society had an income of £21,500 and a total expenditure of £13,500. We estimate that around £6,500 was awarded in grants to individuals.

Applications

Apply in writing to the correspondent. Applications should, preferably, be submitted through a social worker, Citizens Advice or other welfare agency. The trustees usually meet twice a year, but applications can be dealt with outside these meetings. Candidates must clearly demonstrate that they are both sick and poor (such as evidence of Income Support or other state benefits).

Other information

Grants may also be made to organisations.

Winchester

Twyford and District Nursing Association

£18,000

Correspondent: Giselle Letchworth, Trustee, Sunnyside, High Street, Twyford, Winchester SO21 1RG (01962 712158; email: giselleletchworth@btinternet.com)

CC number: 800876

Eligibility

People who are in need and live in the parishes of Twyford, Compton and Shawford, Colden Common and Owslebury, in the county of Hampshire.

Types of grants

One-off grants according to need. In the past, awards have been given for: electrical goods; convalescence; clothing; travel expenses; medical equipment; nursing fees; furniture; disability equipment; and help in the home.

Annual grant total

In 2014 the association had an income of £7,300 and a total expenditure of £20,800. We estimate that the amount of grants given to individuals totalled £18,000.

Exclusions

The association cannot offer long-term care.

Applications

Application forms are available from the correspondent. Applications are usually made through the medical practices in the area (mainly the Twyford Practice) and people can also apply through the social services, a doctor or community nurse, or if they do not have a direct medical contact, directly to the correspondent or through a relevant third party.

Hertfordshire

The Bowley Charity for Deprived Children

£7,000

Correspondent: Kay Rees, Correspondent, 175 Cassiobury Drive, Watford WD17 3AL (01923 226710; email: kayrees@hotmail.com; website: www.bowleycharity.btck.co.uk)

CC number: 212187

Eligibility

Disadvantaged children up to 16 years (or 18 if in full-time education) who live in south-west Hertfordshire.

Types of grants

Small, one-off grants of up to £300 for cookers, beds, bedding, prams, cots and other essential household items. Grants are also given for clothing and shoes for children. Grants should primarily benefit children, rather than adults, and usually come in the form of Argos vouchers.

Annual grant total

In 2013/14 the charity had an income of £11,000 and a total expenditure of £7,300. We estimate that the amount of grants given to individuals totalled £7,000.

Exclusions

Trustees will not normally fund flooring, living room furniture, holidays, school uniform, outings or school trips.

Applications

Application forms are available to download from the charity's website or from the correspondent. Applications should be made through a social worker, Citizens Advice or other welfare agency. The trustees meet quarterly in March,

June, September and December to consider grants. See the website for closing dates for applications.

The Hertfordshire Charity for Deprived Children

£8,000

Correspondent: Diane Hanlon, Acting Clerk, 138 Fairview Road, Stevenage SG1 2NS (email: dianehh@ntlworld.com; website: mgtact0.wix.com/herts-charity-child)

CC number: 200327

Eligibility

Disadvantaged children up to the age of 17 living in Hertfordshire (excluding the Watford area). The charity's website states that it supports children who 'are facing difficulties that compromise their well-being and self-worth'.

Types of grants

One-off grants generally for holidays (not overseas), clothing (such as school or cub/brownie uniforms or general clothing), bedding, furniture and other household items (such as cookers, or washing machines, where this would improve the quality of life for the child). Grants usually range between £30 and £300.

Annual grant total

In 2014/15 the charity had an income of £10,400 and an expenditure of £8,300. We estimate that the amount of grants given to individuals totalled £8,000.

Exclusions

The charity is unable to help looked-after children in residential care or foster placements. Grants are not made towards loan repayments.

Applications

Apply on a form available to download from the charity's website or from the correspondent. Applications should be made through a health visitor, social worker, housing officer or similar third party. Trustees normally meet in May and November, but applications can be considered between meetings and can be approved on the agreement of two trustees.

Hertfordshire Community Foundation

£62,500 (390 grants)

Correspondent: Caroline Langdell, Fund Manager, Foundation House, 2–4 Forum Place, Off Fiddlebridge Lane, Hatfield, Hertfordshire AL10 0RN (01707 251351; fax: 01707 251133; email: caroline.

langdell@hertscf.org.uk; website: www.hertscf.org.uk)

CC number: 299438

Eligibility

For the Hertfordshire Children's Fund: children below the age of 16 who are affected by disability or disadvantage and live in Hertfordshire. Applicants should check the foundation's website for details of eligibility criteria for other funds currently available.

Types of grants

For the Hertfordshire Children's Fund: one-off grants of up to £300 towards, for example, beds and bedding, baby equipment, white goods or specialised equipment for a child with a disability. Check the charity's website for current guidelines, eligible items and amounts available.

The foundation manages a number of funds and applicants should check the website for other funds currently available.

Annual grant total

In 2013/14 the foundation held assets of almost £8.1 million and had an income of almost £1.5 million. A total of £730,500 was awarded in grants through the various funds administered by the foundation, the majority of which were to local organisations. 63 grants were made to families from the Hertfordshire Children's Fund, totalling £12,000. A further 327 grants amounting to £50,500 were made to individuals and families from the Warm Homes/Healthy People Fund.

Exclusions

Grants are not given for: clothing or school uniform; holidays or school trips; carpeting or curtains; general furniture; gardening equipment; debt repayment.

Applications

Apply to the Hertfordshire Children's Fund on a form available from the correspondent or to download from the website, where full guidelines are also provided. Applications can be made at any time and must be made through a recognised professional such as a social worker or health visitor.

Application details for other funds can be found on the website.

Other information

The foundation administers 90 funds which provide grants to organisations and to individuals.

The Hertfordshire Convalescent Trust

£21,000

Correspondent: Janet Bird, Administrator, 140 North Road, Hertford SG14 2BZ (01992 505886; fax: 01992 582595; email: janet_l_bird@hotmail.com)

CC number: 212423

Eligibility

People in need who are convalescing following an operation or period of ill health, chronically sick, terminally ill or children with special needs and their carers. Families suffering from domestic violence or relationship breakdown may also be eligible for assistance. Applicants must live in Hertfordshire.

Types of grants

One-off grants in the range of £300 to £500 for traditional convalescence in a nursing home or for respite breaks and recuperative holidays in hotels and caravans.

Annual grant total

In 2014 the trust had assets of £561,000 and an income of £26,500. Grants totalled £21,000.

Exclusions

There are no grants available for equipment or transport costs.

Applications

Application forms are available from the correspondent. Applications should be sponsored by a health professional, social worker or member of the clergy. They are considered throughout the year.

Other information

The trustees' annual report for 2014 states: 'About 120 adults and children throughout the county of Hertfordshire were able to take a holiday during the year due to receiving a grant from the trust. Grants to each family or individual averaged between £450 and £500.'

Dacorum

The Dacorum Community Trust

£45,500

Correspondent: The Grants and Finance Officer, The Hub Dacorum, Paradise, Hemel Hempstead HP2 4TF (01442 231396; email: admin@dctrust.org.uk; website: www.dctrust.org.uk)

CC number: 272759

Eligibility

People in need who live in the borough of Dacorum.

Types of grants

Generally one-off grants of up to £500 towards domestic equipment; disability equipment; clothes and shoes; funeral expenses; respite breaks and holidays for families; debt relief; and the costs involved in making homes habitable and safe for young and old.

Annual grant total

In 2013/14 the trust had assets of £111,500 and received an income of £104,000. There were 721 grants made totalling £60,500. Direct grants totalled £35,000 and gifts in kind were costed at £26,000. We have estimated the educational grants total to be around £15,000 and grants/gifts in kind for social welfare purposes to total £45,500.

Exclusions

Grants are not normally given for the costs of further or mainstream education and only in exceptional circumstances for gap year travel.

Applications

Apply on a form available from the correspondent or to download from the website. Applications can be submitted by the individual, through a recognised referral agency (such as Social Services or Citizens Advice) or through an MP, GP or school. Applications are considered in March, June, September and December. The trust asks for details of family finances. A preliminary telephone call is always welcome.

Other information

This trust also gives to organisations.

East Hertfordshire
Buntingford Relief-In-Need Charity

£15,000

Correspondent: Eunice Woods, Trustee, 38 Hare Street Road, Buntingford, Hertfordshire SG9 9HW (01763 271974)

CC number: 262264

Eligibility

Older people on state registered pensions who have lived in the parish of Buntingford for at least ten years. Other people in need within the parish may also be helped.

Types of grants

Our research suggests that £20 per household is given in early December towards the cost of fuel.

Annual grant total

At the time of writing (November, 2015) the latest financial information available was from 2011. In 2011 the charity had an income of £9,500 and a total expenditure of £124,000, which is exceptionally high. Both figures vary from year to year. In the past grants to individuals have totalled around £15,000.

Applications

Apply in writing to the correspondent.

Other information

Organisations may also be assisted.

The Ware Charities

£8,000 (11 grants)

Correspondent: Susan Newman, Correspondent, 3 Scotts Road, Ware, Hertfordshire SG12 9JG (01920 461629; email: suedogs@hotmail.com)

CC number: 225443

Eligibility

People in need who live in the area of Ware town council, the parish of Wareside and the parish of Thundridge.

Types of grants

Grants are made towards items or services not readily available from any other source. Awards are not paid to individuals directly, rather through a third party.

Annual grant total

In 2014/15 the charity had an income of £66,000 and a total expenditure of £41,000. Full accounts were not available to view at the time of writing (September 2015). In the past grants to individuals have totalled about 40% of the overall expenditure, on average. We estimate that about £16,500 was paid in grants to individuals and out of that sum about £8,000 for social welfare purposes. Note that grant-making varies annually. On average about 37 awards are made each year to individuals.

Applications

Applications may be made in writing to the correspondent at any time. They should be submitted directly by the individual or a family member. Applications must include brief details of the applicant's income and savings and be supported and signed by a headteacher, GP, nurse, member of the clergy or social worker.

Other information

Grants are also made to local organisations and individuals for educational needs.

North Hertfordshire
The Letchworth Civic Trust

£1,500

Correspondent: Sally Jenkins, Secretary, Broadway Chambers, Letchworth Garden City, Hertfordshire SG6 3AD (07785 104357; email: letchworthct@gmail.com; website: letchworthct.org.uk)

CC number: 273336

Eligibility

People who have lived in Letchworth Garden City for two years or more.

Types of grants

Assistance can be given to people who have disabilities to help with mobility problems.

Annual grant total

In 2013/14 the trust had assets of £725,000 and an income of £71,000. Grants totalled £51,500, the majority of which was distributed to individuals for purposes relating to their education. We estimate that the amount of grants given to individuals for medical support amounted to around £1,500. A total of £8,500 was also paid in grants to ten organisations.

Applications

Application forms can be downloaded from the charity's website and should be returned to the trust by post. Applications are considered in January, March, June, September, October and December and can be submitted by the individual or a third party such as a headteacher, social worker, probation officer or police officer.

Other information

The trust mainly makes grants to schoolchildren and students for purposes relating to their education. In a typical year about 200 grants are given to individuals, mainly for young people. Around 20 organisations also receive support each year.

St Albans
The Harpenden Trust

£51,500 (777 grants)

Correspondent: Dennis Andrews, Secretary, The Harpenden Trust Centre, 90 Southdown Road, Harpenden AL5 1PS (01582 460457; email: admin@ theharpendentrust.org.uk; website: www. theharpendentrust.org.uk)

CC number: 1118870

Eligibility

People in need who live in the AL5 postal district of Harpenden, with a preference for young and older people.

Types of grants

One-off grants are made to assist with household bills, as vouchers for food and clothing, and in the form of new and recycled furniture and white goods. Help can also be given to older people who have difficulty paying their winter utility bills (electricity, gas and water). Christmas parcels are delivered to older people who are housebound during the festive period.

Annual grant total

In 2013/14 the trust had assets of £4 million and an income of £229,000. Grants to individuals totalled £63,000, of which £51,500 was given in 777 awards for what we consider to be social welfare purposes. They were distributed as follows:

General grants	559	£33,000
Utilities grants	78	£16,800
Youth grants	92	£11,300*
Christmas parcels	140	£1,700

*We have taken this figure to represent grants given to young people for educational purposes and, therefore, have not included it in the grant total.

A further £41,500 was awarded to organisations.

Exclusions

Grants are not given to individuals living outside Harpenden.

Applications

Apply in writing to the correspondent, either directly by the individual or, if applicable, through a third party such as a social worker or Citizens Advice. The trust can be contacted by telephone or email, by completing the online contact form, or by dropping into the Trust Centre (between 10am and noon, Monday to Friday).

Other information

The Harpenden Trust was founded in 1948 by Dr Charles Hill. Amongst its activities in the Harpenden community – and with the help of more than 300 volunteers – the trust hosts coffee mornings for older people (Tuesdays at the Trust Centre, 90 Southdown Road and Thursdays at High Street Methodist Church Hall, Lower High Street, both at 10am–11am), organises outings for older people and children, and operates a home visiting service to assist families financially and otherwise. Each year, the trust produces and sells its own calendar, of which it donates 50 units each to around 12 local charities to sell for their own funds.

Watford

The Watford Health Trust

£18,900 (30 grants)

Correspondent: Ian Scleater, Trustee, Allways, 23 Shepherds Road, Watford WD18 7HU (01923 222745; email: ian@scleater.co.uk)

CC number: 214160

Eligibility

People in need who are in poor health, convalescent or who have a disability and live in the borough of Watford and the surrounding neighbourhood.

Types of grants

One-off and recurrent grants to assist recovery or improve quality of life.

Annual grant total

In 2013/14 the trust had assets of £958,000 and an income of £26,000. During the year, individuals received £18,900 in 30 grants. A further £335 was returned to the trust unspent.

Applications

Apply in writing to the correspondent. Grants are generally made through official bodies or practices familiar with the applicant's needs.

Welwyn Hatfield

Wellfield Trust

£14,200

Correspondent: Jenny Bayford, Trust Manager, Birchwood Leisure Centre, Longmead, Hatfield, Hertfordshire AL10 0AN (01707 251018 (Monday to Friday, 9.30am to 3pm); email: wellfieldtrust@aol.com; website: www.wellfieldtrust.co.uk)

CC number: 296205

Eligibility

People in need who are on a low income and have lived in the parish of Hatfield for six months.

Types of grants

One-off grants, usually between £100 and £500, towards a range of welfare needs such as clothing, beds, recliner chairs and school uniforms.

Annual grant total

In 2013/14 grants to individuals amounted to £14,900, with a further £5,200 given in grants to organisations.

The majority of grants are given for social welfare purposes, mostly for household appliances, carpets and beds

and furniture. We estimate that these totalled around £14,200 during the year.

Exclusions

Our research indicates that grants are not made for council tax arrears, rent or funeral costs. Applications are not normally considered from individuals who have received a grant from the trust within the last two years.

Applications

There is an application form available to download from the website, which must be completed by the individual or a member of the household in need and a sponsor. The sponsor should be somebody from an organisation that is familiar with the applicant's personal circumstances such as a social worker, health visitor, housing officer or warden. Applicants who cannot think of an appropriate sponsor should contact the trust for advice.

Unless the application is for household appliances or carpets, it needs to be accompanied by a shop-written estimate (a compliment slip with the details of the item will do). The trust also states this additional information on its website:

If you are applying for a household appliance you just need to state the item you are in need of such [as] a washing machine, fridge or cooker etc. and we will do the rest. If you are applying for carpet, the applicant needs to contact our supplier Colin Stuart of CCS Floorings Ltd. (tel. no. 01727 822776) to arrange for any estimate. Only one type of carpet is considered and usually only for the main priority room.

The trust's committee meets on the second Tuesday of every month to consider applications which, to be considered at the next meeting, must be submitted by the first Monday of every month.

Other information

The trust also gives to organisations and has a room at a local leisure centre which can be hired free of charge to charitable organisations. It also runs the Scooter Loan Scheme, through which 17 motorised scooters are loaned to residents of Hatfield who would otherwise be 'virtually housebound' for as long as is required. The trust manager can be contacted for an initial discussion about the scheme.

Isle of Wight

The Broadlands Fund (Broadlands Home Trust)

£3,300

Correspondent: Mrs M. Groves, Correspondent, 2 Winchester Close, Newport, Isle of Wight PO30 1DR (01983 525630; email: broadlandstrust@btinternet.com)

CC number: 201433

Eligibility

Single women and widows who are over the age of 40, in need and live on the Isle of Wight.

Types of grants

Pensions of around £450 a year and Christmas boxes of between £50 and £100. General relief-in-need grants may occasionally be given.

Annual grant total

In 2013/14 the fund had an income of £11,300 and a total expenditure of £6,800, which is the lowest in the past five years. Grants are given for both educational and social welfare purposes and we estimate the total awarded in welfare grants to be around £3,300.

Exclusions

Grants are not made for married women or graduates.

Applications

Application forms are available from the correspondent and should be submitted either directly by the individual or a family member. Requests are considered quarterly in January, April, July and October. If you are applying by post, enclose an sae.

Other information

Educational support is also given to girls and young single women (under the age of 22) in need who are at school, starting work or are in further or higher education and are resident in the Isle of Wight.

Ryde Sick Poor Fund (Greater Ryde Benevolent Trust)

£7,000

Correspondent: Tricia Cotton, Correspondent, 40 Buckland Gardens, Ryde, Isle of Wight PO33 3AG (01983612913; email: cottontricia1956@gmail.com)

CC number: 249832

Eligibility

People who live in the former borough of Ryde (Isle of Wight) and are on low income and have health problems.

Types of grants

Small, one-off grants only.

Annual grant total

In 2014 the fund had an income of £6,900 and a total expenditure of £7,500. We estimate that grants totalled around £7,000.

Exclusions

Our research indicates that the trust is unable to provide recurrent grants.

Applications

Apply in writing to the correspondent.

Kent

Headley-Pitt Charitable Trust

£6,300

Correspondent: Thelma Pitt, Old Mill Cottage, Ulley Road, Kennington, Ashford, Kent TN24 9HX (01233 626189; email: thelma.pitt@headley.co.uk)

CC number: 252023

Eligibility

Individuals in need who live in Kent, with a preference for those residing in Ashford. There is also a preference for older people.

Types of grants

One-off grants, usually in the range of £100 to £300.

Annual grant total

In 2014/15 the trust had assets of £2.5 million and an income of £82,500. A total of 62 grants were made to individuals, for both social welfare and educational purposes, totalling £12,600. We estimate that social welfare grants to individuals amounted to £6,300.

An additional £27,500 was awarded in 94 grants to organisations.

Applications

Apply in writing to the correspondent, either directly by the individual or through a third party.

Other information

The trust also administers ten bungalows for the benefit of older people.

Kent Community Foundation

£105,500

Correspondent: Grants Team, Office 23, Evegate Park Barn, Evegate, Ashford, Kent TN25 6SX (01303 814500; email: admin@kentcf.org.uk; website: www.kentcf.org.uk)

CC number: 1084361

Eligibility

Children and young people affected by disability or life threatening conditions and adult carers in Kent. Young carers seeking support in the borough of Gravesham and Medway. Young people who are economically disadvantaged.

Types of grants

Grants for respite, equipment, short breaks, holidays, pamper days and days out.

Annual grant total

In 2013/14 the foundation held assets of £12.3 million and had an income of £7 million. Welfare grants to individuals totalled £105,500. Grants awarded to organisations and for other charitable purposes amounted to a further £5.2 million.

Applications

An individual can only be nominated for funding by a doctor, nurse or social worker familiar with the person's situation. A professional wishing to nominate an individual should email or telephone the foundation for an application form. Nominations are reviewed following deadlines, which are specified on the website. **Note:** it may take three months for an applicant to receive a decision.

Other information

The Kent Community Foundation administers a number of funding schemes for both organisations and individuals, including educational and opportunities funding for offenders and ex-offenders and for young people who are economically disadvantaged. See the foundation's informative website for more details.

Kent Nursing Institution

£2,000

Correspondent: Canon R. Stevenson, Trustee, Michaelmas Cottage, Stan Lane, West Peckham, Maidstone, Kent ME18 5JT (01732 842245)

CC number: 211227

Eligibility

People in need who are sick, convalescent, disabled or infirm and live in west Kent.

Types of grants

One-off grants ranging between £200 and £500. Grants have been given to relieve hardship caused by family illness (for example, hospital visiting costs) and to assist with payments for specialist equipment to relieve discomfort (special beds, ultrasound matching, etc.).

Annual grant total

In 2014 the institution had an income of £5,000 and a total expenditure of £4,300. We estimate that the amount of grants given to individuals totalled £2,000, with local organisations also receiving funding.

Exclusions

The charity does not assist with debt or bankruptcy fees.

Applications

Apply in writing to the correspondent either directly by the individual or through a social worker, doctor, priest, Citizens Advice or other welfare agency. Applications are usually considered in March and October.

Littledown Trust

£5,500

Correspondent: Paul Brown, Trustee, Littledown Farmhouse, Lamberhurst Down, Lamberhurst, Tunbridge Wells TN3 8HD (01892 890867; email: paul.g. brown@btinternet.com)

CC number: 1064291

Eligibility

People in need, with a preference for the elderly and disadvantaged or disabled children and adults who live in Kent or Devon.

Types of grants

One-off and recurrent grants are given according to need, ranging between £100 and £500.

Annual grant total

In 2013/14 the trust had an income of £11,700 and an expenditure of £11,700. We estimate that the amount of grants given to individuals totalled £5,500 with funding also awarded to organisations in Devon and Kent.

Applications

Apply in writing to the correspondent, or through Citizens Advice, a social worker or another relevant third party.

Sir Thomas Smythe's Charity

£18,000

Correspondent: Grants Administrator, The Skinners' Company, Skinners' Hall, 8 Dowgate Hill, London EC4R 2SP (020 7213 0562; email: charitiesadmin@ skinners.org.uk; website: www. skinnershall.co.uk)

CC number: 210775

Eligibility

People who are elderly or disabled and live within the 26 parishes of Tonbridge and Tunbridge Wells in their own home, either as a tenant or an owner-occupier. Most successful applicants are in receipt of a combination of benefits, disability allowances or state retirement pension, but each case will be examined individually.

Types of grants

Quarterly pensions (£660 per annum in 2013/14) are distributed personally by a trustee. Pension levels are reviewed every April. One-off crisis grants are typically made for items not covered by benefits, for example, unexpected household repairs or the replacement of domestic appliances.

Annual grant total

In 2013/14 the charity held assets of £1.3 million and had an income of £33,500. Pensions to individuals totalled £18,000.

Exclusions

Grants are not made to people in residential care and cannot be given to cover funeral costs or debt repayments.

Applications

Applications are only recommended via local trustees. For contact details of your local trustee, contact the charity's administrator. The trustees meet twice yearly in April and October, but urgent applications may be dealt with sooner.

Note: The annual report states that in 2013/14 no new applications for pensions were considered 'partly because funds were fully committed but also to allow Trustees to focus on the Charity's strategic options'.

Other information

The Sir Thomas Smythe's Charity was founded in the will of Sir Thomas Smythe in 1625.

The charity has an informative website.

Ashford
The Thanet Charities

£4,500

Correspondent: Patricia Guy, Correspondent, Garden House, Bethersden Road, Hothfield, Ashford, Kent TN26 1EP (01233 612449)

CC number: 213093

Eligibility

People in need who live in the parish of Hothfield.

Types of grants

Small monthly payments to elderly residents of Hothfield village. There are also a limited number of hardship grants available for individuals in need. These come in the form of one-off monetary payments or through the provision of services/facilities.

Annual grant total

In 2013/14 the charity had an income of £6,900 and a total expenditure of £5,400. We estimate that the amount of grants given to individuals totalled £4,500.

The charity also makes a yearly payment to the Thanet Educational Foundation.

Applications

Apply in writing to the correspondent.

City of Canterbury
The Canterbury United Municipal Charities

£3,500

Correspondent: Aaron Spencer, Furley Page Solicitors, 39 St Margaret's Street, Canterbury, Kent CT1 2TX (01227 863140; email: aas@furleypage.co.uk)

CC number: 210992

Eligibility

People in need who have lived within the boundaries of what was the old city of Canterbury for at least two years.

Types of grants

One-off and repeated grants and pensions are given. Small pensions are given to around 20 needy older people. Also at Christmas, vouchers/tokens of around £25 are given for: clothing for children aged 6 to 16 (30 children); and people who are older and in need (120 adults).

Annual grant total

In 2014 the charity had an income of £9,200 and a total expenditure of £7,300. Grants are made for social welfare and educational purposes. We estimate that social welfare grants to individuals totalled around £3,500.

Applications

Applications can be made in writing to the correspondent through the individual's school/college/educational welfare agency or directly by the individual. Applications are considered on an ongoing basis and should include a brief statement of circumstances and proof of residence in the area.

The Lord Mayor of Canterbury's Christmas Gift Fund

£15,000

Correspondent: Jennifer Sherwood, Administrator, MHA MacIntyre Hudson, 31 St George's Place, Canterbury, Kent CT1 1XD (01227 464991; email: christmasgiftfund@gmail.com; website: www.christmasgiftfund.co.uk/about.php)

CC number: 278803

Eligibility

People in need who live in Canterbury and the surrounding area comprised in the former district of Bridge Blean. Preference is given to older people and to families with young children.

Types of grants

Food parcels (worth approximately £25 each) and toy vouchers are distributed before Christmas.

Annual grant total

In 2013/14 the fund had an income of £17,900 and a total expenditure of £15,800 We estimate that Christmas gifts to individuals – including 500 grocery parcels – totalled £15,000.

Applications

A list is compiled over the year from local doctors, clergy, Age UK, direct applications and other sources. Direct applications should be made in writing to the correspondent. Gifts are delivered in person by volunteers.

Other information

The fund's website describes how it 'was set up 60 years ago by members of the business community, who approached the then Mayor, suggesting that they might launch an appeal to give parcels to the elderly and needy at Christmas time. In that first year the appeal raised between £200 and £300.'

Streynsham's Charity

£20,500

Correspondent: The Clerk to the Trustees, PO Box 970, Canterbury, Kent CT1 9DJ (0845 094 4769)

CC number: 214436

Eligibility

People who live in the ancient parish of St Dunstan's in Canterbury.

Types of grants

One-off grants, up to a maximum of about £300.

Annual grant total

In 2014 the charity had an income of £74,000 and a total expenditure of £74,000. A total of £33,500 was awarded to individuals and organisations. Grants to individuals amounted to £24,000, £20,500 of which was given for social welfare purposes. They were distributed as follows:

Lifeline grants	£7,400
Individual specific grants	£6,800
Regular individual grants	£6,100
Educational grants	£3,600*

*We have not included the figure for educational awards in our grants total.

Applications

Apply in writing to the correspondent. Applications should be made directly by the individual. They are usually considered in March and October but can be made at any time and should include an sae and telephone number if applicable.

Dartford

Wilmington Parochial Charity

£3,500

Correspondent: Regina Skinner, Correspondent, 101 Birchwood Road, Dartford DA2 7HQ (01322 662342)

CC number: 1011708

Eligibility

People in need who live in the parish of Wilmington and are receiving a statutory means-tested benefit, such as Income Support, Housing Benefit or help towards their council tax.

Types of grants

Our research suggests that recurrent grants are available as follows:
- Grocery vouchers of £30 redeemable at any grocery shop within the parish
- Cash grants of £10 at Christmas
- Heating grants of £60 at Easter

Annual grant total

In 2013/14 the charity had an income of £13,300 and a total expenditure of £8,800. The charity's record on the Charity Commission's website states that about 15%–17% of the expenditure is given for educational purposes. We estimate that about £3,500 a year is potentially available for welfare needs to individuals.

Applications

Applications should be submitted by the individual or through a social worker, Citizens Advice or other welfare agency. The trustees meet in February and November. Urgent applications can be considered between the meetings in exceptional circumstances.

Other information

Grants are also given to local schools at Christmas and to individuals for educational purposes.

Dover

The Coleman Trust

£50,500

Correspondent: Peter Sherred, Correspondent, Copthorne, Dover Road, Guston, Dover, Kent CT15 5EN (01304 203548)

CC number: 237708

Eligibility

People who live in Dover and the immediate neighbourhood and are sick, convalescing, or living with a mental or physical disability.

Types of grants

One-off grants according to need. In the past, grants have been given for periods in residential care and nursing homes, disability aids, telephone facilities and convalescent holiday breaks.

Annual grant total

In 2014 the trust had assets of £1.2 million and an income of £70,500. Grants to individuals totalled £50,500.

Exclusions

No grants are given for furniture, home repairs or debts.

Applications

Applications should be made through a social worker, Citizens Advice, welfare agency, doctor or consultant and sent to Mrs Barbara Godfrey, Welfare Officer, 41 The Ridgeway, River, Dover, Kent CT16 1RT.

Gravesham

William Frank Pinn Charitable Trust

£161,000 (1,615 grants)

Correspondent: Trust Officer, HSBC Trust Company (UK) Ltd, 10th Floor Norwich House, Nelson Gate, Commercial Road, Southampton SO15 1GX (023 8072 2224)

CC number: 287772

Eligibility

People of pensionable age who live in Gravesham borough. Priority is given to those on lower incomes.

Types of grants

One-off grants averaging £100 are made for specific purposes only, mainly for household expenses and clothing.

Annual grant total

In 2013/14 the trust held assets of £6.6 million and had an income of £259,000. A total of £161,000 was awarded in 1615 grants to individuals.

Exclusions

No more than two grants may be made to any household per calendar year.

Applications

Application forms are available from the correspondent. Applications should be submitted directly by the individual and are considered as received.

Other information

This trust was formed from the estate of Mr William Frank Pinn who died on 18 June 1983.

Maidstone

The Edmett and Fisher Charity

£9,000

Correspondent: Robin Rogers, Correspondent, 72 King Street, Maidstone, Kent ME14 1BL (01622 698000)

CC number: 241823

Eligibility

People in need who are aged over 60 and live in the former borough of Maidstone (as it was before April 1974).

Types of grants

One-off and recurrent grants are given according to need. Christmas gifts have also been distributed in previous years.

Annual grant total

In 2013/14 the charity had an income of £9,200 and a total expenditure of £9,700.

We estimate that the amount of grants given to individuals totalled £9,000.

Applications

Application forms are available from the correspondent. Applications should be submitted directly by the individual. Applications are usually considered twice a year.

Medway

The William Mantle Trust

£3,400

Correspondent: Jane Rose, Clerk to the Trustees, Administrative Offices, Watt's Almshouses, Maidstone Road, Rochester, Kent ME1 1SE (01634 842194; email: admin@richardwatts.org.uk; website: www.richardwatts.org.uk)

CC number: 248661

Eligibility

People in need who are over 60 and were either born in that part of Rochester which lies to the south and east of the River Medway, or have at any time lived in that part of the city for a continuous period of at least 15 years.

Types of grants

Recurrent grants, typically of around £65 per person, per month.

Annual grant total

In 2014/15 the trust had an income of £9,900 and a total expenditure of £3,500. We estimate that the amount of grants given to individuals totalled £3,400.

Applications

Apply on form available from the correspondent. Applications should be submitted directly by the individual or through a third party on their behalf. They are considered on a regular basis.

Richard Watts and The City of Rochester Almshouse Charities

£70,500 (115 grants)

Correspondent: Jane Rose, Clerk and Chief Officer, Administrative Offices, Watts Almshouses, Maidstone Road, Rochester, Kent ME1 1SE (01634 842194; fax: 01634 409348; email: admin@richardwatts.org.uk; website: www.richardwatts.org.uk)

CC number: 212828

Eligibility

People in need who live in the city of Rochester and urban Strood.

Types of grants

The charity offers regular four weekly pension payments to retired people who are resident in the area of benefit. One-off grants are made to people of any age towards a wide variety of needs, including clothing, electrical goods, travel expenses, medical equipment, furniture, disability equipment and subsidised home help. Awards are usually in excess of £50.

Annual grant total

In 2014 the charity had assets of £20.8 million and an income of £1.2 million. Payments to individuals for social welfare purposes totalled £70,500 and were distributed as follows:

Pensions	73*	£58,500
Children and family	24	£7,000
Older people	6	£3,000
Helpline	6	£1,000
Others	6	£800

*This refers to the average number of recipients.

The charity also provided a subsidised home help service for 39 individuals to the cost of £24,000. We have not included this figure in the grants total.

In addition, £9,100 was awarded in 13 educational grants to individuals and organisations received a further £34,500.

Applications

Application forms can be requested from the correspondent and can be submitted at any time directly by individuals. Evidence of the applicant's financial situation is required and a letter of support – from social services, a doctor, school or other care organisation – is needed in most cases. Applications are considered on a regular basis and candidates will be interviewed before the final decision is reached.

Other information

This charity was founded in 1579 and, aside from making grants, also runs almshouses. There are four main sites: Maidstone Road; Reeves House in Watts Avenue; St Catherine's at the top of Star Hill; and Haywards House in Corporation Street.

The charity also offers a subsidised home help service for people who are in need of domestic help. Applications are usually made through referral by social services, doctors or care organisations, for example, or by contacting the charity's office. At the time of writing, the charity's website stated the following: 'The charge for the Home Help Service is £10.50 per hour. If you are on a low income (disposable income of less than £125 per week for a single person, or £175 for a couple) a financial assessment can be carried out to see if you qualify for a free service.' For enquiries about the service, contact Fleur Boyce on 01634 823115.

Sevenoaks

Kate Drummond Trust

£500

Correspondent: David Batchelor, Trustee, The Beeches, Packhorse Road, Sevenoaks, Kent TN13 2QP (01732 451584)

CC number: 246830

Eligibility

People in need who live in Sevenoaks urban district and neighbourhood, with preference given to older people and young girls.

Types of grants

The majority of grants are one-off, given according to need.

Annual grant total

In 2013/14 the trust had an income of £7,000 and a total expenditure of £1,100, which is the lowest in the past five years. We estimate that the amount of grants given to individuals for social welfare purposes totalled around £500.

Applications

Applications may be made in writing to the correspondent. Include an sae if a reply is required.

Other information

The trust owns and operates a residential house offering either a rent-free or subsidised accommodation. Grant-making is available when there is surplus money. The trust can also give grants to organisations and for educational purposes.

The Leigh United Charities

£42,000

Correspondent: Sally Bresnahan, Correspondent, 3 Oak Cottages, High Street, Leigh, Tonbridge TN11 8RW (01732 838544; email: sally@bresnahan.co.uk)

CC number: 233988

Eligibility

People in need who live in the ancient parish of Leigh.

Types of grants

One-off grants according to need.

Annual grant total

In 2013/14 the charity had an income of £47,000 and a total expenditure of £45,000. We estimate grants to individuals totalled £42,000. No

accounts were available to view at the time of writing.

Exclusions

No payment for council tax.

Applications

The individual should apply directly to the correspondent in writing. Applications are considered throughout the year.

Other information

The charity also makes grants to organisations and in 2012/13 awarded a total of £2,500 to Leigh Primary School.

The Dorothy Parrott Trust Fund

£700

Correspondent: Gina Short, 10 The Landway, Kemsing, Sevenoaks TN15 6TG (01732 760263)

CC number: 278904

Eligibility

People in need who live in the area administered by Sevenoaks Town Council and adjoining parishes (the TN13 TN14 and TN15 postcode areas). Preference is given to young children and older people.

Types of grants

Usually one-off grants ranging from £25 to £100 according to need. Previous grants have been given towards a fridge, a school outing for the child of a single parent, house decoration, boots, ballet shoes, a mattress for twins and project trips such as Operation Raleigh.

Annual grant total

In 2014 the fund had an income of £8,900 and a total expenditure of £2,900. Grants are made to individuals and organisations for social welfare and educational purposes. We estimate that social welfare grants to individuals totalled £700.

Applications

Applications can be submitted either directly to the correspondent by the individual or through a social worker, Citizens Advice or similar third party, including a general history of the family. Applications are considered on the last Monday of January, April, July and October.

Shepway

Folkestone Municipal Charities

£88,000

Correspondent: Michael Cox, Administrator, Romney House, Cliff Road, Hythe CT21 5XA (01303 260144; email: gillyjc@btinternet.com)

CC number: 211528

Eligibility

People in need who live in the borough of Folkestone and have done so for at least five years. Preference is usually given to older people and single parent families.

Types of grants

Pensions and one-off relief-in-need grants. Previous grants have been given for telephone installation, help after a burglary, loss of a purse/wallet, shoes for disadvantaged children, gas/electricity bills, beds/bedding, prams, clothing and household repairs. Relief-in-need payments, whenever possible, are made directly to the supplier.

Annual grant total

In 2013/14 the charity held assets of £2.9 million and had an income of £109,000. Grants and pensions totalled £88,000 with £62,000 given towards pensions and £26,000 for welfare.

Other charitable causes received a further £7,500 in grants and donations.

Applications

Application forms are available from the correspondent. Applications should be submitted through a third party such as a social worker, Citizens Advice or similar welfare agency. They are considered on a monthly basis, although urgent requests can be dealt with between meetings.

Anne Peirson Charitable Trust

£2,000

Correspondent: Ina Tomkinson, Trustee, Tyrol House, Cannongate Road, Hythe, Kent CT21 5PX (01303 260779; fax: 01303 238660)

CC number: 800093

Eligibility

People who live in the parish of Hythe and are in need due to, for example, hardship, disability or sickness. Our research suggests that support is primarily given for educational needs but grants for emergency needs will be made if financial hardship is demonstrated.

Types of grants

One-off grants ranging from £100 to £600. Grants have been made towards nursery school fees, special needs for people with children who have disabilities, household goods and so on.

Annual grant total

In 2014 the trust had an income of £14,100 and a total expenditure of £8,300. We estimate the amount given to individuals for social welfare purposes was around £2,000.

Exclusions

Grants are not made where statutory support is available.

Applications

Applications may be made in writing to the correspondent via either Citizens Advice, a social worker, health visitor, school headteacher or other third party. Grants are considered at quarterly meetings of the trustees, but emergency applications can be considered in the interim.

Other information

Grants are awarded to individuals and organisations for both educational and social welfare purposes.

Swale

The William Barrow's Charity

£30,500 (28+ grants)

Correspondent: Stuart Mair, Clerk, George Webb Finn, 43 Park Road, Sittingbourne, Kent ME10 1DY (01795 470556; email: stuart@georgewebbfinn. com)

CC number: 307574

Eligibility

People in need who live in the ancient ecclesiastical parish of Borden, Kent, or have lived in the parish and now live nearby. There is a preference for people of 60 years or over and people who have disabilities.

Types of grants

One-off grants and twice-yearly allowances may be given for pensions, disability and medical equipment, travel expenses and convalescence. Grants typically range from £350 to £500.

Annual grant total

In 2014 the charity had assets of £6.7 million and an income of £242,500. Grants to individuals totalled £72,500, of which £30,500 was given from the eleemosynary fund for social welfare purposes. They were distributed as follows:

Grants to pensioners	£30,500
Grants to students	£29,500
Educational grants	£13,000

An additional £52,000 was paid in grants to schools.

Applications

Application forms are available from the correspondent. Applications are considered in January, April, July and October.

Thanet

Margate and Dr Peete's Charity

£2,600

Correspondent: Dorothy Collins, Correspondent, 31 Avenue Gardens, Cliftonville, Margate, Kent CT9 3AZ (01843 226173; email: dorothy_collins@ talktalk.net)

CC number: 212503

Eligibility

People in need who live in the former borough of Margate (as constituted before 1974).

Types of grants

One-off and recurrent grants generally in the range of £50 to £250.

Annual grant total

In 2013/14 the charity had an income of £9,100 and a total expenditure of £5,500. We estimate that welfare grants totalled £2,600, with funding also awarded to individuals for educational purposes.

Applications

Application forms are available from the correspondent. Applications should be submitted either directly by the individual or, where applicable, through a social worker, Citizens Advice or other welfare agency.

Other information

The charity was established in 1907 following the death of Dr Thomas Peete, who left his entire estate – a total of £50,000 – to the Margate Philanthropic Institution. Since then, the fund has supported many of Margate's neediest residents.

Tunbridge Wells

Miss Ethel Mary Fletcher's Charitable Bequest

£8,000

Correspondent: Trust Administrator, Thomson Snell & Passmore, Ref 1295, 3 Lonsdale Gardens, Tunbridge Wells TN1 1NU (01892 510000)

CC number: 219850

Eligibility

Older people in need who live in the Tunbridge Wells area.

Types of grants

One-off and recurrent grants towards, for example, fuel bills, clothing, medical treatment, food and other necessary comforts.

Annual grant total

In 2013/14 the bequest had an income of £9,300 and a total expenditure of £17,300. We estimate that the amount of grants given to individuals totalled £8,000, with organisations also receiving funding.

Applications

Apply in writing to the correspondent through a social worker, Citizens Advice or other welfare agency. At times when funds are already committed, consideration will only be given to those with exceptional circumstances.

Oxfordshire

The Peter Ward Charitable Trust

£2,000

Correspondent: A. J. Carter and Co., 22B High Street, Witney, Oxfordshire OX28 6RB (01993 703414; email: ajc@ ajcarter.com)

CC number: 258403

Eligibility

People in need who live in Oxfordshire.

Types of grants

One-off and recurrent grants are given according to need.

Annual grant total

In 2014/15 the trust had an income of £7,600 and a total expenditure of £31,900. The majority of grants are made to organisations known to the trustees. We estimate that the amount of grants given to individuals totalled £2,000.

Applications

Apply in writing to the correspondent although unsolicited applications are not encouraged.

Cherwell
The Banbury Charities

£44,000

Correspondent: Nigel Yeadon, Clerk, 36 West Bar, Banbury OX16 9RU (01295 251234)

CC number: 201418

Eligibility

People in need who live within the former borough of Banbury.

Types of grants

One-off and recurrent grants towards living costs, household essentials and appliances, bedding, fuel and domestic help.

Annual grant total

In 2014 the charities had assets of £5.6 million and an income of £418,500. A total of 310 grants were made to individuals for both education and social welfare purposes which, with an average of £285 per grant, amounted to £88,500. We estimate that the amount of grants given to individuals for social welfare purposes totalled around £44,000.

Grants totalling £204,000 were also made to organisations serving the area of benefit.

Applications

Apply in writing to the correspondent. Applicants are encouraged to obtain a letter of support from their social worker, carer or other person in authority to give credence to their application.

Other information

Banbury Charities is a group of eight registered charities. These are as follows: Bridge Estate Charity; Countess of Arran's Charity; Banbury Arts and Educational Charity; Banbury Almshouses Charity; Banbury Sick Poor Fund; Banbury Welfare Trust; Banbury Poor Trust; and Banbury Recreation Charity.

The Souldern United Charities

£3,500

Correspondent: Carol Couzens, Trustee, 2 Cotswold Court, Souldern, Bicester, Oxfordshire OX27 7LQ (01869 346694; email: caroldavidinsouldern@btinternet.com)

CC number: 1002942

Eligibility

People in need who live in the parish of Souldern.

Types of grants

One-off and recurrent grants are given according to need.

Annual grant total

In 2014/15 the charity had an income of £10,500 and a total expenditure of £10,700. We estimate that welfare grants to individuals totalled £3,500, with funding also awarded to local organisations and for educational purposes.

Applications

Apply in writing to the correspondent.

Other information

The charity also provides housing.

City of Oxford
The City of Oxford Charity

£76,500 (317 grants)

Correspondent: David Wright, Clerk, 11 Davenant Road, Oxford OX2 8BT (01865 247161; email: enquiries@oxfordcitycharities.fsnet.co.uk; website: www.oxfordcitycharities.org)

CC number: 239151

Eligibility

People who have lived in the city of Oxford for at least three years and who are in need and hardship. Our research indicates that priority is given to children and people who are older, have disabilities or a medical condition.

Types of grants

The charity can offer one-off relief-in-need grants, generally of up to £600, towards various welfare needs, such as furniture for people moving home, household appliances, washing machines, recuperation holidays for people with disabilities or medical problems and/or their carers, baby equipment, wheelchairs and mobility scooters and so on. Support is also available towards the payment of bankruptcy court fees.

Annual grant total

In 2014 the charity had assets of £5.5 million and an income of £360,500. Grants totalled £92,000, the majority of which was given for social welfare purposes. During the year, 260 grants for the relief of need and sickness were made totalling £68,500. A further 57 grants to help with bankruptcy fees amounted to £8,000.

Applications

Application forms can be downloaded from the charity's website or requested from the correspondent. They can be submitted through welfare services/other organisations or by individuals directly. All applications have to be supported by a letter from a social worker/health visitor/similar professional commenting on the circumstances of the family and the need for a grant. The trustees meet every six weeks to consider applications. Candidates are required to specify exactly what the money is for and the costs involved, as applications without exact costings will be delayed.

Other information

The charity is an amalgamation of a number of charities working for the benefit of the people of Oxford city. It also gives grants to organisations, can support local schools, assists individuals for educational needs, and maintains almshouses in the local area.

The Stanton Ballard Charitable Trust

£1,000

Correspondent: The Secretary, PO Box 81, Oxford OX4 4ZA

CC number: 294688

Eligibility

Individuals in need who live in the city of Oxford and the immediate area.

Types of grants

Small, one-off grants are given according to need.

Annual grant total

In 2013/14 the trust had assets of £2.6 million and an income of £120,000. Grants were made totalling £32,000, 'mainly to Oxfordshire based charities and voluntary organisations'. Previous research indicates that at least £1,000 has been given to individuals, but this figure may be higher.

Applications

Application forms are available from the correspondent on receipt of an sae. Applications should be made through social services, probation officers or other bodies and are considered approximately five times a year.

South Oxfordshire

The John Hodges Charitable Trust

£3,600

Correspondent: Julie Griffin, Administrator, 3 Berkshire Road, Henley-On-Thames RG9 1ND (01491 572621; email: juliegriffin2004@ googlemail.com)

CC number: 304313

Eligibility

People in need living in the parish of St Mary the Virgin, Henley-On-Thames and the surrounding area.

Types of grants

One-off and recurrent grants towards, for example, white goods, carpets and flooring, clothing, mobility aids, bankruptcy fees and heating bills.

Annual grant total

In 2014/15 the trust had an income of £11,900 and a total expenditure of £7,500. We estimate that the amount of grants given to individuals totalled £3,600, with funding also awarded to organisations.

Applications

Apply in writing to the correspondent.

The Thame Welfare Trust

£6,700

Correspondent: John Gadd, 2 Cromwell Avenue, Thame, Oxfordshire OX9 3TD (01844 212564; email: johngadd4@gmail. com)

CC number: 241914

Eligibility

People in need who live in Thame and the immediately adjoining villages.

Types of grants

One-off grants of up to £1,000, where help cannot be received from statutory sources. In the past, grants have been given towards a single parent's mortgage repayments and a wheelchair for a person who has disabilities.

Annual grant total

In 2013/14 the charity had an income of £15,700 and a total expenditure of £28,500. Grants are made to individuals and organisations for a range of purposes. We estimate that social welfare grants to individuals totalled £6,700.

Applications

Apply in writing to the correspondent. Applications are usually made through social workers, probation officers, teachers, or a similar third party, but can also be submitted directly by the applicant.

Wallingford Relief in Need Charity

£3,000

Correspondent: Jamie Baskeyfield, Correspondent, Wallingford Town Council, 9 St Martin's Street, Wallingford, Oxfordshire OX10 0AL (01491 835373; email: queries@ wallingfordtc.co.uk)

CC number: 292000

Eligibility

People in need who live in Wallingford and the neighbourhood (including the former parish of Clapcot).

Types of grants

One-off grants for necessities, including the payment of bills, clothing and shoes, cookers, fridges and so on. Payments are made to local suppliers, cash grants are not made directly to the individual.

Annual grant total

In 2014/15 the charity had an income of £8,500 and a total expenditure of £4,100. We estimate that grants for social welfare purposes totalled about £3,000. Our research indicates that overall grants generally average around £6,500.

Applications

Application forms are available from the correspondent. They should be submitted either directly by the individual or through a local organisation. The trustees meet about every three months, although emergency cases can be considered in between the meetings. Urgent cases may require a visit by a trustee.

Other information

The charity also gives grants for educational purposes; however, the majority of grants are given for relief in need.

The Wheatley Charities

£2,800

Correspondent: R. Minty, Trustee, 24 Old London Road, Wheatley, Oxford OX33 1YW (01865 874676)

CC number: 203535

Eligibility

Residents of Wheatley, Oxford who are in need.

Types of grants

One-off and repeated grants are given according to need.

Annual grant total

In 2014 the charity had an income of £4,100 and a total expenditure of £5,800. Grants are made to individuals and organisations for social welfare and educational purposes. We estimate that social welfare grants to individuals totalled £2,800.

Applications

Apply in writing to the correspondent.

Vale of White Horse

The Appleton Trust (Abingdon)

£2,500

Correspondent: David Dymock, Correspondent, 73 Eaton Road, Appleton, Abingdon, Oxfordshire OX13 5JJ (01865 863709; email: appleton.trust@yahoo.co.uk)

CC number: 201552

Eligibility

People who live in Appleton with Eaton and are in need or suffer from sickness, disability or other hardship.

Types of grants

One-off and recurrent grants in the range of £50 to £100 can be given towards various needs, including fuel and bereavement costs.

Annual grant total

In 2014 the trust had an income of £5,400 and a total expenditure of £5,100. We estimate that individual grants totalled around £2,500.

Applications

Apply in writing to the correspondent. Applications can be made either directly by the individual or through an appropriate third party.

Other information

Grants are also given to local organisations and for educational purposes to former pupils of Appleton Primary School.

The Faringdon United Charities

£3,200

Correspondent: Vivienne Checkley, Bunting and Co., Faringdon Business Centre, Brunel House, Volunteer Way, Faringdon, Oxon SN7 7YR (01367 243789; email: vivienne.checkley@ buntingaccountants.co.uk)

CC number: 237040

Eligibility

People who are in need and live in the parishes of Great Faringdon, Littleworth or Little Coxwell, all in Oxfordshire.

Types of grants

One-off grants towards clergy expenses for visiting the sick, domestic appliances, holidays, travel expenses, medical and disability equipment, furniture and food, etc.

Annual grant total

In 2013/14 the charity had an income of £11,200 and a total expenditure of £13,000. Grants are made to individuals and organisations for both social welfare and educational purposes. We estimate that social welfare grants to individuals totalled £3,200.

Exclusions

Grants cannot be given for nursing/retirement home fees or the supply of equipment that the state is obliged to provide.

Applications

Applications can be made in writing to the correspondent throughout the year. They can be submitted either through Citizens Advice, a social worker or other third party, directly by the individual or by a third party on their behalf for example a neighbour, parent or child.

The Lockinge and Ardington Relief-in-Need Charity

£4,000

Correspondent: Mrs A. Ackland, Correspondent, c/o Lockinge Estate Office, Ardington, Wantage, Oxfordshire OX12 8PP (01235 833200; email: aackland@lockinge-estate.co.uk)

CC number: 204770

Eligibility

People in need who live in the parish of Lockinge and Ardington. Help is given when government sources are not available or adequate.

Types of grants

One-off and recurrent grants between £30 and £60.

Annual grant total

In 2014/15 the charity had an income of £5,000 and a total expenditure of £4,500. We estimate that the amount of grants given to individuals totalled around £4,000.

Applications

Apply in writing to the correspondent by the individual. Applications are considered in March, July and November although urgent cases can be considered at any time.

The Wantage District Coronation Memorial and Nursing Amenities Fund

£3,000

Correspondent: Carol Clubb, Correspondent, 133 Stockham Park, Wantage, Oxfordshire OX12 9HJ (01235 767355)

CC number: 234384

Eligibility

People who are in poor health, convalescent or who have disabilities and live in the Wantage area of Oxfordshire.

Types of grants

One-off and recurrent grants typically ranging from around £20 to £100.

Annual grant total

In 2013/14 the fund had an income of £5,000 and a total expenditure of £3,200. We estimate that the amount of grants given to individuals totalled £3,000.

Exclusions

No grants are given towards the relief of taxes, rates or other public funds, but grants may be applied in supplementing relief or assistance provided out of public funds.

Applications

Apply in writing to the correspondent.

West Oxfordshire

The Bampton Welfare Trust

£4,000

Correspondent: David Pullman, Mill Green Cottage, Bampton, Oxon OX18 2HF (01993 850589; email: david@dpullman.plus.com)

CC number: 202735

Eligibility

People who live in the parishes of Bampton, Aston, Lew and Shifford, of any occupation, who are in need. Preference is given to children, young people and older people.

Types of grants

One-off grants which can be repeated in subsequent years at the discretion of the trustees. Past grants have included food vouchers for families awaiting benefit payment, heating allowance for older people in need and assistance in purchasing a washing machine for a single parent with multiple sclerosis.

Annual grant total

In 2014 the trust had an income of £9,000 and a total expenditure of £8,000. We estimate that the amount of grants given to individuals totalled around £4,000, with organisations also receiving funding.

Applications

Applicants are advised to initially discuss their circumstances with the correspondent, who will advise the applicant on what steps to take. This initial contact can be made directly by the individual, or by any third party, at any time. The trustees meet twice a year.

The Bartlett Taylor Charitable Trust

£5,400 (13 grants)

Correspondent: Gareth Alty, Trustee, John Welch and Stammers, 24 Church Green, Witney, Oxfordshire OX28 4AT (01993 703941; email: galty@johnwelchandstammers.co.uk; website: www.btctrust.org.uk)

CC number: 285249

Eligibility

People in need who live in West Oxfordshire.

Types of grants

Relief-in-need grants range from £100 to £500 and medical support can be of around £500–£750. Loans may also be considered.

Annual grant total

In 2013/14 the trust had assets of £2.3 million and an income of over £83,500. Grants to 13 individuals totalled £5,400, of which six were medical grants (£3,400) and seven relief-in-need grants (£2,000) grants. A further £1,800 was awarded in seven educational grants.

Applications

Apply on a form on the charity's website. The trustees meet bi-monthly.

Other information

Grants are also made to organisations, including national, international and local charities (£39,500 in 2013/14).

The Burford Relief-in-Need Charity

£5,100

Correspondent: Anne Burgess Youngson, Whitehill Farm, Burford, Oxfordshire OX18 4DT (01993 822894)

CC number: 1036378

Eligibility

People who are in need and live within seven miles of Tolsey, Burford.

Types of grants

One-off grants towards hospital expenses, electrical goods, travel costs, convalescence, medical equipment and disability aids.

Annual grant total

In 2014 the charity had an income of £13,200 and a total expenditure of £10,500. We estimate that social welfare grants to individuals totalled £5,100, with funding also awarded to individuals for educational purposes.

Applications

Apply in writing to the correspondent either directly by the individual or, where applicable, through a social worker, Citizens Advice or other welfare agency. Applications should include the individual's full name, address, age, and the number of years they have lived in Burford or their connection with Burford. Receipts are required for grants towards the cost of equipment. Applications are usually considered on a quarterly basis but urgent cases can be dealt with quickly.

The J. I. Colvile Charitable Trust

See entry on page 403

Eynsham Consolidated Charity

£3,100 (21 grants)

Correspondent: Robin Mitchell, Clerk to the Trustees, 20 High Street, Eynsham, Witney, Oxfordshire OX29 4HB (01865 880665; email: robinmitchell255@gmail.com; website: eynsham-pc.gov.uk/a-z_club_detail.asp?ClubID=140)

CC number: 200977

Eligibility

People in need who live in the ancient parish of Eynsham (which covers Eynsham and part of Freeland). The website provides a map marking the area of benefit. In exceptional circumstances grants can be made to people living immediately outside the parish; in practice, residents from most of Freeland may apply.

Types of grants

One-off grants, generally ranging from £50 to £200, can be given for specific items (glasses, furniture, washing machines, cookers, paint, school clothing or special equipment for people with disabilities), services (an insurance premium, heating costs or other utility bills, urgent debts, removal costs, electric rewiring and so on) and for other unforeseen difficulties. The charity notes that where the cost of providing the necessary help will be high help may be given in conjunction with other welfare organisations.

Most awards are made to elderly people in winter.

Annual grant total

In 2014 the charity had an income of £5,600. Grants to 21 individuals totalled £3,100.

Exclusions

Grants are not made to help with payment of rates, taxes or other public charges. Support is not given on a recurrent basis or through personal loans.

Applications

Apply in writing to the correspondent. Applications can be made directly by the individual or on their behalf by a neighbour, friend, family member and so on. Candidates should include details of what the grant is for, the costs involved and their personal circumstances. The trustees meet four times a year, usually in February, May, September and November, although urgent requests can be dealt with in between the meetings.

Other information

This charity also gives grants to organisations helping people in the local area.

The Great Rollright Charities

£2,600

Correspondent: Paul Dingle, Correspondent, Tyte End Cottage, Tyte End, Great Rollright, Chipping Norton, Oxfordshire OX7 5RU (01608 737676; email: paul@pcdingle.plus.com)

CC number: 242146

Eligibility

People who are in need and live in the ancient parish of Great Rollright.

Types of grants

One-off grants towards, for example, fuel payments and to older people at Christmas.

Annual grant total

In 2013/14 the charity had an income of £10,900 and a total expenditure of £10,800. We estimate that welfare grants to individuals totalled £2,600, with funding also awarded to local organisations and for educational purposes.

Exclusions

No grants are given for the relief of rates, taxes or other public funds.

Applications

Apply in writing to the correspondent.

Surrey

The Bookhams, Fetcham and Effingham Nursing Association Trust

£4,000

Correspondent: Jenny Peers, Trustee, 1 Manor Cottages, Manor House Lane, Bookham, Leatherhead, Surrey KT23 4EW (01372 456752; email: j.peers@tiscali.co.uk)

CC number: 265962

Eligibility

People in need who are sick, convalescent, disabled or infirm who live in Great Bookham, Little Bookham, Fetcham and Effingham.

Types of grants

Grants of between £100 and £1,500 for items, services or facilities which will alleviate the discomfort or assist the recovery of such people, where these facilities are not available from any other sources.

Annual grant total

In 2014/15 the trust had an income of £8,000 and a total expenditure of £8,000. We estimate that the amount of grants given to individuals totalled around £4,000, with funding also awarded to local organisations.

Applications

Applications should be referred through medical or social services, not directly from the public.

Leatherhead United Charities

£30,000

Correspondent: David Matanle, Clerk to the Trustees, Homefield, Forty Foot Road, Leatherhead, Surrey KT22 8RP (01372 370073; email: luchar@btinternet.com)

CC number: 200183

Eligibility

People in need who live in the area of the former Leatherhead urban district council (Ashtead, Bookhams, Fetcham and Leatherhead). Preference is given to residents of the parish of Leatherhead as constituted on 27 September 1912.

Types of grants

One-off grants, usually in the range of £100 and £750, are given for general relief in need. Pensions are also distributed.

Annual grant total

In 2014 the charity had assets of £4 million and an income of £306,500. During the year, 30 grants were made, 27 of which were to individuals and the remainder to organisations. 'Pension, grants and other charges' are listed in the annual report and accounts as having totalled £120,000. We estimate that assistance for social welfare purposes totalled around £30,000.

Applications

Application forms can be requested from the correspondent. Our research suggests that they should be submitted through a recognised referral agency, such as a social worker, Citizens Advice or a doctor. Candidates should also provide details of their/their family income and include names of two referees. Awards are considered throughout the year.

Other information

The charity also provides residents of Mole Valley district council with sheltered housing and associated services.

Elmbridge

Jemima Octavia Cooper for the Poor (Stoke D'Abernon Charities)

£2,400

Correspondent: Ron Stewart, Trustee, Old Timbers, Manor Way, Oxshott, Leatherhead, Surrey KT22 0HU (07785 272590; email: ronandjackie@tecres.net)

CC number: 200187

Eligibility

People in need who live in the ancient parish of Stoke D'Abernon (which includes part of Oxshott).

Types of grants

One-off and recurrent grants are given according to need. Grants are made at Christmas and are of around £50 on average. Occasionally smaller distributions are made in the summer.

Annual grant total

In 2014/15 the charity had an income of £2,800 and an expenditure of £2,600. We estimate that around £2,400 was awarded in grants to individuals.

Applications

Applications can be made formally in writing; however in practice many applications are made informally by word of mouth given the small size and catchment area of the charity. If a formal application is to be made the trustees prefer email, where possible.

Smith Charity (Esher)

£2,000

Correspondent: The Parish Office, Christ Church Parish, Church Street, Esher, Surrey KT10 8QS (01372 462282 or 01372 465755; email: christchurch@esher.org)

Eligibility

People in need who live in the ancient parish of Esher.

Types of grants

Annual grants to a number of older people and low-income families.

Annual grant total

The charity generally has an income of about £2,000, allocated by Henry Smith's (General Estate) Charity, all of which is given in grants.

Applications

Apply in writing to the correspondent through a social worker, Citizens Advice or other third party. Details of the applicant's financial circumstances should be included.

Weybridge Land Charity

£41,500 (311 grants)

Correspondent: Howard Turner, Treasurer and Clerk, PO Box 730, Woking, Surrey GU23 7LL (01483 211728; website: weybridgelandcharity.org.uk)

CC number: 200270

Eligibility

People in need who live in Weybridge.

Types of grants

Emergency grants for food, clothing, household appliances and furniture, for example. Christmas grants (including fuel payments for the elderly) which in 2014 ranged between £50 – £270.

Annual grant total

In 2014 the charity held assets of £1.8 million and had an income of almost £66,000. A total of 311 grants were made to individuals, amounting to £41,500. Of these, 13 grants totalling £4,800 were given in emergency payments to individuals who had been referred to the charity by various welfare agencies, and 294 Christmas grants were made, amounting to £36,500.

Exclusions

No funding is given towards credit card or debt relief.

Applications

Applications for emergency grants must be recommended to the charity by the Citizens Advice, North Surrey Primary Care Trust or another approved agency. Direct applications from individuals are not considered. Application forms for Christmas grants are available during September and October at the Weybridge Day Centre and Public Library and should be returned before 31 October for payments in the first week in December.

Other information

The charity also owns and operates allotments in Weybridge.

Epsom and Ewell

Epsom Parochial Charities (Epsom Almshouse Charity)

£3,600

Correspondent: John Steward, Trustee, 26 Woodcote Hurst, Epsom, Surrey KT18 7DT (email: vanstonewalker@ntlworld.com)

CC number: 200571

Eligibility

People in need who live in the ancient parish of Epsom.

Types of grants

One-off grants ranging from £100 to £500 can be given according to need. Awards made include those for clothing, food, medical care and equipment and household appliances.

Annual grant total

In 2014 the charity had assets of £1.7 million (most of which is endowment funds) and an income of

£89,500. Grants to individuals for welfare purposes totalled £3,600.

Applications

Application forms are available from the correspondent.

Other information

Grants are also made for education. The charity also provides residential accommodation through its three almshouses.

The Ewell Parochial Trusts

£28,000

Correspondent: Miriam Massey, Clerk and Treasurer, 19 Cheam Road, Ewell, Epsom KT17 1ST (020 8394 0453; email: mirimas@globalnet.co.uk)

CC number: 201623

Eligibility

People in need who live, work or are being educated in the ancient ecclesiastical parish of Ewell and the domain of Kingswood.

Types of grants

One-off or recurrent grants according to need.

Annual grant total

In 2013 the trusts had an income of £43,500 and a total expenditure of £41,000. We estimate that welfare grants to individuals totalled around £28,000. Grants are also given to organisations and for educational purposes.

Applications

Apply in writing to the correspondent. Applicants are referred from local Citizens Advice, charities, health services and other welfare agencies. Applications which do not meet the eligibility criteria will not be acknowledged.

Guildford

John Beane's Eleemosynary Charity (Guildford)

£23,500

Correspondent: Brian France, Clerk to the Trustees, PO Box 607, Guildford GU2 8WR (01483 572474; email: brian@ accountingfacilities.co.uk)

CC number: 242309

Eligibility

People in need who live in the administrative county of Surrey.

Types of grants

One-off or recurrent grants according to need. Grants have been made for furniture, bedding, clothing, removal expenses and electrical appliances.

Annual grant total

In 2014/15 the charity had an income of £31,500 and grants were made to individuals totalling £23,500.

Applications

Apply on a form available from the correspondent and submit through a social worker, health visitor, Citizens Advice or other welfare agency.

Other information

The charity was founded in 1772 on the death of the Reverend John Beane, who left in trust certain assets 'to be applied, *inter alia* [among other things] to the relief of the needy in Dorking and Guildford'.

The Guildford Poyle Charities

£23,000 (164 grants)

Correspondent: Janice Bennett, Manager, 208 High Street, Guildford GU1 3JB (01483 303678; fax: 01483 303678; email: admin@ guildfordpoylecharities.org; website: www.guildfordpoylecharities.org)

CC number: 1145202

Eligibility

People in need who live in the borough of Guildford as constituted prior to 1 April 1974 and part of the ancient parish of Merrow. A map showing the beneficial area can be viewed on the website.

Types of grants

Mainly one-off grants ranging between £100 and £300 for electrical appliances, kitchen items, second-hand furniture, household items, baby equipment, clothing, second-hand computers and holiday playschemes, for example. Christmas food vouchers are also available to families. Grants for carpets are only considered in special circumstances. Grants are in the form of cheques or vouchers for suppliers with which the charity has arrangements or a cheque made out to the referral agency.

Annual grant total

In 2014 the charity held assets of £4.1 million and had an income of £184,000. A total of 164 grants were awarded to individuals, amounting to £23,000.

A further £77,000 was given in 19 grants to organisations.

Exclusions

Grants are usually not made to pay for basic items such as food, rent and utility bills. No help is given towards helping reduce debt or arrears.

Applications

Application forms are available from the correspondent or to download from the website. Applications can be submitted at any time through a social worker, Citizens Advice or other welfare agency. Individuals may apply directly, although the charity states that an application has more chance of being successful if it is supported by a letter from a health or welfare professional who is familiar with the individual's circumstances. They are considered every two to three weeks and decisions are confirmed in writing.

The charity's office welcomes enquiries.

Other information

The charity is also known as the Henry Smith's or The Poyle Charity.

Applications for school uniforms are now handled through the Home School Link Worker (HSLW) attached to the child's school. Approach them for more details.

The Mayor of Guildford's Christmas and Local Distress Fund

£9,400

Correspondent: Kate Foxton, Civic Secretary, Guildford Borough Council, Millmead House, Millmead, Guildford, Surrey GU2 4BB (01483 444031; fax: 01483 444444; email: civicsecretary@ guildford.gov.uk.; website: www. guildford.gov.uk)

CC number: 258388

Eligibility

People in need who live in the borough of Guildford, with a preference for the elderly and people living with disabilities.

Types of grants

One-off grants of up to £150. There are no specific restrictions on what can be applied for and the purpose of the grant is defined in the application form. Grants have previously been given for purposes such as kitchen appliances, furniture and clothing. Grants are also made for Christmas events.

Annual grant total

In 2014/15 the charity had an income of £8,400 and a total expenditure of £9,600. We estimate that the amount of grants given to individuals totalled £9,400.

Exclusions

Grants are not given for ongoing expenses such as rent, utility bills or debt relief.

Applications

Apply on a form available for download from the Guildford borough council website, to be submitted through a social worker, Citizens Advice, local GP or other relevant third party. Applications are usually considered in January, April, July and October.

The Henry Smith Charity – West Clandon

£2,800

Correspondent: Stephen Meredith, Trustee, 11 Bennett Way, West Clandon, Guildford GU4 7TN

CC number: 200165–1

Eligibility

People in need, mainly older people, who have lived in the parish of West Clandon for at least five years.

Types of grants

One-off cash grants.

Annual grant total

In 2014 the charity had an income of £3,000 and an expenditure of almost £3,100. We estimate that grants totalled around £2,800.

Applications

Apply in writing to the correspondent. The deadline for applications is 31 October. Grants are usually distributed during December.

Other information

This fund is a linked charity to West Clandon Parochial Charities.

The Henry Smith Charity (Ash and Normandy)

£2,100

Correspondent: Alan Coomer, Correspondent, 84 Queenhythe Road, Jacob's Well, Guildford, Surrey GU4 7NX (01483 300103; email: alancoomer@yahoo.co.uk)

CC number: 240485

Eligibility

People in need who live in Ash and Normandy.

Types of grants

One-off or recurrent grants according to need.

Annual grant total

In 2014/15 the charity had an income of £3,600 and a total expenditure of £4,500. We estimate that the amount of grants given to individuals totalled £2,100, with funding also awarded to local organisations.

Applications

Apply in writing to the correspondent, either directly by the individual or through a social worker, Citizens Advice or other welfare agency. Applications are normally considered as they arrive.

The Henry Smith Charity (Effingham)

£2,600

Correspondent: The Clerk, Effingham Parish Council, The Parish Room, 3 Home Barn Court, The Street, Effingham, Leatherhead KT24 5LG (01372 454911; email: clerk2009@effinghamparishcouncil.gov.uk)

CC number: 237703

Eligibility

People in need who live in Effingham.

Types of grants

One-off grants and gift vouchers, generally of £50 to £100; many grants are given at Christmas.

Annual grant total

In 2014/15 the charity had an income of £3,500 and a total expenditure of £2,600. We estimate that the amount of grants given to individuals totalled £2,400.

Applications

Apply in writing to the correspondent. Applications are considered monthly.

The Henry Smith Charity (Send and Ripley)

£4,500

Correspondent: Geoffrey A. Richardson, Trustee, 2 Rose Lane, Ripley, Surrey GU23 6NE (01483 225322; email: janet.a.richardson@hotmail.co.uk)

CC number: 200496

Eligibility

People in need who live in Send and Ripley, and have done so for five years.

Types of grants

One-off grants of around £30 at Christmas to 50 or 60 elderly people in Send and a similar number in Ripley. Other grants according to need are also available from any remaining funds, primarily for the elderly and those with disabilities.

Annual grant total

In 2013/14 the charity had an income of £4,900 and a total expenditure of £5,000. We estimate that the amount of grants given to individuals totalled £4,500.

Applications

Apply in writing to the correspondent. Applications can be submitted directly by the individual or, where applicable, through a social worker, Citizens Advice or any other welfare agency or third party on behalf of the individual. Applications are considered as they arrive.

Worplesdon United Charities

£2,700

Correspondent: Eric Morgan, Trustee, 21 St Michael's Avenue, Fairlands, Guildford GU3 3LY (01483 233344)

CC number: 200382

Eligibility

Individuals, mainly older people, who are in need and live in the parish of Worplesdon.

Types of grants

Grants of around £80 are given to buy fuel, clothing or groceries at Christmas.

Annual grant total

In 2013/14 the charity had an income of £2,700 and a total expenditure of £2,900. We estimate that the amount of grants given to individuals totalled £2,700.

Applications

Apply when the distribution is advertised within the parish (normally in October/November each year). Emergency grants can be considered at any time.

Mole Valley

The Abinger Consolidated Charities

£6,000

Correspondent: Mad Berry, Charity Administrator, The Rectory, Abinger Lane, Abinger Common, Dorking, Surrey RH5 6HZ (01306 737160)

CC number: 200124

Eligibility

People in need who live in the ancient parish of Abinger.

Types of grants

One-off or recurrent grants according to need.

Annual grant total

In 2012/13 the charity had an income of £14,500 and a total expenditure of £11,000. Taking into account that the charity also gives grants to organisations, we estimate that the total amount of grants awarded to individuals was approximately £6,000. At the time of writing (November 2015) the information provided was the latest available.

Applications

Apply in writing to the correspondent.

Betchworth United Charities

£2,300

Correspondent: Andrea Brown, Clerk, 15 Nutwood Avenue, Brockham, Betchworth, Surrey RH3 7LT (01737 843806; email: snowwhite15@btinternet.co)

CC number: 200299

Eligibility

People in need who live in the ancient parish of Betchworth.

Types of grants

One-off grants usually ranging from £60 to £250. The majority of funding is given for welfare purposes but a small amount is also available for educational needs under the Margaret Fenwick Fund.

Annual grant total

In 2014 the charity had an income of £12,200 and a total expenditure of £9,700. We estimate that social welfare grants to individuals totalled £4,000. Grants are also awarded to organisations and to individuals for educational purposes.

Applications

Apply in writing to the correspondent. Applications should be submitted by a third party, such as a doctor, minister or social worker. Applications are considered at trustee meetings.

Ockley United Charities (Henry Smith Charity)

£6,700

Correspondent: Tim Pryke, Trustee, Danesfield, Stane Street, Ockley, Dorking RH5 5SY (01306 711511)

CC number: 200556

Eligibility

People in need who live in Ockley (primarily older people living in sheltered accommodation provided by Ockley Housing Association or rented housing).

Types of grants

Recurrent annual cash gifts of £110. Assistance is also given to local families for nursery fees.

Annual grant total

In 2013/14 the charity had an income of £8,600 and a total expenditure of £7,200. We estimate that the amount of grants given to individuals totalled £6,700.

Applications

Apply in writing to the correspondent. Applications should include details of income, housing and need. They are considered on a regular basis.

Henry Smith and Michael Earle Charities

£2,600

Correspondent: Jeanette Gillespie, The Birches, Ifield Road, Charlwood, Horley, Surrey RH6 0DR (01293 862129; email: gillespie2@btinternet.com)

CC number: 200043

Eligibility

People with disabilities or those over 65 and in need who have lived in the old parish of Charlwood for at least five years.

Types of grants

One-off and recurrent grants are made, usually of up to £80.

Annual grant total

In 2014 the charity had an income of £6,000 and a total expenditure of £5,500. We estimate that the amount of grants given to individuals totalled £2,600.

Applications

Apply using a form available from the correspondent. Applications for one-off (usually larger) grants should be submitted through a recognised referral agency (such as a social worker, Citizens Advice or other welfare agency). Applications for recurrent grants can be submitted directly by the individual and should include details of any disability or special need. Applications are considered in November.

Other information

Help is also given towards the hiring of halls for meetings for older people, hospices and school requirements.

Smith Charity (Capel)

£2,000

Correspondent: Mrs J. Richards, Administrator, Old School House, Coldharbour, Dorking, Surrey RH5 6HF (01306 711885)

Eligibility

People in need who have lived in Beare Green, Capel and Coldharbour, usually for at least five years.

Types of grants

Mostly Christmas vouchers for older people redeemable at several local stores. The vouchers are usually £20 for couples and £15 for single people.

Annual grant total

Grants usually total about £2,000 each year.

Applications

Apply in writing to the correspondent directly by the individual or a family member. Applications should be received by 1 November and are considered in December.

Smith Charity (Headley)

£4,000

Correspondent: Anthony Vine-Lott, Trustee, Broom Cottage, Crabtree Lane, Headley, Epsom KT18 6PS (01372 374728; email: tony.vinelott@btinternet.com)

Eligibility

People in need who live in the parish of Headley.

Types of grants

One-off and recurrent grants are available to help with, for example, groceries and hospital travel.

Annual grant total

In 2013/14 the charity had an income of £5,100 and an expenditure of £4,500. We estimate that grants totalled around £4,000.

Applications

Apply in writing to the correspondent or any trustee, giving the reasons for the application.

The Henry Smith Charity (Leigh)

£4,500

Correspondent: Mrs J. Sturt, Correspondent, 12 Knoll Road, Dorking RH4 3EW (01306 881547; email: notman-janesturt@hotmail.co.uk)

CC number: 237335

Eligibility

People in need who live in Leigh, Surrey.

Types of grants

The charity has a list of all people who are over the age of 65 in the area of Leigh; each receives support at Christmas in the form of food vouchers, or help with household bills. Gifts may also be given at Easter in the years when the charity receives more income. Help is also given to other residents of Leigh who are in need.

Annual grant total

In 2013/14 the charity had an income of £4,900 and a total expenditure of £4,700. We estimate that the amount of grants given to individuals totalled £4,500.

Applications

Apply in writing or by telephone to the correspondent, or through a third party.

Smith Charity (Newdigate)

£5,000

Correspondent: Diana Salisbury, Parish Councillor, Langholm, Village Street, Newdigate, Dorking, Surrey RH5 5DH (website: newdigate.atspace.com/ benefact.htm)

Eligibility

People in need who live in the parish of Newdigate.

Types of grants

One-off grants for a variety of needs. Grants are typically made to help residents with bereavement, health needs and special educational requirements. In addition, just after Christmas each year the charity hosts a special lunch provided in the village hall for all residents over 65 years old.

Annual grant total

Grants usually total around £5,000 per year.

Applications

Apply in writing to the correspondent. Applications should be submitted directly by the individual.

The Henry Smith Charity (Wotton)

£4,000

Correspondent: Rosemary Wakeford, Secretary, 2 Brickyard Cottages, Hollow Lane, Wotton, Dorking, Surrey RH5 6QE (01306 730856)

CC number: 240634

Eligibility

People in need who live in the ancient parish of Wotton.

Types of grants

One-off grants ranging from £100 to £500. Grants have in the past been given to older people of the parish towards fuel and lighting bills and holidays, young people taking part in schemes such as The Duke of Edinburgh Award which will enhance their job prospects, and help towards the cost of independent projects or travel costs.

Annual grant total

In 2014 the charity had an income of £12,000 and a total expenditure of nearly £5,000. We estimate that the total amount of grants awarded to individuals was approximately £4,000.

Applications

Apply in writing to the correspondent. Applications are considered in March and September. They can be submitted directly by the individual or through a third party.

Runnymede

The Egham United Charity

£4,500

Correspondent: Max Walker, Correspondent, 33 Runnemede Road, Egham, Surrey TW20 9BE (01784 472742; email: eghamunicharity@aol. com; website: www.eghamunitedcharity. org)

CC number: 205885

Eligibility

People in need who have lived in Egham, Englefield Green (West and East), Hythe or Virginia Water for at least five years.

Types of grants

One-off grants according to need. Grants are awarded towards, for example, fuel bills, household essentials, mobility aids and for school uniforms, trips and travel fares. Payments are made directly to the supplier/provider (in the case of settling bills) or to the sponsoring agency for distribution.

Annual grant total

In 2014 the charity had an income of £22,000 and a total expenditure of £8,800. We estimate that the amount of grants given to individuals totalled £4,500, with funding also awarded for educational purposes.

Exclusions

No recurrent grants or loans. No funding is given to cover services which should be provided by central or local authorities (though 'top-up' of partial provision may be considered).

Applications

Application forms are available to download from the website. Applications should be submitted through an appropriate third party such as Citizens Advice or a social worker. Ideally applications should include quotations for goods or services required. Applications are only ever considered at trustee meetings which are held every six weeks. Applicants may occasionally be visited.

Other information

The charity has an informative website.

The Henry Smith Charity (I. Wood Estate)

£18,000

Correspondent: Bernard Fleckney, Democratic Services Manager, Runnymede Borough Council, Civic Centre, Station Road, Addlestone KT15 2AH (01932 425620)

CC number: 233531

Eligibility

People over 60 who are in need and live in Chertsey, Addlestone, New Haw and Lyne, Surrey.

Types of grants

Recurrent fuel vouchers which can be used as part-payment of fuel bills.

Annual grant total

In 2013/14 the charity had both an income and expenditure of £21,000. We estimate that the amount of grants given to individuals totalled £18,000.

Applications

Apply in writing to the correspondent either through a social worker, Citizens Advice or other third party or directly by the individual. Applications can be considered at any time during the year.

Spelthorne

The Staines Parochial Charity

£4,400

Correspondent: Carol Davies, Honorary Clerk to the Trustees, 191 Feltham Hill Road, Ashford, Middlesex TW15 1HJ (01784 255432; email: candodavies@tiscali.co.uk)

CC number: 211653

Eligibility

Older people over the age of 60 who live in the parish of Staines; people who are unable to work; people caring for a person with disabilities and occasionally other people in need who live in the area of the former urban district of Staines.

Types of grants

One-off grants according to need to alleviate hardship or distress, for example, the payment of gas or electricity bills. Grants usually range from £80 to £100.

Annual grant total

In 2014/15 the charity had an income of £4,800 and a total expenditure of £4,600. We estimate that the amount of grants given to individuals totalled £4,400.

Exclusions

No grants are given to individuals living outside the beneficial area.

Applications

Apply on a form available from the correspondent including evidence of need, hardship or distress. Applications can be submitted either directly by the individual, through a social worker, Citizens Advice, welfare agency or other third party. The application must be sent via a trustee who must countersign the application. Applications are normally considered in September.

Surrey Heath

Frimley Fuel Allotments (formerly known as The Frimley Fuel Allotments Charity)

£91,500 (234 grants)

Correspondent: Frank Smithin, Trustee, 2A Hampshire Road, Camberley GU15 4DW (01276 23958; email: ffa.office@googlemail.com; website: www.frimleyfuelallotments.org.uk)

CC number: 231036

Eligibility

People in need who live in the parish of Frimley. Priority is given to people who are older or who have a disability, and those who care for them.

Types of grants

One-off grants.

Annual grant total

In 2014 the charity had assets of £1.7 million and an income of £151,500. Grants totalled £121,500, of which £78,000 was awarded as standard grants to individuals with a further £13,500 paid in heating grants.

Applications

Apply on a form available from the secretary or a local Citizens Advice, church or social services centre. Applications for the Christmas heating grants should be returned to the respective social service centre by mid-November and can be made directly by the individual. Applications for other grants can be made at any time and are considered on a regular basis. Applicants may be visited by a trustee before a grant is made.

Other information

Grants are also made to local organisations (£30,000 in 2014).

The Henry Smith Charity (Bisley)

£2,800

Correspondent: Alexandra Gunn, Trustee, 213 Guildford Road, Bisley, Woking, Surrey GU24 9DL (email: sandy213@ntlworld.com)

CC number: 200157

Eligibility

People in need who live in Bisley.

Types of grants

Grants to assist with food costs are distributed twice a year.

Annual grant total

In 2014 the charity had an income of £3,000 and a total expenditure of £3,000. We estimate that the amount of grants given to individuals totalled around £2,800

Applications

Application forms are available from the correspondent. Applications should be submitted directly by the individual.

Henry Smith Charity (Chobham)

£7,500

Correspondent: Elizabeth Thody, Correspondent, 46 Chertsey Road, Windlesham, Surrey GU20 6EP (email: cpa1831@aol.co.uk)

CC number: 200155

Eligibility

People in need who live in the ancient parish of Chobham (roughly the current civil parishes of Chobham and West End) in Surrey.

Types of grants

One-off grants, usually in the form of vouchers worth £20 to £30, to be used to purchase goods from local shops.

Annual grant total

In 2014/15 the charity had an income of £9,500 and a total expenditure of £8,100. We estimate that the amount of grants given to individuals totalled £7.500.

Applications

Application forms are available from the correspondent.

Other information

The origins of this charity date back to 1642.

Windlesham United Charities

£3,600 (28 grants)

Correspondent: Carol Robson, Clerk to the Trustees, 4 James Butler Almshouses, Guildford Road, Bagshot, Surrey GU19 5NH (01276476158; email: jamesbutleroffice@btinternet.com)

CC number: 200224

Eligibility

Mainly the elderly and people with disabilities who are in need and have lived in the parishes of Bagshot, Lightwater and Windlesham (Surrey) for at least two years.

Types of grants

One-off grants, mainly in the form of small heating grants.

Annual grant total

In 2014 the charity had assets of £385,000 and an income of £61,000. Grants to individuals totalled £3,600 distributed to 28 people in Bagshot, Lightwater and Windlesham to cover fuel expenses.

Applications

Apply in writing to the correspondent at any time.

Other information

Windlesham United Charities consists of four separate funds: R E Cooper Educational Fund, The Duchess of Gloucester Educational Fund, Windlesham Poors Allotments and Windlesham United Charities. The charity also maintain allotments for the poor.

Tandridge

The Bletchingley United Charities

£6,100

Correspondent: Christine Bolshaw, Clerk, Cleves, Castle Street, Bletchingley, Surrey RH1 4QA (01883 743000; email: chrisbolshaw@hotmail.co.uk; website: www.bletchingley.org.uk)

CC number: 236747

Eligibility

People in need, hardship or distress who live in the parish of Bletchingley.

Types of grants

One-off and recurrent grants in the range of £20 to £200 towards medical items, welfare support, gas and electricity. Grants are also given for equipment such as cookers, fridges and freezers.

Annual grant total

In 2013/14 the charity had an income of £10,300 and a total expenditure of £10,700. We estimate that the amount of grants given to individuals totalled £5,000, with funding also awarded to local organisations.

Exclusions

Grants are not given for rates, taxes or other public funds.

Applications

Apply in writing to the correspondent. Applications can be submitted either directly by the individual, through a third party such as a social worker, or where applicable, through an organisation such as Citizens Advice or other welfare agency. They are considered throughout the year.

The Godstone United Charities

£6,400

Correspondent: Patricia Bamforth, Administrator, Bassett Villa, Oxted Road, Godstone, Surrey RH9 8AD (01883 742625; email: clerk@godstonepc.org.uk; website: www.godstonepc.org.uk)

CC number: 200055

Eligibility

People in need who live in the old parish of Godstone (Blindley Heath, South Godstone and Godstone Village).

Types of grants

Food vouchers are usually given in December and March. One-off grants are also available.

Annual grant total

In 2013/14 the charity had an income of £6,500 and a total expenditure of £6,600. We estimate that the amount of grants given to individuals totalled £6,400.

Applications

Apply in writing to the correspondent: either directly by the individual, through a relevant third party or, where applicable, via a social worker, Citizens Advice or other welfare agency. Applications should include relevant details of income, outgoings, household composition and reason for request. All grants are paid directly to the supplier.

Other information

The charity may also assist with educational needs.

The Oxted United Charities

£4,800

Correspondent: Christopher Berry, Trustee, 9 Paddock Way, Oxted, Surrey RH8 0LF (01883 818549; email: cjboxted@aol.co.uk)

CC number: 200056

Eligibility

People in need who live in the parish of Oxted.

Types of grants

One-off grants, generally in the range of £20 to £500. In the past, grants have been given for clothing, food, education, utility bills, television licences, furniture and floor covering.

Annual grant total

In 2014/15 the charity had an income of £5,500 and a total expenditure of £5,000. We estimate that the amount of grants given to individuals totalled £4,800.

Applications

Apply in writing to the correspondent. Applications are considered at any time and should be submitted directly by the individual or, where applicable, through a social worker, Citizens Advice or other welfare agency.

The Henry Smith Charity (Horne)

£4,500

Correspondent: Colin Buckley, Correspondent, Nutmeg Cottage, Domewood, Copthorne, Crawley RH10 3HD (01342 713822)

CC number: 201988

Eligibility

Older people and people in need who live in the ancient parish of Horne.

Types of grants

One-off grants are the norm, although recurrent grants can be considered.

Annual grant total

In 2014/15 the charity had an income of £7,600 and a total expenditure of £5,300. We estimate that the amount of grants given to individuals amounted to around £4,500.

Exclusions

Group applications are not accepted.

Applications

Application forms are available from the correspondent. Applications can be submitted either directly by the individual or through a social worker and should include details of the applicant's level of income. Applications are normally considered twice a year (notices are posted around the parish).

Waverley

The Churt Welfare Trust

£2,500

Correspondent: Mrs E. Kilpatrick, Trustee, Hearn Lodge, Spats Lane, Headley Down, Bordon, Hampshire GU35 8SU (01428 712238; email: john@regalarch.f9.co.uk; website: churt.org/ChurtWelfareTrust.html)

CC number: 210076

Eligibility

People in need who live in the parish of Churt and its neighbourhood.

Types of grants

One-off grants in the range of £10 to £1,000. Grants have been given towards: winter fuel bills for the elderly; equipment, furnishings and comforts for the physically or mentally ill; specialist equipment or household assistance for the terminally or temporarily ill; travel or holiday arrangements; medical expenses; taxi or transport costs for the elderly or for long distance medical appointments; and household repairs and maintenance.

Annual grant total

In 2013/14 the trust had an income of £11,500 and a total expenditure of £12,000. We estimate that the amount of grants given to individuals totalled £2,500, with funding also awarded to local organisations and to individuals for educational purposes.

Exclusions

The trust cannot renew or commit to repeat grants.

Applications

Apply in writing to the correspondent.

The Dempster Trust

£5,200

Correspondent: Peter Jeans, Trustee, 21 Broomleaf Road, Farnham GU9 8DG (01252 721075; email: joncurtis@ thedempstertrust.org.uk)

CC number: 200107

Eligibility

People in need, hardship or distress who live in Farnham and the general neighbourhood.

Types of grants

One-off grants or help for limited periods only. In the past, grants have been given towards nursing requisites, to relieve sudden distress, travelling expenses, fuel, television and telephone bills, clothing, washing machines, televisions, radios, alarm systems and so on. Grants usually range from £50 to £500.

Annual grant total

In 2014/15 the trust had an income of £12,200 and an expenditure of £11,100. We estimate that the amount of grants given to individuals totalled £5,200, with funding also awarded to local organisations.

Exclusions

Help is not given towards rent, rates or house improvements.

Applications

Apply on a form available from the correspondent or from the trust's website, to be submitted through a doctor, social worker, hospital, Citizens Advice or another welfare agency. Applications can be considered at any time.

The Margaret Jeannie Hindley Charitable Trust

£7,000

Correspondent: The Trustees, Marshalls Solicitors, 102 High Street, Godalming, Surrey GU7 1DS (01483 416101)

CC number: 272140

Eligibility

Relief of poverty and distress among people in 'reduced or destitute circumstances'. In practice priority is given to people living in the Godalming area.

Types of grants

Some recurrent grants of £40 to £50 each month are made. One-off grants of up to £750 are more usual.

Annual grant total

In 2013/14 the trust had an income of £17,000 and a total expenditure of £14,700. We estimate that the amount of grants given to individuals totalled £7,000, with funding also awarded to local organisations.

Applications

Apply in writing to the correspondent. The trustees meet regularly throughout the year to consider applications.

The Witley Charitable Trust

£1,100

Correspondent: Daphne O'Hanlon, Trustee, Triados, Waggoners Way, Grayshott, Hindhead, Surrey GU26 6DX (01428 604679)

CC number: 200338

Eligibility

Children and young people (normally under the age of 20) and older people (normally aged over 60) who are in need and who live in the parishes of Witley, Milford and small part of Brook.

Types of grants

One-off, modest grants ranging from £25 to £300. Support can be given towards telephone, electricity and gas debts (up to about £150, usually paid via social services), for medical appliances not available through the NHS, in Christmas gifts, food hampers or vouchers, and towards other needs.

Annual grant total

In 2014 the trust had an income of £3,700 and an expenditure of £2,400. We estimate that around £1,100 was awarded in welfare grants.

Exclusions

The trust does not give loans or support for items which should be provided by statutory services.

Applications

Applications can be made in writing to the correspondent. Applications should be submitted through nurses, doctors, social workers, clergy, Citizens Advice and so on but not directly by the individual. Awards are usually considered in early February and September, although emergency applications can be considered throughout the year.

Other information

Grants are also given for educational needs.

The Wonersh Charities

£4,500

Correspondent: Anna Pritchard, Correspondent, 8 Hullmead, Shamley Green, Guildford, Surrey GU5 0UG (01483 894191; email: wonershuc@gmail. com)

CC number: 200086

Eligibility

Older people and people with a disability who live in the parishes of Wonersh, Shamley Green and Blackheath.

Types of grants

Cash grants are given at Christmas. One-off grants are also available.

Annual grant total

In 2013/14 the charities had an income of £5,600 and a total expenditure of £5,100. We estimate that the amount of grants given to individuals totalled £4,500.

Applications

Apply in writing to the correspondent preferably through a third party such as Citizens Advice, trustee of the charity, local clergy or other organisation. Applications are usually considered in early July and early December.

Woking

The Byfleet United Charity

£166,000

Correspondent: Director, 10 Stoop Court, Leisure Lane, West Byfleet, Surrey KT14 6HF (01932 340943; email: buc@ byfleetunitedcharity.org.uk)

CC number: 200344

Eligibility

People in need who have lived in the ancient parish of Byfleet or West Byfleet area for at least a year (normally three years) immediately prior to their application.

Types of grants

Monthly pensions and one-off grants towards essential household items, for example, cookers, heaters, vacuum cleaners and also for nursery school fees.

Annual grant total

In 2014 the charity had assets of £5.9 million and an income of £493,000. Grants were made to 59 individuals totalling £27,500 and a further £138,500 was paid in pensions.

Exclusions

People outside the area of benefit or resident there temporarily can only be assisted in exceptional circumstances.

Applications

Apply in writing to the correspondent. Applications can be made directly by the individual or through a third party, such as a social worker, Citizens Advice, local GP or church. Candidates are usually visited and assessed.

Other information

The charity gives money to local organisations (£27,500 to eight organisations in 2014). It also operates a sheltered housing complex of 24 flats available to people over the age of 55 who are in real need.

This charity is an amalgamation of smaller trusts, including the Byfleet Pensions Fund.

Chobham Poor Allotment Charity

£10,100

Correspondent: Elizabeth Thody, 46 Chertsey Road, Windlesham GU20 6EP

CC number: 200154

Eligibility

People in need who live in the ancient parish of Chobham, which includes the civil parishes of Chobham and West End.

Types of grants

The majority of grants are given in the form of vouchers, ranging between £30 and £50, as payment towards goods in local shops. Assistance is also given to provide stair-lifts and electric scooters.

Annual grant total

In 2013/14 the charity had assets of £429,000 and an income of £47,500. Grants totalled £21,000, of which those to individuals amounted to around £10,700. Grants were distributed as follows:

Organisations	£10,500
Annual distribution	£8,500*
Grants to individuals	£1,200**
Other benefits (stair-lifts and scooters)	£1,000

*The annual distribution for the year saw 1,698 vouchers redeemed for the benefit of 90 parishioners.

**We believe this figure to include educational grants, which we estimate totalled around £600. We have not included this amount in our grants total.

Applications

Applications can be made on a form available from the correspondent. Applications should be submitted directly by the individual for consideration at any time.

Other information

The charity also manages almshouses and an area of allotment land. As well as making grants, the charity also supports local organisations through the provision of interest-free loans.

The Henry Smith Charity (Woking)

£5,800

Correspondent: David Bittleston, Trustee, Pin Mill, Heathfield Road, Woking, Surrey GU22 7JJ (01483 828621)

CC number: 232281

Eligibility

People in need who live in the ancient parish of Woking.

Types of grants

One-off grants only.

Annual grant total

In 2013/14 the charity had both an income and an expenditure of £6,000. We estimate that the amount of grants given to individuals totalled £5,800.

Exclusions

Grants are not given for the relief of rates, taxes and other public funds.

Applications

Apply in writing to the vicar of the parish, either directly by the individual or, where applicable, through a social worker, Citizens Advice or other welfare agency. Successful grants are distributed by the vicars of each of the seven parishes in the area.

West Sussex

Midhurst Pensions Trust

£35,000

Correspondent: Anina Cheng, Trust Administrator, 4th Floor, Swan House, 17–19 Stratford Place, London W1C 1BQ (020 7907 2100; email: charity@mfs.co.uk)

CC number: 245230

Eligibility

People in need who have been employed by the Third Viscount Cowdray, Lady Anne Cowdray, any family company or on the Cowdray Estate, and their dependants.

Types of grants

One-off grants typically in the range of £25 to £2,000.

Annual grant total

In 2013/14 the trust held assets of £4.6 million and had an income of £86,000. Payments to pensioners totalled £35,000.

Applications

Apply in writing to the correspondent.

The Three Oaks Trust

£58,000 (307 grants)

Correspondent: The Trustees, The Three Oaks Family Trust Co. Ltd, 65 Worthing Road, Horsham, West Sussex RH12 1TD (email: contact@thethreeoakstrust.co.uk; website: www.thethreeoakstrust.co.uk)

CC number: 297079

Eligibility

People and families in need who live in West Sussex. There is a particular focus on people with a physical or mental disability (including learning difficulties), and on low-income families, single parents and the long-term sick.

Types of grants

One-off grants of up to £300 towards basic furnishings, clothing, washing machines, fridges, telephone connections and so on.

Annual grant total

In 2013/14 the trust held assets of £6.9 million and had an income of £249,500. 307 grants to individuals totalled £58,000.

Grants were also made to organisations totalling £154,000.

Exclusions

No funding is given for gap year work or similar activities.

Applications

Direct applications by individuals will not be considered. Applications can only be made through Crawley and Horsham Social Services and Citizens Advice and other invited local agencies. Details of the agency to which any cheque should be made payable should be included in the application. Ineligible applications will not be answered.

The trustees have noted in their 2013/14 report that:

> In the case of long-term difficulties, the trustees are more likely to be sympathetic to a request if the person or family on behalf of whom the request is being made, is able to reflect on whether there are any changes they could make to prevent the same problems reoccurring.

Further guidelines are offered on the trust's website, along with an application form for professional agencies.

Other information

The trust also supports a number of social welfare organisations in the UK and overseas through grants. Of the total charitable expenditure in 2013/14, 60% went to UK-registered charities and organisations, 13% to overseas organisations and 27% to individuals.

Crawley

Crawley and Ifield Relief in Sickness Fund

£3,500

Correspondent: Roger Gibson, Trustee, 7 Priest Croft Close, Crawley RH11 8RL (01293 520752; email: roger.gibson7@talktalk.net)

CC number: 254779

Eligibility

People in need who are sick, disabled, convalescent or infirm and live within a three-mile radius of the church of St John Crawley.

Types of grants

One-off grants according to need.

Annual grant total

In 2014 the fund had an income of £2,800 and a total expenditure of £3,800. We estimate that the amount of grants given to individuals totalled £3,500.

Applications

Apply in writing to the correspondent.

Horsham

Ashington, Wiston, Warminghurst Sick Poor Fund

£6,000

Correspondent: Rod Shepherd, Trustee, Sheen Stickland LLP, 7 East Pallant, Chichester, West Sussex PO19 1TR (email: rod.shepherd@btinternet.com)

CC number: 234625

Eligibility

People in need – typically those who are ill – who live, firstly in the villages of Ashington, Wiston and Warminghurst, and secondly in West Sussex.

Types of grants

One-off grants according to need. Most grants are for equipment that will make an ill individual's life easier although trustees award grants towards anything that will improve their well-being. The average grant is £300.

Annual grant total

In 2014 the fund had an income of £740 and a total expenditure of £6,300 We estimate that the amount of grants given to individuals totalled £6,000.

Applications

Application forms are available from the correspondent. Applications can be submitted directly by the individual or a relevant third party.

Mid Sussex

The Chownes Foundation

Correspondent: Sylvia Spencer, Secretary, The Courtyard, Shoreham Road, Upper Beeding, Steyning, West Sussex BN44 3TN (01903 816699; email: sylvia@russellnew.com)

CC number: 327451

Eligibility

Former employees of Sound Diffusion plc who lost their pensions when the company went into receivership. Our research indicates that grants are also made to assist older people who live in mid-Sussex and are in need.

Types of grants

One-off and recurrent grants are given according to need.

Annual grant total

In 2013/14 the foundation had an income of £20,000 and a total expenditure of £110,500. Due to its low income, the foundation was not required to submit its accounts to the Charity Commission and so we were unable to determine a total for grants made during the year.

In the most recent year for which accounts were available to view (2012/13), the foundation awarded £17,000 to assist former employees of Sound Diffusion plc. A further £15,700 was given to individuals for other charitable purposes. We estimate that around half of this was given for social welfare purposes. Based on this, we estimate that social welfare grants to former employees of Sound Diffusion plc and other individuals totalled around £25,000.

Applications

Our research suggests that the trustees prefer a one page document and will request further information if they require it.

Other information

The majority of the charity's funds are committed to long-term support for poor and vulnerable beneficiaries, so only very few applications are successful.

South West

General

Viscount Amory's Charitable Trust

£3,500

Correspondent: Secretary to the Trustees, The Island, Lowman Green, Tiverton, Devon EX16 4LA (01884 254899; email: office@vact.org.uk; website: www.vact.org.uk)

CC number: 204958

Eligibility
People in need in the south west of England.

Types of grants
One-off and recurrent grants are given according to need. Short-term loans may also be awarded.

Annual grant total
In 2013/14 the trust had assets of almost £12.4 million and an income of £433,000. The trust made 16 grants to individuals totalling £7,500, of which £3,500 was awarded for social welfare purposes and £4,000 for educational purposes. A further £324,500 was given to organisations.

Applications
Apply in writing to the correspondent, for consideration every month. Applications should be submitted by post, not email. Details of what should be included are outlined on the website.

Other information
The charity also gives grants to individuals for educational purposes and to organisations.

The Beckly Trust

£3,000

Correspondent: Stephen Trahair, Trustee, 10 South Hill, Stoke, Plymouth PL1 5RR (01752 675071)

CC number: 235763

Eligibility
Children under 18 who live in the city of Plymouth or district of Caradon, Cornwall and who have an illness or a disability and are in need.

Types of grants
One-off grants of around £200 to £300.

Annual grant total
In 2013/14 the trust had an income of £10,600 and a total expenditure of £4,400. We estimate that the amount of grants given to individuals totalled £3,000. Funding is occasionally also awarded to organisations.

Applications
Apply in writing to the correspondent giving brief details of income and outgoings of the applicant's parent/guardian and a description of the child's need. Applications should be made preferably through a social worker, Citizens Advice or other welfare agency but can also be made directly by the individual or through another third party. Applications are considered on an ongoing basis.

The Grateful Society

£20,500

Correspondent: June Moody, Administrator, Kestrel Court Business Centre, Harbour Road, Portishead, Bristol BS20 7AN (0117 929 1929; email: g-s.moody@btconnect.com; website: gratefulsociety.org)

CC number: 202349

Eligibility
Women who are over 50 years old who have lived in Bristol and the surrounding areas (including the unitary authorities of North Somerset, South Gloucestershire or Bath and North East Somerset) for at least ten years and would benefit from financial assistance, typically to pursue an independent life in their own home.

Grants may occasionally be given to men in reduced circumstances.

Types of grants
Regular allowances, paid quarterly. One-off grants can be paid towards, for example, electrical goods, clothing, household bills, food, holidays, travel expenses, heating repairs, medical equipment, furniture and disability equipment.

Annual grant total
In 2014, the society had an income of £118,000 and total assets of £207,500. During the year, grants were paid to 24 beneficiaries totalling £20,500.

Applications
Apply in writing to the correspondent. Applications may be submitted directly by the individual or through a third party.

Other information
The charity also makes grants to organisations with similar aims including day care centres and activities for older people (£36,000 in 2013).

A team of visitors also provides a befriending service to older people.

The Peter Hervé Benevolent Institution

£74,500

Correspondent: June Moody, Hon. Secretary and Treasurer, Suite F11B, Kestrel Court Business Centre, Harbour Road, Portishead, Bristol BS20 7AN (0117 929 1929; email: g-s.moody@ btconnect.com)

CC number: 202443

Eligibility
People aged 60 and over who live within a 25-mile radius of Bristol city centre, own their own homes and have fallen on hard times.

Types of grants
Recurrent grants, averaging £200 a quarter and one-off emergency grants of up to £500 towards, for example, the costs of a new boiler.

Annual grant total

In 2014 the charity held assets of £2.1 million and had an income of £158,000. Grants and annuities to individuals totalled £74,500 and were distributed as follows:

Regular gifts	£40,300
Emergency gifts	£28,000
Annuities	£2,200

Applications

The charity does not accept applications directly but rather invites organisations working with potential beneficiaries to apply for annuities and emergency gifts.

Other information

The Peter Hervé Benevolent Institution is a registered charity and was founded in 1812 by Mr Peter Hervé, a painter of miniatures.

The Pirate Trust

£3,500

Correspondent: Nicholas Lake, Correspondent, Pirate FM Ltd, Carn Brea Studios, Barncoose Industrial Estate, Redruth, Cornwall TR15 3XX (01209 314400; email: piratetrust@ piratefm.co.uk; website: www.piratefm. co.uk/piratetrust)

CC number: 1032096

Eligibility

People in need living within the Pirate FM 102 broadcast area (Cornwall, Plymouth and west Devon). Preference is given to people with disabilities.

Types of grants

One-off and recurrent grants mainly towards disability equipment.

Annual grant total

In 2014/15 the trust had an income of £4,100 and a total expenditure of £7,000. We estimate grants to individuals totalled £3,500.

Applications

Application forms are available to download from the website.

St Monica Trust (formerly known as St Monica Trust Community Fund)

£352,000 (468+ grants)

Correspondent: Community Fund Team, Cote Lane, Westbury-on-Trym, Bristol BS9 3UN (0117 949 4003; email: community.fund@stmonicatrust.org.uk.; website: www.stmonicatrust.org.uk)

CC number: 202151

Eligibility

People who have a physical disability or long-term physical health problem living in Bristol, South Gloucestershire, North Somerset or Bath and North East Somerset. Applicants must have a low income, limited savings and be over 40 years old.

Help is available to people who are in recovery from substance misuse or alcoholism, provided they have been drug or alcohol free for at least six months and also have a physical disability or long-term physical health problem.

Types of grants

Gifts

One-off grants averaging around £300 but never exceeding £500 to help towards mobility aids, home/car adaptations, domestic appliances, furniture and flooring, bedding, clothing, health costs, communication aids, bills and debts.

This list is by no means exhaustive and gifts will be considered for anything that will make a positive difference to the applicant's everyday life.

Short-Term Grants

A period of monthly payments designed to help a person through a time of crisis. For example, help can be given for: debt relief; adjusting to a sudden loss of income; unexpected costs; and, the extra costs involved when undergoing chemotherapy, interferon or similar treatments. Usually up to £25 each week is paid for anywhere between a couple of months up to a maximum of three years. Help is usually given for around six months.

Annual grant total

In 2014 the trust had assets of £236 million and an income of £26.1 million. Charitable expenditure totalled £25.6 million. Grants were made to at least 468 individuals (of 997 applications received) totalling £234,500 and can be categorised as follows:

Gifts	365	£131,500
Short-term grants	179	£92,500
Annuities	8	£10,600

Over 468 individuals were helped directly through grants and more were helped through LinkAge.

Exclusions

No help is given to people with mental health problems or people with a learning disability unless they also have a physical disability or long-term physical health problem (although the trust can help those with dementia). Help is not generally given to people who have more than £3,000 in savings.

Help will not be given for holidays; gardening; bankruptcy fees; funeral expenses; decorating labour costs; respite care and care home fees.

Applications

Apply on a form available to download from the trust's website or by contacting the trust. If possible, applications should be submitted via a social worker, advice worker or a similar professional, although individuals can apply themselves. Depending on the request, a letter may be needed from an occupational therapist confirming the need for a particular item and why it is not available from statutory funds. Individuals should contact the trust if they are having any difficulties in filling out the form, and if needed a home visit can be arranged to help complete the application.

The fund expects you to have applied for statutory funding first, for example community care grants and disabled facilities grants, before applying. They may refer you to a relevant trade or forces benevolent fund where possible before considering your application. The fund's website also advises: 'If you own your own home and are asking for help with repairs or improvements, we would expect you to investigate equity release schemes and charitable interest free loans before you ask us for help.'

Other information

Grants are also made to organisations whose aim is to support a similar group of beneficiaries, with seven organisations receiving a total of £73,000 in 2012. The fund also provides sheltered housing and retirement accommodation; support services; and nursing and residential care. The charity also works in partnership with Bristol city council, the Clinical Commissioning Group and other local charities on a project called LinkAge, supporting older people.

City of Bristol

The Anchor Society

£37,500

Correspondent: Annie Berry, Administrator, 29 Alma Vale Road, Clifton, Bristol BS8 2HL (0117 973 4161; email: admin@anchorsociety.co.uk; website: www.anchorsociety.co.uk)

CC number: 208756

Eligibility

Isolated people over the age of 55 who are in genuine immediate need and live in the Bristol and former Avon postcode area (BS).

Types of grants

One-off and regular grants to help older people stay independent and in their own homes. Grants can be used for essential home repairs and adaptations, mobility aids and helping make homes more accessible and safe.

Annual grant total

In 2013/14 the society had assets of £3.9 million and an income of £150,500. Grants were made totalling £144,500, of which £37,000 was given to individuals and £108,000 to organisations.

Exclusions

The society does not give grants for general living expenses, to pay off outstanding bills, to cover moving costs or travel expenses, holidays or respite breaks, insurance costs or funeral costs.

Applications

Applications should be made through the society's website and should be completed by a third party responsible for referring the individual for a grant.

Other information

The society has also invested in the provision of a new form of day care for elderly people within the region through Link Age, who it supports with an annual grant (£80,000 2013/14) and has close links with other welfare charities in the area. It has also invested in a number of housing projects as well as a robotics laboratory which allows researchers to trial new assisted-living technology.

The Bristol Benevolent Institution

£374,500

Correspondent: Maureen Nicholls, Secretary, 45 High Street, Nailsea, Bristol BS48 1AW (01275 810365 (mobile 07968 434 274); email: admin@ bristolbenevolent.org; website: bristolbenevolent.org)

CC number: 204592

Eligibility

Older people with small fixed incomes and little or no capital. Applicants must be over 60 and have lived in Bristol for 15 years or more. People over the age of 55 who have chronic illness or severe disabilities are also eligible.

Types of grants

Mostly small recurrent grants paid quarterly, usually between £320 and £1,300 per annum. One-off grants may also be made for specific needs, such as household items, repairs or removal fees.

People over the age of 70 who own their own homes, free of mortgage, can apply for small interest-free loans to help supplement a low income or to help

make essential repairs. Loans are repaid from the sale of the property upon the death of the beneficiary, or if the beneficiary sells their home. In the cases of couples, a loan can be transferred to the surviving spouse automatically.

Annual grant total

In 2014 the institution had an income of £485,000 and a total expenditure of £489,435. Grants to individuals totalled £384,500. An average of 233 grants were paid to individuals each quarter and 60 loans were also made during the year.

During the year the trustees also awarded each beneficiary special grants for heating costs after a period of cold weather, in summer and at Christmas.

A further £10,000 was awarded in grants to other charities.

Exclusions

The institution's website states that whilst it 'cannot give grants to people who own their own homes', it can offer interest-free loans to those homeowners over the age of 70.

Applications

Potential applicants should contact the secretary by phone, email or post. A visitor from the institution will then call to complete an application. Applications can be submitted directly by the individuals or through a third party such as a family member, a friend, a social worker or doctor, provided the individual concerned is notified and approves of the application. Applications are considered at quarterly trustees' meetings.

Other information

BBI's accounts state that most of its beneficiaries 'have less than £80 per week for food and clothing after paying their rent, medical bills, heat, light, transport and other standing costs'.

The institution notes that although it gives financial assistance, 'we believe that the most valued assistance we give is friendship and advice, ably provided by our lady visitors'. Newsletters, visits and telephone calls help the institution keep in touch with its beneficiaries.

Bristol Charities

£208,000

Correspondent: Andy Dixon, Correspondent, 17 Augustine's Parade, Bristol BS1 4UL (0117 930 0301; fax: 0117 925 3824; email: info@ bristolcharities.org.uk; website: www. bristolcharities.org.uk)

CC number: 1109141

Eligibility

People in need who have lived in Bristol for more than two consecutive years.

Types of grants

Grants are mainly in the form of vouchers which are used to purchase specific goods. Grants are considered for beds, carpets, clothing for schoolchildren aged 5–15 (where more than one child in the family is at school, one voucher per child), white goods, essential furniture (second hand or reconditioned), safety equipment, washing machines and starter packs.

In recent years, the trustees have introduced a 'retained ownership scheme' for items such as wheelchairs, electric wheelchairs and scooters, by which they are acquired for specific individuals but remain under the ownership of the charities, with the purpose of recycling the equipment should the original recipient no longer require it.

Annual grant total

In 2013/14 the charities had a consolidated income of £1.4 million and a total expenditure of £1.2 million. Welfare grants to individuals totalled £208,000 and grants to individuals for education totalled £3,700.

Exclusions

No grants are given for debts or rent arrears. Only one grant is given per applicant per year and there is a limit of three grants per person.

Applications

Application forms are available from the Bristol Charities website. All applicants require the support of a sponsor who should be a healthcare professional. Applications are considered daily.

Other information

The provision of accommodation for the elderly at four almshouse sites (Perrett House, Red Cross Mews, Manor House and John Foster's) is carried out through 'Orchard Homes', which is a registered provider. The charities also own and manage two day centres (Summerhill in St George and Henbury).

The Lord Mayor of Bristol's Christmas Appeal for Children

£59,000 (1,650 grants)

Correspondent: Bruce Simmonds, Hon. Treasurer, 3 Park Crescent, Frenchay, Bristol BS16 1PD (07768 077 864; website: www.lordmayorofbristolappeal. co.uk)

CC number: 288262

Eligibility

Children under 16 who are in need and who live in the city of Bristol.

Types of grants

One-off grants at Christmas in the form of vouchers. Each child receives two vouchers; one worth £20 to be spent on food, and another worth £20 to be spent on either clothing or toys.

Annual grant total

In 2013/14 the charity held assets of £69,000 and had an income of £44,000. The total value of food, clothing and toy vouchers, awarded to approximately 1,650 children, amounted to £59,000.

Applications

Through a social worker, Citizens Advice, welfare agency or other third party such as a parent or a person who can confirm the individual's needs.

Other information

The Appeal originated in the 1920's, when it was known as the Lord Mayor's Fund, and the money raised was used to provide Christmas dinners and boots for poor children.

The Charity of Thomas Beames

£1,800

Correspondent: Philippa Drewett, 1 All Saints Court, Bristol BS1 1JN (0117 966 5739)

CC number: 245822

Eligibility

People in need who live in the ancient parish of St George with St Augustine, Bristol or the parishes of Christchurch with St George, St Stephen with St James or St John the Baptist with St Michael, Bristol. In exceptional cases, the charity may help people who live outside this area, who produce sufficient good reason why they should be treated as being resident within the parish.

Types of grants

Grants are made at the discretion of the trustees, towards, for example, bedding, food and electrical cookers.

Annual grant total

In 2014 the charity had an income of £6,000 and a total expenditure of £2,000. We estimate that the amount of grants given to individuals totalled £1,800.

Applications

Apply in writing to the correspondent including details of why help is needed. Applications are usually considered quarterly.

The Dolphin Society

£90,500

Correspondent: June Moody, Administrator, Kestrel Court Business Centre, Harbour Road, Portishead, Bristol BS20 7AN (0117 929 9649; email: dolphinsociety@btconnect.com; website: dolphinsociety.org.uk)

CC number: 203142

Eligibility

People in need and/or at risk through poor health, disability or financial difficulty and who live in Bristol. Preference is given to older people who need help in maintaining their independence and security in their own homes.

Types of grants

Help with telephone installations, smoke alarms, pendant alarms and security items such as external security boxes and door and window locks. Payments from the hardship fund can be used to help with home adaptations to enable people to continue to live in their homes while coping with increasing disability. The charity is also developing a project offering tablet computers to help isolated older people in the community to access information, communicate with relatives and so on.

Annual grant total

In 2013/14 the society held assets of £148,000 and had an income of £60,000. Charitable expenditure for individuals totalled £90,500 and was distributed as follows:

Pendant alarms/telephone installation	£60,000
Grants for disability equipment	£12,500
Home security	£12,500
Independent Living fund	£12,500

A further £440 was spent on the society's iPad project.

Exclusions

No grants are given to applicants living outside the area of benefit.

Applications

Application forms are available from the correspondent. Applications can be submitted directly by the individual or family member or by an appropriate third party. There are no deadlines and applications are considered throughout the year.

Other information

In the future, the society hopes to continue its iPad project, which explores the role tablet computers can play in helping isolated older people to live independently in the community.

The Redcliffe Parish Charity

£4,000

Correspondent: Paul Tracey, Trustee, 18 Kingston Road, Nailsea, Bristol, North Somerset BS48 4RD (email: redcliffeparishclerk@mail.com)

CC number: 203916

Eligibility

People in need who live in the city of Bristol, with preference for those who live in the ecclesiastical parish of St Mary Redcliffe with Temple – Bristol, and St John the Baptist – Bedminster.

Types of grants

One-off grants usually of £25–£50. The trustees generally limit grants to families or individuals who can usually manage, but who are overwhelmed by circumstances and are in particular financial stress rather than continuing need. Our research suggests that grants are typically given for electric goods, clothing, living costs, food, holidays, furniture and equipment for people with disabilities.

Annual grant total

In 2013/14 the charity had an income of £8,500 and a total expenditure of £8,400. We estimate that social welfare grants totalled around £4,000.

Exclusions

Grants are not made for bankruptcy fees, debts in respect of council tax, rent arrears, credit debts, recurrent grants, in the form of loans or for school/college fees.

Applications

Awards are made through a third party, for example, social services, housing associations, doctor, health visitor, Citizens Advice or other appropriate body. Applications need to be made in writing on behalf of an individual for consideration each month. Ages of family members should be supplied in addition to financial circumstances and the reason for the request.

Other information

Grants to schoolchildren are also made as part of the charity's wider welfare work.

Cornwall

The Lizzie Brooke Charity

£19,000

Correspondent: Sheila Bates, Administrator, 13 Church Close, Lelant, St Ives TR26 3JX (01736 752383; email: michael@vickers13.co.uk)

CC number: 254764

Eligibility

Older people, people who are sick and those in need who live in West Cornwall.

Types of grants

One-off grants ranging from £100 to £200 for the necessities of everyday living. Grants can be given towards electric goods, clothing, holidays, travel expenses, furniture and hospital expenses.

Annual grant total

In 2014 the charity had an income of £4,800 and a total expenditure of £23,000. We estimate that the amount of grants given to individuals totalled £19,000.

Exclusions

Grants are not made to people living in other parts of Cornwall or for students for fees.

Applications

Apply on a form available from the correspondent, to be completed by a sponsor. Applications should be submitted through a social worker, Citizens Advice or other welfare agency. They are considered at any time.

Cornwall Community Foundation

£119,000 (429 grants)

Correspondent: The Grants Team, Suite 1, Sheers Barton, Lawhitton, Launceston, Cornwall PL15 9NJ (01566 779865 or 01566 779333; email: grants@cornwallfoundation.com; website: www.cornwallfoundation.com)

CC number: 1099977

Eligibility

People in need living in Cornwall.

Types of grants

Usually one-off awards ranging from £50 to about £1,000 (depending on the fund). Grants have been made to alleviate poverty, hardship and distress, provide help in crisis, support young carers or to help young people foster their talent. Grants have also been given to those affected by extreme weather and flooding.

Annual grant total

In 2014 the foundation had assets of £4 million and an income of almost £2 million. Grants to individuals totalled around £139,000. Our research suggests that around £119,000 of this was awarded for welfare purposes to 429 individuals.

Applications

Initial enquiries should be directed to the grants team to discuss which funds are available and further application procedure. Alternatively, a list of open grant schemes together with application forms and separate deadlines are available on the foundation's website. Note that, as with all community foundations, schemes are likely to open and close regularly, so check before applying.

Other information

Grants are mostly made to organisations, groups, clubs and community projects.

The Duke of Cornwall's Benevolent Fund

£500 (2 grants)

Correspondent: Terry Cotter, Administrator, Duchy of Cornwall, 10 Buckingham Gate, London SW1E 6LA (020 7834 7346)

CC number: 269183

Eligibility

People who are in need because of sickness, poverty or age. In practice funds are steered towards the south west of England and areas related to Duchy lands, which are principally in Cornwall.

Types of grants

One-off and recurrent grants are given according to need.

Annual grant total

In 2013/14 the fund had assets of £3.8 million and an income of £64,000. Grants totalled £98,500. During the year two grants were made to individuals, although the amount awarded was not specified. We have used a nominal figure for the total amount of grants given to individuals.

Applications

Apply in writing to the correspondent. The trustees meet quarterly to consider grants.

Other information

The fund's main focus is on awarding grants to registered charities.

Charity of John Davey

£12,400

Correspondent: E. Pascoe, Administrator, Tregenna Lodge, Crane, Camborne TR14 7QX (01209 718853; email: pbfhayle@hotmail.co.uk)

CC number: 232127

Eligibility

Ex-miners over 70 years of age and their widows who are in need and live in the ancient parish of Gwennap, near Redruth in Cornwall. Ex-miners should have worked underground in a mine for at least five consecutive years. Support is also given to miners of any age who are unable to work due to sickness or injury.

Types of grants

Quarterly grants of £10 to £40 for general living expenses.

Annual grant total

In 2013/14 the charity had an income of £11,400 and a total expenditure of £12,600. We estimate that the amount of grants given to individuals totalled £12,000.

Applications

Initial telephone calls to the correspondent are welcome and application forms are available on request. Applications can be submitted directly by the individual or family member.

The Charity of Thomas Henwood

£6,000

Correspondent: Jennifer Moyle, Trustee, Homeleigh, Gunwalloe, Helston TR12 7QG (01326 564806)

CC number: 206765

Eligibility

People who live in the parish of Gunwalloe and are unemployed, sick or retired and in need.

Types of grants

One-off or recurrent grants according to need, and grants for the provision of nurses and to assist people recovering from illness. Grants normally range from £60 to £100. Income is also used to care for graves in the churchyard if no relatives are still alive.

Annual grant total

In 2014 the charity had an income of £10,000 and a total expenditure of £6,300. We estimate that the amount of grants given to individuals totalled £6,000.

Applications

Apply in writing to the trustees. Applications are considered in March and December.

North Cornwall

Blanchminster Trust

£12,100 (30 grants)

Correspondent: Jane Bunning, Clerk to the Trustees, Blanchminster Building, 38 Lansdown Road, Bude, Cornwall EX23 8EE (01288 352851; email: office@ blanchminster.plus.com; website: www. blanchminster.org.uk)

CC number: 202118

Eligibility

People who live in the parishes of Bude, Stratton and Poughill (the former urban district of Bude-Stratton), who are in need.

Types of grants

Assistance may be given in the form of a cash grant, disability equipment or travel costs for hospital visits, for example.

Annual grant total

In 2014 the trust had assets of almost £11 million and an income of £511,500. During the year, 30 grants were made for social welfare purposes, totalling £12,100.

Applications

Applications should be made in writing to the correspondent and outline exactly what assistance is needed and why. The trust does not have a standard application form, although it will send a 'Financial enquiry' form to individuals seeking assistance. Applications must include details of weekly income and expenditure, as well as information on any efforts that have been made to seek help from elsewhere.

Other information

Grants are also made to individuals for educational purposes and for community projects.

Devon

The Barnstaple and North Devon Dispensary Fund

£20,000

Correspondent: Christina Ford, Clerk to the Trustees, 17 Sloe Lane, Landkey, Barnstaple, Devon EX32 0UF (01271 831551; email: bandnddf@gmail.com)

CC number: 215805

Eligibility

People in need who live in the North Devon parishes.

Types of grants

One-off grants towards coal and heating bills, convalescence, medical equipment and other costs, bedding, clothing, travel expenses and food.

Annual grant total

In 2014 the fund had an income of £11,400 and a total expenditure of £22,000. We estimate that the amount of grants given to individuals amounted to £20,000.

Applications

Apply in writing to the correspondent, preferably through a doctor, health visitor, social worker or other third party.

The David Gibbons Foundation

£10,000

Correspondent: Roger Dawe, Trustee, 14 Fore Street, Budleigh Salterton, Devon EX9 6NG (01395 445259; email: enquiries@gibbonstrusts.org; website: www.gibbonstrusts.org)

CC number: 1134727

Eligibility

The elderly, sick, disabled and needy in Devon, with a preference for those from East Devon.

Types of grants

One-off grants according to need, typically ranging between £550 and £650.

Annual grant total

In 2013/14 the foundation held assets of £2.7 million and had an income of £103,500. Grants to 17 individuals totalled £10,000 with 47 organisations receiving a further £95,500.

Applications

On an application form which can be downloaded from the website and posted to the foundation. Applications must be supported by at least one letter from a professional third party such as a social worker, teacher, doctor, etc. Applications without a letter of support will not be considered. It is also helpful, but not essential, to include a copy of personal identification. All applications will be acknowledged by letter or email. Trustees usually meet in January, April, July and October; therefore, it may be three months before the success of an application is confirmed. All grants are paid by cheque and successful applicants should acknowledge receipt of the grant through the foundation's office address, or risk ineligibility for any future applications.

Note the following from the foundation's website: 'Please do not send applications by Recorded Delivery post. Also please ensure you have attached the correct stamps to cover the postage cost.'

Other information

The foundation was established by the will of Mr David Gibbons of Exmouth who passed away in February 2008.

Devonian Fund

£2,000

Correspondent: Grants Administrator, The Factory, Leat Street, Tiverton EX16 5LL (01884 235887; email: grants@ devoncf.com.; website: devoncf.com/ apply/apply-for-a-grant/individual-grants)

CC number: 1057923

Eligibility

People resident in Devon who are experiencing mobility or transport issues due to illness or disability.

Types of grants

Grants of £500 to £1,000 for items that relieve mobility problems, including specialised equipment or specialised transport such as accessible coaches or taxis.

Annual grant total

In 2013/14 grants totalled £26,000. We estimate that the amount of grants given to individuals totalled £2,800.

At least £23,000 was awarded in grants to organisations.

Exclusions

Grants for IT and associated equipment can only be made for up to £400.

Applications

Application forms are available to download from the Devon Community Foundation website. Applications must be made through a health care professional such as an occupational therapist, or a community group working with the individual.

Applications can be made throughout the year.

Other information
This fund is administered by Devon Community Foundation.

The Maudlyn Lands Charity

£2,000

Correspondent: Anthony Golding, Clerk to the Trustees, Blue Haze, Down Road, Tavistock, Devon PL19 9AG (01822 612983)

CC number: 202577

Eligibility
People who live in the Plympton St Mary and Sparkwell areas and are in need.

Types of grants
One-off or recurrent grants, usually ranging between £250 and £500.

Annual grant total
In 2013/14 the charity had an income of £7,500 and a total expenditure of around £8,200. We estimate that about £2,000 was awarded to individuals for educational purposes.

Applications
Applications may be made in writing to the correspondent. They are considered in November.

Other information
This charity also gives grants to individuals for educational purposes, and to organisations.

Northcott Devon Foundation

£188,000 (1,010 grants)

Correspondent: Emma O'Loughlin, Administrator, 1b Victoria Road, Exmouth, Devon EX8 1DL (01395 269204; fax: 01395 269204; email: emma.pat@live.co.uk; website: northcottdevonfoundation.com)

CC number: 201277

Eligibility
People living in Devon who are in need as the result of illness, injury, bereavement or exceptional disadvantages.

Types of grants
One-off and recurrent grants of up to £200 towards, for example, computers for children with physical disabilities, adaptations, repairs, holidays, clothing, furniture and wheelchairs.

Annual grant total
In 2013/14 the foundation held assets of £5.7 million and had an income of £202,500. A total of almost £188,000 was awarded in 1,010 grants to individuals. A further £6,500 was awarded to organisations.

Exclusions
No grants are given towards long-term educational needs, funeral expenses, energy bills or to relieve debts, council tax or other taxes.

Applications
Apply on a form available from the correspondent or to download from the foundation's website. Applicants must be sponsored by a doctor, social worker, Citizens Advice, health visitor, headteacher or a faith leader who is prepared to handle any grant on the applicant's behalf. The application must state the need for the grant, the applicant's income and expenditure, and must be accompanied by a supporting letter from the sponsor, complete with the sponsor's details. Any estimates should also be included. Grants are means-tested and cheques are made to the sponsor.

Note: applicants must have explored all statutory funding options with no success. Successful applicants must wait at least one year before re-applying.

Other information
The foundation was established in 1960 by George Northcott who relocated to Lympstone after World War ll.

City of Exeter

Central Exeter Relief-in-Need Charity

£4,800

Correspondent: Prof. Robert Snowden, Trustee, 50 Wonford Road, Exeter EX2 4LQ (01392 278425; email: r.snowden@blueyonder.co.uk)

CC number: 1022288

Eligibility
People in need who live in the parish of Central Exeter.

Types of grants
One-off grants usually of £50 to £150 for basic needs such as furniture, assistance with heating bills, children's clothing and mobility aids.

Annual grant total
In 2014/15 the charity had an income of £2,400 and a total expenditure of £5,100. We estimate that the total amount of grants awarded to individuals was approximately £4,800.

Exclusions
Grants are not made for educational and training needs.

Applications
Apply in writing to the correspondent with the support of a social worker, health visitor or other welfare agency. Applications are considered in June and December.

Exeter Dispensary and Aid-in-Sickness Fund

£25,000 (111 grants)

Correspondent: Peter Coleman, Applications Secretary, Ridge Farm, Broadhembury, Honiton, Exeter EX14 3LU (01404 841401)

CC number: 205611

Eligibility
People living in Exeter who are in poor financial circumstances and who are sick or have disabilities.

Types of grants
One-off grants for day-to-day needs including convalescence breaks, help with fuel or telephone bills, cooking or heating appliances, clothing, food, medical care, bedding, travel to and from hospitals and so on. The average such grant is £100. Larger grants are made towards medical appliances and aids.

Annual grant total
In 2014 the fund had assets of £910,000 and an income of £36,500. There were 111 grants made to individuals totalling £25,000.

Exclusions
Grants are not given for items which are available from public funds or for structural alterations to property.

Applications
Applications should be made through Citizens Advice, other welfare agency, a social worker or other third party such as a GP. They should include brief details of the medical condition, the financial circumstances and the specific need. Applications are considered throughout the year for day-to-day needs and in March and November for medical appliances and so on.

Other information
Grants are also given to other organisations with similar objectives (2014: £9,000).

The Exeter Nursing Association Trust

£2,100

Correspondent: Helen Hiscox, Trustee, 1 Thompson Road, Exeter, Devon EX1 2UB (01392 211306; email: helen. hiscox@lloydsbanking.com)

CC number: 202314

Eligibility

People in need who are receiving, or in need of, medical/nursing care, or needy employees or ex-employees of the association and the nursing profession, who live in the city and county of Exeter. Grants are also available to supplement nursing services of any kind, nursing amenities, educational facilities and any charity associated with nursing.

Types of grants

Providing and supplementing nursing services of any kind. One-off grants are also made.

Annual grant total

In 2013/14 the trust had an income of £9,100 and a total expenditure of £4,300. We estimate that the amount of grants given to individuals totalled £2,100, with funding also awarded to charities associated with nursing.

Applications

Apply in writing to the correspondent. Patients should write via their attending health visitor or district nurse; nurses should write via a senior nurse at Community Nursing Services Exeter Localities.

The Exeter Relief-in-Need Charity

£5,000

Correspondent: Stephen Sitch, Trustee, The Exeter Municipal Charity, 6 Southernhay West, Exeter, Devon EX1 1JG (01392 421162; email: info@ exetermunicipalcharity.org.uk)

CC number: 1002152

Eligibility

People in need who live in the city of Exeter.

Types of grants

One-off grants of between £50 and £150. Individuals can re-apply in subsequent years for further support. Grants can be made towards household furniture, equipment, floor coverings, bedding, school uniforms and other clothing, essential travelling expenses, heating and lighting bills and so on.

Annual grant total

In 2014 the charity had an income of £8,600 and a total expenditure of £5,800. We estimate that the amount of grants given to individuals totalled around £5,000.

Exclusions

Grants cannot be made for debt repayment, interest on loans, rent, mortgage, or council tax arrears.

Applications

At the time of writing, the charity's website states: 'Unfortunately, we are not processing any applications at present, however, please check our website in future for further updates. If you wish to contact the office to discuss this further, please do not hesitate to do so.'

Other information

This charity is part of Exeter Municipal Charities.

The Charity of John Shere and Others

£4,000

Correspondent: David Tucker, Trustee, 5 Elm Grove Gardens, Topsham, Exeter EX3 0EL (01392 873168; email: tucker-david@talktalk.net)

CC number: 220736

Eligibility

People in need who live in the parish of Topsham.

Types of grants

One-off and recurrent grants in the range of £350 to £400 are given where assistance cannot be obtained from any other means. Other forms of financial assistance are available.

Annual grant total

In 2014 the charity had an income of £9,100 and a total expenditure of £9,600. We estimate that the amount of grants given to individuals totalled around £4,000.

Exclusions

Applicants must have lived in Topsham for at least three years.

Applications

Application forms are available from the correspondent. Applications can be submitted at any time either directly by the individual or through a third party such as a social worker.

City of Plymouth

The Joseph Jory's Charity

£10,500

Correspondent: Jennifer Rogers, Correspondent, c/o Wolferstans, 60–66 North Hill, Plymouth PL4 8EP (01752 292347)

CC number: 235138

Eligibility

Widows over 50 who are in need and have lived in the city of Plymouth for the last seven years.

Types of grants

Small pensions, paid quarterly. Amounts vary according to available income.

Annual grant total

In 2014 the charity had an income of £12,500 and an expenditure of £10,800. We estimate that the amount of grants given to individuals totalled £10,500.

Applications

The trust advertises locally when funds are available; because ongoing grants are made, funds only become available to new applicants when someone leaves the charity's list of beneficiaries. However, any new applications are kept on file.

The Ladies' Aid Society and the Eyre Charity

£8,500

Correspondent: Mrs J. Stephens, Correspondent, Headland View, 14 Court Park, Thurlestone, Kingsbridge, Devon TQ7 3LX (01548 560891; email: joycestephens@onetel.com)

CC number: 202137

Eligibility

Widows and unmarried women in need who live, or have lived, in Plymouth.

Types of grants

Pensions of around £100 are given quarterly to each recipient.

Annual grant total

In 2014 the charity had an income of £12,100 and a total expenditure of £9,000. We estimate that the amount of grants given to individuals totalled £8,500.

Exclusions

Women who are divorced are not eligible for grants.

Applications

Application forms are available from the correspondent. Applications should be submitted through a social worker, Citizens Advice, clergy, doctor, solicitor or similar third party. Before applying to the charity, the applicant should have obtained any statutory help they are entitled to.

Plymouth Charity Trust

£3,000

Correspondent: Samantha Easton, Trust Manager, Charity Trust Office, 41 Hele's Terrace, Prince Rock, Plymouth PL4 9LH (01752 663107; email: info@plymouthcharitytrust.org.uk)

CC number: 1076364

Eligibility

People living in the city of Plymouth who require financial assistance. In exceptional cases individuals who are otherwise qualified but reside outside the city of Plymouth, or are only temporarily resident there, may be supported at the trustees' discretion.

Types of grants

Grants are normally one-off and can be given towards a wide range of welfare needs of families with very limited income and to relieve sudden distress, sickness or infirmity. Awards range between £50 and £100 and can be given for household essentials, clothing, in Christmas gifts and so on. The trust usually makes the payment in the form of vouchers or credit at a relevant shop – payments are not made directly to the applicant.

Annual grant total

In 2014/15 the charity had assets of £2.3 million and an income of £425,000. We estimate that about £3,000 was awarded to individuals for welfare purposes.

Exclusions

Our research suggests that no grants are given to other charities, to clear debts or for any need that can be met by social services.

Applications

Application forms are available from the correspondent. Candidates should normally be referred through a third party, for example, a social worker, health professional or Citizens Advice. Applications are normally considered on the first Monday of every month.

Other information

The charity also gives grants to individuals for educational purposes and provides housing accommodation.

East Devon
Elizabeth Beaumont Charity

£4,000

Correspondent: Paula Land, Administrator, Ford Simey, 118 High Street, Honiton EX14 1JP (01404 540024; email: psl@fordsimey.co.uk)

CC number: 202065

Eligibility

People in need who live in the parish of Gittisham, Devon.

Types of grants

Quarterly pensions and Christmas bonuses.

Annual grant total

In 2014 the charity had an income of £5,400 and a total expenditure of £4,200. We estimate that the amount of grants given to individuals totalled £4,000.

Applications

Apply in writing to the correspondent at any time throughout the year. Applications can be submitted directly by the individual or through a third party such as a social worker and should include details of income and any savings.

Budleigh Salterton Nursing Association

£1,000

Correspondent: B, Tilbury, Hayes End, 1 Boucher Way, Budleigh Salterton, Devon EX9 6HQ (01395 442304; email: jenny@tilbury24.plus.com)

CC number: 204219

Eligibility

People living in the Budleigh Salterton areas (including East Budleigh and Otterton) who are in poor health, convalescent, have disabilities or are caring for sick partners.

Types of grants

One-off grants according to need. Grants have been given for medical items, wheelchairs, raised beds, Propad cushions, mattress elevators, reclining chairs, stair-lifts, audio cassettes, telephone extensions, transport costs to and from hospital and other facilities.

Annual grant total

In 2014/15 the association had an income of £2,100 and an expenditure of £1,100. We estimate that the amount of grants given to individuals totalled around £1,000.

Applications

Apply in writing to the correspondent. Applications can be submitted directly by the individual or through a social worker, Citizens Advice or other appropriate third party.

Other information

Grants may also be given to organisations.

Exmouth Welfare Trust

£8,100

Correspondent: Lynne Elson, Trustee, 23 Hazeldene Gardens, Exmouth, Devon EX8 3JA (01395 264731)

CC number: 269382

Eligibility

People living in the former urban district of Exmouth, comprising the parishes of Withycombe Raleigh and Littleham-cum-Exmouth who are convalescent, disabled, infirm or in need. A fund is available for modest awards for those setting up home on a minimal budget.

Types of grants

One-off grants and gift vouchers towards, for example, dietary needs, childcare, respite costs, safety equipment, hospital expenses, electrical goods, convalescence, clothing, travel expenses, medical equipment, furniture, disability equipment and help in the home. Cheques will be payable to charities, suppliers, service providers and official departments. Payments will not be made personally to individuals.

Annual grant total

In 2014 the trust had an income of 26,000 and a total expenditure of £12,500. Social welfare grants to individuals totalled £8,100.

Exclusions

No grants are given for rents, rates, debts and outstanding liabilities.

Applications

Application forms are available from the correspondent. They should be submitted through an independent third party (not a relative) such as a social worker, Citizens Advice, other welfare agency, or another professional or well experienced person with detailed knowledge. Applications are considered throughout the year.

Fuel Allotment Charity (formerly known as Culmstock Fuel Allotment Charity)

£2,400

Correspondent: Jennifer Sheppard, Rexmead, Culmstock, Cullompton, Devon EX15 3JX (01823 680516; email: jenny@rexmead.eclipse.co.uk)

CC number: 205327

Eligibility

People in need who live in the ancient parish of Culmstock.

Types of grants

Recurrent grants are given towards electricity and heating bills.

Annual grant total

In 2014/15 the charity had both an income and a total expenditure of £5,000. Grants are made for both social welfare and educational purposes. We estimate that welfare grants to individuals totalled £2,400.

Applications

Individuals can apply directly to the correspondent in writing.

Honiton United Charities

£5,500

Correspondent: Paula Land, Administrator, Ford Simey, 118 High Street, Honiton, Devon EX14 1JP (01404 540024; email: psl@fordsimey.co.uk)

CC number: 200900

Eligibility

People in need who live in the borough of Honiton.

Types of grants

One-off and recurrent grants ranging from £50 to £100. Pensions are paid quarterly.

Annual grant total

In 2014 the charity had an income of £11,500 and a total expenditure of £11,600. We estimate that the amount of grants given to individuals totalled £5,500, with organisations also receiving funding.

Exclusions

No grants are given to people living outside the beneficial area or for funding a gap year.

Applications

Apply in writing to the correspondent including details of income and savings. Applications can be submitted directly by the individual or through a social worker, Citizens Advice or other welfare agency, and are considered throughout the year.

Sidmouth Consolidated Charities

£13,200

Correspondent: Ruth Rose, Correspondent, 22 Alexandria Road, Sidmouth, Devon EX10 9HB (01395 513079; email: ruth.rose@eclipse.co.uk)

CC number: 207081

Eligibility

People in need who live in Sidmouth, Sidford, Sidbury or Salcombe Regis.

Types of grants

Our research suggests that one-off grants of up to £1,000 are available towards, for example, new cookers, washing machines and stair-lifts, and to help with travel expenses to visit someone in hospital.

Annual grant total

In 2014 the charity had assets of £1.25 million, almost all of which was permanent endowment and unavailable for distribution. The charity's income was £36,500 and a total of £30,000 was spent in awarding grants, which consisted of 'housing needs based' (£23,000) and 'other local needs' (£6,800). No other details were given; we estimate that the amount of grants given to individuals for social welfare purposes totalled around £13,200.

Applications

Applications may be made in writing to the correspondent, either directly by the individual or through a social worker, Citizens Advice or welfare agency. Applications are considered at monthly meetings.

Other information

The charity supports both organisations and individuals for social welfare and educational needs.

The charity's record on the Charity Commission's website notes that 'the objects of the John Arthur & William Slade branch are the relief of poverty, need or other hardship for beneficiaries over the age of 60 years who are resident in the area'.

Mid Devon

Charity of Edward Blagdon

£7,000

Correspondent: Adrian Richfield, Correspondent, 29 Lime Tree Mead, Tiverton, Devon EX16 4PX (01884 258595)

CC number: 244676

Eligibility

People in need who live in Tiverton and Washfield in Devon.

Types of grants

One-off grants only, ranging from £10 to £500. Grants may be given in monetary form directly to the individual, or through payment for the provision of suitable services/facilities.

Annual grant total

In 2013/14 the charity had an income of £19,300 and a total expenditure of £7,600. We estimate that the amount of grants given to individuals totalled £7,000.

Applications

Apply in writing to the correspondent directly by the individual or through a social worker, Citizens Advice or other welfare agency.

Crediton United Charities

£2,000 (15 grants)

Correspondent: Mike Armstrong, Clerk, 5 Parr House, Lennard Road, Crediton EX17 2AP (01363 776529)

CC number: 247038

Eligibility

People in need who have been resident in Crediton town and the parish of Crediton Hamlets for at least 12 months.

Types of grants

One-off grants of up to £300 towards, for example, nursery school costs, travel expenses, second-hand furniture, medical equipment, food, hospital expenses, electrical goods, household bills and disability equipment. 'General benefit tickets' of £5 each to buy food in local shops are also available from local health visitors.

The charity purchases goods and services from suppliers on behalf of beneficiaries whenever possible. Individuals generally do not receive payments directly.

Annual grant total

In 2013/14 the charity had an income £13,000 and a total expenditure of

£7,300. The sum of £2,000 was awarded in grants to 15 individuals. 'General benefit tickets' were reimbursed to local traders totalling £20.

A further 4 grants were made to local organisations, amounting to £2,200.

Exclusions

Grants are not given towards house improvements or to repay existing debts.

Applications

Application forms are available from the correspondent. Applications can be submitted directly by the individual, or through a third party such as a social worker. Applications are considered on the first working Monday of every month and should be submitted before the end of the previous month. 'A supplementary letter is always useful.'

Other information

Crediton United Charities consists of the Crediton Relief in Need Charity, through which grants are made to individuals and organisations, and the Charity of Humphrey Spurway, which owns almshouses in the form of four flats and four bungalows.

The Heathcoat Trust

£404,500

Correspondent: Mrs C. Twose, Secretary, The Factory, Tiverton, Devon EX16 5LL (email: heathcoattrust@ heathcoat.co.uk)

CC number: 203367

Eligibility

People who are older, in poor health or financial need and live in Tiverton and the mid-Devon area. Applicants need to have a personal connection with either the John Heathcoat or the Lowman Companies.

Types of grants

One-off and recurrent grants are given according to need.

Annual grant total

In 2013/14 the trust had assets of £19.8 million and an income £563,000. Grants totalled £732,000, and included grants to organisations totalling £160,000, and grants to individuals for educational purposes totalling £167,500. Social welfare grants to individuals were distributed as follows:

Consolidated grant	£279,000
Death grants	£63,500
Hospital visiting	£30,500
Chiropody	£20,500
Communication grant	£3,900
In cases of hardship	£3,900
Employees in case of sickness	£3,100

Applications

Apply in writing to the correspondent.

Sandford Relief-in-Need Charity

£5,000

Correspondent: Mrs H. Edworthy, Administrator, 7 Snows Estate, Sandford, Crediton, Devon EX17 4NJ (01363 772550; email: chris@cctheedom.co.uk)

CC number: 235981

Eligibility

People in need who live in Sandford parish. Support is mostly given to pensioners.

Types of grants

One-off grants usually between £10 and £50 towards repair of household utility items, bereavement expenses, fuel bills, also recurrent grants of £12 a month (to about 30 households). Christmas vouchers of £25 are also available.

Annual grant total

In 2014 the charity had an income of £5,300 and an expenditure of £5,200. We estimate that the amount of grants given to individuals totalled £5,000.

Applications

Application forms can be requested from the correspondent. They can be submitted either directly by the individual or through a social worker, Citizens Advice, or other welfare agency. The trustees usually meet in March, September and November, but awards may also be considered outside these times.

Silverton Parochial Charity

£8,100

Correspondent: Michelle Valance, Secretary to the Trustees, 9 Davis Close, Silverton, Devon EX5 4DL (01392 860408; email: secretary@silverton parochialtrust.co.uk; website: www. silvertonparochialtrust.co.uk)

CC number: 201255

Eligibility

People in need who live in the parish of Silverton only.

Types of grants

One-off grants, with no minimum or maximum limit. Awards are towards anything that will help relieve hardship or need, such as alarms for people who are infirm, stair-lifts, domestic replacements, furniture and carpets, hospital travel costs, heating costs, medical equipment, children's clothing and wheelchairs.

Annual grant total

In 2014 the charity had an income of £38,000 and paid grants in aid to individuals and community projects totalling £32,500. We estimate that the amount of grants given to individuals for social welfare purposes totalled around £8,100.

Exclusions

The charity only supports needs that are not provided for by the state schemes such as state benefit programmes. Grants are not normally made towards state or local authority taxes.

Applications

Application forms are available to download from the website and should be returned to the correspondent or the trustees. The forms can also be obtained from the correspondent, Silverton Post Office. The trustees will need details of the applicant's financial situation (including the income and outgoings) as well as any additional information that may assist the application. The trustees meet eight times a year.

Other information

Grants are also made to organisations providing assistance for people in need who live in the parish and may be made for educational needs. The charity has an informative website.

North Devon

Bridge Trust

£3,000

Correspondent: Peter Laurie, Chamberlain, The Bridge Trust, 7 Bridge Chambers, The Strand, Barnstaple EX31 1HB (01271 343995; email: chamberlain@barumbridgetrust.org; website: www.barumbridgetrust.org)

CC number: 201288

Eligibility

People who live in the borough of Barnstaple, Devon, with a preference for people who have disabilities, older and young people. Area of benefit extends within five-mile radius of the Guild Hall at Barnstaple.

Types of grants

Individuals are eligible for Samaritan Grants (emergency grants of up to £400) towards furniture or domestic appliances and Support or Development Grants (for example, towards attendance of a competition, voluntary work, sports, special educational needs or skills development).

Annual grant total

In 2014 the trust had assets of £4.9 million and an income of £346,000.

Most of the charitable expenditure is allocated to organisations. We estimate that around £3,000 a year is available for individuals through The Samaritan Fund.

Exclusions

Recurrent grants are not given.

Applications

Apply in writing to the correspondent. Applications must be made via a third party, such as social worker, Citizens Advice or other welfare agency at any time. Applications should provide full contact information (including telephone and email), amount required, the purpose for which it is to be used and any additional supporting information. Payments are normally made to organisations or the supplier of items/services, not the applicant.

All applications for Support or Development Grants must be supported in writing by the sponsor (such as a school/college or health professional).

Other information

The trust's main priority is the maintenance of 24 properties in Barnstaple and making grants to local organisations.

South Hams

Brixton Feoffee Trust

£5,600

Correspondent: Sally Axell, Clerk, 15 Cherry Tree Drive, Brixton, Plymouth PL8 2DD (01752 880262; email: brixtonfeoffeetrust@googlemail.com; website: www.brixton-village.co.uk/feoffee.htm)

CC number: 203604

Eligibility

People in need who live in the parish of Brixton, near Plymouth.

Types of grants

One-off and recurrent grants are given according to need. Recent grants have been given for disability aids, essential household items, school travel costs, independent living alarms and assistance with rent payments.

Annual grant total

In 2014/15 the trust had assets of £1.3 million and an income of £36,500. Grants were made totalling £24,800, of which £6,400 was given to individuals, £11,700 to St Mary's Church and £6,600 to local organisations and initiatives.

Exclusions

The charity cannot give grants where the funds can be obtained from state sources.

Applications

Apply on a form available from the correspondent or to download from the charity's website. Applications can be submitted directly by the individual or through a social worker, Citizens Advice or other welfare agency or third party. They are considered throughout the year.

Other information

The trust's scheme states that its net income should be shared equally between people in need in the parish of Brixton and a local church, St Mary's in Brixton, for its upkeep and maintenance. If any of the allotted money is unspent at the end of the financial year it is transferred to a third fund which is distributed to charitable schemes that benefit Brixton parish as a whole. The charity also funds a car scheme which provides transport to those in need in the area.

The Dodbrooke Parish Charity (Dodbrooke Feoffees)

£12,500

Correspondent: Jane Balhatchet, Correspondent, Springfield House, Ashleigh Road, Kingsbridge, Devon TQ7 1HB (01548 854321)

CC number: 800214

Eligibility

People in need who live in the parishes of Dodbrooke and Kingsbridge.

Types of grants

One-off grants and pensions to older people.

Annual grant total

In 2014 the charity had an income of £22,000 and a total expenditure of £27,500. We estimate the annual total amount of grants given to individuals to be around £12,500.

Applications

Apply in writing to the correspondent. Applications are normally considered in January, March, June and September.

Other information

The charity also makes grants to organisations, supports the parish church and rents property to local residents.

Parish Lands (South Brent Feoffees)

£11,800

Correspondent: John Blackler, Clerk, Luscombe Maye, 6 Fore Street, South Brent TQ10 9BQ (01364 646180; email: southbrent@luscombemaye.com)

CC number: 255283

Eligibility

Individuals who live or have lived in the parish of South Brent.

Types of grants

One-off or recurrent grants and Christmas gifts. Awards are generally in the range of £50–£300 and can be for a variety of needs, including hospital transport/travel costs and special treatment where the family is in desperate need of help.

Annual grant total

In 2014 the charity had assets of around £67,500 and an income of £55,000. A total of £35,500 was given in grants. We estimate that welfare support to individuals totalled around 11,800.

Applications

Application forms can be requested from the correspondent. They can be submitted at any time either directly by the individual or through a third party, such as a family member, social worker, teacher, or an organisation, for example Citizens Advice or school.

Other information

Grants are also given to organisations and for educational purposes. The trustee's annual report further specifies that one third of the income of the charity is to be applied for upkeep of the parish church, one third for the benefit of deserving people in need living in the parish and one third to form the endowment of the Parish Lands Educational Foundation (to support the education and advancement in life of the parish children).

The Saint Petrox Trust Lands

£4,000

Correspondent: Hilary Bastone, Clerk/Treasurer, 30 Rosemary Gardens, Paignton, Devon TQ3 3NP (01803 666322; fax: 01803 666322; email: hilarybastone@hotmail.co.uk)

CC number: 230593

Eligibility

People in need who live in the parish of Dartmouth and particularly within the ancient parish of St Petrox.

Types of grants

One-off grants of £100 to £500, to people affected by hardship through illness, homelessness, hospitalisation and so on for items including electrical goods, hospital expenses, household bills, travel expenses, medical equipment and furniture.

Annual grant total

In 2013/14 the charity had an income of £62,000 and an expenditure of £63,000. The charity's accounts had been received at the Charity Commission but not published. Grants for social welfare purposes are generally in the region of £4,000.

Exclusions

Recurring grants are not made.

Applications

Apply in writing to the correspondent either directly by the individual or through a social worker, Citizens Advice, other welfare agency, or other third party on behalf of the individual. Applications should include details on the purpose of grant, proof of need and estimates of costs. They are considered in January, April, July and October.

Other information

The trustees recently stated that they would like to support more individuals in need. They have therefore widened the charity's beneficial area to cover the whole of the Parish of Dartmouth. Grants are also given towards the upkeep of ancient buildings within the ancient parish of St Petrox (Ancient Buildings Scheme).

Reverend Duke Yonge Charity

£3,800

Correspondent: Janet Milligan, 8 Chipple Park, Lutton, Ivybridge PL21 9TA

CC number: 202835

Eligibility

People in need who live in the parish of Cornwood.

Types of grants

One-off and recurrent grants are given according to need. In the past, grants have been given to help with playgroup attendance fees, a sit-in shower facility, a support chair and winter heating costs.

Annual grant total

In 2014 the charity had an income of £15,800 and a total expenditure of £15,600. Grants are made to individuals and organisations for both social welfare and educational purposes. We estimate

that social welfare grants to individuals totalled £3,800.

Applications

Apply in writing to the correspondent via the trustees, who are expected to make themselves aware of any need. Applications are considered at trustees' meetings.

Torbay
Paignton Parish Charity

£5,700

Correspondent: Revd Roger Carlton The Revd Prebendary, Trustee, The Vicarage, Palace Place, Paignton, Devon TQ3 3AQ (01803 551866; email: secretary@paigntonparishchurch.co.uk)

CC number: 240509

Eligibility

Individuals who are in need and are long-term residents of Paignton. In exceptional circumstances the trustees may decide to assist somebody who is resident outside Paignton.

Types of grants

Cash payments, usually of £50 to £60, are given twice a year for use as the recipient wishes.

Annual grant total

In 2013/14 the charity had an income of £9,700 and a total expenditure of £11,700. We estimate that the amount of grants given to individuals totalled £5,700, with funding also awarded to organisations.

Exclusions

Payments are not made towards living expenses.

Applications

Application forms are available from the correspondent. Applications are considered in May and November and should be submitted by the end of April and October respectively. They should include the applicant's age and length of residency in Paignton.

The Annie Toll Bequest

£2,000 (7+ grants)

Correspondent: Simon Brookman, Correspondent, Jacks Lane, Torquay, Devon TQ2 8QX (01803 327256; email: brookersstill@live.co.uk)

CC number: 201197

Eligibility

Older women who live in Torquay and are in need, suffer from ill health or other hardship. Preference is given to

women resident in the ecclesiastical parish of St George and St Mary.

Types of grants

Recurrent grants of £400 a year and small, one-off payments for special needs, services or items, ranging from £100 to £300. Our research suggests that awards may be given towards the hire costs of equipment, for example a television.

Annual grant total

In 2014 the charity had an income of £3,400 and an expenditure of £2,000. We estimate that grants totalled around £1,800. The charity states that currently seven individuals are receiving annual payments.

Applications

Apply in writing to the correspondent. Applications can be made directly by the individual or through a third party, such as a social worker, Citizens Advice or other welfare agency, if applicable.

Torridge
Bideford Bridge Trust

£47,000

Correspondent: P. Sims, Steward, 24 Bridgeland Street, Bideford, Devon EX39 2QB (01237 473122)

CC number: 204536

Eligibility

People in need who live in Bideford, Devon and the immediate neighbourhood.

Types of grants

One-off grants usually ranging from £150 to £500. The charity also administers the Torridge Taxi Voucher Scheme, which assists with the travel needs of people who are older or who are ill.

Annual grant total

In 2014 the charity had assets of £15.2 million and an income of £766,000. During the year, £32,000 was paid in social welfare grants to individuals. An additional £15,000 was paid through the Torridge Taxi Voucher Scheme.

Exclusions

Applications from individuals in Barnstaple, Torrington and the areas beyond this are not accepted.

Applications

Application forms are available from the correspondent. Applications should be submitted at any time during the year by the individual, although a sponsor is usually required.

Great Torrington Town and Lands Charity

£63,500

Correspondent: Ian Newman, Steward, 25 South Street, Great Torrington, Devon EX38 8AA (01805 623517; email: greattorringtoncharities@btconnect.com)

CC number: 202801

Eligibility

People in need who live in Great Torrington.

Types of grants

Usually one-off grants according to need. Individual grants are generally up to £200, although may reach up to £400 in extreme cases.

Christmas vouchers are made to residents of Great Torrington who qualify under certain criteria to be used only in local shops. The vouchers are of £15 to each resident.

Annual grant total

In 2013/14 the charity had assets of around £6.2 million and an income of £258,500. The total amount spent on charitable activities for this charity totalled about £453,500, which included £44,500 in the maintenance of its almshouses. Grants were made totalling £374,000; however, unlike in the past, further breakdown was not given. In previous years support to 'sick and aged' has reached on average around 7% of the overall grant total. We estimate grants to individuals for welfare purposes to be around £63,500.

Christmas vouchers totalled £9,600 in the year.

Exclusions

Needs that should be addressed by statutory sources are not funded. The charity cannot make recurrent grants.

Applications

Applications should be made in writing to the correspondent, providing all the relevant personal information.

Other information

The charity is concerned with the provision of almshouse accommodation and affordable rented housing. Grants are provided for organisations with various purposes, local churches, pensioners and other people in need.

West Devon

The Brownsdon and Tremayne Estate Charity (also known as the Nicholas Watts' Gift)

£9,000

Correspondent: Joan Stewart, Correspondent, 17 Chapel Street, Tavistock, Devon PL19 8DX (email: rec-tv@francisclark.co.uk)

CC number: 203271

Eligibility

For the Brownsdon Fund, men in need who live in Devon, with a preference for Tavistock applicants, preferably owner/occupiers. For the Tremayne Estate Charity, people in need who live in Tavistock.

Types of grants

One-off grants of around £300. In addition to general relief in need, the trustees help towards the maintenance of homes owned by beneficiaries, for example, providing new carpets, grants towards the costs of roof repairs and occasionally supplying computers to people with disabilities.

Annual grant total

In 2013/14 the charity had an income of £21,000 and a total expenditure of £9,500. We estimate that the amount of grants given to individuals totalled £9,000.

Exclusions

The charity does not assist with mortgage repayments.

Applications

Application forms are available from the correspondent. The trustees mainly advertise for applications in July, to be considered in September, but will also consider applications for emergencies at other times. Applications can be submitted directly by the individual.

Other information

The charity is known as Nicholas Watts' Gift and is made up of two different funds: the Brownsdon Fund and the Tremayne Estate Charity.

Dorset

Cole Anderson Charitable Foundation

£3,300

Correspondent: Martin Davies, Rawlins Davy, Rowlands House, Hinton Road, Bournemouth BH1 2EG (01202 558844; email: martin.davies@rawlinsdavy.com)

CC number: 1107619

Eligibility

People in need who live in Bournemouth and Poole.

Types of grants

Grants are made to provide or pay for services or facilities which will help to relieve hardship.

Annual grant total

In 2013/14 the foundation had an income of £10,000 and a total expenditure of £6,700. Grants are made to individuals for both social welfare and educational purposes. We estimate that social welfare grants to individuals totalled £3,300.

Applications

Apply in writing to the correspondent.

The MacDougall Trust

£14,500

Correspondent: Diana Ginever, Administrator, 96 Scarf Road, Poole, Dorset BH17 8QL (01202676961; email: macdougalltrust@gmail.com; website: www.macdougalltrust.com)

CC number: 209743

Eligibility

People in need who live in Dorset.

Types of grants

One-off grants of up to £250 for all kinds of personal need. Only in exceptional circumstances will more than £250 be awarded, although the trust can contribute towards larger projects which will be jointly funded.

Annual grant total

In 2013/14 the trust had an income of £15,900 and a total expenditure of £15,000. We estimate that the amount of grants given to individuals totalled £14,500.

Exclusions

No grants are made for education, sponsorship, childcare, debt, people living outside Dorset or to organisations. The trust cannot consider requests for ongoing funding.

Applications

Apply on a form available from the correspondent or to download from the trust's website. Applications should be supported by a recognised agency such as Citizens Advice, a local GP, social services or a similar organisation. Forms should be returned to the administrative secretary. Applications are considered quarterly – usually in March, June, September and late November/early December – although urgent requests may be considered between meetings. For consideration at a quarterly meeting, applications should be received the month before.

Note: if the application is being made on behalf of a minor, then details of the whole family will need to be included.

St Martin's Trust

£2,000

Correspondent: The Revd David Ayton, Trustee, 201 Kinson Road, Bournemouth BH10 5HB (01202 547054; email: davidj. ayton@ntlworld.com; website: www. stmartinsbooks.co.uk)

CC number: 1065584

Eligibility

People who are in need, people who have disabilities and older people who live in Dorset.

Types of grants

One-off and recurrent grants are given according to need.

Annual grant total

In 2013/14 the trust had an income of £6,900 and a total expenditure of £8,700. We estimate that welfare grants to individuals totalled around £2,000.

Applications

Apply in writing to the correspondent. Note that the trust has previously informed us: 'Whilst we have made such grants in the past, our income has dropped significantly during the last year and we are unlikely to be able to make further grants for the foreseeable future.'

Other information

The following information is taken from the trust's website:

> St Martin's Bookshop is a charity bookshop staffed by volunteers in Bournemouth, England. St Martin's Trust is an ecumenical charity, founded in 1997 by a group of Christians who wanted to work together for the good of the local community. The funds raised from book sales are used to support local and other good causes including Michael House (a Bournemouth charity for the homeless).

Christchurch

Legate's Charity

£5,000

Correspondent: Sarah Culwick, Correspondent, 83 Brierley Road, Bournemouth BH10 6EG (01202 495273; email: sculwick@ christchurchandeastdorset.gov.uk)

CC number: 215712

Eligibility

People in need who live in the borough of Christchurch and the immediate surrounding area.

Types of grants

One-off grants for domestic items and clothes and small monthly allowances to help towards household bills. At the time of writing, allowances stand at £8 per week for individuals and £10 per week for couples.

Annual grant total

In 2014 the charity had an income of £8,500 and a total expenditure of £4,000. We estimate that social welfare grants to individuals totalled around £3,800.

Applications

Apply on a form available from the correspondent submitted either directly by the individual or through a friend, relative, social worker, Citizens Advice or other welfare agency.

Mayor's Goodwill Fund

£600

Correspondent: The Mayor's Secretary, Civic Offices, Bridge Street, Christchurch, Dorset BH23 1AZ (01202 495134; email: sroxby@ christchurchandeastdorset.gov.uk)

CC number: 263342

Eligibility

People in need who live in the borough of Christchurch.

Types of grants

One-off grants of grocery parcels, potted plants, sweets and chocolates.

Annual grant total

In 2013/14 the fund had an income of £600 and a total expenditure of £1,400. We estimate that grocery parcels, potted plants and sweets amounted to £600. Grants are also given to organisations for the provision of Christmas activities for people who are in need in the borough.

Applications

Application forms are available from the correspondent. Applications should be submitted through a social worker, Citizens Advice, other welfare agency,

friend, neighbour or clergy. Applications should include the applicant's name and address and details of their circumstances.

East Dorset

The Boveridge Charity

£2,400

Correspondent: Rosemary Hunt, Brinscombe House, Lower Blandford Road, Shaftesbury, Dorset SP7 0BG (01747 852511; email: Rosemary_ Hunt62@hotmail.com)

CC number: 231340

Eligibility

Poor people who are in need and have lived in the ancient parish of Cranborne (which includes the present parishes of Cranborne-cum-Boveridge, Wimborne St Giles, Alderholt, Verwood, Ferndown, West Parley and Edmondsham) for at least two years. People in need who live outside the beneficial area may also be supported in exceptional circumstances.

Types of grants

One-off grants ranging from £100 to £500. Small pensions are also available.

Annual grant total

In 2014/15 the charity had an income of £6,800 and an overall expenditure of £9,700. We estimate that the amount of grants given to individuals totalled £2,400, with funding also awarded to local organisations.

Applications

Apply in writing to the correspondent, submitted directly by the individual, through a third party such as a social worker or through an organisation such as Citizens Advice or other welfare agency. Applications are considered throughout the year and should contain details of the individual's annual income and capital, detail of need, age and occupation.

Brown Habgood Hall and Higden Charity

£16,000

Correspondent: Hilary Motson, Administrator, White Oaks, Colehill Lane, Colehill, Wimborne, Dorset BH21 7AN (01202 886303; email: bhhh. charity@btinternet.com)

CC number: 204101

Eligibility

Usually retired people on low income living in the ancient parish of Wimborne Minster, in Dorset

Types of grants

Mainly recurrent quarterly payments, although one-off grants are also given. Grants are not usually for more than £200, and are mainly for smaller amounts.

Annual grant total

In 2014 the charity had a total income of £16,000 and total expenditure of £17,500. We estimate that grants totalled £16,000.

Applications

Applications should be made in writing to the correspondent, either directly by the individual, through a social worker, Citizens Advice, other welfare agency or through another third party such as a doctor, health visitor or clergy. The applicant's full name, address, age and employment should be included.

North Dorset

John Foyle's Charity

£2,500

Correspondent: Simon Rutter, Administrator, Cann Field House, Cann Common, Shaftesbury, Dorset SP7 8DQ (01747 851881; email: simonrutter@ pwcr.co.uk)

CC number: 202959

Eligibility

People in need who live in the town of Shaftesbury.

Types of grants

One-off and recurrent grants and loans, including those for educational toys for people with disabilities, moving expenses, fuel, equipment, carpets and decoration. Around 15 grants a year are made ranging from £30 to £500.

Annual grant total

In 2014 the charity had an income of £5,500 and a total expenditure of £5,400. Taking into account that the charity also gives grants to organisations, we estimate that the total amount of grants awarded to individuals was approximately £2,500.

Exclusions

No grants are given for items/services that are the responsibility of the state.

Applications

Apply in writing to the correspondent. Applications can be submitted directly by the individual or through an appropriate third party and should show evidence of need, for example, benefit record, and proof of address. They can be submitted at any time, for consideration at the discretion of the trustees.

The William Williams Charity

£39,000

Correspondent: Ian Winsor, Steward, Stafford House, 10 Prince of Wales Road, Dorchester, Dorset DT1 1PW (01305 264573; email: enquires@ williamwilliams.org.uk; website: www. williamwilliams.org.uk)

CC number: 202188

Eligibility

People in need who live in the ancient parishes of Blandford Forum, Shaftesbury or Sturminster Newton.

Types of grants

Grants are usually made to help with the purchase of furnishings or white goods. The charity aims to provide goods or services directly to the applicant; it does not make cash grants.

Annual grant total

In 2014 the charity had assets of £8.2 million and an income of £422,500. Grants totalled £153,000, of which £18,500 was given to organisations. Grants to individuals amounted to £134,500, with £39,000 of this awarded for social welfare purposes.

Exclusions

Grants cannot be made to relieve debt or towards rent/mortgage arrears.

Applications

In the first instance, applicants should write, either to the correspondent or to one of the local town administrative trustees, whose names and contact details are listed on the website. Letters from social services, GPs, Citizens Advice, healthcare workers, Lifestyle or similar organisations are accepted. They should include: the applicant's name, current address, telephone number or email (if preferred); the length of residence in the relevant town (or the previous place of residence if less than a year); some information on the applicant's personal background/situation; the reason for applying; and details on the applicant's financial circumstances, including income and main expenditure and whether or not they are in receipt of benefits. Following receipt of application, the town trustee will arrange to meet with the applicant to discuss their application. Note that evidence of income will be required.

Purbeck

Corfe Castle Charities

£7,300 (57 grants)

Correspondent: Jenny Wilson, Clerk to the Trustees, The Spinney, Springbrook Close, Corfe Castle, Wareham, Dorset BH20 5HS (01929 480873; email: jennybear.wilson@virgin.net)

CC number: 1055846

Eligibility

People in need who live in the parish of Corfe Castle.

Types of grants

One-off grants or interest-free loans according to need. The charity's grant-making policy is to meet 'the needs of the disabled, sick and elderly as well as to mitigate hardship or distress'. Grants can be made for: specialist medical equipment; special furniture; Lifelines (emergency telephone links for older people and people with disabilities), including installation of a telephone line; and convalescence. The trustees will also consider applications for domestic and family expenses.

Annual grant total

In 2013/14 the charity had assets of £3.25 million and an income of £234,000. A total of 57 grants were made to individuals for social welfare purposes, amounting to £7,300.

Applications

Application forms are available from the correspondent. Applications should be submitted directly by the individual. The trustees meet monthly, but emergency requests are dealt with as they arise.

Other information

Grants are also made to individuals for educational purposes and to organisations.

West Dorset

Beaminster Relief in Need Charity

£2,700

Correspondent: John Groves, Correspondent, 24 Church Street, Beaminster, Dorset DT8 3BA (01308 862192; email: jan@hand-n-head. freeserve.co.uk)

CC number: 200685

Eligibility

Individuals in need who live in the parish of Beaminster, Dorset. Preference is given to children.

Types of grants

One-off grants in the range of £50–£1,000. The trustees will consider any application, including those for medical needs, disability and sports and recreation. About 50 grants are made each year.

Annual grant total

In 2014 the charity had an income of £13,800 and a total expenditure of £10,900. These are the highest figures in the past five years. We estimate that the total awarded to individuals for social welfare purposes was around £2,700.

Applications

Applications can be submitted in writing to the correspondent by the individual or through a recognised referral agency, such as social worker, doctor or Citizens Advice. The trustees meet throughout the year.

Other information

Grants are also made to organisations and for educational purposes.

Dorchester Relief in Need Charity

£1,000

Correspondent: Robert Potter, Trustee, 8 Mithras Close, Dorchester, Dorset DT1 2RF (01305 262041; email: robjoy1@talktalk.net)

CC number: 286570

Eligibility

People in need who live in the ecclesiastical parish of Dorchester.

Types of grants

One-off grants according to need.

Annual grant total

In 2014/15 the charity had an income of £3,200 and a total expenditure of £2,200. We estimate that the amount of grants given to individuals for social welfare purposes totalled around £1,000.

Applications

Application forms are available from the correspondent and can be submitted through a social worker, health visitor, Citizens Advice or social services.

Other information

Support may also be given for educational needs.

Gloucester-shire

The J. I. Colvile Charitable Trust

£3,000

Correspondent: John Hankey, 4 Park Lane, Appleton, Abingdon, Oxfordshire OX13 5JT (01865 862668)

CC number: 1067274

Eligibility

People in need who are resident in Gloucestershire, west Oxfordshire and south Warwickshire. Help is regularly given to ex-servicemen and their families via, for example, SSAFA.

Types of grants

One-off grants ranging from £250 to £500.

Annual grant total

In 2014 the trust had an income of £3,100 and a total expenditure of £3,200. We estimate that the amount of grants given to individuals totalled around £3,000.

Applications

Apply in writing to the correspondent. Applications can be submitted directly by the individual or family member, or by an organisation such as Citizens Advice. They are considered as necessary.

Other information

Grants are also made to youth training projects.

The Fluck Convalescent Fund

£290,000

Correspondent: Peter Sanigar, Administrator, c/o Whitemans Solicitors, Second Floor, 65 London Road, Gloucester GL1 3HT (01452 411601; fax: 01452 300922; email: info@whitemans. com)

CC number: 205315

Eligibility

Women of all ages and children under 16 who live in the city of Gloucester and its surrounding area, and are in poor health or convalescing after illness or operative treatment.

Types of grants

One-off grants between £50 and £350 for recuperative holidays, clothing, bedding, furniture, fuel, food, household equipment, domestic help, respite care and medical or other aids.

Annual grant total

In 2013/24 the fund held assets of £1.1 million and had an income of £44,000. Grants were made to individuals totalling £29,000.

Exclusions

No grants are made for the repayment of debts or for recurrent payments such as rent and rates.

Applications

Apply in writing to the correspondent through a 'responsible person' such as a social worker, medical professional or welfare organisation. Applications are considered throughout the year.

Gloucestershire Football Association – Benevolent Fund

£6,500

Correspondent: Tony Stone, Trustee, Gloucestershire Football Association Ltd, Oaklands Park Stadium, Gloucester Road, Almondsbury, Bristol BS32 4AG (01454 615888; email: info@ gloucestershirefa.com; website: www. gloucestershirefa.com/clubs-and-leagues/benevolent-fund)

CC number: 249744

Eligibility

According to the website, support is available to 'players of clubs affiliated to the Gloucestershire Football Association and in membership of the fund, and players of Representative League and county teams, who may be injured whilst playing football in a recognised match'. The fund also helps affiliated referees who are injured whilst officiating at sanctioned matches. Applicants must be unable to work normally for at least two weeks before they will be considered eligible for a grant.

Types of grants

One-off and recurrent grants according to the nature of the accident and the applicant's personal circumstances. Grants may be awarded as a lump sum or in instalments.

Annual grant total

In 2014 the fund had an income of £8,600 and a total expenditure of £6,500. We believe that grants to individuals accounted for the fund's entire expenditure.

Applications

Application forms are available from the correspondent or can be downloaded from the website. Requests must be made within 28 days of the injury unless there are exceptional circumstances. All forms must be signed, include a report by and be countersigned by a member of the Gloucestershire FA Council and provide a medical certificate.

Other information

The website notes:

> The Gloucestershire FA aims to provide 'Football for All', part of this plan includes disability football. This can be through; 'Come and Try It' events, Ability Counts County League Teams, school tournaments and the Gloucestershire FA Player Development Centre. If you are interested in attending a disability football session then the various options are shown [on the website].

Cheltenham

Cheltenham Aid-in-Sickness and Nurses Welfare Fund (Gooding Fund)

£10,500

Correspondent: Patricia Newman, Correspondent, Cheltenham Family Welfare Association, 21 Rodney Road, Cheltenham, Gloucestershire GL50 1HX (01242 522180; email: pat.cfwa@ btconnect.com; website: www. cheltenhamfamilywelfare.co.uk)

CC number: 205340

Eligibility

People in need who are engaged in domiciliary nursing in the Cheltenham area, or retired nurses who were so engaged. Grants may also be made to individuals and families who are in financial need due to illness.

Types of grants

One-off and recurrent grants to those in need.

Annual grant total

In 2014/15 the fund had an income of £18,500 and a total expenditure of £11,200. We estimate that the amount of grants given to individuals totalled £10,500.

Applications

Applications should be made on a form available from the correspondent. Applications should be submitted through a third party such as a health visitor, social worker or Citizens Advice.

The Prestbury Charity (Prestbury United Charities)

£2,000

Correspondent: Brian Wood, Clerk, 2 Honeysuckle Close, Prestbury, Cheltenham, Gloucestershire GL52 5LN (01242 515941; email: puc.clerk@ prestbury.net; website: www.prestbury. net/puc)

CC number: 202655

Eligibility

People in need who live in the ecclesiastical parish of Prestbury and the adjoining parishes of Southam and Swindon village or immediately adjoining areas (most of north Cheltenham).

Types of grants

One-off grants according to need. Previously support has been given towards: heating costs for a person with disabilities; security lights for an elderly person; repairs and decorating costs; and assistance for single parent families.

Annual grant total

In 2014 the charity had an income of £21,500 and an expenditure of £4,100. We estimate that around £2,000 was made in grants to individuals with grants also made to local organisations.

Applications

Application forms are available to download from the charity's website and should be printed and returned directly to the clerk. Applications can be made directly by the individual or via a third party, such as a social worker, Citizens Advice or other welfare agency. Candidates should provide their home address, so that the charity can see that they live in the area of benefit.

Other information

Local organisations, groups and societies are also supported. The charity has an almshouse branch responsible for providing accommodation to those in need.

City of Gloucester

Barnwood House Trust

£286,000 (755 grants)

Correspondent: Gail Rodway, Grants Manager, Ullenwood Manor Farm, Ullenwood, Cheltenham, Gloucestershire GL53 9QT (01452 611292; fax: 01452 634011; email: gail.rodway@ barnwoodtrust.org; website: www. barnwoodtrust.org)

CC number: 218401

Eligibility

People in need who live in Gloucestershire, have a long-term mental or physical disability that affects their quality of life, are on a low income and have little or no savings. Applicants are expected to seek statutory support first.

Types of grants

Wellbeing Fund

One-off grants ranging from £50 to £750 to enable applicants to live independently. Support can be given for purchase of domestic appliances, holidays, personal items, home repairs and adaptations, disability-related equipment, mobility aids, respite care breaks, holidays, computers, clothes, selected bills and so on.

Annual grant total

In 2014 the trust had assets of £85.1 million and an income of £3.28 million. Grants were made totalling £557,000, which consisted of £237,000 given to organisations and £340,500 provided to 821 individuals. A total of 755 people were assisted through the Wellbeing Fund totalling £286,000.

Exclusions

Grants are not usually made for:

- Funeral costs
- Medical equipment
- Private healthcare (for example, assessment, treatment or medication)
- Counselling or psychotherapy
- Top-up nursing home fees
- Private education or university tuition fees
- Council tax
- Court fines
- House purchase, rent deposits or rent in advance
- Regular payments to supplement income
- The needs of non-disabled dependants or carers
- Retrospective requests
- Appeals from people living outside Gloucestershire
- People with problems relating to drugs and alcohol – unless they also have physical disabilities or a diagnosed mental illness

Applications

Application forms can be downloaded from the trust's website or requested from the correspondent. All applications should be made through, or endorsed by, a social or healthcare professional (an occupational therapist, social worker, health visitor, district nurse or community psychiatric nurse). Wherever possible, the trust will visit applicants at home to discuss their needs in greater detail. The trust aims to provide an answer within ten working days of the home visit.

Other information

Small grants (up to £1,000) are made to local organisations with similar aims (£62,000 in 2014). The trust is also engaged in providing housing accommodation. The Small Sparks grants are offered to 'small groups of people throughout Gloucestershire to get together to do something they enjoy and make a difference to where they live' (66 grants totalling over £16,000 awarded in 2014).

The trust's website specifies that the Opportunities Award offers individuals 'the chance to try something new that will enable them to move on to employment, volunteering or give them the ability to help others'.

United Charity of Palling Burgess and Others

£1,200

Correspondent: Margaret Churchill, Administrator, 30 Gambier Parry Gardens, Gloucester GL2 9RD (01452 421304; email: nikkiarthy@btinternet. com)

CC number: 236440

Eligibility

People in need who live in the Gloucester city council administrative area, including people with disabilities, children and young people, and the elderly.

Types of grants

One-off cash grants and grants in kind up to a maximum value of £250.

Annual grant total

In 2013/14 the charity had an income of £1,900 and a total expenditure of £2,400. We estimate that half of the award is given to individuals for general charitable purposes (£1,200) and the other half for educational purposes.

Applications

Apply in writing to the correspondent. Applications should be submitted through a social worker, nurse, health visitor, minister of religion or similar third party and are considered twice a year in March and October. Applications should be submitted by the end of February and September respectively.

South Gloucestershire

Almondsbury Charity

£3,100

Correspondent: Peter Orford, Secretary, Shepperdine Road, Oldbury Naite, Oldbury-on-Severn, Bristol BS35 1RJ (01454 415346; email: peter.orford@ gmail.com; website: www. almondsburycharity.org.uk)

CC number: 202263

Eligibility

Individuals who are in need and have lived in Almondsbury, Bradley Stoke North, Easter Compton, Patchway or parts of Pilning for at least one year.

Types of grants

One-off grants according to need, for instance for household appliances.

Annual grant total

In 2013/14 the charity had assets of £2.3 million and an income of £69,500. Grants totalled £56,000 and were mainly made to organisations. We were able to establish that the amount of grants given to 18 individuals from the Education and Relief Fund amounted to £6,200, but we were unable to determine how they were distributed.

Exclusions

Grants are not given towards fuel bills.

Applications

Applications can be made using the appropriate form. Forms are available to download from the charity's website and should be completed and returned to the correspondent along with any other relevant information. The charity does not make cash awards.

The Chipping Sodbury Town Lands

£9,700 (137+ grants)

Correspondent: Nicola Gideon, Clerk, Town Hall, 57–59 Broad Street, Chipping Sodbury, Bristol BS37 6AD (01454 852223; email: nicola.gideon@ chippingsodburytownhall.co.uk; website: www.chippingsodburytownhall.co.uk)

CC number: 236364

Eligibility

People in need who live in the parish of Sodbury.

Types of grants

One-off and recurrent grants are given according to need. Grants to help with winter heating bills, as well as for equipment for a variety of activities.

Annual grant total

In 2014 the charity had assets of £9 million and an income of £360,500. Grants totalled £92,000, £24,500 of which was given to individuals for both social welfare and educational purposes. Social welfare grants totalled £9,700.

Applications

Apply in writing to the correspondent.

Other information

Grants are also made to schools, clubs and other organisations in the area of benefit.

Thornbury Consolidated Charities (administered by Thornbury Town Trust)

£12,100

Correspondent: Amanda Powell, Clerk, Cliff Farm, Passage Road, Aust, Bristol BS35 4BG (01454 631169; email: amandatowntrust1@talktalk.net)

CC number: 238273

Eligibility

People in need who live in the parish of Thornbury. Beneficiaries are often of pensionable age or disabled but anyone in the parish can apply.

Types of grants

One-off grants of £110 (at the time of writing) to help with the extra expense of Christmas, as well as one-off grants given at other times.

Annual grant total

In 2014 the charities had assets of £894,500 and an income of £42,000. Gifts to individuals totalled £14,100, of which we estimate around £12,100 was given solely for welfare purposes.

A further £6,400 was given to local organisations.

Exclusions

Grants are not given where the need is covered by statutory authorities.

Applications

Apply in writing to the correspondent. Applications can be submitted directly by the individual or through a social worker, Citizens Advice or other welfare agency and should include details of income. They are considered in November for Christmas but applications for special needs can be made at any time.

Other information

The charities also own almshouses.

Stroud

The Ancient Charity of the Parish of Bisley

£3,500

Correspondent: Jane Bentley, Secretary, The Old Post Office, High Street, Bisley, Stroud GL6 7AA (01452 770756; email: bisleycharity.capb@gmail.com)

CC number: 237229

Eligibility
People in need who live in the ancient parish of Bisley.

Types of grants
One-off grants according to need. Grants have included gifts of money to people who are sick and convalescing and have been awarded towards, for example, the costs of hospital visits, help with residential care and the support of young people pursuing work experience.

Annual grant total
In 2013/14 the charity had an income of £9,500 and a total expenditure of £7,600. We estimate that the amount of grants given to individuals totalled £3,500, with organisations also receiving funding.

Exclusions
No grants are given towards the relief of rates or taxes. No recurrent gifts.

Applications
Apply in writing to the correspondent.

Tewkesbury

The Gyles Geest Charity

£8,000

Correspondent: Mrs M. Simmonds, Correspondent, 10 Troughton Place, Tewkesbury GL20 8EA (01684 850697; email: mandnksimmonds@talktalk.net)

CC number: 239372

Eligibility
People in need who live in the borough of Tewkesbury.

Types of grants
Grants usually average around £30 per household and are given as vouchers for use in local shops.

Annual grant total
In 2013/14 the charity had an income of £7,900 and a total expenditure of £8,500. We estimate that the amount of grants given to individuals totalled £8,000.

Applications
Application forms are available from the correspondent and can submitted directly by the individual or through a third party.

Other information
The charity has been in existence since 1551, when Gyles Geest established a fund for the poor of Tewkesbury.

Somerset

Bath and North East Somerset

The Mayor of Bath's Relief Fund

£14,000

Correspondent: James Money-Kyrle, Director of Support Services, c/o St John's Hospital, 4–5 Chapel Court, Bath BA1 1SQ (01225 486400; email: james.money-kyrle@stjohnsbath.org.uk)

CC number: 204649

Eligibility
People in need who live in Bath.

Types of grants
One-off grants ranging from £50 to £350 for carpets, second-hand furniture and appliances, school uniforms and bills. The trust states that its key aim is to ensure that children have 'clean clothes, hot food and a warm house'.

Annual grant total
In 2014 the charity had an income of £13,600 and a total expenditure of £14,500. We estimate that the amount of grants given to individuals totalled £14,000.

Exclusions
No grants are given for tuition fees or rent arrears.

Applications
Application forms are available from local health visitors, social services or Citizens Advice. Applications should be submitted through one of these organisations or a similar third party and are considered throughout the year. **Note:** Grants are only made as a last resort for those who have already exhausted all other funding channels such as social security, social services and other local charities.

Combe Down Holiday Trust

£44,000 (213 grants)

Correspondent: The Trustees, c/o Combe Down Surgery, The Avenue, Combe Down, Bath BA2 5EG (01225 837181; email: ro@cdht.org.uk; website: www.cdht.org.uk)

CC number: 1022275

Eligibility
People who have disabilities, their families and carers, who live in the Bath and North East Somerset area.

Types of grants
One-off grants averaging around £130 towards the cost of a holiday, short break or respite care.

Annual grant total
In 2014 the trust had assets of £1 million and an income of £70,500. Holiday grants totalled £44,000 benefitting 637 people including carers, children and siblings.

Applications
Application forms are available from the correspondent. Applications should be submitted directly by the individual or through a social worker, Citizens Advice or other welfare agency.

Other information
Note, specialised accommodation is usually booked months in advance, so applicants are advised to apply as early as possible to avoid disappointment.

Ralph and Irma Sperring Charity

£28,000

Correspondent: E. Hallam, Company Secretary, Thatcher and Hallam Solicitors, Island House, Midsomer Norton, Bath BA3 2HJ (01761 414646; email: sperringcharity@gmail.com)

CC number: 1048101

Eligibility
People in need who live within a five-mile radius of the church of St John the Baptist in Midsomer Norton, Bath.

Types of grants
One-off and recurrent grants are given according to need.

Annual grant total
In 2013/14 the charity had assets of £6.2 million and an income of £218,000. Awards to local causes amounted to £111,500. The charity makes grants to both individuals and organisations although there is no stipulation as to how the income is divided. We have

estimated the amount awarded to individuals for welfare purposes to be around £28,000.

Applications
Apply in writing to the correspondent. Applications are considered quarterly.

St John's Hospital (Bath)

£160,000 (569 grants)

Correspondent: Carolyn Burgess, Individual Grants Officer, 4–5 Chapel Court, Bath BA1 1SQ (01225 486408; email: carolyn.burgess@stjohnsbath.org.uk; website: www.stjohnsbath.org.uk)

CC number: 201476

Eligibility
People who live in Bath and the surrounding area and are in need due to age, ill health, disability, financial hardship or other circumstances. There are no age restrictions.

Types of grants
Grants can be made up of several payments but generally not for more than a total of £1,500 over three years. Support can be given towards clothing, white goods, rent arrears, utility bills, food, TV licenses, furniture, bedding, carpets, bankruptcy fees or counselling. Other requests may also be considered.

Annual grant total
In 2014 the charity awarded grants to individuals totalling £160,000. 569 applications were received and 497 individuals received grants. 56 grants were awarded from the Mayor of Bath's Relief Fund, which is administered by the charity, totalling £14,500.

Exclusions
Grants are not given for:
▶ DWP loans
▶ Funeral expenses
▶ Magistrates court fines
▶ Deposits or rent in advance for accommodation
▶ Washing machines (unless there is a child in the family or there are medical grounds, in which case medical confirmation must be supplied)

Only one grant per individual/family is considered in any twelve-month period. No family or individual shall receive more than three grants within five years or up to a limit set by the trustees. The charity will not duplicate assistance available from statutory or other external agencies.

Applications
Applications can only be made through recognised local welfare agencies, such as Citizens Advice, Housing Advice Centre, health visitors, Developing Health and Independence (DHI), the Genesis Trust or others. There is an online system where applications can be made on behalf of the individual. Direct applications from those in need are not accepted.

Other information
The charity also provides almshouse accommodation for people over the age of 65 and grants to local organisations. In 2014 grants to community organisations totalled £461,000.

Mendip

Charity of John and Joseph Card (also known as Draycott Charity)

£11,000

Correspondent: Helen Dance, Administrator, Leighurst, The Street, Draycott, Cheddar, Somerset BS27 3TH (01934 742811)

CC number: 203827

Eligibility
People in need who live in the hamlet of Draycott, near Cheddar, with a preference for those who receive a pension from the charity.

Types of grants
Pensions usually range up to £500 a year and are made to people of pensionable age on low incomes (i.e. basic pensions). One-off payments range up to £250 and can be made to people of all ages, for welfare and educational purposes.

Annual grant total
In 2013/14 the charity had an income of £14,300 and a total expenditure of £14,000. We estimate that the amount of grants given to individuals totalled around £11,000.

Exclusions
No grants are given to pay normal household bills.

Applications
For pensions apply on a form available from the correspondent and for hardship grants apply in writing. Applications for pensions are considered in November and hardship grants are considered at any time. Applications can be submitted directly by the individual or by a family member.

North Somerset

Marchioness of Northampton (Wraxall Parochial Charities)

£15,000

Correspondent: Mrs A. Sissons, Clerk and Treasurer, 2 Short Way, Failand, Bristol BS8 3UF (01275 392691)

CC number: 230410

Eligibility
Residents of the parish of Wraxall and Failand, Bristol who are in need due to hardship or disability.

Types of grants
One-off grants in the range of £50–£100.

Annual grant total
In 2014 the charity had assets of £12,600, an income of £38,000 and a total expenditure of £37,500. There were 'discretionary payments' totalling £900 and 'Christmas Distribution' totalling £14,500. We take it that about £15,000 was given for social welfare purposes. The accounts state:

> Discretionary Payments were granted to the Wraxall Entertainments Committee towards the cost of an outing for local residents, to Wraxall School to allow 2 children to attend after school activities and the provision of a washing machine for a disabled resident. John Lewis Vouchers for Grocery and Clothing were issued to 66 households at Christmas to families with children of school age or under, the over 65's, widows, widowers and to two disabled residents.

Applications
Applications may be made in writing to the correspondent, directly by the individual. They are considered in February, June, September and November.

Other information
Grants are made to individuals and organisations for educational and welfare purposes.

A total of £2,900 was spent on the hire of a mini bus once a week for older residents and those with disabilities to get to shops, health centres, libraries and chemists in Nailsea.

Nailsea Community Trust Ltd

£2,100

Correspondent: Ann Tonkin, 1st Nailsea Scouts Training and Activity Centre, Clevedon Road, Nailsea, North Somerset BS48 1EH (email: info@ nailseacommunitytrust.co.uk; website: www.nailseacommunitytrust.co.uk)

CC number: 900031

Eligibility

People of any age or occupation who are in need due, for example, to hardship, disability or sickness, who live in Nailsea, Backwell, Chelvey, Tickenham or Wraxall.

Types of grants

One-off grants, usually up to £500, towards items, services or facilities.

Annual grant total

In 2013/14 the trust had an income of £7,200 and a total expenditure of £8,800. Grants are made to individuals and organisations for social welfare and educational purposes. We estimate that social welfare grants to individuals totalled £2,100.

Exclusions

Applications from outside the area of benefit will not be considered.

Applications

The trust's website states that eligible individuals, or somebody who knows of an individual who may be eligible, should contact the trust by email or in writing. Applicants may be asked for a short interview with a couple of the trustees so a fuller understanding of their situation can be established. All applications are dealt with in confidence.

The Portishead Nautical Trust

£3,900

Correspondent: Liz Knight, Secretary, 108 High Street, Portishead, Bristol BS20 6AJ (01275 847463; email: portisheadnauticaltrust@gmail.com)

CC number: 228876

Eligibility

People in need, usually under 25, who live in Portishead, North Somerset, Bristol and surrounding areas. Preference is given to people who are: homeless; unemployed; experiencing problems related to drug or solvent abuse; being ill-treated; being neglected, in the areas of physical, moral and educational well-being; or 'people who have committed criminal acts, or are in danger of doing so'.

Types of grants

Small grants and bursaries, 'where such a grant will enable a young person to realise their full potential'.

Annual grant total

In 2013/14 the trust had assets of £2 million and an income of £87,500. Grants totalled £57,000, most of which was given to a combination of local and regional organisations, with individuals receiving £7,700. We estimate that around £3,900 of this was given for welfare purposes.

Applications

Application forms are available from the correspondent. Applications must be supported by a sponsor, such as a welfare officer or health visitor. The trustees meet four times a year to consider applications.

Sedgemoor

The Nuttall Trust

£9,500

Correspondent: Nicholas Redding, Trustee, Barrington and Sons, 60 High Street, Burnham-on-Sea, Somerset TA8 1AG (01278 782371; email: nredding@barrington-sons.co.uk)

CC number: 1085196

Eligibility

People in need who live in the parishes of Brent Knoll, East Brent, Mark and Lympsham in Somerset.

Types of grants

One-off grants according to need.

Annual grant total

In 2013/14 the trust had an income of £25,000 and an expenditure of £19,700. We estimate that the amount of grants given to individuals totalled £9,500, with funding also awarded to local organisations.

Applications

Apply in writing to the correspondent. Applications can be submitted directly by the individual or via a third party.

South Somerset

The Ilchester Relief in Need and Educational Charity (IRINEC)

£3,400

Correspondent: Kaye Elston, Clerk, 15 Chilton Grove, Yeovil, Somerset BA21 4AN (01935 421208; website: www. ilchesterparishcouncil.gov.uk/ IlchesterPC/irinec-24745.aspx)

CC number: 235578

Eligibility

People in need who live in the parish of Ilchester only. Preference may be given to people over the age of 50.

Types of grants

One-off grants according to need are given for specific items or services.

Annual grant total

In 2014 the charity had assets of £502,500 (mainly as a permanent endowment) and an income of £32,500. Relief-in-need grants totalled £3,400.

Exclusions

Grants are not available where support should be received from statutory sources.

Applications

Application forms and can be requested from the correspondent and should be submitted directly by the individual. Additional information can be obtained from the correspondent. The trustees consider grants at their monthly meetings (held on the fourth Tuesday of each month). Evidence of financial need will be required.

The website states: 'Phone the clerk to talk through your needs to find out if you qualify to be considered for help by the Trustees.'

Other information

Grants are also given for educational purposes. Organisations may be supported.

Taunton Deane

The Taunton Aid in Sickness Fund

£6,200 (12 grants)

Correspondent: Lynne Durman, The Clerk, Stafford House, Blackbrook Park Avenue, Taunton, Somerset TA1 2PX (01278 661101; email: info@ tauntonaidinsicknessfund.co.uk; website: www.tauntonaidinsicknessfund.co.uk)

CC number: 260716

Eligibility

People in poor health who are in need and live within a four-mile radius of St Mary's Church, Taunton. Priority is given to those living in the former borough of Taunton and the parish of Trull.

Types of grants

One-off grants generally up to £500. Recent grants have been given towards holidays, travel costs, outings and entertainments, laundering, furniture, food for special diets, help with childcare costs, and many other benefits for those in poor health.

Annual grant total

In 2013/14 the fund held assets of £845,000 and had an income of £27,500. Grants were made to 12 individuals totalling £6,200. A further £5,200 was made in grants to organisations.

Exclusions

There can be no grant payment for council tax, other taxes, other public funds or payment of debts. Grants cannot be made on a recurring basis.

Applications

Application forms are available to download from the website. Applications should be completed and signed by a recognised referral agency such as social services or a local NHS trust. If a person needs help and is not in direct contact with any professional workers, Citizens Advice will provide help in making the claim and administering it. Applications can be made at any time.

Taunton Heritage Trust

£63,000

Correspondent: Karen White, Clerk to the Trustees, Huish Homes, Magdalene Street, Taunton, Somerset TA1 1SG (01823 335348 (Mon-Fri, 9am-12pm); email: tauntonheritagetrust@btconnect. com; website: www.tauntonheritagetrust. org.uk)

CC number: 202120

Eligibility

People who live in Taunton Deane borough and are in conditions of need, hardship or distress. Applicants should not have had an application submitted on their behalf in the previous 12 months and should be eligible for/in receipt of housing benefit or another form of low income support.

Types of grants

One-off grants for specific items, for example, furniture, white goods, equipment for babies/children, household repairs/decoration, flooring, holidays, clothing, disability aids, garden equipment, bedding, counselling, computers, etc.

Annual grant total

In 2014 the trust had assets of £5.7 million and an income of £628,500. A total of 332 grants were made amounting to £95,000, both to individuals for social welfare and educational purposes and to organisations. Grants for social welfare purposes totalled £63,000 and were given mainly for white goods, furniture and household items.

Exclusions

Grants are not given: to replace statutory support (supplementary grants may be available, however); for school trips, school bags or stationery; for retrospective applications; or for further/higher education course fees or books/materials.

Applications

Application forms can be downloaded from the trust's website. They must be completed and typed (not handwritten) by a recognised referral agency such as social services or Citizens Advice, for example. Applicants must not complete the forms themselves. Four copies of the completed form must be returned to the trust. The trust asks that, if possible, all information be included on one side of A4 (an accompanying letter should only be sent if absolutely necessary). The referral agency must check and provide details of the type and amount of benefits and/or other income that the applicant is receiving. The applicant's individual/family circumstances must also be described and the need for the grant fully explained. Specific items must be itemised and costed (more information on details to include is listed on the website).

The referral agency officer responsible for submitting the application, and for monitoring the use of any grant, must ensure that they have signed the form. Applications submitted by schools must be signed by the headteacher. If the applicant has moved home in the last 12 months, their previous address should be included. It is also essential (in order to arrange delivery of white goods) to include the applicant's correct telephone number.

Note that the trust cannot accept applications via email.

Other information

The primary role of the charity is to provide sheltered accommodation for people over the age of 60.

West Somerset

The Henry Rogers Charity (Porlock Branch)

£2,200

Correspondent: Mrs C. Corner, Administrator, Tyrol, Villes Lane, Porlock, Minehead, Somerset TA24 8NQ (01643 862645; email: dennis.corner@ talktalk.net)

CC number: 290787

Eligibility

Older people who live in Porlock.

Types of grants

One-off grants and small monthly payments.

Annual grant total

In 2014 the charity had an income of £4,500 and a total expenditure of £2,500. We estimate that social welfare grants to individuals totalled £2,200.

Applications

Application forms are available from the correspondent. Applications should be submitted directly by the individual.

Wiltshire

The Community Foundation for Wiltshire and Swindon

£71,000 (317 grants)

Correspondent: The Grants Team, Ground Floor, Sandcliff House, 21 Northgate Street, Devizes, Wiltshire SN10 1JT (01380 729284; email: info@ wscf.org.uk; website: www.wscf.org.uk)

CC number: 1123126

Eligibility

People in need living in Wiltshire and Swindon.

Types of grants

Welfare help is made through the Surviving Winter fund which offers grants of up to £200 towards, for example, paying fuel bills, purchasing oil or an oil heater, purchasing coal, topping up electricity meters, or purchasing warm slippers and a blanket. Support is mainly given for older people who spend on average 10% of their income on fuel during winter and may also be awarded to those who have a disability or are suffering extreme hardship.

The foundation's priorities are reviewed every three years by the Grants Policy Committee; therefore new or additional funds for individuals may appear in the future.

Annual grant total

In 2013/14 the foundation held assets of £17.35 million and had an income of £2.26 million. During the year a total of £800,000 was awarded in grants to 157 different groups and 391 individuals (totalling £240,000). The Surviving Winter fund awarded 348 households in fuel poverty totalling £71,000.

Applications

Applications for assistance from the Surviving Winter fund must be made through a recognised partner organisation, such as Age UK, Aster

Living, the Credit Unions and Citizens Advice who identify those who need help. For applications for grants from other funds, visit the foundation's website to complete an Expression of Interest form.

As with any community foundation, funds are likely to open and close – for the most up-to-date information on grant schemes currently operating consult the website.

Other information

The foundation also supports a number of organisations and provides educational support through its One Degree More programme aimed at individuals under the age of 25.

The community foundation is an amalgamation of two smaller trusts – the Thamesdown Community Trust and the Wiltshire Community Trust.

Wiltshire

Aldbourne Poor's Gorse Charity

£2,200

Correspondent: Terence Gilligan, Correspondent, Poor's Allotment, 9 Cook Road, Aldbourne, Marlborough, Wiltshire SN8 2EG (01672 540205; email: terrygilliganaldbourne@gmail. com)

CC number: 202958

Eligibility

People in need who live in the parish of Aldbourne, with a preference for those over 65.

Types of grants

One-off grants towards fuel costs.

Annual grant total

In 2014 the charity had an income of £2,800 and a total expenditure of £2,600. We estimate that social welfare grants to individuals totalled £2,200.

Applications

Apply in writing to the correspondent, directly by the individual, usually on the charity's invitation.

The Cecil Norman Wellesley Blair Charitable Trust

£8,000

Correspondent: Matthew Ridley, Administrator, 6 Middle Lane, Trowbridge BA14 7LG (01225 752289; email: redrum.ridley@gmail.com)

CC number: 202446

Eligibility

People in need who live in the civil parish of Trowbridge. Preference is given to those in receipt of income support, job seekers allowance or pension credit.

Types of grants

Small, one-off grants, mainly in the form of vouchers for food, fuel and clothing.

Annual grant total

In 2013/14 the trust had an income of £7,800 and a total expenditure of £8,500. We estimate that welfare grants to individuals totalled £8,000.

Applications

The trust advertises the date of distribution each year in the local press – usually the first Friday in December. It issues vouchers via two distribution points and beneficiaries must go to those points and present proof that they are in receipt of statutory benefits.

Other information

In very exceptional circumstances, when there is surplus money, grants are also available for local charitable organisations.

Charity of William Botley

£8,500

Correspondent: Clerk to the Trustees, Trinity Hospital, Trinity Street, Salisbury, Wiltshire SP1 2BD (01722 325640; email: clerk@almshouses.demon. co.uk; website: www. salisburyalmshouses.co.uk)

CC number: 268418

Eligibility

Women in need who live in the city of Salisbury.

Types of grants

One-off grants ranging from about £100 to £200, to meet all kinds of emergency and other needs which cannot be met from public funds. Recent grants have been made for second hand white goods, clothing for mothers and children, carpets and floor coverings and holiday costs.

Annual grant total

In 2014 the charity had an income of £5,800 and a total expenditure of £9,800. We estimate that around £8,500 was awarded to individuals.

Exclusions

No grants are given for the payment of debts.

Applications

Application forms are available from the Salisbury City Almshouse and Welfare Charities website. Applications are considered during the second week of every month and should be received at least two weeks prior to this. They should be submitted through a recognised professional such as a social worker.

Chippenham Borough Lands Charity

£27,000

Correspondent: The Grants Officer, Jubilee Building, 32 Market Place, Chippenham, Wiltshire SN15 3HP (01249 658180; fax: 01249 446048; email: admin@cblc.org.uk; website: www.cblc. org.uk)

CC number: 270062

Eligibility

People in need who are living within the parish of Chippenham at the date of application, and have been for a minimum of two years immediately prior to applying.

Our research suggests that people applying for mobility equipment will be asked to attend the Independent Living Centre in order for them to assess which equipment would be most appropriate.

Types of grants

One-off, and occasionally recurrent, grants and loans are made according to need. Recent grants have included help with living costs, mobility aids, domestic appliances, debt relief, travel passes, food vouchers, furniture and childcare.

Annual grant total

In 2014/15 the charity had assets of £14.6 million and an income of £452,500. Grants were given to 47 individuals totalling about £37,000. Grants are made to both individuals and organisations for educational, social welfare and other charitable purposes. Grants paid to individuals for social welfare purposes totalled around £27,000.

Exclusions

The charity is unable to help towards:
- Funding of individual sports people
- Direct funding of the local authorities
- Religious organisations (except projects with an entire community benefit)
- First degrees
- The provision of carpets
- Council tax arrears

The charity will not consider an application if a grant has been received within the past two years (or one year for mobility aids) unless the circumstances are exceptional.

Applications

Application forms should be requested from the correspondent. In the first instance get in touch with the charity via phone or email to discuss your requirements. Once received the application will be looked at in detail by the Welfare Officer, Christine Jenkins. It is possible that the charity will visit, or ask applicants to call in at this stage. Applications are considered every month and can be submitted directly by the individual or through a third party, such as Citizens Advice, social worker or GP. The trustees meet monthly.

Other information

The charity was first established in 1554 when Queen Mary granted a Royal Charter to Chippenham. She gave Crown Land to the borough and the income was to be used to pay for two members of parliament and for the upkeep of the bridge over the River Avon. A full history of the charity can be found on its informative and helpful website.

Organisations are also supported. Each of the 14 state schools within the parish is allocated a specific amount annually to enable them to provide activities and/or equipment that they would otherwise be unable to fund and for which they receive no government funding. There is also an annual award, known as the Social Fund, given to each school to help with the provision of school uniform and trips for those families on low incomes.

Note that after the changes made to the parish boundary both the Cepen Park North and Cepen Park South estates are included in the parish of Chippenham.

The Ernest and Marjorie Fudge Trust

£15,000 (17 grants)

Correspondent: Joan Biancoli, Correspondent, 12 Rock Lane, Warminster, Wiltshire BA12 7HD (email: jbiancoli@yahoo.co.uk; website: www.fudgetrust.co.uk)

CC number: 298545

Eligibility

People in need who live in Warminster and surrounding areas, with a preference for people with learning difficulties.

Types of grants

One-off and recurrent grants are given according to need. Recent grants have been made for items such as mobility scooters, stair-lifts and winter fuel payments.

Annual grant total

In 2013/14 the trust had assets of £1.36 million and an income of £49,500. A total of £47,000 was awarded to 17 individuals and 29 organisations. Grants are given for both educational and social welfare purposes. A breakdown of grants distributed was not available. We estimate that welfare grants to individuals totalled £15,000.

Applications

Applications should be made on a form available to download from the website. Applications must be countersigned by a social worker, minister of religion, solicitor or some other professional person who is independent of the applicant. If you wish to discuss your application or eligibility before submitting a form, call the trust's chairperson Fran Pearson on 01985 213440 or fill out the contact form on the website.

Other information

The trust has an informative website. Grants are also given to local organisations.

Salisbury City Almshouse and Welfare Charities

£3,600

Correspondent: Mrs S. Coen, Clerk to the Trustees, Trinity Hospital, Trinity Street, Salisbury, Wiltshire SP1 2BD (01722 325640; fax: 01722 325640; email: clerk@almshouses.demon.co.uk; website: www.salisburyalmshouses.co.uk)

CC number: 202110

Eligibility

People in need who live in the district of Salisbury. Awards are aimed at relieving a temporary hardship.

Types of grants

One-off grants of between £100 and £300 are available to meet all kinds of emergency or other needs that cannot be met from public funds. Awards can be towards, for example, essential items, such as electrical goods, heaters, school and other clothing, shoes, moving costs, beds/bedding, holidays and wheelchairs. Interest-free loans are also available.

Annual grant total

In 2014 the charity had assets of £14.4 million and an income of £1.57 million. Charitable activities totalled over £1.1 million, mainly consisting of almshouse operational costs. During the year a total of 22 welfare grants were considered and approved totalling £8,700. This included grants to both individuals (£3,600) and local organisations helping people in need in Salisbury (£5,100).

Exclusions

Grants are not made to cover debts or where equivalent support is available from the state (although statutory entitlements may be augmented in special circumstances). It is unusual for the charity to make more than one grant to an applicant in any one year. Only in exceptional circumstances will grants be made for holidays taken in consecutive years.

Applications

Application forms and full guidelines are given on the charity's website. Our research indicates that appeals are considered in the second week of each month and they should be submitted at least 15 days before. All applications must be sponsored by a recognised professional who is fully aware of statutory entitlements and is capable of giving advice/supervision in budgeting and so on.

Note the following included in the guidelines: 'The demand on all Charities is ever increasing and making any grant, which exceeds an applicant's minimum essential needs, can result in others in need receiving little or no help.'

Other information

The charity's main concern is the maintenance of almshouses – the charity owns and manages 190 almshouses at 12 sites in and around Salisbury. This mainly includes housing for older people; however, accommodation is also offered to young families, especially single parents.

Educational support is given through Salisbury City Educational and Apprenticing Charity (Charity Commission no. 309523).

Yorkshire

General

The Leonard Chamberlain Trust

£9,900

Correspondent: Alison Nicholson, Secretary, 4 Bishops Croft, Beverley, North Humberside, East Yorkshire HU17 8JY (01482 865726; email: alinicholson4@googlemail.com)

CC number: 1091018

Eligibility

Applicants must live within the area of benefit: East Riding of Yorkshire, particularly Hull and Selby.

Types of grants

In 2014 grants were given primarily to assist with the costs of heating, as well as for Lifeline alarms. One-off grants are also given according to need.

Annual grant total

In 2014 the charity had assets of £6.2 million and an income of £190,500. Grants totalled £52,000, of which £9,900 was given for the relief of hardship. These grants were distributed as follows:

Heating	£7,800
Lifeline	£1,100
Other	£1,000

Applications

Applications can be made in writing to the correspondent.

Other information

The trust's main purpose is the provision of housing for residents in the area of benefit who are in financial need and it also makes a small number of grants for religious and educational purposes.

Yorkshire Water Community Trust

See entry on page 17

East Riding of Yorkshire

The Joseph and Annie Cattle Trust

£10,500

Correspondent: Roger Waudby, Administrator, PO Box 23, Patrington, Hull HU12 0WF (01964 671742; fax: 01964 671742; email: rogerwaudby@ hotmail.co.uk; website: www. jacattletrust.co.uk)

CC number: 262011

Eligibility

Vulnerable people who live in the Hull or East Riding of Yorkshire area. Preference is given to people who are older, who have disabilities or are disadvantaged, and children who have dyslexia.

Types of grants

One-off grants, usually of £200 to £500, for needs such as travel expenses, furniture, medical and disability equipment, electric goods and help in the home.

Annual grant total

In 2013/14 the trust had assets of £8.6 million and an income of £367,000. The annual report and accounts state that £319,000 was distributed during the year, although a breakdown of individual and organisational grants was not provided. In previous years, grants to individuals for both social welfare and educational purposes have totalled around £21,000.

Exclusions

The trust cannot accept applications from, or make grants to, individuals directly. It only deals with charitable organisations or statutory authorities.

Applications

Individuals may not apply directly, but a welfare body (charitable or statutory) may apply on their behalf. Application forms can be downloaded from the website and should be printed and completed by hand before being returned to the trust by post or fax. Supporting papers should accompany the form where necessary.

Note that Hull city council agencies should not use the application form, but should instead contact Hull Advice (01482 300303).

The Hesslewood Children's Trust (Hull Seamen's and General Orphanage)

£27,000

Correspondent: Rex Booth, Secretary to the Trustees, 1 Canada Drive, Cherry Burton, Beverley, North Humberside HU17 7RQ (01946 550474; email: detaylor@duttonmoore.co.uk)

CC number: 529804

Eligibility

People under 25, who are in need and are native to, or have family connections with, the former county of Humberside or the district of Gainsborough and Caistor in Lincolnshire.

Types of grants

One-off and recurrent grants, typically up to £1,000, according to need.

Annual grant total

In 2013/14 the trust had assets of £2.8 million and an income of £88,000. Grants totalled £72,500, of which £34,000 was given to organisations. Grants to or on behalf of specific individuals amounted to £38,000, with those for social welfare purposes totalling £27,000.

Exclusions

Students who have come to the area to study are not eligible. Loans are not made.

Applications

An application form is available from the correspondent. Applications can be made either directly by the individual or through the individual's school/college/

welfare agency or another third party on their behalf. Applicants must give their own or their parental financial details, the grant required, and why parents cannot provide the money. If possible, a contact telephone number should be quoted. Applications must be accompanied by a letter from the tutor or an educational welfare officer (or from medical and social services for a disability grant). The deadlines are 16 February, 16 June and 16 September.

East Riding of Yorkshire

The Garlthorpe Charity

£5,000

Correspondent: John Burman, Correspondent, c/o Hepstonstalls Solicitors, 7–15 Gladstone Terrace, Goole, North Humberside DN14 5AH (01405 765661; email: jeff.leighton@ heptonstalls.co.uk)

CC number: 224927

Eligibility

People in need who live in the parish of Barmby on the Marsh.

Types of grants

One-off grants according to need.

Annual grant total

In 2013/14 the charity had an income of £10,400 and a total expenditure of £5,400. We estimate that the amount of grants given to individuals totalled £5,000.

Applications

Apply in writing to the correspondent.

Other information

The charity uses one sixth of its income to fund the maintenance and repair of the church in the ecclesiastical parish of St Helen, Barmby on the Marsh.

Newton on Derwent Charity

£2,500

Correspondent: The Trustees, Grays Solicitors, Duncombe Place, York YO1 7DY (01904 634771)

CC number: 529830

Eligibility

People who are sick, older or in need who live in the parish of Newton on Derwent.

Types of grants

One-off grants according to need.

Annual grant total

In 2014 the charity had an income of £11,500 and a total expenditure of £10,300. Grants are made to individuals and organisations for both social welfare and educational purposes. We estimate that social welfare grants to individuals totalled £2,500.

Applications

Apply in writing to the correspondent.

Robert Towrie's Charity

£2,500

Correspondent: Debbie Ulliot, Correspondent, The Cottage, Carlton Lane, Aldbrough, Hull HU11 4RA (01964 527255; email: roberttowerytrust@googlemail.com)

CC number: 222568

Eligibility

People in need who live in the parishes of Aldbrough and Burton Constable, especially older people and individuals with disabilities.

Types of grants

One-off and recurrent grants for food and fuel.

Annual grant total

In 2013/14 the charity had an income of £11,300 and a total expenditure of £10,100. We estimate the total amount of grants awarded to individuals for social welfare purposes to be around £2,500.

Applications

Applications may be made in writing to the correspondent, directly by the individual.

Other information

The charity also makes grants to organisations for both educational and social welfare purposes.

Hull

The Hull Aid in Sickness Trust

£16,000 (48 grants)

Correspondent: Dawn Singleton, Correspondent, 34 Thurstan Road, Beverley, Hull HU17 8LP (07835 472 512; email: info@hullaidinsickness.co.uk)

CC number: 224193

Eligibility

People in need, on a low income, who live in the city and county of Kingston upon Hull and are sick, disabled, infirm or convalescent.

Types of grants

One-off grants of £150 to £500 to aid and improve quality of life. This can include grants for electrical goods, medical and disability equipment, food and living costs and so on.

Annual grant total

In 2013/14 the trust had assets of £1.3 million and an income of £48,000. Grants were made totalling £34,000, of which £16,000 was given in grants to individuals.

Exclusions

No grants are given towards helping reduce debts or where funds are available from public funds.

Applications

Application forms are available to download from the website and can be submitted directly by the individual or through a social worker, Citizens Advice, other welfare agency or other third party. Applications must be supported by a doctor's certificate or similar. Applications should also include a quote for requested items and details of who the grant cheque should be made out to. Grant requests are considered at the trustees' quarterly meetings.

The Charity of Miss Eliza Clubley Middleton

£12,000

Correspondent: Trust Administrator, Rollits LLP, Rowntree Wharf, Navigation Road, York YO1 9WE (01904 625790; email: andy.cook@rollits.com)

CC number: 229134

Eligibility

Poor women of the Catholic faith who have lived in the Hull area for over ten years.

Types of grants

Grants are distributed twice a year, at Christmas and in the summer. The typical average value of any individual grant is less than £75.

Annual grant total

In 2013/14 the charity had an income of £4,300 and a total expenditure of £12,600. We estimate that grants totalled £12,000.

Applications

A list of current beneficiaries is circulated to all local priests each year. They then recommend any additions or note changes in circumstances.

The 'Mother Humber' Memorial Fund

£15,000

Correspondent: Malcolm Welford, Correspondent, The Hollies, Meadow View, Bainton, Driffield YO25 9NU (01377 219524)

CC number: 225082

Eligibility

People in need who live in the city of Kingston upon Hull.

Types of grants

One-off grants ranging from £50 to £500.

Annual grant total

In 2013/14 the fund held assets of £485,000 and had an income of £34,000. We estimate that the amount of grants given to individuals totalled £15,000, with funding also awarded to local organisations.

Exclusions

No grants are made for educational appeals and sponsorship e.g. of Duke of Edinburgh Award students, the payment of debts, the payment of wages or administration expenses.

Applications

Application forms are available from the correspondent and should be submitted through a social worker, Citizens Advice or other welfare agency.

The Joseph Rank Benevolent Fund

£72,000 (454 grants)

Correspondent: Debby Burman, Clerk to the Trustees, Artlink Centre, 87 Princes Avenue, Hull HU5 3QP (01482 225542; email: info@josephrankfund.org.uk; website: www.josephrankfund.org.uk)

CC number: 225318

Eligibility

Men aged 65 or over and women aged 60 or over, who are retired and have lived in Hull for at least ten of the last 15 years. If the applicant is married, their partner must also meet these age limits. Applicants should be on a low income and have no more than £6,000 in savings.

Types of grants

Recurrent grants of £30 per quarter to single people and £60 per quarter to married couples.

Annual grant total

In 2014 the fund held assets of £3.5 million and had an income of £131,500. A total of £72,000 was awarded in 454 grants; 404 of which were paid to single beneficiaries, the remaining 50 to married couples.

A further £6,000 was donated to local charities.

Applications

Application forms are available from the correspondent. Applications are considered throughout the year.

Other information

The fund's website states: 'The Joseph Rank Benevolent Fund was founded in 1934 by Joseph Rank, of flour milling fame, to help those in need in the Hull area.'

Wilmington Trust

£4,300

Correspondent: Graham Wragg, Trustee, 16 Caledonia Park, Hull HU9 1TE (01482 223050; email: lindawickins@lindawickins.karoo.co.uk)

CC number: 250765

Eligibility

People in need who live in Kingston upon Hull (east of the river Hull).

Types of grants

Our research suggests that one-off grants ranging from £50 to £100 can be provided towards various needs, including clothing, furniture, white goods and other household items, unforeseen emergencies and, particularly, for holidays benefitting the applicant's health.

Annual grant total

In 2014 the trust had an income of £4,200 and a total expenditure of £8,800. Grants are made to both individuals and organisations. We estimate that social welfare grants to individuals totalled £4,300.

Applications

Application forms are available from the correspondent. Applications must be made through Citizens Advice, social workers or members of the clergy. The trustees usually meet twice a year to consider grants, although decisions can also be made between the meetings.

North Yorkshire

The Olive and Norman Field Charity
See entry on page 323

Reverend Matthew Hutchinson Trust (Gilling and Richmond)

£3,700

Correspondent: Christine Bellas, Oak Tree View, Hutton Magna, Richmond DL11 7HQ (01833 627997; email: cbellas4516@gmail.com)

CC number: 220870/220779

Eligibility

People who are in need and live in the parishes of Gilling and Richmond in North Yorkshire.

Types of grants

One-off grants according to need. Past grants have been given towards medical care, telephone rental, a violin, running shoes and children's nursery fees.

Annual grant total

This charity has branches in both Gilling and Richmond, which are administered jointly, but have separate funding. In 2014 the combined income of the charities was £23,000 and their combined total expenditure was £15,400. Both charities make grants to individuals and organisations for social welfare and educational purposes. We estimate that social welfare grants to individuals totalled £3,700.

Applications

Apply in writing to the correspondent. Applications can be submitted directly by the individual or through a trustee, social worker, Citizens Advice or other welfare agency.

Other information

Grants are made to organisations including local schools and hospitals.

John T. Shuttleworth Ropner Memorial Fund
See entry on page 325

The Teesside Emergency Relief Fund

£3,500

Correspondent: Linda Leather, Client Case Officer, Tees Valley Community Foundation, Wallace House, Falcon Court, Preston Farm Industrial Estate, Stockton-on-Tees TS18 3TX (01642 260860; email: info@teesvalleyfoundtion. org; website: www.teesvalletfoundation. org)

CC number: 1111222–3

Eligibility

People living in Darlington, Hartlepool, Middlesbrough, Stockton on Tees and

Redcar and Cleveland who are facing a crisis.

Types of grants

Grants of up to £250 are available. The fund will provide items to ensure applicants have: something to sleep on; something to cook hot food with; something to store food and medication safely; suitable means to keep warm, dry and healthy.

Annual grant total

In 2013/14 the fund made grants of around £3,500 to individuals.

Exclusions

The fund emphasises that it does not give grants for lifestyle choices such as the desire of new furnishings when moving or non-essential items. The fund is also unable to provide carpets, curtains or other soft furnishings.

Applications

Application forms are available from the Teesside Community Foundation's website. The fund is operated as a third party grant and individuals cannot apply directly. Applications must be submitted by a support organisation which has detailed knowledge of the applicant's circumstances. Any applications for clients in the Stockton-on-Tees area *must* go through Stockton Citizens Advice otherwise applications will be returned. Applicants are considered weekly and decisions are final and cannot be appealed against.

All applications are dealt with on an individual basis, but must show evidence of which of the following circumstances are faced: crisis due to a force of nature – such as a fire or flood or other weather-related poverty such as extreme cold or heat; personal crisis – such as relationship breakdown, domestic violence or prejudice; poverty-related crisis – such as immediate loss of job or income.

Craven

The Gargrave Poor's Land Charity

£8,600

Correspondent: The Trustees, Kirk Syke, High Street, Gargrave, Skipton, North Yorkshire BD23 3RA

CC number: 225067

Eligibility

People who are in need and are permanently resident in Gargrave, Bank Newton, Coniston Cold, Flasby, Eshton or Winterburn.

Types of grants

One-off and recurrent grants for debt relief, travel to hospital, household equipment, furniture, respite care, electrical goods and essential repairs. Christmas gifts are also made each year to permanent residents who are poor, older, disadvantaged or disabled. Loans may also be given.

Annual grant total

In 2013/14 the charity had assets of £427,000 and an income of £32,500. Grants totalled £17,300 and were distributed as follows:

Educational assistance	£8,700*
Hardship relief	£5,500
Christmas distribution	£3,100

*We have not included the figure for educational assistance in the grants total.

Applications

Applications can be made on a form, which is available from the correspondent, and can be submitted at any time.

Hambleton

Bedale Welfare Charity (The Rector and Four and Twenty of Bedale)

£2,600

Correspondent: John Winkle, Correspondent, 25 Burrill Road, Bedale, North Yorkshire DL8 1ET (01677 424306; email: johnwinkle@awinkle. freeserve.co.uk)

CC number: 224035

Eligibility

People who are in need, hardship or distress and live in the parishes of Aiskew, Bedale, Burrill with Cowling, Crakehall, Firby, Langthorne and Rand Grange. Necessitous children and young people, older people suffering from illness or people with disabilities are particularly supported.

Types of grants

One-off grants, usually ranging from £40 to £500, can be given for various items and services according to need.

Annual grant total

In 2013/14 the charity had an income of £15,000 and a total expenditure of £5,500. The charitable expenditure varies each year. We estimate that about £2,600 was distributed in social welfare support to individuals.

Applications

Application forms are available from the correspondent. They can be submitted at any time either directly by the individual or through a third party, such as a social worker or teacher.

Other information

Grants are also made to organisations.

There is a separately registered charity, Bedale Educational and Bedale 750 Charity (Charity Commission no. 529517) known under same working name – The Rector and Four and Twenty of Bedale – and sharing some of the trustees, which supports educational needs. The expenditure of this charity varies annually and in the past five years has fluctuated from £0 to £2,500.

Harrogate

The Knaresborough Relief-in-Need Charity

£7,100

Correspondent: Michael Dixon, Correspondent, 9 Netheredge Drive, Knaresborough, North Yorkshire HG5 9DA (01423 863378; email: thedixongang@btinternet.com)

CC number: 226743

Eligibility

People in need who live in the parish of Knaresborough, with a preference for people who have lived there for at least five years or twenty years for a pension.

Types of grants

Pensions of £30 a year and occasional one-off grants of up to £5,000.

Annual grant total

In 2014, the charity had an income of £28,500 and a total expenditure of £34,000. Grants totalled £33,500, £26,500 of which was given to organisations. Around £7,100 was given to individuals, including pensions of around £30 each to 161 individuals, totalling £4,800, and a further £2,300 in one-off grants to three individuals.

Applications

Apply in writing to the correspondent.

Richmondshire

The Smorthwaite Charity

£3,000

Correspondent: Geoff Clarke, Trustee, Pen Cottage, Main Street, West Witton, Leyburn, North Yorkshire DL8 4LX (01969 624393)

CC number: 247681

Eligibility

Older people in need who live in West Witton.

Types of grants

Annual grants ranging from £100 to £150.

Annual grant total

In 2013/14 the charity had an income of £12,200 and a total expenditure of £11,800. We estimate that the amount of grants given to individuals totalled around £3,000.

Applications

The charity usually advertises in the local post office. Most applications tend to be submitted by word of mouth and through conversations with the trustees rather than through a formal application process.

Other information

Much of the charity's expenditure goes towards the upkeep of the rental properties it owns in the area.

Scarborough

The Scarborough Municipal Charity

£2,500

Correspondent: Elaine Greening, Flat 2, 126 Falsgrave Road, Scarborough YO12 5BE (01723 375256; email: scar.municipalcharity@yahoo.co.uk)

CC number: 2177793

Eligibility

People who have lived in the borough of Scarborough for at least five years and are in need, hardship or distress.

Our research suggests that in exceptional circumstances support may be given to someone resident outside the area of benefit or living in the borough temporarily.

Types of grants

Small, one-off grants according to need. The awards can range between £250 and £1,500 but are usually modest. Support can be given towards livings costs, specific essential items, services and travel expenses.

Annual grant total

In 2014 the charity had assets of £2.1 million and an income of £185,000. Grants are given for social welfare and educational purposes and, during the year, amounted to £4,900. We estimate that social welfare grants totalled around £2,500.

Applications

Application forms are available from the correspondent. Our research suggests that they are considered quarterly.

Other information

The trustees are responsible for both the almshouse and the relief-in-need branches of the charity. The majority of expenditure is spent in direct charitable activities maintaining the almshouses and providing services to the tenants.

York

Norman Collinson Charitable Trust

£13,400 (76 grants)

Correspondent: Dianne Hepworth, Clerk to the Trustees, Fairfield, The Mile, Pocklington, York YO42 1TW (01377 236262; website: www.normancollinsoncharitabletrust.org.uk)

CC number: 277325

Eligibility

People in need in the city of York, or from within a 20-mile radius of the city.

Types of grants

One-off grants for essential costs.

Annual grant total

In 2014 the trust had assets of £955,000 and an income of £37,000. Grants were made to both organisations and individuals, totalling £31,500. 76 grants totalling £13,400 were made to individuals and the remainder was distributed in small grants to 41 organisations.

Exclusions

Grants are not made towards rent arrears or holidays.

Applications

Applications and detailed guidance notes can be downloaded from the trust's website. Applications are considered by the trustees at monthly meetings, usually on the second Tuesday. Applications should be received by the first Tuesday for consideration in the month and will not be accepted by email. Applications should be completed by a third party, such as a social worker, Citizens Advice or voluntary organisation. Grants are not made directly to beneficiaries.

In exceptional circumstances emergency applications up to £250 can be considered outside the monthly trust meeting.

Other information

Grants are distributed through partner agencies in the local area, for example: Leeds and York PFT, City of York Council, NYCC, Ryedale Citizens Advice and Richmond Fellowship.

The Purey-Cust Trust

£2,500 (1 grant)

Correspondent: Kathryn Hodges, Secretary, 5 Grimston Park Mews, Grimston Park, Tadcaster, North Yorkshire LS24 9DB (01378 34730; email: pureycusttrust@hotmail.com; website: www.pureycrusttrust.org.uk)

CC number: 516030

Eligibility

People with medical needs who live in York and the surrounding area.

Types of grants

One-off grants ranging between £100 and £10,000 (to both individuals and organisations) for healthcare equipment, specialist medical equipment and medical education.

Annual grant total

In 2013/14 the trust had assets of £2.6 million and an income of £71,500. The total amount of grants awarded to individuals was £2,500 with the remaining grants, totalling £46,500, awarded to local organisations and City of York Council. Some of these grants were given to organisations for equipment or opportunities for the benefit of an individual.

Exclusions

The trust tries to assist with one-off grants for specific purposes rather than ongoing routine costs, such as rent, rates and salaries.

Applications

Apply on a form which is available on the trust's website. Applications may be emailed or posted. Applications must show evidence of the medical need and can be submitted directly by the individual or through a social worker, Citizens Advice, other welfare agency or third party. Applications are considered throughout the year.

The Charity of St Michael-le-Belfrey

£5,000

Correspondent: Christopher Goodway, Clerk, c/o Grays Solicitors, Duncombe Place, York YO1 7DY (01904 634771)

CC number: 222051

Eligibility

People in need who live in the parish of St Michael-le-Belfrey, York.

Types of grants

One-off and recurrent grants ranging from £50 to £500. Quarterly pensions are available to older people as well as one-off payments to relieve special needs.

Annual grant total

In 2014 the charity had an income of £8,200 and a total expenditure of £10,300. We estimate that the amount of grants given to individuals totalled £5,000, with funding also awarded to organisations.

Exclusions

No grants are given for educational purposes.

Applications

Application forms are available from the correspondent. Evidence of financial circumstances will be required. Applications can be submitted directly by the individual or through a social worker, Citizens Advice, other welfare agency or other third party.

The Charity of Jane Wright

£4,100

Correspondent: Diane Grayson, Clerk, Harland and Co., 18 St Saviourgate, York YO1 8NS (01904 655555; email: cjw@harlandsolicitors.co.uk)

CC number: 228961

Eligibility

People in need who live in the city of York.

Types of grants

One-off grants and vouchers according to need.

Annual grant total

In 2013/14 the charity held assets of £1.37 million and had an income of £64,000. 'Miscellaneous individual grants' totalled £4,100.

A further £11,100 was awarded in relief-in-need grants to York College and Blueberry Academy.

Applications

Applications must be made directly or via recognised welfare agencies. They are considered at or between trustees' meetings.

Other information

The charity was founded on 21 December 1675 by Jane Wright who was born in York. Although she lived and died as a wealthy businesswoman in Whitechapel, London, she left her estate to benefit the poor in her hometown. In the present day, the charity also manages 11 almshouse flats.

York Children's Trust

Correspondent: Margaret Brien, Administrator, 29 Whinney Lane, Harrogate HG2 9LS (01423 504765)

CC number: 222279

Eligibility

Young people under the age of 25 living within a 20-mile radius of the city of York.

Types of grants

One-off grants are given according to need where no statutory funding is available.

Annual grant total

In 2014 the trust had an income of £96,000 and a total expenditure of £91,500. At the time of writing (November 2015) the trust's annual report and accounts for the year were not yet available to view on the Charity Commission register. In the most recent year for which we have a grants figure (2012) social welfare grants to individuals totalled £10,400.

Applications

An application form is available from the correspondent. The trustees meet to consider applications four times a year. More urgent grants of up to £300 may be awarded between meetings.

Other information

The trust was established through the amalgamation of five existing charities: St Stephen's Orphanage, Blue Coat Boys' and Grey Coat Girls' Schools, The William Richard Beckwith Fund, The Charity of Reverend A.A.R. Gill and The Matthew Rymer Girls Education Fund.

Grants are also made to organisations and to individuals for educational purposes.

York Moral Welfare Charity

£1,800

Correspondent: Laura Davis, Correspondent, c/o York CVS, 15 Priory Street, York YO1 6ET (01904 621133; email: laura.davis@yorkcvs.org.uk)

CC number: 216900

Eligibility

Women and girls under the age of 50, who live in York and who are in need.

Types of grants

Generally one-off grants, between £50 and £100, to help with essential household items, fuel bills, furnishings, baby equipment and children's clothes.

Annual grant total

In 2014/15 the charity had an income of £3,600 and a total expenditure of £3,800. We estimate that the amount of grants given to individuals totalled £1,800.

Exclusions

No grants are made for education or travel costs.

Applications

Application forms are available from the correspondent. Applications should be made through a recognised agency and include details of the individual's income. They are considered on an ongoing basis.

Other information

Grants (usually up to £250) may also be made to local organisations which operate with similar aims.

South Yorkshire

Doncaster

Armthorpe Poors Estate Charity

£1,600

Correspondent: Tracey Ellis, 6 The Lings, Armthorpe, Doncaster, South Yorkshire DN3 3RH (01302 355180; email: apecharity@gmail.com)

CC number: 226123

Eligibility

People who are in need and live in Armthorpe.

Types of grants

One-off and recurrent grants, usually of £50 to £500, towards items such as mobility aids, aids for people with visual difficulties, hospital visiting and care of older people.

Annual grant total

In 2013/14 the charity had an income of £10,800 and a total expenditure of £6,800. Grants are made to individuals and organisations for a wide range of purposes. We estimate that social welfare grants to individuals totalled £1,600.

Exclusions

Applications from individuals outside Armthorpe will be declined.

Applications

Contact the clerk by telephone who will advise if a letter of application is needed.

The Cantley Poor's Land Trust

£18,700 (125 grants)

Correspondent: Margaret Jackson, Clerk to the Trustees, 30 Selhurst Crescent, Bessacarr, Doncaster, South Yorkshire DN4 6EF (01302 530566; email: margaret.jackson001@gmail.com)

CC number: 224787

Eligibility

People in need who live in the ancient parish of Cantley with Branton.

Types of grants

One-off grants ranging from £50 to £500 including those towards electric goods, clothing, medical equipment, furniture and disability equipment.

Annual grant total

In 2014/15 the trust had assets of £711,500 and an income of £310,500. 125 grants were made to individuals, totalling £18,700.

Exclusions

Restrictions apply to the relief of rates, taxes and repeat grants.

Applications

Application forms are available from the correspondent and should be submitted directly by the individual or through a welfare agency. Applications are considered on a monthly basis.

The John William Chapman Charitable Trust

£38,500

Correspondent: Rosemarie Sharp, Secretary to the Trust, QualitySolicitors Jordans, 4 Priory Place, Doncaster DN1 1BP (email: info@chapmantrust.org; website: chapmantrust.org)

CC number: 223002

Eligibility

People in need who live in the metropolitan borough of Doncaster.

Types of grants

One-off grants in kind, not cash, up to the value of £500 towards essential items including fridges, cookers, washing machines, beds, cots, carpets and clothing.

Annual grant total

In 2013/14 the trust held assets of £3.7 million and had an income of £186,500. Grants to individuals totalled £38,500, with a further £27,000 awarded to organisations.

Exclusions

No repeat grants are given. No grants are given towards wardrobes, cupboards, drawers, living room suites, TVs, Hi-Fis, video players, educational course fees, funeral expenses, external work to a property, payment of debts (including rent bonds), decorating materials, toys, removal expenses, baby high chairs or gates, structural repairs or heating in tenanted property.

Applicants are expected to have approached all statutory sources of funding available.

Applications

Apply on a form available from the correspondent or to download from the trust's website, or on the charity's online form. Applications must be accompanied by a letter from a social worker, GP or welfare agency as well as evidence of any loans or refusals from statutory services. Applicants who complete an online form must also supply documentary evidence on paper. The trust visits applicants before consideration of their application.

Note: Only one application can be accepted in any 12-month period, except in exceptional circumstances. Incomplete applications will be returned and may not be considered in the intended month's allotment.

Rotherham

The Common Lands of Rotherham Charity

£4,600

Correspondent: Ann Louise Ogley, Correspondent, Barn Cottage, 66 Moorgate Road, Rotherham, South Yorkshire S60 2AU (01709 365032; email: ann@maes-group.co.uk)

CC number: 223050

Eligibility

People in need who live in Rotherham. Preference is usually given to older people.

Types of grants

One-off and recurrent grants are given according to need.

Annual grant total

In 2014, the charity had an income of £14,700 and a total expenditure of £9,800. Taking into account that the charity also gives grants to organisations, we estimate that the total amount of grants awarded to individuals was approximately £4,600.

Applications

Apply in writing to the correspondent following advertisement in September.

The Stoddart Samaritan Fund

£13,000

Correspondent: Peter Wright, 7 Melrose Grove, Rotherham, South Yorkshire S60 3NA (01709 376448; email: charlie0358-stoddartcfund@yahoo.co.uk)

CC number: 242853

Eligibility

People in need who have medical problems and would benefit from financial assistance to help their recovery. Applicants must live in Rotherham or the surrounding area.

Types of grants

One-off grants to assist people recovering from medical problems.

Annual grant total

In 2013/14 the fund had an income of £12,900 and a total expenditure of £13,600. We estimate that the amount of grants given to individuals totalled £13,000.

Applications

Application forms are available from the correspondent and should be submitted by the applicant's doctor. Applications are considered on a regular basis.

Sheffield

Beighton Relief-in-Need Charity

£1,800

Correspondent: Diane Rodgers, Trustee, 41 Collingbourne Avenue, Sothall, Sheffield S20 2QR (email: beigtonrelief@hotmail.co.uk)

CC number: 225416

Eligibility

People in need who live in the former parish of Beighton.

Types of grants

One-off grants according to need. In the past, grants have been given towards bath-lifts and childcare seats for people with disabilities. Winter fuel grants of £15 per household were also given to older people.

Annual grant total

In 2014 the charity had an income of £10,700 and a total expenditure of £7,400. Grants are made to individuals and organisations for social welfare and educational purposes. We estimate that social welfare grants to individuals totalled £1,800.

Applications

Apply in writing to the correspondent. Applications can be submitted directly by the individual or through a social worker, Citizens Advice, other welfare agency or a third party such as a relative, neighbour or trustee.

Sir George Franklin's Pension Charity

£8,600

Correspondent: Tom Preece, Administrator, PKF, Regent House, Clinton Avenue, Nottingham NG5 1AZ (01159629240)

CC number: 224883

Eligibility

People in need aged 50 and over who live in the city of Sheffield.

Types of grants

Annual allowances of £350 paid half-yearly in June and December.

Annual grant total

In 2013/14 the charity had an income of £9,100 and a total expenditure of £8,800. We estimate that the amount of grants given to individuals totalled £8,600.

Applications

Application forms are available from the correspondent. Vacancies arise infrequently and are publicised locally. Applications should only be made in response to this publicity. Speculative applications will not be successful.

Other information

The charity is named after Sir George Franklin (1853–1916), who once served as Lord Mayor of Sheffield and Pro-Chancellor of the University of Sheffield.

Sir Samuel Osborn's Deed of Gift Relief Fund

£2,400

Correspondent: Sue Wragg, Fund Manager, South Yorkshire Community Foundation, Unit 3 – G1 Building, 6 Leeds Road, Attercliffe, Sheffield S9 3TY (0114 242 4294; fax: 0114 242 4605; email: grants@sycf.org.uk; website: www.sycf.org.uk/apply/individuals/sir-samuel-osborns-deed-gift-relief-fund)

CC number: 1140947

Eligibility

Residents of Sheffield, with some preference for those with a connection to the Samuel Osborn Company.

Types of grants

One-off grants are made ranging between £250 and £1,000 for convalescent or recuperative holidays or care, medical comforts or equipment not available through the NHS, other essential needs considered on a case by case basis.

Annual grant total

In 2013/14 the fund had an investment income of £5,500 and made grants totalling £4,900 for social welfare and educational purposes. We estimate that social welfare grants to individuals totalled £2,400.

Exclusions

Grants are not given for medical items available from the NHS or to individuals with large personal reserves of money. Individuals are limited to one grant per year.

Applications

Apply using the form, which is available to download along with guidelines, from the South Yorkshire Community Foundation's website. The foundation welcomes informal approaches about applications prior to submitting. Applicants with a connection to the Osborn company should include written evidence. The foundation aims to assess cases within 12 weeks of receiving the completed application form with all enclosures.

Other information

The fund is now administered by the South Yorkshire Community Foundation.

West Yorkshire

The Charles Brook Convalescent Fund

£12,500

Correspondent: Carol Thompson, Correspondent, Mistal Barn, Lower Castle Hill, Almondbury, Huddersfield HD4 6TA (01484 532183; email: charlesbrooke@hotmail.co.uk)

CC number: 229445

Eligibility

People who are convalescing and live within the old Huddersfield Health Authority catchment area.

Types of grants

One-off grants for special foods, medicines or appliances, household goods such as washing machines and fridges, floor coverings, cleaning services, clothing, bedding and holidays for convalescence.

Annual grant total

In 2013/14 the fund had an income of £13,300 and a total expenditure of £13,000. We estimate that the amount of grants given to individuals totalled £12,500.

Exclusions

No loans.

Applications

Apply on a form available from the social work department at Royal Infirmary, Huddersfield and St Luke's Hospital, Huddersfield. Applications must be submitted through a social worker and include details of weekly income/expenditure and family situation. Applications sent directly to the correspondent cannot be considered.

Radio Aire and Magic 828's Cash For Kids

£440,000

Correspondent: Katy Winterschladen, Regional Charity Manager, 51 Burley Road, Leeds LS1 3LR (0113 283 5555; email: katy.winterschladen@bauermedia.co.uk; website: www.radioaire.co.uk/charity)

Eligibility

Children under the age of 18 who live in Leeds and West Yorkshire, particularly those who are underprivileged, have an illness or disability.

Types of grants

One-off grants for children in need. A large part of the charity's activity is the provision of Christmas gifts to local children who might otherwise not receive anything. Grants have also been made for specialist medical equipment, surgery and therapy, mobility aids, beds and bedding, day trips, kitchen appliances and so on.

Annual grant total

In 2014 the charity raised over £1.1 million to support 64,000 local children in Leeds and West Yorkshire. This amount included a contribution of £936,000 towards the annual Christmas appeal which provided gifts to over 18,730 local children. We have estimated that grants to individuals totalled around £440,000. Grants are also made to organisations working with children.

Applications

Application forms are available from the correspondent or to download from the charity's website. Our research suggests that candidates should attach payslips or other evidence of income and bank statements for the last three months. A supporting letter from a professional such as health visitor or teacher should also be included. The trustees normally meet four times a year to consider applications and applications should be received one month before each trustee meeting, the dates of which can be confirmed by contacting the correspondent.

Other information

Grants are also made to local organisations with similar aims. Funds are not restricted but the charity has previously told us that in practice approximately 60% of funds raised are distributed to organisations and the remaining 40% distributed to individual appeals each year.

Bradford

John Ashton (including the Gift of Hannah Shaw).

£2,100

Correspondent: Ruth Richardson, Trustee, 262 Poplar Grove, Bradford, West Yorkshire BD7 4HU (01274 779455)

CC number: 233661

Eligibility

People in need who are over 65 and live alone in the Great Horton area of Bradford.

Types of grants

Small grants, according to need.

Annual grant total

In 2014, the charity had an income of £2,900 and a total expenditure of £2,300. We estimate that the total amount of grants awarded to individuals was approximately £2,100.

Applications

Application forms are available from the correspondent and should be submitted directly by the individual or through a family member for consideration in June and December.

Bowcocks Trust Fund for Keighley

£2,500

Correspondent: Alistair Docherty, 17 Farndale Road, Wilsden, Bradford BD15 0LW (01535 272657; email: wendy. docherty4@btinternet.com)

CC number: 223290

Eligibility

People in need who live in the municipal borough of Keighley as constituted on 31 March 1974.

Types of grants

One-off grants of no more than £350 are given according to need.

Annual grant total

In 2014/15 the charity had an income of £9,400 and a total expenditure of £10,200. Grants are made to individuals and organisations for both social welfare and educational purposes. We estimate that social welfare grants to individuals totalled £2,500.

Applications

Initial telephone calls are welcomed. Applications should be made in writing to the correspondent by a third party.

Bradford and District Wool Association Benevolent Fund

£2,400

Correspondent: Sir James Hill, Chair, Sir James Hill (Wool) Ltd, Unit 2 Baildon Mills, Northgate, Baildon, Shipley, West Yorkshire BD17 6JX (01274 532200; email: sirjameshill@ btconnect.com)

CC number: 518439

Eligibility

Former workers in the wool trade in Bradford and district or their spouses, who are in need. Preference is given to those who are elderly or disabled.

Types of grants

Normally recurrent grants of up to a maximum of £200 towards heating, electricity and telephone costs. Special cases (such as the need for mobility aids, for example) are considered.

Annual grant total

In 2013/14 the fund had an income of £2,600 and a total expenditure of £2,600. We estimate that the total amount of grants awarded to individuals was approximately £2,400.

Applications

Apply in writing to the correspondent either directly by the individual or through a relative or friend. Applications are considered at any time.

The Bradford Tradesmen's Homes

£6,500

Correspondent: Colin Askew, Trust Administrator, 44 Lily Croft, Heaton Road, Bradford BD8 8QY (01274 543022; email: admin.bth@btconnect. com)

CC number: 224389

Eligibility

Individuals over the age of 60 who are in need, with preference for those who have held a position of responsibility in a profession in Bradford, and their dependants.

Types of grants

Pensions of £65 per quarter, plus a Christmas grant.

Annual grant total

In 2013/14 the charity had assets of £1 million and an income of £211,600. Grants and annuities to individuals totalled £6,500.

Applications

Application forms are available from the correspondent. Applications can be submitted directly by the individual or, where applicable, through a social worker, Citizens Advice, other welfare agency, doctor, clergy or other third party. Applicants will be visited before an award is made and they must provide the names of two referees. Applications are considered throughout the year.

Other information

Bradford Tradesmen's Homes was first established in 1865, with the purpose of building and maintaining 30 homes for elderly tradesmen. Housing is still a priority for the charity and in 2012/13 £112,000 was spent on running its 45 almshouses for elderly men and women.

The charity's social committee organises events and activities for residents.

The William and Sarah Midgley Charity

£3,600

Correspondent: Eileen Proctor, 7 Lachman Road, Trawden, Colne, Lancashire BB8 8TA (01282 862757; email: eileenproctor@talktalk.net)

CC number: 500095

Eligibility

People who are in need, hardship or distress and live in Barcroft, Lees and Cross Roads in the former borough of Keighley, West Yorkshire.

Types of grants

Our research suggests that Christmas hampers are normally given to older people in the area. Occasional one-off cash grants and gifts in-kind have also been made for electrical goods, clothing, food, travel expenses, medical and disability equipment and furniture.

Annual grant total

In 2014/15 the charity had an income of £5,300 and a total expenditure of £3,700.

We estimate that the amount of grants given to individuals totalled £3,600.

Applications

Apply in writing to the correspondent.

The Moser Benevolent Trust Fund

£1,500

Correspondent: Donald Stokes, Correspondent, 33 Mossy Bank Close, Queensbury, Bradford, West Yorkshire BD13 1PX (01274 817414; email: moser@donaldstokes.co.uk)

CC number: 222868

Eligibility

People in need who are 60 or over and have lived or worked in the former county borough of Bradford for at least three years.

Types of grants

On average around ten recipients receive pensions of around £400 a year.

Annual grant total

In 2013/14 the trust had an income of £6,500 and a total expenditure of £1,700 We estimate that the amount of grants given to individuals totalled £1,500.

Applications

Apply in writing to the correspondent. Applicants should include details of income and assets and are accepted at any time.

Other information

The fund is named after Jacob Moser, former Lord Mayor of Bradford. In 1898, the mayor and his wife, Florence, donated £10,000, to establish a 'Benevolent Fund for the Aged and Infirm Workpeople of Bradford', and served the city as well-respected philanthropists throughout their lives.

Joseph Nutter's Foundation

£18,000

Correspondent: John Lambert, Administrator, 2 The Mews, Gilstead Lane, Bingley BD16 3NP (01274 688666; email: john@bradfordtextilesociety.org.uk)

CC number: 507491

Eligibility

People aged 16 or under who live in the metropolitan district of Bradford and have suffered the loss of a parent.

Types of grants

One-off grants of around £100 to £200 are given towards clothing, bedding, beds and other household items that will specifically benefit the child. Other needs may occasionally be considered on an individual basis.

Annual grant total

In 2013/14 the foundation had an income of £20,000 and a total expenditure of £19,500. We estimate that grants totalled £18,000.

Applications

Apply in writing to the correspondent at any time. Applications can be submitted directly by the individual or family member. Potential applicants are welcome to contact the correspondent for further advice before applying.

Paul and Nancy Speak's Charity

£8,000

Correspondent: Malcolm Dixon, Secretary, 10 The Orchards, Bingley, West Yorkshire BD16 4AZ (01274 770878)

CC number: 231339

Eligibility

Women in need who are over the age of 50 and live in Bradford.

Types of grants

Regular allowances of £500 a year, paid quarterly.

Annual grant total

In 2014 the charity had an income of £10,700 and a total expenditure of £8,900. We estimate that the amount of grants given to individuals totalled £8,000.

Applications

Apply in writing to the correspondent.

The Samuel Sunderland Relief-in-Need Charity

£2,200

Correspondent: John Daykin, Clerk, Weatherhead and Butcher Solicitors, 120 Main Street, Bingley BD16 2JJ (01274 562322; email: info@wandb.uk.com)

CC number: 225745

Eligibility

People who live in the former parish of Bingley (as constituted on 14 February 1898) and are in need, hardship or distress.

Types of grants

Emergency payments and annual grants (including Christmas gifts).

Annual grant total

In 2014 the charity had an income of £7,300 and a total expenditure of £4,700. We estimate that the amount of grants given to individuals totalled £2,200, with local organisations also receiving funding.

Exclusions

The charity stresses that it only accepts applications from individuals residing within the boundary of the former parish of Bingley. Applications from those living elsewhere will not be considered.

Applications

Apply in writing to the correspondent through a social worker, Citizens Advice, other welfare agency or any other third party on behalf of the individual. When specific items are required estimates of the cost must be provided. General applications should be submitted before 1 February and are usually considered in mid- to late-February. Applications for Christmas gifts must be submitted by 1 November and are usually considered on the first Thursday in November. Urgent applications from eligible people can be considered throughout the year.

Other information

The charity also makes grants to local organisations.

Calderdale

The Bearder Charity

£32,000

Correspondent: Richard Smithies, Administrator, 5 King Street, Brighouse, West Yorkshire HD6 1NX (01484 710571; email: bearders@btinternet.com; website: www.bearder-charity.org.uk)

CC number: 1010529

Eligibility

Residents of Calderdale, West Yorkshire.

Types of grants

One-off grants according to need. Previously grants have been made for household items, computers and holidays.

Annual grant total

In 2013/14 the charity held assets of £3.7 million and had an income of £137,500. Grants to individuals totalled £32,000.

Applications

Apply in writing to the secretary. Applications may be made directly or through a local third party such as Citizens Advice or Stonham Housing. State what you need and how much it will cost.

The Community Foundation for Calderdale

Correspondent: Grants Department, The 1855 Building (first floor), Discovery Road, Halifax, West Yorkshire HX1 2NG (01422 438738; fax: 01422 350017; email: grants@cffc.co.uk; website: www.cffc.co.uk)

CC number: 1002722

Eligibility

People in need who live in Calderdale.

Types of grants

Grants from the Individual Fund are awarded up to a maximum of £250 to help alleviate personal needs.

Annual grant total

In 2013/14 grants were awarded to 349 individuals. Grants from the Individual Fund amounted to £52,000. We believe that the majority of this was awarded for social welfare purposes, but we were not able to determine an exact figure.

Applications

Individuals should apply through a referring agency, the contact details of which are listed on the foundation's website.

Other information

The foundation also gives to organisations and to individuals for educational purposes.

Mary Farrar's Benevolent Trust Fund

£6,500

Correspondent: Peter Haley, Administrator, P. Haley and Co., Poverty Hall, Lower Ellistones, Saddleworth Road, Greetland, Halifax HX4 8NG (01422 376690)

CC number: 223806

Eligibility

Women of limited means over 55 years of age, who are native to the parish of Halifax, or have lived there for more than five consecutive years.

Types of grants

Pensions, paid quarterly.

Annual grant total

In 2013/14 the fund had an income of £4,900 and a total expenditure of £6,700. We estimate that pensions totalled £6,500.

Exclusions

A maximum 6 grants are available each year for married women and widows.

Applications

Application forms are available from the correspondent. Applications can be submitted by the individual, through a recognised referral agency (such as a social worker, Citizens Advice, or doctor) or another third party such as a relative, friend, minister of religion or trustee.

The Goodall Trust

£3,300

Correspondent: Andrew Buck, 122 Skircoat Road, Halifax HX1 2RE (01422 255880; email: atbuck@tiscali.co.uk)

CC number: 221651

Eligibility

Widows and unmarried women who are in need and live in the present Calderdale ward of Skircoat or the parts of the parishes of St Jude and All Saints (Halifax) which are within the ancient township of Skircoat.

Types of grants

Recurrent grants are given according to need.

Annual grant total

In 2014 the trust had an income of £3,400 and a total expenditure of £3,500. We estimate that the amount of grants given to individuals totalled £3,800.

Applications

Application forms are available from the correspondent. Applications should be submitted by mid-September either directly by the individual; by a relative, friend or neighbour; or through a welfare agency. They are considered in October.

The Halifax Tradesmen's Benevolent Institution

£16,500

Correspondent: Anthony Wannan, West House, Kings Cross Road, Halifax HX1 1EB (01422 352517; email: anthony.wannan@bm-howarth.co.uk)

CC number: 224056

Eligibility

People in need aged 60 or over who have been self-employed or a manager of a business for at least seven years and live in the parish of Halifax and the surrounding area, and their dependants. Applicants should have no other income than a pension and have only modest savings.

Types of grants

Pensions, which in recent years have amounted to around £550 per annum.

Annual grant total

In 2014/15 the charity had assets of £556,500, an income of £44,500 and a total expenditure of £27,000. Pensions paid to individuals totalled £16,500.

Applications

Apply in writing to the correspondent, applications are considered quarterly.

Charity of Ann Holt

£11,000

Correspondent: G. Jacobs, Oak House, 9 Cross Street, Oakenshaw, Bradford, West Yorkshire BD12 7EA (01274 679835; email: oakey9uk@yahoo.co.uk)

CC number: 502391

Eligibility

Single women over the age of 55, who have lived in Halifax for at least five years, and are in need.

Types of grants

Pensions of around £200 a year, paid in quarterly instalments until the recipient dies, moves out of the area or relocates to a residential home.

Annual grant total

In 2013/14 the charity had an income of £15,100 and a total expenditure of £11,700. We estimate that the amount of grants given to individuals totalled £11,000.

Applications

Applications should be made in writing to the correspondent, directly by the individual. Applicants will need to be prepared to provide two referees who are not relations, such as a vicar, ex-employer or someone else they have known for a number of years.

Kirklees

Dewsbury and District Sick Poor Fund

£11,800

Correspondent: John Winder, Correspondent, 130 Boothroyd Lane, Dewsbury, West Yorkshire WF13 2LW (01924 463308; email: alanwwayside@talktalk.net)

CC number: 234401

Eligibility

People who are sick and in need who live in the county borough of Dewsbury and the ecclesiastical parish of Hanging Heaton.

Types of grants

One-off grants according to need for household goods and holidays to aid recuperation after illness. Vouchers are also available for food, clothing and the purchase of medical aids.

Annual grant total

In 2014 the fund had an income of £3,000 and a total expenditure of £12,000 We estimate that the amount of grants given to individuals totalled £11,800.

Applications

Apply in writing to the correspondent including details of illness and residential qualifications. Applications can be submitted either directly by the individual, through a third party such as a social worker or through an organisation such as Citizens Advice.

The H. P. Dugdale Foundation

£55,000 (48 grants)

Correspondent: Thomas Green, Administrator, Bank Chambers, Market Street, Huddersfield, West Yorkshire HD1 2EW (01484 648482; email: thomas.green37@btinternet.com)

CC number: 200538

Eligibility

People in need who live in the county borough of Huddersfield (comprising the urban districts of Colne Valley, Kirkburton, Meltham and Holmfirth). People who have previously lived in the area for a period of ten consecutive years are also eligible for assistance.

Types of grants

One-off and recurrent grants are given according to need.

Annual grant total

In 2013/14 the foundation had assets of £1.7 million and an income of £72,500. Grants were made to 48 individuals totalling £55,000. Of this, £49,000 in regular grants went to 32 beneficiaries, which also included Christmas grants totalling £7,500. A further £6,000 was paid in one-off grants to 17 individuals.

Applications

Application forms are given to local organisations such as social services and churches and may be submitted by or on behalf of the individual.

Leeds
The Bramley Poor's Allotment Trust

£1,800

Correspondent: Marian Houseman, 9 Horton Rise, Rodley, Leeds LS13 1PH (0113 236 0115)

CC number: 224522

Eligibility

People in need who live in the ancient township of Bramley, especially people who are elderly, poor and sick.

Types of grants

One-off grants between £40 and £120.

Annual grant total

In 2014 the charity had an income and expenditure of £3,600. We estimate that grants given to individuals for social welfare purposes totalled around £1,800.

Applications

Apply in writing to the correspondent. The trust likes applications to be submitted through a recognised referral agency (social worker, Citizens Advice, doctor, headmaster or minister). They are considered monthly.

The Community Shop Trust (also known as The Leeds Community Trust)

£25,500

Correspondent: Lynn Higo, Administrator, McCarthy's Business Centre, Suite 23, Enterprise House, Leeds LS7 2AH (0113 237 9685; fax: 0113 278 3184; email: info@ leedscommunitytrust.org; website: www. leedscommunitytrust.org)

CC number: 701375

Eligibility

Families who are in need and live in the Leeds area. Families with children are usually given preference.

Types of grants

The trust provides assistance in a number of forms:

- One-off grants are given for emergency items such as beds, bedding, carpets, washing machines and removal costs, etc. The website states: 'Families with children are usually given priority, but we try to help all families in need who have problems such as physical or mental disabilities, child protection issues, homelessness or similar situations'
- Holiday grants are given to enable children and their families to go away on holiday; this could be for use of a caravan, to go to a bed and breakfast, or even to stay at a guesthouse
- Christmas grants are given to disadvantaged families with children to cover food and gifts. Where funds permit, a grocery voucher is issued before Christmas
- The Millennium Project, whenever funds permit, helps to provide a bed for children who do not have a permanent bed
- Through the Kozy Kids Project the trust works with families who have experienced difficult circumstances in order to help the children furnish their bedroom/s
- Through the Keen Kids Project small, one-off grants are given to children to assist with educational, musical and sports costs

Annual grant total

In 2014 the trust had an income of £23,500 and a total expenditure of £28,500. Due to its low income, the trust was not required to submit its accounts to the Charity Commission and so we were unable to determine how much was given in grants. Based on previous years, we estimate that around £25,500 was given in social welfare grants to individuals.

Applications

Applications can only be submitted by a social worker or care agency on behalf of the individual.

Other information

The trust runs two shops and distributes the profits to local charities, groups and individuals in need, particularly people who are in vulnerable situations.

Kirke's Charity

£1,700

Correspondent: Bruce Buchan, Trustee, 8 St Helens Croft, Leeds LS16 8JY (01924 465860)

CC number: 246102

Eligibility

People in need who live in the ancient parishes of Adel, Arthington or Cookridge.

Types of grants

One-off grants, usually of around £100.

Annual grant total

In 2013/14 the charity had an income of £9,500 and a total expenditure of £7,000. Grants are made to individuals and organisations for both social welfare and educational purposes. We estimate that social welfare grants to individuals totalled £1,700.

Applications

Applications can be submitted directly by the individual or through a social worker, Citizens Advice or other welfare agency.

The Leeds Tradesmen's Trust

£4,500

Correspondent: Grants Team, 1st Floor, 51A St Paul's Street, Leeds LS1 2TE (0113 242 2426; email: info@leedscf.org. uk)

CC number: 1096892

Eligibility

People over 50 who have carried on business, practised a profession or been a tradesperson for at least five years (either consecutively or in total) and who, during that time, lived in Leeds or whose business premises (rented or owned) were in the city of Leeds. Grants are also given to self-employed business/professional people who 'have fallen upon misfortune in business'; normally older people. Widows and unmarried daughters of the former are also eligible.

Types of grants

Quarterly pensions, normally of £10 to £500 a year, plus Christmas grants and spring fuel grants only to those already receiving a pension.

Annual grant total

In 2013/14 pensions totalled £19,000.

Applications

Enquiries should be made to the Leeds Community Foundation's grants team by telephone or email.

Other information

Community Foundation for Leeds took over the administration of the trust in April 2013.

The Metcalfe Smith Trust

£11,900

Correspondent: Geoff Hill, Secretary, c/o Voluntary Action Leeds, Stringer House, 34 Lupton Street, Hunslet, Leeds LS10 2QW (email: secretary@metcalfesmithtrust.org; website: www.metcalfesmithtrust.org.uk)

CC number: 228891

Eligibility

Adults and children who live in Leeds and have 'a physical disability, long-term illness or a mental health difficulty'.

Types of grants

One-off grants ranging from £250 to £2,500 towards items or services that will significantly improve quality of life. Grants are given towards, for example, disability equipment, computers, respite breaks, heating costs, small items of furniture and course fees.

Annual grant total

In 2013/14 the trust had assets of £742,000 and an income of £26,000. Grants to individuals totalled £11,900 with £9,500 given to individuals for relief in need and a further £2,400 given through the emergency fund.

Exclusions

No support is given for individuals outside the area of benefit, general appeals, recurrent grants, fundraising initiatives or research costs.

Applications

Application forms are available on request by completing the 'application request form' on the trust's website. Individual applications must be supported by a social worker or local welfare organisation. They are considered twice a year, normally in May and October/November. See the website for dates of application deadlines and trustees' meetings. Emergency grants of up to £100 can be made at any time and applicants can use the online application form.

Other information

The trust's annual report states that: 'The Metcalfe Smith Trust was established in 1867, by a Victorian banker and benefactor, John Metcalfe Smith, who built Cookridge Convalescent Hospital, in memory of his father, for the benefit of people living and working in the Borough (as it was then) of Leeds.'

Wakefield

The Brotherton Charity Trust

£2,100

Correspondent: Christopher Brotherton-Ratcliffe, Trustee, PO Box 374, Harrogate HG1 4YW

CC number: 221006

Eligibility

People in need who are over 60 years old and live in Wakefield.

Types of grants

Annual pensions.

Annual grant total

In 2014 the trust had an income of £4,300 and a total expenditure of £2,400. We estimate that pensions totalled £2,100.

Applications

Application forms are available from the correspondent. When vacancies arise an advert is placed in the Wakefield Express and a waiting list is then drawn up. Applications can be made directly by the individual or family member.

Advice organisations

The following section lists the names and contact details of voluntary organisations that offer advice and support to individuals in need. The list is split into two sections: 'Welfare' and 'Illness and disability'. Each section begins with an index before listing the organisations by category.

The listings are a useful reference guide to organisations that individuals can contact to discuss their situation and receive advice and support. These organisations will have experience in tackling the sorts of problems that other individuals have faced, and will know the most effective and efficient ways of dealing with them. They may also be able to arrange for people to meet others in a similar situation. As well as providing advice and support, many of the organisations will be happy to help individuals submit applications to the trusts included in this guide. They may also know of other sources of funding available.

Some organisations included in this list have their own financial resources available to individuals. We have marked these with an asterisk (*). This list should not be used as a quick way of identifying potential funding – the organisations will have criteria and policies that may mean they are unable to support all the needs under that category and the guide will include many more potential sources of funding than there are organisations here.

Some organisations have local branches, which are better placed to have a personal contact with the individual and have a greater local knowledge of the need. We have only included the headquarters of such organisations, which will be happy to provide details for the relevant branches.

It is helpful for the organisations listed if any request for information includes an sae.

This list is by no means comprehensive and should only be used as a starting point. It only contains organisations that have a national remit and does not include organisations that provide general advice and support solely to members of a particular religion, country or ethnic group. For further details of groups, look for charitable and voluntary organisations in your local phone book, or contact your local council for voluntary service (CVS) (sometimes called Voluntary Action) which should be listed in the phone book.

The following general welfare section includes 'Benefit and grants information' and 'Debt and financial advice', which may be of particular relevance during these difficult economic times.

There is also a separate section 'Service and regimental funds' (see page 93), which details where support and advice for ex-service men and women and their families in need can be sought.

Welfare

General

Advice NI, 1 Rushfield Avenue, Belfast BT7 3FP (tel: 028 9064 5919; email: info@adviceni.net; website: www.adviceni.net). For information on sources of advice and support in Northern Ireland.

National Association of Citizens Advice Bureaux (NACAB), Myddelton House, 115–123 Pentonville Road, London N1 9LZ (tel: 020 7833 2181 [admin only]; email: info@nacab.org.uk; website: www.nacab.org.uk). For details of your local Citizens Advice office please see the website. Online advice is also available on a range of topics from the Citizens Adviceguide website: www.adviceguide.org.uk.

The Salvation Army, Territorial Headquarters, 101 Newington Causeway, London SE1 6BN (tel: 020 7367 4500; email: info@salvation army.org.uk; website: www. salvationarmy.org.uk)

Samaritans, Freepost RSRB-KKBY-CYJK, Chris, PO Box 90 90, Stirling FK8 2SA (tel: 020 8394 8300; 24-hour helpline: 116 123; see phone book for local number; email: admin@ samaritans.org (general) jo@ samaritans.org (helpline); website: www.samaritans.org)

Benefit and grants information

The Association of Charity Organisations (ACO), 2nd Floor, Acorn House, 314–320 Grays Inn Road, London WC1X 8DP (tel: 020 7255 4480; email: info@aco.uk.net; website: www.aco.uk.net)

Child Benefit, PO Box 1, Newcastle upon Tyne NE88 1AA (helpline: 0300 200 3100 [8am–8pm Monday to Friday and until 4pm Saturday]; textphone: 0300 200 3103; email: Online contact form; website: www. hmrc.gov.uk/childbenefit)

Child Maintenance Options, (tel: 0800 988 0988 [Mon–Fri, 8am–8pm and Saturdays 9am–4pm]; textphone: 0800 988 9888; website: www. cmoptions.org). Contact can also be made through an online live chat feature or by using online form.

Child Trust Fund, Child Trust Funds have been withdrawn. Information about Child Trust Funds can only be given through the company which holds your child's trust fund. You can find out who that is by using the online form on the gov.uk website. See www.gov.uk/child-trust-funds/ overview

Disability Benefits Centre, (Disability Living Allowance helpline: 0345 712 3456 [Mon–Fri, 8am–6pm]; Attendance Allowance helpline: 0345 605 6055; Personal Independence Payment (PIP) helpline: 0345 850 3322; website: www.gov.uk/disability-benefits-helpline)

Gov.uk, general information on money, tax and benefits (website: www.gov.uk)

Jobseekers (Benefit claim line: 0800 055 6688 [Mon–Fri, 8am–6pm]; textphone: 0800 023 4888; website: www.gov.uk/jobseekers-allowance/ overview). You may also make a claim online.

Pension Credit Claim Line; (tel: 0345 606 0265 [Mon–Fri, 8am–6pm]; textphone: 0800 169 0133; website: www.gov.uk/pension-credit/overview) See the website for information on local offices.

Tax Credits helpline, Tax Credit Office, Preston PR1 4AT; (tel: 0345 300 3900 [Mon–Fri, 8am–8pm and Saturdays 8am–4pm]; textphone 0345 300 3909; website: www.gov.uk/ browse/benefits/tax-credits)

Veterans Agency, Ministry of Defence, Norcross, Thornton Cleveleys, Lancashire FY5 3WP; (Veterans helpline: 0808 191 4218 [Mon–Thurs, 7.30am–6.30pm and Fridays 7.30am–5pm] Out of hours calls will be taken by Combat Stress or Samaritans, using same number; email: veterans-uk@mod.uk; website: www.veterans-uk.info)

Winter Fuel Payments, Winter Fuel Payment Centre, Mail Handling Site A, Wolverhampton WV98 1LR; (helpline: 0345 915 1515 [Mon–Fri, 8am–6pm]; textphone: 0345 606 0285; website: www.gov.uk/winter-fuel-payment

Bereavement

Cruse Bereavement Care, PO Box 800, Richmond upon Thames, Surrey TW9 1RG; (tel: 020 8939 9530; helpline: 0844 477 9400; email: info@cruse.org.uk or helpline@cruse.org.uk; website: www. cruse.org.uk)

Natural Death Centre, In The Hill House, Watley Lane, Twyford, Winchester SO21 1QX; (tel: 01962 712690; email: rosie@naturaldeath. org.uk; website: www.naturaldeath. org.uk)

Survivors of Bereavement by Suicide (SOBS), The Flamsteed Centre, Albert Street, Ilkeston, Derbyshire DE7 5GU; (tel: 0115 944 1117; helpline: 0300 1115065 [9am–9pm daily]; email: sobs.admin@care4free.net; website: www.uk-sobs.org.uk)

Children

Child Bereavement UK, Clare Charity Centre, Wycombe Road, Saunderton, Buckinghamshire HP14 4BF; (tel: 0800 028 8840; email: support@ childbereavement.org.uk; website: www.childbereavement.org.uk)

Winston's Wish, 3rd Floor, Cheltenham House, Clarence Street, Cheltenham, Gloucestershire GL50 3JR; (tel: 01242 515157; helpline: 0845 203 0405 [Mon–Fri, 9am–5pm and Wednesday evenings 7pm–9.30pm]; email: info@ winstonswish.org.uk; website: www. winstonswish.org.uk)

Parents

Child Death helpline, Barclay House, 37 Queen Square, London WC1N 3BH; (tel: 020 7813 8416 [admin]; helpline: 0800 282986 or from mobiles 0808 800 6019 [Mon, Thurs and Fri, 10am–1pm; Tues–Wed, 10am–4pm; and every evening 7pm–10pm]; email: contact@ childdeathhelpline.org; website: www. childdeathhelpline.org.uk)

The Compassionate Friends, 14 New King Street, Deptford, London SE8 3HS; (tel: 0345 120 3785; helpline: 0845 123 2304 [10am–4pm and 7pm–10pm daily]; Northern Ireland helpline: 028 8778 8016 [10am–4pm and 7pm–9.30pm daily]; email: info@tcf.org.uk or helpline@tcf.org.uk; website: www.tcf. org.uk)

The Lullaby Trust, 11 Belgrave Road, London SW1V 1RB (tel: 020 7802 3200; helpline: 0808 802 6868 [Mon–Fri, 10am–5pm; weekends and public holidays 6pm–10pm]; email: office@lullabytrust.org.uk or

support@lullabytrust.org.uk; website: www.lullabytrust.org.uk)

Stillbirth and Neonatal Death Society (SANDS), 28 Portland Place, London W1B 1LY (tel: 020 7436 7940; helpline: 020 7436 5881 [Mon–Fri, 9.30am–5.30pm and Tuesdays and Thursdays, 6pm–10pm]; email: support@uk-sands.org [general information] or helpline@uk-sands.org; website: www.uk-sands. org)

Carers

Carers UK, 20 Great Dover Street, London SE1 4LX; (tel: 020 7378 4999; The Carers UK Adviceline: 0808 808 7777 [Mon–Fri, 10am–4pm]; email: advice@carersuk.org; website: www. carersuk.org)

Leonard Cheshire Disability, 66 South Lambeth Road, London SW8 1RL; (tel: 020 3242 0200; website: www. leonardcheshire.org). Contact can also be made by completing an online enquiry form.

Children and young people

Action for Children, 3 The Boulevard, Ascot Road, Watford WD18 8AG (tel: 01923 361500; email: ask.us@ actionforchildren.org.uk; website: www.actionforchildren.org.uk)

Catch 22, 27 Pear Tree Street, London EC1V 3AG (tel: 020 7336 4800; email: using the online form on website; website: www.catch-22.org.uk)

ChildLine, 42 Curtain Road, London EC2A 3NH (tel: 020 7825 2500; 24-hour advice helpline: 0800 1111; website: www.childline.org.uk). A personal inbox can be set up on the site which will allow you to send emails to ChildLine and save replies in similar way to a normal email service. Alternatively, send a message without signing in through the 'send Sam a message' function. You can also chat online with a ChildLine counsellor.

The Children's Society, Edward Rudolf House, Margery Street, London WC1X 0JL (tel: 0300 303 7000; email: supportercare@ childrenssociety.org.uk; website: www.childrenssociety.org.uk)

Coram Children's Legal Centre, Riverside Office Centre, Century House North , North Station Road, Colchester CO1 1RE (tel: 01206

714650 [general]; Civil Legal Advice Education Law Line: 0845 345 4345 [Mon–Fri, 9am–8pm and Saturdays 9am–12.30pm]; Migrant Children's Project Advice Line: 020 7636 8505 [Tues–Thurs, 10am–4pm]) email: info@coramclc.org.uk; website: www. childrenslegalcentre.com)

Get Connected, PO BOX 7777, London W1A 5PD; (tel: 020 7009 2500; helpline: 0808 808 4994 [1pm–11pm daily]; text: 80849; email: only by using online form [general enquiries]; website: www. getconnected.org.uk). There is also a Webchat service available between 1pm and 11pm every day accessible through the website.

National Youth Advocacy Service, Egerton House, Tower Road, Birkenhead, Wirral CH41 1FN (tel: 0151 649 8700; helpline: 0808 808 1001 [Mon–Fri, 9am–8pm and Saturdays 10am–4pm]; email: main@ nyas.net or help@nyas.net; website: www.nyas.net)

NSPCC, Weston House, 42 Curtain Road, London EC2A 3NH (tel: 020 7825 2500 [Mon–Fri, 9am–5pm]; helpline for adults concerned about a child: 0808 800 5000; ChildLine: 0800 1111; email: only by using online form; website: www.nspcc.org.uk)

Save the Children UK, 1 St John's Lane, London EC1M 4AR (tel: 020 7012 6400; email: supporter.care@ savethechildren.org.uk; website: www. savethechildren.org.uk)

The Who Cares? Trust, 15–18 White Lion Street, London N1 9PG (tel: 020 7251 3117; email: mailbox@ thewhocarestrust.org.uk; website: www.thewhocarestrust.org.uk)

Youth Access, 1–2 Taylors Yard, 67 Alderbrook Road, London SW12 8AD (tel: 020 8772 9900 [Mon–Fri, 9.30am–1pm and 2pm–5.30pm]; email: admin@ youthaccess.org.uk; website: www. youthaccess.org.uk; for an online directory of information, advice and support services for young people)

Bullying

The Anti-bullying Alliance, National Children's Bureau, 8 Wakely Street, London EC1V 7QE (website: www. anti-bullyingalliance.org.uk; details of the regional offices are available on the website)

Kidscape, 2 Grosvenor Gardens, London SW1W 0DH (tel: 020 7730 3300; email: info@kidscape.org.uk; website: www.kidscape.org.uk)

Young People Leaving Care, Catch22, National Care Advisory Service (NCAS), 27 Pear Tree Street, London EC1V 3AG; (tel: 020 7336 4800; email: website: www.leavingcare.org)

Debt and financial advice

Age UK Money Matters, provides a range of advice on topics such as pensions, tax, financial management, consumer issues and benefits (website: www.ageuk.org.uk/money-matters; Age UK Advice: 0800 169 2081)

Business Debtline, (tel: 0800 197 6026 [Mon–Fri, 9am–5.30pm]; website: www.businessdebtline.org). The debtline does not provide advice by letter or email.

Gamblers Anonymous (GANON), (website: www.gamblersanonymous. org.uk; they advertise three types of meetings please check their website for further details.)

GamCare, 2nd Floor, 7–11 St John's Hill, London SW11 1TR (tel: 020 7801 7000; helpline: 0808 802 0133 [8am–midnight daily]; email: info@ gamcare.org.uk; website: www. gamcare.org.uk)

The Money Advice Service, Holborn Centre, 120 Holborn, London EC1N 2TD (tel: 0300 500 5000; typetalk: 18001 0300 500 5000 [Mon–Fri, 8am–8pm and Saturdays 9am–1pm]; email: enquiries@ moneyadviceservice.org.uk; website: www.moneyadvice.org.uk; an online chat facility is also available.)

National Debtline, Tricorn House, 51–53 Hagley Road, Edgbaston, Birmingham B16 8TP (helpline: 0808 808 4000 [Mon–Fri, 9am–9pm and Saturdays 9.30am–1pm]; website: www. nationaldebtline.org). Contact can also be made by completing an online enquiry form.

StepChange Debt Charity, Wade House, Merrion Centre, Leeds LS2 8NG (helpline: 0800 138 1111 [Mon–Fri, 8am–8pm and Saturdays 8am–4pm]; email: by using online form; website: www.stepchange.org)

TaxAid, 304 Linton House, 164–180 Union Street, London SE1 0LH (tel: 020 7803 4950 [advice agencies only]; helpline: 0345 120 3779; website: www.taxaid.org.uk). Contact can also be made by completing an online enquiry form.

TPAS (Pensions Advisory Service), 11 Belgrave Road, London SW1V 1RB (tel: 020 7630 2250; pensions advice: 0300 123 1047; helpline for women: 0345 600 0806; helpline for self-employed: 0345 602 7021; email: by using online form; website: www. pensionsadvisoryservice.org.uk). An online chat facility for legal advice is also available from Mon–Fri, 9am–5pm and Tuesdays 7pm–9 pm.

Families

Home-Start UK, Home-Start Centre, 8–10 West Walk, Leicester LE1 7NA (tel: 0116 258 7900; Mon–Fri, 8am–8pm and Saturdays 9am–12pm; email: info@home-start.org.uk; website: www.home-start.org.uk)

Housing

Homes and Communities Agency, Arpley House, 110 Birchwood Boulevard, Birchwood, Warrington WA3 7QH (tel: 0300 1234 500; email: mail@homesandcommunities.co.uk; website: www.homesandcommunities. co.uk)

Shelter, 88 Old Street, London EC1V 9HU (tel: 0300 330 1234; helpline: 0808 301 5978; email: only by using online enquiry form; website: www.shelter.org.uk)

Legal

Advice Services Alliance (ASA), Tavis House (Floor 7), 1–6 Tavistock Square, London WC1H 9NA (tel: 07904 377460; email: by using online form; website: www.asauk.org.uk) Please note: ASA does not give advice to the general public.

Bar Pro Bono Unit, 48 Chancery Lane, London WC2A 1JF (tel: 020 7092 3960 [Mon–Fri, 10am–4pm]; email: enquiries@barprobono.org.uk and emails can also be sent using the online form; website: www. barprobono.org.uk)

Civil Legal Advice, (helpline: 0345 345 4 345 [Mon–Fri, 9am–8pm and Saturdays 9am–12.30pm]; email: by using online form; website: www.gov. uk/civil-legal-advice). An online chat

facility for legal advice is also available.

Law Centres Network, Floor 1, Tavis House, 1–6 Tavistock Square, London WC1H 9NA (tel: 020 3637 1330 [please note: this is not an advice line but LCN's office line]; email: by using online enquiry form; website: www. lawcentres.org.uk). See the website for information on your local law centre.

LGBT

The Lesbian and Gay Foundation (LGF), 5 Richmond Street, Manchester M1 3HF (helpline: 0845 330 3030 [6pm–10pm daily]; email: info@lgf.org.uk; website: www.lgf.org. uk)

Stonewall, Tower Building, York Road, London SE1 7NX (Office (admin): 020 7593 1850; Info Line: 0800 050 2020 [Mon–Fri, 9.30am–5.30pm]; email: info@ stonewall.org.uk; website: www. stonewall.org.uk)

Missing people

Missing People, 284 Upper Richmond Road West, London SW14 7JE; (helpline: 116 000; text: 116 000; email: 116000@missingpeople.org.uk [if you're missing and want to talk about your situation] or use the online enquiry form [to report someone missing]; website: www. missingpeople.org.uk)

Offenders and ex-offenders

APEX Trust, Tontine House, 24 Church Street, St Helens, Merseyside WA10 1BD; (tel: 01744 612898; email: sthelens@apextrust. com)

National Association for the Care and Rehabilitation of Offenders (NACRO), Park Place, 10–12 Lawn Lane, London SW8 1UD (tel: 020 7840 7200; Resettlement Advice Service: 020 7840 1212; email: helpline@nacro.org.uk; website: www.nacro.org.uk)

Prisoners Abroad, 89–93 Fonthill Road, Finsbury Park, London N4 3JH (tel: 020 7561 6820; helpline: 0808 172 0098; email: info@ prisonersabroad.org.uk; website: www.prisonersabroad.org.uk)

UNLOCK; Maidstone Community Support Centre, 39–48 Marsham Street, Maidstone, Kent ME14 1HH (helpline: 01634 247350 [Mon–Fri,

10am–4pm]; text: 07824 113848; Skype: unlockhelpline; email: advice@unlock.org.uk, emails can also be sent using the online form; website: www.unlock.org.uk)

Families of people who have offended

Offenders' Families helpline, c/o Family Lives, 15–17 The Broadway, Hatfield, Hertfordshire AL9 5HZ (helpline: 0808 808 2003 [Mon–Fri, 9am–8pm and Sat–Sun, 10am–3pm]; email: info@offendersfamilieshelpline.org.uk. Information sheets are available on request by post or can be downloaded from the website: www.offendersfamilieshelpline.org.uk)

Partners of Prisoners and Families Support Group, POPS 1079 Rochdale Road, Blackley, Manchester M9 8AJ (tel: 0161 702 1000; helpline: 0808 808 2003 [Mon–Fri, 9am–8pm and Sat–Sun, 10am–3pm]; email: mail@partnersofprisoners.co.uk or by using the online form; website: www.partnersofprisoners.co.uk)

Prisoners' Families and Friends Service, 29 Peckham Road, London SE5 8UA (tel: 020 7735 9535; helpline: 0808 808 3444; email: info@pffs.org.uk or by using the online enquiry form; website: www.pffs.org.uk)

Women offenders and ex-offenders

Creative and Supportive Trust (CAST), Unit 1 Lysander Mews, Lysander Grove, Upper Holloway, London N19 3QP (tel: 020 7281 9928; mobile: 07435 967990; email: info@castwomen.org.uk; website: www.castwomen.org.uk)

Older people

Age UK, Tavis House, 1–6 Tavistock Square, London WC1H 9NA (helpline: 0800 169 2081 [Mon–Fri, 9am–4pm]; email: contact@ageuk.org.uk or by using online form; website: www.ageuk.org.uk)

The Age and Employment Network, Headland House, Jessica House, Red Lion Square, Wandsworth High Street, London SW18 4LS (website: www.taen.org.uk)

Friends of the Elderly, 40–42 Ebury Street, London SW1W 0LZ (tel: 020 7730 8263; email: enquiries@fote.org.uk or by using the online form; website: www.fote.org.uk)

Parenting

Family Lives, 15–17 The Broadway, Hatfield, Hertfordshire AL9 5HZ (tel: 020 7553 3080; 24-hour helpline: 0808 800 2222; website: www.familylives.org.uk). Contact can also be made by using the online chat support service.

Home-Start UK, Home-Start Centre, 8–10 West Walk, Leicester LE1 7NA (tel: 0116 258 7900; [Mon–Fri, 8am–8pm and Saturdays 9am–12pm]; email: info@home-start.org.uk; website: www.home-start.org.uk)

Twins and Multiple Births Association (TAMBA), Manor House, Church Hill, Aldershot, Hampshire GU12 4JU (tel: 01252 332344; helpline: 0800 138 0509 [10am–1pm and 7pm–10pm daily]; email: asktwinline@tamba.org.uk; website: www.tamba.org.uk/home)

Abduction

Reunite (National Council for Abducted Children), PO Box 7124, Leicester LE1 7XX (tel: 0116 255 5345; Advice line: 0116 255 6234; email: reunite@dircon.co.uk; website: www.reunite.org)

Adoption and fostering

Adoption UK, Linden House, 55 The Green, South Bar Street, Banbury OX19 9AB (tel: 01295 752240; helpline: 0844 848 7900 [Mon–Fri, 10am–4pm]; online contact form also available; website: www.adoptionuk.org.uk)

After Adoption, Unit 5 Citygate, 5 Blantyre Street, Manchester M15 4JJ (tel: 0161 839 4932; Action Line: 0800 056 8578; email: information@afteradoption.org.uk; website: www.afteradoption.org.uk)

CoramBAAF Adoption & Fostering Academy, Coram Campus, 41 Brunswick Square, London WC1N 1AZ (tel: 020 7520 0300, email: mail@corambaaf.org.uk; web: corambaaf.org.uk)

Fostering Network, 87 Blackfriars Road, London SE1 8HA (tel: 020 7620 6400; Fosterline: England – 020 7401 9582, Wales – 0800 316 7664, Scotland – 0141 204 1400, Northern Ireland – 028 9070 5056; email: info@fostering.net; website: www.fostering.net)

National Association of Child Contact Centres, Second Floor Offices, Friary Chambers, 26–34 Friar Lane, Nottingham NG1 6DQ (tel: 0845 450 0280 or 0115 948 4557 from mobiles [call for information on nearest centre]; email: contact@naccc.org.uk; website: www.naccc.org.uk)

Post-Adoption Centre, 5 Torriano Mews, Torriano Avenue, London NW5 2RZ (tel: 020 7284 0555; Advice line: 020 7284 5879 [Mon, Tues & Fri, 10am–4pm, Wed and Thurs 2pm–7pm]; email: using online form; website: www.pac-uk.org.)

Childcare

Family and Childcare Trust, The Bridge, 81 Southwark Bridge Road, London SE1 0NQ (tel: 020 7940 7510; email: info@familyandchildcaretrust.org.uk; website: www.familyandchildcaretrust.org)

Family Rights Group, Second Floor, The Print House, 18 Ashwin Street, London E8 3DL (tel: 020 7923 2628; advice line: 0808 801 0366 [Mon–Fri, 9.30am–3pm]; email: using the online contact form; website: www.frg.org.uk)

Divorce

Both Parents Forever, 39 Cloonmore Avenue, Orpington, Kent BR6 9LE (helpline: 01689 854343 [8am–9pm daily])

CAFCASS (Children and Family Court Advisory and Support Service), 3rd Floor, 21 Bloomsbury Street, London WC1B 3HF (tel: 0300 456 4000; email: webenquiries@cafcass.gsi.gov.uk or telephoneenquiries@cafcass.gsi.gov.uk; website: www.cafcass.gov.uk)

Families Need Fathers, 134–146 Curtain Road, London EC2A 3AR (helpline: 0300 0300 363 [7am–midnight daily]; email: fnf@fnf.org.uk; website: www.fnf.org.uk)

National Family Mediation, Civic Centre, Paris Street, Exeter (tel: 0300 4000 636; email: using the online contact form; website: www.nfm.org.uk)

NCDSW (National Council for the Divorced and Separated and Widowed), 68 Parkes Hall Road, Woodsetton, Dudley DY1 3SR (tel: 07041 478120; email: secretary@ncdsw.org.uk; website: www.ncdsw.org.uk)

Grandparents

Grandparents Association, Moot House, The Stow, Harlow, Essex CM20 3AG (helpline: 0300 123 7015 [Mon–Fri, 10am–3pm]; email: advice@grandparentsplus.org.uk; website: www.grandparents-association.org.uk)

Mothers

Mothers Apart from their Children (MATCH), BM Box No. 6334, London WC1N 3XX (email: enquiries@matchmothers.org; website: www.matchmothers.org)

Mumsnet, (email: contactus@mumsnet.com; website: www.mumsnet.com)

Pregnancy

ARC (Antenatal Results and Choices), 345 City Road, London EC1V 1LR (tel: 020 7713 7486; helpline: 0845 077 2290 [Mon–Fri, 10am–5.30pm]; email: info@arc-uk.org or online using the contact form; website: www.arc-uk.org)

British Pregnancy Advisory Service (BPAS), 20 Timothys Bridge Road, Stratford Enterprise Park, Stratford upon-Avon, Warwickshire CV37 9BF (Advice line: 03457 30 40 30; email: info@bpas.org; website: www.bpas.org)

Brook, 50 Featherstone Street, London EC1Y 8RT (tel: 020 7284 6040 [admin]; email: admin@brook.org.uk; website: www.brook.org.uk). You may also use the Ask Brook facility to ask questions via email or text 07537 402024.

Disability Pregnancy and Parenthood International (DPPI), 336 Brixton Road, London SW9 7AA (tel: 020 7263 3088; helpline: 0800 018 4730 [Tues–Thurs, 10.30am–2.30pm; email: info@dppi.org.uk; website: www.dppi.org.uk)

National Childbirth Trust, Alexandra House, Oldham Terrace, London W3 6NH (helpline: 0300 330 0700; website: www.nct.org.uk; email: enquiries@nct.org.uk). Contact can also be made by completing an online enquiry form.

Single parents

Gingerbread, 520 Highgate Studios, 53–79 Highgate Road London NW5 1TL (tel: 020 7428 5420 [admin]; helpline: 0808 802 0925 [Mon, 10am–6pm, Tues, Thurs and Fri 10am–4pm and Wed 10am–1pm and 5pm–7pm]; website: www.gingerbread.org.uk). Contact can also be made by completing an online enquiry form.

Single Parents, The Silai Centre, 176–178 Easton Road, Bristol BS5 0ES (website; www.singleparents.org.uk)

Poverty

Care International, 9th Floor, 89 Albert Embankment, London SE1 7TP (tel: 020 7091 6000; website: www.careinternational.org.uk). Contact can also be made by completing an online enquiry form.

Counselling, 5 Pear Tree Walk, Wakefield, West Yorkshire WF2 0HW (website: www.counselling.ltd.uk)

Family Action, 24 Angel Gate, City Road, London EC1V 2PT (tel: 020 7254 6251; email: info@family-action.org.uk; website: www.family-action.org.uk). Contact can also be made by completing an online enquiry form.

Law Centres Network, Floor 1, Tavis House, 1–6 Tavistock Square, London WC1H 9NA (tel: 020 3637 1330 [admin]; an online enquiry form is also available for non-legal advice; website: www.lawcentres.org.uk). See the website for information on your local law centre.

The Trussell Trust, Unit 9 Ashfield Trading Estate, Ashfield Road, Salisbury SP2 7HL (tel: 01722 580180; email: enquiries@trusselltrust.org; website: www.trusselltrust.org). You can also use the sites search facility to find your nearest foodbank.

Refugees and asylum seekers

Asylum Aid, Club Union House, 253–254 Upper Street, London N1 1RY (tel: 020 7354 9631; advice line: 020 7354 9264 [Mon–Fri, 10am–12pm]; email: info@asylumaid.org.uk; website: www.asylumaid.org.uk)

Migrant Help, Charlton House, Dour Street, Dover, Kent CT16 1AT (tel: 01304 218700; email: info@migranthelpline.org; website: www.migranthelp.org)

Refugee Action, Victoria Charity Centre, 11 Belgrave Road, London SW1V 1RB (tel: 020 7952 1511; asylum advice: 0808 800 0630 website: www.refugee-action.org.uk). See the website for a list of local offices.

Refugee Council, PO Box 68614, London E15 9DQ (tel: 020 7346 6700 [head office]; website: www.refugeecouncil.org.uk. Please visit the website for signposting to a specific service)

Refugee Support Centre, 47 South Lambeth Road, London SW8 1RH (tel: 020 7820 3606; email: rsctherapy47@hotmail.com)

Relationships

Albany Trust Counselling, 239A Balham High Road, London SW17 7BE (tel: 020 8767 1827; email: info@albanytrust.org; website: www.albanytrust.org.uk)

Family Planning Association, 23–28 Penn Street, London EC1Y 8QU (tel: 020 7608 5240; email: general@fpa.org.uk; website: www.fpa.org.uk)

Relate (National Marriage Guidance) Premier House, Carolina Court, Lakeside, Doncaster DN4 5RA (tel: 0300 100 1234; email: using the online contact form; website: www.relate.org.uk; there is also a Live Chat service available on the website)

Social isolation

The Farming Community Network, Manor Farm, West Haddon, Northampton NN6 7AQ (helpline: 0300 011 1999 email: chris@fcn.org.uk; website: www.fcn.org.uk)

The Single Concern Group, PO Box 40, Minehead TA24 5YS (tel: 01643 708008; [Office Hours])

Squatters

Advisory Service for Squatters (ASS), Angel Alley, 84b, Whitechapel High Street, London E1 7QX (tel: 020 3216 0099; email: advice@squatter.org.uk; website: www.squatter.org.uk)

Victims of accidents and crimes

Abuse

Action on Elder Abuse (AEA), PO Box 60001, Streatham SW16 9BY (helpline: 0808 808 8141; email: enquires@elderabuse.org.uk or using the online contact form; website: www.elderabuse.org.uk)

The Clinic for Boundaries, 49–51 East Road, London N1 6AH (tel: 020 3468 4194; email: info@professional boundaries.org.uk; website: www. professionalboundaries.org.uk)

NSPCC, Weston House, 42 Curtain Road, London EC2A 3NH (tel: 020 7825 2500; helpline: 0808 800 5000; email: help@nspcc.org.uk; website: www.nspcc.org.uk)

Crime

Victim Support, Octavia House, 50 Banner Street, London EC1Y 8ST (tel: 020 7336 1730; Supportline: 0845 303 0900 [weekdays 8am–8pm and Sat–Sun, 9am–7pm]; email: supportline@victimsupport.org.uk; website: www.victimsupport.org). For details on the regional offices please see the website.

Disasters

Disaster Action, No. 4, 71 Upper Berkeley Street, London W1H 7DB (email: admin@disasteraction.org.uk; website: www.disasteraction.org.uk)

Domestic violence

Broken Rainbow, PO Box 68947, London E1W 9JJ (tel: 0845 260 5560 [admin]; helpline: 0300 999 5428 [Mondays and Thursdays 10am–8pm, Tuesdays and Wednesdays 10am–5pm]; email: mail@broken-rainbow.org.uk or help@ brokenrainbow.org.uk; website: www. brokenrainbow.org.uk). They also have an online chat service.

Mankind, Flook House, Belvedere Road, Taunton, Somerset TA1 1BT (tel: 01823 334299; helpline: 01823 334244; email: admin@mankind.org. uk; website: www.mankind.org.uk)

Men's Advice Line and Enquiries (MALE), (helpline: 0808 801 0327 [Mon–Fri, 9am–5pm]; email: info@ mensadviceline.org.uk; website: www. mensadviceline.org.uk)

National Centre for Domestic Violence, PO Box 999 Guildford Surrey GU1 9BH (24-hour helpline: 08009702070; text: 'NCDV' to 60777 for call back; email: office@ncdv.org. uk; website: www.ncdv.org.uk)

Women's Aid Federation, PO BOX 3245, Bristol BS2 2EH (tel: 0117 944 4411 [admin]; national 24-hour helpline: 0808 200 0247; email: info@ womensaid.org.uk or helpline@ womensaid.org.uk; website: www.

womensaid.org.uk). For details on the regional offices please see the website.

Medical accidents

Action for Victims of Medical Accidents (AVMA), 117 High Street, Croydon, London CR0 1QG (tel: 020 8688 9555 [admin only]; helpline: 0845 123 2352 [Mon–Fri, 10am–5pm]; email: advice@avma.org. uk; website: www.avma.org.uk)

Rape

Rape Crisis Centre, BCM Box 4444, London WC1N 3XX (helpline: 0808 802 9999 [12pm–2.30pm and 7pm–9.30pm daily); email: rceinfo@ rapecrisis.org.uk; website: www. rapecrisis.org.uk). See website for contact information on local rape crisis centres.

Women Against Rape (WAR) and Black Women's Rape Action Project, Crossroads Women's Centre, 25 Wolsey Mews NW5 2DX (tel: 020 7482 2496 [Mon–Fri, 1.30pm–4pm]; email: war@womenagainstrape.net or bwrap@dircon.co.uk; website: www. womenagainstrape.net)

Road accidents

RoadPeace, Shakespeare Business Centre, 245a Cold Harbour Lane, Brixton, London SW9 8RR (tel: 020 7733 1603; helpline: 0845 450 0355 [Mon–Fri, 9am–5pm]; email: info@ roadpeace.org or helpline@roadpeace. org; website: www.roadpeace.org)

Work issues

Employment Tribunals Enquiry Line, (Public Enquiry Line: 0300 123 1024; minicom: 01509 221564; website: www.gov.uk/employment-tribunals-enquiries). See website for the contact details of local employment tribunals.

Public Concern at Work, 3rd Floor, Bank Chambers, 6–10 Borough High Street, London SE1 9QQ (tel: 020 3117 2520; Whistleblowing Advice Line: 020 7404 6609; email: whistle@ pcaw.org.uk; website: www.pcaw.org. uk)

Women

Refuge, Fourth Floor, International House, 1 St Katharine's Way, London E1W 1UN (tel: 020 7395 7700 (general); 24-hour helpline: 0808 200 0247; email: info@refuge.org.uk; website: www.refuge.org.uk)

Women and Girls Network, PO Box 13095, London W14 0FE (tel: 020 7610 4678; Advice Line: 0808 801 0660 [Mon–Fri, 10am–4pm and Wednesdays 6pm–9pm]; Sexual Violence Helpline: 0808801066 [Please see website for opening times]; email: website: www.wgn.org. uk; an online contact facility is also available)

Women's Health Concern, Spracklen House, Dukes Place, Marlow, Buckinghamshire SL7 2QH (tel: 01628 890199; email and telephone advice is available for a small fee please check the website for more details; website: www.womens-health-concern.org)

Illness and disability

Disability (general)

Action Medical Research, Vincent House, Horsham, West Sussex RH12 2DP (tel: 01403 210406; email: info@action.org.uk; website: www.action.org.uk)

Contact a Family, 209–211 City Road, London EC1V 1JN (tel: 020 7608 8700; helpline: 0808 808 3555; email: info@cafamily.org.uk or by using online enquiry form; website: www.cafamily.org.uk)

Disabled Living Foundation (DLF), 4th Floor, Jessica House, Red Lion Square, 191 Wandsworth High Street, London SW18 4LS (tel: 020 7289 6111; helpline: 0300 999 0004 [Mon–Fri, 10am–4pm]; email: helpline@dlf.org.uk; website: www.dlf.org.uk)

Disabled Parents' Network, Disability Resource Centre, 1A Humphrys Road, Woodside Estate, Dunstable LU5 4TP (email: by using online enquiry form; website: www.disabledparentsnetwork.org.uk)

Disabilities Trust, 32 Market Place, Burgess Hill, West Sussex RH15 9NP (tel: 01444 239123; email: info@thedtgroup.org; website: www.thedtgroup.org)

Disability Law Service (DLS), The Foundry, 17 Oval Way, London (tel: 020 7791 9800; email: advice@dls.org.uk; website: www.dls.org.uk)

Disability Pregnancy and Parenthood International (DPPI), 87 Barrenger Road, London N10 1HU (helpline: 0800 018 4730; website: www.disabledparent.org.uk)

Disability Rights, Ground Floor, CAN Mezzanine, 49–51 East Road, London N1 6AH (tel: 020 7250 8181; email: enquiries@disabilityrightsuk.org; website: www.disabilityrightsuk.org)

I CAN's, Unit 31, Angel Gate (Gate 5), Goswell Road, London EC1V 2PT (tel: 0845 225 4071; email: info@ican.org.uk; website: www.ican.org.uk)

*Jewish Care, Amélie House, Maurice and Vivienne Wohl Campus, 221 Golders Green Road, London NW11 9DQ (tel: 020 8922 2000; helpline: 020 8922 2222; email: helpline@jcare.org; website: www.jewishcare.org)

Kids, 7–9 Elliott's Place, London N1 8HX (tel: 020 7359 3635; email: by using the online contact form; website: www.kids.org.uk)

PHAB England, Summit House, 50 Wandle Road, Croydon CR0 1DF (tel: 020 8667 9443; email: info@phab.org.uk; website: www.phab.org.uk)

Queen Elizabeth's Foundation (QEF), Leatherhead Court, Woodlands Road, Leatherhead, Surrey KT22 0BN (tel: 01372 841100; email: by using online contact form; website: www.qef.org.uk)

RESPOND, 3rd Floor, 24–32 Stephenson Way, London NW1 2HD (tel: 020 7383 0700; helpline: 0808 808 0700 [Thurs 10am–4pm]; email: wvhelpline@respond.org.uk; website: www.respond.org.uk)

Addiction

Addaction, 67–69 Cowcross Street, London EC1M 6PU (tel: 020 7251 5860; email: by using the online contact form; website: www.addaction.org.uk)

Lions Lifeskills (formerly Tacade), 257 Alcester Road South, Kings Heath, Birmingham B14 6DT (tel: 0844 963 2427; email: by using online contact form; website: www.lionlifeskills.co.uk)

Ageing

Age UK, Tavis House, 1–6 Tavistock Square, London WC1H 9NA (helpline: 0800 169 2081; email: by using online contact form; website: www.ageuk.org.uk)

*Independent Age, 18 Avonmore Road, London W14 8RR, (tel: 020 7605 4200; advice line: 0800 319 6789; email: charity@independentage.org; website: www.independentage.org)

AIDS/HIV

National Aids Trust, New City Cloisters, 196 Old Street, London EC1V 9FR (tel: 020 7814 6767; email: info@nat.org.uk; website: www.nat.org.uk)

Terrence Higgins Trust, 314–320 Grays Inn Road, London WC1X 8DP (tel: 020 7812 1600; advice and support: 0808 802 1221 [Mon–Fri, 9.30am–5.30pm]; email: info@tht.org.uk; website: www.tht.org.uk)

Alcohol

Al-Anon Family Groups UK and Eire (AFG), 57B Great Suffolk Street, London SE1 0BB (helpline: 020 7403 0888 [10am–10pm daily]; email: enquiries@al-anonuk.org.uk; website: www.al-anonuk.org.uk)

Alcohol Concern, 25 Corsham Street, London N1 6DR (tel: 020 7566 9800; email: by using online contact form; website: www.alcoholconcern.org.uk)

Alcoholics Anonymous (AA), General Service Office, PO Box 1, 10 Toft Green, York YO1 7NJ (tel: 01904 644026; helpline: 0800 917 7650; email: help@alcoholics-anonymous. org.uk; website: www.alcoholics-anonymous.org.uk)

Drinkline, helpline: 0300 123 1110 [Mon–Fri, 9am–8pm and Sat–Sun, 11am–4pm]

Foundation 66, (Now a subsidiary of Pheonix Futures Group) 68 Newington Causeway, London SE1 6DF (tel: 020 7234 9740; email: 020 7234 9740; website: www. phoenix-futures.org.uk/foundation-66)

Turning Point, Standon House, 21 Mansell Street, London E1 8AA (tel: 020 7481 7600; email: info@ turningpoint.co.uk; website: www. turning-point.co.uk)

Allergy

Action Against Allergy, PO Box 278, Twickenham TW1 4QQ (tel: 020 8892 4949; helpline: 020 8892 2711; email: actionagainstallergy@btconnect. comorby using the online contact form; website: www. actionagainstallergy.co.uk)

Allergy UK, Planwell House, LEFA Business Park, Edgington Way Sidcup, Kent DA14 5BH (helpline: 01322 619898 [Mon–Fri, 9am–5pm]; email: info@allergyuk.org; website: www.allergyuk.org; a live chat facility is also available on the website)

Alopecia areata and alopecia androgenetica

Alopecia UK, PO Box 341, Baildon, Shipley BD18 9EH (email: info@ alopecia.org.uk website: www. alopeciaonline.org.uk)

Alzheimer's disease

*Alzheimer's Society, Devon House, 58 St Katharine's Way, London E1W 1LB (tel: 0330 333 0804; helpline: 0300 222 1122 [Mon–Fri, 9am–5pm and Sat–Sun, 10am–4pm]; email: enquiries@alzheimers.org.uk; website: www.alzheimers.org.uk)

Angelmann syndrome

ASSERT (Angelman Syndrome Support Education and Research), PO Box 4962, Nuneaton CV11 9FD (helpline: 0300 999 0102; email: assert@angelmanuk.org; website: www.angelmanuk.org)

Ankylosing spondylitis

National Ankylosing Spondylitis Society (NASS), 4 Albion Court, Hammersmith, London W6 0QT (tel: 020 8741 1515; email: admin@nass.co. uk; website: www.nass.co.uk)

Arthritis/rheumatic diseases

Arthritis Care, Floor 4, Linen Court, 10 East Road, London N1 6AD (tel: 020 7380 6500; helpline: 0808 800 4050; email: info@arthritiscare.org.uk; website: www.arthritiscare.org.uk)

Arthritis Research UK, Copeman House, St Mary's Gate, Chesterfield S41 7TD (tel: 0300 790 0400; email: enquiries@arthritisresearchuk.org or by using online contact form; website: www.arthritisresearchuk.org)

Arthrogryposis

Arthrogryposis Group (TAG), PO Box 1199, Spalding, Lincolnshire PE11 9EY (helpline: 0800 028 4447; email: help@arthrogryposis.co.ukor by using online contact form; website: www.tagonline.org.uk)

Asthma

Asthma UK, 18 Mansell Street, London E1 8AA (tel: 0300 222 5800; Advice line: 0300 222 5800 [Mon–Fri, 9am–5pm]; email: info@asthma.org. uk; website: www.asthma.org.uk)

Ataxia

*Ataxia UK, Lincoln House, Kennington Park, 1–3 Brixton Road, London SW9 6DE (tel: 020 7582 1444; helpline: 0845 644 0606 [Mon–Thurs, 10.30am–2.30pm]; email: helpline@ataxia.org.uk; website: www.ataxia.org.uk)

Autism

National Autistic Society (NAS), 393 City Road, London EC1V 1NG (tel: 020 7833 2299; helpline: 0808 800 4104 [Mon–Fri, 10am–4pm]; email: nas@nas.org.uk; website: www. autism.org.uk)

Back pain

Back Care, 3rd Floor, Regal House, 70 London Road, Twickenham TW1 3QS (tel: 020 8977 5474; helpline: 0845 130 2704; email: contact@backcare.org.uk; website: www.backcare.org.uk)

Behçet's syndrome

Behçet's Syndrome Society, Kemp House, 152–160 City Road, London EC1V 2NX (tel: 0845 130 7328; helpline: 0845 130 7329; email: info@ behcetsdisease.org.uk; website: www. behcets.org.uk)

Blind/partially sighted

CALIBRE (Cassette Library of Recorded Books), Aylesbury, Buckinghamshire HP22 5XQ (tel: 01296 432339; email: enquiries@ calibre.org.uk; website: www.calibre. org.uk)

International Glaucoma Association (IGA), Woodcote House, 15 Highpoint Business Village, Henwood, Ashford, Kent TN24 8DH (tel: 01233 648164; helpline: 01233 648170; email: info@iga.org.uk; website: www.iga.org.uk)

Listening Books, 12 Lant Street, London SE1 1QH (tel: 020 7407 9417; email: info@listening-books.org.uk; website: www.listening-books.org.uk)

National Federation of the Blind of the UK, Sir John Wilson House, 215 Kirkgate, Wakefield WF1 1JG (tel: 01924 291313; email: admin@ nfbuk.orgor by using online enquiry form; website: www.nfbuk.org)

Partially Sighted Society, 1 Bennetthorpe, Doncaster DN2 6AA (tel: 01302 965195; email: reception@ partsight.org.uk; website: www. partsight.org.uk)

*Royal National Institute for the Blind (RNIB), 105 Judd Street, London WC1H 9NE (helpline: 0303 123 9999 [Mon–Thurs, 8.45am–5.30pm]; email: helpline@ rnib.org.uk; website: www.rnib.org. uk)

RP Fighting Blindness, PO Box 350, Buckingham MK18 5GZ (tel: 01280 821334; email: info@rpfighting blindness.org.uk; website: www. rpfightingblindness.org.uk)

Voluntary Transcribers' Group, 8 Segbourne Road, Rubery, Birmingham B45 9SX (tel: 0121 453 4268; email: braillist@btinternet.com)

Bone marrow

Anthony Nolan Trust, 2 Heathgate Place, 75–87 Agincourt Road, London NW3 2NU (tel: 0303 303 0303; email: by using online contact form; website: www.anthonynolan.org.uk)

Bowel disorders

Children with Crohn's and Colitis (CICRA) Parkgate House, 356 West Barnes Lane, Motspur Park, Surrey KT3 6NB (tel: 020 8949 6209; email: support@cicra.org or by using online contact form; website: www.cicra.org)

National Association for Colitis and Crohn's Disease (NACC), 45 Grosvenor Road, St Albans AL1 3AW (tel: 0300 222 5700; helpline: 0121 737 9931 [Mon–Fri, 1pm–3.30pm and 6.30pm–9pm]; email: info@crohnsandcolitis.org.uk; website: www.crohnsandcolitis.org. uk)

Brain injury

British Institute for Brain-Injured Children (BIBIC), Old Kelways, Somerton Road, Langport, Somerset TA10 9SJ (tel: 01458 253344; email: info@bibic.org.uk; website: www. bibic.org.uk)

Brittle bones

*Brittle Bone Society, Grant-Paterson House, 30 Guthrie Street, Dundee DD1 5BS (tel: 01382 204446; email: bbs@brittlebone.org or by using online enquiry form; website: www. brittlebone.org)

Burns

British Burn Association, Royal College of Surgeons of England, 35–43 Lincoln's Inn Fields, London WC2A 3PE (tel: 020 7869 6923; email: by using the online contact form; website: www.britishburn association.org)

Children's Burns Trust, 2 Grosvenor Gardens, London SW1W 0DH (tel: 020 7881 0902; email: info@cbtrust. org.uk or by using online contact form; website: www.cbtrust.org.uk)

Cancer and leukaemia

Action Cancer, 1 Marlborough Park South, Belfast BT9 6XS (tel: 028 9080 3344; email: info@actioncancer.org; website: www.actioncancer.org)

Cancer Support Scotland, The Calman Centre, 75 Shelley Road, Glasgow G12 0ZE (tel: 0800 652 4531; email; info@cancersupport scotland.org; website: www. cancersupportscotland.org)

*CLIC Sargent Cancer Care for Children, No. 1 Farriers Yard, Assembly London, 77–85 Fulham Palace Road, London W6 8JA (tel: 0300 330 0803; email: by using online enquiry form; website: www. clicsargent.org.uk)

*Leukaemia Care Society, One Birch Court, Blackpole East, Worcester WR3 8SG (tel: 01905 755977; 24-hour helpline: 0808 801 0444; email: care@ leukaemiacare.org.uk; website: www. leukaemiacare.org.uk; online chat facility also available)

*Macmillan Cancer Relief, 89 Albert Embankment, London SE1 7UQ (tel: 020 7840 7840; helpline: 0808 808 0000 [Mon–Fri, 9am–8pm]; email: by using online enquiry form; website: www.macmillan.org.uk)

Marie Curie Foundation, 89 Albert Embankment, London SE1 7TP (helpline: 0800 090 2309; email: supporter.relation@mariecurie.org.uk; website: www.mariecurie.org.uk)

Tenovous Cancer Head Office, Gleider House, Ty Glas Road, Llanishen, Cardiff CF14 5BD (tel: 029 2076 8850; helpline: 0808 808 1010 [8am–8pm]; email: info@tenovus. com or by using their 'ask the nurse' facility online; website: www.tenovus. org.uk)

Cerebral palsy

SCOPE, 6 Market Road, London N7 9PW (tel: 020 7619 7100; helpline: 0808 800 3333 [Mon–Fri, 9am–5pm]; email: helpline@scope.org.uk; website: www.scope.org.uk)

Charcot-Marie-Tooth disease

CMT International United Kingdom, 3 Groverley Road, Christchurch BH23 3HB (tel: 0800 652 6316 email: enquiries@cmtuk.org.uk; website: www.cmt.org.uk)

Chest/lungs

British Lung Foundation, 73–75 Goswell Road, London EC1V 7ER (tel: 020 7688 5555; helpline: 0300 003 0555; email: helpline@blf.org.uk or by using online enquiry form; website: www. blf.org.uk)

Child growth

Child Growth Foundation, 21 Malvern Drive, Sutton Coldfield B76 1PZ (helpline: 020 8995 0257 [Mon–Fri, 9.30am–4pm]; email: info@childgrowthfoundation.org; website: www.childgrowthfoundation. org)

Cleft lip/palate disorder

Cleft Lip and Palate Association (CLAPA), 1st Floor, Green Man Tower, 332B Goswell Road, London EC1V 7LQ (tel: 020 7833 4883; email: info@clapa.com or by using online contact form; website: www.clapa. com)

Coeliac disease

Coeliac UK, 3rd Floor, Apollo Centre, Desborough Road, High Wycombe HP11 2QW (tel: 0118 939 1537; helpline: 0333 332 2033; email: by using online contact form; website: www.coeliac.org.uk)

Colostomy

Colostomy Association (CA), Enterprise House, 95 London Street, Reading, Berkshire RG1 4QA (tel: 0118 939 1537; 24-hour helpline: 0800 328 4257; email: cass@ colostomy association.org.uk or by using online enquiry form; website: www.colostomyassociation.org.uk)

Cot death

Compassionate Friends, 14 New King Street, Deptford, London SE8 3HS (helpline: 0345 123 2304; or 028 8778 8016 in Northern Ireland [Mon–Fri, 10am–4pm and 7pm–10pm]; email: helpline@tcf.org.uk; website: www.tcf. org.uk)

The Lullaby Trust (formerly Foundation for the Study of Infant Deaths), 11 Belgrave Road, London SW1V 1RB (tel: 020 7802 3200; helpline: 0808 802 6868; email: office@lullabytrust.org.uk or support@lullabytrust.org.uk; website: www.lullabytrust.org.uk)

Counselling

British Association for Counselling and Psychotherapy, 15 St John's Business Park, Lutterworth LE17 4HB, (tel: 01455 883300; email: bacp@bacp.co.uk; website: www.bacp.co.uk)

Samaritans, The Upper Mill, Kingston Road, Ewell KT17 2AF (tel: 020 8394 8300; 24-hour helpline: 0845 790 9090; see phone book for local number; email: admin@samaritans.org (general) jo@samaritans.org (helpline); website: www.samaritans.org)

SupportLine, PO Box 2860, Romford, Essex RM7 1JA (tel: 01708 765222; helpline: 01708 765200; email: info@supportline.org.uk; website: www.supportline.org.uk)

Craniosynostosis orcraniostenosis

Headlines Craniofacial Support, 8 Footes Lane, Frampton, Cottrell, Bristol BS36 2JQ (helpline: 01454 850557; email: info@headlines.org.uk; website: www.headlines.org.uk)

Crohn's disease

Children with Crohn's and Colitis (CICRA) Parkgate House, 356 West Barnes Lane, Motspur Park, Surrey KT3 6NB (tel: 020 8949 6209; email: support@cicra.org or by using online contact form; website: www.cicra.org)

National Association for Colitis and Crohn's Disease (NACC), 45 Grosvenor Road, St Albans AL1 3AW (tel: 0300 222 5700; helpline: 0121 737 9931 [Mon–Fri, 1pm–3.30pm and 6.30pm–9pm]; email: info@crohnsandcolitis.org.uk; website: www.crohnsandcolitis.org.uk)

Crying/restless babies

The CRY-SIS Helpline, BM CRY-SIS, London WC1N 3XX (sae required); (helpline: 0845 122 8669 [9am–10pm daily]; website: www.cry-sis.org.uk)

Cystic fibrosis

Butterfly Trust, Swanston Steading, 109/3 Swanston Road, Edinburgh EH10 7DS (tel: 0131 445 5590; email: info@butterflytrust.org.uk; website: www.butterflytrust.org.uk)

*Cystic Fibrosis Trust, One Aldgate, Second Floor, London EC3N 1RE (helpline: 0300 373 1000; email: enquiries@cysticfibrosis.org.uk; website: www.cysticfibrosis.org.uk)

Deafblind

Deafblind UK, National Centre for Deafblindness, John and Lucille Van Geest Place, Cygnet Road, Hampton, Peterborough PE7 8FD (tel/textphone: 01733 358100; email: info@deafblind.org.uk or by using online contact form; website: www.deafblind.org.uk)

*Sense, 101 Pentonville Road, London N1 9LG (tel: 0300 330 9250; textphone: 0300 330 9252; email: info@sense.org.uk; website: www.sense.org.uk)

Deafness/hearing difficulties

Action on Hearing Loss, 19–23 Featherstone Street, London EC1Y 8SL (tel: 020 7296 8000; text: 020 7296 8001; information line: 0808 808 0123 [voice] 0808 808 9000 [text]; email: informationonline@hearingloss.org.uk; website: www.actionhearingloss.org.uk)

British Deaf Association (BDA), 3rd Floor, 356 Holloway Road, London N7 6PA (tel: 020 7697 4140; email: bda@bda.org.uk; website: www.bda.org.uk)

The Guide Dogs for the Blind Association, Burghfield Common, Reading RG7 3YG (tel: 0118 983 5555; email: guidedogs@guidedogs.org.uk; website: www.guidedogs.org.uk)

Hearing Dogs for Deaf People, The Grange, Wycombe Road, Saunderton, Buckinghamshire HP27 9NS (tel and minicom: 01844 348100; email: info@hearingdogs.org.uk; website: www.hearingdogs.org.uk)

*National Deaf Children's Society, Ground Floor South, Castle House, 37–45 Paul Street, London EC2A 4LS (tel: 020 7490 8656; minicom: 020 7490 8656; helpline: 0808 800 8880; email: ndcs@ndcs.org.uk or

helpline@ndcs.org.uk; website: www.ndcs.org.uk)

Royal Association for Deaf People (RAD), Century House South, Riverside Office Centre, North Station Road, Colchester, Essex CO1 1RE (tel: 0845 688 2525; minicom: 0845 688 2527; email: info@royaldeaf.org.uk; website: www.royaldeaf.org.uk)

Dental health

British Dental Association, 64 Wimpole Street, London W1G 8YS (tel: 020 7935 0875; email: enquiries@bda.org website: www.bda.org)

British Dental Health Foundation (BDHF), Smile House, 2 East Union Street, Rugby, Warwickshire CV22 6AJ (tel: 01788 546365; helpline: 01788 539780; email: helpline@dentalhealth.org; website: www.dentalhealth.org)

Depression

Befrienders Worldwide, c/o The Samaritans, Upper Mill, Kingston Road, Ewell, Surrey KT17 2AF (tel: 0845 790 9090; minicom: 0845 790 9192; email: info@befrienders.org; website: www.befrienders.org)

Bipolar UK, 11 Belgrave Road, London SW1V 1RB (tel: 0333 323 3880; email: info@bipolaruk.org.uk; website: www.bipolaruk.org.uk)

Depression Alliance, 20 Great Dover Street, London SE1 4LX (tel: 0845 123 2320; email: info@depressionalliance.org; website: www.depressionalliance.org)

Depression UK, c/o Self Help Nottingham, Ormiston House, 32–36 Pelham Street, Nottingham NG1 2EG (email: info@depressionuk.org; website: www.depressionuk.org)

Samaritans, The Upper Mill, Kingston Road, Ewell KT17 2AF (tel: 020 8394 8300; 24-hour helpline: 0845 790 9090; see phone book for local number; email: admin@samaritans.org (general) jo@samaritans.org (helpline); website: www.samaritans.org)

Diabetes

Diabetes UK, 10 Parkway, London NW1 7AA (tel: 0345 123 2399; [Mon–Fri, 9am–7pm]; email: info@diabetes.org; website: www.diabetes.org.uk)

Disfigurement

Disfigurement Guidance Centre, PO Box 7, Cupar, Fife KY15 4PF (tel: 01337 870281)

Let's Face It, 72 Victoria Avenue, Westgate-on-Sea, Kent CT8 8BH (tel: 01843 833724; email: chrisletsfaceit@aol.com; website: www.lets-face-it.org.uk)

Down's syndrome

Down's Syndrome Association, Langdon Down Centre, 2a Langdon Park, Teddington Middlesex TW11 9PS (helpline: 0333 1212 300 [Mon–Fri, 10am–4pm]; email: info@downs-syndrome.org.uk; website: www.downs-syndrome.org.uk)

Drugs

ADFAM National, 25 Corsham Street, London N1 6DR (tel: 020 7553 7640; email: admin@adfam.org.uk; website: www.adfam.org.uk)

Cocaine Anonymous UK, Talbot House, 204–226 Imperial Way, Rayners Lane, Harrow HA2 7HH (helpline: 0800 612 0225 or 0300 11 2285 [10am–10pm daily]; email: wtf@cauk.org.uk; website: www.cauk.org.uk)

Early Break, Annara House, 7–11 Bury Road, Radcliffe M26 2UG (Bury: 0161 723 3880; East Lancashire: 01282 604022; Rochdale: 0161 723 3880; email: info@earlybreak.co.uk; website: www.earlybreak.co.uk)

Families Anonymous, Doddington and Rollo Community Association, Charlotte Despard Avenue, Battersea, London SW11 5HD (helpline: 0845 120 0660 or 020 7498 4680; email: office@famanon.org.uk; website: www.famanon.org.uk)

FRANK (National Drugs Helpline), (24-hour helpline: 0300 123 6600; text: 82111; website: www.talktofrank.com). Contact can also be made via an online chat facility from 2pm–6pm.

Narcotics Anonymous (NA), 202 City Road, London EC1V 2PH (tel: 020 7251 4007; helpline: 0300 999 1212 [10am–midnight]; website: www.ukna.org)

Turning Point, Standon House, 21 Mansell Street, London E1 8AA (tel: 020 7481 7600; email: info@turning-point.co.uk or by using online contact form; website: www.turning-point.co.uk)

Dyslexia

British Dyslexia Association, Unit 8, Bracknell Beeches, Old Bracknell Lane, Bracknell RG12 7BW (tel: 0333 405 4555; helpline: 0333 405 4567 [Mon–Fri, 10am–1pm and 1.30pm–4pm (but not on Wednesdays)]; email: using contact form on website; website: www.bdadyslexia.org.uk)

Dyslexia Action, Dyslexia Action House, 10 High Street, Egham, Surrey TW20 9EA (email: by using online contact form; website: www.dyslexiaaction.org.uk)

Dyspraxia

Dyspraxia Foundation, 8 West Alley, Hitchin, Hertfordshire SG5 1EG (tel: 01462 455016; helpline: 01462 454986 [Mon–Fri, 9am–5pm]; email: dyspraxia@dyspraxiafoundation.org.uk; website: www.dyspraxiafoundation.org.uk)

Dystonia

Dystonia Society, Second Floor, 89 Albert Embankment, London SE1 7TP (tel: 020 7793 3651; helpline: 020 7793 3650; email: info@dystonia.org.uk; website: www.dystonia.org.uk)

Eating disorders

Eating Disorders Association (Beat), Wensum House, 103 Prince of Wales Road, Norwich NR1 1DW (tel: 0300 123 3355; helpline: 0845 634 1414; Youth helpline: 0845 634 7650; email: help@b-eat.co.uk or fyp@b-eat.co.uk (youth); website: www.b-eat.co.uk)

Eczema

National Eczema Society, Hill House, Highgate Hill, London N19 5NA (tel: 020 7281 3553; helpline: 0800 089 1122 [Mon–Fri, 8am–8pm]; email: helpline@eczema.org; website: www.eczema.org)

Endometriosis

Endometriosis UK, Suites 1&2, 46 Manchester Street, London W1U 7LS (tel: 020 7222 2781; Crisis helpline: 0808 808 2227 [opening times vary depending on volunteer availability, see website for details]; email: support@endometriosisuk.org or by using online contact form; website: www.endometriosis-uk.org)

Epidermolysis bullosa

Dystrophic Epidermolysis Bullosa Research Association (DEBRA), Debra House, 13 Wellington Business Park, Dukes Ride, Crowthorne, Berkshire RG45 6LS (tel: 01344 771961; email: debra@debra.org.uk; website: www.debra.org.uk)

Epilepsy

Epilepsy Action, New Anstey House, Gate Way Drive, Yeadon, Leeds LS19 7XY (tel: 0113 210 8800; helpline: 0808 800 5050 [Mon–Fri, 8.30am–5.30pm]; email: helpline@epilepsy.org.uk; website: www.epilepsy.org.uk)

Epilepsy Society, Chesham Lane, Chalfont St Peter, Buckinghamshire SL9 0RJ (tel: 01494 601300; helpline: 01494 601400 [Mon–Fri, 9am–4pm and Wednesdays 9am–8pm]; website: www.epilepsysociety.org.uk)

Growth problems

Child Growth Foundation, 21 Malvern Drive, Sutton Coldfield B76 1PZ (tel: 020 8912 0723; helpline: 020 8995 0257; email: info@childgrowthfoundation.org; website: www.childgrowthfoundation.org)

Restricted Growth Association (RGA), PO Box 99, Lyndney GL15 9AW (tel: 0300 111 1970; email: office@restrictedgrowth.co.uk; website: www.restrictedgrowth.co.uk)

Guillain Barré syndrome

Guillain Barré & Associated Inflammatory Neuropathies (GAIN), Ground Floor, Woodholme House, Heckington Business Park, Station Road, Heckington, Sleaford NG34 9JH (tel: 01529 469910; helpline: 0800 374803; email: office@gaincharity.org.uk or by using the online form; website: www.gaincharity.org.uk)

Haemophilia

*Haemophilia Society, Wilcox House, 140–148 Borough High Street, London SE1 1LB (tel: 020 7939 0780; email: info@haemophelia.org.uk; website: www.haemophilia.org.uk)

Head injury

Headway – National Head Injuries Association Ltd, Bradbury House, 190 Bagnall Road, Old Basford, Nottingham, Nottinghamshire NG6 8SF (tel: 0115 924 0800; helpline: 0808 800 2244; email: enquiries@headway.org.uk or helpline@headway.org.uk; website: www.headway.org.uk)

Heart attacks/heart disease

British Heart Foundation, Greater London House, 180 Hampstead Road, London NW1 7AW (tel: 020 7554 0000; helpline: 0300 330 3311; website: www.bhf.org.uk). Contact can also be made by completing an online enquiry form.

Coronary Artery Disease Research Association (CORDA), Royal Brompton Hospital, Sydney Street, London SW3 6NP (website: www.corda.org.uk)

HeartLine Association, 32 Little Heath, London SE7 8HU (tel: 0330 022 4466; email: admin@heartline.org.uk; website: www.heartline.org.uk)

Hemiplegia

Hemi-Help, 6 Market Road, London N7 9PW (tel: 0345 120 3713, helpline: 0345 123 2372 [Mon–Fri, 10am–1pm during term time]; email: support@hemihelp.org.uk or helpline@hemihelp.org.uk; website: www.hemihelp.org.uk)

Herpes

Herpes Viruses Association (SPHERE), 41 North Road, London N7 9DP (helpline: 0845 123 2305; email: info@herpes.org.uk; website: www.herpes.org.uk)

Hodgkin's disease

Lymphoma Association, 3 Cromwell Court, New Street, Aylesbury HP20 2PB (helpline: 0808 808 5555 [Mon–Fri, 9am–5pm]; email: information@lymphomas.org.uk; website: www.lymphomas.org.uk). Contact can also be made by completing an online enquiry form.

Huntington's disease

*Huntington's Disease Association, Suite 24, Liverpool Science Park IC1, 131 Mount Pleasant Liverpool L3 5TF

(tel: 0151 331 5444; email: info@hda.org.uk; website: www.hda.org.uk)

Hyperactive children

Hyperactive Children's Support Group, 71 Whyke Lane, Chichester, West Sussex PO19 7PD (tel: 01243 539966 [Mon–Fri, 2.30–4.30pm]; email: hacsg@hacsg.org.uk; website: www.hacsg.org.uk). If writing, the Group requests that you enclose a large sae.

Incontinence

Association for Continence Advice (ACA), Fitwise Management Ltd, Blackburn House, Redhouse Road, Seafield, Bathgate, West Lothian EH47 7AQ (tel: 01506 811077; email: aca@fitwise.co.uk; website: www.aca.uk.com)

Industrial diseases

Mesothelioma UK, Glenfield Hospital, Groby Road, Leicester LE3 9QP (helpline: 0800 169 2409; email: mesothelioma.uk@uhl-tr.nhs.uk; website: www.mesothelioma.uk.com)

RSI Action, 19 Station Road, Steeple Morden, Royston, Hertfordshire SG8 0NW (email: info@rsiaction.org.uk; website: www.rsiaction.org.uk)

Infantile hypercalcaemia

Williams Syndrome Foundation, 161 High Street, Tonbridge, Kent TN9 1BX (tel: 01732 365152; email: enquiries@williams-syndrome.org.uk; website: www.williams-syndrome.org.uk)

Infertility

Infertility Network UK, Charter House, 43 St Leonards Road, Bexhill-on-Sea, East Sussex TN40 1JA (helpline: 01424 732361; email: admin@infertilitynetworkuk.com; website: www.infertilitynetworkuk.com)

Irritable bowel syndrome

The IBS Network 5, Unit 1.12 SOAR Works, 14 Knutton Road, Sheffield S5 9NU (tel: 0114 272 3253; email: info@ttheibsnetwork.org; website: www.theibsnetwork.org)

Kidney disease

*British Kidney Patient Association (BKPA), 3 The Windmills, St Mary's Close, Turk Street, Alton GU34 1EF

(tel: 01420 541424; helpline: 01420 541424; email: info@britishkidney-pa.co.uk; website: www.britishkidney-pa.co.uk)

National Kidney Federation, The Point, Coach Road, Shireoaks, Worksop, Notts S81 8BW (helpline: 0845 601 0209; email: by using the online enquiry form; website: www.kidney.org.uk)

Learning disability

Mencap, Mencap National Centre, 123 Golden Lane, London EC1Y 0RT (tel: 020 7454 0454; helpline: 0808 808 1111; email: help@mencap.org.uk; website: www.mencap.org.uk)

Limb disorder

*Blesma, 185–187 High Road, Chadwell Heath, Romford RM6 6NA (tel: 020 8590 1124; email: ChadwellHeath@blesma.org; website: www.blesma.org)

Limbless Association, Unit 10, Waterhouse Business Centre, 2 Cromar Way, Chelmsford CM1 2QE (tel: 01245 216670; helpline: 0800 644 0185; email: enquiries@limbless-association.org; website: www.limbless-association.org)

Reach – The Association for Children with Hand or Arm Deficiency, Pearl Assurance House, Brook Street, Tavistock, Devon PL19 0BN (tel: 0845 130 6225; email: reach@reach.org.uk; website: www.reach.org.uk)

STEPS (A National Association for Families of Children with Congenital Abnormalities), The Wright House, Wilderspool Business Park, Greenalls Avenue, Warrington WA4 6HL (helpline: 01925 750271; email: using online contact form; website: www.steps-charity.org.uk)

Literacy/learning difficulties

Learning and Work Institute, Chetwynd House, 21 De Montfort Street, Leicester LE1 7GE (tel: 0116 204 4200; email: enquiries@learningandwork.org.uk; website: www.niace.org.uk)

Liver disease

British Liver Trust, 2 Southampton Road, Ringwood BH24 1HY (tel: 01425 481320; information line: 0800 652 7330; email: info@britishliver trust.org.uk; website: www.britishliver trust.org.uk)

Lowe Syndrome Trust (UK Contact Group) (LSA) 77 West Heath Road, London NW3 7TH (tel: 020 7794 8858; email: lowetrust@gmail.com; website: www.lowetrust.com)

Lupus

Lupus UK, St James House, Eastern Road, Romford RM1 3NH (tel: 01708 731251; email: headoffice@lupusuk. org.uk; website: www.lupusuk.org.uk)

Raynaud's and Scleroderma Association, 112 Crewe Road, Alsager, Cheshire ST7 2JA (tel: 01270 872776; Freephone: 0800 917 2494; email: info@raynauds.org.uk; website: www. raynauds.org.uk)

Marfan syndrome

Marfan Association UK, Rochester House, 5 Aldershot Road, Fleet, Hampshire GU51 3NG (tel: 01252 810472; email: contactus@marfan-association.org.uk; website: www. marfan-association.org.uk)

Mastectomy

Breast Cancer Care (BCC), 5–13 Great Suffolk Street, London SE1 0NS (tel: 0845 092 0800; helpline: 0808 800 6000 [Mon–Fri, 9am–5pm and Saturdays 10am–2pm]; email: info@breastcancercare.org.uk; website: www.breastcancercare.org. uk)

Ménière's disease

Ménière's Society, The Rookery, Surrey Hills Business Park, Wotton, Dorking, Surrey RH5 6QT (tel: 01306 876883; email: info@menieres.org.uk; website: www.menieres.org.uk)

Meningitis

Meningitis Now, Fern House, Bath Road, Stroud, Gloucestershire GL5 3TJ (tel: 01453 768000; 24-hour helpline: 0808 801 0388; email: info@ meningitisnow.org or helpline@ meningitisnow.org; website: www. meningitisnow.org)

Menopause

The Daisy Network Premature Menopause Support Group, PO Box 71432, London SW6 9HJ (email: info@daisynetwork.org.uk; website: www.daisynetwork.org.uk)

Mental health

Mental Health Foundation, Colechurch House, 1 London Bridge Walk, London SE1 2SX (tel: 020 7803 1100; website: www.mentalhealth.org. uk). Note that MHF does not offer a help or advice line and should not be contacted unless specific information on its work is required or you wish to collaborate with the foundation in a professional capacity. Its website advises that other organisations such as Samaritans, however, can offer emotional support. Samaritans can be contacted by calling 116 123 or by emailing jo@samaritans.org.

Mind (National Association for Mental Health), 15–19 Broadway, Stratford, London E15 4BQ (tel: 020 8519 2122; Mind information line: 0300 123 3393; email: info@mind.org. uk; website: www.mind.org.uk)

SANE (The Mental Health Charity), St. Mark's Studios, 14 Chillingworth Road, Islington, London N7 8QJ (tel: 020 3805 1790; helpline: 0300 304 7000 [6pm–11pm daily]; email: info@ sane.org.uk; website: www.sane.org. uk; an online contact support service is also available)

Metabolic disorders

CLIMB (Research Trust for Metabolic Diseases in Children), Climb Building, 176 Nantwich Road, Crewe CW2 6BG (tel: 0845 241 2173 or 0800 652 3181; email: contact@climb.org. uk; website: www.climb.org.uk)

Migraine

Migraine Action Association (formerly British Migraine Association), Fourth Floor, 27 East Street, Leicester LE1 6NB (tel: 0845 601 1033; email: info@migraine.org. uk; website: www.migraine.org.uk). Contact can also be made by completing an online enquiry form.

Migraine Trust, 52–53 Russell Square, London WC1B 4HP (tel: 020 7631 6970; email: info@migrainetrust.org; website: www.migrainetrust.org)

Miscarriage

The Miscarriage Association, 17 Wentworth Terrace, Wakefield, West Yorkshire WF1 3QW (tel: 01924 200795; helpline: 01924 200799 [Mon–Fri, 9am–4pm]; email: info@ miscarriageassociation.org.uk;

website: www.miscarriageassociation. org.uk)

Tommy's, Nicholas House, 3 Laurence Pountney Hill, London EC4R 0BB (tel: 020 7398 3400; email: mailbox@tommys.org; website: www. tommys.org)

Motor neurone disease

*Motor Neurone Disease Association (MND), PO Box 246, Northampton NN1 2PR (tel: 01604 250505; helpline: 03457 626 262; email: enquiries@mndassociation.org or mndconnect@mndassociation.org; website: www.mndassociation.org)

Multiple sclerosis

*Multiple Sclerosis Society, MS National Centre, 372 Edgware Road, London NW2 6ND (tel: 020 8438 0700; helpline: 0808 800 8000 [Mon–Fri, 9am–9pm]; email: helpline@mssociety.org.uk; website: www.mssociety.org.uk). Contact can also be made by using the online form.

Muscular dystrophy

Muscular Dystrophy Campaign, 61A Great Suffolk Street, London SE1 0BU (tel: 020 7803 4800; helpline: 0800 652 6352; email: info@ muscular-dystrophy.org; website: www.muscular-dystrophy.org)

Myalgic Encephalopathy/ Chronic Fatigue Syndrome(ME/CFS)

Action for ME, 42 Temple Street, Keynsham BS31 1EH (tel: 0117 927 9551; helpline 0800 138 6544; email admin@actionforme.org.uk or welfare@actionforme.org.uk; website: www.actionforme.org.uk)

Association of Young People with ME, Tickford House, Silver Street, Newport Pagnell MK16 0EX (tel: 01908 379737; helpline 0330 221 1223; email info@ayme.org.uk or helpline@ayme.org.uk; website: www. ayme.org.uk)

ME Association, 7 Apollo Office Court, Radclive Road, Gawcott, Buckinghamshire MK18 4DF (helpline: 0844 576 5326 [10am–12pm, 2–4pm and 7–9pm]; email: meconnect@meassociation.org. uk; website: www.meassociation.org. uk)

Myasthenia gravis

Myasthenia Gravis Association, The College Business Centre, Uttoxeter New Road, Derby DE22 3WZ (tel: 01332 290219; email: info@myaware. org; website: www.myaware.org)

Myotonic dystrophy

Myotonic Dystrophy Support Group, 19–21 Main Road, Gedling, Nottingham NG4 3HQ (tel: 0115 987 5869; helpline: 0115 987 0080; email: contact@mdsguk.org; website: www. mdsguk.org)

Narcolepsy

Narcolepsy Association (UK), PO Box 26865, Kirkaldy KY2 9BX (tel: 0345 450 0394; email: info@ narcolepsy.org.uk; website: www. narcolepsy.org.uk)

Neurofibromatosis

The Neuro Foundation, HMA House, 78 Durham Road, London SW20 0TL (tel: 020 8439 1234; email: info@ nfauk.org; website: www.nfauk.org)

Organ donors

British Organ Donor Society (BODY), Balsham, Cambridge CB21 4DL (tel: 01223 893636; email: body@argonet.co.uk; website: body.orpheusweb.co.uk)

Osteoporosis

National Osteoporosis Society, Camerton, Bath BA2 0PJ (tel: 01761 471771; helpline: 0808 800 0035; email: nurses@nos.org.uk; website: www.nos.org.uk)

Paget's disease

The Pagets Association, Suite 5, Moorfield Road, Swinton, Manchester M27 0EW (tel: 0161 799 4646; nurse helpline: 07713 568197; email: by using online contact form; website: www.paget.org.uk)

Parkinson's disease

*Parkinson's Disease Society of the United Kingdom, 215 Vauxhall Bridge Road, London SW1V 1EJ (tel: 020 7931 8080; helpline: 0808 800 0303 [weekdays 9am–7pm and Saturdays 10am–2pm]; email: hello@ parkinsons.org.uk; website: www. parkinsons.org.uk)

Perthes' disease

Perthes Association, PO Box 773, Guildford GU1 1XN (tel: 01483 447122; helpline: 01483 306637; email: admin@perthes.org.uk; website: www.perthes.org.uk). Contact can also be made by completing an online enquiry form.

Phobias

Anxiety UK (National Phobics Society), Zion Community Resource Centre, 339 Stretford Road, Hulme, Manchester M15 4ZY (tel: 0161 226 7727: infoline 0844 477 5774 [Mon–Fri, 9.30am–5.30pm]: text service: 07537 416905; email: support@anxiety.org.uk; website: www.anxietyuk.org.uk). Contact can also be made by completing an online enquiry form.

Pituitary disorders

Pituitary Foundation, 86 Colston Street, Bristol BS1 5BB (tel: 0117 370 1333; support line: 0845 450 0375 [Mon–Fri, 10am–4pm]; Endocrine Nurse helpline: 0845 450 0377 [Mondays 6pm–9pm and Thursdays 9am–1pm]; email: helpline@pituitary. org.uk; website: www.pituitary.org. uk)

Poliomyelitis

British Polio Fellowship, Eagle Point, The Runway, South Ruislip, Middlesex HA4 6SE (tel: 0800 043 1935; email: info@britishpolio.org.uk; website: www.britishpolio.org.uk)

Post-natal

Association for Post-Natal Illness, 145 Dawes Road, Fulham, London SW6 7EB (tel: 020 7386 0868 [Mon–Fri, 10am–2pm]; website: www.apni.org)

Prader-Willi syndrome

Prader-Willi Syndrome Association, Craegmoor Suite 4.4, Litchurch Plaza, Litchurch Lane, Derby DE24 8AA (tel: 01332 365676; email: admin@ pwsa.co.uk; website: www.pwsa.co.uk)

Pre-eclampsia

Action on Pre-Eclampsia, The Stables, 80B High Street, Evesham, Worcestershire WR11 4EU (tel: 01386 761848; email: info@apec.org.uk; website: www.action-on-pre-eclampsia.org.uk)

Psoriasis

Psoriasis Association, Dick Coles House, 2 Queensbridge, Northampton NN4 7BF (tel: 01604 251620; helpline: 0845 676 0076; email: mail@psoriasis-association.org. uk; website: www.psoriasis-association.org.uk)

Raynaud's and Scleroderma Association, 112 Crewe Road, Alsager, Cheshire ST7 2JA (tel: 01270 872776; Freephone: 0800 917 2494; email: info@raynauds.org.uk; website: www. raynauds.org.uk)

Retinitis pigmentosa

RP Fighting Blindness, PO Box 350, Buckingham MK18 5GZ (tel: 01280 821334; helpline: 0845 123 2354; email: info@rpfightingblindness.org. uk; website: www.rpfightingblindness. org.uk)

Rett syndrome

Rett Syndrome Association UK, Langham House West, Mill Street, Luton LU1 2NA (tel: 01582 798910; helpline: 01582 798911; email: info@ rettuk.org or support@rettuk.org; website: www.rettuk.org)

Reye's syndrome

National Reye's Syndrome Foundation of the UK (NRSF), 15 Nicholas Gardens, Pyrford, Woking, Surrey GU22 8SD (tel: 01932 346843; website: www. reyessyndrome.co.uk). Contact can also be made using by completing the online contact form.

Sacoidosis

SILA (Sacoidosis and Interstitial Lung Association), Studio 1, 240 Portobello Road, London W11 1LL (tel: 020 3389 7221 or 0800 014 8821; website: www.sila.org.uk). The best way to contact the association is by completing the online contact form.

Schizophrenia

Rethink, 15th Floor, 89 Albert Embankment, London SE1 7TP (general enquiries telephone: 0121 522 7007; Advice Service: 0300 5000 927; email; info@rethink.org or advice@rethink.org; website: www. rethink.org). The Advice Team can be contacted Mon–Fri, 10am–2pm, except on bank holidays. Note that Rethink cannot deal with emergency or crisis issues. See the website for a list of emergency contact details.

Scoliosis
Scoliosis Association (UK) (SAUK), 4 Ivebury Court, 325 Latimer Road, London W10 6RA (tel: 020 8964 5343; helpline: 020 8964 1166; email: info@sauk.org.uk; website: www.sauk.org.uk)

Seasonal affective disorder
SAD Association (SADA), PO Box 332, Wallingford OX10 1EP (email: support@sada.org.uk; website: www.sada.org.uk)

Sickle cell disease
Sickle Cell Society (SCS), 54 Station Road, London NW10 4UA (tel: 020 8961 7795; email: info@sicklecellsociety.org; website: www.sicklecellsociety.org). Contact can also be made by completing an online enquiry form.

Sjögren's syndrome
British Sjögren's Syndrome Association (BSSA), PO Box 15040, Birmingham B31 3DP (tel: 0121 478 0222; helpline: 0121 478 1133 [Mon–Wed, 9.30am–4pm and Thurs–Fri, 9.30am–8.00pm]; website: www.bssa.uk.net). Contact can also be made by completing an online enquiry form.

Sleep disorders
British Snoring and Sleep Apnoea Association (BSSAA), Chapter House, 33 London Road, Reigate RH2 9HZ (tel: 01737 245638; email: info@britishsnoring.co.uk; website: www.britishsnoring.co.uk)

Smoking
Fag Ends (Roy Castle Lung Cancer Foundation), The Roy Castle Centre, 4–6 Enterprise Way, Wavertree Tech Park, Liverpool, Merseyside L13 1FB (helpline: 0333 323 7200; website: www.royalcastle.org/how-we-can-help/Prevention/Stop-Smoking)

QUIT (National Society of Non-Smokers), 4 Sovereign Close, St Katharine's & Wapping, London E1W 3HW (tel: 020 7533 2109; email: stopsmoking@quit.org.uk website: www.quit.org.uk)

Solvent abuse
Re-Solv, 30a High Street, Stone, Staffordshire ST15 8AW (tel: 01785 817885; helpline: 01785 810762; email: information@re-solv.org; website: www.re-solv.org)

Speech and language difficulties
Association for All Speech-Impaired Children (AFASIC), 1st Floor, 20 Bowling Green Lane, London EC1R 0BD (tel: 020 7490 9410; helpline: 0300 666 9410; website: www.afasic.org.uk). You can also contact the helpline by completing an online enquiry form.

British Stammering, 15 Old Ford Road, London E2 9PJ (tel: 020 8983 1003; helpline: 0845 603 2001 or 020 8880 6590 [for a geographic number]; email: mail@stammering.org or info@stammering.org [helpline]); website: www.stammering.org). The helpline is open 2pm–5pm and 7pm–9pm on Monday and 2pm–5pm on Thursday.

Royal Association for Deaf People (RAD), Century House South, Riverside Office Centre, North Station Road, Colchester, Essex CO1 1RE (tel: 01908 604191; minicom: 0845 688 2527; email: info@royaldeaf.org.uk; website: www.royaldeaf.org.uk)

Speakability, 240 City Road, London EC1V 2PR, (tel: 020 7566 1516; email: melanie.derbyshire@stroke.org.uk; website: www.speakability.org.uk)

Spina bifida
SHINE, 42 Park Road, Peterborough PE1 2UQ (tel: 01733 555988; email: website: www.shinecharity.org.uk). Contact can also be made by completing an online enquiry form.

Spinal injuries
Spinal Injuries Association, SIA House, 2 Trueman Place, Oldbrook, Milton Keynes MK6 2HH (tel: 01908 604191; advice line: 0800 980 0501; email: sia@spinal.co.uk; website: www.spinal.co.uk)

Stress
Coronary Artery Disease Research Association (CORDA), Royal Brompton Hospital, Sydney Street,

London SW3 6NP (tel: 020 7351 8613)

Stroke
Stroke Information Service, Stroke Association, Life After Stroke Centre, Church Lane, Bromsgrove, Worcestershire B61 8RA (helpline: 0303 303 3100; textphone: 18001 0303 3033 100; email: info@stroke.org.uk website: www.stroke.org.uk)

Thalassaemia
United Kingdom Thalassaemia Society (UKTS), 19 The Broadway, Southgate Circus, London N14 6PH (tel: 020 8882 0011; email: office@ukts.org; website: www.ukts.org)

Thrombocytopenia with absent radii
TAR Syndrome Support Group, for further information contact Susy Edwards (email: SusyEdwards@hotmail.co.uk; website: www.ivh.se/TAR)

Tinnitus
Action on Hearing Loss, 19–23 Featherstone Street, London EC1Y 8SL (tel: 020 7296 8000; text: 020 7296 8001; information line: 0808 808 0123 [voice] 0808 808 9000 [text]; email: informationonline@hearingloss.org.uk; website: www.actionhearingloss.org.uk)

British Tinnitus Association (BTA), Ground Floor, Unit 5, Acorn Business Park, Woodseats Close, Sheffield S8 0TB (tel: 0114 250 9933; helpline: 0800 018 0527; minicom: 0114 258 5694; email: info@tinnitus.org.uk; website: www.tinnitus.org.uk)

Tourette's syndrome
Tourettes Action, Kings Court, The Meads Business Centre, 19 Kingsmead, Farnborough, Hampshire GU14 7SR (helpline: 0300 777 8427; website: www.tourettes-action.org.uk). Contact can also be made by completing the online contact form.

Tracheo-oesophagealfistula
Aid for Children with Tracheotomies (ACT), 75 Sheepcote Lane, Tamworth, Staffordshire B77 3JN. For further information contact Alison Allan (tel: 01827 65778; email:

support@actfortrachykids.com; website: www.actfortrachykids.com)

Tracheo-Oesophageal Fistula Support Group (TOFS), St George's Centre, 91 Victoria Road, Netherfield, Nottingham NG4 2NN (tel: 0115 961 3092; email: info@tofs.org.uk; website: www.tofs.org.uk)

Tranquillizers

Tasha Foundation, 63 Matlock Lane, London W13 9LA (tel: 020 7118 4334; email: enquiries@tasha-foundation. org.uk; website: www.tasha-foundation.org.uk)

Tuberous sclerosis

Tuberous Sclerosis Association, CAN Mezzanine, 32–36 Loman Street, London SE1 0EH (email: admin@ tuberous-sclerosis.org; website: www. tuberous-sclerosis.org). Contact can also be made by completing an online enquiry form.

Turner syndrome

Turner Syndrome Support Society, 12 Simpson Court, 11 South Avenue, Clydebank Business Park, Clydebank G81 2NR (website: www.tss.org.uk)

Urostomy

Urostomy Association, 4 Demontfort Way, Uttoxeter ST14 8XY (tel: 01889 563191; email: secretary@ urostomyassociation.org.uk; website: www.urostomyassociation.org.uk)

Williams syndrome

Williams Syndrome Foundation, 161 High Street, Tonbridge, Kent TN9 1BX (tel: 01732 365152; email: enquiries@williams-syndrome.org.uk; website: www.williams-syndrome.org. uk)

Index